HUMAN
FOOD
USES

HUMAN FOOD USES

A Cross-cultural, Comprehensive Annotated Bibliography

compiled by
ROBERT L. FREEDMAN

GREENWOOD PRESS
WESTPORT, CONNECTICUT • LONDON, ENGLAND

Library of Congress Cataloging in Publication Data

Freedman, Robert L. 1941-
    Human food uses.

    Bibliography: p.
    Includes index.
    1. Food Habits—Bibliography.   2.   Diet—Bibliography.
I. Title.
Z5118.F58F73   [GT2855]   016.3941   81-469
ISBN 0-313-22901-5 (lib. bdg.)   AACR1

This publication was supported in part by NIH
Grant LM 03082 from the National Library of Medicine.

Library of Congress Catalog Card Number: 81-469
ISBN: 0-313-22901-5

First published in 1981

Greenwood Press
A division of Congressional Information Service, Inc.
88 Post Road West, Westport, Connecticut 06881

Printed in the United States of America

10 9 8 7 6 5 4 3 2 1

Contents

Preface

This bibliography has been developed for scholars and scientists requiring data on various aspects of food in human culture. Those acquainted with the literature in the fields of food habit research and nutritional anthropology will recognize that the present selection continues work begun in National Research Council Bulletin 111 (1945), Rossi & Gottlieb (1958) and Gottlieb & Rossi (1961), Mead (1964), and Wilson (1973; 1980), as well as the comprehensive, unpublished bibliographic data compiled by Professor Louis Evan Grivetti (Department of Nutrition and Department of Geography, University of California, Davis). I am in the debt of each of the foregoing for providing motive, inspiration, and direction.

It is particularly hoped that the information in this volume may be found useful by professionals in the areas of health care delivery: physicians, nurses, public health nutritionists, dietitians, and dentists, and also by anthropologists, psychologists, sociologists, social welfare personnel, home economists, botanists, agronomists, and public policy planners. Each of these specialists is frequently called upon to make decisions which directly or indirectly affect the diets of individuals from a wide range of socioeconomic and ethnic contexts; and, practically speaking, these decisions can be more effectively taken in proportion to the decision-makers' understanding of the roles and meanings of food in human societies.

All titles are listed in the bibliography alphabetically by the author's last name. Where a title is issued by a corporate entity, that entity is entered as author. Where the author is a government agency, the name of the political unit (nation, state, province, county, city/town) is given first, followed by the name of the agency. For manuscript material, the city in which the depository (library, archive, or other) is located is given first, followed by the name of the depository institution. These conventions are followed in library cataloging, and are used here to help reduce retrieval time.

Each author entry is preceded by a numeral, beginning with 1 and carrying through to the final entry (9097). Titles for citations in periodical literature are entered in full. Periodical titles are, however, abbreviated. A key to these abbreviations is found preceding the bibliography. The place of issue is included in parentheses, after the full title, in order to assist in hastening the retrieval process.

The bibliography is followed by an index which represents all entries by key words. In addition, key concepts have been entered, so that the theme of any entry, as well as the title, will be represented under as many logical headings as possible. The numerals following each index entry refer to the individual entries in the bibliography.

Annotation, where included, is intended to provide

an indication of the theme and content of the original book or article. In some instances unannotated entries have not been seen by the compiler; every effort has been made to verify the accuracy of these titles through existing bibliographic resources. Initially, the material which formed the basis for this volume was gathered for future reference for the compiler's own research interests. With the passage of time, and a manifold increase in data, thought was given to the coordination of the material for publication. Subsequent to receipt of support for the latter purpose, effort has been made to provide annotation wherever possible. Lack of annotation should in no way be construed as a judgment upon the merit of an entry.

The appropriateness of any kind of data is relative to the varying requirements of persons seeking information. Evaluation has been eschewed in this bibliography, in order to allow researchers to become familiar with material on a first-hand basis without prejudice as to its quality or usefulness.

Wherever possible, the orthography used for ethnic groups is taken from George Peter Murdock's *Outline of World Cultures*, 5th ed. (New Haven, Conn.: Human Relations Area Files, Inc., 1975).

Readers familiar with various of the languages represented in the bibliography will note the absence of diacritical markings. This omission is regretted, resulting from constraints of an economic nature relating to special manufacture of word-processing equipment print-wheels.

A wide range of sources is cited in this volume, and the question of availability immediately arises. Some monographs and serials will be found readily in most college or university libraries, and in major public library collections as well. Other materials may usually be obtained from holding institutions, through Interlibrary Loan. One feature of this bibliography is the inclusion of a substantial number of titles of doctoral dissertations and master's theses. Many dissertations completed in the United States and Canada within the past thirty years may be purchased through University Microfilms (provided the awarding institution has an agreement with this microfilm vendor). Available titles are printed in *Dissertation Abstracts*, which is subscribed to by major university libraries. Dissertations completed before ca. 1950, or at schools not participant in the University Microfilms program, may usually be borrowed through Interlibrary Loan from the awarding institution.

Indexing of master's theses has not been as thorough as for doctoral dissertations. Although the situation has begun to improve over the past fifteen years, it is still probable that greater success will be had in obtaining master's theses through Interlibrary Loan, rather than through University Microfilms.

What of the availability of dissertations completed overseas? Many recent doctoral dissertations are now being indexed in *Dissertation Abstracts International*, and are therefore available through University Microfilms. However, for dissertations written before the mid-1970s, and for those written in nations not indexed by *Dissertation Abstracts International*, the reader is referred to the section "Availability of Dissertations" in *Doctoral Dissertations on China, 1971-1975: A Bibliography of Studies in Western Languages*, by Frank Joseph Shulman (Seattle and London: University of Washington Press, 1978). Although this volume is concerned specifically with China, the mentioned section provides helpful advice for obtaining foreign doctoral monographs of all disciplines.

The entries in this bibliography represent data processed within the first year of the compiler's National Library of Medicine grant support. Soon after beginning the first year of data organization, it became apparent that processing all of the material at hand within one year would not be possible. Approval, by the library, of a second year of support, has permitted the processing of approximately four thousand additional citations. Material sought but not found in the present volume may be included in its supplement.

Acknowledgments

I am deeply appreciative of the support extended me by the National Library of Medicine through its Publication Grant Program, and I am particularly grateful to Mr. Randall Worthington, Program Officer, International Programs Division, National Library of Medicine, for his patience and courtesy in response to my many questions and requests during the period of grant tenure.

To my teachers at the University of Arizona and at the University of Hawaii, particularly Professors Bernard Fontana and Alice G. Dewey, for their guidance in the basics of scholarly research; and to innumerable colleagues whose cooperation is evidenced on each page, my warmest thanks for your time, effort, and interest; I hope that these, the results of your assistance, may be helpful in return.

Thanks also to Professor Lou Grivetti, for sharing his time and his outstanding bibliographic materials;

To Dr. James T. Sabin, Vice President—Editorial at Greenwood Press, for his early interest in the bibliography;

To Dr. Martin M. Cummings, M.D., Director, National Library of Medicine, and Mr. Albert M. Berkowitz, Chief of the Library's Reference Services Division, for courtesies in permitting me access to the Library's collections;

To Mr. Wallace C. Olsen, Chief, Library Operations Division, National Agricultural Library, and Ms. Robyn Frank, Chief of the Library's Food and Nutrition Information and Materials Center, for sharing time, and taking interest in my research, and for permitting me access to the Library's collections;

To Jane M. Palmer, for typing the key to the serial title abbreviations, and much more;

And to Chuck and Linda Buford, proprietors of Executive Suite Office Services, Walnut Creek, California, for their many hours of hard work, patience, and cooperation in rendering the manuscript material on twelve thousand index cards, in a dozen languages, into camera-ready copy.

Without the efforts and cooperation of all of these persons, this book could not have been produced.

Serial Title Abbreviations

AA	*American Anthropologist* (Washington, D.C.)	AA-UC-ES-B	*Addis Ababa. University College. Ethnological Society. Bulletin* (Addis Ababa, Ethiopia)
AAA-M	American Anthropological Association. Memoirs (Menasha, Wisconsin)	AB	*Anales de Bromatologia* (Madrid, Spain)
AAAS-P	*American Association for the Advancement of Science. Proceedings* (Washington, D.C.)	ABB	*Arizona Business Bulletin* (Phoenix, Arizona)
AAAS-SRMD-CDAZR-C	American Association for the Advancement of Science. Southwestern and Rocky Mountain Division. Committee on Desert and Arid Zone Research. Contribution (Arizona State College, Flagstaff, Arizona)	ABJ	*American Bee Journal* (Philadelphia, Pennsylvania)
		ABM	*American Breeder's Magazine* (Washington, D.C.)
		ABN	*Arquivos Brasileiras de Nutricao* (Rio de Janeiro, Brazil)
AAD-R	*Asociacion Argentina de Dietologia. Revista* (Buenos Aires, Argentina)	ABNeer	*Acta Botanica Neerlandica* (Amsterdam, Netherlands)
AAffair	*African Affairs* (London, England)	ABot	*American Botanist* (Binghamton, New York)
AAG-A	*Association of American Geographers. Annals* (Lancaster, Pennsylvania)	ABSFMS	*Agriculture Bulletin of the Straits and Federated Malay States* (Singapore, Malaya)
AAGB	*Afdeling Agrarische Gescheidenis Bijdragen* (Wageningen, Netherlands)	ABT	*American Biology Teacher* (Lancaster, Pennsylvania)
AAH	*Acta Archaeologica Hungaricae* (Budapest, Hungary)	ACA	*Amazonia Colombiana Americanista* (Sibundoy, Colombia)
AAm	*Acta Amazonica* (Manaus, Brazil)	ACCEFN-R	*Academia Colombiana de Ciencias Exactas, Fisicas, y Naturales. Revista* (Bogota, Colombia)
AAng	*Agronomia Angolana* (Luanda, Angola)		
AAnt	*American Antiquarian* (New York, New York)		
AAnth	*Applied Anthropology* (Boston, Massachusetts)	AC-FRI-P	Antioch College. Fels Research Institute. Publications (Yellow Springs, Ohio)
AAnz	*Anatomischer Anzeiger* (Jena, Austria)	ACiba	*Actas Ciba* (Basle, Switzerland)
AAOJ	*American Antiquarian and Oriental Journal* (Chicago, Illinois)	AColon	*See*: IAAI-RMAC
		ACook	*American Cookery* (Boston, Massachusetts)
AAPSS-A	American Academy of Political and Social Science. Annals (Philadelphia, Pennsylvania)	ACP	*Annales de Chimie et de Physique* (Paris, France)
AArb-J	*Arnold Arboretum Journal* (Cambridge, Massachusetts)	ACS-J	*American Chemical Society. Journal* (New York, New York)
AArch	*Acta Archaeologica* (Copenhagen, Denmark)	ActaAm	*Acta Americana* (Washington, D.C.)
AAS-P	*American Antiquarian Society. Proceedings* (Worcester, Massachusetts)	ActaGeog	*Acta Geographica* (Paris, France)

ADC	*Archives of Diseases in Childhood* (London, England)
Adibasi	*Adibasi* (Cuttack, Orissa, India)
ADW	*Arizona Days and Ways*. Magazine of the *Arizona Republic* (Phoenix, Arizona)
AE	*Acta Ethnographica Hungarica* (Budapest, Hungary)
AEH	*Archives of Environmental Health* (Chicago, Illinois)
AEL	*Acta Ethnologica et Linguistica* (Vienna, Austria)
Aequatoria	*Aequatoria* (Coquilhatville, Belgian Congo)
Aesculape	*Aesculape* (Paris, France)
AF	*Afrique Francaise* (Paris, France)
AF-A	*Academia Farmacia. Anales* (Madrid, Spain)
AFC	*Archivos del Folklore Chileno* (Santiago, Chile)
AFFL	*American Forests and Forest Life* (Washington, D.C.)
Affword	*Affword* (Flagstaff, Arizona)
AFJ	*American Food Journal* (Chicago, Illinois)
AFRDCP	*Advances in Flourine Research and Dental Caries Prevention* (Macmillan Pub. Co., New York)
Africa	*Africa. Journal of the International Institute of African Languages and Cultures* (London, England)
Africa(M)	*Africa* (Madrid, Spain)
Africa(T)	*Africa* (Tervuren, Belgium)
Africana	*Africana* (Newcastle-on-Tyne, England)
AFS-M	American Folklore Society. Memoirs (Boston, Massachusetts)
AG	*Annales de Gembloux* (Brussels, Belgium)
AgEco	*Agro-Ecosystems* (Amsterdam, Netherlands)
AGeo	*Annales de Geographie* (Paris, France)
AgHR	*Agricultural History Review* (London, England)
AGNSW	*Agricultural Gazette of New South Wales* (Sydney, Australia)
Agrarwirtschaft	*Agrarwirtschaft* (Hannover, Germany)
AgriMod	*Agricoltore Moderna* (Milan, Italy)
Agron	*Agronomie Tropicale* (Paris, France)
Agros	*Agros* (Lisbon, Portugal)
AgTrop	*Agricultura Tropical* (Bogota, Colombia)
AGW-S-M	*Anthropologische Gesellschaft in Wien. Sitzungsbericht. Mitteilungen* (Vienna, Austria)
AH	*Agricultural History* (Berkeley, California)
AHigh	*Arizona Highways* (Phoenix, Arizona)
AHist	*Amateur Historian* (Windsor, Berkshire, England)
AHLF	*Annales d'Hygiene de Langue Francaise* (Paris, France)
AHPIS	*Annales d'Hygiene Publique, Industrielle et Sociale* (Paris, France)
AHyg	*Archiv fur Hygiene* (Munich, Germany)
AIL	*Agricultural and Industrial Life* (Manila, Philippines)
AIM	*Annals of Internal Medicine* (Ann Arbor, Michigan)
AIM-R	Auckland Institute and Museum. Records (Auckland, New Zealand)
AIowa	*Annals of Iowa* (Des Moines, Iowa)

AISSP-B	*Academie Imperiale des Science de Saint-Petersbourg. Bulletin* (Saint Petersburg, U.S.S.R)
AK	*Archiv fur Kulturgeschichte* (Munster-Koln, Germany)
AL	*Agricultural Ledger* (Calcutta, India)
Ala-AES-B	Alabama. Agricultural Experiment Station. Bulletin (Auburn, Alabama)
AlbHR	*Alberta Historical Review* (Edmonton, Canada)
Alemann	*Alemannisches Jahrbuch* (Freiburg im Breisgan, Germany)
ALing	*Anthropological Linguistics* (Bloomington, Indiana)
Allergy	*Annals of Allergy* (St. Louis, Missouri)
AlMed	*Alaska Medicine* (Anchorage, Alaska)
ALN	*Archivos Latinamericanos de Nutricion* (Caracas, Venezuela)
AlVie	*Alimentation et la Vie* (Paris, France)
AL-VPS	*Agricultural Ledger. Vegetable Products Series* (Calcutta, India)
AM	*Atlantic Monthly* (New York, New York)
AMal-BT	*Academie Malgache. Bulletin Trimestriel* (Tananarive, Madagascar)
AmAn	*American Antiquity* (Menasha, Wisconsin)
Am-B	*Academie de Medicin. Bulletin* (Paris, France)
AMedHyd	*Archives of Medical Hydrology* (London, England)
AMerc	*American Mercury* (New York, New York)
Americas	*Americas* (Pan American Union. Washington, D.C.)
Amerind-P	Amerind Foundation. Publication (Dragoon, Arizona)
AmEth	*American Ethnologist* (Washington, D.C.)
AMFVMUK	*Acta Medicinae Facultatis Vytauti Magni Universitatis Kaunas* (Kaunas, Lithuania)
AMHaiti-B	*Association Medicale Haitienne. Bulletin* (Port-au-Prince, Haiti)
AMH-M	Academia Mexicana de Historia. Memorias.
AMJ	*American Museum Journal* (New York, New York)
AMM	*Australian Museum Magazine* (Sydney, Australia)
AMN	*Acta Medica Nagasakiensia* (Nagasaki, Japan)
AMNHist	*Annals and Magazine of Natural History* (London, England)
AMNH-M	American Museum of Natural History. Memoirs (New York, New York)
AMNH-PA	American Museum of Natural History. Papers in Anthropology (New York, New York)
AMPC	*Annales de Medecine et de Pharmacie Coloniale* (Paris, France)
AMPhil	*Acta Medica Philippina* (Manila, Philippines)
AMPR-B	*Asociacion Medica de Puerto Rico. Boletin* (Santurce, Puerto Rico)
AMS	*Acta Medica Scandinavica* (Stockholm, Sweden)
AmSci	*American Scientist* (Champaign, Illinois)
AMT	*Acta Medica Turcica* (Ankara, Turkey)
AMWEP	*Altneuland Monatsschrift fur die Wirtschaftliche Erschliessung Palastinas* (Berlin, Germany)
AN	*American Naturalist* (New York, New York)

ANA	*Annales de la Nutrition et de l'Alimentation* (Paris, France)
ANA-T	*American Neurological Association. Transactions* (New York, New York)
Anatol	*Anatolian Studies* (London, England)
Andrologia	*Andrologia* (Berlin, Germany)
ANDSC	*Annales de Notre Dame du Sacre Coeur* (Antwerp, Belgium)
AnEtno	*Antropolgia y Etnologia* (Madrid, Spain)
ANH	*Australian Natural History* (Sydney, Australia)
ANI	*Asie Nouvelle Illustree* (Saigon, French Indo-China)
Annales	*Annales; Economies, Societes, Civilisations* (Paris, France)
AnnInd	Annuario Indigenista (Mexico City, Mexico)
ANSBLAB-A	*Academie National des Sciences, Belles-Lettres et Arts de Bourdeaux. Actes* (Paris, France)
ANSEN	*Archives Neerlandaises des Sciences Exactes et Naturelles* (The Hague, Netherlands)
Anthropologia	*Anthropologia* (London, England)
Anthropolgica(H)	*Anthropolgica* (The Hague, Netherlands)
Anthropolgica(O)	*Anthropolgica* (Ottawa, Canada)
Anthropologie	*Anthropologie* (Paris, France)
Anthropos	*Anthropos* (Freiburg, Germany)
AntiqJ	*Antiquaries Journal* (London, England)
Antiquity	*Antiquity* (Gloucester, England)
Antiseptic	*Antiseptic* (Edinburgh, Scotland)
AOAC-J	*Association of Official Agricultural Chemists. Journal* (Baltimore, Maryland)
AOS-J	*American Oriental Society. Journal* (Philadelphia, Pennsylvania)
AO-UP-SERB-B	Agra and Oudh. United Provinces. Statistics and Economic Research Bureau. Bulletin. Published by the Superintendant of Printing and Stationery (United Provinces, India)
APA-J-SE	*American Pharmaceutical Association. Journal. Scientific Edition* (Washington, D.C.)
APAO	*Archaeology and Physical Anthropology in Oceania* (Sydney, Australia)
APC	*Alimentazione; produzione e consumo* (Milan, Italy)
APCG-YB	*Association of Pacific Coast Geographers. Year Book* (Cheney, Washington)
APed	*Acta Pediatrica* (Uppsala, Sweden)
APer	*Asian Perspectives* (Honolulu, Hawaii)
APF	*Archivos Peruanos de Folklore* (Lima, Peru)
APhytS-M	*American Phytopathological Society. Monograph* (Lancaster, Pennsylvania)
APJ	*Acta Pharmaceutica Jugoslavica* (Zagreb, Yugoslavia)
APPC	*L'Agriculture pratique des pays chauds* (Paris, France)
APScan-S	*Acta Paediatrica Scandinavica. Supplement* (Uppsala, Sweden)
APS-P	*American Philosophical Society. Proceedings.* (Philadelphia, Pennsylvania)
APS-Y	*American Philosophical Society. Yearbook* (Philadelphia, Pennsylvania)
APU	*Archivos de Pediatria del Uruguay* (Montevideo, Uruguay)
AQ	*Anthropological Quarterly* (Washington, D.C.)
AQuart	See: QRes
Aquila	*Aquila* (Perugia, Italy)
ARA	*Annuaire Roumain d'Anthropologie* (Bucarest, Romania)
Arbeitsphysiologie	*Arbeitsphysiologie* (Berlin, Germany)
ARBio	*Annual Review of Biochemistry* (Palo Alto, California)
Archaeologia	*Archaeologia* (London, England)
Archaeology	*Archaeology* (Washington, D.C.)
ArchAnth	*Archiv fur Anthropologie* (Brunswick, Germany)
Archeion	*Archeion* (Rome, Italy; Santa Fe, Argentina)
Archivi	*Archivi per l'Antropologia* (Florence, Italy)
Arctic	*Arctic* (Montreal, Canada)
ARev	*Anthropological Review* (London, England)
ARGERG	*Archiv fur Rassen-und Gesellschaftsbiologie Einschiesslich Rassen-und Gesellschafts-hygiene* (Berlin, Germany)
Ariz-AES-B	Arizona. Agriculture Experiment Station. Bulletin (Tucson, Arizona)
Arizona	*Arizona Cattlelog. (Official Publication of the Arizona Cattle Growers' Association.* Phoenix, Arizona)
Army	*Army Magazine* (San Francisco, California)
ARPEM	*Archives Roumaines de Pathologie Experimentale et de Microbiologie* (Paris, France)
ArqB	*Arquivos de Bromatologia* (Rio de Janeiro, Brazil)
Artifact	*Newsletter of the El Paso Archaeological Society* (El Paso, Texas)
AS	*American Scholar* (New York, New York)
ASA-J	*American Society of Agronomy. Journal* (Washington, D.C.)
ASB-J	*Anthropological Society of Bombay. Journal* (Bombay, India)
ASC-B	*Archaeological Society of Connecticut. Bulletin* (New Haven, Connecticut)
ASci	Advancement of Science (British Association for the Advancement of Science. London, England)
ASI	*Agricultural Situation in India* (New Delhi, India)
Asia	*Asia and the Americas* (New York, New York)
AS-IHP-M	*Academia Sinica. Institute of History and Philology. Monographs* (Shanghai, China)
ASJ-T	Asiatic Society of Japan. Transactions (Tokyo, Japan)
ASL-J	*Anthropological Society of London. Journal* (London, England)
ASL-M	Anthropological Society of London. Memoirs (London, England)
ASMU	*Acta Societatis Medicorum Upsalensis* (Uppsala, Sweden)
ASN	*Annales des Sciences Naturalles* (Paris, France)
ASNJ-N	*Archaeological Society of New Jersey. Newsletter* (New Brunswick, New Jersey)
ASORJ-B	*American Schools of Oriental Research in Jerusalem. Bulletin* (Baltimore, Maryland)
ASP-B	*American Society of Papyrologists. Bulletin* (New York, New York)
ASpeech	*American Speech* (New York, New York)

ASR	*American Sociological Review* (Menasha, Wisconsin)
ASRel	*Archives de Sociologie des Religions* (Paris, France)
AStat	*Applied Statistics* (London, England)
ASTP	*Archives Suisses des Traditions Populaires* (Basel, Switzerland)
ASTPTEK	*Archiv fur Schiffs-und Tropenhygiene, Pathologie und Therapie Exotischer Krankheiten* (Leipzig, Germany)
ASTT-P	Agricultural Society of Trinidad and Tobago. Proceedings (Port-of-Spain, Trinidad)
AStudies	*African Studies* (Johannesburg, South Africa)
ASW-T	Anthropological Society of Washington. Transactions (Washington, D.C.)
AS-Z	*Anthropologika Spolechnost. Zapravy* (Brno, Czechoslovakia)
AT	*Agronomie Tropicale* (Nogent-sur-Marne, France)
AtAdv	*Atlantic Advocate* (Frederickton, New Brunswick, Canada)
ATF-B	*Asociacion Tucumana de Folklore. Boletin* (Tucuman, Argentina)
Atherosclerosis	*Atherosclerosis* (Limerick, Irish Republic)
ATP	*Arts et Traditions Populaires* (Paris, France)
ATrop	*Acta Tropica* (Basel, Switzerland)
Auslander	*Auslander* (Stuttgart, Germany)
Australasian	*Australasian* (Melbourne, Australia)
Ave	*Ave Maria* (Notre Dame, Indiana)
AVF-B	*Academie Veterinaire de France. Bulletin* (Paris, France)
AVMA-J	*American Veterinary Medical Association. Journal* (Chicago, Illinois)
AVN	*Archivos Venezolanos de Nutricion* (Caracas, Venezuela)
AVS-BI	*Asociacion Venezolana de Sociologia. Boletin Informativo* (Caracas, Venezuela)
AVSL	*Archiv de Vereins fur Siebenburgische Landeskunde* (Hermannstadt, Germany)
AVSPD	*Archiv fur Verdaungskrankheiten, Stoffwechsel, Pathologie und Diatetik* (Berlin, Germany)
Awake	*Awake.* Publication of Jehovah's Witnesses (Brooklyn, New York)
AWSJ	*American Wine Society Journal* (Royal Oak, Michigan)
A-YM	*Alaska-Yukon Magazine* (Juneau, Alaska)
BAAS-R	British Association for the Advancement of Science. Report (London, England)
BABGPB	*Bulletin of Applied Botany, Genetics and Plant Breeding* (Leningrad, U.S.S.R.)
BACB	*Bulletin Agricole du Congo Belge* (Brussels, Belgium)
BAEI	*Bulletin de l'Agence Economique de l'Indochine* (Paris, France)
Bantu	*Bantu Studies* (Johannesburg, South Africa)
BArch	*Baessler Archiv* (Berlin, Germany)
B-ARSC-CSNM-M	Belgie. Academie Royale des Sciences Coloniales. Classe des Sciences Naturelles et Medecin. Memoir (Brussels, Belgium)
BATuF	*Boletin de la Asociacion Tucumana de Folclore* (San Miguel de Tucuman, Argentina)
BBAA	Boletin Bibliografico de Antropologia Americana (Mexico City, Mexico)

BBZ	*Beihefte zum Botanischen Zentralblatt* (Dresden, Germany)
BCARL	*Biederman's Central-Blatt fur Agrikulturchemie und Rationellen Landwirtschafts-Betrieb* (Leipzig, Germany)
BCGP	*Boletin Cultural da Guine Portuguesa* (Bissau, Portuguese Guinea)
BCS-B	*Board of Celtic Studies. Bulletin* (Cardiff, Wales)
BCSM	*Boston Cooking-School Magazine* (Boston, Massachusetts)
B-DA-B	Burma. Department of Agriculture. Bulletin (Rangoon, Burma)
BDJ	*British Dental Journal* (London, England)
BDVA	*Beitrage zur Deutschen Volk-und Altertumskunde* (Hamburg, Germany)
The Beaver	*The Beaver* (Hudson's Bay Company, Winnipeg, Manitoba)
Bee	*Bee World* (Benson, England)
BeiTrop	*Beihefte zum Tropenpflanzer* (Berlin, Germany)
BES-B	*Brooklyn Entomological Society. Bulletin* (Lancaster, Pennsylvania)
BESM	*Bulletin Economique et Social du Maroc* (Rabat, Morocco)
BEST	*Bulletin Economique et Sociale de la Tunisie* (Tunis, Tunisia)
BG	*Botanical Gazette* (Chicago, Illinois)
BG-BA-J	*British Guiana. Board of Agriculture. Journal* (Georgetown, Guyana)
BGC	*Boletin Geral das Colonias* (Lisbon, Portugal)
BGC-AR	*Botanic Garden of Calcutta. Annual Review* (Calcutta, India)
BGeb	*Brot und Geback* (Erfurt, Germany)
BHA	*Boletin de Historia y Antiguedades* (Bogota, Colombia)
BHMed	*Bulletin of the History of Medicine* (Baltimore, Maryland)
BInd	*Boletin Indigenista* (Mexico City, Mexico)
BioScience	*BioScience* (Arlington, Virginia)
Biotech	*Biotechnology and Bioengineering* (New York, New York)
BIR	*Bulletin de l'Information et Renseignement de l'Afrique Occidental Francaise* (Dakar, Senegal)
BJAAD	*British Journal of Addiction to Alcohol and Other Drugs* (London, England)
BJCS	*British Journal of Children's Diseases* (London, England)
BJI	*British Journal of Inebriety* (London, England)
BJMP	*British Journal of Medical Psychology* (London, England)
BJN	*British Journal of Nutrition* (Cambridge, England)
BKFNF-UFVS	*Bidrag till Kannedom om Finlands Natur och Folk. Utgifna of Finska Vetenskaps Societeten* (Helsinki, Finland)
Blackwood's	*Blackwood's Magazine* (Edinburgh, Scotland)
BMad	*Bulletin de Madagascar* (Tananarive, Madagascar)
BMAOF	*Bulletin Medicale de l'Afrique Occidentale Francaise* (Dakar, Senegal)
BMedSciJnl	*Boston Medical and Scientific Journal* (Boston, Massachusetts)

BMHS-J	*Barbados Museum and Historical Society. Journal* (Bridgetown, Barbados)
BMJ	*British Medical Journal* (London, England)
BMQ	*British Museum Quarterly* (London, England)
BMSJ	*Boston Medical and Scientific Journal* (Boston, Massachusetts)
BMS-T	*British Mycological Society. Transactions* (Cambridge, England)
BND	*Biblioteca Nutritio et Dieta* (Basel, Switzerland)
BNot	*Botaniska Notiser* (Lund, Sweden)
BNR	*Botswana Notes and Records* (Gaberone, Botswana)
BO	*Belgique d'Outremer* (Brussels, Belgium)
BolInd	*Boletin Indigenista Venezolana* (Caracas, Venezuela)
BORI-A	Bhandarakar Oriental Research Institute. Annals (Poona, India)
BPBM-B	Berenice Puahi Bishop Museum. Bulletin (Honolulu, Hawaii)
BPBM-SP	Berenice Puahi Bishop Museum. Special Publications (Honolulu, Hawaii)
BPedag	*Bulletin Pedagogique* (Point-a-Pitre, Guadeloupe)
BR	*Botanical Review* (Lancaster, Pennsylvania)
BRD	*Book Review Digest* (Bronx, New York)
BRev	*Business Review.* See UWash-BR
BRNR	Borden's Review of Nutrition Research (New York, New York)
BSA	*Bulletin Sanitaire de l'Algerie* (Algiers, Algeria)
BSE-T	Botanical Society of Edinburgh. Transactions (Edinburgh, Scotland)
BSNH-P	Boston Society of Natural History. Proceedings. (Boston, Massachusetts)
BS-OP	Botswana Society. Occasional Papers (Gaborone, Botswana)
BSPub	*Boletin de Salud Publica* (Montevideo, Uruguay)
BStud	*Bantu Studies* (Johannesburg, South Africa)
BTech	*Baking Technology* (Chicago, Illinois)
Budstikken	*Budstikken* (Copenhagen, Denmark)
BU-FM-J	*Baghdad University. Faculty of Medicine. Journal* (Baghdad, Iraq)
BV	*Blatter fur Volksgesundheitspflege* (Berlin, Germany)
BW	*Bakers Weekly* (New York, New York)
BZ	*Botanische Zeitung* (Berlin, Germany)
CA	*Chemical Abstracts* (Easton, Pennsylvania)
CAS-T	Connecticut Academy of Sciences. Transactions. (New Haven, Connecticut)
Caducee	*Caducee* (Paris, France)
Cahiers	*Cahiers des Annales* (published by Colin; Paris)
CAJM	*Central African Journal of Medicine* (Salisbury, Southern Rhodesia)
CalAg	California Agriculture (University of California Agriculture Extension Service. Berkeley, California)
CalAnth	*California Anthropologist* (California State University at Los Angeles. Los Angeles, California)
CalHSQ	*California Historical Society Quarterly* (San Francisco, California)
CALR	*Ceylon Antiquary and Literary Register* (Colombo, Sri Lanka)
CaMJ	*Calcutta Medical Journal* (Calcutta, India)
CancerRes	*Cancer Research* (Chicago, Illinois)
CanCJ	*Canadian Congress Journal [Trades and Labor Congress. Journal]* (Toronto, Canada)
Can-DA-B	Canada. Department of Agriculture. Bulletin (Ottawa, Canada)
CAnth	*Current Anthropology* (Chicago, Illinois)
Cape Argus	*Cape Argus* (Capetown, South Africa)
Cape Times	*Cape Times* (Capetown, South Africa)
Carib	*Caribbean Studies* (Rio Piedras, Puerto Rico)
CasAm	*Casa de las Americas* (Havana, Cuba)
CAS-P	*California Academy of Science. Proceedings* (San Francisco, California)
Castalia	*Rivista di Storia dell'Arte Sanitaria* (Milan, Italy)
CathDgst	*Catholic Digest* (St. Paul, Minnesota)
CathUA-AS	Catholic University of America. Anthropological Series (Washington, D.C.)
CathWld	*Catholic World* (New York, New York)
CB	Chronica Botanica (Waltham, Massachusetts)
CCat	*Canadian Cattlemen. Western Stockgrowers Association* (Calgary, Canada)
CCF-B	Comissao Catarinense de Folclore. Boletim (Florianopolis, Brazil)
CCFCS-P	Canadian Center for Folk Culture Studies. Paper (National Museum of Man, Ottawa, Canada)
CChem	*Cereal Chemistry* (St. Paul, Minnesota)
CCM	*Cooking Club Magazine* (Goshen, Indiana)
CColon	*Cahiers Coloniaux* (Marseilles, France)
CCPI	*Canadian Chemistry and Process Industries* (Toronto, Canada)
CCQ	*Ceylon Coconut Quarterly* (Lunawila, Sri Lanka)
CDA-J	*Canadian Dietetic Association. Journal* (Ottawa, Canada)
C-DM-GS-M-AS	*Canada. Department of Mines. Geological Series. Memoirs. Anthropological Series* (Ottawa, Canada)
CE	*Ceskoslovenska Etnografie* (Prague, Czechoslovakia)
CEA	*Cuadernos de Estudios Africanos* (Madrid, Spain)
CEAfr	*Cahiers d'Etudes Africaines* (Paris, France)
CEd	*Childhood Education* (Washington, D.C.)
CEHS-AOF-B	Comite d'Etudes Historiques et Scientifiques. Afrique Occidentale Francaise. Bulletin (Paris, France)
CEJ	*Chinese Economic Journal and Bulletin* (Peking, China)
Celtica	*Celtica* (Dublin, Irish Republic)
CEM	*Chinese Economic Monthly* (Peking, China)
Centaurus	*Centaurus* (Copenhagen, Denmark)
Century	*Century Magazine* (New York, New York)
Cesky Lid	*Cesky Lid* (Prague, Czechoslovakia)
CF	*Ceylon Forester* (Colombo, Sri Lanka)
CFI	*Cahiers Francais d'Information* (Paris, France)
CGGSP-B	*Commisao Geographica e Geologica de Sao Paulo. Boletim* (Sao Paulo, Brazil)
CGM-B	*Canadian Geological Museum. Bulletin* (Ottawa, Canada)

CGNF	*Country Guide and Nor'west Farmer* (Winnipeg, Manitoba, Canada)
Chacra	*Chacra* (Buenos Aires, Argentina)
CHAS-J	*Cork Historical and Archaeological Society. Journal* (Cork, Irish Republic)
Chatelaine	*Chatelaine* (Montreal, Canada)
CHB	*Child Health Bulletin* (New York, New York)
CH-CP	*Children's Hospital. Clinical Proceedings* (Washington, D.C.)
CHE	*Cahiers d'Histoire Egyptienne* (Cairo, Egypt)
Children	*Children* (United States Department of Health, Education and Welfare. Washington, D.C.)
CHM	*Child Health Magazine* (New York, New York)
Chronique	*Chronique d'Egypte* (Brussels, Belgium)
ChronMed	*Chronique Medical* (Asniers-sur-Seine, France)
Chronobiologia	*Chronobiologia.* (Milan, Italy)
ChronOkla	*Chronicles of Oklahoma* (Oklahoma City, Oklahoma)
CHS-J	*Columbus Horticultural Society. Journal* (Columbus, Ohio)
CI	*Chemistry and Industry* (London, England)
Ciencia	*Ciencia* (Mexico City, Mexico)
CInd	*Chemie en Industrie* (Amsterdam, Netherlands)
CinLancet	*Cincinnati Lancet and Clinic* (Cincinnati, Ohio)
CIS-B	*Cranbrook Institute of Science. Bulletin* (Bloomfield Hills, Michigan)
Civilizations	*Civilizations* (Brussels, Belgium)
CIW-DG-R	Carnegie Institute of Washington Department of Genetics. Report (Washington, D.C.)
CIW-DMB	Carnegie Institute of Washington. Department of Marine Biology (Washington, D.C.)
CIW-NSB	*Carnegie Institute of Washington. News Service Bulletin* (Washington, D.C.)
CIW-P	Carnegie Institute of Washington. Publications (Washington, D.C.)
CIW-SP	Carnegie Institute of Washington. Supplementary Publication (Washington, D.C.)
CJ	*China Journal* (Shanghai, China)
CJP	*Chinese Journal of Physiology* (Peking, China)
CJPH	*Canadian Journal of Public Health* (Ottawa, Ontario, Canada)
CL	*Country Life* (Garden City, New York)
CLA	*Country Life in America* (Garden City, New York)
Classic	*Classical Journal* (Ann Arbor, Michigan)
CleveMNH-SP	Cleveland Museum of Natural History. Scientific Publication (Cleveland, Ohio)
ClioMed	*Clio Medica* (Amsterdam, Netherlands)
ClujMed	*Clujul Medical Clinica Dermatologica* (Cluj, Romania)
CMA-J	*Canadian Medical Association. Journal* (Montreal, Canada)
CMD	*Current Medicine and Drugs* (London, England)
CMJ	*Chinese Medical Journal* (Shanghai, China)
CMM-AMM	Casopis Moravskeho Musea v Brne. Acta Musei Moraviae (Brno, Czechoslovakia)

C-MNH-CM-SCE-D	Canada. Musee National de l'Homme. Collection Mercure. Service Canadien d'Ethnologie. Dossier (Ottawa, Canada)
CN	*Canadian Nurse* (Ottawa, Canada)
CNA	*China News Analysis* (Hong Kong)
CND	*Cahiers de Nutrition et de la Dietetique* (Paris, France)
CNHM-B	*Chicago Natural History Museum. Bulletin* (Chicago, Illinois)
C-NMM-CE-B	Canada. National Museum of Man. Contributions to Ethnology. Bulletin (Ottawa, Canada)
CNN	*Canadian Nutrition Notes* (Ottawa, Canada)
CNord	*Cahiers Nord-Africains* (Paris, France)
Collier's	*Collier's* (Springfield, Ohio)
ComCan	*Commerce Canada* (Ottawa, Canada)
ComInd	*Commerce and Industry* (Government Printer. Pretoria, South Africa)
CompAir	*Compressed Air Magazine* (Easton, Pennsylvania)
ConCong	*Conseiller Congolais* (Brussels, Belgium)
ConJ	*Contemporary Japan* (Tokyo, Japan)
ConMed	*Concours Medical* (Paris, France)
Cons	*Conservationist* (Madison, Wisconsin)
Consommation	*Consommation* (Paris, France)
Construire	*Construire* (Paris, France)
CoopMelk	*Cooperatieve Melkcentrale* (The Hague, Netherlands)
Cornhill	*Cornhill Magazine* (London, England)
Corriere Sanitario	*Corriere Sanitario* (Milan, Italy)
CorU-AES-B	Cornell University. Agricultural Experiment Station. Bulletin (Ithaca, New York)
CorU-BH	Cornell University. Bulletin for Homemakers (Ithaca, New York)
CorU-CRC-FHS	Cornell University. Cornell Reading Course. Farm House Series (Ithaca, New York)
CorU-CRC-RLS	Cornell University. Cornell Reading Course. Rural Life Series (Ithaca, New York)
CorU-HEMRR	Cornell University. Home Economics and Management Research Report (Ithaca, New York)
CorU-INMS	Cornell University. International Nutrition Monograph Series (Ithaca, New York)
CPAP	Colonial Plant and Animal Products (Colonial Products Laboratory. Colonial Products Advisory Bureau: Plant and Animal. London, England)
CPHJ	*Canadian Public Health Journal* (Toronto, Canada)
CPro	*Cooking for Profit* (Madison, Wisconsin)
CPS-BT	*Commission du Pacifique-Sud. Bulletin Trimestriel* (Noumea, New Caledonia)
CQPR-B	*Colegio del Quimicos de Puerto Rico. Boletin* (San Juan, Puerto Rico)
Craftsman	*Craftsman* (Eastwood, New York)
CRev	*Contemporary Review* (London, England)
C-RGCB-BSBEC	Congo. Revue Generale de la Colonie Belge et Bulletin de la Societe Belge d'Etudes Coloniales (Brussels, Belgium)
Critic	*Critic* (New York, New York)
C-RS-TP	Canada. Royal Society. Transactions and Proceedings (Ottawa, Canada)
CS	*Child Study* (New York, New York)
CSB	*Central States Bulletin* (Ann Arbor, Michigan)

CSB-J	*Cumann Seanchais Bhreifne. Journal* (Dublin, Irish Republic)
CSH-BL-SQB	Cold Spring Harbor. Biological Laboratory. Symposia on Quantitative Biology (Cold Spring Harbor, New York)
CSJ	*Cactus and Succulent Journal* (Pasadena, California)
CSJ-ABS	*Cactus and Succulent Journal. Amateur Bulletin Section* (Pasadena, California)
CSM	*Christian Science Monitor* (Boston, Massachusetts)
CSM-M	*Christian Science Monitor Magazine* (Boston, Massachusetts)
CSPB	Communications on the Science and Practice of Brewing (Wallerstein Laboratories, New York)
CSPSR	*Chinese Social and Political Science Review* (Peking, China)
CST	*Cereal Science Today* (St. Paul, Minnesota)
CSTM-B	*Calcutta School of Tropical Medicine. Bulletin* (Calcutta, India)
CTo	*Ceylon Today* (Colombo, Ceylon)
CTunisie	*Cahiers de Tunisie* (Tunis, Tunisia)
CU-CA	Columbia University. Contributions to Anthropology (New York, New York)
CurrLit	*Current Literature* (New York, New York)
CurSci	*Current Science* (Bangalore, India)
CU-SHEPL	Columbia University. Studies in History. Economics and Public Law (New York, New York)
CU-TCB-TEB	Columbia University. Teachers College Bulletin. Technical Education Bulletin (New York, New York)
CU-TCR	*Columbia University. Teachers College Record* (New York, New York)
CVen	*Cultura Venezolana* (Caracas, Venezuela)
CWAS-J	*Colorado-Wyoming Academy of Science. Journal* (Boulder, Colorado)
CypressMJ	*Cypress Medical Journal See:* Cyprus MJ
Cyprus MJ	*Cyprus Medical Journal* (Nicosia, Cyprus)
CZ	*Chemischer Zeitung* (Heidelberg, Germany)
CZen	*Chemiker Zentralblatt* (Berlin, Germany)
Daedalus	*Daedalus* (Boston, Massachusetts)
DAI	Dissertation Abstracts International (Ann Arbor, Michigan)
DAI-RGK-B	Deutsches Archaeologisches Institute. Romisch-Germanische Kommision. Berichte (Frankfurt am Main, Germany)
DAKM	*Deutsche Archiv fur Klinische Medicin* (Leipzig, Germany)
DalRev	*Dalhousie Review* (Halifax, Nova Scotia)
DAM-L	Denver Art Museum. Leaflet (Denver, Colorado)
DBG-B	Deutsche Botanische Gesellschaft. Berichte (Stuttgart, Germany)
DC	*Dental Cosmos* (Philadelphia, Pennsylvania)
DeriMuz	*A Deri Muzeum Evkonyve* (Debrecen, Hungary)
DesEc	*Desarrollo Economico* (New York, New York)
DGAEU-CB	*Deutschen Gesellschaft fur Anthropologie, Ethnologie und Urgeschichte. Correspondenz-Blatt* (Munich, Germany)
DGIM-V	*Deutschen Gesellschaft fur Innere Medizin. Verhandlungen* (Munich, Germany)
DGNVOT-M	*Deutschen Gesellschaft fur Natur-und Volkerkunde Ostasiens in Tokio. Mitheilungen* (Tokyo, Japan)
DGU	*Danmarks Geologiske Undersogelse* (Copenhagen, Denmark)
DHG	*Dietetic and Hygiene Gazette* (New York, New York)
DI	*See:* DISSSR
DietAdTher	*Dietary Administration and Therapy* (Cleveland, Ohio)
DifSoc	*Difesa Sociale* (Rome, Italy)
Diplomat	*Diplomat Magazine* (New York, New York)
Directions	*Directions* (Asheville, North Carolina)
DISSSR	*Dekorativnaya Iskusstvo Soyuz Sovietskykh Sosialistichiskikh Respublik* (Moscow, U.S.S.R.)
DJA	*Davidson Journal of Anthropology* (Seattle, Washington)
DJV	*Deutsches Jahrbuch fur Volkskunde* (Berlin, Germany)
DLG-M	*Deutsche Landwirtschaftsgesellschaft Mitteilungen* (Berlin, Germany)
DLR	*Deutsche Lebensmittel-Rundschau* (Stuttgart, Germany)
DM	*Desert Magazine* (El Centro, California)
DMus-B	Dominion Museum. Bulletin (Wellington, New Zealand)
DMW	*Deutsche Medizinische Wochenschrift* (Leipzig, Germany)
DMZ	*Deutsche Monatsschrift fur Zahnheilkunde* (Berlin, Germany)
DN	*Dialect Notes* (New Haven, Connecticut)
DNIMT	*Documenta Neerlandica et Indonesica Morbis Tropicis* (Amsterdam, Netherlands)
DNS	*Diseases of the Nervous System* (New York, New York)
DQJMS	*Dublin Quarterly Journal of Medical Science* (Dublin, Irish Republic)
DVNI-M	*Dienst der Volksgezondheid in Nederlandsch-Indie. Mededeelingen* (Batavia, Java)
DZA	*Dietschland Zuid-Afrika* (Steenbrugge, Belgium)
EAAJ	*East African Agricultural Journal* (Nairobi, Kenya)
EAlm	*Estudos Almeidas* (Rio de Janeiro, Brazil)
EAMJ	*East African Medical Journal* (Nairobi, Kenya)
EAnth	*Eastern Anthropologist* (Lucknow, India)
EA-ES	*English Association. Essays and Studies* (London, England)
EAP-R	*Ecole d'Anthropologie de Paris. Revue* (Paris, France)
E-AZ	*Ethnographisch-Archaologische Zeitschrift* (Berlin, Germany)
EB	*Economic Botany* (Lancaster, Pennsylvania)
EBJahr	Engler Botanische Jahrbucher (Leipzig, Germany)
ECN	*Estudios de Cultura Nahuatl* (Mexico City, Mexico)
Ecology	*Ecology* (Silver Spring, Maryland)
EColonias	*Estudos Colonias* (Lisbon, Portugal)
EDCC	*Economic Development and Cultural Change* (Chicago, Illinois)
Edoth	*Edoth* (Jerusalem, Israel)

EE	*Economia y Estadistica* (Bogota, Colombia)
EEI	*Eveil Economique de l'Indochine* (Hanoi, French Indo-China. Imprimerie Tonkinois)
EFN	*Ecology of Food and Nutrition* (London, England)
EFolk	*Etnologia y Folklore* (Havana, Cuba)
EG	*Economic Geography* (Worcester, Massachusetts)
EGJ	*Ethiopian Geographical Journal* (Addis Ababa, Ethiopia)
EHR	*Edinburgh Hospital Reports* (Edinburgh, Scotland)
EInt	*Economia Internazionle* (Genoa, Italy)
EJ	Explorers Journal (New York, New York)
ElPal	*El Palacio* (Santa Fe, New Mexico)
EMA-J	*Egyptian Medical Association. Journal* (Cairo, Egypt)
EMed	*Europe Medicale* (Paris, France)
EMEVEK	*Erdelyi Muzeum Egyesulet Vandorgyuleseinek Emlekkonyve Kolozsvar* (Kolozsvar, Hungary)
EMOM	*Encyclopedie Mensuelle d'Outre-Mer* (Paris, France)
Empire	*Empire Review* (London, England)
EMS	*Experimental Medicine and Surgery* (Brooklyn, New York)
EMSJ	*Edinburgh Medical and Scientific Journal* (Edinburgh, Scotland)
EMT	*Enfant en Milieu Tropical* (Dakar, Senegal)
EMVW	*Enquetes du Musee de la Vie Wallonne* (Liege, Belgium)
Endeavor	*Endeavor* (London, England)
EntB	*Entomologische Berichten* (Haarlem, Netherlands)
EntN	*Entomological News* (Philadelphia, Pennsylvania)
Entomologist	*Entomologist* (London, England)
Environment	*Environment* (St. Louis, Missouri)
EO	*Etnograficeskoe Obozrenie* (Moscow, U.S.S.R.)
EO-M	*Etudes d'Outre-Mer* (Marseilles, France)
EPHA-J	*Egyptian Public Health Association. Journal* (Cairo, Egypt)
Epicure	*Epicure* (London, England)
EPol	*Etnografia Polska* (Wroclaw, Poland)
EPreg	*Etnoloski Pregled* (Beograd, Yugoslavia)
Equilibre	*Equilibre* (Paris, France)
ER	*Evergreen Review* (New York, New York)
Erdball	*Erdball* (Berlin-Lichterfelde, Germany)
Erdely	*Erdely Muzeum* (Kolzsvar, Hungary)
ERev	*Ecclesiastical Review* (Philadelphia, Pennsylvania)
Ernahr	*Ernahrungsforschung* (Potsdam-Rehbrucke, East Germany)
ERur	*Etudes Rurales* (Paris, France)
ESA-B	*Entomological Society of America. Bulletin* (Columbus, Ohio)
E-SAnt-A	*Egypte. Service des Antiquites. Annales* (Cairo, Egypt)
EScan	Ethnologia Scandinavica (Lund, Sweden)
ESL-T	*Ethnological Society of London. Transactions* (London, England)
ESO-AR	Entomological Society of Ontario. Annual Report (Toronto, Canada)

ESoc	*Economies et Societes* (Paris, France)
EStud	*Ethnologische Studien* (Leipzig, Germany)
Estudio	*Estudio* (Bucaramanga, Colombia)
Estudos	*Estudos Afro-Brasileiros* (Rio de Janeiro, Brazil)
ESW-B	Entomological Society of Washington. Bulletin (Washington, D.C.)
ESW-P	Entomological Society of Washington. Proceedings (Washington, D.C.)
Etc.	*Etc. A Review of General Semantics* (Chicago, Illinois)
Ethnografia	*Ethnografia* (Budapest, Hungary)
Ethnographie	*Ethnographie* (Paris, France)
Ethnology	*Ethnology* (Pittsburgh, Pennsylvania)
Ethnomedizin	*Ethnomedizin* (Hamburg, Germany)
Ethnopsychologie	*Ethnopsychologie* (Le Havre, France)
Ethnos	*Ethnos* (Stockholm, Sweden)
Etnoiatria	*Etnoiatria* (Naples, Italy)
Etnolog	*Etnolog* (Ljubljana, Yugoslavia)
EU	*Ernaehrungs Umschau* (Frankfort am Main, Germany)
Euphytica	*Euphytica* (Wageningen, Netherlands)
Experientia	*Experientia* (Basle, Switzerland)
F-A	*France-Asie* (Saigon, French Indo-China)
F-AES-B	*Florida. Agricultural Experiment Station. Bulletin* (Gainesville, Florida)
FAnth	*Florida Anthropologist* (Gainesville, Florida)
FAOReview	*Food and Agriculture Organization of the United Nations Review* (Rome, Italy)
Farol	*El Farol* (Caracas, Venezuela)
FASEB-FP	*Federated American Societies for Experimental Biology. Federation Proceedings* (Washington, D.C.)
Fataburen	*Fataburen* (Stockholm, Sweden)
Fauna	*Fauna* (Sao Paulo, Brazil)
FB	*Farm Bulletin* (Indian Council of Agricultural Research. New Delhi, India)
FC	*Food in Canada* (Toronto, Canada)
FCI	*Folia Clinica Internacional* (Barcelona, Spain)
FCIAFAD-AR	Food and Container Institute for the Armed Forces Acceptance Division. Activities Report (Chicago, Illinois)
F-DA-AJ	*Fiji. Department of Agriculture. Agricultural Journal* (Suva, Fiji)
FE	*Food Engineering* (New York, New York)
FFH	*Freedom from Hunger* (FAO; Rome, Italy)
FFHCN	*Freedom from Hunger Campaign News* (FAO; New York)
FI	*Food Industries* (New York, New York)
Field-Anth	Fieldiana: Anthropology. (Chicago Museum of Natural History. Chicago, Illinois)
Figaro	*Figaro* (Paris, France)
FISA	*Food Industries of South Africa* (Cape Town, South Africa)
FL	*Field and Laboratory* (Southern Methodist University, Dallas, Texas)
FLH	*Finska Lakavesallskapets Handlingar* (Helsinki, Finland)
FMA-J	*Formosan Medical Association. Journal* (Taipei, Taiwan)
FMan	*Food Manufacture* (London, England)
FMed	*Folia Medica* (Naples, Italy)

FMNH-AL	Field Museum of Natural History. Anthropology Leaflets (Chicago, Illinois)		*Laboratorium voor de Praktijk* (Haarlem, Netherlands)
FMNH-P-AS	Field Museum of Natural History. Publications. Anthropological Series (Chicago, Illinois)	GB-MA-J	*Great Britain. Ministry of Agriculture. Journal* (London, England)
FMSM-J	*Federated Malay States' Museum. Journal* (Kuala Lumpur, Malaya)	GB-MOD-ORP	Great Britain. Ministry of Overseas Development. Overseas Research Publication (London, England)
FMVT-A	*Facolta di Medicina Veterinaria di Torino. Annali* (Turin, Italy)	GB-PC-MRC-SRS	Great Britain. Privy Council. Medical Research Council. Special Report Series (London, England)
FN	*Food and Nutrition* (United States Department of Agriculture. Food and Nutrition Service. Washington, D.C.)	GB-PP	Great Britain. Parliamentary Papers (London, England)
FNNR	*Food and Nutrition Notes and Reviews* (Canberra, Australia)	GB-RBGK-BMI	*Great Britain. Royal Botanical Garden at Kew. Bulletin of Miscellaneous Information* (Kew, England)
Folk	*Folk* (Copenhagen, Denmark)		
Folkeminder	*Folkeminder* (Copenhagen, Denmark)	GB-RBGK-BMI-AS	*Great Britain. Royal Botanical Garden at Kew. Bulletin of Miscellaneous Information. Additional Series* (Kew, England)
Folklife	*Folklife* (Cardiff, Wales)		
Folk-liv	*Folk-liv* (Stockholm, Sweden)		
Folk Lore (C)	*Folk Lore* (Calcutta, India)	GB-RBGK-KB	*Great Britain. Royal Botanical Garden at Kew. Kew Bulletin* (Kew, England)
Folk-Lore (L)	*Folk-Lore* (London, England)		
FO-M	*Fruits d'Outre-Mer* (Paris, France)	GB-RSA-J	*Great Britain. Royal Society of Arts. Journal* (London, England)
ForAg	*Foreign Agriculture* (United States Department of Agriculture, Washington, D.C.)	GBull	*Garden's Bulletin* (Singapore, Malaya)
Fornvardaren	*Fornvardaren* (Ostersund, Sweden)	GBVI	*Giornale di Batteriologia, Virologia ed Immunologia* (Turin, Italy)
FortMed	*Fortschritte der Medizin* (Berlin, Germany)	GCAG	*Gardeners Chronicle and Agricultural Gazette* (London, England)
FP	*Folia Primatologica* (Basel, Switzerland)		
FPF	*Forschung Praxis Fortbildung* (Berlin, Germany)	GC-DA-B	*Gold Coast. Department of Agriculture. Bulletin* (Accra, Gold Coast/Ghana)
FPQ	*Food Preservation Quarterly* (Sydney, Australia)	GC-DA-N	*Gold Coast. Department of Agriculture. Newsletter* (Accra, Gold Coast/Ghana)
FQ	*Farm Quarterly* (Cincinnati, Ohio)	GeoMed	*Geographia Medica* (Budapest, Hungary)
FR	*Food Research* (Champaign, Illinois)	Geriatrics	*Geriatrics* (Minneapolis, Minnesota)
Friend, The	*The Friend* (Honolulu, Hawaii)	Gerontologia	*Gerontologia* (Basel, Switzerland)
FS	*Food Science* (Mysore, India)	GGBB-J	*Gesellschaft fur die Geschichte und Bibliographie des Brauwesens Jahrbuch* (Berlin, Germany)
FSA	*Farming in South Africa* (Pretoria, South Africa)		
FSAC	Folia Scientifica Africae Centralis (Bukavu/Costermansville, Belgian Congo)	GGD	*Glasnik Geografskog Drustva* (Beograd, Yugoslavia)
FSSI-TP	Fiji Society of Science and Industry. Transactions and Proceedings (Suva, Fiji)	GH	*Good Health* (Battle Creek, Michigan)
FS-TP	*Fiji Society. Transactions and Proceedings* (Suva, Fiji)	GIETH-B	*Geobatanischen Institut der Eidgenossische Technische Hochschule. Berichte* (Zurich, Switzerland)
FTA	*Food Technology in Australia* (Sydney, Australia)	GimKras	*Gimtasis Krastas* (Vilna, Lithuania)
FTech	*Food Technology* (Chicago, Illinois)	GK	Gastronomisk Kalender (Stockholm, Sweden)
FTop	*Food Topics* (New York, New York)	Globus	*Globus* (Braunschweig, Germany)
FU-FS-B	*Fuad University. Faculty of Science. Bulletin* (Cairo, Egypt)	GLS-J	*Gypsy Lore Society. Journal* (London, England)
FW	*Farmer's Work* (Bloemfontein, South Africa)	GMB	*Gardeners Magazine of Botany* (London)
GA	*Gazeta do Agricultor* (Lourenco Marques, Mozambique)	Gourmet	*Gourmet* (New York, New York)
		GPM	*Genetic Psychology Monographs* (Worcester, Massachusetts)
GAA	*Gazeta Agricola de Angola* (Lisbon, Portugal)	GR	*Geographical Review* (New York, New York)
G-AES-B	Georgia. Agricultural Experiment Station. Bulletin (Athens, Georgia)	Grandgousier	*Revue de Gastronomie Medicale* (Paris, France)
Gard Chron	*Gardeners' Chronicle* (London, England)	Grands Lac	*Grands Lac* (Namur, Belgium)
Gastroenterology	*Gastroenterology* (Baltimore, Maryland)	GRI	*Geographical Review of India* (Calcutta, India)
Gastronomo, Il	*Il Gastronomo* (Milan, Italy)	GRS-B	*Gujarat Research Society. Bulletin* (Bombay, India)
GB-CO-CRS	Great Britain. Colonial Office. Colonial Research Studies (London, England)	GRS-J	*Gujarat Research Society. Journal* (Bombay, India)
GB-II-B	*Great Britain. Imperial Institute. Bulletin* (London, England)	GSan	*Gazzeta Sanitaria* (Milan, Italy)
GBKLP	*Geneeskundige Bladen uit Kliniek en*	GSC-B	*Geological Society of China. Bulletin* (Peking, China)

GSND	*Glasnik Skopskog Naucnog Drustva* (Skopje, Yugoslavia)
GTNI	*Geneeskundig Tijdschrift voor Nederlandsch-Indie* (Batavia, Java)
GVES-B	*Gesellschaft fur Volker und Erdkunde zu Stettin. Bericht* (Stettin, Germany)
GV-M	*Gesellschaft fur Volkerkunde. Mitteilungen* (Leipzig, Germany)
G-VSL	*Gradina. Via Si Livada* (Bucarest, Romania)
Gwerin	*Gwerin* (Oxford, England)
HAd	*Honolulu Advertiser* (Honolulu, Hawaii)
Hai-BE-B	Haiti. Bureau d'Ethnologie. Bulletin (Port au Prince, Haiti)
Hai-SNHAPS-B	*Haiti. Service National d'Hygiene et d'Assistance Publique et Sanitaire. Bulletin* (Port au Prince, Haiti)
Harefuah	*Harefuah* (Tel Aviv, Israel)
Harper's	*Harper's Magazine* (New York, New York)
HAS	*Harvard African Studies* (Cambridge, Massachusetts)
HawPlant	*Hawaiian Planter Record* (Honolulu, Hawaii)
HB	*Human Biology* (Baltimore, Maryland)
HBild	*Historiska Bilder* (Stockholm, Sweden)
HBV	*Hessische Blatter fur Volkskunde* (Leipzig, Germany)
HCNews	*Hotel and Club News. See:* Hotel Voice
HCQ	*Hospital Corps Quarterly* (Washington, D.C.)
HD	*Hoard's Dairyman* (Fort Atkinson, Wisconsin)
HE	*Home Economics* (Manila, Philippines)
Health	*Health* (Wellington, N.Z.)
HEcol	*Human Ecology* (New York, New York)
Heimatland	*Heimatland* (Hannover, Germany)
Heimatleben	*Heimatleben* (Zurich, Switzerland)
HEJ	*Health Education Journal* (London, England)
Herbarist	*Herbarist* (Boston, Massachusetts)
Hereditas	*Hereditas* (Lund, Sweden)
HFHMB	*Henry Ford Hospital Medical Bulletin* (Detroit, Michigan)
HH	*Harofe Haivri [Hebrew Medical Journal]* (New York)
Hi-AES-AR	Hawaii Agriculture Experiment Station. Annual Report (Honolulu, Hawaii)
Hi-AES-B	Hawaii. Agricultural Experiment Station. Bulletin (Honolulu, Hawaii)
Hi-AES-MP	University of Hawaii. Agricultural Experiment Station. Miscellaneous Paper (Honolulu, Hawaii)
Hi-AES-TB	University of Hawaii. Agricultural Experiment Station. Technical Bulletin (Honolulu, Hawaii)
HiFS	*Hawaii Farm Science* (Hawaii Agricultural Experiment Station. Honolulu, Hawaii)
Hilgardia	*Hilgardia* (Berkeley, California)
HInd	*Hotel Industry* (Mt. Morris, New York)
Hippokrates	*Hippokrates* (Stuttgart, Germany)
Hispania	*Hispania* (Madrid, Spain)
Historia	*Historia* (Paris, France)
HJAS	*Harvard Journal of Asiatic Studies* (Cambridge, Massachusetts)
HJBKM	*Hooker's Journal of Botany and Kew Miscellany* (London, England)
HJH	*Hawaiian Journal of History* (Honolulu, Hawaii)

HJSL	*Historisches Jahrbuch der Stadt Linz* (Linz, Austria)
HKG	*Heimatjahrbuch des Kreises* (Gelnhausen, Germany)
HKN	*Hong Kong Naturalist* (Hong Kong)
HMD	*Hommes et Migrations Documents* (Paris, France)
HMedJ	*Hawaii Medical Journal* (Honolulu, Hawaii)
HMM	*Harper's Monthly Magazine* (New York, New York)
Homme, L'	*L'Homme* (Paris, France)
Hospitals	*Hospitals* (Chicago, Illinois)
Hotel Voice	*Hotel Voice* (Publication of Hotel, Motel and Club Employees Union, Local 6. New York, New York)
HPBCA	*Human Problems in British Central Africa* (Lusaka, Zambia)
HPR	*Hawaiian Planters' Record* (Honolulu, Hawaii)
HR	*Human Relations* (Cambridge, Massachusetts)
HRNews	*Hotel and Restaurant News* (Boston, Massachusetts)
HS	*Hindusthan Standard* (Calcutta, India)
HS-B	*Honolulu Star-Bulletin* (Honolulu, Hawaii)
HSLC-T	Historic Society of Lancashire and Cheshire. Transactions (Liverpool, England)
HSpec	*Hamilton Spectator* (Hamilton, Ontario, Canada)
HSS	*Hospital Social Service* (New York, New York)
HSZPC	*Hoppe-Seyler's Zeitschrift fur Physiologische Chemie* (Strasbourg, France)
HU-BI-B	*Harvard University. Bussey Institution. Bulletin* (Jamaica Plain, Massachusetts)
HU-BM-L	Harvard University. Botanical Museum. Leaflets (Cambridge, Massachusetts)
HU-CLCBFH	Harvard University. Contribution from the Laboratories of Cryptogamic Botany and the Farlow Herbarium (Cambridge, Massachusetts)
HU-PMAAE-P	Harvard University. Peabody Museum of American Archaeology and Ethnology. Papers (Cambridge, Massachusetts)
HW	*Harper's Weekly* (New York, New York)
Hygeia	*Hygeia* (Chicago, Illinois)
HZ	*Hemera Zoa* (Bogor, Indonesia)
IAAI-RMAC	*Istituto Agronomico per l'Africa Italiana. Relazionie Monografie Agrario-Coloniale* (Florence, Italy)
Ia-AS-J	*Iowa. Archaeological Society. Journal* (McGregor, Iowa)
I-AC	*Indo-Asian Culture* (New Delhi, India)
IAC-EB	Idaho Agricultural College. Extension Bulletin (Moscow, Idaho)
IAE	*Internationales Archiv fur Ethnologie* (Leyden, Netherlands)
IAEP-P	Instituto de Antropologia et Etnologia do Para. Publicacoes. (Museo Paraense Emilio Goeldi. Belem-Para, Brazil)
I-AES-B	Iowa. Agricultural Experiment Station. Bulletin (Ames, Iowa)
IAg	*L'Italia Agricola* (Milan, Italy)
I-AS-B	India. Anthropological Survey. Bulletin (Calcutta, India)

IAS-P	Indiana Academy of Science. Proceedings (Indianapolis, Indiana)	IJAL	*International Journal of American Linguistics* (Bloomington, Indiana)
IB-B	*See:* HU-BI-B	IJAS	*Indian Journal of Agricultural Sciences* (Calcutta, India)
IBECC-CNF-CEFRGS-P	Instituto Brasileiro de Educacao Ciencia e Cultura. Comissao Nacional de Folclore. Comissao Estadual de Folclore do Rio Grande do Sul. Publicacao (Porto Alegre, Brazil)	IJDS	*Indian Journal of Dairy Science* (Bangalore, India)
		IJGPB	*Indian Journal of Genetics and Plant Breeding* (New Delhi, India)
IBG-TP	Institute of British Geographers. Transactions and Proceedings (London, England)	IJHE	*International Journal of Health Education* (Geneva, Switzerland)
Ibis	*Ibis* (London, England)	IJHM	*Indian Journal of the History of Medicine* (Madras, India)
IBPTESV	*Internationale Beitrage zur Pathologie und Therapie der Ernahrungsstorungen, Stoffwechsel und Verdauungskrankheiten* (Berlin, Germany)	IJMR	*Indian Journal of Medical Research* (Calcutta, India)
		IJMS	*Israel Journal of Medical Sciences* (Jerusalem, Israel)
I-BSA-AR	India. Board of Scientific Advice. Annual Report (New Delhi, India)	IJND	*Indian Journal of Nutrition and Dietetics* (Coimbatore, India)
ICJ	*Indian Coconut Journal* (Ernakulam, India)	IJNPS-B	*Instituto Joaquim Nabuco de Pesquisas Sociais. Boletim* (Recife, Brazil)
ICMR-SRS	Indian Council of Medical Research. Special Report Series (Cawnpore, India)		
ICR	*Ice Cream Review* (Milwaukee, Wisconsin)	IJOrth	*International Journal of Orthodontia* (St. Louis, Missouri)
ICUAER-B	International Committee on Urgent Anthropological and Ethnological Research. Bulletin (Vienna, Austria)	IJPed	*Indian Journal of Pediatrics* (Calcutta, India)
		IJSPsych	*International Journal of Social Psychiatry* (London, England)
ID	*Indian Dairyman* (Bangalore, India)	IJSW	*Indian Journal of Social Work* (Bombay, India)
I-DA-B	India. Department of Anthropology. Bulletin. (Calcutta, India)		
IDSUS-C	Institute of Development Studies at the University of Sussex. Communications (Brighton, England)	IL-A	Instituto de Linguistica. Anales (Mendoza, Argentina)
		IllAm	*Illustrated American* (New York, New York)
IE-B	*Institut de l'Egypte. Bulletin* (Cairo, Egypt)	ILN	*Illustrated London News* (London, England)
IEC-B	*Institut des Etudes Centrafricaine. Bulletin* (Brazzaville, Congo-Brazzaville)	IMAJ	*Indian Medical Association Journal* (Calcutta, India)
IEF-A	*Instituto de Estudios Africanos. Anales* (Madrid, Spain)	Imago	*Imago* (Leipzig, Germany)
IEO-A	Institut de l'Extreme Orient. Annales.	IMed	*Imprensa Medica* (Rio de Janeiro, Brazil)
IF	*Indian Forester* (Dehra Dun, India)	I-MFG-FIU-DE-B	*India. Ministry of Food and Agriculture. Farm Information Unit. Directorate of Extension. Bulletin* (New Delhi, India)
IFAN-B	*Institut Francais de l'Afrique Noire. Bulletin* (Dakar, Senegal)		
IFAO-B	*Institut Francais d'Archeologie Orientale. Bulletin* (Cairo, Egypt)	IMG	*Indian Medical Gazette* (Calcutta, India)
IFarm	*Indian Farming* (New Delhi, India)	IMig	*International Migration* (Geneva, Switzerland)
IF-B	*Instituto de Folklore. Boletin* (Caracas, Venezuela)	IMT-A	Instituto de Medicina Tropical. Anais (Lisbon, Portugal)
IFC	*Industry of Free China* (Taipei, Taiwan)	IN	*Indian Notes* (New York, New York)
IFT-P	*Institute of Food Technologists. Proceedings* (Champaign, Illinois)	INAH-A	Instituto Nacional de Antropologia e Historia. Anales (Mexico City, Mexico)
IH	Information Historiques (Paris, B. Bailliere)	INAH-DIA-P	Instituto Nacional de Antropologia e Historia. Departamento de Investigaciones Antropologicas. Publicacion (Mexico City, Mexico)
IHPET-T	*Institut d'Hygiene Publique de l'Etat Tchecoslovaque. Travaux* (Prague, Czechoslovakia)		
IHQ	*Indian Historical Quarterly* (Calcutta, India)	Independent	*Independent* (New York, New York)
I-I	*Indo-Iranica* (Calcutta, India)	Indica	*De Re Indica* (Caracas, Venezuela)
IIALC-M	International Institute of African Languages and Cultures. Memorandum (London, England)	Indoors	*Indoors* (London, England)
		IndustMed	*Industrial Medicine* (Beloit, Wisconsin)
		INI	*Ingenieur in Nederlandsch Indie* (Bandung, Indonesia)
IIAPI-B	*Instituto Internacional Americano de Proteccion a la Infancia. Boletin* (Montevideo, Uruguay)	INIA-B	*Instituto Nacional de Investigaciones Agronomicas. Boletin* (Madrid, Spain)
		INIF-C	Instituto Nacional de Investigaciones Folkloricas. Cuadernos (Buenos Aires, Argentina)
IIEH-BT	*Institut Indochinois pour l'Etude de l'Homme. Bulletin et Travaux* (Hanoi, French Indo-China)		
		INM	Indian Notes and Monographs (New York, New York)
IIN-B	*Instituto Interamericano del Nino. Boletin* (Montevideo, Uruguay)	Inplant	*Inplant Food Management* (Pontiac, Illinois)

InPro	*Investigacion y Progresso* (Madrid, Spain)
InSoc	*Informacao Social* (Lisbon, Portugal)
Institutions	*Institutions* (Chicago, Illinois)
Internist	*Internist* (Berlin, Germany)
INT-R	*Instituto Nacional de la Tradicion. Revista* (Buenos Aires, Argentina)
IO	*Inter Ocean* (Batavia, Java)
IPA-A	Institut Pasteur d'Algerie. Archives (Algiers, Algeria)
IP-A	*Institut Pasteur. Annales* (Paris, France)
IPAOF-R	Institut Pasteur de l'Afrique Occidentale Francaise. Rapport (Dakar, Senegal)
IPFC-RS	Indo-Pacific Fisheries Council. Regional Studies (Food and Agriculture Organization of the United Nations. Bangkok, Thailand)
IPGTI-A-P	Institut Pasteur de la Guyane et du Territoire de l'Inini. Archives. Publication (Cayenne, French Guiana)
IPI-A	*Institut Pasteur de l'Indochine. Archives* (Hanoi, French Indo-China)
IPT-A	*Institut Pasteur de Tunis. Archives* (Tunis, Tunisia)
IRA	*International Review of Agriculture* (International Institute of Agriculture. Rome, Italy)
IRCB-ARSC-SSNM-M	Institute Royale Colonial Belge. Academie Royale des Sciences Coloniales. Section des Sciences Naturelles et Medicales. Memoirs (Collection in 8°. Brussels, Belgium)
IRCB-B	Institut Royale Coloniale Belge. Bulletin (Brussels, Belgium)
IRES-B	Institut de Recherches Economiques et Sociales. Bulletin (Louvain, Belgium)
IRMGPC	*International Record of Medicine and General Practice Clinics* (New York, New York)
IRS-T	Institut de Recherches Sahariennes. Travaux (Algiers, Algeria)
IS	*Indian Sentinel* (Bureau of Catholic Indian Missions. Washington, D.C.)
ISA-A	Istituto Sperimentale Agronomico. Annali (Bari, Italy)
IRSAC-C	Institut pour la Recherche Scientifique en Afrique Centrale. Chroniques (Bukavu, Belgian Congo/Zaire)
ISCA-P	Indian Science Congress Association. Proceedings (Calcutta, India)
ISCJS	*Iowa State College Journal of Science* (Ames, Iowa)
ISET-R	*Instituto de Salubridad y Enfermedades Tropicales. Revista* (Mexico City, Mexico)
Isis	*Isis* (History of Science Society. Smithsonian Institution. Washington, D.C.)
IslenForn	Islenzka Fornleifafelag. Arbok (Reykjavik, Iceland)
IUO-A	Instituto Universitario Orientale. Annali (Naples, Italy)
I-UP-AB	India. United Provinces of Agra and Oudh. Agricultural Bulletin (Allahabad, India)
IVita	*Igiene e la Vita* (Turin, Italy)
IWel	*Ireland of the Welcomes* (Dublin, Republic of Ireland)
IZV	*Internationale Zeitschrift fur Vitaminforschung* (Berlin, Germany)
JADA	*Journal of the American Dietetic Association* (Chicago, Illinois)
JADentA	*Journal of the American Dental Association* (Chicago, Illinois)
JAF	*Journal of American Folklore* (Bloomington, Indiana)
JAFC	*Journal of Agricultural and Food Chemistry* (Easton, Pennsylvania)
JAgEcon	*Journal of Agricultural Economics* (Reading, England)
JAH	*Journal of African History* (London, England)
JAIE	*Journal of American Indian Education* (Tempe, Arizona)
JAMA	*Journal of the American Medical Association* (Chicago, Illinois)
JAN	*Journal of Applied Nutrition* (La Habra, California)
JAnthRes	*Journal of Anthropological Research* (Albuquerque, New Mexico)
Janus	*Janus* (Leiden, Netherlands)
JAP	*Journal des Americanistes de Paris* (Paris, France)
JAppPhys	*Journal of Applied Physiology* (Washington, D.C.)
JAPrat	*Journal d'Agriculture Pratique* (Paris, France)
JAPsych	*Journal of Applied Psychology* (Worcester, Massachusetts)
JAR	*Journal of Agricultural Research* (Washington, D.C.)
JArizH	*Journal of Arizona History* (Tucson, Arizona)
JASP	*Journal of Abnormal and Social Psychology* (Albany, New York)
JATBA	*Journal d'Agriculture Tropicale et de Botanique Applique* (Paris, France)
JATrop	*Journal d'Agriculture Tropicale* (Paris, France)
JBact	*Journal of Bacteriology* (Baltimore, Maryland)
JBC	*Journal of Biological Chemistry* (Baltimore, Maryland)
JBot	*Journal de Botanique* (Paris, France)
JCEd	*Journal of Chemical Education* (Easton, Pennsylvania)
JConch	*Journal of Conchology* (Manchester, Leeds, England)
JConP	*Journal of Consulting Psychology* (Lancaster, Pennsylvania)
JCPP	*Journal of Comparative and Physiological Psychology* (Baltimore, Maryland)
JCS	*Journal of the Chemical Society* (London, England)
JDAM	Jahrbucher fur die Deutsche Armee und Marine (Berlin, Germany)
JDev	*Journal of Developmental Studies* (London, England)
JDR	*Journal of Dental Research* (New York, New York)
JDS	*Journal of Dairy Science* (Baltimore, Maryland)
JEA	*Journal of Egyptian Archaeology* (London, England)
JEAS	*Journal of East Asiatic Studies* (Manila, Philippines)
JEE	*Journal of Economic Entomology* (Menasha, Wisconsin)
JEGP	*Journal of English and German Philogy* (Urbana, Illinois)

JEP	*Journal of Experimental Psychology* (Princeton, New Jersey)
JESHO	*Journal of the Economic and Social History of the Orient* (London, England)
JESoc	*Journal of Educational Sociology* (New York, New York)
Jez-mis	*Jezuiten-missies* (Anderlecht, Belgium)
JFE	*Journal of Farm Economics* (Lafayette, Indiana)
JFS	*Journal of Food Science* (Champaign, Illinois)
JG	*Journal of Gerontology* (Springfield, Illinois)
JGeog	*Journal of Geography* (Lancaster, Pennsylvania)
JH	*Journal of Hygiene* (Cambridge, England)
JHE	*Journal of Home Economics* (Washington, D.C.)
JHer	*Journal of Heredity* (Washington, D.C.)
JHH-B	*Johns Hopkins Hospital. Bulletin* (Baltimore, Maryland)
JHM	*Journal of the History of Medicine and Allied Sciences* (New York, New York)
JHN	*Journal of Human Nutrition* (London, England)
JHRel	*Journal of Human Relations* (Wilberforce, Ohio)
JHSB	*Journal of Health and Social Behavior* (Fort Worth, Texas)
JHUSHPS	*Johns Hopkins University Studies in Historical and Political Science* (Baltimore, Maryland)
JIB	*Journal of the Institute of Brewing* (London, England)
JIH	*Journal of Indian History* (London, England)
JIMA	*Journal of the Indian Medical Association* (Calcutta, India)
JIR	*Journal of Irreproducible Results* (Chicago, Illinois)
JJN	*Japanese Journal of Nutrition* [Eiyo-gaku zasshi] (Tokyo, Japan)
JKind	*Jahrbuch fur Kinderheilkunde* (Berlin, Germany)
JLan	*The Journal Lancet* (Minneapolis, Minnesota)
JLM	*Journal de Lux et des Modes* (Paris, France)
JLS(B)	*Journal of the Linnean Society (Botany)* (London, England)
JMBA	*Journal of the Marine Biological Association of India* (Mandapam Camp, India)
JMF	*Journal of Marriage and the Family* (Minneapolis, Minnesota)
JMFT	*Journal of Milk and Food Technology* (Albany, New York)
JN	*Journal of Nutrition* (Springfield, Illinois)
JNE	*Journal of Nutrition Education* (Berkeley, California)
JNE-S	*Journal of Nutrition Education. Supplement* (Berkeley, California)
JNegro	*Journal of Negro Education* (Washington, D.C.)
JNES	*Journal of Near Eastern Studies* (Chicago, Illinois)
JO	*Journal of Orthopsychiatry. See:* AJO
JOMed	*Journal of Occupational Medicine* (Chicago, Illinois)
JPChim	*Journal de Pharmacologie et de Chimie* (Paris, France)
JPE	*See:* JPolEcon
JPed	*Journal of Pediatrics* (St. Louis, Missouri)
JPGA-M	*Justus Perthes Geographischer Anhalt. Mittheilungen* (Gotha, Germany)
JPolEcon	*Journal of Political Economy* (Chicago, Illinois)
JPS	*Journal of the Polynesian Society* (Wellington, New Zealand)
JPS-M	*See:* PS-M
JPSP	*Journal of Personality and Social Psychology* (Durham, North Carolina)
JQR	*Jewish Quarterly Review* (London, England)
JSciM	*Journal des Sciences Militaires* (Paris, France)
JSFA	*Journal of the Science of Food and Agriculture* (London, England)
JSH	*Journal of Southern History* (Baton Rouge, Louisiana)
JSIR	*Journal of Scientific and Industrial Research* (New Delhi, India)
JSMed	*Journal of State Medicine* (London, England). *See also:* RIPHH-J
JSO	*Journal de la Societe des Oceanistes* (Paris, France)
JSP	*Journal of Social Psychology* (Worcester, Massachusetts)
J-SRC-IB	Jamaica. Scientific Research Council. Bulletin (Kingston, Jamaica)
JSS	*Journal of the Siam Society* (Bangkok, Thailand)
JT	*Journal of Tibetology* (Sikkim, India)
JTB	*Journal of Theoretical Biology* (London, England)
JTG	*Journal of Tropical Geography* (Singapore, Malaya)
JTM	*Journal of Tropical Medicine* (London, England)
JTMH	*Journal of Tropical Medicine and Hygiene* (London, England)
JTPECH	*Journal of Tropical Pediatrics and Environmental Child Health* (London, England)
JTPECH-M	Journal of Tropical Pediatrics and Environmental Child Health. Memoirs (London, England)
JTS	*Journal of Texture Studies* (Dordrecht, Netherlands)
JVATM	*Journal des Voyages et des Aventures de Terre et de Mer* (Paris, France)
JWest	*Journal of the West* (Los Angeles, California)
JZ	*Jinruigaku Zasshi* (Tokyo, Japan)
Kaogu	*Kaogu* (Peking, China)
KAS-P	Kroeber Anthropological Society. Proceedings (Berkeley, California)
KAWA-VGVW N-A	Koninklijke Akademie van Wetenschappen te Amsterdam. Verslagen van de Gewone Vergaderingen der Wis-en Natuurkundige. Afdeeling (Amsterdam, Netherlands)
KAWW-PHK-S	Koniglich Akademie der Wissenschaften in Wien. Philosophisch und Historisch Klasse. Sitzungsberichte (Vienna, Austria)
KBGMB-D-N	Koniglich Botanische Gartens und Museums zu Berlin-Dahlem. Notizblatt (Berlin, Germany)

KDVS-AKM	Kongelige Danske Videnskabernes Selskab. Archaeologisk, Kunsthistoriske Meddedelser (Copenhagen, Denmark)
KDVS-HFM	Kongelige Danske Videnskabernes Selskab. Historisk-Filologiske Meddedelser (Copenhagen, Denmark)
KEAMJ	*Kenya and East African Medical Journal* (Nairobi, Kenya)
KFLQ	*Kentucky Foreign Language Quarterly* (Lexington, Kentucky)
KFQ	*Keystone Folklore Quarterly* (Lewisburg, Pennsylvania)
KFR	*Kentucky Folklore Record* (Bowling Green, Kentucky)
KHKM	*Kwartalnik Historii Kultury Materialnej* (Warsaw, Poland)
Khoa	*Khoa hoc* (Saigon, French Indo-China)
Kiva	*Kiva* (Tucson, Arizona)
KJFLGD	Koch's Jahresberichte uber die Fortschritte in der Lehre von den Gahrungs-Organismen (Leipzig, Germany)
KKenkyu	*Kagakushi Kenkyu [Journal of the History of Science]* (Tokyo, Japan)
KKGAW-Z	*Kaiserliche Konigliche Gesellschaft der Aerzte in Wien. Zeitschrift* (Vienna, Austria)
KL	*Karntner Landsmannschaft* (Klagenfurt, Germany)
KKHP	*K'ao Ku Hsueh Pao [Chinese Journal of Archeology]* (Peking, China)
KMJ	*Kenya Medical Journal* (Nairobi, Kenya)
KNOIMK-T	*Kostromskogo Naucnogo Obshchestvo po Izucheniyu Mestnogo Kraya. Trudy* (Kostroma, U.S.S.R.)
Konservenzeitung	*Konservenzeitung* (Leipzig, Germany)
Kosmos	*Kosmos* (Stuttgart, Germany)
Kotiseutu	*Kotiseutu* (Helsinki, Finland)
KPAW-B-S	*Koniglich Preussische Akademie der Wissenschaften. Berlin. Sitzungsberichte* (Berlin, Germany)
KRund	*Koloniale Rundschau* (Berlin, Germany)
KU-AS	Kyoto University. African Studies (Kyoto, Japan)
Kuml	*Kuml* (Aarhus, Denmark)
Kush	*Kush* (Khartoum, Sudan)
KW	*Klinische Wochenschrift* (Berlin, Germany)
KZ	*Keizai Zasshi* (Tokyo, Japan)
LA	*Living Age* (Boston, Massachusetts)
LAlpha	*Lambda Alpha. Journal of Man.* (Department of Sociology and Anthropology, Wichita State University. Wichita, Kansas)
LancCAS-T	Lancashire and Cheshire Antiquarian Society. Transactions (Manchester, England)
Lancet	*Lancet* (London, England)
Landbrukstidende	*Landbrukstidende* (Trondheim, Norway)
Language	*Language* (Baltimore, Maryland)
Laos	Comparative Studies of Folklore and Regional Ethnography (Stockholm, Sweden)
Lares	*Lares* (Florence, Italy)
Laryngologie	*Laryngologie, Rhinologie, Otologie und Ihre Grenzgebiete* (Stuttgart, Germany)
Lasso	*Lasso* (Buenos Aires, Argentina)
LCHS-P	Lebanon County Historical Society. Papers (Lebanon, Pennsylvania)
LD	*Let's Dance* (San Francisco, California)
Lejeunia	*Lejeunia* (Liege, Belgium)
LH	*Leisure Hour* (London, England)
LHeim	*Lauenburgische Heimat* (Lauenberg, Germany)
LHJ	*Ladies Home Journal* (Philadelphia, Pennsylvania)
LHQ	*Louisiana Historical Quarterly* (New Orleans, Louisiana)
Liasons	*Liasons* (Leopoldville/Kinshasa, Zaire)
Lichtgang, Der	*Der Lichtgang* (Denzlingen, Germany)
LInd	*Lebensmittel Industrie* (Leipzig, Germany)
Lippincott	*Lippincott's Magazine* (Philadelphia, Pennsylvania)
LMed	*Lisboa Medica* (Lisbon, Portugal)
LMV-J	Leipzig Museum fur Volkerkunde. Jahrbuch (Leipzig, Germany)
LMV-M	*Leipzig Museum fur Volkerkunde. Mitteilungen* (Leipzig, Germany)
LN-HO-B	League of Nations. Health Organization. Bulletin (Geneva, Switzerland)
Lore	*Lore* (Milwaukee, Wisconsin)
LQR	*London Quarterly Review* (London, England)
L-RS-PT	London. Royal Society. Philosophical Transactions (London, England)
LSJ	*Lingnan Science Journal* (Canton, China)
LSL(B)-J	*Linnean Society of London (Botany). Journal* (London, England)
LSL-P	Linnean Society of London. Proceedings (London, England)
LSNSW-P	Linnean Society of New South Wales. Proceedings (Sydney, Australia)
LT-LS	*London Times. Literary Supplement* (London, England)
LW	*Living Wilderness* (Washington, D.C.)
LYH	*Living for Young Homemakers* (New York, New York)
LZ	*Landwirtschaftliche Zeitung* (Halle, Germany)
Maasgouw	*Maasgouw* (Maastrecht, Netherlands)
MACNBR-PECD	Museo Argentina de Ciencias Naturales "Bernardino Rivadavia." Publicaciones de Extension Cultural y Didactica (Buenos Aires, Argentina)
MAd	*Mensario Administrativo* (Luanda, Angola)
M-AES-B	Missouri. Agricultural Experiment Station. *Bulletin* (Columbia, Missouri)
M-AES-C	Missouri. Agricultural Experiment Station. Circular (Columbia, Missouri)
Mainlande	*Mainlande* (Wurzburg, Germany)
MalayMJ	*Malayan Medical Journal* (Singapore)
Man	*Man* (London, England)
MANews	*Medical Anthropology Newsletter* (Miami, Florida)
Mankind	*Mankind* (Sydney, Australia)
MAnnals	*Medical Annals* (Washington, D.C.)
Manpower	*Manpower* (Pretoria, South Africa)
March	*March of India* (New Delhi, India)
Marseille	*Marseille* (Marseilles, France)
MarsMed	*Marseilles Medicale* (Marseilles, France)
MASAL-P	Michigan Academy of Sciences, Arts and Letters. Papers (Ann Arbor, Michigan)
Mass-AES-B	Massachusetts. Agricultural Experiment Station. Bulletin (Amherst, Massachusetts)

MassDPH-P	Massachusetts Department of Public Health. Publication (Boston, Massachusetts)
MAT-J	*Medical Association of Thailand. Journal* (Bangkok, Thailand)
Mayo	*Mayo Clinic. Proceedings* (Rochester, Minnesota)
MBET	*Madagascar Bulletin Economique Trimestriel. See: AMAL-BT*
MBG-A	*Missouri Botanical Gardens. Annals* (St. Louis, Missouri)
MC	*Missions Catholiques* (Lyon, France)
MC-A(B)	Musee du Congo. Annales (Botanique) (Tervuren, Belgium)
MC-B	*Menninger Clinic. Bulletin* (Topeka, Kansas)
MCen	*Mycologisches Centralblatt* (Jena, Germany)
MCFTRI-B	*Mysore Central Food Technological Research Institute. Bulletin* (Mysore, India)
MCM	*Mois Coloniale et Maritime* (Paris, France)
MCM-A	*Musee Coloniale de Marseilles. Annales* (Marseilles, France)
MCMonde	*Marches Coloniaux du Monde* (Paris, France)
MCNA	Medical Clinics of North America (Philadelphia, Pennsylvania)
MColon	*Materiel Coloniale* (Brussels, Belgium)
MC-PC-T	Montgomeryshire Collections. Powys-land Club. Transactions (London, England)
Me-AES-B	Maine. Agricultural Experiment Station. Bulletin (Orono, Maine)
MEB-B	*Musee Ethnographique Beograd. Bulletin* (Beograd, Yugoslavia)
MedAnth	*Medical Anthropology* (Pleasantville, New York)
Medicina	*Medicina* (Mexico City, Mexico)
MedJnlRec	*Medical Journal and Record* (New York, New York)
MedKlin	*Medizinische Klinik* (Berlin, Germany)
MedOfficer	*Medical Officer* (London, England)
MedRec	*Medical Record* (New York, New York)
Meehan's	*Meehan's Monthly* (Philadelphia, Pennsylvania)
MemphisSU-ARC-OP	Memphis State University. Anthropological Research Center. Occasional Papers (Memphis, Tennessee)
MexAnt	*Mexico Antiguo* (Mexico City, Mexico)
MF	*Midwest Folklore* (Bloomington, Indiana)
MFisch	*Mitteilungen fur die Fischindustrie* (Lubeck, Germany)
MFolk	*Mexican Folkways* (Mexico City, Mexico)
MGT-M	*Medizinische Gesellschaft zu Tokio. Mitteilungen* (Tokyo, Japan)
MGuard	*Manchester Guardian* (Manchester, England)
MHJ	*Medical History Journal* (London, England)
MHN-R	*Museo Historico Nacional. Revista* (Santiago, Chile)
MHosp	*Modern Hospital* (St. Louis, Missouri)
MHyg	*Mental Hygiene* (New York, New York)
MichArch	*Michigan Archeologist* (East Lansing, Michigan)
Micronesica	*Micronesica* (Agana, Guam)
Mid-Am	*Mid-America* (Chicago, Illinois)
Milling	*Milling* (Chicago, Illinois)
Millstone	*Millstone* (Indianapolis, Indiana)
Mil-PM-B	Milwaukee. Public Museum. Bulletin (Milwaukee, Wisconsin)
MIndia	*Man in India* (Ranchi, India)
MinMed	*Minerva Medica* (Turin, Italy)
Minn-AES-AR	University of Minnesota. Agricultural Experiment Station. Annual Report (Delano, Minnesota)
Minn-AES-MJS-P	Minnesota. Agricultural Experiment Station. Miscellaneous Journal Series. Papers (Delano, Minnesota)
MinnAS-P	Minnesota Academy of Sciences. Proceedings (Minneapolis, Minnesota)
Mirror	*Mirror* (Manila Times Publishing Co., Manila, Philippines)
Missionario	*Missionario* (Verona, Italy)
Miss-AES-B	Mississippi. Agricultural Experiment Station. Bulletin (State College, Mississippi)
Missou-AES-B	Missouri. Agricultural Experiment Station. Bulletin (Columbia, Missouri)
MIZ	*Manshu Igaku Zasshi [Journal of Oriental Medicine]* (Dairen, Shimmeicho, South Manchuria)
MJA	*Medical Journal of Australia* (Sydney, Australia)
MJA-S	Medical Journal of Australia. Supplement (Sydney, Australia)
MJR	*Medical Journal and Record* (New York, New York)
MJZ	*Medical Journal of Zambia* (Ndola, Zambia)
MK	*Minzokugaku Kenkyu [Japanese Journal of Ethnology]* (Tokyo, Japan)
MKey	*Masterkey* (Los Angeles, California)
MKunst	*Monatshefte fur Kunstwissenschaft* (Leipzig, Germany)
ML	*Mondo del Latto* (Milan, Italy)
MLeaves	*Medical Leaves* (Chicago, Illinois)
ML-PM-SE	Museum w Lodzi. Prace i Materialy. Seria Etnograficzna (Lodz, Poland)
MMed	*Maroc Medicale* (Casablanca, Morocco)
MMFQ	*Milbank Memorial Fund Quarterly* (New York, New York)
MMir	*Medical Mirror* (St. Louis, Missouri)
MMJ	*Maharashtra Medical Journal* (Poona, India)
MMTT	Men en Maatschappij Tweedmandelijks Tydschrift (Groningen, Netherlands)
MMW	*Munchen Medizinische Wochenshrift* (Munich, Germany)
MN	*Museum News* (W. H. Over Dakota Museum, University of South Dakota. Vermillion, South Dakota)
MNA-B	Museum of Northern Arizona. Bulletin (Flagstaff, Arizona)
MNA-MN	Museum of Northern Arizona. Museum Notes (Flagstaff, Arizona)
MNHist	*Magazine of Natural History* (London, England)
MNMPSP	Museum of New Mexico Popular Series Pamphlet (Sante Fe, New Mexico)
MNutr	*Modern Nutrition* (Los Angeles, California)
MNyelv	*Magyar Nyelvtudomany* (Budapest, Hungary)
Montana	*Montana* (Helena, Montana)
MPEG-PA	Museu Paraense Emilio Goeldi. Publicacoes Avulsas (Belem, Brazil)
M-PMag	*Mid-Pacific Magazine* (Honolulu, Hawaii)

M-PM-B	Milwaukee. Public Museum. Bulletin (Milwaukee, Wisconsin)	NGRU-B	New Guinea Research Unit. Bulletin (Port Moresby, Papua, New Guinea)
MPM-PA	Milwaukee Public Museum. Publications in Anthropology (Milwaukee, Wisconsin)	NGS	Nieuw Guinea Studien (The Hague, Netherlands)
M-PM-YB	Milwaukee. Public Museum. Year Book (Milwaukee, Wisconsin)	NH	Natural History (New York, New York)
MP-R	Museu Paulista. Revista (Sao Paulo, Brazil)	NHA	New Hampshire Archaeologist (Newport, New Hampshire)
MRS-P	Marine Research Society. Publication (Salem, Massachusetts)	NHP	Nevada Highways and Parks (Carson City, Nevada)
MSurg	Military Surgeon (New York, New York)	NI	Nicaragua Indigena (Managua, Nicaragua)
MTimes	Medical Times (London, England)	Nigeria	Nigeria (Lagos, Nigeria)
MTT	Medicine Today and Tomorrow (Richmond, Surrey, England)	Nigrizia	Nigrizia (Missioni Africane in Verona. Verona, Italy)
MVHR	Mississippi Valley Historical Review (Lincoln, Nebraska)	NJESS	Nigerian Journal of Economic and Social Studies (Ibadan, Nigeria)
MVN	Mesa Verde Notes (Mesa Verde, Colorado)	NJournal	Nyasaland Journal (Blantyre, Nyasaland)
M-WHR	Mid-West Hotel Reporter (Omaha, Nebraska)	NK	Nordisk Kultur (Stockholm, Sweden)
MWJ	Medical Woman's Journal (Cincinnati, Ohio)	NLGKGS	Neues Leben durch Gesundung von Korper, Geist und Seele (Dornbirn, Austria)
MWorld	Muslim World (New York; London)		
NA	Notes Africaines (Dakar, Senegal)	NMSTCS	Northwest Missouri State Teachers College Studies (Marysville, Missouri)
NAB	Northern Affairs Bulletin (Ottawa, Canada)	NM-AES-B	New Mexico. Agricultural Experiment Station. Bulletin (Las Cruces, New Mexico)
Nada	Southern Rhodesia Native Affairs Department Annual (Salisbury, Rhodesia)		
NAf	Nieuw Afrika; missietijdschrift der Witte Paters Missionarissen van Afrika (Antwerp, Belgium)	NMBR	New Mexico Business Review (Albuquerque, New Mexico)
Nahrung	Institut Ernahrung Bulgarische Akademie fur Wissenschaft (Sofia, Bulgaria)	NMCBP	Notas Mimeografadas do Centro de Biologia Piscatoria (Lisbon, Portugal)
Nanpo	Nanpo Dozuku (Taihoku, Japan)	NMC-PE	National Museums of Canada. Publications in Ethnology (Ottawa, Canada)
NARev	Nutrition Abstracts and Reviews (Aberdeen, Scotland)	NME	Neprajzi Muzeum Ertesitoje (Budapest, Hungary)
NARN	Northwest Anthropological Research Notes (Department of Sociology/Anthropology, University of Idaho, Moscow, Idaho)	NMed-A	Nordisk Medicinhistorisk. Arsbok (Stockholm, Sweden)
NatNouv	Nations Nouvelles (Yaounde, Cameroun)	NMex	New Mexico (Santa Fe, New Mexico)
Nature(L)	Nature (London, England)	NMFR	New Mexico Folklore Record (Albuquerque, New Mexico)
Nature(P)	Nature (Paris, France)		
NatWoch	Naturwissenschaftliche Wochenschrift (Jena, Austria)	NMill	Northwestern Miller (Minneapolis, Minnesota)
		NMP	Native Medical Practitioner (Suva, Fiji)
Nautilus	Nautilus (Philadelphia, Pennsylvania)	NMUAH-M	Nordiska Museet utigifna af Artur Hazelius. Mededelanden (Stockholm, Sweden)
Nawa	Nawa Pacha (Department of Anthropology, University of California-Berkeley, Berkeley, California)	NN	Nutrition News (Manila, Philippines)
		NNA-AR	Northern Nut Growers Association. Annual Report (Ithaca, New York)
NCan	Naturaliste Canadien (Cap Rouge, Quebec, Canada)	NNews	Nutrition News (Manila, Philippines)
NDA	Nachrichten ueber Deutsche Alterthumskunde (Supplement to Zeitschrift fur Ethnologie. Berlin, Germany)	NNGA-RP	Northern Nut Growers Association. Report of the Proceedings (Ithaca, New York)
NDHealth	Nutrition and Dental Health (Lavoris Company. St. Paul, Minnesota)	NNLet	Nutrition Newsletter (Food and Agriculture Organizaton of the United Nations, Rome, Italy)
Neb-AES-B	Nebraska. Agricultural Experiment Station. Bulletin (Lincoln, Nebraska)	NNyelv	Neprajzi es Nyelvtudomany (Szeged, Hungary)
NEJM	New England Journal of Medicine (Boston, Massachusetts)	NO	Nursing Outlook (New York, New York)
NeKoz	Neprajzi Kozlemenyek (Budapest, Hungary)	NObs	Nouvel Observateur (Paris, France)
Neprajzi	Neprajzi Ertesito (Budapest, Hungary)	NOH-A	Nordisk Oldkyndighed og Historie. Aarboger (Copenhagen, Denmark)
NEQ	New England Quartery (Portland, Maine)	NOMSJ	New Orleans Medical and Scientific Journal (New Orleans, Louisiana)
Neurobiologia	Neurobiologia (Pernambuco, Brazil)		
NewShet	New Shetlander (Lerwick, Scotland)	Norveg	Norveg
NField	Nigerian Field (London, England)	NQ	Notes and Queries for Readers and Writers, Collectors and Librarians (London, England)
NGJ	Nigerian Geographical Journal (Ibadan, Nigeria)	NQE-B	North Queensland Ethnography. Bulletin (Brisbane, Australia)
NGM	National Geographic Magazine (Washington, D.C.)	NR	Nutrition Reviews (New York, New York)

NRC-B	National Research Council. Bulletin (Washington, D.C.)
NRev	*New Review* (London, England)
NS	*Nation's Schools* (Chicago, Illinois)
NSci	*New Scientist* (London, England)
NSIS-PT	Nova Scotia Institute of Science. Proceedings and Transactions (Halifax, Nova Scotia, Canada)
NSoc	*New Society* (London, England)
NSM-AP	Nevada State Museum. Anthropological Papers (Carson City, Nevada)
NT	*Nutrition Today* (New York, New York)
NTNI	*Natuurkundig Tijdschrift voor Nederlandsch Indie* (Batavia, Java)
Nutriologia	*Nutriologia* (Mexico City, Mexico)
Nutrition(L)	*Nutrition* (London, England)
Nutrition(P)	*Nutrition* (Paris, France)
NVBBDVA-M	*Nederland Vereniging tot Bevordering Biologische-Dynamische Landbouwmethode. Mededelingen* (Heemstede, Netherlands)
NWG	*National Wool Grower* (Salt Lake City, Utah)
NWIG	*Nieuw West Indische Gids* (Amsterdam, Netherlands)
NY-AES-AR	New York. Agricultural Experiment Station. Annual Report (Albany, New York)
NYAM-B	*New York Academy of Medicine. Bulletin* (New York, New York)
NYAS-A	New York Academy of Sciences. Annals (New York, New York)
NYAS-T	New York Academy of Sciences. Transactions (New York, New York)
NYBG-J	*New York Botanical Gardens. Journal* (Bronx, New York)
NyelKoz	*Nyelvtudomanyi Kozlemenyek* (Budapest, Hungary)
NYFQ	*New York Folklore Quarterly* (Ithaca, New York)
NYJD	*New York Journal of Dentistry* (New York, New York)
NYRevB	*New York Review of Books* (New York, New York)
NYSAS-T	New York State Agricultural Society. Transactions (Albany, New York)
NZAA-N	*New Zealand Archaeological Association. Newsletter* (Christchurch, New Zealand)
NZDJ	*New Zealand Dental Journal* (Wellington, New Zealand)
NZG	*New Zealand Geographer* (Christchurch, New Zealand)
NZI-TP	New Zealand Institute. Transactions and Proceedings (Wellington, New Zealand)
NZJST	*New Zealand Journal of Science and Technology* (Wellington, New Zealand)
NZL	*New Zealand Listener* (Wellington, New Zealand)
NZM	*Neue Zeitschrift fur Missionswissenschaft* (Beckenreid, Switzerland)
NZMJ	*New Zealand Medical Journal* (Wellington, New Zealand)
O-AES-B	Ohio. Agricultural Experiment Station. Bulletin (Wooster, Ohio)
OArch	*Ohio Archaeologist* (Plain City, Ohio)
OAS-P	Oklahoma Academy of Sciences. Proceedings (Norman, Oklahoma)
Oberfalz	*Oberfalz* (Kallmunz, Germany)
OC	*Open Court* (Chicago, Illinois)
Oceania	*Oceania* (Melbourne, Australia)
OEA-ES	Oxford English Association. Essays and Studies. *See:* EA-ES
OFWR	*Ontario Fish and Wildlife Review* (Publication of Ontario Department of Lands and Forests. Toronto, Canada)
OG	*Obstetrics and Gynecology* (New York, New York)
OHN	*Occupational Health Nursing* (New York, New York)
OHQ	*Oregon Historical Quarterly* (Salem, Oregon)
OHSQ	*Oregon Historical Society Quarterly* (Portland, Oregon)
OIHP-B	*Office International d'Hygiene Publique. Bulletin* (Paris, France)
OKAS-N	*Oklahoma Anthropological Society. Newsletter* (Norman, Oklahoma)
OL	*Orientalische Literaturzeitung* (Berlin, Germany)
Oleagineux	*Oleagineux* (Paris, France)
OM	*Objets et Mondes. La revue du Musee de l'Homme* (Paris, France)
OMSG	*Oxford Medical School Gazette* (Oxford, England)
ON	*Ottawa Naturalist* (Ottawa, Canada)
OP	*Occupational Psychology* (London, England)
OpAth	*Opuscula Atheniensia* (Lund, Sweden)
OPM-AR-[Ap.EDR]	Ontario Provincial Museum. Archaeological Report [Appendix to Education Department Report] (Ottawa, Canada)
Opportunity	*Opportunity. A Journal of Negro Life* (New York, New York)
ORANA-R	*Organisation de Recherches pour l'Alimentation et la Nutrition Africaines. Rapport* (Dakar, Senegal)
ORev	*Occult Review* (London, England)
OrHet	*Orrosi Hetilap* (Budapest, Hungary)
Orientalia	*Orientalia Suecana* (Uppsala, Sweden)
OSP-B	*Oficina Sanitaria Panamericana. Boletin* (Washington, D.C.)
OTNE	*Old Time New England* (Boston, Massachusetts)
Oudtestament	*Oudtestamentliche Studien* (Leyden, Netherlands)
Outre-Mer	*Outre-Mer* (Paris, France)
PAfric	*Presence Africaine* (Paris, France)
PAg	*Philippine Agriculturist* (Manila, Philippines)
PAGPMT	*Pflugers Archiv fur die Gesamte Physiologie des Menschen und der Tiere* (Bonn, Germany)
Paideuma	*Paideuma* (Frankfurt am Main, Germany)
PakHS-J	*Pakistan Historical Society. Journal* (Karachi, Pakistan)
Palaeohistoria	*Palaeohistoria* (Groningen, Netherlands)
Palimpsest	*Palimpsest* (Iowa City, Iowa)
PAnth	*Practical Anthropology* (Tarrytown, New York)
PAR	*Politisch-Anthropologische Revue* (Leipzig, Germany)
Parassitologia	*Parassitologia* (Rome, Italy)
PArch	*Pennsylvania Archaeologist* (Pittsburgh, Pennsylvania)

PARev	*Philippine Agricultural Review* (Manila, Philippines)
P-AS-CRH	*Paris. Academie des Sciences. Comptes Rendues Hebdomadaires* (Paris, France)
PAU-B	*Pan American Union. Bulletin* (Washington, D.C.)
PB	*Psychological Bulletin* (Princeton, New Jersey)
PBM	*Perspectives in Biology and Medicine* (Chicago, Illinois)
PCJEB	*Pomona College Journal of Economic Botany* (Pomona, California)
P-DAF-AL	*Palestine. Department of Agriculture and Forests. Agricultural Leaflets* (Jerusalem)
P-DANR-BA-B	*Philippines. Department of Agriculture and Natural Resources. Bureau of Agriculture. Bulletin* (Manila, Philippines)
PDG	*Pacific Dental Gazette* (San Francisco, California)
PDisc	*Pacific Discovery* (San Francisco, California)
PE	*Professional Engineer* (Chicago, Illinois)
Pediatria	*Pediatria* (Naples, Italy)
Pediatrics	*Pediatrics* (Springfield, Illinois)
Penn-AES-B	*Pennsylvania. Agricultural Experiment Station. Bulletin* (University Park, Pennsylvania)
PennGer	*Pennsylvania German* (Lebanon, Pennsylvania)
PennHR	*Pennsylvania Hotel Record* (Harrisburg, Pennsylvania)
PennSU-DA-OPA	Pennsylvania State University. Department of Anthropology. Occasional Papers in Anthropology (University Park, Pennsylvania)
PES-B	Palestine Economic Society. Bulletin (Jaffa, Palestine)
PFJ	*Punjab Fruit Journal* (Lyallpur, Pakistan)
Pflanzer	*Pflanzer* (Dar-es-Salam, Tanganyika)
PFNS	*Progress in Food and Nutrition Science* (Elmsford, New York)
PFolk	*Pennsylvania Folklife* (Lancaster, Pennsylvania)
PFPMP-J	*Philippine Federation of Private Medical Practitioners. Journal* (Manila, Philippines)
PGM-E	*Petermann's Geographische Mitteilungen. Ergänzungsheft* (Gotha, Germany)
PH	*Pacific Historian* (Stockton, California)
Pharmazie	*Pharmazie* (Berlin, Germany)
PHCurr	*Public Health Currents* (Publication of Ross Laboratories. Columbus, Ohio)
PhilMag	*Philippine Magazine* (Manila, Philippines)
PhilStat	*Philippine Statistician* (Manila, Philippines)
PHM	*Philippine Herald Magazine* (Manila, Philippines)
PHN	*Public Health Nursing* (New York, New York)
PHR	*Pacific Historical Review* (Glendale, California)
PHSoc	*Prehistoric Society. Proceedings* (London, England)
Phytochemistry	Phytochemistry (New York, New York)
PI	*Peru Indigena* (Lima, Peru)
PI-BA-B	Philippine Islands. Bureau of Agriculture. Bulletin (Manila, Philippines)
PI-DANR—BF-B	Philippine Islands. Department of Agriculture and Natural Resources. Bureau of Forestry. Bulletin (Manila, Philippines)
Piltdown	Piltdown Newsletter (Department of Anthropology, University of California, Riverside, California)
PIM	*Pacific Islands Monthly* (Sydney, Australia)
PIMA-J	*Philippine Islands Medical Association. Journal* (Manila, Philippines)
P-INH-B	Paris. Institut National d'Hygiene. Bulletin (Paris, France)
Pittonia	*Pittonia* (Berkeley, California)
P-JIU-EED	Portugal. Junta de Investigacoes do Ultramar. Estudos Ensaios e Documentos (Lisbon, Portugal)
PJN	*Philippine Journal of Nutrition* (Manila, Philippines)
PJS	*Philippine Journal of Science* (Manila, Philippines)
PJSIR	*Pakistan Journal of Science and Industrial Research* (Peshawar, Pakistan)
Plateau	*Plateau* (Flagstaff, Arizona)
PMan	*Primitive Man* (Washington, D.C.)
PMArg	*La Prensa Medica Argentina* (Buenos Aires, Argentina)
PMHB	*Pennsylvania Magazine of History and Biography* (Philadelphia, Pennsylvania)
PMJ	*Postgraduate Medical Journal* (London, England)
P-MNHN-B	Paris. Museum National d'Histoire Naturelle. Bulletin (Paris, France)
PMono	Psychological Monographs (Princeton, New Jersey)
PNGAJ	*Papua and New Guinea Agricultural Journal* (Port Moresby, Papua, New Guinea)
PNGSS-T	Papua and New Guinea Scientific Society. Transactions (Port Moresby, Papua, New Guinea)
PNHB	*Peking Natural History Bulletin* (Peking, China)
PNorth	*Problems of the North* (Ottawa, Canada)
PNQ	*Pacific Northwest Quarterly* (Seattle, Washington)
PNS	*Proceedings of the Nutrition Society* (Cambridge, England)
Policlinico	*Policlinico* (Rome, Italy)
Polynesian	*Polynesian* (Honolulu, Hawaii)
Population	*Population* (Paris, France)
PP	*Pure Products* (New York, New York)
PPac	*Paradise of the Pacific* (Honolulu, Hawaii)
PPA-J	*Philippine Pharmaceutical Association. Journal* (Manila, Philippines)
PPrax	*Pharmaceutische Praxis* (Vienna, Austria)
PPRI-J	*Pan-Pacific Research Institute. Journal* (Honolulu, Hawaii)
PQuart	*Philological Quarterly* (Iowa City, Iowa)
PR	*Polar Record* (Cambridge, England)
Prensa, La	*La Prensa* (Buenos Aires, Argentina)
PresMed	*La Presse Medicale* (Paris, France)
PRev	*Partisan Review* (New York, New York)
Print	*Printer's Ink* (New York, New York)
PRJPHTM	*Puerto Rico Journal of Public Health and Tropical Medicine* (San Juan, Puerto Rico)
PRund	*Pharmaceutische Rundschau* (Prague, Czechoslovakia; Berlin, Germany)
P-SB-CRHSM	*Paris. Societe de Biologie. Comptes Rendues-*

	Hebdomadaires des Seances et Memoires (Paris, France)
PSC	*Problemes Sociaux Congolais* (Elisabethville, Belgian Congo)
PSci	*Pacific Science* (Honolulu, Hawaii)
PSC-TB	*Peulvruchten Studie Combinatie. Technische Berichten* (Wageningen, Netherlands)
PSeg	*Prevision y Seguridad* (Monterrey, Mexico)
PS-M	*Polynesian Society. Memoirs* (Wellington, New Zealand)
PSMed	*Pagine di Storia della Medicina* (Rome, Italy)
PSMo	*Popular Science Monthly* (New York, New York)
PSNH-B	Peking Society of Natural History. Bulletin (Peking, China)
PS-P	*Prehistoric Society. Proceedings* (London, England)
PSR	*Philippine Sociological Review* (Manila, Philippines)
Psychiatry	*Psychiatry* (Washington, D.C.)
PsychMed	*Psychosomatic Medicine* (Washington, D.C.)
Psychologie	*Psychologie* (Centre d'Etudes et de Promotion de la Lecture. Paris, France)
Psychopathology	*Psychopathology and Pictorial Expression* (Basel, Switzerland)
PsychQt	*Psychiatric Quarterly* (Utica, New York)
PsychRep	*Psychological Reports* (Louisville, Kentucky)
PsychRev	*Psychological Review* (Lancaster, Pennsylvania)
PWeek	*Pharmaceutisch Weekblad* (Amsterdam, Netherlands)
PWorld	*Plant World* (Binghamton, New York)
QFF	*Quick Frozen Foods* (New York, New York)
QJS	*Quarterly Journal of Science* (London, England)
QJSA	*Quarterly Journal of Studies on Alcohol* (New Haven, Connecticut)
QJSA-LS	*Quarterly Journal of Studies on Alcohol. Lay Supplement* (New Haven, Connecticut)
QJTM	*Quarterly Journal of the Taiwan Museum* (Taipei, Taiwan)
QN	*Quaderni della Nutrizione* (Rome, Italy)
QPMV	*Qualitas Plantarum et Materiae Vegetabiles* (The Hague, Netherlands)
QR	*Quarterly Review* (London, England)
QRP	*Quarterly Review of Pediatrics* (Washington, D.C.)
QRes	*Quartenary Research* (London, England)
Quartar	*Quartar-Hominiden* (Bonn, Germany)
RAFS-J	*Royal African Society. Journal* (London, England)
RAHS-N	Royal Australian Historical Society. Newsletter (Sydney, Australia)
RAIGBI-J	*Royal Anthropological Institute of Great Britain and Ireland. Journal* (London, England)
RAIGBI-OP	Royal Anthropological Institute of Great Britain and Ireland. Occasional Papers (London, England)
RAnth	*Revue Anthropologique* (Paris, France)
RASB-J	*Royal Asiatic Society of Bengal. Journal* (Calcutta, India)
RASC-J	*Royal Asiatic Society of Ceylon. Journal* (Colombo, Sri Lanka)
RASGBI-J	*Royal Asiatic Society of Great Britain and Ireland. Journal* (London, England)
RAS-NCB-J	*Royal Asiatic Society. North China Branch. Journal* (Shanghai, China)
RAS-P	*Rochester Academy of Science. Proceedings* (Rochester, New York)
RAuc	*Revue de l'Aucam* (Louvain, Belgium)
RBAAT	*Revue International de Botanique Applique et d'Agriculture Tropical* (Paris, France)
RBF	*Revista Brasileira de Folclore* (Rio de Janeiro, Brazil)
RBQ	*Revista Brasileira de Quimica* (Rio de Janeiro, Brazil)
RCAnt	*Revista Colombiana de Antropologia* (Bogota, Colombia)
RCB	*Revue Coloniale Belge* (Brussels, Belgium)
RCF	*Revista Colombiana del Folclore* (Bogota, Colombia)
RCHMP	*Revista Chilena de Higiene y Medicina Preventiva* (Santiago, Chile)
RCM	*Review of Czechoslovak Medicine* (Prague, Czechoslovakia)
RCMG	*Revista del Colegio de Medicina de Guatemala* (Guatemala City, Guatemala)
RCol	*Revue Coloniale* (Paris, France)
RCong	*Recherches Congolaises* (Brazzaville, Belgian Congo)
RD	*Reader's Digest* (Pleasantville, New York)
RDAA	*Revista Dominicana de Arqueologia y Antropologia* (Santo Domingo, Dominican Republic)
RDM	*Revue des Deux Mondes* (Paris, France)
RE	*Revista de Etnografia* (Museu de Etnografia e Historia. Porto, Portugal)
REA	*Revue de l'Ecole d'Anthropologie. See:* RMEAP
Realites	*Realities* (Paris, France)
REC	Recherches et Etudes Camerounaises (Yaounde, Cameroun)
REd	*Revista de Educacion* (La Plata, Argentina)
REEADN	*Revista Espanola de las Enfermedades del Aparato Digestivo y Nutricion* (Madrid, Spain)
REFran	*Revue Economique Francaise* (Paris, France)
Relics	*Relics* (Austin, Texas)
REMA-J	*Royal Egyptial Medical Association. Journal* (Cairo, Egypt)
REMVPT	*Revue de l'Elevage et du Medecin Veterinaire des Pays Tropicaux* (Paris, France)
RESL-T	Royal Entomological Society of London. Transactions (London, England)
RETP	*Revue d'Ethnographie et des Traditions Populaires* (Paris, France)
RevHist	*Revue Historique* (Paris, France)
RevIndo	*Revue Indochinoise* (Hanoi, French Indo-China)
RevMyc-S	*Revue Mycologique. Supplement* (Paris, France)
RevNou	*Revue Nouvelle* (Brussels, Belgium)
RevPsic	*Revista Psicologia* (La Plata, Argentina)
RevRev	*Review of Reviews* (New York, New York)
RF	*Revista de Folklore* (Organo de la Comision Nacional de Folklore. Bogota, Columbia)
RFEE	*Revue Francaise de l'Elite Europeene* (Paris, France)

RFQ	*Revista de la Facultad de Quimica* (Lima, Peru)
RGA	*Revista Geografica Americana* (Buenos Aires, Argentina)
RGB	*Revue Generale de Botanique* (Paris, France)
RGPSO	*Revue Geographique des Pyrenees et du Sud-Ouest* (Toulouse, France)
RHMS	*Revue d'Hygiene et de Medecines Sociales* (Nancy, France)
RHNA	*Revue d'Histoire Naturelle Appliquee* (Paris, France)
Rhodora	*Rhodora* (Boston, Massachusetts)
RHPS	*Revue d'Hygiene et de Police Sanitaire* (Paris, France)
RHS-L-J	*Royal Horticultural Society. Journal* (London, England)
RHS-L-T	Royal Historical Society. Transactions (London, England)
Rig	*Rig* (Stockholm, Sweden)
RIPHH-J	*Royal Institute of Public Health and Hygiene. Journal* (London, England)
Riso	*Riso* (Milan, Italy)
Riz	*Riz et Riziculture et Culture Vivrieres* (Paris, France)
RJ	*Rice Journal* (New Orleans, Louisiana)
R-LI-J	*Rhodes-Livingstone Institute. Journal* (Manchester, England)
R-LP	Rhodes-Livingstone Papers (Lusaka, Northern Rhodesia)
RMA	*Revista de Medicina y Alimentacion* (Santiago, Chile)
RMC	*Revista Medica de Chile* (Santiago, Chile)
RMCuba	*Revista Medica Cubana* (Havana, Cuba)
RMEAP	*Revue Mensuelle de l'Ecole d'Anthropologie de Paris* (Paris, France)
RMN	*Revista del Museo Nacional* (Lima, Peru)
RMPeru	*Revista Medica Peruana* (Lima, Peru)
RMQO	*Revista Medico Quirurgia de Oriente* (Santiago de Cuba)
RMS	*Revista Mexicana de Sociologia* (Mexico City, Mexico)
RMSAS	*Revista del Ministerio Sanitario y Asistencia Social* (Caracas, Venezuela)
RMSR	*Revue Medicale de la Suisse Romande* (Geneva, Switzerland)
RMV	*Recueil de Medicine Veterinaire* (Paris, France)
RMY	*Revista Medica de Yucatan* (Merida, Mexico)
RNFS	*Review of Nutrition and Food Science* (London, England)
ROMM	*Revue de l'Occident Musulman et de la Mediterranee* (Aix-en-Provence, France)
RParis	*Revue de Paris* (Paris, France)
RPC	*Revue des Produits Chimiques* (Paris, France)
RPP	*Revue de Psychologie des Peuples* (Le Havre, France)
RPR	*Review of Philosophy and Religion* (Poona, India)
RPVEAF	*Revue du Pathologie Vegetale et Entomologie Agricole Francaise* (Paris, France)
RPZH	*Roczniki Panstwowego Zakladu Higieny* (Warsaw, Poland)
RR	*Regional Review* (United States Department of the Interior. National Park Service. Region One. Richmond, Virginia)
RRel	*Race Relations* (Johannesburg, South Africa)
RSci	*Revue Scientifique* (Paris, France)
RSC-PT	Royal Society of Canada. Proceedings and Transactions (Ottawa, Canada)
RSE-T	Royal Society of Edinburgh. Transactions (Edinburgh, Scotland)
RSI-J	*Royal Sanitary Institute. Journal* (London, England)
RSL-NR	*Royal Society of London. Notes and Records* (London, England)
RSL-P	*Royal Society of London. Proceedings* (London, England)
RSMed	*Revista Stiintelor Medicale* (Bucarest, Rumania)
RSNA	*Revue des Sciences Naturelles Appliquees* (Paris, France)
RSO	*Rivista degli Studi Orientali* (Rome, Italy)
RSQ-P	Royal Society of Queensland. Proceedings (Brisbane, Australia)
RSSA-TP	Royal Society of South Australia. Transactions and Proceedings (Adelaide, Australia)
RSTMH-T	Royal Society of Tropical Medicine and Hygiene. Transactions (London, England)
RStorMed	*Revista di Storia della Medicina* (Rome, Italy)
RST-PP	Royal Society of Tasmania. Papers and Proceedings (Hobart, Tasmania)
Runa	*Runa*. Archivo para las Ciencias del' Hombre (Buenos Aires, Argentina)
RV	*Rheinische Vierteljahresblatter* (Bonn, Germany)
RV-BM	Rijksmuseum voor Volkskunde. Bijdragen en Mededelingen (Arnhem, Netherlands)
RVol	*Recherches Voltaiques* (Paris, France)
RWZV	*Rheinisch Westfalische Zeitschrift fur Volkskunde* (Bonn, Germany)
SA	*Scientific American* (New York, New York)
SAAB	*South African Archaeological Bulletin* (Capetown, South Africa)
SAA-M	Society for American Archaeology. Memoirs (Menasha, Wisconsin)
SAB-B	*Societe de l'Academie de Brest. Bulletin* (Brest, France)
SABrux-B	Societe d'Anthropologie de Bruxelles. Bulletin (Brussels, Belgium)
SAC-B	Southeastern Archaeological Conference. Bulletin (Lexington, Kentucky)
SAGMN	*Sudhoff's Archiv fur Geschichte der Medizin und der Naturwissenschaft* (Leipzig, Germany)
SAH-B	*Sociedad Argentina de Horticultura. Boletin* (Buenos Aires, Argentina)
SA-J	*Societe des Africanistes. Journal* (Paris, France)
SAJE	*South African Journal of Economics* (Johannesburg, South Africa)
SAJMS	*South Afican Journal of Medical Sciences* (Johannesburg, South Africa)
SAJS	*South African Journal of Science* (Johannesburg, South Africa)
SAM-A	*South African Museum. Annals* (Cape Town, South Africa)

SAMJ	*South African Medical Journal* (Cape Town, South Africa)
SAmP-J	*Societe des Americanistes de Paris. Journal* Paris, France)
SAM-R	*South Australian Museum. Records* (Adelaide, Australia)
SAN	*Saskatchewan Archaeology Newsletter* (Regina, Canada)
SANat	*South Australian Naturalist* (Adelaide, Australia)
Sankhya	*Sankhya* (Calcutta, India)
SANorm-B	Societe des Antiquaires de Normandie. Bulletin (Paris, France)
SAN-P	Science Association of Nigeria. Proceedings (Ibadan, Nigeria)
SAP-B	*Societe d'Anthropologie de Paris. Bulletin* (Ibadan, NIgeria)
SAP-BM	Societe d'Anthropologie de Paris. Bulletins et Memoires (Paris, France)
SAP-J	*Societe d'Anthropologie de Paris. Journal* (Paris, France)
SarMJ	*Sarawak Museum Journal* (Kuching, Sarawak)
SA-RS-TP	South Africa. Royal Society. Transactions and Proceedings (Cape Town, South Africa)
SA-S	*Scientific American. Supplement* (New York, New York)
SAS-P	Society of Antiquaries of Scotland. Proceedings (Edinburgh, Scotland)
SAS-TS-B	Sultanic Agricultural Society. Technical Section. Bulletin (Cairo, Egypt)
SAV/ASTP	*Schweizerische Archiv fur Volkskunde/Archives Suisses des Traditions Populaires* (Basel, Switzerland)
SAVMA-J	*South African Veterinary Medical Association. Journal* (Johannesburg, South Africa)
SBF-B	*Societe Botanique de France. Bulletin* (Paris, France)
SBJ	*School Board Journal* (Milwaukee, Wisconsin)
SBMT-A	Societe Belge de Medecine Tropicale. Annales (Anvers, Belgium)
SBP-A	*Sociedad de Biologia de Pernambuco. Anales* (Pernambuco, Brazil)
SC-AES-B	South Carolina. Agricultural Experiment Station. Bulletin (Clemson, South Carolina)
SCB-B	*Societe Chimique de Belgique. Bulletin* (Gand, Belgium)
SciCoun	*Science Counsellor* (Duquesne University, Pittsburgh, Pennsylvania)
Science	*Science* (Lancaster, Pennsylvania)
SciHist	*Scientiarium Historia* (Antwerp, Belgium)
SCI-J	*Society of the Chemical Industry. Journal* (London, England)
ScotMag	*Scotland's Magazine* (Edinburgh, Scotland)
ScotRev	*Scottish Review* (London, England)
Screenings	*Screenings* (Oregon Archaeological Society. Portland, Oregon)
SCult	*Science and Culture* (Calcutta, India)
SD-AES-B	South Dakota. Agricultural Experiment Station. Bulletin (Brookings, South Dakota)
SD-AS-P	South Dakota. Academy of Sciences. Proceedings (Vermillion, South Dakota)
SDigest	*Science Digest* (Chicago, Illinois)

S-DL-B	Suriname. Departement Landbouwproefstation Bulletin (Paramaraibo, Surinam)
SEAEP-AM	Sociedad Espanola de Antropologia, Etnografia y Prehistoria. Actas y Memorias (Madrid, Spain)
SEAJTMPH	*South East Asia Journal of Tropical Medicine and Public Health* (Bangkok, Thailand)
Search	*Search* (Seattle, Washington)
SEBM-P	Society for Experimental Biology and Medicine. Proceedings (New York, New York)
SEHR	*Swedish Economic History Review* (Stockholm, Sweden)
SEIAAOF-B	*Services de l'Elevage et des Industries Animales de l'Afrique Occidentale Francaise. Bulletin* (Dakar, Senegal)
SEIC-B	*Societe des Etudes Indo-Chinoises. Bulletin* (Saigon, French Indo-China)
Sel'skoBiol	*Sel'skohozyaistvenna Biologia* (Moscow, U.S.S.R.)
SemMed	*Semaine Medicale* (Paris, France)
SEO-B	*Societe d'Etudes Oceaniennes. Bulletin* (Papeete, Tahiti)
SES	*Social and Economic Studies* (Kingston, Jamaica)
SEst	*Svio-Estonica* (Lund, Sweden)
Set	*Set* (New Zealand Council for Educational Research.Wellington, New Zealand)
SEtno	*Slovenski Etnografia* (Ljubljana, Yugoslavia)
SEU	*Studia Ethnographica Uppsaliensia* (Uppsala, Sweden)
Sewanee	*Sewanee Review* (Sewanee, Tennessee)
SF	*Social Forces* (Chapel Hill, North Carolina)
SFarm	*Science for the Farmer* (Agricultural Experiment Station. Pennsylvania State University. University Park, Pennsylvania)
SFB	*Shetland Folk Book* (Lerwick, Scotland)
SFChron	*San Francisco Chronicle* (San Francisco, California)
SFHM-B	*Societe Francaise d'Histoire de la Medicine. Bulletin* (Paris, France)
SFM-A	Sociedad Folklorica de Mexico. Annuario (Mexico City, Mexico)
SFT	*Svensk Farmaceutisk Tidskrift* (Stockholm, Sweden)
SG	*Science Gossip* (London, England)
SGAE-B	*Schweizerische Gesellschaft fur Anthropologie und Ethnologie. Bulletin* (Bern, Switzerland)
SGC-B	*Sociedad Geografica de Colombia. Boletin* (Bogota, Colombia)
SGHG-A	Sociedad de Geografia e Historia de Guatemala. Anales (Guatemala City, Guatemala)
SGI-B	*Societa Geografica Italiana. Bolletino* (Rome, Italy)
SGM	*Scottish Geographical Magazine* (Edinburgh, Scotland)
SHF-HT	Svenska Historiska Foreningen. Historisk Tidskrift (Stockholm, Sweden)
SHHGG-R	*Societe Haitienne d'Histoire, Geographie et Geologie. Revue* (Port-au-Prince, Haiti)
SH-MHV	*Schleswig-Holstein. Monatsheft fur Heimat und Volkstum* (Flensburg, Germany)
SI	*Shima Isseido* (Tokyo, Japan)

SIA-B	*Societe Imperial d'Acclimation. Bulletin* (Paris, France)
SI-AR	Smithsonian Institution. Annual Report (Washington, D.C.)
SI-ARBR	Smithsonian Institution. Annual Report of the Board of Regents (Washington, D.C.)
SI-BAE-AR	Smithsonian Institution. Bureau of American Ethnology. Annual Report (Washington, D.C.)
SI-BAE-B	Smithsonian Institution. Bureau of American Ethnology. Bulletin (Washington, D.C.)
SI-BE-AR	Smithsonian Institution. Bureau of Ethnology. Annual Report (Washington, D.C.)
SIBS-B	*Societa Italiana di Biologia Sperimentale. Bollettino* (Naples, Italy)
SI-CA	Smithsonian Institution. Contributions to Anthropology (Washington, D.C.)
SI-CK	Smithsonian Institution. Contributions to Knowledge (Washington, D.C.)
SI-ISA-P	Smithsonian Institution. Institute of Social Anthropology. Publication (Washington, D.C.)
SIll	*Sports Illustrated* (Chicago, Illinois)
SI-MC	Smithsonian Institution. Miscellaneous Collection (Washington, D.C.)
SI-MC-P	Smithsonian Institution. Miscellaneous Collection. Publication (Washington, D.C.)
SI-P	Smithsonian Institution. Publication (Washington, D.C.)
SItalBS-B	See SIBS-B
SI-USNH-C	Smithsonian Institution. United States National Herbarium. Contributions (Washington, D.C.)
SIWBS	Smithsonian Institution War Background Series (Washington, D.C.)
SiegerHeim	*Siegerlander Heimatkalender* (Siegen, Germany)
SJA	*Southwest Journal of Anthropology* (Albuquerque, New Mexico)
SJGVV	Schmollers Jahrbuch fur Gesetzgebung, Verwaltung und Volkswirtschaft (Berlin, Germany)
SJin	*Shakai Jinruigaku [Social Anthropology]* (Tokyo, Japan)
SLife	*Suburban Life* (New York, New York)
SLL-BM	*Societe Linneenne de Lyon. Bulletin Mensuel* (Lyon, France)
SLS	*Sierra Leone Studies* (Freetown, Sierra Leone)
SM	*Scientific Monthly* (Washington, D.C.)
SMag	*Scribner's Magazine* (New York, New York)
SMan	*Science of Man* (Sydney, Australia)
SMedJ	*Southern Medical Journal* (Birmingham, Alabama)
SMF-B	*Societe Mycologique de France. Bulletin* (Paris, France)
SMFW-B	*Society of the Medical Friends of Wine. Bulletin* (San Francisco, California)
SMJ	*Sind Medical Journal* (Karachi, Pakistan)
SMMF-B	*Societe de Medecine Militaire de France. Bulletin* (Paris, France)
Smoke	*Smoke Signals* (Newark, New Jersey)
SM-P	Southwestern Museum. Papers (Los Angeles, California)
SMSJ	*Southern Medical and Surgical Journal* (Augusta, Georgia)
SMVD-AB	*Staatlichen Museum fur Volkerkunde Dresden. Abhandlungen und Berichte* (Dresden, Germany)
SMW	*Schweizerische Medizinische Wochenschrift* (Basel, Switzerland)
SN	*Slovensky Narodopis* (Bratislava, Czechoslovakia)
SNAF-B	*Societe Nationale d'Acclimatation de France. Bulletin* (Paris, France)
SNCS-B	*Societe Naturale de Chalon-sur-Saone. Bulletin* (Chalon-sur-Saone, France)
SNews	*Sindri News* (Publication of Fertilizer Corporation of India, Ltd. Dhanabad, Bihar)
SNight	*Saturday Night* (Toronto, Canada)
SNL	*Science News Letter* (Washington, D.C.)
SNN-B	*Societa di Naturalisti di Napoli. Bolletino* (Naples, Italy)
SNS	*Stare i Nowe Siokowice* (Wroclaw, Poland)
SNSNMC-M	Societe Nationale des Sciences Naturelles et Mathematiques de Cherbourg. Memoires (Cherbourg, France)
SoIS	*Southern Indian Studies* (Archaeological Society of North Carolina. Chapel Hill, North Carolina)
SOR	*Springfield Ohio Republican* (Springfield, Ohio)
SouthLore	*Southwestern Lore* (Boulder, Colorado)
SouthM-L	*Southwest Museum. Leaflet* (Los Angeles, California)
Southwesterner	*Southwesterner* (El Paso, Texas)
SP	*South Pacific* (Sydney, Australia)
SPB	*South Pacific Bulletin* (Noumea, New Caledonia)
SPBA-A	*Sociedad de Puericultura de Buenos Aires. Anales* (Buenos Aires, Argentina)
SPC-QB	*South Pacific Commission. Quarterly Bulletin* (Noumea, New Caledonia)
SPC-TIC	South Pacific Commission. Technical Information Circular (Noumea, New Caledonia)
SPC-TP	South Pacific Commission. Technical Papers (Noumea, New Caledonia)
SPCYB	Soap, Perfumery and Cosmetics Year Book (London, England)
SPE-B	*Societe de Pathologie Exotique. Bulletin* (Paris, France)
Speculum	*Speculum* (Cambridge, Massachusetts)
SPH	*Social Process in Hawaii* (Department of Sociology. University of Hawaii. Honolulu, Hawaii)
Spotlight	*Spotlight* (Central News Agency. Johannesburg, South Africa)
SR	*Saturday Review* (London, England)
SRC-B	*Societe de Recherche Congolaise. Bulletin* (Brazzaville, Belgian Congo)
SRev	*Saturday Review* (New York, New York)
SrpAN[Medicine]-G	Srpska Akademia Nauk. Glacnik (Belgrade, Yugoslavia)
SRur	*Sociologia Ruralis* (Assen, Netherlands)
SS	*Scottish Studies* (Edinburgh, Scotland)
SSC-ZS-BLC	Scientific Society of China. Zoological Series. Biological Laboratory Contribution.
SSed	*Saga och Sed* (Uppsala, Sweden)
SSHAARH-B	*Societe Scientifique d'Hygiene Alimentaire et d l'Alimentation Rationnelle de l'Homme. Bulletin* (Paris, France)

SSM	*School Science and Mathematics* (Chicago, Illinois)
SSMed	*Social Science and Medicine* (Long Island City, New York)
SSR	*Sociology and Social Research* (Los Angeles, California)
STA-J	*Society for Tropical Agriculture. Journal [Nettai Nogaku Kwaishi]* (Publication of Taihoku University. Taipei, Japan)
ST-MS	*Seattle Times. Magazine Section* (Seattle, Washington)
Stocharstvo	*Stocharstvo* (Zagreb, Yugoslavia)
Stone Age	*Stone Age* (Farmingdale, New York)
ST-PS	*Seattle Times. Pictorial Section* (Seattle, Washington)
SU-FRI-S	Stanford University. Food Research Institute. Studies (Palo Alto, California)
SUMCJ	*Severance Union Medical College Journal* (Seoul, Korea)
Sumer	*Sumer* (Baghdad, Iraq)
SurLan	*Surinaamse Landbouw* (Paramaraibo, Surinam)
Susswaren	*Susswaren* (Werner Benecke Verlag. Hamburg, Germany)
SVie	*Science et la Vie* (Paris, France)
SW-HMM	*Sunday World-Herald Magazine of the Midlands* (Omaha, Nebraska)
Synergy	*Synergy* (San Francisco, California)
SZAPB	*Schweizerische Zeitschrift fur Allgemeine Pathologie und Bakteriologie* (Basel, Switzerland)
SZS	*Sibirskaya Zhivaya Starina* (Irkutsk, Siberia)
TAC-EB	Texas Agricultural College. Extension Bulletin (College Station, Texas)
TAE	*Trabalhos de Antropologia e Etnologia* (Porto, Portugal)
Tage-Buch	*Tage-Buch* (Berlin, Germany)
TAH	*Te Ao Hou* (Christchurch, New Zealand)
TAM	*Terre, Air, Mer* (Paris, France)
Tane	*Tane* (Journal of the Auckland University Field Club. Auckland, New Zealand)
Tararua	*Tararua* (Publication of Tararua Tramping Club, Inc. Wellington, New Zealand)
TArbok	Thisted Arbok (Thisted Amt County, Denmark)
TArch	*Tennessee Archaeologist* (Knoxville, Tennessee)
TAS-MP	*Tennessee Archaeological Society. Miscellaneous Papers* (Knoxville, Tennessee)
TBC-B	*Torrey Botanical Club. Bulletin* (New York, New York)
TCTJ	*Tea and Coffee Trade Journal* (New York, New York)
Tebiwa	*Tebiwa* (Pocatello, Idaho)
Tech	*Technology and Culture* (Detroit, Michigan)
TechQtly	*Technical Quarterly* (Master Brewers Association of America. Chicago, Illinois)
TermKoz	*Termeszettudomanyi Kozlony* (Budapest, Hungary)
Tex-AES-B	Texas. Agricultural Experiment Station. Bulletin (College Station, Texas)
TF	*Tierra Firme* (Madrid, Spain)
TFA	*Turk Folkloru Arastirmalari Yilligi. Belleten* (Ankara, Turkey)

TFSP	Texas Folklore Society Publication (Austin, Texas)
TGM	*Tropical and Geographical Medicine* (Haarlem, Netherlands)
TH	*Today's Health* (Chicago, Illinois)
THA	Thrum's Hawaiian Annual (Honolulu, Hawaii)
TI	*Tribuna Israelita* (Mexico City, Mexico)
Timehri	*Timehri* (Georgetown, Guyana)
TITBD	*Turk Ijiyen ve Tecrubi Bijoloji Dergisi* (Ankara, Turkey)
T-IU-CA-B	*Tokyo. Imperial University. College of Agriculture. Bulletin* (Tokyo, Japan)
T-IU-CA-J	*Tokyo. Imperial University. College of Agriculture. Journal* (Tokyo, Japan)
TIZ	*Taiwan Igakkai Zashi* [Journal of the Medical Association of Formosa] (Government Medical College. Taipei, Taiwan)
TJEM	*Tokushima Journal of Experimental Medicine* (Tokushima, Japan)
TNLaeg	*Tidsskrif for den Norske Laegeforening* (Dar-es-Salaam, Tanganyika)
Totem Pole	*Totem Pole* (Detroit, Michigan)
TP	*Trabalhos e Pesquisas. See UFRJ-IN-TP*
TPac	*Trans Pacific* (Tokyo, Japan)
TPBGS	Trudy po Prikladnoi Botanike, Genetike i Selektsii (Leningrad, Russia)
Tramontane	*Tramontane* (Perpignan, France)
Travel	*Travel* (New York)
TropAg	*Tropical Agriculture* (Port of Spain, Trinidad)
TropAgMag	*Tropical Agriculturalist and Magazine* (Ceylon Agriculture Society. Colombo, Sri Lanka
Tropenpflanzer	*Tropenpflanzer* (Berlin, Germany)
TropHort	*Tropical Horticulture* (Taipei, Taiwan)
T-RPC	*Tradicion. Revista Peruana de Cultura* (Cuzco, Peru)
True West	*True West* (Austin, Texas)
TSMA-J	*Tennessee Medical Association. Journal* (Nashville, Tennessee)
TTalk	*Tavern Talk* (Kansas City, Missouri)
TTechC-B-SS	Texas Technological College. Bulletin. Scientific Series (Lubbock, Texas)
TT-DA-M	Trinidad and Tobago. Department of Agriculture. Memoirs (Port of Spain, Trinidad)
TU	*Trait d'Union* (Paris, France)
TU-HI-Comm	Taihoku University. Horticulture Institute. Communications (Taipei, Taiwan)
TU-HI-Con	Taihoku University. Horticulture Institute. Contributions (Taipei, Taiwan)
TulU-MARS-P	Tulane University. Middle American Research Series. Publications (New Orleans, Louisiana)
TVie	*Terre et la Vie* (Paris, France)
UAE-B	*Union des Agriculteurs d'Egypte. Bulletin* (Egypt, Cairo)
U-AES-B	Utah. Agricultural Experiment Station. Bulletin (Logan, Utah)
U-AES-C	Utah. Agricultural Experiment Station. Circular (Logan, Utah)
UAlas-AP	University of Alaska. Anthropological Papers (College, Alaska)
UAlas-EB	University of Alaska. Extension Bulletin (College, Alaska)
UBCol-GS	University of British Columbia. Geography Series (Vancouver, Canada)
UC	*UNESCO Courier* (Paris, France)

UCal-AR — University of California. Anthropological Records (Berkeley, California)

UCal-AS-R — University of California. Archaeological Survey. Reports (Berkeley, California)

UCal-AS-UCARF — University of California. Archaeological Survey. University of California Archaeological Research Facility (Berkeley, California)

UCalD-CAR-P — University of California at Davis. Center for Archaeological Research. Publications (Davis, California)

UCal-PAAE — University of California. Publications in American Archaeology and Ethnology (Berkeley, California)

UCal-PG — University of California. Publications in Geography (Berkeley, California)

UCape-SAS-C — University of Cape Town. School of African Studies. Communications (Cape Town, South Africa)

UChi-SAOC — University of Chicago. Studies in Ancient Oriental Civilization (Chicago, Illinois)

UChild — *Understanding the Child* (Boston, Massachusetts)

UCLA-AS-AR — University of California at Los Angeles. Archaeological Survey. Annual Report (Los Angeles, California)

UConn-AES-B — University of Connecticut. Agricultural Extension Service. Bulletin (Storrs, Connecticut)

UCS-SA — University of Colorado Studies. Series in Anthropology (Boulder, Colorado)

UFRJ-IN-TP — Universidade Federal do Rio de Janeiro. Instituto de Nutricao. Trabalhos e Pesquisas (Rio de Janeiro, Brazil)

UHi-CES-HEC — University of Hawaii. Cooperative Extension Service. Home Economics Circular (Honolulu, Hawaii)

UHi-RP — University of Hawaii. Research Publication (Honolulu, Hawaii)

UIll-B — University of Illinois. Bulletin (Urbana, Illinois)

UJ — *Uganda Journal* (Kampala, Uganda)

UKy-AES-SCS-B — University of Kentucky. Agricultural Experiment Station. Southern Cooperative Series. Bulletin (Lexington, Kentucky)

ULaeg — *Ugeskrift for Laeger* (Copenhagen, Denmark)

ULF — Uppsala Lakarforenings Forhandlinger (Uppsala, Sweden)

UMich-MA-AP — University of Michigan. Museum of Anthropology. Anthropological Papers (Ann Arbor, Michigan)

UMich-MA-OC — University of Michigan. Museum of Anthropology. Occasional Contributions (Ann Arbor, Michigan)

UMinn-B-SSS — University of Minnesota. Bulletin. Social Science Series (Minneapolis, Minnesota)

UMontr-IB-C — Universite de Montreal. Institut de Botanique. Contributions (Montreal, Canada)

Umschau — *Umschau* (Frankfurt am Main, Germany)

UNacMex-IB-A — Universidad Nacional de Mexico. Instituto de Biologia. Anales (Mexico City, Mexico)

UNacMex-IB-FDC — Universidad Nacional de Mexico. Institute de Biologia. Folletos de Divulgacion Cientifica (Mexico City, Mexico)

UNap-FSA-A — *Universita di Napoli. Facolta di Scienza Agronomica. Annali* (Naples, Italy)

UNCol-MA-MS — University of Northern Colorado. Museum of Anthropology. Miscellaneous Series (Greeley, Colorado)

UNM-B-AS — University of New Mexico. Bulletin. Anthropological Series (Albuquerque, New Mexico)

UNM-B-BS — University of New Mexico. Bulletin. Biological Series (Albuquerque, New Mexico)

UNM-PB — University of New Mexico. Publications in Biology (Albuquerque, New Mexico)

UNMSML-FFB-A — Universidad Nacional Mayor de San Marcos de Lima. Facultad de Farmacologia y Bioquimica. Anales (Lima, Peru)

UNMSML-FM-A — Universidad Nacional Mayor de San Marcos de Lima. Facultad de Medicina. Anales (Lima, Peru)

UN-P-CAF-B — University of Nanking. Publications. College of Agriculture and Forestry. Bulletin (Nanking, China)

UOkla-DA-PA — University of Oklahoma. Department of Anthropology. Papers in Anthropology (Norman, Oklahoma)

UOtago-DA-SPA — University of Otago. Department of Anthropology. Studies in Prehistoric Anthropology (Dunedin, New Zealand)

UParis-IE-TM — Universite de Paris. Institut d'Ethnologie. Travaux et Memoires (Paris, France)

UPenn-AES-B — *See* Penn-AES-B

UPenn-BL-CBLMA — University of Pennsylvania. Botanical Laboratory. Contributions from the Botanical Laboratory and the Morris Arboretum (Philadelphia, Pennsylvania)

UPenn-UM-AP — University of Pennsylvania. University Museum. Anthropological Publications (Philadelphia, Pennsylvania)

UPenn-UM-MM — Universtiy of Pennsylvania. University Museum. Monographs (Philadelphia, Pennsylvania)

UPhil-NASB — *University of the Philippines. Natural and Applied Science Bulletin* (Diliman, Quezon City, Philippines)

UPhil-SE-IED-DP — University of the Philippines. School of Economics. Institute of Economic Development. Discussion Paper (Diliman, Quezon City, Philippines)

UQn-AM-OP — University of Queensland. Anthropology Museum. Occasional Papers (St. Lucia, Brisbane, Australia)

Urania — *Urania* (Jena, Austria)

URead-IAH-RP — University of Reading. Institute of Agricultural History. Research Paper (Reading, Berkshire, England)

USA-FCI-RDA-AR — United States Army. Food and Container Institute. Research and Development Association. Activity Report (Chicago, Illinois)

USA-RCG — United States Army. Report of the Commissary General (Washington, D.C)

USAfr-DAF-DBPP-BSB — Union of South Africa. Department of Agriculture and Forestry. Division of Botany and Plant Pathology. Botanical Survey. Bulletin (Pretoria, South Africa)

USAfr-DA-DB-M — Union of South Africa. Department of Agriculture. Division of Botany. Memoir (Pretoria, South Africa)

USAfr-DAF-DB-PIS-B — Union of South Africa. Department of Agriculture and Forestry. Division of Botany. Plant Industry Series. Bulletin (Pretoria, South Africa)

USAfr-DA-R	Union of South Africa. Department of Agriculture. Report (Pretoria, South Africa)
USAfr-DA-SB	Union of South Africa. Department of Agriculture. Science Bulletin (Pretoria, South Africa)
USCarl-PT	*Universidad de San Carlos. Publicacion Trimestral* (Guatemala City, Guatemala)
USCFF-RC	United States Commission on Fish and Fisheries. Report of the Commissioner (Washington, D.C.)
USDA-AH	United States Department of Agriculture. Agricultural Handbook (Washington, D.C.)
USDA-BAE-AEB	United States Department of Agriculture. Bureau of Agricultural Economics. Agricultural Economics Bibliography (Washington, D.C.)
USDA-BAI-AR	United States Department of Agriculture. Bureau of Animal Industry. Annual Report (Washington, D.C.)
USDA-BAI-B	United States Department of Agriculture. Bureau of Animal Industry. Bulletin (Washington, D.C.)
USDA-BAI-C	United States Department of Agriculture. Bureau of Animal Industry. Circular (Washington, D.C.)
USDA-BBS-B	United States Department of Agriculture. Bureau of Biological Survey. Bulletin (Washington, D.C.)
USDA-BPI-B	United States Department of Agriculture. Bureau of Plant Industry. Bulletin (Washington, D.C.)
USDA-C	United States Department of Agriculture. Circular (Washington, D.C.)
USDA-DB-B	United States Department of Agriculture. Division of Botany. Bulletin (Washington, D.C.)
USDA-DB-USNH-C	United States Department of Agriculture. Division of Botany. United States National Herbarium. Contributions (Washington, D.C.)
USDA-DHE-FES/DD-OCD	United States Department of Agriculture. Department of Home Economics. Federal Extension Service & Department of Defense. Office of Civil Defense (Washington, D.C.)
USDA-ERS-AER	United States Department of Agriculture. Economic Research Service. Agricultural Economic Report (Washington, D.C.)
USDA-ERS-MRR	United States Department of Agriculture. Economic Research Service. Market Research Report (Washington, D.C.)
USDA-ERS-MTS	United States Department of Agriculture. Economic Research Service. Marketing and Transport Situation (Washington, D.C.)
USDA-ESC	United States Department of Agriculture. Extension Service Circular (Washington, D.C.)
USDA-FB	United States Department of Agriculture. Farmer Bulletin (Washington, D.C.)
USDA-HB	United States Department of Agriculture. Hand Book (Washington, D.C.)
USDA-HGB	United States Department of Agriculture. Home and Garden Bulletin (Washington, D.C.)
USDA-L	United States Department of Agriculture. Leaflet (Washington, D.C.)
USDA-L-BC	United States Department of Agriculture. Library. Bibliographic Contributions (Washington, D.C.)
USDA-MP	United States Department of Agriculture. Miscellaneous Publications (Washington, D.C.)
USDA-OC-FHN	United States Department of Agriculture. Office of Communications. Food and Home Notes (Washington, D.C.)
USDA-OES-B	United States Department of Agriculture. Office of Experiment Stations. Bulletin (Washington, D.C.)
USDA-OESC	United States Department of Agriculture. Office of Experiment Stations. Circular (Washington, D.C.)
USDA-PMA-PA	United States Department of Agriculture. Production and Marketing Administration. Program Aid (Washington, D.C.)
USDA-RC	United States Department of Agriculture. Report of the Commissioner (Washington, D.C.)
USDA-TB	United States Department of Agriculture. Technical Bulletin (Washington, D.C.)
USDA-YB	United States Department of Agriculture. Year Book (Washington, D.C.)
USDCL-DCTR	United States Department of Commerce and Labor. Daily Consular Trade Reports (Washington, D.C.)
USDCL-MCR	United States Department of Commerce and Labor. Monthly Consular Reports (Washington, D.C.)
USDCL-USDA-B	United States Department of Commerce and Labor & United States Department of Agriculture. Bulletin (Washington, D.C.)
USDHEW-PHR	United States Department of Health, Education and Welfare. Public Health Reports (Washington, D.C.)
USDI-BF-RCF	United States Department of the Interior. Bureau of Fisheries. Report of the Commissioner of Fisheries (Washington, D.C.)
USDI-FWS	United States Department of the Interior. Fish and Wildlife Service (Washington, D.C.)
USDI-FWS-FL	United States Department of the Interior. Fish and Wildlife Service. Fishery Leaflet (Washington, D.C.)
USDI-USGGSRMR-CNAE	United States Department of the Interior. United States Geographical and Geological Survey of the Rocky Mountain Region. Contributions to North American Ethnology (Washington, D.C.)
USDL-CBP	United States Department of Labor. Children's Bureau Publications (Washington, D.C.)
USGGS-ST-UP	United States Geological and Geographical Survey. Survey of the Territories. Unclassified Publications (Washington, D.C.)
US-NAS-NRC-B	United States. National Academy of Sciences. National Research Council. Bulletin (Washington, D.C.)
USNI-P	*United States Naval Institute. Proceedings* (Washington, D.C.)
USPHR	*United States Public Health Reports* (Washington, D.C.)
USVI-DH-ND-B	United States Virgin Islands. Department of Health. Nutrition Department. Bulletin (Charlotte Amalie, Virgin Islands)
UTex-B-BRSS-S	University of Texas. Bulletin. Bureau of Research in Social Sciences. Study (Austin, Texas)
UTo-FS-J	*University of Tokyo. Faculty of Science. Journal* (Tokyo, Japan)

UU-AP	University of Utah. Anthropological Papers (Salt Lake City, Utah)		WASci	*Western American Scientist* (San Diego, California)
UWashBR	*University of Washington Business Review* (Seattle, Washington)		WAS-J	*Washington Academy of Science. Journal* (Washington, D.C.)
UWash-PA	University of Washington. Publications in Anthropology (Seattle, Washington)		WAust	*Wildlife in Australia* (Brisbane, Australia)
UWash-PE	University of Washington. Publications in Ethnography (Seattle, Washington)		WC	*World Crops* (London, England)
UWT	*Umschau in Wissenschaft und Technik* (Frankfurt am Main, Germany)		WCB	*Wisconsin Conservation Bulletin* (Madison, Wisconsin)
Vanyajati	*Vanyajati* (New Delhi, India)		WCBRS-J	*West China Border Research Society. Journal* (Chengtu, Szechuan, China)
Vasabladet	*Vasabladet*		WE	*What to Eat. The National Food Magazine* (Chicago, Illinois)
VC	*Virginia Cavalcade* (Richmond, Virginia)		West, The	*The West* (Freeport, New York)
Ven-MAG-DG-C	Venezuela. Ministerio de Agricultura y Ganaderia. Departamento de Genetica. Circular (Caracas, Venezuela)		WF	*Western Folklore* (Berkeley, California)
			WFood	*Wine and Food* (London, England)
			WG	*Weekly Graphic* (Quezon City, Philippines)
VFPA	Viking Fund Publication in Anthropology (New York, New York)		WH	*World Health* (Geneva, Switzerland)
VGJ	*Victorian Geographical Journal* (Melbourne, Australia)		WHC	*Woman's Home Companion* (Springfield, Ohio)
VH	*Volk und Heimat* (Eisenstadt, Germany)		WHH	*Woman and Her Home* (Pretoria, South Africa)
VHM	*Victorian Historical Magazine* (Melbourne, Australia)		WHO-B	*World Health Organization. Bulletin* (Geneva, Switzerland)
VI	*Veterinaria Italiana* (Teramo, Italy)		WHO Chronicle	*World Health Organization Chronicle* (Geneva, Switzerland)
VicQ	*Victoria Quarterly* (Kingston, Jamaica)			
Vie	*Vie et Sante* (Dammarie-les-Lys, France)		WHO Features	*World Health Organization Features* (Geneva, Switzerland)
Vie, La	*La Vie* (Paris, France)			
VJ	Vestisches Jahrbuch (Racklinghausen, Germany)		WHQ	*Washington Historical Quarterly* (Seattle, Washington)
VJA	*Victoria Journal of Agriculture* (Publication of the Victoria Department of Agriculture. Melbourne, Australia)		Wiad Lek	*Wiadomsci Lekarskie* (Warsaw, Poland)
			WIG	*West-Indische Gids* (Amsterdam, Netherlands)
VL	*Vie et Langage* (Paris, France)		WIMJ	*West Indian Medical Journal* (Mona, Jamaica)
VL-J	Vorarlberger Landesmuseumsvereins. Jahrbuch (Bregenz, Austria)		Wine	See: WFood
VM-HR	*Vegetarian Messenger and Health Review* (Manchester, England)		Wira	*Wira Kocha. Revista Peruana de Estudios Antropologicos.* (Lima, Peru)
VN	*Var Naring* (Stockholm, Sweden)		WKW	*Wiener Klinische Wochenschrift* (Vienna, Austria)
VNat	*Victorian Naturalist* (Melbourne, Australia)		WM	*War Medicine* (Chicago, Illinois)
VNews	*Vegetarian News* (London, England)		WMission	*World Mission* (New York, New York)
Voeding	*Voeding* (Utrecht, Netherlands)		WMon	*Westermann's Monatshefte* (Berlin, Germany)
Voedingsnieuws	*Voedingsnieuws* (Zoetmeer, Netherlands)		WMQ	*William and Mary Quarterly* (Williamsburg, Virginia)
Voprosy Pitania	*Voprosy Pitania* (Moscow, U.S.S.R.)			
Vt-AES-B	Vermont. Agricultural Experiment Station. Bulletin (Burlington, Vermont)		WMW	*Wiener Medizinische Wochenschrift* (Vienna, Austria)
VW	*Virginia Wildlife* (Publication of the Commission of Game and Inland Fisheries. Blacksburg, Virginia)		WorldArch	*World Archaeology* (Henley on Thames, England)
			World's Work	*World's Work* (New York, New York)
VZ	*Vitalstoffe Zivilisationskrankheiten* (Hanover, Germany)		WP	*Waman Puma. Revista Mensuel de Cultura Folklore* (Cuzco, Peru)
WA	*Washington Archaeologist* (Seattle, Washington)		WRND	World Review of Nutrition and Dietetics (Basel, Switzerland)
WAJBC	*West African Journal of Biological and Applied Chemistry* (Ibadan, Nigeria)		WSE-M	*Wernerian Society of Edinburgh. Memoirs* (Edinburgh, Scotland)
Walkabout	*Walkabout* (Melbourne, Australia)		WVAS-P	*West Virginia Academy of Science. Proceedings* (Morgantown, West Virginia)
WAN	*Western Australian Naturalist* (Perth, Australia)		WW	*Wyoming Wildlife* (Cheyenne, Wyoming)
WArch	*Wisconsin Archaeologist* (Milwaukee, Wisconsin)		WWM	*Wide World Magazine* (London, England)
			YDS-T	*Yorkshire Dialect Society. Transactions* (York, England)
WASA-J	*West African Science Association. Journal* (Achimoto, Ghana)		Yeda'am	*Yeda'am* (Tel Aviv, Israel)
WASAL-T	Wisconsin Academy of Sciences, Arts, and Letters. Transactions (Milwaukee, Wisconsin)		YLM	*Yn Lioar Manninagh*
			YMT	*Yikal Maya Than* (Merida, Yucatan, Mexico)

YN	*Young Naturalist* (London, England)
YNN	*Yosemite Nature Notes* (United States National Park Service. Yosemite National Park, California)
YUPA	Yale University Publications in Anthropology (New Haven, Connecticut)
ZAEU	*Zeitschrift fur Anthropologie, Ethnologie und Urgeschichte. See ZE*
Zaire	*Zaire* (Brussels, Belgium)
ZASA	*Zeitschrift fur Aegyptische Sprache und Altertumskunde* (Leipzig, Germany)
ZAssyr	*Zeitschrift fur Assyriologie* (Berlin, Germany)
ZBPIH	*Zentralblatt fur Bakteriologie, Parasitenkunde, Infektionskrankheiten und Hygiene* (Jena, Austria)
ZDPV	*Zeitschrift fur Deutschen Palastina-Vereins* (Weisbaden, Germany)
ZE	*Zeitschrift fur Ethnologie* (Berlin, Germany)
ZEM	*Zentralblatt der Experimentellen Medizin* (Berlin, Germany)
ZErn	*Zeitschrift fur Ernahrungswissenschaft* (Darmstadt, Germany)
ZErn-S	*Zeitschrift fur Ernahrungswissenschaft. Supplementa* (Darmstadt, Germany)
ZFMH	*Zeitschrift fur Fleisch- und Milch-Hygiene* (Berlin, Germany)
ZMHil	*Zeitschrift des Museums zu Hildesheim* (Hildesheim, Germany)
ZG	*Zentralblatt fur Gynakologie* (Leipzig, Germany)
ZHVS	*Zeitschrift des Historischen Vereins fur Stiermark* (Graz, Austria)
ZK	*Zeitschrift fur Kulturgeschichte* (Berlin, Germany)
ZLUF	*Zeitschrift fur Lebensmittel-Unterschungen Forschung* (Berlin, Germany)
ZLVO	*Zeitschrift fur Landwirtschaftliches Versuchs wesen in Osterreich* (Vienna, Austria)
ZMOT	*Zeitschrift fur Morphologie und Okologie der Tiere* (Berlin, Germany)
ZMS	Zbornik Matice Srpske za Knijizevnost i Jezik (Novy Sad, Yugoslavia)
ZOC	*Zeitschrift fur Oeffentliche Chemie* (Weimar, Germany)
Zoe	*Zoe* (San Francisco, California)
Zoologist	*Zoologist* (London, England)
ZOV	*Zeitschrift fur Osterreichische Volkskunde* (Vienna, Austria)
ZP	Zambia Papers (University of Zambia. Lusaka, Zambia)
ZSpir	*Zeitschrift fur Spiritusindustrie* (Berlin, Germany)
ZTZ	*Zeitschrift fur Tierzuchtung und Zuchtungsbiologie* (Berlin, Germany)
ZUL	*Zeitschrift fur Untersuchung und Lebensmittel* (Berlin, Germany)
ZUNG	*Zeitschrift fur Untersuchungen der Nahrungs- und Genusmittel* (Berlin, Germany)
ZVV	*Zeitschrift des Vereins fur Volkerkunde* (Berlin, Germany)

BIBLIOGRAPHY

1.   A. 1891.   Flour from jak-seeds?   Trop Ag 11:62

   Inquiry concerning feasibility of producing flour from seeds of Artocarpus heterophyllus, and its potential nutritional value.

2.   Aaronsohn, Aaron.   1909.   Contribution a l'histoire des cereales.   [Contribution to the history of cereals.]   SBFB 56:196-203; 237-245; 251-288.

3.   Aaronsohn, Aaron & Schweinfurth, Georg. 1906.   Die auffindung des wilden Emmers (Triticum dicoccum) in Nordpalastina.   [The discovery of wild emmer in northern Palestine.] AMWEP Nos. 7-8:213-220.

4.   Abarbanell, Albert.   Nutrition, health, and sexuality.   In The encyclopedia of sexual behavior.   Edited by Albert Ellis & Albert Abarbanell.   1964.   Vol. 2.   Pp. 776-787.   New York: Hawthorn Books.

5.   Abbatucci, S. L'alimentation des Chinois d'Indochine et de la Chine du sud.   [Diet of the Chinese in Indochina and South China.]   In L'alimentation indigene dans les colonies francaises.   Protectorats et territoires sous mandats. Edited by G. Hardy & C. Richet. 1933. Pp. 330-335. Paris: Vigot Freres.

   Superficial sketch of Chinese diet.

6.   Abbott, Isabella Aiona   & Williamson, Eleanor Horswill.   1974.   Limu.   An ethnobotanical study of some edible Hawaiian seaweeds. Lawai, Kauai: Pacific Tropical Botanical Garden.

7.   Abbott, O.D.; Townsend, R.O. & French, R.B.   1952.   A survey of food preferences of Florida men.   F-AES-B No. 500.

8.   Abbott, P.H. 1950.   A survey of signs of nutritional ill-health among the Azande of the southern Sudan.   RSTMH-T 43:477-492.

9.   Abbott, W.L. 1892. Ethnological collections in the U.S. National Museum from Kilimanjaro, East Africa.   SI-AR for the year 1891.   Pp. 381-428.

   Culinary utensils: pp. 410-416.

10.   Abe, Koryu   & Tsuji, Shigemitsu.   1974. Tofu no hon.   [Book of tofu]   Tokyo: Murata Shoten.

   Includes historical material on tofu, a curd prepared from soybeans.

11.   Abel, Mary White Hinman. 1890. Practical sanitary and economic cooking, adapted to persons of moderate and small means.   New York [?]: American Public Health Association.   Reviewed BMJ 2: 736-737 [1890].

12.   Abelman, Max. 1933.   Better food and satisfied patient.   MHosp 40: 47-50.

   Brief description of the Dietetics Department, Brooklyn Jewish Hospital. Reviewed in JSS 28:95,96.

13.   Abelson, Philip H.   1975.   Food: politics, economics, nutrition and research.   Washington, D.C.: American Association for the Advancement of Science.

14.   Abrams, Jr., H. Leon.   Sugar - a cultural complex and its impact on modern society.   Paper presented at 67th Annual Meeting of the American Anthropological Association.   21 November, 1968. Seattle, Washington.

15.   Abrams, Jr., H. Leon.   The sociocultural syndrome of milk.   Paper presented at 69th Annual Meeting of the American Anthropological Association. 19 to 22 November 1970. San Diego, California.

16.   Abrams, Ira. Formation of complex fishing organizations as a recent adaptation to a new environment in Xaibe, Belize. Paper presented at 73rd Annual Meeting of the American Anthropological Association.   19-24 November, 1974. Mexico City.

17.   Abreu, Velho H. de L.G. 1954.   Estudo da alimentacao dos indigenas em Angola. [Study of

the food habits of Angola natives.] A Ang 9:117-186.

18.   Abrol, Y.B.; Uprety, D.C. & Swaran, T. Browning of chapatties. Research communication. In First Asian Congress on Nutrition. 22 January -2 February 1971. Hyderabad. India. Proceedings. Edited by P.G. Tulpule & Kamala S. Jaya Rao. 1972. Pp. 803-804. Hyderabad: Nutrition Society of India.

A recently introduced hybrid dwarf wheat produces a flour the dough of which browns immediately, thus making the staple bread produced from it less acceptable to consumers. This report indicates the chemical basis of the coloring reaction.

19.   Accum, Fredric. 1820. A treatise on adulterations of food and culinary poisons. Exhibiting the fraudulent sophistications of bread, beer, wine, spiritous liquors, tea, coffee, cream, confectionery, vinegar, mustard, pepper, cheese, olive oil, pickles and other other articles employed in domestic economy. And methods of detecting them. Philadelphia: Ab'm Small.

20.   Acker, P.; Leclerc, A.-M.; & Ramel, P. 1968. Quelques aliments traditionnels du Congo (Brazzaville) envisagees sous l'angle de leur apport lipidique [Some traditional Congo (Brazzaville) foods, seen from the perspective of their lipid supply.] ANA 22:17-34.

21.   Acosta, Jose de. 1604. The natural and morall historie of the East and West Indies. In treating of the remarkable things of heaven, of the elements, metals, plants and beast, which are proper to that country together with the manners, ceremonies, lawes, governments and warres of the Indians. Translated by Edward Grimestone. London: Printed by V. Sims for E. Blount and W. Apsley.

Contains notes on a Peruvian indigenous bread tauta; melindre, a maize flour confection; and a description of the preparation of chicha, a maize beer.

22.   Acosta, Phyllis B. & Aranda, Robert G. Mexican - American low-income groups. Cultural determinants of food habits in children of Mexican descent in California. In Practices of low-income families in feeding infants and small children with particular attention to cultural subgroups. Edited by Samuel J. Fomon & T.A. Anderson. 1972. Pp. 75-87. Washington, D.C.: U.S. Department of Health, Education and Welfare.

Looks at attitudes toward food, and goes on to examine food practices in Agua Prieta and Esqueda, Sonora, Mexico; San Ysidro, California; East Los Angeles, California and Hanford, California

23.   Adachi, Isamo. 1950. Kaitei Nihon Shokumotsu-shi. [History of Japanese food.] 2 Vols. Tokyo: Yuzan - kaku.

24.   Adair, John. Alcoholism through Navaho eyes. Film screened at 75th Annual Meeting of 21 November, 1976. Washington, D.C.

25.   Adama, William Y. 1966. The vintage of Nubia. Kush 14: 262-283.

26.   Adametz, L. 1892. Ueber die herstellung und zusammensetzung des bosnischen trappisten kases. [On the manufacture and composition of Bosnian Trappist cheeses.1 M Zeit 2]: 310-313.

27.   Adamovic, Lujo. 1911. Die Pflanzenwelt. [The plant world.] Leipzig: W. Klinkhardt.

28.   Adams, Jeanne Marion. North American Indian maize preparation and its implications for archaeology. Masters thesis. Anthropology. Florida Atlantic University, 1972.

29.   Adams, John W. The politics of feasting among the Gitksan. Ph.D. dissertation. Harvard University. 1969.

A study of the potlatch in a contemporary, Pacific Northwest Native American group. Rejects previous theories of the potlatch as an institution facilitating the redistribution of food and material wealth, in favor of the hypothesis that potlatching is, rather, a social mechanism which has evolved to promote the redistribution of individuals to corporate groups by regulating population flow through, for example, marriage ties which are used to counteract conflicts arising within the social structure.

30.   Adams, Mabel E. A study of the food consumption habits of a group of farm families in Alabama. Master's thesis. University of Alabama. 1943.

31.   Adams, Ramon F. 1972. Come an' get it: the story of the old cowboy cook. Norman: University of Oklahoma Press.

32.   Adams, Richard N. A nutritional research program in Guatemala. In Health, culture, and community. Case studies of public reactions to health programs. Edited by Benjamin D. Paul & W. Miller. 1955. New York: Russell Sage Foundation.

In order to obtain blood samples for biochemical analyses, the anthropologist had to confront local concepts of blood loss as weakening. Using the same logic, it was explained that, since blood was considered a measure of weakness or strength, predisposed a person to be sick or well, it would follow that the blood could also be a measure of sickness or well-being. Thus, the anthropologist was able to rationalize the need for taking samples from local children.

33.   Adams, Richard N. 1959. Nutrition, anthropology and the study of man. NR 17:97-99.

Influence of anthropology in applied public health nutrition programs and complementary nature of both disciplines when working together.

34. Adams, Richard N. Food habits in Latin America: a preliminary historical survey. In Human nutrition: historic and scientific. Edited by Iago Galdston. 1960. Pp. 1-22. New York Academy of Medicine. Institute of Social and Historical Medicine. Monograph 3. New York: International Universities Press.

35. Adams, Richard N. Cultural aspects of infant malnutrition and mental development. In Malnutrition, learning and behavior. Edited by Nevin S. Scrimshaw & John E. Gordon. 1968. Pp. 465-474. Cambridge, Massachusetts, London, England: Massachusetts: Institute of Technology Press.

Calls for diachronic study of the variables which impinge upon nutritional status, learning, and behavior, but stresses that "Cultural content is to be distinguished from relevant socioeconomic and psychobiological elements". Introduces the concept of "adaptive cycle" to characterize the effective relations of causal variables over time during human psychophysiological development.

36. Adams, Suzanne F. 1959. Use of vegetables in infant feeding through the ages. JADA 35:692-703.

37. Adams, W.R. 1949. Food animals used by the Indians at the Angel site. IAS-P 59:19-24.

38. Addington, James. Collectors or farmers dental attrition and pathology as related to subsistence in the Ohio Valley. Paper presented at 72nd Annual Meeting of the American Anthropological Association. 1 December, 1973. New Orleans, Louisiana.

39. Adelson, Sadye F. 1960. Some problems in collecting dietary data from individuals. JADA 36: 453-461.

40. Adelson, Sadye F. & Blake, E.C. 1950. Diets of families in the open country: A Georgia and an Ohio County, Summer, 1945. USDA-MP No. 704.

41. Adkin, G.L. 1942. Former food stores (pataka) in Lake Horowhenua. JPS 51:181-186.

New Zealand Maori.

42. Adolph, William Henry. 1924. A study of North China dietaries. JHE 17: 1-7. Includes tables of kinds, quantities, and food value of foods eaten by 340 adults, and 114 children under 12 years of age. Observations on reaction of Chinese students in United States to North American diet.

43. Adolph, William Henry. 1926. Analyses of Chinese food materials. PJS 30:287-293.

44. Adolph, William Henery. 1937-1938. Oddities in nutrition. PNHB 12: 199-212.

An informal review of the history of dietetics, food uses, and food fads.

45. Adolph, William Henry. 1951. Nutrition under the Chinese Communist government. SM 73: 128-130.

Reviews mandated changes in dietaries, research programs, and health status in relation to nutrition.

46. Adolph, William Henry. 1954. Nutrition in the Near East. JADA 30:753-756.

Basic cereal diet; limited animal protein; value of rural Lebanese diet; variation in economic status; foods unique to the area; feeding of Palestinian refugees.

47. Adriaens, E.L. 1951. Recherches sur l'alimentation des populations au Kwango. [Research on the diet of the populations of Kwango.] BACB 42:227-270, 473-552.

48. Adriaens, E.L. 1952. A propos d'enquetes alimentaires. [Concerning dietary investigations.] BACB 43:45-54.

49. Adriaens, E.L. 1957. L' alimentation, probleme d' Afrique Centrale. [Diet, a Central African problem.] PAC no.35. Pp. 23-27.

Suggests rich protein sources not be exported, but consumed domestically.

50. Adriaens, E.L. & Lozet, F. 1951. Contribution a l' etude des boissons fermentees indigenes au Ruanda. [Contribution to the study of native Ruanda fermented beverages.] BACB 42:933-950.

51. Adriano, F.T. & Guzman, M.S. de 1932. The proximate chemical analysis of some Philippine food products. PAg 20:580-592.

52. Adriano, F.T.; Ramos, H.T.; Ynalvez, L.A. 1932. The proximate analysis of Philippine food and feeding stuffs. 3. PAg 20:530-534.

53. Aerboe, Friederich; Ballod, Karl; & Beyschlag, Franz. 1914-1915. Die deutsche Volkernahrung und der englische aushundersplan. [Diet of the German people and the English starvation plan. Edited by Paul Eltzbacher. Braunschweig: Vieweg & Sohn.

54. Agathon, M. 1976. Les therapies comportementales dans les troubles due comportement alimentaire. [Behavioral thera-pies in the treatment of human dietary problems.] ANA 30:281-288.

55. Agee, James Evans Walker. 1970. Let us now praise famous men. New York: Ballantine Books. No. 122.

Description of a rural Alabama kitchen: pp. 375; rural Alabama dietary: pp. 377-378.

56.   Aggarwal, J.S. 1961. L'alimentation des populations rurales du delta vif du Niger et de l'Office du Niger. [Diet of the rural populations of the Niger shifting delta and of the Department of Niger.] Secretariat d'Etat aux Relations avec les Etats de la Communaute. Vol. 1. Paris: P. Dupont.

57.   Aggarwal, V. A study of the food habits of the people in a selected rural community. Master's thesis. Lady Irwin College University of Delhi. 1967.

> The community studied is Nangloi, in Delhi Union Territory. Goal of this study was to determine the influence, if any, between patterns of food consumption and various socio-economic variables e.g., caste, ownership of cattle, land, prestige items, age and gender. Conclusion was that food patterns seemed to be determined more by cultural norms than by socio-economic factors. No differences in meal patterns were reported on the basis of age or gender.

58.   Aguilar - Santos, C. & Doty, M.S. 1968-1969. Caulerpa as food in the Philippines. PAg 52:447-482.

59.   Aguilera, Miguel. 1973. La antropofagia de las tribus americanas [Cannibalism among Native American tribes.] BHA 24:162-185.

60.   Ahmann, Chester F., Abbott, Ouida Davis & Westover Georgia. 1930. A nutritional study of the white school children in five representative counties of Florida. F-AES-B No. 216.

> The counties involved in this survey are Alachua, Jackson, Hillsborough, Columbia, and Indian River, each representing a different geographic area of the State. Two-day dietary intake was recorded for 2,110 children.

61.   Ahmed, Myrna M. A sociological approach to a qualitative dietary survey and food habit study in an Andea community. Master's thesis. Cornell University, 1967.

62.   Ahmed, Myrna J.M. & van Veen, Andre G. 1969. A sociological approach to a dietary survey and food habit study in an Andean community. TGM 20:88-100.

> Contains data on changing food habits and food beliefs in the Peruvian village of Yungay (9.08S, 77.73W). Fifty-one households were interviewed.

63.   Ahuja, P.N. 1936. Diet factor in human economy. SMJ 8:170-174.

64.   Aichinger, E. 1966. Food habits and taboos. RLCT 21:16-17.

65.   Aimez, P. 1976. Modifications des comport ements alimentaires pathogenes; techniques de groupe. [Modification of pathogenic dietary behavior; group techniques] ANA 30:289-300.

66.   Albino, R.C. & Thompson, V.J. 1956. The effect of sudden weaning on Zulu children. BJMP 29: 177.

67.   Albrecht, F.W. No date. The natural food supply of the Australian Aborigines. Adelaide: Aborigines' Friends' Association.

> A small pamphlet discussing sources of water, animal and vegetable food of Central Australia's native groups.

68.   Albrecht, William A. Nutrition and the climatic pattern of soil development. In Centennial: collected papers presented at the Centennial celebration. Washington, D.C., September 13-17, 1948. 1950. Pp. 85-96.

> Relationship between climate, soil quality, food quality and disease is explored. Correlations between certain soil types and certain diseases are illustrated on maps.

69.   Alcott, William A. 1838. Vegetable diet: as sanctioned by medical men, and by experience in all ages. New York: Fowler & Wells.

70.   Aldebrandin. Medecin de Roy de france. ca. 1484. Le livre de Maistre Aldebrandin pour la sante du corps garder et du chacun membre, pour soi garder et conserver en sante, compose a la requete du roi de France.

> Includes chapters on how to eat and drink; as well as on the use of various foods such as bread, wine and different meats.

71.   Aldrich, C. Anderson. 1942. Ancient processes in a scientific age. Feeding aspects. AJDC 64:714-722.

> Comments on successful breast feeding, and on hospital practices which are inimical to it.

72.   Alexander, A.B. 1902. Notes on the boats, apparatus, and fishing methods employed by the natives of the South Sea Islands and results of fishing trials by the Albatross. USCFF-RC for the year 1901. Pp. 743-829.

> Areas visited include the Marquesas, Paumotu, Society, Gilbert, Marshall and Caroline Islands. Details of fishing procedures are extensive and accompanied by drawings of equipment as well as black and white photographs.

73.   Alexander, D. 1970. Retailing in England during the Industrial Revolution. London: Athlone Press.

74.   Alexander, Jeanette. Evaluation as a means of determining the content and procedures for teaching foods and nutrition. Master's thesis. University of Oklahoma. 1943.

75. Alford, B.B. & Nance, Emma B. 1976. Customary foods in the Navajo diet. JADA 69:538-539.

76. Alireza, Marianne. 1971. At the drop of a veil. Boston: Houghton Mifflin.

Saudi Arabian food and food habits. Communal water bowl: pp. 6,7; variety in meals: p. 41; breakfast: p. 57; goat cheese: p.75; dining etiquette: pp.91-92; confections: p. 112; seeds as snacks: p. 185; lamb's head stew: p. 87; spiced zweiback: p. 220; whole lamb; banana pastry: p.234; Ramadan foods: p. 289.

77. Allard, D. 1896. Le beurre. Production du lait, ecremage, travail de la creme, fabrication du beurre...et les fromages, e'tude des principaux types. [Butter. Production of milk, removing and working the cream, manufacture of butter...and cheese. Study of the principal types.] Paris: les fils d'E. Deyrolle.

78. Allen, Alberta J.S. Food consumption of 86 families in Carlsbad, New Mexico. Master's thesis. Prairie View Texas: Prairie View University. 1945.

79. Allen, K.W. 1955. The monotonous diet of the African. EAMJ 32:95-97.

80. Allen, O.H. & Allen, Ethel K. 1933. The manufacture of poi from taro in Hawaii, with special emphasis upon its fermentation. Hi-AES-B No. 70.

Poi is a paste prepared from the boiled corm of Colocasia esculenta. It was the staple starch food of the islands before European contact.

81. Aller, Wilma F. 1954. Aboriginal food utilization of vegetation by the Indians of the Great Lakes region, recorded in the Jesuit Relations. WArch 35:59-73.

Reference here is to the Historical introduction to the Jesuit Relations and allied documents. Edited by Reuben Gold-Thwaites. 1896-1901. Cleveland: Burrows Brothers Co.

82. Allgeir, R.J.; Nickol, G.B. & Conner, H.A. 1974. Vinegar: history and development. FPD 8:69-71.

83. Almaral, F.P. 1945. Politica alimentar. [Politics of nutrition] Sao Paulo: Editora Brasiliense.

84. Altheer, J.J. 1857. Eetbare aardsoorten en geophagie. [A geophagous edible earth] NTNI 13:83-100.

85. Altschul, Aaron M. 1965. Proteins: their chemistry and politics. New York: Basic Books.

86. Altus, W.D. 1949. Adjustments and food versions among Army illiterates. JConP 13:429-432.

Posits the validity of food aversions related to socio-economic level, and further that the number of an individual's food aversions may be a partial index to psychological adjustment.

87. Alum, Rolando A. The "retail stores system" of a Dominican plantation community. Paper presented at 76 Annual Meeting of the American Anthropological Association. 29 November to 3 December, 1977. Houston, Texas.

This report presents ethnographical data on the internal marketing system of small retail stores (colmados) in a typical cane-workers' community located in a state-owned plantation in the Dominican Republic. Data are presented on plantation social organization, as well as nutritional patterns. The study also tests some of the dimensions of Sidney Mintz's proposed definition of the "rural proletariat".

88. Alvarado, Lisandro. 1919. Antropofagia. CVen 3:295-301.

89. Alvarez, L.E. Cuevas. 1957. La alimentacion del pueblo dominicano. [Diet of the Dominican people] USDom-A nos. 81-82. Pp. 181-230.

90. Amados, Enrique S. Contribucion al estudio de alimentos mexicanos (Amaranths paniculatus). [Contribution to the study of Mexican foods (Amaranthus paniculatus).] Thesis. Faculty of Chemical Sciences. Universidad de Mexico.

91. Amanolahi, Sekandar. The herder-gatherers of Iran. Paper presented at 76th Annual Meeting of the American Anthropological Association. 29 November to 3 December, 1977. Houston, Texas.

This paper explores the ecological adaptation of the herder-gatherers in the Zagros Mountains, and also makes speculations about early Neolithic communities in this part of the world. The herder-gatherers have adapted themselves by raising goats and by gathering fruits from partially-wild, privately-owned trees. Providing pasture and gathering fruit have led the herder-gatherers to pursue a tentless, semi-nomadic existence during part of each year. Ethnographic evidence from these herder-gatherers suggests that plants and animals were originally domesticated by populations while still pursuing a hunting mode of subsistence, and that pastoral nomadism developed independently of intensive agriculture.

92. Ambro, Richard D. 1967. Dietary - technological - ecological aspects of Lovelock Cave coprolites. In Papers on Great Basin archaeology. UCal-AS No. 70. UCARF Pp. 37-47.

In this paper, the author considers the

advantages and problems of using prehistorical human fecal remains as a basis for reconstructing dietary patterns. The material referred to is from the Nevada cave site. Conclusions regarding the persistence of dietary pattern at the site are offered.

93.   American Peanut Research and Education Association 1973. Peanuts, culture, and uses. A symposium. Raleigh, North Carolina State University.

94.   American Can Company. 1972. Carbonated beverages in the United States. Greenwich, Connecticut: American Can Company.

95.   American Dietetic Association. 1944. Selected list of references on national food patterns and recipes. Chicago: American Dietetic Association.

96.   American Frog Canning Company. 1934. Frog recipe book. New Orleans: American Frog Canning Company.

97.   American Manufacturing Company. 1883. The American fruit drier, or pneumatic evaporator. Waynesboro, Pennsylvania: American Manufacturing Company.

98.   American Philosophical Society. 1958. Benjamin Franklin: the art of eating. Princeton: Princeton University Press.

99.   American Public Health Association. 1955. Nutrition practices: a guide for public health administrators. New York: American Public Health Association.

    Contents include: nutrition confronts the administrator; nutrition's place in public health practice; determining opportunities for nutrition services: program planning; interdepartmental and inter-agency relationships; Federal and state financial aid; assessing nutrition service gains

100.   Ames, Genevieve M. The problem drinker housewife: changes in role and role behavior. paper presented at 77 Annual Meeting of the American Anthropological Assocaition. 14 to 18 November, 1978. Los Angeles, California.

101.   Ames, Oakes. 1939. Economic annuals and and human cultures. Reprint. Cambridge: Botanical Museum of Harvard University, 1953.

    Contains extensive historical data.

102.   Amin, Galal. 1966. Food supply and economic development with special reference to Egypt. London: Frank Cass.

103.   Amoreux, P-J. 1784. Triate de l'olivier, contenant l'histoire et la culture des arbres, les differentes manieres d'exprimer l'huile dolive, celle de la conserver, etc. 2nd edition. [Treasise on the olive, containing the history and the cultivation of the trees, the different manners of pressing the oil of the olive, of its preservation, etc. 2nd

edition] Montpellier: the widow Gontier.

104.   Amsden, Diana Avery. Fasting as a culture trait. Paper presented at 77th Annual Meeting of the Anthropoligical Association. 29 November to 3 December, 1977. Houston, Texas.

    After discussing animal fasting, which the author believes to be a precursor of certain forms of human fasting, a history of fasting is proposed beginning with the Lower Paleolithic. Generalizations are made about fasting as a cultural trait, and definitions of fasting are presented. The paper concludes with an examination of political and contemporary medical fasting.

105.   Anderson, Raoull R. Trawler cook as mother. Paper presented at 68th Annual Meeting of the American Anthropological Association. 20 to 23 November, 1969. New Orleans, Louisiana.

    This paper examines the process by which men become trawler cooks - a traditionally feminine role, in the context of the otherwise traditionally highly masculine society of Grand Banks trawler fishermen of Newfoundland. A consideration of trawler crew behavior reveals that the trawler cook plays a distinctively anomalous part in this masculine context, and an examination is made of the factors implicated in the special kinds of persisting strains in role relationships faced by the cooks primarily while at sea. An attempt is then made to comprehend the techniques or strategies employed by the cook in coping with these strains.

106.   Andersen, Raoul. That's my fish° Spatial access and competition in Newfoundland fishing. Paper presented at 9th International Congress of Anthropological and Ethnological Sciences. 28 August to 8 September, 1973. Chicago, Illinois.

    Examines strategies developed by Newfoundland fishermen since the 19th Century, in response to competition for acess to marine resources in in-shore and off-shore waters. The effects of modern technologies on fishing, and community economic and socio-spatial variables are considered.

107.   Anderson, A.W. 1955. Maori food plants. 2. The introduced species. Gard Chron 137:88-89.

108.   Anderson, Edgar. 1944. Maize reventador. MBG-A 31:301-312.

    Technical description of a primitive popcorn from western Mexico, including two archaeological ocurrences of the same or a similar variety.

109.   Anderson, Edgar. 1944. Two collections of prehistoric corn-tassels from southern Utah. MBG-A 31:345-350.

110.   Anderson, Edgar. The maize collectins from Painted Cave. In Painted Cave, northeastern Ari-

zona. Edited by Emil Haury. 1945. Amerind-P No. 3 Pp. 77-85.

111.   Anderson, Edgar. 1947. Corn before Columbus. Des Moines, Iowa. Pioneer Hi-Bred Corn Co.

112.   Anderson, Edgar. Racial indentity of the corn from Castle Park. In The Archaeology of Castle Park, Dinosaur Natonal Monument. Edited by R.F. Burg & C.R. Scoggin. 1948. UCS-SA No. 2 Pp. 91-92.

113.   Anderson, Edgar. Zapalote chica: an important chapter in the history of maize and man. In 33 Congreso Internacional de Americanistas. 20-27 Julio 1958. San Jose, Costa Rica. Actas. Vol. One. 1959. Pp. 230-237.

     Zapalote chico is a variety of Zea mays which matures rapidly and is relatively independent of day length [i.e. amount of available sunlight]. The author observes that most varieties of maize have been unconsciously selected to fit the day length of the region in which they are grown. The characteristics of Zapalote chico are such as to raise the possibility that when dent varieties first moved up into the Great Plains and Southwestern United States they might have done so in less than a decade rather than by the slow selection of strains adapted to longer and longer summer days, since their ability to mature early endowed them with a potential to cross with varieties and inbreds from the northern part of the maize belt with little or no difficulty.

114.   Anderson, Edgar & Barlow, R.H. 1943. The maize tribute of Moctezuma's empire. MBG-A 30L413-420.

     Quantities, and contributing areas are studied.

115.   Anderson, Edgar & Blanchard, Frederick D. 1942. Prehistoric maize from Canon del Muerto. AJB 29:832-835.

116.   Anderson, Edgar & Cutler Hugh C. 1942. Races of Zea mays l: their recognition and classification. MBG-A 29: 69-89.

     Pima-Papago, and Pueblo maize.

117.   Anderson, Edgar & Cutler Hugh C. 1950. Methods of popping corn and their historical significance. SJA 6: 303-308.

118.   Anderson, Edgar & Finan, John Jay. 1945. Maize in the Yanhuitlan Codex. MBG-A 32:361-366.
     This codex, produced after contact, (ca. 1550-1570) recounts the history of the town of Yanhuitlan, located in the Mixteca Alta, half-way between Nochistlan and Tepozcolula, in the present State of Oaxaca. Descriptions of the drawings of maize in the Codex are given, together with mention of maize granaries used, and the tumpline method of transporting the grain.

119.   Anderson, Jr., Eugene Newton. The ethnoicthylogy of the Hong Kong boat people. Ph.D. dissertation. University of California, Berkeley. 1967.

120.   Anderson, Jr., Eugene Newton. 1970. Reflexions sur la cuisine. [Reflections on food.] L'Homme 10:122-123.

     Encourages greater attention to food and nutrition among anthropologists.

121.   Anderson, Jr., Eugene Newton. Chinese fishermen in Hong Kong and in Malaysia. Paper presented at 9th International Congres of Anthropological and Ethnological Sciences. 28 August to 8 September, 1973. Chicago, Illinois.

     Study of South Chinese coastal fishing communities, both traditional and those more recently established by in-migrants.

122.   Anderson, Jr., Eugene Newton & Anderson, Marja L. Folk dietetics in two Chinese communities, and its implications for the study of Chinese medicine. In Medicine in Chinese cultures: comparative studies of health care in Chinese and other societies. Papers and discussions from a conference held in Seattle, Washington, U.S.A. February, 1974. Edited by Arthur Kleinman; Peter Kunstadter; E. Russell Alexander & James L. Gale. 1975. Pp. 143-175. A publication of the Geographic Health Studies, John E. Fogarty International Center for Advanced Study in the Health Sciences. United States Department of Health, Education and Welfare. Public Health Service. National Institutes of Health, DHEW Publication No. (NIH) 75-653. Washington, D.C.: Government Printing Office.

     Contribution includes discussion of food beliefs and classifications (hot-cold-neutral); food as a religious and social marker; nutritional considerations and food beliefs; food in Chinese and Western medicine.

123.   Anderson, Jr., Eugene Newton. Changing food patterns in rural Hong Kong. Paper presented at 4th Asian Conference of Southern California. 1977.

     This paper recounts changes in the economy in Castle Peak Bay, in the rural New Territories of Hong Kong, which occurred between the author's stay in the area in 1965-1966 and his return during 1974-1975. Most noticeable were an increase in the standard of living with increased purchases of favored foods; the disappearance of certain former staples (e.g. dried and salt fish) and a slow incorporation of selected Western vegetables and snack (e.g. highly sugared) foods.

124.   Anderson, Jr., Eugene Newton. Eating at the Ngs. Paper presented at Annual Meeting of the Southwestern Anthropological Association. 1977.

     A descriptive account of the food habits of a Hong Kong working class family. The author and his family shared a refrigerator with the family a factor which aided the research upon which this paper is based. Everyday diet, and foods served on special occasions are accounted for, although intensive questionnaires were not employed, therefore, no mention is included of foods eaten away from home - either at restaurants or at the homes of others.

125. Anderson, Jr., Eugene Newton. No date. Rural to urban in Hong Kong foodways. Typescript. Riverside, California.

Describes and contrasts food habits at Castle Peak Bay (New Territories) in its rural days (1965-1966) when the author resided there and again in 1974-1975 on a return visit. Most apparent were changes in the direction of greater variety of Chinese as well as Western foods, with concommitant improvement in nutritional quality of diets. An increase in social activities associated with food was observed; as was a decline in the overall availability of fresh foods (e.g. fish, vegetables) due to greater demand (associated with improved standard of living) and the resulting requirement to provide larger quantities of food from further away.

126. Anderson, Jr., Eugene Newton. Edible boundary lines: foods as ethnic markers among Chinese. Paper presented at Annual Meeting of the Association for Asian Studies. 1977.

A description of regional Chinese dietaries, and a review of the factors which may govern those menu items which become well-known and distinctive. The author concludes that it is not possible to give a full explanation of how a given food becomes a marker, but lists a number characteristics of such foods: they should be reasonably common; typical; a protein food; not a poverty food; be expensive; and be complex in preparation: the latter two characteristics observed as bestowing prestige upon the marker.

127. Anderson, Jr., Eugene Newton. "Hot" and "cold" foods in Hong Kong. Paper presented at Meeting of West Coast Nutritional Anthropologists. March, 1978. San Francisco, California.

This paper investigates the place of traditional food classification in contemporary South China and how it compares with the humoral concepts current elsewhere (e.g. Mexico). The history of food categorization is informally examined, and its intimate relationship to states of disease is reviewed. A list of foods and their categories (based upon the physical effets they are held to generate upon the system) is appended: i.e. "hot", "cooling", "dry", "wet", "neutral", "poison-potentiating", "supplementing".

128. Anderson, Jr., Eugene Newton. Special eating occasions in Cantonese culture. Paper presented at 10th International Congress of Anthropological and Ethnological Sciences. December 1978. New Delhi.

Based on observational data collected in the Castle Peak Bay area of Hong Kong's New Territories. This paper classifies special eating occasions (e.g. New Years, Moon Festival, memorial feasts of departed ancestors, birthdays, weddings, conclusion of business contract) and constructs a tentative model for the occurrence of special meals (vide supra) and what general sorts of foods may be eaten there at.

129. Anderson, Jr., Eugene Newton & Anderson, Marja L. 1969. Cantonese ethnohoptology. Ethnos 34:107-117.

Food uses among Hong Kong populations.

130. Anderson, Jr., Eugene Newton & Anderson, Marja L. 1972. Panang Hokkien ethnohoptology. Ethnos 37:137-147.

Food uses among a Chinese population in Malaysia.

131. Anderson, G.W. 1944. Notes on cassava preparation in north Kavirondo and Samiya. EAAJ 10:110-112.

Kenya.

132. Anderson, J.P. 1939. Plants used by the Eskimo of the northern Bering Sea and Arctic regions of Alaska. AJB 26:714-716.

133. Anderson, James N. Dietary changes of West Coast Malays: context and consequence. Paper presented at 75th Annual Meeting of the American Anthropological Association. 17 to 21 November, 1976. Washington, D.C.

Diet and nutrition have assumed increasing importance as factors affecting diseases, disorders and deaths. Diets are the dynamic product of ecological, boological and cultural factors, thus, they can be understood adequately only when approached in an integrated, multifactorial way. This paper proposes a conceptual framework for the identification and integration of relevant factors related to diet and nutrition. It employs the concept of "dietary strategy", a construct developed on the basis of an intensive analysis of ecological, biomedical, demographic, ethnohistorical and sociocultural materials. The integrating framework proposed is illustrated with case data deriving from comparative studies carried out in rural populations in Negri Sembilan and Malacca. Data are presented relating to specific dietary changes with contingent changes in ecology, demography, economy, history and culture of west coast Malaysia.

134.   Anderson, Jay N.   A solid sufficiency: an ethnography of yeoman foodways in Stuart England.   Ph.D. dissertation.   University of Pennsylvania. 1971.

135.   Anderson, Marja.   1971.   An answer to a Piltdown request - dog recipe.   Piltdown 2(3):8.

A recipe for stewing dog, collected in Malaya.

136.   Anderson, O. William.   1958.   Breast feeding in the culture of the United States.   QRP 13:203-211.

Follows the decline of breast feeding in the United States.   No explanation is offered. Artificial feeding is likened to wet nursing, and is termed "substitute" feeding.

137.   Anderson, Robert.   Social impacts of abrupt phaseout of the pineapple industry on the island of Molokai.   Paper presented at 73rd Annual Meeting of the American Anthropological Association.   19 to 24 November, 1974.   Mexico City.

138.   Anderson, T.F. 1937.   Kikuyu diet.   EAMJ 149:120-131.

139.   Anderson, Richmond K.; Calvo, Jose; Serrano, Gloria; & Payne, George C. 1946.   A study of the nutritional status and food habits of Otomi Indians in the Mezquital Valley of Mexico.   AJPH 36:883-903.

Concerned largely with health as related to general nutritional status.   The clinical data are complemented and qualifed by a brief introduction to ecology, life style, and food habits.   Extensive analytic reports are included based on nutrient intake and clinical observations.

140.   Anderson, R.Y. 1955.   Pollen analysis.   A research tool for the study of cave deposits.   Am An 21:84-85.

141.   Andrade, Margarette Sheehan de. 1965.   Brazilian cookery, traditional and modern.   Rutland, Vermont: Charles E. Tuttle Co.

142.   Andre, Jacques. 1933.   Dix livres de cuisine d' Apicus.   [The ten cookbooks of Apicius.]   Paris: B. Guegan.

French translation of the surviving collection of classical Roman recipes.

143.   Andre', Jacques. 1961.   L'alimentation et la cuisine a Rome.   [Diet and cooking in the Roman Empire.]   Paris: Klincksieck.   Collection E'tudes et Commentaires.

144.   Andree, Richard. 1886.   Die anthropophagie. Eine ethnographische studie.   [Anthrophagy.   An ethnographic study.]   Leipzig: Veit.

145.   Andrews, Alfred C.   1951.   From seeds of grass to staff of life.   Sci Coun 14:41-42.

146.   Andres, Alfred C. 1956.   Sage as a condiment in the Graeco-Roman era.   EB 10:263-266.

147.   Andrews, E.W. IV. 1969.   The archaeological use and distribution of Mollusca in the Maya lowlands.   Middle American Research Institute, Publication 34.   New Orleans: Tulane University.

148.   Andres, Julia C.   1859-1869.   Breakfast, dinner, and tea: viewed classically, poetically, and practically.   Containing numerous curious dishes and feasts of all times and all countries.   Besides three hundred modern receipts.   New York: D. Appleton.

149.   Andrews, Margaret S. [1976?]   Two decision models of household food behavior.   Paper 76-1. Silver Spring, Maryland: Intech, Inc.

Provides an optimzation framework for decision-making behavior in households.   Two diet models are used: (1) households not producin food, and (2) households producing food.   Food budget, and prices are considered to play the determining role in food selection.   Model is applied to the Dominican Republic.   [After Foster.   1978.   P. 47.]

150.   Andrieu, P. 1955.   Histoire du restaurant en France.   [History of the restaurant in France.] Paris: Journees Vinicoles.

151.   Andrieu, P.   1975.   Historique de la naissance des restaurants en France au 18e siecle. [History of the birth of restaurants in France in the 18th Century.]   Historia No. 42. Pp. 71-72.

152.   Andry, Nicolas. 1704.   Le the de l'Europe ou les proprietes de la veronique, tirees des observations des meilleurs auteurs et surtout de celles de M. Francus, medecin allemand.   [The 'tea' of Europe or the properties of veronica taken from the observations of the best authors and especially from those of M. Francus, German physician.] Paris: Imprimerie de Boudot.

A plant of the botanical family Scrophulariaceae.

153.   Andry, Nicolas.   1710.   La regime du Caresme considere par rapport a la nature du corps, et des alimens.   En trois parties ou l'on examine le sentiment de ceux qui pretendent que les alimens maigres sont plus convenable a l'homme que la viande; ou l'on traite a ce sujet, de la qualite et de l'usge des legumes, des herbages, des racines, des fruits, du poisson, etc.   Et ou l'on eclarcit plusieurs questions touchant l'abstinence, et le jeune suivant les principes de la physique et de la medecine, entre autres si l'on doit defendre en caresme l'usage de la macreuse et du tabac, par M. Nicolas Andry, Docteur, Regent de la Faculte de Medecine de Paris, lecteur et professeur royal. [The diet of Caresme considered in terms of congruence with the nature of the body, and of foods.   In three parts, in which are examined the feeling of those who assert that vegetable food is more fitting for humans; and where are treated the subjects of the qualities and uses of vegetables,

grasses, roots, fruits, and of fish, etc. And where are cleared up numerous important questions touching on abstemiousness and fasting, following the principles of physiology and medicine, among others if one may defend the use of duck and tobacco during Lent.] Paris: chez Jean Baptiste Coignard.

154.   Anell, B. & Lagercrantz, S. 1958. Geophagical customs. SEU 17:1-84.

155.   Angladette, A. 1961. Nutrition et production agricole en Afrique tropicale d'expressin francaise. [Nutrition and agriculture in French-speaking tropical Africa.] Agron 16:179-220.

156.   Angress, Shimon & Reed, Charles A. 1962. An annotated bibliography on the original and descent of domestic mammals, 1900-1955. Field-Anth 54(1).

157.   Ann Arbor. University of Michigan. Ethnobotanical Laboratory. Some Hopi plant uses and plant names. [by Volney Hurt Jones.] 1932.

158.   Ann Arbor. University of Michigan Museum of Anthropology. Ethnobotanical Report No. 371. Seeds from an early Pueblo pithouse near Albuquerque [by Volney Hurt Jones.] 1957.

159.   Annegers, John F. Geographic patterns of diet and nutritional status in West Africa. Ph.D. dissertation. East Lansing: Michigan State University. 1972.

160.   Annegers, John F. 1973. Ecology of dietary patterns and nutritional status in West Africa. 1. Distribution of starchy staples. EFN 2:107-119.

This study maps the geographical patterns of starchy staple consumption, in terms of their relative dietary importance. The foods covered are millet (Pennisetum spp.); sorghum (sorghum spp.); fonio (Digitaria exilis, D. iburua); rice (Oryza sativa, O. glaberrima); maize (Zea mays); cocoyam (Colocasia esculenta, Xanthosoma saggitifolium); plantain (Musa paradisiaca); manioc (Manihot utilissima); wheat (Triticum spp.). These staples were found to have regional patterns of usage resulting from plant ecology and historical diffusion.

161.   Annegers, John F. 1973. Seasonal food shortages in West Africa. EFN 2:251-257.

The phenomenon of seasonal food shortage occurs in parts of the Sudanic zone of West Africa, where there is reliance on one relatively short harvest. Without irrigation or flood plain irrigation, multiple harvests cannot occur, and the lack of use of root crops for food deprives the populations this zone of a calorie source which could provide the energy required to extend the harvest period.

162.   Annegers, John F. 1974. Protein quality of West African foods. EFN 3:125-130.

Maps the relative content of key amino acids: cystine, isoleucine, lysine, and methionine, which tend to limit the quality of West African diets. In humid areas, sulfur-containing amino acids were extremely limited, with total amino acid and protein intake low. In some regions, isoleucine was found to be equally as limiting as the sulfur-containing amino acids. The relative lysine content of most West African diets was found to be marginal.

163.   Anonymous. 1500. This is the boke of cokery. Here beginneth a noble boke of festes royalle and cokery a boke for a pryncis housholde or anyother estates; and the making thereof accordynge as ye shall fynde more playnly within this boke. The feste of Kynge Harry the fourth to the herawldes and Frenchmen whan they hadde justed in smythefelde. The feste of the Erle of Hunlynton at Caleys. The erle of Warynkes feste vnto the Kynge at London. The stallacion of Clyfforde byshop of London. The feste of my lord Chaunceler archibysshop of Yorke at his stallcyon in Yorke: the yere of our Lorde 1465...London: Emprynted without Temple Barre by [Ri] charde Pynson.

164.   Anonymous. 1574. Discours sur les causes de l'extreme cherte qui est ajourdhuy en France et sur les moyens d'y remedier. [Discourse on the causes of the extremely high cost-of-living in France today and on the means to remedy it.] Paris: a l'Olivier de Pierre l'Huilier.

This booklet contains data on the costs of a number of agricultural products, as well as observations on manners and customs of private life related to food, dining and restaurants.

165.   Anonymous. 1618. Arrest de la Cour de Parlement pour la subvention de nourriture des pauvres de la province de Normandie. [Judgement of the Court of Parliament for aid and provision of food for the needy in the Province of Normandy.] Rouen: Mart. le Mesgissier.

166.   Anonymous. 1629. Arrest sur le traffic de vin des hostelleries et tavernes. [Judgement on the trading in wine by inns and taverns.] No place or publisher cited.

France.

167.   Anonymous. 1656. Arrest de la Court de Parlement, conformemet suyvante le vouloir et intention du Roy sur le faict de la police, des suprfluitez de toutes sortes d'abits: et reiglement des maistres jurez des mestiers, taverniers et cabarestiers, et vacabons estants in ceste ville. [Judgement of the Court of Parliament conforming to and following the will and intention of the King on the business of the police, of excesses in dress, and orders for master guild foremen, tavern-keepers, cabaret-proprietors, and those without fixed occupation being in this city.] Paris: pour Iean Dallier libraire, demourant sur le pont Sainct Michel, a l'enseigne de la Rose blanche.

168. Anonymous. 1682. Articles, statuts, ordonnances et reglements des jurez anciens bacheliers, et maistres vinaigriers. [Articles, statutes, orders and regulations for guild foremen, former knights and master vinegar-makers.] Paris: de l'Imprimerie de Garbriel Martin.

169. Anonymous. 1694. Arrest notable rendu au profit de la communaute des maistres vinaigriers, contre les limonadiers (26 mars 1694). [Royal judgement rendered in favor of the corporatins of vinegar-makers against the lemonade makers.] (26 March, 1694.] no place cited: De l'imprimerie de la veuve de Charles Coignard.

170. Anonymous. 1696. Arrest de la Covrt de Parlement du vingt Septieme mars 1696 qui confirms les Mes de la communaute des vinaigriers, distilateurs d'eau de vie et esprit de vin, dans le droit et possession de vendre et debiter de l'eau de vie en gros et en detail, et d'en donner a boire dans leur boutiques et maisons, dans de petits verres ou tasses: et qui juge que les limonadiers ne peuvent sous aucun pretexte demander d'aller en visite dans les maisons des Mes vinaigriers. (27 mars 1696). [Judgement of the Court of Parliament of 27 March, 1696 sanctioning and investing the corporation of vinegar-makers, brandy and liquer-distillers' right to sell and supply brandy in wholesale and retail, and to make it available in their shops and places of commerce in small glasses or cups; and which adjudges against lemonade-makers from visiting - under any pretext - the shops of the vinegar-makers.] No place or publisher cited.

171. Anonymous. 1710. Arret du 29 novembre qui defend aux charcuitiers de paris de faire leurs achats de porcs ailleurs que dans les marches de Paris, Poissy et Sceaux, etc. [Judgement of 29 November, which prohibits Parisian pork butchers from making their purchases of pork anywhere but in the markets of Paris, Poissy, and Sceaux, etc.] No place or publisher cited.

172. Anonymous. 1740. Arrest de la Cour de Parlement qui fait deffense a tous patissier et boulangers de fabriquer ni vendre a l'occasion de la fete des rois, aucuns gateaux de quelques nature qu'ils soient. Du 31 decembre 1740. [Judgement by the Court of Parliament which prohibits all pastry-makers and bakers from making and selling on Twelfth Night any kind of cakes whatsoever. 31 December 1740.] No place or publisher cited.

France.

173. Anonymous. 1741. Arrest de la Cour de Parlement, rendu en faveur de la communaute des maitres chaircutiers de Paris, contre la communaute des maitres traiteurs. Portant defenses aux maitres traiteurs de vendre et debiter au public du jambon de pays, meme de Bayonne et de Mayence, entiers par morceaux, a la livre, ou autrement, a peine d'amende et de confiscation. Du dix-sept juillet, 1741. [Judgement by the Court of Parliament rendered in favor of the community of master pork butchers, against the community of master caterers. Prohibiting the master-caterers from publicly selling or supplying local ham, or ham of Bayonne or Mayence, by the piece, pound, or

otherwise, on pain of fine and confiscation. 17 July 1741. No place cited: De l'Imprimerie de Thiboust.

174. Anonymous. 1743. Arrest du Conseil d'Etat du Roy, du 25 decembre 1742. Qui ordonne l'execution de l'ordannance de 1680 et de l'Arrest du Conseil du 20 juillet 1728. Fait defenses aux chaircuitiers forains de faire entrer a Paris des marchandises de porcs frais, hors les jours de marches et avant l'heure prscrite par l'ordonnance, etc. [Judgement by the King's Council of State, of 25 December, 1742. Which orders the execution of the order of 1680 and of the Council's judgement of 20 July, 1728. Prohibits non-resident pork butchers from entering Paris to sell fresh pork on non-market days, and before the hour prescribed by the order, etc.] Paris: de l'Imprimerie de Mesnier.

175. Anonymous. 1757. Arrest de la Cour de Parlement, concernant le boulangers de la ville et fauxbourgs de Paris, et les boulangers forains de ladite ville (23 September 1757). [Judgement by the Court of Parliament, concerning the bakers of the city and suburbs of Paris, and non-resident bakers of said city (23 September 1757. Paris: chez P.G. Simon, imprimeur du Parlement.

176. Anonymous. 1759. Arret du 21 juillet 1759 concernant la communaute des fruitiers-orangers. [Judgement of 21 July 1759 concerning the corporation of fruiterers-orange-suppliers.] no place or publisher cited.

France.

177. Anonymous. 1775. Arret de la Cour de Parlement de Rouen, qui fait defenses a toutes personnes d'inserer dans les cidres aucuns ingrediens ou corps etrangers, de quelque nature et qualite qu'ils soient, sous peine d'etres poursouivies extraord., et punies de peines pecuniaires ou corporelles, meme de mort, suivant l'exigence de cas; 7 juillet 1775. [Judgement by the Court of Parliament of Rouen, which prohibits anyone from including in cider any foreign matter or ingredients of whatever nature or quality under plain of being uncommonly prosecuted and by subject to fine, corporal punishment or death, as occaision may require. 7 July, 1775.] Rouen: Rich-Lallemant.

178. Anonymous. 1786. Arret du 28 juin 1786 qui permet aux traiteurs-restaurateurs de recevoir du monde dans leurs salles et y donne a manger jusqu'a onze heures en hiver et minuit en ete, etc. [Judgement of 28 June 1786 which allows caterers-restaurateurs to receive the public in their rooms and provide food until eleven o'clock in winter and midnight in summer.] Paris: no publisher cited.

179. Anonymous. 1790. Etrennes a tous les amateurs de cafe pour tous les temps ou Manuel de l'amateur de cafe; contenant: l'histoire, la description, la culture, les proprietes de ce vegetal, le commerce qui se'n fait en France, etc.; l'introduction de son usage parmi les Mahometans & les Europeens; la meilleur maniere de le preparer pour en rendre la boisson saine, agreable & meme utile, semees de traits, d'anecdotes, d'observations les plus propres a faire connoitre les effets et les proprietes du cafe, & suivies de differentes analy-

ses chimiques, etc., etc... [Gift for all connoisseurs of coffee for all time, or handbook for coffee lovers; containing the history, description, cultivation, and properties of this plant, its commerce in France, etc; introduction to its use among Mohammedans and Europeans; the best way to prepare it in order to make the drink wholesome, pleasing and beneficial as well, filled with facts, anecdotes, and observations on the most suitable way to make known the properties and effects of coffee, followed by different chemical analyses, etc. etc...] Paris: Hotel Bouthillier.

180. Anonymous. 1799. La chair des animaux ne doit pas servir d'aliment a l'homme; il est urgent de cesser cet usage. [The flesh of animals must not serve as food for humans; it is urgent to cease its use.] Paris: Maret.

181. Anonymous. 1812. Chansons de table, choisies de meilleurs auteurs anciens et modernes. [Dinner-table songs, chosen from the best ancient and modern authors.] Paris: Le Fuel.

182. Anonymous. 1821. L'art de faire la biere. Ouvrage elementaire, theorique et pratique, donnant les moyens de faire la biere en toute saison avec nombre de vegetaux et produits de vegetaux, soit racines, tiges, fruits, semences, etc. [The art of making beer. Basic, theoretical and practical work, giving the means of making beer in all seasons with a number of vegetables, and vegetable products: roots, stems, fruits, seeds, etc.]. Paris: Carilian-Goeury.

183. Anonymous. 1846. Comment une ordonnance de police changera la Societe francaise en changeant les heurs des repas. [How a police ordinance will change French society by changing dining hours.] In Almanach de la table. Paris: V. Bouton.

184. Anonymous. 1846. A manual of homoeopathic cookery, designed chiefly for the use of such persons as are under homoeopathic treatment. By the wife of a homoeopathic physician. New York: W. Radde.

185. Anonymous. 1849. English cookery five hundred years ago: exhibited in sixty "nyms" or receipts. From a manuscript, compiled about 1390, by the master cooks of King Richard the Second, entitled "The Forme of Cury", & c. Printed (verbatim) in black letter. [Gothic type], with the addition of a running glossary and notes. Great Totham: Printed by C. Clark at his private press.

186. Anonymous. 1850. Toddy men and toddy implements. HJBKM 2: 23-27.

Palm wine sap extraction in Madras.

187. Anonymous. 1864. Bantingism. BMJ 2:469,470.

Comments on the system of weight reduction of William Banting.

188. Anonymous. 1866. Note on prison dietaries in Scotland. BMJ 2:45.

Adequacy of milk as a substitute for meat.

189. Anonymous. 1868. Cheap food for the working classes. BMJ 1:226.

Reference to a plan of Mr. Corbet, of Glasgow, for providing wholesome and well-cooked food to the working classes at nominal cost.

190. Anonymous. 1868. Dietary tables. BMJ 1:12, 13.

Editorial questioning the validity of the concept of "average" man, and of the variables employed in the construction of recommended allowances of foods.

191. Anonymous. 1868. BMJ 2:33.

Review of a Society of Arts committee concerned with improvement of popular alimentation. Noted are: dissemination of information on edible mushrooms; importation of meat; poultry and fish-raising; and a steam-jacketed cooker developed by Captain Warren.

192. Anonymous. 1869. Dinners for working men. BMJ 2:640.

Proposal for establishing dining rooms in poor neighborhoods to provide inexpensive meals. One is mentioned at Norton Folgate, which fed about one thousand men daily.

193. Anonymous. 1870. Almanach des assieges pour l'an de guerre 1871. [Almanac for the besieged for the war year 1871.] Paris: aux bureaux du Petit Monifeur.

Includes description of the food eaten during the Siege of Paris, with recipes for dogmeat and horse meat.

194. Anonymous. 1871. La cuisiniere assiegee ou l'art de vivre en temps de siege par un femme de menage. [The siege cookbook, or the art of living in times of siege by a homemaker.] Paris: Laporte.

This book includes a list of uncommon edibles that one might obtain during the Siege of Paris. Recipes are included for dog, horse, and rat.

195. Anonymous. 1875. Agricultural dietary. BMJ 1:616.

Includes articles of diet consumed by a farm family at Crowton, England.

196. Anonymous. 1875. A new article of diet. BMJ 1:452.

Report on a leguminous weed mulmunda, the seeds of which are ground into flour for bread by the poorer classes of the Deccan, and southern Mahratta. Analysis showed the seed to contain "nearly as much nitrogenous substances as some of the chief varieties of Indian peas and beans."

197.   Anonymous. 1878. German army food. BMJ 2:480.

A commercial ration composed of beef, vegetables, with pea or bean flour, in a dry, powered form. A gelatine capsule containing fat was included.

198.   Anonymous. 1878. Prison dietaries. BMJ 1:935, 936.

Costs; foods used; nutritional considerations. (Great Britain).

199.   Anonymous. 1879. A campaign against first fallacies. BMJ 2:466, 467.

Criticizes excessive meat consumption. Advocates greater use of legumes, and other vegetables.

200.   Anonymous. 1879. Moral dietaries. BMJ 2:134.

Contra tea, coffee, alcoholic beverages, and flesh.

201.   Anonymous. 1880. The dietary in Coldbath Fields prison. BMJ 2: 53, 54.

Description of rations in an English short-term prison.

202.   Anonymous. 1880. A vegetarian restaurant. BMJ 1:449.

Notice of opening; favorable review of meals, and critical note regarding over-consumption of meat, generally.

203.   Anonymous. 1881. Lloyd's Universal Food. BMJ 1:1007.

A malted, farinaceous food based on cereal grains and pulses, with malt-meal.

204.   Anonymous. 1881. The Pure Food Company's preparations. BMJ 1:278.

Beef tea; proprietary milk-based infant formula; and a malted-milk food based on Egyptian lentils.

205.   Anonymous. 1882. Diet of the Japanese. BMJ 2:1044.

Brief enumeration of foods.

206.   Anonymous. 1883. Prior to introduction of beef, fish and othr sea food was used by natives. HAd 7 July:2.

Hawaiian Islands.

207.   Anonymous. 1884. Anthropophagy. B Med Sci Jnl 111:185-186.

Informal article on use of human flesh as food during famine, and in cannibalism.

208.   Anonymous. 185. The dietary of hospital nurses. BMJ 1:1066.

Suggests quality and variety of diets of British hospital nurses be improved.

209.   Anonymous. 1885. Dietetic education. BMJ 1:244.

Encourages greater use of vegetables, and reduction of meat consumption.

210.   Anonymous. 1886. Starving London. BMJ 1:512.

Economic advantages of vegetarianism.

211.   Anonymous. 1886. Vegetarianism and poetry. BMJ 1:604.

Notes on the English poets Edward Fitzgerald and Alfred Tennyson as vegetarians.

212.   Anonymous. 1887. The consumption of vegetables in Paris and London. BMJ 2:842.

Per capita consumption of selected fruit and vegetables.

213.   Anonymous. 1887. Tree tomato. GB-RBGK-BMI No. 8 Pp. 2-6. August.

Cyphomandra betacea. Native to the Andean region. Use as food: p. 4.

214.   Anonymous. 1889. Lily flowers and bulbs used as food. GB-RBGK-BMI No. 29. Pp. 116-118.

Describes use of lily flowers Hemerocallis gramineae, Lilium bulbiferum and Lilium cordifolium roots in China, and among the Ainu, and Japanese.

215.   Anonymous. 1890. The follies of food reformers. BMJ 2:743-744.

Response to the 'Bread and Food Reform League', which urged consumption of whole grain bread, and vegetarianism.

216.   Anonymous. 1892. Food in literature. AM 70:856-858.

217.   Anonymous. 1892. Mim. PMHB 16:472.

Mimbo: a beverage prepared from rum, water, and loaf sugar.

218.   Anonymous. 1896. People's food - a great national inquiry. Professor W.O. Atwater and his work. Rev Rev 13:679-690.

219.   Anonymous. 1898. Gastronomy in fiction. Cur Lit 26: 373-375.

220.   Anonymous. 1901. Insects as food. SA 52 [Supp.] 21725. 21 December.

Cockroaches, caterpillars, locusts.

221. Anonymous. 1903. Fruits and nuts as food. SA 89:255. 10 October.

Used in dietary experiments. Peanuts are recommended as a high protein source.

222. Anonymous. 1904. Curious foods. SA 91:242-243. 8 October.

Insects (Ephydra sp., Lake Mono, California); seafood.

223. Anonymous. 1909. Pickled tea. Trop Ag Mag 32 [Supp.4]: 491-492.

A fermented tea leaf product, used in Burma and neighboring areas. Preparation method, packaging for export, and wholesale prices are noted. The tea is prepared with sesame seed and oil, fried garlic, grated green ginger and salt.

224. Anonymous. 1909. The varieties of the oil palm in West Africa (Elaeis guineesis, Jacq.) GB-RBGK-BMI No. 2. Pp. 33-49.

225. Anonymous. 1913. Diet and electricity. SA 108:10. 4 January.

Reports on experimentation in which diathermy current is used to replace caloric heat produced by nutrient metabolism.

226. Anonymous. 1913. Prehistoric bread from Sweden. PP 9:505.

227. Anonymous. 1913. Reindeer milk and cheese. PP 9:566.

Its use among Lapps. Notes the high percentage of milk solids (37% to 38%); and 9% to 11% protein content.

228. Anonymous. 1919. The sweetest leaf known. JHer 10:331.

Note on the properties of Stevia rebaudiana, called kaahee, a plant native to the Paraguayan prairies.

229. Anonymous. 1919-1920. A pictorial history of tea. Part 1. In the early days of China. TCTJ 36:417-418. Part 2. The introduction of tea into Japan. 36: 512-515; Part 3. Introduction of tea into Continental Europe. 37:30-32; Part 4. Introduction of tea into Great Britain. 37: 250-253; Part 5. Tea in Britain in the Eighteenth Century. 38:34-37.

Documented historical narrative accompanies the illustrations.

230. Anonymous. 1930. Legends of the rice grain. IO 11:233-240.

231. Anonymous. 1931. Dental diseases controlled by diet. Science 74 (1907 [Supp.]): 12.

Report of an experiment with three groups of children, in which elimination of refined dietary sugar (and use of a mouth rinse)

practically eliminated caries activity from the control group.

232. Anonymous. 1932. Arizona Indians ate turkey 1000 years ago. SNL 22:335. Also in El Pal 33:230 (1932).

233. Anonymous. 1932. Cannibal remains on Alaskan Island. Science 75 [Supp.] :9-10. 15 January.

Discoveries of human osteological material on Kodiak Island, by Professor Ales Hardlicka. Cracked bones suggest possibility that marrow was eaten.

234. Anonymous. 1932. Dr. Hrdlicka finds proof of cannibalism. El Pal 32:81-82.

Investigation on Kodiak Island, Alaska, by Ales Hrdlicka, revealed human bones, cracked open apparently for extraction of marrow.

235. Anonymous. 1932. Soft drinks of the Nebraska pioneer. A Speech 7:391-392.

236. Anonymous. 1933. Food carts a part of the night here. T Pac 21:14.

237. Anonymous. 1936. Food and nutrition of African natives. BMJ 1:1224-1225.

A review of April, 1936 number of the journal Africa, devoted to food habits and nutritional status in sub-Saharan Africa.

238. Anonymous. 1939. Story of food and water prepared by early Polynesian voyagers. HS-B 2 March. Pp. 3, 24; March. P.13; 7 August. P. 7.

239. Anonymous. 1941. Taro products are good food. HS-B 24 December. P. 6.

Hawaiian Islands.

240. Anonymous. 1942. Italian food patterns. JADA 18:684.

A summary of research done by the staff of the National Research Council's Committee on Food Habits.

241. Anonymous. 1942. Sugar from cactus. CSJ-ABS 1:32.

Notice reprinted from the Los Angeles Times, 22 February, 1942, concerning a consulting chemist W.D. Hoppie (217 W. 47th Street) who developed a process for extracting sugar from an unidentified ("the most common") cactus.

242. Anonymous. 1943. Th development of the nutrition project in Pleasantville, New Jersey. SBJ 106:38.

Organization of small lunch-room projects.

243.   Anonymous. 1943. Pigeon pea meal may be substituted for imported soy bean meal. HS-B 23 April.

244.   Anonymous. 1943. Some Central European food habits. JADA 19: 702-706.

> Prepared by the Committee on Food Habits of the United States National Research Council Ethnic groups included are Polish, Hungarian, Czech and Slovak. Although unsigned, this may have been prepared by Sula Benet and Natalie Joffee. See also Benet & Joffee (1943).

245.   Anonymous. 1946. Food used by Filipinos in Hawaii is subject of fascinating booklet. HS-B 15 May. P. 20.

> Refers to Miller, Louis & Yanazawa (1946).

246.   Anonymous. 1951. History of the sandwich. JADA 27:27.

> Anecdotal data, derived from sources indicated as in the collections of the American Institute of Baking.

247.   Anonymous. 1951. Soda fountain progress matches ice cream industry growth. ICR 34:52-54.

> Data on origin of the ice cream soda at the Franklin Institute Exposition, in Philadelphia, October, 1874.

248.   Anonymous. 1951. Origin of the chocolate coated ice cream bar. ICR 35:132.

> Invented by Christian K. Nelson, a Danish immigrant to the United States, in 1922. Called the "Eskimo Pie".

249.   Anonymous. 1952. Centuries of mince pie. JADA 28:1172.

> Informal historical data, based on sources held by the American Institute of Baking.

250.   Anonymous. 1954. The ice cream cone observes its fiftieth anniversary. ICR 37:58-59.

> Extensive account of its composite invention at the St. Louis World's Fair, of 1904.

251.   Anonymous. 1955. Ancient seed plants: the Cycads. MBG-A 43:65-80.

> Food use of Cycads in South Africa, and the Malay peninsula, with description of methods of toxin removal: pp.73-76.

252.   Anonymous. 1955. Baked beans. Gourmet November: Pp. 56, 59.

> Historical.

253.   Anonymous. 1955. The first ice tea. M-WHR 15 October: P.30.

254.   Anonymous. 1955. First spectacular use of gas for cooking. CPro November: P.25.

255.   Anonymous. 1955. Frozen foods in 97 B.C. QFF February. P. 158.

256.   Anonymous. 1955. How food habits develop. JADA 31:56.

> Rust prevented the successful cultivation of wheat in the South Atlantic colonies of the United States. Maize, which was not prey to this disease, was selected instead, and became the staple food crop.

257.   Anonymous. 1955. Old Romans valued sesame seed. M-WHR 15 January. P. 20.

258.   Anonymous. 1955. Shircliffe collection of menus, records early eating habits in U.S. MHor 15 September. P.22-23. Also in: HC News September. Pp. 3, 12; T Talk 17 September. Pp.8, 4-17; H Ind September-October: P.8; HR News 3 September. Pp. 2; 10 September. P. 2. Hotel 10 October. P. 5; Penn HR 21 September: P.4.

259.   Anonymous. 1955. Traces genealogy of the 'compleat kitchean'. Institutions. April. Pp. 52, 53; May. 26-27; September: P. 56.

260.   Anonymous. 1956. Origin of doughnuts. M-WHR 15 July: P. 25. Also in C Pro July: P. 19.

261.   Anonymous. 1956. Indians developed art of making maple sugar. Institutions. June. P. 133.

262.   Anonymous. 1956. Russian inplant cafeteria. Inplant September: Pp. 15, 16-18.

263.   Anonymous. 1957. Encouraging Zulus to eat eggs. JADA 33:21.

> Report of Dr. John Cassell's comments on the Polela Native Reserve Health Project [See also Cassell. 1955, 1957.

264.   Anonymous. 1958. Changes in eating habits affect restaurant industry. C Pro October. P. 11.

265.   Anonymous. 1958. Food processors study family eating habits. Hospitals 1 September. P. 88.

266.   Anonymous. 1958. La cucina Siciliana. [The Sicilian kitchen.] Gastronomo Autonno. 20-25.

267.   Anonymous. 1958. Nutrition among children. Nigeria No. 57. Pp. 98-109.

268.   Anonymous. 1959. Ingredients for a faster mile, diet for Herbert Elliott, miler from Australia. SIll 9 February: P. 26-27.

269.   Anonymous. 1959. Nationwide nutrition survey. CMJ 79:204.

> People's Republic of China.

270.   Anonymous. 1960. Economic value of the Great Leap (4). Food. Edible oil, vegetables, staple food. CNA 8 July.

271.   Anonymous. 1961. Store site selection: a new dimension: economic and marketing geography. FTop 16: 6-25.

272.   Anonymous. 1963. Negative results in treating pica. NR 21:287.

    Study of twenty-four Black American children in Washington, D.C.

273.   Anonymous. 1965. Sake water baffles scientists. PHM 16 January: P. 30-31.

    Japanese rice wine.

274.   Anonymous. 1966. The cycle of rice. FFH January-February: P. 16-17.

    A collection of Eighteenth Century engravings showing production procedures titled "The Rice Manufacturing in China.

275.   Anonymous. 1966. Voedingsgewoonten in Turkije. [Food habits in Turkey.] Voeding 27: 95-98.

    Recipes for popular Turkish foods.

276.   Anonymous. 1968. Fresh food is now flying into Biafra. MGuard 13 August: P.3.

    Insects as food: Hymenoptera.

277.   Anonymous. 1968. Seasonal hunger in underdeveloped countries. NR 26:142-145.

278.   Anonymous. 1969. Algae, three times as nourishing as steak. UC March. P. 11.

    Short account of use of Spirulina as food in Chad. Includes photograph of drying algae.

279.   Anonymous. 1970. Savor the Chinese flavor. Awake 51: 20-22.

    Taiwan food markets; Chinese methods of cookery; recipes.

280.   Anonymous. 1971. Navajos bring food closer to home. FN 1:2-4.

281.   Anonymous. 1971. Nutrition and infection: cannibalism. NR 29:226-227.

    Kuru, a slow-acting virus, associated with eating human brains, among the Fore, of New Guinea.

282.   Anonymous. 1972. Mountain cookery. Directions 1:31.

    Various breads, including soda biscuits and hoe cakes of the U.S. southern highlands.

283.   Anonymous. 1973. Malnutrition and intellectual competence. MJA 2:46.

284.   Anonymous. 1977. An Islamic twist. Lancet 30 July. P. 232.

    Occurences of primary, small-bowel volvulus among Pushtoon tribe of Afghanistan. Attributed to observance of the Islamic proscription for abstinence from food during daylight hours of Ramadan, with subsequent consumption of single, large meal after sunset. Pushtoons are unusually susceptible to small-bowel volvulus, resulting from strict adherence to Ramadan dietary requirements, and very high fibre diets.

285.   Anthonio, Q.B.O. & Akinwumi, J.A. 1971. The supply and distribution of smoked fish in Ibadan markets. NGJ 14: 151-164.

286.   Antonini. 1938. Les chenilles comestibles dans la Haute-Sangha. [Edible worms of Upper Sanga.] R Cong 25: 133-145.

    Groups mentioned include the Baya, Sango, Banda, Balali, Bateke, Loango, and others.

287.   Antonio, Q.B.O. 1967. The supply and distribution of yams in Ibadan markets. NJESS 9:33-49.

288.   Antoun, R. 1968. The social significance of Ramadan. M World 58: 36-42.

289.   Apicius. 1958. The Roman cookery book. A critical translation of the Art of Cooking, for use in the study and in the kitchen. Translated by Barbara Flower & Elizabeth Rosenbaum. London: George C. Harrap.

290.   Apicius, Marcus Gavius. 1933. Les dix livres d' Apicius. [The ten books of Apicius.] Translated by Bertrand Guegan. Paris: Rene Bonnel.

    Contains commentary by the translator.

291.   Appert, Charles. 1811. L'art de conserver, pendant plusiers annees, toutes les substances animales, vegetales. [The art of preserving for many years, all animal and vegetable substances.] Paris: Patris. Reprint. Paris: Gauthier-Villar. 1950.

    N.B. Volume 3 of the French Catalogue Generales des Livres Imprimees de la Bibliotheque National (p.735) gives the author's first name as 'Charles'; the reprint gives 'Nicolas'. Vicaire (1890:34) gives 'Francois'.

292.   Appert, Maurice. 1928. L'arachide et le manioc au Senegal. [Peanut and manioc in Senegal.] RE Fran No. 6. P. 179-182.

293.   Apgriffith, G. 1938. Clay in a vegetable diet. Nature (L) 141:793.

    Geophagy among pregnant Baganda women.

294. Arago, Jacques. 1842. Comme on dine a Paris. [How they dine in Paris.] Paris: Berquet et Petion.

Amusing anecotes about Parisian restaurants of different classes; of their food and its service.

295. Arago, Jacques. 1842. Comme on dine partout. [How they dine everywhere.] Paris: a la librairie curieuse de Bohaires.

A humorous work on the food habits of such groups as the Patagonians, Hottentots, Kaffirs, and others, including cannibals.

296. Aranzadi, T de. 1920. La pierre a chocolat en Espagne. [The chocolate stone in Spain.] RETP 1: 169-173.

A hand mill for grinding cocoa.

297. Arauz, Reina Torres de. 1972. Habitos dietarios y dieta cuantitativa de los indios Chocoes (Panama). [Dietary habits and dietary quantity of Choco Indians (Panama).] Am Ind 32:169-178.

298. Arbellot, Simon. 1964. Du mamoul aux pommes de terres. VL No. 142. Pp. 45-46.

Raw sheep organs consumed in Langogne France; also historical data concerning potatoes.

299. Arbellot, Simon. 1964. Le Clafoutis. VL No. 153. Pp. 709.

A type of cherry flan.

300. Arbellot, Simon. 1964. Les truffes. [Truffles]. VL No. 145. Pp. 192.

301. Arbellot, Simon. 1965. Culinographe, gastronomade, architriclan. VL No.165. Pp. 668-669.

Neologisms coined by the French gourmand Curnonsky, pseudonym of Maurice Edmond Saillans.

302. Arbellot, Simon. 1966. Curnonsky, prince de gastronomes. [Curnonsky, prince of gastronomes.] Paris: Productions de Paris.

Biography of Maurice Edmond Saillans (pseud. Curnonsky).

303. Archaestratus. Poetic fragments on gastronomy. In Poetae bucolici et didactici, Theocritus, Bion, Moschus, et al. Collection des Auteurs Grecs. 1846. Paris: Ambroise Firmin-Didot.

Archaestratus was a Greek poet, who flourished towards the middlle of the Fourth Century B.C. His poem on gastronomy survives only in sixteen fragments.

304. Archibald, J.G. 1934. Evolution of nutrition. JCED II: 601-608.

305. Arenander, E.O. 1911. Die altertumliche Milchwirtschaft in Nordschweden (Norrland). [The old time dairy economy in north Sweden (Norrland).] Stockholm: Haegstroms.

306. Arens, Richard. 1957. Notes on camote ritual in Leyte and Samar Islalnds, Philippines. PJS 85: 343-347.

Camote, or sweet potato, is an important staple food in these islands. Its importance is emphasized by the ritual practices associated with the preparation of land prior to planting: with planting itself, and with harvest. These rituals are described in this article. Leyte Island is located at approximately between 10.0 and 11.45 N, and 124.20 and 124.35 Samar Island is located at approximately between 11.3 and 12. 25 and 124. and 125.25.

307. Aresty, Esther. 1964. The delectable past. New York: Simon & Schuster.

Informal history of food habits in the Western Hemisphere, particularly Europe.

308. Argenti, Philip Pandely & Rose, Herbert Jennings. 1949. The folklore of Chios. Vol. One. Cambridge University Press.

Cooking at the Kampochora: 126-128; cooking and baking in the Kentrochora and Voreiochora: 151-152.

309. Aribaud, A. 1968. La cuisine, image des civilizations. (Cookery, reflection of civilization.) Paris: Guyenne & Gascogne.

310. Arie, T.H.D. 1959. Pythagoras and beans OMSG 2:75.

311. Ariyapala, M.B. 1956, Society in Medieval Ceylon. (The state of Society in Ceylon as depicted in the Saddharmaratndvaliya and other literature of the Thirteenth Century). Colombo, and Kandy: K.V.G. De Silva.

Food: pp. 314-320.

312. Arlington, L.C. & Lewisohn, William. 1935. In search of old Peking. Peking: Henri Veitch, The French Bookstore.

A list of famous Peking restaurants, and the specialties is given on pp. 269-272.

313. Armelagos, George J.; Goodman, Alan; & Jacobs, Kenneth. The role of infections and nutritional disease in populational growth. Paper presented at 74th Annual Meeting of the American Anthropological Association. 2 to 6 December, 1975. San Francisco, California.

314. Armillas, Pedro. Chinanpas and terrace systems in the Valley of Mexico. Paper presented at 67th Annual Meeting of the American Anthropological Association. 21 to 23 November, 1968. Seattle, Washington.

315.   Armitage, F.P. 1922. Diet and race. An-thropological essays. London, New York, Bombay, Calcutta, Madras: Longmans, Green, & Co.

This volume comprises three essays: 'Diet and physique', in which the author discusses dietary pattern as a determining factor in stature. Essay Two: 'Diet and color' posits a relationship between skin pigmentation and the presence of sodium chloride in the blood. Essay Three: "Diet and cranial form' corelates cephalic index with dietary intake.

316.   Armour, R. 1891-1892. The coile-colle: a fern used as food by the Ceylon villager. Trop Ag 11:207.

317.   Armstrong, Lillie Mae. Habits of cereal consumption of one hundred Texas families. Master's thesis. Denton: Texas State College for Women. 1943.

318.   Armstrong, Wiliam. 1944. Drying buffalo meat after the hunt. The Beaver December: p.15.

An illustration.

319.   Arnold, Pauline & White, Percival. 1959. Food: America's biggest business. New York: Holiday House.

320.   Arnold, R. Contribution a le'etude des laits fermentes. Le leben. [Contribution to the study of fermented milks. Leben.] Thesis. Universite de Montpellier. 1899. Abstracted in KJFLGO 10:226 (1899).

Leben is a kind of yoghurt made in the Near East.

321.   Arnoldo, M. 1954. Geweekte en nuttige planten van de Nederlandse Antilen. Uitgiven van de Natuurwetenschappelijke Werkgroep Nederland-se Antillen. [Cultivated and useful plants of the Dutch Antilles. Published by the Natural Science Working Group of the Dutch Antilles.] The Hague: Martinus Nijhoff.

322.   Arnott, Margaret Louise. 1955. Ein greichi-sches Weinachtsbrot. [A Greek Christmas bread.] SAV-ASTP 51:243-245.

323.   Arnott, Margaret Louise. Bread for the dead. In 6e Congres International des Sciences Anthropologiques et Ethnologiques 30 juillet - b aout 1969. Vol. 2. Ethnologie. (Vol. 2). 1964. Pp. 135-139. Paris: Musee de l'Homme.

Small, round breads marked with the Church seal, commemorating the dead on official Greek religious, and traditional days. Also described is the boiled wheat dish (kolyva) prepared in memory of the martyr. Theodo-ros Tiro, who commanded his people to eat only boiled wheat, in order to avoid food poisoned by Julian the Apostate (A.D. 62).

324.   Arnott, Margaret Louise. A look into Phila-delphia's bread basket: a survey. Paper presented at First International Symposium on Ethnological Food Research. 21 August to 25 August, 1970. Lund: Folklivsarkivet. Lund University.

Surveys history, production, and availability of ethnic breads.

325.   Arnott, Margaret Louise. The breads of Mani. Paper presented at 9th International Con-gress of Anthropological and Ethnological Sciences. 28 August to 8 September, 1973. Chicago, Illinois.

Ceremonial breads and related customs of Mani, a remote mountainous area of the Greek Pelopennese. Comparison is made with bread customs in other areas of Greece.

326.   Arnott, Margaret Louise. The breads of Mani. In Gastronomy. The anthropology of food and food habits. Edited by Margaret Louise Arnott. 1975. Pp. 297-304. Paris; the Hague: Mouton Publishers. World Anthropology.

Breads, and a the customs surrounding their preparation and use in Mani, a region of the southern Peloponesus of Greece, on the slo-pes of Mount Tygetos.

327.   Arnould, Maurice A. 1954. Les gateaux de Noel et leur decoration en Hainaut. [Christians cakes and their decoration in Mainaut.] EMVW 7:1-74.

Hainaut is a southeastern province of Bel-gium.

328.   Arnous, L. & Meunier, A. 1976. Relations psycho-socio-economiques au sein es systemes de consommation. [Psycho-socio-economic relations within consumption systems.] ANA 30:379-388.

329.   Aron, Hans. 1909. Diet and nutrition of the Filipino people. PJS 4 [B]:195-202.

Based on a study of rations provided inmates of Bilibid Prison, in Manila.

330.   Aron, Hans. 1909. Medical survey of the town of Taytay. 6. The food of the people of Taytay from a physiological point of view. PJS 4 [B]:225-231.

Review of dietary pattern; food intake sur-vey; analysis of common protein foods; ratio of nutrient value to market cost.

331.   Aron, J.P. Biologie et alimentation a l'aube du 19 siecle. [Biology and diet at the dawn of the 19th Century.] In Pour une histoire de l'alimenta-tion. Edited by J.J. Hemardinguer. 1970. Pp. 23-28. Paris: Colin.

332.   Aron, J.P. 1973. Exagerations alimentaires des mangeurs gourmands du 19 siecle. [Dietary excesses of gourmands of the 19th Century.] Reali-tes. No. 334. Pp. 108-115.

333.   Aron, J.P. 1973. Le mangeur du 19 siecle. [The eater in the 19th Century.] Paris: Laffont.

334. Arrington, L.R. 1959. Foods of the Bible. 1959. JADA 35:816-820.

Fruits, vegetables and legumes, cereals and cereal products; dairy products; meat, poultry, fish; oils and fats; nuts; honey; herbs and spices; "manna".

335. Arrington, Leonard J. 1966. Beet sugar in the West: a history of the Utah-Idaho Sugar Company, 1891-1966. Seattle: University of Washington Press.

History of a Mormon Church enterprise.

336. Artes de Mexico. 1968. La cocina Mexicana. [Mexican cookery.] 2 vols. Mexico: Artes de Mexico.

Historical.

337. Arvelo-Jimenez, Nelly. Ye'cuana ethnobotany and ethnomedicine: a preliminary case study of inter-influences with the Guianas. Paper presented at 70th Annual Meeting of the American Anthropological Association. 20 November, 1971. New York City.

Paper focuses on the characteristics which make the two sub-systems part of Venezuelan Ye'cuana symbolic and religious systems; and their role in politics. Comparison is made between Ye'cuana and Guyanese societies' symbolic systems in order to elucidate their mutual influences.

338. Aschmann, Homer. 1952. A primitive food preparation technique in Baja, California. SJA 8:36-39.

Describes parching of the grains of Antigonon leptopus, a process which pops the grains, and renders them digestible.

339. Asenjo, C.F. 1953. Story of the West Indian cherry. (Malpighia punicifolia, L.) CQPR-B 10:1-11.

340. Asenjo, C.F. & Gusman, A.R. Freire de. 1946. The high ascorbic acid content of the West Indian cherry. Science 103:219.

Malpighia punicifolia.

341. Ash, A.S.F. 1954. Seaweed as food. FPQ 14:71-73.

Brief review of history, and nutritive value.

342. Ashford, Bailey K. Tropical sprue in Porto Rico - a synthesis of fifteen years' work of investigation and 2,200 cases. In International Conference on health problems in tropical America. Kingston, Jamaica, 22 July to 1 August, 1924. Proceedings. Pp. 686-708. Boston: United Fruit Co.

Puerto Rican diet: pp. 695-697.

343. Cultural anthropology and nutrition. In The Tamil Nadu nutrition study. Vol. 2. Report to the United States Agency for International Development. Contract AID-NESA-399. Mission to India. Haverford, Pennsylvania: Sidney Cantor Associates, Inc. July 6.

344. Ashley, William James. 1928. The bread of our forefathers: an inquiry into economic history. Oxford: The Clarendon Press.

British grain trade.

345. Ashmead, A.S. 1892. On the absence of cow's milk from Japan; its beneficial consequences. Science 20:211-212.

346. Ashton, A.F. 1900. Salt supply of northern India. AL No. 13. Pp. 119-141.

347. Ashton, Edmund Hugh. 1939. A sociological sketch of Sotho diet. SA-RS-TP 27:147-214.

Includes data on food preparation, staple foods, and quantitative food intake.

348. Ashton, John. 1904. The history of bread from prehistoric to modern times. London: The Describes parching of the grains of Antigonon leptopus, a process which pops the grains, and renders them digestible.

349. Athenaeus of Naucratis. 1927-1941. The Deipnosophists. Translated by Charles Burton Gulick. 6 vols. Loeb Classical Library. New York: G.P. Putnam's Sons.

Discusses food habits and dietaries of eastern Mediterranean peoples, drawn from accounts of ancient authors. Athenaeus was an Egyptian Greek who lived from A.D. 170-A.D. 230.

350. Atkinson, Frank. 1960. Oatbread of northern England. Gwerin 3:44-55.

351. Atwater, Wilbur Olin. 1895. Methods and results of investigations on the chemistry and economy of food. USDA-OES-B No. 21.

A comprehensive review of nutritional studies done in Asia, Europe, and the United States between 1865 and 1890. Many of the publications synopsized contain socio-anthropological data. The author, himself, encouraged the inclusion of such data in nutrition studies as a complement to statistical reports (p. 198).

352. Atwater, Wilbur Olin. 1895. Chapter Five. Preparation of food - cooking. In Methods and results of investigations on the chemistry and economy of food. USDA-OES-B No. 21.

353. Atwater, Wilbur Olin & Woods, C.D. 1897. Dietary studies with reference to the food of the Negro in Alabama in 1895 and 1896. Conducted with cooperation of the Tuskeegee Normal and Industrial Institute and the Agricultural and Mechanical College of Alabama. USDA-OES-B No. 38.

The first part of this monograph comprises an analysis of common Alabama foods. Staple foods of Black Alabamans is described on pp. 19-21; cooking, on p. 21. The remainder of the monograph is given over to records of the dietaries of various Black farm families. A comparison of the dietaries of Blacks surveyed is made with diets of New England, European, and Asian groups. Dietary standards for various types of work are included in the comparative table.

354.   Aucapitaine, Henri. 1857. Les Yam-yem, tribu anthropophage de l'Afrique centrale. [The Yam-yem, anthropophagous tribe of Central Africa.] Paris: A. Bertrand.

355.   Auchter, E.C. 1939. The interrelation of soils and plant, animal and human nutrition. Science 89:421-427.

The author, a chief of the United States Department of Agriculture's Bureau of Plant Industry, reviews the variables related to soil quality, and their potential effect on plant quality. The suggestion is made that effects of fertilizers, sprays, dusts and the like upon plants be investigated as these may definitely modify their composition so that the plants are either more nutritious or toxic to the humans or livestock which consume the plants.

356.   Aucoin, D. et. al. 1972. A comparative study of food habits: influence of age, sex and selected family characteristics. CJPH 63:143-151.

357.   Auffret, Charles & Tanguy, F. 1949. Sur la valeur alimentaire des termites. [On the food value of termites.] IPAOF-R 1947:110-112. Also in: BMAOF 4:395.

358.   Aulagnier, A.F. 1839. Dictionnaire des alimens et des boissons en usage dans les divers climats et chez tous les peuples. Cet ouvrage contient l'histoire naturelle de chaque substance alimentaire, etc., precede de considerations generales sur la nourriture de l'homme. [Dictionary of foods and beverages used in various climates and among various peoples. This work contains the natural history of each food substance, etc., preceded by general considerations on human nourishment.] Paris: Cosson.

359.   Aurencon, Marguis d'. 1914. Vegetable butters. PP 10:550.

Notes on two African and one Indian source of possible culinary use. Illipe butter, derived froms seeds of Bassia Donsifolia. Dika butter, derived from seeds of Irvingia Gabonensis; Muscade butter, extracted from Myristica moschata.

360.   Auriac, Eugene d'. 1861. Essai historique sur la boucherie de Paris. [Historical essay on Parisian butcheries.] Paris: Dentu.

361.   Austen, Leo. 1946. Notes on the food supply of the Turamarubi of Western Papua. Mankind 3:227-230.

362.   Australia. Army. 1943. Friendly fruits and vegetables. Prepared by the General staff, L.H.Q. Australia, and issued under the authority of the Commander, Allied Land Forces, S.W.P.A. May 31st. Melbourne: Arbuckle, Waddell Pty, Ltd.

363.   Australia. Parliament. Joint Library Committee. 1922. Historical records of Australia. Series 1. Governor's dispatches to and from England. Vol. 15. June 1829-December 1830. Sydney:

The Library Committee of the Commonwealth Parliament.

Notes on Aboriginal diet: pp. 376, 378.

364.   Autret, Marcel. Nutrition et aimentation tropicales. [Tropical nutrition and diet.] In Conferences du Deuxieme Cours de Nutrition pour l'Afrique Noire. 4 Octobre a 15 Decembre, 1955. Marseilles. Recueil 1957. Pp. 606-629. Rome: Food and Agriculture Organization of the United Nations.

365.   Autret, Marcel. 1968. Applied nutrition IJMS 4:443-456.

Proceedings of a symposium, with an international panel of discussants.

366.   Avcin, M. 1956. Lebens - und Ernahrungsprobleme der Zigeuner. [Life-style and nutrition problems among gypsies.] MMW 107:1502-1507.

Gypsies of northeast Slovenia manifesting vitamin B complex deficiencies.

367.   Avery, A.C. 1952.   Preservation of very small fish in the Philippine Islands. F Tech 6:4-5.

368.   Avila, Maria Teresa.   1952.   Las plantas en el folklore del Tucuman.   Las cactaceas.   [Plants in Tucuman folklore.   The cactuses.]   BATuF 2:4-11.

Argentina.

369.   Axelrod, Paul & Ktona-Apte, Judit.   The effect of a food help program on a Nevada Indian community.   Paper presented at 75th Annual Meeting of the American Anthropological Association. 17 to 21 November, 1976. Washington, D.C.

The effectiveness of a United States Government food help program on a Shoshone Indian reservation in Nevada is assessed. The policies of the government agencies toward the feeding of Indians are examined and are compared to program implementation in the community.   The analysis of the dietary patterns shows that the food provided by the food help program is not consistent with Shoshone dietary habits.

370.   Axford, Lavonne Brady, ed., comp.   1976. English language cookbooks, 1600-1973.   Detroit: Gale Research Company.

Includes comprehensive listing of periodical publications.

371.   Ayabe, Tsuneo.   1959.   The concept of "grain spirit" among the peoples of Southeast Asia.   [In Japanese.] S Jin 2:32-49.

372.   Ayensu, Dinah Ameley.   1972.   The art of West African cookery.   Garden City, New York: Doubleday.

373.   Ayerton, Elizabeth.   1974.   The cookery of England.   London: Andre Deutsch.

374.   Ayeva, Ryssalatou.   1965.   Les habitudes alimentaires au Togo.   [Food habits in Togo.]   EMT 23:18-23.   Also in Nat Nouv 5:26-29.

375.   Ayim, E.N.   1966.   Ernahrungs probleme Westafrikas zwischen gestern und heute.   [West African nutrition problems: past and present.]   EU 13:129-134.

376.   Aykroyd, Wallace Ruddell.   1937.   Les travaux sur l'alimentation dans l'Inde.   [Work on diet in India.]   OIHP-B 24:2388-2392.

377.   Aykroyd, Wallace Ruddell.   Malnutrition and the rice problem.   In Fourth International Congresses on Tropical Medicine and Malaria.   10 May to 18 May, 1948.   Washington, D.C.   Proceedings. Vol. 2.   Pp. 1172-1180.   Washington, D.C.: Department of State.

378.   Aykroyd, Wallace Ruddell.   Prologue 1.   The Nutrition Research Laboratories, Coonor.   In The work of Sir Robert McCarrison.   Edited by H.M. Sinclair.   1953.   Pp. xi-xxix.   London: Faber & Faber, Ltd.

Account and verification of comparative regional diets fed to laboratory animals: pp. xvi-xvii.   See McCarrison. (1928).

379.   Aykroyd, Wallace Ruddell.   1962.   Reflections of human food patterns.   FNNR 19:21-27. Also in Nutrition (L) 15:65-70.

380.   Aykroyd, Wallace Ruddell.   1963.   The nutritive value of Indian foods and the planning of satisfactory diets.   Revised by C. Gopalan & S.C. Balasubramanian.   6th edition.   New Delhi: Indian Council on Medical Research.

381.   Aykroyd, Wallace Ruddell; Alexa, I. & Nitzulescu, J.   1935.   Dietary study of peasants in a pellagrous area of Moldavia (Roumania).   [In French.] ARPEM 8:407-423.

382.   Aykroyd, Wallace Ruddell & Krishnan, B.G. 1937.   Diet surveys in South Indian villages.   IJMR 24:667-688.

383.   Aylward, Francis.   1953.   The indigenous foods of Mexico and Central America.   PNS 12:48-58.

384.   Aylward, Francis.   1966.   Food habits in western tropical Africa.   CI 39:1624-1627.

385.   Ayoub, A.   Les etats du Levant (sous mandat Francais).   [Levantine states (under French mandate).   In L'alimentation indigene dans les colonies francaises.   Protectorats de territoires sous mandats.   Edited by G. Hardy & C. Richet.   1933.   Pp. 338-350.   Paris:Vigot Freres.

Largely given over the geographical dta, a very brief description of food patterns is contained on pp. 349, 350.

386.   Ayres, William S.   Marine subsistence base for prehistoric Easter Island.   paper presented at 74th Annual Meeting of the American Anthropo-

logical Association. 2 to 6 December, 1975. San Francisco, California.

387. Ayrout, Henry. 1952. Fellahs d'Egypte. [Egyptian peasants.] Cairo: Sphynx.

Diet: pp. 106-110.

388. Azevedo, R. Pelagra. Contribuicao ao seu estudo. [Pelagra Contribution to its study.] Thesis. Universidade do Recife. 1935.

389. S.B. 1966. The soul of the rice. FFH January-February. Pp. 11-14.

Overview of ritual, custom and myth relating to rice in east and Southeast Asia.

390. Baader, R. ed. 1949. Der Fisch. [Fish.] M Fisch. 4:1-647.

Worldwide descriptions of fishing methods, and industry.

391. Baba, H. Ishibashi, T. 1969. On the vitamin D of fermented sea-food shiokara. JJN 27:45-48.

392. Babayan, Silvia Y.; Budayer, Bushra; et. al. 1966. Age, sex and culture as variables in food aversion. JSP 68:15-17.

Rejection of food declines with age; young females reject food to a greater extent than young males.

393. Babb, L.A. 1970. Food of the gods in Chattisgarh: some structural features of Hindu ritual. SJA 26: 287-304.

394. Babb, Marle Spies. Diets of 50 families in Tuscaloosa, Alabama supplemented by (a) whole wheat bread or (b) equivalent in money. Master's thesis. University of Texas. 1944.

395. Babcock, Charlotte G. 1948. Food and its emotional significance. JADA 24:23-31.

396. Babcock, Charlotte G. 1961. Attitudes and the use of foods. JADA 38:546-551.

397. Babeau, Albert. 1885. Le artisans et les domestiques d'autrefois. [Artisans and domestics of former times.] Paris: Firmin-Didot.

Included is a chapter on feeding.

398. Babeau, Albert. 1886. Les bourgeois. d'autrefois. [The middle-class of former times.] Paris: Firmin-Didot.

Chapter Eight is devoted exclusively to meals, but throughout the book are notes on food, feasts, and banquets.

399. Babel, E. 1961. La viande de boeuf et le lait dans le bilan alimentaire malgache. [Beef and milk in Malagasy nutrition.] B Mad No. 181. Pp. 477-491.

400. Babelon, J.; Carcopino, J.; Champigneulle, B.; Heron de Villefosse; et al. 1951. La cuisine considered as one of the fine arts. [Cookery consideree comme un des beaux-arts.] Paris: Tambourinaire.

401. Bachsetz, Marcel & Aragon, Attagracia. 1942. Notes on Mexican drugs 2. Characteristics and composition of the fatty oil from "gusanos de maguey" ["maguey worms"] (Caterpillars of Acentrocneme hesperiaris) APA-J-SE 31:145-146.

An Aztec food insect, called "meoculin" in Nahuatl.

402. Bachsetz, Marcel & Arragon, Altagracia. 1945. Notes on Mexican drugs, plants, and foods 3. Ahuautl: the Mexican caviar. APA-J-SE 34:170-172.

Historical review of use of certain water-insect larvae as food; with chemical analysis of larvae.

403. Back, E.H. 1961. The dietary of small farmers in Jamaica. WIMJ 10:28-43.

404. Back, Kurt W. Food, sex and theory. In Nutrition and anthropology in action. Edited by Thomas K. Fitzgerald. 1976. Pp. 24-34. Assen, Amsterdam: Van Gorcum.

Compares and contrasts two physiological drives i.e. sexuality, and hunger. Emphasizes that tolerence appears to be greater toward differences in sexual patterns than toward eating habits. Suggests that eating has an identity function (in terms of ethnicity and its associated variables) which takes on greater significance than its survival (physiological-hunger) value.

405. Backhouse, J. 1843. Appendix D. Remarks on the indigenous vegetable productions of Tasmania, available as food for man. In A narrative of a visit to the Australian colonies. London: Adams & Co.

406. Bacon, Raymond F. 1908. Starch production of the Philippine Islands. PJS 3 [A. General Science] :93-96.

Discusses various plant sources, including cassava (Manihot utilissima Pohl); arrowroot (Maranta arundinacea L.), sincamas (Pachyrhizus bulbosus Britton), Tacca pinnatifida Forst.; Dioscorad sp.; seeds of Cyeas circinalis, L.; and tubers of Amorphophallus campanulatus Blume.

407. Baden-Powell, Fletcher Smyth. 1868-1869. Handbook of the economic products of the Punjab. 2 vols. Roorkee: Thomason Civil Engineering College Press.

408. Baeder, John. 1978. Diners. New York: Harry N. Abrams.

Paintings of a genre of eating establishments which has all but disappeared from the American scene. This type of restaurant characteristically served low-cost, quickly prepared and served food.

409. Baegert, Jacob. 1864. Chapter Three. Of their food and the manner of preparing it. In An account of the aboriginal inhabitants of the California peninsula, as given by Jacob Baegert, a German Jesuit missionary, who lived there seventeen years during the second half of the last century. Translated by Charles Rau. SI-Ar for the year 1863. Pp. 352-369.

410. Baehr, H.A. 1950. Wheat processing and uses in the Far East. For Ag 14:204-208.

411. Baer, Jr., Arthur B. 1974. The evolution of the soft drink industry. New York: Faulkner, Daukins & Sullivan.

412. Bagge, Frederic. 1956. Om matsedlar. [On menus] Fataburen Pp. 67-84.

413. Baglioni, S. 1927. Dietetics of the ancients. [In Italian] Archaeion 8:9-16.

414. Baglioni, S. 1937. Jacopo Bartolomeo Beccari (1682-1766) founder of modern chemical doctrine of dietetics. [In Italian] P Alim 1:2-8.

415. Bai, R.G. 1965. Report of a community nutrition project conducted in a village Kalappanaickenpalayam near Coimbatore. Madras: University of Madras.

Records brief data concerning food expenditure; cooking methods, food preservation and storage, and home production of foods. Village studied is in Tamil Nadu State, South India. Coimbatore is situated at 11ON, 76.5E.

416. Bai, R.N. Report on a community nutrition project carried out in Nanjundapuram village, Coimbatore District. Master's thesis. University of Madras. 1966.

Project combines diet survey and nutrition education program in a semi-urbanized village 16km from Coimbatore City, in the south Indian State of Tamil Nadu. Changes in food use frequency, and nutrient intake were observed following a seven day nutrition education program. Data are recorded for food expenditure patterns; frequency of food use; cooking methods; dietary restrictions; food preservation and storage techniques.]

417. Bailey, Adrain, 1969. The cooking of the British Isles. New York: Time-Life Books. Foods of the World.

418. Bailey, Elizabeth. "Malnutrition": a film produced for the Agency for international Development, together with background papers. Master's thesis. Anthropology. University of Wisconsin. 1966.

419. Bailey, Flora L. 1940. Navaho foods and cooking methods. AA 42:270-290.

Cooking equipment and utensils: pp. 273-275; food preparation techniques: pp. 275-278; etiquette and eating customs: p. 278; beliefs and practices concerning food: pp. 278-279; recipes: pp. 279-290; food storage: p. 290.

420. Bailey, Herbert S. & Le Clerc, J.A. 1918. The peanut, a great American Food. USDA-YB for the year 1917. Pp. 289-301.

Uses of peanut flour, and peanut butter as food substitutes during World War I. A variety of recipes is included.

421. Bailey, K.V. Rural nutrition studies in Indonesia. Medical dissertation. University of Melbourne. 1960.

A series of articles incorporating these data are found in TGM 13:216-254; 289-315; 14:1-19; 111-139; 230-237 (1961-1962). The following villages are studied: Djatiredjojoso (Central Java).; Djimbaran, Sempol, Sukodadi, Talong Agung (east Java); Wonogiri (Gunung Kidul Regency, Togjakarta); Kedungsari, Patemon, Timbulhardjo, Triwadadi (Jogjakarta).

422. Bailey, K.V. 1963. Team studies in infant nutrition in New Guinea Highlands. SPB 13:38-40.

423. Bailey, K.V. Protein malnutrition and peanut foods in the Chimbu. In An integrated approach to nutrition and society. The case of the Chimbu. Report of the symposium held at the Thirty-seventh Congress of the Australian and New Zealand Association for the Advancement of Science, 20-24th January. Edited by Eben H. Hipsley. 1964. NGRU-B No. 9.

Background to the interdisciplinary applied nutrition project in the New Guinea highlands, concerned with alleviating infant malnutrition among Chimbu infants.]

424. Bailey, K.V. 1964. Synopsis of rural nutrition studies in Indonesia. MJA 1:669-676.

425. Bailey, K.V. & Whiteman, Josephine. 1963. Dietary studies in the Chimbu (New Guinea highlands). TGM 15:377-388.

Includes discussion of foods; meal patterns; and infant feeding patterns.

426. Bailey, Liberty Hyde, ed. 1922. Cyclopedia of farm crops. A popular survey of crops and crop-making methods in the United States and Canada. New York: Macmillan.

427. Bailey, Liberty Hyde. 1930. Development and use of the baking powder and baking chemicals. USDA-C No. 138.

Includes brief data on historical development of leavening agents.

428.   Bainton, Barry R. Ecological factors in the drinking patterns of the rural aged. Paper presented at 76th Annual Meeting of the American Anthropological Association.   29 November to 3 December. 1977. Houston, Texas.

Draws on data from a recently completed state-wide survey of alcohol usage patterns of rural elderly in Arizona. Examines the effects of isolation from the general population and from age peers; and the effects community type and length-of-residence.

429.   Baker, E. Allan, & Foskett, D.J. 1958. Bibliography of food. A select international bibliography of nutrition, food and beverage technology and distribution, 1936-1956. London: Butterworth Scientific Publications.

430.   Baker, Herbert George. 1962. Comments on the thesis that there was a major centre of plant domestication near the headwaters of the River Niger. JAH 3:229-233.

431.   Baker, Herbert George. 1965.   Plants and civilization. Belmont, California: Wadworth Publishing Co.; London: Macmillan.

432.   Baker, Paul T., & Mazess, Richard B. 1963. Calcium: Some unusual sources in the highland Peruvian diet. Science 142: 1466-1467.

A survey done in the vicinity of Nunoa (14 degrees 29S, 70 39W) at an altitude of between 4000-5000 meters, revealed two edible earths cal or catahui, and cha'go. Cal is prepared by burning, and then pulverizing calcium-containing rocks; it is most often eaten mixed with quinua (Chenopodium quinoa) or canihua (Chenopodium pallidicaule) in the form of a porridge. Cha'go is a clay, used in water suspension as a sauce for potatoes. Calcium content of two samples of cal were 36.3% and 42.0% respectively. Cha'go has no calcium, but contains some iron. A product called llipta is chewed together with coca leaves; it is prepared from the ashes of the stalks and grains of quinua, and canihua, mixed with water and sun-dried into a small cake. An average of 2gm of llipta is ingested daily by men and women over the age of fifteen years, providing between 200 mg and 500 mg of calcium daily. When calcium is taken in combination with normal dietary sources, it appears that calcium intake in this area meets or exceeds recommended daily allowances.

433.   Balasubramanian, S.C., & Basu, K.P. 1955. The nutritional significance of milk and some indigenous milk products. ID 7:99-104.

434.   Balasubramanyan. 1963. Diet and culture. MMJ 10:45-49.

435.   Balavady, B., & Gopalan, C. 1959. Studies in lactation and dietary habits in Nilgiri Hill tribes. IJMR 47:234.

Tamil Nadu State, India.

436.   Baldaggi, O. 1956. La geofagia in Sardegna. [Geophagy in Sardinia] SGI-B 9:152-157.

437.   Baldwin, Richard S. 1975. Robert R. Williams (1886-1965) - biographical sketch. JN 105:3-14.

A professional history of the biochemist who identified and synthesized vitamin B1; pioneered in bread and cereal grain enrichment; and whose philanthropy, through the Williams-Waterman Fund, has made a significant contribution to nutrition research.

438.   Bales, Robert Freed. 1963. Attitudes toward drinking in the Irish culture. In Society, culture, and drinking patterns. Edited by David Joshua Pittman & Charles R. Snyder. 1963. New York: John Wiley & Sons.

439.   Balfet, Helene. Bread in some regions of the Mediterranean area: a contribution to the studies on eating habits. In Gastronomy. The anthropology of food and food habits. Edited by Margaret Louise Arnott. 1975. Pp. 305-314. Paris; The Hague: Mouton Publishers. World Anthropology.

Based on data collected as part of a survey of cultural unity or diversity in the Mediterranean area. The region studied includes southern France (Languedoc, Provence); southern Italy; parts of Turkey; Malta; North Africa (the Maghreb) and some areas of Corsica, Lebanon, and Syria. Types of bread and the utensils used for baking them are described, as are the various preparations based on breads of the regions surveyed.

440.   Balintfy, Joseph L. 1964 Menu planning by computer. Association for Computing Machinery. Communication No.7. New York: Association for Computing Machinery.

441.   Ball, Carleton R. 1910. The history and distribution of sorghum. USDA-BPI- B No. 175.

442.   Ball, J. Dyer. 1903. Things Chinese or notes connected with China. Hong Kong: Kelly & Walsh.

Includes recipes for bird's nest soup: pp. 90-91; shark fins; chicken with fermented rice liquor; and 'genii duck' (cooked with rice wine or rice liquor): pp. 287-292.

443.   Ball, J. Dyer. 1912. The Chinese at home, or the man of tong and his land. New York, Chicago; Toronto: Fleming H. Revell.

Food habits, etiquette, preparation: pp. 158-171.

444.   Ball, J.W., & Eaton, J.D. 1972. Marine resources and the prehistoric lowland Maya: a comment. AA 74:772-776.

445.   Balland. 1906. Concerning edible earths. [In French.] JPChim 6 [series 23] : 181-183.

Discusses the absence of nutrients in these earths. Abstracted in ZUNG 13:433 (1907).

446.   Baloch, A.K. & Hujjutullah, S. 1966. Nutritive value of edible wild plants in the frontier region of West Pakistan. PJSIR 9:87-90.

447.   Balls, Edward K. 1962. Early uses of California plants. Berkeley: University of California Press Paperbacks.

448.   Balsdon, J.P.V.D. 1969. Life and leisure in ancient Rome. New York, St. Louis, San Francisco: McGraw-Hill.

Dinners: pp. 32-53.

449.   Bamber, M.K. 1913. Report on Palmyra fruit paste (pinadu). Trop Ag 40:95.

450.   Bancroft, J. 1884. Food of the aborigines of central Australia. RSQ-P 1: 104-107.

451.   Bancroft, Thomas L. 1894. Note on bungwall (Blechnum serrulatim, Rich), an aboriginal food. LSNSW-P 9:25-26.

A freshwater swamp fern, common in Queensland. The rhizome is pounded and eaten with oysters, crab and fish.

452.   Bandyopalhyaya, No., & Pal, S.S. 1962. Studies in rural change: reports on re-surveys of villages. Mohisgot (1957-1962). Agro-Economic Research Centre. Santiniketan, West Bengal: Visva-Bharati University.

Includes detailed expenditure data for several foods by occupational group. Village studied is located in Howrah District, West Bengal, approximately 10 km - 15 km northwest of Calcutta.

453.   Banerji, Niant Dhan. 1929. Indian dietaries in United Provinces. IMG 64:183-186.

454.   Banik, Allen E. & Taylor, Renee. 1960. Chapter Four. Hunza food and farming. In Hunza land. Long Beach, California: Whitehorn Publishing Co. Pakistan.

455.   Banning, C. & Den Hartog, C. 1936. Nutrition and dietary habits in various provinces of the Netherlands. LN-HO-B 5:560-563.

456.   Bansil, P.C. 1958. India's food resources and population: a historical and analytic study. Bombay: Vora.

457.   Bansil, P.C. 1960. Food resources and population of India: a historical study. Sankhya 22:183-208.

458.   Bantje, Han. Sociological aspects of nutrition education in Jamaica. In Nutrition and anthropology in action. Edited by Thomas K. Fitzgerald. 1976. Pp. 94-105. Assen, Amsterdam: Van Gorcum.

Provides suggestions for ways in which anthropologists can improve the effectiveness of applied programs of health-care delivery. These include use of epidemiological data correlated with socio-economic variables, and in-depth study of specific occurrences of malnutrition - both calculated to increase the relevant specificity of intervention programs. Finally, the author suggests that failure of applied public health programs may derive from discontinuity in perception of needs and methods in communities on the part of health care administrators, and emphasizes the need to study the sociology of the delivery system itself, as a means toward improving its effectiveness.

459.   Barakat, M.R., & Mohamed, G. 1951. A comparison of food consumption of industrial and agricultural labourers in rural Egypt. REMA-J 34:462-469.

460.   Baranov, A.I. 1962. On the uses of wild plants in N.E. China. QJTM 18:107-116.

461.   Barber, Edith M. 1948. The development of the American food pattern. JADA 24:586-591.

462.   Barber, Edwin A. 1878. Moqui food preparation. AN 12:456-458.

Describes Hopi piki bread; tum-i-lak-i-ni: a mixture of dried fruits, chopped meat and straw, formed into cakes and sun-dried; and a tamale.

463.   Barber, H.S. 1928. Thomas Say's unrecorded journey in Mexico. Ent N 39:17.

Food use of the rove beetle (Oxytelus rugulosos) in Mexico City.

464.   Barberet, J. 1886-1887. Le travail en France. Monographies professionelles. [Work in France. Professional monographs.

Vol. 1. includes butchers and bakers. Vol 2. includes brewers. Volume 3. includes pork butchers. Vol. 4. includes chocolate and candy makers.

465.   Barbosa, Jose Joao. 1952. Estudo comparativo entre o pao "saps" e o pao popular. [Comparative study between "saps" bread and regular bread.] Colecao Estudo e Pesquisas Alimentar, No. 27. Rio de Janeiro: Servico de Alimentacao de Previdenecia Social.

466.   Barden, Howard. The association of vitamin A with health status and dental enamel abnormalities in Down's syndrome and other mentally retarded subjects. Ph.D. dissertation. Anthropology. University of Wisconsin, Madison. 1974.

467.   Bardsley, William A. 1957. Will science save the saguaros. P Disc 10:24-29.

Contains illustration of Arizona Papago woman carrying a basket of the fruit of the cactus Carnegeia gigantea.

468.   Bareis, Charles. 1957.   Comments on pre-historic corn samples. OKAS-N 6:7-8.

469.   Barette, Christian. Ethno-ecologie d'un village Andin. [Ethnoecology of an Andean village.[Master's thesis. Anthropology. Universite de Montreal. 1972.

470.   Barghoorn, Elso S. 1944.   Collecting and preserving botanical materials of archaeological interest. Am An 9:289-294.

471.   Barghoorn, Elso S.; Wolfe, M.K.; & Clisby, K.H. 1954.   Fossil maize from the Valley of Mexico. HU-BM-L 16:299-240.

472.   Barjona de Freitas, Augusto Sant'iago. 1908.   Indice a obra Plantas uteis da Africa Portugueza. [Index to the work useful plants of Portuguese Africa.] Lisbon: Imprensa Nacional.

   Food uses of plants noted.

473.   Barker, P.T.P. 1902.   Samsu, a fermented drink of eastern Asia and its characteristic fungus. BAAS-R Pp. 818-819. Also in Lancet 163:881 (1902).

474.   Barker, J. 1943. The part played by legumes in the diet of the Nyasaland African with notes on the cooking and palatability of a number of different kinds. EAAJ 8:212-218.

475.   Barker, J. 1950.   Nyasaland native foods. Blantyre: Nyasaland Times.

476.   Barker, Theodore Cardwell, McKenzie, John C.; & Yudkin, John, eds. 1966. Our changing fare: two hundred years of British food habits. London: MacGibbon & Kee.

477.   Barker, T.C. Dr. Edward Smith and the first large-scale British dietary surveys, 1862-3. In The dietary surveys of Dr. Edward Smith, 1862-3. Edited by T.C. Barker; Derek J. Oddy; & John Yudkin. 1970. London: Staples Press.

478.   Barker, T.C. Changing patterns of food consumption in the United Kingdom. In Diet of man: needs and wants. Edited by John Yudkin. 1978. Pp. 163-186.

   An historical consideration of British food supply and nutrtional quality, largely concerned with the 18th and 19th Centuries. Includes an analysis of mid - 19th Century working class diets; and discussion on the uses of major food commodities, bread, fish, alcoholic beverages, and cereals.

479.   Barker, T.C. & Yudkin, John. 1971. Fish in Britain. Trends in its supply, distribution and consumption during the past two centuries. Department of Nutrition. London: Queen Elizabeth College.

480.   Barlow, Joel. 1796. The hasty-pudding, a poem in three cantos. Written at Chambery, in Savoy. January, 1793. He makes a good breakfast who mixes pudding with molasses. New Haven, Connecticut: Tiebout & O'brien.

481.   Barlow, Joel. 1850. The hasty puddings; a peom in three cantos. Written at chamvery [sic[; in Savoy, January, 1793, by Joel Barlow, minister plenipotentiary to France. Omne tulit punctum qui miscuit utile dulce. He makes a good breakfast who mixes pudding with molasses. New York: C.M. Saxton.

   Copies held by Ammerican Antiquarian Society, Worcester, Massachusetts; Brown University, Providence, Rhode Island; New York Public Library.

482.   Barmes, David Edward. Dental disease patterns related to dietary patterns in primitive peoples in the Territory of Papua and New Guinea. D.D.Sc. dissertation.   University of Queensland. 1963.

483.   Barnes, Richard H. 1971.   Nutrition and man's intellect and behavior. FASEB-FP 30: 1429-1433.

   Cites evidence indicating the probability that individuals experiencing early, severe malnutrition will manifest changes in emotionality and elevated response levels to adverse stimuli as adults.

484.   Barnett, Homer G. 1955 The Coast Salish of British Columbia. Eugene: The University of Oregon Press.

   Some food preparations are described: pp. 61-64.

485.   Barnett, Milton L. Alcoholism in the Cantonese of New York City: an anthropological study. In Etiology of chronic alcoholism. Edited by Oskar Diethelm. 1955. Pp. 179-227. Springfield, Illinois: Charles C. Thomas.

486.   Baron, Kathleen. Protein nutrition of expectant mothers in American Samoa and its effect upon the health of the infant. Master's thesis. Montana State University. 1971.

487.   Baron, Stanley. 1962. Brewed in America: a history of beer and ale in the United States. Boston: Little, Brown.

488.   Baroni, W. 1969. Nicolas Andry, un ortopedico dietologo. [Nicolas Andry, an orthopedic dietitian] R Stor Med 13:200-209.

489.   Barra, P. 1676. L'usage de la glace, de la neige et du froid. [The use of ice, snow, and cold.] Lyon: Chez Antoine Cellier fils.

   Uses related to food.

490.   Barrau, Jacques. 1950. Preliminary list of economic plants in New Caledonia. SPC-TO No. 6.

491.   Barrau, Jacques. 1956. L'agriculture vivri-ere indigene aux Nouvelle Hebrides. Indigenous subsistence agriculture of the New Hebrides.] JSO 12:181-216.

492.   Barrau, Jacques. 1956. L'arrowroot Poly-nesien. [Polynesian arrowroot.] TVie 103:80-82.

493.   Barrau, Jacques. 1956. Les ignames alimen-taires des iles du Pacifique sud. [The edible yams of the South Pacific Islands.] JATBA 3:385-401.

494,   Barrau, Jacques. 1956. Legumineuses a tubercule alimentaire de la Melanesie. [Edible leguminous tubers of Melanesia.] TVie 103:11-16.

495.   Barrau, Jacques. 1956. Plantes alimen-taires de base des Melanesiens. [Staple food plants of the Melanesians.] JATBA 3:32-49.

496.   Barrau, Jacques. Polynesian and Microne-sian subsistence agriculture.   Mimeographed. Noumea, New Caledonia: South Pacific Commis-sion. 1956.

497.   Barrau, Jacques. 1956. Quelques plantes alimentaires des rivages marins du Pacifique sud. [Some edible plants of South Pacific sea shores.] TVie 103: 77-79.

    Mangrove; algae.

498.   Barrau, Jacques. 1957. Les aracees a tuber-cules alimentaires des iles du Pacifique sud. [Edi-ble tuber of Araceae of the South Pacific.] JATBA 4:34-53.

499.   Barrau, Jacques. 1957. L'arbre a pain en oceania. [Breadfruit in oceania.] JATBA 4:117-124.

    Artocarpus incisa, L.

500.   Barrau, Jacques. 1957. L'enigme de la patate douce en oceanie. [The enigma of the sweet potato in Oceania.] EOU 40:83-87.

501.   Barrau, Jacques. 1958. Ethnobotanique et traversees du Pacifique en radeau. [Ethnobotany and Pacific raft crossings.] JATBA 5:665-667.

502.   Barrau, Jacques. Edible yams of the South Sea Islands. Species present, vernacular names, and distributions. In Pacific Science Congress. Ninth. 18 November to 9 December, 1957. Chula-longkorn University, Bangkok. Proceedings. Vol-ume Four. 1962. (Botany). Pp. 309-311.

503.   Barrau, Jacques. Les plantes alimentaires de l' Oceanie, origines, distributions et usages. [Food plants of Oceania, origins, distribution and uses.] Ph.D dissertation Universite d' Aix -Marseil-le. 1962. Also published in MCM-A Vol. 3-9. (1955-1961). Fascicule unique.

504.   Barrau, Jacques. 1965. Histoire et prehis-toire horticoles de l' Oceanie tropicale. [History and prehistory tropical Oceanic horticulture.] JSD 21:55-78.

505.   Barrau, Jacques. 1965. Witnesses of the past: notes on some food plants of Oceania. Ethnology 4:282-294.

506.   Barrau, Jacques.   Relationships between food processing and agricultural techniques re-examined in the light of the cooking habits of Australian and Malayo - Oceanian food gatherers. Paper read at the Annual Meeting of Northeastern Anthropological Association, April, 1968, Provi-dence, Rhode Island.

507.   Barrau, Jacques & Peeters, Alice. 1972. Histoire et prehistoire de la preparation des ali-ments d'origine vegetale. [History and prehistory of the preparation of plant foods.] JSO 35:141-152.

508.   Barrett, Mary F. 1947. The sycomore fig of ancient lineage. NYBG-J 48:254-262.

    Reference to use of Ficus sycomorus fruit as food among [unspecified] ancient peo-ples (probably in the circum-Mediterranean area): p. 255.

509.   Barrett, O.W. 1910. Promising root crops for the South. 1. yautias, taro, and dasheens. UADA-BPI - B No. 164.

510.   Barrett, Ward Judson. Agriculture of West-ern Samoa.   Ph.D. dissertation.   University of California, Berkeley. 1959.

511.   Barrick, Mary Jean. Evaluation of three types of audio-visual materials for teaching nutri-tion to freshman college women. Master's thesis. Iowa State College. 1947.

512.   Barringer, Maria Massey. 1867. Dixie cook-ery: or, how I managed my table for twelve years. A practical cookbook for Southern housekeepers. Boston: Loring.

513.   Barros, Souza. 1961. Tabus e habitos alimentares. [Taboos and food habits.] ABN 17:39-50.

514.   Barrow, Mark Velpeau; Niswander, Jerry D.; & Fortune, Robert. 1972. Health and disease of American Indians north of Mexico. A bibliography, 1800 - 1969. Gainsville: University of Florida Press.

    Diet, nutrition and growth: pp. 12-16.

515.   Barrows, Anna; Shapleigh, Bertha E.; with Blitz, Anne D. 1915. An outline on the history of cookery. CU-TCB [6th series] No. 11 TEB No. 28.

516.   Barrows, David Prescott. 1900. The ethno-botany of the Cahuilla Indians. Chicago: Universi-ty of Chicago Press. The author's 1897 Ph.D. dissertation.   Reprint.   New York: AMS Press. 1977. Banning, California: Malki Museum Press; Morongo Indian Reservation Press. 1977.

517.   Barry, C.B. 1925. Rates of food consump-tion by Zamindars in the Tallagang Tahsill of the

Attock District. Publication No. 6. Rural Section. Lahore, India: Punjab Board of Economic Inquiry.

518.   Barry, III, Herbert; Child, Irvin L.; & Bacon, Margaret K. 1959. Relation of child training to subsistence economy. AA 61:51-63.

Using Murdock's world ethnographic sample, a correlation is sought between personality orientation and survival demands in societies with a "low accumulation economy".

519.   Barthelemy, J.-J. 1824. Voyage du jeune Anacharis en Grece vers le milieu du quatrieme siecle avant l'ere vulgaire. 7 vols. [The journey of young Anacharsis in Greece toward the middle of the 4th century B.C.] Paris: chez Jaunet et Cottelle.

Food: (Athens): Vol.2. Chapter 25; (Sparta): Vol. 4. Chapter 48.

520.   Barthelemy, Pierre Eugene Gabriel. 1908. L'alimentation du soldat. Considerations -theoriques et pratiques a l'usage des officiers, suivies de quelques notions sur l'expertise de la viande de boucherie de la viand de conserve et du porc sale'. [The food of soldiers. Theoretical and practical considerations, for the use of officers, followed by a few ideas on the skill of meat butchering, on preserved meat, and on unclean pork.] Paris: Maloine.

521.   Barthes, Roland. Pour une psychosociologie de l'alimentation contemporaine. [Towards a social psychology of contemporary diet.] In Pour une historie de l'alimentation. Edited by J.J. Hemardinguer. 1970. Pp. 307-315. Paris: Colin.

522.   Barthes, Roland. Towards a psychosociology of contemporary food consumption. In European diet from pre-industrial to modern times. Edited by Robert Forster & Elborg Forster. 1975. New York: Harper & Row. Harper Torchbooks No. 1863.

523.   Bartlett, Alden Eugene. 1925. Chapter Thirteen. Enchiladas and chili con carne. In Least known America. New York: Fleming H. Revell.

Contains informal but explicit directions for preparing various New Mexican foods, e.g. chili bean soup, enchiladas, and tortillas.

524.   Bartlett, Katherine. 1931. Prehistoric Pueblo foods. MNA-MN 4:1-4.

525.   Bartlett, Katherine. 1933. Pueblo milling stones of the Flagstaff region and their relation to others in the Southwest. MNA-B No. 3.

526.   Bartlett, Katherine. 1936. The utilization of maize among the ancient pueblos. In Symposium on prehistoric agriculture. UNM-B No. 296 AS 1 (5):29-34.

527.   Bartlett, Katherine. 1943. Edible wild plants of northern Arizona. Plateau No. 1.

528.   Bartlett, Peggy F. Evolution theory and agricultural development: a Costa Rican case. Paper presented at 74th Annual Meeting of the American Anthropological Association. 2 to 6 December, 1975. San Francisco, California.

529.   Bartolozzi, E. 1939. Nota sulla apicultura e sulla produzione del miele nell' Africa Orientale Italiana. [Note on bee culture and on the production of honey in Italia East Africa.] A Colon 33:28-31.

530.   Barton, D.R. 1939. Food the world over. NH 44:308-311.

Popular survey of exotic food items, and preparation techniques. Poorly documented.

531.   Barton, Roy Franklin. 1911. The harvest feast of the Kaingan Ifugao. PJS 6 [D]:81-103.

532.   Barton-Wright, E.C. 1955. A historical survey of the nutritive value of fermented drinks, with special reference to beer. CSPB 18:95-105.

533.   Barton-Wright, E.C. 1956. Fermented drinks and nutrition. F Man 31:321-325.

534.   Bartram, Willliam. Travels through North and South Carolina, Georgia and west Florida. Philadelphia: James & Johnson.

Alachua preparation of fish: p. 157; tortoise as food: pp. 158-159; Alachua feast: p. 164; tripe soup: p. 168.

535   Bas, J.W. 1957. Nutrition ou alimentation? Commentaires sur l'enquete mondiale de l' Organization des Nations Unies. [Nutrition or diet? Commentary on the world survey by the United Nations Organization.] R Anth 3:136-146.

536.   Bascom, William R. 1946. Ponape: a Pacific economy in transition. Economic survey of Micronesia. Vol. Eight. Honolulu: U.S. Commercial Company.

Basic foods, cooking techniques, food preparation, and fishing methods: pp. 71-78; notes on eating times: pp. 164-166 (passim.); note on wild food plants: p. 166; special terms for persons performing food-related tasks: p. 168. A very extensive section is given over to Ponapean agriculture (pp. 170-238) with thorough details on cultivation techniques, taboos, food preparation and use, plant varieties, and harvesting. Fishing techniques, processing, and associated taboos: pp. 239-258. Domestic animals, and hunting: pp. 258-264.

537.   Bascom, William R. 1948. Ponapean prestige economy. SJA 4:211-221.

Caroline Islands.

538.   Bascom, Willliam R. 1949. Subsistence farming on Ponape. NZG 5:115-129.

Caroline Islands.

539. Basile, C. 1954. Ligurian gastronomy. [In Italian] APC 4:34-37.

540. Basler, Adolph. 1932. Ueber die Ernaehrung und die wichtigsten Nahrungsmittel in China. [On nutrition and the staple foods of China.] Canton: Verlag der Sun Yat - Sen Universitaet.

541. Bassir, O. 1949. The food habits of the Mende. Africana Nos. 1-2. Pp. 23-24.

542. Bassir, O. 1961. Une dietetique Africaine [An African diet.] P Afric Nos. 34-35. Pp. 207-210.

543. Bassir, O. 1962. Observations on the fermentation of palm wine. WAJBC 6:20-25.

544. Basso, Ellen B. 1972. The Kalapalo dietary system. In 40 Congresso Internazionale degli Americanisti. 40th. Atti. Edited by Ernesta Cerulli & Gilda della Ragione. Pp. 629-637. Genoa:Tilgher.

The Kalapalo are a Carib - speaking group, living in Mato Grosso State, Brazil.

545. Basso, Ellen B. The Kalapalo dietary system. In Carib - speaking Indians. Culture, society and language. University of Arizona. Anthropology Papers. No. 29. Edited by Ellen B. Basso. 1977. Pp. 98-105.

A classification of living animals, based on the criterion 'eaten' or 'not eaten'.

546. Bastide, Roger. 1952. A cozinha dos deuses (alimentacao e candombles.) [Cookery of the gods. Food and vodun.] Rio de Janeiro: Servico de Alimentacao da Previdencia Social.

547. Basu, Chunilal. 1929. Food. Adharchandra Mookerjee Lecture. Calcutta: University of Calcutta.

Role of food in Indian life.

548. Bataillard, J. 1869. Histoire de la boulangerie. [History of baking.] Besancon: Imprimerie de J. Roblot.

549. Bataillard, J. 1870. Histoire et legislation de la boucherie et de la charcuterie. [History and legislation of butchery and pork-butchery.] Besancon: Imprimerie de J. Roblot.

550. Batavia. Institute of Sea-Fisheries. 1941. De Vischery-Producten van Indo-China. [Fish products of Indo-China.] Communication No. 6. Batavia, Java: Institute of Sea-Fisheries.

Review of the literature on fish products.

551. Batchelder, Helen, 1951. The Jerusalem artichoke (Helianthus tuberosus). Herbarist No. 17. Pp. 24-29.

552. Batchelor, John. 1901. Chapter Twenty. Food. In The Ainu and their folklore. London: Religious Tract Society.

Latin plant names are given, with comments on food preparation, meal etiquette; millet and its role as deity. Bear festival foods: pp. 486, 493-495; food offerings to bear cub: pp. 491-492; 496.

553. Batchelor, John 1927. Ainu life and lore: echoes of a departing race. Tokyo: Kyobunkwan.

The following foods are noted: ash-cooked eggs: p. 61, arrowroot (Lilium glennii) cakes: p. 77, general diet: pp. 89-90, 93-94; Trichiurus japonicus: p. 404; chestnut-salmon roe paste: p. 410.

554. Batchelor, John. 1932. The Ainu bear festival. ASTJJ-T 9:37-44.

555. Batchelor, John & Miyabe, Kingo. 1893. Ainu economic plants. ASJ-T 21:198-240.

Edible plants are described on pp. 214-236, together with Ainu, Japanese, and Latin nomenclatures.

556. Bates, Daisy M. 1921. Aboriginal cannibalism. Australasian 6 August.

557. Bates, Daisy M. 1927. Aboriginal cannibals: mothers who eat their babies. AReg 8 March.

558. Bates, Marston. 1957 - 1958. Man, food, and sex. AS 27:449-458.

559. Bates, Marston. 1959 - 1960. Insects in the diet. AS 29:43-52.

Orthoptera, Isoptera, Homoptera, Lepidoptera, Hymenoptera.

560. Bates, Marston. 1967. Chapter 1. Food and sex. Chapter 2; Three square meals. Chapter 3. Insects in the diet. In Gluttons and libertines. New York: Random House.

561. Bates, Marston. 1970. Eating and being eaten. S Digest 68:20-24.

562. Bates, O. 1917. Ancient Egyptian fishing. HAS 1:199-271.

563. Batky, Isigmond. 1907. A foldevesrol. [Earth-eating.] Term Koz 39:129-132.

564. Battad, Josephine R. 1976. Determinants of nutritional status in rural Philippines households. U Phil S E IED-RDP No. 76-16. 29 July.

Influence of income and education in different age groups.

565. Battle, Herbert B. 1922. The domestic use of oil among the Southern aborigenes. AA 24:171-182.

Sources of cooking oil among Native American groups in the southeastern United States.

566. Bauby, C. 1948. Gastronomie de Noel. [Christmas gastronomy.] Tramontane 32:327-329.

567.   Baud, Theodore. 1859. Histoire des champignons comestibles et veneneux. [History of edible
and poisonous mushrooms.] Borganeuf: Imprimerie Buisson.

568.   Baudet, Florence E.J.M. 1904. De maaltijd
en de Reuken in de middeleeuwen. Geillustreerd
met authentieke afbeeldingen. [Mealtime and
cooking in the Middle Ages. Illustrated with authentic pictures.] Leiden: A.W. Sijthoff.

569.   Baudon, A. 1912. Sur quelques plantes alimentaires indigenes du Congo francais. [About
several indigenous food plants of the French Congo.] Paris: Challamel.

570.   Baudon, A. 1913. Les cultures indigenes de
la region du Gribingui. [Indigeneous cultigens of
the Gribingui region.] MCM-A 1 [Series 3]: 203-
254.

> An area located in the Central African
> Republic at approximately 7 degrees ON,
> 19. degrees OE.

571.   Baudoin, H. 1962. Bierbrouwerijn en bier-
verbruik te Maastricht in de eerste helft van de
18c eeuw. [Breweries and beer consumption at
Maestricht in the first half of the 18th Century.]
Maasgouw 81:5-16.

572.   Bauer, Max. 1903. Der deutsche Durst.
Mythologischen Skizzen aus der deutschen Kulturgeschichte. [German thirst. Mythological sketches
from German culture history.] Berlin: H.
Seemann.

573.   Baumann, E.D. 1960. Hippokrates over
voeding. [Hippocrates on nutrition.] Voeding
21:89-95. Abstracted in NA Rev 30:1418.

574.   Baumann, E.D. 1961. Diet in the Netherlands in Roman times derived chiefly from Pliny
the Elder. [In Dutch.] Voeding 22:7-14.

575.   Baumgarten, Karl. 1965. Die Tirschordnung
im alten meeklenburgischen Bauernhaus. [Table
arrangement in old Mecklenburg farmhouses.] DJV
2:1-15.

576.   Bautista, Alicia P. 1967. On Filipino recipes. PJN 20:31-35.

> Regional and sectional variation.

577.   Bavly, Sarah. Family food consumption in
Palestine. Ph.D. dissertation. Teachers College.
Columbia University. 1947.

578.   Bavly, Sarah. 1960. Food consumption and
levels of nutrition of urban wage and salary earners' families in Israel (1956 - 1957). Central
Bureau of Statistics. Special Series No. 10. Jerusalem: Ministry of Education and Culture.

579.   Bavly, Sarah. 1966. Changes in food habits
in Israel. JADA 48:488-495.

580.   Bavly, Sarah. 1968. Nutritional patterns
among seven rural communities in Israel, 1963.
WRND 9:32-35.

581.   Bayer, G. 1959. Die Erdmandel [The earth
almond.] Berliner Gartner Bucher. Vol. 35. Berlin: Deutscher Bauerverlag.

> Chufa (Cyperus esculenta, L.).

582.   Bayerl, Marie. 1901. Die Koch-Kunst im
Bohmewalde. [Bohemian Forest cookery.] ZOV
7:183-185.

> German rural cookery.

583.   Bayley, Iris. 1949. The bush teas of Barbados. BMHS-J 7:161-170.

584.   Bayne-Powell, Rosamund. 1956 Chapter 7.
Food. Chapter 8. Drink. Chapter 9. Entertaining,
meals. In Housekeeping in the eighteenth century
London: John Murray.

585.   Bazore, Ellen Katherine. 1940. Hawaiian
and Pacific foods, a cookbook of culinary customs
adapted for the American hostess. New York:
Barrows & Co.

586.   Beadle, G.W. 1939, Teosinte and the origin
of maize. J Her 30:245-247.

587.   Beaglehole, Ernest. 1937. Chapter 3: Foods.
In Some modern Hawaiians UHi-RP No. 19.

588.   Beaglehole, Pearl. 1938. Foods and their
preparation. In Notes on Hopi economic life, by
Ernest Beaglehole. YUPA No. 15. Pp. 60-71.

589.   Beale, Bessie V. A study of the food habits
and practices of a selected group of women war
workers in Washington, D.C. Master's thesis.
Washington, D.C.: Howarad University. 1945.

590.   Beals, Alan R. 1964. Food is to eat: the
nature of subsistence activity. AA 66:134-136.

> A critique of traditional classifcatory term-
> inology related to subsistence activities, and
> a suggestion for refinement of the terms
> employed in George Peter Murdock's Ethno-
> graphic Atlas.

591.   Beals, Ralph L. 1934. Material culture of
the Pima, Papago, and western Apache. United
States Department of the Interior. National Park
Service. Berkeley, California: Field Division of
Education.

> Wildplants: pp. 10-13; animal foods: pp. 13-
> 14, cooking: p. 14.

592.   Beals, Ralph L. 1946. Cheran: a Sierra
Tarascan village. SI-ISA-P No. 2.

> Food data: pp. 47-58.

593.   Bean, Lowell. 1960 - 1961. An ethnobotanical report sheet, a field technique. UCLA-AS-AR
3:233-236.

Drawn up for use in study of the Cahuilla, a Native American group of southern California.

594.   Bean, Lowell John & Saubel, Katherine. 1961. Cahuilla ethnobotanical notes: the aboriginal use of the oak. UCLA-AS-AR. 3:237-245.

595.   Beardsley, Richard K. 1948. Three instances of Japanese wartime cannibalism: problems in psychiatry, or culture history? CSB 2:2-3.

596.   Beasley, Walter L. 1903. The secret cannibal society of the Kwakiutl. SA 89:120-122.

597.   Beattie, G.R. 1961. The fragrant clove and its many uses. SPCYB 34:541-544.

Clove production in Zanzibar, with historical background and on use as a condiment.

598.   Beaubier, Jeff. High life expectancy on the island of Paros, Greece. New York: Philosophical Library.

Nutrition: pp. 55-60. Describes the basic diet of the island; attitudes of islanders towards commerical foods; effects of food scarcity during World War II; and average nutrient intake per capita.

599.   Beauchamp, William Martin. 1885. The Iroquois White Dog feast. A ANT 7:235-239.

Contains brief mention of cooking the sacrificial animal, and its use as food.

600.   Beauchamp, Willliam Martin. 1898. Indian corn stories and customs. JAF II:195-202.

Mythic material, with notes on ritual practice.

601.   Beaudry-Darisme', Micheline N.; Hayes-Blend, Lesly C.; & Van Veen, Andre G. 1972. The application of sociological research methods to food and nutrition problems on a Caribbean Island. EFN 1:103-119.

A frequency of food intake survey was carried out in two hundred households in two villages and one suburban area of the island of St. Vincent, over a period of two months. Analysis of the data recorded indicated that, on an area basis, an increase in the complexity of the way of life (from rural to urban), as well as an increase in the complexity of the pattern of food intake, appeared associated with a lower incidence of malnutrition in children between the ages of one and five years; a lower child mortality ratio, and a shorter period of breast feeding. The authors see the process of "modernization" as exerting a positive influence in health-related areas. Infant feeding practices, beliefs related to the efficacy of food in OB/GYN contexts Tables of commonly eaten foods are included.

602.   Beauregard, Ollivier; Le Tourneau; Magilot; Royer, Clemence; Fauvelle. 1888. Suite sur la discussion sur l'anthropophagie. [Continuation of the discussion on anthropophagy.] SAP-B 11:123-136.

Anthropophagy in ca. Egypt B.P. 5600; anthropophagy and human dentition; anthrophagy in the Palaeolithic in relation to food supply.

603.   Beaver, W.-N. 1914. Some notes on the eating of human flesh in the Western Division of Papua. Man 14:145-147.

604.   Beccari, O. 1917. The origin and dispersal of Cocos nucifera. PJS 12 [Section Botany]: 27-43.

Criticizes the theory of Orator Fuller Cook which holds a New World origin for the coconut. Examines as well the nature of the possible mutual evolutionary influences exerted by the land crab Birgus latro and Cocas nucifera upon one another. Supports the probability of dissemination of C. nucifera by ocean currents, and posits an Asiatic or Polynesian origin for the tree.

605.   Becher, Hans. 1967. Die endokannibalistischen Riten als fruheste Erscheinungs form der Anthropophagie. [Endocannibalistic rites as the earliest manifestation of anthropophagy.] ZE 92:248-253.

606.   Becker, Johan Hermann. 1810-1822 Versuch einer allgemeinen und besondern Nahrungsmittel Runde. Mit einer Vorrede von Dr. S.G. Vogel. 5 vols. [A general and particular study on the science of nutrition. With a foreword by Dr. S.G. Vogel.] Stendal: Franzen und Grosse.

Copy held by British Museum. Only three volumes published.

607.   Becker, Marion Rombauer. 1969. Little acorn. The story behind The Joy of Cooking, 1931 - 1966. Indianapolis: Bobbs-Merrill.

608.   Beckerman, Stephen. Ecological aspects of the anthropological study of nutrition. Paper presented at 76th Annual Meeting of American Anthropological Association. 29 November to 3 December, 1977. Houston, Texas.

Nutrition is connected with the distribution and abundance of human populations through the feedback channels of the differing needs of populations with distinct age-gender distributions, climates, and activity levels for different diets. Demands of labor and/or status may place other constraints on what must or should be eaten, and certain items in the diet may necessitate or proscribe certain others. Environmental change can cause dietary change, and dietary change may affect reproductive rate. Examples of these relationships suggest hypotheses for field testing and underscore the intricacy of the biology -culture interaction.

609.   Beckwith, Martha Warren. 1927. Notes on Jamaican ethnobotany. Poughkeepsie, New York: Vassar College.

Part Two. Food Plants.

610.   Beckwith, Martha Warren. 1940. Hawaiian mythology. New Haven: Yale University Press.

Tree of food: tree once contained all food: people needed only to pick it (Hawaii): p. 286; acquisition of vegetables and cereals (Samoa): p. 439; (Isabel Island): p. 504; origin of yams (sweet potato, taro) New Zealand, Tonga, Samoa): p. 101; (Cook Islands-Manihiki): p. 256; gods provide drinkable water (Hawaii): p. 63f.

611.   Beckwith, Mary. 1959. Life from the earth. DM 22:4-7.

Includes data on wild foods of the prehistoric Anasazi culture of Arizona. Includes illustration of Papago maize storage vessels.

612.   Beddoe, John. 1865. On hospital dietaries. DQJMS 72:46-72.

Reviews hospital diets in England, Ireland, and Scotland, with tabular analysis preceded by a 'Standard Table of Composition of Food'. Prison diets are also reviewed. Fourteen 'Experiments on convalescent Diet in Bristol Infirmary' are given.

613.   Bedford. P.W. 1959. Sea Dyak diet: a lonnghouse survey. SarMJ 9:203-214.

614.   Beede, Laurence. Teen-age drinking in Seattle and King County. Master's thesis. Anthropology. University of Washington. 1968.

615.   Beel, T.A.L. 1913. Notes on the history of preserving fish. [In German] ZHMH 24:129-133.

Herring industry.

616.   Beeley, Brian W. 1970. The Turkish village coffeehouse as a social institution. GR 60:475-493.

617.   Beemer, Hilda. 1939. Notes on the diet of the Swazi in the Protectorate. B Stud 13:199-236.

618.   Beetle, Alan A. 1950. Bulrushes and their multiple uses. EB 4:132-138.

Nutritive value of Scirpus grains, roots, and shoots: pp. 135,136.

619.   Beeuwkes, Adelia M. 1960. Studying the food habits of the elderly. JADA 37:215—218.

620.   Beeuwkes, Adelia M.; Todhunter, E. Neige; & Weigley, Emma Seifrit, compilors. 1967. Essays on history of nutrition and dietetics, reprinted on the occasion of the 50th anniversary of the founding, in 1917, of the American Dietetic Association. Chicago: The American Dietetic Association.

Part two contains a history of food and cookbooks. Articles originally published in JADA.

621.   Begrie, I. Christine. 1963. Food and food habits in Uganda. RNFS 3:8-11.

622.   Bequez y Cesar, A. 1939. Feeding of Cuban infants from time of weaning to age of thirty months. [In Spanish.] RM Cuba 5-:311-329.

623.   Behrman, Daniel. 1960. Laboratory for desert living. UC January:32-33.

Contains a review of food service and dietary conditions in the Sahara oil town of Hassi-Messaoud, Algeria (31 52 N, 5 57 E).

624.   Behar, Moises. Food and nutrition of the Maya before the conquest and at the present time. In Biomedical challenges presented by the American Indian. Pan American Health Organization. 1968. Pp. 114-119. Scientific Publication No. 165. Washington, D.C.: Pan American Health Organization.

625.   Behar, Moises. 1976. Nutrition: a social problem. Who Features No. 35.

Emphasizes need for equal distribution of food supply; criticizes economic development schemes which only benefit elites; and agricultural programs which fail to meet the needs of poor farmers.

626.   Behar, Moises & Scrimshaw, Nevin S. 1962. Effect of environment on nutritional status. AEH 5:257-264.

Biological, socioeconomic, food production, population, and plant and animal domestication are the factors considered.

627.   Behn, H. 1934. Tausend jahre speiszettel; weltgeschichte im Kochhopf. [A thousand-year-old menu; world history in a cookpot.] W Mon 152:329-332.

628.   Behrend, Gary. Dental attrition and subsistence change. Paper presented at 76th Annual Meeting of the American Anthropological Association. 29 November to 3 December, 1977. Housto, Texas.

Characteristic patterns of attrition along the dental arcade result from exposure to abrasive materials and occlusal friction. These patterns represent relatively permanent records of tooth function and of the interaction between teeth and certain elements of the environment, especially the diet. This study tests the hypothesis that: where changes occur in subsistence strategy, changes may also be expected to occur in the pattern of severity of tooth wear. Prehistoric Woodland and Mississippian skeletal populations, representing hunting and gathering and horticultural adaptions, respectively, from the lower Illinois Valley, are utilized.

629.   Behura, N.K. 1962. Meals and food habits in rural India. IAS-B ll:111-137.

630.   Beidelman, Richard G. 1952. Ethnozoology of the Pueblo Indians. CWAS-J 4:19-20.

631.   Beidelmlan, Thomas O. 1961. Beer drinking and cattle theft in a Tanganyika chiefdom. AA 63:534-549.

632.   Beidelman, Thomas O. 1964. Some Kaguru plants: terms, names, uses. Man 64:79-82.

Contains a list of wild and cultivated plants used for food, by this Tanganyikan group.

633.   Bejarano, Jorge. 1949. Alimentacion y nutricion en Colombia. [Diet and nutrition in Colombia.] Bogota: Editorial Cromos.

634.   Belbeuf, Marquis de. 1856. Histoire des Grands - Panetiers de Normandie et du francfief de la grande paneterie. [History of the Grand Panetiers of Normandy and of the fief of the Grand Panetier.] Paris: J.-B. Dumoulin.

The office of the Grand-Panetier of France was instituted, probably under the reign of Philllipe-Auguste, and was filled only by the King's powerful lords, who were in charge of the distribution of bread in the royal household. The Grand Panetier had authority over the bakers of France. After 1749, the Grand-Panetier fulfilled his function only on New Year's Day, and on the four principal feasts of the year, being elsetimes replaced by gentlemen-servants.

635.   Belderok, B. 1965. Johan Rudolf Katz, 1880 -1938, en zijn onderzockingen over het oud-bakken worden van brood. [Johan Rudolf Katz, 1880 - 1938, and his research on the old words for bread.] Voeding 26:485-492.

636.   Belding, L. 1892. Some of the methods and implements by which the Pacific Coast Indians obtained game. Zoe 3:120-124.

Throwing stones, snares, nets; notes the Eskimo method of hunting with a 'coil' of sharpened whale-bone. The whale-bone is soaked in warm water and when soft is bent in half, tied, and allowed to dry. When dry, the tying cord is removed. The 'coil' is covered with tallow, and laid out as wolf-bait. The trap is literally 'wolfed-down' and the coil responds to the warmth and digestive juices in the animal's stomach by straightening out and piercing the animal internally, either causing fatal injury, or so incapacitating the animal that it is a ready ready prey for the hunter on its trail.

637.   Belfrage. S.H. 1935. Diet and race. In The new health guide. Edited by William Arbuthnot Lane, London: Geoffrey Bles.

638.   Bell, E.J. 1950. Far Eastern food preferences. For Ag 14:161-163.

639.   Bell, F.L.S. 1931. The place of food in the social life of Polynesia. Oceania 2:117-135.

Conspicuous   consumption (ostentatious feasting); cultural functions of feasts; relationship between food production and kinship; food and religious offerings; sumptuary restrictions; totemic relationships; ritual purity of chiefs' agricultural rites; food preparations.

640.   Bell, F.L.S. 1946 - 1948. The place of food in the social life of the Tanga. Oceania 17:139-172; 310-326; 18:35-59; 233-237; 19:51-74.

Part One describes the subsistence gardening of a Melanesian group inhabiting the Bismack Archipelago. Part Two discusses beliefs and practices associated with fishing. Part Three discusses the central role of pigs in the subsistence economy and includes a unique discussion of ethnobotanical veterinary practices relating to pigs. Part Four discusses methods of hunting and trapping, and includes a list of fruits, nuts, and vegetables collected for food. Part Five concludes with a discussion of food beliefs, etiquette, ceremonial role of food, menus, "recipes", and feasting behavior.

641.   Bell, H.C.P. 1883. Sinhalese customs and ceremonies connected with paddy cultivation in the low country. RASC-J Pp. 44-93.

Ceylon.

642.   Bell, H.C.P. 1889. Paddy-cultivation ceremonies in the four Korales, Legalla district. RASC-J Pp. 67-77.

Ceylon.

643.   Bell, Marjorie. 1932. The nutritionist and the home. HSS 26:298-302.

Decries the failure of physicians, and homemakers to apply knowledge of nutrition; and the effects of poor diet on public health.

644.   Bell, Martin L. 1962. A portrait of progress: a business history of Pet Milk Company from 1885-1960. St. Louis, Missouri: Pet Milk Co.

645.   Bell, Willis H. & Castetter, Edward Franklin. 1937. Ethnobiological studies in the American Southwest 5. The utilization of mesquite and screwbean by the aborigines in the American Southwest. UNM-B No. 314. BS 5 No. 2.

646.   Bell, Willis H & Castetter, Edward Franklin. 1941. Ethnobiological studies in the American Southwest 7. The utilization of yucca, sotol and beargrass by the aborigines in the American Southwest. UNM-B No. 372. BS No. 5.

647.   Belle, F.P., comp. 1925. California cook book. Chicago: Reagan Publishing Corp.

Contains old Spanish recipes.

648.   Belle, Gustave.   1886.   La cuisine pour les infants, les malades, les convalescents et les viellards.   [Cooking for infants, the ill, convalescents, and old persons.]   Paris: L. Sauvaitre; the author.

649.   Belloni, L.   1965.   La dietetica nella medicina del passato.   [Dietetics in medical practice in the past.]   G San 36:3-7.

650.   Bellows, Albert Jones.   1868.   The philosophy of eating.   2nd. ed. New York: Hurd & Houghton.

651.   Beltran, Enrique.   1949.   Plantas usadas en la alimentacion por los antiguos mexicanos.   [Plants used in the diet by the ancient Mexicans.]   Am Ind 9:195-204.

Staple foods (maize, chile, legumes, maguey etc.) are mentioned, with notes on their botanical history, archaeology, and nutritive values.

652.   Beltran, Gonzalo Aguirre.   1955.   Capitulo Tres. Cultura y nutricion.   [Chapter Three. Culture and nutrition.]   In Programas de salud en la situacion intercultural.   Mexico: Ediciones del Instituto Indigenista Interamericano.

Section One ('La dieta indigena' - 'Native diet') provides evidence to dispel the myth of the general inadequacy of rural Mexican food patterns. Section Two ('Contexto cul tural' - 'Cultural context') discusses the economic basis of diet, and dietary change: applied and spontaneous, as a result of culture contact, and changes from peasant status to urban wage laborer. Section Three ('Valores y patrones de alimentacion' -'Dietary values and patterns') refers to ritual food consumption, differences in cultural attitudes toward food; food systems (e.g. "hot" and "cold" categorizations). Section Four ('Programas nutriologias -'Nutritional programs') considers the significance of ecological, biological and cultural factors in applied nutrition programs in relation to reevalution of native foods from a compositional point-of-view; increasing the quantity of existing food resources; the reintroduction of known foods to supplement monocropping; secularization of ceremonial foods; and introduction of new foods.

653.   Bement, Lewis.   1950.   The cutlery story.   Deerfield, Massachusetts: Associated Cutlery Industries of America.

654.   Bender, Donald R.   Population and the agricultural productivity of bush fallow systems in tropical forest habitats.   Paper presented at 68th Annual Meeting of the American Anthropological Association.   20 to 23 November, 1969.   New Orleans, Louisianna.

It is commonly assumed that environmental factors determine the agricultural productivity necessary to either allow or else bring into existence large populations and densi-ties. The purpose of this paper is to show that, under some circumstances with bush fallow systems in tropical forest habitats, increased populations can bring into existence increased agricultural productivity.

655.   Bender, Alfred E.   1976.   Food preferences of males and females.   35:181-189.

Concludes that it is uncertain as to whether there are any clear differences in food preferences where gender is the determining variable.

656.   Bender, Alfred E., & Doell, B.H.   1960.   The nutritionist in industry.   CI no. 29. Pp. 908-911.

657.   Bender, Barbara.   1975.   Farming in prehistory.   From hunter-gatherer to food producer.   New York: St. Martin's Press.

Transition to food production; theoretical approaches; recognition of domestication; significance of climatic change; distribution of potential domesticates; southwest Asia; Meso-America; Peru.

658.   Bender, G.   1931.   Geographie der Hirsen.   [Geography of millet.]   K Rund 7:79-87.

Dispersal, cultivation, and use of millet.

659.   Benedict, Francis Gano; Miles, Walter R.; Roth, Paul; & Smith, H. Monmouth.   1919.   Human vitality and efficiency under prolonged restricted diet.   CIW-P No. 280.

660.   Benedict, Francis Gano & Steggerda, Morris.   1936.   The food of the present-day Maya Indians of Yucatan.   CIW-CAA 3:155-188.   Publication no 436.

Describes individual foods, with Maya, Spanish, English and Latin names; indicates methods of preparation. Food consumption tables for thirty persons are recorded. Comments on food hygiene; historical recap of Maya diet since European colonialization; report on nutritional value of Maya dietary.

661.   Benet, Sula.   1951.   Festival menus 'round the world.   New York: Abelard-Schuman.

662.   Benet, Sula M. & Joffe, Natalie F.   Some Central European food patterns and their relationship to wartime problems of food and nutrition.   Polish food patterns.   Mimeographed.   Committee on Food Habits.   Washington, D.C.:   National Research Council.   1943 February.

663.   Benetato, G.   1936.   Nutrition of rural population in the community of Maguri.   [In Roumanian.]   Cluj Med 17:661-662.

664.   Beni, C.   1883.   Il pulque (neutli) dei Messicani.   [Pulque (neutli) of the Mexicans.]   Archivi 13:13-23.

An alcoholic beverage derived from the root of the maguey plant (Agave sp.)

665. Bennett, Jr., Charles F. 1962. The Bayono Cuna Indians of Panama: an ecological study of livelihood and diet. AAG-A 52:32-50.

Comprehensive description of climate, geography, health, ethnobotany, architecture, transportation, animal domestication, hunting, fishing, and food preparation. Results of a brief dietary survey is included with an accompanying evaluation of nutritional status.

666. Bennett, F.J.; Jelliffe, Derrick Brian; Jelliffe, E.F.P.; & Moffat, M. 1968. The nutrition and disease pattern of children in a refugee settlement. EAMJ 45:229-246.

667. Bennett, F. J., Mugalula-Mukiibi, A. A. ; Lutwama, J. S. W., & Nansubuga, G. 1965. An inventory of Kiganda foods. UJ 29: 45-53.

Contains a list of food plants, with notes on uses, preparation, and tabus.

668. Bennett, G. 1832. Botany of the South Sea Islands. MN Hist 5: 483-486.

Remarks on several edible plants and edible beverages.

669. Bennett, John W. 1943. Food and status in a rural society. ASR 8:561-569.

Prestige role of foods in a rural-to-urban transitional area of southern Illinois.

670. Bennett, John W. 1946. An interpretation of the scope and implications of social scientific research in human subsistance. AA 48: 553-573.

A review of research in nutritional anthropology from ca: 1932 through 1944. Attempts to define the concepts of theoretical and applied research as these relate to the study of human food habits.

671. Bennett, John W. Subsistence economy and foodways in a rural community: a study of socio-economic and cultural change. Ph.D. dissertation. University of Chicago. 1946.

Study of a Southern Illinois Community.

672. Bennett, John W.; Passin, Herbert; & Smith, H. 1943. Food and culture in southern Illinois. ASR 7: 645-660.

673. Bennett, K. H. 1883. Notes on methods of obtaining water from Eucalyptus roots as practiced by the natives of the country between the Lochlan and Darling Rivers. LSNSW-P 8: 213-215.

Australian Aborigines.

674. Bennett, Linda A. & Wolin, Stephen J. The development and maintenance of family rituals under the impact of parental alcoholism. Paper presented at 77th Annual Meeting of the American Anthropological Association. 14 to 18 November, 1978. Los Angeles, California.

675. Bennett, Merrill Kelly. 1941. International contrasts in food consumption. GR 31:365-376.

676. Bennett, Merrill Kelly. 1955. The food economy of the New England Indians. 1605 - 1675. JPE 43:369-397.

677. Bennett, Merrill Kelly. 1960. A world map of food crop climates. SU-FRIS 1:285-295.

678. Bennett, Merrill Kelly & Pierce, R.H. 1961. Change in the American national diet, 1879 - 1959. SU-FRIS 2:95-119.

679. Bennett, Richard & Elton, John. 1898. History of corn milling. 4 vols. Reprint. New York: Burt Franklin. 1964.

Vol. 1. Handstones, slaves, and cattle mills. Vol. 2. Watermills and wind mills. Vol. 3. Feudal laws and customs; Vol. 4. Some fuedal laws.

680. Bennett, Wendell Clark & Zingg, Robert M. 1935. The Tarahumara. Chicago. University of Chicago Press.

Food habits: pp. 30-47; 111-144; 163-180.

681. Benson, P.H. & Peryam, David R. 1958. Preferences for foods in relation to cost. JAP 42: 171-174.

682. Benton, A.A. 1894. Classical cookery. Sewanee 2:413-424.

683. Bentz, T. 1952. Chip steaks - how they started. QFF 14: 177-178.

684. Bentzen, R.C. 1929. Dental conditions among Mimbres people of southwestern United States previous to year 600 A.D., original study of teeth and jaws from series of skeletons unearthed by Jenks Expedition. DC 71:1068-1073.

685. Bequaert, J. 1921. Insects as food. NH 21:191-200.

Historical and recent ethnographic data.

686. Beranard, R.-J. Peasant diet in 18th Century Gevaudan. In European diet from pre-industrial to modern times. Edited by Robert Forster & Elborg Forster. 1975. New York: Harper & Row. Harper Torchbooks No. 1863.

Gevaudan is a region in southeastern France.

687. Berardinelli, Waldemar. 1958. Tipos humanos e alimentacao. Ensaio e debate alimentar, No. 8. [Human types and diet. Food essay and debate, No. 8.] Rio de Janeiro: Servico de Alimentacao da Previdencia Social.

688. Bercaw, Louise O.; Hannay, Annie M.; & Larson, Nellie G.; Lacy, Mary G., coordinator. 1940. Corn in the development of the civilization of the Americas. A selected and annotated bibliography. USDA- BAE-AEB No. 9-87.

689. Berchoux, J. 1805. La gastronomie. Poeme, suivi des poesies fugitives de l'auteur. [Gastonomy. A Poem, followed by fleeting poetry by the author.] Paris: Giguet & Michaud.

Copy held by the Library of the Food and Agriculture Organization of the United Nations, Rome.

690. Berdichevsky, Bernardo. Die Kjokken moddings der chilenischen Zentralkuste. [Kitchen-middens of the central coast of Chile.] In 5 Internationale Kongress fur vor - und Frugeschichte. 24 bis 30 August 1958. Hamburg. Edited by Gerhard Bersu. 1961. Pp. 93-96. Berlin: Verlag Gebruddern Mann.

691. Berdichevsky (Berday), Norman. The cultural geography of coffee and tea preferences: a study in perception and diffusion. Master's thesis. Geography. University of Wisconsin. 1971.

692. Berdichevsky (Berday), Norman. 1976. A cultural geography of coffee and tea preferences. AAG-A 8:24-29.

693. Bereczki, Gabor. 1963. Cseremisz KH. 'melena', u. 'melna' 'pfannkuchen', 'fladen'. Nyel Koz 65:175-176.

Cheremis 'melena' glossed as 'pancake'.

694, Berg, Gosta. 1941. Drinking tubes: some notes from Europe. Ethnos 6:97-108.

695. Berg, Gosta. 1949. Faret som mjolkdjur. Nagra anteckningar till den primitiva boskapsskotselns historia. [The sheep as a milk animal. Some notes toward the history of live-stock raising.] Rig 32:50-65.

696. Berg, Gosta. 1957. Om ostron. [On oysters.] Fataburen Pp. 15-18.

697. Berg, Gosta. 1962. Det svenska smorgabordet. [The Swedish smorgasbord.] S Sed Pp. 9-21.

698. Berg, Gosta. 1963. Kringlor och pepparkakor. [Cracknel and peppercake.] Fataburen Pp. 61-80.

Kringlor is a brittle cake or biscuit.

699. Berg, Gosta. Die Kartoffel und die Rube. [The potato and the sugar beet.] Paper presented at First International Symposium on Ethnological Food Research. 21 to 25 August, 1970. Lund: Folklivsarkivet, Lund University.

700. Bergamin, Fransisco Vivanco. Nutrition problems and programs in the Spanish civil population. In Fifth Armed Forces International Nutrition Conference. April 24-30, 1962. Madrid. Proceedings. 1963. Pp. 101-114. Alto Estado Mayor, Spain: Interdepartmental Committee on Nutrition for National Defense (United States of America).

701. Bergasse, Alphonse. 1852. Recherches sur la consommation de la viande et du poisson a Rouen depuis 1300. Memoire. [Research on meat and fish consumption in Rouen since 1300. Memoir.] Rouen: Imprimerie A. Peron.

702. Bergen, F.D. 1900. Some homely viands. JAF 13:292-294.

703. Bergeret, B.; Masseyeff, R.; Perisse, Julien & Le Berre. 1957. Table de composition de quelques aliments tropicaus. [Composition tables for some tropical foods.] ANA 11:45-89.

Animal and vegetable foods representing almost the entire tradtional dietary of the southern Cameroun forest zone.

704. Berggren, J. 1844. Guide francais-arabe vulgaire des voyageurs et des francs en Syrie et en Egypte, avec carte physique et geographique de la Syrie et plan geometrique de Jerusalem ancien et moderne comme supplement aux voyageurs en Orient. [Colloquial French-Arabic guide for travellers and for Frenchmen in Syria and Egypt, with a physical and geographical map of Syria and a geometric plan of old and new Jerusalem as a supplement for travellers in the East. Uppsala: chez Leffler & Sebell.

Under the entry Cuisine, columns 259-270, are included details concerning Arabic cookery and of the various foods used in Arabic countries.

705. Bergier, Emile. 1941. Peuples entomophages et insects comestibles. [Insect-eating peoples and edible insects.] Avignon: Imprimerie Rulliere Freres.

706. Bergman, Stan. 1963. My father is a cannibal EJ 41:35-37.

707. Bergmann, John F. The cultural geography of cacao in aboriginal Middle America and its commercialization in early Guatemala. Ph.D. dissertation. Geography. University of California, Los Angeles. 1959.

708. Bergmann, John F. 1969. The distribution of cacao cultivation in pre-Columbian America. AAG-A 59:85-96.

709. Bergner-Rabinowitz, Sarah. 1947-1948. Hygiene, education and nutrition among Kurdish, Persian and Ashkenazic Jews in Jerusalem. [In Hebrew.] Edoth 3:117-123.

710. Berkes, Fikret & Farkas, Carol S. 1978. Eastern James Bay Cree Indians: changing patterns of wild food use and nutrition. EFN 7:155-172.

The purpose of this study is to assess and evaluate the use of wild foods in relation to the nutrition and health of the seven bands of eastern James Bay Cree of northeastern Quebec. Tradtional diet is described, together with a consideration of the availability of wild foods, past and contemporary. Representative nutrient values of selected wild foods are given, and the potential in-put of these foods as a future dietary resource is considered in relation to changing Cree life-style.

711. Berkman, Boris. 1949. Milkweed. EB 3:223-239.

Used as food: pp. 224.

712. Berland, Lucien. 1953. Les Araignees comestibles. [Edible spiders.] RBAAT 33:71-72.]

Use as food as recorded in historical and entomological literature. Specific mention of Nephila edulis.

713. Berleant-Schiller, Riva. Subsistence and social organization in Barbuda, West Indies. Ph.D. dissertation. Anthropology. State University of New York, Stony Brook. 1974.

714. Berlin, Brent. 1967. Categories of eating in Tzeltal and Navajo. IJAL 33:1-6.

715. Berlin, Brent. Establishing classes of manioc in Aguaruna. Paper presented at 72nd Annual Meeting of the American Anthropological Association. 29 November, 1973. New Orleans, Louisiana.

716. Berlin, Brent. The perceptual basis of Aguaruna botanical cosmology. Paper presented at 75th Annual Meeting of the American Anthropological Association. 17 to 21 November, 1976. Washington, D.C.

An important aspect of the ethnobiological cosmology of the Aguaruna, of Peru's Upper Maranon River drainage, concerns a mythical figure called nungkui, from whom most cultigens were derived, but who later changed them into inedible wild counterparts. These wild counterparts share numbers of features in common with their associated cultivated forms, many pairs representing species of the same botanical genus or family. This aspect of Aguaruna ethnobotanical cosmology may be partially explained by positing an implicit recognition of biological affinity that is consonant with Western botanical analysis, and which is based on the same perceptual considerations of gross morphology.

717. Berlin, Elois Ann. Nutritional status: some factors in the interaction of diet and health. Paper presented at 76th annual meeting of the American Anthropological Association 29 November 1977. Houston, Texas.

Physical well-being, as demonstrated by an anthropometric measurement and medical evaluation, is an essential correlate of diet. Activity, infection, ecological setting and cultural practices may assume crucial importance in determination of dietary adequacy. Nutritional needs are determined not by a simple formula, universally applied, but by the interaction of minimum need with myriad biological and cultural factors the sums of which are manifested in health status. This paper discusses sources and mechanisms of stress on nutrient needs and their impact on health.

718. Berlin, Elois Ann & Markell, Edward K. Parasites and nutrition: the dynamics of health among the Aguaruna Jivaro. Paper presented at 75th Annual Meeting of the American Anthropological Association. 17 to 21 November, 1976. Washington, D.C.

An evaluation of the nutritional adequacy of the traditional Aguaruna Jivar diet demonstrates sufficiency and balance in nutriet intake. Assessment of the health status in terms of anthropometric measurements, clinical examination, as well as follow-up blood tests confirms the positive health picture. Two unanticipated and significant findings, however, are: (1) incidence of parasite infection is among the highest reported; and (2) dietary intake is extremely high in terms of bulk and nutriets. Parasite toleration is seen as being due, in large measure, to dietary quality and quantity.

719. Berlin, Elois Ann & Markell, Edward K. 1977. An assessst of the nutritional and health status of an Aguaruna Jivaro community, Amazonas, Peru. EFN 6:69-81.

The Aguaruna are a widely-dispersed manioc-cultivating people, inhabiting a tropical rain forest environment along the Upper Maranon River and most of its major tributaries in north-central Peru. Included in the evaluation of the nutritional adequacy of the traditional diet is a discussion of food preparation, and a listing of cultivated food plants. Animal foods are also described.

720. Bernard, Augustin. L'alimentation des indigenes en Algerie et en Tunisie. [Diet of natives in Algeria and Tunisia.] In L'alimentation indigene dans le colonies francaises. Protectorats et territoires sous mandat. Edited by G. Hardy & c. Ricket. 1933. Pp. 115-124. Paris: Vigot Freres.

721. Berman, Louis. 1932. Food and character. Boston: Houghton Mifflin Co.

722. Bernard, Juana T. A contribution to the study of rice in the Philippines. Master's thesis. Pharmacy. University of Santo Tomas. 1935.

723. Bernard, Theos. 1939. Penthouse of the gods. A pilgrimage into the heart of Tibet and the sacred city of Lhasa. New York, London: Charles Scribner's Sons.

Meal of a wealthy Tibetan family: pp. 82-83.

724. Bernatzik, Hugo Adolph. 1947. Akha und Meau. Probleme der angewand ten volkekunde in Hinterindien. [Hakka and Miao. Problem of applied ethnography in farther India.] 2 vols. Innsbruck: Kommissionsverlag Wagner'sche Univer-

sitat Buchdruckerdai,. Translated into English by Ardis Nagler, for the Human Relations Area Files.

Food habits, utensils: pp. 103;409;417-419; 421;467-473; 503-508. Field work done in 1936 - 1937.

725. Berndt, Emil A. 1941. Food and diseases a century ago. The Friend October. P.203.

726. Berndt, Ronald, & Berndt, Catherine H. 1964. The World of the first Australians. Chicago: University of Chicago Press; Sydney: Ure Smith Pty.

Food habits and preparations: pp. 92-101.

727. Bernhardt, Joshua. 1920. Government control of the sugar industry in the United States. New York: Macmillan.

728. Bernheim, Samuel, & Rousseau, P. 1908. Le cheval aliment. [Horse flesh as food.] Paris: Rousset.

729. Bernier, G. 1961. Les vegetaux dans la vie quotidienne des populations rurales du Haut Katanga. [Vegetables in the daily life of the rural populations of Upper Katanga.] Lejeunia No. 2. Pp. 1-8.

Part 1 of this article contains a list of plants, with their uses, with Kisanga, French, and Latin names.

730. Bernier, G. 1963. Les vegetaux dans la vie quotidienne des populations rurales du Haut-Katanga. [Vegetables in the daily life of the rural population of Upper Katanga.] PSC No. 66. Pp. 43-59.

Plants used in cooking.

731. Bernier, G. & Lambrechts, A. 1959. Etude sur les boissons fermentees indigenes du Katanga. [Study of the indigenous fermented beverages of Katanga.] B-ARSC-CSNM No. 9.

Introduction. Estimate of the quantity of beer produced, and consumption per caput. Techniques of preparation of beers, i.e. maize beer munkoyo, preparation of base, gathering of roots of the shrubs eg. Erminia polyadenia Hauman & E. harmsiana De Wild., preparation of the beer, other beers (munkoyo) from sorgho flour; preparation of eleusine, manioc and sweet potato flour. Palm wine, hydromel, kibuku of the Basanga; wild fruit beverages; maize-stalk beer; kinseke; agents of fermentation. Nutritive value of beers. Importance of beer in terms of use of available time and in native budget (beer as basis for income for women; the consumption of beer as an expense for men and women). Conclusions.

732. Bernier, G. & Lambrechts, A. 1960. Etude sur les boissons fermentees indigenes du Katange. [Study of the indigenous fermented beverages of Katanga.] PSC 48: 5-42.

733. Bernot, Lucien. 1967. Les paysans Arakanais du Pakistan Oriental, l'histoire, le monde vegetal et l'organisation sociale des refugies Marma (Mog.) [Arakanai peasants of East Pakistan, history, plant world, and social organization of Marma refugees (Mogh.)] Le Monde Outre-Mer. Passe et Present. Premiere Serie. Etude 16. The Hague; Paris: Mouton & Co.

Food habits: pp. 307-377.

734. Bernoulli, R. Geschichte der Soldatenernahrung der militarisch wichtigsten volker Europas. [History of soldiers' nutrition among the militarily important peoples of Europe.] Dissertation Universitat Basel. 1943.

735. Berquist, Eric Harry. 1965. Sodertaljekringlor. [Southern cut-out cookies.] GK 5:81-92.

Sweden.

736. Berreman, Gerald Duane. 1963. Hindus of the Himalayas. Los Angeles and Berkeley: University of California Press.

Preparation and consumption of food: pp. 49-50.

737. Berry, R.M. 1907. Fruit recipes. New York: Doubleday, Page & Co.

Information on tropical and little-known fruit.

738. Berthaud, Paul. 1934. De l'hippophagie et du cheval de boucherie. [Of horse-meat eating and horse-meat butchering.] Saint-Nazaire: Imprimerie Ouvriere.

The author's thesis for the degree in Veterinary Medicine.

739. Berthelet, D. Greg. 1731. Traite historique et moral de l'abstinence de la viande et des revolutions qu'elle a cues depuis la commencement du monde, parmi les Hebreux, les Payens, les chretiens, etc. [Historical and moral treatise on abstinence from meat and of the revolutions there have been since the beginning of the world, among the Hebrews pagans, Christians, etc.] Rouen: no publisher cited.

740. Berthelot, P.E. 1893. The discovery of alcohol and distillation. PSMO 43:95.

741. Bertholet, C.J.L. & Benchadiswar. Housing and food patterns in eleven villages in northeast Thailand. Mimeographed Ubol: United Nations Education, Scientific and Cultural Organization. Thailand Fundamental Education Centre.

742. Berthrong, Donald John. 1963. The Southern Cheyenne. Norman: University of Oklahoma Press.

Pemmican: p. 103.

743. Bertillon. 1867. Investigaciones generales sobre las enfermedades de las razas que no padecen

le fiebre amarilla. [General investigations on the illness of the races which are not susceptible to yellow fever.] SAP-B 2 [Second series]: 36,37.

Contains details of a pathologic condition called hinchasan (swelling) occuring among adult Black males working in sugar factories and as honey gatherers. The disease observed Dr. Henri Dumont, and characterized as a kind of leukemia, with hydroemy and adenopathy. Details of symptoms are included.

744.   Bertin, L.   1954.   Les poisson du Nil au temps des pharaons.   [Nile fish in Pharaonic times.]   RFEE 54:35-40.

745.   Berton, Pierre Francis de Marigny & Berton, Janet.   1966, The Centennial food guide; a century of good eating.   Comprising an anthology of writings about food and drink over the past two hundred years, together with divers recipes, helpful suggestions, curiosa, and illustrations culled from old records, the whole being seasoned with the personal prejudices and enthusiasms of the authors. Toronto: Canadian Centennial Puplishing Co.

746.   Bertoni, Guillermo Tell.   La yerba mate. Una planta simbolica de Ameria.   [Yerba mate. An American symbolic plant.]   In Vigesimo Congreso Internacional de Americanistas.   20 a 30 de Agosto de 1922, Rio de Janeiro.   Annaes.   1924. Vol. 1.   Pp. 91-93.   Rio de Janeiro: Imprensa Nacionel.

Paraguay.   Use as beverage, and medicine; its place in Guarani legend and tradition.

748.   Bertsch, Karl, & Bertsch, Franz.   1947. Geschichte unserer Kulturpflanzen.   [History of our cultivated plants.] Stuttgart: Wissenschaffliche Verlagsgesellschaft.

749.   Bervoets, W.; Lassance, M. et al.   1959. Modes et coutumes alimentaire des Conglais en milieu rural.   Resultats d'une enquete portant sur le Congo Belge et le Ruanda-Urundi a l'exclusion du Katanga, 1955 - 1957.   [Food manners and customs of rural Congolese.   Results of a survey carried out in the Belgian Congo and Ruanda Urundi, excluding Katanga.   1955 - 1957.]   B-ARSC-CSNM-M No. 9.

Carbohydrate foods, animal protein resources, traditional lipid sources, alcoholic and fruit beverages in Congolese diet, milk consumption, salt, dietary pattern, weaning, infant feeding practices, geoghagy.   taboos, food consumption.

750.   Besant, Walter.   1903.   London in the Eighteenth Century.   The survey of London.   London: Adam and Charles Black.

Food and drink: pp. 289-302.

751.   Besant, Walter.   1903.   London in the time of the Stuarts. London: Adam and Charles Black.

Food and drink: pp. 287-297.

752.   Best, Elsdon.   1902.   Food products of the Tuhoeland. NZI-TP 35: 45-111.

Food supplies, food interdictions, and customs of non-agricultural tribes of New Zealand.

753.   Best, Elsdon.   1907 - 1908.   Maori forest lore. NZI-TP 40:185-254; 41:231-286; 42:433-481.

References to food sources throughout.

754.   Best, Elsdon.   1916.   Maori storehouses and kindred structures. DMus-B No. 5.

755.   Best, Elsdon.   1918.   Shell-middens of the Wellington district. Welligton, New Zealand: Government Printer.

756.   Best, Elsdon.   1922.   The taro, Colocasia antiquorum.   Wellington, New Zealand: Government Printer.   Also NZJST 5(4) (1922).

757.   Best, Elsdon.   1923.   An eel feast.   NZJST 5:1-08-109.

Maori, New Zealand.

758.   Best, Elsdon.   1924.   The Polynesian steam oven. NZJST 6:54-56.

759.   Best, Elsdon.   1925. Maori agriculture. The cultivated food plants of the natives of New Zealand, with some accounts of the native methods of agriculture, its ritual and myths. D MUS B No. 9.

760.   Best Elsdon.   1928.   The Story of Ngae and Tutununui. JPS 37:261-270.

Maori myth on origin of cannibalism: pp. 262-267.

761.   Best, Elsdon.   1942.   Forest lore of the Maori; with methods of snaring, trapping, and preserving birds and rats, uses of berries, roots, fern--root, and forest products, with mythological notes on origins, karakia used, etc. PS-M No. 19.

762.   Bethune, C.J.S.   1876.   The western locusts. ESO-AR for the year 1875. Pp. 45-54.

Locusts as food: pp. 52-54.

763.   Better Homes and Gardens.   1975.   Heritage cook book. n.p.: Meredith Corporation.

An historical-regional review of American foods, with recipes, and unusual full color photographs and reproductions of paintings.

764.   Bettis, F.P. & Burton, H.B. 1955. A nutritional study of a community of Kiowa Indians. OAS-P 34:110-114.

765.   Betts, William, 1965. Indian whale hunters. The West 3:44-46.

766.   Bevel, M.L. 1937.   L'alimentation chez le Basonge.   [Food among the Basongo.]   Con Cong 2:34.

Cannibalism; food habits; dried meat.

767.   Bey, Mahmoud.   Un banquet de medecins arabes au 11e siecle.   [An 11th Century Arabic physician's banquet.]   In Congres international de medecin tropical et d' hygiene. Cairo. December, 1928. Comptes Rendus. 1929. Vol. 1. Pp. 237-239.

Menu includes chickory, boiled beef (madyara), roast lamb, and a rice-milk confection (falouzag, or mahalabiah).

768.   Beybey, Eyidi R.; Pierme, J.-L.; & Masseyeff, R. 1961-1962. Une enquete sur l'alimentation a Douala: quartier New Bell. [Inquiry into diet in Douala: New Bell quarter.] REC No. 5. Pp. 3-46.

769.   Beyer, H. Otley. 1912. Report on the use of a fermented rice drink in northern Luzon. PJS 7 [A]: 97-119.

770.   Beyerinck, Martinus W. 1899. Sur le Kefir. [On Kefir.] ANSEN 23: 428-444.

A fermented dairy product.

771.   Bhanja, P.K., & Roy, N.K. 1966 [?]. Studies in rural change: reports on re-surveys of villages.   Jungul (1958-1966).   Agro-Economic Research Centre.   Santiniketan, West Bengal: Visva-Bharati University.

Includes detailed expenditure data for several foods by occupational group. Village studied is located in Birbhum District (approximately 23. 50N, 87. 50E.) in West Bengal.

772.   Bhardwaj, K.S. & Virmani, Ranjna. 1971. A note on the age at menarchy of Delhi girls. EAnth 29: 83-86.

Among variables studied is diet (vegetarian/non-vegetarian), and nutritional status.

773.   Bhatti, A,N, 1964. Modern Muslim cooking of India-Pakistan. Lahore: Indus Publishing House.

774.   Bicchieri, M.G. A study of the ecology of food gathering peoples: a cross-cultural analysis of the relationship of environment, technology and bio-cultural viability. Ph.D dissertation. Anthropology. University of Minnesota. 1966.

775.   Bickel, Adolf. 1938. Die Ernahrung der olympischen Kampfer in vergangenheit und gegenwart. [Diet of Olympian contestants, past and present] Bucher der Hygiene und Volksernahrung. No. 3. Berlin: Deutsche Verlagsgesellschaft.

776.   Bickford, R.A. The traditional economy of the Aborigenes of the Murray Valley. Bachelor's honors thesis. University of Sydney. 1966.

777.   Bicknell, Algernon Sidney. 1868. Hippophagy: the horse as food for man. London: William Ridgway.

778.   Bidwell, Norma. 1976. Even prisoners want to learn good nutrition. HSpec 15 January.

Describes reactions of women inmates to experimental nutrition education sessions in a Canadian short-term prison detention facility.

779.   Bidyalankarana [Prince]. 1930. The ambrosial confection. Bangkok: Bangkok Times Press.

780.   Bidyalankarana [Prince]. 1932. The ambrosial confection. JSS 25: 79-81.

A Thai thanksgiving ceremony performed around a preparation containing all available vegetable foods of the season, as well as milk, butter, fruit juices and other liquids. It was by custom presented first to the King, and then to Buddhist monks.

781.   Biebuyck, Daniel & Mateene, Kahombo C, eds. and translators. 1969. The Mwindo epic from the Banyanga (Congo Republic).   Berkeley, Los Angeles: University of California Press.

Food; eating: Pp. 6, 13, 25-29, 34, 44, 50-51, 64, 74, 75, 80-81, 84, 88, 94, 97, 100-102, 107, 111, 113, 115, 118, 124, 126; bananas: passim.

782.   Biel, J. 1874.   Untersuchungen uber der Kumys, und der Stoffwechsel wahrend der Kumyskur. [Investigation on kumis and on the material changes during Kumiss therapy.] Vienna: Faesy & Frick.

783.   Bielenstein, A. 1904. Das Kochen und der Kesselhaken der alten Letten. Auj einem in Arbeit befindlichen Werke ubes die alteste Kulturgeschichte der Letten. [Kitchens and kettle hooks of old Latvia. From a work-in-progress on the oldest culture history of Latvia.] Globus 85: 181-183.

784.   Bien, Karen S. 1966. Food habits and nutrient intake of Head Start children in Baltimore County. Maryland State Department of Health. Baltimore: Baltimore County Department of Health. August.

785.   Bierdrager, J. 1936. Mass poisoning in New Guinea caused by eating turtle meat. [In Dutch.] GTNI 76: 1933-1944.

786.   Bierens de Haan, J.A., & Heubel, F. 1939. Uber Futtervorlieber dei Affen und die Bestimmung ihrer Grose und Starke. [Food preferences in apes and the determination of its extent and strength.] ZMOT 34: 89-120.

787.   Biesanz, John Berry & Biesanz, Mavis Hitunen. 1945. Costa Rican life. New York: Columbia University Press.

Food: Pp. 31-32.

788.   Biesanz, John Berry & Biesanz, Mavis Hitunen. 1955. The People of Panama. New York: Columbia University Press.

Food: Pp. 242, 243; 252; 268-269.

789. Biester, Charlotte E. 1955. Milestones in American cookery literature. JADA 31: 1214-1217.

790. Bigford, M. E. Malnutrition: its potential impact on the individual's and family's adaptive responses to childbearing and nurturing. Presented at 74th Annual Meeting of the American Anthropological Assn. Dec. 1975. San Francisco, Ca.

791. Biggar, H. Howard. 1919. The old and the new in corn culture. USDA-YB for the year 1918. Pp. 123-126.

Contains excellent photographs of American Indian maize processing equipment, planting methods, and includes historical and ethnographic data relating to maize in the United States.

792. Biggs, H.E. 1960. Mollusca from prehistoric Jericho. J Conch 24: 379-387.

793. Bigwood, E.J.; Jaequemyns, G.; & Levy, Paul M.G. 1940. Une experience alimentaire en Belgique. [A Nutritional experiment in Belgium.] Brussels: Imprimerie Vronans.

An account of a feeding program in Brussels, among 600 Belgian school children, comparing and contrasting the results of a breakfast program, or supplementary milk feeding only.

794. Bigwood, E.J. Influence of the Belgian agricultural pattern upon the nutrition habits of the country. In A brief review of food and nutrition in five countries. 1944. Pp. 11-17. United States Department of Agriculture. War Food Administration. Washington, D.C.: Government Printing Office.

Agricultural production, nutrient intake, school feeding, and the effects of military occupation on nutritional status, during the early 1940's.

795. Billington, B.P. The health and nutritional status of the aborigenes. In Records of the Australian-American Scientific Expedition to Arnhem Land. Volume 2. Anthropology and nutrition. Edited by Charles P. Mountford. 1960. Pp. 27-59. Melbourne: Melbourne University Press.

796. Billioud, J. 1968. Comment Marseille fut sauvee de la famine pendant la peste de 1720. [How Marseille was saved from famine during the pestilence of 1720.] Marseille 72: 27-31.

797. Binder, R.M. 1925. Man is what he eats; how food affects physiology, mentality, and the destiny of races. SA: 133: 374.

798. Binford, Lewis R. Archaeological and ethno historical investigation of cultural diversity and progressive development among aboriginal cultures of coastal Virginia and North Carolina. Ph.D. dissertation. University of Michigan. 1961.

Includes tables of edible flora and fauna of mid--Atlantic coastal plain during present and past periods.

799. Bing, Franklin C. 1967. Lydia Jean Roberts -a biographical sketch (June 30, 1879 - May 28, 1965). JN 93: 3-13.

800. Binger, C.A. 1942. A word to teachers about eating habits. UChild 11:3-6.

801. Binney, G.A. 1968. The social and economic organization of two White Meo communities in northern Thailand. Advanced Projects Agency APA-T10. No. 811. Washington, D.C.: United States Department of Defense.

Brief description of foods, meal and eating habits, methods of food preparation for the communities of Khae, and Mae Nai, in the northern Thai province of Chiengmai. [After Schofield. 1975:206.]

802. Biot. 1839. Note sur des matieres pierreuses employees a la Chine dans les temps de famine, sous le nom de farine de pierre. [Note on stony substances used during times of famine in China, under the name rock flour.] ACP 62: 215-219.

Includes translations of Chinese texts.

803. Birch, H.G., & Gussow, Joan Dye. 1970. Disadvantaged children: health, nutrition, and school failure. New York: Harcourt, Brace & World.

804. Bird, Alan R. 1962. Surplus...the riddle of American agriculture. New York: Springer Publishing Co.

805. Bird, Junius B. 1948. America's oldest farmers. NH 57: 296-303.

806. Birkas, Maria. An historical geography of paprika in Hungary. Master's thesis. Geography. University of California, Los Angeles. 1976.

807. Birket-Smith, Kaj. 1929. Drinking tube and tobacco pipe in North America. E Stud 2: 29-39.

808. Birket-Smith, Kaj. 1943. The origin of maize cultivation. KDVS - HFM 29. No. 3.

809. Birket-Smith, Kaj. 1952. The rice cultivation and rice harvest feast of the Bontoc Igorot. KDVS -HFM 32. No. 8.

810. Birket-Smith, Kaj. 1965. The paths of culture. Translated by Karin Fennow. Madison, & Milwaukee: University of Wisconsin Press.

Food and drink: pp. 111-115.

811. Birmingham, Stephen. 1972. Chapter Twenty-one. An altogether different sort. In The grandees. The story of America's Sephardic elite. New York: Dell Publishing Co. Dell Book 3013.

Contains descriptions of foods of the Jews of Greece, and Turkey.

812. Bishop, Charles A. Ojibwa cannibalism. Paper presented at International Congress of Anthropological and Ethnological Sciences. 28 August to 8 September, 1973. Chicago, Illinois.

Relates the 'Windigo Psychosis' to cultural and ecological changes occurring after European contact. Notes the possible existence of a 'cannibal-giant' myth in pre-contact times, but acknowledges the innability to demonstrate a relationship between such a myth and the Windigo psychosis. Rather, the phenomenon seems to have been extended to include situations arising from the fear of starvation and the real potential of becoming a cannibal. A distinction is made between famine cannibalism, and Windigo cannibalism.

813. Bishop, George. 1965. A soggy saga of man in his cups. Los Angeles: Sherbourne Press.

814. Bishop, Isabella L. Bird. 1891. Journeys in Persia and Kurdistan, including a summer in the Upper Karun region and a visit to the Nestorian Rayahs. 2 vols. New York: G.P. Putnam's Sons; London: John Murray.

Rose water, walnut, and sugar paste Vol. 1. P. 234.

815. Bismuth, H.; Menage, C.; Toury, J.; Bocat, R.; & Giorgi. 1961. Les boissons alcooliques en A.O.F. [Alcoholic drinks in French West Africa.] IFAN-B 23: 60-118.

Gives geographic distribution of native alcoholic beverages, together with their methods of preparation. Described are palm wines, raphia wines, palmyra. [Borrasus flabelliformus, Murr.] Wine; cereal beers; hydromel; fermented fruit beverages; distilled beverages, and stills. Includes chemical analyses of the prodcts described.

816. Biswas, Prophilla Chander. 1956. Santals of the Santal Parganas. Delhi: Bharatiya Adimjati Sevak Sangh.

Bihar. Food: Pp. 36-42.

817. Bitting, Arvil Wayne. 1937. Appertizing; or, the art of canning: its history and development. San Fransisco; The Trade Pressroom.

818. Bitting, Avrill Wayne, & Bitting, Katherine Golden. 1915. Ketchup: methods of manufacture; microscopic examination by Katherine Golden Bitting. Lafayette, Indiana: Murphy - Bivins Co. Press.

819. Bitting, Katherine Golden. 1920. The Olive Chicago: Glass Container Association.

820. Bivins, S. Thomas. 1912. The Southern cookbook; a manual of cooking and list of menus, including recipes used by noted colored cooks and prominent caterers. Hampton, Virginia: Press of the Hampton Institute.

821. Bixler, Raymond Walter. 1972. The West African cocoa story. New York: Vantage Press.

822. Bizal, Rachel Sanders & Monsch, Helen. A study of infant feeding practices as found by a survey of 702 New York State babies. Master's thesis. Home Economics. Cornell University. 1933.

823. Bjerre, Jens. 1957. The last cannibals. Translated by E. Bannister. New York: Willliam Morrow.

824. Black, G.A. 1933. Prehistoric American diet. IMH 29: 96-103.

825. Black, Laura Sue. Food management practices of Headstart families. Master's thesis. University of Arizona. 1970.

Includes Native American families.

826. Black, W.A.P. 1953. Seaweeds and their value in foodstuffs. PNS 12: 32-39.

827. Blackburn, Roderick, Honey in Okiek personality, culture and society. Ph.D dissertation Anthropology. Michigan State University. 1971.

Kenya.

828. Blacke, E.C. 1969. Can one cook in a skin? Antiquity 43: 217-218.

829. Blackham, R.J. 1937. Infant feeding in warm climates. JS Med 45: 462-473.

830. Blackman, J. The corner shop: the development of the grocery and general provision trade. In The making of the modern British diet. Edited by Derek J. Oddy & D.S. Miller. 1976. London: Croom Helm.

831. Blackman, Margaret B. Ethnohistoric changes in the Haida pottatch complex. Paper presented at 73rd Annual Meeting of the American Anthropological Association. 19 to 24 November, 1974. Mexico City.

832. Blackman, Ruth Nina. A survey of food habits of 11th and 12th grade students in two North Carolina communities. Master's thesis. Greensboro: Women's College of the University of North Carolina. 1946.

833. Blackstone, J.H., & Inman, B.T. 1942. Food habits of consumer groups in small towns of Alabama that effect farmer's markets. Ala - AES-B No. 252.

834. Blackwood, Beatrice. Use of plants among the Kukukuku of southwest-central New Guinea. In Sixth Pacific Science Congress. 1939. Berkeley, California. Proceedings. Volume Four. (Anthropology, zoology, entomology, botany, forest resources, soil resources, climatology). 1940. Pp. 111-126. Berkeley: University of California Press.

Indicates part of plant eaten, manner of eating. Gives Kukukuku and Latin nomenclature.

835.   Blair, R. The food habits of the East Slavs. Ph.D. dissertation. University of PA. 1956.

836.   Blair, T.L.V. 1966. Continuity and change in African food habits. F Tech 20: 757-762.

837.   Blaisdell, James Pershing. Seasonal development and yield of native plants on the Upper Snake River plains of Idaho and their relation to climatic factors. Ph.D. dissertation. University of Minnesota, Minneapolis. 1956.

838.   Blake, Edith. 1890. Norbrook kitchen midden. Vic Q 2: 26-33.

839.   Blake, John H. 1903. Tea hints for retailers. Denver: Willliamson-Haffner Engraving Co.

840.   Blake, Sidney Fay. 1922. Native names and uses of some plants of eastern Guatemala and Honduras. SI-USNH-C 24: 87-100.

841.   Blakeslee, Albert F. 1935. Dinner demonstration of threshold differences in taste and smell. Science 81: 504-507.

842.   Blanc, Honore (du Fuguret). Le guide des dineurs ou statistiques des principaux restaurans de Paris; ouvrages indispensable aux etrangers, necessaire aux personnes qui ne tiennent pas menage, utile a tous les gens de gout, et dans lequel on trouve: 1. les cartes raisonnees, et les demeures des meilleurs restaurateurs de Paris; 2. des observations sur les qualites, quantite, prix des mets et portions dites pour un; sur l'elegance des salons, l'heureuse et sage disposition des cabinets particuliers et sur la promptitude dans le service; 3. enfin l'indication des cafe's les plus renomes. [Guide for diners or statistics of principal Parisian restaurants. An indispensable work for foreigners, a necessity for those who do not keep a household, useful for persons of good taste, and in which are found: 1. descriptive menus, and the lodgings of the best restaurateurs of Paris; 2. Some observations on the qualities, quantities, and prices of foods and portions served for one person; on the style of dining rooms; the wise disposition of specific rooms; the promptness of the service; 3. lastly, the most well-known cafes.] Paris chez les Marchands de Nouveautes.

843.   Blanco, Anat. Nutritional studies in Puerto Rico. Master's thesis. University of Chicago. 1944.

844.   Blankhart, D.M. Two surveys on the nutritional status and the feeding of children under three around Chogoria, Meru, Kenya. Mimeographed. Nutrition Department. Nairobi: Medical Research Centre. [1974.]

The villages studied are Mukui, and Gitombani, located at approximately 0. 12 S, 37. 40 E. Patterns of breast and infant feeding, and weaning patterns are described and con-

trasted. Length of breast feeding differed markedly between the villages.

845.   Blasedale, Walter C. 1899. A description of some Chinese vegetable food materials and their nutritive and economic value. USDA-OEA-B No. 68.

Includes extensive documentation relating to chemical analyses of Chinese food, materials, purchased at Chinese markets in San Francisco, California.

846.   Blatin. 1864. Usage alimentaire de viande de cheval. [Food use of horse meat.] Paris: Imprimerie de Soye & Bouchet.

847.   Blatz, W.E. 1928. A study of eating habits in a nursery school. In observation and training of the fundamental habits in young children, by E.A. Bott; W.E. Blatz; N. Chant; & H. Bott. GPM No. 1. Part 4. Pp. 89-115.

848.   Blazdeck, Leda Francis. Food habits and living conditions of Mexican families on four income levels in the Upper Rio Grande Valley. Master's thesis. Austin: University of Texas. 1938.

849.   Bleibtreu, Hermann K. 1973. An anthropologist views the nutrition professions. JNE 5: 11-13.

Emphasizes need to recognize the relativity of cultural values, in this instance, as regards food habits, when planning nutrition education programs. Stresses the need to greatly increase social and behavioral science training for students of human nutrition, and advocates increased need to attract students from such disciplines as medicine, law, and business.

850.   [Blelloch, David H.] Industrial canteens in Great Britain. In Nutrition in industry. International Labour Office. 1946, Pp. 113-117. Studies and Reports. New series No. Four. Montreal: International Labour Office.

Includes data on the history of canteen feeding. Food patterns, and sample menus are also given.

851.   Bleuel, M.T. 1923.   Some unusual food plants. SSM 23: 369-376.

852.   Blevans, Stephen. A critical review of the anthropological literature on drinking drunkenness, and alcoholism. Master's thesis. Anthropology. University of Washington. 1967.

853.   Blind, Karl. 1895. Ale-drinking in old Egypt and the Thrako-Germanic race. Scot. Rev 25: 23-41.

854.   Bloch, M. Les aliments de l'ancienne France. [The foods of ancient France.] In Pour une histoire de l'alimentation. Edited by J.J. Hemmardinguer. 1970. Pp. 231-235. paris: Colin.

855. Bloch, M.R. 1963. The social influence of salt. SA 209: 89-99.

856. Blom, Frans. 1956. On Slotkin's "Fermented drinks in Mexico". AA 58: 185-186.

857. Blond, Georges & Blond, Germaine. 1961. Histoire pittoresque de notre alimentation. 2 vols. [Pictorial history of our eating habits.] Montreal: Cercle du Livre de France. Also: Paris: Fayard. 1960.

858. Blond, George & Blond, Germaine. 1975. Description des habitudes alimentaires des francais qui vecurent sous la Revolutin de 1789. [Description of the food habits of French who lived through the Revolution of 1789.] Historia No. 42. Pp. 73-83.

859. Blondel. 1934. La cuisine indigene a labe. [Native food at Labe.] EA No. 87. Pp. 173-185.

Guinea. Located at 11.17 N, 12.11 W.

860. Blum, Richard H., & Blum, Eva M. 1964. Drinking practices and controls in rural Greece. BJAAD 60: 93-108.

861. Blunt, Edward Arthur Henry. 1931. The caste system of northern India with special reference to the United Provinces of Agra and Oudh. London and Madras: Oxford University Press.

862. Blunt, Katharine & Wang, Chi-che. 1916. Chinese preserved eggs - pidan. JBC 28: 125 - 134.

Method of preparation and chemical analysis.

863. Blyn, George. 1961. Controversial views on the geography of nutrition. EG 37: 72-74.

864. Bo, G., Meloni, C., & Zinardi, A. 1962. Observations on the food habits in three rural zones of Lombardy. [In Italian.] AN 22: 77-92.

Contains a summary in English.

865. Boalt, C. & Zotterman, Y. 1943. Rations and food consumption in Sweden during 1941 -1943. Nature (L) 152: 635-636.

866. Boas, Franz. 1916, Tsimshian mythology. Based on texts recorded by Henry W. Tate. SI-BAE-AR for the year 1909-1910. Pp. 29-1037.

Food: Pp. 44,45; giant learns to cook olachen (myth): p. 66; fishing, hunting, and food gathering; seasons and months; seasonal occupations; sea hunting; eagles; food-gathering; specific food items; food preparation; winter provisions; boiling with stones; steamings; cooking   olachen; rich and poor food; meals: Pp. 404-406.

867. Boas, Franz. 1921. Ethnology of the Kwakiutl. Based on data collected by George Hunt. SI-BAE-AR for the year 1913-1914. Pp. 43-794.

This corpus of material is possibly the most extensive dealing with food to be found in the ethnographic literature. (One exception may be Gast's Ahaggar material.) Under the head 'Industries', the manufacture of various implements for hunting and gathering food is described. Hunting, fishing, and food-gathering procedures are outlined, followed by details relating to food preservation. A section of nearly three hundred pages is devoted to recipes for fish and other aquatic foods, mountain goat, and a variety of plant foods. Contained in the recipe narration is a wealth of data concerning sociological aspects of food-related behavior. Beliefs and customs relating to eating, and huckleberry picking: p. 607. Feasts centering about specifics kinds of foods: pp. 750-776.

868. Boccassino, Renato. 1962. La vendetta del sangre praticata dagli Acioli dell' Uganda: riti e canibalismo guerreschi. [The blood feud carried out among the Achioli of Uganda: war-related rites and cannibalism.] Anthropos 57: 357-373.

869. Bodecker, C.F. 1930. Defects in enamel of teeth of ancient American Indians. JDR 10: 313-322.

870. Bodei, J. 1943. Contributions to the gathering economy of Zalabaksa. [In Hungarian.] NME 35: 69-96.

Hungary. Located at 46 44 N, 16 34 E.

871. Bodenheimer, Friederich Simon. 1951. Insects as human food. The Hague: W. Junk. Reviewed in FMan 28: 318 (1953).

872. Bodenheimer, Friederich Simon. 1956. L'entomophagie, phenomene d'ecologie humaine. [Entomophagy, phenomenon of human ecology.] Nature (P) March. Pp. 92-96.

873. Bodenheimer, Friederich Simon & Theodor, Oskar., eds. 1929. Ergebnisse der Sinai-Expedition 1927 der hebraischen Universitat, Jerusalem. [Results of the 1927 Sinai Expedition of the Hebrew University at Jerusalem.] Leipzig: J.C. Hinrichs.

874. Boek, Jean K. 1956. Dietary intake and social characteristics. AJCN 4: 239-245.

875. Boettiger, M. 1797. Carte ou menu d'nn repas de l'ancienne Rome. Menu or bill of fare for an ancient Roman meal. Translated from German by F.-J. Bast. JLM 12: 587-598.

Reprint. Paris: Didot. 1801.

876. Boez, L., & Guillerm, J. 1930. Le facteur microbien dans la fabrication de la saumure indochinoise. Nuoc mam. [The microbial factor in the fabrication of the Indochinese condiment Nuoc mam.] P-AS-CRH 190: 534-535.

877. Bogair, Nahum. 1951. Favism in Israel. In Hebrew. HH 2: 72-81., 190-191.

878.   Boggs, E.G. Nutrition of 50 colored families in Chicago. Master's thesis. University of Chicago. 1929.

879.   Boggs, Ralph Steele. 1960. La industria del pulque en elestado de Mexico.[The pulque industry in the State of Mexico.] E Alm Pp. 279-281.

880.   Bogic, G. 1939. Prilozi za istoriju geografiju ishrane u Jugoslaviji za razdoblje od 1932-do1925 godu. Prilozi za istoriju i geografiju gladi na territoriju Jugoslavije od 12 veka da danas. [Contribution to the history and geography of nutrition in Yugoslavia between 1923 and 1925. Contribution to the history of famine in the territory of Yugoslavia from the 12th century until the present.] Beogradi Biblioteka Centralnog Higienskog Azvoda.

881.   Bohlen, Diedrich. 1937. Die Bedeutung der ficherei fur die antike Wirtschaft. Ein Bietrag zur Geschichte der antiken fischerei. [The significance of fishing in ancient economy. A contribution to the history of ancient fishing.] Hamburg: Hans Christian.

882.   Bohrer, Vorsila L. 1954. Punch cards applied to ethnobotanical research. AA 56: 99-104,

883.   Bohrer, Vorsila L. 1960. Zuni agriculture EL Pal 67:181-202.

    Provides several lists indicating ceremonial relationship of certain bean varieties, as well as distribution of Zuni bean varieties in the Southwestern United States, according to archaeological site provenience.

884.   Boiko, N.N., Kliooshkina, N.C., & Kondrat'iev, Y. 1963. The use of monocellular algae for the alimentation of man. [In Russion.] VP 22: 3-8.

885.   Boileau, Etienne. 1837. Reglemens sur les arts et metiers de Paris, rediges au 13e siecle et connus sous le nom du Livre de Metiers d' Etienne Boileau; publies pour la premiere fois en entier, d'apres les manuscrits de la Bibliotheque du Roi et des Archives du Royaume...[Regulations on the arts and crafts of Paris, edited in the 13th Century and known by the name Book of Crafts of Etienne Boileau; published for the first time in its entirety, from manuscripts in the Bibliotheque du Roi and in the Archives du Royaume.] Paris: de l'Imprimerie de Crapelet.

    Included are: tavern-keepers; brewers; fruit and spice merchants; cooks; fish and poultry sellers; bakers; pastry makers; broilers, and other food-related occupations.

886.   Bois, Desire Georges Jean Marie. 1920. Coleus tubereux alimentaires, introduction aux iles Marquises. [Edible tuberous Coleus; their introduction to the Marquesas.] RHNA 1: 22-26.

887.   Bois, Desire Georges Jean Marie. 1927 - 1937. Les plantes alimentaires chez tous les peuples et a tranvers les ages; histoire, utilization, et culture. [Edible plants of all peoples, through the ages; history, use, and cultivation.[Encyclopedie Biologique 1, 3, 7, 17. Paris: P.. Lechevalier.

888.   Bois, Desire Georges Jean Marie & Diguet, Leon. 1914. Une plante alimentaire peu connue du Mexique, la Jicama de Baryta (Delembertia populifolia), euphorloiacee. [A little-known Mexican food plant, the Jicama de Baryta (Delembertia populifolia) Euphorbiaceae.] Paris: Societe des Editions Geographiques, Maritimes et Coloniales.

889.   Bois, E. 1944. A propos de la legende du grain de riz. [Concerning the legend of the rice grain.] IIEH-BT 6: 339-342.

890.   Boisset, E. 1838. Notice sur la fecule de pommes de terres, ses divers proprietes et usages dans l'economie domestique, la medecine et les arts. [Note on potato starch, its diverse properties and uses in domestic economy, medicine and the arts.] Lyon: de l'Imprimerie de Delueze.

891.   Bojarski, Edmund A. 1958. The last of the cannibals in Tanganyika. TNR 51: 227-231.

892.   Bokonyi, Sandor. Effects of environmental and cultural changes on prehistoric fauna assemblages. In Gastronomy. The anthropology of food and food habits. Edited by Margaret Louise Arnott. 1975. Pp. 3-12. Paris, The Hague: Mouton Publishers. World Anthropology.

    Examines the significance animal husbandry, and hunting on archaeological interpretation of animal osteological material.

893.   Bokonyi, Sandor & Janossy, D. 1958. Data about the occurrence of the turkey in Europe before the time of Columbus. Aquila 65: 265-268.

894.   Bolian, Charles E. Manioc cultivation in periodically flooded areas. Paper presented at 70th Annual Meeting of the American Anthropological Association. November 18, 1971. New York City.

    Historical records indicate that the Omagua Island dwellers of the upper Amazon Basin used underground storage facilities for manioc during floods. Modern Ticuna, who are currently occupying the use the same underground storage system when flooding occus; however, this involves not only manioc storage, but a rearrangement of crop priorities with maize temporarily replacing the role of manioc in the diet. The normal system of gardens being predominantly located in the flood plains also changes with many new gardens being placed in the less fertile but dry areas of old alluvium.

895.   Bolitho, Hector. 1929. The glorious oyster. His history in Rome and in Britain. How to cook him, and what various writers and poets have written in his praise. London, New York: Alfred A. Knopf.

896.   Bollavista-Torres, Carmen.   The work of the nutritionist in state departments of public health. Master's thesis. Cornell University. 1943.

897.   Bollig, Laurentius.   1927.   Die Bewohner der Truk-Inseln. Religion, Lebben und Kurze Grammatik eines Mikronesievolkes. [The natives of Truk Island. Religion, life and a short grammar of a Micronesian people.] Munster: W. Aschendorf.

Myth: Acquisition of food supply for human race (myth): p.5

898.   Bollman, Marlon C. Influence of food preparation methods on acceptance in the Army. In Conference on Food Acceptance Research. 6 December to 7 December, 1945. Washington, D.C. Quartermaster Corps Manual 17-9. United States War Departent. United States Army. 1946. Pp. 16-19. Washington, D.C.: Quartermaster Food and Container Institute. Research and Development Branch. Military Planning Division. Committee on Food Research.

Available in microform from United States Library of Congress. Microform Division. Item PB-53-883.

899.   Bollman, Marlon C.   1958.   Historical reflections reveal progress in military feeding. USA-FCI-RDA-AR 10: 10-15.

900.   Bolton, J.M. 1972. Food taboos among the Orang Asli in west Malaysia; a potential nutritional hazard. AJCN 25: 789-799.

901.   Bolton, Ralph. Qolla aggression: the hypoglycemia hypothesis. Paper presented at 9th International Congress of Anthropological and Ethnological Sciences. 28 August to 8 September, 1973. Chicago, Illinois.

The Qolla (Aymara) are a highland Peruvian and Bolivian people, who have been described in the literature as highly aggressive and violence-prone. Numerous social, cultural, and environmental factors have been advanced as to the cause of Qolla behavior and personality. The present paper postulates a physiological mechanism which might generate their behavior, suggesting that low blood-glucose levels may be the cause.

902.   Bommer, Sigwald & Bommer-Lotzin, Lisa. 1961. Die Gabe der Demeter. Die Geschichte der greichischen und romischen Ernahrung. [The gift of Demeter. The history of Greek and Roman food.] Krailing bei Munchen: Georg Muller.

903.   Bona, Julia. 1963. Harszti taplalkozasi hagyomanyai. [Traditional food in Haraszti.] N Nyelv 7:1441-144.

Hungary.

904.   Bonafous, Matthieu. 1828. Excursion dans le pays de Gruyeres, ou memoire sur les fromages de cette contree. [Excursion in the Gruyeres country, or memoir on the cheeses of this district.] Paris: Madame Huzard.

905.   Bonafous, Matthieu. 1833. Memoire sur la fabrication du fromage du Mont-Cenis. [Memoir on the manufacture of the cheese of Mont-Cenis.] Paris: Madame Huzard.

France.

906.   Bonafous, Matthiew.   1836.   Histoire naturelle agricole et economique du mais. [Natural, agricultural, and economic history of maize.] Paris: Mme. Huzard.

907.   Bonavia, Emanuel. 1886. On the probable wild source of the whole group of cultivated true limes. JLS (B) 22: 213-218.

908.   Bonavia, Emanuel. 1888. The fruits of India. GB-RSA-J 36: 941-947; 953-959.

909.   Bonavia, Emanuel. 1894. The flora of the Assyrian monuments and its outcomes. Westminster: Archibald Constable & Co.

On the basis of representations of plants on Assyrian sculpture and cylinder seals, the author identifies a variety of fruiting plants including the date (Phoenix dactylifera), vine (Vitis vinifera), pomegranate (Punicia granatum), fig (Ficus carica), banana (Musa sapientum), melon (Cucumis melo or Citrullus vulgaris), and the baobab (Adansonia digitata). Chapter Three is given over to an analysis of the 'cone fruit', and a comparison of various speculations as to the identity of this representation. The final section of conclusions offers an explanation as to the origin of a number of common sacred symbols and their derivation from fruiting plants.

910.   Bonfil Batalla, Guillermo. 1962. Diagnostico sobre el hambre in Sudzal, Yucatan (un ensayo de antropologia aplicada). [Diagnosis of hunger in Yucatan (an attempt at applied anthropology).] INAH-DIA-P No. 11.

911.   Boni, Ada. 1969. Italian regional cooking. Translated by Maria Langdale and Ursula Whyte. New York: Bonanza Books.

The introductory material to each region contains limited data on food use per se; however, the excellent color photography of the food provides a striking document of the imagination and variety of people whose cuisine is little-known in its entirety.

912.   Bonnafont, J. 1976. Le comportement alimentaire comme acte social et facteur de socialisation. [Food behavior as social act and agent of socialization.] ANA 30: 369-378.

913.   Bonnain-Moerdijk, R. Elements pour une sociologie de la cuisine contemporaine. [Elements

of a sociology of contemporary diet.] Ph.D. dissertation. Universite de Paris-X-Nanterre. 1972.

914. Bonnain-Moerdijk, R. 1975. Examen des caracteristiques de l'alimentation paysanne en France entre 1850 et 1936, degages lors d'une enquete menee en 1935 par l'Encyclopedie Francaise. Etude de l'importance des manifestations sociales dans l'evolution du systeme alimentaire de la paysannerie francasie durnat cette periode. [Examination of some characteristics of peasant diet in France between 1850 and 1936, drawn from an inquiry conducted in 1935 by the Encyclopedie Francaise. An important study of social indicators in the evolution of the French peasant diet during this period.] ERur No. 58. Pp. 29-49.

915. Bonnell, M. 1966. Cave Creek cooks along the ol' Hohokam Trail. ADW 21 August. Pp. 8-10.

916. Bonnerjea, B. 1938. Cannibalism: theories and facts. NQ 275: 176.

917. Bonnet, E. 1897. Le haricot (Phaseolus vulgaris L.) etait-il connu dans l'ancien monde avant la decouverte de l'Amerique? [The string-bean (Phaseolus vulgaris L.): was it known in the Old World before the discovery of America?] J Bot 11: 14-20.

918. Bontou, A. 1899. De la cuisine dans les temps anciens et de l'utilite' de la cuisine au gaz dans les temps moderne, conference faite le 10 juin 1899 a la Societe' de patronage des ecoles du groupe de Nansouty. [Of cookery in ancient times and of the usefulness of gas cookery in modern times, conference held on 10 June 1899 at the Society of School Patros of the Nansouty Group.] Bordeaux: Imprimerie G. Gounouilhou.

Copy held by Biblioteque Nationale (Paris). Piece 13303.

919. Bonwick James. 1870. Daily life and origin of the Tasmanians. London: Sampson Low, Son & Marston.

Food, cookery, cannibalism: Pp. 14-23.

920. Booher, Margaret. A study of the dietary habits of Mexican families in Tucson, Arizona. Master's thesis. University of Arizona. 1937.

Records consumption patterns of purchased food in twelve Spanish-American families, during a two week period. Also included are responses to a questionnaire distribted to 178 Spanish-American elementary school children.

921. Boon, James A. One rice cult for two ecologies. Paper presented at 74th Annual Meeting of the American Anthropological Association. 2 to 6 December, 1975. San Francisco, California.

922. Boorman, Sylvia. 1962. Wild plums in brandy. A cookery book of wild foods in Canada. New York: McGraw-Hill.

923. Booth, Sally Smith. 1971. Hung, strung and potted: a history of eating in Colonial America. New York: Crown Publishers.

924. Boots, J.L. 1935. A preliminary study of the diet and customs of the Korean people with relation to their oral conditions. SUMCJ 3: 35-62.

925. Booz, Allen & Hamilton, Inc. 1976. Energy use in food system. Office of Industrial Programs. Washington, D.C.: Federal Energy Administration.

The following analytic results are published: agricultural production accounts for less than three percent of total U.S. energy consumption; fishing accounts for one-half of one percent; manufacturing food and kindred products: ca. four percent; whole-sale trade: less than one percent; retail trade: under one percent; consumption (in-home preparation = four percent; out-of-home prepartion = over two percent); trans-portation: ca. two percent. Approximately seventeen percent of all U.S. energy requirements are related to the food system.

926. Bopp-Oeste, Monica. Sinopsis de los estudios sobre la paleobotanica en la Republica Mexicana. [Synopsis of studies on paleobotony in the Republic of Mexico.] In 5 Internationale Kongress fur Vor- und Frugeschichte. 24 bis 30 August 1958. Hamburg. Edited by Gerhard Bersu. 1961. PP. 112-119. Berlin: Verlag Gebruddern Mann.

A review of the pertinent literature, and a consideration of problems directions for re-search.

927. Borah, Adelaide. 1929. Trees of the Bible. Part 3. The date palm and the pomegranate. AFFL 35: 89-92; Part 4. The olive tree and the fig. 35: 155-157; Part 5. The tamarisk and the syca-more. 35: 231-233. Part 6. The sycamine and the almond. 35: 293-295.

928. Borcsok, V. 1963. A szolo es must a szegedi tanyal nepenek teli taplalkozasaban. [The role of grapes and must in the winter food of the people of the Szeged farmsteads.] N Nyelv No. 7. Pp. 135-139.

Hungary.

929. Bord, Gustave. 1887. Histoire du ble en France. Le pacte de famine. Histoire.legende. [History of wheat in France. The famine pact. History. Legend.] Parts: A. Sauton.

930. Borden Company. 1953. Food in fiction in the American tradition from "The Song of Hiawatha" to "The Yearling". With notes on uses in schools and York: The Borden Company

931. Bordier. 1888. L'anthropophagie. [Anthropophagy.] SAP-B 11 62-71.

A theoretical discussion of the origins of anthhropophagy, and environmental and bio-logical (dentition) factors associated there-with. Introduces the term 'anthropoexopha-

gy' for the pracatice of cannibalizing enemies killed in warfare.

932.   Borgaux, Albert. 1935. Quatre siecles d'
histoire du cacao et du chocolat. [Four centuries
of the history of cacao and chocolate,] Bruxelles:
Office International du cacao et du chocolat.

933.   Borgstrom, George. 1961-1963, Fish as
food. New York, London: Academic Press.

934.   Borgstrom, George. 1973. The food and
people dilemma. Belmont, California: Wadsworth
Publishing Co.; North Scituate, Massachusetts:
Duxbury Press.

935.   Borie, Victor. 1857. La question du pot-au-
feu. Organisation du commerce des viands. [The
question of the soup-pot. The organisation of food
commerce.] Paris: Librairie agricole de la maison
rustique.

936.   Borja, Arturo Jiminez. 1953. La comida en
el antiguo Peru. [Eating in ancient Peru.] RMN
22: 113-134.

    Origins of food in ancient Peru; food consid-
    eredas as something alive; imagery of food
    in the context of gender, prestige, and psy-
    chological illness.

937.   Bornet, Liesl. 1968. Food and their place in
folklore. LD 35: 8-10.

938.   Bornstein, Anika. 1972. Some observations
on Yemeni food habits. Nutr News 10: 1-9.

    Eight villages were studied: Al Maleka
    (Midlands), Al Homrah, Al Zohrah, 'Arb, Dar
    al-Olefi Hamami (Highlands). Ibn Abas (Tih-
    ama), and Sana'a. Infant and child feeding
    habits are described, with emphasis on
    breast and bottle-feeding, and weaning pra-
    ctices.

939.   Bornstein, Annika. Sorghum in the Yemen.
Paper presented at 9th International Congress of
Anthropological and Ethnological Sciences. 28
August to 8 September, 1973. Chicago, Illinois.

    Describes methods of sorghum cultivation,
    tools, reckoning of seasons astronomically,
    individual and collective planting, harvest-
    ing, and threshing systems. Preparation of
    sorghum bread, and porridge; kitchen ute-
    nsils, baking and cooking methods; consump-
    tion factors; place of sorghum in the diet;
    sorghum combined with other grains, and
    legumes, preferred varieties; songs and pro-
    verbs referring to the culture of sorghum
    and its consumption.

940.   Bornstein - Johanssen, Annika. Sorghum and
millet in Yemen. In Gastronomy. The anthropology of food and food habits. Edited by Margaret L.
Arnott. 1975. Paris, The Hague: Mouton Publishers. World Anthropology.

    Methods of cultivation, work patterns, sorg-
    hum and millet in the diet, preparation of

bread and porridge, utensils, changes in food
habits.

941.   Borrchardt, Ludwig. 1932. Ein Brot. [A
bread.] ZASA 68: 73-79.

942.   Borsook, H. & Halverson, W.L. 1940. Nutrition and health in Pasadena. AJPH 30: 895-900.

943.   Bosch, E.F. 1964. Studies in Spanish nutrition, No. 34. Inquiry on the population of Mahon
(Menorca). [In Spanish] AB 16: 273-294.

    English summary.

944.   Bose, Saradindu. 1964, Economy of the
Onge of Little Andaman. M. India. 44: 298-310.

    Analysis of the carrying capacity of the
    coastal and forest areas under primitive
    conditions. Hunting-fishing-gathering acti-
    vities are recorded, and food preparation
    and quantitative consumption data provided.
    Gross nutrient intake is indicated for one
    month.

945.   Bosley, Bertlyn. 1959. Nutrition in the
Indian Program. JADA 35: 905-909.

    Native American.

946.   Bossard, James H. 1943. Family table talk
-an area for sociological study. ASR 18: 295-301.

947.   Bossen, Laurel. Household work patterns in
an urban shantytown in Guatemala. Paper presented at 74th Annual Meeting of the American
Anthropological Association. 2 to 6 December,
1975. San Francisco, California.

948.   Botha, Colin Graham. 1927. Social life in
the Cape Colony in the 18th century. Capetown:
Juta.

    Description of foods: pp. 41, 56-57, 66, 87,
    100.

949.   Botkin, Benjamin Albert, ed. 1956. New
York City folklore. Legends, tall tales, anecdotes,
stories, sagas, heroes and characters, customs,
traditions and sayings. New York: Random House.

    Old saloon days: pp. 107-131; integration of
    Puerto Rican foods into previously Eastern
    European Jewish neighborhood: pp. 208-209.

950.   Botkin, C.W., & Shires, L.B. 1948. The
composition and value of pinon nuts. NM-AES-B
No. 344.

952.   Botta, Paul-Emile. 1841. Relations d'un
voyage dans 1 'Yemen, enterpris en 1837 pour le
Museum a histoire naturelle de Paris. [A narrative
of travels in the Yemen, undertaken by the
Museum of Natural History of Paris.] Paris: B.
Duprat.

952.   Botte, F. 1953. Gastronomia parmense.
[Gastronomy of Parma.]   Parma: Scuola
Tipografia Benedettina.

953.   Bouchal, Leo. 1899. Geophagie. [Geopha-
gy.] AGWS-M 29(1): 11.

    A brief review of the literature on geophagy
in Indonesia.

954.   Bouchal, Leo. 1900. Noch einige Belegstel-
len fur Geophagie in Indonesien und Melanesien.
[Still another quotation for earth-eating in Indonesia and Melanesia.] AGWS-M 30: 180-181.

955.   Boucher, Nicole D. Prehistoric subsistence
at the Helen Point site. Master's thesis. Anthropology. Burnaby, British Columbia: Simon Frazer
University.

956.   Boucherie, Maurice. 1872. Etude sur les
boissons fermentees. Histoire du vin, culture de la
vigne, les vendanges, la fermentation, vins blancs,
vins rouges, vins de liqueurs, vins d' Europe,
d'Amerique, d'Asie, de Turquie, d'Afrique, vins des
colonies Anglaises. [Study of fermented drinks.
History of wine, vine cultivation, vintages, fermentation, white and red wines; wines and liqueurs;
wines of Europe, America, Asia, Turkey, Africa;
wines of the English colonies.] Paris: E. Lacroix.

957.   Boudreaux, Maydell C. Food preservation
methods used by a select group of one hundred
rural families in St. Landry Parish, Louisiana.
Master's thesis. Louisiana State University. 1947.

958.   Boulenger, Edward George. 1927. Naturalist at the dinner table. London: Duckworth.

959.   Boulos, C. 1954. Une enquete alimentaire
en Haiti. [A dietary inquiry in Haiti.] AM Haiti-
B 6: 185-188.

960.   Bouquet, A., & Kerharo, J. 1950. Les vegetaux condiments de l'Afrique du Nord dans l'alimentation, la therapeutique et la magie. [North
African vegetable condiments in diet, medicine,
and magic.] A Trop 7: 237-274.

    Plants mentioned include conifers (pine
    nuts); monocotyledons ("lagmi" vinegar),
    cyperous, garlic, onions, saffron, ginger,
    malaquetta pepper; apetaliferous archich-
    lamidae (hazel nuts, peppers, cubeb); dipe-
    taliferous thalamiflores (cinnamon, laurel,
    nutmeg, capers, hibiscus, rue, citron, mas-
    tic, and raisins.)

961.   Bourdaire. 1914. L 'alimentation des
armees dans les guerres modernes. Conference
fait a l'ecole d' instruction des officiers de reserve
de l' armee territoriale de la 20e region. [Feeding
armies in modern wars. Conference held at the
school of Instruction of territorial reserve army
officers of the 20th Region.] Levrault: Berger.

962.   Bourdin, Francois-Jean-Isidore. Geophagie.
[Geophagy.] Medical thesis. No.897. Universite
de Toulouse. 1910.

964.   Bourgeat, J. 1963. Les plaisirs de la table
en France des Gaulois a nos jours. [Pleasures of
the table in France from the times of the Gauls to
our own days.] Paris: Hachette.

965.   Bourgnon De Layre, Antonin. 1846. De la
fabrication du pain chez la classe agricole et dans
ses rapports avec l'economie publique. [Of the
manufacture of bread by the agricultural class and
its relation to the economy-at-large.] Poitiers:
Imprimerie Dupre.

966.   Bourgoin, Edme. 1870. De l'alimentation
des enfants et des adultes dans une ville assiegee
et en particulier de la viande de cheval. Conference faite le 25 Novembre 1870 a l'Ecole de
Pharmacie de Paris. [Of the diet of children and
adults in a besieged city and in particular of horse
meat.   Conference held the 25th of
Novembre,1870, at the School of Pharmacy of
Paris.] Paris: A. Delahaye.

967.   Bourgoin, Edme. 1871. Du ble, de sa valeur
en temps de siege et de disette Conference faite le
27 decembre 1870, a l'Ecole de Pharmacie de Paris.
[Of wheat, and its value in times of siege and
scarcity. Conference held on the 27th December,
1870, at the School of Pharmacy of Paris.] Paris:
A. Delahaye.

968.   Bourguignon, Erika. 1959. The persistence
of folk beliefs: some notes on cannibalism and
zombis in Haiti. JAF 72: 36-46.

969.   Bourke, John Gregory. 1892. The medicine
men of the Apache. SI-BAE-AR No. 9: pp. 445-
603.

    Includes notes on ritual foods, ceremonial
    use of maize meal, and maize pollen.

970.   Bourke, John Gregory. 1894. Distillation by
early American Indians. AA 7: 297-299.

971.   Bourke, John Gregory. 1895. Folk-foods of
the Rio Grande Valley and of northern Mexico.
JAF 8: 41-71. Also in TFSP 9: 85-117. (1931).

972.   Bourke, John Gregory. 1934. Chapters
Five, Six, Seven. Coprophagia. Chapter Fourteen.
Onions. In Scatalogic rites of all nations. New
York: American Anthropological Society.

973.   Bourne, Geoffrey H. 1946. Nutrition in
Japan. Nature (L) 157: 177-178.

974.   Bourne, Geoffrey H. 1953. The food of the
Australian aboriginal. PNS 12: 58-65.

    Includes insects, e.g. Isoptera, Homoptera,
    Lepidoptera, Hymenoptera.

975.   Bourne, Henry E. 1919. Food control and
price-fixing in Revolutionary France. JPol Econ
27: 73-94; 108-209.

976.   Bourret, Dominique. Etude ethnobotanique
des dioscoracees alimentaires, ignames de Nouvel-
le-Caldeonie. [Ethnobotanical study of edible Dio-
scoraceae, yams of New Caledonia.] Ph. D
dissertation. Universite de Paris. 1973.

977.   Boutigny, P.-H. 1827. Du chocolat, de sa
fabrication, des moyens de reconnaitre sa falsification, et de ses proprietes alimentaires et medi-

cales. [Of chocolate, of its manufacture, means for recognizing its falsification, and of its dietary and medicinal properties.] Evreux: Imprimerie d'Ancelle.

978.   Bowden, Shirley. Nutritional beliefs and food practices of Mexican-American mothers. Master's thesis. Home Economics. Fresno, California: Fresno State College. 1968.

979.   Bowdidge, Elizabeth. 1935. The soya bean: its history, cultivation and uses. London: Oxford University Press.

980.   Bowen, David James. 1953. Y Gwasanaedr bwrad. [Table service.] BCB-B 15: 116-120.

Two 16th Century Welsh texts on table manners.

981.   Bowen, Joanne. The Mott Farm: zooarchaeology and Colonial New England foodways. Master's thesis. Brown University. 1975.

982.   Bowles, M.E. 1845. The last of the cannibals: a legend of Mangea. Polynesian 1(48). 19 April.

983.   Bowers, W. 1964. A further note on a recently reported root crop from the New Guinea Highlands. JPS 73: 333-335.

984.   Boxer, C.R. 1952. Maize names. UJ 16: 178-178.

Africa.

985.   Boyce, W. Scott. 1917. Economic and social history of Chowan County, North Caroline, 1880-1915. CU-SHEPL 76 (1).

Food habits of fisherfolk: Pp. 104, 105, mentions "black yeopon" i.e. tea without milk or sugar; cooking utensils, and food preparation: Pp. 222-225; 230-232.

986.   Boyd, E. 1958. Fireplaces and stoves in colonial New Mexico. El Pal 65: 219-224.

987.   Boyd, Grace M. Food preferences of women students at the Iowa State College as a basis for menu planning in the college dining halls. Master's thesis. Institutional Management. Ames: Iowa State College. 1947.

988.   Boyd, J.D. 1938. The nature of the American diet. J Ped 12: 243-254.

989.   Boyd, Minnie Clare. 1931. Alabama in the Fifties; a social study. CU-SHEPL No. 353.

Diet of slaves: pp. 44, 45; foods in Southern hotels, homes, restaurants: pp. 112-116.

990.   Boyd-Orr, John. 1936. Problems of African native diet. Forward. Africa 9: 145-146.

991.   Boyd-Orr, John. 1954. Nutrition on an international scale. BRNR 15: 17-32.

992.   Boylan, Patricia. 1964. Bread with an Irish flavor. I Wel 13: 12-14.

993.   Brace, C. Loring & Mahler, Paul E. More chews to increase: or evidence for ongoing dental reduction. Paper presented at 69th Annual Meeting of the American Anthropological Association. 19 to 22 November, 1970. San Diego, California.

994.   Bracke, A. & De Rumer, E. 1917. Nos plantes sauvages comestibles. [Our edible wild plants.] Brussels: Jos. Jouffroy & Cie.

995.   Bracken, F.J. 1953. Infant feeding in the American colonies. JADA 29: 349-358.

996.   Bradbury, John P. & Puleston, Dennis E. A palynological investigation of Maya agriculture. Paper presented at 73rd Annual Meeting of the American Anthropological Association. 19 to 24 November, 1974. Mexico City.

997.   Bradfield, R. 1971. The changing pattern of Hopi agriculture. RAIGBI-OP No. 20.

998.   Bradfield, Robert B. & Brun, T. 1970. Nutritional status of California Mexican-Americans. A review. AJCN 23: 798-806.

Nutritional status and food beliefs: P. 800.

999.   Bradfield, Robert B. & Lauriault, James. 1961. Diet and food beliefs of Peruvian jungle tribes. 1. The Shipibo (Monkey People). JADA 39: 126-128.

1000.   Bradley, Lawrence. Subsistence strategy at a late Archaic site in south-central Kansas. Master's thesis. University of Kansas. 1973.

1001.   Braidwood, Robert J. 1960. Preliminary investigations concerning the origins of food production in Iranian Kurdistan. AS 17:214.

1002.   Braidwood, Robert J. 1962. Further investigations of the paleo-ecological aspects of the appearance of food production on the Hilly Flanks of the Fertile Crescent in southwestern Asia. Report to the National Science Foundation of the United States of America.

1003.   Braidwood, Robert J., & Howe, B. 1960. Prehistoric investigations in Iraqi Kurdistan. UChi-SAOC No. 31.

1004.   Braidwood, Robert J. & Reed, Charles A. 1957. The achievement and early consequences of food production: a cosideration of the archaeological and natural-historical. CSH-BL-SQB 22: 19-31.

1005.   Braidwood, Robert J.; Sauer, Jonathan D.; Helbaek, Hans; Mangelsdorf, Paul C.; Cutler, Hugh C.; Coon, Carleton S.; Linton, Ralph; Steward, Julian; & Oppenheim, A. Leo. 1953. Symposium: Did man once live be beer alone? AA 55:515-526.

Addresses the question was the earliest utilization of the domesticated cereals for the preparation of beer, rather than for the manufacture of bread.

1006. Brain, C.K. 1974. Human food remains from the Iron Age at Zimbabwe. SAJS 70: 303-309.

1007. Bramwell, E.M. 1961. Diet of London busmen. A sample study. PNS 20 30-35.

1008. Brancourt, Andre'-Alfred-Pierre. 1934. Le lait dans le delta Tonkinois. [Milk in the Tonkin Delta.] Bourdeaux: Imprimerie de Delmar.

Indochina. The author's thesis for the degree in Pharmacy.

1009. Brand, Donald. 1951. Quiroga, a Mexican municipio. SI-ISA-P No. 11.

Wild food plants: pp. 160-162; diet: pp. 222-224; beverages: pp. 224-225.

1010. Brandegee, T.S. 1900. A new Tapirira from Baja California. Zoe 5: 78-79.

Tapirira edulis. The ripe fruit indicated as eaten in the Cape Region of Baja California, during August and September. Common name is given as ciruela (Spanish=plum).

1011. Brandes, Raymond S. Frank Hamilton Cushing: pioneer Americanist. Ph.D. dissertation. University of Arizona. 1965.

Cushing is the author of the classic food ethnography Zuni Breadstuff.

1012. Brandreth, C.J.B. 1919. A "rice wedding" in Java. WWM 42: 261-266.

1013. Brandt, Edward. 1927. Untersuchungen zum Romischen Kochbuche. Versuch eines Losung der Apicius Frage. [Investigations on a Roman cookbook. An attempt at a solution of the Apicius question.] Leipzig: Dietrich'sche Verlagsbuchhandlung.

1014. Brandt, K. 1948. Brot herstellung in Vest in vor-und fruhgeschichtlicher Zeit. [Bread production in Vest in pre-and early historical times.] VJ 50: 7-14.

1015. Brandt, Karl. 1940. Whale oil; an economic analysis. Stanford University, Food Research Institute. Palo Alto: Stanford University Press.

1016. Brandt, Karl. 1948. Whaling and whale oil during and after W.W.II. War-Peace Pamphlet No. 11. Stanford University, Food Research Institute. Palo Alto: Stanford University Press.

1017. Branthoover, B. 1962. Game cookery guide. IAC-EB No. 373.

1018. Bratanic, Branimir. Orace sprave u Hrvata. [Ploughing implements among the Croats.] University of Zagreb. 1947.

1019. Brauer, Erich. 1934. Ethnologie der Jemenitischen Juden. [Ethnology of Yemeni Jews.] Kulturgeschichtliche Bibliothek. 1. Reihe: Ethnologische Bibliothek No. 7. Heidelberg: Carl Winters Universitats-buchhandlung.

Food habits: pp. 97-113.

1020. Braun, A. 1877. 1877. Ueber die im K[oni]gl[iche] Museum zu Berlin. Aufbewahrten Pflanzenreste aus altagyptischen Grabern. [On the fossil plants from ancient Egyptian graves preserved in the Royal Museum at Berlin.] ZE 9: 289-310.

1021. Braungart. 1912. Die Urheimat der Landwirtschaff aller indogermanischen Volker an der Geschichte der Kulturpflanzen und Ackerbaugerate in Mittel und Nordeuropa nachgeweisen. [The original home of agriculture of all Indogermanic peoples and the history of cultivated plants and agricultural implements in Central and Northern Europe.] Heidelberg: C. Winters.

1022. Braunholtz, H.J. 1928. Wooden food trough from Santa Cruz. BMQ 3: 26-27.

Solomon Islands.

1023. Brautigan, Richard. 1966. The menu. ER No. 42. Pp. 30-32.

Food served to inmates awaiting execution in the San Quentin federal penitentiary, Marin County, California.

1024. Brautlecht, Charles Andrew. 1953. Starch: it sources, production and uses. New York: Rheinhold.

1025. Bravo Letelier, Virginia. 1950. La comida tradicional chilena. [The traditional Chilean meal.] SFM-A Pp. 463-470.

Survey of historical influences on Chilean foods; lists foods adopted from France, Spain, England and Germany. Data on meal times; typical meal menus; beverages, confections; Sunday and feast meals.

1026. Bray, George W. Dietary deficiency on Nauru. M.D. dissertation. University of Sydney. 1927.

Nauru is an independent island republic in the Pacific Ocean, at approximately 0.31 S, 166. 56 E.

1027. Brebion, Jean-Francois-Antoine. 1909 Une distillerie indochinoise. [An Indo-chinese distillery.] SNCS-B Extrait. [Reprint.] Chalon-sur-Saone: Bertrand.

1028. Brebion, Jean-Francois-Antoine. 1913. Boissons et mets cochinchinois. [Beverages and food preparations of Cochinchina.] RevIndo 5 mars [March] Extrait. [Reprint.] Hanoi: Imprimerie d' Extreme Orient.

Cochin is an area in the Republic of Vietnam southwest of Saigon.

1029. Brehm, Jack W. & Cohen, Arthur P. 1962. Explorations in cognitive dissonance. New York & London: John Wiley & Sons.

Cognition of hunger a function of dissonance reduction (description of an experiment): Pp. 133-137

1030.   Bremer, Michele K.   1976.   Body composition differneces in animals fed two American diets. EFN 6:63-68.

Laboratory mice fed a highly processed, standard American diet from weaning showed significant differences in body composition at maturity compared with mice fed an apparently similar but minimally processed "natural foods" diet, and mice fed laboratory "chow". Mice fed the processed diet had significantly greater mean body weight, proportion of body fat, and proportion of carcass weight lost in drying. An experiment with rats produced similar differences in dried carcase weight. A food preference study suggests that overeating might partially explain these differences.

1031.   Bremmer, J.M.   The bread industry in New Zealand.   Master's thesis.   Economics.   Auckland University.   1938.

1032.   Bremond, H.M.L.   Recherches sur quelques condiments azotes d'Extreme-Orient.   [Research on some pickled condiments of the Far East.]   Ph.D. dissertation.   Medicine and Pharmacy, Universite de Bourdeaux.   1919.

1033.   Bremond, H.M.L. & Rose, E.   1919.   Condiments azotes solides en Indochine [Solid salted condiments in Indochina.]   IPI-A 33: 282-291.

1034.   Brenneman, Joseph.   1932.   Psychological aspects of nutrition in childhood.   J Ped 1: 145-171.

Contains extensive commentary on childhood anorexia.

1035.   Brenninkmeijer, C.M.   1963.   Nutrition of Gypsies living in caravans.   [In Dutch.]   Voeding 24: 16-23.

1036.   Bresard, M.   1957.   La consommation des matieres grasses et du pain a Saint Etienne.   [Consumption oils and bread in Saint Etienne.]   P-INH-B 12: 313-381.

France.

1037.   Bresard, M.   1959.   La consommation des boissons en France: Marseille.   [The consumption of beverages in France: Marseille.]   P-INH-B 14:95-163.

1038.   Bresard, M.; Maujol; & Varlot.   1964.   Consumption of beverages in rural areas.   (Two districts, Tarn-et-Garonne, and Main-et-Loire).   [In French.]   P-INH-B 19: 203-231.

1039.   Breton, Yvan.   The role of petty commodity production among Venezuelan fisherman.   Paper presented at 74th Annual Meeting of the American Anthropology Association.   2 to 6 December, 1975. San Francisco, California.

1040.   Bretschneider, Emili Vasilevich.   1871.   On the study and value of Chinese botanical works, with notes on the history of plants and geographical botany from Chinese sources.   Foochow: Rozario, Marcal & Co.

1041.   Bretschneider, Emil Vasilievich.   1898.   History of European botanical discoveries in China.   2 vols. in one.   London: Sampson Low, Marston.   Reprint.   Leipzig: K.F. Koehler's Antiquarium.   1935.

Biographies of plant explorers, with lists of their botanical discoveries.

1042.   Bretschneider, Emilii Vasilevich.   1890.   Botanicon Sinicum.   Notes on Chinese botany from native and western sources.   3 Vols.   London: Trubner.

Extensive references to food plants and their uses.   Volume one contains bibliography which includes a number of entries for older works on 'dietetics': Pp. 138-216.

1043.   Brew, J.O.   The hunters.   In 5 Internationale Kongress fur Vor-und Frugeschichte.   24 bis 30 August 1958.   Hamburg.   Edited by Gerhard Bersu.   1961.   Pp. 157-158.   Berlin: Verlag Gebruddern Mann.

Review of several ethnographic films recording the food guest of a band of Kung Bushmen in the Nai Nai region of the Kalahari Desert.

1044.   Brewer, Lucille & Cannon, Helen.   1916.   Dandelions as food.   CorU-CRC-FHS 5: 79-91.

1045.   Briand, M. (pseud. M.C.D.).   1750.   Dictionnaire des alimens, vin et liquers, leurs qualites, leurs effets, relativement aux differens ages, & aux differens temperamens; avec la maniere de les appreter, ancienne et moderne, suivant la methode des plus habiles chefs d'office & chefs de cuisine, de la cour, & de la ville.   Ouvrage tres-utile dans toutes les familles.   [Dictionary of foods, wine and liquors, their qualities and their effects relative to different ages and different temperaments; with the manner of learning this latter, ancient and modern, following the methods of the most able cooks, household chefs, head chefs, chefs of court & city.   A very useful work for every family.]   Paris: chez Gissey.

1046.   Briault, M.   1944.   Y-a-t-il encore une anthropophagie africaine?   [Is there still cannibalism in Africa?]   Construire 11: 181-201.

1047.   Bridges, B.J.   1971.   Aboriginal cannibalism. RAHS-N No. 109-7-8.

1048.   Bridgland, L.A.   1959.   Cocoa processing-history and principles.   PNGAJ 12: 49-85.

1049.   Briffault, Eugene.   1846.   Paris a table. [Paris at the table.]   Paris: J. Hetzel.

Includes a history of dining in Paris, from the time of Charlemagne to the 1840's.

1050. Briggs, Hazel F. 1956. Changing food habits and restaurant fare. CPro March. Pp. 9-11.

1051. Brighetti, A. 1968. Diete per gli infermi dell' Arcispedale di Santo Spirito in Sassia nella Seconda meta del secolo 16. [Diet for the sick in the Chief Hospital of the Holy Spirt in Sassia during the second half of the 16th century.] Policlinico 75: 1140-1145.

1052. Brillat-Savarin, Jean Anthelme. 1826. Physiologie du gout, ou meditations du gastronomie transcendante. 2 vols. [The physiology of taste, or meditations on transcendental gastronomy.] Paris: A. Sautelet.

1053. Brim, John A. Paddy agriculture and lineage land in Hong Kong's New Territories. Paper presented at 68th Annual Meeting of the American Anthropological Association. 20 to 23 November, 1969. New Orleans, Louisiana.

1054. Bringeus, Nils-Arvid. 1970. Lundasymposiet for etnologisk matforskning. [The Lund Symposium for Ethnological Food Research.] Rig 1970. Pp. 114-116.

    This Symposium was convened in Lund, Sweden, from 21-25 August, 1970. Twenty-two of the papers prepared for the Symposium are published in E Scan (1971).

1055. Bringeus, Nils-Arvid. Problems, and methods in ethnological food research. Paper presented at First International Symposium on Ethnological Food Research, 21 to 25 August, 1970. Folklivarkivet, University of Lund, Lund, Sweden.

1056. Bringeus, Nils-Arvid. Food and folk beliefs: on boiling blood sausage. In Gastronomy. The anthropology of food and food habits. Edited by Margaret Louise Arnott. 1975. Pp. 251-273. Paris; The Hague: Mouton Publishers. World Anthropology.

    Discusses sausage cookery; taboos related to sausage preparation and cookery; cooking the sausage with hog spleen; incantations recited over cooking sausages; smacking the sausage against the stove to prevent splitting of the uncooked sausage; magic dialogue recited in connection with sausage boiling.

1057. Brinton, Daniel G. 1897. Cannabalism in Europe. Science 5: 688.

1058. Brinton, William. 1861. On food and its digestion; being an introduction to dietetics. London: Longman, Green, Longman & Roberts.

    Covers: need for food; the nature of food; digestive organs; varieties of food, animal and vegetable; condiments; tea and coffee; alcohol; cookery; choice of food or diet. Reviewed in BMJ 2: 282-284 (14 September, 1861).

1059. Briones, Jose de Jesus Montoya. 1964. Atla: etnografia de un pueblo Nahuatl. [Atla: ethnography of a Nahuatl village.] INAH-DIA-P No. 14.

1060. Brisseau. 1745. Dissertation sur les mauvaises et pernicieuses qualitez du cuivre employe pour la construction des ustensiles qui servent a l'usage de la cuisine et de la pharmacie, et des bonnes et salutaires qualitez du fer qu'on doit lui substituer pour le meme usage. [Dissertation on the injurious and hurtful qualities of copper used in the manufacture of utensils used in cooking and pharmacy and the favorable and salutary qualities of iron which may be substituted for the same use.] Tournay: Jovenau.

1061. Bristol, Melvin L. 1964. Philoglossa - a cultivar of the Sibundoy of Colombia. HU-BML 20: 325-333.

    A pot-herb, used in the Colombian Andes.

1062. Bristol, Melvin L. Sibundoy ethnobotany. Ph.D. dissertation. Harvard University. 1965.

    Colombia.

1063. Bristowe, W.S. 1932. Insects and other invertebrates for human consumption in Siam. RESL-T 80: 387-404.

    Lists eight arachnids (spiders and scorpions); and thirty-five species of insects. Orthoptera, Odonata, Isoptera, Hemiptera, Homoptera, Coleoptera, Lepidoptera, Hymenoptera, Arthropods other than insects.

1064. Bristowe, W.S. 1953. Insects as food. PNS 12: 44-48.

    Isoptera, Hemiptera, Homoptera, Coleoptera, Lepidoptera, Hymenoptera, Arthropods other than insects. The author recounts his experiences with edible insects in various cultures throughout the world. Methods of preparation and uses are described.

1065. Brito, J.C. 1948. La pelagra y la la extincion de la civilizacion Maya. [Pelagra and the extinction of the Maya civilization.] USC-PT 11: 87-102.

1066. Brittin, Helen C. & Zinn, Dale W. 1977. Meat buying practices of Caucasians, Mexican-Americans and Negroes. JADA 71: 623-628.

1067. Broach, Rebecca Agnes. A study of the use of peanut butter as shortening in cakes. Master's thesis. University of Georgia. 1944.

1068. Brock, J. F. & Autret, Marcel. 1952. Kwashiorkor in Africa. Geneva: World Health Organization.

1069. Brockmann, C. Thomas. Subsistence and nutrition in the Maya Lowlands: past and present. Paper presented at 73rd Annual Meeting of the American Anthropological Association. 19 to 24 November, 1974. Mexico City.

Preparation and consumption of foods: Pp. 70-74.

1070.   Brode, John. 1969. The process of modernization. An annotated bibliography on the sociocultural aspects of development. Cambridge: Harvard University Press.

Includes numerous citations for articles concerned with village economics and market systems.

1071.   Brodie, W. 1901. Animal remains on Indian village sites. OPM-AR Pp. 44-51.

Canada.

1072.   Broeg, William E. 1944. Some interesting factors for consideration by food technologists in the postwar period: the influence of odor on palate acceptance. IFT-P Pp. 141-148.

1073.   Brokensha, David & Riley, Bernard W. Mbeere wild foods. Paper presented at 77th Annual Meeting of the American Anthropological Association. 15 November, 1978. Los Angeles, California.

The Mbeere are linguistically related to the Kikuya, Embu, Meru, and Kamba. They occupy an area east of Mount Kenya, and southwest of the Tana River in Kenya. This paper includes, in addition to an enumeration of wild plant foods, data on preparation, time, location, manner, of gathering, as well as who gathers plants, and the extent of knowledge concerning edible plants.

1074.   Bronson, Bennett. 1966. Roots and subsistence of ancient Maya. SJA 22: 251-279.

1075.   Bronson, Bennett. Roots and the subsistence of the ancient Maya. Master's thesis. Anthropology. University of Pennsylvania. 1968.

1076.   Brook, Ralph Vernon. 1966. They didn't barter to fill the larder. Artifact 4 (3) 1-11.

Excavation at the Hot Well site, located about two thousand yards south of the Texas-New Mexico border, thirteen miles east of Newman, Texas, revealed egg shells, maize cobs and a variety of other botanical and osteological material. The site is considered pre-Spanish. Identification of egg shell material suggests that the turkey may have been domesticated for egg production but that the animal itself was not used for food. Background on Mogollon dietary is given, derived from the archeological literature.

1077.   Brooke, Clarke. 1967. The heritage of famine in Central Tanzania. TNR No. 67. Pp. 15-22.

1078.   Brooke, Clarke. 1967. Types of food shortages in Tanzania. GR 57: 333-357.

1079.   Brooke, Clinton L. 1954. Historical highlights of bread enrichment. BW 162: 31-34.

United States.

1080.   Broster, John B. Identification of manioc from archaeological ceramics. Paper presented at 70th Annual Meeting of the American Anthropological Association. 18 November, 1971. New York City.

Through chemical and microscopic analysis of ceramic shard collections from Venezuela, Mexico, and Central America, it is proposed that manioc, maize and other vegetal materials can be identified as residue on these ceramics. This approach may provide a test for determining functions of archaeological ceramics and aid in establishing temporal placement of cultigens, such as manioc, in a certain regional sequence.

1081.   Brothwell, Don R. 1959. Teeth in earlier human populations. PNS 18: 59-65.

1082.   Brothwell, Don R. 1961. Cannibalism in early Britain. Antiquity 35: 304-307.

1083.   Brothwell, Don & Brothwell, Patricia. 1969. Food in antiquity. A survey of the diet of early peoples. Ancient peoples and places series, No. 66, London: Thames and Hudson; New York: Frederick A. Praeger.

1084.   Broughton, Thomas Duer. 1813. Letters written in a Mahratta camp during the year 1809, descriptive of the character, manners, domestic habits, and religious ceremonies of the Mahrattas. London: John Murray.

1085.   Broumische, Edouard. 1856. Notes sur l'etat actuel de Taiti. [Notes on the present condition of Tahiti.] RCol 16: 653-666.

Contains a list of locally used plants.

1086.   Brousse, H. 1961. La consommation des boissons. [The consumption of beverages.] Consommation 8:47-70.

1087.   Brosseur, G. 1961. Etude de geographie regionale: le village de Tenentou (Mali). [Regional geographic study: the village of Tenentou (Mali). IFAN-B 23 [series B]: 607-675.

Foods, preparation techniques, meal patterns, and variation in seasonal availability are described.

1088.   Browman, David L. Some aspects of prehistoric nutrition in the Lake Titicaca Basin. Paper presented at 77th Annual Meeting of the American Anthropological Association. 14 to 18 November, 1978. Los Angeles, California.

1089.   Brown, A. & Whitmarsh, P. 1909. Social life in the Philippines. CCM No. 4. Pp. 291-298; No. 5. Pp. 395-401.

Data on food supply and preparation.

1090.   Broun, Alfred Forbes & Masey, Reginald Ernest. 1929. Flora of the Sudan. With a conspectus of groups of plants and artificial key to families.

Obtainable from the Controller, Sudan Government. London: Made by Thomas Murby & Co.

Data on uses of plants as food is included.

1091. Brown, Alice Cooke. 1966. Chapter Four. Culinary use of herbs. In Early American herb recipes. Rutland, Vermont: Charles E. Tuttle Co.

1092. Brown, Almeda Perry. 1929. Food habits of Utah farm families. U-AES-B No. 213.

1093. Brown, Almeda Perry. 1930-1931. Diet as an index to living level in some Utah farm homes. U-AS-P 8:111-114.

1094. Brown, Almeda Perry. 1934. Types of greens or pot-herbs used in rural Utah homes. U AES-C No. 104.

1095. Brown, Almeda Perry. 1943. Food habits of rural school children in relation to their well-being. U-AES-B No. 246.

1096. Brown, Antoinette B. Bone strontium content and the hominid diet. Paper presented at 69th Annual Meeting of the American Anthropological Association. 19 to 22 November, 1970. San Diego, California.

1097. Brown, Antoinette. Bone strontium content as a dietary indicator in human skeletal populations. Ph.D. dissertation. Anthropology. University of Michigan, Ann Arbor. 1973.

1098. Brown, Bob. 1932. Let there be beer. History and anecdote, and recipes. New York: Harrison Smith & Robert Haas.

1099. Brown, Bob & Brown, Eleanor Parker. 1961. Culinary Americana. Cookbooks published in the cities and towns of the United Stats of America during the years from 1860 through 1960. Edited by Alice G. Hansen. New York: Roving Eye Press.

1100. Brown, D.K. 1954. Vitamin, protein, and carbohydrate content of some Arctic plants from Fort Churchill, Manitoba Region. Report No. 23. Ottawa: Canadian Defense Research Board.

1101. Brown, Dale. 1968. The cooking of Scandinavia. New York: Time-Life Books. Foods of the World.

Food customs, preparations and uses of Norway, Denmark, Sweden, and Finland illustrated with excellent color photographs.

1102. Brown, E.L. 1976. Factors influencing food choices and intake. Geriatrics 31: 89-92.

1103. Brown, Elsworth. 1957. Indian invention of New-World foods, and breakfast at Tanaqui. TAS-MP No. 1.

1104. Brown, J.W. 1957. Science and the art of cooking. IRMGPC 170: 357-360.

Discusses the contribution of food technology to nutritional well-being in what the author refers to as "...a shift of the responsibility for choosing and blending basic food ingredients from the homemaker to the food processing industry."

1105. Brown, John Hull. 1966. Early American beverages. Rutland, Vermont: Charles E. Tuttle.

1106. Brown, Judith K. 1969. Cross-cultural ratings of subsistence activities and sex division of labor: retrospects and prospects. BSN 4:281-290.

Reviews the strengths and weaknesses of George Peter Murdock's Ethnographic atlas (1967), and Robert B. Textor's A cross-cultural summary (1967) and concludes that, based on the noted weaknesses, "Rating the sex division of labor for categories of subsistence activities on a large sample of societies is probably not a fruitful procedure at the present time". Suggestions are made for improving Murdock's, and Textor's analyses.

1107. Brown, Judith K. A cross-cultural study of making a living: subsistence variables in Textor's A cross-cultural summary. Paper presented at 68th Annual Meeting of the American Anthropological Association. 20 to 23 November, 1969. New Orleans, Louisiana.

Geographers such as Sauer, and Bobek and anthropologists such as Forde and Murdock have suggested that the interrelationships among subsistence activities, dietary staples and division of labor by gender are far from arbitrary. These interrelationships among the subsistence variables themselves are examined together with their relationships with other variables such as inflation rites.

1108. Brown, Judith K. 1970. Subsistence variables: a comparison of Textor and Sauer. Ethnology 9: 160-164.

Uses the statistical data in Robert B. Textor's A cross-cultural summary (1967) to test hypotheses related to subsistence variables put forward by Carl O. Sauer in Agricultural origins and dispersals (1952)

1109. Brown, Myrtle L. & Adelson, Saydie F. 1969. Infant feeding practices among low- and middle-income families in Honolulu. TGM 21: 53-61.

A predominant pattern of artificial feeding and early feeding of solid foods was observed among the majority of low and middle-income families. Overall incidence of breast-feeding, in a sample of 249 mothers and 281 children, was 25 percent. Greater incidence of breast-feeding occurred among middle-income and Japanese women. Feeding of solid foods during the first three months of life did not appear to be related to ethnicity.

1110. Brown, Myrtle L. & Ho, Claire Hughes. Low-income groups in Hawaii. Infant and childhood feeding practices among low-income families in urban Hawaii. In Practices of low-income families in feeding infants and small children, with particular attention to cultural sub-groups. Edited by Samuel J. Fomon & T.A. Anderson. 1972. Pp. 91-95. Washington, D.C.:   U.S. Department of Health, Education and Welfare.

Covers introduction to solid foods, vitamin and mineral supplementation, and nutrient intakes.

1111.   Brown, M.L.; Worth, R.M., & Shah, N.K. 1968. Food habits and food intake in Nepal. TGM 20: 217-224.

1112.   Brown, P.T. & Bergan, J.G.   1975.   The dietary status of practicing macrobiotics: a preliminary communication. EFN 4: 103-107.

The macrobiotic diet is a vegetarian regimen and a component of a larger philosophical system with roots in traditional Japanese religious thought. This paper analyzes the nutritional inadequacies of the diet, for children and adults.

1113.   Brown, Paula. 1972. The Chimbu: a study of change in the New Guinea highlands. Cambridge, Massachusetts: Schenckman Publishing Co.

1114.   Brown, R. 1868. On the vegetable products used by the Northwest American Indians as food and medicine, in the arts, and in superstitious rites. BSE-T 9: 378-396.

1115.   Brown, Roy E.   1978.   Weaning foods in developing countries. AJCN 31: 2066-2072.

Importance of weaning foods; definitions; cultural influences; weaning foods, their preparation, and contamination.

1116.   Brown, Sanborn C. 1954. Count Rumford: a bicentennial review. Am Sci 42: 113-127.

Biographical sketch of the Colonial American expatriate who, among other accomplishments, invented the antecedent of the modern kitchen range; the drip coffee pot; developed a school-lunch program in the Munich work-house he established; introduced the New World potato to Germany; and initiated a public feeding program, the basis of which was the 'Rumford' soup, still served in Europe.

1117.   Brown, William H. 1920. Wild food plants of the Philippines. In Minor products of Philippine forests. PI-DANR-BF-B No. 21.

Food plants are listed by botanical family, genus and species. Part of plant used, and method of preparation are given.

1118.   Brown, William H. & Fischer, Arthur F. 1918. Philippine mangrove swamps. P-DANR-BF-B No. 17. Pp. 119-1127.

1119.   Brown, William L.; Anderson, Edgar G.; & Tuchawena, Jr., Roy. 1952. Observations on three varieties of Hopi maize. AJB 39: 597-609.

1120.   Browne, Daniel Jay, comp. 1847. Memoir on maize or Indian corn. New York: W.H. Graham.

Recipes: Pp. 49-56.

1121.   Browne, Marva Z. & Nomani, M.Z.A. 1978. Nutritional assessment of Virgin Islands school children. JADA 73: 411-415.

1122.   Browning, Clara W. & Munsell, Edith J. 1913. A story of certain table furnishings. CorU-CRC-RLS 3 No. 4.

History of table ware, napkins, and porcelain.

1123.   Browning, K.C. & Symons, C.T.   1916. Coconut toddy in Ceylon. SCI-J 35: 1138-1142.

Production, use, and chemical analysis of sap of Cocos nucifera. Products derived from sap include crude sugar, vinegar, alcoholic and non-alcoholic beverages.

1124.   Brozek, Josef. 1950. Psychology of human starvation and nutritional rehabilitation.   SM 70:270-274.

1125.   Brozek, Josef. 1953. Measuring nutriture. AJPA 11: 147-180.

1126.   Brozek, Josef. 1955. Nutrition and psyche with special reference to experimental psychodietetics. AJCN 3: 101-113.

1127.   Brozek, Josef, ed. 1956. Body measurements and human nutrition. Detroit: Wayne State University Press.

1128.   Brozek, Josef. 1959. Experimental studies on the impact of deficient diet on behavior. BRNR 20: 75-88.

1129.   Bruch, Hilda. 1944. Food and emotional security. NC 3: 165-173.

1130.   Bruch, Hilda. 1978. The golden cage: the enigma of anorexia nervosa. Cambridge, Massachusetts: Harvard University Press.

Considers the sociological environment in which this psychological problem is usually generated. Case histories, and comments on medical treatment are included.

1131.   Brues, C.T. 1936. Aberrant feeding behavior among insects and its bearing on the development of specialized food habits. QRB 11: 305-309.

1132.   Brugge, David M. 1965. Navajo use of agave. Kiva 31: 88-98.

Traces the origins of Navajo mescal use, its preparation and food use, and variations in the latter as compared with other southwestern United States groups utilizing the plant.

1133. Brugsch, Heinrich Karl. 1890. Die Kosten des Haushalts in alter Zeit. [Household fare in olden times.] Berlin: L. Simon.

1134. Bruhn, Crhistine M. & Pangborn, Rose Marie. 1971. Food habits of migrant farm workers in California. Comparison between Mexican-Americans and Anglos. JADA 58: 347-355.

1135. Bruhn, Christine M., & Pangborn, Rose Marie. 1971. Reported incidence of pica among migrant families. JADA 58: 417-420.

1136. Bruhn, F. 1906. Kefir und Kumys. [Kefir and Kumiss.] ZFMH 16: 181-184.

Two fermented milk products.

1137. Bruman, Henry John. Aboriginal drink areas in New Spain. Ph.D dissertation. University of California. Berkeley. 1940.

1138. Bruman, Henry John. 1944. Some observations on the early history of the coconut in the New World. Acta Am 2: 228-243.

1139. Brunet, Diane Clarabel. The influences of the cultural milieu upon choices in infant feeding. Master's thesis. Syracuse, New York: Syracuse University. 1970.

1140. Bruneton, Ariane. Bread in the region of the Moroccan High Atlas: a chain of daily technical operations in order to provide daily nourishment. In Gastronomy. The anthropology of food and food habits. Edited by Margaret Louise Arnott. 1975. Pp. 275-285. Paris, The Hague: Mouton Publishers. World Anthropology.

Describes grains used; milling, winnowing, ovens, baking, and bread types and their uses among the Ait Mgun, a Berber tribe of the Infdwak group, inhabiting the Tessaout Valley.

1141. Bruniguel. Madagascar. In L'alimentation indigene dans les colonies francaises. Protectorats et territoires sous mandats. Edited by G. Hardy & C. Richet. 1933. Pp. 227-240. Paris: Vigot Freres.

Concise ethnography of native food uses.

1142. Bruniquel. La Reunion. [Reunion.] In L'alimentation indigene dans les colonies francaises. Protectorats et territoires sous mandats. Edited by G. Hardy & C. Richet. 1933. Pp. 241-243. Paris: Vigot Freres.

Notes that the food of this Indian Ocean islands is a combination of European, African, and East Indian. Describes briefly the food pattern, and the use of locally produced rum.

1143. Brunow, G. de. 1824. Traite sur les effets du cafe. [Treatise on the effects of coffee.] Translated from German by G. de Brunow. Dresden: Arnold.

1143. Brunson, Rose T. Socialization experiences and socio-economic characteristics of urban Negroes as related to use of selected southern foods and medical remedies. Ph.D dissertation. Michigan State University. 1962.

1144. Brunton, Ruth Carolyn. Effect of a good diet in pregnancy on a woman and her infant. Masters's thesis. University of Colorado. 1948.

1145. Brunvand, Jan. 1962. Milk recipes for 'planked' game. WF 21: 45-46.

Four jesting recipes for cooking game, on a plank, of the type foisted on greenhorns.

1146. Brush, Edward F. no date. Kumyss. Mt. Vernon, New York: the author.

Medical uses of a fermented milk product.

1147. Brush, Edward F. 1903. Kumyss of the Kirghis steppes. Mt. Vernon, New York: the author.

Historic, ethnographic, and etymological study of a Central Asian fermented milk product.

1148. Brush, Stephen B. Subsistence strategies and vertical ecology in an Andean community: Uchucmarca, Peru. Ph.D dissertation. Anthropology. University of Wisconsin, Madison. 1973.

1149. Brush, Stephen B. 1976. Man's use of an Andean ecosystem. HEcol 4: 147-166.

This article discusses the natural and crop zonation in one valley of the Chachapoyas region of northeastern Peru. The entire valley is exploited by the community of Uchucmarca. Land use patterns are described and the boundaries of food crop cultivation are enumerated, together with characteristic hazards which jeopardize the crops of planted beyond the boundaries.

1150. Bryan, A.H. & Anderson, E.L. 1960. Retrospective dietary interviewing. JADA 37: 558-561.

1151. Bryan, Julian. 1969. Preparing a meal. Food preparation and eating a meal. Bozo tribe, Niger River. New York: Harper & Row.

A super-8 mm color film loop; running-time: 3 minutes, 40 seconds.

1152. Bryan, M.S. & Lowenberg, Miriam E. 1958. The father's influence on young children's food habits. JADA 34: 30-35.

1153. Bryan, William Alanson. 1915. Natural history of Hawaii. Honolulu: Hawaiian Gazette Co.

Native consumption of edible fish and manner of preparation: pp. 349; edible mussels: p. 443.

1154.   Bryant, A.T.   1907.   A description of native foodstuffs and their preparation.   Maritzburg: Printed for the Natal Government.

South Africa.

1155.   Bryant, Carol.   Impact of social network members and health professionals on infantile obesity among Cubans, Puerto Ricans and Anglos in Dade County, Florida.   Paper presented at 76th Annual Meeting of the American Anthropological Association. 29 November to 3 December, 1977.   Houston, Texas.

Values, norms, and feeding practices associated with infantile obesity are described for the three groups.   Compared with Anglo mothers, Latins perceive fatter babies as the cutest, the healthiest, and the best reflection of good maternal care.   The impact of social network members and health care professionals on infantile obesity and infant weight norms is assessed.   Social networks are shown to play a critical role in mothers' compliance with recommendations to control their babies' weights.

1156.   Bryant, Charles.   1783.   Flora diaetetica; or history of esculent plants, both domestic and foreign.   London: B. White.

1157.   Bryant, J.P.   1925.   The six cardinal points. N Mill 141: 325.

Important factors in judging bread quality: flavor, texture, moisture, bloom, volume, general appearance.

1158.   Bryant, L.S.   1913.   School feeding, its history and practice at home and abroad.   Philadelphia: J.B. Lippincott.

1159.   Bryant, Vaugh.   1974.   Prehistoric diet in southwest Texas: the coprolite evidence.   A Ant 39: 407-420.

Ca. 800 B.C. to ca. A.D. 500.

1160.   Bryant, Walter E.   1891.   The "reed birds" of the San Fransisco markets.   Zoe 2: 142-145.

Methods of marketing, hunting and serving. The birds here identified as "reed" birds (Dolichonyx oryzivorous) are presumed atually to be a horned lark (Octoris), and several species of sparrow.   (Zonotrichia), house finch (Carpodacus), blackbirds. (Agelaius, and Scolecophagus), and sandpipers (Tringa minutilla) and Ereunetes occidentalis).

1161.   Bryce, Alexander.   1912.   World theories of diet.   London: Longmans, Green.

1162.   Bryce, Peter H.   1919.   Year's changes in food habits.   AJPH 9: 108-113.

Effects of World War I on U.S. and Canadian food consumption.

1163.   Bryden, W. Chapter Fifteen.   Aborigines.   In Biogeography and ecology in Tasmania.   Edited by William David Williams.   1974.   Pp. 417-433.   The Hague: W. Junk.

Food of Tasmanian Aborigines: p. 425.

1164.   Bryusov, Alexander Ia.   The problem of drinking water in antiquity.   In 5 Internationale Kongress fur Vor-und Frugeschichte.   24 bis 30 August 1958.   Hamburg.   Edited by Gerhard Bersu. 1961.   Pp. 159-162.   Berlin: Verlag Gebruddern Mann.

Conjectural and archeological evidence for techniques used to obtain pure water with reference to the White Sea area.

1165.   Buccieri, Theresa F. 1966.   Feasting with nonna Serafina.   (A guide to the Italian kitchen). New Brunswick, New Jersey: A.S. Barnes & Co.

1166.   Buchanan, J.C.R., comp.   1947.   A guide to Pacific Island dietaries.   Souva, Fiji: South Pacific Health Services.   Another edition: Wellington: H.H. Tombs.

1167.   Buchbinder, Georgeda.   Maring microdaptation: a study of demographic, nutritional, and phenotypic variation in a Highland New Guinea population.   Ph.D dissertation.   Columbia University. 1973.

1168.   Buchbinder, Georgeda.   Endemic cretinism among the Maring: a by-product of culture contact. In Nutrition and anthropology in action.   Edited by Thomas K. Fitzgerald.   1976.   Pp. 106-116.   Assen, Amsterdam: Van Gorcum.

Describes the unanticipated consequences of replacement of iodine-rich salt of native manufacture by uniodized trade salt.   The Maring are swidden horticulturalists, who inhabit the central Sibai and Jimi Valleys, in the Bismarck Mountain region of the central New Guinea Highlands' northern fringe.

1169.   Buchbinder, Georgeda.   They are what they eat: the social significance of food taboos among the Maring of New Guiniea.   Paper presented at 76th Annual Meeting of the American Anthropological Association.   29 November to 3 December, 1977.   Houston, Texas.

The Maring have an elaborate and highly developed system of food taboos.   There are three major categories of such avoidances. The first regualtes food sharing and interdining with enemies.   The second relates to clan totems, and the third to mourning.   In addition to these, there are other sets of avoidances related to age, sex, and ritual status.   All of these avoidances carry a high degree of affect as well as supernatural sanctions.   Because of the crosscutting nature of these sets of taboos, each adult suffers under a unique set of restrictions.

Thus, a Maring adult may be socially defined by what and with whom he or she eats.

1170. Buchinger, O. 1968. Das Heilfasten und Seine Hillfsmethoden als biologischner Weg. [The healthfast and its therapeutic methods as a biological procedure. Stuttgart: Hippokrates Verlag.

History of health fasting: pp. 13-30.

1171. Buc'hoz, Joseph-Pierre. no date. Dissertation analytique sur l'histoire generale et economique de trois regnes de la nature, principalement sur l'histoire naturelle de l'homme, et sur les differens ouvrages de medicine et de matiere alimentaire. [Analytic dissertation on the general and economic history of three realms of nature, principally on the natural history of man, and on the different works of medicine and food materials.] Paris: Prevost et Barrois.

Held by the Bibliotheque Nationale, Paris. No. 51403 (23).

1172. Buc'hoz, Joseph-Pierre. no date. Dissertation sur la bandure, plante des plus rares et de plus curieuses...qui distille continuellement de l'eau dans un resrvoir place a l'extremite de ses feuilles pour appaiser la soif des voyageurs. [Treatise on the pitcher plant, most rare and curious of plants...which continuously distills water in a reservoir placed at the extremity of its leaves to appease the thirst of travellers.] Paris: the author.

1173. Buc'hoz, Joseph-Pierre. no date. Dissertation sur le durion, arbre des Indes orientales, qui donne un fruit bon a manger et qui merite d'etre cultive dans nos colonies. [Dissertation on the durian, an East Indian tree, which produces a fruit which is good to eat, and which merits being cultivated in our colonies.] Paris: the author.

Held by the Bibliotheque Nationale, Paris. No. S1425 (17).

1174. Buc'hoz, Joseph-Pierre. 1771. Manuel alimentaire des plantes tant indigenes qu' exotiques qui peuvent servir de nourriture et de boisson aux differens peuples de la terre; cotenant la connoissance exacte de tous les vegetaux qui croissent sous les deux hemispheres, leurs noms triviaux et botaniques, suivant les auteurs les plus celebres, l'utilite qu'on en peut tirer dans la vie animale et les differentes manieres de les preparer pour la cuisine, l'office, la distillation et pour les differens usages de l'economie domestique. [Food manual of indigenous as well as exotic plants which can serve as food and drink among different peoples of the earth; containing knowledge of all the vegetables which grow under the two hemispheres, their common and botanical names, following the most celebrated authors; the use one can make of them in animal life and the different ways of preparing them for cooking, food service, distilling and for different uses in domestic economy.] Paris: J.-P. Costard.

1175. Buc'hoz, Joseph-Pierre. 1774-1780. Histoire universelle du regne vegetal, ou nouveau dictionnaire physique et oeconomique de toutes les plantes qui croissent sur la surface du globe. 26 vols. [Universal history of the vegetable kingdom, or a new physical and economic dictionary of all the plants which grow on the surface of the globe.] Paris: Costard (Brunet).

1176. Buc'hoz, Joseph-Pierre. 1783. L'art alimentaire ou methode pour preparer les alients les plus sains pour l'homme. [The art of cookery or method of preparing the most wholesome food for humans.] Paris: no publisher cited.

1177. Buc'hoz, Joseph-Pierre. 1785. Dissertation sur le cacao, sur sa culture et sur les differents preparations du chocolat. [Dissertation on cacao, on its cultivation and on the different preparations of chocolate. Paris: the author.

1178. Buc'hoz, Joseph-Pierre. 1785. Dissertation sur le cafe; sa culture, ses differentes preparations & ses proprietes tant alimentaires, que medicinales. [Dissertation on coffee; its cultivation, different methods of preparation and alimentary as well as medicinal properties.] Paris: the author.

1179. Buc'hoz, Joseph-Pierre. 1787. Dissertatioin sur l'abre au pain de premiere necessite pour la nourriture d'un grand nombre d' habitants et qui merite d'etre cultive dans nos colonies. [Dissertation on the bread-fruit tree, staple food for a large number of inhabitants and which merits being grown in our colonies.] Paris: the author.

1180. Buchoz, Joseph-Pierre. 1804. Memoire sur le ble de smyrne, autrement ble d'abondance, sur le ble de Turquie, le millet d'Afrique et la po-herbe [sic] d'Abyssinie. [Memoir on Smyrna wheat, formerly abundant, Turkish wheat, African millet and the poherb of Abyssinia.] Paris: Aux frais de la dame Buc'hoz.

1181. Buc'hoz, Joseph-Pierre. 1806. Histoire naturelle du the de la Chine, de ses differentes especes, de sa recolte, de ses preparations, de sa culture en Europe, de l'usage qu'on en fait, comme boisson, chez differenes peuples, pricipalement en Angleterre. A laquelle on a joint un memoire sur le the du Paraguay, de Labrador, des Isles, du Cap, du Mexique, d'Oswego, de la Martinique, etc., etc. [Natural history of Chinese tea, its different species, its harvest, its preparation, the use that is made of it as a beverage among different peoples, principally in England. To which is joined a memoir on the teas of Paraguay, Labrador, the Islands [sic], the Cape, Mexico, of the Oswego, of Martinique, etc., etc.] Paris: by Madame Buc'hoz, the author's wife.

1182. Buc'hoz, Joseph-Pierre. 1812. Traite usuel du chocolat...Edition redigee par l'editeur (et composee en partie par J.P. Buc'hoz.) [Common treatise on chocolate...Edition drawn up by the publisher (and composed in part by. P.J. Buc'hoz).] Paris: Chambon.

1183. Buck, John Lossing. 1926. An economic and social survey of 150 farms, Yenshan County, Chihli Province, China. UN-P-CAF-B No. 13.

1184. Buck, John Lossing. 1930. Chinese farm economy. A study of 2866 farms. Shanghai: University of Nanking.

One chapter pertains to food consumption.

1185.   Buck, Peter Henry. (Te Rangi Hiroa). 1921. Maori food supplies of Lake Rotorua, with methods of obtaining them, and usage and customs appertaining thereto. NZI-TP. 53:433-451.

1186.   Buck, Peter Henry. (Te Rangi Hiroa). 1925. The pre-European diet of the Maori. NZDJ 20:203-217.

1187.   Buck, Peter Henry. [Te Rangi Hiroa] 1927. Maori health. MJA 2 [Supp. 5]: 146-150. 10 September.

Meat; fish; plant foods; fruit; berries. Meals; variety in diet; mastication of food.

1188.   Buck, Peter Henry. (Te Rangi Hiroa). 1932. Ethnology of Manihiki and Rakahang. BPBM-B No. 99.
Food habits: pp. 83-101.

1189.   Buck, Peter Henry. (Te Rangi Hiroa). 1938. Vikings of the sunrise. New York: Frederick A. Stokes Co.

Origin of cooking. In the Australs and Tubuai (myth): p. 168.

1190.   Buck, Peter Henry. (Te Rangi Hiroa). 1950. Material culture of Kapingamarangi. BPBM-B No. 200.

Food: Pp. 3-50, cookhouses: p.75.

1191.   Buck, Peter Henry. (Te Rangi Hiroa). 1964. Arts and crafts of Hawaii. Section 1. Food. BPBM-SP No. 45.

Historic foods of the Hawaiian Islands; utensils; preparation techniques; customs.

1192.   Buckland, Anne Walbank. 1893. Our viands, whence they come and how they are cooked, with a bundle of old recipes from cookery books of the last century. London: Ward and Downey.

Traces the history of certain preparations and their ingredients.

1193.   Buckner, Dorothy. 1933. A study of the economic status of undernourished children in the Boston Dispensary, 1930-19331. HSS 27: 607-612.

Relationship of economic depression and low income to under nutrition.

1194.   Budin, K.Z. 1971. Ispolzovanie mirovoi kolektsii v seleksii vuisokoproduktivnikh i vuisokokachestvennich sortov i gibridov. [Use of the world's collection of plants for breeding high-productive and high quality varieties and hybrids.] Sel'sko Biol 6: 328-337.

Collection includes wild species, ancient and native varieties and all principal farm crops. Collection is located at N.I. Vavilov All-Union Scientific Research Institute of Plant Breeding.

1195.   Buehr, Wendy. 1968. The horizon cookbook and illustrated history of eating and drinking through the ages. New York: American Heritage Publishing Co.

1196.   Bugbee, James M. 1885. Cocoa and chocolate; a short history of their production and use, and with a full and particular account of their properties, and of the various methods of preparing them for food. Dorchester, Massachusetts: Walter Baker & Company.

1197.   Builder, A. 1939. L'eau potable. [Drinking water.] Paris: Payot.

1198.   Buisson, Emile. 1941. Enquete sur les vegetaux dans et l'ethnographie. [Inquiry upon vegetables in folklore and ethnography.] Ethnographie No. 39. Pp. 93-118.

1199.   Buisson, Emile. 1943. Suite de l'enquete sur les vegetaux dans le folklore et l'ethnographie Tatuages du Cameroun, representatifs de vegetaux. 2. Une plante fetiche du Haut-Cameroun. 3. Plantes medicinales utilisees dans l'Oubangui meridional. [Continuation of the inquiry on vegetables in folklore and ethnography. 1. Cameroon tatoo depicting vegetables. 2. A fetish plant of Upper Cameroon. 3. Medicinal plants used in Central Oubangui]. Ethnographie No.43. Pp. 93-100.

1200.   Buisson-Lefresne, J. 1968. Some exotic fruits on the French market - their nutritional value. [In French.] Al Vie 56: 5-16.

1201.   Bukasov, S.M. 1954. The cultivated plants of Mexico, Guatemala and Colombia. Translated by H.J. Kidd. MBG-A 41: 271-299.

1202.   Bullock, R.A. Population and nutrition in central and Western Kenya. Ph.D. dissertation. University of London. 1969.

1203.   Bunge, G. 1885. Der Vegetarianismus: ein Vortrag. [Vegetarianism: a discourse.]. Berlin: Hirschwald. Reviewed in BMJ 1: 352 (1885).

1204.   Bulmer, R. 1964. Edible seeds and prehistoric stone mortars in the Highlands of New Guinea. Man 64: 147-150.

1205.   Bunzel, Ruth. 1940. The role of alcoholism in two Central American cultures. Psychiatry 3: 361.-387.

1206.   Buonassisi, Vincenzo. 1973. Pasta. Translated by Elisabeth Evans. Wilton, Connecticut: Lyceum Books.

The Introduction contains a brief history. The book is illustrated throughout by color plates on exhibition at the historic museum of pasta at Pontedassio, Imperia.

1207.   Burch, Jr., Ernest S. 1972. The caribou/wild reindeer as a human resource. Am An 37:339-368.

Food use of Rangifer tarandus: pp. 362-363.

1208. Burch, Tillie. 1944. In the Pueblo kitchen. N Mex 22:18.

Native American cookery in New Mexico.

1209. Burchard, Roderick E. Coca and food exchanges in Andean Peru: or how to turn one sack of potatoes in eight. Paper presented at 70th Annual Meeting of the American Anthropological Association. 21 November, 1971. New York City.

Examines strategies developed by a Peruvian highland peasant community for maximizing scarce resources through exchange. Food and coca exchanges are studied as well as the socioeconomic alliances which develop between the community members themselves and with peasants from different ecological zones outside the community. In such a network, it is theoretically possible for a peasant to maximize one sack of potatoes to eight; however, this can only be done by violating traditional norms of reciprocity.

1210. Burchard, Roderick E. A new perspective of coca and food. Paper presented at 9th International Congress of Anthropological and Ethnological Sciences, 28 August to September, 1973. Chicago, Illinois.

Argues that access to coca has meant and continues to mean access to food for Andean peasants and that peasants are able to maximize limited food production through a long-standing strategy of cocoa and food exchange between peasants located in different ecological zones at different altitudes producing different resources.

1211. Burchard, Roderick E. Coca leaf, food, work and peasant health in the Andes. Paper presented at 77th Annual Meeting of the American Anthropological Association. 14-18 November, 1977. Los Angeles, California.

1212. Burdsall, Richard L. & Emmons, Arthur B. 1935. Men against the clouds. The conquest of Minya Konka. New York, London: Harper & Brothers.

Food of mountain climbing expedition: Pp. 75, 152, 177, 186-187, 193, 276-277.

1213. Burema, L. 1953. De voeding in Nederland van de middeleeuwen tot de twingtigste eeuw. [Food in the Netherlands from the Middle Ages to the Twentieth Century.] Ph.D dissertations, Amsterdam. Assen: Van Gorcum.

1214. Burger, Henry G. Ethnorama: directing subsistent transculturation by schoolroom simulation. Paper presented at 70th Annual Meeting of the American Anthropolocial Association. 21 November, 1971. New York City.

Modeling and gaming enrich cognitive overemphasis with affect and sensorimotion; statics with diachrony; certitude with environmental risk. Recent crossethnic simula-

tion by game designers, however, serves mostly Western world middle class. It should expand to serve Third World students confronting Western impact. Nonindustrial cultures already use audiovisuals for teaching navigation, herding, etc. Western presentations, including flashbacks and pannings, must accommodate bicultural individuals. Hybird seed can be dramatized with hot-housing; butchering allotment charts with carvable plastic; etiquette with videotaped crises, literacy with printing kits. The result is ethnopedagogy by diorama.

1215. Burgess, Anne P. 1961 - 1962. Nutrition and food habits. IJHE 4: 55-58.

1216. Burgess, Anne P., & Dean, Reginald Francis Alfred. 1962. Malnutrition and food habits. Report of an internation and interprofessional conference. New York: Macmillan.

Edited proceedings of the classic interdisciplinary meeting at Cuernavaca, which delineated the scope, procedures, and goals of social science in applied nutritional change and nutrition education.

1217. Burgess, Anne P., Morton, Christine; & Burgess, H.J.L. 1962. Diet of some Uganda schoolgirls. EAMJ 39: 464-477.,

1218. Burgess, H.J.L. 1962. Cereal foods used in Uganda. 1. Millets and sorghum. EAMJ 39: 437-442. 2. Maise. 39: 443-448.

Both parts make mention of food uses.

1219. Burgess, H.J.L. 1962. Notes on the possible use of wild game as a source of food in Uganda. EAMJ 39: 431-436.

1220. Burgess, H.J.L., & Wheeler, E. Lower shire nutrition survey. A report of a nutritional status and dietary survey carried out in Ngabu Area, April - May. 1970. Mimeographed. Lilongwe [?] Malawi: Ministry of Health. 1970.

The villages studied are Billey, Chamanga, Chapamoka, Chindoko, Mandele, Masache, N'Chacha, Nguluwe, Salabene, and Zwake. The Ngabu Area is located at approximately 16. 27 S, 34. 55 E. Correlation is attempted for children's nutritional status and family data. Food consumption frequency meal pattern; production and consumption data are provided.

1221. Burgess, R.C. & Laidin, Bin Alang Musa. 1950. A report on the state of health, the diet and the economic conditions of groups of people in the lower income levels in Malaya. Kuala Lumpur: Institute of Medical Research.

1222. Burgstaller, Ernst. 1957. Brauchtumsgebacke und Weihnachtsspeisen. [Traditional baked goods and Christmas foods.] Linz: Zentralstelle fur des Volkskundeatlas in Osterreich.

1223.   Burian, V. 1961. Lidova strava na Vyskovsku v polovine devatenacteho stoleto. [Folk diet in Vijskov region in the middle of the Nineteenth Century.] CE 9: 192-194.

1224.   Burk, Marguerite C. 1958. An economic appraisal of change in rural food consumption. JFE 40: 572-590.

1225.   Burkart, Arturo & Bruchner, H. 1953. Phaseolus aborigineus, Burkart, die muttmassliche andine Stammform der Kulturbohne. [Phaseolus aborigineus, Burkart, the supposed Andean original form of the cultivated bean.] DZ 23: 65-72.

1226.   Burke, Georgine S. & Allan, Lindsay H. Methodological issues in the measurement of dietary complexity. Paper presented at 77th Annual Meeting of the American Anthropological Association. 14 to 18 November, 1978. Los Angeles, California.

1227.   Burkill, Isaac Henry. 1904. The tapioca plant, its history, cultivation and uses. AL No. 10 Pp. 123-148.

1228.   Burkill, Isaac Henry. 1906. Goa beans in India. AL No. 4 Pp. 51-64.

1229.   Burkill, Isaac Henry. 1911. Edible frogs. AL No. 4. Pp. 11-15.

Frogs used as food in India.

1230.   Burkill, Isaac Henry. 1935. A dictionary of the economic products of the Malay Peninsula. With contributions by Frederick W. Foxworthy, J.B. Scrivener, and J.G. Watson. Published on behalf of the Governments of the Straits Settlements and Federated Malay States. London: Crown Agents for the Colonies.

1231.   Burkhill, Isaac Henry. 1937-1938. The contact of the Portuguese with African food plants which gave words such as 'yam' to Europoean languages. LSL-P 150th Session. Pp. 84-95.

An etymological study of the relationship between Colocasia esculentum and the West African Temne (Sierra Leone) word enyame.

1232.   Burkill, Isaac Henry. 1953. Habits of man and the origins of cultivated plants of the Old World. LSL-P 164th Session. Pp. 12-42.

1233.   Burkill, Isaac Henry. 1953. The vegetables eaten with rice in two typical Malay households of the neighborhood of Telok Anson, southern Perak. G Bull 14: 17-29.

1234.   Burnet, E. 1938. L'alimentation en Tunisie. [Food in Tunisia.] IPT-A 27-89-95.

1235.   Burnet, E., E Visconti, M. 1939. Composition of some Tunisian dishes. [In French.] IPT-A 28: 339-349.

1236.   Burnett, J. The history of food adulteration in Great Britain in the Nineteenth Century, with special reference to bread, tea and beer. Ph.D. dissertation. University of London. 1958.

1237.   Burns, H.A. & Ching, Ah-Gwah. 1942. The American Indian's contribution. Food and drugs. J Lan 62: 12-15.

1238.   Burrill, W.M. & Alsop, B. 1955. Food habits of South Dakota women. SD-AES-B No. 451.

1239.   Burrill, W.M.; Alsop, B,; Schuck, C.; Swanson, P.; Ohlson, M.A.; Biester, A., Leverton, Ruth M.; Reynolds, M.S.; & Mangel, M. 1959. Evaluation of the self-chosen diets of 402 women 30-97 years of age in seven north central States. SD-AES-B No. 478.

1240.   Burris, Evadene A. Frontier homes and management. Master's thesis. University of Minnesota. 1933.

Minesota during the 1850's.

1241.   Burris, Evadene. 1933. Frontier food. MH 14: 378-392.

This article is a chapter from the author's Master's thesis. It is an example of utilization of the literature in local history and personal reminiscence. The article describes food and beverages commercially available during the 1850's, in Minnesota territory; maple-sugaring techniques of the Chippewa; food substitutes; recipes; grain production statistics, and typical dietaries of poor, and well-to-do settlers.

1242.   Burrows, Fredrika Alexander A. 1976. Cannonballs and cranberries. Taunton, Massachusetts: William S. Sullwold.

History and technology of cranberry industry in Massachusetts: pp. 51-91.

1243.   Burrows, W. 1953. Notes on molluscs used as food by the Fijians. FS-TP 2:12-14.

1244.   Burton, John. 1963. The introduction of the potato in Ireland and England. HEJ 21: 71-78.

1245.   Burton, Jr., Warren Hepburn. The agriculture problem of the Navajo Indian Reservation. Master's thesis. Worcester, Massachusetts: Clark University. 1954.

1246.   Burtt-Davy, Joseph. 1910-1911. Poisonous properties of Rhadi-ferment. USAfr-DA-R: P. 244.

The root of Mesembrianthemum mahoni. after paring, drying, and powdering, is used to some extent in South Africa as a substitute for yeast in bread making and for fermenting Kaffir beer. Its hazardous quality, due to presence of 3% oxalic acid content, is considered.

1247.   Burtt-Davy, Joseph. 1913. Maize. Its history, cultivation, handling, and uses. With special reference to South Africa. A text-book for farmers, students of agriculture, and teachers of nature study. London, New York, Bombay, Caluctta: Longmans, Green & Co.

History, including its possible presence in the Old World prior to 1492, etymologies of and vernacular terms: pp. 9-24; maize as human food, with special reference to native South African groups: pp. 673-701. Includes excerpts from the historical literature; and several brief inexact recipes, for use as a base for fermented and non-fermented beverages.

1248.   Buschan, Georg. 1891. Ein Blick in die Kuche der Vorzeit. [A look into the kitchen of ages past.] Arch Anth 23: 23-24.

1249.   Buschan, Georg. 1893. Chenopodium-Samen als Nahrungsmittel. [Chenopodium seeds as foodstuff.] ZE: 25:28.

1250.   Buschan, George. 1895. Vorgeschichtliche Botanik der Kultur-und Nutzpflanzer der Alten Welt auf Grund Prahistorischen Funde. [Prehistoric botany of cultivated and useful plants of the Old World from archaeological finds.] Breslau: J.U. Kern's Verlag.

1251.   Buschmann, J. Ottokar von. 1909. Das salz, dessen Vorkommen und Verwertung in Samtlichen staten der Erde. [Salt, its occurrence and use in all the nations of the world.] Leipzig: W. Engelmann.

1252.   Bushnell, Jr., David I. 1909. The Choctaw of Bayou La Comb, Louisiana. SI-BAE-B No. 48.

Food supply: Pp. 8-10.

1253.   Bushnell, John H., & Bushnell, Donna D. Cultural and psychological aspects of the food complex in a Matlatzinca village, 1950 - 1970. Paper presented at 69th Annual Meeting of the American Anthropological Association. 19 to 22 November, 1970. San Diego, California.

1254.   Buskirk, Winfred. Western Apache subsistence economy. Ph.D. dissertation. University of New Mexico. 1949.

1255.   Busse, W. & Pilger, R. 1902. Ueber Culturformen der Sorghum-hirse aus Deutsch Ost-africa und Togo. [On the methods of cultivation of sorghum-millet in German East Africa and Togo.] EB Jahr 32: 182-189.

1256.   Busson, F. A chemical and biological study of food plants in West Africa, in their relation to the geographical and human environment. [In French] Ph.D. dissertation. Universite de Marseille. 1965.

1257.   Bustamente, M.E. & Herrera, J.R. 1942. Sanitation among the Maya about the years 436-534. [In Spanish.] I SET-R 3: 251-253.

1258.   Bustrillos, N.R. 1963. The family meal and the child in a rural area. HE 1: 41-55.

1259.   Buszek, Beatrice Ross. 1978. The cranberry connection. Cranberry cookery with flavour, fact, and folklore, from memories, libraries, and kitchens of old and new friends and strangers. 2nd ed. Brattleboro, Vermont: Stephen Greene Press.

1260.   Butler, Eva L. A preliminary outline of Algonkian culture and use of maize in southern New England. Master's thesis. University of Pennsylvania. 1946.

1261.   Butler, Eva L. 1946. A preliminary outline of Algonkian culture and use of maize in southern New England. ASC-B 22: 3-39.

1262.   Butler, Helen S. 1967. Hospital feeding of immigrants from India and Pakistan. Nutrition (L). 21: 28-34.

Observations on the need for considering religious restrictions. Recipes given for curry and chutney.

1263.   Butterfield, Harry M. 1963. A history of subtropical fruits and nuts in California. University of California. Division of Agricultural sciences. Agricultural Extension Service. Berkeley: University of California Agricultural Experiment Station. [Limited distribution]

1264.   Buttes, Henry. 1599. Dyets dry dinner: consisting of eight several courses: 1. fruits. 2. Hearbes. 3. Flesh. 4. Fish. 5. Whitemeats. 6. Spice. 7.Sauce. 8. Tobacco. All served in the order of Time universall. London: Tho. Creede for William Wood.

Held by British Museum, London. No. C.31 b.8.

1265.   Buyckx, E.J. & Decelle, J. 1957. Resultats d'une enquete sur la conservation des denrees au Congo Belge. [Results of an inquiry concerning the preservation of comestibles in the Belgian Congo.] BACB 48: 1163-1171.

1. Preservation among native groups. 2. Principles and methods; means of preserving maize, rice, sorghum, peanuts, green beans, manioc. 3. Commercial aspects of the harvest. a. warehousing among middlemen; b. stocking among distributors.

1266.   Buzina, R.; Ferber, E.; Keys, A.; Brodarel, A.; Agneletto, B.; & Horvat, A. 1964. Diets of rural families and heads of families in two regions of Yugoslavia. Voeding 25: 629-639.

1267.   Buzzo, A.; Agostini de Munoz, A.; & Calabrese, A. 1939. Causes of diversion for maternal breast, with special reference to alcoholism. [In Spanish,] SPBA-A 5: 183-186.

1268.   Bylund. H.B. 1957-1958. Socio-economic status, national origin help determine liking for mushrooms. S Farm 5:13.

1270.   Byrd, James W. 1968. Review of Let noon be fair, by Willard Motley. New York: Dell Distributing Company. TFSB 34:31-32.

Notes on culinary discriptions in Motley's novel, set in Mexico.

1271. Byrne, Muriel Saint Clare. 1957. Elizabethan life in town and country. London: Metheun;
New York: Barnes & Noble. University Paperbacks.

Food: pp. 59-62; 121, 162, 252, 294; cost of
food: pp. 169, 233-234, 308, 309, 312;
school meals: p. 205; wine: pp. 60, 61, 101,
150, 309,

1272. Cabello, E. & Cervini, P.R. 1942. Psychic
development of infants in the city of Buenos Aires
in relation to type of feeding. [In Spanish.] SPBA-
A 8: 29-46.

1273. Cabras, C.; Guiso, F.; & Peretti, G. 1956.
Food habits of the agricultural population of Sardin-
ia: a study on the families of farm laborers of
Mamilla and of peasants of Nurra.   [In Italian.]
SItal BS B 32: 1440-1442.

1274. Cardart, Jean. 1955.   Les escargots
[Snails.] Paris: Les Editionis Paul Chevalier.

An encyclopedic survey, covering biology,
technology, and gastronomy. Includes recipes.

1275. Cadart, Jean. 1957. The edible snail; the
French now eat more than 8000 tons of snails a
year. SA 197: 113-114.

1276. Cadet-de-Vaus, Ant. - Alexis. 1814. De
l'economie alimentaire du peuple et du soldat ou
moyen de parer aux disettes et d'en prevenis a
jamais le retour; d'assurer constamment et dans
toutes les contrees, d'excellent pain et de fixer,
pour les camps et armees, la nourriture la plus
economique, la plus salutaire et qui, la plus appropr-
iee a l economie animale, la preserve de ces maladies contagieuses provenant du vice du regime alimentiare. [Dietary economy of the people and the
soldier, or means to ward off scarcity and prevent
its reutrn; to assure excellent bread continually in
all areas and to establish, for the camps and armies,
the most economical and wholesome nutriture
which, most appropriate for the physical constitu-
tion, can defend it from contagious illnesses deriving from the evil of diet.]

1277. Cadol, Edouard. 1871.   Paris pendant le
siege. [Paris during the siege.] Brussels: Office de
Publicite.

Diet in Paris during the siege: P. 69 et seq.

1278. Cador, L. 1850. Subsistences et populations. [Food supplies and populations.] Paris: Guillaumin.

1279. Cadzow, Donald A. 1294. Eskimo lamps
and cooking vessels. IN 1:26-28.

1280. Cahill, K.M. & Ley, A.B. 1962. Favism and
thalassemia minor in a pregnant woman. JAMA 180:
119-121.

1281. Cail, Odile. 1972.   Peking. New York:
David McKay.

A traveler's guide. Chinese cuisine: pp. 49-
59. Discusses regional cuisines; kinds of
meals; drinks; structure of a Chinese meal;
principal Chinese food preparations. Restaurants of Peking: pp. 77-87.

1282. Calavan, Michael M. Diet and nutrition in a
north Thai village. Paper presented at 69th Annual
Meeting of the American Anthropological Association. 19 to 22 November, 1970. San Diego, California.

1283. Calavan, Michael M. Decisions against nature: crop choice in a northern Thai village. Ph.D.
dissertation. Anthropology. University of Illinois,
Urbana. 1973.

1284. Calavan, Michael M. Food use patterns as
indices of adaptative process: a prospecutus. Paper
presented at 73rd Annual Meeting of the American
Anthropological Association.l   19-24 November,
1974. Mexico City.

1285. Calder, Ritchie. 1963. Gastronomy for the
bold. UC 16: 21-24.

1286. Caldwell, Joseph R. Primary forest effici-
ency. In Twenty-first Southeastern Archaelogical
Conference. November 6-7, 1964. New Orleans,
Louisiana.   Proceedings.   Edited by Stephen
Williams. 1965. Pp. 66-69. SAC-B No. 3.

Discusses forest food resources as a phase in
the archaeological record of eastern North
America.

1287. Caldwell, M.J. 1972. Ascorbic acid content
of Malaysian leaf vegetables. EFN 1: 313-317.

Forty-four species of plants, many of which
grow wild, were analyzed for ascorbic acid
content.   Most contained significant
amounts of this nutrient, and would be useful supplements to rural diets where intake
of ascorbic acid is marginal.

1288. Caldwell, M.J. & Enoch, I.C. 1972. Riboflavin content of Malaysian leaf vegetables. EFN 1:
309-312.

Forty-six plants are analyzed, and their use
suggested as a means for increasing intake
of riboflavin in Southeast Asia, where deficiency of this nutrient is widespread.

1289. Calera, Ana Maria. Chapter One. La
cocina vasca tipical y cocina vasca normal. [Tradi-
tional and every-day Basque cookery.] Chapter two.
Los condimentos.   [Seasonings.] Chapter Three.
Las setas.   [Edible mushrooms.] Chapter Four.
Utensilos de cocina - el fuego. [Cooking utensils -
the fire.] Chapter Five. La materia prima. [Basic
ingredients.] Chapter Six. Menus.   [Menus.]
Chapter Seven. Terminologia. [Terminology.] In
La Cocina Vasca [Basque cookery.] 1971. Bilbao:
Editorial "La Gran Enciclopedia Vasca".

1290.   Calinanos, Theodore.   Development of regional canning projects in Greece.   Master's thesis.   University of Massachusetts.   1948.

1291.   Caliendo, M.A.   An ecological analysis of the dietary and nutritional status of pre-school children.   Ph.D dissertation.   Nutritional Sciences.   Cornell University.   1975.

1292.   California.   Senate.   1943.   Final report of the joint legislative fact-finding committee on agricultural and industrial labor.   Sacramento: California State Printing Office.

   Use of prisoners-of-war in crop harvesting during World War II: pp. 15,16.

1293.   Caliwag, Felix.   1963.   The origin of rice.   WG 29:28.

1294.   Call, Cora Pinkeley.   1950.   From my Ozark cupboard.   A basic Ozark cook book.   Kansas City, Missouri: Allan Publications.

1295.   Call, David.   1965.   An examination of caloric availability and consumption in the United States, 1909 - 1963.   AJCN 16: 374-379.

   Food consumption statistics are not precise scientific measures but, rather, rough approximations of the amount of food taken off the retail market.   No attempt is made to adjust for kitchen or plate waste.   Suggestions are offered for improving the accuracy of these data.

1296.   Callahan, Errett.   Gathering without hunting: non-violent subsistence ecology in action.   Paper presented at 77th Annual Meeting of the American Anthropological Association.   17 November, 1978.   Los Angeles, California.

   Report of a project in experimental gathering of wild flora and fauna in and around the reservation of the Pamunkey tribe, in Virgina.

1297.   Callbeck, Lorne C.   1967.   A faithfull friend -the potato.   At Adv 57: 53-57.

1298.   Callcott, Maria.   1842.   A scriptural herbal.   London: Longman, Brown, Green, and Longman.

   Foods used in the Near East during Biblical times.   Data on famine foods, e.g. Vicia sativa; Ornithogallum umbellatum.

1299.   Callen, Eric O.   1965.   Food habits of some pre-Columbian Mexican Indians.   EB 19: 335-343.

1300.   Callen, Eric O.   1967.   The first new world cereal.   Am An 32: 535-538.

   Setaria sp. (foxtail millet) was eaten in quantity in Tamaulipas, prior to the introduction of maize (ca.   4000 B.C. - 3500 B.C.) as well as in Tehuacan, southern Pueblo, Mexico (ca. 5500 B.C.).

1301.   Callen, Eric O. & Cameron, T.W.M. 1960. A prehistoric diet revealed in coprolites. N Sci 8: 35-40.

1302.   Calloway, Doris Howes & David. Lore Rose.   1961.   Nutrition and radiation injury: an annotated bibliography.   United States Army.   Quartermaster Food and Container Institute for the Armed Forces.   Chicago: Quartermaster Nutrition Branch.

1303.   Calloway, Doris H. & Gibbs, J.C.   1976.   Food patterns and food assistance programs in the Cocopah Indian community.   EFN 5: 183-196.

   Studies factors affecting participation rates in United States Federal food relief programs and the possible effect of such programs on food intake.   The Cocopah are a Native American group of Yuman linguistic stock, inhabiting reserve lands at Somerton, and Yuma, Arizona.

1304.   Calmus.   1851.   Plus de disette possible ou panification du marron d'Inde, de l'Arum maculatum et de la bryone.   [Further famine possible, or the use of the horse chestnut, Arum maculatum, and Bryonia for bread.]   Paris: Imprimerie Leautey.

   A. maculatum is commonly called Cuckoo-pint, Lords-and-Ladies, and Adam-and-Eve.   Bryony is of the family Cucurbitaceae.   The species in question here may be either Bryonia alba, L., or Bryonia dioica, Jacq., called wild hop.

1305.   Calonne, Alberic de.   1880.   L'alimentation de la ville d'Amiens au 15e siecle, etude historique.   [Dietary of the city of Amiens in the 15th Century, historical study.]   Amiens: Imprimerie Douillet.

1306.   Calvert, T.C.   1946.   The story of Wenslydale cheese.   Clapham, Lancaster: Dalesman Publishing Co.

1307.   Calvo, Jose; Serrani, Gloria; Millan, Rafael Segura; Miranda, Fransisco de P. & Anderson, Richmond K.   1946.   Nutritional status of economically poor families fed in a government operated dining room in Mexico City. JADA 22: 297-302.

1308.   Calvo, Jose & Salazar, Dolores.   1952.   Estudio sobre el estado de nutricion de un grupo de habitantes del pueblo de Chamilpa, Estado de Morelos.   [Study of the nutritional status of a group of citizens of the village of Chamilpa, State of Morelos.]   Nutriologia 1: 57-81.

1309.   Cambaceres, Jules.   1841.   Des moyens de faire cesser dans Paris l'usage clandestin de la chair de cheval.   [Means for ending the clandestine use of horse flesh in Paris.]   Paris: Imprimerie Ducessois.

1310.   Cameron, Ludovick Charles Richard Duncombe-Jewell.   1917.   The wild foods of Great Britain, where to find them and how to cook them...London: G. Routledge & Sons.

1311.   Camp, H.M.   A study of anorexia in children.   Master's thesis.   Denton: Texas State College for Women.   1937.

1312. Campa, Arthur L.   1932.   Pinons - an important custom. NMBR 1: 144-147.

Compares the pinon in New Mexico and Arizona to the Virginia peanut, and the Texas pecan. Statistics on picking, processing and marketing are given. A local recipe for 'sopa de pinon' (pinon soup) is described, calling for toasted bread, cheese, pinons, and milk sweetened with caramel sugar which is oven-baked.

1313. Campbell, A.J.   1952.   Miarasa: New Guinea's last cannibal outpost. PIM 22: 69-70.

1314. Campbell, Alastair H.   1965.   Elementary food production by the Australian aborigenes. Mankind 6: 206-211.

1315. Campbell, Alastair H.   1965.   Addenda to elementary food production by the Aborigenes. Mankind 6: 288.

Australia.

1316. Campbell, Ake.   1951.   Notes on a Swedish contribution to the folk culture atlas of Europe. Laos 1: 111-120.

Conclusions drawn from mapping distribution of Swedish bread types.

1317. Campbell, Andrew.   1956.   The book of beer. London: Dennis Dobson.

History, manufacture, customs, quotations.

1318. Campbell, Angus.   Interviewing for food habit surveys.   In Conference on food acceptance research.   6 December, 1945.   United States War Department.   Quatermaster Food and Container Institute. Research and Development Branch. Military Planning Division.   Committee on Food Research.   1946. Pp. 52-54. Quartermaster Corps Manual 17-9.

1319. Campbell, Clara Mae. The use of peanuts as an important food.   Master's thesis.   University of Georgia. 1944.

1320. Campbell, H.B. 1917. Foodstuffs imported into the Hawaiian Islands. Haw Plant 16: 446-449.

Imports, both foreign and domestic, are contrasted against principal exports of food for the year 1916.

1321. Campbell, Henry. 1903. Observations on mastication. 1. Effects of mastication. BMJ 2: 84-86. 2. Changes which the jaws and teeth of man have undergone during man's evolution from his anthropoid ancestors 2: 150-152. 3. Evils resulting from inefficient mastication. 2: 216-220. 4. Means of insuring adequate mastication. 2: 375-377.

1322. Campbell, Henry. 1905. The diet of the precibiculturists. MBJ 2: 40-41. (Tasmanian); 208-209 (Australian); 350-352 (Australian); 406-409 (California Digger Indians); 665-666 (Brazilian Botocudo;

Fuegian groups); 813-815 (Bushmen, Pygmies); 979-981 (Andaman Islanders, Philippine and Malay Negritos); 1217-1219 (Palaeolithic diets); 1658-1659 (Neolithic diets). Food habits of prehistoric and historic non-urbanized groups, based largely on travellers' accounts (except for Palaeolithic and Neolithic data).

1323. Campbell, Joan M.   Famine and culture in East Africa. Paper presented at 68th Annual Meeting of the American Anthropological Association. 20 to 23 November, 1969. New Orleans, Louisiana.

1324. Campbell, R.M. & Cuthbertson, D.P. Factors in influencing man's selection of food. In Progress in nutrition and allied sciences. Edited by D.P. Cuthbertson. 1963. Pp. 395-420. Edinburgh: Oliver & Boyd.

1325. Campbell, T.N. 1959. Choctaw subsistence: ethnographic notes from the Lincecum manuscript. FAnth 12 (1): 9-24.

Data derived from material recorded, by Gideon Lincecum (1793-1874), a Nineteenth Century physician and naturalist, from an elderly Choctaw between 1823-1825. Contains information on hunting, fishing, gathering, and horticulture.

1326. Campbell, Thomas G. 1926. Insect food of the aborigenes. AMM 2: 407-410.

1327. Campo, Juan Comas Y. 1942. El regimen alimenticio y el mejoramiento indigena. [Diet and the betterment of native groups.] AmInd 2: 51-56.

1328. Campo, Rafael Martin del. 1938. El pulque en el Mexico pre-Cortesiano. [Pulque in Mexico before the arrival of Cortes.] UNM-IB-A 9:5-23.

Opens with a review of ancient Mexican knowledge of Agave sp., and its uses, (including dietary). The place of intoxicating beverages among Native Mexicans is explored, and the mythological origin of pulque, the fermented secretion of the maguey, is recounted. The psychology of drunkness, and the goddess of maguey and gods of inebriation are also considered.

1329. Campos, M.A. Pourchet. 1963. As especiarias na alimentacao do homem Brasileiro. [The Brazilian's food spices.] ABN 19: 51-62.

Study of thirty-six Brazilian seasonings, their regional use and distribution, and mineral content.

1330. Camus, Jose S. 1921. Rice in the Philippines. P-DANR-BA-B No. 37.

1331. Candee, Richard M. 1968. The re-discovery of milk-based house paints and the myth of 'brick-dust and buttermilk' paints. OTNE 58: 79-81.

1332. Candolle, Alphonse Louis Pierre Pyramus. 1885. Origin of cultivated plants. International Science Series. Vol. 48. New York: D. Appleton & Co.

Part One opens with a consideration of the time of origin of agriculture, followed by a discussion of methods for discovering or proving the origins of plant species. Part Two comprises detailed entries for numerous plants, arranged according to the criterion of which part of the plant cultivation is undertaken, with data on their origins, early cultivation, and subsequent diffusion. Part Three contains a tabular summary of the data in Part Two, and conclusions.

1333. Canet, J. 1943. Note sur l'alimentation des coolies de plantations. Quelques mesures recentes prises a ce sujet par les grand exploitations. [Note on the diet of plantation coolies. Some recent measures taken in this regard by the large planters.] IIEH-BT 5: 58-88.

1334. Cannel, B. 1940. Jewish dietary laws and food customs. PHN 32: 683-687.

1335. Canon, Helen & Brewer, Lucille. 1915. The fireless cooker and its uses. CorU-CRC-FHS No. 9: 273-296.

Pp. 274-275 contain historical data on these cookers.

1336. Cannon, Poppy. 1964. Revolution in the kitchen, with some notes on the anthropology of food. S Rev 47: 54-57.

1337. Cant, John G.H. Feeding ecology of spider monkeys. Paper presented at 76th Annual Meeting of the American Anthropological Association. 29 November to 3 December,1977. Houston, Texas.

Field observations of spider monkeys at Tikal, Guatemala, reveal a general pattern of frugivory; however, the study population also shows unusual concentration on the product of one tree species including its unripe seeds. The evenness of food species representation in monthly diet positively correlates with diversity, tentatively suggesting that the animals eat edible items approximately in proportion to a rate at which they encounter them. Selection ratios, relating consumption to rough measures of resource availabilty, are much lower than ratios reported for red colobus monkeys, reflecting different coevolutionary processes that have affected the various types of food.

1338. Canto, Borges do. 1961. A pesca na Lagoa Panguila e de fumacao do peixe. [Fish and fish-smoking at Lake Panguila.] Luanda: Instituto de Angola.

1339. Capelovici, Jacques. 1960. Beefsteak o biftec? [Beefsteak or biftec?] VL No. 104. Pp. 579-582.

Etymological study.

1340. Capelovici, Jacques. 1961. Suivons le boeuf...[Let's follow the steer.] VL No. 109. Pp. 214.

Etymology of the word steak.

1341. Capinpin, J.M. & Pancho, J.V. 1961. Note: wild species of rice in the Philippines. PAg 44: 523-524.

1342. Capitan, L. 1910. Les sacrifices humains et l'anthropophagie rituelle dans l'Amerique ancienne. [Human sacrifice and ritual anthropophagy in ancient America.] EAP-R 20: 170-179.

1343. Capitan, L. 1920. Les sacrifices humains et l'anthropophagie rituelle chez les anciens Mexicans. [Human sacrifices and ritual anthropophagy among the ancient Mexicans.] S Am P-J 12: 211-217.

1344. Capot-Rey, R. 1960. Le sel et le commerce au Borkou-Ennedi-Tibesti. [Salt and the salt trade at Borkou de l' l'Ennedi et du Tibesti.] IRS-T 18: 187-193.

This is a division of northern Chad, south of the Libyan border.

1345. Captain, O.B. 1969. A study in Omaha, Nebraska: cost and quality of food in poverty and non-poverty areas. JADA 55: 569-571.

1346. Caramelea, V.V.: Remus, Anghel; Nastaseanu, Lili; Berchina, Doina; Bortun, D., Calin, Ioana; Cojocaru, Silvia; Goian, I.; Lupei, I.; Negoescu, F.; & Voinea, Maria. 1973. Aspects of the enculturation and socialization process in the Berivoesti Pilot Station (Department of Arges). ARA 10: 111-117.

Changes in food habits: p. 112.

1347. Cardenas, J. & Gibbs, C.E.; & Young, E.A. 1976. Nutritional beliefs and practices in primigravid Mexican-American women. JADA 69: 262-265.

1348. Cardona, Miguel. 1954. Cocina y dulceria. [Cookery and confectionery.] IF-B 1: 150-161.

Notes and recipes on numerous Venezuelan tradtional foods and sweets.

1349. Cardona, Miguel. 1957. Biografia del casabe, el pan del pobre. Biography of casabe, the bread of the poor.] El Farol 19: 34-38.

A round, flat, unleavened Venezuela bread.

1350. Cardona, Miguel. 1959. Una bebida Venezolana: la chicha. [A Venezuelan beverage: chicha.] Elite No. 1775. Pp. 10-13.

1351. Cardona, Miguel. 1960. El casabe. [Casabe.] El Universal 11 de Julio.

1352. Cardona, Miguel. 1964. Temas de folklore Venezolano. [Venequelan folklore themes.] Caraccas: Ediciones del Ministerio de Educacion. Direccion de Cultura y Bellas Artes.

Cocina y dulceria [Cookery and confectionery] : pp. 361-383. Biografia del casabe. [Biography of casabe] ; pp. 173-191.

1353.   Cardozo, M.   1959.   A mo e a farinha, o forno e o pao. Nota etnographica. [Grindstone and flour, oven and bread... Ethnographic note.] TAE 17:235-248.

1354.   Careme, Antonin.   La table de quelques souverains. [The dinner table of various sovereigns.] In Les classiques e la table. Anonymous. 1844. Paris: Dentu; Tresse: J. Renouard.

1355.   Carey, Henry. 1970. A learned dissertation on dumpling. Pudding and dumpling burnt to pot; or a compleat key to the dissertation on dumpling. Los Angeles: William Andrews Clark Memorial Library.

1356.   Carillo, Gil, A. 1935. Deficient feeding and its consequenes in Yucatan. [In Spanish.] RMY 18: 101-116.

1357.   Carles, William Richard.   1888.   Life in Corea. London: Macmillan & Co. Data

     Data on preparation of oats; and eating postures.

1358.   Carlier. 1912. L'elevage au Kivu. (Congo Belge). [Cattle herding in Kivu (Belgian Congo).] BACB 3: 775-798.

     Use of cheese, butter, and meat.

1359.   Carlile, William K.; Olson, Helen Ger; Gorman, Jean; McCracken, Clayton; Vanderwagen, Robert; & Connor, Hillary. Contemporary nutritional status of North American Indian children. In Nutrition, growth and development of North American Indian children. Based on a conference co-sponsored by the National Institute of Child Health and Human Development, Indian Health Service, American Academy of Pediatrics Committee on Indian Health. Edited by William M. Moore; Marjorie M. Silverberg, & Merrill S. Read. 1972. Pp. 47-64. Department of Health, Education, and Welfare. Publication No. (NIH) 72-26. Washington, D.C.: Government Printing Office.

1360.   Carlson, G.G. & Jones, Volney Hurt. 1940. Some notes on the uses of plants by the Comanche Indians. MASAL-P 25: 517-542.

1361.   Carlson, V., comp. 1927. A bibliography for cookery investigation problems. Bureau of Publications. New York: Columbia University Teachers College.

1362.   Carmignani, R. 1954. Il cannibalismo degli Asande (o Niam-Niam). [Cannibalism among the Azande (or Niam-Niam]. Rome: Collana di Studi Etnografice.

1363.   Carmignani, R. 1957. Il cannibalismo degle Asande. [Cannibalism among the Azande.] Africa 27: 397-400.

1364.   Carneiro, J. Fernando. 1947. A antropofagia entre os indios do Brasil. [Anthropophagy among the Indians of Brazil.] Acta Am 5: 159-184.

1365.   Caron, Raymond. 1966. Fete de la banane et du can-oui-o chez les indiens Tapirapes (Bresil). [Banana and 'can-oui-o' feast among the Tapirape Indians (Brazil).] OM 6:213-244.

1366.   Carapino, Jerome. 1955. Daily life in ancient Rome. The people and the city at the height of the empire. Edited by Henry T. Rowell. Translated by E.O. Lorimer.   New Haven: Yale University Press.

     Dinner: Pp. 263-276.

1367.   Carpenter, J.A. 1956. Species differences in taste preferences. JCPP 49: 139-144.

1368.   Carpenter, Thorne M. & Steggerda, Morris 1939. The food of the present-day Navajo Indians of New Mexico and Arizona. JN 18: 297--305.

     Describes typical diet. Contains compositional analysis of such foods as blue corn cakes, clay, tansy mustard, and acorns.

1369.   Carr, Elizabeth Ball. 1972. Da kine talk. From pidgin to standard English in Hawaii. Honolulu: University of Hawaii Press.

     References to ethnic foods are inlcuded in the section on loanwords: Pp. 81-109.

1370.   Carr, Kurt W. A game-processing station, 44WR50. Paper presented at 72nd Annual Meeting of the American Anthropological Association.   29 November, 1973. New Orleans, Louisiana.

1371.   Carr, L.C. 1943.   Survival foods of the American aborigines. JADA 19: 845-847.

1372.   Carr, Lucien. 1895. Food of certain American Indians and their methods of preparing it.   AAS 10: 155-190.

     Extensively documented from the historical narrative and travel literature relating to North America. Reprint. Worcester, Massachusetts: Charles Hamilton (1895).

1373.   Carr, W.R.   1956.   The preparation and analysis of some African foodstuffs. CAJM 2: 334-339.

     Side dishes and relishes used by Rhodesian natives. A constituent chemical analysis of nineteen African foods is given, on wet and dry basis.

1374.   Carr, W.R. 1957. Notes on some Southern Rhodesian indigenous fruits with particular reference to their ascorbic acid content. FR 22: 590-596.

1375.   Carr, W.R. 1958. Southern Rhodesia, its food economy in review. F Tech 12(5): 10-18.

African methods of food processing; dietary patterns: Pp. 16,18.

1376.   Carranza, F. 1955. Aspectos de la bromatologia en el Peru.   [Aspects of food science in Peru.] AB 7: 5-12.

1377.   Carrasco Saiz, J.F. 1966. La alimentacion en Fernando Poo y Rio Muni. [Diet in Fernando Poo and Rio Muni.]   Africa (M) 23: 7-11.

Former Portuguese West African colonies.

1378.   Carreira, A. 1963. Do arrancamento da pele aos cadaveres e da necrofagia na guine portuguesa. [Peeling the skin of cadavers and necrophagia in Portuguese Guinea.] P-JIU-EED No. 102. Pp. 103-129.

Although cannibalism and necrophagy have all but disappeared under European influence, there is still some practice of necrophagy among the Felupe and Bayole.

1379.   Carrick, George L. 1891. Koumiss. London: Blackwood & Sons.

A fermented mare's milk product, native to the nomadic groups of Central Asia.

1380.   Carrington, Mereward. 1931. The occult side of diet. O Rev 52: 312-319.

1381.   Carson, Gerald. 1954. The old country store.   Fairlawn, New Jersey: Oxford University Press.

1382.   Carson, Gerald. 1957. Cornflake crusade. New York: Rinehart & Co.

Life and times of John Harvey Kellogg, physician, and developer of early instant breakfast cereal in the United States.

1383.   Carson, Rachel. 1943. Food from the sea: fish and shellfish of New England.   USDI-FWS-CH No. 33.

1384.   Carter, G. Malnutrition and the administrator. In First Asian Congress of Nutrition.   22 January - 2 February 1971.   Hyderabed, India. Proceedings. Edited by P.G. Tulpule & Kamala S. Jaya Rao. 1972. Pp. 895-901. Hyderabad: Nutrition Society of India.

Calls for a systematic briefing of administrators, in Asian nations, from national planning bodies to district and local levels, on the essential facts of malnutrition, on the basic principles of nutrition, on solutions which are possible, on their own country's programme, and on their specific role.

1385.   Carter, George Francis 1945. Plant geography and culture history in the American Southwest. VFPA No. 5.

Covers maize, tepary bean, kidney bean, lima bean, cucurbita, with additional material on climate, irrigation, and agriculture.

1386.   Carter, Goerge Francis. 1945. Some archaeological cucurbit seeds from Peru.   Act Am 3: 163-172.

1387.   Carter, George Francis. 1946. Some Hopi Indian food herbs.   Herbarist No. 12. Pp. 32-36.

1388.   Carter, George Francis. 1948. Sweet corn among the Indians. GR 38: 206-221.

1389.   Carter, George Francis. 1950. Plant evidence for early contacts with America. SJA 6: 161-182.

1390.   Carter, George Francis. 1963.   Maize to Africa. AJC 8:1-3.

1391.   Carter, George Francis. 1964. The turkey in pre-Colombian Europe? C Anth 5: 453-454.

1392.   Carter, George Francis. Pre Colombian chickens in America. In Man across the sea: problems of pre-Colombian contacts. Edited by Carroll L. Riley. 1971. Pp. 178-218. Austin: University of Texas Press.

1393.   Carter, George Francis & Anderson, Edgar. 1945. A preliminary survey of maize in the Southwestern United States.

1394.   Carter, Herbert Dyson. 1942. Let them eat grass. SNight 58: 12.

Nutrition problems in Germany during World War II.

1395.   Carvalho, Jose dos Santos. 1953. Composicao de algunas alimentos exoticos e seus nomes vulgares. [Composition of some foreign foods and their common names.] IMT-A 10: 1525-1561.

Vernacular and Latin names and composition of food plants grown in Portuguese colonies.

1396.   Carvalho, Marceline de. 1963. A arte de beber assim falava Baco). [The art of drinking (Thus spake Bacchus). Sao Paulo: Editorial Civilizacao Brasileira.

1397.   Carvalho, Maria da Conceicao & Burger, Osmar Neves. 1960. Contribuicao ao estudo do pequi de Brasilia. Estudo e pesquisa alimentar. No. 50. [Contribution to the study of the pequi of Brasilia. Diet study and research. No. 50. Rio de Janeiro: Servico de Alimentacao de Previdencia Social.

The pequi is a Brazilian tree of the genus Caryocar.

1398.   Cary, R.L. 1920. Child-feeding work in Germany under the American Friends' Service Committee co-operating with the American Relief Administration and the European Children's Fund, Herbert C. Hoover, Chairman. AAPSS-A 92: 157-162.

1399.   Casal, U. 1940. Some notes on the sakazuki and on the role of sake drinking in Japan. ASSJ-T Vol. 19.

An ethnographic study of sake utensils and rice wine.

1400.   Casalini, G.   1932.   Dietary of ancient Greeks and Romans.   [In Italian]   I Vita 15: 225-257.

1401.   Casco, O.E.   El marchitamento del mani. [The marketability of the peanut.]   Thesis.   La Plata, Argentina: Universidad de la Plata. 1940.

1402.   Cascudo, Luis da Camara. 1963. Historia do alimentacao no Brasil.   [History of diet in Brazil.] RE 1: 47-53.

1403.   Cascudo, Luis da Camara.   1964.   O bom paladar e dos ricos ou dos pobres?   [Who are the gourmets, the rich or the poor?] RE 2:255-258.

1404.   Cascudo, Luis da Camara.   1967.   Chapter Four. Bebidas e alimentos popular. [Popular beverages and foods.]   In Folclore do Brasil.   Rio de Janeiro: Editora Fundo de Cultura.

1405.   Cascudo, Luis da Camara. 1977. Antologia da alimentacao no Brasil.   [Anthology of Brasilian food habits.] Rio de Janeiro: Livros Tecnicos e Cientificos Editora.

Sixty-two extracts from a wide range of literatures (scientific, travel, sociological, literary) providing a retrospective view of Brazilian foods, food habits, and attitudes toward food, from the Eighteenth through the Twentieth Centuries.

1406.   Case, L.A.   1925.   Finickiness and food. CHM 6:5-7.

1407.   Casella, D.   La frutta nella pitture Pompeiana.   [Fruit in the Pompeian murals.]   In Raccolta di studi per il secondo centenario degli scavi di Pompeii.   1950.   Pp. 355-386.   Naples. Gaetano Maccharioli:

Notes the representation of a fruit resembling pineapple.

1408.   Caseneuva, Paul.   1883.   Alimentation among savage and civilized peoples. Cin Lancet 10: 550-559.

Informal, anecdotal review.

1409.   Casey, J. 1947. Food from flowers. Cath Dgst 11: 106-108.

1410.   Casoti, L.   1951.   L'alimentazione nell antico Egitto. [Food in ancient Egypt.] Castalia No. 4.

1411.   Cassady, Jr.., Ralph & Jones, W.L. 1949. The changing competitive structure in the wholesale grocery trade. Berkeley: University of California Press.

1412.   Cassalis, Eugene. 1859. Les Bassoutos, ou vingt-trois anees de l'Afrique au sud.] The Basuto, or twenty-three years in South Africa.]   Paris: C. Meyrueis. Reprint. Cape Town: C. Struik. 1965.

Food and its preparation: Pp. 142-146.

1413.   Cassel, B. Jewish dietary laws and food customs. PHN 32: 682-687.

1414.   Cassel, John.   1957.   Social and cultural implications of food and food habits. AJPH 47: 732-740.

Additional data on an extended applied community health program in Polela, a Zulu community in Natal, Union of South Africa.

1415.   Cassel, John. A comprehensive health program among South African Zulus. In Health, culture and community. Case studies of public reactions to health programs.   Edited by Benjamin D. Paul & Walter B. Miller. 1955. New York: Russell Sage Foundation.

Includes description of nutrition intervention program in the village of Polela, southwest Natal, designed to improve maternal-child health, and upgrade overall village nutritional status.   One of the earliest applied nutrition programs, this study illustrates how knowledge of the history of a group's food habits can be obtained and used to create receptiveness for nutrition education and improvement of community diet.

1416.   Cassidy, Claire M.   "Benign neglect" of children as a factor in population control. Paper presented at 76th Annual Meeting of the American Anthropological Association.   29 November to 3 December, 1977. Houston, Texas.

Certain institutionalized methods of child care, by exposing weanlings to excessive nutritional and psychological stress, permit their early death or and thus act to limit population size, although effecting such consequences is not the primary or expressed funtion of these methods. Family food supply is not available to weanlings in pro portion to their needs. Food seeking by weanlings is often further frustrated by psychological rejection by adults.   Weanlings react with signs of overwhelming stress. Parental "neglect" is "benign" because parents are concurrently loving and depriving apparently without fully realizing the latter.

1417   Cassidy, Claire M. & Stavrakis, Olga. Subsistence system, diet and nutrition in a Lowland Maya Village. Paper presented at 73rd Annual Meeting of American Anthropological Association. 19-24 November, 1974. Mexico City.

1418.   Cassidy, Frederick G. 1961. Some footnotes on the 'Junjo question. A Speech 32: 101-103.

A Jamaican folk-word for mushroom.

1419.   Cassina Garden Club of St. Simon's Island. 1937.   Coastal cookery recipes of the coastal section of Georgia. St. Simon's Island, Georgia: Cassina Garden Club of St. Simon's Island.

1420.   Castaing, A. De l'importance de la nourriture sur le caractere et le developpment des peuples. De la distribution des cereales et de leur succedanees. [Of the influence of food on the character and development of peoples.   Of the distribution of cereals and of their usefulness.] congres International des Sciences Ethnographiques, tenu a Paris du 15 au 17 juillet, 1878. Ministere de l' Agriculture et du Commerce. 1881. Pp. 216-224.

1421.   Castaneda, Rafael Romero. 1961.   Frutas silvestres de Columbia. [Forest fruits of Columbia.] Bogota: Editorial Juan Eudes.

1422.   Castanheira, A.C. 1948-1949. Tabu alimentacao dos Cuanhamas. [Dietary tabu of the Kwanyama.] E Colon 1: 84-85.

      Angola.

1423.   Castanie, H. 1950. Le lait vegetal. [Vegetable millk.] RIPCMC 25: 39-40.

      Soy milk, its use and preparation. Notes other plants of the families Euphorbiaceae, Asclepiadceae, Urticaceae, and Apocynaceae from which 'milk' can be derived.

1424.   Castellanos, F.E. 1943. Valor dietetico de un menu tipico Cubano. [Nutritive value of a typical Cuban menu. RMQO 4: 12-16.

1425.   Castelot, A. Bref historique du decor, des ustensiles et des horaires qui ont caracterise l'evolution de la cuisine et des repas au cours des siecles. [Short history of decor, utensils, and timers which have characterized the evolution of cooking and meals through the centuries.] Historia No. 42. Pp. 9-17.

1426.   Castetter, Edward Franklin. 1935. Ethnobiological studies in the American Southwest 1. Uncultivated native plants used as sources of food. UNM-B No. 266 BS 4(1).

1427.   Castetter, Edward F. 1944. Domain of ethnobiology. AN 78: 158-170.

      Review of ethnobotanical and ethnozoological work by United States' scholars, with an outline for fieldwork procedures.

1428.   Castetter, Edward Franklin & Bell, Willis H. 1937.   Ethnobiological studies in the American Southwest 4. The aboriginal utilization of the tall cacti in the American Southwest. UNMB-B No. 307 BS 5(1).

1429.   Castetter, Edward Franklin & Bell, Willis H. 1942. Pima and Papago Indian agriculture. Albuquerque: University of New Mexico Press.

1430.   Castetter, Edward F. & Bell, Willis H. 1951. Yuman Indian agriculture. Primitive subsistence on the lower Colorado and Gila Rivers. Alburquerque: University of New Mexico Press.

      Yuma, Maricopa, Mohave, and Cocopa tribes in what is the present State of Arizona.

1431.   Castetter, Edward Franklin; Bell, Willis H.; & Grove, Alvin R. 1938. Ethnobiological studies in the American Southwest 6. The early utilization and the distribution of Agave in the American Southwest. UNMB- No. 335 BS 5(4).

1432.   Castetter, Edward Franklin & Erwin, Arthur Thomas. 1929. A systematic study of squashes and pumpkins. I-AES-B No. 244.

1433.   Castetter, Edward Franklin & Opler, Morris Edward. 1936. Ethnobiological studies in the American Southwest 3. The Ethnobiology of the Chiricahua and Mescalero Apache. The use of plants for foods, beverages and narcotics. UNM-B No. 297 BS 4(5).

1434.   Castetter, Edward Franklin & Underhill, Ruth M. 1935. Ethnobiological studies in the American Southwest 2. The ethnobiology of hte Papago Indians. UNM-B No. 275 BS 4(3).

1435.   Castro, Josue de. 1936. Alimentacao e raca. [Diet and race.] Rio de Janeiro: Civilizacao Brasileira.

1436.   Castro, Josue de. 1937. A alimentacao Brasileira a luz da geografia humana. [Diet in Brazil in the light of human geography.] Porto Alegre: Livraria do. Glabo.

1437.   Castro, Josue de. 1938. Fisiologia dos tabus com un apendice contendo varios tabus alimentares brasileiros. [Physiology of tabus, with an appendix listing various Brazilian food taboos.] Ofrecido pelo "Nestle". Sao Paulo: Companhia Melhoramentos.

1438.   Castro, Josue de. 1939. O problema da alimentacao no Brasil. [The problem of diet in Brazil.] Sao Paulo: Companhia Editora Nacional.

1439.   Castro, Josue de. 1941. Fisiologia dos tabus. [Physiology of taboos.] Rio de Janeiro: Edicao oficina Grafica Manua Limitida.

1440.   Castro, Josue de. 1945. Areas alimentares do Brasil. [Diet areas of Brazil.] AmInd 5: 191-205.

1441.   Castro, Josue de.   1948.   Areas alimenticias do Brasil. [Diet of Brazil.] UB-In-TP 1: 19-45.

1442.   Castro, Josue de. 1949. La alimentacion en el area Amazonica. [Diet in the Amazon area.] AmInd 9: 113-142.

1443.   Castro, Josue de. 1952. The geography of hunger. Boston: Little, Brown & Co.

A standard study of causes and patterns of world food shortage and nutritional deficiencies.

1444.   Castroviejo, J. & Junqueiro, A. 1962. Viaje por los montes y chimenes de Galicia. Caza y cocina gallegas. [Voyage through the peaks and chimneys of Galicia. Galician game and cookery.] Madrid: Espasa-Calpe.

The use of the word 'chimney' gives a double-entendre, with an implication of the colloquial sense of 'gullet'.

1445.   Cathcart, E.P. & Murray, A.M.T. 1951. A study in nutrition. An inquiry into the diet of 154 families of St. Andrews. GB-PC-MRC-SRS No. 151.

1446.   Catley, A. 1963. Notes on insects as food for native peoples in Papua and New Guinea. PNGSS-T 4: 10-12.

1447.   Catlin, I.N. 1897. Beverages of Mexico. SA-S 43: 17519.

1448.   Cattle, Dorothy Jean. Protein patterns in a coastal Miskito Indian village, eastern Nicaragua. Paper presented at 73rd Annual Meeting of the American Anthropological Association. 19 to 24 November, 1974. Mexico City.

1449.   Cattle, Dorothy Jean. An alternative to nutritional particularism. In Nutrition and anthropology in action. Edited by Thomas K. Fitzgerald. 1976. Pp. 35-45. Assen, Amsterdam: Van Gorcum.

This paper examines the shortcomings of a monovalent approach to problem-oriented research, (biological, evolutionary, ecological, and socio-cultural) model which is seen as both theoretically, and descriptively more productive (dynamic) than the former (static) view.

1450.   Cattle, Dorothy Jean. Dietary diversity and nutritionial security in a coastal Miskito Indian village, eastern Nicaragua. In Frontier adaptations in lower Central America. Edited by Mary W. Helms & Franklin D. Loveland. 1976. Pp. 117-130. Philadelphia: Institute for the Study of Human Issues.

Studies the effects of wage labor upon a subsistence economy. Harvesting of the subsistence protein staple Chelonia mydas (green sea turtle) provides cash for the purchase of a variety of store bought food, but in spite of increased diversity, nutritional quality of Miskito diet declines. The author suggests that the possible over-harvesting of the green turtle will not cause immediate nutritional problems, and will be replaced by efforts at terrestrial animal husbandry. Only if population increase exceeds subsistence capabilities will new forms of adaptation be required.

1451.   Caudell, A.N. 1916. An economic consideration of Orthoptera directly affecting man. ESW-B 18: 84-93.

Orthoptera as human food: pp. 89-91.

1452.   Cave, Hugh Barnett. 1952. Haiti, highroad to adventure. New York: Henry Holt.

Contains scattered material on Haitian cookery.

1453.   Cazanove, J.L.F. 1936. L'alimentation des indigenes en [Afrique] [Occidentale] [Francaise]. [Food habits of natives in French West Africa.] AF mai: 288-293; juin: 339; juillet: 383-386.

1454.   Cazanove, J.L.F. 1936. La questioin du lait dans les colonies africaines. [The question of milk in the African colonies.] Africa 9: 227-236.

1455.   Cazzuola, F. 1880. Le piante utili e nocive agli uomini e agli animale che crescono in Italia. Useful and poisonous plants for humans and animals growing in Italy.] Turin: Loescher.

1456.   Cedillo, Valentin C. 1952. Cassava rice, or ladang. PAg 35: 428-440.

1457.   Centre Latino-Americano de Recherches en Sciences Sociaux. 1965. Quelques aspects sociaux de la consommation de produits alimentaires en Amerique Latine. [Some social aspects of the consumption of food products in Latin America.] Civilizations 15: 270-279.

1458.   Cepede, Michel. 1972. Nutrition et sociologie. [Nutrition and sociology.] SRur 12: 37-41.

1459.   Cepede, Michel; Grond, Linus; & Houtart, Francois. 1964. Population and food. New York: Sheed & Ward.

1460.   Cepede, Michel & Lengelle, Maurice. 1953. Economie alimentaire du globe. Essai d'interpretation. [Global food economy. Interpretative essay.] Paris: Librairie de Medicis. Editions M-Th. Genin.

An encyclopedic work, touching on the physical, economic, social, political, moral, psychological, historical, and geographical aspects of diet. The authors have been conscientious in providing supportive documentation, maps, statistics, and diagrams.

1461.   Cepede, Michel & Lengelle, Maruice. 1964. L'economie de l'alimentation. [Food economy.] Paris: Presses Universitaires Francaises. Series Que sais-je?

1462.   Cereceda, Juan Dantin. 1937. Primeros contactos entre los tipos de alimentacion antillano y mediterraneo. [First contacts between Antillean and Mediterranean food habits.] TF 2: 383-412.

1463.   Ceriotti, A. 1936. Edible coconut oil. [In Spanish.] RFQ 0: 27-35.

A review of the properties and uses of coconut oil. Abstracted in CA 30: 7370.

1464.   Cervio, Vincenzo. 1581. Il trinciante. [Carving.] Venice: Giovanni Varisco.

Instructions for cutting all kinds of meats, fish and fruit.

1465. Cerwin, Herbert, 1947. Chapter Fourteen. The great corn god. Chapter Nineteen. Too much tequila. Chapter Twenty. What Mexico eats. In These are the Mexicans. New York: Reynal & Hitchcock.

1466. Ceylon. Department of Agriculture. Peradeniya. 1952. The cashew nut. Circular No. 5. Colombo: Ceylon Government Press.

1467. Chabon, R.S. 1967. Kwashiorkor in a Navajo Indian child. In Second Joint Meeting of the Clinical Society and Commissioned Officers' Association. Atlanta: Department of Health, Education and Welfare. Public Health Service.

1468. Chafetz, Morris E. 1964. Consumption of alcohol in the Far and Middle East. NEJM 271-301.

1469. Chadoutand, L. 1959. Sur le favisme. [On favism.] Pres Med 67: 132-133.

1470. Chagnon, Napoleon A. 1968. The feast. NH 77: 34-41.

Yanomamo tribe; Brazil.

1471. Chagnon, Napoleon A. 1968. Yanomamo, the fierce people. Case studies in Cultural Anthropology. New York: Holt, Rhinehart and Winston.

Food preparation: pp. 29-32; food in myth: pp. 47, 92, 108, 112; other uses: p. 50.

1472. Chakravarti, Chintaharan. 1965. Beef in Hindu folklore of Bengal. Folklore (C) 6: 18-19.

1473. Chakravorty, S.K. & Pal, S.S. 1962 [?]. Studies in rural change: reports on re-surveys of villages. Nachangacha (1955-1962). Agro-Economic Research Centre. Santiniketan, West Bengal: Visa-Bharati University.

Includes detailed expenditure data for several foods by occupational groups. Village studied is in Birbhum District (approximately 23 50 N, 87 50 E), in West Bengal.

1474. Chalot, C. 1904. Note sur une nouvelle plante alimentaire d'Afrique centrale. [Note on a new food plant from Central Africa.] APPC 4: 104-106.

A tuber called dazo (Coleus dazo), with chemical analysis.

1475. Chalover, W.H. 1960. Food and drink in British history. A Hist 4: 315-319.

1476. Chamberlain, Alexander F. 1891. The maple amongst the Algonkian tribes. AA [old series] :39-43.

Reviews data in the historical literature; mythological references to the maple tree in Algonkian oral literature; explores the etymology of various Algonkian terms pertaining to the maple, its sweet sap and derived products.

1477. Chamberlain, Alexander F. 1895. Beitrag zur pflanzen kunde der Naturvolker Amerikas. [Contribution to the study of Native American botany.] ZE 27:551-556.

1478. Chamberlain, Narcissa & Chamberlain, Narcisse. 1960-1964. The flavor of France, in recipes and pictures. 2 vols. New York: Hastings House.

1479. Chamberlin, Ralph Vary. 1909. Some plant names of the Ute Indians. AA 11: 27-40.

After a brief introduction covering the nature of the Ute language, an extensive list of plants is recorded. Latin and vernacular names are given, together with food use of plant, where appropriate.

1480. Chambers, T. King. 1875. A manual of diet in health and disease. London: Smith, Elder & Co. Reviewed in BMJ 2: 299-301. (1875).

Subjects covered include: physiology; selection of mixed diet; diet in athletic training; diet while traveling; diet and climate; diet for fevers, hysteria, alcoholism, insanity, consumption, circulatory disorders.

1481. Chambers, William & Chambers, Robert. 1842. Chambers's information for the people. Vol. Two.

Article on dairy husbandry contains information on the use of cow's stomach in setting milk in 19th Century Scotland.

1482. Chambless, Marion Agnes. A study of methods of preparation used for certain fruits and vegetables by fifty families in Richland Parish, Louisiana. Master's thesis. Louisiana State University. 1944.

1483. Chambliss, Charles E. 1941. The botany and history of Zizania aquatica. L. (Wild rice). SI-P No. 3622. Pp. 369-382.

1484. Chandler, Asa C. 1953. The relation of nutrition to parasitism. EMA-J 36: 533-552. Egypt.

Effects of host nutritional status upon parasitic survival; effect of host nutritional status upon host defense mechanisms.

1485. Chandler, Julia D. 1905. Food and cookery in Jamaica. BCSM 9: 348.

1486. Chandler, R.W. 1954. The value of the oak tree to West Virginia, particularly as food. WVAS-P 26: 99-101.

1487. Chandrapono, A. 1955. Food consumption of the Thai people. MAT-J 38: 115-159.

1488. Chaney, Ralph W. 1935. The food of 'Peking Man'. CIW-NSB 3: 199-202.

1489.   Chang, Kwang-chih. 1963. The archaeology of ancient China. New Haven and London: Yale University Press.

Cultivated crops of the Neolithic Yangshao stage: p. 59. Reference to ceramic food vessels: passim.

1490.   Chang, S. African game ranching as a form of land use. Master's thesis. Geography. University of California, Los Angeles. 1969.

1491.   Chang, Te-tzu. 1976. The origin, evolution, cultivation, dissemination and diversification of Asian and African rices. Euphytica 25: 425-441.

Posits a Gondwanaland origin for the progenitor of Asian (oryza sativa) and African (Oryza glaberrima). with dispersal occuring subsequent to fracture of the supercontinent. Anthropological and historical evidence are brought forward in a discussion of earliest domestication in Asia.

1492.   Chantre, E. 1904. Recherches anthropologiques dans l'Afrique orientale: Egypte. [Anthropological researchers in East Africa: Egypt.] Lyon: A. Rey.

Food of the Egyptian peasant: pp. 168-169.

1493.   Chao, Buwei Yang. 1963. How to cook and eat in Chinese. 3rd edition. New York: Random House. Vintage Books V-703.

Includes discussion of Chinese foods; utensils; preparation techniques; meals; menus; and an epilogue on tea.

1494.   Chao, Buwei Yang. 1974. How to order and eat in Chinese to get the best meal in a Chinese restaurant. New York: Random House. Vintage Books V-983.

Between-meal foods; table etiquette; formal and informal dinners; regional cuisines; and translation of Chinese ideographs most frequently encountered in Chinese restaurant menus.

1495.   Chao, Yuen Ruen. 1953. Popular Chinese plant words. A descriptive lexico-grammatic study. Language 29: 379-414.

1496.   Chapelle, Mary Lou. 1972. The language of food. AJN 72: 1294-1295.

Significance of food as a means of expresion among staff and patients in Osawatomie State Hospital, Kansas.

1497.   Chapman, A.C. & Baker, F.G.S. 1907. Kaffir beer. JIB 13: 638-645.

Analysis of South African indigenous maize beers.

1498.   Chapman, V.J., ed. 1970. Chapter 5. Algae as food for man. In Seaweeds and their uses. Edited by V.J. Chapman. Pp. 86-118. London: Metheun & Co.

1499.   Charette, E. 1883. Restaurateurs et restaures. [Restaurant proprietors and their customers.] Paris: Le Chevalier.

1500.   Charlesworth, Mildred B. A study to determine the nutritionial backgrouund and needs of students in order to plan a functional unit at the Senior High school level. Master's thesis. Home Economics. Philadelphia: Drexel Institute of Technology. 1947.

1501.   Charmet, P. 1976. La publicite' et les media comme facteurs de modification du comportment alimentaire. [The influence of advertising and mass media in changing food habits.] ANA 30: 481-490.

1502.   Charnock, Richard Stephen. 1866. Cannibalism in Europe. ARev No. 12. Pp. xxii-xxxi.

1503.   Charpentier, Henri & Sparkes, Boyden. 1934. Life a la Henri; being the memoirs of Henri Charpentier. New York: Simon & Schuster.

Gourmet chef; inventor of crepes suzettes.

1504.   Chartkoff, Joseph C. Cause of adaptive change and the origins of food production. in the Near East, Ph.D. dissertation. Anthropology. University of California, Los Angeles. 1974.

1505.   Charvat, Frank J. 1961. Supermarketing. New York: Macmillan.

1506.   Chase, Joseph Smeaton. 1919. California desert trails. Boston, New York: Houghton Mifflin.

Numerous references to edible plants of the Mojave Desert used by Native Americans. Includes an Appendix listing plants and their uses. Mentions use of ocotillo (Fouquieria splendens) flowers as food.

1507.   Chassy, Judith Price; Van Veen, A.G.; & Young, F.W. 1967. The application of social science research methods to the study of food habits and food consumption in an industrializing area. AJCN 20: 56-64.

Study in a five year old "planned" industrial city: Ciudad Sahagun, Hidalgo, Mexico.

1508.   Chastagnol, A. 1953. La ravitaillement de Rome en viande au Ve Siecle. [Rome's meat supply during the Fifth Century.] Rev Hist 77: 13-22.

1509.   Chatillon-Plessis. 1894. La vie de la table a la fin du 19e siecle. Theorie, pratique et historique de gastronomie moderne. [Dining at the close of the 19th Century. The theory, practice and history of modern gastronomy.] Paris: Firmin-Didot.

1510.   Chatterjee, I. 1948. Khesari (Lathryus sativus) as human food. I Farm 9: 328-331.

Reviews history, research, and the literature reports on toxic and non-toxic varieties.

1511.   Chatterjee, N.K.   1962.   Letter on beef eating. Folklore (C) 6: 21-22.

1512.   Chatterjee, P. & Gettman, J.H. 1972. Lead poisoning: subculture as a facilitating agent. AJCN 25: 324-330.

Pica.

1513.   Chattopadhyay, A. 1968. Flowers and dried meat in medicine in ancient India. IJHM 13: 45-47.

1514.   Chattopadhyay, Basantakumar. 1962. Letter on beef eating. Folklore (C) 6:20.

1515.   Chattopadhyay, Basantakumar. 1962. On beef-eating among the Aryans. HS 6, 7 September; 29, 30 September.

1516.   Chaudhuri, R.N.; Chetri, M.; Saha, T.K.; & Mitra, P. 1963. Lathyrism: a clinical and epidemiological study. JIMA 41: 169-173.

1517.   Chaudhuri, S.K., & Sengupta, S.C. [1967?]. Studies in rural change: reports on re-surveys of villages. Daksinsija (Birbhum District) (1960-1967.) Agro-Economic Research Centre.   Santiniketan, West Bengal: Visva-Bharati University.

Includes detailed expenditure data for several foods by occupational groups. Village studied is located in the Birbhum District (approximately 23 50 N, 87. 50 E) of West Bengal.

1518.   Chaussin, E.   1934.   Comment et pourquoi manger du sel.   [How and why salt is eaten.] Nature (P) No. 2931. Pp. 562-564.

1519.   Chaussin, E.   1934.   Comment et pourquoi nous devons manger du sel?   [How and why must we eat salt?] Paris: Le Francois.

1520.   Chaves, Nelson. 1965.   Tropico, nutricao e desinvolvimento. [The tropics, nutrition and development.] Recife: Imprenta Universitaria.

1521.   Chavez, A.B.   1957.   Cultivo de la oca; preparacion de la caya.   [Cultivation of oca and preparation of caya.] V Agri Mayo Pp. 375-376.

Oca is an Andean tuber Oxalis tuberosa Molina) which is frozen, leached, and dried to produce an edible product caya.

1522.   Chavez, Joaquin; Pechnik, E.; & Matosso, L.V. 1950. Estudo da constituicao quimica e do valor alimenticio pupunha. [Study of the chemical composition and nutritive value of pupunha.] TP 3: 209.

Spiny Peach Palm, Guilielma speciosa.

1523.   Cheek, E.B.   1955.   Good health through good feeding.   A Malayan guide to good health through balanced diet. London: Macmillan.

1524.   Chelus, D.   1719.   Histoire naturelle de cacao et du sucre, divisee en deux traites. Edited by Nicolas Mahundel.   [Natural history of cacao and sugar, divided into two treatises.] Paris: L d'Houry.

1525.   Chemorin, Julien.   1958.   Une activite rurale en voie de disparition dans le Haut Jura: la fabrication fermiere du fromage bleu.   [A rural activity on its way to diappearing in the Upper Jura: farm manufacture of bleu cheese.] ATP 6: 51-56.

1526.   Chen, Jack.   1973.   A year in Upper Felicity.   Life in a Chinese village during the Cultural Revolution. New York: Macmillan.

Ethnography of village subsistence pattern: Pp. 49-55; 220-221; 257-261; 313.

1527.   Chen, Jung-pei & Tung, Ta-cheng. 1955. Observations on the applicability of "premix" enriched rice to social customs in Taiwan. FMA-J 54: 113-120.
Pre and post-trial response of target population in suburban Taipei to B vitamin-enriched rice.   Rice cooking methods are described.

1528.   Chen, Ta. 1940.   Emigrant communities in South China. A study of overseas migration and its influence on standards of living and social change. New York: Institute of Pacific Relations. Secretariat.

Changes induced by returned emigres, in various communities in east Kwangtung, and south Fukien (commencing at Chao An, formerly Chao Chou, through Swatow, and Amoy and ending at Chuan Chou (south Fukien). Changes in food habits: Pp. 96-99. In Swatow and Amoy an increase in the consumption of fresh fruit had occurred, which formerly was only eaten occasionally, or at elaborate feasts. Pepper and coffee were also introduced. Cold drinks (iced coffee, orange squash) were introduced into Fukien and Kwangtung by returned emigres from the Philippines, Indonesia, and Indochina, in spite of a tradition of hot beverages.

1529.   Chen, T'ien-hsi (F.T.).   1954.   Musings of a Chinese gourmet.   Food has its place in culture. London: Hutchinson.

Aesthetics; methods; and regional variation in Chinese cookery. Includes recipes.

1530.   Chen, Tung-pai. 1935. The oyster industry of Chung-shan. LSJ 14: 65-72.

Describes production of oyster sauce, and dried oysters, used in Chinese cookery: pp. 68-69.

1531.   Cheney, Ralph H. 1947. The biology and economics of the beverage industry. EB 1: 243-275.

Contains references to the use of cocoa in Native Honduran courtship; mate among Argentine gauchos; and manzanilla fruit drinks in Ecuador.

1532. Cheng, L.T. & Ku, H.C. 1939. A dietary study of the middle-class Chinese and Mohammedans in Sungpan. SSC-ZS-BLC 13: 99-101.

1533. Cheng, L.T.; Tao, H.; & Chu, C.K. 1935. A study of the winter dietary in Nanking. SSC-ZS-BLC 10: 291-302.

1534. Chenier, Louis. 1787. Recherches historiques sur les Maures et histoire de l' Empire du Maroc. [Historical research on the Moors and history of the Moroccan Kingdom.] Paris: the Author.

1535. Cheo, Ying-mei-tsang. A study of methods for detecting malnutrition in children. Master's thesis. Oakland, California: Mills College. 1946.

1536. Cheong, Phyllis S.Y. & Gopaul, Marilyn. 1965. Feeding of immigrants. Nutrition (L) 47: 224.

Review of Chinese, and West Indian (Caribbean) food preparation techniques for use in hospitals.

1537. Cherniak, Lawrence. 1979. Cooking with bhang. Stone Age No. 2 (Spring). Pp. 32-37.

Cannabis sativa in foods and beverages, and the shops in India where these are sold.

1538. .Chervin, Arthur. 1908. Anthropologie Bolivienne. [Bolivian anthropology.] Paris: Imprimerie Nationale; Librairie H. Le Soudier.

Vol. One: includes chemical analysis of edible clay.

1539. Chestnut, Victor King. 1927. Primitive manufacture and use of acorn meal. NNA-PR 18:43-45.

1540. Chevalier, Alphonse (fils). 1848. Notice historique et chronologique sur l'emploi de la pomme de terre et de sa fecule dans la panification. [Historical and chronological note on the use of potatoes and potato starch in bread making.] Paris: Imprimerie de Vve Bouchard-Huzard.

1541. Chevalier, Alphonse. 1851-1982. Dictionnaire des alterations et falsifications des substances alimentaires, medicamenteuses et commerciales, avec l'indication des moyens de les reconnaitre. [Dictionary of a alterations and falsification of food, medical, and commercial substances, with indication of the means for recognizing them.] Paris: Bechet jeune.

1542. Chevalier, Alphonse (fils) & Chevalier, Alphonse (pere). 1858. Recherches chronologiques sur les moyens appliques a la conservation de substances alimentaires de nature animale et de nature vegetale. [Chronological research on the means used to preserve animal and vegetable substances.] Paris: J.-B. Bailliere.

1543. Chevalier, Alphonse. 1862. Du cafe, son historique, son usage, son utilite', ses alterations, ses succedanses, et ses falsifications...[Of coffee, its history, its use, its usefulness, its alterations, its falsification...] Pairs: J.-B. Bailliere.

1544. Chevalier, Auguste. 1906. Les baobabs (Adansonia) de l'Afrique continentale. [The baobabs (Adansonia) of continental Africa.] SBF-B Pp. 480-495.

1545. Chevalier, Auguste. 1908. A propos du Manihot Teissonieri, A. Chev. [Concerning Manihot Teissonieri, A. Chev.] JA Trop 8: 110-111.

1546. Chevalier, Auguste. 1910. Sur une nouvelle legumineuse a fruits souterrains cultivee dans le Moyen-Dahomey (Voandzeia poissoni, A. Chev.). [On a new underground fruiting legume cultivated in Middle-Dahomey (Voandzeia poissoni, A. Chev.). P-AS-CR-HS 4 juillet.

1547. Chevalier, Auguste. 1911. Le riz sauvage de l'Afrique tropicale. [Wild rice of tropical Africa.] JATBA 11: 1-3.

1548. Chevalier, Auguste. 1922. Les Salicornes et leur emploi dans l'alimentation. Etude historique, botanique, economique. [Salicornia sp. and their use as food. Historical, botanical and economic study.] RBAAC 2: 697-785.

As food: Pp. 709-714; 762-765.

1549. Chevalier, Auguste. 1933. Plantes nouvelles ou peu connues de l'Afrique tropicale. 3. Sur une Rutaceae utile de Soudan francais. [New or little-known plants of tropical Africa. 3. On a useful Rutaceae from French Sudan.] P-MHN-B 5: 408-410.

1550. Chevalier, Auguste. 1952. De quelques Dioscorea d'Afrique Equitoriale toxiques dont plusieurs varietes sont alimentaires. [On several toxic Dioscorea of Equatorial Africa, some of which are edible.] RBAAT 32: 14-18.

1551. Chevalier, Auguste. 1953. Une curiosite biologique: l'usage ancien de quelques Araignees pour l'alimentation humaine. [A biological curiosity: former use of several spiders as human food.] RBAAT 33: 70.

Mentions use of Aranea edulis in New Caledonia, during late Eighteenth Century.

1552. Chi, Y.F. & Read, Bernard Ems. 1935. Vitamin C content of Chinese foods. CJP 9: 47-61.

1553. Chiang, T'ien Tse. 1934. Chia Ming's 'Elements of Dietetics.' A summary of the first volume with an introduction. Isis (Washington, D.C.) 20: 324-334.

1554. Chiao, Hsiao-hui. 1949. Microbiology of paw-tsay. 1. Lactobacilli and lactic acid. fermentation. FR 14: 405-412.

Investigatio n of a fermented Chinese vegetable. Preparation is described.

1555. Chiappella, A.R. 1907. Concerning a little-known edible mushroom. [In German.] ZUNG 13: 384-389.

Boletus bellini.

1556. Chibnik, Michael. The value of subsistence production. Paper presented at 77th Annual Meeting of the American Anthropological Association. 18 November, 1978. Los Angeles, California.

Observes that most anthropologists and economists studying peasant agriculture have either not attempted to place a monetary value on crops consumed at home or have valued such production at market (selling) price. This paper takes the view that the foregoing can lead to incomplete or erroneous analysis of agricultural behavior, since a sensible farmer should often value subsistence production near retail (buying) price. Theoretical problems associated with assigning monetary values to subsistence production are discussed. Some evidence on how farmers actually value crops consumed at home is presented, and suggestions for needed research are made.

1557. Chicago. Newberry Library. Everett D. Graff collection of western Americana. United States Army. Headquarters. Department of New Mexico. Santa Fe, New Mexico. March 25, 1864. General orders No. 8. By command of Brigadier General Carleton.

Relates to food supplies for some seven thousand captive Native Americans.

1558. Chicago. University of Chicago. Department of Anthropology. Hopi foodways. A study in the cultural, nutritional and environmental factors in the diet of the Hopi people. [By James B. Watson.] 1942.

1559. Chicago. University of Chicago Library. Department of Photographic Reproduction. Manuscripts on Middle American cultural anthropology. No. 21. Notes on the Indians of finca Nueva Granada [by Antonio Goubaud Carrera]. 1949.

Diary of a month's stay at a coffee plantation in connection with the Carnegie Institution of Washington survey of food habits in Guatemala (under the direction of Sol Tax). Text in Spanish. [After Peabody Museum Library Catalogue. Item MS C 432 m case 9. No. 21.]

1560. Chicago. University of Chicago Library. Department of Photographic Reproduction. Manuscripts on Middle American cultural anthropology, No. 22. Notes on the Indians of eastern Guatemala [by Antonio Goubaud Carrera]. 1949.

Diary of a two-months' stay in San Luis Jilotepeque (14. 40 N, 89 .42 W), among the Pokomam; and in Jocotan (14. 50 N, 89. 32 W). among the Chorti, in connection with the Carnegie Institution of Washington survey of food habits in Guatemala (under

the direction of Sol Tax). Text in Spanish. [After Peabody Museum Library Catalogue. Item MS C 432 m case 9. No. 22.]

1561. Chicago. University of Chicago Library. Department of Photographic Reproduction. Manuscripts on Middle American cultural anthropology, No. 23. Notes on San Juan Chamelco, Alta Verapaz [by Antonio Goubaud Carrera.] 1949.

Diary of a three months' stay in San Juan Chamelco, a Kekchi community of Alta Verapaz, in connection with the Carnegie Institution of Washington survey of food habits in Guatemala (under the direction of Sol Tax). Text in Spanish. [After Peabody Museum Library Catalogue. Item MS C 432 m Case 9 No. 23.]

1562. Chicago. University of Chicago Library. Department of Photographic Reproduction. Manuscripts on Middle American cultural anthropology, No. 24. Notes on Aguacatan by Juan de Dios Rosales No. & Augustin Pop]. 1949.

Diary and notes of a three months' stay in Auguacatan, Huehuetenango, Guatemala...in connection with the Carnegie Institution of Washington survey of food habits in Guatemala (under the direction of Sol Tax. In addition, there is a systematic descriptioin of various aspects of the culture. Text in Spanish. [After Peabody Museum Library Catalogue. Item MS C 432 m case 9 No. 24.]

1563. Chick, H. 1935. Diet and climate. Cantor Lectures. London: Royal Society of Arts.

1564. Child, Irvin L. 1969. Esthetic preference and other correlatives of active versus passive food preference. JPSP 11: 75-84.

1565. Childs, A. 1933. Some dietary studies of Poles, Mexicans, Italians, and Negroes. CHB 9: 84-91.

1566. Chiltoskey, Mary Ulmer. Cherokee foods and cooking methods. Paper read at the 9th International Congress of Anthropological and Ethnological Sciences. 28 August to 8 September, 1973. Chicago, Illinois.

Descriptions based on the author's residence among North Carolina Cherokee.

1567. Chiltosky, Mary Ulmer. Cherokee Indian food. In Gastronomy. The anthropology of food and food habits. Edited by Margaret Louise Arnott. 1975. Pp. 235-244. Paris; The Hague: Mouton Publishers. World Anthropology.

Informal account of contemporary and recent historic foods; and food in Cherokee oral tradition. Includes description of food preparation techniques.

1568.   China. Bureau of Economoic Information. 1924. Wine-making in China. CEM No. 8. Pp. 11-13.

1569.   China.   Statistical Department.   1888. Teas. The Maritime Customs. Special Series. No. 11. Shanghai: Statistical Department of the Inspectorate General of Customs.

1570.   China. Statistical Department. 1911. The soja bean of Manchuria. The Maritime Customs. Special Series. No. 31. Shanghai: Statistical Department of the Inspectorate General of Customs.

1571.   Chiriboga, Carlos Collazos. 1954. La dieta del Indio. [Indian diet.] AVN 5: 343-346.

    Analysis of Native Peruvian diet. Save for the staple quinoa (Chenopodium quinoa) rich in protein, iron, phosphorus, and some B vitamins, nutrient intake is found insufficient.

1572.   Chittenden, G. The effect of mid-morning lunch on anger and irritability in nursery school children. Master's thesis. University of Nebraska. 1936.

1573.   Chiu, Y.T.   1931.   Analyses of Chinese foods. 1. Chinese wines. LSJ 10: 391-398.

1574.   Chiva, M. 1976. Facteurs genetiques et environnementaux dans les conduites alimentaires normales et deviantes chez l'enfant. [Genetic and environmental factors in normal and deviant food habits among children.] ANA 30: 255-262.

1575.   Cho, Hae-joang. The myth of the sexual division of labor. Paper presented at 77th Annual Meeting of the American Anthropological Association.   14 to 18 November, 1978. Los Angeles, California.

1576.   Chopra, Jogjinder G., & Gist, CA.A 1966. Food practices among Trinidadian children. JADA 49: 497-501.

1577.   Chopra, R.N. & Chopra, G.S. 1933. Some country beers of India. IMG 68: 665-675.

1578.   Choremis, K. 1947. The child's nutrition in Greece. A Ped 36: 120-128.

1579.   Chotel, Jean-Baptiste. 1900. L'alimentation de l'armee. [The army's food.] Paris: R. Chapelot.

1580.   Chou, Eric.   1972.   The dragon and the phoenix. The book of Chinese love and sex. New York: Bantam Books.

    The interrelation between food and sex: Pp. 156-160.

1581.   Chowdry, B. 1958. Food habits in India. SNews 6: 8-9.

1582.   Chowdhury, B.K.   1961.   Studies in rural change: first-point village surveys. No. 1 Kanrsar (Burdwan District), 1957-1968. Agro-Economic Research Centre. Santiniketan, West Bangal: Visva-Bharati University.

    Contains detailed food expenditure data for religious and occupation groups.   Village studied is located approximately one hundred km northwest of Calcutta.

1583.   Chowdhury, K.A. 1965. Plant remains from pre-and proto-historic sites and their scientific significance. S Cult 31: 177-178.

1584.   Chrispeels, Maarten J. & Sadava, David. 1977. Chapter Three. Plants as a resource of food. Chapter Eleven.   Alternative sources of food.   In Plants, food, and people.   San Francisco: W.H. Freeman.

1585.   Christensen, M. Reliability of dietary questionnaire to measure food habits. Master's thesis. Iowa State University. 1974.

1586.   Christian, Eugene & Griswold, Molly. 1904. Uncooked foods and how to use them. A treatise on how to get the highest form of animal energy from food. New York, Passaic, New Jersey: [?] The Health-Culture Co.

1587.   Christian, John. 1891. Behar proverbs classified and arranged according to their subject matter and translated into English with notes illustrating the social customs, popular superstitions and every day life of the people. London: Trubner. Trubner's Oriental Series.

1588.   Christensen, J.J. 1963. Corn smut caused by Utsilago maydis. A PhytS-M No. 2. Also published as Minn-AES-MJS-P No. 1119.

1589.   Christian, G. 1971. La vie quotidienne de la society gourmande au 19e siecle. [Daily life among gourmands of the 19th Century.] Paris: Hachette.

1590.   Christie, C.D. 1923. The relation of a dietetic department to the medical service of a hospital. Diet Ad Ther 1: 8-12.

    Refers to nutritional medicine, and the relevance of dietetics to the amelioration of certain diseases.

1591.   Christie, Emerson B. 1912. Report on the drinking customs of the Subanuns. PJS 7 [A]: 114-117.

    Philippines.

1592.   Christopherson, J.B. 1910. Earth eating in the Egyptian Sudan. JTM 13: 3-7.

    Includes references to the occurrence of geophagy throughout the world which are documented, and do not appear in the general literature on the subject.

1593.   Ch'u, Chih-Sheng. 1954. Chung-kuo liang-tsang chih-tu kai-lun. [The Chinese system of food storage.] Taipei: Chung-wang-wen-wu-kung-ying-shu.

1594.   Chubbock, Levi.   1914.   Alaska's reindeer industry. JH 5: 149-154.

   Notes on reindeer milk: p. 152.

1595.   Chung, H.L. & Ripperton, J.C. 1929. Utilization and composition of Oriental vegetables in Hawaii. Hi-AES-B No. 60.

   Includes botanical, Chinese, and Japanese designations (with ideographs), and directions for preparation.

1596.   Chuquet, Alphonse.   1868.   Gulyas hus. [The gulash of Hungary.] Strasbourg: Imprimerie de veuve Berger-Levrault.

   Includes 'historico-culinary' comments, and notes on the history and use of Hungarian red pepper (paprika).

1597.   Church, A.H. 1880. Food, some account of its sources, constituents and uses. Published for the Committee of Council on Education. London: Chapman & Hall.

1598.   Church, A.H. 1886. Food grains of India. South Kensington Handbooks. London: Chapman.

1599.   Church, A.H.   1896.   Euryale ferox: the Gorgon fruit. AL No. 39. Pp. 1-3.

1600.   Church, Margaret B. 1923. Soy and related fermentations. USDA-DB No. 1152.

   A report on experimentation with soy sauce and related East Asian fermented soy products, such as miso, and natto. Photographs of apparatus, in China and Japan, are contained in the report, including one of the ripening of soy sauce mash at Ichang, Hupeh Province, taken by the U.S.D.A. plant explorer Frank N. Meyer, in 1917.

1601.   Church, M. & Doughty, Joyce. 1976. Value of traditional food practices in nutrition education. JHN 30: 9-12.

   Discusses effect of fragmentation of knowledge on nutrition education; the cultural gap and nutrition education; mixtures of foods in traditional diets; cultural context and nutrition education; also included are verses from the traditional 'Song of Lawino' expressing cultural attitudes toward food in East Africa.

1602.   Churchill-Taylor, Samuel E. 1975. Tea and sects. Tarzana, California: Moore-Taylor.

1603.   C.I.L.E.A.C.   (Centro de Investigaciones Linguisticas y Etnograficas Amazonas de Colombia). 1945.   Contribucion provisional a la bibliografia etnobotanica.   [Provisional contribution to ethnobotanical bibliography.] ACA 3:48-52.

   Contains a list of sixty-six studies. Serial is held by Staatsbibliothek, Berlin.   No. 204/L-1.

1604.   Cilento, R.W.   1927.   Diet and nutrition in northern Melanesia. MJA-S 5: 150-153.

1605.   Des Cilleuls, J. 1965. A propos des vivres de reserve et de la conservation des aliments aux armees de la monarchie (17e et 18e siecles). [Concerning reserve rations and the preservation of foodstuffs in the armies of the Monarchy (17th and 18th Centuries.] SMMF-B 59: 3-10.

   France.

1606.   Cintra, Antonio Barros de Ulhoa.   Nutritional deficiencies in the American tropics.   In International Congresses on Tropical Medicine and Malaria. Washington, D.C., 10 May to 18 May, 1948. Proceedings.   Vol. 2. Pp. 1229-1236.   Washington, D.C.: Department of State.

   Article discusses food habits and nutritional status, focusing largely on Brazil.

1607.   Cipriani, Lidio.   1966.   The Andaman Islanders.   Translated by D. Taylor Cox & Linda Cole. London: Weidenfeld & Nicolson.

1608.   Cissoko, S.M. 1968 Famines et epidemies Tombouctou et dans la boucle du Niger du 16e au 18e siecles.   [Famines and epidemics at Tombouctou and at the bend of the Niger from the 16th to the 18th Centuries.] IFAN-B 30 [series B]: 806-821.

1609.   Citizens' Board of Inquiry into Hunger and Malnutrition in the United States. 1968. Hunger, U.S.A. Washington, D.C.: New Community Press.

   Report of investigations on dietary adequacy in several hundred counties in the continental United States. Reviews specific examples of failures to meet the nutritional needs of low-income groups. Analyzes food and welfare programs and makes recommendations designed to bring food aid within the reach of all who are qualified to receive it.

1610.   Citizens' Board of Inquiry into Hunger and Malnutrition in the United States. 1972. Hunger U.S.A. revisited.   Atlanta: Southern Regional Council. [?]

   Reviews progress made in providing nutrition programs to low income populations since the Citzens' Board's previous report on malnutrition in several hundred counties in the United States.

1611.   Claasen, Walter.   1911.   Beitrage zur Feststellung der Ernarungsverhaltnisse des deutschen Land- und Stadtvolkes. [Essay on the establishing of nutritional requirements for rural and urban Germans.] ARGERG 8: 458-487.

1612.   Clairmont, Donald H. 1962. Notes on the drinking behaviour of the Eskimos and Indians in the Aklavik area. A preliminary report. Northern Coordination and Research Centre. Ottawa: Canada. Department of Northern Affairs and National Resources.

Examines drinking patterns ("splurge and binge"); beverage preferences; use of home brew, and alcohol-containing non-beverage products (shave lotion, perfume); age, gender, and ethnic variables; community attitudes toward drinking; crime, law enforcement and drinking behavior.

1613.   Clapier-Valladon, M. 1971. Les Ksouriens de Nema. [The Ksourien of Nema.] Ethnopsychologie 1: 43-72.

Diet of a Mauritanian group: Pp. 63-64.

1614.   Clark, Jr., Mrs. Arthur. 1970. Bayou cuisine; its tradition and transition. Indianola, Mississippi: St. Stephen's Episcopal Church.

1615.   Clark, C., comp., ed. 1849. English cookery five hundred years ago: exhibited in sixty "nyms" or receipts. From a manuscript compiled about 1390 by the master cooks of King Richard the Second, entitled "The forme of cury", & c. Printed (verbatim) in black letter, with the addition of a running glossary and notes. Totham, England: Printed by C. Clark at his private press.

1616.   Clark, Colin & Haswell, Margaret. 1967. The economics of subsistence agriculture. New York: St. Martin's Press.

1617.   Clark, E.H. 1956. Who invented the bottle screw? Indoors January. Pp. 23-25.

1617.   Clark, E. Phylis. 1946. West Indian cookery. Published for the Government of Trinidad and Tobago. Edinburgh: Thomas Nelson & Sons.

1618.   Clark, G.F. & Lombard, P.M. Description of and key to American potato varieties. USDA-C No. 741.

1619.   Clark, Grahame. 1942. Bees in antiquity. Antiquity 16: 208-211.

Honey as food and beverage: pp. 210-211.

1620.   Clark, Grahame. 1948. Fowling in prehistoric Europe. Antiquity 22: 116-130.

1621.   Clark, H.H. 1967. The origin and early history of the cultivated barleys - a botanical and archaeological synthesis. AgHR 15: 1-18.

1622.   Clark, Leslie L. Appendix D. Preliminary coding system for nutrition materials. In Cross-cultural studies of factors related to differential food consumption. Final Report. United States Public Health Service Grant No. 3557. New Haven, Connecticut: Human Relations Area Files.

1623.   Clarke, H.V.A. 1954. Food in Barbados. Nutrition (L) 8: 79-82.

1624.   Clark, H. Walton & Southall, John B. 1919. Freshwater turtles: a source of meat supply. USDI-BF-RCF for the year 1919.

Nineteen recipes collected from Illinois and Missouri residents: pp. 18-20.

1625.   Clark, J. Desmond. 1948. The development of fishing in prehistoric Europe. Antiq J 28: 440-485.

1626.   Clark, J. Desmond. 1962. The spread of food production in sub-Saharan Africa. JAH 3:211-228.

1627.   Clark, J. Desmond. 1971. A re-examination of the evidence for agricultural origins in the Nile Valley. PS-P 37: 34-79.

1628.   Clark, John. 1956. Hunza. Lost kingdom of the Himalayas. New York: Funk & Wagnalls.

Recounts, among other experiences, the author's observations while operating a dispensary. Provides evidence which contradicts the popular image of Hunza as a region characterized by a disease-free population living on a 'perfect' diet. Descriptions of Hunza foods: pp. 73, 139, 149, 203-205.

1629.   Clark, Kate McCosh. 1896. Maori tales and legends collected and retold by Kate McCosh Clark. London: D. Nutt.

Origin of cannibalism (myth): p.15.

1630.   Clark, Margaret. 1959. Health in the Mexican-American culture. A community study. Los Angeles, Berkeley: University of California Press.

Hot-cold classification of foods: pp. 164-167.

1631.   Clark, Taliaferro. 1924. A plea for more attention to the nutrition of the school child. Med. Officer 32: 213-215.

Discusses the relationship of nutrition to growth. Encourages health and nutrition education in schools. Emphasizes the importance of lunch, especially in rural areas, where breakfast may be hurried, and lunches for school children poorly prepared.

1632.   Classen, T.E.A. 1946. The tuna industry of southern Spain. USDI-FWS-FL No. 188.

Preservation and preparation of tuna, with recipes: pp. 13-21.

1633.   Clastres, Pierre & Sebag, Lucien. 1963. Cannibalisme et mort chez les Guayakis (Achen). [Cannabilism and death among the Guayaki; (Achen).] MP-R 14: 174-181.

Paraguay.

1634.   Claudian, Jean. 1964. Propositions pour l'analyse du comportement alimentaire de l'homme. [Proposals for the analysis of dietary behavior in humans.] Paris: Fondation Internationale pour le Progres de l' Alimentation.

1635.   Claudian, Jean [1967?] Final technical report on factors of food selection. Factors of food selection other than nutritional and palatability i.e. psychosociological factors of food preference and consumption. Public Law 480 Grant No. FG-Fr-122. Project No. E9-SRS-1 (c). Hopital Bichat. Paris: Unite de Recherches de Dietetique de l' I.N.S.E.R.M.

A unique monograph, covering in detail cultural patterns; traditional foods; variables determining food choice; meal length; relative importance of the three meals within family; feasts meals and prestige foods; attitudes toward food; mealtime atmosphere; meal structure; food likes and dislikes; economic variables affecting food consumption; meal and menu planning; role of radio and televison during meals.

1636.   Claudian, Jean. 1972. L'homme et son pain. [Man and his bread.] CND 7: 265-274.

1637.   Claudian, Jean. 1973. Reflexioins sur le cannibalisme de famine. [Reflections on cannibalism during famines.] CND 8: 299-302.

1638.   Claudian, Jean & Serville, Yvonne. Les aliments du dimanche et vendredi. Etudes sur le comportement alimentiare actuel en France. [Sunday's and Friday's foods. Studies on current eating behavior in France.] In Pour une histoire de l'alimentation. Edited by J.J. Hemardinguer. 1970. Pp. 300-306. Paris: Colin.

1639.   Claudian, Jean & Serville, Yvonne. Aspects de l'evolution recente du comportement alimentaire en France: composition des repas et urbanisation. [Aspects of the recent evolution of eating behavior in France: urbanisation and components of meals.] In Pour une histoire de l'alimentation. Edited by J.J. Hemardinguer. 1970. Pp. 174-187. Paris: Colin.

1640.   Claudian, Jean & Serville, Yvonne. 1970. Evolution recente des coutumes alimentaires en France. [Recent evolution of dietary practices in France.] CND 5: 41-53.

1641.   Claudian, Jean & Serville, Yvonne. 1973. L'homme de l'ere industrielle et ses aliments. [Man in the industrial era, and his food.] CND 8: 227-234.

Considers adaptation to new economic conditions, and adaptation to a new, urban life style, and the relation of these variables to diet and food habits.

1642.   Claudian, Jean; Vinit, F.; & Audollent, F.C. 1956. Enquete sur la consommation alimentaire en Vendee. [Inquiry upon food consumption in Vendee.] P-INH-B 11: 359-371.

The Department of Vendee is located in west-central France.

1643.   Clausen, Lucy W. 1954. Insect fact and folklore. New York: Macmillan.

Insects as food in Burma, and elsewhere: pp. 18-19; Greece and Thailand: p. 29;

China, Malabar, Argentina, Peru, Barbados, ancient Greece and Rome: pp. 32-33; Burma: p. 63; Modoc Tribe (California): p. 82; Mexico City: p. 124; Miskito, Jicaque, and Jivaro Tribes, Mexico City: p. 139; Bali p. 143.

1644.   Clavigero, Fransisco Javier Mariano 1787. History of Mexico, collected from Spanish and Mexican histories, from manuscripts and ancient painting of the Indians. 2 vols. Translated by Charles Cullen. London: G.G.J. & J. Robinson.

Reference to a food made from the eggs of the insect axayacatl, called tecuitlatil, observed to taste like cheese.

1645.   Cleaver, Harry. The origins of the Green Revolution. Ph.D dissertation. Stanford University. 1975.

1646.   Cleene, N. de. 1940. Les problemes de l'alimentation des indigenes du Congo Belge. [Dietary problems of Belgian Congo natives.] Africa (Madrid) 13: 72-73.

Concerns work done by the Foundation Reine Elisabeth pour l'Assistance Medicale aux Indigenes (acronym: FOREAMI).

1647.   Clein, M.W. 1952. Acerola juice - the richest known source of vitamin C. JPed 48: 140-145.

1648.   Cleland, Charles E. The prehistoric animal ecology and ethnozoology of the Upper Great Lakes region. Ph.D. dissertation. University of Michigan. 1966.

1649.   Cleland, J.B. 1932. Botanical notes of anthropological interest from Macdonald Downs, central Australia. RSSA-TP 56: 36-38.

1650.   Cleland, J.B. 1936. Ethnobotany in relation to the Central Australian Aboriginal. Mankind 2: 6-9.

1651.   Cleland, J.B. 1957. Our natives and the vegetation of southern Australia. Mankind 5: 149-162.

1652.   Cleland, J.B. 1964. Food of the aborigenes. Letter to the editor. VNat 80: 273.

1653.   Cleland, J.B. & Johnston, T.H. 1933. The ecology of the Aborigenes of central Australia: botanical note. RSSA-TP 58: 113-124

1654.   Cleland, J.B. & Johnston, T.H. 1937. Notes on native names and uses of plants in the Musgrave Range region. Oceania 8: 208-215.

1655.   Cleland, J.B. & Johnston, T.K. 1939. Aboriginal names and uses of plants at The Granites, central Australia. RSSA-TP 63: 22-26.

1656.   Cleland, J.B. & Johnston, T.H. 1939. Aboriginal names and uses of plants in the northern Flinders Ranges. RSSA-TP 63: 172-179.

1657.   Cleland, J.B. & Tindale, Norman B. 1954. The ecological surroundings of Ngalia natives in central Australia, and native names and uses of plants. RSSA-TP 77: 81-86.

1658.   Clements, F.W.   1959.   Changing food habits. SP 10: 173-177.

1659.   Clements, Frederick E. & Chaney, R.W. 1937. Environmental and life in the Great Plains. CIW-SP No. 24.

1660.   Clemmer, Donald. 1940. The prison community. Boston: The Christopher Publishing House.

Food in various contexts of prison life: pp. 163-168.

1661.   Clemont-Janin. 1875. Notes sur les prix des denrees en Bourgogne. [Notes on costs of foodstuffs in Burgundy.] Dijon: Imprimerie Marchand.

1662.   Clerc, Louis. 1828. Manuel de l'amateur de cafe ou l'art de cultiver le cafier, de le multiplier, d'en recolter son fruit et de preparer agreablement et economiquement sa boisson par des procedes tant anciens que nouveaux, suivi des proprietes physiologiques et medicales de cette boisson et de la maniere de cultiver la chicoree et d'en preparer la poudre; ainsi que d'un autre cafe' indigene compose' par l'auteur comme ayant un arome et une saveur beaucoup plus agreable. [Manual for the connoisseur of coffee or the art of coffee-tree cultivation, and multiplication, harvesting its fruit, and of preparing the beverage agreeably and economically by old and new processes, followed by the physiological and medicinal properties of the drink and of cultivating chicory and preparing a powder from it; as well as another indigenous coffee developped by the author having a very highly agreeable aroma and taste.] Paris: the author.

1663.   Clerc, Louis. 1828. Manuel de l'amateur de fromage et de beurre, ou l'art de preparer a peu de frais toutes les especes de fromages connues soit en France, soit dans les pays etrangers. [Manual for the connoisseur of cheese and butter, or the art of preparing at little cost all the kinds of cheeses known in France as well as in foreign countries. Paris: chez l'editeur; Metz: Imprimerie d'Hadamard.

1664.   Clifcorn, L.E. & Peterson, G.T.   1954. Trends in the development of foods for the upper age groups. F Tech 8: 277-279.

United States of America. Foods for older adults.

1665.   Cline, Beryl Mae. The development of units for teaching nutrition in the elementary grades. Master's thesis. Lubbock: Texas Technological College. 1947.

1666.   Cline, J.A. & Godfrey, R.S. 1927. Unusual meats. M-AES-C No. 162.

Cooking viscera, backbone, spareribs.

1667.   Cline, Walter; Commons, Rachel S.; Walters, L.V.W.; Mandelbaum, May; & Post, Richard H. The Sinkaietk, or southern Okanagon of Washington. Edited by Leslie Spier. LA-CGSA No. 6.

The subsistence quest: pp. 11-34: the seasonal round; salmon fishing; salmon drying; first-salmon ceremony; small fish; deer hunting; preparation of deer, bear and other game animals; berries; roots, and other plant foods; starvation foods; plant names; storage; first-fruit ceremonies.

1668.   Close, J. 1955. Enquete alimentaire au Ruanda-Urundi: [Dietary survey in Ruanda-Urundi.] IRCB-ARSC-SSNM No. 2.

1669.   Close, J. 1955. Une grand enquete alimentaire au Ruanda-Urundi. [A large-scale dietary survey in Ruanda-Urundi.] FSAC 1: 3-5.

1670.   Cloudsley - Thompson, J.L. 1953. Caterpillars eaten by a Zulu. Entomologist 86: 51-52

1671.   Clow, Bertha. Food preferences in four areas of Montana. Department of Home Economics. Typescript. Bozeman, Montana: Montana State College 1946-1947.

Results of a questionnaire returned from nine hundred ninety persons, throughout Montana of high school age and older. Most liked foods included white wheat flour bread, oranges, butter, white potato, chicken, canned peaches, fresh apples, iceberg lettuce, fresh tomatoes, beef, ice cream, whole milk, fresh peaches, canned pears. Least liked foods were kidney, brains, canned milk, buttermilk, margarine, mutton, tongue, skim milk, rabbit, dandelion greens, egg plant, hominy, oysters, and rutabaga.

1672.   Clubb, Henry Stephen. 1905. Unpolished rice, the staple food of the Orient. A lecture by the Rev. Henry S. Clubb to the vegetarian Society of America; to which is added over one hundred receipts for cooking unpolished rice, rice flour, rice polish; and testimonials of eminent food reformers. Philadelphia: Vegetarian Society of America.

1673.   Cluff, Helen Novak. Cross cultural food problems of Iranian college students. Ph.D. dissertation.l Columbia University. 1963.

Three hundred seventy-nine students, in two hundred five colleges and universities in forty states responded to questionnaires. Analytic variables used are gender and age. Major areas of food-related conflict are religious belief, tradition, and ethnic habits. Women students initially showed fewer problems in the new cultural environment. Health and nutritional status were affected by dietary change, poor food selection, and insufficient nutritional knowledge. Lack of adequate preparation for participation in U.S. culture is identified. Includes suggestions for orientation of Iranians to U.S. culture.

1674.   Clum Woodworth. 1936. Apache agent, the story of John P. Clum. New York, Boston: Houghton Mifflin.

Food: p. 147.

1675.   Clute, Willard N.   1918.   Food from wild plants. A Bot 18: 131-139.

Arranged by botanical family.

1676.   Cobb, John N. 1902. Commercial fisheries of the Hawaiian Islands. USCFF-RC for the year 1901. Pp. 383-499.

A comprehensive report which touches on the lore of Hawaiian fishermen; types of boats and nets, lines, hooks, bait and bait preparation equipment; fish ponds; preparation of fishery products; imports, introduction of new aquatic life; fishing activity by island; and background of early whaling. A number of black-and-white photographs are included.

1677.   Cobley, Leslie S. 1956. An introduction to the botany of tropical crops. London: Longmans, Green & Co.

1678.   Cockayne. Thomas Oswald.   1864-1866. Leechdoms wortcunning, and starcraft of early England. London: Longmans.

References to Anglo-Saxon food.

1679.   Cockrell, Wilburn A.   Glades I and pre-Glades settlement and subsistence patterns on Marco Island (Collier County, Florida). Masters thesis. Anthropology. Florida State University. 1970.

1680.   Codd, L.E.W. 1951. Trees and shrubs of the Kruger National Park. ASAAfr-DA-DBPP-BSM No. 26.

Passing references to fruit used as native foods.

1681.   Codrington, Robert Henry. 1891. The Melanesians. Studies in their anthropology and folklore. Oxford: Oxford University Press.

Acquisition of food supply for human race (New Hebrides; myth): p. 170.

1682.   Coelho, Joao.   1936.   Habitudes alimentaires. [Food habits.] Pres Med 44: 1186.

Importance of diet, with examples from the Arctic, Africa, and South America.

1683.   Coffin, R.   1960.   Changing food habits among Alaska natives. Al Med 2: 5-7.

1684.   Coffman, Franklin A. 1946. The origins of cultivated oats. ASA-J 38: 983-1002.

1685.   Coffman, Kathlyn L.   Navajo student food preferences. Master's thesis. Utah State University. 1966.

1686.   Coggins, Jack. 1962. Arms and equipment of the Civil War. New York: Doubleday & Co.

The Quartermaster Corps subsistence department: Pp. 120-123.

1687.   Coggs, Maud. The food likes of boys and girls in Nebraska. Master's thesis. University of Nebraska. 1947.

1688.   Cohen, B.G.   Emotions and food therapy. Master's thesis. Boston: Simmons College. 1939.

1689.   Cohen, Barbara S. Intravillage transactions and social relations: tortilla exchange among women in a Zapotec village of Oaxaca, Mexico. Paper presented at 76th Annual Meeting of the American Anthropological Association.   29 November to 3 December, 1977. Houston, Texas.

Tortilla exchange consists of specific processes of interaction through which goods and services are transferred from one person to another. An examination of tortilla production and distribution makes it possible to identify and define social groups of women. The nature and content of exchange transactions reinforce social relationships based on kinship and class. Land ownership, family structure and occupational status are factors which influence participation in these exchange activities. Attention is given to whether or not there is a regional aspect to tortilla exchange relations.

1690.   Cohen, Malka. 1972. Rikiki hag hashevuot bi-nosayah yihudei Tripoli. [Shevuot biscuits prepared by the Jews of Tripoli.] Yeda?am 16:63.

1691.   Cohen, Mark Nathan. Settlement pattern and subsistence analysis on the Peru coast. Ph.D. dissertation. Anthropology. Columbia University. 1971.

1692.   Cohen, Mark Nathan. 1972-1974. Some problems in the quantitive analysis of vegetable refuse illustrated by a Late Horizon site on the Peruvian coast. Nawa 10-12: 49-60.

1693.   Cohen, Mark Nathan. Pleistocene population growth and the origins of agriculture. Paper presented at 74th Annual Meeting of the American Anthropological Association.   2 to 6 December, 1975. San Fransisco, California.

1694.   Cohen, Mark Nathan. 1977. The food crisis in prehistory: overpopulation and the origins of agriculture. New Haven, Connecticut, London: Yale University Press.

The major thrust of this book is to demonstrate the similarity of events in different areas of the world which led up to the emergence of agriculture and to demonstrate that these events are plausibly linked with agriculture. There is strong reliance on archaelogical evidence in support of the author's hypothesis. The study begins with a discussion of agricultural origins, and moves on to examine the theory of archaeological measurement of population growth and population pressure. Concluding chapters consider the Old and New World evidence.

1695.   Cohen, Saul B.   1961.   Store location research for the food industry. New York: National-American Wholesale Grocer's Association.

1966.   T. & Gitman, L. 1959. Oral complaints and taste perception in the aged. JD 14: 294-298.

1697.   Cohn, Ferdinand. 1884. Prahistorische pflanzenfunde in Schleisen. [Prehistoric plant findings in Schleisen.] DGAEU-CB 9: 101-109.

1698.   Coindet, Leon. 1867-1869. Le Mexique considere au point de vue medico-chirurgical. [Mexico considered from a medico-surgical point of view.] 3 vols. Paris: Victor Rozier.

Refers to food use of the insect eggs axayacatl, called ahuautl when cooked, and sold under the the term 'mosco para los pajaros'.

1700.   Cole, Richard L. 1913. Sacramental wine: intoxicating or non-intoxicating? A study in scriptural principles. London: C.H. Kelly.

1701.   Coleman, B. 1953. Ojibwa and the wild rice problem. AQ 26: 79-88.

1702.   Coleman, Edith. 1938. One man's meat Walkabout 1 September. Pp. 36-38.

Australian Aboriginal food.

1703.   Colenso, William. 1878. Notes, chiefly historical, on the ancient dog of the New Zealanders. NZI-TP 10: 135-155.

Uses as food noted.

1704.   Colenso, William. 1880. Contributions toward a better knowledge of the Maori race. NZI-TP 12: 108-147.

Proverbs related to food and eating: nos. 2, 4, 5, 6, 7, 18, 19 (reedible Freycinetia banksii bracts); 20-24; 29, 38, 45-46, 80 (reuse of Typha angustifolia pollen in confection); 99-101, 117, 126, 127, 129, 131, 158.

1705.   Colenso, William. 1880. On the vegetable food of the ancient New Zealanders before Cook's visit. NZI-TP 13: 3-38.

1706.   Colenso, William. 1892. Some reminiscences of the Maoris: of the fine smelling sense and taste of the ancient Maoris for perfume. Nature (L) 47: 43.

1707.   Coles, Robert & Clayton, Al. 1968. Still hungry in America. New York: World.

Malnutrition in low-income areas of the United States.

1708.   Coll, Armengo. 1907. Los indigenas de Fernando-Poo. [The natives of Fernando-Poo.] Anthropos 2: 387-391.

Foods: pp. 389.

1709.   Collazos, C.; et al. 1954. Dietary survey in Peru. 3. Chacan and Vicos. Rural communities in the Peruvian Andes. JADA 30: 1222-1230.

1710.   Collazos, C.; White, P.L.; White, H.; et al. 1957. La composicion de los alimentos peruanos. [The composition of Peruvian foodstuffs.] UNMSML-FM-A 40: 232-266.

1711.   Colle, Royal D. & Colle, Susana Fernandez de. The pila communication project. Final report. Xerographed [?] Ithaca, New York: Cornell University. October. 1975.

Account of a nutrition education program in Guatemala. Using a cassette tape recorder, programs were developed of interest to women living on a coffee and rubber plantation near Guatemala's Pacific Coast. As all the women spend some time daily at the outdoor public laundering center (pila), this locus was chosen as the site for the education program. Content or message was structured in dramatic or novela form, with reinforcing 'reminders' similar to public service announcements and interviews with medical or other health authorities. Program length was thirty minutes. The authors include an evaluation of the response to the project, together with indications as to the most effective means for carrying such a program out in terms of over-all exposure to message, and in different cultural and social contexts.

1712.   Collier, John & Collier, Mary. 1948. Navajo farmer. FQ 3:17-25.

1713.   Collins, C.W. 1891. Cookery. Blackwood's 150: 166-178.

1714.   Collins, E.J.T. The "consumer revolution" and the growth of factory foods: changing patterns of bread and cereal-eating in Britain in the Twentieth Century. In The making of the modern British diet. Edited by Derek J. Oddy & D.S. Miller. 1976. London: Croom Helm.

1715.   Collins, G.N. 1909. A new type of Indian corn from China. USDA-BPI-B No. 161.

1716.   Collins, G.N. 1911. Dumboy, the national dish of Liberia. NGM 22: 84-88.

1717.   Collins, G.N. 1912. The origin of maize. WAS-J 2: 520-530.

1718.   Collins, G.N. 1914. Pueblo Indian maize breeding. JH 5: 255-272.

Author believes Hopi and Navajo may have selectively bred for drought-resistant varieties.

1719.   Collins, G.N. 1918. Maize: its origins and relationship. WAS-J 8: 42-43.

1720.   Collins, G.N. 1919. A fossil ear of maize. JHer 10: 170-172.

1721.   Collins, Jr., Henry B.; Clark, Austin H.; & Walker, Egbert H. 1945. The Aleutian Islands: their people and natural history (with keys for the identification of the birds and plants). SI-WBS No. 21.

>   Food and food gathering: pp. 24-26. Reviews animal and plant foods. Unique is reference to an early account of meat and fish having been boiled in springs of hot water on Kanaga Island in the Andreanof group.

1722.   Collins, J.L. 1951. Antiquity of the pineapple in America. SJA 7: 145-155.

1723.   Collins, Thomas W. Economic change and the use of alcohol among American Indians. Paper presented at 69th Annual Meeting of the American Anthropological Association. 19 to 22 November, 1970. San Diego, Califoria.

1724.   Collins, Varnum. 1865. Sorgo, or north Chinese sugar cane. RAS-NCB-J 2: 85-98.

1725.   Collinson, John. 1870. The Indians of the Mosquito territory. ASL-M 3: 148-156.

>   Inebriation rituals, and an intoxicating fruit beverage mishla: pp. 151-152.

1726.   Collis, W.R.F.; Dema, J.; & Omololu, A. 1962. On the ecology of child health and nutrition in Nigerian villages. 2. Dietary and medical surveys. TGM 14: 201-229.

>   Food habits: pp. 201-203; seasonal changes in food supply: pp. 203-204.

1727.   Collomb, H. Maladies psychosomatiques au Senegal. [Psychosomatic illness in Senegal.] Contribution a la Semaine Psychosomatique Internationale. Rome. 11 September to 16 September, 1967. Copy on file at the Library of the Food and Agriculture Organization of the United Nations.

>   Emphasizes the need to consider the weaning practices; the relationship between the mother and infant; and the nature of the maternal substitute to which the child is introduced, during and after weaning, in the etiology of kwashiorkor.

1728.   Colombie, Auguste. 1895. Philosophie de l'Ecole de cuisine. Histoire du repas a travers les ages. [Philosophy of the School of Cookery. History of dining through the ages.] Paris: the author.

>   Held by the Bibliotheque Nationale, Paris. No. 8o V. 26703.

1729.   Colomer, L. Gutierrez, 1966. Costumbres, medicamentos y alimentos precolombinos en el Peru. [Customs, medicaments and foods in pre-Columbian Peru.] AF-A 32: 382-413.

1730.   Colon, E.D. 1930. Datos sobre la historia de la agricultura de Puerto Rico antes de 1898. [Facts about the history of Puerto Rican agriculture prior to 1898.]   San Juan: Tipografia Cantero Fernandez & Co.

1731.   Coloquio Internacional de Estudos Luso-Brasileiros. 1959. Uma festa de Xango. [A Xango feast.]   Salvador: Universidad de Bahia. Fundo Goncalo Moniz.

1732.   Colson, Anthony. Kenduri and Selematan: a comparison of Malay and Javanese ritual feasts. Paper presented at 69th Annual Meeting of the American Anthropological Association. 19 to 22 November, 1970. San Diego, California.

1733.   Colson, Elizabeth Florence. 1958. Plateau Tonga diet. R-LIJ No. 24. Pp. 51-67.

1734.   Comas, Juan. 1942. El regimen alimenticio y el mejoramiento indigena.   [Diet and native betterment.] AM Ind 2 (2): 51-56.

>   Indicates the existence of nutritional defiency among Native American populations, and suggests a systematic investigation of native dietary, to be undertaken by anthropologists and nutritionists.

1735.   Combris, P.; Lassaut, B.; & Sylvander, B. 1976. Incidences sur le comportement alimentaire de l'homme de l'evolution des relations producteur-distributeur-consommateur. [Impact of producer-distributor-consumer relations on the evolution of human food behavior.] ANA 30: 491-504.

1736.   Comhaire-Sylvain, Suzanne. 1950. Chapter Three. Food and diet. In Food and leisure among the African children of Leopoldville (Belgian Congo). A study in the adaptation of Congo youth to urban life. U Cape-SAS-C No. 25.

>   Includes data on effects of internal migration upon food habits change among Bakongo tribe.

1737.   Comhaire-Sylvain, Suzanne & Comhaire-Sylvain, Jean. 1952. La alimentacion en la region de Kenscoff. Haiti. [Diet in the Kenscoff region of Haiti.] Am Ind 12: 177-203.

1738.   Comite Organizador de los Juegos de la 19 Olimpiada. [1968]. Mexico 68. Markets today and yesterday. Pictorial review. No. 19. Mexico: Departmento de Publicaciones.

1739.   Commission International des Industries Agricoles. 1953. Bibliographie sur l' huile de noix de coco dans la physiologie humaine et animal. [Bibliography on coconut oil in human and animal physiology.] Paris: Commission International des Industries.

1740.   Common Council for American Unity. What's cooking in your neighbor's pot? Mimeographed. New York: Common Council for American Unity. 1944.

1741.   Concepcion, I. 1937. A study of the food intake of the inmates of Welfareville. PIMA-J 17: 197-210.

1742.   Concepcion, I. 1941. Significance of the soybean in the dietary of Filipinos. AMPhil 2: 479-495.

1743.   Concepcion, I. & Samson, D.D. 1931. A study on the nutritive value and cost of the fiambrera lunch. UPhil-NAPS 1: 257-263.

1744.   Conde, Charles. 1950. Conferencia interafricain sobre a alimentacao e nutricao. Relatoris final. [Interafrican conference on diet and nutrition. Final report.] BGC No. 302-303. Pp. 47-68.

1745.   Condit, Ira J. 1939. A bibliography on the avocado (Persea americana, Miller). Riverside, California: University of California Citrus Experiment Station.

   History and accounts previous to 1800: pp. 7-12; uses, food values, recipes: pp. 176-186.

1746.   Condominas, Georges & Haudricourt, A. 1952. Premiere contribution a l'ethnobotanique indochinoise. Essai d' ethnobotanique Mnong gar (Proto-indochinois du Vietnam). Initial contribution to the ethnobotany of Indo-China. Essay on Mnong gar ethnobotany (Proto-Indochinese of Vietnam).] RBAAT 32: 19-27; 168-180.

   Cultivated food plants: pp. 23-26; non-cultivated food plants: pp. 169-173.

1747.   Condon, Edward V. 1934. Food and the theory of probability. USNI-P 60: 75-78.

1748.   Cone, Jane M. 1957. Food in 17th Century Virginia. VW 18: 16-19.

1749.   Conger, R.M. The effect of diet on activity. Master's thesis. Iowa State College. 1929.

1750.   Congo Belge. Direction Generale de l' Agriculture. 1913. L'agriculture du Congo Belge. [Agriculture in the Belgian Congo.] BACB Vol. 4. No. 4(1).

1751.   Connell, Neville. 1957. Punch drinking and its accessories. BMHS-J 25: 1-17.

1752.   Connoly, Charlene & Eckert, Nan. 1970. The archaeological significance of the desert tortoise. NSM-AP 14: 81-93.

   Nutritional analysis; implications of dietary value to early southern Nevada Native Americans.

1753.   Conrad, Agnes. 1937. The attitude toward food. AJO 7: 360-367.

1754.   Conrad, R. Die Haustiere in den fruhen Kulturens Indiens. [Domesticated animals in early Indian cultures.] Ph.D. dissertation. Ludwig-Maximilians-Universitat Munchen. 1966.

1755.   Constantin, A. Question de folklore matrimonial et sexuel. [A question relating to the folklore of matrimony and sexuality.] In 15e Congres International d' Anthropologie & d' Archeologie Prehistorique. 21-30 Septembre 1930. Coimbre & Porto, Portugal. Actes du Congres. 1931. Pp. 646-649. Paris: Librairie E. Nourry.

   The history and meaning of nougat caramel candy, bearing the likeness of a goat's head, which is broken off by the husband at marriage banquets in Lorraine and offered to his bride.

1756.   Constantin, Marc. 1857. Histoire des cafes de Paris, extraite des memoires d' un viveur, cafes du Palais-Royal, des boulevards, de ville, etc. [History of Parisian cafes, extract from the memoirs of a rake; cafes of the Palais-Royal. of the boulevards, the city, etc.] Paris: Desloges.

1757.   Constantin, J. & Bois, D. 1910. Sur les graines et tubercules des tombeaux peruviens de la periode Incaique. [On the grains and roots of Peruvian tombs of the Incaic period.] RGB 22: 242-246.

1758.   Constantin Cesar. 1543. Les 20 livres de Constantin Cesar, ausquels sont traictez les bons enseignements d' agriculture: traduictez en francoys par Anthoine Pierre. [The 20 books of Constantin Cesar, to which are added good instructions in agriculture: translated into French by Antoine Pierre.] Poitiers: Jehan & Enguilbert de Marnef freres.

   The twenty books contain numerous references to food such as for an unleavened bread; care and preservation of vegetables; recipes for olive preserves, honey; and an entire book on fish and fishing (the 20th).

1759.   Conteneau, Georges. 1954. Everyday life in Babylon and Assyria. Translated by K.R. Maxwell-Hyslop & A.R. Maxwell-Hyslop. London: Edward Arnold.

   Food: pp. 71-79.

1760.   Continental Baking Corporation. 1925. The story of bread. New York: Continental Baking Corporation.

   In two parts, historical and statistical.

1761.   Continental Can Company. 1967. Merchandising ideas to help sell soft drinks in convenience stores. Metal Division. New York: Continental Can Company.

1762.   Conzemius, Edouard. 1932. Ethnographical survey of the Miskito and Sumu Indians of Honduras and Nicaragua. SI-BAE-B No. 106.

   Food: pp. 88-101.

1763.   Cook, D.H.; Rivera, Trinita; & Torres Diaz, L. 1928. Preliminary study of a common Puerto Rican diet. PRJPHTM 4: 253-255.

1764.   Cook, D.H. & Rivera, Trinita. 1929. Rice and beans as an adequate diet. PRJPHTM 5: 16-20.

Also includes discussion of yautia and platano.

1765.   Cook, Della Collins. Changes in subsistence base: the human skeletal evidence. Paper presented at 74th Annual Meeting of the American Anthropological Association. 2 to 6 December, 1975. San Francisco, California.

1766.   Cook, Della Collins. Human growth: a perspective on subsistence base change. Paper presented at 76th Annual Meeting of the American Anthropological Association. 29 November to 3 December. 1977. Houston, Texas.

The biological impact of changes in subsistence base, strategies of exploitation, and density on human populations is most directly measured in the immature skeleton. Disturbances of growth in individuals dying between one and four years are a particularly sensitive index, in that these deaths generally reflect nutritionally mediated disease in modern primitive groups. A model for these effects is tested using Woodland and Mississippian [skeletal material to provide evidence of] growth retardation, growth arrest, enamel defects, and interactions with nutritionally-mediated diseases, suggesting higher biological costs in the terminal Late Woodland populations of the region.

1767.   Cook, Della Collins. 1979. Subsistence base and health in prehistoric Illinois Valley: evidence from the human skeleton. Med Anth 3: 109-124.

This paper presents a model for the interactions among demographic, skeletal, and nutritional variables across the transition from hunting and gathering to maize agriculture-based societies. Data on population composition, growth retardation, growth arrest markers, cortical bone dynamics, and nutritional-related dental variables are examined, with a quantification of the biological impact hypothesized for the transition from Woodland to Mississippian economies in the lower Illinois Valley region from ca. O to A.D. 1000. Population pressure is suggested as having precipitated agriculture.

1768.   Cook, Edwin A. & Pflanz-Cook, S.M. Predicting a pig festival. Paper presented at 73rd Annual Meeting of the American Anthropological Association. 19-24 November, 1974. Mexico City.

New Guinea highlands.

1769.   Cook, Edwin A. & Pflanz-Cook, Susan M. Nobody will feed me. Paper presented at 76th Annual Meeting of the American Anthropological Association. 29 November to 3 December, 1977. Houston, Texas.

This paper is concerned with food taboos among the Manga, a New Guinea highland group; the societal level of taboo application; their genesis, and elimination. Manga society is seen structured into subsets of overlapping exchange networks, the boundaries of which are demarcated by food taboos. Case history data are adduced to support the analysis.

1770.   Cook, Harriet N. 1846. The trees, fruits, and flowers of the Bible. New York: American Tract Society.

1771.   Cook, N. Small food stores in metropolitan Victoria. Master's thesis. Geography. Edmonton, Alberta, Canada: University of Alberta.

1772.   Cook, Orator Fuller. 1904. Food plants of ancient America. In SI-AR for the year 1903. Pp. 481-497.

1773.   Cook, Orator Fuller. 1909. Vegetation affected by agriculture in Central America. USDA-BPI-B No. 145.

Refers to prehistoric agricultural terracing.

1774.   Cook, Orator Fuller. 1910. History of the coconut palm in America. SI-USNH-C Vol. 14. Part Two.

Rich in references to the literature on voyages and travels; reference to use as food; etymological data: pp. 314-316.

1775.   Cook, Orator Fuller. 1913. Wild wheat in Palestine. USDA-BPI-B No. 274.

Historical data on wheat, and other cereals, and their origins.

1776.   Cook, Orator Fuller. 1919. Olneya beans: a native food product of the Arizona desert worthy of domestication. JHer 10: 321-331.

Suggests the fruit of the Sonoran desert plant Olneya tesota be utilized for human and/or animal food. Notes these fruit were not eaten by Native Americans.

1777.   Cook, Orator Fuller. 1920. Foot-plow agriculture in Peru. SI-AR for the year 1918. Pp. 487-491.

1778.   Cook, Orator Fuller. 1921. Milpa agriculture, a primitive tropical system. SI-AR for the year 1919. Pp. 307-326.

Guatemala. Nature of the milpa system; effects of repeated clearing; limits of population under the milpa system; migration to new lands; centers of population; precautions against the spread of fires; periods of reforestation; maize plantings in uncut bush; artificial grasslands and deserts; pastoral periods; secondary, permanent and temporary systems; limitations of native agriculture in Central America.

1779.   Cook, Orator Fuller. 1925. Peru as a center of domestication. Part One. Tracing the

origin of civilization through domesticated plants. J
Her 16: 33-46;

> Part Two.   Endemic crop plants of the
> peruvian region. 16: 95-110. Part one is
> concerned with agriculture, and plant
> domestication. Part two covers specific
> food plants, with excellent black-and-white
> photographs.

1780.   Cook, Orator Fuller. 1932. Debt of agriculture to tropical America. SI-AR for the year 1931.
Pp. 491-501.

> Domestication of American plants; inter-
> change of crops; tropical agriculture in the
> United States; maize; difficulty in changing
> food habits.

1781.   Cook, Orator Fuller. 1935. The Maya
breadnut in Southern Florida. Science 82: 615-616.

1782.   Cook, Orator Fuller. 1942. Etnobotanica:
plantas endemicas domesticadas por los antiguos
peruanos. [Ethnobotany: native plants domesticated by the Ancient Peruvians.] RMN 11: 25-30.

> Twenty-one grains, fruit, and roots used for
> food.

1783.   Cook, Orator Fuller & Collins, G.N. 1903.
economic plants of Puerto Rico. SI-USNH-C 8:57-
280.

1784.   Cook, P.H. & Wyndham, A.J. 1953. A study
of industrial workers patterns of eating behavior.
HR 6:141-160.

> Sociological analysis of status grouping; cul-
> ture, and personality variables in an Aus-
> tralian engineering factory.

1785.   Cook, R.   1966.   The general nutrition
problems of Africa. A Affair 65: 329-340.

1786.   Cook, Sarah Louise. The ethnobotany of the
Jemez Indians. Master's thesis. University of New
Mexico. 1930.
A Rio Grande Pueblo group.

1787.   Cook, Sherburne Friend. 1975. Subsistence
ecology of Scovill. Am An 40: 354-356.

> Analyzing animal protein and nut residues
> from a Terminal Middle Woodland village
> site in Illinois, the author estimates the
> population carrying capacity of the area
> adjacent to the site, in terms of protein and
> calories.

1788.   Cooke, E. 1964. Fair to show Indian cooks.
ADW 15 March. P. 37.

1789.   Cooke, E. 1966. The conversation of chuck
fire cooking. ADW 20 March. Pp. 26-29.

1790.   Cooke, F.C. 1951. The coconut palm as a
source of food. CCQ 2: 153-154.

1791.   Cooley, J.S. 1951. The sweet potato: its
origin and primitive storage practices EB 5:378-386.

1792.   Coombs, Gary. A network model of food
distribution and exchange. Paper presented at 76th
Annual Meeting of the American Anthropological
Association. 29 November to 3 December, 1977.
Houston, Texas.

> This is a progress report on continuing re-
> search by the author, into the nature of
> distribution and exchange systems involving
> food resources. The research utilizes the
> network concept and network analytical
> methods to isolate the characteristics of
> various abstract [i.e. modeled] exchange-
> distribution systems involving food resour-
> ces. A mathematical simulation of selec-
> tive retention is also employed to evaluate
> the viability of the various abstract system's
> different and changing environments. It is
> anticipated that the research will provide
> valuable insights into the evolutionary sys-
> tems for the exchange and distribution of
> subsistence resources as well as suggesting
> reasons for cross-cultural differences in
> such systems.

1793.   Coon, Carleton S. 1959. Race and ecology
in man. CSH-BL-SQB 24: 153-159.

1794.   Cooper, E.H.; Reasonover, F.; Tribble, M.; &
Cox, M. 1962. Wildgame-care,cooking. TAC-EB
No. 987.

1795.   Cooper, Elizabeth. 1914. The women of
Egypt. London: Hurst & Blackett.

> Food: pp. 146-149.

1796.   Cooper, G. 1954. Food of the middle west.
Nutrition [L] 8: 131-134.

> England.

1797.   Cooper, Joe E. 1952. With or without
beans; being a compendium to perpetuate the inter-
nationally-famous bowl of chili [Texas-style] which
occupies such an important place in modern civilization. Dallas: W.S. Henson.

1798.   Cooper, Marcia Mann. 1957. Pica: a
survey of the historical literature as well as reports
from the fields of veterinary medicine and anthropology, the present study of pica in young children,
and a discussion of its pediatric and psychological
implications. Springfield, Illinois: Charles C.
Thomas, Publisher.

1799.   Cooper, R.M.; Bilash, I.; & Zubeck, J.P.
1959. The effect of age on taste sensitivity. JG 14:
56-59.

1800.   Cooper, Robert. The Maori and his plants.
Paper read at the meeting of the Auckland District
Council of the Royal New Zealand Institute of
Horticulture. 25 September, 1963.

1801.   Cooper, Virginia M. 1941. Creole kitchen
cook book. San Antonio, Texas: The Naylor Company.

1802.   Coose, Lois. The Texan's necessities of life, 1821-1845.   Master's thesis.   San Antonio: St. Mary's University. 1941.

References to Native American foods.

1803.   Coote, H.C. 1868. The cuisine bourgeoise of ancient Rome. Archaeologia 41: 283-324.

Devoted largely to the reproduction and translation of recipes from the Roman cookery book of Apicius, accompanied by bibliographic notes relating thereto.   Contains other relevant data and documentation from classical authors.

1804.   Copping, A.M. 1964. Sir Jack Cecil Drummond, F.R.S. Biographical sketch, January 12, 1891 to August 4, 1952. JN 82: 3-9.

1805.   Copping, A.M. 1968. Planning nutrition education in developing countries. JADA 53: 127-129.

1806.   Coquillet, M. 1959. Les glands du chene dans l'alimentation des hommes prehistoriques. [Acorns in the diet of prehistoric people.] SLL-BM 28: 28-32

1807.   Corbett, Thomas H. 1968. Iron deficiency anemia in a Pueblo Indian village. JAMA 205: 186.

Letter regarding occurence among infants and young children, examined May through July, 1966. Acoma Pueblo New Mexico.

1808.   Cordemoy, P. 1932. Le nuocmam. [Nuocmam] BAEI No. 54. Pp. 200-205.

Nuoc-mam is the Vietnamese name for a fermented fish condiment used throughout Southeast Asia.

1809.   Cordeu, Edgardo J. 1969-1970. Aproximacion al horizonte mitico de los Tobas. [Bringing the mythical horizon of the Toba nearer.] Runa 12: 67-176.

The myth of the origin of cultivation: pp. 141-143. Argentina.

1810.   Cordier, Francois-Simon. 1826. Guide de l'amateur de champignons ou precis de l'histoire des champignons alimentaires, veneneux et employes dans les arts, qui croissent sur la sol de la France; contenant la description des caracteres particuliers a chacune de ces plantes; des generalites sur leur emploi dans les arts; sur la preparation culinaire des especes; sur les moyens de distinguer ces especes des especes veneneux; sur les moyens de remedier aux accidens qui produisent ces derniers etc. [Guide for the connoisseur of mushrooms or synopsis of the history of edible and poisonous mushrooms, and those used in the arts, which grow on French soil; containing the description of the particular characters of each of these plants; generalities on the use of these plants in the arts; on the culinary preparations of the edible species; on the means of distinguishing the edible from the poisonous species; on the means for remedying accidents

produced by the latter, etc.] Paris: Galerie de Bossange pere; and the author.

1811.   Core, Earl E. 1967. Ethnobotany of the Southern Appalachian aborigenes. EB 21: 199-214.

1812.   Corkill, N.L. 1946. The feeding of Sudanese infants. Khartoum: Sudan Medical Service.

1813.   Corkill, N.L. 1949. Malnutrition and snake poisoning in the Sudan. RSTMH-T 42: 613-616.

1814.   Corkill, N.L. 1950. Malnutrition in Sudanese millet eaters; a follow-up. JTMH 53: 125-136.

1815.   Corkill, N.L. 1954. Seasonal dietary change in a Sudan desert community. JTMH 57: 257-269.

1816.   Corkill, N.L.; Creditor, H.; & Stewart, G.E.S. 1948. Millet beer and peanuts as remedial foods in polyhypovitaminosis. JTMH 51: 160-168.

1817.   Corley, T.A.B. 1972. Quaker enterprise in biscuits: Huntley and Palmers of Reading, 1882-1972. London: Hutchinson. England.

1818.   Corley, T.A.B. Nutrition, technology and the growth of the British biscuit industry.   In The making of the modern British diet. Edited by Derek J. Oddy & D.S. Miller. 1976. London: Croom Helm.

1819.   Cornell, Ralph D. 1934. Desert associations -the mesquite. Mkey 8: 109-114.

1820.   Cornely, P.B. & Bigman, S.K. 1961. Cultural considerations in changing health attitudes. MAnnals 30: 191-199.

1821.   Cornely, P.B.; Bigman, S.K.; & Watts, D.D. 1963. Nutritional beliefs among a low-income urban population. JADA 42: 131-135.

1822.   Cornwall, Edward. 1927.   The remarkable case of Luigi Cornaro and how he balanced his diet. Med Jnl Rec 126: 309-310.

Therapeutic effects of diet modification in advanced disease; effects of diet in prolonging life.

1823.   Cornwall, Edward. 1937. What the ancient Greeks ate. AmHist 9: 30-33.

From literary sources, including Homer, and Aristophanes.

1824.   Corres, Antonio Agusto Mendes. 1952. Palestras sobre a alimentacao. [Talks on diet.] TAE 13: 270-302.

1825.   Correa, Manuel Pio. 1926-1975. Diccionario das plantas uteis do Brasil e das exoticas cultivadas. [Dictionary of the useful plants of Brazil and of non-indigenous cultigens.] 6 vols. Ministerio de Agricultura, Industria e Commercio. Rio de Janeiro. Imprensa Nacional

1826.   Correll, Donovan S. 1944. Vanilla: its history, cultivation and importance. Llyodia 7: 236-264.

Devoted largely to botanical, cultural, and economic aspects. The early history of its use as flavoring and medicament in Europe are found on pp. 243-246.

1827. Correll, Donovan S. 1948. Wild potato collecting in Mexico. FL 16: 94-112.

Food use: p. 103.

1828. Correll, Donovan S. 1962. The potato and its wild relatives. Renner, Texas: Texas Research Foundation.

1829. Corrigan, R.S.C. 1946. Scurvy in a Cree Indian. CMAJ 54: 380-383.

1830. Cortes, E. Gonzalez. 1941. Consideraciones sobre la alimentacion rural. [Considerations on rural dietary.] RMS 69: 299-303.

Chile.

1831. Cortes, Efrain. La economia de subsistencia entre los tejedores de palma en una comunidad Mixteca. [Subsistence economy among palm weavers in a Mixtec Community.] Paper presented at 73rd Annual Meeting of the American Anthropological Association. 19 to 24 November, 1974. Mexico City, Mexico.

1832. Cosentino, Geraldine & Stewart, Regina. 1977. Kitchenware. A guide for the beginning collector. Racine: Western Publishing Co.

Largely historical, with sections on collecting, purchasing, care and display.

1833. Cosminsky, Sheila, 1975. Changing food and medical beliefs and practices in a Guatemalan community. EFN 4: 183-191.

This article examines the relationship between food and illness, as part of the interaction between indigenous and Western medicine in the Quiche-speaking, Mayan community of Santa Lucia Utatlan, located in the southwestern highlands of Guatemala. The conceptual significance of food quality terms ["hot", "cold", "highly nutritive", "fresh" or "cooling"] is examined in relation to local acceptance of the idea that certain foods maintain health and prevent illness. Includes tables of foods and medicines indicating the variation in elicited individual classification according to the system of qualitative categories.

1834. Costa, Angyone. 1943. A alimentacao de nossos indios. [The diet of our Indians.] Am Ind 3: 221-226.

Study based on historical documentation.

1835. Costa, Dante. 1948. Pesquisas de nutricao na Amazonia. [Nutrition investigations in Amazonia.] IMed 24: 3-13.

1836. Costa, Dante. 1960. Problemas de educacao alimentar em paises de pouco desinvolvi-

mento economico. [Problems of nutrition education in economically underdeveloped countries. Estudo e Pesquisa Alimentar No. 38. Rio de Janeiro: Servico de Alimentacao de Previdencia Social.

1837. Costa, Dante; Mota, Salatiel; & Carvalho, Maria da Conceicao. 1960. Sobre o valor nutritivo do doce de capuacu. Estudo e pesquisa alimentar No. 14. [On the nutrive value of capuacu confection. Diet study and research No. 14.] Rio de Janeiro: Servico de Alimentacao de Previdencia Social.

Cupuacu is a tree related to cacao [Theobroma grandiflora].

1838. Costa, Dante & Carvalho, M. Conceicao. 1954. Contribuicao ao estudo do caju e doces de caju. [Contribution to the study of the cashew and of cashew confections.] Colecao estudo e pesquisa alimentar No. 36. Rio de Janeiro: Servico de Alimentacao da Previdencia Social.

1839. Costanzo, G. 1963. Arachnids and annelids used as an alimentary additive among the Piaroa Indians of the Middle Orinoco. Parasitologia 5: 221-223.

Venezuela.

1840. Cotgreave, W. 1898. Gastronomic Germany. Lippincott 61: 853-855.

1841. Cott, Hugh B. 1953. The exploitation of wild birds for their eggs. Ibis 95: 409-449; 96: 129-149.

1842. Cotte, Jules, & Cotte, Charles. 1912. Etude sur les bles de l'antiquite. [Study on the wheats of antiquity.] Paris: J.-B. Bailliere et fils.

1843. Cotting, J.R. 1837. Analysis of a species of clay found in Richmond County which is eagerly sought after and eaten by many people, particularly children. SMSJ 1: 288-292.

1844. Cottingham, John O. 1951. Mycophagy. IAS-P 61: 78-80.

Author's comments on personal experience eating various kinds of mushrooms.

1845. Coughenour, C. Milton. 1972. Functional aspects of food consumption activity and family life cycle stages. JMF 34: 656-664.

Food consumption is seen as a social [group] process. The study further discusses markers useful for identifying the stage at which the food consumption process becomes a primary developmental-role task for the homemaker.

1846. Couperie, Pierre. 1964. L'alimentation au XVIIe siecle. Les marches de pourvoirerie. [Diet in the 17th Century. The purveyors' markets.] Annales 19: 467-479.

1847. Couperie, P. Les marches de pourvoirerie: viands et poissons chez les Grands du 17e siecle.

[The markets of supply: meat and fish among the Great Powers of the 17th Century.] In Pour une histoire de l'alimentation. Edited by J.J. Hemardinguer. 1970. Pp. 241-254. Paris: Colin.

1848.   Coursey, David G. 1968. The edible aroids. WC 20(4): 25-30.

Discusses the following Araceae: cocoyam, dasheen, taro, yautia, ocumo, macabo, maffaffa, kulokasi, elephant yam, and chou-dachine.

1849.   Coursey, David G. 1972. The cultivation of the yam: interrelationship of man and yams in Africa and the Indo-Pacific region APAO 7: 215-233.

1850.   Coursey, David G. The ethnobotany of the West Africa yam culture. Paper presented at the 9th International Congress of Anthropological and Enthological Sciences. 28 August to 8 September, 1973. Chicago, Illinois.

Presents botanical evidence that the main species of yam [Dioscorea spp.] cultivated in West Africa are of indigenous origin. Suggests that domestication of these species is also indigenous. Notes also that Dioscorea sp. of Asiatic origin may have been introduced to the East African littoral in comparatively early times.

1851.   Coursey, D.G. The origins and domestication of yams in Africa. In Gastronomy. The anthropology of food and food habits. Edited by Margaret Louise Arnott. 1975. Pp. 187-212. Paris, the Hague: Mouton Publishers. World Anthropology.

The domestication of the yam is seen as an indigenous, slowly evolving process culminating in a complex of ritual socioreligious sanctions which regulated the behavior of cultures toward the yam plant in such a way as to facilitate the emergence of staple cultivars and cultigens.

1852.   Coursey, D.G. & Coursey, Celia K. 1971. The new yam festivals of West Africa. Anthropos 66: 444-484.

Comparative study of yam harvest celebrations, with reference to comparable ceremonies in other parts of the world. Includes discussion of survival of the festival in Afro-America.

1853.   Coutinho,Rui. 1935. Alimentacao e estado nutricional do escravo no Brasil. [Diet and nutritional status of slaves in Brazil.] Estudos 1: 199-213.

1854.   Coutinho, Rui. 1937. Valor social da alimentacao. [Social value of diet] Rio de Janeiro: Civilizacao Brasileira Editora.

Tropical nutrition; disease, and hygiene.

1855.   Coutinho, Rui, 1939. Findings of investigation on common diet in Pernambuco. [In Portugese.] Neurobiologia 2: 9-26.

1856.   Covarrubias, Miguel. 1937. The good food of Bali. Asia 37: 334-339.

1857.   Coville, Frederick Vernon. 1897. Notes on the plants used by the Klamath Indians of Oregon. SI-USNH-C 5: 87-108.

1858.   Coville, Frederick Vernon. 190. Wokas, a primitive food of the Klamath Indians. SI-AR for the year 1902.

Pod of the yellow water lily. Nymphaea polysepala. The pods are buried in pits, partially fermented, and removed. The seeds may be dried and roasted, after being separated from other portions of the pod.

1859.   Coville, Frederick Vernon. 1904. Desert plants as a source of drinking water. SI-AR for the year 1903. Pp. 499-505.

1860.   Cowan, Frank, 1865. Curious facts in the history of insects; including spiders and scorpions. A complete collection of the legends, beliefs and ominous signs connected with insects, together with their uses in medicine, art, and as food, and a summary of their remarkable injuries and appearances. Philadelphia: J.B. Lippincott.

1861.   Cowan, James. 1909. The last of the cannibals. LH 5: 568-573.

Maori.

1862.   Cowan, Richard A. 1967. Lake-margin ecologic exploitation in the Great Basin as demonstrated by an analysis of coprolites from Lovelock Cave, Nevada. In Papers on Great Basin archaelogy. UC-AS No. 70. UCAL-ARF Pp. 21-35.

This paper is a report on prehistoric Great Basin Indian diets as reconstructed from an analysis of human coprolites. The findings differ with the generalized picture of Great Basin subsistence patterns as previously perceived, particularly as regards the use of fish.

1863.   Cowgill, Ursula M. 1961. Soil fertility and the ancient Maya. CAAS-T 42:1-56.

The author examines the nature of maize milpa agriculture in the area of central Peten, Guatamala, and concludes that, for this region, at least, the collapse of Classic Maya culture cannot be attributed to a material decrease in food supply. Planting, harvesting, and storage techniques currently practiced are described, together with details on crop yield; soil chemistry; and land use; weed occurrence, water availability, and supplementary food crops. A review is included of the literature pertaining to soil fertility and agriculture in northern Yucatan, and Guatemala in relation to Classic Maya demise.

1864.   Cowles, M.L. 1935. A study of winter food consumption in Wisconsin farm families. JADA 11: 322-330.

1865.   Cox, Kathryn. A study of sixty Tennessee home kitchens. Master's degree University of Tennessee. 1947.

1866.   Cozine, June. 1944. Missouri history depicted through food customers. NMSTCS Vol 8. No. 1.

1867.   Cragin, F.W. 1835. Observations on cachexia africana or dirt-eating. AJMS 17: 356-364.

1868.   Craik, Brian. Fur trapping and food sharing in Fort George, Quebec. In Sixth Algonquian Conference. 1974. Papers. Edited by William Cowan. 1975. Pp. 223-236. C-MNH-CM-SCE-D No. 23.

1869.   Crain, Carlton. Distribution of fish hooks in the primitive world. Master's thesis. Anthropology. San Francisco State College. 1963.

1870.   Crain, Jay B. Ngerufan: ritual process in a Bornean rice harvest. Paper presented at 72nd Annual Meeting of the American Anthropolocial Association. 30 November, 1973. New Orleans, Louisiana.

1871.   Craplet, C. 1971. Alimentation d'aujourd'hui et de demain. [Food of today and of tomorrow.] Paris: Vigot.

1872.   Cravioto, Joaquin. 1961. Ciertos aspectos socioculturales de la educacion en nutricion. [Certain socio-cultural aspects of nutrition education.] FAO-WHO-UNICEF Seminario Sobre Educacion en Nutricion para Mexico, Centro America, Panama, Cuba, y la Republica Dominicana. 11-21 Octubre 1961. Guanajuato, Gto.: Mexico.

Cultural factors contributing to resistance to changing food habits.

1873.   Cravioto, Rene O. 1955. El pozol. [Posole.] Ciencia 15: 27-30.

Posole is a form of hominy [maize kernels soaked in lye solution until softened and expanded], used as a cereal base for stews, in Mexico, and some areas of the Southwestern United States.

1847.   Cravioto, Rene O.; Anderson, Richmond K.; Lockhart, Ernest E.; Miranda, Fransisco de P.; & Harris, Robert Samuel. 1945. Nutritive value of the Mexican tortilla. Science 102: 91-93.

In addition to chemical analysis, preparation and food use data are briefly included.

1875.   Cravioto, Rene O.; Lockhart, Ernest E.; Anderson, Richmond K.; Miranda, Francisco de P.; Harris, Robert S.; Aguilar, Estela; Tapia, Elizabeth W.; Lockhart, Helen S.; Nutter, Mary K.; & Guild, Louise P. 1945. Composition of typical Mexican foods. JN 29: 309-329.

List of vegetable products. Spanish and English names; areas of cultivation, and nutritive values.

1876.   Cravioto, Rene O.; Massieu, G.; & Guzman, G.J. 1955. Investigaciones bromatologicas en alimentos mexicanos. [Chemical investigations into Mexican foods.] OSP-B 38: 26-33.

Maize, tortillas, beans. and other foods.

1877.   Crawford, Gary Willian & Yarnell, Richard A. The paleoethnobotany of two Indian Knoll sites. Paper presented at 75th Annual Meeting of the American Anthropological Association. 17-21 November, 1976. Washington, D.C.

Analysis of plant remains from the Carlston Annis and Bowles sites provides new evidence for Late Archaic subsistence adaptations. Comparisons with Salt's Cove, Kentucky, Late Archaic-Early Woodland subsistence ecology are made. It is apparent from carbonized squash rind remains that the earliest evidence for plant husbandry in eastern North America has been recovered from both Indian Knoll sites.

1878.   Crawford, I.M. 1966. An aboriginal meal. WAN 10 [3]: 69-71.

Australia.

1879.   Crawford, J. et al. 1971. Nutritional status of young Gilbertese children in a transitional economy. TGM 23: 249-257.

The center of the Gilbert chain is approximately at the Equator at 105 E.

1880.   Crawford, John. 1866. On cannibalism in relation to ethnology. ESL-T 4: 105-124.

1881.   Crawford, M.S. 1896. Jungle products used as food in Mannar District. CF 2 [old series] (9): 142-144.

1882.   Crawford, Mary Caroline. 1924. Old New England Inns. New edition. Boston: L.C. Page.

Inn food: pp. 220-227; passim.; beer. p. 225, passim.

1883.   Crawford, Mary Mazeppa. 1943. Student folkways and spending at Indiana University, 1940-1941; a study in consumption. CU-SHEPL No. 499.

Food: pp. 64-97.

1884.   Crawley, Alfred Ernest. 1931. Chapter Two. Drinks, drinkers, drinking. In Dress, drinks, and drums. Edited by Theodore Besterman. London: Methuen & Co.

1885.   Cree, A.W. 1903. What one eats in the Philippines. LHJ 20:10.

1886.   Cremer, H.D. 1967. International cooperation of various disciplines to improve nutrition in developing countries. In Seventh International Congress of Nutrition. Hamburg. 1966. Proceedings. Vol. 3 [Nutrition under various geographical and climatic conditions.] Pp. 220-221.

Recapitulates details of an interdisciplinary nutrition study carried out in Kenya, in 1964. Indicates how multiple perspectives in nutrition intervention can effect health. Cites, as example, agronomic/botanic function of weed control, in an area where wild plants ["weeds"] are gathered and eaten. Suggests possibility of cultivation hitherto wild plants, for their vitamin content, instead of importing vegetables.

1887. Cresta, M.; Fiorentini, M.; Mancini, F.; & Raimondi, A.M. 1963. Consumi alimentari di 266 famiglie di una zona rurale italiana. [Food intake of 266 families in a rural area of Italy.] QN 23: 337-360.

1888. Crete, L. 1975. Description des habitudes alimentaires des francais qui vecurent sous Louis Philippe. [Description of the food habits of the French under Louis Philippe.] Historia No. 42. Pp. 96-112.

1889. Crevost, Charles. 1918. Matieres alimentaires du Tonkin. [Food of Tonkin.] Hanoi Imprimerie d'Extreme-Orient.

1890. Crevost, Charles. 1932. Quelques preparatifs culinaires annamites a base de rix. [Some rice foods of Annam.] EEI No. 729. 20 mars.

Annam is a region in Vietnam located at approximately 18 N, 106 E.

1891. Crevost, Charles. 1934. Le lait artificiel de soja. [An artificial milk from soy beans.] BAEI 76: 140-141.

1892. Crew, Mary Esther. Relation between sink dimensions and posture of the worker. Department of Household Economics and Management. New York State College of Home Economics. Ithaca, New York: Cornell University. Unpublished report. 1948.

1893. Cribb, A.B. 1966. Don't starve in the bush. W Aust 3: 50-53.

Wild foods: peanut tree [Sterculia quadrifida]; screw pine, pandanus [Pandanus pedunculata]; cabbage tree [Livistona australis]; Kruse's mallee [Eucalyptus kruseana]; Lillypilly [Eugenia coalminians]; walking-stick palm [Linospadix monostachyus]; native cherry [Exocarpus latifolius]; coral fungus [Hericium sp.]; Bunya nut [Araucaria bidwillii].

1894. Crile, George W. & Quiring, D.P. 1939. Indian and Eskimo metabolism. JN 18: 361-368.

1895. Critchell, James Towbridge & Raymond, Joseph A. 1912. A history of the frozen meat trade; an account of the development and present day methods of preparation, transport and marketing of frozen and chilled meats. London: Constable & Co.

1896. Crocco, G. 1963. Contributo alla conoscenza della distribuzione del favismo in Italia. Considerazioni clinico-pato-genetiche. [Contribution to the study of the distribution of favism in Italy. Clinico-pathogenetic considerations.] PNap 71: 592-601.

1897. Crocker, H.E. 1944. Among the cannibals of the Congo. RAFS-J 43: 75-79.

1898. Cronwright, B.C. 1953. A diet of worms. FW 86: 14-15.

Reference to use of Gonimrasia belina as food among native peoples in the northern Transvaal.

1899. Crosby, Eleanor Beatric Vane. Maori fishing gear, a study of the developing of Maori fishing gear, particularly in the North Island. Master's thesis. University of Auckland. 1966.

1900. Crosse-Upcott, A.R.W. 1958. Ngindo famine subsistence. TNR No. 50. Pp. 1-20.

1901. Crowfoot, Grace Mary & Balden-Sperger, Louise. 1932. From cedar to hyssop. A study in the folklore of plants in Palestine. New York, and Toronto: Macmillan Co.; London. Sheldon Press.

1902. Crowley, Daniel J. & Crowley, Pearl Ramcharan. Differential diets of Trinidad Creoles and Indians. Paper presented at 68th Annual Meeting of the American Anthropological Association. 20 to 23 November, 1969. New Orleans, Lousiana.

It is hypothesized that the diet of "lower-class" Creoles more nearly approximates adequate nutritional standards than the diet of East Indians of the same class. Historical, psychological and environmental factors such as the diverse origins of Trinidad Creole culture and cuisine, its relatively open attitude toward innovation and lack of interest in local products is contrasted to the East Indians' religious prejudices against meat and in favor of vegetables, their conservatism toward the introduction of new foods and their greater willingness to use locally-grown or wild foods. Traditional recipes of both groups are cited, especially those using similar ingredients to produce preparations of varying nutritional value. The daily diet of the lowest class in each group is described, along with the tools, utensils and methods of cooking. Suggestions are made regarding needed innovations to improve both diets.

1903. Croy, Homer. 1943. Country cured. New York: Harper Brothers.

Reminiscences of rural life in the Missouri-Iowa border area. Contains descriptions of farm food processing.

1904.   Croy Homer.   1947.   <u>Corn country</u>.   New York: Duell, Sloan & Pearce.

Non-fiction on American folkways, and maize.

1905.   Crum, M. 1940.   <u>Gullah: Negro life in the Carolina Sea Islands</u>.   Durham: Duke University Press.

Scattered references to food habits.

1906.   Crumbine, Samuel J. & Tobey, James A. 1929.   <u>The most nearly perfect food</u>.   Baltimore: Williams & Wilkins.

Cow's milk.

1907.   Csatkai, Endre. 1948.   A marc.   Egy eltunt nepi csemege.   [Marc, a lost folk delicacy.]   <u>Ethnografia</u>

1908.   Cu, H.T.   <u>Enquete sur la nutrition au village de Vinh Hai, Province de Kank Hoa</u>.   [Nutrition survey in Vinh Hai village.   Kanh Hoa Province.]   Ph.D. dissertation. Saigon University.

1909.   Cuatrecasas, Juan, & Sager, Nejam L. de. 1966.   Psicogenesis del fenomeno antropofagico.   [Psychogenesis of the phenomenon of anthropophagy.]   <u>Rev Psic</u> 3: 27-31.

Cites examples of modern-day cannibalism to support the thesis that it is not an individual aberration but, rather, a proto-symbolic rite of primitive communities. From an anthropological viewpoint, it derives from an archetypal image in the psychic evolution of the species.

1910.   Cueto, J.M.   1961.   Rice terraces in Batangas.   <u>PFP</u> 54:34.

Philippines.

1911.   Culwick, Geraldine Mary.   1943.   Nutrition work in British African colonies since 1939.   <u>Africa</u> 14: 24-26.

1912.   Culwick, Geraldine Mary.   1944.   Nutrition in East Africa.   <u>Africa</u> 14: 401-410.

Encourages continued use of local foods and food preparation techniques.

1913.   Culwick, Geraldine Mary. 1950.   <u>A dietary survey among the Zande of the Southwestern Sudan. With a clinical note by P.H. Abbott</u>.   Agricultural Publications Committee.   Khartoum: Ministry of Agriculture. Sudan Government.

Chapter Six. The foods and their treatment. Chapter Seven. Feeding: includes material on food attitudes, commensalism; etiquette; estimate of time devoted to food preparation, foods for the sick, infants and lactating women.   Cites <u>bameranda</u> plant as external galactogogne.   Chapter Nine describes preparation of beer and other alcoholic beverages. Appendix One [List One] enum-

erates Zande food plants.   Appendix Two contains notes on production, storage and utilization of Zande foods. Appendix Three describes maize flour preparation.

1914.   Culwick, Geraldine Mary. 1951.   <u>Diet in the Gezira irrigated areas, Sudan</u>.   Publication No. 304. Khartoum: Sudan Survey Department. February.

Typical foods and food preparations are recorded on pp. 58-116; with information also given regarding Islamic fasts, and feasts. Dietaries of children and women during pregnancy are included. Additional description of foods and food preparation is contained on pp. 150-190.   Appendix Five lists Gezira foods classified by nutrient content per 100gm.

1915.   Culwick, Geraldine Mary. 1955. Social factors affecting diet.   In <u>Annual Conference of the Philosophical Society of the Sudan.   1953.   Khartoum.   1955</u>. Khartoum.   M. McCorquodale.

Includes discussion on role of taboos in Azande diet, and their nutritional ramifications.

1916.   Culwick, A.T. & Culwick, Geraldine Mary. 1939.   Factors governing food supply in Ulanga, Tanganyika Territory.   <u>EAMJ</u> 16: 43-61.

1917.   Cummings, Richard Osborn.   1941.   <u>The American and his food: a history of food habits in the United States</u>.   Revised edition.   Chicago: University of Chicago Press.

1918.   Cummings, Richard Osborn.   Historical influence and regional differences in United States food habits.   In <u>Conference on food acceptance research. 6 December to 7 December, 1945</u>.   United States War Department.   Quartermaster Food and Container Institute.   Research and Development Branch. Military Planning Division. Committee on Food Research.   1946.   Pp. 99-103. Quartermaster Corps manual 17-9.

Available in microform from Library of Congress as item PB-53-883.

1919.   Cummings, T.C.   1907.   Our ancestor's plum-pudding. <u>SLife</u> 5: 372.

1920.   Cunningham, Keith. 1973.   Ethno-cuisine: goat roast.   <u>Affword</u> 2: 44.

1921.   Cunningham, Roberta L.   <u>A Vitamin B study particularly adapted for use in high school teaching</u>. Master's thesis. Washington State College.   1943.

1922.   Curran, C.H. 1937.   Insect lore of the Aztecs.   <u>NH</u> 39: 196-199.

Brief mention of use of insects as food.

1923.   Curran, C.H. 1939.   On eating insects.   <u>NH</u> 43: 84-89.

Survey of food use of insects worldwide. Orthoptera, Isoptera, Lepidoptera, Diptera, Hymenoptera.

1924. Curran, C.M. 1951. Insects in your life. New York: Sheridan House.

Insects as human food: pp. 205-224; insect foods of the Native Americans. pp. 271-285.

1925. Currens, Gerald E. The Loma farmer: a socioeconomic study of rice cultivation and the use of resources among a people of northwestern Liberia. Ph.D. dissertation. Anthropology. University of Oregon. 1974.

1926. Currier, Richard L. 1966. Hot-cold syndrome and symbolic balance in Mexican and Spanish-American folk medicine. Ethnology 5: 251-263.

1927. Currier, W.D. 1957. Nutritional aspects of stress. JAN 10: 588-592.

1928. Curtin, Leonora Scott Muse. 1957. Some plants used by the Yuki Indians of Round Valley, California. Los Angeles: Southwestern Museum.

1929. Curtin, Leonora Scott Muse. 1967-1968. Preparation of sacred corn meal in the Rio Grande pueblos. Mkey 41: 124-130; 42: 10-16.

1930. Curtin, Leonora Scott Muse. 1968. Preparation of sacred corn meal in Rio Grande pueblos. Los Angeles: Southwest Museum.

1931. Curtis, Natalie. 1904. A bit of American folk music: two Pueblo Indian grinding songs. Craftsman 7: 35-41.

Includes musical notation.

1932. Curtis-Bennett, Francis Noel. 1949. The food of the people, being a history of industrial feeding. London: Faber & Faber.

1933. Curwen, Eliot Cecil & Hatt, Gudmund. 1953. Plough and pasture: the early history of farming. New York: Schuman.

1934. Cusa, Salvatore. 1873. La palma nella poesia; nella scienza e nella storia Siciliana. [The palm in poetry, science and Sicilian history.] Palermo: Lao.

1935. Cushing, Frank Hamilton. 1884-1885. Zuni breadstuff. Millstone Vol. 9 No. 1 through Vol. 10 No. 8.

1936. Cushing, Frank Hamilton. 1920. Zuni breadstuff. New York: Museum of the American Indian. Reprint. New York: Museum of the American Indian. 1974.

One of the classic studies of the food habits of a Native American group. Cushing lived among the Zuni, being adopted into the Macaw clan.

1937. Cushman, Ella M. 1936. The development of a successful kitchen. CorU-BH No. 354. Revised: 1946.

1938. Cussler, Margaret T. Cultural sanctions of the food pattern in the rural southeast. Ph.D. dissertation. Cambridge, Massachusetts: Radcliffe College. 1943.

1939. Cussler, Margaret T. 1943. Foods and nutrition in our rural southeast. JHE 35: 280-282.

1940. Cussler, Margaret T. & De Give, Mary L. 1941. Interrelations between cultural pattern and nutrition. USDA-ESC No. 366.

1941. Cussler, Margaret T. & De Give, Mary L. 1942. The effect of human relations on food habits in the rural southeast. AAnth 1: 13-18.

Effects of food self-sufficiency and social status upon nutritional well-being and food attitudes.

1942. Cussy, Louis de. La gastronomie historique. [Historic gastronomy.] In Les classiques de la table. Anonymous. 1844. Paris: Dentu; Tresse: J. Renouard.

1943. Cuthbertson, D.P. Chapter Eight. Food Selection. In Nutrition. A comprehensive treatise. Vol. 2. Vitamins, nutrient requirement, and food selection. Edited by George H. Beaton, & Earle Willard McHenry. 1964. New York, London: Academic Press.

Extensive ethnographic data, largely from non-specific anthropological sources. Covers Europe, sub-Saharan Africa, and briefly, Asia. Orientation is medico-nutritional.

1944. Cuthbertson, W.F.J. 1966. Problems of introducing new foods to developing countries. FT 20: 634-636.

Notes importance of understanding local food beliefs.

1945. Cutler, Hugh C 1944. Medicine men and the preservation of a relict gene in maize. JHer 35: 290-294.

Suggests a possible relationship between petroglyphs found in the southwestern United States depicting the character called Kocopelli the "hunch-backed flute player", and the discovery of an ear of pod [tunicate] maize at the Betatakin ruin, in Arizona. Kocopelli bears an impressionistic resemblance to the travelling Callahuayo medicine men of Bolivia, who are known to have traveled throughout South America, and into Central America, carrying on their backs blankets containing their remedies. The pack-blankets may give the characteristic "hunch-backed" appearance. These healers also carried the grains of the pod maize which, although not now cultivated in Bolivia, are used in Quechua medicine as a cure for respiratory illness. The author suggests that perhaps Callahuayo medicine men brought the tunicate maize to the southwestern United States, at about A.D. 1300, and had their image preserved in the likeness of Kocopelli, thereby introducing to North America a characteristic of maize which had not been introduced earlier in ears selected for food.

1946.   Cutler, Hugh C.   1944.   A preliminary survey of plant remains of Tularosa Cave. Field-Anth 40: 461-479.

1947.   Cutler, Hugh C. 1951.   The oldest corn in the world. CNHM-B 22: 4-5.

1948.   Cutler, Hugh.   1960.   Cultivated plant remains from Waterfall Cave, Chihuahua. AmAn 26: 277-279.

Maize [Pima-Papago race]; common beans; bottle gourd, and squash.

1949.   Cutler, Hugh. C. Cultivated plants. In The McGraw site, a study in Hopewellian dynamics. Edited by Olaf H. Prufer. 1965. Cleve MNH-SP 4, 4(1): 107-112.

1950.   Cutler, Hugh & Blake, Leonard. Analysis of corn from the Banks Site.   Crittendon County, Arkansas.   In Twenty-first Southeastern Archaeological Conference.   November 6-7, 1964.   New Orleans, Louisiana. Proceedings. Edited by Stephen Williams. 1965. Pp. 75-77.

Description of the morphological characteristics of maize excavated from a site dated by the Carbon-14 method, at A.D. 1535.

1951.   Cutler, Hugh C. & Cardenas, Martin. 1947. Chicha, a native South American beer. HU-BM-L 13: 33-60.

1052.   Cutolo, A. 1910. Composition and nutritive value of taralli, a special bread made in Naples. [In Italian.] SNN-B 2: 158-164.

1953.   Cutright, Paul Russell. 1940. Great naturalists explore South America. New York: Macmillan.

Use of insects as food: pp. 310-314.

1954.   Cutting, Charles L.   1955.   Chapter One. Antiquity.   Chapter Two.   Fish in pre-industrial times. In Fish saving. A history of fish processing from ancien to modern times. London: Leonard Hill [Books] Limited.

1955.   Cutting, Charles L. 1958. Some consumer aspects of fish as food. PNS 17: 147-153.

1956.   Cuypers, E. 1959. Flitsen uit het lande der Wanande. [Flashes from the land of the Banande.] OA 82: 8-14.

Aspects of Nande cultivatiion, diet and attitudes.

1957.   Cuzacq, Rene. 1949. Triptygue bayonnaise. [Bayonne triptych.] Mont-de-Marsaon: Imprimerie J. Gliac.

Bayonnaise ham; chocolate.

1958.   Cuzent, Gilbert. 1873-1874. De boissons envirantes en usage chez les different peuples. [Stimulating beverages used by various peoples.] SAB-B 1: 141-230.

Kava [Piper methysticum], and other beverages used by native people of French Polynesia.

1959.   Czadek, O. Von. 1906. Midzu ame, a new foodstuff. [In German.] ZLVO 9: 891.

Analysis of a Japanese food product prepared usually from rice by malting. The sample analyzed gave an appearance and taste similar to honey.

1960.   Czajkowski, Janina M.   1961.   Hawaiian foods and traditions. U Conn-AES-B No. 60-25.

1961.   Czajkowski, Janina M. 1964. Mexican foods and traditions. U Conn-AES-B No. 64.

1962.   Czajkowski, Janina M. 1971. Puerto Rican foods and traditions. U Conn-AES-B November.

1963.   A.D., & F.T. 1934. The uses of banana. UJ 2: 116-119.

East Africa.

1964.   Da Costa Pereira, Carlos. 1957-1958. Da cebola do alho. [Onion and garlic.] CCF-B 8: 4-9.

In dynastic Egypt; Imperial Rome; in beliefs, proverbs, riddles, figures of speech.

1965.   Dadswell, I.W. 1934. The chemical composition of some plants used by Australian aborigines as food. AJEBMS 12: 13-18.

1966.   D'Agostino, Mary Ann. Diet of the Italian people. Mimeographed. Detroit, Michigan: Detroit Department of Public Welfare. Undated.

1967.   Dahlgren, B.E. & Standley, Paul C. 1944. Edible and poisonous plants of the Caribbean region. Bureau of Medicine and Surgery. Washington, D.C.: United States Navy.

1968.   Dahlquist, Paul A. Food producing complex in a Ponapean community. Paper presented at 70th Annual Meeting of the American Anthropological Association. 21 November, 1971. New York City.

Describes ongoing food complex in a community facing heavy pressure for change in the Eastern Caroline Islands. Compares the present situation to that described for about twenty-six years earlier (approximately the commencement of United States Trust Territory administration).

1969.   Dahlquist, Paul A.   Khodo Mwenge: the food complex in a changing Samoan community. Ph.D. dissertation.   Anthropology.   Ohio State University.   1972.

1970.   Daigre, R.P.   1927.   Plantes alimentaires du pays Banda.   [Food plants of the Banda area.]   SRC-B No. 8.   Pp. 123-124.

French Equatorial Africa.

1971.   Daigre, R.P.   1932.   Les Bandas de l'Oubangui-Chari [Afrique Equatorials Francaise].   [The Banda of Ubangi-Chari [French Equatorial Africa]]   Anthropos 27: 153-181.

1972.   Dale, Ivan R.   1955.   The Indian origins of some African cultivated plants and African cattle. UJ 19: 68-72.

1973.   Dallenbach, John W. & Dallenbach, Karl M. 1943.   The effects of bitter-adaptation on sensitivity to the other taste qualities.   AJPsy 56: 21-31.

1974.   Dallet, Charles.   1874.   Histoire de l'eglise de Core.   [A history of the church in Korea.]   Paris: Victor Palme   Translated for the Human Relations Area Files by Charles A. Messner.

Brief data on food: raw fish; meat; intestines; spicy sauce eaten with fish.

1975.   Dalton, G.   1912.   Pepper growing in Upper Sarawak.   Sar MJ 1: 53-61.

1976.   Daly, Patricia.   Micro-structure of animal bone as a diagnostic of domestication.   Paper presented at 70th Annual Meeting of the American Anthropological Association.   20 November, 1971. New York City.

Compares several archeological sites and several species of animals in both wild and domesticated form; discusses evidence indicating that earliest domestication affected osteal structure, and that wild animals of different species resemble each other more than they do their domestic relatives. Offers suggestions about processes involved in the changes noted, and on the applications of archeology evidence to a study of the beginnings of animal husbandry throughout the world.

1977.   Damn, Hans.   1961.   Die Susser-Kartoffel [Batate] im Leben der Volker Neuguineas.   [The sweet potato [Batata] in the life of New Guinea natives.]   ZAEU 86: 208-223.

1978.   Dando, W.A.   1976.   Man-made famines: some geographical insights from an exploratory study of a millennium of Russian famines.   EFN 4: 219-234.

Historical study of the causes of seventy-seven famines from A.D. 971 to A.D. 1970.

1979.   Danish Cheese Export Board.   1955.   Danish cheese.   Aarhus, Denmark: Danish Cheese Export Board.

1980.   Dann, Jeffrey.   A study of an Indian tavern on skid row.   Master's thesis.   Anthropology.   University of Washington.   1967.

Native American; alcohol use.

1981.   Dantrine, M.   1937.   Le palmier-dattier et les arbres sacres.   [Date palms and sacred trees.] Paris: Librairie Orientaliste Paul Geuthner.

1982.   Danziger, A.   1898   Jewish gastronomy.   Cur Lit 26: 373.

1983.   Darboo, S.H.   A historical review of the hygiene of shipboard food service in the United States Navy, 1775-1965.   Ph.D. dissertation.   University of California, Los Angeles.   1966.

1984.   Darby, William J.   1959.   Protective effects of certain natural foods against whole body irradiation.   Quartermaster Food and Container Institute for the Armed Forces.   Contract N-1130.   Progress Report 1, 1959.

Dietary supplementation with green plant materials is under study.   Final report will be available in 1961.

1985.   Darby, William J.   1965.   This hungry world: a responsibility of preventive medicine.   AJCN 16: 509-516.

1986.   Darby, William J.; Adams, Catherine M.; Pollard, Artha, Dalton, Etta,; & McKinley, Pauline. 1956.   A study of the dietary background and nutriture of the Navajo Indian.   Part 2.   Dietary patterns.   JN 60 [Supplement 2]: 19-33.

1987.   Darby, William J.; Gahlioungui, Paul; & Grivetti, Louis Evan.   1977.   Food: the gift of Osiris.   2 vols. New York, London: Academic Press.

A panoramic, scholarly view of foods in Classical Egypt, in the contexts of social, religious, political, historical and medical usage.

1988.   Darby, William J.; McGanity, William J.; & Bridgforth, Edwin B.   1956.   A study of the dietary background and nutriture of the Navajo Indian.   5. Interpretation.   JN 60 [Supplement 2]: 75-79.

1989.   Darby, William J.; Salsbury, Clarence G.; McGanity, William J.; Johnson, Heward F.; Bridgforth, Edward B.; & Sandstead, Harold R.   1956.   A study of the dietary background and nutriture of the Navajo Indian.   Part 1.   Background and food production.   JN 60 [Supplement 2]: 3-17.

1990.   Darcet, J.P. Joseph.   1822.   Description d'un forneau de cuisine construit de maniere a pouvoir y preparer toute espece d'aliment, sans etre incommode par la vapeur du charbon, par la fumee du bois ou par l'odeur desagreable qui se repand ordinairement dans les cuisines lorsqu'on y fait griller de la viande ou du poisson, lorsqu'on y emploie de la friture ou lorsqu'on y brule des os, de plumes, des aretes, etc., etc.   [Description of a cooking oven constructed in a manner which allows the preparation of every kind of food without being annoyed by carbon fumes, wood smoke or disagreeable odors which are ordinarily given off in kitchens when meat or fish are grilled, when frying, or when broiling by bones, feathers, fish-bones, etc., etc. Paris: Bachelier.

1991.   Dare, R. 1974. The ecology and evolution of food sharing Cal Anth 2: 13-25.

Hypothesis concerning socio-behavioral and ecological variables in primate life predisposing toward cooperative behavior and sharing.   Contains documentation on primate feeding behavior.

1992.   Darenne, E. 1904. Histoire des metiers de l'alimentation. [History of food professions.] Meulan: Imprimerie de a Rety.

1993.   Darling, Charles William. 1886. Anthropophagy. Utica, New York: Book and Job Printer.

Poorly documented collection of historical accounts relating to cannibalism.

1994.   Darling, F. Fraser. 1960. Wildlife husbandry in Africa. SA 203: 123-134.

1995.   Darlington, William. 1859. American weeds and useful plants: being a second and illustrated edition of Agricultural Botany. Revised with additions by George Thurber. New York: A.O. Moore & Co.

1996.   Darre, Richard Walther Oskar. 1933. Die Schwein als Rriterium fur nordische Volker an Semiten. [The pig as criterion for Nordic and Semitic peoples.] Munich: Wolf & Rasse.

1997.   Dart, Raymond. The carnivorous propensity of baboons. In The primates. The proceedings of the symposium held on 12th-14th April, 1962. 1963. Pp. 49-56. Symposia of the Zoological Society of London No. 10. London: published by the Society.

1998.   Das, Abinas Chandra. 1925. Rgvedic culture. Calcutta, Madras: R. Cambray.

Food: pp. 200-210.

1999.   Das, Nityananda. 1959. A note on markets in the Saoraland of Orissa. Vanyajati 7: 98-103.

India.

2000.   Das, Amal Kumar. 1959. Food habits and dietaries of the Orans and their nutritional efficiency. Vanyajati 7: 53-58.

2001.   Das, Tarakchandra. 1931. The cultural significance of fish in Bengal. M India 11: 275-303.

2002.   Das, Tarakchandra. 1932. The cultural significance of fish in Bengal. M India 12: 96-115.

2003.   Dasmann, Raymond F. 1964. African game ranching. Oxford: Pergamon Press.

2004.   Dastre, M.A. 1902. Salt and its physiological uses. [Translated from French.] SI-AR for the year 1901. Pp. 568-595. Also in RDM 1: 197-227 [1901].

2005.   Dastur, Jehangir Fardunji. 1951. Useful plants of India and Pakistan: a popular handbook of trees and plants of industrial economic and commercial utility. 2nd ed. Bombay: D.B. Taraporevala & Sons.

Indicates edible plants, fruit.

2006.   Daudin, Pierre. La gallette des rois. The king's tart.] VL No. 165. Pp. 678-683.

2007.   Daum, Ida Vintes. The politics of malnutrition: an example from urban Kingston, Jamaica. Paper presented at 74th Annual Meeting of the American Anthropological Association. 2 to 6 December, 1975. San Francisco, California.

2008.   Daum, Ida Vintes. Barriers to breast feeding in urban Jamaica. Paper presented at 76th Annual Meeting of the American Anthropological Association. 29 November to 3 December, 1977. Houston, Texas.

In a Kingston shantytown setting, those mothers who did not breast feed their infants appeared to be more dependent upon the urban political economy and to hold values motivated by the urban mainstream or middle class, whereas mothers who did breast feed appeared to be less identified with these influences.   The decision to breast feed or not to breast feed does not have a community-cultural context. Rather, it reflects individual consciousness in each household; the controlling variable is the extent to which the mother and father of the infant have become part of the urban market economy and absorbed its commodity dependence.

2009.   Daunys, S. 1943. Valgomojo aliejaus spaudimas, gruces grudimas ir suriu gambya. [On the production of edible oils and the preparation of groats and cheese.] Gim Kras No. 31. Pp. 264-271.

2010.   Dauwe, Ferdinand. Le regime alimentaire des prisons en Belgique.   [The diet in Belgion prisons.] In Deuxieme Congres Internationale d'Hygiene Alimentaire et de l'Alimentation Rationelle de l'Homme. 4-8 Octobre, 1910. Bruxelles. 1910. Vol. 1. Section 2. Pp. 49-65.

An analysis of menu items; consideration of monotomy in prison dietary, and reference to rations in several German prisons.

2011.   Dauzvardis, Josephine J. 1955 [1958]. Popular Lithuanian recipes. 2nd edition, revised. Chicago: no publisher cited.

2012.   Davenport, Charles Benedict. 1947. The dietaries of primitive peoples. AA 47: 61-82.

Description of dietary patterns for major world geographic regions.

2013.   Davenport, William H. A comparative study of two Jamaican fishing communities. Ph.D. dissertation. Anthropology. Yale University. 1956.

2014.   Daver, M.B. 1942. Observations on dietary habits and nutritional conditions in Hyderabad State. IMAJ 12: 42-45.

2015.   David, Elizabeth. 1970. Spices, salt, and aromatics in the English cooking, ancient and moderns. Volume 1. Harmondsworth, England: Penguin Books.

2016.   David-Schwarz, H. 1929. Aus der psychologischen Beratungspraxis. [From the practice of psychological counseling.] PRund 1: 314-316.

   Food rejection by children, and means for overcoming the problem.

2017.   Davidson, Anne L.   Nutrition and Social identification. Paper presented at 77th Annual Meeting of the American Anthropological Association. 14 to 18 November, 1978. Los Angeles, California.

2018.   Davidson, Charles S. 1954. Guiding principles for solution of dietary problems of an aging population. F Tech 8: 271-273.

2019.   Davidson, Janet M. 1964. Processing and analysing midden samples. NZAA-N 7: 152-163.

2020.   Davidson, Janet M. 1967. Midden analysis and the economic approach in New Zealand archaeology. AIM-R 6: 203-208.

2021.   Davidson, Sidney G. 1930. The value of a dietitian in an out-patient clinic HSS 21: 57-60.

   Strongly favors a more influential role in medical treatment.

2022.   Davidson, William D. 1953. A brief history of infant feeding. JPed 43: 74-87.

2023.   Davies, Esther S. 1928. The food consumption of rural school children in relation to their health. Mass-AES-B. No. 241.

   This very thorough monograph, studies two towns in Massachusetts: Carver, located west of Plymouth, approximately ten miles inland from the Atlantic seaboard and Southwick, located along the western part of the southern border of the State, in the Connecticut River Valley. Ethnically, Carver's population is composed of Finns, French-Canadians, Portuguese, and Anglo-Saxon groups. Southwick's population is composed of Anglo-Saxons, Poles, Swedes, and Italians, predominantly, with a few Black Americans. Very detailed data are included for food consumption, by food type, and meals. The possible influence of Finnish whole-wheat bread consumption pattern upon the community of Carver is observed: p. 114.

2024.   Davies, H.J. 1916. Notes on the history and uses and cultivation of the papaya. I-UP-AB No. 37.

2025.   Davies, H.R. 1909. Yun-nan. The link between India and the Yangtse. Cambridge: Cambridge University Press.

   Tsamba, a roasted barley flour, buttered tea: p. 386.

2026.   Davies, J.N.P., ed. 1954. Second Inter-African Conference on Nutrition. [C.C.T.A.] 1952. Gambia. Report. Malnutrition in African mothers, infants, and young children. Great Britain, Colonial Office. London: Her Majesty's Stationery Office.

2027.   Davies, J.N.P. 1955. Nutritional states as causal factors of cancer. SZAPB 18: 416-423.

   Cancer and malnutrition in African groups.

2028.   Davies, O. 1968. The origins of agriculture in West Africa. CAnth 9: 479-482.

2029.   Davies, P. 1961. Favism. PMJ 37: 477-480.

2030.   Davis, Aud Greta Lundberg. The Two-Head-of--the-Rio village Maya: some changes in drinking patterns in a Maya Indian community. Master's thesis. Anthropology. University of Illinois. 1965.

2031.   Davis, C. Noel. Observations on beriberi. In Far Eastern Association of Tropical Medicine. Biennial Congress. Second. Hong Kong. 1912. Transactions. [1912] Pp. 23-30. Hong Kong: Noronha & Co.

   Provides details of diets provided prisoners in the Shanghai Municipal Goal, and to Chinese police recruits.

2032.   Davis, Clara M. 1928. Self-selection of diets. AJDC 36: 651-679.

   Experiments with healthy infants. Includes list of foods offered and selected; methods of preparation; growth charts; serum calcium and phosphorous values.

2033.   Davis, Clara M. 1934. Studies in the self selection of diet by young children. J ADent A 21: 636-640.

2034.   Davis, Clara M. 1935. Choice of formulas made by three infants throughout the nursing period. AJDC 50: 385-394.

2035.   Davis, Clara M. 1939. Results of the self-selection of diet by newly-weaned infants. CMAJ 41: 257-261.

2036.   Davis, Herbert. 1919. The rediscovery of an old dish. USDA-YB for the year 1918. Pp. 269-276.

   Cottage cheese; its use in the United States as a food substitute, during World War I. Historical information is included.

2037.   Davis, J. Merle, ed. 1933. Modern industry and the African. London: Macmillan.

Brief note on basic foods of Northern Rhodesian mine workers: pp. 62-63.

2038.   Davis, James Richard Ainsworth. 1931. Cooking through the centuries. London: J.M. Dent & Sons; New York: E.P. Dutton & Co.

British cookery.

2039.   Davis, John Francis. 1845. The Chinese: a general description of China and its inhabitants. Vol. 2. London: Charles Knight & Co.

Food and eating habits: pp. 18-30.

2040.   Davis, Michael. 1925. What the dietitian can contribute to the effectiveness of the medical man. Diet Ad Ther 3: 47-49.

Encourages closer relationship between dietitians and physicians, nursing, and public health personnel.

2041.   Davis, William Stearns. Chapter Six. Food and drink. How the day is spent. The dinner. In A day in old Rome. A picture of Roman life. 1925. Boston, New York: Allyn & Bacon. Reprint. New York: Biblo & Tannen. 1962.

2042.   Davis, William Stearns. 1945. Chapter Eighteen. Athenian cookery and the symposium. In A day in old Athens. New York: Allyn & Bacon.

2043.   Day, Elizabeth Phillips. Undirected and directed food choices in a new school cafeteria. Master's thesis. University of Oklahoma. 1945.

2044.   Day, H.H. 1954. About yoghurt. London: Thorsons.

2045.   Day, Mary-Lou; Lentner, Marvin; & Jaquez, Shirley. 1978. Food acceptance patterns of Spanish-speaking New Mexicans. JNE 10: 121-123.

2046.   Daye, V.L. 1963. Poutines rapees...the story of a favourite Acadian delicacy. Atl Adv 54: 57-59.

2047.   Dayton, Charles & Mansfield, Edward R. 1904. Studies of food of Maine lumbermen. USDA-OES-B No. 49.

2048.   De, S. & Ray, S.C. 1952. Studies on the indigenous method of khoa-making. IJDS 5: 147-165.

Khoa is a heat-coagulated, semi-dehydrated whole milk product used as a base and filler for Indian milk sweets.

2049.   De, S.S. 1967. Traditional foods: their present production and use. IJND 4: 331-341.

Short descriptions of the household methods of preparing common foods of Asia, Africa, and the Near East. The foods are described under the following categories: soya products, peanut, coconut, fish, milk, beans, vegetables and fruits and cereals. A discussion of the nutritive values, modern production methods, and research relating to these traditional items is included.

2050.   Deacon, H.J. Demography, subsistence and culture during the Middle Pleistocene in southern Africa. Paper presented at 9th International Congress of Anthropological and Ethnological Sciences. 28 August to 8 September, 1973. Chicago, Illinois.

2051.   Dean, Reginald Francis Alfred. 1959. Infant feeding in Uganda. QRP 14: 182-183.

2052.   Dean, Stella M. 1925. Nutrition in a nursing association. HSS 11: 156-161.

Training and outreach activities of the Public Health Nursing Association of Rochester, New York.

2053.   Deane, Shirley. 1961. The road to Andorra. New York: William Morrow & Co.

Food preparation techniques: pp. 112-113; 120.

2054.   Death, James. 1887. The beer of the Bible. One of the hitherto unknown leavens of Exodus. (A confirmation of biblical accuracy) with a visit to an Arabic brewery, notes on the Oriental ferment products, etc., and a map of the routes of the Exodus, with description of the different authors' contentions. London: Trubner & Co.

2055.   De Baudricourt, Sire. 1903. Le manuel culinaire aphrodisique. [The culinary aphrodisiac manual.] Paris: Editions Photographique.

Also: an Italian translation by Omero Rompini. 1926. La cucina dell'amore. Catania: F. Guaitolini.

2056.   Debay, Auguste. 1860. Hygiene alimentaire, histoire simplifice de la digestion des aliments et des boissons a l'usage des gens du monde. [Alimentary hygiene, simplified history of the digestion of foods and beverages used by peoples throughout the world.] Paris: Dentu.

2057.   Debay, Auguste. 1864. Les influences du chocolat, du the et du cafe sur l'economie humaine. Leur analyse chimique, leurs falsifications, leur role important dans l'alimentation. [The influences of chocolate, tea, and coffee on human economy. Their chemical analysis, their falsifications, their important role in diet.] Paris: E. Dentu.

2058.   De Beniparell, C. 1954. Los problemas alimenticios del continente africano. [Dietary problems of continental Africa.] CEA 28:19-28.

2059.   Debien, Gabriel. 1964. La nourriture des esclaves sur les plantations des Antilles Francaises aux 17e at 18e siecles. [Diet of slaves on plantations in the French Antilles during 17th and 18th Centuries.] Carib 4: 3-27.

2060. Debo, Angie. 1941. The road to disappearance. Norman: University of Okalahoma Press.

Creek foods and utensils: pp. 20, 109, 302-303.

2061. De Bondt, Jakob, 1642. De medicina Indorum. [The medicine of the Indies.] Lugduni, Batavia: F. Hackium.

Observations relating to the botany and natural history of the East Indies, especially the vegetables used in medicine and diet. Robert Watt, in his Bibliotheca Britannica, Edinburgh: Constable & Co. Vol. 1: 133, 134 notes that James [sic] Bontius, M.D. was a physician to the Dutch settlement at Batavia [Java], a native of Leyden who flourished about the middle of the 15th [sic] Century.

2062. Debry, G. 1976. Validite des methodes d'enquetes alimentaires. [Validity of nutrition surveys.] ANA 30: 115-128.

2063. Debry, G. & Feron, R. 1976. Evolution de la consommation humaine de proteines en France au cours des dix dernieres annees. [Evolution of protein intake in France during the past ten years.] ANA 30: 161-174.

2064. Decary, Raymond. 1928. Contribution a l'etude de l'anthropophagie a Madagascar. [Contribution to the study of anthropophagy in Madagascar.] SAP-BM 9: 116-121.

2065. Decary, Raymond. 1946. Plantes et animaux utiles de Madagascar. [Useful plants and animals of Madagascar.] MCM-A 55 [series 6]. No. 4.

Food plants: pp. 1-44; oil plants; pp. 45-53; sweetener and beverage plants: pp. 54-62.

2066. Decary, Raymond. 1956. La vanille a Madagascar. [Vanilla in Madagascar.] EMOM No. 65. Pp. 32-34.

2067. Dechend, Hertha Von. Die Kultische und mythische Bedeutung des Schweines in Indonesien und Ozeanien. [The significance of pigs in myth and cult in Indonesia and Oceania.] Ph.D. dissertation. Frankfurt: Goethe Universitat. 1943.

2068. Decker, Bryce. Plants, man and landscape in Marquesan valleys. Ph.D. dissertation. University of California. Berkeley. 1965.

2069. Decroix, Emile-Francois. 1864. L'alimentation par le viande de cheval. [Horse meat as food.] Paris: Asselin.

2070. Decroix, Emile-Francois. 1870. Alimentation des armees en compagne, viande de cheval. [Feeding armies in the field, horse meat.] Paris: A Chaix.

2071. Decroix, Emile-Francois. 1873. Note sur la consommation de la viande de cheval en France. [Note on the consumption of horse meat in France.] Paris: Imprimerie de E. Martinet.

2072. Decroix, Emile Francois. 1879. L'hippophagie et les viandes insalubres. [Horse-flesh eating and unsanitary meats.] Paris: Asselin.

2073. Decroix, Emile-Francois. 1895. Avantages de l'hippophagie. [Advantages of eating horse meat.] Paris: [the author?] [?]

2074. Decroix, Emile Francois. 1895. Avantages de l'hippophagie. Un dernier mot sur la question. [Advantages of eating horse flesh. A final word on the question.] RSNA 42: 657-682.

History; first horse flesh butcher in Paris, during the siege of Paris; consumption of horse-flesh in the provinces; present state of use of horse-flesh as food in France, and elsewhere.

2075. De Coutouly, Francois. 1925. Gros et petit gibier en Afrique Occidentale. [Large and small game in West Africa.] CEHS-AOF-B Pp. 217-569.

2076. Deer, Noel. 1949-1950. History of sugar. 2 vols. London: Chapman & Hall.

2077. De Faria, Oswaldo Lamartine: 1963. Conservacao de alimentos nos sertoes do Serido. [Food preservation in the Serido wilderness.] IJNPS-B 12: 83-152.

Serido is located at approximately 7 S., 37 E.

2078. Deffner, Karen M. Mammalian material from Cahokia, Illinois: a preliminary analysis. Master's thesis. University of Wiconsin. 1968.

2079. De Ficalho, Conde. 1947. Plantas uteis da Africa Portuguesa. [Plants used in Portugese Africa.] Agencia Geral das Colonias. Divisao de Publicacoes e Biblioteca. Lisbon: Ministerio das Colonias.

2080. Deflesselle, Constant. L'alimentation des indigenes dans les iles du Pacifique oriental. [Diet of the natives in the eastern Pacific islands.] In L'alimentation indigene dans les colonies francaises. Edited by Georges Hardy and Charles Richet [fils]. 1933. Pp. 361-370. Paris: Vigot Freres.

Society, and Marquesas Islands, Tahiti, Tubuai, Gambier, and Tuamotu. Describes staple foods, food preparation, and eating etiquette. Notes a food classification system of two categories: maa, or essential food, such as banana, breadfruit; and hinei, or accompanying foods, e.g. meat, fish, and shellfish.

2081. De Friedemann, Nina S. The feast of the Indian in Quibdo, Colombia. Paper presented at 9th International Congress of Anthropological and Ethnological Sciences. 28 August to 8 September, 1973. Chicago, Illinois.

2082.   Degener, Otto. 1932. Koko'olau, the Hawaiian tea. PPRI-J 7: 2-16.

2083.   De Girardot, Auguste-Theodor Baron. 1858. Les fetes de la Revolution, 1790-an 8. [The festivals of the Revolution, 1790 - year 8.] Nantes: Imprimerie de Vre C. Mellinet. Held by the Bibliotheque National, Paris. No. 8 LK7,5477.

2084.   De Give, Mary L. Social interrelations and food habits in the rural Southeast. Ph.D. dissertation. Cambridge, Massachusetts: Radcliffe College. 1943.

2085.   De Give, Mary L. & Cussler, Margaret T. Outline of studies on food habits in rural Southeast. In The problem of changing food habits. Report of the Committee on Food Habits. 1941-1943. National Research Council. 1943. Pp. 109-112. NRC-B No. 108.

> Three communities: Bath, North Carolina; Dutch Fork, South Carolina; and Nuberg and Flat Rock Georgia were studied to determine relationships, if any, between sociocultural pattern and food-related behavior. Patterns in food intake, attitudes, and related behavior were found to configure around cultural (Black as contrasted with Anglo) economic [landlord, tenant, wage labor], and residential (neighborhood) lines. A variety of data are recorded for each community, in relation to the specific focus of the three studies. An interesting distinction between "light" and "heavy" foods is recorded.

2086.   De Give, Mary L. & Cussler, Margaret T. Bibliography and notes on German food patterns. Mimeographed Committee on Food Habits. Washington, D.C.: National Research Council. February, 1944.

2087.   De Gubernatis, Angelo. 1878-1882. La mythologie des plantes, ou les legendes du regne vegetale. [The mythology of plants, or the legens of the vegetable kingdom.] 2 vols. Paris: C. Reinwald.

2088.   De Haas, J.H.; Posthuma, J.H.; Ruzette, E.M.; & Meulmans, O. 1941. Infant feeding in the tropics during the first six months. [In Dutch.] GTNI 81: 355-372.

2089.   Dehoux, J.-B. 1884. Du sacrifice humaine et de l'anthropophagie dan Vaudou. [On human sacrifice and anthropology in Vodun.] SAP-B 7: 206-216.

> Account of a case of sacrificial anthropophagy in Port-au-Prince, Haiti, in February, 1864.

2090.   De Jong Osborne, Lilly. 1944. Ensayo sobre la alimentacion de los indigenas en Guatemala. [Essay on the food habits of native Guatemalans.] SGHG-A 19: 365-370.

> Miscellaneous descriptive remarks on various foods, both daily and special; food-related folklore; preparation and serving.

2091.   De Jongh Osborne, Lilly. 1944. Guatemala: on Indian foods. Bol Ind 4: 42-47.

2092.   De Knight, Freda. 1948. A date with a dish. A cookbook of American Negro recipes. New York: Hermitage Press.

> Reprinted as The Ebony Cookbook. Chicago: Johnson Publishing Co. 1962. Revised ed. 1973.

2093.   Dekowski, Jan Piotr. 1963. Kaszarze Stobieccy brzezniccy i dziatoszniscy. [The groat producers of Stobiecko, Brzeznica and of Dziatoscyn.] ML-PM-SE 7: 129-149.

> Three towns on the Warta River in southeast-central Poland.

2094.   Dekowski, Jan Piotr. 1963. Pozywiene ludu radomszczankiego. [Food of the inhabitants of the Radomsko regions.] ML-PM-SE 7: 103-127.

> Radomsko is a town located about 48km due south of Lodz.

2095.   Dekowski, Jan Piotr. 1964. Z badan nad pozywieniem ludu Leczyckiego. [Food of the people of the Leczyca region.] ML-PM-SE 7: 185-197. [Summary in French]

> Leczyca is a town about 45km southeast of Warsaw.

2096.   Delafontaine. 1850. Le chocolat par Delafontaine et Detwiller, successeur de M. Masson. [Chocolate, by Delafontaine and Detwiller, successors to Mr. Masson.] Paris: the authors.

2097.   Delaimy, Khalaf S. al- & Barakat, M.M.F. Antimicrobial and preservative activity of garlic extract on camel meat. Paper submitted to Third Internatonal Congress of Food Science and Technology. 9 to 14 August, 1970. Washington, D.C.

2098.   De la Malle, Dureau. 1826. The ancient history, origin and fatherland of the cereals, particularly wheat and barley. [In French.] ASN 9: 61-82.

2099.   Delamare. 1719. Traite de la police ou l'on trouvera l'histoire de son etablisement, les fonctions et les prerogatives des ses magistrats, toutes les lois et tous les reglemens qui la concernent: on y a joint une description historique et topographique de Paris et huit plans gravez qui represent son ancien Etat et ses divers accroissemens; avec un recueil e tous les statuts et reglemens des six corps des marchands et de toutes les communautez des arts et metiers. [Treatise on the police, in which will be found the history of its establishment, its functions and the prerogatives of its magistrates, all the laws and regulations which conern it; added to this is an historical and topographical description of Paris and eight engraved plans which represent its former condition and its various extensions; with a collection of all the statutes and regulations of the six companies of merchants and of all the corporations of arts and trades. Vol. 3 Paris: Michel Brunet.

> The fifth book covers bread, meat, freshwater, dried, and salted fish; sweetwater fish; eggs, butter, and cheese; fruit and vegetables; wine and beer; wood and charcoal fuel, etc. Also included are observations on the life and manners of various food-related professionals, e.g. bakers, grillers.

2100.   De la Torre-Buena, J.R. 1942. A bibliographical note on aquatic Hemiptera used as food in Mexico. BES-B 37: 168-169.

2101.   De la Torre-Buena, J.R. 1944. Why not eat insects. BES-B 39: 122-131.

> Worldwide survey of use of insects as food.

2102.   Delbetz, P. Theodore. 1856. Du topinambour culture, panification et distillation de ce tubercule. [The jerusalem artichoke, its culture, use in bread-making, and distillation of this root.] Paris: August Goin.

2103.   Delcourt, Pierre. 1888. Ce qu'on mange a Paris. [What Paris eats.] Paris: Librairie Illustree.

> Part One of this book covers food products and their falsification; Part Two covers commercial products, pharmaceuticals, etc.

2104.   Delf, E. Marion. 1943. Nature and uses of seaweeds. Nature [L] 152: 149-153.

2105.   Delgado, Graciela; Brumback, C.L.; & Deaver, Mary Brice. 1961. Eating patterns among migrant families. US-DHEW-PHR 76: 349-355.

2106.   Delgado, Juan Alvarez. 1946. Sobre la alimentacion indigena de Canarias. El Gofio. Nota linguisticas. [On the diet of Canary Islands indigenes. El Gofio. Linguistic notes.] SEAEP-AM 21: 20-58.

2107.   Dellenbaugh, Frederick S. 1900. The North-American Indians of yesterday. New York, London: G.P. Putnam's Sons.

> Three indigenous Mexican beverages: p. 360.

2108.   Delmarcel, V. L'alimentation du detenu. [Prisoner's diet.] In Deuxieme Congres International d'Hygiene Alimentaire et de l'Alimentation Rationnelle de l'Homme. 4-8 Octobre, 1910. Bruxelles. 1910. Vol. 1. Section 2. Pp. 39-48. Brussels: M. Weissenbruch.

> Describes the diet for prisoners in the central prison of Louvain, and for secondary prisons. Food values are given.

2109.   Del Monte Corporation. 1978. There's no taste like home. Vol. One. [San Francisco]: Del Monte Corporation.

> This illustrated booklet contains a number of ethnic recipes adapted to North American food uses and patterns. It is an excellent example of how a composite culture absorbs and modifies the food combinations of its component cultural groups.

2110.   Delolme, Antoine. 1936. Contribution a l etude des riz de la region e Sikasso [Soudan]. [Contribution to the study of the rices of the Sikasso region [Sudan]. Nancy: Imprimerie de G. Thomas.

> The author's Ph.D. dissertation, from the Universite de Nancy. Faculte de Sciences. Laboratoie de Botanique Agricole et Coloniale.

2111.   Delon, Charles. 1881. Parmentier et la pomme de terre. [Parmentier and the potato.] Paris: Hachette.

> A. Parmentier was an Eighteenth Century French food researcher, who published works on breadmaking and food substitutes suitable for times of shortage.

2112.   Deloria, Ella c. 1967. Some notes on the Santee. MN 28: 10-13.

> Includes data on wild rice (Zizania aquatica).

2113.   De Loureiro, J.A.M. 1942. Estimation of available food of Portugal. [In Portuguese.] Am Lus 1: 442-457.

2114.   De Lucy-Fossarieu, P. Les langues Indiennes de la Californic. Etude de philologie enthographique. [Indian languages of California. Philological ethnographic study.] In Congres International des Sciences Ethnographiques tenu a Paris du 15 au 17 juillet, 1878. Ministere de l'Agriculture et du Commerce. 1881. Paris: Imprimerie Nationale.

> Food: p. 520.

2115.   Delvaille, Camille, ed. compilor. 1856. De l'usage alimentaire de la viande de cheval. Lecons faites au Museum d'Histoire Naturelle par M. Isidore Georffroy Saint-Hilaire. [The food use of horse meat. Lessons given at the Museum d'Histoire Naturelle by Mr. Isidore Geoffroy Saint-Hilaire.] Paris: Imprimerie de Gros.

2116.   Delvau, Alfred. 1862. Histoire anecdotique des cafes et cabarets de Paris, etc. [Anecdotal history of the cafes and cabarets of Paris.] Paris: Dentu.

2117.   Delvert, Jean. 1961. Le paysan Cambodgien [The Cambodian peasant.] Le Monde d'Outre-Mer. Passe et Present. Premiere Serie. Etudes. No. 10. Paris; the Hague: Mouton & Co.

> Food: pp. 149-156.

2118.   Dema, I.S. An experimental study of the protein values of Nigerian diets and the relation of the results to the devlopment of the native food economy. Ph.D. dissertation. University of London. 1959.

> Four Nigerian villages are studied: Bida, located at 9. .06 N., 5. .59 E.; Illu, Kanui, Otukwang, and Sorugbemi and the quality of their diets compared.

2119.   Dema, I.S. 1965. Review of recent nutritional surveys in Nigeria as a guide to social action. SAN-P 6: 73-86.

2120.   Demarchi, M. 1963. Family food consumption survey of workers belonging to the brick industry. BU-FM-J 5: 173-178.

2121.   Demarchi, M.; Isa, A.; Al-Saidi, M.; Al-Azzawee, M.; Ali, M.; & Elmilli, N. 1966. Food consumption and nutritional status of pregnant women attending a maternal-child health center in Baghdad. BU-FM-J 8: 20-30.

2122.   Demarchi, M.; Mohanty, M.; Ali, M.; Al-Azzawee, M.; Al-Saidi, S., & Isa, A. 1962. A dietary survey in rural areas of Baghdad. BU-FM-J 4: 140-149.

2123.   Dembinska, Maria. 1961. Z badan nad konsumpcja zywnosciowa w Polsce sredniowiecznej. [Food consumption in medieval Poland.] EPol 4: 93-106.

2124.   Dembo, Isaac Alexandrovich. 1894. Jewish method of slaughter compared with other methods, from the humanitarian, hygienic, and economic points of view. Translated from the German with the author's ammendments. Published by the trustees of the late J.A. Franklin. London: Kegan Paul.

2125.   De Mendizabal, Miguel O. 1946. La distribucion geografica de la sal. [The geographic distribution of salt.] In Mexico prehispanico. Antologia de "Esta Semana" [Prehispanic Mexico. Anthology of "This Week".] Edited by Jorge A. Vivo. Pp. 742-753. Mexico City: Editorial Emma Hurtado.

2126.   Demerson, L. 1826. Histoire naturelle de la vigne et du vin, suive de considerations relatives a l'influence du vin sur l'homme. [Natural history of vine and wine, followed by considerations relative to the influence of wine upon man.] Paris: Carpentier.

2127.   Demetrio, Fransisco. R. 1970. Dictionary of Philippine folk beliefs and customs. Book 1. Museum and Archives Publication. No. 2. Cagayan de Oro City: Xavier University.

> Cookery: pp. 23-25, eating: pp. 39-49.

2128.   Demeunier. 1776. L'esprit des usages et des coutumes des differens peuples, ou observations tirees des voyageurs et des historiens. [The character of practices and customs of different nations, or observations drawn from travellers and historians.] Paris: chez Tisson.

This volume is composed of eighteen sections or 'books'. The first book is composed of six chapters devoted to foods and meals among different peoples of the world.

2129.   Demory, Barbara. Where quantity is quality: Ponapean child feeding. Paper presented at 74th Annual Meeting of the American Anthropological Association. 2 to 6 December, 1975. San Francisco, California.

> Caroline Islands.

2130.   Denevan, William M. & Parsons, James J. Aboriginal cultivation of the South American wetlands: review and new evidence. Paper presented at 67th Annual Meeting of the American Anthropological Association. 21 to 24 November, 1968. Seattle, Washington.

> Ridged and platform fields have been found in the Mojos Savannahs of northeastern Bolivia, the San Jorge flood plain of northern Colombia, the Guayas Basin of coastal Ecuador, the coastal savannahs of Surinam, Lake Titicaca Basin, and the Sabana de Bogota. Traces of ridged fields have also been found in the Rio Apure area of the Venezuelan llanos. Questions of chronology, culture, demography, technology, and function remain to be answered.

2131.   Denevan, William M. 1971. Campa subsistence in the Gran Pajonal, eastern Peru. GR 61: 496-518.

> Relation of subsistence patterns to population density; settlement stability; food productivity and resources; and cultural evolution in the Amazon basin.

2132.   Dengler, Harry William. 1958. The folklore of walnuts. NNA-AR No. 49. Pp. 96-100.

2133.   Den Hartog, Adel P. Some aspects of food habits in Pantang [a farming community in the coastal savannah of Ghana]. Mimeographed. Regional Food and Nutrition Commission for Africa. [Rome?]: Food and Agriculture Organization of the United Nation. 1970.

> Frequency of food use for males and females is given, by meals, age group, own produced and purchased items. Also described are food preparation and distribution, infant feeding practices, food preferences and taboos, and ceremonial foods.

2134.   Den Hartog, Adel P. 1973. Dietary habits of northern migrant labourers in Accra, Ghana. Voeding 34: 282-299.

2135.   Hartog, Adel P. den. 1973. The use of rodents as food in tropical Africa. NNLet 11(2): 1-14.

2136.   Den Hartog, Adel P. 1974. A suggested reading list on food habits. NNLet 12(1): 31-38.

Selected books and articles on food habits and their place in the social context of human culture; changing food habits; food habits of vulnerable groups; food avoidances; and methods of food habits research.

2137.   Den Hartog, Adel P. 1977. Field guide on food habits. A practical introduction to social surveys on food and nutrition in third world communities. International Course in Food Science and Nutrition Papers. No. 1. Department of Human Nutrition. Wageningen, The Netherlands: Agricultural University.

Part One of this manual provides a background for the study of human food behavior in relation to socio-anthropological variables. Part Two examines in detail procedures for the collection and presentation of field data. Both sections are supported by references to much of the classic literature in the area of human food habits. Recommended to researchers contemplating field work in nutritional anthropology.

2138.   Den Hartog, C. & Kooy, G. 1965. Voeding en sociale verandering. [Nutrition and social change.] Voeding 26: 87-93.

2139.   Denis, Hector. 1887. L'alimentation et la force de travail. Etude de sociologie biologique comparee. [Diet and work strength. Comparative socio-biological study.] Brussels: Imprimerie des Travaux Publics.

2140.   Dennett, R.E. 1898. Notes on the folklore of the Fjort [French Congo]. London: Published for the Folklore Society.

Song of hunger: pp. 162-163, Loango Province. Relates to famine periods.

2141.   De Noter, Raphael Ferdinand Edouard David Marie. 1931. La bonne cuisine aux colonies Asia-Afrique-Amerique. [The good food of the Asian, African and American colonies.] Paris: Depot General a l'Art Culinaire.

2142. Densmore, Frances. 1914. A study of Sioux music. SI-MC-P Vol. 68. No. 2275

Contains an illustration of paunch-boiling.

2143.   Densmore, Frances. 1918. Study of Chippewa material culture. SI-MC-P Vol. 68 No. 2494.

Contains description of gathering and parching wild rice [Zizania aquatica].

2144.   Densmore, Frances. 1928. Uses of plants by the Chippewa Indians. SI-BAE-AR- for the year 1926-1927. Pp. 275-397.

2145.   Dentan, Robert Knox, ed. A preliminary guide to the collection of information on food behavior. Final report. United States Public Health Service Grant No. A-3557. New Haven: Human Relations Area Files. 1961.

2146.   Dentan, Robert Knox. Some Senoi Semai dietary restrictions: a study of food behavior in a Malayan hill tribe. Ph.D. dissertation. Anthropology. Yale University. 1965.

2147.   Dentler, Mame & Huenemann, Ruth. 1943. Case studies of nutrition. Five Chicago cases. AAPSSA 225: 58-61.

Brief sketches of typical diets of Swedish-American, Polish-American, and Italian-American individuals, with additional descriptions of a bachelor railroad worker's food habits, and an eight year old girl's diet of refined carbohydrates.

2148.   Deonna, Waldemar & Renard, Marcel. 1961. Croyances et superstions de table dans la Rome antique. [Ancient Roman beliefs and superstitions relating to eating.] Bruxelles: Collection Latomus.

2149.   Depaire, J.B. 1896. Hydromel et produits derives de la fermentation de miel. [Hydromel and products derived from the fermentation of honey.] Bruxelles: M. Lamertin.

2150.   De Pauw, L.-F. 1893-1894. Contribution a l'etude de l'alimentation de l'homme et des anthropomorphes. [Contribution to the study of the food habits of humans and primates.] SA Brux-B 12: 139-144; 218-221.

2151.   De Pomiane Pozerski, E. 1933. La cuisine aux 4 points cardineaux. [Food in the four corners of the world.] SSHAARH-B 21: 401-441.

2152.   Depositario, W.C. 1965. Food from wood. Mirror 30 July. P. 30.

2153.   De Quatrefages, A. 1893. The moas and the moa-hunters. Translated by Laura Buller. NZI-TP 25: 17-49.

Moa and dog as food [New Zealand]: pp. 38-40; [Paris, 1873]: p. 38 footnote.

2154.   Derman, William. Metropolis and periphery, drought and famine: the case of the Sahel. Paper presented at 74th Annual Meeting of the American Anthropological Association. 2 to 6 December, 1975. San Francisco, California.

2155.   De Rougemont, Denis. 1898. Cannibal blacks of north-western Australia. SA-S 46: 1937.

2156.   Descamps, P. 1925. Le cannibalisme, ses causes et ses modalites. [Canniablism, its causes and forms.] Anthropologie 35: 321-341.

2157.   Descola, Jean. 1968. Daily life in colonial Peru. Translated by Michael Heron. New York: Macmillan.

Foods: pp. 127-133.

2158.   Descourtilz, Michelle Etienne. 1837. Des champignons comestibles, suspects et veneneux. [Edible, questionable, and poisonous mushroms.] Paris: Chappron.

2159. De Silva, W.A. 1889-1890; 1890-1891; 1891-1892. Indigenous food products; cultivated and wild. Trop Ag 9: 302;, 373, 374; 444, 445; 587; 658; 659; 721, 722; 795, 796, 866; 10: 67, 146, 147; 266; 307; 387; 531, 532; 607, 608; 679; 815; 11: 371, 372; 520, 521; 607; 695, 696; 792, 793; 872, 873.

India.

2160. De Silva, W.A. 1891-1892. The madu tree [Cycas circinalis]. Trop Ag 11: 83.

2161. De Silva, W.A. 1903-1904. The edible root crops of Ceylon. Trop Ag 23: 499, 500, 571, 572, 716.

2162. Desjardins, E. 1970. Montreal aux prises en 1847 avec les victimes de la faim. [Montreal at close quarters in 1847 with the victims of the famine.] UMC 99: 306-313.

2163. De Sola, Ralph & De Sola, Dorothy. 1969. A dictionary of cooking; approximately eight thousand definitions of culinary ingredients, methods, terms and utensils. New York: Meredith Press.

2164. Des Ombiaux, Maurice. 1928. L'art de manger et son histoire. [The art of eating and its history.] Paris: Payot; Abbeville: Imprimerie F. Paillard.

2165. Despaux. [Physician de Crony sur Ourcq.] Du pain blanc et du pain bis ou de menage. [White bread and brown (or household bread.) Meaux: Destouches.

2166. Desplanques, Jules. 1883. Des origines de la pomme. [The origins of the apple.] Alencon: Imprimerie A. Lepage.

A review of authors who have mentioned apples, and cider, from the Hebrews and Romans to later times.

2167. Destamnil. 1871. La cuisine pendant la siege, recettes pour accomoder les viands de cheval et d'ane... suivies des conseils sur la conservation ou l'utilisation de diverses substances. [Food during the siege, recipes for adaptation to horse and mule meat...followed by directions on the preservation and use of diverse substances.] Paris: Librairie des Villes et des Campagnes. Held by the Bibliotheque National [Paris] No. 8. Lb57 793.

2168. Detienne, M. 1970. La cuisine de Pythagore. [The dietary regimen of Pythagoras.] AS Rel 29: 141-162.

2169. Dettweiler. 1914. Aryan agriculture. JHer 5: 473-481.

Early plant and animal domestication. Includes illustration of a prehistoric Swedish petroglyph depicting yoked oxen pulling a plough guided by a ploughman.

2170. De Tussac, F. 1808, 1818, 1824, 1827. Flora Antillarum, seu historia generalis botanica, ruralis, oeconomica, vegetabilium in Antilis indigenorum et exoticorum indigenis cultura adiscriptorum. [Flora of the Antilles, or a general botanic, rural, and economic history of the indigenous Antillean vegetables, and of the exotic ones that have become naturalized there.] 4 vols. Paris. Vol. 1. the author & F. Schnoell; Vol. 2. the author & D.'Hautel; Vol. 3. the author; Vol. 4. the author.

2171. De Veer-Ahn, C. 1958. En enquete naar de voeding en voedingsgewoonten in enkele Woonoorden voor Ambonezen in Nederland. [An investigation of the nutrition and food habits of the Amboinese living in the Netherlands.] Voeding 19: 365-386.

Ambon is located in the southern Moluccas, in the Indonesian archipelago.

2172. Devitt, Napier. 1945. People and places. Cape Town: Unie-Volkpers.

Derivation and evolution of traditional South African cookery: pp. 13-16.

2173. De Voe, Thomas, Farrington. 1862. The market book, containing a historical account of the public markets in the cities of New York, Boston, Philadelphia, with a brief description of every article of human food sold therein, the introduction of cattle in America, and the notices of many remarkable specimens. Printed for the author.

Only one volume publishd which relates to New York. Held by U.S. Library of Congress, Washington, D.C. No. HF 5472. U7N6.

2174. De Voe, Thomas Farrington. 1866. The market assistant, containing a brief description of every article of human food sold in the public markets of the cities of New York, Boston, Philadelphia, and Brooklyn; including the various domestic and wild animals, poultry, game, fish, vegetables, fruit, etc., etc., with many curious incidents and anecdotes. New York: Orange, Judd & Co.

Held by U.S. Library of Congress, Washington, D.C. No. TX 353. D48.

2175.   Devore, Irven. Ethnoarchaeology: Bushman ecology and hunting patterns. Paper presented at 70th Annual Meeting of the American Anthropological Association. 19 November, 1979. New York City.

Discusses the relationship between group composition, hunting, and foraging strategies, with particular reference to the representation of these activities in the artifact remains of contemporary Bushman campsites.

2176.   De Vries, Arnold P. 1952. Primitive man and his food. Chicago: Chandler Book Co.

2177.   De Waal, M. 1955. Zuivel, ei en honing door alle eeuwen heen. [Dairy products, eggs and honey throughout the centuries.] Zutphen: W.J. Thieme.

2178.   De Wahlens, Paul. 1963. Le toteman [patisserie de Noel a Tirlemont]. 'Toteman' [a Christmas pastry from Tirlemont]. FBrab 160: 476-484.

Tirlemont is a city east of Brussels, in Brabant. Tirlemont is modernly called Tiuen.

2179.   Dewalt, Kathleen Musante. Nutritional assessment in peasant societies. Paper presented at 74th Annual Meeting of the American Anthropological Association. 2 to 6 December, 1975. San Francisco, California.

2180.   Dewalt, Kathleen Musante & Dewalt, Billie Richard. Economic diversification and patters of food use in a Mexican ejido. Paper presented at 76th Annual Meeting of the American Anthropological Association. 29 November to 3 December, 1977. Houston, Texas.

This paper investigates the nutritional effects of economic diversification resulting from various development efforts in a Mexican ejido. As a result of these projects, different ejidatorios follow a number of agricultural adaptive strategies, including traditional subsistence maize production, cash maize production using "green revolution" techniques, livestock production and cash cropping of forage crops. Using a number of twelve-hour dietary recall interviews, day-longobservations, with food weighment, anthropometry, and hair-root mineral analysis for a sample of families, patterns of food use and nutritional status are outlined for families following each of the adoptive strategies.

2181.   Dewalt, Kathleen Musante & Pelto, Gretel H. Food use and household ecology in a Mexican community. In Nutrition and anthropology in action. Edited by Thomas K. Fitzgerald. 1976. Pp. 79-93. Assen, Amsterdam: Van Gorcum.

Analyzes factors influencing food intake in the community of Nopalcingo, on the Rio Lerma, in the northwest part of the Mexican State of Mexico. Dietary patterns are described, together with a discussion of concepts of flavor and healthfulness of foods and the influences of these variables upon food consumption and the meaning of the results of this research for nutritional change programs. Concludes that efforts toward improvement of health and nutritional status must take into account household ecology in relation to the economic and political structure of the community and the region.

2182.   Dewevre, Alfred. 1894. Les plantes utiles du Congo. [Useful plants of the Congo.] 2nd revised and corrected edition. Brussels: Vanderouwera; Lamertin; Paris: G. Carre.

Annotated list of cultivated and wild plants, classified according to use.

2183.   Dewey, Kathryn. The impact of agricultural change on diet and nutrition in Tabasco, Mexico. Paper presented at 77th Annual Meeting of the American Anthropological Association. 14 to 18 November, 1978. Los Angeles, California.

2184.   Dhalla, Manecki Nusservanji. 1922. Zoroastrian civilization. From the earliest times to the downfall of the last Zoroastrian empire 651 A.D. New York: Oxford University Press.

Food and drink [Kianian period]: pp. 187-189; [Median period]: p. 205; [Achaemenian period]; pp. 260-261; [Sasanian period]: pp. 370-372.

2185.   Dharma, P.C. 1938. Women during the Ramayana Period. JIH 17: 1-28.

India. Alcoholic beverages: p. 20.

2186.   Dharma, P.C. 1949. The status of women during the Epic period. JIH 27: 69-90.

India. Food-related activities: p. 83.

2187.   D'Hoye. 1937. Maniok, het brood der zwartzen. [Manioc, the bread of the Blacks.] Jezmis 9: 327-331.

Africa. This periodical is held by the Staatsbibliothek, Berlin.

2188.   Dia, Ibrahim Maleck. Le role du poisson dans l'alimentation et l'economie senegalaises. [The role of fish in Senegalse diet and economy.] Thesis No. 73. Allfort, France: Ecole Nationale Veterinaire. 1963.

2189.   Dick, Everett N. Food of our fathers. Paper read at the 36th Annual Meeting of Mississippi Valley Historical Association, 24 April, 1943. Cedar Rapids, Iowa.

Notes on frontier food in the United States.

2190.   Dickie, J. 1940. Note on a salt substitute used by one of the inland tribes of New Guinea. JPS 49: 144-147.

2191.   Dickins, Dorothy. 1926. Negro food habits in the Yazoo, Mississippi delta. JHE 18: 523-525.

2192.   Dickins, Dorothy. 1927. A study of food habits of people in two contrasting areas of Mississippi. Miss-AES-B No. 245.

2193.   Dickins, Dorothy. 1928. A nutrition investigation of Negro tenants in the Yazoo Mississippi Delta. Miss-AES-B No. 254.

A study in rural nutritional sociology. Opens with a discussion of methodology used in the study; nutritive value of diets is given. Food uses, combinations, preparation techniques, and preferences are recorded. Use of home-grown foods, typical menus, and expenditures for food included.

2194.   Dickins, Dorothy. 1943. Case studies of nutrition. Three Mississippi Negro families. AAPSS-A 225: 55-56.

Three cases: a low-income share cropper family; a low-income urban family, and a well-fed farm family. Brief dietary, and food preparation data are recorded.

2195.   Dickins, Dorothy. 1943. Food preparation of owner and cropper farm families in the shortleaf pine area of Mississippi. SF 22: 56-63.

2196.   Dickins, Dorothy. 1945. Changing pattern of food preparation of small town families in Mississippi. Miss-AES-B No. 415.

Data for this monograph were gathered by personal interview with a total of one thousand one hundred and fifty-eight families-Black and Caucasian. Trends in the consumption and preparation techniques of new foods are recorded and analyzed, and the variables influencing receptiveness to innovation are examined. Implications of the foregoing are enumerated for use in food education programs.

2197.   Dickins, Dorothy. 1945. Traditional food preparation rules. Miss-AES-B No. 418.

Responses to a survey among Black American, and Caucasian homemakers in rural Mississippi. This monograph appears to be unique in the literature; the data are carefully analyzed from a socio-anthropological perspective; as well as from that of the home economist.

2198.   Dickins, Dorothy. 1946. Menu planning and food habits. JADA 22: 890.

Emphasies the value in studying menus as indicators of food preparation techniques, food combinations in "culturally determined clusters" and individual, family and regional preferences. The article is illustrated with practical examples from the author's experience as a home economics researcher. Provides suggestions for the introduction of previously un-tried foods, and gives reasons

which may account for slow-up in efforts to change food habits, particularly among lower income, tradition-oriented groups.

2199.   Dickins, Dorothy. A regional approach to food habits and attitude research: some implications of recent food preparation studies in Mississippi. In Conference on Food Acceptance Research. 6 December to 7 December, 1945. Washington, D.C. Quartermaster Corps Manual 17-9. United States War Department. United States Army. 1946. Pp. 27-37. Washington, D.C.: Quartermaster Food and Container Institute. Research and Development Branch. Military Planning Division. Committee on Food Research.

Available in microform from United States Library of Congress. Microform Division. Item PB-53-883.

2200.   Dickins, Dorothy & Ford, R.N. 1942. Geophagy [dirt-eating] among Mississippi Negro school children. ASR 7: 59-65.

2201.   Dicks, Catherine. Food management practices and food habits of Anglo-American and Spanish-American girls in New Mexico. Master's thesis. Colorado A&M College. 1944.

2202.   Dickson, Evelyn Marthena Hogue. Food plants of the western Oregon Indians. Master's thesis. Palo Alto: Stanford University. 1946.

2203.   Diener, Paul & Robkin, Eugene E. 1978. Ecology, evolution, and the search for cultural origins: the question of Islamic pig prohibition. CAnth 19: 493-540.

Separates evolutionary and functional types of explanations. Includes a highly detailed consideration of both perspectives, with comments by sixteen internationally-known scholars. Offers an historical-political hypothesis as tentative explanation, citing fluctuations in socio-cultural stability.

2204.   Dieng, D. 1955. Une enquete su l'alimentation chez les Sarakolle. [An inquiry into the diet of the Sarakole.] TU No. 8 Pp. 21-22.

Mali.

2205.   Dierbach, Johann Heinrich. 1831. Flora Apiciana. Ein Beitrag Zur naheren Kentniss der Nahrungsmittel der alten Romer: mit besonderer Rucksicht auf die Bucher des Caelius Apicius de opsoniis et condimentis sive Arte Coquinaria. [The flora of Apicius. A contribution to food knowledge: the foodstuffs of the ancient Romans: with particular regard to the book of Caelius Apicius Heidelberg, Leipzig: Neue Akademische Buchhandlung von Karl Groos.

2206.   Dieterlien, G. & Calame-Griaule, G. 1960. L'alimentation Dogon. [Dogon food habits.] CEAfr No. 3. Pp. 46-89.

West Africa.

2207.   Dietz, Lawrence.   1973.   Soda pop; the history, advertising, are, and memorabilia of soft drinks in America.   New York: Simon & Schuster.

2208.   Dieu-Minh.   1931.   Sach nau an chay.   [Culinary art among Buddhist monks.]   2nd edition. Bentre: Imprimerie Bui-van-Nha.

2209.   Digby, William.   1902.   The food of the Indian people... with some diagrammatic presentments by W. Pollard Digby.   London: A. Bonner.

2210.   Diguet, Leon.   1895.   Le jojoba, Simondsia californica.   [The jojoba, Simondsia californica.] RSNA 42: 685-687.

> Prepared for food, by Baja California natives: infused; mixed with sugar [and formed] into a table [sic]. Fruit produces an edible oil which does not become rancid.

2211.   Diguet, Leon.   1928.   Les cactacees utiles de Mexique. Ouvrage posthume revise par Andre Guillaumin. Avec une notice necrologique sur Leon Diguet, par D. Bois.   [The useful cacti of Mexico. Posthumous work revised by Andre Guillaumin. With an obituary of Leon Diguet, by D. Bois.] Achives d'Histoire Naturelle No. 4. Societe Nationale d'Acclimation de France. Paris: au siege de la Societe. Rouen: Imprimerie Lecerf fils.

> Use of cactus seeds and fruit as food: pp. 382-386.

2212.   Dill, David Bruce.   1944.   Food technology problems in the North African and European theatres of operation.   IFT-P 1944. Pp. 13-16.

2213.   Dillingham, Frank T.   1907. The staff-tree: Colastrus scandends as a former food supply of starving Indians.   AN 41: 391-393.

> Describes and documents the use of the bark of a climbing shrub, as a famine food, by Native American groups.

2214.   Di Lullio, Orestes.   Popular foods and their preparation.   [In Spanish.]   In Sociedad Argentina de Patologia Regional del Norte. Octava Reunion. 1934. Pp. 360-391. Beunos Aires: Universidad de Buenos Aires.

2215.   Di Lullio, Orestes.   1941.   Supersticiones relativas a la alimentacion.   [Superstitions relating to diet.]   La Prensa 13-7 Seccion tercera. [Third section.]

2216.   Dimock, Ana Margarita.   1973.   Food preparation of the Guambianos, an indigenous tribe of Colombia.   Minn AS-P 39: 24-25.

> Residing on reserve land, this Native Colombian group retains certain traditional food habits, but is slowly acculturating to modern Columbian dietary. Protein, fresh fruit and vegetables are lacking in Guambiano diet.

2217.   Dion, Roger.   1959.   Histoire de la vigne et du vin en France, des origines, au 19e siecle.

[History of vines and wine in France, from their origin to the 19th century.] Paris: the author.

2218.   Directorate-General.   1953.   Iraqi dates. Culture, industry, trade, and delicious recipes. Baghdad: Date Association.

2219.   Dirks, Robert.   Effects of hunger on social behavior. Paper presented at 75th Annual Meeting of the American Anthropological Association. 17 to 21 November, 1976. Washington, D.C.

> Generalization concerning the effects of hunger on social behavior is hampered by a descriptive literature that presents a confusing and often contradictory composite. In an effort to achieve some coherence, sources bearing on social response to food deprivation are reviewed and analyzed, with special attention to political implications. The cycle of famine and relief is examined, in terms of progressive stages; and concomitant behavioral transformations are described. It is concluded that these transformations can be viewed as attempts to achieve equilibrium between conflicting demands of the organism and the environment.

2220.   Dishman, Clara B.   A study of the modification of the food habits of the preschool child. Master's thesis. Denton: Texas State College for Women. 1931.

2221.   Ditmer, E.E.   1929-1930.   K voprosy o proiskhozhdenii kul'turnich fasolei.   [Contribution to the question of the origin of Phaseolus.] BABGPB 23: 309-402.

> Aztec use of Phaseolus: pp. 351-353.

2222.   Dittrick, H. 1939. Nursing can; early American feeding device. BH Med 7: 696-704.

2223.   Divale, William T. Kapauku warfare, calories and population. Paper presented at 70th Annual Meeting of the American Anthropological Association. 19 November, 1971. New York City.

> Primitive warfare was part of a system that regulated population to available energy. Crossculturally, this is demonstrated by warfare's effects on the age-sex ratios of 460 populations representing 150 different cultures. A case study of the New Guineea Kapauku is made using Pospisil's data on their economy, nutrition and demography, and Carneiro's formular for carrying capacity. It is demonstrated that the Kapauka were at optimum density given their per capita rate of energy harnessing and caloric/protein requirements. Population remained stable despite high birth rates, and it is argued that warfare and disease regulated the excess. Since 'pacification', population has increased.

2224.   Diwakar, Ranganath Ramachandra.   1958. Bihar through the ages.   Calcutta: Orient Longmans.

Food: late Gupta age: p. 288; A.D. 750-1200: p. 344; A.D. 1206-1526 [Hindu]: pp. 428, 461-462; A.D. 1526-1707 [Hindu]: p. 528; [Muslim]: pp. 533-534.

2225.   Dixon, James Main.   1885.   Japanese etiquette. ASJ-T 13: 1-21.

Arrangement of table service, food gifts, dinner table etiquette.

2226.   Dixon, Keith A. 1963. The inter-American diffusion of a cooking technique: the culinary shoepot. AA 65: 593-619.

Ceramic vessel.

2227.   Dixon, Roland B. 1932. The problem of the sweet potato in Polynesia. AA 34: 40-46.

2228.   Dizon, Leticia E.   The leguminosae of the University area and vicinity, Quezon City.   Master's thesis Botanay.   Diliman, Quezon City: University of the Philippins. 1953.

Includes leguminous plants used as food.

2229.   Doane, C.F. & Lawson, H.W.   1908. Varieties of cheese. Descriptions and analyses.   USDA-BAI-B 105.

2230.   Dobell, Horace. 1864. A manual of diet and regimen for physician and patient.   London: J. Churchill & Sons.

Includes thirty-nine rules for the promotion of health among adults in the United Kingdom, together with tables of essentials of a normal diet.   Reviewed in BMJ 1: 675 [22 May, 1864].

2231. Documentary Educational Resources & Pennsylvania State University. 1968. The feast. 16mm film, sound and color.   Thirty minutes. Watertown, Massachusetts: Documentary Educational Resources; University Park, Pennsylvania: Pennsylvania State University.

Includes footage on food preparation for feast related to group alliance formation among the Yanomamo of Amazonian Brazil.

2232.   Documentary Eductional Resoures & Pennsylvania State University. 1974. Climbing the peach palm. 16mm film, sound and color. Nine minutes. Watertown, Massachusetts: Documentary Educational Resources; University Park, Pennsylvania: Pennsylvania State University.

Footage depicts climbing palm and gathering of rasha fruit by Yanomamo man of Amazonian Brazil.

2233. Documentary Educational Resources & Pennsylvania State University. 1975. Bride service. 16mm film, sound and color. Ten minutes. Watertown, Massachusetts: Documentary Educational Resources; University Park, Pennsylvania: Pennsylvania State University.

Contains footage showing young woman carrying fruit and meat for her husband. Filmed among the Yanomamo of Amazonian Brazil.

2234.   Documentary Educational Resources & Pennsylvania State University. 1975. Tapir distribution.   16mm film, sound and color.   Fifteen minutes. Watertown, Massachusetts: Documentary Educational Resources; University Park, Pennsylvania: Pennsylvania State University.

Hunting and meat distribution among the Yanomamo of Amazonian Brazil.

2235.   Documentary Educational Resources. 1977. Misa Colombiana.   16mm film, sound, black-and-white. Twenty minutes. Watertown, Massachusetts: Documentary Educational Resources.

Contains footage of squatters in Medellin, Colombia, scavenging from city refuse dump.

2236.   Dodd, George. 1856. The food of London; a sketch of the chief varieties, sources of supply...and machinery of distribution of the food for a community of two million and a half. London: Longman.

2237.   Dodds, Kenneth S. 1966. The evolution of the cultivated potato. Endeavor 25: 83-88.

2238.   Dodge, Ernest Stanley.   1943.   Gourd growers of the South Seas.   An introduction to the study of the Lagenaria gourd in the culture of the Polynesians. Ethnographical Series. No. 2. Boston: Gourd Society of America.

Lagernaria vulgaris is cited as the only probable Polynesian autochthonous food plant. Only food use in Oceania is cited for the Maori, who ate the young fruit. It was baked in an earth oven and eaten in large quantities during the summer season. Elsewhere, Lagenaria may have been eaten only during times of famine.

2239.   Dodge, Fay.   The nature and extent of Indian agriculture in North America.   Master's thesis. Sociology. University of Kansas. 1911.

2240.   Dohrs, Fred E. & Sommers, Lawrence M. 1967. Cultural geography: selected readings. New York: Thomas Y. Crowell.

2241.   Doke, Clement M. 1931. The Lambas of northern Rhodesia. London: George G. Harrap.

Food and its preparation: pp. 99-108.

2242.   Dolan, J.R. 1964. Peddlars of food. In The Yankee peddlars of early America: an affectionate history of life and commerce in the developing colonies and the young republic.   New York: Charles N. Potter.

2243.   Dole, Gertrude. Techniques of preparing manioc flour as a key to cultural history in tropical America.   In Men and cultures. Selected papers of the International Congress of Anthropological and

Ethnological Sciences. 1-9 September, 1956. Philadelphia, Pennsylvania. Edited under the chairmanship of Anthony F.C. Wallace. 1960. Pp. 241-248. Philadelphia: University of Pennsylvania Press.

> Distribution of devices used to express moisture from manioc pulp, by type, tribe, and linguistic group. Notes devices are not meant for removing toxic component [hydrocyanic, or Prussic acid] of manioc, as expression technique is used for both non-toxic and toxic types. Other means for toxicity neutralization are used, i.e. artificial heating, or exposure to sunlight, and fermentation.

2244.   Dole, Gertrude. 1962. Endocannibalism among the Amahuaca Indians. NYAS-T 24: 567-593.

> Brazil.

2245.   Dole, Gertrude E.   A final stage in the development of the tipiti. Paper presented at the 70th Annual Meeting of the American Anthropological Association. 18 November, 1971. New York City.

> New evidence bearing on the development of the tipiti (sleeve press for expression of toxic factors in manioc) is presented. A plaited mat press used by the Witoto of Colombia is described and illustrated. The relation of the mat-type press to the sleeve type press is considered.

2246.   Doman, Leila. 1937. A study of the price differences in retail grocery stores in New York State. Cor U-AES-B No. 665.

> An in-depth, scientific analysis of the variables involved in comparative food shopping.

2247.   Dombrowski, Joane. Plant domestication in Ethiopian culture history. Master's thesis. Anthropology. Yale University. 1966.

2248.   Domenig, Lina. 1964. Die Kost auf der "Stor". [Food from sturgeon.] KL No. 1. Pp. 5-6.

2248.   Dominguez, Juan A. & Autran, Eugenio. Archivos ineditos de Aime Bonpland existentes en el Instituto de Botanico y Farmacologia de la Facultad de Medicina de la Universidad. [Unpublished manuscript material of Aime Bonpland in the Institue of Botany and Pharmacology of the Department of Medicine of the University.] 17 Congreso Internacional de Americanistas. 17-23 de Mayo de 1910. Buenos Aires. Actas. 1912. Pp. 599-602. Buenos Aires: Imprenta de Coni Hermanos.

> Includes reference to "...numerosas notas sobre la yerba mate..." ["...numerous notes on yerba mate..."]

2249.   Don, George. 831-1838. A general history of dichlamydeous plants, arranged according to the natural system. 4 vols. London: J.G. & F. Rivington. Also published under the title A system of gardening and botany.

2250.   Donahue, Wilma T. 1951. Psychological aspects of feeding the aged. JADA 27: 461-466.

2251.   Donath, W.F. 1957. Summary of the historical development of research on nutrition in the Netherlands Indies over a century. [In Dutch.] Voeding 18: 349-355.

2252.   Donath, W.F.; Koolhaas, D.R.; & Van Veen, Andre G. 1935. Tables showing chemical composition of native food products in Netherlands East Indies. [In Dutch.] GTNI 75: 426-446.

2253.   Donley, Erma J. A study of the integration of nutrition in the curriculum of the Fifth grade of Upper Arlington School. Master's thesis. University of Minnesota at St. Paul. 1947.

2254.   Donoso, G.; Hedayat, H.; Khayatian, H. 1969.   Favism with special reference to Iran. WHO-B 40: 513-519.

2255.   Doolittle, Justus. 1867. Social life of the Chinese: with some account of their religious, governmental, educational, and business customs and opinions, with special but not exclusive reference to Fuchou. New York: Harpers Brothers.

> Scattered references to festival food contained throughout.

2257.   Dor. 1937. Explication Zoologiques des prescriptions alimentaires de la bible et du talmud. [Zoological explanation of Biblical and Talmudic food taboos. SAP-BM 8: 63-70.

> Concludes that only vegetable-eating terrestrial vertebrates and invertebrates are permitted, in the belief that exclusion of predators will avoid transmission of infection borne by scavengers.

2258.   Dorcus, Roy M. 1942. Food habits: their origin and control. JADA 18: 738-740.

2259.   Doran, John. 1854. Table traits, with something on them. 2nd edition. London: R. Bentley.

2260.   Doreau, M. 1962. Current considerations on the nutrition of the native in Sahara. [In German.] VZ 7: 252-255.

> Summary in English.

2261.   Dornstreich, Mark D. A study of subsistence ecology: the Gadio Enga of mid-montane New Guinea. Paper presented at 68th Annual Meeting of the American Anthropological Association. 20 to 23 November, 1969. New Orleans, Louisiana.

2262.   Dornstreich, Mark D. 1972. A comment on lowland Maya subsistence. AA 74: 776-779.

2263.   Dornstreich, Mark D. An ecological study of Gadio Enga (New Guinea) subsistence. Ph.D. dissertation. Anthropology. Columbia University. 1973.

2264.   Dornstreich, Mark D. 1973. Food habits of early man: balance between hunting and gathering. Science 179: 306-307.

2265.   Dorrell, Sheila. The preservation of organic material in the tombs of Jericho. In Excavations at Jericho.   Report of the joint expedition of the British School of Archaeology in Jerusaleum, the Palestine Exploration Fund, the British Academy, in collaboration with the American School of Oriental Research in Jerusalem. Vol. 2. The tombs excavated in 1955-1958.   Edited by Kathleen Mary Kenyon. 1960-1965. Pp. 704-717. London: Published by the British School of Archaelogy in Jerusalem.

2266.   Dorschel, Edith.   Speise und Trank in Vorderindien. [Food and drink in East India.] Ph.D. dissertation. Geography. Universitat Heidelberg.

2267.   Dorsey, J. Owen. 1884. Omaha sociology. SI-BE-AR for the year 1881-188. Pp. 205-370.

        Food and its preparation: Pp. 303-309; includes mention of various vegetables, fruit, nuts, roots, and seasonings.

2268.   Doubleday, Thomas. 1842. The true law of population, shewn to be connected with the food of the people.   3rd edition.   London: Simpkin, Marshall.

2269.   Doudiet, Ellenore W. Coastal Maine cooking: foods and equipment from 1760. In Gastronomy. The anthropology of food and food habits. Edited by Margaret Louise Arnott. 1975. Pp. 215-232. Paris; The Hague: Mouton Publishers.

        Data derived from local histories, museum archives, early cookbooks. Includes recipes.

2270.   Douet-D'Arcq, M.L.   1865.   Comptes de l'hotel des rois de France aux 16e et 17 siecles, publie pour la Societe de l'Histoire de France. [Accountings of the residences of the Kings of France for the 16th and 17th Centuries, published by the French Historical Society.] Paris: chex Mme veuve Jules Renouard.

        Contains details of expenses for the royal households: tithes, bread, and wine; fruit.

2271.   Douglas, Charles Edward. 1925. Rice: its cultivation and preparation. Pitman Common Commodities and Industries series. London: Isaac Pitman's Sons.

2272.   Douglas, Charles Edward. 1929. Report on the cultivation and preparation of rice in Egypt. Hasting: F.J. Parsons.

2273.   Douglas, Frederic H. 1931. Iroquois foods. DAM-L No. 26 Reprinted: 1968.

2274.   Douglas, Mary. 1972. Deciphering a meal. Daedalus 101: 61-81.

        The 'semantics' of food-related categories: meals, dietary proscriptions. Exemplifies, in particular, the Hebraic dietary code in the Old Testament of the Bible; analyzes its structure, and notes its persistence up to the present time.

2275.   Douglas, Mary. 1974. Food as an art form. SInt 188: 83-88.

2276.   Douglas, Mary.   1977.   Structure of gastronomy.   In Russell Sage Foundation Annual Report for the year 1976-1977. Pp. 55-81. New York: Russell Sage Foundation.

        This paper brings together much of the author's thought on structural analysis of food-related behavior and the light which it may cast on socio-anthropological considerations of cultural food habits. Results of completed research, as well as methodological details are given. Under 'New Directioins for Research', suggestions are made for determining systematization of a number of food-related variables, including organoleptic, aesthetic, socio-economic, and architectural. Recommended as a basic reading for researchers contemplating field-work in nutritional anthropology.

2277.   Douglas, Mary, & Nicod, Michael. 1974. Taking the biscuit: the structure of British meals. NSoc 30: 744-747.

2278.   Douglas, Norman [psued. Pilaff Bey]. 1952. Venus in the kitchen. London: William Heineman.

2279.   Dournes, Jacques. 1969. Modele structural et realite ethnographique (a propos du "Triangle" culinaire").   [Structural model and ethnographic reality (concerning the "culinary triangle)]. L'Homme 9: 42-48.

        Reference here is to the theoretical work of Claude Levi-Strauss, in the area of covert cultural structuring of organoleptic characteristics and methods of cooking food.

2280.   Dove, William Franklin. 1939. A study of individuality in the nutritive instincts and of the causes and effects of variation in the selection of food. AN 69: 469-544.

2281.   Dove, William Franklin. 1943. Appetite levels of food consumption: a technique of measuring food in terms of psychological and nutritional values combined. HB15 199-220.

2282.   Dove, William Franklin. 1943. On the linear arrangement of palatability of natural foods with an example of varietal preference in Leguminosae and Cruciferae by a new, rapid laboratory method. JN 25: 447-462.

2283.   Dove, William Franklin. 1943. The relative nature of human preference with an example in the palatability of different varieties of sweet corn. JCCP 35: 219-226.

2284.   Dove, William Franklin.   Techniques for measuring changes in flavor acceptability. Technical papers from the Quartermaster Food and Container Institute for the Armed Forces. Chicago:

Quartermaster Food and Container Institute. April, 1945.

2285. Dove, William Franklin. 1946. Developing food acceptance research. Science 103: 187-190.

2286. Dove, William Franklin. The process of developing food acceptance research. In Conference on Food Acceptance Research. 6 December to 7 December, 1945. Quartermaster Corps Manual 17-9. United States War Department. United States Army. 1946. Washington, D.C.: Quartermaster Food and Container Institute. Research and Development Branch. Military Planning Division. Committee on Food Research.

Available in microform from United States, Library of Congress. Microform Division. Item PB-53-883.

2287. Dove, William Franklin. 1947. Food acceptability. Its determination and evaluation. FTech 1: 39-50.

2288. Dovey, E.R. 1913. The composition of carabao's milk. PJS 3 [Section A]: 151-157.

Includes data on composition carabao-milk cheese.

2289. Dower, A.R. 1943. Muckindiak: the eats and drinks of Timor. Walkabout July. Pp. 14-16.

2290. Downes, T.W. 1926. Maori rat-trapping devices. JPS 35: 228-234.

Rats as an item of food, cooking techniques: pp. 229-230.

2291. Downing, Glenn R. & Furniss, Lloyd S. 1968. Some observations on camas digging and baking among present day Nez Perce. Tebiwa 11: 48-59.

2292. Doyle, Christina Inez. Food practices and nutritional status of some rural Alabama school children. Master's thesis. University of Alabama. 1948.

2293. Drachman, A.G. 1932. Ancient mills and presses. KDVS-AKM Vol. 1. No. 1. Copenhagen: Levin and Munksgaard.

2294. Dragoni, Carlo, & Burnet, E. 1938. L'alimentation popular au Chili; premiere enquete-generale de 1935; texte complet presente au Gouvernement du Chili; en execution du plan de cooperation entre le Gouvernement du Chili et la Section d' Hygiene de la Societe des Nations; rapport redige par le Prof. Carlo Dragoni, avec la cooperation du Doc Et. Burnet. [Popular diet in Chile; first general survey of 1935; complete text presented to the government of Chile; in fulfillment of the cooperative plan between the government of Chili and the Hygiene Section of the League of Nations; report edited by Prof. Carlo Dragoni with the cooperation of Doc. Et. Burnet.] RCHMP 1: 407-611. Reprint. Santiago de Chile: Universo. 1938.

2295. Drake, B.K. The biorheological process of mastication. In Rheology and texture of foodstuffs. Society of Chemical Industry Monograph No. 27. Society of Chemical Industry. 1968. Pp. 29-39. London: Society of Chemical Industry.

Physiologial aspects of chewing food; comments on subjective terms for food textures.

2296. Drake, T.G.H. 1933. Antiques of pediatric interest. JPed 3: 374-375.

Hugh Smith's feeding pot.

2297. Drake, T.G.H. 1933. Antiques of pediatric interest. Early feeding bottles. JPed 3: 779-780.

2298. Drake, Phyllis. A survey of food practices of sixty-three families in Lubbock, Texas. Master's thesis. Lubbock: Texas Technological College. 1943.

2299. Drake, P.; Roach, F.E.; & Watson, E.S. 1955. Use of milk by rural families in South Carolina, 11953. SC-AES-B No. 431.

2300. Drake, Phyllis & Lamb, M.W. 1944. Study of the dietary and food practices of 63 families in Lubbock, Texas. JADA 20: 528-529.

2301. Drake, William D. & Fajardo, Luis F. 1976. The Promotora program in Candelaria: a Colombian attempt to control malnutrition and disease, 1968-1974. Cali, Colombia: Community Systems Foundation. July 25.

Report of a combined health-public nutrition program.

2302. Draper, Patricia. The hunting and gathering mode of subsistence and its relation to child rearing: a review of the Bacon, Barry and Child hypothesis. Paper presented at 70th Annual Meeting of the Amercian Anthropological Association. 19 November, 1971. New York City.

Discusses the concepts of self-reliance, achievement, independence, and evaluates the applicability of these categories of behavior to data gathered among Kung Bushman children.

2303. Drefus, Simone. 1963. Les Kayapo du Nord. Etat de Para-Bresil. Contribution a l'etude des Indiens Ge. [The Northern Cayapo. Para State, Brazil. Contribution to the study of the Ge Indians.] Le Monde d'Outre-Mer. Passe et Present. 24. Paris; the Hague: Mouton & Co.

Diet and cookery: pp. 34-36.

2304. Dress, Michael G. 1964. Shopping behavior of customers in modified and conventional layouts of retail food stores. USDA-ERS-MTS No. 153.

2305. Dressler, Robert L. 1953. The pre-Columbian cultivated plants of Mexico. HU-BML 16: 115-172.

Over fifty food plants are listed, and each entry is annotated in terms of its distribution, center of diversity, and relevant archaelogical, historical, and linguistic data.

2306.   Drexel, Theodor.   1885.   Catalog der Kochbucher Sammlung.   Als Manuscript gedrukt. [Catalogue of cook book collection.   Printed from manuscript.]   Frankfurt   am   Main: August Osterreith.

Catalogue lists two hundred ninety-one items: German: nos. 1-123; French: nos. 124-188; English: nos. 189-216; Latin, Italian, Spanish: nos. 217-242; Dutch, and Swedish: nos. 243-258; Supplement: nos. 259-291.

2307.   Drieberg, C.   1914.   Origin and varieties of the banana.   Trop Ag   43: 114,115.

2308.   Driver, Harold E.   1953.   The acorn in North American Indian diet.   IAS-P   62: 56-62.

2309.   Driver, Harold E.   1954.   Alcoholic beverages in native North America.   IAS-P   64:50.

Abstract of a paper read before the Anthropology Section.

2310.   Drohojowska,   Antoinette   Josephine Francoise Anne.   1886.   Les savants modernes et leurs oeuvres: Parmentier, Rumfort [sic], Liebig. Alimentation publiques.   [Modern scientists and their works: Parmentier, Rumford, Liebig.   Public feeding.]   Lille: J. Lefour.

2311.   Dronne, L.-F.   1885.   Charcuterie ancienne et   moderne.   Traite   historique   et   pratique renfermant tous les preceptes qui se rattachent a la charcuterie proprement dite et a la charcuterie-cuisine.   Suivi des lois, ordonnances et statuts concernant cette profession, etc.   [Ancient and modern pork-butchery.   Practical and historical treatise filled with all the precepts connected with charcuterie itself and charcuterie-cuisine.   Followed by the laws, ordinances, and statutes concerning this profession.   Paris: Eugene Lacroix.

2312.   Drummond, Jack Cecil, et al.   1939.   Historic tinned foods.   International Tin Research Council. Technical Publication No. 85.   Columbus, Ohio: Battelle Memorial Institute.

2313.   Drummond, Jack Cecil & Wilbraham, Anne. 1939.   The Englishman's food, a history of five centuries of English diet.   London: Jonathon Cape; Toronto: Nelson.

2314.   Drummond, Jack Cecil & Wilbraham, Anne. 1958.   The Englishman's food, a history of five centuries of English diet.   Revised edition.   Edited by Dorothy Hollingsworth.   London: Jonathon Cape.

2315.   Drummond, Therese.   1975.   Using the method of Paulo Freire in nutrition education: an experimental plan for community action in northeast Brazil.   Cor U-INMS No. 3.

The Freire approach consists in raising the consciousness of non-literate peasants regarding their cultural heritage, and of teaching them to read and write.   The author has adapted Freire's model as a vehicle for the nutrition educator in the Third World.

2316.   Dryepondt.   L'alimentation du blanc au Congo.   [Diet of the European in the Congo.]   In Deuxieme Congres International d'Hygiene Alimentaire et de l'Alimentation Rationnelle de l'Homme. 4-8 Octobre, 1910.   Bruxelles.   1910.   Vol.   1. Section 2. Pp. 66-78.   Brussels: M. Weissenbruch.

A guide for Europeans living in tropical areas, this article discusses which foods should be eaten, and in what proportions; how they should be selected and cooked; how to purify local cooking fats and oils; times meals should be eaten; and the most favorable beverages, including native palm wine and sugar cane beer.   Warning is made regarding the need to filter and boil local water before drinking.

2317.   Drysdale, C.R.   1882.   The influence of the food supply on the death-rate.   BMJ   2: 515, 516.

Over population, poverty, wages, and disease in relation to availability of food, and influence of these factors on the public health.

2318.   Du, S.D.   1952.   Favism in West China.   CMJ 70: 17-26.

2319.   Dubarry, Armand.   1882.   Histoire anecdotique des aliments.   [Anectodal history of foods.] Paris: H. Paulin.

2320.   Dubarry, Armand.   1884.   Le boire et le manger, histoire anecdotique des aliments.   [Drinking and eating, anecdotal history of foods.]   Paris: Furne, Jouvet.

This book is divided into the following sections: bread; meat; milk; vegetables; fruit; condiments; beverages.

2321.   Du Bois, Cora.   Attitudes toward food and hunger in Alor.   In Language, culture and personality; essays in memory of Edward Sapir.   Edited by Leslie Spier;   A. Irving Hallowell & Stanley S. Newman. 1941.   Pp. 272-281.   Menasha: Sapir Memorial Publication Fund.

Alor is an island in the Indonesian archipelago located at approximately 8 15 S, and between 124. 15 and 125. 5 E.   Discusses personality effects of cultural factors which demand feeding self-sufficiency early in childhood.

2322.   Dubois, M.-M.   1961.   Slang et cuisine. 1961. [Slang and food.]   VL No. 114. Pp. 469-473.

2323.   Dubois, Urbain.   1868.   Cuisine de tous les pays, etudes cosmopolites.   Avec 220 dessins composes pour la demonstration par Urbain Dubois, chef de cuisine de leurs majestes royales de Prusse. [Cookery of all nations, cosmopolitan studies. With 200 drawings composed by Urbain Dubois, head cook for their royal majesties of Prussia.] Paris: E. Dentu.

2324. Dubos, Rene. 1965. Man adapting. New Haven: Yale University Press.

Man's food: pp. 63–87, discusses malnutrition, and the relationship between nutrition and growth.

2325. Ducomet, V. 1917. Les plantes sauvages, resources de la flore francaise. [Edible wild plants, resources of French flora.] Paris: J.-B. Bailliere & fils.

2326. Dufougere, W. Alimentation des indigenes de la Martinique, de la Guadeloupe et de la Guyane. [Diet of natives in Martinique, Guadeloupe and French Guiana.] In L'alimentation indigene dans les colonies francaises. Protectorats et territories sous mandats. Edited by G. Hardy & C. Richet. 1933. Pp. 350–370. Paris: Vigot Freres.

Informal account of available foods, and diet on Martinique and Guadeloupe. With regard to French Guyana, at the time little more than a penal colony, brief mention is made of prisoners' diet.

2327. Dufour, Phillippe-Sylvestre. 1685. Tractatus hovi de potu caphe, de Chinensium the et de chocolata. [New treatise on the coffee beverage, Chinese tea, and chocolate.] Paris: P. Muguet.

2328. Dufour, Phillippe Sylvestre. 1685. Traitez nouveaux et curieux du cafe, du the et du chocolate. Ouvrage egalement necessaire aux medecins, et a tous ceux qui aiment leur sante. [Curious new treatise on coffee, tea, and chocolate. A work equally necessary to physicians and all those who love their health.] Lyon: chez Jean Girin.

2329. Dufour, Valentin. 1868. Une question historique, 1720–1868. Dissertation historique sur la defense de manger de la chair de cheval. [An historic question, 1720–1868. Historic dissertation in defense of eating horse flesh.] Paris: Librairie de P. Rouquette.

2330. Dugast, Idlette. 1955. Monographie de la tribu des Ndiki (Banen du Cameroun). [Monograph on the Ndiki tribe [Banen of the Cameroon]. Volume 1. UParis-IE-TM No. 58.

Diet: pp. 411–567.

2331. Dugat, H. & Girard, A.L. 1908. Les produits alimentaires. Les aliments animaux; les aliments vegetaux; les boissons, les sucres, le cacao, le cafe, le the. 4 vols. [Food products. Animal foods; vegetable foods; beverages; sweeteners; cacao, coffee; tea.] Paris: Balliere.

2332. Dugelli, Max. 1905. Bakteriologische untersuchungen uber das armenische Mazun. [Bacteriological investigation on Armenian madzoon.] ZBPIH 15: 577–600.

Armenian yoghurt.

2333. Duke, J.A.; Aulik, D.; & Plowman, T. 1975. Nutritional value of coca. HU-BML 24: 113–119. Erythroxylon coca.

2334. Dukes, Clement. 1884. A remarkable case of a juvenile earth eater. Lancet 2: 822.

Association of roundworm [Ascaris lumbricoides] with geophagia.

2335. Dumas, Alexandre. 1873. Grand dictionnaire de cuisine. [Grand dictionary of cookery.] Paris: Alphonse Lemerre.

2336. Dummet, R.E. The social impact of the European liquor trade on the Akan of Ghana (Gold Coast and Asente), 1875. 1910: the use of anthropological insights in historical interpretation. Paper presented at 9th International Congress of Anthropological and Ethnological Sciences. 28 August to 8 September, 1973. Chicago, Illinois.

Denies that European liquor was responsible for disruptive social change in the period studied; argues, rather, that strong corporate kinship structures and traditional constraints militated against over-indulgence and aberrant behavior subsequent to heavy drinking to continued as a potent controlling force throughout the period breaking down only in recent decades.

2337. Dumont, Louis. 1957. Une sous-caste de l'Inde de sud. Organisation sociale et religion des Pramalai-Kallar. [A sub-caste of South India. Social organization and religion of pramalai-Kallar. Le Monde d'Outre-Mer. Passe et Present. Premier Serie. Etudes. 1. Paris; the Hague: Mouton & Co.

Cookery: Pp. 75–80.

2338. Dumont, Remi. 1935. La culture du riz dans le Delta du Tonkin; etude et propositions d'amelioration des techniques traditionnelles de riziculture tropicale. [Rice cultivation in the Tonkin Delta; study and proposals for improvement of traditional, tropical rice cultivation.] Paris: Societ de'Editions Geographiques, Maritimes et Coloniales.

2339. Dunare, N. Milchprodukte im rumanischen Hirtenwesen. [Milk products in Roumanian pastoral life.] In Viehwirtschaft and Hirtenkultur. Enthnographische Studien. Edited by L. Foldes. 1969. Pp. 603–639. Budapest: Akademiai Kiado.

2340. Dunbar, H.F. 1938. Emotions and bodily changes. New York: Columbia University Press.

2341. Duncan, A.C. 1947. Diet and disease in the subarctic. Lancet 253: 919–921.

2342. Duncan, Daniel. 1705. Avis salutaire a tout le monde, contre l'abus des choses chaudes, et particulierement du cafe, du chocolat, et du the. [Salutary advice for everyone, against the abuse of hot things especially of coffee, tea, and chocolate.] Rotterdam: chez Abraham Acher.

2343. Duncan, J.R. 1933. Native food and culinary methods. Nada 11: 101-106.

Notes on the foods of some northern Rhodesian populations.

2344. Duncan, Lawnzina Prince. A study of the dietary habits and nutritional status of forty-six Negro and Mexican children from two parochial schools in the Maxwell Street area of Chicago. Master's thesis University of Chicago. 1948.

2345. Duncan, Marion H. 1964. Chapter Five. The land of tsamba and buttered tea. In Customs and superstitions of Tibetans. London: Mitre Press.

Detailed enumeration of staple Tibetan foods; food combinations; preparation techniques; and seasonal variation in dietary. Also: etiquette of tea drinking: p. 195; monastery food: p. 171; foods of the harvest festival [Yonnecham]: p. 131; picnic foods: p. 127; butter-barley ritual images: p. 115; post-natal food: p. 84; kitchen and cookstoves: p. 38.

2346. Duncher, K. 1938. Experimental modification of children's food preferences through social suggestion. JASP 33: 489-507.

2347. Dungdung, V. Economic life of the Hos of Salipura. Master's thesis. Ranchi University. 1961.

Bihar State, India.

2348. Dunham, E.C., et al. 1937. Physical status of 219 Pueblo Indian children. AJDC 53: 739-749.

2349. Dunn, H. Percy. 1885. The influence of diet upon cancer. BMJ 2: 728.

Implicates over-eating.

2350. Dunstant, W.R. 1899. Edible oils used in India. AL No. 12.

2351. Dupeyrat, Andre. 1958. Le cannibalisme en Papouasie et ailleurs. [Cannibalism in Papua and elsewhere.] ANDSC: 82[?] Pp. 194-197.

2352. Dupin, Henri. 1976. Les erreurs les plus frequemment commises dans l'alimentation du nourrison; effects pathogenes eventuels. [The most frequent errors in infant feeding practices; possible pathogenic effects.] ANA 30: 263-276.

2353. Dupin, Henri & Dupin, M. 1962. Nos aliments. Manuel a l'usage des educateurs de l'ouest Africain. [Our foods. Manual for the use of educators of West Africa.] Organisme de Recherches sur l'Alimentation et la Nutrition Africaine [O.R.A.N.A.] Paris: Editions Sociales Francaises.

2354. Dupont, E. Sur les animaux domestiques pendant les temps prehistoriques. [On domestic animals in prehistoric times.] In 7e Congres International d'Anthropologie & d'Archeologie Prehistoriques. 1874. Stockholm. Compte Rendu. Vol. 1. 1876. Pp. 818-833. Stockholm: P.A. Norstedt & Soner.

Review of archeological evidence and historical documentation.

2355. Dupont, Edouard. 1893-1894. Le regime frugivore est le regime natural de l'homme. [In La discussion sur l'influence du regime alimentaire artificiel.] [Fruitarian diet is the natural diet for Man. [In Discussion on the influence of artificial food diet.] SA Brux-B 12: 50-57.

2356. Du Pont de Nemours & Co., E.I. 1953. Every second counts. A study of consumer bakery shopping habits. Wilmington, Delaware.

Frequency study of bakery items purchased in Supermarkets. Average time and average number of purchases calculated. Item is out-of-print and no reference copy available according to correspondence with Du Pont.

2357. Dupuis, Jacques. 1970. Coutumes alimentaires, societes et economies. Le cas de la repartition de la consommation de lait en Asie tropicale. [Dietary customs, societies and econcomies. The case of the distribution of milk consumption in Asia.] AGeo 79: 529-544.

2358. Dupuy, Aime. 1963. La vigne, le vin et le vigneron dans le language francais. [Vine, wine and vineyard in the French language.] VL No. 135. Pp. 282-289; No. 138. Pp. 458-464.

A regional linguistic survey.

2359. Dupuy, Lola E. 1953. El maiz en la alimentacion popular del norte. [Maize in the folk diet of the north.] ATF-B 2: 73-76. Argentina.

2360. Duran, Pierre. 1967. La consomation ostentoire en milieu rurale a Madagascar. [Conspicuous consumption in rural Madagascar.] L'Homme 7: 30-47.

2361. Durand, C. 1877. Le cuisinier Durand. Cuisine du Midi et du Nord. [The Durand cookbook. Cookery of Midi and of the north.] Paris: Garnier Freres.

2362. Durand, Jr., Loyal. 1949. The American dairy region. J Geog 48: 1-20.

2363. Durand, Jr., Loyal. 1956. Mountain moonshining in east Tennessee. GR 46: 168-181.

2364. Durand-Forest, Jacqueline de. 1967. El cacao entre los aztecas. [Cocoa among the Aztecs.] ECN 7: 155-181.

Botanical and historical background: pp. 163-167; social aspects: pp. 167-172; ritual role: pp. 173-175; as tribute: pp. 175-178; as money: pp. 178-181.

2365. Durant, N.S. 1889. Leprosy and food. BMJ 2: 690.

Comment on leprosy in Grenada, West Indies. Suggests salt fish as possible source of leprosy baccilus.

2366. Dureteste, Andre. 1933. La question du nuoc-mam en Indochine. [The question of nuoc-mam in Indochina.] RP Pp. 521-531.

Nuoc-mam is a fermented fish condiment widely used, under different names in Southeast Asia.

2367. Durey, L. 1934. Le massage dans les troubles de la nutrition. [Massage in nutrition problems.] Nutrition (P) 4: 433-450.

2368. Durey d'Harnoncourt, P. 1763. Dissertation sur l'usage de boire a la glace. [Dissertation on the custom of drinking ice water.] Paris: Imprimerie de Valleyre.

2369. Durgin, Edward. Brewing and boozing: a study of the drinking habits among the Hare Indians. Ph.D. dissertation. Anthropology. University of Oregon. 1974.

The Hare are a northern Canadian tribe.

2370. Durham, Elizabeth. A study of the dietary habits and nutritional status of 500 Negro children. Ph.D. dissertation. Ellen H. Richards Institute. Pennsylvania State College. 1948.

2371. Dutcher, B.H. 1893. Pinon gathering among the Panamint Indians. AA 6 [old series]: 377-380.

Describes a shelter camp on a mountain ridge between Saline and Panamint Valleys, in Inyo County, California; and the techniques involved in harvesting and proessing the nuts of Pinus monophylla. A native camp meal is recorded. Data were gathered in September, 1891.

2372. Duthie, John Firminger & Fuller, J.B. 1882-1893. Field and garden crops of the northwestern provinces and Oudh. 3 vols. Roorkee: Printed at the Thomason Civil Engineering College Press.

India.

2373. Dutta, Parul C. 1956. Food and drink of the Oraons. ISC-P 43: 330.

India.

2374. Dutta, Parul C. 1959. The Tangsas of the Namchik and Tirap Valleys. Shillong: North-East Frontier Agency. India.

Foods, and preparation techniques: pp. 39-48. The Tirap Valley is located in northeastern India, on the Burma frontier, at approximately 96. E, 25. N.

2375. Duval, Mathias. 1885. Sur les oeufs pourris comme aliment en Chine. [Decayed eggs as food in China.] SAP-BM 18: 299.

2376. Dwivedi, M.P. & Prasad, B.G. 1964. An epidemiological study of lathyrism in the District of Rewa, Madhya Pradesh. IJMR 52: 81-116.

Seven villages in the Rewa District [approximately 60km south of Allahabad] were chosen for a dietary survey. The incidence of lathyrism was correlated with the mean consumption per unit of daily intake of Lathyrus sativus, and with social status of villagers. Scanty irrigation left the farmers dependent upon rainfall and forced them to cultivate L. sativus as a safeguard against drought. [After Schofield 1975: 118.]

2377. Dy. 1940. Maniok. [Manioc.] CR 3: 1088.

Neutralization of toxic factor, and preparation of manioc food food use.

2378. Dyson-Hudson, Rada & Dyson-Hudson, Neville. 1969. Subsistence herding in Uganda. SA 220: 76-89.

2379. Dyson-Hudson, Rada & Dyson-Hudson, Neville. The food production system of a semi-nomadic society: the Karimojong: Uganda. In Food in Africa. Edited by P. McLaughlin. 1970. Pp. 94-123. Baltimore: John Hopkins Press.

2380. Dyson-Hudson, Rada & Dusen, Roxann van. 1972. Food sharing among young children. EFN 1: 319-324.

Girls and boys aged five years to eight years attending a city day camp were observed for two weeks. Girls tended to share food more frequently with other girls and boys, than boys did. Implications of the finding are considered in relation to friendship and network development among children.

2381. Earle, Alice Morse. 1893. Chapter Six. Supplies of the larder. Chapter Seven. Old colonial drinks and drinkers. In Customs and fashions of old New England. New York: Charles Scribner's Sons. Reprint. Detroit: Singing Tree Press. 1968.

2382. Earle, Alice Morse. 1896. Chapter Seven. The Dutch larder. In Colonial days in old New York. New York: Charles Scribner's Sons. Reprint. Detroit: Singing Tree Press. 1968.

2383, Earle, Alice Morse. 1897. Old Colonial drinks. Cur Lit 22: 256-257.

2384. Earle, Alice Morse. 1927. Chapter Three. The kitchen fireside. Chapter Four. The serving of meals. Chapter Five. Food from forest and sea. Chapter Six. Indian corn. Chapter Seven. Meat and drink. In Home life in colonial days. New York: Macmillan.

2385. Earle, Timothy. Control hierarchies in the traditional irrigation economy of the Halelea District, Kauai, Hawaii. Ph.D. dissertation. Anthropology. University of Michigan, Ann Arbor. 1973.

2386. Early, Daniel K. The effects of dependence: the impact of New York coffee market price fluctuations on remote Nahuatl communities. Paper presented at 75th Annual Meeting of the American Anthropological Association. 17-21 November, 1976. Washington, D.C.

> The structure of the coffee economy is traced from remote Nahuatl producers to market-town buyers, regional exporters, and United States corporate importers. Changes in village economy, technology, and fiesta patterns over the past twenty-five years respond to New York price fluctuations. The structural effects of the recent intervention of the Mexican Coffee Institute are also examined.

2387.   Early, Daniel K. Effects of the New York coffee market on Nahuatl subsistence agriculture. Paper presented at 76th Annual Meeting of the American Anthropological Association. 29 November to 3 December, 1977. Houston, Texas.

> The relationship between cash crop and subsistence agriculture is examined in a number of "open" communities of the Zongolica Veracruz Sierra. Cash crop coffee production was found to subsidize subsistence maize production in such a manner that a price increase in the New York coffee market and, by extension, the local market, would provoke an increase in maize production and vice versa.

2388.   Early, Daniel K. Hautli: the revival of Aztec amaranth, an appropriate technology food. Paper presented at 77th Annual Meeting of the American Anthropological Association. 17 November, 1978. Los Angeles, California.

> A review of the historical and current modes of propogation, and food use of Amaranthus sp. in Mexico; and the results of experimental field trials in the United States.

2389.   East, E.M. 1913. A chronicle of the tribe of corn. PSM 82: 225-236.

2390.   Eastwood, Alice. 1900-1901. Plants used for poisoning fish. Zoe 5: 136.

> Notes the use of the seeds Mennispermum cocculas L., in the Philippines. Indicates that fish poisoned in this manner may be eaten without harmful effects.

2391.   Eaton, John W. The 'taste blindness' phenomena among the primates. Master's thesis. Anthropology. University of Florida. 1964.

2392.   Ebbs, J.H.; Tisdall, F.F.; Moyle, W.J.; & Bell, M. 1941. Influence of prenatal diet on the mother and child. JN 22: 515-526.

2393.   Eberhardt, Charles C. 1910. Indians of Peru. SI-MC 53: 181-194.

> Earth eating; fermented yucca [masato], and banana beverages: Pp. 190-191.

2394.   Eckstein, Eleanor F. 1973. Menu planning. Westport, Connecticut: AVI Publishing Co.

> Section Four: Foodways of American Subgroup cultures; and Appendix 1: Literature search summary reports: foodways; are excellent introductions for professionals involved in cross-cultural food preparation or research.

2395.   Eddy, Frank W. 1964. Metates and manos. The basic corn-grinding tools of the Southwest. MNM-PSP No. 1.

> United States.

2396.   Eddy, T.P. 1970. Food habits as a barrier. RNFS 20: 10-12.

2397.   Edelstein, L. 1966. Antike Diatetik. [Ancient dietetics.] JMH 1: 162-174.

2398.   Eder, James F. 1978. The caloric returns to food collecting: disruption and change among the Batak. HEcol 6: 55-69.

> The changing economy of a group of Veddoid tropical forest hunter-gatherers is described. The Batak currently number about three hundred and sixty persons and inhabit the interior of central Palawan Island northeast of Puerto Princesa (9.50 N, 188.10 E), in the Philippines. The Batak now participate in an external market system, gathering and selling Manila copal (a tree resin) to earn cash to purchase rice. Digging wild yams (Dioscorea hispida, Dennst.; and D. luzonensis, Schauer.) is no longer the major subsistence activity. Entering the market system is shown to have a comparatively unfavorable caloric cost-benefit for the Batak, and has further apparently had a negative effect on nutritional status.

2399.   Edgard, C. 1900. Ernahrung der Soldaten in Niederland-Ostindien. [Nutrition of soldiers in the Netherlands East Indies.] JDAM 103: 220-229.

2400.   Edge-Partington, James. 1903. Food trough from Rubiana, New Georgia. Man 3: 161-162.

> Description of bowl; the food used to dedicate it, and its use in cannibalism. New Georgia is an island of the Solomon group.

2401.   Edge-Partington, T.W. 1906. Note on the food bowl from Rubiana, New Georgia. Man 6: 121.

> Rejects the cannibalistic association contained in Edge-Partington, J. [1903].

2402.   Edlin, H.L. 1969. Plants and man. The story of our basic food. Garden City, New York: The Natural History Press.

> Chapters One throught Nine are concerned with food; Ten through Sixteen cover industrial products. The book is well-illustrated

and provides concise botanical, historic, geographic, and economic information about basic world food crops.

2403. Edmundo, Luiz. 1936. Rio in the time of the Viceroys. Translated by Dorothea Momsen. Rio de Janeiro: J.R. de Olveira & Co.

Food habits: pp. 236-264.

2404. Edmundson, Wade C. 1972. Land, food, and work in three Javanese villages. Ph.D. dissertation. Geography. University of Hawaii. 1972.

2405. Edmundson, Wade C. 1976. Land, food and work in east Java. New England Monographs in Geography. No. 4. Department of Geography. Armidale, New South Wales: University of New England.

Strongly criticized in a review by Van Veen in EFN 6: 129, 130 (1977).

2406. Edozien, Joseph C. Ethnic differences in growth rate of preschool children. Paper presented at 75th Annual Meeting of the American Anthropological Association. 17 to 21 November, 1976. Washington, D.C.

A new national study has confirmed recent reports of ethnic differences in the growth rate of pre-school children in the United States. Black infants were smaller than Anglo infants of comparable socioeconomic status at birth. But, by six months of age, they had surpassed the Anglo children in height and weight and, by the age of forty-eight months, there was a difference of nearly 2.5 cm between their adjusted heights. These differences emphasize the need for ethnic-specific growth standards for the proper use of height and weight measurements in the assessment of nutritional status.

2407. Edwards, C.D. & Dodds, M.L. 1965. Diet and eating practices of school children in Ghana. JADA 46: 463-464.

2408. Edwards, Cecile Hoover; McDonald, S.; Mitchell, J.R.; Jones, L.; Mason, L.; Kemp, D. Laing; & Trigg, L. 1959. Clay- and cornstarch-eating women. JADA 35: 810-815.

2409. Edwards, Cecile Hoover; McDonald, S.; Mitchell, J.R.; Jones, L.; Mason, L.; & Trigg, L. 1964. Effect of clay and cornstarch intake on women and their infants. JADA 44: 109-115.

2410. Edwards, Cecile Hoover; McSwain, Hattie, & Haire, Susie. 1954. Odd dietary practices of women. JADA 30: 976-981.

A survey among Black women in Louisiana, Alabama, Kentucky, South and North Carolina. Includes data on food superstitions, pre- and post-partum diets, geophagy, and corn-starch consumption.

2411. Edwards, Everett E. 1933. Agriculture of the American Indians: a classified list of annotated historical references. USDA-L-BC No. 23.

2412. Edwards, L.D. & Craddock, L.J. 1973. Malnutrition and intellectual development: a study in school-age Aboriginal children at Walgett, N.S.W. MJA 1: 880-884.

Australia.

2413. Edwards, William E. The postulated Indonesian island origin of food producing. Paper presented at 69th Annual Meeting of the American Anthropological Association. 19 to 22 November, 1970. San Diego, California.

2414. Edwards-Randall, Nancy. Cognitive ethnography of cooking. Paper presented at 76th Annual Meeting of the American Anthropological Association. 29 November to 3 December, 1977. Houston, Texas.

This paper contrasts the "diet survey" approach with the "ethnoscience" approach to the ethnography of cooking. The conclusion drawn is that neither approach leads to an understanding of why the Muslim Samal of southwestern Mindanao eat the meals they do. Meal-planning is actually a mental activity; a logical and hierarchical ordering of activity forms. Samal morning meal-planning is discussed as an example. The meal-plan is compared with data from a diet survey of one family.

2415. Eels, Myron. 1883. The potlatches of Puget Sound. Am An 5: 135-147.

2416. Eels, Myron. 1889. Indians of the Washington Territory. SI-AR for the year 1887. Pp. 605-681.

Subsistence: pp. 617-620; 621-622; potlatch: pp. 658-664.

2417. Eerden, Lucia van der. Maternity care in a Spanish-American community of New Mexico. Ph.D. dissertation. Catholic University of America. 1947. Also published as CathUA-AS No. 13. (1948).

Based on field work at Rancho de Taos, during the late 1940's, this study is concerned with the death rate among Spanish-American mothers. It looks at the possibility of achieving improved maternity care, with specific recommendations such as the development of a nurse-midwidery delivery service with a small number of Spanish-American midwives specially trained for this work. Food in exchange for midwife service: p. 37; traditional post-partum foods (maternal): p. 47; (infant): p. 48; lactation: p. 48.

2418. Efimov, I. 1959. Pekarskaja skul'ptura. [Baker's sculpture.] DI 3: 40-42.

2419. Egan, M.F. 1892. Dinners with novelists. Critic 20: 358.

2420.   Egardt, Brita. 1964. Da svampen blev mat. [When fungus becomes food.] GK 4: 84-91.

2421.   Eggan, Fred & Pijoan, Michel. 1943. Some problems in the study of food and nutrition. Am Ind 3: 9-22.

Review of the Southwest Project, a survey of Native American and Hispanic-American food habits and nutritional status in the Southwestern United States undertaken in the early 1940's. The origins, participants, interdisciplinary framework, goals, and results are reviewed. Includes a report of Michel Pijoan's nutrition research among the Papago, Navajo, Hopi and Hispanic-American populations during the period February-May, 1942.

2422.   Eggers, I.M. Elsdon Best, man and writer. Master's thesis. History. Dunedin University. 1935.

Elsdon Best was a student of Maori culture. Several of his studies on Maori food uses are entered in the present bibliography.

2423.   Egidi, V.N. 1907. La tribu di Kuni. [The Kuni tribe.] Anthropos 2: 107-115.

Papua New Guinea. Food habits: pp. 108-115.

2424.   Ehrenfels, Omar Rolf Leopold Werner. 1959. Hippopotamus flesh as food. TNR 52: 139-140.

2425.   Ehret, C. 1967. Cattle-keeping and milking in eastern and southern African history: the linguistic evidence. JAH 8: 1-17.

2426.   Ehrstrom, Robert. 1933. Diet of northern countries from a historical point of view; survey of diet in prehistoric times; study of introduction of salt into diet, and discussion of avitaminoses. [In Swedish]. FLH 75: 931-957.

2427.   Ehrstrom, Robert. 1934. Die Diat- und Kostfuhring der nordischen Lander in historische Beleuchtung. Ein Beitrag zur Geschichte der Kost-furhing in vorhistorischer Zeir, des Kochsalzes und der Avitaminoses. [Diet and food patterns in Scandinavia from an historical perspective. History of diet in prehistoric times with reference to salt and avitaminosis.] AMS 81: 583-610.

Part One. Introduction. Part Two. Archaeological review. Part Three. Food patterns in hunting and fishing cultures of the Palaeolithic. Part Four. Transition to cattle breeding and farming since the Neolithic. Part Five. Adaptation and food patterns in different cultural periods. Part Six. The role of vitamin content in the transition from one food pattern to another. Part Seven. Final conclusions and summary.

2428.   Eidlitz, Kerstin. 1969. Food and emergency food in the circumpolar area. Studia Ethnographica Upsaliensia. No. 32. Uppsala: Almqvist & Wiksells.

2429.   Eimer, K. 1933. Rohkost und Sport. [Raw foods and sport.] ZErn 3: 193-198.

2430.   Eindhoven, Jan. 1957. Research planning for the study of food combination. Conference Notes. United States Army Quartermaster Corps. Chicago: Quartermaster Food and Container Institute for the Armed Forces.

2431.   Eindhoven, Jan & Peryam, David R. 1959. Measurement of preferences for food combinations. FTech 13: 379-382.

2432.   Eiselen, Eliabeth. 1956. Quinoa, a potentially important food crop of the Andes. JGeog 55: 330-333.

2433.   Eisenberg, Azriel. 1965. Feeding the world: a biography of David Lubin. New York: Abelard-Schuman.

Founder of the International Institute of Agriculture, in Rome, which later became the basis for the Food and Agriculture organization of the United Nations.

2434.   Ekvall, Robert B. 1963. A note on 'live blood', as food among the Tibetans. Man 63: 145-146.

2435.   Ekvall, S. 1940. On the history and conditions of life of the West Bothnian nomad Lapps, their food and health conditions. AMS 105: 329-359. Also in PR 4: 338-339 [1946].

Sweden.

2436.   Elaut, L. 1964. Het dieetboekje van J.B. Fiera (1498) en zijn betekenis als voorloper van de geneeskundige Renaissance. [The diet book of J.B. Fiera (1498) and its significance as a precursor of the medical Renaissance.] Sci Hist 6: 169-177.

2437.   Elaut, L. 1965. La dietetique versifiee de J.-B. Fiera (1498) prodrome de la renaissance medicale. [The dietetics-in-verse- of J.-B. Fiera (1498), annunciator of the medical renaissance.] Janus 52: 289-296.

2438.   Elaut, L. 1968. Les regles d'une gastronomie hygienique, exposees par le medicin-humaniste Georgius Pictorius. [The rules of an hygienic-humanist Georgius Pictorius.] Clio Med 3: 349-359.

2439.   Elia, Eugenio d'. 1948-1949. Riflessi delle condizioni di prigenia su alcuni caratteri fisici dei prigioneri italiani in Germania. [Observations on prision conditions and some physical characteristics of Italian prisoners in Germany.] Riv Ant 36: 159-173.

Includes data on dietary.

2440.   Elichondo, Margarita. 1966. Folklore del sabor. [Folklore of flavor.] SFC 1: 47-50.

Notes on regional Argentine foods gathered mostly from literary sources, with a few texts of coplas (songs) about food. Two recipes are given.

2441. Eliot, Abigail A. 1933. Eating habits in relation to personality development of two- and three-year old children. GPM 13: 399-479.

2442. Eliot, Elisabeth. 1961. Chapter Seven. Menu: manioc, monkey and Nescafe. In The savage my kinsman. New York: Hodder & Stoughton.

The Auca of eastern Ecuador.

2443. Eliot, Martha M. 1933. Some effects of the Depression on the nutrition of children. HSS 28: 585-598.

Overview of selected Atlantic Coast communities, based on data gathered by the Child Hygiene Committee of the State and Provincial Health Officers of North America, and from other sources.

2444. Elkon, Juliette. 1955. The honey cookbook. More than 250 recipes, some from early Egypt. New York: Alfred A. Knopf.

2445. Ellacombe, Henry N. 1884. The plant-lore and garden craft of Shakespeare. London: W. Satchell & Co.

2446. Ellacott, S.E. 1953. The story of the kitchen. London: Methuen.

2447. Ellinger, E. 1957. Hopi harvest. AHigh 33: 30-33. August.

2448. Elliott, Harriet. Nutrition and consumer protection in defense. In National Nutrition Conference for Defense, May 26, 27, and 28, 1941. Called by Presiden Franklin Delano Roosevelt. Proceedings. 1942. Pp. 57-62. Office of the Director of Defense Health and Welfare Services. Federal Security Agency. Washington, D.C.: Government Printing Office.

2449. Ellis, Aytoun. 1957. The penny universities: a history of coffee houses. New York: Macmillan.

2450. Ellis, David V. The advent of food-production in West Africa. Paper presented at 9th International Congress of Anthropological and Ethnological Sciences. 28 August to 8 September, 1973. Chicago, Illinois.

Based on archeological data from several West African sites from the pre-Neolithic and eolithic Periods, a strong Saharan influence was revealed in the assemblages from savannah and forest sites. On the basis of this evidence (and an alternative interpretation of Binford's model for the development of food production), it is hypothesized that extensive contacts between Saharan cultivators and savannah peoples were established by 3000 B.C., in the area south of 'Air-ou-Azbine. The migration of populations southward into this same area as a result of

Saharan dessication created demographic pressures stimulating the development of plant cultivation, probably between 2500 B.C. and 2000 B.C.

2451. Ellis, George E. 1882. The red man and the white man in North America. Boston: Little, Brown & Co.

Tripe de roche [rock tripe], a fungus or moss eaten with meat or marrow-bone: p. 149; pemmican: p. 178.

2452. Ellis, Henry. 1946. These birds sometimes appeared on the menu of the Indians who traded at York Factory: 1. The horned owl; 2. The white-tailed eagle. The Beaver, March. P. 41.

Illustration. York Factory is located in Manitoba, at 57. 30 N, 97. 30 W.

2453. Ellis, Henry. 1956. Occasionally encountered on the menu of Indians of York Factory: 1. The pelican; 2. The heathcock and partridge. The Beaver March. P. 42.

Illustration.

2454. Ellis, J.E.; Wiens, J.A.; Rodell, C.F.; & Anway, J.C. 1976. A conceptual model of diet selection as an ecosystem proess. JTB 60: 93-108.

2455. Ellis, Rhoda. The value of an education program for changing food habits. Ph.D. dissertation. New York University. 1944.

2456. Ellwanger, George Herman. 1902. The pleasures of the table. An account of gastronomy from ancient days to present times, with a history of its literature, schools, and most distinguished artists together with some special recipes and views concerning the aesthetics of dinners and dinner-giving. New York: Doubleday, Page & Co.

2457. Elmendorf, F.L. 1925. How the hospital dietitian may cooperate with the restaurant manager. Diet Ad Ther 3: 307-3

Explains the nature of fast food service, and reviews [unsuccessful] efforts of restaurants to provide limited nutrition education. Reasons for failure of these programs are offered. Predicts that in future, dietetics will play a greater role in public eating.

2458. Elmore, Francis H. 1938. Food animals. The Navajo. El Pal 44: 149-154.

Includes supplementary vegetable foods, and methods of cooking.

2459. Elting, Mary & Folsom, Michael. 1967. The mysterious grain, science in search of the origin of corn. New York: M. Evans & Co. New world maize.

New World maize.

2460. Embree, John F. 1941. <u>Acculturation among the Japanese of Kona, Hawaii.</u> AAA-M No. 59.

Food at banquets, weddings, funerals: pp. 30, 31; kitchens, rice: p. 32. foods at <u>kumi</u> (cooperative group) meetings: p. 45; photo (Fig. 5) of food preparation: facing p. 47; funeral foods: p. 66, 70, 71; festival foods: 124, 125, 126. adoption of Japanese food customs by local caucasians: p. 146; cost of certain funeral banquet foods: p. 150.

2461. Embrey, Hartley & Wang, Tsan-ch'ing. 1921. Analyses of some Chinese foods. CMJ 35: 247-257.

Foods studies include green mung bean and its fresh sprouts; mung bean starch; various forms of tofu (bean curd), and the locust seed huaitzu [Robinia pseudoacacia]. In addition, some fruits and cereal grains are also included.

2462. Emerson, Edward Randolph. 1902. <u>A lay thesis on Bible wines.</u> New York: Merrill & Baker.

2463. Emerson, Edward Randolph. 1902. <u>The story of the vine.</u> London; New York: G.P. Putnam's Sons.

Wines of antiquity; wines of England, France, Spain, Portugal, Africa, Persia, India, China, Russia, Turkey, Hungary, Italy, Germany, Switzerland, and America.

2464. Emerson, Edward Randolph. 1908. <u>Beverages, past and present.</u> 2 vols. New York: G.P. Putnam's Sons.

Historical sketches of beverage production, by country, with data on the customs associated with their consumption.

2465. Emerson, R.A. 1953. A preliminary survey of the milpa system of maize culture as practiced by the Maya Indians of the northern part of the Yucatan Peninsula. MBG-A 40: 51-62.

Studies undertaken at Piste, about 120 kilometers from Merida, between Merida and Chichen Itza; at Peto, at about 150 kilometers southeast of Merida, and 180 kilometers southwest of Merida to Campeche. Short excursions from these points were also made to outlying milpas. This article describes the topography, geography, meteorology and botany of the area briefly; followed by a description of <u>milpa</u> agriculture; maize yields; effects of population density. Suggests significant crop increases could be achieved using the <u>milpa</u> system by increasing the percentage of land under cultivation. Based on the requirements of <u>milpa</u> agriculture, the author believes the <u>milpa</u> system was capable of having supported the classic Maya centers and providing sufficient surplus to permit the kinds of specializations characteristic of the ceremonial centers.

2466. Emmerling, Oskar. 1898. Uber armenisches Mazun. [On Armenian madzoon.] ZBPIH 4: 418-421.

Armenian yoghurt.

2467. Emmons, George T. 1910. The potlatches of the North Pacific Coast. AMJ 10: 229-237.

2468. Emory, Kenneth. 1943. Meet coconut meat -potential life saver. P Pac 55: 21-22.

2469. Endicott, William. 1923. <u>Wrecked among cannibals in the Fijis.</u> MRS-P No. 3

2470. Endle, Sidney. 1911. <u>The Kacharis.</u> London: Macmillan.

Assam. Food habits: pp. 14-16.

2471. Endriss, Gerhard. 1953. Speis und Trank in Ulm an der Donau. [Food and drink in Ulm-on-the-Donau.] Alemann Pp. 349-378.

2473. Engle, Fannie & Blair, Gertrude. 1954. <u>The Jewish festival cookbook.</u> New York: David McKay.

2474. Engelbrecht, Thiess Hinrich. 1914. <u>Die Feldfruchte Indiens in Ihrer geographischen Verbreitung.</u> [Geographical distribution of Indian agricultural products]. Hamburg: L. Friedrichsen.

2475. Engelbrecht, Thiess Hinrich. 1928. <u>Die Feldfruchte des Deutschen reichs in ihrer geographischen verbreitung.</u> [Geographical distribution of agricultural products of the German Empire.] Berlin: Deutsche Landwirtschafts-Gesellschaft.

2476. Engelhardt, Christian Moritz. 1818. <u>Herrad von Landsperg, Aebtissin zu Hohenburg, oder St Odilien, im Elsatz, im zwolften Jahrhundert; und ihr Werk: Hortus deliciarum. Ein Beytrag zur Geschichte der Wissenschaften, Literatur, Kunst, Kleidung, Waffen und Sitten des Mittelaters.</u> [Harrad of Landsperg, Abbess of Hohenburg or Saint Odilia in Alsace in the Twelfth Century, and her work entitled "Hortus Deliciarum" [Garden of Delights]. An essay on the history of Medeival arts and sciences, of literature, dress, weapons, and customers.] Stuttgart; Tubingen: F.G. Cotta.

2477. Enock, C. Reginald. 1909. <u>Mexico, its ancient and modern civilization.</u> New York: Charles Scribner's Sons.

Food: pp. 213-218.

2478. Epine, C. de l'. 1929. Historique des famines et disettes dans l'Urundi. [History of famines and scarcity in Urundi.] BACB 20: 440-442.

Covers the period 1905-1926.

2479. Epple, George M. "The heavy thumb" in a West Indian fish market. Paper presented at 72nd Annual Meeting of the American Anthropological Association. 1 December, 1973. New Orleans, Louisiana.

2480.   Eppright, Ercel S. 1947. Factors influencing food acceptance. JADA 23: 579-587.

2481.   Eppright, Ercel S. 1950. Food habits and preferences: a study of Iowa people of two age groups. I-AES-B No. 376.

2482.   Epstein, H. 1971. The origin of the domestic animals of Africa. New York: Africana Publishing Co.

2483.   Erhard, Darla. 1974. The new vegetarians. Part 2. The Zen macrobiotic movement and other cults based on vegetarianism. NT 9: 20-27.

2484.   Erihi, R. 1964. What's wrong with our Maori foods? TAH No. 46. Pp. 5-7.

2485.   Erixon, Sigurd. 1955. Durfangst och jakt samt insamling av vegetabiliska fodoamnen under nyare tid [Hunting and gathering in recent times.] NK 11-12a. Pp. 110-119.

2486.   Erixon, Sigurd. 1964. An innovation among the Lapps viewed in the light of northern Scandinavian practice. SEU 21: 71-80.

Seasoning coffee with salt.

2487.   Erkol, Blanche Fearing. The effects of 12 lessons in food and nutrition on the food habits of certain women patients at Ingham County tuberculosis sanitarium. Master's thesis. Michigan State College. 1945.

2488.   Erman, Adolf. 1894. Life in ancient Egypt. Translated by H.M. Tirard. London: Macmillan. Reprint. New York: Dover Publications. 1971.

Food habits: pp. 185-193.

2489.   Ernle, Rowland Edmund Prothero. 1961. English farming. Past and present. 6th ed. Chicago: Quadrangle Books.

Two sections: the historiography of English farming: pp. xci-cxv; and Appendix One: Select list of agricultural writers down to 1700 valuable as starting points for research. Also useful for general background on food economics are Chapter Twelve: The English corn laws; and Appendix Three - Corn laws, providing annual average annual prices for various grains, taxation rates, and details on the Assize of bread, which regulated food and beverage prices from ca. 1266 through 1836.

2490.   Ernst, A. 1886. Ethnographische mittheilungen aus Venezuela. 1. Nahrungs-und Genussmittel. [Ethnographic communication from Venezuela. 1. Food and stimulants. ZE pp. 514-521.

2492.   Ernster Mark. 1976. Investigation of dietary changes in the Gezira, Sudan. EFN 5: 217-223.

This item is an extended review and appreciation of Culwick [1951].

2493.   Ernster, Mark; McAleenan, Michael; & Larkin, Frances. 1976. Social research methods applied to nutritional assessment. EFN 5: 143-151.

Using as a model a case study of a Tanzanian population, this paper exemplifies procedures followed in collecting, coordinating, analyzing and evaluating data concerning attitudes and beliefs about nutrition as a research phase preceeding implementation of an Under Five's Clinic. The purpose of the paper is to demonstrate to nutritionists in field situations that it is possible to use social data that are easily collected, in order to explore and evaluate factors which influence nutritional status.

2494.   Erwin, A.T. 1934. A rare specimen of Zea mays var. saccharata. Science 79: 589.

From Aztec Ruin, New Mexico, ca. A.D. 1200-A.D. 1300.

2495.   Erwin, A.T. 1947. Sweet corn not an important Indian food plant in pre-Columbian period. ASA-J 39: 117-121.

2496.   Escalante, Roberto & Lopez, Antonio. Ethnomycological data on the Matlatzinca Indians. Paper presented at 72nd Annual Meeting of the American Anthropological Association. 1 December, 1973. New Orleans, Louisiana.

2497.   Escudero, P. 1943. La alimentacion de las poblaciones rurales Argentinos hacia 1750. [The diet of rural Argentine populations since 1750.] AAD-R 1: 152-155.

2498.   Esdorn, Ilse. 1961. Die Nutzpflanzen der Tropen und Subtropen der Weltwirtschaft. [The useful plants of the tropics and subtropics in world economy.] Stuttgart: G. Fischer.

2499.   Eskew, Garnett L. 1948. Salt, the fifth element. Chicago: J.G. Ferguson & Associates.

2500.   Essig, Edward Oliver. 1931. History of entomology. New York: Macmillan.

Insects as human food: pp. 23-24. Orthoptera, Homoptera, Coleoptera, Lepidoptera, Diptera, Hymenoptera.

2501.   Essig, Edward Oliver. 1934. The value of insects to the California Indias. SM 38: 181-186.

Orthoptera, Isoptera, Homoptera, Coleoptera, Lepidoptea, Diptera, Hymenoptera.

2502.   Estes, Rufus. 1911. Good things to eat, as suggested by Rufus; a collection of practical recipes for preparing meats, game, fowl, fish, puddings, pastries...etc., by Rufus Estes...Chicago: the author.

From the author's practical experience with dining car and restaurant cookery. Recipes included.

2503.   Estes, Valerie. Nutrition education for rural Colombian women. Paper presented at 75th Annual

Meeting of the American Anthropological Association. 17 to 21 November, 1976. Washington, D.C.

Rural development projects have generally focused more on woman's role as mother and wife and less on her role as producer of agricultural goods and services. A current project in a rural area of the Colombian highlands, in which women are in training as nutrition analysts and educators, takes these multipe roles into account. In this region of mixed subsistence and cash crop farming, women are involved in decisions about the land as well as the home, and it is hypothesized that changes resulting from participation in a nutrition education program affect not only family eating patterns but also agricultural production.

2504.   Estrada G., Manuel. 1953. La contribucion indigena de Mexico en la cultura mundial. [The contribution of indigenous Mexico to world culture.] YMT No. 16. Pp. 9-12.

2505.   Etiennez, Hippolyte. 1852. Le livre de la phagotechnie universelle, ou l'art de manger chez tous les peuples. [The book of universal 'phagotechny', or the art of eating among all people.] Bibliotheque de la Maitre de la Maison. Paris: C. Plocke.

2506.   Eubank, Mary W. A study of the interrelationships of the authentication of Zapotec urns and the evolution of maize. Master's thesis. Anthropology. University of North Carolina at Chapel Hill. 1973.

2507.   Euler, Robert C. & Jones, Volney Hurt. 1956. Hermetic sealing as a technique of food preservation among Indians of the American Southwest. APS-P 100: 87-99.

2508.   Eustis, Celestine. 1903. Cooking in old Creole dats. La cuisine creole a l'usage de petits menage. [Creole cookery for use by small households.] New York, R.H. Russell. Reprint. New York: Arco Press. 1973.

2509.   Eva, C.P. 1961. Etel es etkezes a magyar nephitben es nepzokasban. Modszer, feladatok problemak. [Food and meal times in Hungarian folk belief and custom. Research problems.] Neprajzi 43: 31-54.

2510.   Evangelista, Alfredo. The function of the Nipa Palm beverage "tuba" in a Philippine community. Master's thesis. Anthropology. University of Chicago. 1959.

2511.   Evans, D.T. 1973. A preliminary evaluation of tooth tartar among the preconquest Maya at the Tayasal area, El Peten. Am An 38: 489-493.

2512.   Evans, Emyr Estyn. 1942. Irish heritage. The landscape, the people and their work. Dundalk: W. Tempest.

Note on a honey wine metheglin: p. 78.

2513.   Evans, I.B.P. 1910-1911. Fungus flora of South Africa. USAfr-DA-R

Edible fungus: p. 259.

2514.   Evans, Ivor H.N. 1923. Studies in religion, folk-lore and customs in British North Borneo and the Malay Peninsula. Cambridge: at the University Press.

Food tabus. Dusun: p. 15; Jakun: p. 261; Negrito: pp. 175; 181-182; 187; Sakai: pp. 232-237.

2515.   Evans, Robert K. An analysis of concepts and assumptions about Neolithic horticulturalists. Paper presented at 72nd Annual Meeting of the American Anthropological Association. 29 November, 1973. New Orleans, Louisiana.

2516.   Evans, Walter H. 1900. Notes on edible berries of Alaska. P World 3: 17-19; 4: 67-68.

2517.   Evans-Pritchard, Edward Evans. 1956. Cannibalism: a Zande text. Africa 26: 73-74.

2518.   Evans-Pritchard, Edward Evans. 1960. Zande cannibalism. RAIGBI-J 90: 238-258.

2519.   Evelyn, John. 1699. Acetaria: a discourse of sallets. London: B. Tooke. Reprinted. Brooklyn: Women's Auxiliary. Brooklyn Botanic Gardens. 1937.

2520.   Evelyn, John. 1958. Recipe for pickling walnuts. NNA-AR No 49. P. 103.

Ca. A.D. 1706.

2521.   Everett, Michael. Cowboys, Indians and "Alcoholism": White Mountain Apache interethnic drinking. Paper presented at 72nd Annual Meeting of the American Anthropological Association. 30 November, 1973. New Orleans, Louisiana.

2522.   Everett, Michael W. Time and place in Apache drinking activities. Paper presented at 73rd Annual Meeting of the American Anthropological Association. 19 to 24 November, 1974. Mexico City.

2523.   Evers. 1935. Der Mensch, ein Fruchte und Wurzel esser. [Man, a fruit and root-eater.] Fort Med 53: 497-506.

Holds that the jaws and teeth of humans are made for fruit and root-eating, by comparison with those of the wild cat, stonemarten, badger, roebuck, hare, wild boar, and chimpanzee.

2524.   Evers. 1935. Human instinct and the problem of natural diet. [In German.] Fort Med 53: 519-521.

2525.   Evers. 1936. Nutrition of prehistoric man and classification of human foods according to their nutritional value. [In German.] Fort Med 54: 156-160.

2526.   Evreinoff, V.A. 1956. Contribution a l'etude du dattier. [Contribution to the study of the date palm.] JATBA 3: 328-329.

2527. Ewbank, Thomas. [pseud. Habakuk O. Westman.] 1844. Transactions of the Society of Literary and Scientific Chiffoniers; being essays on primitive arts in domestic life. The spoon: primitive, Egyption, Roman, Medieval, and modern, with upwards of one hundred illustrations. New York: Harper and Brothers.

2528. Ewers, John C. 1937. Teton Dakota ethnology and history. United States Department of the Interior. Berkeley, California: U.S. National Park Service.
    Foods: pp. 14-19.

2529. Ewers, John C. 1944. Food rationing is nothing new to the Blackfoot. MKey 18: 73-80.

2530. Ewing, Joseph Franklin. 1963. Food and drink among the Tawsug; with comparative notes from other Philippine and near-by groups. A Quart 36: 60-70.

2531. Exell, A.W. The introduction of food plants into Africa by the Portugese. Paper presented to Third Conference on African History and Archaeology, 3-7 July, 1961. School of Oriental and African Studies, University of London.

2532. Eykman, Christiaan. 1911. De voeding der Trappisten. [Diet of trappist monks.] KAWA-VVWNA 19: 1406-1407.

2533. Eyre, John D. 1959. Sources of Tokyo's fresh food supply. GR 49: 455-474.

2534. F... 1845. Dejeuner. Le lait, le cafe. Examen critique et approfondi. [Breakfast. Milk, coffee. Thorough critical examination.] Paris: Mlle. Laignier.

2535. Fa'atiga, Togama'u. 1935. Infant feeding in native villages. NMP 2: 255-262.

    Samoa.

2536. Fabianek, J. & Fournier, P. 1967. Lucie Randoin - a biographical sketch. JN 91: 3-8.

    Retrospective appreciation of the late French nutritionist, whose work often dealt with sociologist aspects of diet.

2537. Fabre. [Erbaf]. 1909. Alimentation et ravitaillement des troupes en campagne. [Feeding and provisioning of troops in the field.] 2nd edition. Angouleme: Imprimerie de L. Couquemard.

2538. Fairbanks, Charles H. 1941. Hunting 500 years ago. To Georgia Indians it was a business. RR 6: 3-6.

2539. Fairbanks, Charles H. Gulf complex subsistence economy. In Twenty-first Southeastern Archaeological Conference. November 6-7, 1964. New Orleans, Louisiana. Proceedings. Edited by Stephen Williams. 1965. Pp. 57-63. SAC-B No. 3.

    Discussion of evidence from excavations in the southeastern coastal United States as to the practice of agriculture before Early Mississippian times. Major focus of this paper is on the Weeden Island Phase, on the Florida Gulf Coast.

2540. Fairbridge, Rhodes W. 1976. Shellfish-eating, preceramic Indians in coastal Brazil. Science 191-353-359; 192: 322.

2541. Fairburn, G.E. 1965. Dining out in Illyria. NZL 53:22.

    Yugoslav cookery.

2542. Fairchild, David. 1918. The palate of civilized man and its influence on agriculture. FIJ 185: 299-316.

    Discusses world wide food habits, and observes the possibility of United States agriculture being inhibited by an eccentric U.S. palate.

2543. Fairchild, David. 1919. Testing new foods. JHER 10: 17-28.

    Describes in some detail experiments in breeding various tropical fruit, and vegetables, by the United States Department of Agriculture, for the purpose of evaluating their potential for domestication.

2544. Fairchild, David. 1938. Chapter Thirty-five. The war and dried vegetables. In The world was my garden. New York, London: Charles Scribners' Sons.

    Account of efforts to commercialize the drying of foods, in the United States, during World War I.

2545. Fakacelli, N.M. & Konstantinidu, S. 1951. Le favisme en Turquie. [Favism in Turkey.] AMT 3: 149-150.

2546. Falls, A.E. 1942. The culinary art of the Navajos. PHE 20: 349-350.

2547. Fanning, Robert Joseph, comp., annotator. 1951. Pacific Islands nutrition bibliography. Honolulu: University of Hawaii Press.

2548. Farabee, William Curtis. 1922. Indian tribes of eastern Peru. HU-PMAAE-P Vol. 10.

    Macheyenga: hunting, fishing, preparation of game, household utensils, drinks: pp. 2-7. Piro: food supply, and food preparation: pp. 55-57. Conebo: food supply: p. 83. Sipibo: food, utensils: p. 96. Jivaro: foods, hunting techniques: pp. 116-117. Witoto: food, hunting: pp. 138-139; Jaliko, Feast of the Pole: pp. 139, 140. Tiatinagua: foods, preparation, hunting: pp. 154-156.

2549. Farabee, William Curtis. 1924. The Central Caribs. UMich-MA-AP No. 10.

    Contains data on food, beverages, and food preparation of the Macusi of the British Guiana (Guyana) - Venezuela border region.

2550. Farga, Amando. 1968. Historia de la comida en Mexico. [History of eating in Mexico.] Mexico City: Costa-Amic.

2551. Faria, L. de. 1949. Antropofagia. [Anthropophagy.] M Ad 18: 17-18.

2552. Farmer, Ann P. 1960. Malnutrition as an ecological problem. EAMJ 37: 399-404.

2553. Farrar, W.V. 1966. Tecuitlatl: a glimpse of Aztec food technology. Nature (L) 211: 341-342.

A review of the historical literature in support of the view that the tecuitlatl eaten by the Aztec populace of Tenochtitlan (modern Mexico City) was a blue-green alga (Cyanophyta) of unknown species, which was non-toxic. Excerpts from the literature mentioned described harvesting and preparation.

2554. Fathauer, George H. 1960. Food habits - an anthropologist's view. JADA 37: 335-338.

2555. Faublee, Jacques. 1942. L'alimentation des Bara (sud de Madagascar). [Diet of the Bara (southern Madagascar).] SA-J 12: 157-201.

2556. Faulkner, Charles H., & Graham, J.B. Plant food remains on Tennessee sites: a preliminary report. In Twenty-second Southeastern Archaeological Conference. November 12-13, 1965. Macon, Georgia. Proceedings. Edited by Bettye J. Broyles. 1967. Pp. 36-40. SAC-B No. 5.

Covers Archaic, Woodland, and Mississippian sites.

2557. Faulks, Philip James. 1958. Chapter Thirty-six. Relation between the nature of cultivated plants and social structure. Chapter Thirty-seven. Relations of beliefs and customs to plant culture. In Introduction to economic botany. London: Moredale Publishers.

2558. Faull, Lesley. 1969. Rice recipes and curries in Southern Africa. Edited by Vida Heard. Cape Town: Books of Africa.

2559. Faure, M. 1946. Feeding the African farmer. EAAJ 12: 71-73.

2560. Faust, Katherine. Peasants and potatoes: a study of cognitive variability. Paper presented at 76th Annual Meeting of the American Anthropological Association. 29 November to 3 December, 1977. Houston, Texas.

Potatoes are of extreme importance in the diet and economy of most Andean peasants whose knowledge in the botanical domain is extensive and complex. This paper studies intracultural variation in cognition in this domain. The hypothesis is tested that common group membership will enhance the degree of concordance in cognitive patterns, based on data derived from eighteen informants in the Canchis village of Santa Barbara, Peru. The analysis is based on naming, attribute ranking and triad tasks. Differences in extent of concordance across individuals are found to be related to cognitive area as well as group membership.

2561. Faust, Richard Allen. A comparative study of anthropophagy among the tribes north of Mexico. Master's thesis. University of Pennsylvania. 1935.

2562. Fauvel, Camille. 1957. Truffles and foies gras. [Truffles and goose livers.] Rev Myc 22: 88-95.

Costs, shopping for these foods, recipes, anecdotes.

2563. Favre, Joseph. 1889-1891. Dictionnaire universel de cuisine et d'hygiene alimentaire. Modification de l'homme par l'alimentation. Le dictionnaire comprend: l'etymologie, la synonimie en trois langues, l'histoire, l'analyse chimique de tous les aliments...les cuisines vegetarienne, asyrienne, grecque, romaine, francaise...la biographie de tous les cuisiniers illustrees. [Universal dictionary of cookery and food hygiene. Modification of homo sapiens through diet. The dictionary includes: etymology, synonyms in three languages, history, chemical analyses of all foods; vegetarian, Assyrian, Greek, Roman, French..with biographies of illustrious cooks.] Paris: les libraries.

2564. Fawcett, William, compilor. 1891. Economic plants. An index to economic products of the vegetable kingdom in Jamaica. Kingston: Government Printing Establishment.

2565. Fawkes, J.W. 1923. Ancient bread of Arizona. BTech 2: 314-317.

2566. Federacao dos Clubes Agricolas do Estado de Sao Paulo. 1959. Vinagre e geleia de caqui. Industrias rurais caseiras. [Vinegar and Japanese persimmon jelly. Rural cottage industries.] Sao Paulo: Direccion de Publicidade Agricola.

2567. Federal Writers' Project. 1940. Early Nebraska cooking. Nebraska folklore pamphlet 28. Lincoln: Federal Writers' Project in Nebraska.

2568. Fehily, Lydia. 1946. What the Russians eat. BMJ 1: 769.

Whole grain cereal staples; dairy products; occurrence of xerophthalmia among Russian Orthodox Church members as a result of repeated religious fasts. Use of preserved vegetables during winter.

2569. Fehlinger, H. 1928. Bauernahrung der Naturvolker. [Peasant food of primitive peoples.] Erdball 2: 157-160.

2570. Fiebelman, Peter S. 1969. The cooking of Spain and Portugal. New York: Time-Life Books. Foods of the World.

2571. Feibelman, Peter S. 1971. American cooking: Creole and Acadian. New York: Time-Life Books. Foods of the World.

2572. Feit, Harvey Allan. Mistasini hunters of the Boreal Forest. Ecosystem dynamics and multiple subsistence patterns. Master's thesis. McGill University. 1969.

2573. Feit, Harvey Allan. The ethno-ecology of the Waswanipi Cree; or how hunters can manage their resources. In Cultural ecology. Edited by B. Cox. 1973. Pp. 115-125. Toronto: Mc Clelland and Stuart.

2574. Feldman, Lawrence. A tumpline economy: production and distribution systems of early central-east Guatemala. Ph.D. dissertation. Pennsylvania State University. 1971.

2575. Felger, R.S. & Moser, M.B. 1976. Seri Indian food plants: desert subsistence without agriculture. EFN 5: 13-27.

The Seri are Mexican group, who inhabit the eastern area of the Gulf of California. This paper is a highly detailed ethnobotany, providing details on plant environment, preparation, and use as food.

2576. Felt, E.P. 1918. Caribou warble grubs edible. JEE 11: 482.

Note on Eskimo food use of grubs infesting Caribou skin.

2577. Fennell, Joseph L. 1948. Cocona - a desirable new fruit. For Ag 12: 181-182.

Solanum topiro, Humb. & Bonpl. This fruit is native to the Orinoco River region.

2578. Fenton, Alexander. Oatmeal and barley meal: a main element in Scottish food research. Paper presented at First International Symposium on Ethnological Food Research. 21 August to 25 August, 1970. Lund: Folklivsarkivet, Lund University.

2579. Fenton, William N. 1963. The Seneca green-corn ceremony: a revealing glimps into the life and mind of New York Indians. Cons 18: 20-22.

2580. Ferguson, J. 1873. Symbolism of the vine. GCAG for 1873. Pp. 1048-1050.

2581. Ferguson, J.H. & Keaton, A.G. 1950. Studies of diets of pregnant women in Mississippi; ingestion of clay and laundry starch. NOMSJ 102: 460-463.

2582. Ferguson, W. 1881-1882. Manihot utilissima. Trop Ag 1: 853.

Historical information on cassava.

2583. Fernald, Merritt Lyndon. 1910. Notes on the plants of Wineland the Good. Rhodora 12: 17-38.

The three plants which have been most depended on to locate Wineland the Good, i.e. "vinber"; "hveiti" and "mosurr" wood —— instead of being the grape, Indian corn or wild rice, and the maple - are, in reality, the Mountain Cranberry (or possibly one of the native currants) Strand Wheat, and Canoe Birch.

2584. Fernald, Merritt Lyndon; Kinsey, Alfred Charles; & Rollins, Reed C. 1958. Edible wild plants of eastern North America. New York: Harper Brothers.

2585. Fernandes, Jose Loureiro. 1964. Sobrevivencias de tecnologia arcaica portuguesa nas prensas da mandoca brasileiras. [Overview of old Portuguese technology in Brazilian manioc presses.] Departamento da Antropologia. Curitiba: Universidade do Parana.

2586. Fernandez, Nelson A. 1975. Nutrition in Puerto Rico. Cancer Res 35: 3272-3291.

A very comprehensive study of production, consumption, and utilization food, with data on nutritional status, and possible dietary etiology in cancer.

2587. Fernandez, Nelson A.; Burgos, J.C.; Roberts, Lydia Jean; & Asenjo, C.F. 1968. Nutritional status of people in isolated areas of Puerto Rico: Survey of Barrio Montones 4, Las Piedras. JADA 53: 119-126.

2588. Fernandez, Renate. Policy implications of the abandonment of breast feeding in northern Spain. Paper presented at 76th Annual Meeting of the American Anthropological Association. 29 November to 3 December, 1977. Houston, Texas.

A radical change in infant feeding patterns has come about over the past four years in rural northern Spain, focused around abandonment of breast for bottle feeding. The most frequently cited reasons given in the infant nutrition literature for shift from breast to bottle - urbanization, female employment, undernutrition, decline of social fabric - are, in this setting, ruled out as causal factors. Field data are used in support of the view that it is the interplay of cultural values and national policies that influence the individual mother's decision on infant feeding in northern Spain. The explanatory prominence of values, belief systems and policies are stressed in this analysis.

2589. Feron, R. 1976. Consommation lipidique des francais. [Lipid consumption among the French.] ANA 30: 141-160.

2590. Ferrando, R. 1968. On the primacy of diet. [In French.] MMed 48: 678-682.

2591. Ferrao, J. & Xabregas, J. 1960. African nutrition and diet. [In Portuguese.] AAng 12: 61-69.

2592. Ferrarese, M. 1949. Distillazione agraria pratica moderna. [Modern practical agricultural distilling.] Milan: Hoepli.

History and principles of distilling wines and spirits.

2593. Ferro-Luzzi, G. 1962. Food patterns and nutrition in French Polynesia. AJCN 11: 299-311.

2594. Ferro-Luzzi, G. 1964. La situation alimentaire et nutritionelle en Mauretanie. [Dietary and nutritional situation in Mauritania.] QN 24: 245-266.

2595. Ferro-Luzzi, G. Eichinger. 1973. Food avoidances of pregnant women in Tamilnad. EFN 2: 259-266.

Over a period of six months, twelve hundred women in South India were interviewed. Although many different kinds of foods are avoided, the most important are fruit and grains. These food avoidances were dominated primarily by fear of abortion, and less significantly by concern about painful birth, diseases and malformation of the fetus.

2596. Ferro-Luzzi, G. Eichinger. 1973. Food avoidances at puberty and menstruation in Tamilnad. An anthropological study. EFN 2: 165-172.

One thousand two hundred women of fifty four castes and fifty-five tribal women were interviewed during six months. Most significant menarcheal avoidances related to foods of animal origin; eggs, though considered impure, were eaten at puberty, because of their reputed "strengthening" effect on a young woman's body for future pregnancies. The role of the "hot"/"cold" classification system in relation to food avoidances is referred to; and examples of specific foods and reasons for their avoidance are recorded.

2597. Ferro-Luzzi, G. Eichinger. 1974. Food avoidances during the puerperium and lactation in Tamilnad. EFN 3: 7-15.

Twelve hundred women in South India, from fifty-four cases; and fifty-five tribal women were interviewed over a span of six months. Avoidances included meat, fish, eggs, buttermilk, curds, certain fruit, gourds, green vegetables, sweet potatoes and ground nuts, and were practiced from a belief that specific foods are associated with some other polluting factor, and that ingestion of such foods could transmit disease-producing qualities to the infant through the mother's breast-milk.

2598. Festinger, Leon. Effect of container on food preferences. Mimeographed. Committee on Food Habits. Washington, D.C.: National Research Council. March, 1944.

2599. Fewkes, Jesse Walter. 1896. A contribution to ethnobotany. AA 9 [old series]: 14-21.

A listing of sixty-eight Hopi plants, some of which are used for food, and others for medicinal or ceremonial purposes.

2600. Fewkes, Jesse Walter. 1897. Tusayan katcinas. SI-BAE-AR for the year 1893-1894. Pp. 245-349.

Foods given by katcinas to spectators: p. 295; food passed into kiva: p. 301; ceremonial foods (Anakatcina celebration at Hano, in the Niman of 1892): p. 303; ingestion of human urine: p. 303.

2601. Fewkes, Jesse Walter. 1898. Archaeological expedition to Arizona in 1895. SI-BAE-AR for the year 1895-1896. Pp. 519-744.

The section entitled 'Pottery', pp. 650-728 is concerned with food bowls, and the variety of decorations they exhibit. Numerous illustrations are included, including pen and ink drawings, photographs, and color plates. Food contents of mortuary food bowls: pp. 741-742.

2602. Fewster, W. Jean. The development of an instrument to assess dimensions of the connotative meaning of foods. Ph.D. dissertation. Mass Communications. University of Wisconsin. 1969.

Uses semantic differential, and twelve dimensions of meaning drawn from the literature in nutrition, social psychology, and anthropology. Comparative ratings were obtained from upper and lower income homemakers for seven food concepts (meat, dairy products, steak, green beans, fresh, and powdered milk.) Results of administering the instrument developed herein indicated the latter was capable of revealing differences in food concept meaning between population groups. Objective of the research is to isolate socio-psychological factors that act as determinants of, or deterrents to the changing food habits through nutrition information programs.

2603. Ficalho, Fransisco Manuel Carlo de Mello. 1884. Plantas uteis da Africa Portugueza. [Useful plants of Por ugues Africa.] Lisbon: Imprensa Nacional.

2604. Fidanza, F. 1915. The action of Sardinian lactic acid on human metabolism. [In Italian.] AIS 25: 411-420.

Gioddu, a Sardinian fermented milk product.

2605. Fiebrig, C. Nomenclatura Guarani de vegetales del Paraguay. [Paraguayan Gaurdni plan nomenclature.] In 20 Congreso Internacional de Americanistas. 20 a 23 Agosto de 1922. Rio de Janeiro. Annaes. 1932. Pp. 305-329. Rio de Janeiro: Imprensa Nacional.

The first section of this paper lists Guardni plants by botanical family, genus, and species, and by vernacular name: pp. 303-317; a second section lists animals, terms of quality, fruit; woods; words for taste, odor, uses, abstract or figurative significance, and habitat - all analyzed etymologically.

2606. Fiedler, Alfred. 1963. Zur Frage des privaten und kommunalen Backens in den Dorfen Sachsens wahrend des 18. und zu Beginn des 19 Jahrhunderts. Ein Beitrag zur Sachsischen Haus and Dorffschung. [On the question of private and communal bakeries in village Saxony during the 18th and beginning of the 19th Centuries. A contribution to the Saxon household and village research.] SMVD-AB 22: 181-201.

2607. Field, H. 1952. The diet of the prehistoric Indians of northeast Iowa. Ia-AS-J 1: 8-13.

2608. Fife-Hamill Memorial Health Center. 1956. Food habits in America - racial groups on low incomes. Health Education Division. Philadelphia: Fife-Hamill Memorial Health Center.

2609. Figuiere, Eugene. 1936. Plantes qui nourrisent, plantes qui querissent. [Plants which nourish, plants which cure.] Paris: Editions Sanitaire & Sociale (l'auteur).

2610. Filby, Frederick Arthur. 1934. A history of food adulteration and analysis. London: G. Allen & Unwin.

2611. Filho, Artur Pinto de Lemos. 1960. Cla do acucuar (Recife: 1911-1934). [The sugar clan (Recife: 1911-1934). Rio de Janeiro: Livraria Sao Jos.

2612. Filipovich, Milenko S. 1956. Kiselitsa i booza. [Groats and liquor.] ZMS 15: 1-7.

2613. Filippi, Filippo de. 1909. Ruwenzori. An account of the expedition of H.R.H. Prince Luigi Amadeo of Savoy, Duke of the Abruzzi. New York: E.P. Dutton.

Contains data on food habits of groups of the area of equatorial Africa known as the Mountains of the Moon.

2614. Les Films de la Pleiade. 1955. Les maitres fous. 16mm film, sound and color. Thirty-five minutes. Paris: Les Films de la Pleiade.

Includes footage on food use of dogs, in Ghana.

2615. Finan, John J. 1948. Maize in the great herbals. MBG-A 35: 149-191.

Originally presented as a Master's thesis, at Washington University, St. Louis Missouri. This article reviews mention of maize in the herbals of Sixteenth and Seventeenth Century Europe. Two types of maize are described in the herbals: a flint-type, similar to those common to eastern North America, and a type similar to the maize used in the Caribbean area. The author discusses the comments in the herbals regarding the geographical provenience of these types relative to their arrival in Europe.

2616. Finck, Henry T. 1886. Gastronomic value of odors. C Rev 50: 680-695.

2617. Finck, Henry T. 1895. Lotos-time in Japan. New York: Charles Scribner's Sons.

Koicha: a thick tea-based beverage: pp. 60-61; a riverside picnic: p. 70; a restaurant meal in Shimbashi: pp. 79, 80, 84-86; food in an Oginohama teahouse: p. 130; food vended on a railway station platform: p. 253.

2618. Finck, Henry T. 1911-1912. The future of cooking and eating. Century 83: 439-448.

2619. Finck, Henry T. 1911-1912. Multiplying the pleasures of the table. Century 83: 220-228.

2620. Finck, Henry T. 1911-1912. Ungastronomic America, with a theory of wholesome eating. Century 83: 28-36.

2621. Finck, Henry T. 1924. Food and flavor. New York, London: Harper & Brothers.

2622. Fincke, Heinrich. 1962. Pfefferbrot und honigbrot als Bestandteile Siegburger alkoholischer Getranke un die Wende des Mittelalters. [Gingerbread and honeybread as permanent parts of Siegburg alcoholic liquors at the turn of the Middle Ages.] RWZV 9: 248-252.

2623. Fincke, Heinrich. 1963. Uber die Bennenungen honigkuchenahnlicher Gebacke als Lebkuchen und Lebzelten sowie als Biber und Bibenzelten. [On the naming of honey-cake-like pastries gingerbread and flat honey-cakes; as well as "beavers" and "beaver cakes".] DLR No. 6. Pp. 159-167.

2624. Fincke, Heinrich. 1963. Was war "Pfefferbrot" im 15. Jahrhundert? [What was "gingerbread" in the 15th Century?] Susswaren 7: 680-682.

2625. Fincke, Heinrich. 1964. Beitrage zur Kentnis honighalter Gebildbackwaren. 5. Laubinger und Leipziger Lebzelten von Orstsnammen abgeleitete Bennenungen des Ausgehenden Mittelalters. [Contribution to knowledge of shaped, honey-cakes. Part Five. Laubingen and Leipzig 'Nuremberg gingerbreads.' derived from late Medeival place-name signs.] Susswarren 7: 680-682.

2626. Fincke, Heinrich. 1964. Beitrage zur kentnis honighaltiger Gebildbackwaren. 3. Aufden S uren alter Schweizer Gebild-backwaren. [Contribution to the knowledge of honey-filled decorated pastries. 3. On the symbols of old Swiss decorated pastries.] Susswaren 8: 836-842.

2627. Fincke, Heinrich. 1964. Zur bildung des Names Biber einer Schweizer honig-kuchenahnlichen Gebackart. [On the development of the name "beaver" for a honey-cake-like Swiss pastry.] DLR Part 6. Pp. 168-170.

2628. Finkler, Kaja. Economic activities of a Mexican village with special reference to the role of domesticated animals. Master's thesis. Anthropology. Hunter College of the City of New York. 1968.

2629. Finney, B.R. 1969. New Guinea entrepreneurs. Indigenous cash cropping, capital formation and investment in the New Guinea Highlands. NGRU-B No. 27.

> As part of this survey, each household in Natauka, Goroka sub-district (approximately 6. 02 S. 145. 22 E) was visited at or near meal times and all foods consumed and the number of people eating were recorded (p. 72). Susbistence foods were found to predominate, although some imported foods we in common use, especially tinned meats. Consumption of imported foods is highest from May to September, because of the ready cash flow from the sale of coffee beans, and owing to the scarcity of local foods in the dry season. [After Schofield. 1975: 228.]

2630.   Firth, Raymond. 1925. Maori storehouses of today. RAIGBI-J 55: 363-372.

2631.   Firth, Raymond. 1931. Totemism in Polynesia Oceania 1: 291-321; 377; 399.

> Clans and plant foods: pp. 293-298.

2632.   Firth, Raymond. 1934. The sociological study of native diet. Africa 7: 401-414.

> Based on discussions at the London School of Economics, in 1933. Urges a multi-disciplinary approach in applied nutrition programs, and discusses these in detail, enumerating specific foci. Believes nutrition intervention can be achieved through concerted cooperation between biochemistry, agriculture, anthropology, and economics, and local administrators. Also recommends establishment of a committee for the study of native diet, under the aegis of International Institute of African languages and Cultures.

2633.   Firth, Raymond. 1950. Economics and ritual sago extraction in Tikopia. Mankind 4: 131-142.

> Tikopia is an island in the Santa Cruz group, located at 12. 10S, 168.50E.

2634.   Firth, Raymond. 1965. Chapter 2. Food and population in Tikopia. In Primitive Polynesian economy. London: Routledge & Kegan Paul.

2635.   Firth, Rosemary. 1966. Housekeeping among Melay peasants. London School of Economics Monographs on Social Anthropology. No. 7. London: Athlone Press.

> This book studies the household of a fishing family in Perupok, Kelantan State, Malaysia. Extensive data on food patterns and practices, food and meal costs, children's diets, weaning practices, meal patterns. Cooking, and household recipes are described. [After Schofield 1975: 192.]

2636.   Fischel, Walter J. 1957. The spice trade in Mamluk Egypt. JESHO 1: 157-174.

2637.   Fischer, Eugen. 1955. Insektenkost beim Menschen. Ein Beitrag zur Urgeschichte meschlichen Ernahrung und der Bambutiden. [Insects as human food. An essay on human nutritional prehistory and the Bambuti pygmies.] ZE 80: 1-37.

> Covers the following: insect food among animals and among humans; nutritional value of insects; flavor aspects of insects as food; nutritional status of the insect eater; quantity of insects available for food; the caloric value of insects and Bambuti diet; calorimetric balance, and its implications for the pygmy's small stature; vitamins; prehistory of human diet; hunting on prehistory; from the diet of the ape to human diet; the origin of Bambuti; pygmy diet.

2638.   Fischer, Fred William. Early and middle Woodland Settlement, subsistence and population in the central Ohio Valley. Ph.D. dissertation. Anthropology. St. Louis, Missouri: Washington University. 1974

2639.   Fischer, H. 1912. Southwest Africa camp food. [In German.] LZ 32: 246, 247.

> Native foods and uses described.

2640.   Fischer, J.L.; Fischer, Ann; & Mahony, Frank. 1959. Totemism and allergy. IJSPsych 5: 33-40.

> Compares disorders attributed to allergens in the United States with symptoms attributed to violations of totemic food tabus in Ponape, Caroline Islands, United States Trust Territories of the Pacific.

2641.   Fischer, Josef. 1960. Das Bauernbrot. [Farm bread.] Oberfalz 48: 236-238.

2642.   Fischer, R.; Griffin, F.; England.; & Garn, Stanley M. 1961. Taste thresholds and food dislikes. Nature (L) 191: 1328.

2643.   Fischer, Theobald. 1881. Die Dattepalme ihre geographische Verbreitung und cultur historische Bedeutung. [The date-palm, its geographical distribution and cultural-historial significance.] PGM-E No. 64. Pp. 1-85.

2644.   Fischer-Harriehausen, Hermann. Das Bonito-Ritual in Zentralmelanesien. [The bonito ritual in central Melanesia.] Ph.D. dissertation. Gottingen: Georg-August-Universitat.

2645.   Fischler, C. 1976. Are culinaire et changement social; quelques remarques [A few remarks on culinary and social change.] ANA 30: 415-426.

2646.   Fish, Suzanne K. Palynology of some cultural contexts. Paper presented at 73rd Annual Meeting of the American Anthropological Association. 19 to 24 November, 1974. Mexico City.

2647.   Fish, Warren Richard. Constraints on the dietary status of rural man in the Paraiba Valley region, Sao Paulo, Brazil. Ph.D. dissertation. Geography. Urbana: University of Illinois. 1972.

2648.   Fisher, Alton Kindt; Kuhm, Herbert W.; & Adami, George C. 1931. Dental pathology of the prehistoric Indians of Wisconsin. Mil-PM-B 10[3]: 331-374.

2649.   Fisher, Harold Henry. 1927. The famine in Soviet Russia, 1919-1923; the operations of the American relief administration.   New York: Macmillan.

2650.   Fisher, Irving. 1907. The effect of diet on endurance; based on an experiment, in thorough mastication, with nine healthy students at Yale University,   January to June, 1901.   New Haven: Tuttle, Morehouse & Taylor.

2651. Fisher, Mary Frances Kennedy. 1968. The cooking of provincial France. New York: Time-Life Books. Foods of the World.

2652.   Fisher, Vardis & Holmes, Opal Laurel. 1968. Gold rushes and mining camps of the early American West. Caldwell, Idaho: Caxton Printers.

Food: pp. 137-145.

2653. Fisher, W.E.G.   1900.   Feasts in fiction. Cornhill 82: 377-389.

2654.   Fitzgerald, C.P.   1941.   The tower of the five glories. London: Crescent Press.

Min Chia peoples of Yunnan Province , China. Dining, and the social function of restaurants.

2655. Fitzgerald, Claudia. 1918. Food administration cafeteria. JHE 10: 411-413.

Describes the origins, operation, menus, and physical plant of the Federal Food Administration cafeteria in Washington, D.C.

2656.   Fitzgerald, Thomas K. Anthropological approaches to the study of food habits: some methodological issues.   In Nutrition and anthropology in action. Edited by Thomas K. Fitzgerald. 1976. Pp. 69-78. Assen, Amsterdam: Van Gorcum.

Describes anthropological methods used in the study of changing nutritional patterns in the community of Whitsett, North Carolina. Of major significance is elaboration on the use of the Food Choice Game, devised by the author. This research instrument, using a scaled "game" board, and food cards with representations of local foods, each informant ('player') sorts the cards to pre-determined dimensions, or scales: e.g. personal preference   or   dislike;   healthfulness; frequency of use. This instrument may be less intimidating than direct questioning.

2657.   Fitzgerald, Thomas K. 1976. Ipomoea batatas: the sweet potato revisited. EFN 5: 107-114.

This article investigates the decline in popularity of a once popular food. A small community of six hundred persons, in the State of North Carolina, in transition from a rural to suburban life-style was studied. The author concludes that the sweet potato has lost prestige for a number of reasons, being retained in the diet largely as a ritual (holiday) food. Reasons for decline in popularity are examined in detail, based on questionnaire responses.

2658.   Fitzgerald, Thomas K. 1978.   The eating habits of New Zealand school children. Set (1). Item 3. 4pp.

Describes the author's research in New Zealand; and the uses of his Food Choice Game, an instrument he developed for instructional and research purposes.

2659.   Fitzgerald, Thomas K. 1979. Southern folks' eating habits ain't what they used to be...if they ever were. NT 14(4): 16-21.

Study of dietary patterns and nutritional knowledge of middle class Black and Anglo-Americans in a North Carolina town undergoing rural-to-urban transition.

2660.   Fitz Gibbon, Theodora. 1968. A taste of Ireland: Irish traditional food. London: J.M. Dent. Boston: Houghton Mifflin (1969). Reprint.   New York: Ballantine Books (1971).

2661.   Fitz Gibbon, Theodora. 1970.   A taste of Scotland: Scottish traditional foods. London: J.M. Dent. Boston: Houghton Mifflin [1971].

2662.   Fitz Gibbon, Theodora. 1971. A taste of Wales: Welsh traditional food. London: J.M. Dent.

2663.   Fitz Gibbon, Theodora. 1972. A taste of England - the West Country: traditional food. London: J.M. Dent.

2664.   Fitz Gibbon, Theodora. 1973. A taste of London: traditional food. London: J.M. Dent.

2665.   Fitzmaurice, H.G. 1937. Appendix One. Observations on native foodstuffs and diet in the Kola-Kota District.   Rhodesia.   Annual Medical Report for the year ending 31st December, 1936. Pp. 79-83. Bomba: Government Printer.

2666.   Fitzpatrick, Mary Brigetta. A dietary study of a group of religious women with special reference to vitamin C nutrition. Master's thesis. Ohio State University. 1944.

2667.   Fitzroy, V.M. 1950. Eat and be merry; a book about people and food. Cape Town: Timmins.

Traditional South African recipes, with additional information about food.

2668.   Fizeliere, Albert de la. 1866. Vins a la mode et cabarets au 17e siecle. [Stylish wines, and cabarets of the 17th Century.] Paris: Rene Pincebourde.

2669. Fjellstrom, Phoebe. 1964. Angelica archangelica in the diet of the Lapps and the Nordic people. SEU 21: 99-115.

Longwort.

2670. Flack Jean R. The spread and domestication of the pecan (Carya illinoensis) in the United States. Ph.D. dissertation. Geography. University of Wisconsin. 1970.

2671. Flack, Katherine E. 1954. Food service training in New York State mental institutions. JADA 30: 476.

2672. Flanagan, Gertrude Catherine. A study of the dietary habits of three generations of the Eastern Cherokee Indians. Master's thesis. Home Economics. University of Kansas. 1938.

2673. Flannery, Kent V. 1965. The ecology of early food production in Mesopotamia: prehistoric farmers and herders exploited a series of adjacent but contrasting climatic zones. Science 147: 1247-1256.

Characterizes the food-producing revolution in southwestern Asia as the consequence of a long process of changing ecological relationships between populations at various altitudes and the plants and animals they had been exploiting transhumantly. Discusses environmental contexts; local climatic sequence; pre-agricultural subsistence pattern; beginnings of food production; biological obstacles to early food production; effects of food production on human life and cultural ecology.

2674. Flannery, Regina. 1953. The Gros-Ventre of Montana - social life. Cath UA-AS No. 15.

Food habits: pp. 56-61.

2675. Flanzy, M. & Causeret, J. 1954. Les vitamins du vin. [The vitamins in wine.] OIV-B 27: 20-24.

2676. Fleck, Martin. Notes on the origin and development of Zea mays. Master's thesis. University of New Mexico. 1939.

2677. Fleckles, Ferdinand. 1880. Das diabetische Regimen mit 60 Menus fur Diabetiser. [Diabetic diet with 60 menus for diabetics.] Carlsbad: Schippang and Knauer.

2678. Fleischmann-Mathes, Ute. 1971. Some aspects of nutritional problems in a village of Gujarat, C. India. ICUAER-B 13: 83-91.

2679. Fletcher, Alice C. & La Flesche, Francis. 1911. The Omaha tribe. SI-BAE-AR for the year 1905-1906. Pp. 17-672.

Chapter Seven. 'The quest for food' (Pp. 261-312) begins with a detailed account of maize planting ritual, and its song, and includes information on maize cultivation, the names of parts and of preparation of maize, the largest portion of this chapter focuses on hunting, principally buffalo, with numerous ritual songs reproduced. Details on butchering are included. A brief section is given over to fishing. A list of flora and fauna, including food items, is listed on pp. 103-107. Omaha terms for taste are given on p. 110-111. Specific foods, and their methods of preparation are described on pp. 340-342. Food in the Watha'wa (Feast of the Count): pp. 499-500; food in Shell Society ritual: pp. 537-538. Food as a ritual offering on the grave of a departed person: p. 592. Psychological effect of change in traditional food supply: pp. 634-635. Terms for newly-introduced foods are given on p. 620.

2680. Fleuret, Anne. The role of wild foliage plants in the diet. A case study from Lushoto, Tanzania. Paper presented at 77th Annual Meeting of the American Anthropological Association. 16 November, 1978. Los Angeles, California.

Indicates that vegetable relishes prepared from wild plants are not supplementary or peripheral in Shambaa diet; rather they form an integral and essential element in the diet, and are not being superseded by introduced, cultivated vegetables.

2681. Fleuret, Anne. 1979. Methods for evaluation of the role of fruits and wild greens in Shambaa diet: a case study. Med Anth 3: 249-269.

The utilization of complementary field observation techniques in shown to resolve an apparent paradox of good nutritional health found in conjunction with extremely low intakes of certain nutrients reported in the literature. Earlier reports employed data gathering techniques which overlooked significant consumption of edible, wild plants which provide the nutrients erroneously observed as deficient.

2682. Flinders-Petrie, William M. 1897. Eaten with honor. CRev 71: 819-828.

Presents archeological evidence of apparent anthropophagy in Dynastic Egypt.

2683. Floch, Herve Alexandre. 1953. Analyses of some fruits and vegetables of French Guiana. [In French.] IPGTI-A-P. No. 286.

2684. Floch, Herve Alexandre & Lecuiller, A. 1951. Nutritive value of some French Guiana products. [In French.] IPGTI-A-P No. 242.

2685. Floch, Herve Alexandre & Gelard, A. 1955. La cerise ronde de Cayenne Malpighia punicifolia, L. Sa richesse exceptionelle en vitamine C. [The Cayenne round cherry Malpighia punicifolia, L. Its exceptional richness in Vitamin C. IPGTI-A-P No. 368.

2686. Floore, F.B. 1948. School lunches in Palestine. JADA 24: 872-874.

2687.   Flores, Mariana. Food patterns in Central America and Panama. In Third International Congress of Dietetics. 10-14 July, 1961. Proceedings. 1961 Pp. 23-27. London: William Byles & Sons.

2688.   Flores, Mariana. Dietary habits and food consumption levels in Central America. Paper presented at 9th International Congress of Anthropological and Ethnological Sciences. 28 August to 8 September, 1973. Chicago, Illinois.

Report based on family dietary surveys. Notes the persistence of Mayan, African, Caribbean, and Spanish influences. Rural diets are characterized by cereal,legume, and wild greens. Urban diet is composed mainly fresh vegetables and fruit and some meat, eggs, and milk. In terms of nutritional adequacy, such diets show that calories and protein reach the recommended levels on the average but are very low for some 25-35 percent of the population in each country. Vitamin A and riboflavin intake is extemely low in rural areas due to the virtual absence of consumption of milk and other animal food products. Since seasonal fruits are not essential items of the food pattern of some groups, some intakes of Vitamic C are also low.

2689.   Flores, Mariana; Flores, Z.; & Lara, Marta Yolanda. 1966. Food intake of Guatemalan Indian children ages 1-5. JADA 48: 480-487.

2690.   Flores, Mariana, Flores Z.; & Meneses, Berta. 1957. [Estudios de habitos dieteticos en poblaciones de Guatemala. [Studies of dietary habits in Guatemalan populations.] AVN 8: 57-82.

2691.   Flores, Mariana & Garcia, B. 1960. The nutritional status of children of pre-school age in the Guatemalan community of Amatitlan. Part 1. Comparison of family and child diets. BJN 14: 207-215.

2692.   Flores, Marina; Garcia B.; & Gularte, Y. 1963. Food habits in Guatemala. 11. Livingston. AVN 13: 61-83.

2693.   Flores, Mariana; Garcia, Berta; Flores, Zoila; & Lara, Marta Yolanda. 1964. Annual patterns of family and children's diet in three Guatemalan Indian communitieis. BJN 18: 281-293.

Survey of food consumption and nutrient intake in highland Guatemalan-Maya towns: Santa Catarina Barahona, Santa Maria Caugue, and Santa Cruz Balanya. Major deficiencies are of Vitamin A, riboflavin, and calcium.

2694.   Flores, Mariana; Meneses, Berta; Flores, Zoila; & Leon, Marta de. 1956. Estudios de habitos dieteticos en pobliaciones de Guatemala. [Study of dietary habits in Guatemalan populations.] OSP-B 40: 504-520.

Food habits: pp. 509-510.

2695.   Flores, Mariana & Reh, Emma. 1955. Estudios de habitos dieteticos en poblaciones de Guatemala. [Study of dietary habits in Guatemalan populations.[Part One. Magdalena Milpas Alta. OSP-B Supp. No. 2. Pp. 90-128. Part Two. Santo Domingo Xencoj. Pp. 129-148. Part Three. San Antonio Aguas Calientes y su aldea San Andreas se ballos. Pp. 149-162. Part Four. Santa Maria Cauque. Pp. 163-173.

2696.   Florez C., Aurora. Adjusting theory to the community: 1. The implementation of an early childhood stimulation program for children at risk of malnutrition in southern barrios of Colombia. Paper presented at 73rd Annual Meeing of the American Anthropological Association. 19 to 24 November, 1974. Mexico City.

2697.   Florez, Luis. 1948. Alimentacion en Coyaima, Tolima. [Food habits in Coyaima, Tolima.] Colombia. RF 1: 173-229.

Gives background notes on the area. Describes typical foods, mealtime hours, and menus. Also includes special foods, drinks, condiments, and beliefs and verses related to food.

2698.   Flowers, Michelle. Breakfast for children. Paper presented at 69th Annual Meeting of the American Anthropological Association. 19 to 22 November, 1970. San Diego, California.

2699.   Fogelman, Billye Y.S. Nutrition and American medicine. Paper presented at 76th Annual Meeting of the American Anthropological Association. 29 November to 3 December, 1977. Houston, Texas.

It is recognized that the etiology of many diseases can be attributed to nutritional deficiencies. Accompanying this knowledge is a re-examination of the role of nutrition in medical school curricula. This on-going research project is aimed at compiling, for the first time, nationwide data on the extent of nutritional training of physicians currently in practice and the extent to which those physicians have integrated nutritional concepts into their practice. Such data will be valuable in planning future medical school curricula and post-graduate seminars and in identifying factors associated with the degree of integration of nutritional concepts into a physician's practices.

2700.   Fogerty, A.P. The biscuit and confectionery industry in New Zealand. Master's thesis. Economics. Auckland University. 1939.

2701.   Fohn-Hansen, L. 1956. The hunter returns with the kill. UAlas-EB 41.

Preparation and cookery of wild game.

2702.   Fokker. 1879. Have drugs a direct influence on nutrition? BMJ 2: 465.

Concludes drugs do not affect nutrition. Rejects the pharmacodynamic systems of Kohler and Rabuteau.

2703. Folan, William J. The community, settlement and subsistence patterns of Nootka Sound area: a diachronic model. Ph.D. dissertation. Anthropology. Southern Illinois University. Carbondale. 1972.

2704. Follett, W.I. 1967. Fish remains from coprolites and midden deposits at Lovelock Cave, Churchill County, Nevada. In Papers on Great Basin archeology. UCal AS No. 70. UCARF. Pp. 93-115.

Material analyzed is estimated to date at ca. A.D. 1000 to A.D. 1500. Evidence indicates the used of small minnows (Gila bicolar); and cui-ui [Chasmistes cujus] probably transported from some distance. No evidence was found indicating use of trout.

2705. Fonssagrives, Jean Baptiste. 1861. Hygiene alimentaire des malades, des convalescents et des valetudinaires; ou de regine envisage comme moyen therapeutique. [Alimentary hygiene for the sick, convalescent and invalids; or diet as a form of therapy.] Paris: J.-B. Bailliere.

2706. Food and Agriculture Organization of the United Nations. 1948-1950. Classified catalogue of the Library of the International Institute of Agriculture. 4 vols. Rome: Food and Agriculture Organization of the United Nations.

2707. Food and Agriculture Organization of the United Nations. 1953. Maize and maize diets. Rome: Food and Agriculture Organization of the United Nations.

2708. Food and Agriculture Organization of the United Nations. 1959. Tabulated information on tropical and sub-tropical grain legumes. Plan Production and Protection Division. Rome: Food and Agriculture Organiation of the United Nations.

Includes plants used as human food.

2709. Food and Agriculture Organization of the United Nations. 1962. Preparing cassava flour. FFHCN 3[13].

Illustration.

2710. Food and Agriculture Organization of the United Nations. 1964. Inter-African Conference on Food and Nutrition. Douala Cameroun. September 4-13, 1961. FAO Nutrition Meeting Report Series, No.33. Rome: Food and Agriculture Organization of the United Nations.

2711. Food and Agriculture Organization of the United Nations. 1964. Bibliography of food consumption surveys. Nutrition Division. Food Consumption and Planning Branch Rome: Food and Agriculture Organization of the United Nations.

Contains 118 entries.

2712. Food and Agriculture Organization of the United Nations. 1965. Bibliography of food consumption surveys. Supplement. Nutrition Division. Food Consumption and Planning Branch. Rome: Food and Agriculture Organization of the United Nations.

2713. Food and Agriculture Organization of the United Nations. 1966. The soul of rice. FFHCN 7: 11-14.

Customs and beliefs relating to rice.

2714. Food and Agriculture Organization of the United Nations. 1976. Methodology of nutritional surveillance. Report of a joint FAO/UNICEF/WHO expert committee. Technical Report Series No. 593. Geneva: World Health Organization.

An outgrowth of the World Food Conference (Rome 1974). Considered information essential for the design of a nutrition surveillance system (who, when, where, why), and the data sources already available for nutritional surveillance. Indicators for nutritional surveillance are considered, both predictive and indicators of nutritional outcome. Basic practical principles for the planning and development of the nutritional surveillance system are presented. Recommendations for future research and for implementation of national and international nutrition surveillance systems are included. [After Foster. 1978. P. 53.]

2715. Foote, A.W. 1867. On the form of depraved appetite known as pica. DQJMS 43: 306-313.

2716. Forbes, Jack D. 1963. Indian horticulture west and northwest of the Colorado river. J West 2: 1-14.

Covers Paiute, Vanyume, Cahuilla, Kamia, and Yuki tribes, and northern Baja California; Los Angeles basin; San Joaquin, and Willamette valleys. Source materials include manuscripts, diaries, and local histories.

2717. Forbes, Hamish A. From ox to equine: ploughing techniques and population pressure in modern Greece and medieval northwest Europe. Paper presented at 74th Annual Meeting of the American Anthropological Association. 2 to 6 December, 1975. San Francisco, California.

2718. Forbes, Mari H. Clark. Wild herbs in the market place: economic success or ecological threat? Paper presented at 74th Annual Meeting of the American Anthropological Association. 2 to 6 December, 1975. San Francisco, California.

2719. Forbes, Mari H. Clark. Farming and foraging in prehistoric Greece: the nutritional ecology of wild resource use. In Nutrition and anthropology in action. Edited by Thomas K. Fitzgerald. 1976. Pp. 46-61. Assen, Amsterdam: Van Gorcum.

Based on contemporary ethnographic observations on the peninsula of Methana, in the eastern portion of the Greek Argolid (located at approximately 37. 35N, 23. 23. E), an extrapolation is made to possible wild plant and animal use in the area, using as comparative data the archeological record for Franthi Cave, the only excavated Neolithic site in the area. Ecological, seasonal, organizational, nutritional, and technological considerations relating to wild food exploitation are made concerning contemporary populations and on this basis potential conditions posited for the Franthi site populations of Mesolithic and early Neolithic times.

2720.   Forbes, R.H. 1921. Moki lima beans. SAS-TS-B 9: 1-22.

Development of a new commercial variety derived from a variety grown by the Hopi.

2721.   Forbes, W.A.   1963.   De oudhollandsche Keuken.   [Old Dutch cooking.]   Bussum, Netherlands: C.J.A. van Dishoeck.

2722.   Forbes, W.A.   1965.   De antieke Keuken. [Ancient cookery.]   Bussum, Netherlands: C.A.J. van Dishoeck.

2723.   Forbis, Stephen D. The relative importance of the buffalo and corn among certain riverine Plains Indians.   Master's thesis.   Anthropology. Austin, Texas: University of Texas. 1976.

2724.   Ford, Findlay J.   1958.   Infant-feeding in South Africa. QRP 13: 245-249.

2725.   Forde, C. Daryll.   1931.   Hopi agriculture and land ownership. GB-RAIGBI-J 61: 357-405.

2726.   Forder, Archibald.   1912.   Chapter Two. Bread baking and cooking. In Daily life in Palestine. London: Marshall Brothers.

2727.   Forman, Martin J. 1973. Planning national nutrition programs: a suggested approach.   Vol. One.   Summary of the methodology.   Office of Nutrition. Bureau for Technical Assistance. Washington, D.C. Agency for International Development. January.

2728.   Formisano, M. 1957-1958. Contribution to the knowledge of fermented milk drinks [second note]. [In Italian.] UNap-FSA-A 23: 63-94.

Summary in English.

2729.   Forien de Rochesnard, Jean-George. 1949. Histoire du rationnement alimentaire au cours des ages. [History of food rationing through the ages.] Auxerre: Imprimerie Moderne.

2730.   Forni, Gaetano. The origin of grape wine: a problem in historical-ecological anthropology. Gastronomy. The anthropology of food and food habits. Edited by Margaret Louise Arnott. 1975. Pp. 67-78. Paris, The Hague: Mouton Publishers. World Anthropology.

Hypothesizes that fermented beverages had their beginnings in the temporary storage of sugary saps of plants the sprout ends of which were cut to obtain the exudate. With the development of storage techniques and sedentary life styles, longer storage and preservation became possible.

2731.   Forot, Charles. 1964. Odeurs de foret et fumets de table. [Forest odors and table aromas.] Saint Felicien: Le Pigeonnier.

The region in France called Vivarais [formerly Languedoc].

2732.   Forrest, Denys Mostyn. 1973. Tea for the British: the social history and economic history of a famous trade. London: Chatto & Windus.

2733.   Forsman, John. 1972. Recipe index, 1970; the eater's guide to periodical literature. Detroit: Gale Research Co.

2734.   Forster, Robert & Ranum, Orest, eds. 1975. Food and drink in history. Selections from "Annales, Economies, Societies, Civilisations".   Baltimore: Johns Hopkins Press.

2735.   Forster, Ruth Heywood. A study of the dietary habits of the people of the United States Virgin Islands in the low income group with a view towards an improved program in these habits. Master's thesis. Washington, D.C.: Howard University. 1957.

2736.   Fortes, Meyer & Fortes, Sally L. 1936. Food in the domestic economy of the Tallensi. Africa 9: 237-276.

2737.   Fortune, Roger. 1961. Les bons plats chez nous. [Our tasty foods.] Rev Guad No. 45. Pp. 27-29.

French West Indies.

2738.   Fosberg, F.R. 1960. Plant collecting as an anthropological field method. El Pal 67: 125-139.

Detailed description of nature of herbarium specimens, their selection, collecting and processing equipment, recording data, pressing plants, drying, storage, shipping, botanical identification. Also included is a list of major herbaria in the United States, and list of basic plant collecting equipment.

2739.   Foster, George Mc Lelland. 1948. Empire's children, the people of Tzintzuntzan. SI-IS-P No. 6.

Foods, and food categories [hot-cold]: pp. 48-52.

2740.   Foster, George Mc Clelland. 1960. Public health and behavioral science: the problem of teamwork. AJPH 51: 1286-1291.

Mutual understanding of disciplinary value systems, and sharing of research methodologies and goals are emphasized.

2741.   Foster, George Mc Clelland. Social anthropology and nutrition of the pre-school child especially as related to Latin America. In Pre-school child malnutrition. Primary deterrent to human progess. An international conference on prevention of malnutrition in the pre-school child. December 7-11, 1964. Washington, D.C. National Academy of Sciences-National Research Council. 1966. Pp. 258-266. Publication 1282. Washington, D.C.: National Academy of Sciences - National Research Council.

Reviews the socio-anthropological characteristics of peasant society; particular reference follows to food behavior in the Mexican town of Tzintzuntzan, and the social function of food elsewhere in Latin America. The relationship of food to health and illness is examined, followed by recommendations for anthropological considerations in nutrition-oriented program planning.

2742. Foster, George Mc Clelland. 1967. The Institute of Anthropology of the Smithsonian, 1943-1952. Ann Ind 27: 173-192.

Describes the program, and U.S. personnel associated with its field projects.

2743. Foster, George Mc Clelland & Anderson, Barbara Gallatin. Chapter Fifteen. Anthropology and nutrition In Medical anthropology. 1978. Pp. 263-279.

Food symbolism in language: pp. 270-271.

2744. Foster, Phillips. 1978. Agricultural policies and rural malnutrition. Occasional Paper No. 7. Technical Assistance Bureau. Office of Agriculture. Economics and Sector Planning Division. Washington, D.C.: United States [Department of State]. Agency for International Development. February.

An annotated bibliography concerned with the impacts of agricultural policies and programs on the nutrition of the rural poor in least developed countries. The literature survey includes material on the relation between malnutrition and poverty; the economic implications of malnutrition, and the controversy over food quantity vs. food quality (protein-calorie controversy).

2745. Fouchard, Jean. 1955. Les joies de la table a Saint-Domingue. [The pleasures of the table at Santo-Domingo.] SHHGG-R 27: 59-63.

Data from historical documents on food and drink in colonial Haiti, chiefly Eighteenth Century.

2746. Fouque, A. 1972. Essai sur la consommation des Indiens de la zone forestiere en Guyane Francaise. [Essay on the food intake of Indians in the forest zone of French Guiana.] FO-M 27: 51-58.

2747. Fournel, Victor. 1858. Ce qu'on voit dans les rues de Paris. [What one sees in the streets of Paris.] Paris: Adolphe Delahays.

Includes a chapter on wine merchants, cafes and restaurants.

2748. Fournie, E. 1934. Native children of American countries and work being done for them; resume of answers to questionnaire. [In Spanish.] IIAPI-B 8: 113-263.

2749. Fowler, Bertram, Baynes. 1952. Men, meat and miracles. New York: Julian Messner.

History of United States meat industry.

2750. Fowler, Don D., & Fowler, Catherine S., eds. 1971. Anthropology of the Numa: John Wesley Powell's manuscripts on the Numic peoples of Western North America, 1868-1880. SI-CA No. 14.

Means of subsistence: pp. 39-49. Plant foods are considered at length, particularly the technology involved in seed gathering and preparation. Storage, and cooker techniques are described, as are the sources of animal protein. Suicide by starvation among old women considered meritorious: p. 61.

2751. Fowler, Henry W. 1955. Archaeological fish bones collected by E.W. Gifford in Fiji. BPBM-B No. 214.

2752. Fowler, Melvin L. Cultivated fields of the Mississippian tradition, eastern North America. Paper presented at 67th Annual Meeting of the American Anthropological Association. 21 to 24 November, 1968. Seattle, Washington.

Aerial photography has revealed areas of Middle Mississippian sites that can be interpreted as prehistoric cultivated fields, an interpretation verified by the distribution of artifacts such as flint hoes and house locations. The discovery of similar fields and houses under a mound at the Macon Plateu of Georgia confirms this interpretation. It is proposed that this type of ridge field system was used to reclaim low-lying riverbottom land and may have been a technological innovation that made possible the rapid expansion of population in Middle Mississippian times and the establishment of agriculture as the dominant subsistence base in the eastern United States.

2753. Fowler, W. Warde. 1965. Social life at Rome in the age of Cicero: London: Macmillan; New York: St. Martin's Press.

Food: pp. 270-271.

2754. Fox, Francis William. 1934. Diet in relation to health in South Africa. Biochemical aspect. SAMJ 8: 3-15. 13 January.

2755. Fox, Francis William. 1936. Diet and health in South Africa. SAMJ 10: 25-36.

2756. Fox, Francis William. 1939. Bantu studies. Some Bantu recipes from the eastern Cape. Johannesburg: University of the Witwatersrand Press.

2757. Fox, Francis William. 1939. Nutritional problems amongst the rural Bantu. R Rel 6: 5-7.

2758. Fox, Francis William. 1939. Some nutritional problems amongst the Bantu in South Africa. SAMJ 13: 87-95.

2759. Fox, Francis William. Nutritionalists and the food chain. SAMJ 41: 1232-1237.

2760. Fox, Francis William & Stone, W. 1938. The anti-scorbutic value of Kaffir beer. SAJMS 3: 7-14.

A beer brewed from maize.

2761. Fox, H. 1958. The composition of food stuffs commonly used in Jamaica. WIMJ 7: 84-92.

2762. Fox, James J. 1977. Harvest of the palm. Cambridge, Massachusetts & London: Harvard University Press.

A study of the subsistence economies of the islands of the Outer Arc of the Lesser Sunda group (Timor, located at approximately between 10.3 5. and 9.0 S and 123.0 E and 127. 50E; Sumba, at approximately 10. 25S and 9. 25, and 119. 15E and 121. 0E; Roti, located immediately southeast of Timor, and Savu at approximately 10. 40S and 121. 15E). The populations of Roti and Savu depend heavily upon the lontar palm [Borassus sundaicus] for food and feed, supplement this source with swine husbandry, fishing, and gardening. The peoples of Timor and Sumba are Swidden agriculturalists. Utilization of B. Sundaicus is described, and compared with two other economies focussing on Borassus sp. i.e. the island of Madura at approximately between 7. 0S and 7. 10S, and 112. 45E and 114. 2E; and Sri Lanka.

2763. Fox, R.H. A study of the energy expenditure of Africans engaged in various rural acitivies; with special reference to some environmental and physiological factors which may influence the efficiency of their work. Ph.D. dissertation. University of London. 1953.

Considers the relationship, between energy expenditure in agricultural tasks (ridging land, planting peanuts, clearing land, weeding, and hoeing) and food intake in Genieri, a village in the Kiang East District, The Gambia. Seasonal food scarcity and energy expenditure are examined in connection with food intake and deficits. Genieri is primarily a millet and rice growing village, where slash and burn agriculture is practiced.

2764. Frajlich, Harvey. The marked bean motif in pre-Colombian Peru. Master's thesis. Anthropology. Hunter College of the city of New York. 1968.

2765. Franca, Eduardo Ferreira. Essai sur l'influence des aliments et des boissons sur le moral de l'homme. [Essay on the influence of foods and beverages on man's morals]. Thesis. Faculte de Medecin de Paris. 1834.

Portuguese translation by Joao Ferreire de Bittencourt e Sa. 1851. A influença dos alimentos e das bebidas sobre o moral do Homen. Bahia, Brasil.

2766. France, 1546. Edict du roy nostre sire sur les vivres que les hosteliers, faverniers et cabaratiers vendront aux passans et repassans. [Decree by the King our Lord concerning the groceries sold by inn-keepers, tavern owners, and cabaret-men to passers-by.] Paris: No publisher cited.

2767. France. 1564. Declaration de Roy pour l'obseration et entetenement de son ordonnance faicte sur le reglement des hosterliers, taverniers, et cabaretiers. [Proclamation by the King regarding the observation and support of his Order made on regulations relating to inn-keepers, tavern-proprieters and cabaret-owners.] Paris: Robert Estieen.

2768. France. 1962. Declaration du Roy, portant reunion a la communaute de maistres vinaigriers, moutardiers, distillateurs en eau-de-vie et esprit de vin, des Offices de Jurez de la dite communaute, creez par Edit du mois de mars 1691. Donnee au camp devant Namur, le 4 juin 1692. [Proclamation by the King, bringing together the cooperation of master vinegar-makers, mustard-makers, brandy and liqueur-distillers, with the foremen of said community, done by Edict of the month of March, 1961. Published at the encampment in front of Namur, 4 June, 1692..] Paris: Estienne Michallet, premier Imprimeur du Roy.

2769. France. 1964. Edits et reglements pour la communaute des cent cinquante marchands privilligiez de cidre et poire en gros et en detail de cette ville. [Edicts and regulations for the corporation of one hundred and fifty licensed wholesale and retail cider and fermented pear-nectar merchants in this city.] Rouen: Julien Courant.

2770. France. 1729. Declaration du Roy portant suppression des droits qui se percoivent aux entrees de Paris sur les oeufs, beurres et fromages. Donne a Versailles le 22 mars 1729. Registree en parlement. [Proclomation by the King cancelling the tax collected at the gates of Paris, upon eggs, butter and cheese. Published at Versailles, 22 March, 1729. Registered in Parliament.] No place of publisher cited.

2771. France. 1733. Declaration du Roy concernant les cafez provenant des plantations et cultures de la Martinique et autres isles francoises de l'Amerique y denommes. [Declaration by the King concerning coffee originating from plantations of Martinique and other French islands of America there named.] No place or publisher cited.

2772. France. Cooperation (Ministere). 1961. Les poissons de fleuve dans l'ouest africain. [River fish in West Africa.] Paris: Imprimerie Servant-Crouzet.

2773.   France. Ministere de la Guerre. Direction des Affaires de l'Algerie. 1855. Catalogue explicatif et raisonne de 1 exposition permanente des produits de l'Algerie....suivi du catalogue methodique des produits algeriens a l'Exposition Universelle de Paris, en 1855. [Explanatory and descriptive catalogue of the regular exhibit of Algerian products...followed by the systematic catalogue of Algerian products at the Paris World's Fair, in 1855.] Paris: Imprimerie de F. Didot.

Contains a classified and annotated list of useful plants.

2774.   France. Ministere de la Marine et des Colonis. 1886. Les plantes utiles des colonis francaises. [Useful plants of the French colonies.] Edited by Jean Marie Antoine de Lanessan. Bibliotheque biologique international. Paris: Imprimerie National.

2775.   Francis, Clarence A. 1937. A history of food and its preservation, a contribution to civilization, an address delivered before Princeton University on March 9, 1937, in the Cyrus Fogg Brackett lectureship in applied engineering and technology. Princeton, New Jersey: the Guild of Brackett Lecturers.

An account of the latest development in food preservation (quick frozen Birds Eye foods).

2776.   Francis, F.J. The relationship of color to food acceptability. Paper presented at Third international congress of food science and technology. 9 August to 14 August, 1970. Washington, D.C.

2777.   Franco, Guilherme; Berger, Osmar Neves; & Carvalho, Maria da Concecao. 1958. A jabuticaba, composicao quimica e valor nutricional. [Jabuticaba, chemical composition and nutritive value.] Estudo e Pesquisa Alimentar No. 40. Rio de Janeiro: Servico de Alimentacao de Previdencia Social.

Fruit of Myrciaria sp.

2778.   Frank, Tenney. 1933-1940. An economic survey of ancient Rome. 4 vols. Baltimore: Johns Hopkins Press.

2779.   Franke, Paul R. & Watson, Don. 1936. An experimental corn field in Mesa Verde National Park. In Symposium on prehistoric agriculture. UNM-B No. 296. AS 1(5): 35-41.

The field was planted to provide visitors with an actual example of the way in which Native American maize was produced without irrigation. The Park is located in Colorado, due west of the town of Durango, adjacent to the Utah State line.

2780.   Frankle, Reva T. & Heussanstam, F.K. 1974. Food zealotry and youth: new dilemmas for professionals. AJPH 64: 11-18.

Reviews contemporary non-standardized dietaries: vegetarianism; emphasis on un-refines foods, grown without industrial fertilizers; and the macrobiotic diet, based on theories propounded by George Ohsawa. The social and psychological environment is examined which has generated interest in these regiments. Suggestions are included for nutrition education approaches useful in working with persons who may have suffered nutritionally from following non-scientific diets.

2781.   Franklin, Alfred, editor. 1874. Les rues et les cris de Paris au 13e siecle, pieces historigues publiees d'apres les manuscrits de la Bibliotheque Nationale et precedees d'une etude sur les rues de Paris au 13e siecle. [The streets and cries of Paris of the 13th Century, historical pieces published on the basis of manuscripts in the Bibliotheque Nationale, and preceded by a study of the streets of Paris.] Paris: Willem; Paul Daffis.

Among the street cries mentioned are those of the pastry, anise, wine, and cress sellers; onion, prune, and herring vendors.

2782.   Frankowski, Eugenjusz. La Lagenaria vulgaris s. et son importance pour la culture humaine. [Lagenaria vulgaris S. and its importance in human culture.] In 15e Congres International d'Anthropologie & d'Archeologie Prehistorique. 21-30 Septembre 1930. Coimbre & Porto, Portugal. Actes du Congres. 1931. Pp. 639-646. Paris: Librairie E. Nourry.

Use as food: p. 641.

2783.   Frankul, W., & Pellet, P.L. 1959. The nutritive value of Kushak, an Iraqi fermented milk-wheat product. PNS 18:xxxvi-xxxvii. (Abstract.)

2784.   Fransisco, Anacleto, D. 1930. Analysis and food value of some unusual Philippine fruits. PJS 43:655-663.

2786.   Fraser, Agnes, R. 1932. The teaching of health to African Women. London: Longmans, Green.

Includes a section on nutrition education.

2787.   Fraser, Henry Malcolm. 1931. Beekeeping in antiquity. London: University of London Press.

2788.   Fraser, Henry Malcolm. 1958. History of beekeeping in Britain. London: Bee Research Association.

2789.   Fraser, John. 1978. Delights of East Wind Market. China turns to convenience foods. SFChron 30 August. P. 10.

Describes the Market's four eating places, as well as the recent availability of Western-style leavened bread, in Peking.

2790.   Fratto, Toni. 1970. Cooking in red and white. PFolk 19:2-15.

Interviews with first and second generation Italian-Americans regarding food habits and food preparation techniques.

2791. Frayser, Mary E. 1929. Children of pre-school age in selected areas of South Carolina. SC-AES-B No. 260.

Investigation was carried out in Beaufort, Dillon, Greenville, and Richland Counties. An extensive review of children's dietary habits, and nutritional status is contained on pp. 28-74.

2792. Frayser, Mary E. & Moser, Ada M. 1930. The diet of school children in relation to their health. (A study of rural children eight, nine, and ten years of age in Laurens County, South Carolina). SC-AES-B No. 268.

Includes data on food preparation equipment; food supply, infant feeding; school lunches, home meals; a qualitative nutritional evaluation of food intake concludes the study.

2793. Frazer, James George & Achariyar, K.R. 1919. Milk customs of the Todas. Man 19:43-46.

India.

2794. Frazier, Ripple Pauline. A suggested method of compiling a modern cookbook. Master's thesis Denton: Texas State College for Women. 1948.

2795. Frederick, Justus George. 1935. The Pennsylvania Dutch and their cookery. Their history, art, accomplishments, also a broad collection of their food recipes. New York: Business Bourse.

Cookery section reprinted as Pennsylvania Dutch cookbook. New York: Dover Publications. 1971.

2796. Frederikson, J.D. 1925. The story of cheese; a short treatise on the manufacture of various kinds of domestic and foreign cheese. Little Falls, New York: Hansen's Laboratory.

2797. Freedman, J.D. Social factors in the etiology of infantile pluricarencial syndrome (kwashiorkor) in Guatemala. Mimeographed. World Health Organization Report No. 13. 1957.

2798. Freedman, Robert Louis. 1968. Wanted: a journal in culinary anthropology. CAnth 9(1)62,63.

Brief review of a variety of articles on human food habits. Suggests the possibility of a publication for reporting data on anthropological aspects of food preparation.

2799. Freedman, Robert Louis. 1971. Directions in food habits research. EScan 1971. Pp. 37-40.

Suggests areas for investigation including little-known food plants; food uses of medicinal plants; and coordination of unedited manuscript and archival material relating to food uses.

2800. Freedman, Robert Louis. 1971. The state of food habits research in the United States of America. BBAA 33-34:167-193.

A chronological, topical bibliography of anthropological and related food habits studies, covering pre-Columbian periods through the Twentieth Century.

2801. Freedman, Robert Louis, comp., ed. 1972. Famine foods. Little-known food-plant resources. A monograph. Berkeley, California: the author.

A listing of nine hundred seventy food plants used primarily during times of famine and scarcity. Latin and vernacular names, as well as part of plant used and method of preparation are given. Also included are chemical analyses and nutritional values of the plants, where this information is available. Plants are arranged according to Western botanical nomenclature, by family, genus, and species.

2802. Freedman, Robert Louis. 1973. Nutrition problems and adaptation of migrants in a new cultural environment. IMig 11:15-31.

A study of the physiological and psychological effects of dietary acculturation among migrating peoples throughout the world. Reviews the relevant literature in nutrition, international migration, anthropology, public health, sociology, psychology and physiology.

2803. Freedman, Robert Louis. 1974. Nutrition and anthropology: each can help the other. CNI-WR 4(3):3-6.

Discusses the complementary roles of these two disciplines and reviews university courses in which the cultural and social dimensions of human food behavior are studied. Comments on the need for health professionals concerned with applied nutrition to understand the significance of the cultural meanings of food in different ethnic groups.

2804. Freedman, Robert Louis. Nutritional anthropology: an overview. In Nutrition and anthropology in action. Edited by Thomas K. Fitzgerald. 1976. Pp. 1-23. Assen, Netherlands: Van Gorcum.

Reviews historical relationships between anthropology and nutrition. Cases studies of applied nutrition incorporating an anthropological component are synopsized. Other significant reports in the literature are also reviewed.

2805.   Freedman, Robert Louis. 1978. Review of recently published work dealing with nutrition research in Mainland China. WRND 30:1-22.

Review of the literature available in English or in English translation reporting on pure and applied research in the Peoples Republic of China since 1950.

2806.   Freeman, D. 1970.   Report on the Iban. London School of Economics Monographs on Social Anthropology No. 41. London: Athlone Press.

Account of Iban Bilek dry rice cultivation in Rumah Nyala (Baleh Region, Sarawak). The nutrition survey component included measurement of the amount of rice cooked for each meal, and an estimation of left-over food, among five families. Response to periods of food shortage, and use of paddy rice in religious function are described. [After Schofield. 1975:193.]

2807.   Freeman, George F. 1912.   Southwestern beans and teparies. Ariz-AES-B No. 68.

2808.   Freeman, George F. 1913. The tepary, a new cultivated legume from the Southwest. BG 56:395-417.

Distinction between legume types among Native Americans, and Mexicans in Arizona, and northern Mexico: p. 397; Papago, and Yaqui terms for beans: pp. 397-398; food use of teparies among Mexicans and Native Americans: pp.414-415.

2809.   Freeman, George F. 1915.   Papago sweet corn, a new variety. Ariz-AES-B No. 75.

2810.   Freeman, J.G. 1922.   The introduction of breadfruit into the West Indies. TT-DA-B 19:224-249.

Artocarpus incisa, L.

2811.   Freeman, J.G. & Williams, R.O. 1928. The useful and ornamental plants of Trinidad and Tobago. TT-DA-M. No. 4

2812.   Freeman, Margaret B. 1943. Herbs for the medeival household for cooking, healing and divers uses. New York: Metropolitan Museum of Art.

Herbs for cooking: pp. 1-16.

2813.   Freiday, Dean. 1939. The story of coffee. NH 44: 281-287.

Popular artical; undocumented.

2814.   French, Cornelia. 1914. A comparison of methods of cooking. JHE 6: 131-135.

Fireless cookery. Extract of the author's thesis for the Senior Normal Work, School of Household Science and Arts, Pratt Institute. (1913).

2815.   French, M.H. 1936. Some observations of the methods of making clarified butter (ghee) with some notes on a new method. GB-II-B 34: 32-44. Also in MBET No. 8. Pp. 345-353 as: "La methode de fabrication du beurre clarifie." [1936].

2816.   French, M.H. 1936-1937. Some notes on the common foodstuffs used in the diets of East African natives. EAMJ 13: 374-378.

2817.   French, Richard Valpy. 1884. Nineteen centuries of drink in England: a history. London: Longman's.

2818.   Freuchen, Dagmar, ed. 1961. Freuchen's book of the Eskimo. Cleveland, New York: World Publishing Co.

Eating and visiting: pp. 135-160.

2819.   Freyre, Gilberto. 1939. Asucar, algumas receitas de doces e bolos dos engenhos do nordeste. [Sugar, some recipes for confections and cakes from the sugar plantations of the northeast.] Rio de Janeiro: Jose Olympio.

2820.   Freyre, Gilberto. 1963. The mansions and the shanties. Translated by Harriet de Onis. New York: Alfred Knopf.

Brazilian food: 19th Century: pp. 118-122; 159-162; of slaves: pp. 130-131; 185-186.

2821.   Friedberg, Claudia. 1958-1959. Contribution a l'etude ethnobotanique des tombes precolombiennes de Lauri [Perou]. [Contribution to the ethnobotanic study of some precolumbian tombs of Lauri [Peru]. JATBA 5: 397-428; 6: 405-435.

2822.   Friederici, Georg. 1936. Die Susser-kartoffel in der Sudsee. [The sweet potato in the South Seas.] GV-M No. 7. Pp. 2-7.

2823.   Friedlander, Benedict. 1898. Notes on the palolo. JPS 7: 44-46.

The sea worm Palolo viridis, eaten in Samoa.

2824.   Friedman, Harriet U. Food supply and power relations: James Bay Cree and the Hudson's Bay Company. Paper presented at 73rd Annual Meeting of the American Anthropological Association. 19 to 24 November, 1974. Mexico City.

2825.   Friedmann. 1871. Der Anthropophagismus der Bataker auf Sumatras Westkuste. [Anthropophagy among the Batak, of the west coast of Sumatra.] ZE 3: 313-325.

2826.   Frikel, Protasio. 1968. Os Xikrin; equipamento e tecnicas de subsistencia. [Xikrin subsistence equipment and techniques.] MPEG-PA No. 7.

Brazil.

2827.   Frisch, Rose E. 1970. Present status of the supposition that malnutrition causes permanent mental retardation. AJCN 23: 189-195.

2828. Frishie, Theodore Robert. An archaeo-ethnologial interpretation of maize deity symbols in the greater Southwest. Ph.D. dissertation. Anthropology. Southern Illinois University. 1971.

Traces origin of maize ceremonialism, in Pueblo culture, which appeared in ca. A.D. 1000, to a hypothesized contact with Meso-american (Pochteca) group, which established an exploitative colony within Chaco Canyon, New Mexico.

2829. Frison, G.C. 1976. Cultural activity associated with prehistoric mammoth butchering and processing. Science 194: 728-730.

2830. Frissell, H.B. & Bevier, Isabel. 1899. Dietary studies of Negroes in eastern Virginia, 1897-1898. USDA-OES-B No. 71.

2831. Fritz, John M. The Hay Hollow site subsistence system: east central Arizona. Ph.D. dissertation. Anthropology. University of Chicago. 1974.

2832. Fritz, Martin F. 1934. A classified bibliography of psychodietetics. P Monog. 46. No. 206.

2833. Fritz, Martin F. 1935. The effect of diet on intelligence and learning. PB 32: 355-363.

Positive correlation concluded.

2834. Fromm-Reichmann, F. 1927. Jewish food ritual. Imago 13: 235-246.

2835. Fromshon, S.N.D. Charlotte. Rainfall and subsistence patterns: the Haya and Ankole. Master's thesis. Anthropology. Catholic University of America. 1973.

East and West Lacustrine Bantu. The Haya reside in Tanzaniz; the Ankole in Uganda.

2836. Froogatt, W.W. 1903. Insects used as food by the Australian natives. S Man 6: 11-13.

2837. Frost, J. 1826. Remarks on Phytolacca dodecandra, or the mustard tree of the Scriptures. QJS 20: 57-59.

2838. Frost, Joel & Payne, Billy L. 1969. Nutrition and intellectual growth in children. Washington, D.C.: Association for Childhood Education International.

2839. Fruitet, Edouard Irad. Le scorbut au penitencier depot de l'Ile Nou (Nouvelle-Caledonie). Scurvy in the penal settlement of Nour Island (New Caledonia). Medical dissertation. Academie de Montpellier.

2840. Fry, Gary Federick. Prehistoric diet at Danger Cave, Utah, as determined by the analysis of coprolites. Master's thesis. Anthropology. University of Utah. 1968.

2841. Fry, Gary Federick. Prehistoric human ecology in Utah; based on the analysis of coprolites. Ph.D. dissertation. Anthropology. University of Utah. 1970.

2842. Fry, Peggy Crooke. 1957. Dietary survey on Rarotonga, Cook Island. 1. General description, methods, and food habits. AJCN 5: 42-50.

Data on meal patterns, foods, and food habits in the villages of Arorangi (21. 13S, 159. 49) and Titikaveka (21. 16S, 159. 45W).

2843. Fry, Peggy Crooke. 1957. Dietary survey on Rarotonga, Cook Islands. 3. Feeding practices and growth of Rarotongan children from birth through six years. AJCN 5: 634-643.

Includes data on traditional and contemporary methods of infant feeding. Notes influence of European contact on infant feeding practices.

2844. Fuchs, Helmuth. La agricultura en la communidad indigena de Santa Clara de Aribi, [Carina]. Estado Anzoategui, Venezuela. [Agriculture in the native settlement of Santa Clara de Aribi, [Carina], Anzoategui State, Venezuela.] In 6e Congres International des Sciences Anthropologiques et Ethnologiques. 30 juillet - 6 aout 1960. Paris. Vol. 2. Ethnologie [Vol. 2]. 1964. Pp. 27-32. Paris: Musee de l'Homme.

Description of the detailed terminology of plants and soils, and cultivated fields, and of the elaborate planting calendar based on a chronology relating to rains, lunar phases, maturation time of plants, and topographic distribution of the fields.

2845. Fuchs, Stephen. 1960. Chapter Four. Food and Meals. In The Gond and Bhumia of eastern Mandla. New York, Bombay: Asia Publishing House.

Indian tribes of Madhya Pradesh.

2846. Fuente, Julio de la. 1945. Sobre nutricion y enfermedades de Indios. [On nutrition and infirmities of Indians.] Am Ind 5: 235-239.

2847. Fuhrmann, Franz. 1907. Uber yoghurt. ZUNG 13: 598-604. [On yoghurt.]

2848. Fuhse, F.L. Sitten and Gebrauch der Deutschen beim Essen und Trinken von den altesten Zeiten bis zum Schlusse des XI. Jahrhunderts. Eine germanistisch-antiquarische Abhandlung. [Manners and customs of the Germans relating to eating and drinking from ancient times to the close of the Eleventh Century. A Germanic-antiquarian essay.] Ph.D. dissertation. Georg-August-Universitat Zu Hamburg. 1898. Wolfenbuttel: Gedruck bei O. Wollerman. 1891. Leipzig: G. Fock. 1891.

2849. Fujioka, Ryoichi. 1973. Tea ceremony utensils. Translated by Louise Cort. Arts of Japan series. No. 3. New York: Weatherhill.

2850. Fulbert-Dumonteil, Jean Camille. 1900. Le cuisine francaise. L'art du bien manger. Fins et joyeux croquis gastronomiques, ecrits pour les gourmets. Annote et redige par Marie-Ernest-Edmond Richardin. [French cooking. The art of dining well.

Refined and pleasant gastronomic sketches, written by the gourmets. Annotated and edited by Marie-Ernest-Edmond Richardin. Paris: Nilsson.

Contains famous preparations from Parisian and Provincial restaurants, writers, and amateur chefs; local, old French recipes. Twelve hundred recipes collected and annotated by the editor.

2851. Funk, H.H. 1908. Some old time breakfast cakes. Penn Ger 9: 37.

Pennsylvania Dutch.

2852. Funnell, Esther H. An investigation of vitamin B and vitamin G values in some seeds used as food. Ph.D. dissertation. Columbia University. 1935.

2853. Furnas, Clifford Cook & Moore, Sparklee. 1937. Man, bread, and destiny. The story of man's food. New York: Reynal & Hitchcock.

2854. Furnas, Clifford Cook & Moore, Sparklee. 1942. The story of man and his food. New York: New Home Library.

2855. Furlow, Richard Harold. The diet and nutrition of North American and African tribes: a comparative study. Master's thesis. Indiana University. 1962.

2856. Furnivall, Frederick James. 1931. Early English meals and manners: John Russell's Boke of Nurture; Wynkyn de Worde's Boke of Keruynge; The Boke of Curtasye; R. West's Booke of Demeanor; Seager's Schoole of Vertue; The Babee's Book; Aristotle's ABC; Urbanitatis; Stans Puer ad Mensam; The Lytylle Childrene Lytil Boke; For to serve a Lord; Old early England. Original series 32. London: Early English Text Society.

2857. Furst, Peter T. 1968. The parching of the maize: an essay on the survival of Huichol ritual. AEL No. 14.

2858. Furst, Peter T. Ecology and nutrition in late pre-conquest central Mexico. Paper presented at 76th Annual Meeting of the American Anthropological Association. 29 November to 3 December, 1977. Houston, Texas.

Harner [1977] has hypothesized that Aztec human sacrifice, "disguised as ritual", was a function of protein starvation. Examination of the Sixteenth Century sources and recent nutritional studies fail to support: (1) Harner's estimate of the extent of sacrifice and his one-to-one equation of sacrifice with cannibalism; and (2) his view of Mesoamerican ecology and Aztec nutrition. Aztec food sources were rich and varied, adequately fulfilling needs for protein, essential vitamins, and minerals. His assertion of cannibalism as "the only possible solution" for the satisfaction of protein requirements is thus rendered invalid and, with it, his reduction of Aztec civilization to a "cannibal empire".

2859. Furst, Peter T. & Furst, Jill Leslie. The god in the flower: Blas Pablo Reko's contribution to Mesoamerican mythobotany. Paper presented at 75th Annual Meeting of the American Anthropological Association. 17 to 21 November, 1976. Washington, D.C.

Oaxacan botanical nomenclature and the cosmological, astronomical, and mythological associations of many plants of medicinal and ritual importance often correspond closely to those of Nahuatl and Maya-speakers. The late Pablo Blas Reko's work on Zapotec plant lore is reexamined and found to demonstrate a certain unity in Mesoamerican mythobotany, suggesting common roots and borrowing in early times.

2860. Furukawa, Y. 1904. Un note sur l'ame. [A note on ame.] Translated by S. Takaki. IB-B 3: 95-97.

A Japanese food indicated to be composed of a mixture of maltose and dextrin.

2861. Furuseth, Jr.; Owen J. Geophagy in eastern North Carolina. Master's thesis. Greenville, North Carolina: Eastern Carolina University. 1973.

2862. Fussell, G.E. 1953. Food manufacture under Elizabeth I. F Man 28: 227-229.

2863. Fussell, G.E. 1955. Old-time potted meats. F Man 30: 418.

England.

2864. Fussell, G.E. & Fussell, K.R. 1953. The English countrywoman; a farmhouse social history, A.D. 1500-1900. London: Melrose.

2865. Fyles, Faith. 1920. Wild rice. Can DA-B No. 4.

2866. Fysh, Catherine F.; Hodges, K.J.; & Siggins, Lorraine Y. Analysis of naturally-occurring foodstuffs in Arnhem Land. In Records of the American-Australian Scientific Expedition to Arnhem Land. Edited by Charles P. Mountford. Vol. 2. 1960. Pp. 136-143. Melbourne: Melbourne University Press.

2867. Gachot, Henri. 1955. Manuel des jus de fruits. [Manual of fruit juice.] Strasburg: P.-H. Heitz.

Includes historical information.

2868. Gade, Daniel W. 1967. The guinea pig in Andean folk culture. GR 57: 213-224.

2869. Gade, Daniel W. Plant use and folk agriculture in the Vilcanota Valley of Peru: a cultural-historical geography of plant resources. Ph.D. dissertation. Geography. University of Wisconsin, Madison. 1967.

2870. Gade, Daniel W. 1976. Horsemeat as human food in France. EFN 5: 1-11.

Documents the historical bases for acceptance of horse flesh as human food in France, and socio-economic contexts of its consumption. A very concise sketch of the demand, quality, use, and marketing.

2871.   Gade, G. 1971.   Grist milling with the horizontal water wheel in the central Andes.   Tech 12: 94-109.

2872.   Gagliano, Sherwood M.   Point Bar agriculture.   In Twenty-second Southeastern Archaeological Conference.   November 12-13, 1965.   Macon, Georgia. Proceedings. Edited by Bettye J. Broyles. 1967. Pp. 13-14. SAC-B No. 5.

Contains an excerpt from Page du Pratz Histoire de la Louisiane (Paris, 1758) Vol. 3. P. 9. conerning planting of wild rice by the Natchez and other groups.

2873.   Gai, B.M. 1956.   Wine in the Orient and its prohibition. I-I 9: 31-46.

2874.   Gaitan, Cloria & Gomez, Hernando. Adjusting theory to the community: 2. The implementation of a preschool program for malnourished children in barrios of Cali. Paper presented at 73rd Annual Meeting of the American Anthropological Association. 19 to 24 November, 1974. Mexico City.

2875.   Galan, P. 1951. Contribution a l'etude du probleme alimentaire au Hoggar. [Contribution to the study of the dietary problem at Hoggar.] IPA-A 29: 230-243.

Hoggar is a region in southern Algeria, close to the Mali, Niger border.

2876.   Galdston, Iago. 1952. Nutrition from the psychiatric viewpoint. JADA 28: 405-409.

2877.   Galdston, Iago, ed. 1960. Human nutrition: historic and scientific. New York: International Universities Press.

2878.   Galinat, Walton C. & Gunnerson, James H. 1963. Spread of eight-rowed maize from the prehistoric Southwest. HU-BML 20: 117-160.

2879.   Galinat, Walton C.; Mangelsdorf, Paul C.; & Pierson, L. 1956. Estimates of teosinte introgession in archaeological maize. HU-BML 19: 163-181.

2880.   Galinat, Walton C. & Rupe, Reynold J. 1961. Further archaeological evidence on the efforts of teosinte introgression in the evolution of modern maize. HU-BML 19: 163-181.

2881.   Galkin, V.A. 1961. Some features particular to the diet of the population of Yemen.   [In Russian.] VP 22: 82-83.

2882.   Gallahue, Edward E. 1946. The economy of the Mariana Islands. Economic study of Micronesia. Vol. Five. Honolulu: U.S. Commercial Company.

A post-World War II evaluation of islands formerly under Japanese administration. The survey was under the direction of Professor Douglas L. Oliver [cf. p. [vi]]. Native Chamorro foods are described on pp. 14-16, and 30-33. A sample list of foods provided to the population of Guam is given on pp. 105, 106.   These are all Western items. Cooking utensils are mentioned on p. 85, together with brief reference to methods of cooking.

2883.   Gallesio, Georges. 1811. Traite du citrus. [Treatise on citrus.] Paris: L. Fintin.

2884.   Gallez, A. 1960. Contribution a l'etude des populations indigenes congolaises en milieu sous-developpe. [Contribution to the study of indigenous Congolese populations in an underdeveloped area.] SBMT-A 40: 481-510.

Covers dietary habits of the Nkutshu and Binji groups, in the Belgian Congo.

2885.   Gallop, R.A. 1970. Redirecting food habits. A food scientist's viewpoint. CDA-J 31: 9-16.

2886.   Galutira, Ernesta C. & Velasquez, Gregorio T. 1963.   Taxonomy, distribution and seasonal occurrence of the edible marine algae in Ilocos Nortes, Philippines. PJS 92: 483-522.

2887.   Galvao, Henrique. 1947. Antropfagos. [Anthropoghages.] Lisbon: Editorial Jornal de Noticias.

2888.   Gamarra, Leonidas Cuentas. Impact of diet on morbidity and mortality patterns.   Paper presented at 77th Annual Meeting of the American Anthropological Association.   14 to 18 November, 1978. Los Angeles, California.

2889.   Gamble, D.P. Economic conditions in two Mandinka villages: Kerewan and Keneba. Mimeographed. Great Britain. Colonial Office. Research Department Report. London: Her Majesty's Stationery Office. 1955.

Kerwan and Keneba are two villages in the Gambia. Kerewan is located in Lower Baddibu, at 130. 29N, 16. 10W. Keneba is located in Western Kiang. A survey was made of lunches and dinners monthly throughout the year 1950-1951. Methods of food preparation and types of foods consumed are described. Of interest is the observation that diets improved during periods of food scarcity when wild leaves, seeds and roots were gathered.

2890.   Gamble, Sydney D. 1927-1928.   Human environments' food. PSNH-B 2: 13-15.

Note on causes of fluctuation in Peking food prices during the year 1924-1925.

2891.   Gamble, Sidney D. Chapter Four. Expenditure-Food. Chapter Five.   Food details.   In How Chinese families live in Peiping. A study of the income and expenditure of 283 Chinese families receiving from $8 to $550 silver per month. 1933. New York, London: Funk & Wagnals.

> Chapter Four is largely a comparative analysis of food expenditures by socio-economic levels. Chapter Five looks at prices and consumption trends of specific food types, i.e. grain, meat, vegetables, dairy products, condiments and fruit.

2892.   Gamerith, Anni. 1953. Bauerliche Tischsitten. [Peasant table customs.] NLGKGS 8: 240-244; 372-377.

2893.   Gamerith, Anni. 1954. Zwischenmahl-zeiten in Bauernhaus. [Between-meal times in farm homes.] NLGKGS 9: 121-124.

2894.   Gamerith, Anni. 1956. Lebendiges Ganzkorn. Neune Sicht Zur Getride frage gewonnen aus die Urwissen bauerliches Uberlieferung. [Live, whole grain. A new view on the cereal question gained from early traditional rural knowledge.] Bad Goisern, Austria: Verlag Neues Leben.

2895.   Gamerith, Anni. 1963. Die Nahrung des Stierischen Bauern. [Stiermark peasant dietary.] ZHVS 7: 80-90.

2896.   Gamerith, Anni. Feuerstatten bedingte Kochtechniken und Speisen. [Cooking on the hearth: techniques and foods.] Paper presented at First International Symposium on Ethnological Food Research 21 to 25 August, 1970. Lund: Folklivsarkivet, University of Lund.

2897.   Gamerith, Anni. Bericht uber den stand der Volksnahrungsforschung in Osterreich. [Report on the state of ethnographic food research in Austria.] Paper presented at First International Symposium in Ethnological Food Research. 21 to 25 August 1970. Lund: Folklivsarkivet, University of Lund.

2898.   Gamio, Manuel. 1948. Reforma de la dieta de Indios y Mestizos. [Dietary reform for Indians and Mestizos.] BInd 8: 186-195.

2899.   Gamio, Manuel. 1951. Introduccion de nuevos alimentos para complementar la dieta indigena. [Introduction of new foods to complement native diet.] Am Ind 11: 5-8.

2900.   Ganapin, J.G. 1962. The rice terraces of Bandwe. PFP 55: 28.

> Philippines.

2901.   Gandhi, Mohan Karamchand. 1949. Diet and diet reform. Ahmedabad: Navaijivan Publishing Co.

> Part One contains Gandhi's writings; Part Two contains writings by other authors.

2902.   Gandilhon, Rene. 1959. Le pain d epice de Rheims. [The spice bread of Rheims.] ATP 7: 20-50.

2903.   Gangulee, N. 1940. Bibliography of nutrition in India. Oxford: Humphrey Milford, Oxford University Press.

2904.   Gann, Thomas W.F. 1918. The Maya Indians of southern Yucatan and northern British Honduras. SI-BAE-B No. 64.

> Procuring food, cooking: Pp. 21-22; 34. Ritual foods in maize agricultural cycle celebration: Pp. 42-47.

2905.   Ganong, William Francis. 1910. The identity of the animals and plants mentioned by the early voyagers to eastern Canada and Newfoundland. RSC-PY 3 [series 3]: 197-242.

2906.   Ganora, R. 1930. Drinks and foods used by inhabitants of Yemen. [In Italian.] AISMC 11: 272-274.

2907.   Gantner, Teo. Essen und Trinken in Zeilung und Kalendern des 19. Jahrhunderts. Beispiel: Basel 1850. [Food and drink in newspapers and calendars in the Nineteenth Century. Example: Basel, 1850.] Paper presented at First International Symposium on Ethnological Food Research. 21-25 August, 1970. Lund: Folklivsarkivet. University of Lund.

2908.   Gantt, W.H. 1938. Extension of a conflict based upon food to other physiological systems and its reciprocal relations with sexual functions. AJP 123: 73-74.

2909.   Garb, J.C. & Stunkard, A.J. 1974. Taste aversions in man. AJPsy 131: 1204-1207.

2910.   Garber, Clark M. 1938. Eating with Eskimos. Hygeia 16: 242-245.

2911.   Garcia, Payon Jose. 1936. Amaxocoatl, o libro del chocolate. [Amaxocoatl, or the book of chocolate.] Toluca: Tipografia Escuela de Artes.

2912.   Garcia-Sabell, Domingo. 1966. Notas para una antropologia del hombre Gallego, [Notes toward an anthropology of the Gallicians.] Coleccion Iberica, 9. Madrid: Ediciones Peninsula.

> Contains an essay "Notas sobre el hambre Gallega" ["Notes on Gallician hunger"], which explores the physiological and psychological phenomena associated with hunger and starvation, both in Gallicia, and elsewhere. The section "Antropologia de hambre" ["Anthropology of hunger"] discusses starvation - with examples from the experimental literature, and from experiences of individuals interned in concentration camps during the World War II.

2913.   Gardeton, Cesar. 1825. Nouveau dictionnaire de menages, de sante, de cuisine et d economie. [New dictionary of householding, health, cookery and economy.] Paris: Corbet aine.

2914.   Gardeton, Cesar. 1826. Dictionnaire des alimens, precede d une hygiene des temperamens, de reflexions sur la digestion et les maladies de l'estomac. [Dictionary of foods, preceded by a hygiene of temperaments, reflections on digestion, and sickness of the stomach.] Paris: J.-J.-Nandin.

2915. Gardeton, Cesar. 1827. La gastronomie pour rire, ou anecdotes, reflexions, maximes et folies gourmandes sur la bonne chere...suivi de principes generaux de politesse. [Humorous gastronomy, or anecdotes, reflections, maxims, and gourmand follies of the good life... followed by general principles of good breeding.] Paris: J.-G. Dentu.

2916. Gardeton, Cesar. 1828. Le nouveau guide des dineurs, ou repertoire des restaurants - a l'usage des bon vivants. [New guide for diners, or repertoire of restaurants...for the use of bon vivants.] Paris: J. Breaute.

2917. Gardiner, L. 1898. Cakes and customs. ILN 113: 106.

2918. Gardiner, P.A. 1956. Observations on the food habits of myopic children. BMJ No. 4994. Pp. 699-700.

   Observed refusal of high protein sources among myopes.

2919. Gardner, Gail I. 1971. Ethnocuisine: cooking in a Dutch oven. Affword 1: 21-22.

   Sore-finger bread.

2920. Gardner, J.L. 1965. Native plants and animals as resources in arid lands of the Southwestern United States. AAAS-SRMD-CDAZR-C No. 8.

2921. Garelli, Guevara E. Los problemas de la alimentacion infantil en el medio rural. [The problem of infant diet in the rural millieu.] Thesis. Universidad Autonoma de Mexico. 1952.

2922. Garine, Igor de. Rapport sur les habitudes alimentaires dans la region de Khombole (Senegal). [Report on the food habits in Khombole Region (Senegal).] FAP Document 60149-60 MR. Rome: Food and Agriculture Organization of the United Nations. 1960.

2923. Garine, Igor de. Budgets familiaux et alimentation a Khombole (Senegal). [Family budgets and diet at Khombole (Senegal).] Report to the food and Agriculture Organization of the United Nations. Rome - Dakar. 1961.

2924. Garine, Igor de. 1962. Usages alimentaires dans le region de Khombole (Senegal). [Dietary practices in the Khombole region (Senegal).] CEAfr 3: 218-265.

2925. Garine, Igor de. 1964. Le Massa du Cameroun. Vie economique et sociale. [The Massa of Cameroon. Economic and social life.] Paris: Presses Universitaires de France pour l'Institut International Africain.

2926. Garine, Igor de. 1969. Pour une anthropologie de l' alimentation. [Toward an anthropology of food habits.] L' Homme 9: 125-126.

2927. Garine, Igor de. 1969. Socio-cultural aspects of food behaviour. Essay on classification of food prohibitions. In Food and Agriculture organization of the United Nations. Scientific, Technical, and Research Commission Report. No. 7 Pp. 3-20. Rome: Food and Agriculture Organization of the United Nations.

2928. Garine, Igor de. Food and nutrition in urban areas. Communication a la reunion de l'OMS sur les consequences sanitaires de l'urbanisation. [Communication at the meeting of the World Health Organization on the health consequences of urbanisation.] Document OMS/RECS/BHS/706. Geneva: World Health Organization. 1970.

2929. Garine, Igor de. Rapport sur les aspects socio-culturels de la transformation industrielle des mils au Niger. [Report on the socio-cultural aspects of the industrial processing of millet in Niger.] Rome: Food and Agriculture Organization of the United Nations. 1970.

2930. Garine, Igor de. 1971. Nutrition, culture et developpement. [Nutrition, culture and development.] FAO Review 4: 46-51.

2931. Garine, Igor de. 1972. The socio-cultural aspects of nutrition. EFN 1: 143-163.

   This article is an excellent introduction to the complex subject of the interrelationship between the qualitative and quantitative dimensions of human subsistence. The author touches on the major areas of cultural influence upon food-related behavior, with appropriate illustrative examples from his own ethnographic research, and from the wide literature relating to human food habits. A basic reading for students and professionals.

2932. Garine, Igor de. 1976. Le comportement alimentaire dans les pays non-industrialises. [Dietary behavior in non-industrialized countries.] ANA 30: 453-466.

2933. Garland, M.A., ed. 1931. From upper Canada to New York in 1835. Extracts from the diary of the Rev. Willliam Proudfoot. MVHR 18: 378-396.

   Native American toothpicks: p. 385.

2934. Garland, Robert F. 1979. Application of business science to the food industry. A case study. JIR 25(2): 7-9.

   A satire of consultancy, market research, and efficiency studies.

2935. Garn, Stanley M. 1966. Nutrition in physical anthropology. AJPA 24: 289-292.

2936. Garn, Stanley, M. Biological correlates of malnutrition in Man. In Nutrition, growth and development of North American Indian children. Based on a conference co-sponsored by the National Institute of Child Health and Human Development, Indian Health Service, American Academy of Pediatrics Committee on Indian Health. Edited by William M. Moore; Marjorie M. Silverberg; & Merrill S. Read. 1972. Pp. 129-138. Department of Health, Education, and Welfare. Publication No. (NIH) 72-26. Washington, D.C. Government Printing Office.

Included are sections on ecological and nutritional diversity in pre-European contact times; post-contact food acculturation and its presumptive relationship to new forms of malnutrition.

2937.   Garn, Stanley M. & Block, Walter D. 1970. The limited nutritional value of cannibalism. AA 72: 106-107.

2938.   Garner, Beatrice. Ute acculturation and dietary adaption. Master's thesis. Michigan State University. 1954.

2939.   Garneret, Jean. 1959. Un village Comptois-Lantenne, ses coutumes, son patois. [A Comptois-Lantenne village, its customs and vernacular.] Publication de l'Institut de Linguistique Romane de Lyon, Vol. 14. Paris: Societe de'Editions "Les Belles Lettres".

2940.   Garnet, J.R. 1968. Honeydew from Cymbidium canaliculatum (Orchidaceae). VNat 85: 165-166.

2941.   Garnier. 1942. Aliments crus chez les Bambara. [Raw foods among the Bambara.] NA No. 13. Pp. 18-19.

2942.   Garrett, Cheryl Ritenbaugh. An analysis of the distribution of diabetes mellitus among Pima Indians of central Arizona. Ph.D. dissertation. Anthropology. University of California, Los Angeles. 1974.

2943.   Garvan, John M. 1912. Report on drinks and drinking among the Mandaya, Manbo, and Mangguangan tribes. PJS 7: 106-114.

Philippines.

2944.   Gaskins, Ruth L. 1968. Introduction. In A good heart and a light hand. Ruth L. Gaskins' collection of traditional Negro recipes. Alexandria, Virginia: Fund for Alexandria. Reprint. New York: Simon & Schuster. 1968.

Traditional foods of southern Black Americans. Attitudes toward food, eating, and cookery.

2945.   Gassaway, Alexander Ramsey. The geography of food supply of Finnmark Fylke, northernmost Norway. Ph.D. dissertation. Geography. Worcester, Massachusetts: Clark University. 1971.

2946.   Gast, Marceau. 1963. Partage de la viande a Ideles. [Apportioning of meat at deles.] Libyca 11: 235-244.

Detailed account of the butchering of a camel, its ritual aspects, and distribution of the butchered parts. Ideles is located at 23.50N and 5.55E, in Algeria.

2947.   Gast, Marceau. 1968. Alimentation des populations de l' Ahaggar. Etude ethnographique. [Food habits of Ahaggar populations.] Centre de Recherches Anthropologiques, Prehistoriques et Ethnographiques. Algers Memoires. No. 8. Paris: Arts et Metiers Graphiques.

One of, if not the most thorough and detailed food habits ethnographies in the literature. Ahaggar is a region in southeastern Algeria inhabited by Tuareg peoples.

2948.   Gast, Marceau. 1969. Persistence protohistorique dans l'alimentation des populations du Sahara central. [Persistence of protohistoric food habits in central Saharan populations.] ROMM 6: 89-93.

2949.   Gast, Marceau & Adrian, Jean. 1965. Mils et sorgho en Ahaggar; etude ethnologique et nutritionnelle. [Millets and sorghum in Ahaggar; an ethnologic and nutritional study.] Centre de Recherche Anthropologiques, Prehistoriques et Ethnographiques, Algers. Memoires. No. 4. Paris: Arts et Metiers Graphiques.

2950.   Gast, Marceau; Maubois, J.L.; Adda, J.; et al. 1969. Le lait et les produits laitiers en Ahaggar. [Milk and its products in Ahaggara.] Centre de Recherches Anthropologiques, Prehistoriques et Ethnographiques, Algers. Memoire No. 14. Paris: Arts et Metiers Graphiques.

2951.   Gaston, E.P. 1905. How they cook in Mexico. WHC 32: 47.

2952.   Gates, Richard. Historical geography of salt in the old Northwest. Master's thesis. Geography. University of Wisconsin. 1966.

2953.   Gatschet, Albert S. 1891. The Karankawa Indians. HU-PMAAE-P Vol. 1. No. 2.

Food and its preparations: pp. 12, 17, 58-59.

2954.   Gaudry, Mathea. 1929. La femme Chaouia de l'Aures. Etude sociolograques Berbere. [The Chaouia woman of Aures. Sociological study of the Berber.] Paris: Librairie Orientaliste Paul Geuthner.

Food habits: pp. 138-146. The Aures Mountains are located in northeastern Algeria.

2955.   Gaudry, Mathea. 1963. La societe feminine au djebel amour et au Ksel. Etude de sociologie rurale Nord-Africaine. [Women of Djebel Amour and Ksel. Study in North African rural sociology.] Paris: Geuthner.

Cookery and food preparation: pp. 225-231; meals: pp. 231-232; butter and cheese making: pp. 232-237. Djebel Ksel is a mountain in northeastern Algeria, located at 33. 44 North, 1. 05E; Djebel Amour are mountains located in the same area.

2956.   Gauducheau, A. 1923. Faut-il faire chauffer les aliments? [Is it necessary to heat food?] Figaro 21 avril.

2957. Gauducheau, A. 1925. Sur la nourriture naturelle de l'homme d' apres l'observation d 'usages alimentaires exotiques primitifs. [On the natural diet of Man, after observations of exotic primitive eating customs.] SPE-B 18: 365-377.

2958. Gauducheau, A. 1933. La riz dans l'alimentation d' Extreme-Orient. [Rice in the diet of the Far East.] SPE-B 26: 677-687.

2959. Gauducheau, A. 1937. L'alimentation d'origine animale. [Diet of animal origin.] Pres Med 45: 1077-1078.

2960. Gauducheau, A. 1937. L'alimentation et l'homme moderne. L' evolution de l'alimentation humaine. [Diet and modern man. The evolution of human diet.] Pres Med 45: 903-905.

2961. Gauducheau, A. 1937. Dans quelle mesure est-il possible de transformer les races humaines par l'alimentation et l'hygiene. Projet d'une experience exotique. [In what measure is it possible to change human groups through diet and hygiene? Overseas experimental project.] SPE-B 30: 496-500.

Proposes nutrition intervention among Third World populations suffering from malnutrition.

2962. Gauducheau, A. 1938. Aliments fermentes. [Fermented foods.] Pres Med 46: 1851-1853.

2963. Gauducheau, A. 1939. Artificial biologic conditions of civilization. [In French.] AHPIS 17: 102-120.

2964. Gauducheau, A. 1941. Le probleme de la nutrition et l'influence du millieu. [The problem of nutrition and the influence of environment.] SSHAARH-B 29: 249-262.

2965. Gaulin, Steven J.C. 1979. A Jarman-Bell model of primate feeding niches. HEcol 7: 1-20.

Extrapolates from the principle which suggests that body size is a fundamental tactic in an animal's feeding strategy to speculations concerning Pleistocene hominid ecology. After a review of what is known of modern primate diet, and a discussion of human diet as a feeding strategy together with archaeological evidence of hominid size and dentition, the conclusion is offered that Pleistocene hominids were characteristically omnivores.

2966. Gaussel, A. 1971. Cuisine et migration. [Food and migration.] HMD No. 813. P. 14.

2967. Gavazzi, Milovan. Die Volkernahrung in Jugoslavien. Quellen und Forschungen. [National diet in Yugoslavia. Sources and research.] Paper presented at First International Symposium on Ethnological Food Research. 21 to 25 August, 1970. Lund: Folklivsarkivet, University of Lund.

2968. Gavin. 1934. A study of diet and social customs in Scotland, changes that have occurred in the past fifty years. Milling 123: 739-740.

2969. Gavrielides, Nicolas. Humour in a Greek village tavern. Paper presented at 72nd Annual Meeting of the American Anthropological Association. 29 November, 1973. New Orleans, Louisiana.

2970. Gedney, Elizabeth. 1942. Food at Fort Clatsop in 1805-1806. OHQ 43: 145-148.

Oregon.

2971. Geerts, A. 1883. Observations on Kinch's list of plants used for food. ASJ-T 11: 31-38.

2972. Gehring, Clara. A review of the literature pertaining to the modification of the intelligence quotient through environmental changes, particularly through changes in nutritional status. Master's thesis. Greensboro: Woman's College of the University of North Carolina. 1943.

2973. Gehrmann, G.; Sturm, A.; & Amelung, D. 1963. Favismus in Deutschland. [Favism in German.] DMW 88: 1865-1869.

2974. Gelfand, Michael. 1945. Geophagy and its relation to hookworm disease. EAMJ 22: 90-103.

Discounts a connection between the two. Recounts an African myth in which earth has the mystical quality of preserving life. Contains unusual ethnographic data pertaining to earth in customs and beliefs of various African groups.

2975. Gelfand, Michael. 1971. Diet and tradition in an African culture. Edinburgh & London: E & S Livingstone.

Mashonaland. Rural Mashonaland, feeding and education of children, the village; the munda (land, or garden) and its crops; preparation of food; fruit; domestic stock and other sources of protein; insects; water; beer; avoidance rules; the Shona meal; assessment of the Shona traditional diet; clinical disorders related to nutrition; influences of customary practices and beliefs on food uses; glossary of Shona plant, animal, bird, and insect names.

2976. General Headquarters. Supreme Allied Commander for the Allied Powers. 1946. Foodstuffs used in the manufacture of alcoholic beverages in Japan. Natural Resources Section. Report No. 24. Tokyo: General Headquarters. Supreme Commander for the Allied Powers.

Available in xerographic form from United States National Archives.

2977. Gensch, Hugo. 1908. Worter verzeichnis der Bugres von Santa Catarina. [Linguistic notes on the Bugre of Santa Catarina. ZE 40: 743-759.

Food habits: p. 746. The Bugre inhabit the State of Santa Catarina in southwestern Brazil.

2978. Geoffroy Saint-Hilaire, Isidore. 1856. Lettre sur les substances alimentaires et particulairement sur la viande de cheval. [Letter on foodstuffs and particularly on horse meat.] Paris: V. Masson

2979.   Georg. Carl. 1888. Verzeichnis der literatur uber Speise und Trank bis zum Jahre 1887. [Catalogue of literature on food and drink up to the year 1887.] Hannover: Klindworth's Verlag.

This bibliography contains 1,704 entries. Most titles are in German, with a number of titles in Latin, French, and English. The bibliography is not annotated. It is a good resource for early (15th, 16th and 17th Century) European books on food, cookery and diet. In addition, it has extensive entries for the subject areas of beer and wine manufacture; housekeeping; and German-language cookery books. Additional subjects listed include table setting; table-servants' guides; carving; and serial publications devoted to housekeeping, hotelkeeping, and to the food industry.

2980.   Gerald, Rex E. Social system responses to famine stress. Paper presented at 74th Annual Meeting of the American Anthropological Association. 2 to 6 December, 1975. San Francisco, California.

2981.   Geralin, Henri. 1953. L' alcoolisme en Afrique Noire. [Alcoholism in Black Africa.] Population avril-juin. Also in RPP 9: 404-414.

2982.   Gerard, Charles Alexandre Claude. 1862. L'ancienne Alsace a table, etude historique et archeologique sur l'alimentation, les moeurs et les usages epulaires de l'ancienne province d' Alscace. [Old Alsace at table, historical and archaeological study on food habits, meal-time customs and practices of the former province of Alsace.] Colmar: Imprimerie de C. Decker.

2983.   Gerarde, John. 1630. The herball or generall historie of plantes...Very much enlarged and amended by Thomas Johnson. London: Adam Isliop, Joice Norton and Richard Whitakers.

2984.   Gerber, Hilda. 1951. Feast of the orange or rose leaves. Cape Argus 17 February.

Includes recipes traditional to this Cape Malay festival. South Africa.

2985.   Gerber, Hilda. 1951. South African herbs make piquant dishes. Spotlight August.

Description of the gardens of the Dutch East India company; uses of herbs in recipes.

2986.   Gerber, Hilda. 1951. Traditional Malay recipes. Cape Times 27 July.

Cape Malay of South Africa.

2987.   Gerber, Hilda. 1957. Traditional cookery of the Cape Malays: food customs and 200 old Cape recipes. Cape Town: A.A. Balkema.

2988.   Gerfeldt, Ewald. 1966. Ernahrungs-Soziologie im 20. Jahrhundert. [Nutritional sociology in the 20th Century.] EU 13: 172-176.

Changes in food consumption patterns in Europe.

2989.   Gerhold, Caroline. 1967. Food habits of the valley people of Laos. JADA 50: 493-497.

2990.   Gerlach, Luther P. 1961. Economy and protein malnutrition among Digo. Minn As-P 29: 3-13.

Malnutrition, particularly kwashiorkor, occurs frequently among this northeast coastal Bantu group, living along the Kenya and Tanganyika Coast. The syndrome is attributed by Digo to the transgression of tabus which prohibit intercourse between parents between birth and weaning of the child. The actual cause rests in traditional food proscriptions which do not allow infants certain categorical relish foods, e.g. non-starchy vegetables, fruit, meat, fish, or eggs, call chitoweo; chakula being the category including staple maize or cassava meal porridge. As a result, the infant is fed only breast milk (or animal milk, if the mother cannot lactate), and a thin maize or cassava gruel. The relationship between diet, and malnutrition (termed chirwa) is unrecognized. The article suggests a better understanding of Digo terminology relating to food in efforts to affect changes in Digo infant feeding practices through explanation of the causes and effects of the chirwa syndrome.

2991.   Gerlach, Luther P. 1964. Socio-cultural factors affecting the diet of the norhteast coast Bantu. JADA 45: 420-424.

2992.   Gerlach, Luther P. 1965. Nutrition in its sociocultural matrix: food getting and using along the East African coast. In Ecology and economic development in tropical Africa. Edited by David Brokensha. Berkeley: University of California Press. 1965. Pp. 245-268.

2993.   Germain, J.R. 1973. Caracteristiques de l'alimentation en France a travers l'histoire. [Characteristics of diet in France throughout history.] SVie No. 664. Pp. 51-53.

2994.   Gernet, Jacques. 1962. Daily life in China on the eve of the Mongol invasion, 1250 - 1276. Translated by H.M. Wright. New York: Macmillan Co.

Cookery: pp. 133-140; 142-143.

2995.   Gershenfeld, L. 1935. Medical works of Maimonides and his treatise on dietetics. AJPharm 107: 14-28.

2996.   Gershon, Jack. Food for life: a case study in applied anthropology. Master's thesis. Anthropology. California State University at San Diego. 1972.

2997. Gerste, A. 1910. Notes sur la medicine et la botanique des anciens Mexicains. [Notes on the medicine and botany of the ancient Mexicans.] Rome: Imprimerie Polyglotte Vaticane.

2998. Gerstenberger, H.J.; Haskins, H.D.; McGregor, H.H.; & Ruh, H.O. 1915. Studies in the adaptation of an artificial food to human milk. AJDC 10: 249-265.

Report of a mixture of various animal and vegetable fats producing a mixture low in volatile fatty acid glycerides, with saponification and iodine numbers nearly identical to human milk fat.

2999. Gerstner, Andreas P. 1939. Der Yams-Anbau in But-Bezirk Neuguineas. [Yam cultivation in the But district of New Guinea.] Anthropos 34: 246-266.

3000. Gervais, F. 1937. Alimentation des indigenes en Algerie. [Diet of native Algerians.] BSA 32: 1461.

3001. Gesmundo, Artemio E. 1932. The nutritive value of gallan, Cytosperma merkusii (Hassk) Schott. Pag 21: 106-126.

Uses as food in Leyte, Philippines: p. 107.

3002. Gessell, Arnold. 1938. El factor psicologico en la alimentacion del nino. [The psychological factor in the feeding of children.] IIAPI-B 11: 479.

3003. Gesell, Arnold & Ilg, Frances L. 1937. Feeding behavior of infants. A pediatric approach to the mental hygiene of early life. Philadelphia, London, Montreal: J.B. Lippincott Co.

Covers foundational patterns of behavior; motor mechanisms of feeding; implements, techniques and behavior; breast and bottle behavior; cup behavior; hygiene; and the adult-infant relationship.

3004. Gewertz. Deborah. The politics of breaking food taboos among the Chambri. Paper presented at 76th Annual Meeting of the American Anthropological Association. 29 November to 3 December, 1977. Houston, Texas.

Using data collected from the Chambri people of the East Sepik Province of Papua New Guinea, this paper describes how food taboos can be manipulated for political ends. Chambri food taboos are nearly always broken, and the ceremonies that can be initiated to compensate for breaking them furnish a context for the exchange of foodstuffs and valuables between wife-givers and wife-takers. An adept Chambri can initiate these ceremonies to force an exchange that will benefit him politically by raising his status within the village.

3005. Ghena, N. 1964. Fromm the history and uses of walnut (Juglans regia) [In Rumanian.] G-VSL 13: 14-19.

3006. Ghidinelli, Azzo. 1971. The alimentation of the Maya. Ethnos 36: 23-31.

Review of diet in first and second stages of the Archaic period; in the Early Classic and Full Classic periods; food sources, preparations.

3007. Ghosh, M.G. 1962 [?]. Studies in rural change: reports on resurveys of villages. Shahajapur (1956-1961). Agro-Economic Research Centre. Santiniketan, West Bengal: Visva-Bharati University.

Includes detailed expenditure data for several foods by occupational groups. Village studied is located in Birbhum District (approximately 23. 50N, 87. 50E), in West Bengal.

3008. Ghoshal, R. 1954. Lathyrism. CaMJ 51: 181-204.

3009. Gibbons, Lulu, compilor. 1966. Indian recipes from Cherokee Indians of eastern Oklahoma. Muskogee, Oklahoma: Creek-Seminole Tribes.

3010. Gibbs, H.D. 1911. The alcohol industry of the Philippine Islands. Part 1. A study of some palms of commercial importance with special reference to the saps and their uses. PJS 6 [A]: 99-206.

Nipa palm, coco palm, buri palm, and sugar palm. Contains historical, ethnographic, and production data.

3011. Gibbs, H.D. & Agcaoli, F. 1912. The alcohol industry of the Philippine Islands. Part 3. Fermented beverages which are not distilled. PJS 7 [A]: 97-117.

Sugar cane, fermented rice; drinks and drinking among the Mandaya, Debabon, Manoba and Mangguangan of Mindanao; and among the Subanun.

3012. Gibbs, H.D. & Agcaoli, F. 1912. Soja-bean curd, an important Oriental food product. PJS 7 [A]: 47-51.

3013. Gibbs, H.D.; Agcaoli, F; & Shilling, G.R. 1912. Filipino foods. PJS 7 [A]: 383-400.

Fish sauce; dried fish; locusts; balut (duck eggs containing partially formed embryos); rice and wheat pasta; soy sauce. Chemical analyses are included.

3014. Gibbs, Walter M. 1909. Spices and how to know them. Dunkirk, New York: the author.

Historical, descriptive, and sociological data.

3015. Gibson, J. 1964. What do you like to eat? U.S. Army food tastes survey. Cath Dgst 28: 60-62.

3016. Gibson, James R. 1968. Food for the fur traders: the first-farmers in the Pacific Northwest. J West 7: 18-30.

Effects of climate and topography on subsistence in Russian Alaska, Canadian Northwest Territory, and British Columbia. Discusses provisioning and local agriculture.

3017.   Gibson, Jon L. Archaeological checklist of edible flora in the lower Mississippi Valley. In The Poverty Point culture. Edited by Bettye J. Broyles & Clarence H. Webb. 1970 [1975]. Pp. 90-98. SAC-B No. 12.

Plants are identified by Latin and common names, with edible parts and seasonality listed. Their preparation is indicated under eight formal categories, however, the sources of these data are not included, and the text references were omitted at the conclusion of the article.

3018.   Gibson, W. Hamilton. 1895. Our edible toadstools and mushrooms and how to distinguish them. New York, London: Harper & Brothers.

3019.   Giddings, Jr., J.L. 1956. Forest Eskimos. An ethnographic sketch of Kobuk River people in the 1880's. UPenn--UMB 20(2). June.

Data derived from narrations of four persons interviewed in 1940, 1941, and 1947, and who were born before contact with Europeans. The monograph is structured in accordance with the activities of the seasons. Food: pp. 9, 10, 14-15, 17, 33, 47; food prohibitions of menarche: p. 48. The Kobuk River headlands are located in the Brooks Range, of northern Alaska ; the Kobuk flows for about two hundred miles westward along the base of the mountains, just north of the Arctic Circle.

3020.   Gidon, F. 1937. Notes sur l'archeologie de l'alimentation. [Notes on the archeology of diet.] SANorm-B 44: 290-309.

Discussion of food plants of antiquity which have fallen into disuse, but which still grow in parts of France. Reviewed by Auguste Chevalier in RBAAT 13: 30-33 [1938] .

3021.   Giffen, Naomi Musmaker. 1930. The roles of men and women in Eskimo culture. University of Chicago Press.

Food: pp. 11-20.

3022.   Gifford, Edward Winslow, compilor. 1924. Tongan myth and fables. BPBM-B. No. 8.

Myth: acquisition of vegetables and cereals: p. 194; origin of coconut: p. 182; origin of drinking ceremonies: pp. 35, 47, 72, 74; origin of eating tabus: p. 80.

3023.   Gifford, Edward Winslow. 1931. The Kamia of Imperial Valley. SI-BAE-B No. 97.

Food use of seeds and herbs: p. 24. A River Yuman tribe of California.

3024.   Gifford, Edward Winslow. California balanophagy. In The California Indians. Edited by Robert

Fleming Heizer & Mary Hune Whipple. 1936. Pp. 237-241. Berkeley, Los Angeles: University of California Press.

Use of acorns among California Native American tribes.

3025.   Gifford, Lorraine. 1973. If you can't stand to cook; easy-to-fix recipes for the handicapped homemaker. Grand Rapids, Michigan: Zondervan.

3026.   Gigault de la Bedolliere, Emile. 1847-1849. Histoire des moeurs et de la vie privee des francais. [History of the manners and private life of the French.] 3 vols. Paris: V. Lecou.

3027.   Gilbert, B. Miles. Some aspects of diet and butchering techniques among prehistoric Indians of South Dakota. Master's thesis. University of Kansa. 1968.

3028.   Gilbert, Christine & Gillman, Joseph. 1944. Diet and disease in the Bantu. Sciene 99: 398-399.

3029.   Gilbert, Fabiola Cabeza de Vaca. 1949. The good life: New Mexican food. Santa Fe: San Vicente Foundation.

3030.   Gilbert, M. Jean. A five week alcoholism ethnography conducted in three Spanish-speaking communities. Paper presented at 76th Annual Meeting of the American Anthropological Association. 29 November to 3 December, 1977. Houston, Texas.

This research review outlines strategies used in the rapid development of ethnographic data focused on one behavioral complex: alcohol-related behavior among segments of an ethnic subculture. Using detailed reporting forms and participant-observer teams, and substantive evidence were obtained on variation among Spanish-speakers in drinking behavior, norms and settings, rural and urban. These techniques are advanced as a partial solution to problems posed by the extremely short field times allocated to anthropological research under contracts which request ethnographic contexts as background for the quantitative surveys of other disciplines.

3031.   Gildersleve, Elena. 1937. Baby epicure. Appetizing dishes for children and invalids. New York: E.P. Dutton & Co.

3032.   Giles, Dorothy. 1940. Singing valleys, the story of corn. New York: Random House.

3033.   Giles, K.A. Wheat as human food. In Symposium on the Great Plains of North America. Edited by Carle C. Zimmerman, & Seth Russell. 1967. Pp. 82-86. Fargo, North Dakota: North Dakota Insitute for Regional Studies.

Origins, history, chemical, and organoleptic qualities of wheat types. Economic factors influencing international wheat trade.

3034.   Gilges, W.   1964.   Some African poison plants and medicines of northern Rhodesia.   RLMOP No. 11.

Use of Croton megalobotrys, by Lunda, Lovale, and Luchazi groups: infusion of root given to infants to promote weight gain.

3035.   Gilks, J.L.   1933.   Dietetic problems in East Africa.   EAMJ 10: 254-265.

3036.   Gilks, J.L. & Orr, John Boyd.   1931.   Studies of nutrition.   The physique and health of two African tribes.   GB-PC-MRS-SRS 155.

Compares two East African groups' [Aikikuyu, vegetarians; and Masai, carnivores] relative nutritional status.   Study is concerned largely with the report of biochemical findings, but also emphasizes the important influence of anthropological factors on nutrition status.

3037.   Gilks, J.L. & Boyd-Orr, John.   1932.   The nutritional condition of the East African native.   EAMJ 9: 160-175; 193-204.

3038.   Gill, L.T.   1934.   Migrations of food plants in the Pacific.   PPRI-J 9: 7-9.

3039.   Gill, William Wyatt.   1876.   Myths and songs from the South Pacific.   London: H.S. King & Co.

Myth: acquisition of food supply for human race [Cook Islands, Mangaia]: p. 14; origin of the domestic hearth: p. 130.

3040.   Gill, William Wyatt.   1912.   A cannibal story of Rarotonga.   JPS 21: 62-64.

3041.   Gillespie, William H.   1969.   Edible wild plants of West Virginia.   New York: Scholar's Library.

3042.   Gillet, Just. & Pague, Egide.   1910.   Plantes principales de la region de Kisantu Leur nom indigene, leur nom scientifique, leurs usages.   [Notes botaniques sur la region du Bas-et Moyen-Congo, fascicule 1].   [Principal plants of the Kisantu region.   Their native and scientific names and their uses.   [Botanical notes on theLower-and Middle-Congo region, fascicule 1] MC-A[b] 5. Fascicule 1.

3043.   Gillett, Lucy H.   1931.   Food at low cost.   New York: American Child Health Association.

3044.   Gillett, Lucy H.   1947.   Nutrition in public health.   Philadelphia: W.B. Saunders.

3045.   Gillett, Lucy H. & Rice, P.   1931.   Influence of education on the food habits of some New York City families.   New York: New York Association for Improving the Condition of the Poor.

Concludes that education is not causal of specific food habits.

3046.   Gillette, Helen.   1925.   The nutrition program-in relation to other public health activities.   HSS 11: 162-164.

Reviews nutritional status of the U.S. public; role of public health nurses and Red Cross in nutrition outreach.

3047.   Gillin, John.   1943.   Houses, food and contact of cultures in a Guatemalan town.   Acta Am 1: 344-359.

3048.   Gillion, K.L.   1962.   Fiji's Indian immigrants. A history to the end of indenture in 1920.   Oxford: Oxford University Press.

Plantation diets: p. 105.

3049.   Gillman, J. & Gillman, T.   1951.   Perspectives in human malnutrition.   New York: Grune & Stratton.

3050.   Gilmore, Melvin Randolph.   1919. Uses of plants by the Indians of the Missouri River region.   SI-BAE-AR for the year 1911-1912. Pp. 43-154.

3051.   Gilmore, Melvin Randolph.   1921.   The ground bean and the bean mouse and their economic relations.   A Iowa 12: 666-669.

Falcata comosa, and Microtus pennsylvanica: their roles in life and folklore of the Native American Dakota tribe.

3052.   Gilmore, Melvin Randolph.   1930.   Indian lore and Indian gardens.   Ithaca, New York: Slingerman-Comstock Co.

Held by United States Library of Congress. No. G3. G34.

3053.   Gilmore, Melvin Randolph.   1931. Vegetal remains of the Ozark Bluff-Dweller culture.   MASAL-P 14: 83-102.

3054.   Gilmore, Melvin Randolph.   1932.   The ethnobotanical laboratory at the University of Michigan.   UMich-MA-OC No. 1.

3055.   Gilmore, Raymond M.   1950.   Fauna and ethnozoology of South America.   SI-BAE-B No. 143. Vol. 6. Pp. 345-364.

3056.   Ginger, Bertha Haffner Palmer, 1914. California Mexican-Spanish cookbook. Selected Mexican and Spanish recipes.   Los Angeles: Citizen Print Shop.

Includes illustrations of Native American cooking techniques, ovens, and kitchens.

3057.   Gini, Bruno; Enright, J.J.; Byrne, A.F.; Burton, T.; Strietelmeier, D.M.; & Koch, Robert B. 1960.   Space feeding.   A closed ecological system for extended travel.   A review of pertinent literature. United States Army. Quartermaster Food and Container Institute for the Armed Forces. Library Bulletin No. 2. Chicago: Quartermaster Research and Engineering Command.

Focuses mainly on algae, with brief reference to experiments concerned with growing tissues of higher plants.

3058.   Ginsberg, Ben. 1960. Let's talk soft-drinks: the story of a great industry. Springfield, Missouri: Mycroft Press.

History and development of soft drink industry; technology; promotion; problems of competition.

3059.   Ginzberg, L. 1932. Whether unfermented wine may be used in Jewish ceremonials AJYB 25. Appendix.

3060.   Girard, Francoise & Barrau, Jacques. 1957. Quelques plantes alimentaires et rituelles en usage chez les Buang. District de Morobe, Nouvelle Guinee, sous toutelle Australienne. [Some food and ceremonial plants used by the Buang, of Morobe District, Australian New Guinea.] JATBA 4: 212-227.

3061.   Girard, de Rialle, Julien. 1872. De l'anthropophagie, etude d'ethnologie comparee. [Anthropophagy, comparative ethnologic study.] Paris: E. Leroux.

3062.   Giradot, Auguste-Theodor, Baron de. 1854. Des subsistances de 1789-1795. [Food provisions from 1789 - 1795.] Paris: P. Dupont.

Food supplies during the period of the French Revolution. Copy held by the Bibliotheque Nationale, Paris. No. R37310.

3063.   Girdhari, Lal & Jain, N.L. 1947. Preservation of water-melon juice. I Farm 9: 67-69.

3064.   Girija, K. Impact of Balwadi feeding of selected children and their mothers in a village under the Applied Nutrition Programme. Master's thesis. University of Madras. 1969.

Twenty-five pre-school children and their mothers, from the village of Samichettipalayam, in the Coimbatore District of Tamil Nadu State, South India, were selected as subjects. Frequency of food purchases, cooking methods, attitudes towards foods and changes in food habits are documented.

3065.   Gispen, W.H. 1948. The distinction between clean and unclean. Oudtestament 5: 190-196.

Jewish dietary rules.

3066.   Githens, Thomas Stotesbury & Wood, Caroll E. 1943. The food resources of Africa. African handbooks, issued by the African section of the University Museum of the University of Pennsylvania, in collaboration with the Committee on African Studies, No. 13. Philadelphia: University of Pennsylvania Press.

3067.   Gizelis, Gregory. 1971-1972. Foodways acculturation in the Greek community of Philadelphia. PFolk 20: 9-15.

3068.   Glacken, Clarence J. Scientific investigations in the Ryukyu Islands. Studies of Okinawan village life. Mimeographed. Pacific Science Board. Washington, D.C.: National Research Council. 1953.

Rice processing, type preferences, and uses: pp. 184-185; vegetable foods: pp. 191-192; tuna: p. 205; lobster: p. 212; daily diet: p. 226; bean curd, miso: p. 303; mochi rice: p. 326.

3069.   Glaman, Kristof. 1962. Beer and brewing in pre-industrial Denmark. SEHR 10: 128-140.

3070.   Glaman, Kristof. 1962. Bryggeriets historie i Danmark indtil slutningen af det 19. arhundrede. [History of brewing in Denmark up to the end of the 19th Century.] Copenhagen: Glydendal.

3071.   Glander, Kenneth. Leaves and leaf-eating primates. Paper presented at 76th Annual Meeting of the American Anthropological Association. 29 November to 3 December, 1977. Houston, Texas.

A comparison of howling monkey feeding behavior with the results of chemical testing of both food and nonfood items indicates prefernetial food selection that is based on the presence or absence of certain secondary compounds. Data will reveal the complex interplay of seasonal variation of food resources, nutritional needs of a primate population, and secondary (toxic) compounds in the environment. The potential food supply of herbivorous primates must be assessed in terms of these dynamic interrelationships, particularly in terms of a plant's defenses (secondary compounds) and the ability of herbivores either to detoxify those compunds or avoid them. Any assumptions of an unlimited food supply (leaves) for leaf-eating primates is severly suspect.

3072.   Glaser, J., et al. 1967. Poi - its use as a food for normal, allergic and potentially allergic children. Allergy 24: 496-500.

Poi is a fermented paste made from the boiled cormes of Colocassia esculenta. It was a stople food in western Polynesia, including Hawaii where it is still eaten in large quantities.

3073.   Glasse, Robert M. 1967. Cannibalism in the Kuru region of New Guinea. NYAS-T 29: 748-754.

3074.   Glasse, Robert M. 1968. Cannibalisme et kuru chez les Fore de Nouvelle Guinee. [Cannibalism and kuru among the Fore of New Guinea] L'Homme 8: 22-36.

Relationship between eating human flesh, especially the brains, and contraction of a slow-acting neurological virus.

3075.   Glassner, Martin I. 1969. Feeding a desert city. Antofagasta, Chile. EG 45: 339-348.

3076. Glatzel, H. 1967. Die Ernahrung gestern, heute und morgen. [Nutrition: past, present, and future.] Hippokrates 38: 749-756.

3077. Glaumont., 1897. La culture de l'igname et du taro en Nouvelle-Caledonie. Travaux gigantesque des indigenes. [Cultivation of yam and taro in New Caledonia. Monumental work of the natives.] L'Anthropologie 8: 41-50.

Detailed description of plantations, with mention of associated ceremonies.

3078. Glegg, C.G. 1945. Native foodstuffs in Tanganyika. The preparation and use of local foodstuffs in the Shinyanga District of Sukumalnad, Tanganyika Territory. Trop Ag 22: 32-38.

Covers staple foods, and cooking methods; wild and cultivated plants (cooking and storage); meat, fish, dairy products, native beer, condiments, grains. An appendix provides Latin, native, and common English names, seasons of availability, and notes on palatability of foods.

3079. Glenn, Viola. 1935. The eating habits of Harlem. Opportunity 13: 82-85.

New York City's oldest Black-American district.

3080. Glick, Carl. 1941. Chapter Eleven. They eat seaweed, Chapter Twelve. Drinks on the house. In Shake hands with the dragon. New York: McGraw-Hill Book Co.

Chinese life in New York City.

3081. Glozer, William K. & GLozer, Liselotte F. 1960. California in the kitchen. As essay upon, and a checklist of California imprints in the field of gastronomy from 1870.-1932. Los Angeles.

3082. Gluckman, Max. 1945. How the Bemba make their living: an appreciation of "Land, labour and diet in Northern Rhodesia." AA 47: 57-75.

Reference is to the classic ethnography written by Professor Audrey Richards (1939).

3083. Govert, E.G. 1940. Usages et rites alimentaires des Tunisiens. Leur aspect domestique, physique et social. [Dietary customs and rites of Tunisians. Their domestic, phyiological, and social aspects. IPT-A 29: 475-489.

3084. Gobert, E.G. 1955. Les references historiques de nourritures tunisiennes. [Historical references to Tunisian foods.] CTunisie 3: 501-542.

Changes in primarily vegetable dietary with the adoption of Western food preparation methods.

3085. Godard, Charles. 1949-1950. Les cultures vivrieres du Tchad. [The food crops of Chad.] In Afrique Equatorial Francais Encyclopedie Maritime et Coloniales. Vol. 1. Pp. 302-307. Paris: Editions de l'Union Francaise.

3086. Goddard, Leon. 1860. Description et histoire de Maroc, comprenant la geographie et la statistique de ce pays, d'apres les renseignenents les plus recents, et le tableau du regne des souverains qui l'ont gouverne depuis les temps les plus anciens jusqua la paix de Tetouan en 1860. 2 vols. [Description and history of Morocco, comprising the geography and statistics of this country, after the latest accounts, and a table of the reigns of the sovereigns who have governed since the most ancient, times up to the Peace of Tetouan in 1860.] Paris: Tanera.

Includes description of the preparations of locusts for human consumption.

3087. Gode, P.K. 1942. A topical analysis of the Bhojana Kutu hala, a work on dietetics, composed by Raghunatha, between A.D. 1675 and 1700. BORI-A for 1941. Pp. 254-263.

3088. Gode, P.K. 1953. Studies in the history of Indian plants - history of fenugreek and alfalfa (Lucerne) in Indian and other countries (between ca. 700 B.C. and A.D. 1800). BORI-A for 1952. Pp. 171-181.

3089. Godelier, Maurice. 1965. Objets et methodes de l'athropologie economique [Goals and methods in economic anthropology.] L'Homme 5: 32-91.

3090. Godelier, Maurice. 1969. La monnaie de sel des Baruya. [Baruya salt money.] L'Homme 9: 5-37.

New Guinea.

3091. Godelier, Maurice. Salt currency and the circulation of commodities among the Baruya of New Guinea. In Studies in economic anthropology. Edited by George Dalton. 1971. Pp. 52-73. Anthropological Studies No. 7. Washington, D.C.: American Anthropological Association.

3092. Godfrey, Elizabeth. [Bedford, Jessie]. 1903. Home life under the Stuarts, 1603-1649. London: Grant Richards; New York: E.P. Dutton.

3093. Godshall, Ammon B.; Lindsay, Walter R.; & Ward, M.F. 1942. Edible, poisonous, and medicinal fruits of Central America. Panama Canal Zone: Canal Zone Experiment Gardens.

3094. Goebel, A. 1863. Uber das Erde-Essen in Persien, und mineralogisch-chemische untersuchung Zwier dergleichen zum Genuss verwendeter Substanzen. [On the practice of earth eating in Persia; complete with a mineralogical-chemical examination of two such substances in the diet.] AISSP-B 5: 397-409.

3095. Goering, George O., et al. 1976. Integrating nutrition planning concerns into agriculture and health sector analysis. A report prepared for the Agency for International Development under Contract No. AID-TA-C-115. Silver Spring, Maryland: Intech Inc. September.

Analyzes factors affecting quantity and quality of food ingested, and factors affecting the biological utilization of food.

3096.   Goertz, Grace Edyth.   The utilization of portions of turkey as food. Master's thesis. Kansas State College, Manhattan. 1947.

3097. Goetz, Wilhelm. 1882. Speise und Trank verganger Zeiten in deutschen Landen. Offentliche Vortrae gehalten in der Schweiz. [Food and drink of by-gone times in German lands; public lectures given in Switzerland.[Basel: Schweighauserische Verlagsbuchhandlung.

Held by Bibliotheque Nationale, Paris. No. 8 Z. 1041.

3098.   Goffile. 1939. Un apercu de l'alimentation indigene au Dahomey. [A glace at native diet in Dahomey.] BIR No. 218. Pp. 229-232.

3099.   Goggin, John M.   1960.   The Spanish olive jar. An introductory study. YUPA No. 62.

The amphorae-shaped pottery containers studied in this monograph were used to ship olive oil, olives in brine, and wine, as well as possibly beans and chick peas [Cicer arietanum] from Spain to its colonies. The present study focuses on the evolution and typology of these jars as revealed by archeological evidence and surviving examples in the Caribbean area.

3100.   Goins, John B. 1914.   The American waiter. Instruction in American and European plan service banquet and private pastry work.   3rd edition. Chicago: The Hotel Monthly Press.

3101. Gokulanathan, Karakat S.   Dysnutrition— nutritional deprivation due to socio-cultural factors. Paper presented at 67th Annual Meeting of the American Anthropological Association.   21 to 24 November, 1968. Seattle, Washington.

This paper reports a preliminary evaluation of the effects of partial industrialization upon infant nutrition and growth in a primarily traditional agrarian community in South India. The observed clinical paradox of substandard growth of children in middle and upper income groups is emphasized. Causal factors are explored. Infant feeding patterns in pre-industrial times are reviewed.   Food taboos and their effects upon children's caloric intake are noted. The importance of research in the anthropological and socio-cultural aspects of infant nutrition in these ancient communities is emphasized, as is the projection of modern technological knowledge over traditional methods, and the advantages of the former for the community.

3102.   Gokulanathan, Karakat S. Conceptualization of obesity as a socio-somatic phenomenon. Paper presented 69th Annual Meeting of the American Anthropological Associaton.   19 to 22 November, 1970. San Diego, California.

3103.   Gokulanathan, Karakat S. & Verghese, Kannarkat, P.   1969.   Socio-cultural malnutrition (growth failure in children due to socio-cultural factors). JTPECH 15:118-24.

Study done in South India (Errakulam-Alwaye industrial area of Kerala).

3104.   Goldberg, Molly & Waldo, Myra. 1959. The Molly Goldberg Jewish cookbook.   New York: Doubleday.

3105.   Goldblith, Samuel A.   Food habits and taboos and the potential of Twentieth Century food science and technology. In Evaluation of novel protein products. Proceedings of the International Biological Programme and Wenner-Gren Center Symposium held in Stockholm.   September 1968. Edited by Alfred E. Bender; R. Kihlberg; B. Lofqvist; & L. Munck. 1970. Pp. 23-32. New York: Pergamon Press.

3106.   Goldenberg, Lora. Wild plant consumption in Mexico: anthropology and nutrition. Honors thesis. Anthropology. University of Michigan. 1974. Includes assessment of amino acid composition of Amaranthus hybridus, and Crotolaria pumila. Isoleucine-leucine ratio in both plants is close to 1:1. Other amino essential amino acids exist in small quantities. [After Messer. 1976:123]

3107.   Golder, F.A. & Hutchinson, Lincoln. 1927. On the trail of the Russian famine.   Palo Alto, California: Stanford University.

Post-World War I food shortage.

3108.   Goldhizer, Ignaz. 1897. Uber Kannibalismus aus Orientalischen Quellen. [Cannibalism in Oriental sources.] Globus 70: 240-242.

Persia and Mongolia.

3109.   Goldman, M.E. A study of the adequacy-economy of some Mexican dietaries.   Master's thesis. University of Texas. 1929.

3110.   Goldsmith, Grace A. The challenge of malnutrition - U.S.A. and the world. Paper presented at 68th Annual Meeting of the American Anthropological Association. 2 to 23 November, 1969. New Orleans, Louisiana.

The most serious nutritional problem is protein-calorie malnutrition, in infants and young children, which retards physical growth and development and may affect mental development. Programs must be developed to ensure more even distribution of food, to reduce food wastage, to increase quantity and quality of food production, and to assist in overall economic development.

3111. Goletshoge, Motsei Doreen. Possibility of meeting human nutritional needs through agricultural development in Bechuanaland. Ph.D dissertation. Home Economics. Queen Elizabeth College. University of London. 1966.

Botswana.

3112. Gomensoro, I. 1941. Dangers in group consumption of mate. [In Spanish.] BSPub 2: 168-171.

3113. Gonczi, Ferencz. 1907. A goceseji s hetesi nep etele, itala es etkezese. [Food, drink, and mealtimes of the people of Gocsej and Hetes.] MNMNOE 8: 232-237.

3114. Gonzalez, Bienvenido. 1914. The macapuno coconut. PAF 3: 31-32.

Philippines.

3115. Gonzalez C., Gustavo. Social policy implications of programs to fight malnutrition and its consequences. Paper presented at 73rd Annual Meeting of the American Anthropological Association. 19 to 24 November, 1974. Mexico City.

3116. Gonzalez, M. 1956. Una encuesta alimentaria en 103 familias de la parroquia de El Valle (Distrito Federal). [A dietary inquiry among 103 families of El Valle Parish (Federal District).] AVN 7: 167-209.

Venezuela.

3117. Gonzales, Natividad A. 1966. Filipino culture and food habits. PJN 19: 194-201.

3118. Gonzales, Natividad A. & Jayme, Josefina B. 1965. A study on food preferences. PJN 18: 114-130.

Philippines.

3119. Gonzalo, Bilbao F. 1952. Estudio de la alimentacion de las ordenas religiosas sometidas al ayuno. [Study of the diet of the humble religious orders while fasting.] AB 4: 219-235.

3120. Goodale, Jane Carter. 1971. Tiwi wives; a study of the women of Melville Island, north Australia. Seattle: University of Washington Press.

Chapter Six: 'Economic role of the Tiwi wife' includes data on women's foods; food gathering and preparation; distribution of food; famine foods; and food-related beliefs.

3121. Goodall, Jane. Feeding behavior of wild chimpanzees. In The Primates. The proceedings of the symposium held on 12th and 14th April, 1962. 1963. Pp. 39-47. Symposia of the Zoological Society of London. No. 10. London: Published by the Society.

3122. Goode, G. Brown. 1880. The use of agricultural fertilizers by the American Indians and the early English colonists. AN 14: 473-479.

Fish as fertilizer.

3123. Goode, G. Brown. 1892. First draft of a system of classification of the World's Columbian Exposition. SI-AR for the year 1891. Pp. 649-735.

Food and its accessories: pp. 699-703.

3124. Goode, Judith. The Philadelphia food project: a study of culture and nutrition. Paper presented at 73rd Annual Meeting of the American Anthropological Association. 19 to 24 November, 1974. Mexico City.

3125. Goode, Judith G. Ethnic dietary change: variation in nutritional consequences. Paper presented at 76th Annual Meeting of the American Anthropological Association. 29 November to 3 December. 1977. Houston, Texas.

In a project focusing on ethnic dietary change, a model has been developed to predict such change. Eating events are scaled according to degree of rule structure. Change occurs least in the highly rule-structured events. This paper examines the consequences of variations in change for the gross nutritional status of individuals. While patterns of change are uniform, household variations in the more open segments of the diet have major consequences for health. Thus, agents of nutritional change should concentrate on the "open" segments of the diet and avoid highly structured food events where choice is restricted.

3126. Goode, Jr., Nat J. 1968. The professional geographer's contribution to the retail food idustry. PG 20: 396-397.

3127. Goodhart, C.B. 1972. Early man's food habits. Science 177: 833-835.

A letter to the editor concerning the use of fire for cooking foods; a reply by A. Carl Leopold and Robert Ardrey is appended.

3128. Goodhart, Robert Stanley. The wartime food and nutrition programme for industrial workers in the United States. In Nutrition in industry. International Labor Office. 1946. Pp. 47-110. Studies and Reports. New Series No. Four. Montreal: International Labour Office.

In addition to providing a detailed general account of national activity in industrial food service, during W.W. II, this study contains interesting information on vitamin supplementation in relation to employee absenteeism from illness (p.82). Also noted are statements from management and union leadership on the favorable effects of in-plant food service on production, morale, health (pp. 83-86, 98-100). Food requirements for special groups e.g. loggers, and miners, are mentioned.

3129. Goodrum, Janet. 1972. Acorns and baskets. PH 16: 19-34.

A photo-ethnography illustrating the food uses of acorns in California Native American cultures. Brief introductory text contains a Yokuts oak tree myth; and notes on acorn-processing techniques.

3130.   Goodrum, Janet. 1973. Food of the Indians -acorn bread. PH 17: 77-80.

Photo study of acorn bread which is wrapped in leaves and baked overnight on ashes. Directions are given for preparation of acorn biscuits, mush, soup, and for toasting acorns. Recipes are from a member of the Native American Maidu tribe.

3131.   Goodrum, Janet. 1973. Indian manzanita cider. PH 17: 85-87.

Preparation described, with photographs.

3132.   Goosen, Jean. Market women's festivities in Guadeloupe. Paper presented at 72nd Annual Meeting of the American Anthropological Association. 30 November, 1973. New Orleans, Louisiana.

3133.   Goodwin, A.J.H. 1939. The origin of certain African food plants. SAJS 47: 283-286.

3134.   Gopalan, C. 1950. The lathyrism syndrome. RSTMH-T 44: 333-338.

A syndrome of spastic paraplegia among poor South Indians subsisting on grossly inadequate diets, not containing Lathyrus sativus, is described. The similarities between this syndrome and lathyrism are pointed out. The role of malnutrition in the causation of the syndrome is examined.

3135.   Gopalan, C. Pellagra in sorghum eaters. In First Asian Congress of Nutrition. 22 January - 2 February 1971. Hyderabad, India Proceedings. Edited by P.G. Tulupe & Kamala S. Jaya Rao. 1972. Pp. 661-669. Hyderabad: Nutrition Society of India.

Although pellagra is classically associated with maize diets, one percent of admissions to hospitals in the Deccan plateau area of India are cases of pellagra, during the winter sorghum season. Dietary causes are examined, and symptoms compared with the maize-generated form.

3136.   Gordon, Edmund I. 1959. Sumerian proverbs. Glimpses of everyday life in ancient Mesopotamia. UPenn-UM-MM.

Grains, vegetables, fruit, by-products: pp. 289-290; food: pp. 304,305; eating and drinking: pp. 315,316.

3137.   Gordon, I. 1942. Social aspects of infant feeding (especially the decline of breast feeding). ADC 17: 139-146.

3138.   Gordon, J.A. 1971. Planning ethnic menus. Hospitals 45: 87-91.

3139.   Gordon, Jean. 1958. Rose recipes: customs, facts, fancies. Woodstock, Vermont: Red Rose Publications.

3140.   Gordon, John E. Social implications of nutrition and disease. In Food, Science and Society. A symposium held in February, 1968, sponsored by the Nutrition Foundation, Inc., the Northern California Section of the Insitiue of Food Technologists, and the University of California, Berkeley. Department of Nutritional Sciences. 1969. Pp. 3-17. New York: The Nutrition Foundation.

3141.   Gordon, Jr., John L. Slingins and high shots: moonshining in the Georgia mountains. Paper presented at 68th Annual Meeting of the American Anthropological Association. 20 to 23 November, 1969. New Orleans, Louisiana.

3142.   Gordon, Karen. Infant care behaviors of Appalachian women. Paper presented at 76th Annual Meeting of the American Anthropological Association. 29 November to 3 December, 1977. Houston, Texas.

The health status of mothers and infants in rural southeastern Kentucky is described, drawing upon the present and past midwifery and medical records of the Frontier Nursing Service of Leslie County. Evidence of shifts in infant feeding practices and related areas of infant management are also described. Data on the current and past health status of mothers and infants are also drawn from a current stratified random sample of mothers who delivered babies under the aegis of the Frontier Nursing Service during 1974-1975. The infant feeding behavior of these mothers and their mothers mirror the fluctuation in the economic conditions of Leslie County.

3143.   Gordon, Kathleen D. Scanning electron microscope study of dental attrition. Paper presented at 75th Annual Meeting of the American Anthropological Association. 17 to 21 November, 1976. Washington, D.C.

Many problems in reconstructing human evolution cannot be resolved without further information about the nature of changes in hominid feeding behavior. The microscopic analysis of tooth-wear facets is presented as a method for obtaining data from teeth, upon which inferences about the dietary behavior and environments of fossil species may be made. Scanning Electron Microscope investigation of enamel abrasion patterns in living primate species are providing background data about the range of normal variability within species, where diet and environment are known. Resulting correlations between abrasion pattern and diet are applied to fossil hominoid species Ramapithecus and Dryopithecus.

3144.   Gordon, Mollie Elizabeth. The ethnobiology of the salmon food area of North America. Master's thesis. University of New Mexico. 1939.

3145.   Gore, J.Howard 1883. Tuckahoe, or Indian bread. SI-AR for the year 1881. Pp. 687-701.

A fungus, Pachyma cocos, Fries., used by Native American groups in Virginia and the Carolinas.   Article reviews the historical literature. A chemical analysis is given. ·

3146.   Gorer, Geoffrey. Chapter Three. Getting food.   In Himalayan vilage, an account of the Lepchas of Sikkim. London: Michael Joseph.

3147.   Gorman, Chester F. Hoabinhian: a pebble-tool complex with early plant associations in Southeast Asia.   Mimeographed. Department of Anthropology. University of Hawaii. 9 October 1968.

3148.   Gorman, Chester F. Hoabinhian transformations in early Southeast Asia: a cultural-chronological sequence circa 12,500 to 7400 BP.   Paper presented at 68th Annual Meeting of the American Anthropological   Association.   20-23 November, 1979. New Orleans, Louisiana.

Until recently, knowledge of prehistoric Southeast Asia has been most complete concerning relatively late (ca. 400 B.C. and later) food-producing cultures and relatively early Homo erectus-related materials. Little is known concerning the human occupation of Southeast Asia between these two extremes.   Early French research in Vietnam discovered and briefly described a "Mesolithic" Southeast Asian expression which they termed Hoabinhian. At present, these assemblages are thought to be the remains of post-Pleistocene hunters and gatherers. Almost no information has been available concerning Hoabinhian cultural ecology; in addition, there have been no Carbon-14 or other chronological sequences associated with these deposits. This paper reports on the excavation and interpretation of Spirit Cave, a small, well-stratified rock shelter site in northwestern Thailand.   A cultural chronology bracketing the Pleistocene-Hololocene "transition" is anchored in time by a reliable radiocarbon sequence. A number of carbonized, botanical macro-fossils suggest that plant domestication had occurred in Southeast Asia by at least 7000 B.C. Other archeological remains fit well with recent linguistic reconstructions, both suggesting that early Southeast Asia was a progressive, emanating center of cultural developments.

3149.   Gorman, Chester F. Beginnings of agriculture in Southeast Asia. Paper presented at 9th International Congress of Anthropological and Ethnological Sciences. 28 August to 8 September, 1973. Chicago, Illinois.

3150.   Gorman, Chester F. Early plant cultivation and agricultural developments in Southeast Asia. Paper presented at 73rd Annual Meeting of the American Anthropological Association.

3151.   Gorman, Martin W. 1896. Economic botany of southeastern Alaska. Pittonia 3: 64-85.

3152.   Gorter, A. 1960. Documentatie op voedingsgebied.   [Documentation in nutrition research,] Voeding 21: 514-517.

3153.   Goslin, Robert M. 1952. Cultivatd and wild plant food from aboriginal sites in Ohio. OArch 2: 9-29.

3154.   Goslin, Robert M. Food of the Adena people.   In The Adena people.   No. 2 Edited by W.S. Webb and Ray S. Baby. 1957. Pp. 41-46. Columbus: Ohio State University Press.   Ohio Historical Society.

3155.   Goss, Arthur. 1897. Dietary studies in New Mexico in 1895. USDA-OES-B No. 40.

One of the earliest studies to place diet in its socio-anthropological perspective. Describes, briefly, economic life; architecture; indicators of acculturation of several low-income Hispanic-American families. Nutritional analyses of diets are given and compared with other regional U.S. dietaries.

3156.   Gott, Philip P. 1958. All about candy and chocolates. Chicago: National Confectioners Association.

3157.   Gottlieb, David & Rossi, Peter H. 1961. A bibliography and bibliographic review of food and food habit research. Library Bulletin No. 4. Library Branch. Technical Services Office. Quartermaster Research and Engineering Command.   Chicago: Quartermasters Food and Container Institute for the Armed Forces. January.

This publication is the first major topical work of its kind. Part A (pp. 1-41) reviews the literature by category, highlighting significant research and research trends. Part B (pp. 42-112) contains the bibliographic entries; by category: physiological bases of food habits; field studies of food consumption patterns; nutritional surveys; feeding problems (psychological and psychoanalytical interpretation); food acceptance in the U.S. Armed Forces; problems of food habits change. The entries are not annotated.

3158.   Gottlieb, Dinny. Aspects of nutrition and food preparation in two Costa Rican towns. Paper presented at 73rd Annual Meeting of the American Anthropological Association.   19 to 24 November, 1974. Mexico City.

3159.   Gottschalk, A. 1948. Hisotire de l'alimentation et de la gastronomie depuis la prehistoire jusqu a nos jours. [History of food and gastronomy since prehistory until our own day.] Paris: Le Francois.

3160.   Gottschalk, A. 1948. Tourisme gastronomique en Languedoc, Aveyron et Rouerque. [Gastronomic   tourism   in   Languedoc,   Aveyron,   and Rouerque.] Grandgousier 15: 14-22.

3161.   Gough, H. 1946. An additional study of food aversions. JASP 41: 86-88.

3162. Gouineau, Andree-Yvette. 1956. La cuisine lao. [Loatian cuisine.] F-A 12: 900-906.

3163. Gould, A.N. 1876. A case of pica. MBSJ 94: 417-418.

Craving for sand by a forty-three year woman.

3164. Gould, Peter R. & Sparks, Jack P. 1969. The geographical context of human diets in southern Guatemala. GR 59: 58-82.

3165. Gould, R.A. 1969. Subsistence behavior among Western Desert Aborigenes of Australia. Oceania 39: 253-274.

3166. Gould, R.E. 1946. Yankee storekeeper. McGraw-Hill. Reprint. New York: Bantam Books. 1948.

3167. Gonelle, R., et al. Research on new foods in states of malnutrition. [In French.] ERmed 3: 161-166.

3168. Gourley, James Edwin, comp. 1937. Eating 'round the world. Foreign recipe books and magazine articles in English. New York: the compiler.

3169. Govil, K.K.; Bhatnagar,, D.P.; & Pant, K.C. 1956. Dietary habits in Uttar Pradesh in relation to income. JIMA 26: 138-170.

3170. Govil, K.K.; Gupta, B.M.; Kapur, S.D., Chakravarty, N.C.; Bhatnagar, D.P.; & Pant, K.C. 1959. Field investigations of lathyrism in Uttar Pradesh. JIMA 33: 499-506.

India.

3171. Gower, R.H. 1948. The effect of a change of diet on Masai school-boys. TNR No. 26. Pp. 77-79.

3172. Goy, Sylvain Claudius. 1915. La cuisine Anglo-Americain. [Anglo-American food.] New York: L. Weiss & Co.

3173. Grabham, M.C. 1921. Subtropical esculents. Lancet 2: 1357-1362.

Dietary of the population of the island of Madeira.

3174. Gradmann, Robert. 1909. Der Getreidebau im Deutschen und Romischen Altertums. Beitrage zur Verbreitungsgeschichte der Kulturgewachse. [Cereal cultivation in German and Roman antiquity. Contribution to the history of the dispersal of cultivated plants.] Jena: Costenoble.

3175. Graebner, Friederich. 1913. Der Erdofen in der Sudsee. [The earth oven in the South Seas.] Anthropos 8: 801-809.

3176. Grafe, H.K. & Schmidt, H.E. 1964. Illustrative nutritional balances. Description of the nutritional situation in large geographical areas. 4. The balance of nutritional sociology, with Potsdam District as an example. [In German.] Ernahr 9: 518-520.

3177. Grafitau, F. 1908. Russian kvass. [In French.] AG 19: 233-248.

Directions for preparing a variety of fermented milk products.

3178. Graham, David Crockett. 1942. The customs of the Ch'iang. WCBRS-J 14 [A]: 68-100.

Diet and food preparation: p. 71, 77-79; Sino-Tibetan border area.

3179. Graham, David Crockett. 1961. Folk religion in southwest China. SI-MC Vol. 142 No. 2 P No. 4457.

Animal and plant foods in southwest China: pp. 18, 19. Diet of the Ch'uan Miao (Szechwan, Kweichow, and Yunnan border areas): p. 69; Tibetan foods: p.95.

3180. Graham, George. 1922. Rua-Kopiha. A peculiar type of kumara store-pit. JPS 31: 122-124.

Maori sweet potato storage.

3181. Graham, George. 1948. He kai, he kai: Some food (for) some food° JPS 57: 64-47.

3182. Graham, S. 1854. Philosophy of sacred history considered in relation to human aliment and the wines of scripture. New York: S.R. Wells & Co.

3183. Grandjean-Hirter, E.A. 1932. Diet among prehistoric races in Switzerland. [In French.] Chron Med 39: 197-206.

3184. Grandjean-Hirter, E.A. 1932. Diet among prehistoric peoples in Switzerland during glacial and lacustrine periods. [In German.] SMW 62: 284-288.

3185. Grant, Faye W. 1955. Nutrition and health of Gold Coast children. 1. Food in four communities. JADA 31: 685-702.

Project methodology; food uses; nutritive value of diets; laboratory test values.

3186. Grant, Faye & Groom, Dale. 1958. A dietary study among a group of southern Negroes. JADA 35: 910-918.

Meal patterns, food costs, dietary intake of selected groups of rural Black-Americans living near Charleston, South Carolina.

3187. Grant, Florence & O'Connor, Joseph A., compilers. 1952. Odors and the sense of smell. A bibliography 320 B.C. - A.D. 1947. New York: Airkem.

3188. Grant, J.W. & Williams, A.N.P. 1949. Burma fruits and their cultivation. B-DA-B No. 30.

3189. Grant, K.F. Food habits and food shopping patterns of Greek immigrants in Vancouver, British

Columbia. Master's thesis. University of British Columbia. 1971.

3190. Grant, K.F. Food habits and food shopping patterns of Greek immigrants in Vancouver. In Peoples of the living land: geography of cultural diversity in British Columbia. Edited by Julia V. Mighi. 1972. Pp. 125-144. UBCol-GS No. 15.

3191. Grant, Marjorie. 1943. Case studies in nutrition. Rural Kentucky. AAPSS-A 225: 52-55.

Three cases indicating nutritional deficiencies. Diets are described briefly.

3192. Grant, Rebecca. Wild foods used by the Cherokee Indians. In Gastronomy. The anthropology of food and food habits. Edited by Margaret Louise Arnott. 1975. Pp. 245-247. Paris; The Hague: Mouton Publishers. World Anthropology.

An informal account by a Native Cherokee.

3193. Grattan, F.J.H. 1948. Chapter Seven. Food and meals. Chapter Eight. Ceremonial presentation of food. In Introduction to Samoan customs. Apia: Samoan Printing and Publishing Co.

3194. Graubard, Mark. 1942. Food habits of primitive man. Part 1. Food and the cultural pattern. SM 55: 342-349; Part 2. Biology of beliefs. 55: 453-460.

3195. Graubard, Mark. 1944. Nutrition education in labor organizations. AAnth 3: 26-37.

In order to achieve trade union support of nutrition education early in World War II, it was necessary to find an approach which would interest the target audience, and make them aware of certain erroneous food-related concepts without being pedantic or alienating. This article describes how historical anecdotes concerning different groups' food patterns, and careful but sensitive objectification of erroneous beliefs about food were successful in winning the support of labor in defense-related nutrition programs in the United States.

3196. Gravielides, Nicolas. Olives, grain, grapes, goats, sheep and ships: adaptive strategies of intensive olive growing. Paper presented at 74th Annual Meeting of the American Anthropological Association. 2 to 6 December, 1975. San Francisco, California.

3197. Graves, Alvin. Portuguese dairymen in the San Joaquin Valley of California: a cultural geography. Master's thesis. Fresno State College. 1970.

3198. Graves, Robert. 1927. Mushrooms, food of the gods. AM 200: 73-77.

3199. Gray, D. 1968. A copy of Lydgate's Dietary at Lille. MQ 15: 245-246.

3200. Gray, Ernest. 1945. Notes on the salt making industry of the Nyanja people near Lake Shirwa. SAJS 41: 465-475.

3201. Gray, James. 1954. Business without boundary: the story of General Mills. Minneapolis: University of Minnesota Press.

General Mills is one of the United States' largest producers of wheat flour products.

3202. Gray. Sarah V. A history of the publication of cookbooks in the United States, 1796-1896. Master's thesis. University of North Carolina. 1964.

3203. Great Britain. Colonial Office. 1954. Malnutrition in African mothers, infants and young children. Report of Second Inter-African (C.C.T.A.) Conference on Nutrition, held under the auspices of the Commission for Technical Co-operation in Africa south of the Sahara, 19-27 November, 1952, at Fajara, Gambia. Publication 88-359.

3204. Great Britain. Economic Advisory Council. 1938. Summary of information regarding nutrition in the Colonial empire. London: Economic Advisory Council.

3205. Great Britain. Ministry of Food. 1944. What do they eat in the United States, Canada, and Great Britain today? London: His Majesty's Stationery Office.

3206. Great Britain. Ministry of Food. 1953. Report of the Committee of Inquiry into the Slaughter of Horses. Cmd. 8925. London: Her Majesty's Stationery Office.

Includes comments on the trade in horse flesh for human consumption.

3207. Grebinger, Paul. Innovation in agriculture: a problem in archeological visibility. Paper presented at 74th Annual Meeting of the American Anthropological Association. 2 to 6 December, 1975. San Francisco, California.

3208. Green, John W. 1966. Useful plants in ancient America. Family cactaceae. Artifact 4(1): 7-10.

Ethnographic and archeological data on food use of cactus. Two recipes are also given: one for nopalitos (Opuntia sp; prickly pear pads); and one for a preserve based on the fruit of the same plant.

3209. Green, Judith Strupp & Jones, Anita. 1968. Los Panecitos Beneditos: clay eating in Oaxaca. Ethnic Technology Notes. San Diego Museum of Man. San Diego: San Diego Museum of Man.

3210. Green, Laura S. & Beckwith, Martha Warren. 1928. Hawaiian household customs. AA 30: 1-17.

Eating customs: pp. 3-4.

3211. Green, Lena. 1962. Some seaweeds of economic importance growing in Jamaican waters. J-SRC-IB 3: 35-36.

3212. Green, Mary E. 1902. Food products of the world. Chicago: The Hotel World.

An encyclopedia, compiled on the basis of foods exhibited at the World's Columbian Exposition, held in Chicago, in 1893. Supplementary written sources were also consulted (see p. vi); however documentation is entirely absent in text.

3213. Greenbaum, Florence Kreisler. 1918. The international Jewish cookbook. A modern "kosher" cookbook. New York: Bloch Publishing Co.

Traditional holy day, and other recipes from Eastern Europe.

3214. Greenberg, Leon A. Alcohol and emotional behavior. In Alcohol and civilization. 1963. Pp. 109-121. New York, San Francisco, Toronto, London: McGraw-Hill.

3215. Greenberg, Leon A. & Carpenter, John A. 1957. The effect of alcoholic beverages on skin conductance and emotional tension. 1. Wine, whiskey and alcohol. QJSA 18: 190-204.3216.Greene, Felix. 1962. China, The country Americans are not allowed to know. New York: Ballantine Books.

Communal dining rooms: p. 134, 160-161; food rationing: pp. 394-395; food supply, and nutritional status: pp. 433-441.

3217. Greene, R.E. 1936. The composition and uses of the giant cactus (Carnegeia gigantea) and its products. JCEd 13: 309-312.

3218. Greenfield, Sidney M. 1965. More on the study of subsistence activities. AA 67: 737-744.

Suggestion regarding the refinement of terminology used in describing subsistence activity. Three categories (1) production; (2) distribution; and (3) consumption, or use are given, with additional qualification for methodological employment of terms.

3219. Greengo, Robert Eugene. Aboriginal use of shellfish as food in California. Master's thesis. Berkeley: University of California. 1951.

3220. Greengo, Robert Eugene. 1952. Shellfish foods of the California Indians. KAS-P No. 7.

3221. Greenway, P.J. 1944. Origin of some East African food plants. Part 1. EAAJ 10: 34-49.

Covers Kenya, Uganda, Tanganyika, ad Zanziber.

3222. Greenway, P.J. 1947. Khat. EAAJ 13: 98-102. Catha edulis (Celastraceae).

Shoots used by Bushman as food.

3223. Greenway, P.J. 1947. Yeheb. EAAJ 12: 216-219.

Nut of Cordeauxia edulis, Hemsl., eaten by Somalis. Nut is boiled or stewed; has a high sugar and oil content, and has been recorded to be a staple food of poorer desert groups, and in the southern frontier region of the former Somaliland Protectorate.

3224. Greenwall, Amy B.H. 1947. Taro-with special reference to its culture and uses in Hawaii. EB 1: 276-289.

3225. Greenwood, William F. Diets and ecology of crop-raiding baboons. Master's thesis. Anthropology. University of Florida. 1971.

3226. Greer, Louise Evangeline. Efficiency in the arrangement of equipment and materials for the performance of a common task in food preparation. Master's thesis. Ithaca, New York: Cornell University. 1938.

3227. Gregory, Jr., H.F. Maximum forest efficiency: swamp and upland potentials. In Twenty-first Southeastern Archaeological Conference. November 6-7, 1964. New Orleans, Louisiana. Proceedings. Edited by Stephen Williams. 1965. Pp. 70-74. SAC-B No. 3.

Discusses swamp and upland food resources in the archeological record for the Lower Mississippi Valley.

3228. Gregson, Ronald E. Beer and communal labor among the Henga of northern Malawi. Paper presented at 68th Annual Meeting of the American Anthropological Association. 20 to 23 November, 1969. New Orleans, Louisiana.

Data gathered in the Henga Valley, northern Malawi indicate that communal agricultural work group which receive finger millet beer as partial compensation are more efficient than most other types of work group. Comparisons are made with other examples of communal work groups recorded in the ethnographic literature.

3229. Greiner, Ted. 1975. The promotion of bottle feeding by multinatinal corporations: how advertising and the health professions have contributed. CorU-INMS No. 2.

3230. Greiner, Ted. Infant food advertising and malnutrition in developing societies. Paper presented at 75th Annual Meeting of the American Anthropological Association. 17 to 21 November. 1976. Washington, D.C.

One of the detrimental events often accompanying economic development is the shift in infant feeding from breast to bottle. Gastroenteritis and marasmus result from the contaminated, dilute, milk-based feeds typically given. Marketing activities of companies producing foods for infants have been implicated as a powerful influence in the increase in bottle feeding. This paper reviews relevant international business data and published infant feeding surveys, examines infant food advertisements from developing areas, reports on data gathered in mic-1975 from interviews with both Caribbean advertisers of infant foods, and with two hundred mothers of infants in St.

Vincent, West Indies, and discusses policy implications.

3231. Grey, Egerton Charles. 1928. The food of Japan. League of Nations. Publication 1928. Series 3. No. 2 Geneva" League of Nations.

3232. Grey, M. 1975. Notes biographiques sur Francois Appert qui mit au point un procede de la conservation des aliments au 19c siecle et sur Charles Albert Tellier qui imposa le principe de la congelation dans le meme but. [Biographical notes on Francois Appert who perfected a process for the preservation of food during the Nineteenth Century and on Charles Albert Tellier who set down the principle of freezing toward the same end. Historia No. 42. Pp. 86-94.

3233. Gribble, Henry. 1883-1884. The preparatio of Japan tea. ASJ-T 12: 1-33.

3234. Griebel, C. 1948. Gesundheilsschadliche Leguminonsensamen, Lathyrus tingitanus, L [Leguminous seeds injurious to health, ZLUF 88: 872-974.

3235 Grieg, S. 1959. Tre norske drikkehorn fra middeladeren. [Three Norse drinking horns from the Middle Ages. Viking 23: 87-109.

3236. Grierson, Philip James Hamilton. 1903. The silent trade; a contribution to the early history of human intercourse. Edinburgh: W. Green & Sons.

Salt in early historical trade.

3237. Gries, Charles-Pierre-Paul. 1905. Association des officiers de la reserve et de l'armee territoriale, Nancy. Conference sur l'alimentation du soldat en general et l'alimentation du soldat en campagne. [Association of reserve officers of the territorial Army, Nancy. Conference on feeding the soldier in general, and feeding th solder in action.] Nancy: Imprimerie de L. Kreis.

3238. Grieve, John, 1788. An account of the method of making a wine by the Tartars, called kumyss, and its uses in medicine. RSE-T 1 [Part 2, Section 1]: 178-190.

3239. Griffen, William B. 1959. Notes on Seri Indian culture - Sonora, Mexico. Latin American Monograph Series, No. 10. Gainesville: University of Florida.

Food habits: pp. 12-13.
3240. Griffin, James B. 1963. A radiocarbon date on prehistoric beans from William Island, Hamilton County, Tennessee. T Arch 19: 43-46.

3241. Griffin, James B. & Yarnell, Richard A. 1963. A new radiocarbon date on corn from the Davis site, Cherokee County, Texas. AmAn 28: 396-397.

3242. Griffin, P. Bion. Agta Negrito women hunter-gatherers. Paper presented at 77th Annual Meeting of the American Anthropological Association. 14 to 18 November, 1978. Los Angeles, California.

Luzon Island, Philippines.

3243. Griffith, F.L. 1926. A drinking syphon from Tell el-gharanah. JEA 12:22.

3244. Griffiths, David & Thompson, Charles Henry. 1929. Cacti. USDA-C No. 66.

Cactus as food: pp. 10-13.

3245. Griffiths, J.L. 1911. Paper bag cookery. USDCL - DCTR 14: 206.

3246. Griffiths, Percival Joseph. 1967. The history of the Indian tea industry. London: Weidenfeld & Nicolson.

3247. Grigoroff, Stamen. 1905. Etude sur un lait fermente comestible. Le Kisselomleko du Bulgarie. [Study on an edible fermented milk. Burgarian kisselomleko.] RMSR 25: 714-721.

3248. Grimble, Arthur. 1933-1934. Migrations of a pandanus people. PS-M No. 12.

Inculdes description of pandanus flour preparation.

3249. Grime, William Ed. 1979. Ethnobotany of the Black Americans. Algonac, Michigan: Reference Publications.

Includes list of food plants.

3250. Grimme, C. 1914. The soybean and its use for food and condimental purposes. [In German.] Konservenzeitung 15: 1-3.

Composition and uses of soybean milk, curd, bread, sauce, and other items.

3251. Grimshaw, Beatrice. 1934. The world's worst cannibal island (Rossell). Asia 34: 348-351.

Rossel Island is located to the southeastern portion of the Louisiade Archipelago at approximately 11. 40S, 154. 5E.

3252. Grindon, Leo H. 1883. Chapter Tenth. Cultivated fruits, esculent vegetables and medicinal herbs. Chapter Thirteenth. The market place and the shops. In The Shakespeare flora. Manchester: Palmer & Howe.

3253. Grinnel, Elizabeth. 1958. Making acorn bread. UCal-AS-R No. 41. Pp. 42-45.

3254. Grisebach, A.H.R. 1864. Flora of the West Indian Islands. London: Lovell Reeve & Co.

3255. Grivetti, Louis Evan. 1973. Information on culture, food and good health for nurses and MCH/FP educators in the Republic of Botswana. Subject: basic references on diet, food, and nutrition: the Botswana literature. DTB 1(1).

3256. Grivetti, Louis Evan. 1973. Information on culture, food and good health for nurses, and MCH/FP educators in the Republic of Botswana. Subject: recent accounts of Batswana diet, extracts from nine sources - 1933 through 1972. DTB 1(3).

3257.   Grivetti, Louis Evan. 1974. Information on culture, food, and good health for nurses, and MCH/FP educators in the Republic of Botswana. Subject: food distribution mechanisms among the baTswana. DTB 2(2).

3258.   Grivetti, Louis Evan. 1975. The importance of flavors in the Middle East. F Tech 29 (6): 38,40.

A concise sketch of Middle Eastern food patterns from the perspective of flavor, followed by a discussion of the problems of cross-cultural analyses of food acceptance. This latter is illustrated with three examples of culture-contact in the context of food sharing.

3259.   Grivetti, Louis Evan. Dietary resources and social aspects of food use in a Tswana tribe. Ph.D. dissertation. Geography. University of California, Davis. 1976.

3260.   Grivetti, Louis Evan. 1976. Nutritional success in a semi-arid land: examination of Tswana agro-pastoralists of the eastern Kalahari, Botswana. AJCN 31: 1204-1220.

The cultural and environmental factors affecting the food quest and nutritional status of the Moshaweng Tlokwa are examined. Data are presented on methods of food procurement, storage, preparation, and preservation; dietary prohibitions and general diet of all age groups. The author concludes that the Tlokwa have coped satisfactorily with drought, and recommends continued diversification of their food quest in order to maintain nutritional well-being in future.

3261.   Grivetti, Louis Evan. 1978. Culture, diet, and nutrition: selected themes and topics. Bio Science 28: 171-177.

Discusses the origin of diet; antiquity of nutritional disease; pica; religion and nutritional status; fasting and nutritional quality; carrion; alcohol and nutritional status; and toxic foods.

3262.   Grivetti, Louis Evan. 1979. Kalahari agro-pastoral-hunter-gatherers: the Tswana example. EFN 7: 235-256.

A thorough study of the historical, ecological, and medico-nutritional aspects of a Bantu-speaking group which has been able to maintain general well-being despite the stresses to which they are subject by a semi-arid environment. An extensive listing of plant and animal foods is provided for the Tlokwa Moshang among whom the author resided for two years (1973-1975).

3263.   Grivetti, Louis Evan & Mogome, Frederick. 1974. A survey of food availability among baTlokwa-ba-Moshaweng of Tlokweng, southeast district, Republic of Botswana. Occasional Reports on food and diet, presented to the Director of Medical Services, Ministry of Health, Labour and Home Affairs, No. 1. Gaborone: Republic of Botswana.

Includes lists of wild flora and fauna used as food; as well as non-traditional foods consumed.

3264.   Grivetti, Louis Evan & Pangborn, Rose Marie. 1973. Food habit research: a review of approaches and methods. JNE 5: 204-208.

Evaluation of seven categories of food habit research, with representative examples from the literature illustrating each: environmentalism; cultural ecology; regionalism; culture-history; fuctionalism, quantitative approaches; clinical approaches. The authors conclude that no one approach alone would be satisfactory for a comprehensive description of a culture's food-related behavior; however, a particular approach may be useful for the solution of a specific problem.

3265.   Grivetti, Louis Evan & Pangborn, Rose Marie. 1974. Origin of selected Old Testament dietary prohibitions. An evaluative review. JADA 65: 634-638.

3266.   Grivetti, Louis Evan & Paquette, Marie B. 1978. Food choices among first generation Chinese in California. Cal Ag 32 (12): 6-8.

3267.   Grivetti, Louis Evan & Paquette, Marie B. 1978. Nontraditional ethnic food choices among first generation Chinese in California. JNE 10: 109-112.

Reminds that nutrition educators should recognize food preferences in ethnic groups ought not to be stereotyped.

3268.   Grlic, Ljubisa. 1954. Vitamin value of edible wild plants common in Yugoslavia. 1. Ascorbic acid and carotene content of edible wild greens. APJ 4: 115-118.

3269.   Grlic, Ljubisa. 1956. The ascorbic acid and carotene contents in leaves as a common characteristic of botanically related species. Experientia 12: 230-231. Abstracted in CA 51: 5567.

3270.   Groen, J. 1958. Cultuur, voedingsgebruiken en misbruiken. [Culture, food use and misuse.] Voeding 19: 599-615.

3271.   Groen, J.J. & Witt, C. de. 1964. Martine Wittop Koning en Jeannette Polak-Kiek, twee pioneersters van de dietistenopleiding in Nederland. [Maritime Wittop and Jeannette Polak-Kiek, two pioneers of education in the Netherlands.] Voeding 25: 244-247.

3272.   Groen, J.J.; Balogh, Miriam; Levy, Mina; Yaron, E.; Zemach, Ruth; & Benaderet, Sarah. 1964. Nutrition of Bedouins in the Negev Desert. AJCN 14: 37-46.

Extensive discussion of food habits.

3273.   Groff, Elizabeth H. 1919. Soy sauce manufacturing in Kwangtung, China. PJS 15: 307-316.

> After historical reference to use of sauces in China, this article goes on to describe production, in the town of Sainam, fifty miles southwest of Canton. Equipment is illustrated, and the various qualities of soy sauce enumerated. The author includes observations on the problems encountered in obtaining information for her research.

3274.   Groff, William S. 1960. California Indian cannibal tales. Mkey 34: 152-165.

> Categorical analysis, by Native American group.

3275.   Gros, H. 1903. Les perversions de l' appetit chez les infants musselmans du premiere age en Algerie. [Perversions of appetite among Algerian Muslim infants.] Caducec 3: 248-249.

> Pica, malacia, geophagy.

3276.   Gross, Daniel R. & Underwood, Barbara A. 1971. Technological change and caloric costs: sisal agriculture in northeastern Brazil. AA 73:725-740.

> Examines the process by which sisal leaves are transformed into exportable fiber, through expenditure of human caloric energy. Concludes the energy costs of sisal laborers are so great in relation to wages that systematic deprivation of adequate calories to their non-productive dependents occurs, resulting in retardation in growth rate among their children.

3277.   Gross, I.H. 1925. A survey of food habits in a Hungarian mining town. JHE 17: 315-321.

3278.   Grossack, Martin M. 1964. Understanding consumer behavior. Boston: Christopher Publishing House.

> How social science can help the marketing and advertising practitioner asses new product acceptance; measure television commercials; problems of social class, hosehold decision-making; new product innovation.

3279.   Grossi, Vincenzo. Antropofagia e sacrifizi nell' America precolombiana. [Anthropophagy and human sacrifice in pre-Colombian America.] In Congres International des Americanistes. Huitieme session. Tenue a Paris en 1890. Compte-rendus. 1892. Pp. 366-371. Paris: Leroux; Laval: Imprimerie et Ster. E. Jamin.

3280.   Grottanelli, V.L. 1949. Antropofagia reale e imaginaria nel mondo camitico. [Real and imaginary anthropophagy in the Hamitic world.] IVO-A 3: 187-202.

3281.   Groundwater, Henrietta. 1962. Everyday food in 19th Century Orkney. SHC 38: 105-106.

3282.   Groves, W.C. 1906. A native feast in Melanesia. Walkabout 1 October. Pp. 31-35.

Tatau village, New Guinea.

3283.   Grubb, Eugene H. & Guilford, W.S. 1913. The potato. London: Constable & Co.

3284.   Grube, F.W. 1934. Cereal foods of the Anglo-Saxons. PQuart 13: 140-158.

3285.   Grube, F.W. 1935. Meat foods of the Anglo-Saxons. JEGP 34:511-529.

3286.   Gruelle, Katherine Bazore. 1946. Effect of the war on food habits in Hawaii. JHE 38: 91-94.

> A rather unusual, first-hand commentary on the response of Hawaiian home-makers to food shortages, and the nature of substitutions and home food processing. The unavailability of numerous imported foods appears to have resulted in a shift toward typical North American foods; consequently, the war-time experience in Hawaii, despite an absence of rationing, was strongly influential in changing the food habits of traditional Oriental and Oceanian populations.

3287.   Grum, Andreja. 1964. Slovenskje narodnje jedi. [Slovenian national food.] Ljubljana: Centralni Zavod za Napredek Gospodinjstva.

3288.   Grumet, Robert Steven. The Coast Tsimshian potlatch in the Nineteenth Century: a systems appproach. Paper presented at73rd Annual Meeting of the American Anthropological Association. 19-24 November, 1974. Mexico City.

3289.   Grunder, M.U. 1968. Etude de possibilites de transformation et d'utilisation industrielles des cereales et legumineuses locales au Senegal. [Study of the possibilities of processing and industrially utilizing local cereals and legumes in Senegal.] United Nations Development Program/S.F. SEN/5. Dakar: Institute of Food Technology.

3290.   Gruner, B. 1908. Il pane pei contacini. [Bread used by peasants.] Agri Mod 14: 71-72.

> Maize meal, and wheat flour bread commonly eaten in many regions of Italy.

3291.   Gruner, O. Cameron. 1970. A treatise on the Canon of Medicine of Avicenna, incorporating a translation of the First Book. New York [i.e. Clifton, New Jersey.]: Augustus M. Kelly, Publishers.

> Dietetics, the influence of food and drink: pp. 214-220; the various kinds of drinking waters: pp. 221-229.

3292.   Grunfeld, B. 1967. De dietetiske forskrifter i det gamle testamente. Myte elle empiri? [Old Testament dietary regulations. Myth or empiricism?] TN Loeg 87: 2023-2027.

3293.   Gruss, Johannes. 1932. Untersuchungen von Broten aus der Agyptische Sammlung der Staatliche Museum ze Berlin. [Research on bread from the Egyptian collection of the State Museum, at Berlin.] ZASA 68: 79-80.

3294. Gudeman, Stephen. Subsistence and the production of surplus. Paper presented at 75th Annual Meeting of the American Anthropological Association. 17 to 21 November, 1976. Washington, D.C.

If the semantics of the words "subsistence" and "surplus" have been a focus of contention in anthropology, much the same is true of economics. The problem becomes acute in the case of a peasantry which produces for its own consumption. By following certain recent interpretations of Ricardo, however, the analysis of use-value production may be brought back within an encompassing economic theory. The enigma of a "subsistence system" is not whether it produces a surplus, but why the surplus it does produce is not "accumulated". Yet, the very conditions which militate against accumulation make such a system ripe for the extraction of surplus by modern organization.

3295. Gudgeon, W.E. 1893. Maori tradition as to the kumura. JPS 2: 99-102.

Sweet potato in New Zealand.

3296. Gudhjonsson, S.V. 1935. Diet of old Nordic peoples. [In German] DMW 61: 1507-1510.

Data derived from old Icelandic literature.

3297. Gudhjonsson, S.V. 1941. Folkekost og sundhedsforhold i gamle Dage. Belyst i gennem oldnordiske Litteratur. [National diet and the state of health in former days. Light from old Scandinavian literature.] In Uitgiven med Stolte fra Carlsbergfonden. Copenhagen: Nyt Nordisk Forlag.

3298. Guedon, Marie-Francoise. Activites feminés esquimades [Eskimo Women's activities.] Master's thesis. Anthropology. Universite de Montreal.

3299. Guerin-Menneville, F.-E. 1857. Memoire sur trois especes d'insectes Hemipteres des punaises aquatique dont les ouefs servent a faire une sorte de pain nomme 'hautle', au Mexique. [Memoir on three species of Hemipterous water-insects, the eggs of which are used to make a kind of 'bread' called 'hautli', in Mexico.] SIA-B 4: 578-581.

3300. Guerrier, Edith. 1941. We pledged allegiance: a librarian's intimate stoary of the United States Food Administration. Hoover Library on War, Revolution, and Peace, Miscellaneous Publication 1. Stanford: Palo Alto, California: Stanford: Stanford University Press.

The author recounts her personal experiences in organizing and administering a program for mobilizing the resources of the libraries of the nation in support of food conservation during World War I.

3301. Guesde, Mathieu-Theodore-Pierre. 1913. La question de l'acool au Tonkin et dans le Nord-Annam. Notre action en Indochine. [The question of alcohol in Tonkin and northern Annam. Our action in Indochina.] Paris: Chaix.

3302. Guetzkow, H.S. & Bowman, P.H. 1946. Men and hunger: a psychological manual for relief worker. Elgin, Illinois: Brethren Publishing House.

3303. Guevarra, A. 1946. El poliedro de la nutricion: aspectos economico y social del problema de la alimentacion en Venezuela. [The polyhedron of nutrition: social and economic aspects of food habits in Venezuela.] Caracas: Editorial Grafolit.

3304. Guevara, Dario. 1960. Expresion ritual de comida y bebidas ecuatorianas. [Ritual context of food and beverages in Ecuador.] Quito: Editorial Universitaria.

3305. Guggenheim, K. & Drefuss, F. 1959. Food habits and food consumption of Jews from Cochin in Israel. AJCN 7: 519-525.

Cochin is located in the Indian State of Kerala, on the coast of the Arabian Sea, at 9. 56N, 76. 19E.

3306. Guggenheim, K.; Kark, S.L.; & Abramson, J.H. 1964. Diet, social class, and neighborhood in Jerusalem, Israel. A study of pregnant women. JADA 45: 429-432.

3307. Guilday, John E.; Parmalee, Paul W.; & Tanner, Donald P. 1962. Aboriginal butchering techniques at the Eschelman Site [36 La 12], Lancaster County, Pennsylvania. P Arch 32: 59-83.

3308. Guillard, Joanny. 1965. Chapitre 5. Alimentation [Chapter Five. Diet.] In Golonpoui. Analyse des conditions de modernisation d'un village du Nord Cameroun. [Golonpoui. Analysis of conditions of modernization in a north Cameroon village.] Le Monde d'outre-mer, passe et present. Deuxieme serie. Documents 7. Ecole pratique des hautes etudes-Sorbonne. 6th Section: Science, economiques et sociales. Paris; the Hague: Mouton.

Chapter includes nutritional information; data on salt, millet beer, dogs as food; and food taboos.

3309. Guillarmod, A. Jacot. 1966. A contribution toward the economic botany of Basutoland. SEN 119: 209-212.

3310. Guillaumin, A. Les plantes cultivees en Nouvelle Caledonie. [Cultivated plants in New Caledonia.] In Ninth Pacific Science Congress. 18 November to 9 December, 1957. Chulalongkorn University, Bangkok. Proceedings. Volume Four [Botany]. 1962. Pp. 253-268.

3311. Guillerm, J. 1928. Le nuoc-mam et l'industrie saumuriere Indochine. [Nuoc-mam and the Indochinese pickling industry.] AIPI No. 7: 21-60.

3312. Guillerm, J. L'explication scientifique d'un phenomene impirique, la production du nuoc-mam. [Scientific explanation of an empirical phenomenon, the production of nuoc-mam.] In Far Eastern Association of Tropical Medicine. Eighth congress. Transactions. Vol. One. 1931. Pp. 122-131.

3313. Guillerm, J. 1931. L'industrie du nuoc mam en Indochine. [The nuoc mam industry in Indochina.] Saigon: Albert Portail.

Salted, fermented fish sauce. Reviewed in IPI-A No. 16. Pp. 309-311. (1932).

3314. Guinaudeau, Z. 1964. Fes vu par sa cuisine. [Fez seen from the point of view of its food.] Rabat, Morocco: J.E. Laurent.

3315. Gunda, Bela. 1949. Plant gathering in the economic life of Eurasia. SJA 5: 369-378.

3316. Gunda, Bela. 1964. Olasz sajtkeszitok Magyarorszagon. [Italian cheese-making in Hungary.] Ethnografia 75: 599-600.

The relationship between Italian puina and Hungarian pujna sour milk cheese.

3317. Gunda, Bela. 1967. Tejolto novenyek a Karpatokban. [Milk-rennet plants in the Carpathians.] Ethnografia 78: 162-175.

3318. Guinee. Service de la Statistique et de la Mecanographie et al. 1957. Etudes agricoles et economiques de quatre villages de Guinee Francaise. 4. Guinee forestiere: village de Niehen. [Agricultural and economic studies of villages in French Guinea. 4. The forest zone: the village of Niehen.] Conakry [?]: Mission Demographique de Guinee 1954-1955.

Niehen is located in the Cercle de N'zere-kore [about 7. 49N, approximately 8. 48W]. Meal patterns, food preparation, and seasonal dietary variations are described.

3319. Gunn, Elizabeth. 1927. Diet. MJA [Supp. 5]: 2: 160. September 10; [Supp. 6]: 161-162, September 17.

Diet in Whanganui, New Zealand.

3320. Gunther, Erna. 1945. Ethnobotany of western Washington. UWash-PA 10. No. 1.

3321. Gunther, M. 1952. Breast-feeding and diet. Lancet 1: 367.

3322. Gunther, R.T. 1897. The oyster culture of the ancient Romans. JMBA 4: 360-365.

3323. Gunther, R.T., ed. 1959. The Greek herbal of Dioscorides. Reprint. New York: Hafner Publishing Co.

3324. Gupta, Biman Kumar Das. 1969. A note on the Rajbanshi (Rajbansi) of eastern India, with special reference to social movements. ASI-B 18: 1-44.

Popular verse referring to rice and curds: p. 23; foods as ritual offerings; pp. 29-31.

3325. Gupta, P.N.S. 1952. Investigations into the dietary habits of the aboriginal tribes of the Abor Hills (north-eastern frontier). IJMR 40: 203-218.

3326. Gupta, P.N.S. 1955. Nutrition problems of the tribes of Abor Hills [Assam]. ISCA-P 42: 386.

Abstract of a paper.

3327. Gupta, Sisir Sen. 1962. Letter of beef eating. Folklore [C] 6: 21.

3328. Gurdon, Philip Richard Thornhagh. 1914. The Khasis. 2nd edition. London: Macmillan.

Assam. Food habits: pp. 51-54.

3329. Gursky, M.J. Dietary survey of three Peruvian highland communities. Master's thesis. Anthropology. Pennsylvania State University. 1969.

3330. Gushchina, S.F. 1928. Materialy po narodnoj kulinarii; Russkoe naselenje tunklinskogo kraya. [Material on the popular culinary art of the Russian population of Tunklinsk Province] SZS 7: 28-46.

Siberia.

3331. Gushchina, S. & Miljus, V. Pishcha i domashnyaya utvar litovskih krest'yan v 19-20 godu. [Food habits and house-hold utensils of Lithuanian peasants in the 19th and 20th centuries.] Ph.D. dissertation. Institute of Ethnography. Academy of Sciences of the U.S.S.R. 1954.

3332. Gussler, Judith D. Nutrition and behavior: ecological factors and ritualized illness in South Africa. Paper presented at 68th Annual Meeting of the American Anthropological Association. 20 to 23 November, 1969. New Orleans, Louisiana.

The hypothesis is offered of a convergence of environmental, biological and cultural factors in the development of institutionalized behavioral patterns, interpreted as illness due to spirit possession. The discussion includes a review of the nervous and mental disorders associated with the diet of the Southern Bantu. A relationship between the endemic nutritional syndromes (primarily pellagra), and the condition known as ukuth-wasa, is proposed.

3333. Gussler, Judith D. Covert food sharing in a Kittitian community. Paper presented at 73rd Annual Meeting of the American Anthropological Association. 19-24 November, 1974. Mexico City.

3334. Gussler, Judith D. The adaptivity of the mixed feeding practices of the mothers of St. Kitts. Paper presented at 76th Annual Meeting of the American Anthropological Association. 29 November to 3 December, 1977. Houston, Texas.

The adaptivity of the mixed infant feeding practices of mothers in St. Kitts, West Indies, are described. St. Kitts' history of slavery, perpetual poverty and fluctuation of economic fortunes, have inhibited the development of group structures and have stimulated migration. Thus, two prominent features of the island's present sociocultural system are its individuation of interpersonal ties and the utilization of multiple natural and social resources by individuals in the system. Infant feeding practices reflect the mothers' attempts to meet the demands of flexible social network strategies.

3335. Gussow, Joan. 1972. Contranutritional messages of the TV ads. aimed at children. FN 29: 122-131.

Abstract from testimony to the United States Senate Commerce Committee Subcommittee on the Consumer. 2 March 1972.

3336. Gustav, Bonnie. Effects of nutritional stress on pelvic sexual dimorphism in three Dickson Mound populations. Paper presented at 72nd Annual Meeting of the American Anthropological Association. 29 November, 1973. New Orleans, Louisiana.

3337. Gustchin G.-G. 1938. Le riz. Origine et histoire de sa culture. [Rice. Origin and history of its cultivation.] Riz 12: 61-98.

3338. Gusten, Rolf. 1968. Studies in the staple food economy of western Nigeria. Munich: Welt-forum Verlag.

3339. Gutelius, M.F.; Millican, F.K.; Layman, E.M.; Cohen, G.J.; & Dublin, C. 1962. Nutritional studies of children with pica. 1. Controlled study evaluating nutritional status. Pediatrics 29: 1012-1017.

A population of thirty Black-American children in Washington, D.C.

3340. Guthe, Carl E. History of the Committee on Food Habits. In The problem of changing food habits. 1941-1943. National Research Council. 1943. Pp. 9-19. US--NAS-NRC-B No. 108.

Establishment, goals; membership; activities; and accomplishments of the first coordinated team of U.S. social scientists entrusted with providing recommendations for national dietary modification, during World War II.

3341. Guthrie, Helen A. 1962. Infant feeding practices in the Philippines. TGM 14: 164-170.

A study which compares the differences in infant feeding in terms of degree of urbanization. Five community groups living in the rice-eating area of Luzon, the largest of the Philippine Islands, are included.

3342. Guthrie, Helen A. 1967. Infant feeding practices in a corn eating area in the Philippines. TGM 19: 48-55.

Comparative study of rural-urban infant feeding.

3343. Guthrie, Helen A. Infant and maternal nutrition in four Taglog communities. In Modernization, its impact in the Philippines, 4. Edited by W.F. Bello & A. de Guzman, II. 1969. Pp. 60-92. Institute of Philippine Culture Papers. No. 7. Quezon: Institute of Philippine Culture.

Includes data on diet during pregnancy and lactation, infant and pre-school feeding practices, food expenditure and food production.

3344. Gutebock, Hans G. 1968. Oil plants in Hittite Anatolia. AOS-J 88: 66-71.

3345. Gutierrez, M. & Santos, F.O. 1938. The food consumption of one hundred families in Paco District, Manila. PJS 66: 397-416.

3346. Gutierrez, M. & Santo, F.O. 1939. Diet of low-income family in Tondo district, Manila. AM Phil 1: 171-193.

3347. Guy, Christian. 1962. An illustrated history of French cuisine, from Charlemagne to Charles de Gaulle. Translated by Elizabeth Abbott. New York: Orion Press.

3348. Guy, Christian. 1962. Une histoire de la cusiine francaise. [A history of French cuisine]. Paris: Productions de Paris.

3349. Guy, Christian. 1975. Caracteristiques des habitudes alimentaires des Francais qui vivaient sous la Renaissance. [Characteristics of the food habits of the French at the time of the Renaissance.] Historia No. 42. Pp. 45-51.

3350. Guy, R.A. 1936. Diets of young children in Peking. CMJ 50: 434-442.

3351. Guy, R.A. & Yeh, K.S. 1938. Peking diets. CMJ 54: 201-222.

3352. Guy, R.A. & Yeh, K.S. 1938. Soybean "milk" as food for young infants. CMJ 54: 1-30.

China.

3353. Guzman, Miguel A.; Ascoli, Werner; & Scrimshaw, Nevin S. Nutrition research in Spanish-Portuguese-Speaking countires. In Recent advances in nutrition. With special reference to clinical medicine. Edited by J.F. Brock. 1961. Pp. 226-251. Boston: Little, Brown & Co.

Nutritive value of foods; assessment of nutritional status; endemic goitre; kwashiorkor; specific nutrient deficiencies.

3354. Gwinn, Alice E. & Hibbard, Esther L. 1966. Fun and frolic from Japan. 2nd edition. New York: Friendship Press.

Food habits and food-related behavior: pp. 20-26.

3355. Gyorgy, P. 1961. The nutritional value of tempeh. National Academy of Science. Publication No. 843. Washington, D.C.: National Research Council.

A fermented soy food manufactured in Indonesia.

3356. Ha, Tae-hung. 1968. Guide to Korean culture. Seoul: Yonsei University Press.

Festival foods and customs: pp. 148, 156, 169-171.

3357. Haag, William G. 1955. Aboriginal influences in Southern diet. US-DHEW-PER 70: 920-921.

Native American food plants. Refers also to African, Spanish, and French cookery techniques.

3358. Haas, A. Das Schlacht-und Viehwesen der Freien Reichstadt Schwabisch-Hall. [Cattle breeding and slaughtering in the Free Imperial City of Schwabisch-Hall.] Ph.D. dissertation. Ludwig-Maximillians Universitat Munich. 1968.

3359. Hackenberg, Robert. 1964. Changing diet of Arizona Indians. JAIE 3: 27-32.

3360. Hacker, Dorothy B. 1951. Food patterns in New Mexico. PHCurr 43: 589-591.

Ethnicity in relation to food intake, preference, and nutritional adequacy.

3361. Hacker, Dorothy B.; Franks, Marilyn S.; Fisher, Viola; Grass, Rebecca J.; Hotopp, Marion; & Lantz, Edith M. 1954. A study of food habits in New Mexico, 1949-1952. NM-AES-B 384.

3362. Hacker, Dorothy B. & Miller, E.D. 1959. Food patterns of the Southwest. AJCN 7: 224-229.

3363. Hackley, S.B. 1904. Table fare of the Virginia mountains. WL 17: 78-79.

3364. Hackwood, Frederick William. 1909. Inns, ales and drinking custom of old England. New York: Sturgis & Walton.

3365. Haddon, Alfred C., ed. 1907. Report of the Cambridge Anthropological Expedition to the Torres Straits. 6 vols. Cambridge: Cambridge University Press.

Food and its preparation, Vol. Four. pp. 130-145. Myth: acquisition of food supply for humankind: Vol. Five; pp. 59-61. Myth: origin of coconut: Vol. Five; p. 103. Myth: origin of eating customers Vol. 5. p. 32.

3366. Hage, Karl Per. A structural analysis of Munchnerian beer terms and beer drinking. Master's thesis. Anthropology. University of Washington. 1968.

3367. Hagerty, Michael. 1940. Comments on writings concerning Chinese sorghum. HJAS 5: 234-260.

3368. Hagood, Margaret Jarman. 1977. Mothers of the south. Portraiture of the white tenant farm woman. New York: W.W. Norton.

3369. Hahn, Fritz. Arbeitstudien als Hilfsmittle der Nahrungsforschung. [Time and motion studies as an aid to nutrition research.] Paper presented at First International Symposium on Ethnological Food

Research   21-25   August,   1970.   Lund: Folklivsarkivet, University of Lund.

3369. Hahn, W. Cockburn, William: an account of the nature, causes, symptoms and cure, of the distempers that are incident to seafaring people. With observations of the diet of the sea-men in His Majesty's Navy. London, 1696. Ph.D. dissertation. Universitat Dusseldorf. 1969.

3371. Haime, Jules. 187. The history of fish-culture in Europe from its earlies records to 1854. USCFF-RC for 1872 and 1873. Pp. 465-492.

3372. Halain, C. 1960. Les poissons dans l'alimentation des habitants de l'Afrique Belge. [Fish in the diet of the inhabitants of Belgian Africa.] BC 15: 148-150.

3373. Halasz, Z. 1963. Hungarian paprika through the ages. Budapest: Corvina Press.

Hungarian red pepper.

3374. Hale, Edwin M. 1891. Ilex cassine: the aboriginal North American tea. USDA-DB-B No. 14

3375. Halim, 'asma. 1944. Thamaniyah ghayyamfial-sayeed. [Thirty days in Upper Egypt.] Cairo: Dar el Fajr.

Egyptian peasant diet: pp. 25-27.

3376. Hall, C.W. & Trout, G.M. 1968. Milk pasteurization. Westpot, Connecticut: AVI Pub. Co.

Historical data: pp. 1-21, passim.

3377. Hall, E.C. 1943. The nutritive value of Australian tropical fruits. AGNZV 1 December: 568-569.

Avocado [Persea sp.], banana [Musa sp.], passion fruit [Passiflora sp.], custard apple [Annona sp.], guava [Psidium guajava], jujube [Zizyphus jujuba], mango [Mangifera indica], pawpaw [Asimina triloba], pineapple [Ananas comosus], persimmon [Diospyros sp.], bread fruit [Artocarpus altilis], roselle [Hibiscus sabdarifa].

3378. Hall, Harrison. 1813. Hall's distiller, containing 1. Full and particular directions for mashing and distilling all kinds of grain, and imitating holland gin and Irish whiskey. 2. A notice of the different kind of stills in use in the United States and of the Scotch skills which may be run off 480 times in 24 hours. 3. A treatise on fermentation, containing the latest discoveries on the subject. 4. Directions for making yeast, and preserving it sweet for any length of time. 5. The Rev. Mr. Allison's process of rectification with improvement; and mode of imitating French brandy, & c, 6. Instructions for making all kinds of cordiels, compound waters, & c.; also for making cider, beer and various kinds of wines. & c. Adapted to the use of farmers, as well as distillers. Philadelphia. John Bioren.

3379. Hall, Irene S. & Hall, Calvin S. 1939. A study of disliked and unfamiliar foods. JADA 15: 540-548.

3380. Hall, L. 1959. Case report: two cases of gout among the Kikuyu. EAMJ 36: 616-617.

It is likely that as Africans' dietary and drinking habits change under the influence of civilization, more are likely to develop the overt disease. Both cases are civil servants with far more protein intake than is common to the Kikuya diet.

3381. Hall, O. 1898. Samoan feast of Pilaui. Lippincott 63: 338-343.

3382. Haller, Konrad. 1960. Das Ende der alten Kommunbrauereien. [The end of the old communal breweries.] Oberpfalz 48: 93-96.

3383. Halley, E. 1946. A recent dietary study of a rural community in Greece. JADA 22: 977-983.

3384. Hallion, L. 1900. Le kefir. [Kefir.] Pres Med 8: 265-267.

A fermented milk.

3385. Hallock, Grace T. 1931. Travels of a rolled oat. Chicago: The Quaker Oats Co.

3386. Hallock, Grace T. & Wood, Thomas D. Grain through the ages. Chicago: The Quaker Oats Company.

3387. Halsell, Grace. 1976. Los viejos. Secrets of long life from the sacred valley. Emmaus, Pennsylvania: Rodale Press.

Diet of longevous population in Vilcabamba, Ecuador: pp. 91-110.

3388. Halseth, Odd S. 1931. Prehistoric irrigation systems revealed by aerial survey in Arizona. PE 16: 7, 26 [July].

3389. Halsted, James A. 1968. Geophagia in man. Its nature and nutritional effects. AJCN 21: 1384-1393.

History; incidence; as a clinical nutrition problem; theories regarding cause.

3390. Hambright, Dudley Ben. A nutritional study of Latin-American children. Master's thesis. Denton: Texas State College for Women. 1943.

3391. Hambruch, Paul. 1915. Nauru. Hamburgische Wissenschaftliche Stiftung. Ergebnisse der Südsee-Expedition 1908-1910. 2. Ethnographie: B. Mikronesien. Vol 1. [Nauru. Hamburg Science Foundation. Results of the South Sea Expedition 1908-1910. Vol. 1. Part 2. Ethnography: B. Micronesia.] Hamburg: L. Friederichsen & Co.

Foods and stimulants: pp. 103-121. Obtaining food: pp. 122-157.

3392. Hambruch, Paul & Eilers, Annaliese, 1936. Ponape. Ergebnisse der Südsee Expedition 1908-1910. [Ponape. Results of the South Sea Expedition 1908-1910.] Hamburg: Friederichsen, de Gruyter & Co.

Food tabus [myth]: pp. 147-149; 165-167.

3393. Hamburger, W.W. 1958. The occurrence and meaning of dreams of food and eating. 1. Typical food and eating dreams of four patients in analysis. Psych Med 20: 1-16.

Freudian interpretations of dreams.

3394. Hamburger, W.W. 1958. The psychology of dietary change. AJPH 48: 1342-1348.

3395. Hamilton, Agus 1908. Fishing and sea-foods of the ancient Maori. DMus-E No.2.

3396. Hamilton, D.J. 1883. Remarks on nutrition and growth. BMJ 2: 1271-1277.

3397. Hamilton, Herbert. 1961. The problem of food acceptance in the military establishment. United States Army. Quartermaster Food and Container Institute for the Armed Forces. Research and Engineering Command. Report no. 3. Contract DA 19-129-qm-1117. Project No. 7-84-15-007. Chicago: United States Army. Quartermaster Food and Container Institute.

3398. Hamilton, Herbert. 1961. Social bases of food attitudes in the military establishment. United States Army. Quartermaster Food and Container Institute for the Armed Forces. Research and Engineering Command. Chicago: United States Army. Quartermaster Food and Container Institute.

3399. Hamilton, Lucy. 1955. Indigenous versus introduced vegetables in the villag dietary patterns. PNGAJ 10: 54-47.

European vegetables are being grown in native gardens in Papua and New Guineas; however, the author notes that indigenous greens have higher nutritive values; and should be encouraged. A food composition table in included.

3400. Hamilton, Lucy & Wilson, Winifred. 1957. Dietary survey in Malaguna village, Rabaul. SP 9: 400-406.

New Britain, Bismarck Archipelago.

3401. Hammarsten, Olof. 1886. Untersuchungen von Kefir. [Investigation on kefir.] ULF 21: -32.

A fermented milk product. Abstracted in BCARL 17: 413-417. [1888].

3402. Hammond, R.J. 1956. History of the Second World War: food. Vol. 2. Great Britain Cabinet Office. United Kingdom Civil Series. Publication No. 63-111-32-4. Studies in Administration and Control. London: Her Majesty's Stationery Office & Longmans, Green & Co.

3403. Hammond, R.J. 1962. History of the Second World War: food. Vol. 3. Great Britain. Cabinet Office. United Kingdom Civil Series. Publication No. 63-111-33-4. Studies in Administration and Control. London: Her Majesty's Stationery Office & Longman's, Green & Co.

3404. Hammond, T.G. 1894. The taro [Colocasia antiquorum] JPS 3: 105-106.

3405. Hampe, Jr., Edward C. & Wittenberg. Merle. 1964. The lifeline of America. Development of the food industry. New York, Toronto, London: McGraw-Hill.

A text book on the history of agriculture, food processing, preservation, transportation, distribution, and marketing.

3406. Hampson, John. 1944. The English at table. Britain in Pictures. London: William Collins.

3407. Hamy, Ernest-T. & Sauvage, Emile. 1867. Sur un kjokkenmodding decouvert à l'embouchure de la Canche. [On a kitchenmidden discovered at the month of the Canche.] SAP-B 2 [second series]: 362-366.

A French site, north of the town of Etaples [Pas-de-Calais], in western France.

3408. Hamy, Ernest T. 1899. Les geophages du Tonkin. [The earth-eaters of Tonkin.] P-MNHN-B 5: 64-66.

3409. Han, Sang-bok. A study of Korean peasant fishing economy. Paper presented at 9th International Congress of Anthropologicals and Ethnological Sciences. 28 August to 8 September, 1973. Chicago, Illinois.

Discusses changes in communal use of seaweed collecting grounds toward individual ownership. Shows the important influence of the entrepreneur, together with political and legal forces at the local level, upon technological and institutional change in Korean maritime economy.

3410. Hanausek, T.F. 1914. A tea from Asia Minor. [In German.] ZUNG 28: 259-263.

An infusion made from the leaves of Orginanum vulgare var. albiflorum, C. Koch; which resembles the Chinese souchong teas.

3411. Hand, D.B. 1959. Part 3. Food habits and technology. In A nutrition survey of the armed forces of Pakistan. JN 69 [Supp. 2]: 19-22. July.

3412. Hand, D.B.; Schaefer, Arnold E.; & Wilson, Christine S. A comparative study of food consumption patterns in Latin American. Middle Eastern, and Far Eastern countries. In Food science and technology. Proceedings of the First International Congress of Food Science and Technology. September 18-21, 1962. London. Edited by James Mui Leitch. Vol. 5. 1967. Pp. 251-270.

This paper is a synopsis of data gathered by the United States Interdepartmental Committee on Nutrition for National Defense which comprised the Departments of State, Defense, Health, Education and Welfare, Agriculture; as well as the Agency for International Development, the Atomic Energy Commission and the Food for Peace Organization. Country comparisons are given with complementary analyses of dietaries.

3413. Handler, Jerome S. 1965. The history of arrowroot production in Barbados and the Chalky Mount Arrowroot Growers Association, a peasant marketig experience that failed. BMHS-J 31: 131-152.

3414. Handy, Edward Smith Craighill. 1939. Marquesan legends. BPBM-B No. 69. Myth: gods teach how to seek and prepare food: P. 114.

3415. Handy, Edward Smith Craighill. 1940. The Hawaiian planter. Vol. 1. His plants, methods, and areas of cultivation. BPBM-B No. 161.

3416. Handy, Edward Smith Craighill, & Handy Willowdean Chatterton. 1924. Samoan housebuilding, cooking, and tatooing. BPBM-B No. 15.

3417. Handy, Edward Smith Craighill; Pukui, Mary Kawena, & Livermore, Katherine. 1934. Outline of Hawaiian physical therapeutics. BPBM-B 126.

Included are data on diets prescribed for pregnancy, and in illness.

3418. Hanes, Phyllis. 1972. Morocco—dining with your fingers. CSM 3 October. P. 9.

Couscous, a bulgur-wheat based casserole; varieties, preparation methods, ingredients; handwashing.

3419. Hanish, Otoman Zar-Adusht. 1914. Mazdaznan dietetics and cookery-book. London: Mazdaznan Publishing and supply Co.

Food regulations of the modern Parsi religion.

3420. Hanizawa, J. 1913. Notes on preserving egg in China. [In German] ZBPH 36: 418-419.

Description of three ways of preserving duck eggs, i.e. pidarn, hueidarn, tsaudarn, in Chihchiang and Kiangsu Provinces.

3421. Hanks, Lucien M. 1972. Rice and man. Chicago: Aldine-Atherton, Inc.

3422. Hanlon, Capistran J. 1970. A Papago barbecue. Kiva 36: 11-13.

Arizona.

3423. Hanna. 1887. Des Soldaten Kochbüchlein. Pramiirt auf der Austellung für Volksernahrung zu Leipzig. [The soldier's little cookbook. Awarded first prize at the Exhibition for Popular Nutrition in Leipzig.] Hildburghausen: Kesselring.

3424. Hannemann, Manfred. A culture-historical geography of the plow cattle complex in the Near East. Master's thesis. Geography. University of California, Los Angeles. 1967.

3425. Hanover, New Hampshire. Dartmouth College Library. Stefansson Collection. Dried meat [by Edward N. Wentworth.] 1955.

3426. Hansen, C.C. 1910. Foodstuffs in Siam. USDCL-DCTR No. 3679. P. 12.

3427. Hansen, H.P. 1941. Hyrdeliv paa Heden. [Shepherds' life on the heath.] Danmarks Folkeminder, No. 49. Copenhagen: Munksgaard.

Scattered references to food.

3428. Hansen, H.P. 1954. Bondens brod, primitiv brodbagning. [Peasant's bread, primitive breadbaking.] Copenhagen: Andersens Forlag.

3429. Hanson, C. 1913. The Kachins. Rangoon American Baptist Mission Press.

Burma. Food: pp. 55-56.

3430. Hanson, Earl. 1933. Malnutrition in the Amazon basin. Science 78: 36-38.

3431. Hanson, H.C. & Gagnon, A. 1964. Hunting and utlization of wild geese by the Indians of Hudson Bay lowlands of northern Ontario. OFWR 3(2): 2-11.

3432. Hanzawa, J. 1912. Fungi and composition of Japanese tamari-kojii. MCen 1: 163-166.

3433. Hapgood, I.F. 1900. Russian breakfast dishes. Independent 52: 2213-2216.

3434. Harako, R. 1976. The Mbuti as hunters——a study of ecological anthropology of the Mbuti pygmies. 1. KU-AS 10: 37-99.

3435. Harbinger, Lucy Jane. The importance of food plants in the maintenance of Nez Perce cultural identify. Master's thesis. Anthropology. Washington State University. 1964.

3436. Harcum, Cornelia G. Roman cooks. Ph.D. dissertation. Johns Hopkins University. 1913.

Cooks and cooking in the early Roman period.

3437. Harden, Arthur. 1932. Alcoholic fermentation. London: Longman's, Green.

3438. Hardesty, Donald L. 1975. The niche concept: suggestions for its use in human ecology. H Ecol 3: 71-85.

The concept of niche is defined in terms of the distinctive ways of using such a Euclidean hyperspace's resources for subsistence that set "cultural species" apart. Distinctiveness [of species] is defined by subsistence variety, the number of resources used for subsistence, and how much each resource is relied upon. Examples illustrating the facets of nich parameters are provided from Bushman, Cree, Tsembaga Maring (New Guinea) Tasbapauni Miskito, Baja California, Busamo (New Guinea) Chimbu (New Guineas), Kapauku (New Guinea), Washo (Nevada), and numerous other groups.

3439. Hardin, James Walker. 1969. Human poisoning from native and cultivated plants. Durham, North Carolina: Duke University Press.

3440. Harding, Robert S.O. The baboon as a predator of small animals. Paper presented at 72nd Annual Meeting of the American Anthropological Association. 1 December, 1973. New Orleans, Louisiana.

3441. Harding, T. Swann. 1931. Food prejudices. MJR 133: 67-70.

3442. Harding, T. Swann. 1935. It was something they had eaten. Med Rec 142: 471-472.

Notes on dietaries of famous men, including: Charles V, Henry II, F. di Medici, Napoleon, Victor Hugo, Herbert Spencer, Charlemagne, James I, and others.

3443. Harding, T. Swann. 1942. A pig is no hog-humans may be. AJPharm 114: 88-95.

Comments on the human tendency to overeat.

3444. Harding, T. Swann. 1948. Native foods of the Western Hemisphere. JADA 24: 609-614.

3445. Hardinge, Mervyn G. & Crooks, Hulda. 1963. Non-flesh dietaries. JADA 43: 545-549.

3446. Hardy, Georges. 1932. L'alimentation des indigenes au Maroc. [Diet of Moroccan natives.] TAM 48: 143-158.

3447. Hardy, G. L'alimentation des indigenes au Maroc. [Diet of natives in Morocco.] In L'alimentation indigene dans les colonies francaises. Protectorats et territories sous mandat. Edited by G. Hardy & C. Richet. 1933. Pp. 125-137. Paris: Vigot Freres.

3448. Hardy, Georges & Richet, Charles [fils]. 1933. L'alimentation indigene dans les colonies francaises. Protectorats et territoires sous mandat. [Native diet in the French colonies. Protectorates and territories under mandate.] Paris: Vigot Freres.

3449. Hare, R.F. & Griffiths, David. 1907. The tuna as food for man. NM-AES-B 64.

Fruit of the Opuntia sp. cactus. Gathering, processing, chemical analysis.

3450. Harford, Charles Forbes. 1904. The drinking habits of uncivilized and semi-civilized races. BJI 2: 92-103.

3451. Harfouche, Jamal Karam. 1965. Chapter
One. Breast feeding and maternal attitude in perin-
atal period. Chapter Two. Maternal diet in pregnancy and birthmarks. Chapter Three. Maternal diet in
post partun period. Chapter Four. Breast feeding
during early neonatal period. Chapter five. Dietary, emotional and other factors affecting lactation.
In Infant health in Lebanon. Customs and taboos.
Beirut: Khayats.

3452. Hariot, P. & Patouillard, N. 1910. Champignons de la region de Timbouctou et de la Mauritan-
ie recuellis par M.R. Chudeau [Mushrooms of the
Timbuctou region and of Mauritania gathered by
Mr. R. Chudeau.] SMF-B 26: 205-209.

3453. Hark, Joseph Maximillian. 1916. Cooking
utensils and cookery of our grandmothers. LCHS-P
7: 225-231.

        Pennsylvania Dutch.

3454. Hark, Milla Theresa Crosta. 1914. Cooking
utensils and cookery of our grandmothers. Lebanon,
Pennsylvania: Lebanon County Historical Society.
3455. Harlan, Jack R. 1967. A wild wheat
harvest in Turkey. Archaeology 20: 197-201.

        Recounts the author's experiments in hand
        harvesting and processing grains of wild
        einkorn [Triticum boeoticum var thaoudar]
        discovered in the region of Karacadag
        (Black Mountain) in the Turkish Province of
        Diyarbakir. Comparisons with domesticated
        einkorn are made.

3456. Harlan, Jack R. 1971. Agricultural origins:
centers and non-centers. Agriculture may originate
in discrete centers or evolve over vast areas without
definable centes. Science 174: 468-474.

        Questions Vavilov's concept of centers of
        origin of cultivated plants, of which there
        were eight. In place of Vavilov's model, the
        author proposes three 'systems' with a cent-
        er of origin and a non-center in which
        activities of domestication occurred and
        cultivated plants dispersed over an area of
        five to ten thousand kilometers. Both cent-
        er and non-center are viewed as having
        interacted, although crops did not necessari-
        ly originate in centers, nor did agriculture
        necessarily develop in a geographical cent-
        er.

3457. Harland, B.F. & Peterson, M. 1978. Nutritional status of lacto-ovo-vegetarian Trappist
monks. JADA 72: 259-264.

3458. Harlow, H.F. & Yudin, H.C. 1933. Social
behavior of primates. 1. Social facilitation of
feeding in the monkey and its relation to attitudes
of ascendance and submission. JCCP 16: 171-185.

3459. Harms, H. von. Ubersicht der bisher in al-
tperuanischen Graben gefunden Pflanzenreste. [Up
to date review of the plant remains founds in
ancient Peruvian burials.] In Eduard Seler darge-
bracht Zum 70 Geburtstag von Freunden, Schulern

und Verehrern. Edited by Walter Lehmann. 1922.
Pp. 157-186. Stuttgart: Strecker & Schroder.

3460. Harner, Michael. 1977. The ecological
basis for Aztec survival. AM Ett 4: 117-135.

3461. Harner, M. 1977. The enigma of Aztec
sacrifice NH 136: 47-51.

        Suggests cannibalism may have been prac-
        ticed in response to a felt need for animal
        protein.

3462. Harney, William Edward. 1951. Australian
aboriginal cooking methods. Mankind 4: 242-245.

        Kangaroo, turtle, bandicoot, opossum, flying
        fox, game, reptiles, fish, vegetable foods.

3463. Harney, William Edward. 1960. Bill
Harney's cookbook, in collaboration with Patricia
Thompson. Melbourne: Lansdowne Press.

        Includes references to cookery of Australian
        aborigines.

3464. Harp, Harry H. & Marshall, E. 1965. Convenience foods: the relationship between sales
volume and factors influencing demand. USDA-
ERS-AER No. 81.

        Cost per serving; competition among similar
        products; importance in overall consumer
        purchase pattern; product availability;
        marketing success.

3465. Harper, Edward B. 1961. Cultural factors in
food consumption: an example from India. EB 15:
289-295.

        Effect of caste status upon food restric-
        tions, and food availability; "hot" -"cold"
        classification; ritual pollution; introduction
        of new foods; attitudes regarding basic
        foods constituting a meal; socio-cultural
        vaiables involved in food habits change. Re-
        ference area is the Malnad (hilly country) on
        the west coast of South India.

3466. Harper, R. 1955. Fundamental problems in
subjective appraisal of foodstuffs. A Stat 4: 145-
160.

3467. Harper, R. 1960. Food assessment and food
acceptance as a psychological theme. OP 34: 233-
240.

3468. Harper, R. 1962. Psychologist's role in food
acceptance research. FTech 16: 70.

3469. Harper, R. 1963. Some attitudes to vegetables and their implications. Nature [L] 200: 14-18.

3470. Harper, R. Texture and consistency from
the standpoint of perception: some major issues. In
Rheology and texture of foodstuffs. Society of
Chemical Industry Monograph No. 27. Society of
Chemical Industry. 1968. Pp. 11-27. London:
Society of Chemical Industry.

Psychophysiological aspects of food textures; texture preferences among consumers; descriptive terminology; the language of flavor.

3471.   Harrington, Harold David.   1967.   Edible native plants of the Rocky Mountains. Albuquerque: University of New Mexico Press.

3472. Harrington, Mark Raymond. 1908. Some Seneca corn-foods and their preparation. AA 10: 575-590.

3473.   Harrington, Mark Raymond.   1945.   Bug sugar. MKey 19: 95-96. the

South Paiutes gathered certain aphids which contained a sweet excresence.

3474.   Harrington, Mark Raymond.   1956.   Indians gather wild rice. Mkey 30: 28-29.

3475.   Harris, Ben Charles. 1969. Eat the weeds. Barre, Massachusetts: Barre Publishers.

Guide to edible wild plants in North America.

3476.   Harris, David R.   1967.   New light on plant domestication and the origins of agriculture. GR 57: 90-107.

3477.   Harris, David R. The origins of agriculture: alternative pathways toward agriculture.   Paper presented at 9th International Congress of Anthropological and Ethnological Sciences.   28 August to 8 September, 1973. Chicago, Illinois.

3478.   Harris, E.L. & Wallace, T.R.   1908. Food in Asiatic Turkey. USDCL-DCTR No. 3297. Pp. 8-10.

Diets of populations in Asia Minor, and Palestine.

3479.   Harris, George.   1873-1876.   Domestic everyday life, manners and customs in the ancient world. RHS-L-T 2: 393-438; 4: 364-415.

3480.   Harris, George.   1877-1882.   Domestic every-day life, and manners and customers in this country, from the earliest period to the end of the last century. RHS-L-T 5: 83-116; 6: 86-130; 7: 176-211; 8: 36-63; 9: 224-253; 10: 203-231.

England.

3481.   Harris, George Henry.   1890.   The Indian bread root of the Senecas. Waterloo, New York: Observer Electric Print.

Held by New York Public Library, Hanford Collection. No. HBC p.v. 170.

3482.   Harris, George Henry. 1891. Root foods of the Seneca Indians. RAS-P 1: 106-117.

3483.   Harris, H.A.   1966.   The diet of Greek athletes. PNS 87-90.

Feeding the earliest Olympic games contestants.

3484.   Harris, Henry Wilson. 1919. The peace in the making. London: Swarthmore Press.

The feeding of Europe during W.W.I.: pp. 179-190.

3485.   Harris, Margaret B. 1946. An introduction to the Chontal of Tabasco, Mexico. AM Ind 6: 247-255.

Diet: p. 249-250.

3486.   Harris, Margaret B. & Nashiro, H. 1958. Diets of families in the Ryukyu Islands. JHE 50: 89-91.

3487.   Harris, Marvin. The myth of the sacred cow. In: Man, culture, and animals AAAS-P No. 78. Edited by Anthony Leeds and Andrew P. Vayda. 1965. Pp. 217-228.

3488.   Harris, Robert Samuel. 1945. An approach to the nutrition problems of other nations. Science 102: 42-44.

3489.   Harris, Robert Samuel. 1946. The nutrition problem of Mexico. JADA 22: 974-976.

3490.   Harris, Robert Samuel. 1948. Food composition and nutritional acceptance programs. NR 6: 33-35.

Concludes "It appears that the food problems other nations will not be solved by imposing our food habits upon them. A long step can be made toward a practical solution of the nutrition problems by an analysis of the food plants and dietaries of each area, and by the production and consumption of the most nutritious indigenous foods. In this sense, food analysis is basic to the solution of the nutrition problems of the world." P. 35.

3491.   Harris, Robert Samuel. 1953. Plantas comestivas nativas da America Central. [Native edible plants of Central America.] ABN 9: 14-26.

3492.   Harris, Robert Samuel. Influences of culture on Man's diet. Paper read at the Symposium on Nutrition and Oral Health. 24 September 1961, at the University of Pennsylvania School of Dentistry, Philadelphia. Mimeographed. Also in AEH 5: 144-152 [1962].

3493.   Harris, Robert Samuel & Munsell, Hazel E. 1950. Edible plants of Central America. JHE 629-631.

3494.   Harris, Robert Samuel; Wang, Florence K.C.; Ying, H. Wu; Tsao, Chi-hsuen; & Loo, Lenore Y.S. 1949. Composition of Chinese foods. JADA 25: 28-38.

3495.   Harris, Seale. The food factor in pellagra. In International conference on health problems in tropical America. Kingston, Jamaica, 22 July to 1

August, 1924. Proceedings. Pp. 709-727. Boston: United Fruit Co.

> Believes infection, as well as diet to be implicated in pellagra.

3496.   Harris, W.E.   1904.   The Caribs of Guiana and the West Indies.   O-ED-AAR   1903.   pp. 139-145.

> Anthropophagy: p. 140, 143; fasting: p. 143.

3497.   Harris, W. Victor.   1940.   Some notes on insects as food.   TNF.   No. 9.   Pp. 45-48.

3498.   Harrison, B.   1971.   Drink and the Victorians. The temperance question in England, 1815-1872.   London: Faber.

3499.   Harrison, Gail Grigsby & Rathje, William L. Nutrient waste in an urban population and the Garbage Project.   Paper presented at 73rd Annual Meeting of the American Anthropological Association.   19 to 24 November, 1974.   Mexico City.

3500.   Harrison, Gail Grigsby.   Sociocultural correlates of food utilization and waste in a sample of urban households.   Ph.D. dissertation.   Anthropology.   University of Arizona.   1976.

3501.   Harrison, John B. & Bancroft, C.K.   1917. Food plants of British Guiana.   BG-BA-J   10: 143-177.

3502.   Harrison, John B. & Bancroft, C.K.   1926. Food plants of British Guiana.   BG-BA-J   19: 18-51.

3503.   Harrisson, Tom.   1949.   Notes on some nomadic Punans.   Sar MJ   5: 130-146.

> Sago processing: p. 146.

3504.   Harrisson, Tom & Salleh, A.K. Marican. 1960.   Nuts and Malays on Tanjong Datu.   Sar MJ   9: 655-669.

> Recipes for uses of oil expressed from indigenous nuts: pp. 664-665.

3505.   Harrison, S.G.   1952.   Edible pine kernels. GB-RBGK-KB   No. 3.   1951.   Pp. 371-375.

> Includes economic, historical, and distributional information.   Reference to use as food in Italy, and among Native Americans in the southwestern United States.   Contains descriptions of harvesting procedures in Italy, Russia, Baluchistan, Afghanistan; and notes its preparation into paste, and cakes by the Navajo.

3506.   Harrow, Benjamin & Funk, Casimir.   1925. Instinct as a guide to food.   A Merc   4: 489-494.

3507.   Harshberger, Jonathan William.   Maize: a botanical and economic study.   Ph.D. dissertation. University of Pennsylvania.   1892.

3508.   Harshberger, Jonathon William.   1893. Maize: a botanical and economic study.   UPenn-BL-CBLMA   1: 75-202.

3509.   Harshberger, Jonathan William.   1896.   The purposes of ethnobotany.   BG   21: 146-154.

3510.   Hart, Ann Boggess.   A study of food habits of families in three urban communities in Texas. Master's thesis. University of Texas.   1948.

3511.   Hart, Charles P.   Paiute herbalist.   Paper presented at the Thirty-fifth meeting of the American Association for the Advancement of Science. 1886. Buffalo, New York.

3512.   Hart, Constance C.   1943.   Plate lunches in war time.   NS   31: 48-49.

> Meat substitutes and extenders used in school lunches in the United States during World War II.

3513.   Hart, Donn V.   1955.   Hunting and food gathering activities in a Bisayan barrio.   JEAS   4: 1-13.

> Includes information on food preparation and famine foods. Philippines.

3514.   Hart, Edmund H.   1930.   Hart's Hawaiian Homes cook book.   Honolulu: Advertiser Press.

3515.   Hart, Ernest.   1879.   The doctor in the kitchen.   BMJ   2: 505, 506:

> Suggestions for inexpensive meals; methods of preparation: 546, 547; criticism of British practice of boiling vegetables; suggestions for improving vegetable preparation: pp. 594,585: Comments on the favorable quality of buttermilk, Zea mays, closed stoves; criticism of the quality of British pottery. Urges attention to other ethnic cuisines: pp. 671-673: soups, breakfast cereals, fuel economy; use of fat; mint sauce, river fish.

3516.   Hart, John A.   1978.   From subsistence to market: a case study of the Mbuti net hunters. HEcol   6: 325-353.

> This article describes the recent transition from subsistence to market hunting of a nomadic society of the Ituri Forest of Zaire. The Mbuti trade with local swidden agriculturalists, exchanging meat, and other forest products for tools, tobacco and cultivated food.   Exchanges of meat for other foods and goods with traders is generally by barter, although cash is occasionally involved. This article poignantly illustrates the pressures which are slowly affecting Mbuti society as it is drawn into a non-traditional economic system as a result of its desire for non-traditional commodities.

3517.   Hartman, C. V. Die Baumkelebasse im tropischen Amerika, ein beitrag zur ethnobotanik. [The tree gourd in tropical America, a study in ethnobotany.]   In Boas anniversary volume.   [Edited by

Berthold Lauffer.] 1906. Pp. 196-207. New York: C.E. Stecher & Co.

Contains references to uses as food containers.

3518. Hartmann, G. 1958. *Alkoholische Getranke bei den Naturvolkern Sudamerikas. [Alcoholic beverages among Native South Americans].* Berlin: Walter de Gruyter. Reviewed by D. Maybury-Lewis in *Man* April: 64 (1960).

3519. Hartmann, G. 1960. Gegorene Getranke bei den Naturvolkern Sudamerikas. [Fermented drinks among the aborigenes of South America.] GGBB-J 80: 77-91. Also in E Arch 39: 31-78 (1960) as Alkoholische Getranke bei den Naturvolkers Sudamerikas.

3520. Hatmann, Wilhelm. 1901. *Theorie und Praxis der Backerei. Gesamtdarstellung des heutigen Backeriebetriebes, mit besonderer Berucksichtigung ihrer Entwicklungsgeschicte. Mit anhang. [Theory and practice of baking. Complete presentation of modern baking operations, with particular consideration to its historical development. With appendix.]* Berlin: W. Hartmann.

3521. Hartson, Margaret. *A study of the influence of color on children's choice of cooked vegetables.* Master's thesis. Pennsylvania State University. 1946.

3522. Hartwich, Carl. 1911. *Die menschlichen Genussmittel, ihre Herkunft, Verbreitung, Geschichte, Anwendung, Bestandteile und Wirkung. [Human stimulants, their origins, distribution, history, uses, composition, and effects.]* Leipzig: C.M. Tauchnitz.

3523. Hartwich, C. & Hakanson, G. 1905. Floating manna grass [Glyceria fluitans], an almost forgotten native cereal. [In German.] ZUNG 10:473-478.

Used occasionally as food in Germany. Also found in the United States. Protein content given as 9.69%.

3524. Harvey. A. 1945. Food preservation in Australian tribes. *Mankind* 3: 191-192.

3524. Harwell, Richard Barksdale. 1975. *The mint julep.* Charlottesville: University Press of Virginia.

History of a traditional rum drink of the southeastern United States.

3525. Harwood, Alan. 1971. The hot-cold theory of disease: implications for treatment of Puerto Rican patients. *JAMA* 216: 1153-1158.

Many Puerto Ricans classify illnesses, medicines and foods according to a system which derives historically from the Hippocratic humoral theories of disease. Adherence to this system can influence the way in which a patient complies with therapeutic regimens, infant feeding, and ante- and post-partum recommendations. The author provides advice for physicians treating Puerto Rican patients on how to work with the therapeutic choices inherent in the system, thereby respecting the cultural values of the patient, and allowing the development of a treatment regimen which does not contravene deeply held ideas about illness and jeopardize chances of ameliorating illness.

3526. Harwood, Jim & Callahan, Ed. 1969. *Soul food cookbook.* Concord, California: Nitty-Gritty Productions.

Cookery of Black-American culture.

3527. Hassan, Khwaja A. 1967. *The cultural frontier of health in Village India.* Bombay: Manaktalas.

Eighty families were randomly sampled in the village of Chinaura, Lucknow District, in the north Indian State of Uttar Pradesh. Detailed data were recorded concerning food habits, and food taboos. Additional information is included regarding food sources, food preservation and storage techniques, and methods of cooking.

3528. Hasan, Khwaja A. 1971. The Hindu dietary practices and culinary rituals in a North Indian village. An ethnomedical and structural analysis. *Ethnomedicine* 1: 43-70.

The effects of cognitive categories (hot-cold; raw-cooked; pure-impure) in Hindu dietary. Explanation of dietary changes based on Firth's organizational approach.

3529. Hasan, Khwaja A. Hindu fasting and related rituals in a North Indian village. Paper presented at 70th Annual Meeting of the American Anthropological Association. 20 November, 1971. New York City.

The various dietary customs and culinary rituals of the Hindus explain the nature of their cosmological ideas and their notions of what a person's proper conduct in this life is. There is no universal code of conduct for all Hindus but there is an intimate relationship between their system of categorical properties, such as "hot" and "cold" and "raw" and "cooked", "pure" and "impure" foods and their group-forming tendencies as exemplified by castes, sub-castes, and the "holy" men as against the ordinary individual. Fasting has also been developed in Hindu religion to an extent unknown elsewhere, and shows a wide range from specific designation for reducing full diet by degree to no food intake at all; and avoiding staple foods like cereals during or after breaking the fast and eating only fruit or milk products. This paper examines Hindu fasting and the rituals and restrictions connected with it and analyzes the symbols they represent in Hindu society.

3530. Hasan, Khwaja A. Social aspects of the use of cannabis in India. Paper presented at 9th Intern-

ational Congress of Anthropological and Ethnological Sciences. 18 August to 8 September, 1973.
Chicago, Illinois.

Reference to use of cannabis leaves in ice
cream, and in a beverage called thandail.
Cannabis is also cermonially offered tothe
diety Shiva on Shivaratri day in temples as
'food of the gods.'

3531. Haslund-Christensen, Henning. 1934. Tents
in Mongolia [Yabonah]. Adventures and experiences among the nomads of Central Asia. Translated
from the Swedish by Elizabeth Sprigge & Charles
Napier. New York: E.P. Dutton.

Mongol dairy products: pp. 113-114; types
of bricks of tea: P. 30.

3532. Hassal, W.O., comp. 1962. How they lived,
55 B.C. - 1485. An anthology of original accounts.
Oxford: Basil Blackwell.

3533. Hassan, Ali. Nutritional problems in Egypt.
In A brief review of food and nutrition in five
countries. 1944. Pp. 6-10. United States Department of Agriculture. War Food Administration.
Washington, D.C.: Government Printing Office.

Data on regional food patterns; nutritional
deficiencies; school feeding; and a review of
nutrition surveys carried out.

3534. Hassan, Fekri A. Nutrition and early agri-
culture in the Near East. Paper presented at 74th
Annual Meeting of the American Anthropological
Association. 2 to 6 December, 1975. San Francisco
California.

3535. Hassan, Fekri A. Early food production in
the Nile Valley. Paper read at 77th Annual Meeting
of the American Anthropological Association. 14 to
18 November, 1978. Los Angeles, California.

Questions the traditional sequencing of pre-
dynastic culture stages. Comments on the
climate of pre-dynastic occupations, and
notes coincidence of declining Nile level.
Patterns of settlement, and the nature of
the subsistence base are described. Climatic influences on agricultural yield are
examined, and the results of the former on
the evolution of social and political organization are considered.

3536. Hassrick, Royal B. 1964. The Sioux. Norman: University of Oklahoma Press.

Food habits: pp. 179-180; 189-190.

3537. Haszard, H.D.M. 1890. Notes on some
relics of cannibalism. NZI-TP 22: 104-105.

Maori, New Zealand.

3538. Haranaka, Sachiko. From the hunter and
gatherer to the subsistence farmer in the New
Guinea highlands. Paper presented at 9th International Congress of Anthropological and Ethnological

Sciences. 28 August to 8 September, 1973. Chicago, Illinois.

Study of the transition of the Sisimin of
West Sepik from semi-nomadic hunter-gatherers to horticulturists. First contacted by
Australians in 1966, the Sisimin, by 1973,
had begun to change their settlement pattern; the composition of their kin group had
become more flexible and the territorial
group more clearly defined.

3539. Hatanaka, Sachiko & Bragge, Laurence W.
1973. Habitat, isolation and subsistence economy in
the Central Range of New Guinea. Oceania 44: 38-
57.

3540. Hatchell, G.W. 1959. Hippopotamus flesh
as food. TNR 52: 13-19.

3541. Hatt, Gudmund. 1951. The corn mothers in
America and Indonesia. Anthropos Pp. 853-908.

Comparison of anthropomorphic agricultural
fertility concepts.

3542. Hauck, Hazel M. 1961. Dietary studies in a
Nigerian secondary school. JADA 34: 467-472.

3543. Hauck, Hazel M. & Sudsaneh, Saovanee.
1956. Dietary study in a Thai rice village. FASEB-
FP 15: 555.

Abstract of paper.

3544. Hauck, Hazel M.; Susaneh, Saovanee; Hanks,
Jane R.; Rajatasilpin, Anusith; Indrasud, Sapha;
Campbell, Mary B.; and Thorangkul, Dana. 1958.
Food and habits and nutrient intakes in a Siamese
rice village. Studies in Bang Chan, 1952-1954.
Cornell Thailand Project. Interim Report Series.
No. 4. Department of Far Eastern Studies. South-
east Asia program. Ithaca: Cornell University.

Data recorded include dietary patterns, ceremonial foods, food beliefs, cooking techniques, eating techniques, food sources, methods of rice milling.

3545. Hauck, Hazel M. & Tabrah, F.L. 1963.
Infant feeding and growth in Awo Omamma, Nigeria. JADA 43: 327-330.

Includes description of food types, infant
feeding practices, and home diets.

3546. Haudricourt, A. 1941. Les colocasiees
alimentaires (taros et yautias). [Edible Colocasia
(taros and yautias)]. RBAAT 21: 40-69.

3547. Haudricourt, Andre G. Le mais n'est pas
originaire de l'Indochine. [Maize is not native to
Indo-China.] In Thirtieth International Congress of
Americanists. 18-23 August, 1952. Cambridge,
England. Proceedings. [1953]. Pp. 160-161. Lon-
don: The Royal Anthropological Institute.

Rejects the hypothesis of Anderson & Stonor
that maize was produced as a result of
genetic crossing of sorghum and coix, being

afterwards transported, in prehistoric time, across the Pacific to Peru, where it was crossed again with tripsacum to produce teosinte.

3548. Haughton, Samuel. 1868. On the relation of food to work done by the body; and its bearing upon medical practice. Introduction. BMJ 2: 163-166; Part Two. BMJ 2: 185-188.

3549. Haughton, Samuel. 1871. Relation of food to work, and its bearing on medical practice. SI-AR for the year 1870. 269-294.

3550. Haupt, P. 1922. Manna, nectar, and ambrosia. APS-P 61: 227-236.

3551. Hauten, Leona V. Food value in relation to food cost. Master's thesis. University of Chicago. 1943.

3552. Hautvast, J.G.A.G. 1971. Fish farming and fish consumption in a rural Tanzanian community. Voedin 32: 123-127.

A study carried out to evaluate the number of household fishponds, attitudes toward fish, and the frequency of its use as food. Area surveyed is in the northern part of Rungwe District of the southern highlands. Brief background on local dietary practices; fishing; sources of fish and taboos. The relationship of fish ponds to the potential breeding of malaria vectors is noted.

3553. Havard, Valery. 1884. The mezquit. AN 23: 451-453.

3554. Havard, Valery 1895. The food plants of the North American Indians. TBC-B 23: 33-46; 83-123.

3555. Havard, Valery. 1896. Drink plants of the North American Indians. TBC-B 23: 33-46.

3556. Havinga, B. 1964. Uit de geschiedenis van het haringkaken. [On the history of herring curing.] Voeding 25: 495-498.

3557. Havemeyer, Loomis. 1916. Chapter Two. Ceremonies connected with the animal foods. Chapter Three. Ceremonies dealing with plant food. In The drama of savage peoples. New Haven: Yale University Press.

3558. Hawaii. Department of Health. Bureau of Nutrition. Racial foods in Hawaii. Mimeographed. [Honolulu: State Department of Health.] 1958.

3559. Hawaii. City and Council of Honolulu. Chamber of Commerce. Public Health Committee. Nutrition sub-Committee. 1953. Foods used in Hawaii. Comparative nutritive values. Honolulu: Chamber of Commerce.

3560. Hawes, W.A.P. 1953. Seaweeds and their value in foodstuffs. PNS 12: 32-39.

After a brief discussion of the use of sea vegetation as food in various areas of the world, different types of algae are described in terms of chemical composition, and their contribution to human nutritional requirements.

3561. Hawkes, E.W. 1916. Food. C-DM-GS-M-AS 91: 29-36.

Labrador Eskimo food habits.

3562. Hawks, J.E. 1931. Diet of Chinese-American children. JALA 7: 202-203.

3563. Hawks, J.E. 1936. Preparation and composition of food served in Chinese homes. JALA 12: 136-140.

3564. Hawkes, J.G. 1947. On the origin and meaning of South American potato names. JLS(B) 53: 205-250.

3565. Hawkes, J.G. The ecology of wild potato species and its bearing on the origin of potato cultivation. In Huitieme Congres International de Botanique. 1954. Paris. Rapports et Communications. Parvenus avant le Congres aux Sections 14, 15 & 16. 1954. Pp. 49-50.

3566. Hawley, Edith. 1932. Economics of food consumption. 1st ed. New York, London: McGraw-Hill.

3567. Hawley, Florence M. Ellis; Pijoan, Michel; & Elkin, C.A. 1943. An inquiry into food economy and body economy in Zia Pueblo. AA 45: 547-556. New Mexico.

Studies surviving traditional food habits and effects of acculturation to European food patterns upon nutritional status of a Keresan-speaking village. A nutritional status report is given, and recommendations for improvement are made within the context of Zia economic capabilities and food practices.

3568. Hay, T.H. 1971. Windigo psychosis: psychodynamic, cultural, and social factors in aberrant behavior. AA 73: 1-19.

3569. Hayakawa, Kotaro. 1942. No to matsuri [Agriculture and rites.] Tokyo: Gloria Society.

Agricultural celebrations; agricultural gods; agrarian rites in various celebrations such as New Year, and Bon. Gods of mountain, and water, and their relation to agriculture; dosojn; gods of fertility and roads.

3570. Hayam, G. 1940. Animal foods of the Australian aborigines. VMat 57: 119-139.

3571. Hayashi, Harutaku. 1942. Nihon no sake. [Japanese wine]. Tokyo: Ichijo shobu.

Patone. Brewing. Part Two. Drinking customs.

3572. Hayashi, Yoshishige. 1961. Ainu no noasa-ku-motsu riyo. [Observations on Ainu techniques of cooking agricultural products.] MK 25: 21-33.

3573. Hayashiya, Tatsuaburo. 1975. Japanese arts and the tea ceremony. Translated by Joseph P. Macadam. Heibonsha survey of Japanese artseries, No. 15. New York: Weatherhill.

Cha-no-yu, the Japanese tea ceremony, and its related utensils.

3574. Hayden, Brian & Beattie, Owen. Resource overexploitation and prehistoric populations. Paper presented at 74th Annual Meeting of the American Anthropological Association. 2 to 6 December, 1975. San Francisco, California.

3575. Hayes, Richard J. 1965. Manuscript sources for the history of Irish civilization. Vol. 5. Boston: G.K. Hall.

Famines: pp. 346-348.

3576. Haynes, Henry W. 1884. Agricultural implements, New England Indians. BSNH-P 22: 437-443.

3577. Haynes, Henry W. 1884. Some new evidences, of cannibalism among New England Indians, from Mount Desert, Maine. BSNH-P 22: 60-63.

Human osteological material in association with animal skeletal material in context of evidence of a cooking fire.

3578. Hays, Wilma Pitchford & Hays, R. Vernon. 1973. Foods the Indians gave us. New York: I. Washburn.

3579. Hayward, Harry. 1904. Facts concerning the history, commerce and manufacture of butter. USDA-BAI-C No. 56.

Uses of butter in ancient times: pp. 177-178. Also in USDA-BAI-AR No. 20 for the year 1903.

3580. Hazelton, Nika Standen. 1969. The cooking of Germany. New York: Time-Life Books. Foods of the World.

3581. Hazlitt, William Carew. 1886. Old cookery books and ancient cuisine. The Book Lover's Library, Popular edition. London: Elliott Stock. Reprint. Detroit: Gale Research Corp. 1968.

Contains a brief overview of cuisine in the ancient classical world [i.e. Greece, Rome], and then concentrates on a history of English food, cookery, and a description of Old English kitchens and cooking utensils. Several recipes, and a list of old cookbooks is included.

3581. Head, Brandon. 1974. Cocoa: the food of the gods. Brooklyn, New York: Revisionist Press.

3582. Headland, Isaac Taylor. 1914. Chapter Nineteen. Food. In Home life in China. London: Methuen; New York: Macmillan.

Fruit; vegetables; banquet menus; preparation; etiquette.

3583. Healy, D.J. 1964. The story of Irish whiskey. IWel 13: 14-17.

3584. Heard, C.R.C. 1955. Palm wine in human nutrition. PNS 14: xi-xii.

3585. Heard, Vida & Faull, Lesley. 1970. Cookery in southern Africa; traditional and today. Cape Town: Books of Africa.

3586. Hearn, Lafcadio. 1885. La cuisine Creole; a collection of culinary recipes from leading chefs and noted Creole housewives, who have made New Orleans famous for its cuisine. New York: William H. Coleman.

3587. Heartman, Frederick, comp. 1942. Aphrodisiac culinary manual, being in part, the Squire of Baudricourt's Cuisine de l'Amour, in use for many centuries, especially designed for physical regeneration, vigor, and health, renewed through the appropriate use of condiments and aromatics in the preparation of dishes and beverages; containing a modern adaptation of nearly two hundred selected historical recipes from originating from many countries and chosen from famous cooking manuals and herbal lore. Also perfumes and diversified dainties. New Orleans: Gourmets' Company.

3588. Heath, D.B. 1958. Drinking patterns in the Bolivian Camba. CJSA 19: 491-508.

3589. Heath, John. 1948. An anthropological investigation in central Australia. BDJ 84: 207-210.

Implicates Western food in Aboriginal dental degeneration.

3590. Heber, A. Reeve & Heber, Kathleen Mary. 1926. In Himalayan Tibet. London: Seeley, Service.

Food habits: pp. 116-120.

3591. Hebert, Alexandre. Etude chimique des fruits de Sorindeia oleosa. [Chemical study of the fruits of Sorindeia oleosa.] In Eighth International Congress of Applied Chemistry. September 4 to 13, 1912. Washington and New York. Original Communications. Volume 18. Section 8c: Bromatology. Pp. 139-141.
The pulp of this fruit is fermented into a kind of cider in the Sudan.

3592. Hebert, M.A. 1842. Les substances alimentaires et des moyens d'en regler le choix et l'usage. [Food substances, and means of regulating their selection and use.] Paris: J.-B. Bailliere.

3593. Hecker, Howard M. Goat domestication at early Neolithic Beidha [Jordan]. Paper presented at 70th Annual Meeting of the American Anthropological Association. 20 November, 1971. New York City.

Most methods for ascertaining the presence of domesticated animals at an archeological site are open to criticism. A recently discovered microscopic technique has been devised which can distinguish between wild and domestic forms of the same species. Using this technique, we have been able to prove the presence of domesticated goat at the early Neolithic site of Beicha, Jordan (6700 B.C.). Because we are dealing with a very large sample (more than 12,000 identifiable bones) in which domestication has been shown by an independent method, we have an excellent opportunity to evaluate the various methods proposed in the past. A side benefit has been to throw light on domestication at nearby, contemporaneous Jericho.

3594. Hecker, Howard M. The faunal analysis of the primary food animals from pre-pottery Neolithic Beicha (Jordan). Ph.D. dissertation. Anthropology. Columbia University. 1975.

3595. Hedar, S. 1949. Gustav Vasa och det saltgröna smöret. [Gustavus Vasa and the salt-green butter.] SHF-HT No. 3. Pp. 253-262.

3596. Hedayat, H.; Khayetian, H.; Ghavifekr, M.; & Donoso, G. 1970. Substances toxiques naturelles des aliments. Cas de la fève et du favisme. [Naturally-occurring toxicants in foods. The case of the broad bean and favism.] CND 5: 23-29.

3597. Hediard, F. 1889. Les produits coloniaux dans l'alimentation. [Colonial products in the diet.] Paris: Cerf.

Contains recipes for preparing these foods.

3598. Hedin, L. Les sources françaises d'ethnobotanique. [French sources in ethnobotany.] In Huitieme Congres International de Botanique. 1954. Paris. Rapports et Communications. Parvenus avant le Congres aux Sections 14, 15, & 16. 1954. Pp. 31-33.

Reviews work of major researchers in the field.

3599. Hee, Marjorie Wong. 1954. Ways of using milk in the Chinese dietary. JALA 30: 788.

Reviews techniques of Chinese cookery, and lists fifteen recipes containing milk approved by a chinese taste-taste panel.

3600. Heeger, Fritz. 1964. Hirsebrei, ein frankisches Kuchenaltertum. [Fried millet, a French culinary antique.] Mainlande 15: 11-12.

3601. Hegyi, Imre. 1964. A lisztmino segek es a tesztfaetelek osszefuggese. [Communication on types of flour and farinaceous foods.] Ethnografia 75: 362-383.

3602. Hehn, Viktor. 1873. Das Salz. Eine kulturhistorische Studie. [Salt. A culture-historical study.] Berlin: Gebruder Borntraeger. Reprint. Darmstadt: Wissenschaftlichen Buchgesellschaft. 1964.

3603. Hehn, Viktor. 1911. Kulturpflanzen und haustiere in ihren Übergang aus Asien nach Griechenland and Italien sowie in das übrige Erops. Historische-Linguistik Skizze. [Cultivated plants and dometicated animals: their crossing from Asia to Greece and Italy as well as their remnants in Europe.] Berlin: Gebruddern Borntraeger. Reprint. Hildesheim: Georg Olms. 1963.

3604. Heiberg, M.E. 1901-1902. Les geophages. Analyse de deux terres mangeables de l'Afrique Centrale. [Earth eaters. Analysis of two edible earths of Central Africa.] Caducee 2: 287-289.

3605. Heichelheim, Fritz. 1930. Wirtschaftliche Schwangkungen der Zeit von Alexander bis Augustus. [Agricultural fashions from the time of Alexander to Augustus.] Jena: G. Fischer.

3606. Heidecker, Lorraine. The effect of dietary protein and light cycle on sexual maturation: an interaction study. Ph.D. dissertation. Anthropology. City University of New York. 1974.

3607. Heidecker, Lorraine. The hunted-hunter shift; meat eating in early hominids. Paper presented at 75th Annual Meeting of the American Anthropological Association. 17 to 21 November, 1976. Washington, D.C.

The problem of the amount of meat included in the diets of plio-pleistocene hominids is analyzed in terms of the caloric and nutritive requirements of these early hominids, and the degree to which these requirements could be met by vegetable resources of a savannah environment. The data suggest the early hominids may have hunted not only because of caloric need but because other nutrients were lacking in the vegetable material available to them. These nutrients could be found in sufficient quantity for a larger primate only in game animals, especially in marginal regions of the savannah.

3608. Heidelman, Richard G. 1952. Ethnozoology of the Pueblo Indians. CWAS-J 4: 19-20.

3609. Heinbecker, Peter. 1928. Studies on the metabolism of Eskimos. JBC 80: 461-475.

3610. Heine-Geldern, Robert. [Southeast Asia.] In Die Volker Asiens, Australiens und der Sudseeinsein. Edited by Georg Buschan. [1935.] Berlin: Globus Verlag.

Food, agriculture, livestock, hunting, and fishing: pp. 803-811.

3611. Heine-Geldern, Robert. 1958. Kulturpflanzengeographie und das Problem vorkolumbischer Kulturbeziehungen szwischen Alter and Neuer Welt. [The geography of cultivated plants and the question of culture contact between the Old and New Worlds.] Anthropos 53: 361-402.

3612. Heineman, Paul G. 1921. Milk. Philadelphia: W.B. Saunders.

3613. Heinen, H. Dieter & Ruddle, Kenneth. 1974. Ecology, ritual, and economic organization in the distribution of palm starch among the Warao of the Orinoco Delta. JAR 30: 116-138.

Covers the food quest, palm sources, seasonal and regional variation in palm starch availability; economic aspects of palm starch in the nahanamu ritual; other rituals involving food sharing. The nahanama ritual occurs during seasons of scarcity, and is seen as an institutionalization of strategies directed toward establishment of a stable supply of essential foods.

3614. Heiner, Mary Koll. The relationship of the work areas as a criterion for functional kitchen design. Master's thesis. Ithaca, New York: Cornell University. 1949.

3615. Heiner, Mary Koll & Mc Cullough, Helen E. 1948. Functional kitchen storage. CorU-AES-E No. 846.

Parameters of the study include family size and income, active and temporary storage (one week's use) of packaged food and related utensils.

3616. Heiner, Mary Koll & Steidl, Rose E. An analysis of memomotion films of breakfasts served in two U-shaped kitchen arrangements to determine the significance of the trips and distances. Department of Household Economics and Management. New York State College of Home Economics. Ithaca, New York: Cornell University. Unpublished report. 1950.

Memomotion refers to a slow-motion film technique used to record activities in time and motion studies.

3617. Heiner, Mary Koll & Steidl, Rose E. 1951. Guides for arrangement of urban family kitchens. CorU-AES-E No. 878.

The number of trips and resulting travel distances for three types of dinner menus were obtained to determine some guidelines for efficient kitchen arrangements. Trips and distances were separated into those for preparation and clearing for three types of dinner menus for a city household of four members of moderate income. In an L-shaped layout, the sink was the area of most frequent use, followed by the cooking range, the mix area, and ranking about equally: the refrigerator, table service, and dining room areas. The relationships most important to a particular area are in turn ranked. Based on the foregoing, and on ancillary variables, suggestions are made with regard to efficiency in planning and design.

3618. Heinz, H.J. & Maguire. 1974. The ethnobotany of the Xo Bushmen. Their ethnobotanical knowledge and plant lore. BS-OP No. 1.

3619. Heischel-Artelt, E. 1967. Eating and drinking in the ancient world. [In German] EU 14: 2-8.

3620. Heischel-Artelt, E. 1969. Kaffee und Tee in Spiegel der medizinischen Literatur des 17 bis 19. Jahrhunderts. [Coffee and tea reflected in the medical literature of the 17th throught the 19th Centuries. MHJ 4:250-260.

3621. Heiser, Jr., Charles Bixler. 1951. Some like it hot: peppers that soothe your palate have burned their names into the pages of history. NH 60: 307-311.

3622. Heiser, Jr., Charles Bixler. 1951. The sun flower among the North American Indians. APS-P 95: 432-448.

3623. Heiser, Jr., Charles Bixler. 1955. The origin and development of the cultivated sunflower. ABT 17: 161-167.

3624. Heiser, Jr., Charles Bixler. 1964. Sangorache, an amaranth used ceremonially in Ecuador. AA 66: 136-139.

Use of the pulverized inflorescence of Amaranthus quitensis H.B.K. as a food coloring for chicha (a maize beer), and a sweet maize soup prepared for the celebration of Dia de Difuntos.

3625. Heiser, Jr., Charles Bixler. 1969. Some considerations of early plant domestication. Bio Science 19: 228-231.

3626. Heiser, Jr., Charles Bixler. 1973. Seed to civilization - the story of man's food. San Francisco: W.H. Freeman.

3627. Heizer, Robert F. 1945. Honey dew sugar in western North America. Mkey 19: 140-145.

Insect secretion used as sweetener.

3628. Heizer, Robert F. 1967. Analysis of coprolites from a dry Nevada cave. In Papers on Great Basin archaeology. UC-AS No. 70 UCARF Pp. 1-20.

Coprolites are a generic term for (prehistoric) dried human fecal matter. Such material can, after proper treatment, provide data concerning human diet. This paper discusses briefly the history of, and analytic procedures involved in coprolite research, together with description of dietary material found in the sample herein studied. The sites yielding the coprolites are located near Lovelock, Nevada.

3629. Heizer, Robert F., ed. 1968. The Indians of Los Angeles County. Hugo Reid's letters of 1852. SM-P No. 21.

Food: pp. 22, 23; as medicine: pp. 33, 34; cooking utensils: pp. 44-45.

3630. Heizer, Robert F. Man, the hunter-gatherer: food availability vs biological factors. In Progress in human nutrition. Vol. 2. Edited by Sheldon Margen & Richard A. Ogar. 1978. Pp. 10-26.

A review of the archeological evidence indicating patterns of human food use in prehistoric times, and indicators of nutritional status.

3631. Helbaek, Hans. 1950. Tollun mandens sidste maaltid. [Tollund man's last meal.] NOH-A Pp. 311-341.

3632. Helbaek, Hans. 1951. Ukrudtsfro so Naeringsmiddel romersk Jernalder. [Weed seeds as food; pre-Roman Iron Age.] Kuml 1951. Pp. 65-71.

3633. Helbaek, Hans. 1952. Early crops in southern England. PPSoc 18: 194-233.

3634. Helbaek, Hans. 1952. Spelt (Triticum spelta, L.) in Bronze Age Denmark. AArch 23: 97-107.

3635. Helbaek, Hans. 1954. Prehistoric food plants and weeds in Denmark. A survey of archaeobotanical research, 1923-1954. DGU 2: 250-261.

3636. Helbaek, Hans. 1958. Garuballemandens Sidste Maltid. [Grauball man's last meal.] Kuml 1958. Pp. 83-116.

3637. Helbaek, Hans. 1959. Domestication of food plants in the Old World. Science 130: 365-372.

3638. Helbaek, Hans. 1959. How farming began in the Old World. Archaeology 12: 183-189.

The development of wheat and barley is the primary subject of this article. The author also emphasizes the needless waste of palaeoethnobotanic materials in C 14 analysis noting that, where carbonized grain is found, carbonized wood is also associated and would be more appropriately used than irreplaceable grain material.

3639. Helbaek, Hans. 1960. Ancient crops in the Shahrzoor Valley in Iraqi Kurdistan. Sumer 16: 79-81.

3640. Helbaek, Hans. 1960. Comment on Chenopodium album as a food plant in prehistory. GIETE-B 1959. Pp. 16-19.

3641. Helbaek, Hans. The palaeoethnobotany of Near East and Europe. In Prehistoric investigations in Iraqi Kurdistan. Edited by Robert J. Braidwood & B. Howe. 1960. Pp. 99-118. Chicago: University of Chicago Press.

3642. Helbaek, Hans. 1961. Late Bronze Age and Byzantine crops at Beycesultan in Anatolia. Anatol 11: 77-97.

3643. Helbaek, Hans. 1961. Studying the diet of ancient man. Archaeology 14: 95-101.

Reviews food remains from various Old World archaeological sources. Most plant material described is preserved grain.

3644. Helbaek, Hans. 1962. Late Cypriote vegetable diet at Apliki. Op Ath 4: 171-186.

3645. Helbaek, H. 1964. The Isca grain. A Roman plant introduction in Britain. N Phyt 63: 158-164.

Debris surrounding a deposit of carbonized grain found at the Roman fortress of Isca, Caerleon, Wales, was examined. Various seeds, grasses, and weeds were identified, providing evidence of weed introductions new to Britain; and of the use of cereals in brewing.

3646. Helbaek, Hans. 1965. Isin-Larsan and Horian food remains at Tell Bazmosian in the Dokan Valley. Sumer 19: 27-35.

Iraq.

3647. Helbaek, Hans. 1966. Vendeltime farming products at Eketorp on Oland, Sweden. A Arch 37: 216-221.

3648. Helbaek, Hans. The plant husbandry of Hacilar. In Excavations at Hacilar. 1. Edited by James Mellaart. 1970. Pp. 189-244. Edinburgh: Edinburgh University Press.

3649. Held, Gerrit Jan. 1957. The Papuans of Waropeni. Kinonklijk Instituut voor Taal-Land-en Volkerkunde. Translation Series 2. The Hague: Martinus Nijhoff.

Food: pp. 346-352.

3650. Hellbom, Anna-Britta. 1968. Cultural continuity and differentiated acculturation as revealed in language. Some examples from Mexico's mestizo groups, previously Nahuatl-speaking. Folk 10: 28-36.

Food preparation: Pp. 31, 32.

3651. Hellegouarch, R., et al. Enquete de consommation alimentaire des deux villages de Senegal a 3 periods de l'annee. [Food intake survey in three Senegalese villages at three periods during the year.] Mimeographed. Dakar: Organisme de Recherches sur l'Alimentation et la Nutrition Africaines (O.R.A.N.A.). 1967 [?].

Includes description of meal patterns and food taboos. The villages studies are Keur Assane Fall, and Sinou Macoumba.

3652. Hellendoorn, C.W. 1970. Onbewerkte en bewerkte peulvruchten in onze voeding. [Raw and cooked legumes in our diet.] Voeding 31: 1-14.

3653. Heller, Christine A. 1943. Regional patterns of dietary deficiency: Spanish-Americans in New Mexico and Arizona. AAPSS-A 225: 49-51.

A brief review of the historical bases of the diets of Spanish-speaking Americans in the southwestern United States, and a very general evaluation of then current food practices and nutritional status. Notes that New Mexico and Arizona have infant mortality rates nearly twice that of the southern States.

3654. Heller, Christine W. 1958. Wild edible and poisonous plants of Alaska. UAlas-EE No. 40.

3655. Heller, Christine A. 1964. The diet of some Alaskan Eskimos and Indians. JADA 45: 425-428.

3656. Heller, Christine A. & Scott, Edward M. 1967. Chapter Four. The diet of the infant. Chapter Five. Food use and preparation. Chapter Six. Season food quest activities. Appendices 1 through 6. In The Alaska dietary survey, 1956-1961. Public Health Service Publication No. 999-AH-2. Washington, D.C.: United States Department of Health Education and Welfare.

This monograph contains extensive ethnographic data on Eskimo [and Native American] diet, food preparation, plant and animal foods. Nutritive values of specific indigenous foods, and of dietaries are recorded; some recipes are included and information is given on utensils, food service, food portioning, and children's food habits. Illustrative photographs supplement the text.

3657. Hellersberg, Elizabeth F. 1946. Food habits of adolescents in relation to family training, and present adjustment. AJO 16: 34-51.

3658. Hellman, E. 1934. The importance of beer-brewing in an urban native yard. Bantu 8: 39-60. South Africa.

3659. Hellman, E. 1936. Urban native food in Johannesburg. Africa 9: 277-290.

3660. Hellmuth, Nicholas. Seventeenth Century Chorti-Lacandon Maya of Chiapas, Mexico. Paper presented at 70th Annual Meeting of the American Anthropological Association. 20 November, 1971. New York City.

Includes data derived from Spanish and Guatemalan archives indicating that there were lowland Maya who subsisted largely on root and tree crops, hunting, fishing, and gathering, and not solely on maize and beans.

3661. Helm, June & Lurie, Nancy O. 1961. The subsistence economy of the Dogrib Indians of Lac la Martre in the Mackenzie District of the N[orth] W[est] T[erritories]. Northern Co-ordination and Research Centre. Ottawa: Canada. Department of Northern Affairs and Resources.

Part One of this monograph describes the socio-anthropological aspects of the community. Part Two-Chapters Four and Five are concerned with subsistence activities. Included are: use of birch wood for food-related utensils; wild plant gathering; hunting; preparation; distribution and consumption. A chart records the weekly incidence

of 'country' (i.e. hunted, animal) foods for various families over the period of eleven months. Food preparation and cookery techniques are described, followed by observations on food preservation. The authors data on eating behavior and attitudes toward eating are thorough and unusually extensive compared with the general food habits literature. Included also are data on breast feeding; food waste; feasting; and alcoholic beverage intake. The report concludes with recommendations for resolving problems of food supply.

3662. Helms, R. 1895. Bogong moth; in Omeo Blacks. LSNSW-P 10: 394.

Used as food by Australian Aborigine group.

3663. Helmuth, Hermann. 1968. Kannibalismus in Palaoanthropologie und Ethnologie. [Cannibalism in paleoanthropology and ethnology.] E-AZ 9: 101-119.

3664. Hemardinguer, J.J. Du nouveau sur le ravitaillement de Paris à la fin du 18e siecle et au debut du 19e siecle. [Once again on the provisioning of Paris at the end of the 18th Century and the beginning of the 19th Century.] In Pour une histoire de l'alimentation. Edited by J.J. Hemardinguer. 1970. Pp. 66-70. Paris: Colin.

3665. Hemphill, Henry. 1891. Edible mollusks of western North America. Zoe 2: 134-139.

Reports the location, common name, and cooking characteristics. Notes ethnic uses, where data is available.

3666. Henane, Rene. 1964. L'alimentation en zone desertique saharienne. Etude medico-physiologie. [Diet in a Sahara Desert zone. Medical-physiological study.] ND 6: 46-60.

Includes descriptive data on typical food preparations; comments on the influence of economy, diet and religious factors on nutritional status.

3667. Hendle, G.M.; Burk, M.C.; & Lund, L.A. 1965. Socioeconomic factors influence children's diets. JHE 57: 205-208.

3668. Henderson, Avery Mack. Dental field theory: an application to primate dental evolution. Ph.D. dissertation. Anthropology. University of Colorado, Boulder. 1975.

3669. Henderson, James D. "Meals by Fred Harvey": a phenomenon of the American West. Master's thesis. University of Arizona. 1965.

3670. Henderson, Junius & Harrington, John Peabody. 1914. Ethnozoology of the Tewa Indians. SI-BAE-B No. 56.

Data derived primarily from San Juan Pueblo, New Mexico.

3671. Henderson, L.L. 1972. Nutritional problems growing out of new patterns of food consumption. AJPH 62: 1194-1198.

3672. Henderson, Neva Isom. A study in improving food habits and attitudes of a selected group of second grade pupils. Master's thesis. Denton: Texas State College for Women. 1948.

3673. Henderson, Randall. 1951. Mescal roast. DM 14: 8.

3674. Henderson, Ruth Elaine. A study of dish-washing as a routine task. Master's thesis. Ithaca, New York: Cornell University. 1937.

3675. Henderson, W.W. 1931. Crickets and grasshoppers in Utah. U-AES-C No. 96.

Documented historical references to Native American use of the locust as food.

3676. Hendley. 1888. Cancer among vegetarians. BMJ 2: 29.

Cites cases of cancer operated upon, among East Indian vegetarians in Jeypore [Jaipur].

3677. Hendrickse, R.G. 1966. Some observations on the social background to malnutrition in tropical Africa. A Affair 65: 341-349.

3678. Henisch, Bridget Ann. 1977. Fast and feast. Food in Medieval society. University Park: Pennsylvania State University Press.

Chapter headings include: mealtimes; fast and feast; cook and kitchen; methods and menus; laying the table.

3679. Henning, Hans. 1916. Der Geruch; ein Handbuch fur die Gebiete der Psychologie, Physiologie, Zoologie, Botanik, Chemie, Physik, Neurologie, Ethnologie, Sprachwissen-schaft, Litteratur, Aesthetik, und Kultur-geschichte. [Smell, a handbook for the areas of psychology, physiology, zoology, botany, chemistry, physics, neurology, ethnology, linguistics, literature, aesthetics and culture history.] Leipzig: Johann Ambr. Barth.

3680. Henning, Hans. 1921. Physiologie und psychologie des Geschmacks. [Physiology and psychology of taste.] E Phys 19: 1-30.

3681. Henninger, Josef. 1940-1941. Kannibalismus in Arabien? Eine quellenkritische Untersuchung im Anschluss an eine neue Monograph uber den Kannibalismus. [Cannibalsim in Arabia? An investigative criticism of sources in connection with a new monograph cannibalism.] Anthropos 35-36: 631-646.

3682. Henriksson, F. Kosthallet hos den dalslandska allmogen for 100 ar sedan. [Food habits among the Dalsland peasantry, one hundred years ago.] In Hembygden. Utgiven av Dalslands fornminnes-och hembygdsforbund. 1930. Goteborg: Dalslands fornminnes-och henbygdsforbunds forlaget.

3683. Henry, Albert. 1920. L'oeuvre du Comite National de Secours et d'Alimentation pendant la guerre. [The work of the National Commission for Relief and Feeding during the war.] Brussels: Office de la Publicite du Comite.

3684. Henry, Augustine. 1893. Notes on the economic botany of China. Shanghai: Presbyterian Mission Press.

3685. Henry, Jules. 1951. The economics of Pilaga food distribution. AA 53: 187-219.

Analysis of food distribution of Argentine hunters-gatherers, based on field data recorded in mid 1930's. The apparent inequality of food exchange is examined in detail. This research might be reexamined from the perspective of input -output analysis, and nutritional cost benefit to high -and low - producers.

3686. Henry, T. & Munia, G. 1959. Special report on the diet of the Sepik River people. PNGAJ 12: 41-43.

3687. Henry, Teuira. 1928. Ancient Tahiti. Based on material recorded by J.M. Orsmond. BPBM-B No. 48.

Myth [Tuamotu]: origin of cannibalism: p. 350.

3688. Henry, Yves & Ammann, Paul. 1913. Mais, ignames et patates. [Maize, yams and potatoes.] Paris: Auguste Challamel.

3689. Henry, Yves. [pseud. C. Farmer.] 1921. Les plantes a huile. [Oil-bearing plants.] Paris: Colin.

3690. Henshaw, H.W. 1890. Indian origin of maple sugar. AA 3 [old series]: 341-351.

3691. Henslow, George. 1905. The uses of British plants traced from antiquity to the present day. London: L. Reeve & Co.

3692. Henslow, George. 1908-1909-1910. The origin and history of our garden vegetables and their dietetic values. RHS-L-J 34: 15-23; 36: 115-126; 345-357; 590-595; 37: 108-114.

3693. Henson, Mariano. 1960. The tastes and ways of a Pompango. Mimeographed. 1960. Angeles, Pompango, Philippines.

Southwestern Luzon regional food habits, with recipes. Held by University of Hawaii, Hamilton Library.

3694. Herbert, Arthur Robert Kenney. Cookery of the hare. In The Hare. By Hugh Alexander Mac Pherson. 1896. Fur and Feather and Fin Series. London: Longmans & Co.

3695. Herbert, Charles W. 1955. Sahuaro harvest in the land of the Papagos. DM 18: 14-17. November.

3696.   Herdi, Ernst Paul [of Holziken, Kanton Aargau.] 1918. Die Herstellung und verwertung von Käse in greichischen-romischen Altertum. [The manufacture and use of cheese in ancient Greece and Rome.] Frauenfeld: Druck von Huber & Co.

3697.   Heringa, J. 1874. Eetbare aarde van Sumatra. [Edible earth of Sumatra.] NTNI 34: 185-189.

3698.   Herklots, Gerhard Andreas & Lin. S. 1940. Common marine food fishes of Hong Kong. Hong Kong: the author.

3699.   Herman, Judith & Herman, Marguerite Shalett. 1973. The cornucopia: good reading and good cookery from more than 500 years of recipes, food lore & c. [1390-1899]. New York: Harper & Row.

3700.   Hermann, H. 1969. La dietetica en la Biblia y el Talmud. [Dietetics in the Bible and Talmud.] FCI 19: 175-186; 400-411; 439-445.

3701.   Heron de Villefosse, R. 1956. Histoire et geographie gourmande de Paris. [A gourmand history and geography of Paris.] Paris: Éditions de Paris.

3702.   Herraia, Elizabeth A. 1960. Change of incidence of dental caries with dietary changes in prehistoric Indian populations. IAS-P 70: 47.

    Abstract of a paper read before the Anthropology Section of the Indiana Academy of Science.

3703.   Herrera, F.L. 1942. Etnobotanica: plantas tropicales cultivadas por los antiguos peruanos. [Ethnobotany: tropical plants cultivated by the ancient Peruvians]. RMN 175-195.

    Names, nature, diffusion, preparation, and use of maiz (Zea mays); mani (Arachis hpogaea = peanut); caigua (Cyclanthera pedata); tomate (Lycopersicum esculentum = tomato); camote (Ipomoea batatas = sweet potato); racacha (Arracacha xanthorrhiza); yuca (Manihot sp.); aji (Capsicum sp. = pepper); chirimoya (Annona sp.), guanabana (Annona sp.); guayaba (Psidium gajava) = guava; palta (Persea americana). = avocado; papaya (Carica papaya); granadilla (Passiflora sp.); jiguima (Pachyrhizus erosus = yam bean); pina (Ananas sp.); tuna (Opuntia sp.).

3704.   Herrera, F.L. 1942. Plantas endemicas domesticadas por los antiguos Peruanos. [Native plants domesticated by the ancient Peruvians.] RMN 11: 25-30.

3705.   Hershey, Lewis B. Selective service and its relation to nutrition. In National nutrition conference for defense, May 26, 27, and 28, 1941. Called by President Franklin Delano Roosevelt. Proceedings. 1942. Pp. 63-67. Office of the Director of Defense Health and Welfare Services. Federal Security Agency. Washington, D.C.: Government Printing Office.

    Possibly the only official statement by Selective Service explicitly acknowledging the physical unfitness of U.S. G.I.'s in World War II and the probably implications of poor diet in this regard.

3706.   Hertz, H. 1947. Notes on clay and starch-eating among Negroes in southern urban communities. SF 25: 343-344.

3707.   Hertz, Rebecca Susskind. 1896. Die praktische israelitische kochin Grundlage Anweisung alle Arten Speisen vorzuglich die Originalgerichte der israelitische kuche nach dem Ritualgestezen zu bereiten. [The practical Jewish cookbook. Basic instructions for preparing all types of foods, and specifically the original foods of Jewish cusine, according to ritual law.] Hamburg: Berendsohn.

3708.   Hervey de Saint-Denys, Marie-Jean-Leon d', translator. 1871. Ethnographie de Ma-touan-lin. Le royaume de Piao. [Ethnography of Ma-touan-lin. The kingdom of Piao.] Paris: Maisonneuve.

3709.   Hervey de Saint-Denis, Marie-Jean-Le d'. 1871. Recherches sur l'agriculture et l'horticulture des Chinois et sur les vegetaux, les animaux et les procedes agricoles que l'on pourrait introduire...dans l'Europe occidentale et le nord de l'Afrique. [Researches on Chinese agriculture and horticulture, and on the vegetables, animals, and agricultural processes that one could introduce...into western Europe and North Africa.] Paris: Allouard & Kaeppelin.

3710.   Herxheimer, H. 1951. Make the most of your precious ...penguin. Cape Argus 21 March.

    Culinary uses of penguin eggs.

3711.   Hess, Alfred Fabian. 1920. Chapter One. History of scurvy. In Scurvy, past and present. Philadelphia, London: J.B. Lippincott.

3712.   Hess, C.D.E. 1965. Cacti and succulents in the diet. [In Spanish.] SAH-B 23: 63-70.

3713.   Hess, John L. & Hess, Karen. 1977. The taste of America. New York: Grossman Publishers.

    A critical examination of U.S. food industry, food writers, restaurateurs, and international food policy.

3714.   Hesse, F.G. 1959. A dietary survey of the Pima Indian. AJCN 7: 532-537.

3715.   Hesse, Zora Getmansky. 1973. South-western Indian recipe book. Volume 1. Apache, Papago, Pima, Pueblo & Navajo. Palmer Lake, Colorado: Filter Press.

3716.   Hesseltine, C.W. & Wang, Hwa L. 1967. Traditional fermented foods. Biotech 9: 275-288.

    Foods mentioned are shoyo, miso, tempeh, suyu, hamanatto, ontjom, katsuobushi, bago'ong. [Filipino fish paste], and nuoc-mam [fish sauce].

3717.   Hesseltine, C.W. & Wang, Hwa L. Fermented soy bean food products. In Soybeans: chemistry and technology. Edited by Allan K. Smith & Sidney J. Circle. 1972. Vol. 1. Pp. 389-419. Westport, Connecticut: AVI.

Discusses history, nutritional value, and technology of miso, shoyu, tempeh, tofu, koji, natto, hamanatto, and sufa.

3718.   Hester, J.A. Natural and cultural bases of ancient Maya subsistence economy. Ph.D. dissertation. University of California at Los Angeles. 1954.

3719.   Heuer, Berys N. Rose. Maori women in traditional family and tribal life. Master's thesis. University of Hawaii. 1966.

3720.   Heun, Eugen. 1962. Nutrition and abstention in primitive peoples. MMir No. 1. Pp. 1-4.

3721.   Heupke, W. 1963. The rapid increase of vegetarianism in the world. [In German.] MMW 105: 2244-2248.

3722.   Heusinger, Carol Frid. 1852. Die sogenannte Geophagie oder tropische (besser: Malaria-) Chlorose-Krankheit aller Lander and Klimate dargestellt. (A description of so-called geophagy or tropical [more appropriately malarial) chlorosis encountered in all countries and climates.] Cassel: Hotop.

3723.   Heuze-Louis, Gustave. 1873. Les plantes alimentaires des pays chauds et des colonies. [Food plants of the and of the colonies.] 2 vols. Paris: Librairie Agricole de la maison rustique.

3724.   Heuze-Louis, Gustave. 1893-1895. Les plantes industrielles. [Industrial plants.] 3rd edition. 4 vols. Paris: Librairie Agricole de la Maison Rustique.

Volume Three includes spice and condiment plants. Volume Four includes quasi-food plants.

3725.   Hewes, Agnes Danforth. 1942. Spice ho. A story of discovery. London: G. Routledge.

3726.   Hewes, Gordon Winant. Aboriginal uses of fishery resources in northwestern North America. Ph.D. dissertation. University of California, Berkeley. 1947.

3727.   Hewes, Gordon Winant. 1961. Food transport and the origin of hominid bipedalism. AA 63: 687-709.

A change from gallery-forest habitat to open country and associated changes in diet (e.g. to carrion, and small-game) are suggested as having required a freeing of arms and hands for carrying food in certain infra-human primates. The necessity of reducing vulnerability by transporting food to shelters may have stimulated bipedal locomotion and therefore maximal transportation efficiency.

3728.   Hewitt, Allie G. 1973. Cape cookery: simple yet distinctive. Edited by Robert Ellis. South African yesterdays No. 3. Capetown: D. Philip.

3729.   Hewitt, Graily. 1883. The question of food in obstetric and gynaecological practice. BMJ 2: 224-226.

Importance of adequate protein during adolescence; emphasizes need for meat in uterine complaints where abstinence from meat is practices. Urges attention to diet for safe childbirth.

3730.   Hewitt, J. 1908. One some vegetable fats native to Sarawak. ABSFMS 6: 173-175.

Culinary fats, their chemistry, and methods of preparation.

3731.   Heyerdahl, Thor. 1964. Plant evidence for contacts with America before Columbus. Antiquity 38: 120-133.

3732.   Heyle, Essie M. 1920. Selected apple recipes. Missou-AES-B No. 93.

3733.   Heyne, K. 1950. Die nuttige planten van Indonesia. [The useful plants of Indonesia.] 2 vols. The Hague: W. Van Hoeve.

3734.   Heyns, Jozef. 1963. Bakhuis en broodbakken in Vlaanderen. [Bakeries and bread baking in Flanders.] Sint-Martens-Latem: Verbond voor Heemkunde.

3735.   Hiatt, Betty. Some aspects of the economy of the Tasmanian Aborigenes. Bachelor's honor thesis. University of Sydney. 1965.

3736.   Hiatt, Betty. 1968. The food quest and the economy of the Tasmanian Aborigenes. Oceania 38: 99-137; 190-219.

3737.   Hibben, Frank Cummings. 1967. The gatherers. Chicago: Rand McNally.

3738.   Hicking, Arobati F. 1939. Foodstuffs in the Gilbert Islands. NMP 3: 432-437.

Describes meal times, fish, shellfish, birds, and various coconut and pandanus preparations.

3739.   Hicking, Arobati F. 1949. Coconut milk: substitute for dextrose in normal saline. HCQ 22: 20-25.

Use of fresh coconut water, administered intramuscularly or intravenously, in cases of sever malnutrition among Gilbert Islanders, during World War II. Includes Gilbertese terminology for stages of coconut development.

3740.   Hickling, C.F. 1948. Fish farming in the Middle and Far East. Nature [L] 161: 748-751.

3741. Hidalgo, Guillermo Perkins. 1961. La cocina tradicional de Corrientes. [The traditional food of Corrientes.] INIF-C 2: 31-48.

Recipes; notes on utensils; beliefs and superstitions relating to food. Corrientes is a Province in northeastern Argentina, close to Paraguay.

3742. Hiernaux, Jean. 1954. Etat de nutrition des Kuba [Kasai]. [Nutritional status of the Kuba [Kasai].] Zaire 8: 719-729.

3743. Hiernaux, Jean. Influence de la nutrition sur la morphologie des Bahutu du Ruanda. [The influence of nutrition on the morphology of the Bahutu of Ruanda.] In 4e Congres International des Sciences Anthropologiques et Ethnologiques. 1-8 Septembre 1952. Vienna. Vol. 1. Anthropologica. 1954. Pp. 157-162. Vienna: Verlag Adolf Holzhausens NFG.

Concludes that genetics determine a development "optimum" which may be attained only under certain environmental conditions. There are "nutristable" characteristics and "nutrilabile" characteristics: in general, proportions are more stable that linear dimensions.

3744. Higgs, E.S. 1962. A metrical analysis of some prehistoric domesticated animal bones from Cyrenaican Libya. Man 62: 119-122.

Excavations at the cave site Hana Fteah.

3745. Higgs, E.S. & White, J.P. 1963. Autumn killing. Antiquity 37: 282-289.

3746. Highland, Joseph. 1976. PCB's in food: a look at federal government responsibility. Environment 18 (2)12-16.

Polychlorinated biphenyl toxicity.

3747. Hiiemae, Karen M. & Kay, R.F. Evolutionary trends in the dynamics of primate mastication. In Symposia of the Fourth International Congress of Primatology. Vol. 3. Craniofacial biology of primates. Edited by M.R. Zingeser. 1973. Pp. 28-64. Basel: S. Karger.

3748. Hijman, A.J. 1939. Purine content of native food products in Java. [In Dutch.] GTNI 79: 5000-5002.

3749. Hilchey, Florence M., comp. 1974. Treasury of Nova Scotia heirloom recipes. Halifax: Nova Scotia Communications and Information Center.

Recipes brought by settlers from France, England, Scotland, Ireland, Germany.

3750. Hildebrand, Karl-Gustav. 1954. Salt and cloth in Swedish economic history. SEHR 2: 74-102.

3751. Hildebrand, Patricio von. 1975. Observaciones preliminares sobre utilizacion de tierras y fauna por los indigenas Miriti-Parana. [Preliminary observations on land and animal use by natives of Rio Miriti, Parana.] RCAnt 18: 183-291.

A large portion of the study is taken up by schematic drawings of garden areas, with qualifactory information on crops, soils, harvest, individuals supported by, and working with crops, and length of growing period. Brief discussion of soil use; fallow, and protection of gardens against animals, is included. Brief mention is also made of domestic animals, i.e. chickens, cattle, and swine.

3752. Hilger, Inez, 1936. Chippeweys prenatal food and conduct tabus. P Man 9: 46-48.

3753. Hill, Albert F. 1939. The nomenclature of the taro and its varieties. HU-BML 7: 113-118.

3754. Hill, Albert F. Ethnobotany in Latin America. In Plants and plant science in Latin America. Edited by Frans Verdoorn. 1945. Pp. 176-181. Waltham, Massachusetts: The Chronica Botanica Company.

A general review of the literature, together with specific reviews for Mexico, Central America, West Indies, Argentina, British Guiana, Chile, Colombia, Ecuador, and Peru.

3755. Hill, Arthur W. 1929. The original home and mode of disperal of the coconut. Nature (L) 124: 133-134.

Presents historical linguistic, and distributional data, and discusses various theories concerning the point of origin. It is concluded that Polynesia or East Indian Islands are the original home of Cocos nucifera.

3756. Hill, Arthur W. 1929. The original home and mode of dispersal of the coconut. Nature [L] 124: 507-508.

A letter to the Editor, adducing further documented evidence concerning observations of coconuts by early post-Renaissance explorers.

3757. Hill, J. 1937. Feeding and personality disorders; study of early feeding in its relation to emotional and digestive disorders. Psych Qt 11: 356-382.

3558. Hill, Janet M. 1904. A short history of the banana and a few recipes for its use. Boston: United Fruit Company.

3559. Hill, Jason. 1944. Wild foods of Britain. London: A.C. Black.

3760. Hill, L.B. & Cambournac, F.J.C. 1941. Diet of five rural families in the province of Alentejo. [In Portuguese] LLmed 18: 691-702.

West-central Portugal.

3761. Hill, Willard W. Agricultural and hunting methods of the Navajo Indians. Ph.D. dissertation. Yale University. 1934.

3762. Hill, Willard W. 1938. The agricultural and hunting methods of the Navajo Indians. YUPA No. 18.

3763. Hille, Helen M. & Reeves, Mary M. 1964. The battle against mental retardation: the dietitian's share. Hospitals 38: 101-102. November 16.

   Role of dietetics in contributing to maternal-child health before and during pregnancy, as a possible preventive measure; and as a resource providing information to parents of mentally-handicapped children.

3764. Hiller, Elizabeth O. 1907. The corn cookbook. Chicago, New York, Toronto: P.F. Volland Co.

   Recipes for maize meal, hominy, maize starch, green maize.

3765. Hilliard, Sam B. Hog meat and hoecake: a geographical view of food supply in the heart of the old South, 1840-1860. Ph.D. dissertation. University of Wisconsin. 1966.

3766. Hilliard, Sam B. 1969. Hog meat and corn pone: food habits in the ante-bellum South. APS-P 113: 1-13

3767. Hilliard, Sam B. 1969. Pork in the antebellum South. AAG-A 59: 461-480.

3768. Hillier, John Masters [?]. 1909. Quinoa or quinua [Chenopodium quinoa]. GB-KBGK-BMI 1909. No. 10. Pp. 425-427.

   Notes on its preparation and use as food in Bolivia, Peru and Ecuador. Comments on methods of cultivation are included, together with an observation on its keeping quality, owing to a naturally-occurring bitter principle which is removed by cooking.

3769. Hills, J.L. 1922. Dairying in Vermont in the '70's and '80's. JDS 6: 87-94.

   Nineteenth Century.

3770. Hilmo, W. Food retailing and consumer behavior in Waterloo. Master's thesis. Geography. Waterloo, Ontario, Canada: Wilfred Laurier University. 1971.

3771. Hindus M. 1962. House without a roof. Garden City. Doubleday.

   Reference to a "milk", prepared in the Siberian forest region from pine kernels.

3772. Hinsworth, J.B. 1953. Story of cutlery from flint to stainless steel. London: Ernest Benn.

3773. Hinton, Thomas B. 1956. A description of the contemporary use of an aboriginal Sonoran food. Kiva 21: 27-28.

   Atole de pechita, mesquite bean gruel manufactured in the Mexican village of Tepupa, on the Moctezuma River, east of Hermosillo, Sonora.

3774. Hintze, Kurt. 1933. Zurgeschichte der deutschen Volksernahrung. [Historical view of German national diet.] ZErn 3: 39-42.

   Notes a rise in meat consumption, and decline in millet consumption. Oats and rye, and potatoes have been added to the diet.

3775. Hintze, Kurt. 1934. Geographie und Geschichte der Ernahrung. [Geography and the history of nutrition.] Leipzig: G. Thieme.

3776. Hintze, Kurt. 1935. La alimentacion en los diversos pueblos a traves de los tiempos. [Diet among various peoples through time.] In Pro 9: 141-145.

3777. Hipsley, Eben H. 1950. The feeding of New Guinea infants. SP 4: 181-187.

3778. Hipsley, Eben H. Some perspectives on food and nutrition of Melanesian people. In R.J. May, ed. 1972. Priorities in Melanesian development. Papers delivered at the 6th Waigani Seminar. Port Moresby: University of Papua New Guinea Press.

3779. Hipsley, Eben H. 1976. Concerning the adaptation of Paua New Guineans to low protein diets. FNNR 33: 37-43.

   Growth rate in relation to protein intake; influence of medical immunization upon growth rate. Asks if, for humans, the 'best' biological growth is necessarily the 'fastest' growth.

3780. Hipsley, Eben H. & Clements, F.W., eds. 1947. New Guinea Nutrition Survey Expedition. Report. Canberra: Australia. Department of External Territories.

   Sociology and diet patterns; food habits and taboos; storage: Pp. 19-24. Villages included in study are: Busama, near Lae; Kaiapit, in the Upper Markham Valley; Patep No. 2, fifty miles inland from Lae; Kavataria, on the Trobriand Island of Kiriwina; Koraegi, on the Purari Delta.

3781. Hipsley, Eben H. & Langley, Doreen. A nutritional study of New Guinea natives. In Seventh Pacific Science Congress. 1949. Christchurch, New Zealand. Proceedings. 1953. Vol. 3. Pp. 418-427.

3783. Hiralel, R.B. 1925. Some notes about marriage, food, drink and occupations of caste affecting social status in the Central Provinces. M India 5: 56-68.

3784. Hirohata, R. & Kamizawa, O. 1934. Nutrition of Formosan savages; value of chief food products. [In Japanese.] TIZ 33: 111.

3785.   Hirth, F. 1887. Notes on the early history of the salt monopoly in China. RAS-NCB-J 12: 53-66.

3786.   Hisar, R. 1949. Lathyrisme. [Lathyrism.] TITBG 9: 78-87.

3787.   Hitchcock, N.E., & Oram, N.D. 1967. Rabia camp. A Port Moresby migrant settlement. NGRU-B No. 14.

Includes detailed information on staple foods, food preparation and cooking techniques, food preservation and storage, food patterns, and infant-feeding patterns. Port Moresby, Papua is located at 9. 30S, 147. 07E.

3788.   Hitchcock, S.W. 1962. Insects and Indians of the Americas. ESA-B 8: 181-187.

As food: Orthoptera, Anoplura, Homoptera, Diptera, Hymenoptera.

3789.   Hjelmqvist, H. 1969. Dinkel und Hirse aus der Bronzezeit sudschwedens nebst einigen Bemerkungen uber ihre spatore Geschichte in Schwened. [Spelt and Panicum from the southern Swedish Bronze Age together with a comment on later history in Sweden. BNot 122: 260-270.

Several impressions of spelt (Triticum spelta L.) and millet (Panicum miliaceum L.) were found in pot sherds and other clay material from the early Bronze Age of Skane. The former species is previously not known in Bronze Age Sweden, the latter species known incompletely for the time. An impression of barnyard millet (Echinochloa crus-galli L. Beauv.) was observed on pottery from the Roman Iron Age of Skane, and numerous grains of Panicum miliaceum were found in contexts of early Medeival time in Lund. It is thus unquestionable that spelt and millet were cultivated in Sweden during the early Bronze Age, and it is possible that cultivation of one or the other species of millet took place in Sweden during the later periods when climate was more favorable for their growth.

3790.   Hladik, C.M.; Hladik, A.; Bousset, J.; Valdebouze, P.; Virben, G.; & DeLort-Laval, J. 1971. Le regime alimentaire des primates de l'ile de Barro Colorado (Panama): resultats des analyses quantitatives. [The diet of primates on the island of Barro-Colorado (Panama): results of some quantitative analyses.] Folia Prim 16: 85-122.

3791.   Ho, Genevieve Po-ai. Factors affecting adaptation to American dietary patterns by students from the Oriental countries. Ph.D. dissertation. Pennsylvania State University. 1961.

One hundred twenty university students (fourteen females, one hundred six males) were studied, from India, China, Japan, Korea, Thailand, Indonesia, Ceylon and Pakistan. Twenty-four hour recall, and dietary attitudes and practices data were collected. Positive relationships were found beteen nationality and degree of adaptation to North American food. Indian groups had the highest and Chinese the least apparent degree of dietary acculturation. Other positive correlations were found between ability to speak English; participation in formal and informal extracurricular activities; length of residence in the United States; cooking experience in home country; and age of respondent.

3792.   Ho, Genevieve Po-ai; Nolan, Francena; & Dodds, Mary L. 1966. Adaptation to American dietary patterns by students from Oriental countries. JHE 58: 277-280.

Synopsis of the senior author's doctoral dissertation.

3793.   Ho, Ping-ti. 1955. The introduction of American food plants into China. AA 57: 191-201.

Plants are peanut, sweet potato, and maize.

3794.   Ho, Ping-ti. 1956. Early-ripening rice in Chinese history. EHR 9: 200-218.

3795.   Hoben, Allan. Eating, seating, and greeting among the Amhara: a formal analysis. Paper presented at 70th Annual Meeting of the American Anthropological Association. 19 November, 1971. new York City.

3796.   Hobson, Abigail K. Dietary habits and health conditions among rural Alabama Negroes. Master's thesis. University of Chicago. 1946.

3797.   Hocart, A.M. 1929. Lau Islands, Fiji. BPBM-B No. 62.

Myth: acquisition of food supply for human race: p. 211.

3798.   Hochstein, Georgianna. Pica: a study in medical and anthropological explanation. In Essays on medical anthropology. Edited by Thomas Weaver. 1968. Pp. 88-98. Southern Anthropological Society. Proceedings. No. 1. Athens: University of Georgia Press.

3799.   Hocking, B. & Matsumura, F. 1960. Bee brood as food. Bee 41: 113-120.

3800.   Hocking, Blanche Miller. Nutrition guidance at the Third grade level. Master's thesis. University of Alabama. 1945.

3801.   Hodge, Walter Henricks. 1942. Plants used by the Dominica Caribs. NYBG-J 43: 189-201.

Food plants are mentioned on pp. 191, 193; kitchen architecture: p. 198.

3802.   Hodge, Walter Henricks. 1946. Three neglected Andean tubers. NYBG-J 47: 214-224. Oca (Oxalis tuberosa); melloco (ullucu) [Ullucus tuberosus]; anu (Tropaelum tuberosum).

3803.   Hodge, Walter Henricks.   1947.   The plant resources of Peru.   EB   1: 119-136.

3804.   Hodge, Walter Henricks.   1949. Tuber foods of the old Incas.   NH   58: 464-470.

Oca [Oxalis tuberosa], ullucu [ullucus tuberosus], anu [Tropaeolum tuberosum].

3805.   Hodge, Walter Henricks & Taylor, Douglas Macrae.   1957.   The ethnobotany of the Island Caribs of Dominica.   Webbia   12: 513-644.

Food plants and their uses indicated throughout.

3806.   Hodgson, R.E.   General problems of human nutrition in the tropics in relation to animal husbandry.   In Fourth International Congresses on Tropical Medicine and Malaria.   10 May to 18 May, 1948. Washington, D.C. Proceedings.   Vol. 2. Pp. 1181-1188. Washington, D.C.: Department of State.

Role of animal products in diet, especially among some agricultural groups.

3807.   Hodous, Lewis.   1929.   Chapter Thirteen. The feast of cold food [Han shih ching yen].   In Folkways in China.   Probstains Oriental Series vo. 18. London: Arthur Probsthain.

An ancient custom of extinguishing fires in celebration of the vernal equinox, during which celebration food was eaten cold.

3808.   Hoebel, Ernest Adamson. 1960. Chapter Six. Hunting and gathering. In The Cheyennes. Indians of the Great Plains.   New York: Holt, Rinehard & Winston. Case studies in Cultural Anthropology.

Chapter is written from the perspective of division of labor by gender.

3809.   Hoelzel, F.   1944.   An explanation of appetite.   AJDD   4: 71-76.

3810.   Hoeven, Jan Arie van der.   Resultaten von een onderzoek naar voeding en deficientie-verschijnselen bij autochtone in Nederlands Nieuw-Guinea. [Results of an investigation on diet and deficiency phenomena among Netherlands-New Guinea natives.] Medical dissertation. Reijksuniversitet te Leiden. 1965.

3811.   Hoffman, I.; Nowosad, F.S.; & Cody, W.J. 1967. Ascorbic acid and carotene values of native eastern Arctic plants.   CJB   45: 1859-1862.

3812.   Hoffman, J.J.   Honey vinegar.   [In Dutch.] PWeek 42: 704-705.
A commercial Dutch food.   Abstracted in ZUNG 11: 349.

3813.   Hoffman, Walter James.   Miscellaneous ethnographic observations on Indians inhabiting Nevada, California and Arizona.   USGGS-ST-AR No. 10 for 1876.

Food: pp. 461-478.

3814.   Hoffman, Walter James.   1896.   The Menomini Indians.   SI-BAE-AR for the year 1892-1893. Pp. 1-328.

Food habits: pp. 286-292.   This section opens with a brief review of then current diet, which already highly Westernized. Comments on the effects of government rationing are made.   The technology of maple sugar collecting is described.   One section each is devoted to a discussion of wild rice harvesting, and berry-gathering. Foods included with burials: p. 239. Hunting and fishing: pp. 272-273.

3815.   Hoffman, William E.   1947.   Insects as human food.   ESW-P   49: 233-237.

In Burma, China, Malaya, and Mexico. Orthoptera,   Hemiptera,   Coleoptera, Lepidoptera.

3816.   Hoffman, Frederick Ludwig. 1937. Cancer and diet. Baltimore: Williams & Wilkins.

3817.   Hoffman, Maria Mullerliele. 1939. Ueber die Konservierung von Nahrungsmitteln und ihren Einfluss auf die Ausnutzung im menschlichen Darm. [Food preservation and its effect on the function of the human intestine]. Gelnhausen: Kalbfleish.

3818.   Hoffman, Mortiz. 1956. Funftausend jahre Bier. [Five thousand years of beer.]   Frankfut am Main: Metzner.

3819.   Hoffs, Joshua A. 1963. Anthropophagy: its relation to the oral stage of development.   Psych Rev 50: 27-54.

3820.   Hofstra, S. 1937. The social significance of the oil palm in the life of the Mende.   [In German.] IAE 34: 105-118.

Sierra Leone.

3821.   Hofstrand, Richard H.   1970.   Wild ricing. NH 79: 50-55.

Harvesting Zizania aquatica by Native Americans in Minnesota.

3822.   Hofvander, Yngve & Eksmyr, R. 1971. An applied nutrition program in an Ethiopian rural community. AJCN 24: 578-591.

3823.   Hogbin, H. Ian.   1938-1939.   Tillage and collection: A New Guinea economy.   Oceania 9: 127-151; 286-325.

3824.   Hogendorn, Jan Stafford. The origins of the groundnut trade in northern Nigeria. Ph.D. dissertation. University of London. 1966.

3825.   Hogg, Garry. 1958. Cannibalism and human sacrifice. London: Hale.

Covers Polynesia, Melauesia, and Maori New Zealand.

3826. Hoh, Pik-wan; Chapman, Jessamine Williams; & Pease, Charles S. 1934. Possible sources of calcium and phosphorous in the Chinese diet. 1. The determination of calcium and phosphorus in a typical Chinese dish containing meat and bone. JN 7: 535-546.

Shows that sweet and sour pork spare ribs can provide RDA for calcium but not for phosphorus. Notes absence of dairy products in Chinese dietaries. Describes spare rib preparation. Also refers to a traditional post-partum food prepared from pig's feet and ginger, fed to lactating women, in China.

3827. Hohenadel, M. 1913. Studies of yoghurt with special reference to dried preparations. [In German.] AHB 78: 193-217.

History of use of milk fermented with Bacterium bulgaricum, used in diets for gastric and intestinal disorders. Briefly describes preparation of yoghurt in Eastern Europe.

3828. Holbrook, Abigail Curlee. 1973. A glimpse of life on antebellum slave plantations in Texas. SHQ 76: 361-383.

Mentions specific slave foods, rations, their distribution and preparation. Child slaves some thought, should have butter milk or clabber, but not sweet milk or molasses. Post partum allowances included extra coffee and sugar for two weeks.

3829. Holbrook, Carey. 1943. Dehydration is old stuff. Comp Air 48: 7006-7009.

Sun drying of foods by Native American groups in the southwestern United States. Foods mentioned include chili peppers (Capsicum sp.); melons (Cucurbita sp.); and meat.

3830. Holden, G.K. & Lamb, M.W. 1962. Early foods of the Southwest. JADA 40: 218-223.

3831. Holden, William Curry. Chapter Five. Household economy. In Studies of the Yaqui Indians of Sonora, Mexico. 1936. Pp. 67-71. TTech C-B 12(1). SS No. 2.

Inventory of fourteen kitchens is included.

3832. Holemans, K. & Martin, H. 1954. Etude de l'allaitement maternel et des habitudes alimentaires du sevrage chez les indigenes du Kwango. [Study of maternal lactation and food-related weaning habits among the Kwango natives.] SBMT-A 34: 915-923.

3833. Holland, J.H. 1919. Food and fodder plants. GB-KBGK-BMI No. 1 & 2.

3834. Holland, Lois. A dietary study of twenty-two students in a Red Cross nutrition class. Master's thesis. Denton: Texas State College for Women. 1945.

3835. Holland, P.E. & Bonney, W. 1912. Cost of living in Mexico. USDCL-DCTR 15: 966-969.

Includes description of preparation of tortillas, enchiladas, and tamales.

3836. Holle, H.G. 1913. Ernahrungsfragen 1.2. [Nutrition problems 1.2.] PAE 12: 126-141; 182-197.

3837. Holleman, L.W.J. 1964. Report to the government of the Dominican Republic on a survey on cassava production and processing. Rome: Food and Agriculture Organization of the United Nations.

Cassava in human diet: pp. 13-14.

3838. Holleman, L.W.J. & Aten, A. 1956. Processing of cassava and cassava products in rural industries. Food and Agriculture Organization of the United Nations. Paper No. 54. Rome: Food and Agriculture Organization of the United Nations.

Use of cassava in human diet: pp. 9-15.

3839. Holleman, L.W.J.; Koohaas, D.R.; & Nijholt, J.A. 1939. Composition of diet of Chinese in Batavia. [In Dutch.] DVNI-M 28: 306-320.

3840. Hollen, Evelyn A study of the dietary habits and nutritional status of school children of different national and racial backgrounds in an anthracite coal region of Pennsylvania. Master's thesis. Pennsylvania State College. 1942.

3841. Hollingsworth, Dorothy F. 1961. The changing patterns in British food habits since the 1939-45 war. PNS 20: 25-30.

Discusses increases in consumption of various staple foods; increase in the habit of eating away from home, and an upward trend in the use of food vending machines.

3842. Hollis, W.S. 1914. Syrian food products exported to United States. USDCL-DCTR 17: 284.

Describes native Syrian foods.

3843. Hollister, Will C. 1971. Dinner in the diner. Great railroad recipes of all time. Pictures, maps, recipes from famous railways. 3rd edition. Corona del Mar, California: Trans-Anglo Books.

3844. Holloway, Laura C. 1886. The Buddhist diet book. New York: Funk & Wagnalls.

3845. Holm, Bill. Modern Carrier potlatching and matriclan adoption. Paper presented at 73rd Annual Meeting of the American Anthropological Association. 19 to 24 November, 1974. Mexico City.

The Carrier are a Native American group of British Columbia.

3846. Holman, E. & Sybalsky, E. 1953. Parties change food habits. JADA 29: 928.

Report on cooking parties to which Puerto Rican residents of New York City were invited for the purposes of introduction of new foods and provision of nutrition education.

3847. Holmberg, Allan R. 1969. Chapter Five. Food and drink. In Nomads of the long bow. The Siriono of eastern Bolivia. American Museum Science Books. B20. Garden City, New York: The Natural History Press.

Describes diet, food consumption frequency (meat); taboos; food preservation; food storage; food preparation; meal-times; food distribution at meals; food portions (quantity eaten); water sources; alcoholic beverages [based on manioc, sweet potato, and honey) and their cultural significance.

3848. Holmberg, Henrik J. 1856. Ethnographische skizzen uber die volker des Russischen Amerika. [Ethnographic sketches of the natives of Russian America.] SSF-A 4: 281-422.

Food plants of Koniag Eskimo: p. 372.

3849. Holmes, E.M. 1920. The manna of the Scripture. AJ Pharm 92: 174-179.

3850. Holmes, George K. 1905. Consumers fancies. In USDA YB for the year 1904. Pp. 417-434.

Considers consumers' preferences for various foods, with reference to a variety of selection criteria.

3851. Holmes, Maybell Marion. A source book of Chinese food habits. Ph.D. dissertation. Cornell University. 1948.

3852. Holmes, S. 1953. Social habits and nutrition. Nutrition (L)7: 28-30.

3853. Holmes, Susan. 1955 [?] Report of nutritional surveys in three villages in the Cook Islands, August-October, 1954. Suva, Fiji: South Pacific Health Service.

Describes local foods, cooking methods, food storage practices, and dietary patterns for the villages of Tutakimore, and Pue, on Rarotonga Island [21. 15S, 159. 45W]; and for Tahunu, Manihiki Island [10. 24S, 161. 01W].

3854. Holmes, Susan. 1956. Public health nutrition programmes in the Pacific Islands. SPC-QB 6: 13-15.

3855. Holmes, Jr., Urban Tigner. 1952. Daily living in the Twelfth century. Madison: University of Wisconsin Press.

Food habits, cookery: pp. 86-94.

3856. Holt, J.M. & Sladden, R.A. 1965. Favism in England - two more cases. ADC 40: 271-273.

3857. Holt, Vincent M. 1885. Why not eat insects. London: Field & Tuer. The Leadenhall Press.

3858. Holwerda, I.K. 1925. Researches on boiled foods in Batavia. [In Dutch.] DVNI-M Pp. 250-276.

3859. Homber, Jean-Marie. The distribution of food plant names in the Camerounian grassfields. Paper presented at 77 Annual Meeting of the American Anthropological Association. 14 to 18 November, 1978. Los Angeles, California.

3860. Home Makers Guild of America. 1967. Profiles in preference: a consumer survey on soft drinks. Toledo, Ohio: Owens-Illinois.

Purchasing patterns; brand preferences; container evaluation; trends in use.

3861. Hongladarom, Gail C. The health food movement as an alternative medical system. Paper presented at 72nd Annual Meeting of the American Anthropological Associaiton. 1 December, 1973. New Orleans, Louisiana.

3862. Honigmann, John Joseph. 1946. Ethnography and acculturation of the Fort Nelson Slave. YUPA No. 33.

Aboriginal Fort Nelson Slave. Technical culture. The food quest: pp. 35-42. Details on hunting, trapping, fishing; cannibalism; diet, food preparation and eating. Contemporary Fort Nelson Slave culture. The foodways: pp. 104-112; includes discussion of hunting, distribution of game; purchase of non-native foods; collecting, gardening; fishing; meals and food preparation; alcoholic beverages.

3863. Honigmann, John J. 1961. Foodways in a Muskeg community. An anthropological report on the Attawapiskat Indians. Northern Co-ordination and Research Centre. Ottawa: Canada. Department of Northern Affairs and National Resources.

This monograph studies a Cree group on the west coast of James Bay, Ontario. Field work extended from July 27, 1947 to June 6, 1948. The first three chapters are focused on methodology, community and community background data, and psychological characteristics of the Attawapiskat. The author notes the general tendency of personality to be characterized by anxiety, with specific anxiety relating to food. Chapter Four contains detailed information on seasonal diets, with menus; sources of food (Government welfare, trading post, gardening, hunting and gathering.)

3864. Honolulu. Hawaii State Archive. Food found on Islands by Captain Cook. Address delivered before the Royal Hawaiian Agricultural Society. 12 August, 1850.

3865. Hood, Allen. 1938. Sago, a New Guinea staple food. Walkabout 1 July. Pp. 41-42.

3866. Hoogewerf, L.W. 1958. A psychological elucidation of food selection. [In Dutch.] NVBBDVA 16: 26-29.

3867.   Hooper, David.   1904.   Analyses of Indian pot herbs of the natural orders Amarantaceae, Chenopodiaceae, and Polygonaceae. AL-VPS 84: 61-72.

3868.   Hooper, David. 1906. The uses and value of the root Costus speciosus as a foodstuff. AL No. 2: Pp. 19-21.

3869.   Hooper, David. 1907. The uses and composition of tamarind seeds. AL No. 2: Pp. 13-16. Tamarindus indica.

3970.   Hooper, David. 1911-1912. Food substances. Accessories to human food. I-BSA-AR Pp. 17-19.

    Analyses of bamboos seed; salep (corm or tuber of a species of orchid); Amorphophallus sp. tubers; tea; Abor tea.

3871.   Hooper, David. 1911. Some Asiatic milk products. RASB-J 7: 63-67. India.

    Products mentioned are karut, chhana, and dahi.

3872.   Hooper, David. 1912. Oils and fats of vegetable origin produced in India. AL No. 5. Pp. 107-168.

3873.   Hooper, David & Mann, H.H. 1906. Earth-eating and the earth-eating habit in India. RASB-M 1: 249-270.

3874.   Hoover, C.L. 1913. The popular cooking fat in Austria. USDCL-DCTI 16: 687.

    Speisfett, from palm-oil.

3875.   Hoover, Robert L. 1971. Food plants of the California Indians. P Disc 24: 11-17.

3876.   Hope M. & Catalan, M.P. 1970. Neolitische Getreide funde in der hohle von Nerja [Prov. Malaga] [Neolithic grain discovered in Nerja Cave [Malaga Province].] Madrider 2: 18-34.

3877.   Hopf, Maria. Bearbeitung und Auswertung vorgeschichtlicher pflanzlicher Funde. [Preparation and analysis of prehistoric plant finds.] 5 Internationale Kongress fur Vor-und Frugeschichte. 24 bis 30 August 1958. Edited by Gerhard Bersu. 1961. pp. 404-407. Berlin: Gebruddern Mann.

3878.   Hopffe, A. 1917. Uber infusorienerde (Bergmehl). [On diatomaceous earth (Bergmehl).] Nat Woch 16: 286-287.

    Geophagy.

3879.   Hopkins, Edward Washburn. 1901. On the Hindu custom of dying to redress a grievance. AOS-J 21: 146-159.

    Specifically, suicide by starvation.

3880.   Hopkins, III, Joseph W. Irrigation and the Cuicatec eco-system: a study of agruelture and civilization in north central Oaxaca, Mexico. Ph.D.

dissertation.   Anthropology University of Chicago. 1974.

3881.   Hopper, Susan V.   Living with diabetes: stigma and chronic illness among the urban poor. Paper presented at 77th Annual Meeting of the American Anthropological Association.   14 to 18 November, 1978. Los Angeles, California.

3882.   Hoppner, K.; McLaughlin, J.M.; Shah, B.G.; Thompson, J.N.; Beare-Rogers, J.; Ellestad-Sayed, J.; & Schaefer, O. 1978. Nutrient levels of some foods of Eskimos from Arctic Bay. N.W.T., Canada. JADA 73: 257, 261.

    Food samples comprised caribou, seal, and char.

3883.   Horder, Thomas Jeeves, et al. 1954. Bread: the chemistry and nutrition of flour and bread, with an introduction to their history and technology. London: Constable.

3884.   Horkheimer, Hans.   1960.   Nahrung und nahringsgewinnung im vorspanischen Peru. [Food and food production in pre-Hispanic Peru.] Biblioteca Ibero-Americana 2. Berlin: Colloquiam Verlag, Otto H. Hess.

3885.   Harriet, van. 1966. Teepee cuisine (and tortillas too). Diplomat 17: 24.

3886.   Horne, Louise. 1960. The evolution of dietary habits in the West Indies. Nutrition (L)14: 158-162.

    Briefly traces African, Chinese, and European influences; six typical Caribbean recipes are given.

3887.   Hornedo, Eduardo. 1953. Utilidad del maguey, planta mitologica. [The usefulness of maguey, mythological plant.] Bol Ind 13: 355-359.

    A species of Agave, from the root of which a fermented beverage is prepared.

3888.   Hornell, James. 1946. How did the sweet potato reach Oceania? LSL[B]-J 53: 41-62.

    Based on the assumption of New World nativity for the sweet potato (Ipomoea batatas), and similarity of the name in Peru and Oceania [kumar, kumal], the author reviews in depth the possibilities of trans-Pacific contact which would account for the dispersal of the sweet potato in the Pacific Islands.

3889.   Horner, J.H. 1942. Early Wallowa Valley Settlers. OHQ 43: 215-227. Oregon.

    Sourdough bread and starter: p. 219.

3890.   Horton, Ann Elizabeth. A study of the diets of a group of pregnant Negro women patients attending the maternity clinic of the Leon County Health Unit in relation to certain social, economic and health factors. Master's thesis. Florida State College for Women. 1946.

3891.   Horton, Donald. 1943. Functions of alcohol in primitive societies: a cross-cultural study. QJSA 4: 199-320.

Offers a theory of psychological and social function to explain certain aspects of the drinking customs of non-industrialized groups.

3892.   Horton, Frances. Food habits and living conditions of Mexicans dwelling in the Rio Grande between Roma and Mercedes. Master's thesis. Austin: University of Texas. 1936.

3893.   Horton, Lucy. 1972. Country commune cooking. New York: Coward, Mc Cann & Geoghegan.

During the middle and late 1970's, a back-to-the land movement among young U.S. Americans resulted in the proliferation of communal residences in many States. This book provides a representative sample of the foods prepared in these communes, with some relevant sociological data.

3894.   Horvath, A.A. 1927. The soybean as human food. China. Bureau of Economic Information. Booklet series 3. Also in CEM 3: 392-400; 513-518 (1926) CEJ 1: 24-32; 175-192; 298-309; 415-425.

3895.   Hose, C. 1900. Cannibalism in Sarawak. AA 2: 403.

Review of a comment made at a meeting of the Anthropological Institute, in London, concerning instances of ingestion of human flesh.

3896.   Hoskins, Michael. Ceremonialism of subsistence cycles among North American Indians. Master's thesis. Anthropology. University of Cincinnati. 1970.

3897.   Hossner, H. 1941. In a Chinese grocery store. CJ 35: 104-110.

3898.   Hostos, Adolfo de. 1923. Three-pointed stone zemi or idols from the West Indies: an interpretation. AA 25: 56-71.

The zemi was believed to have an influence on the growth of the yuca plant, in the Taino culture areas (Haiti-Puerto Rico.). The author suggests a similarity in form between certain growth phases of the yautia (Xanthosoma sp.), and the zemi stone, and its amplification into a more general fertility idol.

3899.   Hostos, Adolfo de. Antillean fertility idols and primitive ideas of plant fertilization elsewhere. In Twenty-first International Congress of Americanists. August 12-16, 1924. The Hague. Proceedings. 1924. Part One. Pp. 247-252. Leiden: E.J. Brill.

Studies the occurrence of inanimate objects used to influence plant growth. Includes two excerpts from Frazer's Golden Bough

relating to breadfruit (New Caledonia) and taro [Colocassia esculenta].

3900.   Hou, Hsiang-ch'uan. 1938. Dietary principles in ancient Chinese medicine. CMJ 53: 347-352.

3901.   Hou, Hsiang-ch'uan; Mar, P.G.; Ni, T.G.; & Read, Bernard Emms. [1940?] Nutritional studies in Shanghai. Divisional of Nutritional Sciences. Shanghai: Henry Lester Institute of Medical Research.

Report on nutritional status of certain Shanghai groups, 1937-1939; dietary surveys, and a study of the value of various supplementary foods.

3902.   Hou, Hsiang-ch'uan, & Yu, C.L.. 1940. Beriberi in ancient Chinese medical literature. CMJ 58: 302-313.

3903.   Houang, K.; Loost, G. & Van Kuyckwolfers. 1934. Quelques considerations d'hygiene alimentaire et sociale sur la consommation du riz en chine. [Some considerations on nutritional hygiene relative to the consumption of rice in China.] SSEAAFE-B 22: 216-224.

Loss of carbohydrate and vitamin and mineral value resulting from discard of water rice is rinsed in. Advocates improved cooking procedures.

3904.   Hough, Walter. 1892. The Bernadou, Allen, and Jouy Korean collections, in the U.S. National Museum. SI-AR for the year 1891. Pp. 429-488.

Kitchen and dining room: pp. 443-446.

3905.   Hough, Walter. 1897. The Hopi in relation to their plant environment. AA 10 [old series]: 33-44. Also in TBC-B 10: 33-44. (1897).

3906.   Hough, Vera A. The bibliography of the ethnobiology of the Southwest Indians. Master's thesis. University of New Mexico. 1931.

3907.   Houghton, W. 1885. Notices of fungi in Greek and Latin authors. AMNHist 5: 22-49.

3907.   Houseman, P.A. 1944. Licorice. Putting a weed to work. Twenty-sixth Streatfield Memorial Lecture. London: Royal Institute of Chemistry of Great Britain and Ireland.

3908.   Houston, Charles O. 1954. Customs associated with rice cultivation in the Philippines. JEAS 3: 287-296.

3909.   Houston, Charles O. 1955. Nutrition and public health in the Philippines: 1934-1950. JEAS 4: 119-136.

3910.   Houze, Emile. 1894-1895. Les progres de l'intelligence sont dus a la selection naturelle; celle-ci depend de la difference de nutrition des organismes dans leur totalite ou dans certaines de leurs parties. L'evolution constante du cerveau est demontree par l'evolution morphologique; elle a ete favorisee par l'acquisition du regime artificiel. [Progress in intelligence is due to natural selection. This depends on differences in nutrition of the total organism or to certain of its parts. The constant evolution of the brain is demonstrated by morphological evolution; it has been favored by the acquisition of artificial dietary.] SABrux-B 13: 32-44.

3911. Howard, Kajorn Lekhakul. Diet and achievement among school children in a depressed community. Master's thesis. University of Hawaii. 1966.

The community studied is Nanakuli, on the Island of Oahu.

3912. Howard, Kajorn Lekhakul. 1967. Food choices and acculturation among some ethnic groups in Hawaii. H Med J 26: 209-212.

Chinese cuisine has made the largest contribution to the regular eating habits of other ethnic groups in Hawaii, while itself remaining conservative with regard to adopting non-traditional food items. Least used by other ethnic groups in the Islands is American food. Chinese have taken over the use of some native Hawaiian food items; six Japanese foods appeared on a list of ten most-liked food preparations.

3913. Howard, L.O. 1916. Insects as food for man. JEE 9: 452.

Note on the experimental use as for of Lachnosterna larvae (in salad), and Cerambycid larvae, fried in butter, at the Office of Home Economics.

3914. Howe, Paul E. Regional food habits as related to food acceptance. In Conference on Food Acceptance Research. 6 December to 7 December, 1945. Washington, D.C. Quartermaster Corps Manual 17-9. United States War Department. United States Army. 1946. Pp. 55-57. Washington, D.C.: Quartermaster Food and Container Institute. Research and Development Branch. Military Planning Division. Committee on Food Research.

Available in microform from United States Library of Congress. Microform Division. Item PB-53-883.

3915. Howe, Paul E. Food storage and preservation in the tropics. In Fourth International Congresses on Tropical Medicine and Malaria. Washington, D.C. 10 May to 18 May, 1948. Proceedings. Vol. 2. Pp. 1189-1196. Washington, D.C.: Department of State.

Effects of storage and preservation techniques on various tropical food products.

3916. Howe, Paul E. & Schiller, Maria. 1952. Growth responses of the school child to changes in diet and environmental factors. J AppPhys 5: 51-61.

Study of height and weight of students in Stuttgart's Volksschule and Oberschule from 1915-1948.

3917. Howe, James & Sherzer, Joel. Semantic analysis of Sappi Turpa "fruit" in San Blas. Paper presented at 72nd Annual Meeting of the American Anthropological Association. 30 November, 1973. New Orleans, Lousiana.

3918. Howe, Sonia Elizabeth. 1946. In quest of spices. London: Herbert Jenkins, Ltd.

3919. Howeler-Coy, J.F. 1966. An account of food and drink in Tasmania, 1800-1900. 'Slippery Bob' and 'Blow-My-Skull.' RST-PP 100: 81-88.

3920. Howes, F.N. 1930. Chenopodium Nuttalliae, a Mexican cereal. GB-RBGK-KB 1930. No. 7. Pp. 332-333.

Refers to the use of Chenopodium quinoa. Willd. grains, cultivated and wed for bread in Germany, during World War I. Additional data on the use of C. Nuttalliae as food in Mexico is given, specifically for the grains, leaves, and young shoots. A recipe for the food use of the unripe inflorescences is given: the spikes are washed and dipped in a batter of egg, flour, and grated cheese, then fried in lard. The ends of several spikes are held together and drawn between the teeth, thereby detaching the green buds. This food is called uauhtzontli.

3921. Howes, F.N. 1948. Nuts, their production and everyday uses. London: Faber and Faber.

In addition to a review of the better-known commercially available nuts, a section is included on lesser-known, edible types.

3922. Howitt, Alfred William. 1904. Native tribes of south-east Australia. London: Macmillan.

Food rules: pp. 756-770.

3923. Hoygaard, Arne. 1937. Untersuchungen uber die Ernahrung und die Physiopathologie des Eskimos Vergenommen in Angmagssalik, Ostgronland. [Investigations on the nutrition and physiopathology of Eskimos at Angmagssalik, east Greenland.] Utgiven av det Koniglich Departement for handel, sjofart, industri, handverk og fiskeri [ved] Norges Svalbard-og Ishavsunder sokelser, No. 4. Oslo: A.W. Broggers boktrikkeri a/s.

3924. Hrdlicka, Ales. 1904. Tesvino among the White River Apaches. AA 6: 190.

A fermented maize beer.

3925. Hrdlicka, Ales. Cannibalism. In Handbook of American Indians north of Mexico. SI-BAE-B No. 30. Edited by Frederick Webb Hodge. Vol. 1. 1907. Pp. 200-201.

3926. Hrdlicka, Ales. 1908. Physiological and medical observations among the Indians of the Southwestern United States and northern Mexico.

SI-BAE B No. 34.

Food: pp. 19-29; 257-266.

3927.   Hrdlicka, Ales.   1945.   The Aleutian and Commander Islands.   Philadelphia: Wistar Institute of Anatomy and Biology

Food: pp. 90-94.

3928.   Hsu, L. & Tung, T.   1977.   Nutritional concepts and dietary practices in China.   PFNS   2: 499-503.

3929.   Hsu, L.C.   1974.   Commentary: Nutrition—from China to the West: art-science duality of nutrition.   EFN 3: 303-314.

A comparison of traditional Chinese attitudes toward food as qualitative and aethetic; and modern Western attitudes seems as quantitative, processed, and objectively managed to achieve health and appearance-related goals. This article offers the reader the opportunity to consider a non-Western-er's impression of Western concepts of the uses of food, as well as a wide variety of references to the place of food in Chinese history and literature.

3930.   Hus, Shiu-ying.   1948.   Shien-some noteworthy edible herbs of China.   Herbarist No. 14.   Pp. 30-36.

3931.   Hu, Shiu-ying.   1956.   Malva - an herb of high nutritive value.   Herbarist No. 22.   Pp. 22-30.

Malva (mallow) in Chinese cookery, with recipes. Reference to high vitamin and mineral content.

3932.   Hu, Ssu-hui.   194-?   Yin san cheng yao. [The importance of a proper diet.]   [In Chinese.]

Photostat copy of a book written in the third year of the reign of Emperor Tien-li, Yuan dynasty (1330), the book being a reproduction made with woodblock printing in the seventh year of the reign of the Emperor Chin tai, Ming dynasty (1456). Held by the United States Department of Agriculture National Agricultural Library. Call number 389 H86.

3933.   Huaco, S.A.   1943.   Los Incas fueron los primeros que desidrataron los comestibles emplea-ban procedimentos naturales y artificiales.   [The Incas were the first to dehydrate food using artificial processes.]   Chacra 13: 18-19.

3934.   Huan, Chang-chen.   1911.   The economic principles of Confucius and his school.   CU-SHEPL No. 44. 2 vols.

Chinese cookery, from the "Record of Rites." Vol. 1. Pp. 251-253.

3935.   Huber, E.   1930. Kampf den alkool im wandel der kultur.   [Struggle with alcohol in culture change.] Berlin: Trowitzch & Sohn.

3936.   Hubert, Henry.   1911.   Les mangeurs d'argi-le.   [Clay eaters.]   Aesculape 1: 111-112.

Among the Bobo-Oule of Diekuy, Upper Senegal and Niger, the Bambara, and the Agni-Ashanti.

3937.   Hubert, Paul.   1911.   Le palmier a huile. [The oil palm.]   Bibliotheque Pratique du Colon, Agriculture, Industrie, Commerce. Paris: H. Dunod et E. Pinat.

3938.   Hubert, Paul.   1912. Fruits des pays chauds. [Fruits of the tropics.]   Bibliotheque pratique du colon, agriculture, industrie, commerce.   Vol. 1. Etude general des fruits.   Paris: H. Dunod & E. Pinat.

3939.   Hubert, Paul & Dupre, Emile.   1910.   Le manioc.   [Manioc.]   Bibliotheque Pratique.   Du Colon, Agriculture, Industrie, Commerce. Paris: H. Dunod et E. Pinot.

3940.   Huch, Richard.   1938. Die Japanische Ern-ahrung und ihre Fragen unter Beruksichtigung neue-rer japanische Literatur. [The question of Japanese nutrition in light of recent Japanese publications.] Verofentlichungen des Seminars fur Sprache und Kultur Japans an der Hanischen Universitat. No. 5. Hamburg: Friederichsen, de Gruyter & Co.

3941.   Huckabee, Eunice. Vegetables in the diet of pre-school children.   Master's thesis.   Denton: Texas State College for Women. 1945.

3942.   Hudson, J.W.   1900.   Preparation of acorn meal by Pomo Indians.   AA 2: 775-776.

Use of Madaria, Arcostaphylos, Querus agri-folia. Quercus densiflora, in the preparation of a type of bread, and mush (pinole). The 'bread' is made with solute red earth. The Pomo are a California Native American group.

3943.   Hudson, Peter J.   1939. Chocktaw Indian dishes. Chron Okla 17: 333-335.

3944.   Huenemann, Ruth Lois. 1954. Nutrition and care of young children in Peru.   1.   Purpose, methods, and procedures of study. JADA 30: 554-558.

3945.   Huenemann, Ruth Lois; Bruch, Hans L.; & Scholes, Robert.   1957.   A dietary survey in the Santa Cruz area of Bolivia. AJTMH 6: 21-31.

3946.   Huenemann, Ruth Lois & Collazos, Carlos C. 1954. Nutrition and care of young children in Peru.   2.   San Nicolas, a cotton hacienda; and Corquin, a fishing village, in the Coastal Plain. JADA 30: 559-569.

3947.   Huenemann, Ruth Lois & Collazos, Carlos C. 1954. Nutrition and care of young children in Peru.   3.   Yurimaguas, a jungle town.   JADA 30: 1101-1109.

3948.   Heunemann, Ruth Lois; French F.E.; & Bier-man, Jesse M.   1961. Diets of pregnant women in

Kauai, Hawaii; two dietary survey methods compared. JADA 39: 569-577.

3949. Huenemann, Ruth Lois; Shapiro, L.; & Hampton, M. 1968. Food and eating practices of teen-agers. JADA 53: 17-24.

3950. Huenemann, Ruth Lois & Turner, D. 1942. Methods of dietary investigation. JADA 18: 562-568.

3951. Huff, Elizabeth Willis de. 1939. Fiesta foods. NMex 17: 21.

3952. Hughes, Phyllis, compilor, ed. 1972. Pueblo Indian cookbook. Recipes from the Pueblos of the American Southwest. Santa Fe: Museum of New Mexico Press.

Contemporary foods from New Mexico Native American Groups.

3953. Hughes, Thomas Patrick. 1885. Dictionary of Islam, being a cyclopedia of the doctrines, rites..and theological terms of the Muhammadan religion. London: W.H. Allen.

Food: pp. 103-104; 130.

3954. Huizinga, B. 1970. Les habitudes alimentaires dans la region du project pour l'amelioration de la nutrition par la creation de jardins familiaux au sud-est du Dahomey. [Food habits in the region of the project for improving nutrition by the establishing family gardens in south-east Dahomey.] Foundation NEDERF. Amsterdam. Royal Tropical Institute.

3955. Huke, Robert E. Rice in Burma: a geographical analysis of three agricultural villages. Ph.D. dissertation. Geography. Syracue, New York: Syracuse University. 1953.

3956. Hulstaert, Gustaaf. 1944. L'alimentation de l'indigene. [Native diet.] Aequatoria 7: 155-157.

3957. Human Relations Area Files. Joint Staff. Cross-cultural studies of factors related to differential food consumption. Final report. United States Public Health Service Grant No. A-3557. New Haven: Human Relations Area Files. 1961.

3958. Human Relations Area Files. Joint Staff. A cross-cultural study of protein consumption: the role of cultural taboos in the differential use of animal protein in a sample of one hundre societies. In Cross-cultural studies of factors related to differential food consumption. Final report. United States Public Health Service Grant No. A-3557. New Haven: Human Relations Area Files. 1961.

3959. Human Relations Area Files. 1964. Food habits survey. 3 vols. New Haven, Conntecticut: Human Relations Area Files.

Surveys food patterns, nutritional status, and areas of major nutritional deficiency. A basic reference source. Available on microfiche from United States Department of Commerce. National Technical Information Service, Springfield, Virginia. Order Nos. AD 817-507; 817-508; & 817-509.

3960. Hume, Audrey Noel. 1978. Food. Colonial Williamsburg Archaeological Series, No. 9. Williamsburg, Virginia: Colonial Williamsburg Foundation.

Food technology; diet; utensils; archaeological reconstruction.

3961. Hume, Ivor Noel. 1969. A guide to artifacts of Colonial America. New York: Alfred A. Knopf.

Glass liquor bottles: pp. 60-71; cooking vessels: pp. 177-183; drinking glasses and decanters: pp. 184-202.

3962. Humphrey, Norman D. 1945. Some dietary and health practices of Detroit Mexicans. JAF 58: 255-258.

3963. Hundley, James M. Nutritional problems associated with food habits and environment. In Borden Centennial Symposium on Nutrition. April 12, 1958. New York City. Proceedings. Pp. 1-11. [New York: The Borden Company Foundation.]

Impact of physical environment and social systems on nutritional status. Effects of culture contact on nutritional status of traditional societies. Problems involved in nutrition intervention programs.

3964. Hunn, Eugene. The abominations of Leviticus revisited: a critique of symbolic anthropology. Paper presented at 75th Annual Meeting of the American Anthropological Association. 17 to 21 November, 1976. Washington, D.C.

The animal prohibitions detailed in Leviticus and Deutoronomy of the Old Testament are used by Mary Douglas to exemplify her claim that apparently arbitrary distinctions of primitive cosmology may be understood by reference to a pan-human inclination to impose logical order on the phenomenal world. In this critique, Douglas' own dictum against piecemeal interpretation is followed by examining the animals singled out by the Biblical texts from the total faunal context of the Hebrew environment. An attempt is made to show that folk classifications of nature cannot be understood as logical products of the characteristics of nature classified.

3965. Hunt, Jeffrey W. Limu recipes. Botany 181: Plant life of the sea. Kailua, Hawaii: Windward Community College. Mimeographed. April, 1977.

3966. Hunter, G. & Pett, L.B. 1941. A dietary survey in Edmonton. CPHJ 32: 259-265.

Canada.

3967. Hunter, Helen Virginia. The ethnography of salt in aboriginal North America. Master's thesis. University of Pennsylvania. 1940.

3968. Hunter, John Desmond. Diet, body build, blood pressure, serum cholestorol levels and cardiovascular disease in Cook Island Polynesians: a comparative study of two Polynesian groups on different diets. M.D. dissertation. University of Otago. 1962.

3969. Hunter, John M. 1967. Seasonal hunger in a part of the West African savannah: a survey of body weights in Nangodi, north east Ghana. IBG-TP 4: 167-185.

3970. Hunter, John M. 1973. Geophagy in Africa and in the United States: a cultural-nutritional hypothesis. GR 63: 170-195.

Hypothesizes that geophagy, as it has evolved in parts of Africa, offers a wide range of mineral supplementation that is nutritionally significant under conditions of dietary deficit.

3971. Hunter, Margaret. A rat growth study of typical low-cost Texas diets. Master's thesis. Denton: North Texas State College. 1942.

3972. Huntingford, G.W.B. 1955. The Galla of Ethiopia and the kingdoms of Kafa and Janjero. Ethnographic survey of Africa. Northeastern Africa. Part two. London: International African Institute.

Galla food: pp. 28-29; Kafa food: p. 109; Janjero food: p. 138.

3973. Hunziker, Armando T. 1943. Los especias alimenticias de Amaranthus y Chenopodium cultivados por los indios de America. [Edible species of Amaranth and Chenopods cultivated by the Indians of America.] RAA 10: 297-354.

Includes North, Meso-, and Latin America.

3974. Hunziker, Armando T. 1952. Los pseudo-cereales de la agricultura indigena de America. [The pseudo-cereals of indigenous American agriculture.] Buenos Aires: Acme Agency.

Mexico, and South America; ethnobotany. Chapter One provides a history of huautli [Chenopodium Nuttalliae Safford]; quinoa [Chenopodiu quinoa Willdenow.]; and canagua [Chenopodium pallidicaule Aellen]. Chapter Two is concerned with taxonomic, distributional, and cultivation data of various edible amaranths and chenopods. Chapter Three describes preparation, food uses, and includes nutritional analyses.

3975. Husain, Afzal. 1951. The nutrition problem of the villager. In Developing Village India: studies in village problems. By various contributors. Pp. 147-153. Bombay, Calcutta, Madras. Longman's.

3976. Husson, Armand. 1856. Les consommations de Paris. [What Paris consumes.] Paris: Guillaumin.

3977. Husson, Camille [fils]. 1879. Etude sur le cafe, le the et les chicorees. [Study on coffee, tea, and chickories.] Paris: V.-A. Delahaye.

3978. Husson, Camille [fils.] 1880. Note sur l'absinthe. [Note on absinthe.] Paris: V.-A. Delahaye.

3979. Husson, Camille [fils]. 1881. L'alimentation animale, ce quelle a ete, ce quelle doit etre, ce quelle devient, ce quelle produit, comment on la prepare; la viande, son histoire, ses caracteres, son utile, ses dangers, statistique, hygiene, police, sanitaire. [Meat diet: what it has been, what it should be, what it is becoming, what it produces, how to prepare it; meat, its history, characteristics, its use, dangers, statistics, hygiene, monitoring, sanitation.] Paris: Dunod.

3980. Husson, Camille [fils]. 1883. Etude sur les epices, aromates, condiments, sauces, et assisonnements, leur histoire, leur utilite, leur danger. [Study on spices, aromatics, condiments, sauces and seasonings, their history, their use, their danger.] Paris: Dunod.

3981. Husson, Camille [fils]. 1884. Champignons comestibles et veneneux dans l'arrondissement de Toul. [Edible and poisonous mushrooms of the Toul neighborhood.] Nancy: Imprimerie de P. Sordoillet.

Toul is a town in France, approximately 20km west of Nancy.

3982. Husson, Camille [fils]. 1887. Histoire du pain a toute les epoques et chez tous les peuples, d'apres un manuscrit de G [sic] Husson. [History of bread over time and among all peoples, after a manuscript by G. Husson.] Tours: A. Cattier.

3983. Hutchinson, John & Melville, Ronald. 1948. Section Two. Plants and early man. Section Five. The harvest of the earth. Section Six. Beverages. In The story of plants and their uses to man. London: P.R. Gawthorn.

3984. Hutchinson, Joseph, ed. 1965. Essays on crop plant evolution. Cambridge: University Press.

3984. Hutchinson, R.C. 1959. Food for survival after a disaster. Carlton, Victoria, New South Wales: Melbourne University Press.

3985. Hutchinson, William B. Nutrition and development in a Peruvian highland community. Paper presented at 70th Annual Meeting of the American Anthropological Association. 21 November, 1971. New York City.

It has been stated that a prerequisite for social and economic development in underdeveloped countries in the breakdown of traditional ties among peasants. In contradiction to this, data from one town in the Peruvian Andes shows that standards of nutrition have declined as a result of the breakdown of subsistence agriculture and an increase of contacts with the marketing system.

3986.   Hutchison, Robert.   1940   Food and the principles of dietetics.   Baltimore: Williams & Wilkins.

3987.   Hutton, John Henry.   1921.   The Angami Nagas. London: Macmillan.

Utensils: pp. 57-60; food: pp. 91-98; food taboos, and ritual foods: passim.

3988.   Hutton, John Henry.   1921. The Sema Nagas. London: Macmillan.

Food, and food interdictions: Pp. 89-99.

3989.   Hutton, John Henry.   1943.   The cannibal complex. Folk-lore (L)54: 274-276.

3991.   Huxley, E.J. 1942. They call them "British restaurants." SNight 57: 32.

3992.   Hvarfner, Harald.   Hunger at fixed times: an ethnic accumulation with biological consequences? Paper presented at First International Symposium for Ethnological Food Research. 21-25 August, 1970. Lund: Folklivsarkivet, Lund University.

Effects of cultural and environmental variables upon   circadian rhythms related to hunger and appetite.

3993.   Hyades, Paul. 1884. Notes hygieniques et medicales sur les Fuegians de l'archipeldu Cap Horn. [Medical and hygiene notes on the Fuegians of Cape Horn.] RHPS 6: 550-590.

Foods, condiments, beverages: pp. 562-566.

3994.   Hyams, Edward S. 1965. Dionysius: a social history of the wine vine. New York: Macmillan.

3995.   Hyamson, M. 1897. Another word on the dietary laws. JQR 9: 294-310.

Jewish religious dietary restrictions.

3996.   Hyatt, Bob. 1972. Foods the Indians gave us. Cath Dgst 37: 47-50.

Native American staple foods in modern world food supply.

3997.   Hyderbad. Nutrition Research Laboratories. 1964. Diet atlas of India. Indian Council of Medical Research. Special Report Series No. 48.

Food consumption statistics represented graphically.

3998.   Ibanez, Felix Mari. 1947. Hacia una ciencia del buen comer. Pobreza y enriquecimiento de la nutricion anglosajona. Notas sobre la psicobiologia alimenticio del mundo actual. [Towards a science of proper eating.   Poverty and improvement of Anglo-Saxon nutrition. Notes on the dietary psychobiology of the modern world.] USC-PT No. 8. Pp. 113-134.

3999.   Ibanez G., Juan. 1935-1936. La alimentacion de los aborigenes de Chile. [Diet of Native Chileans.] RMA 2: 337-350; 3: 15-26.

Historical data on foods of native tribes. Chemical analyses of certain foods is given.

4000.   Ibanez G., Juan. 1939. La alimentacion de los aborigenes de Chile. [Food habits of Chilean native peoples.] RGA 11: 199-215.

4001.   Idosugie, Ephraim O. Role of improved methods of food technology in the nutrition of Nigerian peoples. Paper read at the Third International Congress of Food Science and Technology. 9 to 14 August, 1970. Washington, D.C.

4002.   Idyll, Clarence P. 1970. Chapter Five. The harvest of seaweed. In The sea against hunger. Harvesting the oceans to feed a hungry world. New York: Thomas Y. Crowell.

Documents uses of seaweed as food in South Wales, Britany, Soviet Union, Canadian Maritime Provinces, Polynesia, and Japan.

4003.   Igbozurike, Matthias U. 1971. Ecological balance in tropical agriculture. GR 61: 519-529.

Food supply crises and nutritional crises recur in developing tropical nations where rapid population growth and traditional farming are the norms. The socio economic merits and importance of mixed cropping as an adaptation to natural ecosystems are emphasized.

4004.   Igoin, L. 1976. Les resistances a la modification du comportement alimentaire humain. [Resistance to change in eating behavior.] ANA 30: 301-310.

4005.   Ilg, Karl. 1954. Vorarlberg Nahrungs-volkskunde. [Food folklore of Vorarlberg.] VL-J Pp. 87-101.

Vorarlberg is a province in northwestern Austria.

4006.   Imanishi, Kinji. 1957. Social behavior in Japanese monkey, Macaca fuscata. Psychologia 1: 47-54.

Behavior at feeding places.

4007.   Immink, Maarten D.C. & Viteri, Fernando E. Energy intake during the life cycle and worker productivity in Guatemalan sugar cane cutters. Paper presented at 77th Annual Meeting of the American Anthropological Association. 14 to 18 November, 1978. Los Angeles, California.

4008.   Imperato, Pascal James. 1977. African folk medicine; practices and beliefs of the Bambara an dother peoples. Baltimore: York Press.

Treatment of kwashiorkor, marasmus, diarrhoea: pp. 129-133.

4009. Imray, J. 1843. Observations on the mal d'estomac or cachexia africana, as it takes place among the negroes of Dominica. EMSJ 59: 304-321.

4010. Inaba, I. 1907. The diet of Japanese farmers. [In German.] MGT-M 21: 1-8.
4011. India. Census of India. 1961. 1962-1968. Vol. 2. Gujarat. Part 6. Village Survey Monographs. Nos. 1-13. Delhi: Indian Government Publications.

Meal frequency, and types of food are described, for thirteen villages.

4012. India. Census of India, 1961. 1964-1969. Vol. 2. Andhra Pradesh. Part 6: Village Survey Monographs. Nos. 2-46. Delhi: Indian Government Publications.

For each village, dietary pattern and staple food items are described. Food prohibitions are also mentioned.

4013. India. Census of India. 1961. 1962-1963. Vol. 16. West Bengal. Part 6. Village Study Monographs Nos. 1-3. Delhi: Indian Government Publications.

The villages of Kodalia; Ghatampur [Hooghly District, approx. fifty kilometers northwest of Calcutta]; and Kamnara [Burdwan District, approximately one hundred kilometers northwest of Calcutta], in West Bengal, are included in this study. Data are recorded regarding foods consumed, and food restrictions (i.e. fish, meat, eggs.). [After Schofield. 1975: 176.]

4014. India. National Council of Applied Economic Research. 1963. Socio-economic conditions of primitive tribes of Madhya Pradesh. New Delhi: National Council of Applied Economic Research.

4015. India. Mysore. Central Food Technological Research Institute. 1955. The Indian sago industry. Mysore: Central Food Technological Research Institute.

4016. Infantes-Vera, Juana G. Vegetales que los antiguos Peruanos usaron para comidas y bebidas y que se usan actualmente. [Food and beverage plants used by the ancient Peruvians and being used today.] In 35 Congreso Internacional de Americanistas. Mexico. Acta y Memoria. 1962. Pp. 153-168. Mexico: Editorial Libros de Mexico, S.A. Vol. Three. 1962.

Part One is grouped as follows: cereals, tubers, fruits, legumes, condiments, with botanical and vernacular terms; archeological sites yielding representations of plant foods in ceramic form; and food uses. Part Two contains illustrations (pen and ink sketches) of the ceramic representations.

4017. Inglett, George E. Chapter Eight. Food uses of corn throughout the world. In Corn: culture, processing, products. Edited by George E. Inglett. 1970. Westport, Connecticut: AVI Publishing Co.

Modern maize processing is carried out mainly in countries that are undergoing an industrial revolution, or are already highly industrialized. In many of the developing countries, where maize is a staple food, preparation methods involve such techniques as parching, boiling, and grinding, with variations depending upon culture and geography. Mexico, Central America, South America, and Africa are the major areas where maize is widely eaten. An estimated 100 million persons in the world consume maize as their main food, or as a major item of diet, consuming it in the form of thin, round flat unleavened cakes, or as porridge.

4018. Institute for Government Research. 1928. The problem of Indian administration. Report of a survey made at the request of Honorable Hubert Work, Secretary of the Interior, and submitted to him, February 21, 1928. Studies in Administration. Baltimore: The Johns Hopkins Press.

Food in Federal schools for Native Americans: pp. 321, 327-331; food among Native American families (Southwestern groups) 555-557; food for infants and invalids: pp. 557-559; expenditures for food by San Carlos Apache and Sacaton Pima: p. 665; food preparation and selection: pp. 684-686.

4019. Instituto de Nutricion de Centro America y Panama. 1952. Tabla provisional de composicion de alimentos de Centro America. [Provisional food composition table for Central America.] Guatemala City: Instituto de Nutricion de Centro America y Panama.

4020. Intengan, Carmen. 1953-1954-1955. Composition of Philippine foods. PJS 82: 227-252; 83: 187-216; 84: 263-273.

4021. International Cooks' Association. 1933. Brief encyclopedia of foods, historical data. Chicago: International Cooks Association Section.

4022. International Institute of African Languages and Cultures. 1937. The food and nutrition of African natives. International Institute of African Languages and Cultures. Memorandum No. 13. London: Oxford University Press.

4023. International Labor Organization of the League of Nations. 1936. Workers' nutrition and social policy. London: P.S. King & Son.

4024. International Tin Research and Development Council. 1939. Historic tinned foods. London: International Tin Research and Development Council.

4025. Ipasescu, Alexandru. 1968. Presence de la geopghagie en Roumanie; deductions etnoiatriques sur la geophagie. [Presence of earth-eating in Rumania; ethnoiatric deductions on earth-eating.] Etnoiatria 2: 29-33.

4026. Ireland. Local Government Board. 1913. Handbook of cookery for Irish workhouses. Dublin: Printed for His Majesty's Stationery Office.

4027. Ireland, William W. 1908. Climate or diet. BMJ 2: 1408.

4028. Irvine, F.R. 1948. Indigenous food plants of West Africa. NYBG-J 49: 225-236; 254-267.

4029. Irvine, F.R. 1952. Food plants of West Africa. Lejeunia 16: 27-51.

4030. Irvine, F.R. 1952. Supplementary and emergency food plants of West Africa. EB 6: 23-40.

4031. Irvine, F.R. 1957. Wild and emergency foods of Australian and Tasmanian Aborigines. Oceania 28: 113-142.

4032. Irving, J.T. 1953. Nutritional uses of seaweed: source of dietary elements. FISA 6: 33-35.

4034. Irwin, A.T. 1950. The origin and history of popcorn. EB 4: 294-299. Also in: AJ 53-55. [1949].

4035. Isaac, Erich. 1959. The citron in the Mediterranean: a study in religious influences. EG 35: 71-78. Also in Cultural geography: selected readings. Edited by Fred E. Dohrs & Lawrence M. Sommers. New York: Thomas Y. Crowell.

4036. Isaac, Erich. 1959. Influence of religion on the spread of citrus. Science 129: 179-186.

4037. Isaac, Glynn L. 1971. The diet of early man: aspects of archeological evidence from Lower and Middle Pleistocene sites in Africa. World Arch 2: 278-199.

4038. Isaac, William Edwin. 1942. Seaweeds of possible economic importance in the Union of South Africa. JSAB 8: 225-236.

Potential edible algae: pp. 232-234.

4039. Isch, C. 1964. A history of hospital fare. JADA 45: 441-446.

4040. Ishige, Naomichi. Comparative study of kitchen utensils. Paper presented at 9th International Congress of Anthropological and Ethnological Sciences. 28 August to 8 September, 1973. Chicago, Illinois.

Utensils in eight cultures: four in Tanzania: Hadza (hunter gatherer); Datoga (pastoralist); Iraqw (agro-pastoralist); and Swahili (agricultural); one Libyan group: Megarha (agricultural); the Moni, of New Guinea (agricultural); Tongan (agricultural); and two Japanese communities, one urban, and one fishing.

4041. Ishikawa, Motsuke. 1948. Coconuts and human life: ecology of the Tolai in the Gazelle Peninsula of northern New Britain. [In Japanese.] MK 13: 50-66.

4042. Itani, J. 1958. On the acquisition and propagation of a new food habit in the natural group of the Japanese monkey at Takasaki-Yama. Primates 1: 84-98.

4043. Ivanosky, Alexis. 1923. Physical modifications of the population of Russia under famine. Translated from the original manuscript by Waldemar Jochelson. AJPA 6: 331-353. Also as Die anthropometrischen Veränderungen russischer Volker unter des Einfluss der Hungersnot. Arch Anth 48: 1-13 [1925].

4044. Ivy, A.C. 1933. The effect of worry on digestion. SM 37: 266-269.

4045. Iwai, Charles K. The rice industry in Hawaii. Master's thesis. University of Hawaii. 1933.

4046. Izumi, Seuchi. 1948. Sago culture: ethnobotany of New Guinea [In Japanese.] MK 13: 346-359.

Includes vocabularies, and data on implements.

4047. Jablonka, Allison & Jablonko, Mare K. Rigidity and fluidity: the process and performance of a meal in the New Guinea Highlands. 16 mm, 10 min. sound-color film screened at the 68th Annual Meeting of the American Anthropological Association. 20-23 November, 1969. New Orleans, Louisiana.

The intersection of personal rhythms of people preparing a meal (hypothesized to be fluid-i.e. relatively variable) with the technical process required (hypothesized to be rigid) is examined in terms of spacing and timing. The film was made in the winter of 1968-1969, in a Maring village in the Simbai Valley.

4048. Jack, J.D.M. Food resources of animal origin in the Sudan. In Conference on food and society in the Sudan. 1953. Khartoum. 1954. Khartoum: Philosophical Society of the Sudan.

4049. Jackson, A.V. Williams. 1906. Persia past and present. A book of travel and research. New York, London: Macmillan.

Food and dining etiquette of Yezd Zoroastrians: p. 356; prohibition against Zoroastrians as food merchants: p. 374; raw eggs as travel food: p. 402; foods as ritual offerings in Zoroastrian religious observances: pp. 369-372; similarity of a Feridun festival practice with Jewish passover custom: p. 372.

4050. Jackson, C.O. Food and drug law reform in the New Deal. Ph.D. dissertation. Emory University. 1967.

Studies the legislation effected during the administration of President Franklin D. Roosevelt.

4051.   Jackson, Herbert Edward Peanuts and pea-nut oil; with special reference to the trade of San Francisco. Master's thesis. University of California. Berkeley. 1924.

4052.   Jackson, James Grey. 1811. An account of the Empire of Marocco and the Districts of Suse and Tafilelt..To which is added an account of shipwrecks on the Western Coast of Africa and an interesting account of Timbuctoo. 2nd ed..corrected, enlarged. London: Cadell.

Reference to use of boiled, fried locusts by Muslims; and to salted locusts by Jewish population. The Jews ate these with a food called tafina made by placing meat, fish, eggs, tomatoes or other food in a jar which was placed in an oven on Friday night, then removed-cooked-on the Sabbath, so that the people got a hot meal without the sin of lighting a fire on that day.

4053.   Jackson, James Grey. 1820. An account of Timbuctoo and Housa, territories in the interior of Africa, by El Hage abd Salan Shabeeny; with notes, critical and explanatory. Tho which is added, let-ters descriptive of travels through west and south Barbary, and across the mountains of Atlas; also; fragments, notes, and anecdotes, specimens of the Arabic epistolary style, etc. etc. London: Printed for Longman, Hurst, Rees, Orme, and Brown.

A breakfast in Haha Province: p. 153; barley gruel (el hassua) as breakfast food: pp. 242-243; 317; kuscasoe [couscous]: pp. 316-317; el haseeda: a roasted barley flour, mixed with water and used as a travelling food: p. 317; preserved butter, dried meat: p. 349.

4054.   Jackson, Lillie. 1969. "Soulin'". Synergy October-November. Pp. 7-8.

Describes soul food and restaurants serving soul food, in the San Francisco Bay Area. Refers to the traditional food of Black-Americans.

4055.   Jacquot, r. & Nataf, Berthe. 1936. Cassava et son utilisation commen aliment. [Cassava and its use as a food.] Paris: Hermann.

4056.   Jacob, H.E. 1935. The saga of coffee. Translated by E. Paul & C. Paul]. London: Allen and Unwin.

4057.   Jacob, H.E. 1944. Six thousand years of bread. Its holy and unholy history. Translated by Richard Winston. New York: Doubleday, Doran.

4058.   Jacob, H.E. 1955. Zes duizend jaren brood; de geschiedenis van ons dagelijks brood van de Egyptenaren tot in de 20 eeuw. [Six thousand years of bread; the history of our daily bread from Egypt-ian times to the 20th Century.] Utrecht: W. de Haan.

4059.   Jacobs, A.H. 1950. Favism in two children in California. Pediatrics 6: 51-54.

4060.   Jacobs, Harry L. & Sharma, Kamal L. 1969. Taste versus calories: sensory and metabolic signals in the control of food intake. NYAS-A 157: 1084-1125.

4061.   Jacobs, Morris B. 1959. Manufacture and analysis of carbonated beverages. New York: Chemical Publishing Co.

Historical development, soda-water period: pp. 16-21.

4062.   Jacoby, H. 1947. The toxic effect of teora [khesari] on man. Protection of the public by legislation and conversion of teora into fodder. IMG 82: 122-125. Lathyrus sativus.

4063.   Jacques Felix H. 1940. L'agriculture des Noirs au Cameroun: enquete sur les plantes cultivees, les outils agricoles et les greniers. [Native agriculture in the Cameroun; survey of cultivated plants, agricultural tools and graineries.] RBAAT 20: 815-838.

Includes illustrations of tools, and grain-storage structures; cultivated and gathered plants are listed, by village.

4065.   Jacques-Felix, H. 1947. Ignames sauvages et cultives au Cameroun. [Wild and cultivated yams of the Cameroun.] RBAAT 27: 119-133.

4066.   Jacquier, Henri. 1936. Etude de l'alimenta-tion des indigenes aux Etablissements francais d'Oceanie. [Study of the native diet in French Polynesia.] AMPC 34: 280-286.

Comments on the physical degeneration re-sulting from abandonment of the traditional diet.

4067.   Jacquier, Henri. 1949. Contribution a l'etude de l'alimentation et de l'hygiene alimentaire en Oceanie Francaise. [Contribution to the study of diet and hygiene in French Polynesia.] SEO-B 7: 584-606.

4068.   Jacquot, R. & Nataf, B. 1937. Le manioc et son utilisation alimentaire. [Manioc and its use as food.] Paris: Hermann.

4069.   Jaffa, Morris E. 1901. Nutrition investiga-tions among fruitarians and Chinese at the Califor-nia Agricultural Experiment Station, 1899-1901. USDA-OES-B No. 107.

4070.   Jaffa, Morrie E. 1907. Nuts and their uses as food. USDA-YB Pp. 295-311.

Nuts as food in various parts of the world: pp. 296-298; 303-307.

4071.   Jagendorf, Moritz A. 1962. Apples in life and lore. NYFQ 18: 278-283.

Includes five recipes for apple wine.

4072. Jagendorf, Moritz A. 1963. Folk wines, cordials, and brandies. Ways to make them together with some lore, reminiscences, and wise advice for enjoying them. New York: Vanguard Press.

4073. Jaghfar, Sharif. 1921. Islam in India; or the Qanum-i-Islam. New edition, revised and rearranged, with additions by William Crook. Translated by Gerhard Andreas Herklots. London: Humphrey Milford.

Contains a chapter on food and drink.

4074. Jai, V. 1961. Our food habits. GRS-J 28: 237-239.

India.

4075. Jain, S.K. 1964. The role of a botanist in folklore research. Folklore (C)5: 145-150.

4076. 'Jakseed.' 1891. Jakseed flour. Trop Ag 11: 63.

Reply to an inquiry (see A. 1891) concerning feasibility of producing jack-seed flour.

4077. Jalso, Shirley B. Relationships between nutritional beliefs and practices and some demographic and personal characteristics. Master's thesis. Cornell University. 1964.

4078. Jalso, Shirley, E.; Burns, Marjorie M.; & Rivers, Jerry M. Nutritional beliefs and practices. 1965. JADA 47: 203-208.

Nutrition education as a means for counteracting food faddism.

4079. Jamalian, J. & Pellet, P.L. 1968. Nutritional value of Middle Eastern foodstuffs. 4. Amino acid values. JSFA 15: 799-805; 19: 378-381.

4080. James, George Wharton. 1903-1904. The Indians of the Fransiscan missions: number three of the series, the Spanish missions of the Southwest. Craftsman 5: 599-616.

Photograph of a Pima woman grinding meal on a metate: p. 602; photograph of a Pima woman winnowing wild seeds: p. 605.

4081. James, George Wharton. 1903-1904-1905. Primitive inventions. Craftsman 5: 124-137.

Contains the following photographs: parching in woven basket (Havasupai): p. 129; handmills (mano) of varying coarseness: p. 133; pounding mesquite beans (Mohave): p. 134; lava stone metate (Walapai): p. 135; stone mortar and basket hopper (southern California): p. 136; boiling water in basket (Native American): p. 137.

4082. James, George Wharton. 1905. Aboriginal American homes: cave, cliff and brush dwellings in New Mexico, Arizona, and California. Craftsman 8: 459-471.

Photograph: use of metate (hand stone grinder) [Cahuilla]: p. 470.

4083. James, George Wharton. 1905. Aboriginal American homes: brush, mud, and willow dwellings. Craftsman 8: 640-649.

Mentions practice of dedicating a Navajo hogan by burning sacred maize meal.

4084. James, Margery Kirkbride. 1971. Studies in the medieval wine trade. Oxford: Clarendon Press.

4085. James, Neill. 1942. Petticoat vagabond in Ainu land and up and down Eastern Asia. New York: Charles Scribner's Sons.

Meal at Jozaneki spa: p. 59; meal at Noribetsu spa: pp. 75, 76; sake as a present to Ainu: p. 80; meal at a Penakori eating house: pp. 145, 146; foods of the Ainu bear festival: pp. 166-168; regulations regarding expenditures and charges for food in public dining places: pp. 241-242.

4086. James, Virginia E. 1892. La Creole cookbook. Memphis, Tennessee: Van Fleet-Mansfield.

4087. James, W.S. 1956. A vegetarian in Central Africa. V New 35: 5-9.

4088. Jamuh, George. 1954. Some Borneo native food preserves. Sar MJ 6: 9-19.

4089. Jamuh, George. 1956. Melanau infant feeding. SarMJ 7: 221-225.

Borneo.

4091. Jamuh, George & Harrison, Tom. 1966. Bornean cooking. 1. (Maloy, Melanau, Sea Dayak). Sar MJ 14: 158-182.

4092. Jandolo, M. 1968. Dall'antica brassicoterapia alla vitamina U. [From ancient cabbage therapy to vitamin U.] GBVI 61: 278-280.

4093. Jank, Joseph K. 1915. Spices: their botanical origin. Their chemical composition. Their commercial use. St. Louis, Missouri: the author.

4094. Janlekha, Kamal Odd. 1968. Saraphi: a survey of socio-economic conditions in a rural community in north-east Thailand. World Land Use Survey. Occasional Papers No. 8. Geographical Publications. Bude (Cornwall): International Geographical Publications.

Community studied is Ban Saraphi (Chok Chai Distric, Nakhon Ratchasimar Province). Describes foods, meal patterns, and cooking practices. [After Schofield 1975: 209.]

4095. Jansen, Adriaan Abraham Jacobus. Nutrition, infections, and serum proteins in Papuans of Netherlands New Guinea. Medical dissertaiton. Rijksuniversitetit te Leiden. 1959.

4096.   Jansen, E.G.   The economic life of the present-day Maori.   Master's thesis.   Economics. Dunedin University. 1934.

4097.   Janstein, Elisabeth.   1930.   Gericht uber Kannibalen.   [Judgement on cannibalism.]   Tagebuch 11: 1999-2001.

4098.   Janvier, Thomas Allibone.   1902.   Feast day on the Rhone.   In The Christmas kalends of Provence and some other Provencal festivals.   New York & London: Harper Brothers.

4099.   Janz, Guilhermo Jorge.   1961.   A etnografia no campo da saude publica e da nutricao.   [Ethnography in the field of public health, and nutrition.]   P-JIU-EED No. 84.   Pp. 311-335.

   The author points out the significance of cultural anthropology in providing a background for professionals in public health, particularly in the area of nutrition. A brief outline is given of the food habits of the Mankanya of Guinea-Bissau, as well as a questionnaire on food habits in use by the Nutrition Section of the Portuguese Institute for Tropical Medicine.

4100.   Janz, Guilhermo Jorge.   1967.   Alguns aspectos da nutricao como problema social.   [Some aspects of nutrition as a social problem.]   In Soc 2: 78-85.

4101.   Janz, Guilhermo Jorge, et al.   1963.   Contribuicao para o estudo do estado de nutricao dos povos da Guine portuguesa.   [Contribution to the study of the nutritional status of the population of Portuguese Guinea]   IMT-A 20: 43-60.

   Inventory of foods eaten; preparation; and distribution of meals; dietaries; beverages; taboos; and rites associated with eating.

4102.   Japanese   National   Commission   for UNESCO.   1958. Japan. Its land, people and culture. Tokyo: Ministry of Finance.

   Food: staple foods, frequency of meals; tea and liquor; typical food and the meals at which they are eaten: pp. 911-913. Rice, and typical rice-based foods: pp. 913-914. Flour, vegetables, meat, fish, sea food, seasonings: pp. 915-917. Characteristics of the Japanese diet; tableware and table manners; history of Japanese diet: pp. 917-919.

4103.   Jara, Sergio Quijada.   1963.   La olla y el porongo en el uso domestico. Del folklore del Valle del Mantaro.   [The stewpot and the gourd in domestic use. From the folklore of the Mantar River Valley.   PI 10: 76-78.

   Southeastern Peru.

4104.   Jaramillo, Gabriel Giraldo.   1947.   Aspectos historicos de la alimentacion indigena.   [Historical aspects of native diet.]   AM Ind (3):48-53.

   Reviews the general nature of pre-Columbian diet in the New World. Data is derived from classical historical sources, and reference to modern ethnographic literature.

4105.   Jaramillo, Y. Mora de. 1962. Chichas de una region rural de la Costa Atlantica colombiana. [Maize beers of a rural region of the Atlantic Coast of Colombia.]   RCF 3: 233-242.

4106.   Jardas, F. 1948. Preradba ovcjeg mlijeka na podrucju Ucke gore. [The production of sheeps' milk in the Ucka region.]   Stocarstvo 2: 16-19.

4107.   Jarde, August F.V. 1925. Les cereales dans l'antiquite grecque.   [Cereals in Greek antiquity.] Paris. E. de Boccard.

4108.   Jardin, Manuel G. 1967.   That old-time Portuguese bread. HJH 1: 83-85.

4109.   Jarvis, Norman D. 1944. Some South American fish recipes. USDI-FWS-FL No. 31.

   Twenty-four recipes collected by the author from original sources in Peru.

4110.   Jasny, Naum. 1944. The wheats of classical antiquity. JHUSHPS 63[3].

   Diets of Roman slaves, and jailed debtors: p. 115. Scholarly historical survey documented on basis of classical authors of Rome, and of modern era.

4111.   Jaspar, R. 1956. Le riz, alimentation de base des population congolaises?   [Rice, staple foods of the Congolese population?]   RCB 11: 219-222.

4112.   Jathar, V.S., et al. 1976. Dietetic habits and quality of semen in Indian subjects. Andrologia 8: 355-358.

4113.   Jatt, A.S. 1948. Food and food problems in Pakistan. 1. Rice and rice husking. Lahore: Western Pakistan Chamber of Commerce and Industry.

4114.   Jaubert, Georges F. 1900.   Les parfums comestibles.   [Edible perfumes.]   Encyclopedie scientifique des Aide-memoires, publiee sous la direction de M. Leaute. Section de l'Ingenieur, No. 256B. Paris: Gauthier-Villars.

4115.   Jeafferson, John Cordy.   1875.   A book about the table. 2 vols in one. London: Hurst & Blackett.

4116.   Jeancon, Jean Allard & Douglas, Frederick. 1930. Pueblo Indian foods. DAM-L No. 8. Reprinted. 1968.

4117.   Jeanselme, E. 1935. Conseils de regime et d'hygiene donnes aux pelerins qui s'achemennaient vers la Terre Sainte. [Advice on diet and hygiene given to pilgrims on their way to the Holy Land.] SFHM-B 29: 17-39.

4118.   Jefferson, Dorothy L. 1954. Child feeding in the United States in the Nineteenth Century. JADA 30: 335-344.

Books on child care; first milk laboratory; controversy over milk modifications; feeding routines; pasteurization; canned milk and baby foods.

4119. Jeffreys, J. 1954. Retailing trade in Britain, 1850-1950. Cambridge: Cambridge University Press.

4120. Jeffreys, Mervyn David Waldegrave. 1953. Pre-Columbian maize in Africa. Nature (L)172: 965.

4121. Jeffreys, Mervyn David Waldegrave. 1954. The history of maize in Africa. SAJS 50: 197-200.

4122. Jeffreys, Mervyn David Waldegrave. 1955. Pre-Columbian maize in Asia. E Anth 9: 21-28.

Maize in the Indian Archipelago.

4123. Jeffreys, Mervyn David Waldegrave. 1956. Muhindi or grain of Arabia. UJ 20: 198-201.

4124. Jeffreys, Mervyn David Waldegrave. 1957. Maize names round the Indian Ocean. AJC 3: 2-11.

4125. Jeffreys, Mervyn David Waldegrave. 1964. Congo, maza = Portguese, maize? Ethnos Nos. 3-4: 191-207.

Rejects the etymological relationship between the homophones on historical grounds, but notes that "the Bushongo have a tradition that maize reached them from the east long before the arrival of Portuguese while other immigrant tribes from the Sudan had arrived in the Congo region before the discovery of the Congo River by the Portuguese in 1482. These immigrants, judging from their names for maize, brought maize and its Sudanic names with them."

4126. Jeffreys, Mervyn David Waldegrave. 1965. Maize and the ambiguity in Columbus's letter. AJC 3: 2-11.

Attempt to resolve the passage in a letter by Christopher Columbus of 18 October 1498, in which it is implied maize already existed in Castile before the Columbian voyages. Includes additional discussion of possible Arabic and other contact with the New World.

4127. Jeffreys, Mervyn David Waldegrave. 1967. Pre-columbian maize in Southern Africa. Nature (L)215: 695-697.

4128. Jeffreys, Mervyn David Waldegrave. Pre-Columbian maize in the Old World from Portuguese sources. Paper presented at 9th International Congress of Anthropological and Ethnological Sciences. 28 August to 8 September, 1973. Chicago, Illinois.

The Portuguese have never claimed to have introduced Zea mays into the Old World. On the contrary, the Portuguese state that maize entered the Iberian peninsula first from Morocco and secondly from Guinea, before Columbus discovered America. Contemporary records yield ample evidence of the unambiguous use of Portuguese terms for maize when America was discovered. The Portuguese evidence is supported by Negro traditions of their use of maize before the arrival of the Europeans. A study of Old World names for maize suggests its introduction by Arabs.

4129. Jeffreys, Mervyn David Waldegrave. Pre-Columbian maize in the Old World: an examination of Portuguese sources. In Gastronomy. The anthropology of food and food habits. Edited by Margaret Louise Arnott. 1975. Pp. 23-66. Paris, The Hage: Mouton Publishers. World Anthropology.

Based on linguistic evidence, and travellers' accounts, the author suggests that maize existed in Spain, prior to the voyages of Columbus, as well as elsewhere in the Old World.

4130. Jellema, Bouwo M. Analysis of the world market for groundnuts and groundnut products. Ph.D. dissertation. Raleigh: North Carolina State University. 1972.

4131. Jelliffe, Derrick Brian. 1955. Infant nutrition in the subtropics and tropics. WHO Chronicle 9: 217-228.

4132. Jelliffe, Derrick Brian. Cultural factors and protein malnutrition in early childhood. In Second International Congress of Dietetics. 10-14 September, 1956. Rome. Proceedings. 1956. Pp. 90-94.

Exemplifies Bengali (Hindu) peasant farmer. Includes data on food classification system.

4133. Jelliffe, Derrick Brian. 1957. Social culture and nutrition. Cultural blocks and protein malnutrition in early childhood in rural West Bengal. Pediatrics 20: 128-138.

Contains description of local food uses, and food classification system.

4134. Jelliffe, Derrick Brian. 1962. Culture, social change, and infant feeding. AJCN 10: 19-45.

Trends in tropical regions; methods of investigating practices; cultural food patterns; animal milk; milk drinkers; non-milk drinkers; variation with local ecology and culture pattern; failing lactation; bottle-feeding; tinned milks.

4135. Jelliffe, Derrick Brian. Cultural and anthropologic factors in infant and maternal nutrition. In International child health. Report of the Forty-seventh Ross Conference on pediatric research. 4-5 April, 1963. Tulane University. New Orleans, Louisiana. Edited by Samuel J. Fomon. 1964. Pp. 52-56.

Examples from a wide variety of cultures, illustrating favorable and unfavorable beliefs and practices relating to food preparation, meal patterns, food interdictions; and

non-feeding practices which impinge directly upon maternal-child nutritional status.

4136. Jelliffe, Derrick Brian. 1966. Chapter
Four. Assessment of ecological factors. In The
assessment of the nutritional status of the community (with special reference to field surveys in developing regions of the world). World Health Organization Monograph Series No. 53. Geneva: World
Health Organization.

   Provides detailed guidelines for obtaining
   data bearing upon nutritional status. Of
   special interest to social scientists in the
   section on cultural influences, cross-cultural
   survey problems, and socio-economic factors: pp. 121-127.

4137. Jelliffe, Derrick Brian. 1967. Parallel food
classification in developing and industrialized countries. AJCN 20: 279-281.

   Introduces the concept of cultural super-
   foods (i.e. foods with acknowledged significance and interrelationship with religion,
   mythology, and history.) Prestige foods, and
   body-image foods are described -the latter
   in relation to diet as well as illness. The
   significance of taboos on protein-rich foods
   is emphasized in relation to at-risk groups in
   the populations of developing areas of the
   world.

4138. Jelliffe, Derrick Brian. 1968. Chapter
Four. Customs and food. In Child nutrition in
developing countries. Public Health Service. Publication No. 1822. Washington, D.C.: United States
Department of Health, Education and Welfare.

   Discusses food taboos and the importance of
   understanding them in order to develop a
   rapport in cross-cultural health care delivery.

4139. Jelliffe, Derrick Brian. 1968. Infant nutrition in the subtropics and tropics. 2nd edition.
Geneva: World Health Organization.

   Under the section 'Local customs and practices', the author cautions "Customs that
   appear strange and possibly unaesthetic to a
   pediatrician trained, for example, in Europe
   or North America must be examined critically and without prejudice" (p. 155). A
   model for the qualitative categorization of
   infant feeding practices is given also: pp.
   157, 158. Composition and preparation
   methods for infant foods used in Buganda,
   and in some parts of Uganda (ettu pastes,
   composed of the staples plantain and sweet
   potato) are given, with additional protein
   foods, e.g. legumes, eggs, milk to increase
   their nutritional benefit: pp. 261, 262.

4140. Jelliffe, Derrick Brian. 1968. The pre-
school child as a bio-cultural transitional. JTPECH
14: 217-227.

   Vulnerability of tropical child to environmental factors (infection, malnutrition) dur-

ing development from the exerogestate fe-
tal state to mobile childhood.

4141. Jelliffe, Derrick Brian. Cultural factors
and breastfeeding. Paper presented at 77th Annual
Meeting of the American Anthropological Association. 14 to 18 November, 1978. Los Angeles,
California.

4142. Jelliffe, Derrick Brian & Bennett F. John.
1961. Cultural and anthropological factors in infant
and maternal nutrition. FASEB-FP 20 [Part 3. No.
7.]: 185-187.

   Reference is made to the Baganda, a Bantu-
   speaking people of Uganda. Women's food:
   p. 186; children's food: p. 186.

4143. Jelliffe, Derrick Brian & Bennett, F. John.
1962. Cultural problems in technical assitance.
Children 9: 171-177.

   Stresses the need for overcoming ethnocentrism when working in a culture other than
   one's own.

4144. Jelliffe, Derrick Brian & Jelliffe, E.F. Pat-
rice. 1961. The nutritional status of Haitian
children. ATrop 18: 1-45.

4145. Jelliffe, Derrick Brian & Jelliffe, E.F. Pat-
rice. Human milk as an ecological force. In First
Asian Congress of Nutrition. 22 January - 2 February, 1971. Hyderabad, India. Proceedings. Edited
by P.G. Tulupe & Kamala S. Jaya Rao. 1972. Pp.
592-602. Hyderabad: Nutrition Society of India.

   The characteristics of human milk from a
   biochemical perspective are examined, as
   contrasted with cow's milk; the economic,
   convenience, maternal, and psychological
   aspects of breast feeding are considered,
   together with a discussion of causes and
   effects of lactation failure. The impact of
   Western patterns of infant feeding are evaluated, and suggestions offered for re-establishment of breast feeding as the most ad-
   vantageous form of infant nourishment.

4146. Jelliffe, Derrick Brian & Jelliffe, E.F. Pat-
rice. Cultural interaction and child nutrition. (Toward a curvilinear compromise?) Paper presented
at 74th Annual Meeting of the American Anthropological Association. 2 to 6 December, 1975. San
Francisco, California.

4147. Jelliffe, Derrick Brian; Jelliffe, E.F. Pa-
trice; Garcia, L.; & Barrios, G. de. 1961. The
children of the San Blas Indians of Panama: an
ecological field study of health and nutrition. J Ped
59: 271-285.

4148. Jelliffe, Derrick Brian & Maddocks, I. 1964.
Notes on ecologic malnutrition in the New Guinea
Highlands. CP 3: 432-438.

4149. Jelliffe, Derrick Brian; Morton, C.; & Nansubuga, G. 1962. Ettu pastes in infant feeding in
Buganda. JTMH 65: 43-44.

Recipes for preparation of steamed plaintain and sweet potato. Ettu refers to the banana leaf packet in which the plaintain and sweet potato are steamed.

4150. Jelliffe, Derrick Brian; Williams, L.L.; & Jelliffe, E.F.P. 1954. A clinical nutrition study in a rural Jamaican village. JTMH 57: 27-40.

4151. Jellinek, E.M. 1955. Distribution of alcohol consumption and of calories derived from alcohol in various selected populations. PNS 14: 93-97.

4152. Jellinek, Gisela. 1964. Introduction to and critical review of modern methods of sensory analysis (odour, taste and flavour evaluation) with special emphasis on descriptive sensory analysis (flavour profile method). IJND 1: 219-260.

4153. Jenkins, Felisha. A critical study of the diets of preschool children in their homes: Group 1: meals at the family table; Group 2: meals alone or at a separate table. Master's thesis. Oakland, California: Mills College. 1932.

4154. Jenkins, J.A. 1948. The origin of the cultivated tomato. EB 2: 379-392.

The ancestral form of the cultivated tomato (Lycopersicon esculentum) was originally confined to the Peru-Ecuador area. After spreading northward, possibly as a weed, in pre-Columbian times, it was not extensively domesticated until it reached Mexico, from whence the cultivated forms were disseminated.

4155. Jenks, Albert Ernest. The wild rice gatherers of the Upper Lakes; a study in American primitive economics. Ph.D. dissertation. University of Wisconsin. 1899.

4156. Jenks, Ernest Albert. 1900. Chapter Five. Consumption. In the wild rice gatherers of the Upper Lakes. A study in American primitive economics. BAE-AR for the years 1897-1898.

Includes nutrient analysis of Zizania aquatica, and possibly the first technical reference to the comparative nutritive quality of an indigenous North American food. Reviewed in Man 3: 124-126 [1903].

4157. Jenks, Albert Ernest. 1900. Faith as a factor in the economic life of the Amerine. AA 2: 676-689.

Beliefs affecting food consumption with notes on food taboos of the Omaha, Arizona Apache, Navajo, and Southern California groups: pp. 683-685.

4158. Jenner, Alice. 1968. Social, emotional and cultural influences as related to eating patterns and malnutrition. CNN 24: 37-43.

Social influences, malnutrition in Central America, western China; social prestige of foods and traditional acceptance; psychological acceptance or rejection of food; dental health; health education. Mentions premastication of infants' food and other food habits in Szechuan, Malaysia and Africa.

4159. Jenness, Diamond & Ballantyne, A. 1926. Language, mythology and songs of Bwaidoga, Goodenough Islands, S.E. Paupa. JPS 36: 303-310.

New Britain. Myth: gods teach people how to seek and prepare food; origin of the coconut.

4160. Jensen, Arlene. A field study of the Nunamiut Eskimos: the last surviving group of inland Eskimos in Alaska whose economy is based upon the caribou. Master's thesis. Geography. Monmouth: Oregon College of Education. 1967.

4161. Jensen, Lloyd B. 1949. Meat and meat foods. New York: Ronald Press.

Historical study.

4162. Jensen, Lloyd B. 1953. Man's foods, nutrition and environments in food gathering times and food producing times. Champaign, Illinois: Garrard Press.

4163. Jensen, Magny Landstad. 1947. Cook book; Norwegian recipes. Brooklyn, New York: Norwegian News Co.

4164. Jenyns, Soame. 1931. Tea. HKN 2: 90-91.

Brief historical, botanic, and ethnographic data.

4165. Jerome, Norge Winifred. Food habits and acculturation. Dietary practices and nutrition of families headed by Southern-born Negroes residing in a northern metropolis. Ph.D. dissertation. University of Wisconsin. 1967.

4166. Jerome, Norge Winifred. American culture and food habits. In Dimensions of nutrition. Proceedings of the Colorado Dietetic Association Conference. 1969. Fort Collins, Colorado. Edited by Jacqueline Dupont. 1970. Pp. 223-229. Boulder: Colorado Associated University Press.

Attempts to correlate certain food behaviors with characteristics of national psychology.

4167. Jerome, Norge Winifred. Acculturation and diet: the case of the Afro-American immigrant. Paper presented at 72nd Annual Meeting of the American Anthropological Association. 1 December, 1973. New Orleans, Louisiana.

4168. Jerome, Norge Winifred. On determining food patterns of urban dwellers in contemporary U.S. society. Paper presented at 9th International Congress of Anthropological and Ethnological Sciences. 28 August to 8 September, 1973. Chicago, Illinois.

4169. Jerome, Norge W. Early dietary experience with sweet taste among human neonates. Paper presented at 73rd Annual Meeting of the American

Anthropological Association. 19 to 24 November, 1974. Mexico City.

4170. Jerome, Norge Winifred. 1975. Flavor preferences and food patterns of selected U.S. and Caribbean Blacks. FTech 29 [6] : 46, 48, 50-51.

An analysis of food patterns, and flavor preferences, illustrated with charts indicating core, secondary, and peripheral foods for basic meals in both groups. Latter concepts derived from Bennett (1942, 1943).

4171. Jerome, Norge Winifred. On determining food patterns of urban dwellers in contemporary United States Society. In Gastronomy. The anthropology of food and food habits. Edited by Margaret Louise Arnott. 1975. Pp. 91-111. Paris, The Hague: Mouton Publishers. World Anthropology.

This paper examines the process by which new foods from the widely varied food supply of an industrialized nation are incorporated into individual diets. Using the concepts of core, secondary, peripheral and marginal foods suggested by Bennett (1942, 1943), the author suggests the occurrence of a continuous two-phase cyclic incorporation of foods into the diet. The cycle commences with experimentation through incorporation of non-core food items into the diet at a low-frequency rate followed by continuous incorporation of preferred food items into the established diet.

4172. Jerome, Norge Winifred. Future of medical anthropology: medical anthropologists and nutrition. Paper presented at 77th Annual Meeting of the American Anthropological Association. 14 to 18 November, 1978. Los Angeles, California.

4173. Jerome, Norge Winifred; Cochran, W.E.; Staugh, L.G. 1968. Changing meal patterns among Southern-born Negroes in a Midwestern city. Learning nutrition through living. Nutrition outreach through home supervision. N News 31: 9-12.

4174. Jerome, Norge Winifred; Kiser, Barbara B.; & West, Estella A. Infant and child feeding practices in an urban community in the north-central region. In Practices of low-income families in feeding infants and small children, with particular attention to cultural sub-groups. Edited by Samuel J. Fomon & T.A. Anderson. 1972. Pp. 49-58. Bethesda, Maryland: United States Department of Health, Education and Welfare. Maternal and Child Health Service (DHEW Publication No. 72-5605).

The community surveyed is Kansas City, Kansas.

4175. Jerome, Norge Winifred & Pelto, Gretel H. Intracultural diversity and nutritional status: an overview. Paper presented at 74th Annual Meeting of the American Anthropological Association. 2 to 6 December, 1975. San Francisco, California.

4176. Jerrold, J. 1897. Chinese dinner in New York. Ill Am 22: 312-313. Also in Curr Lit 22: 444 (1897).

4177. Jessen, John M. A fisherman out of water: a network analysis of the participatory behavior of New England fishermen. Paper presented at 77th Annual Meeting of the American Anthropological Association. 14 to 18 November, 1978. Los Angeles, California.

4178. Jesus, Pascuala de. Improvement of the present method of cooking rice, and standardization of formula for cooking rice recipes. Master's thesis. Home Economics Manila: Philippines Women's University. 1949.

4179. Jiggets, J. Ida. 1949. Religion, diet, and health of Jews. New York: Block Publishing Co.

This monograph is devoted to a study of foods in Jewish religious culture. The Scriptural bases for religious food practices are first reviewed: pp. 5-46. Preparation of foods follows: pp. 47-66. A final section is devoted to Nutritional analysis of the orthodox Jewish diet: pp. 67-92.

4180. Jipp, Shirley E. 1974. Popcorn's popularity. SW-H-MM 25 August.

Account of Popcorn Days in North Loup, Nebraska, a center of popcorn production in the United States Midwest, where a yearly festival is held.

4181. Jocano, F. Landa. 1958. Corn and rice rituals among the Sulod of central Panay, Philippines. PJS 87: 455-472.

Describes how these rituals are related to planting and harvesting activities among the Sulod, a mountain people in central Panay. These rituals are seen as techniques for interacting with, and influencing the supernaturals. Texts are included, and the article concludes with an analysis of the sociological, and psychological role of these rituals in Sulod life. Panay Island is located between ca. 10. 25N and ca. 11. 50N; and between ca. 122. 0E and ca. 122. 10E, northwest of the island of Negros, and southeast of the Island of Mindoro.

4182. Jocano, F. Landa. 1967. The relevance of anthropology to nutrition research. PJN 20: 202-210.

4183. Jochelson, Waldemar. Kumiss festivals of the Yakut and the decoration of kumiss vessels. In Boas anniversary volume. [Edited by Berthold Lauffer.] 1906. Pp. 257-271. New York: G.E. Stechert & Co.

Customs, production, and ceremonials relating to fermented mare's milk among Siberian group.

4184. Joel, Judith. The Yuman word for bean as a clue to prehistory. Paper presented at 76th Annual Meeting of the American Anthropological Association. 29 November to 3 December, 1977. Houston, Texas.

Internal linguistic evidence suggests that the pan-Yuman word for cultivated kidney bean (Phaseolus vulgaris) is borrowed. Archeology indicates that farming was adopted late, in the Colorado River region, after having been already well-established in regions to the east. The two most likely sources from which farming and cultigens reached the Colorado River Yumans were the Anasazi and the Hohokam. Linguistic evidence centering on the words for "bean" may tell us from which of these sources this cultigen was derived.

4185. Joest, W. 1896-1897. Lause-Essen und Eau de Cologne-Trinken. [Louse-eating and Eau-de-cologne drinking.] Globus 69: 145-146.

Unusual items of 'food': examples from Paraguay; Texas; Germany; Austria; among Cossacks; Madeira; Marquesas Islands; New Hebrides.

4186. Joffe, Natalie F. Food habits of selected subcultures in the United States. In The problem of changing food habits. Report of the Committee on Food Habits. 1941-1943. National Research Council. 1943. NRC-B No. 108. Pp. 97-103.

Brief descriptions of the staple foods, dietary patterns, and attitudes toward food of Italian-Americans, Polish-, Hungarian-, and Czechoslovak-Americans, and Black-Americans.

4187. Joffe, Natalie F. 1948. Food and food habits. ASNJ-N No. 5. Pp. 14-15.

4188. Joffe, Natalie F.; Janis, M.; Shippee, E.; & Woodward P. Role of milk in American culture. Mimeographed. Committee on Food Habits. Washington, D.C.: National Research Council. October, 1943.

4189. Joffee, Natalie F. & Walker, T.T. Some food patterns of Negroes in the United States of America, and their relationship to wartime problems of food and nutrition. Mimeographed. Committee on Food Habits. Washington, D.C.: National Research Council. April, 1944.

4190. Johannessen, Carl L. 1970. The dispersal of Musa in Central America: the domestication process in action. AAG-A 60: 689-699.

4191. Johannessen, Carl, L., et al. 1970. The domestication of maize: process or event? GR 60: 393-414.

4192. Johari, Pratapchandra. Tribal economy in Kumaon. Ph.D. dissertation. Economics. Agra University. 1965.

India.

4193. Johnsen, B. 1968. Food in Iceland, 874-1550. N Med-A Pp. 66-76.

4194. Johnson, Allen W. Computer simulation of swidden agriculture. Paper presented at 69th Annual Meeting of the American Anthropological Association. 19 to 22 November, 1970. San Diego, California.

4195. Johnson, Charles Pierpoint. 1861. The useful plants of Great Britain: a treatise upon the principle native vegetables capable of application as food, medicine, or in the arts and manufactures. London: R. Hardwicke.

4196. Johnson, Dennis B. The cashew of northeast Brazil: a geographical study of a tropical tree crop. Ph.D. dissertation. Geography. University of California, Los Angeles. 1972.

4197. Johnson, Denis B. Chapter Six. Food store-dwelling linkages in selected areas of Calgary. In Calgary. Metropolitan structure and influence. Edited by Brenton M. Barr. 1975. Pp. 193-228. Victoria, British Columbia: University of Victoria Press.

Analyzes variables responsible for mutual accessibility between food stores and their custom. Study includes descriptive geographical, and interview response data.

4198. Johnson, Eileen. Preliminary faunal analysis -Lubbock Lake site. Paper presented at 72nd Annual Meeting of the American Anthropological Association. 29 November, 1973. New Orleans, Louisiana.

4199. Johnson, Elden. 1969. Archaeological evidence for utilization of wild rice. Science 163: 276-277.

4200. Johnson, F.A. A study of the reaction to food of country children of preschool age, and factors influencing it. Master's thesis. University of Chicago. 1926.

4201. Johnson, Irma Y. A study of certain changes in the Spanish-American family in Bernalillo County, 1915-1946. Master's thesis. University of New Mexico. 1948.

4204. Johnson, J.D.; Simoons, Frederick J.; Kurwitz, R.; Grange, A.; Mitchell, C.H.; Sinatra, F.R.; Sunshine, P.; Robertson, W.V.; Bennett, P.H.; & Kretchmer, Norman. 1977. Lactose malabsorption among the Pima Indians of Arizona. Gastroenterology 73: 1299-1304.

4203. Johnson, Laurces A. & Ray, Marcia. 1961. Over the counter and on the shelf. Country-store-keeping in America, 1620-1920. New York: Bonanza Books.

4204. Johnson, Lois S. 1969. What we eat. The origins and travels of foods 'round the world. Chicago; New York; San Francisco: Rand McNally & Co.

Poorly documented.

4205. Johnson, Marjorie. Effect of size of initial food serving on the eating efficiency of a group of preschool children. Master's thesis. Iowa State University. 1942.

4206. Johnson, M.O. 1935. The pineapple. Honolulu: Paradise of the Pacific Press.

4207. Johnson, Orna Rothbaum. Eating arrangements and the structure of male/female relations among Machinguenga Indians. Paper presented at 73rd Annual Meeting of the American Anthropological Association. 19 to 24 November, 1974. Mexico City.

4208. Johnson, Robert E. Tropical deterioration and nutrition: a discussion based on observations on troops. In Fourth International Congresses on Tropical Medicine and Malaria. Washington, D.C, 10 May to 18 May, 1948. Proceedings. Vol. 1. Pp. 148-167. Washington, D.C.: Department of State.

Concludes that evidence indicates caloric requirements decrease as mean temperature increases.

4209. Johnson, Robert E. & Kark, Robert M. Feeding problems as related to environment. An analysis of United States and Canadian army ration trials and surveys. In Conference on food acceptance research. 6 December to 7 December, 1945. United States War Department. Quartermaster Food and Container Institute. Research and Development Branch. Military Planning Division. Committee on Food Research. 1946. Quartermaster Corps Manual. 17-9.

Available in microform from United States Library of Congress. Microform Division. Item PB-53-883.

4210. Johnson, Robert E. & Kark, Robert M. 1947. Environment and food intake in man. Science 105: 378-379.

4211. Johnson, B.M. & Raymond, W.D. 1956. The sago palm. CEAP 6: 20-32.

4212. Johnston, Alexander. 1958. Native plants in Blackfoot culture. CCat 21: 21-23.

4213. Johnston, Alexander. 1960. Uses of native plants by the Blackfoot Indians. Alb HR 8: 8-13.

4214. Johnston, Alexander. 1962. Chenopodium album as a food plant in Blackfoot Indian prehistory. Ecology 43: 129-130.

4215. Johnston, Alexander. 1969. The old Indian's medicine. SAN No. 26. Pp. 1-36.

4216. Johnston, B.F. 1956. Staple food crops in West Africa and the Congo. Trop Ag 33: 214-220.

4217. Johnston, B.F. 1958. The staple food economies of western tropical Africa. Stanford: Stanford University Press.

4218. Johnston, Charles. 1847. Travels in Southern Abyssinia, through the country of Adal to the kingdom of Shoa. 2 vols. London: J. Madden.

Vol. One. Use of camel's milk products by Dankalli (Danakil): pp. 271-272; slaughter, Grain mills: pp. 27-28; manner of brewing tedj a fermented honey: pp. 170-171; a meal of teff bread and its condiments wort, or dillock, thalah, an ale; meal etiquette: pp. 172-177; use of raw meat: pp. 224-226; salt as currency: pp. 232-237; foods sold in the market of Aliv Amba: pp. 240-241; food of slaves of slave-merchants: p. 241; manner of selling honey, and preserved butter: pp. 242-243; baking bread and the use of pulverized cotton seed meal: pp. 253-254; manufacture of drinking horns: pp. 332-334; manufacture of ale and beer: pp. 345-350; butchering goat meat: pp. 368-370.

4219. Johnston, J.H. & Cleland, J.B. 1942. Aboriginal names and uses of plants in the Ooldea region, South Australia. RSSA-TP 66: 93-103.

4220. Johnston, J.H. & Cleland, J.B. 1943. Native names and uses of plants in the northeastern corner of South Australia. RSSA-TP 67: 149-173.

4221. Johnston, Judith C. The household context of infant feeding practices in South Trinidad. Paper presented at 76th Annual Meeting of the American Anthropological Association. 29 November to 3 December, 1977. Houston, Texas.

Change in infant feeding patterns of a rural East Indian community in Trinidad, during the last decade [sic], are described, drawing on feeding interviews with new mothers in 1969 and 1976. A stable pattern of "mixed" feeding predominates during this decade, with no trend toward the exclusive use of either breast or bottle. However, a significant shift has occurred in the content of bottle formulas. Sago and flour pap have been replaced by imported milk powders. Decisions regarding infant feeding are embedded in a larger strategy for the economic survival and comfort of the infant's household group. Infant survival, while desired, is not given precedence of the interests of the group as a unit.

4222. Johnston, T. Harvey & Tryon, Henry. 1914. Report of prickly-pear Travelling Commission. 1 November, 1912-30 April, 1914. Brisbane: Government Printer.

Investigations on methods for eradication of Opuntia sp. a pest cactus, wherever introduced. Its use as human food: India: p. 27; South Africa: pp. 37-38; Canary Islands: p. 44; Europe and the Mediterranean: pp. 51-52; Mexico: Pp. 88-89; Brazil: p. 108.

4223. Johnston, Thomas Frederick. The stress-reducing function of Tsonga beer-songs. Master's thesis. California State University at Fullerton. 1972.

This study consists of an examination of one hundred forty song texts collected in Mozambique and southern Transvaal, during 1968-1970. Each call and response is shown in indigenous language, and English translation. Purpose of the research is to explain the song-texts by reference to comparative texts and ethnographic data, and to understand further the nature of ceremonial beer drinking. It is concluded that ceremonial beer drinking, rather than being solely a recreational pastime, fulfills an important pragmatic role in the reduction of stress. A further conclusion is that different categories of song-text subject-matter can be arranged on a scale according to the degree with which, in the context of beer-drinking, they serve this stress-reducing function.

4224. Johnstone, G.W. The growth of the sugar trade and refining industry. In The making of the modern British diet. Edited by Derek J. Oddy & D.S. Miller. 1976. London: Croom Helm.

4225. Joeklainen, Aili; Pekkarinen, Maija; Roine, Paavo, & Meitinnen, Jorma K. 1962. Diet of Finnish Lapps. ZErn 3: 110-117.

4226. Joelaud, L. 1924. Le boeuf de Madagascar. Son origine, son role dans les coutumes Sakalaves. [The ox of Madagascar, its origins, its role in Sakalava cust ns.] Anthropologie Nos. 1-2: 103-108.

4227. Jolians, J.L. 1959. Meat preferences of people in the Central region of Ghana. WASA-J 5: 64-78.

A survey of 658 persons living in and around the Kumasi area (6. 45W, 1. 35W).

4228. Jolly, Clifford J. 1970. The seed-eaters: a new model of hominid differentiation based on a baboon analogy. Man 5: 5-26.

4229. Joly, F.I. 1938. Sur quelques plantes cultivees du Haut Oubangui d'origine americaine. [Several cultivated plants of Upper Oubangi of American origin.] R Cong 26: 67-77.

4230. Jonas, Clara E. Kitchen storage in relation to management. Master's thesis. Ithaca, New York: Cornell University. 1938.

4231. Jones, E. Baker. 1942. The food of the Rhodesian native from the dietetic point of view. Nada No. 19. Pp. 34-39.

4232. Jones, E. Baker. 1956. Some nutritional problems in Central Africa. CAJM 2: 60-72.

4233. Jones, Eric Lionel. 1963. Seasons and prices. The role of the weather in English agricultural history. London: Allen & Unwin.

Based on Records of the seasons, prices and agricultural produce and phenomena observed in the British Isles, by T.H. Baker. 1883. London: Simpkin, Marshall.

4234. Jones, J.L. 1954. Seaweed for the table. CL 116: 2106-2107.

4235. Jones, Jana W. Child feeding in the rural low-income family. In Practices of low-income families in feeding infants and small children, with particular attention to cultural subgroups. Proceedings of a national workshop. Airlie Conference Center, Warrenton, Virginia, March 17-18, 1971. Edited by Samuel J. Fomon & Thomas A. Anderson. 1972. Pp. 37-42. Bethesda, Maryland: United States Department of Health, Education, and Welfare. Maternal and Child Health Service. (DHEW Publication No. 72-5605).

Family differences among rural low-income groups; breast versus bottle feeding; solid foods.

4236. Jones, Martha R.; Larsen, Nils P.; & Pritchard, George. 1947. Le taro, et la patate contre les cereales alimentaires et leur influence sur la sante et la carie dentaire aux Hawaii. [The taro, and potato compared with food cereals and their influence on health and dental caries in Hawaii.] SEO-B 7: 386-405.

4237. Jones, Michael Owen. Perspective in the study of eating behavior. Paper presented at International Centenary Conference of the Folklore Society. 17 July to 21 July, 1971. Royal Holloway College, University of London, Egham, Surrey.

A review of Audrey I. Richards' Hunger and work in a savage tribe (1932) and Mary Douglas' "Deciphering a meal" (Daedalus 101: 61-81 1972), with additional supportive documentation from the ethnographic, and folklore literatures. A brief synthesis of physiological, and socio-psychological studies on food in culture.

4238. Jones, Rex L. & Jones, Shirley Kurz. 1976. The Himalayan woman. Palo Alto: Mayfield Publishing Co.

Food: pp. 14-21.

4239. Jones, Sonya M. 1963. A study of Swazi nutrition. Report of the Swaziland nutrition survey, 1961-1962, for the Swaziland administration. Institute for Social Research. Durban: University of Natal.

Food preparation and consumption: pp. 62-88.

4240. Jones, Trandailer. 1952. Impressions of nutrition habits in the Virgin Islands. USVI-DH-ND-B No. 2.

4241. Jones, Trandailer. 1953. Where tea means breakfast and breakfast means lunch. JADA 29: 918.

An overview of typical U.S. Virgin Islands foods, and eating habits.

4242. Jones, Volney Hurt. The ethnobotany of the Isleta Indians. Master's thesis. University of New Mexico. 1931.

A Rio Grande Pueblo culture of New Mexico.

4243.   Jones, Volney Hurt.   1936. The vegetable remains of Newt Kash Hollow Shelter. In Rock Shelters in Menifee County, Kentucky. By W.S. Webb & W.D. Funkhouser. UK-RAA 3 [4].

4244. Jones, Volney Hurt. 1942. A native southeastern tea plant. El Pal 49: 272-280.

Thelesperma longipes, and Thelesperma gracile.

4245. Jones, Volney Hurt. 1945. The use of 'honeydew' as food by Indians. Mkey 19: 145-149.

A sweet insect secretion.

4246. Jones, Volney Hurt. 1948. Notes on Indians maize. PArch 13: 23-24.

4247. Jones, Volney Hurt. Maize from the Davis site: its nature and interpretation. In The George C. Davis site, Cherokee County, Texas. Edited by H. Perry Newell & A.D. Krieger. 1949. SAA-M No. 5. Pp. 241-249.

4248. Jones, Volney H. 1951. Material from the Hemenway Archaeological Expedition (1887-1888) as a factor in establishing the American origin of the garden bean. 29th International Congress of Americanists. 1951. Chicago. Proceedings. 1956. Vol. 3. Pp. 177-184. Chicago: University of Chicago Press.

4249. Jones, Volney Hurt. The bark of the bittersweet vine as an emergency food among the Indians of the Western Lakes region. In Papers in honor of Emerson F. Greenman. Edited by James E. Fitting. 1965. Mich Arch 11(3-4): 170-180.

4250. Jones, V.K. 1944. Snake steak with relish: abridged. Cath Dgst 8: 31-34.

Popular account of some Latin American foods.

4251. Jones William O. 1957. Manioc: an example of innovation in African economics. EDCC 5: 97-117.

4252. Jones, William O. 1959. Manioc in Africa. Stanford: Stanford University Press.

4253. Jones, William O. 1961. The food and agricultural economics of tropical Africa: a summary view. SU-FRI-S 2: 3-20.

4254. Jongh, Gerrit. Sociological acceptance of cereal foods products. Introductory paper read at the Symposium 'Sociological Acceptance of Cereal Foods' convened at Sixth International Cereal and Bread Congress, 17 September to 22 September, 1978. Winnipeg, Manitoba.

Examples of historical, technological, organoleptic and foreign trade variables as influences on food acceptance.

4255. Jordahl, Harold C.& Curran, George A. 1956. Manomin: good grain. WCB 21: 17-21.

Wild rice.

4256.   Jordan, Brigitte. One the analyzability of social relationships in magazine advertisements for hard liquor. Paper presented at 76th Annual Meeting of the American Anthropological Association. 29 November to 3 December, 1977. Houston, Texas.

Advertisements which appear in popular U.S. magazines are here considered as folk productions which draw for their intelligibility on common cultural understandings about social structure and social relationships. A photographic slide-support analysis is presented which identifies the types of social relationships portrayed in liquor ads, specifies the iconographic devices by which such relationships are made visible in liquor ads, and suggests cultural notions about product-specific problems as the constraint which operates on the selection of particular social relationships as hosts for product consumption.

4257.   Jordan, David Starr & Evermann, Barton Warren. 1902. Preliminary report of an investigation of the fishes and fisheries of the Hawaiian Islands. USCFF-RC for the year 1901. Pp. 353-380.

Lists food fishes; rules and regulations relating to fishing; introduction of new species; fish ponds; operation of fish markets in Honolulu, Hilo, Wailuku and Lahaina; and the nature of commercial fisheries.

4258.   Jordan, Julia Anne. Ethnobotany of the Kiowa Apache. Master's thesis. Anthropology. University of Oklahoma. 1965.

4260.   Joret, Charles. 1904. Les plantes dans l'antiquite et au Moyen Age. [Plants in antiquity and in the Middle Ages.] Paris: Emille Bouillon.

4261.   Joseph, Frances A. 1896. The dietary laws from a woman's point of view. JGR 8: 643-651.

Jewish food regulations.

4262.   Joseph, S.A.; Goldberg, A.; & Guggenheim, K. 1962. Composition of Israeli mixed dishes. JADA 40: 125-129.

4263.   Josephs, H.W. 1944. Favism. JPE-B 74: 295-298.

4264.   Joshi, V.H. 1966. Economic development and social change in a south Gujarat village. Baroda: University of Baroda.

Brief description of effects of urbanization upon diet. The village studied is Haria, located at approximately 21. 10N, 72. 54E.

4265.   Jouan, Henri. 1875. Les plantes alimentaires de l'Oceanie. [Food plants of Oceania.] Cherbourg: Debelfontaine et Seyffert.

4266.   Jouan, Henri. 1875. Les plantes alimentaires de l'Oceanie. [Food plants of Oceania.] SNSNMC-M 19: 33-83.

4267. Joy, Leonard. 1966. The economics of food production. AAffair 65: 317-328.

Africa.

4268. Joy, Leonard. Economic aspects of food and nutrition planning. In First Asian Congress of Nutrition. 22 January - 2 February 1971. Hyderabad, India. Proceedings. Edited by P.G. Tulupe & Kamala S. Jaya Rao. 1972. Pp. 267-274. Hyderabad: Nutrition Society of India.

In this paper, the author speaks against unqualified linear programming as a basis on which to develop least-cost diets as components of national nutrition programs. The concerns of a successful nutrition plan would be consideration of distribution and the consumer; consideration of individual, group and regional problems; and concern for appropriate available foods rather than categorically 'least expensive'. Detailed suggestions for improvement of India's national nutrition program are made.

4269. Joy, Leonard. 1973. Economics of nutrition planning. IDSUS-C 107.

4270. Joy, Leonard. 1973. Food and nutrition planning. JAgEcon 24: 165-192.

Points up that errors in nutrition policy planning are made based on the false perception that major nutrient deficiency is of protein, whereas it is, in fact, one of calories. In addition, the foregoing arises as a result of inadequate effective demand for, rather than insufficient supply of food. The author concludes that effective policies will seek to eliminate malnutrition through generating income in poverty contexts. Reference is India. The important role of the economist in nutrition planning is emphasized.

4271. Joy, Leonard & Payne, P.R. 1975. Nutrition and national development planning. IDSUS-C No. 83.

4272. Joyce, Arthur T. 1952. Changing food habits and their effects on bakery products consumption. BW 156: 45-48.

Discussion of trends away from baked foods.

4273. Joyce, Gail Jane. The between meal eating habits of high school students in Alabama. Master's thesis. University of Alabama. 1948.

4274. Joyner, Charles W. 1971. Soul food and the Sambo stereotype: folklore from the slave narrative collection. KFQ 16: 171-178.

4275. Judd, J.E. 1957. Century-old dietary taboos in 20th Century Japan. JADA 33: 489-491.

Food combinations; sequence of foods in meals; food avoidances of specific festival days; influence of military occupation following World War II.

4276. Judd, L.C.R. Chao Dai: dry rice farming in northern Thailand. Ph.D. dissertation. Cornell University 1961.

4277. Judge, Arthus I., ed. 1914. A history of the canning industry by its most prominent men. Baltimore: The Canning Trade.

4278. Julius, Charles. Anthropologist's report. In New Guinea Nutrition Survey Expedition. Report. Edited by Eben H. Hipsley & F.W. Clements. 1947. Pp. 31-71. Canberra: Australia. Department of External Territories.

Background material relating to village life.

4279. Jumelle, Henri Lucien. 1900. Le cacaoyers, sa culture et son exploitation dans tous les plays de production. [Caccao, its cultivation and exploitation in all the countries producing it.] Paris: Challamel.

4280. Jumelle, Henri Lucien. 1901. Les cultures coloniales. 1. Plantes alimentaires. [Colonial cultigens. 1. Food Plants.] Paris: Bailliere et fils.

4281. Jumelle, Henri Lucien. 1910. Les plantes a tubercules alimentaires des climate temperes et des pay chauds. [Edible root plants of temperate and tropical climates.] Encyclopedie Scientifique. Bibliotheque de Botanique Appliquee. No. 35. Paris: O. Doin.

4282. Jumelle, Henri Lucien. 1912-1915. Les plantes coloniales. 2. Legumes et fruits. 3. Plants a surce; cafe, cacao, the, mate. 4. Plantz a condriments et plantes medicinales. [Colonial plants. 1. vegetables and fruits. 3. Sources of sugar; coffee, cocoa, tea, mate. 4. Condiment plants, and medicinal plants.] Paris: J.-B. Bailleres.

4283. Junemann, Joachim. 1964. Gastfreundschaft and heimische Kost in Sudhannover. [Hospitality and home-cooking in south Hannover.] Heimatland Pp. 103-106.

4284. Jung, Robert. 1952. Alt-Siegerlander Brot und Geback. [Old Siegen bread and baked goods.] Sieger Heim Pp. 121-122.

Siegen is a city in northeastern Germany, located at 50. 52N, 8. 02E.

4285. Junod, Henri A. 1930. L'alcoholisme chez les noirs africains. [Alcoholism among Black Africans.] Geneva: Bureau Internationale d'Ethnologie pour la Defense des Indigenes.

4286. Jungueira, Oswaldo Gomes. 1954. A farinhada. [Manioc-flour production.] IBECC-CNF-CEFRGS No. 5.

4287. Juritz, C.F. 1914. Notes on some indigenous and other food plants. USA-DA-SB No. 6.

4288. Justice, Catherine Leirer. A study of some factors influencing the food intake of preschool chilren. Master's thesis. Lafayette, Indiana: Purdue University. 1944.

4289.   Justin, M.M.; Rust, L.O.; & Vail, G.E. 1956. Chapter Five. What may influence the food eaten. In Foods. An introductory college courses. Cambridge, Massachusetts: Riverside Press.

4290.   Jyothi, K.K.; Dhakshayani, R; Swaminathan, M.C.; & Venkatachalam, P.S. 1963. A study of the socio-economic diet and nutritional status of a rural community near Hyderabad. TGM 15: 403-410.

Diet patterns, staple foods, infant feeding, and special diets for illness, pregnancy, and lactation are described. The villages are studied in the State of Himachal Pradesh; Muthangi; and Chitkul (31. 21N. 78. 24E).

4291.   Kahn, Jr., E.J. 1960. The big drink: the story of Coca-Cola. New York: Random House.

4292.   Kajaba, I. 1969. Development of research on the nutrition of the population of Slovakia. RCM 15: 185-197.

4293.   Kajewski, S. Frank. 1946. Plant collecting in the Solomon Islands. A Arb-J 27: 292-304.

Food plants, methods of cultivation, and preparation: pp. 297-303.

4294.   Kakeya, M. 1974. Subsistence ecology of the Tongwe. A Quat 5: 3-99.

Tanzania.

4295.   Kale, D.V. Life and manners of 18th Century Maharashta. Master's thesis. Sociology. University of Bombay. 1928.

4196.   Kale, F.S. 1937. Soya bean, its value it dietetics, cultivation and uses with 300 recipes. Baroda: F. Doktor & Co.

History of soybean; preparation methods from Europe, U.S., China, Japan, and India: pp. 253-336.

4297.   Kaloyev, B.V. Ethnic traditions in agriculture in the northern Caucasus. Paper presented at the 9th International Congress of Anthropological and Ethnological Sciences. 28 August to 8 September, 1973. Chicago, Illinois.

Proposes the view that agriculture among different peoples is marked by certain ethnic features such as implements, technology and expertise. Examples from the north Caucasus region.

4298.   Kamal, Hassan. 1967. [?]. A dictionary of Pharaonic medicine. Cairo: The National Publication House.

[Under the heading 'Food' (pp. 179-187) the following subjects are covered: ovens, flour-making, diet, corn (i.e. wheat, barley), bread, meat, herbs, fruits, preserved fish, cooking, meals, and paleopathology under which latter are described food remains found in the intestines of mummified bodies from dynastic to Coptic periods.

4299.   Kamen, Joseph M. & Peryam, David R. 1960. Monotony characteristics of food. Ftech 14(6):44. (Abstract 180).

A twenty-four day experiment involving seventy-two soldiers was performed in order to determine how the number of different foods in a dietary, and the type of menu, affect food preferences and intake. Results indicated some evidence that preference ratings and intake of a food depend upon the other foods served with it.

4300.   Kamen, Joseph M. & Peryam, David R. 1961. Acceptability of repetitive diets. FTech 15(4):173-177.

4301.   Kandel, Randy F. Dietary assessment in urban and suburban settings. Paper presented at 74th Annual Meeting of the American Anthropological Association. 2 to 6 December, 1975. San Francisco, California.

4302.   Kandel, Randy Frances & Kandel, Joel. Ritual and repersonalization in American medicine: Lamaze childbirth and macrobiotic diets. Paper presented at 70th Annual Meeting of the American Anthropological Association. 19 November, 1971. New York City.

4303.   Kaneda, H. & Johnston, B.F. 1961. Urban food expenditures in tropical Africa. SU-FRI-S 2: 229-275.

4304.   Kang, Younghill. 1931. The grass roof. New York: Scribner's Sons.

Notes on Korean wedding feast foods, including rice cakes. kook-soo, and kimchee.

4305.   Kantawala, S.T. 1954. The second report of health, economic and nutrition survey of 35 families at Khar (Greater Bombay). GRS-B 16: 124-141.

4306.   Kao, Lois Teresa. 1946. Cookery book on local foods. Singapore: Straits Printers.

Malay.

4307.   Kapadia, H.R. 1933. Prohibition of flesh-eating in Jain. RPR 4: 232-239.

4308.   Kapla, Lawrence. 1956. The cultivated beans of the prehistoric Southwest. MBG-A 43: 189-251.

Phaseolus lunatus (lima); Phaseolus latifolius (tepary); Phaseolus vulgaris (garden; kidney; snap; field); Phaseolus coccineus (scarlet runner).

4309.   Kaplan, Lawrence. Beans. In Basket Maker III sites near Durango, Colorado. Edited by R.L. Carlson. 1963. UCS-SA No. 8. P. 47.

4310.   Kaplan, Lawrence. 1963. Archaeoethnobotany of Cordova Cave, New Mexico. EB 17: 350-359.

4311.   Kaplan, Lawrence. Identifications and comments on bean seeds from a cave in the Trigo Mountains, Yuma County, Arizona. In A prehistoric twined-woven bag from the Trigo Mountains, Arizona. Edited by Wilma A. Kaemlein. 1963. Kiva 28: 10-12.

4312. Kaplan, Lawrence. Ethnobotanical and nutritional factors in the domestication of American beans. In Man and his foods. Studies in the ethnobotany of nutrition-contemporary, primitive, and prehistoric non-European diets. Edited by Claude Earle Smith, Jr. 1973. Pp. 75-85. Birmingham: University of Alabama Press.

4313. Kaplan, Lawrence. The ethnobotany of food grain legumes. Paper presented at 9th International Congress of Anthropological and Ethnological Sciences. 28 August to 8 September 1973. Chicago, Illinois.

This paper assembles evidence to study the mutually adaptive human-plant relationships that resulted in as many as seven independent regional domestications of grain legumes in both Old and New Worlds. Historic and ethnographic data on legume preparation and use are examined to determine the status of these plants in certain indigenous diets significant in understanding the basis for human selection of food legumes.

4314. Kaplan, Lawrence & MacNeish, Richard S. 1960. Prehistoric bean remains from caves in the Ocampo region of Tamaulipas, Mexico. HU-BL 19: 33-56.

4315. Kappler, Ernst. Nahrungs-und Genussmittel in Vorderasien. [Food stuffs and stimulants in the Near East.] Ph.D. dissertation. Geography. Universitat Heidelberg. 1924.

4316. Kapungan, Rosalia O. Determination of the food value of some of the Philippine bananas. Master's thesis. Pharmacy. Manila: University of Santo Tomas. 1936.

4317. Kare, M.R. & Halpern, B.P., eds. 1961. The physiological and behavioral aspects of taste. Chicago: University of Chicago Press.

4318. Kargbo-Reffell, A. 1968. Nutrition in Sierra Leone. RNFS 10: 17-19.

4319. Kariel, Herbert G. 1966. A proposed classification of diet. AAG-A 56: 68-79.

This article offers a model for ordering world food consumption and dietary patterns, taking into account both the adequacy and nutritional variety of staple dietary items. Twenty classes of foods are delineated, based on the following criteria: 1) major sources of calories derived from protein (e.g. meat, legumes), and 2) other major sources of calories (e.g. food grains, fats). The major foods and the locations of each class are described, and their spatial distribution indicated on a world map.

4320. Kark, Robert M.; Johnson, Robert E.; & Lewis, J.S. 1945. Defects of pemmican as an emergency ration for infantry troops. WM 7: 345-352.

4321. Kark, Sidney L. & Le Riche, H. 1944. The nutrition and health of South African Bantu school children. (Somatometrical and clinical study.) Field work and report of findings. Manpower 3: 2-141. Bilingual article (English/Afrikans).

Data gathered during the years 1938 and 1939. Areas surveys are Transvaal (Pretoria, Bochem, and Letaba); Natal (Pietermaritzburg, Nqutu); and Orange Free State (Bloemfontein, Witzieshoek).

4322. Karstrom, L. 1976. Les travaux effectuees depuis le 19e siecle sur les proprietes et avantages du vegetarisme. [Work accomplished since the 19th Century on the nature and advantages of vegetarianism.] Vie 87: 16-19.

4323. Kastenbaum, Robert. 1965. Wine and fellowship in aging: an exploratory action program. JHRel 13: 266-271.

4324. Kastenbaum, Robert & Slater, Philip E. Effects of wine on the interpersonal behavior of geriatric patients: an exploratory study. In New thoughts on old age. Edited by Robert Kastenbaum, Ruth Aisenberg, et al 1965. New York: Springer Co.

4325. Katona, Imre. 1963. Szeszfogyasztas - kocsmazas - mulatozasok kubikmunkan. [Alcohol consumption -pubs - carousing among navvies.] Ne Koz 8: 378-411.

4326. Katona-Apte, Judit. A cross-cultural study of attitudes and behavior toward food consumption. Paper presented at 68th Annual Meeting of the American Anthropological Association. 20 to 23 November, 1969. New Orleans, Lousiana. Hypothesizes that the extent to which a non-native accepts new food habits is highly correlated with the extent of internalization of a new normative system. This study concentrates on individuals and families from South Asia residing in the United States and investigates their beliefs and behavior patterns regarding their own as well as American food habits.

4327. Katona-Apte, Judit. Dietary aspects of acculturation. Paper presented at 9th International Congress of Anthropological and Ethnological Sciences. 18 August to 8 September, 1973. Chicago, Illinois.

A study of Maharashtra migrants to South India.

4328. Katona-Apte, Judit. A look at nutritional adaptation. Paper presented at 73rd Annual Meeting of the American Anthropological Association. 19 to 24 November, 1974. Mexico City.

4329. Katona-Apte, Judit. Dietary aspects of acculturation: meals, feasts, and fasts in a minority community in South Asia. In Gastronomy. The anthropology of food and food habits. Edited by

Margaret Louise Arnott. 1975. Pp. 315-326. Paris, The Hague: Mouton Publishers. World Anthropology.

This paper studies the changes in food habits of Marathi speakers in the South Indian State of Tamilnadu. Changes which have occurred are examined against the perspective of the practices of meal patterns, fasting and feasts.

4330. Katz, D. 1933. Die Gesetz der Nahrungsaufnahme in ihrer grundsatzlichen Bedeutung fur die Bedurfnis psychologie. [The laws of food intake in their fundamental significance for the psychology of need.] I Psych 10: 28-29.

4331. Katz, S.H. The anthropological and nutritional significance of traditional maize processing techniques in the New World. Paper presented at the 9th International Congress of Anthropological and Ethnological Sciences. 28 August to 8 September, 1973. Chicago, Illinois.

Provides evidence showing that all Western Hemisphere societies with a major dietary dependence on maize practiced dilute-alkali processing to soften the grain. This practice also effectively released protein-bound lysine and niacin. Two processes universally practiced were cooking or soaking maize in a solution consisting of either water and pulverized limestone or water and wood-ash.

4332. Katz, Sol; Schall, J.; Sundick, P.; & Coleman, J. Evolutionary significance of fava bean consumption in the Circum-Mediterranean area. Paper presented at 77th Annual Meeting of the American Anthropological Association. 14 to 18 November, 1978. Los Angeles, California.

4333. Kaufman, Mildred. 1957. Adapting therapeutic diets to Jewish food customs. AJCN 5: 678-681.

4334. Kaufman, Mildred; Lewis, Eugene; Hardy, Albert V.; & Proulx, Joanne. 1973. Families of the fields. Their food and their health. Report of the Florida migrant nutrition project. Monograph series No. 13. Jacksonville: State of Florida. Division of Health. Department of Health and Rehabilitation Services.

4335. Kaunitz, Hans. 1956. Causes and consequences of salt consumption. Nature 178: 1141-1144.

Reviews the medical literature which indicates that sodium chloride is a metabolic stimulant, and unnecessary as an additive to food. The historical and ethnographic literatures are cited to provide observations as to the role of salt in various human cultures.

4336. Kaunitz, Hans. 1968. Magische und Wissenschaftliche Elemente in der Ernahrung. [Magical and scientific elements in nutrition.] WKW 80: 260-263.

4337. Kaunitz, Hans & Johnson, Ruth Ellen. 1962. Manipulations of food intake by man. EMS 20: 50-54.

Based on data derived from the Human Relations Area Files, this paper reviews the food habits of twenty-six Oceanic, and sixteen African societies. Among patterns discovered were: the agricultural character of most groups; derivation of 50% -80% of calories from carbohydrate sources e.g. rice, yams, sweet potatoes, taro, tapioca [i.e. cassava], millet, maize, and breadfruit; desire for condiments, stimulating beverages, and sweets; and a wide range of food interdictions. Perhaps most notable is the fact that this article is written by medical personnel, and was published in the medical literature.

4338. Kaunitz Hans & Johnson, Ruth Ellen. 1979. Chapter Eight. Craving for salt. In Biological effects of salt. ZErn-S No.22.

This chapter contains a number of references to the use of salt in human cultures.

4339. Kawagoe, S. 1925. The market fungi of Japan. BMS-T 10: 201-206.

4340. Kawamura, Wataru. 1958. Miso enkakushi. [Historical chronicles of miso.] Tokyo: Zenkoku Miso Rengokai.

4341. Kawamura, Wataru. 1973. Misoshiru fudoki. [Miso soup in the provinces.] Tokyo: Mainichi Shimbun.

Recipes, and information on history of miso, a fermented soybean paste, in the culture of the Japanese provinces.

4342. Kawamura, Wataru & Tatsumi, Hamako. 1972. Miso no hon. [Book of miso.] Tokyo: Shibata Shoten.

Part 1 contains a detailed history of miso, a fermented soy bean paste, in China and Japan.

4343. Kay, Allison. 1949. Some edible mollusks of Kauai, Hawaiian Islands. Nautilus 62: 119-121.

4344. Kay, G. 1964. Chief Kalaba's village. RL-P No. 55.

Includes notes on food preparation in this Zambian village.

4345. Kay, N.B. 1970. Meat production from wild herbivores. PNS 29: 271-278.

4346. Kay, Robert. 1962. More Shetland dishes. New Shet 60: 33.

4347. Kaye, Shirley, ed. 1969. Yorkshire cooking. Halifax, Yorkshire: Halifax Courrier.

4348. Kayser, D. 1971. A Navajo Julia Child. El Pal 77: 37-40.

4349.   Kearney, Michael. Alcoholism and religious conversion in Oaxaca, Mexico. Paper presented at 67th Annual Meeting of the American Anthropological Association. 21 to 24 November, 1968. Seattle, Washington.

4350.   Keegan, Marcia. 1977. Pueblo and Navajo cookery. Dobbs Ferry, New York: Morgan & Morgan. Earth Books.

This book contains recipes collected from contemporary Native Americans in Arizona and New Mexico. It includes color photographs, and traditional food lore.

4351.   Kefford, J.F. 1956. Food storage in Antarctica. FPQ 16: 47-49.

Reviews the results of tests of various techniques of food preservation at the Australian National Antarctic Reserach Expedition Station at Mawson.

4352.   Kehoe, Thomas F. New interpretations of prehistoric Plains economy. Paper presented at 75th Annual Meeting of the American Anthropological Association. 17 to 21 November, 1976. Washington, D.C.

Early Twentieth Century anthropologists viewed the prehistoric Plains as uninhabited, impoverished, or a barren, marginal land of low population surrounded by high population pressure areas. Interviews with native informants, a search of historical records, and excavations of bison-drive sites in northern Plains during the second half of the century [sic] have revealed the contrary. From Paleo-Indian to the historic bison hunters, there was development of communal efforts; bison drives resulting in larger kills and meat supplies and consequent industrialization; increased meat processing; eventual commercialization and near-domestication.

4353.   Keimer, L. 1939. Boutargue dans l'Egypte ancienne. [Caviar in ancient Egypt.] IE-B 21: 215-243.

4354.   Keister, Mary Elizabeth. The relationship of mid-morning feeding to certain types of social-emotional behavior in nursery school children. Ph.D. disseration. University of Chicago. 1949.

4355.   Keith, Louis; Evenhouse Henry; & Webster, Augusta. 1968. Amylophagia during pregnancy. OG 30: 415-418.

Incidence of amylophagia (starch eating) among nine hundred eighty-seven obstetric patients at Cook County Hospital, Chicago, Illinois, was thirty-four and six-tenths percent. There was a noticeable correlation between the quantity of starch ingested, and the degree of anemia diagnosed. An apparent relationship between dirt eating in childhood and amylophagia during pregnancy.

4356.   Keleny, G.P. 1962. Origin and introduction of the basic food crops of the New Guinea people. PNGAJ 15: 7-13.

4357.   Kelleny, E. 1958. Vegetarianism in Hungary. V New 37: 101-105.

4358.   Keller, Wolfgang. 1965. Studie zur Ernahrung be zwei Stammen in Nord-Tanganyika. [Study of nutrition among two tribes in North Tanganyika.] Forschungsbericht des Landes Nordrhein-Westfalen No. 1445. Koln u. Opladen: Westdt. Verlag.

4359.   Kellerman, W.A. 1895. The primitive corn. Meehan's 5:44.

4360.   Kellogg, John Henry. 1877-1878. The household manual. Hygiene, food and diet. Battle Creek, Michigan: Office of the Health former.

4361.   Kellogg, Vernon Lyman. 1917. Feeding Belgium via canals. World's Work 35: 92-98. November.

Food relief to Belgium during World War I.

4362.   Kellogg, Vernon Lyman. 1917. How Belgium was fed. World's Work 34: 528-541.

Food relief in Belgium during World War I.

4363.   Kellogg, Vernon Lyman. 1918. Fighting starvation in Belgium. Garden City, New York: Doubleday, Page & Co.

Food relief in Belgium during WW1.

4364.   Kellogg, Vernon Lyman. 1918. How north France has been fed. World's Work 35: 299-305.

Food relief in France during World War I.

4365.   Kelly, Isabel T. 1958. Cambios en los patrones relacionados con la alimentacion. [Changes in dietary patterns.] IIN-B 32: 205-208.

Examples of situations in which directed nutritional change was attempted.

4366.   Kelly, Isabel T. La antropologia, la cultura y la salud publica. [Anthropology, culture, and public health.] Mimeographed. Institute of Interamerican Affairs. La Paz: United States Mission to Bolivia. 1959. Reprint. Lima: Ministry of Public Health and Social Welfare, 1960.

4367.   Kelly, Isabel T. 1964. Southern Paiute ethnography. UU-AP No. 69.

Food: Kaibab: pp. 39-55; Kaiparowits: pp. 152-158; San Juan: pp. 170-172; Panguitch: pp. 179-183.

4368.   Kelly, Isabel T. & Anderson, Edgar. 1943. Sweet corn in Jalisco. MBG-A 30: 405-412.

Discusses differences between sweet and dent types of maize. Data suggest Jalisco sweet maize is not a recent introduction. It is used in pinole, a thick, maize flour cereal preparation eaten with milk; and in ponte duro, a kind of candy brittle to which squash seeds, roasted maize kernels, and peanuts are added.

4369.   Kelly, Isabel T. & Palerm, Angel.   1952. The Tajin Totonac.   Part 1.   History, subsistence, shelter and technology. SI-ISA-P No. 13.

Food: pp. 150-175; kitchen equipment: p. 195.

4370.   Kelly, Phyllis B. What shall I feed my child? Infant feeding patterns in a Mexican town.   Paper presented at 73rd Annual Meeting of the American Anthropological Association.   19 to 24 November, 1974. Mexico City.

4371.   Kelly, Phyllis B. Nutritional assessment in horticultural societies.   Paper presented at 74th Annual Meeting of the American Anthropological Association. 2 to 6 December, 1974. San Francisco, California.

4372.   Kelly, Phyllis & Dewalt, Kathy. Nutritional correlates of socioeconomic differentiation in a community in highland Mexico. Paper presented at 72nd   Annual   Meeting   of   the   American Anthropological Association.   1 December, 1973. New Orleans, Lousiana.

4373. Kelly, William H.   1977.   Chapter Three. Subsistence. In Cocopa ethnography. UA-AP 29.

Baja, California. Describes: yearly round of activities: agriculture, water-control systems; land use; crops; clearing land, planting, harvesting; gathering; mesquite (Prosopis juliflora, Schwarts, DC.); screwbean (Prosopis odorata, Torr. & Frem.) wild rice (Uniola palmeri Vasey); quelite (pigweed) (Amaranthus palmeri, s.   wats.; Amaranthus caudatus, L.); wild grass seeds planted and harvested (Dactyloctenium aegypticum (L.) Richt.); and Panicum sp. (probably Panicum hirticaule, Presl, or Panicum stramineum, Hilchc.); wild onion (Sagittaria lattifolia, wild.); tule (Typha lattifolia, L. Typha angustifolia, L.); other Delta food plants; desert and mountain food plants; storage; fishing and hunting.

4374. Kelso, Jack. 1962. Dietary differences as a possible selective mechanism in ABO blood frequencies. South Lor 28: 48-56.

4375. Kelso, Jack & Armelagos, George.   1963. Nutritional factors as selective agencies in the determination of ABO blood group frequencies. South Lore 29: 44-48.

4376. Kemp, William B. 1971. The flow of energy in a hunting society. SA 225: 105-115.

An input-output analysis of subsistence activities in two Eskimo village households on Baffin Island. The influence of modern technology on traditional hunting practices is described, and the place of imported, non-traditionl foods in the diet examined. Per

tinent information on food habits is included. Essential quantitative input-output data is plainly diagrammed.

4377.   Kempton, J.H. 1936. Maize as a measure of Indian skill. In Symposium on prehistoric agriculture. UNM-B No. 296. AS 1[5]:19-28.

Origins and food uses of maize in North America; history and distribution of maize.

4378.   Kempton, J.H. 1938. Maize - our heritage from the Indian. SI-AR for the year 1937. Pp. 385-408.

4379.   Kempton, Willett M. Category grading in the classification of household items. Paper presented at 75th Annual Meeting of the American Anthropological Association.   17 to 21 November, 1976. Washington, D.C.

Classification of the domain of handmade ceramic tableware is elicited from Spanish-speaking campesinos in central Mexico, and English-speaking students in Texas.   The interview technique is based on the assumption that there is a grading of category membership: that is, that membership in a category is not simply all or none, but may be more or less. The resulting "fine-grained" data allow a close examination of the taxonomic relations of inclusion and contrast, and of informant variation in classificatory systems.

4380.   Kennard, William C. & Freyre, Reuben H. 1957. The edibility of shoots of some bamboos growing in Puerto Rico. EB 11: 235-243.

Bambusa polymorpha, Munro; and Dendrocalumua membranaceous, Munro.

4381.   Kennard, William C. & Winter, H.F. 1960. Some fruits and nuts for the tropics. USDA-MP No. 801.

4382.   Kennedy, Diana. 1972. Cuisines of Mexico. New York; Evanston; San Francisco; London: Harper & Row.
This book is an extensive survey of regional Mexican cookery, with a large number of recipes, and sociological data throughout, including quotations from old accounts of travelers concerning food.

4383.   Kennedy, J.G. 1963. Tesguino complex: the role of beer in Tarahumara culture. AA 65: 620-640.

Fermented maize beer.

4384.   Kennedy, John G. 1970. Circumcision and excision in Egyptian Nubia. Man 5 [new series]: 175-191.

Food associated with ritual, surgery: pp. 177, 178, 179, 180

4385.   Kennedy, K.A.R. 1960. The dentition of Indian crania of the Early and Late archaeological horizons in central California. UCal-AS-R No. 50. Pp. 41-50.

Includes comments on influence of diet on condition of teeth.

4386.   Kennedy, P. Beveridge. 1900. Saltbushes. USDA-FB No. 108.

Atriplex, sp. Cultural and nutritional data. Some species have been used as food, e.g. Atriplex canescens, A. Nuttallii.

4387.   Kennett, R.H. 1933. Lecture 2. Food. In Ancient Hebrew social life and custom as indicated in law, narrative, and metaphor. The Schweich lectures of the British Academy, 1931. London: Oxford Unversity Press.

4388.   Kenninger, Josef. 1944. Kannibalismus in Arabien. [Cannibalism in Arabia.] Anthropos 35-36: 631-646.

4389.   Kensinger, Kenneth M. Manioc and the Cashinahus (Peru). Paper presented at 70th Annual Meeting of the American Anthropological Association. 18 November, 1971. New York City.

Sweet manioc is one of three major vegetable staples in Cashinahua diet, and its production represents a significant investment of both time and energy. This paper will present data on the technology and ideology of manioc cultivation and usage in relation to the semantic/cultural domains of which it is a part.

4390.   Kent, Roland G. 1929. The cookery inscriptions from Praeneste. Language 5: 19-22.
Intepretation of illustrated bronze cista depicting the processing of meat. Decipherment of inscription is included.

4391.   Kenyon, A.S. 1912. Camping places of the aborigines of South East Australia. VHM November. Pp. 99-10.

4392.   Keown, Aribe Joseph Wayne. The family grocery: an analysis of entrepreneurship in a Mexican-American community. Master's thesis. Anthropology. California State University at Long Beach. 1973.

Small family groceries represent a form of entrepreneurial activity that has been associated with almost every Mexican-American community in the Southwestern United States. Frederik Barth has suggested that study of entrepreneurial activity would be of interest to the anthropologist because of its implications in the areas of community leadership, culture brokerage, and culture stability and change. It is along the lines of the latter suggestion that this study is oriented. Community focus is in southern California.

4393.   Kephart, Horace. 192 Our southern highlanders. New York: Macmillan

Bear grease as bread shortening: p. 98; liquor manufacture: pp. 126-166; foods: pp. 250-252.

4394.   Kermorgant, M. 1907. Alimentation de l'Indo-Chine. [Diet in Indo-China.] AHPML 4: 411-431.

Dietay habits of native and foreign residents, Notes on cultivated plants and domestic animals.

4395.   Kern, C.A. 1903. Sources of sugar. DHG 19: 522-524.

4396.   Kerr, M.J. Food habits and social organization at Rupert's House; preliminary report to the National Committee for Community Health. Typescript. Toronto. 1948.

4397.   Kerr, Norman Shanks. 1882. Unfermented wine a fact: a review of the latest attempt to show that the existence of unfermented wine among the ancients was impossible. 5th edition. London: National Temperance Depot.

4398.   Kerr, Norman Shanks. 1885. Wines of the Bible. London: National Temperance Depot.

4399.   Kerr, Norman Shanks. 1882. Wines: scriptural and ecclesiastical. Expanded edition. New York: National Temperance Society.

4400.   Kervegant, D. 1943. Valeur nutritive des aliments en usage a la Martinique. [Nutritive value of foods in use on Martinique.] Fort-de-France: Imprimerie Officielle.

4401.   Keszi-Kovacs, L. Die traditionelle Milchwirtschaft bei den Ungarn. [Traditional dairy economy in Hungary.] In Viehwirtschaft und Hirtenkultur. Ethnographische Studien. Edited by E. Foldes. 1969. Pp. 640-695. Budapest: Akademiai Kiado.

4402.   Kettner, Auguste. 1877. Kettner's book of the table. A manual of cookery. Translated by Enaeas S. Dallas. London: Dulan & Co.

Includes historical data on cookery.

4403.   Keyland, Nils. 1919. Svensk allmogekost: bidrag till den svenska folkhushallningens historia. Swedish peasant diet: a contribution to the history of Swedish home economics.] Stockhold: Svenska Teknologforeningens forlag.

4404.   Keys, Ancel; Aravanis, Chris & Sdrin, Helena. 1966. The diets of middle-aged men in rural areas of Greece. Voeding 27: 575-586.

Diets of men aged 40-59, on the islands of Crete, and Corfu.

4405.   Keyter, Carl. 1962. Feeding customs and food habits of urban Africans. Fact Paper 11. Johannesburg: South African Institute of Race Relations.

Describes food etiquette; hygiene; color schemes for canteens; food consumption; attitudes toward food. Includes observations on seating arrangements at meals. Reference group is Bantu.

4406. Khaleque, K.A.; Muazzam, M.G.; & Chowdhury. 1961. Stress in Ramadan fasting. JTMH 64: 277-279.

4407. Khaleque, K.A.; Muazzam, M.G.; & Ispahani, P. 1960. Further observations on the effects of fasting in Ramadhan. JTMH 63: 241-243.

4408. Khan, Bazlur Rahman. 1969. Royal dishes and drinks under Akbar and Jahangir. PakHs-J 17: 145-160.

4409. Khare, Ravindra. Inequalities: some structural and culinary interrelationships in northern India. Paper presented at 70th Annual Meeting of the American Anthropological Association. 21 November, 1971. New York City.

Draws on field data on normal, special and normative food transactions in northern India to analyze the inequalities of the Hindu concepts of the raw, the uncooked and the cooked (including the kacca and pakka) in relation to those of Hindu marriage, kinship and rituals. The study presents internally consistent structures and meanings of culinary inequalities. Included are systematic abstraction, paradigmatic arrangement of the presented data, and a preliminary application of the mathematics of inequality providing axioms and propositions for ranked relationships.

4410. Khare, R.S. Ideology and reality: cultural genesis of "food problems" in India. Paper presented at 74th Annual Meeting of the American Anthropological Association. 2 to 6 December, 1975. San Francisco, California.

4411. Khayat, Marie Karam, & Keatinge, Margaret Clarke. 1961. Food from the Arab world. Beirut: Khayat's Cookbook.

4412. Khouhestanik, A.H.; Ghavifekr, H.; Rahmanian, M.; Mayurian, H.; & Sarkissian, N. 1969. Composition and preparation of Iranian breads. JADA 55: 262-266.

4413. Kidd, Dudley. 1904. The essential Kafir. London: Adam & Charles Black South Africa.

Notes on a Bantu porridge of maize ("mealie pap"), and maize beer: pp. 326-327. Etiquette: p. 330.

4414. Kight, Mary Ann; Reid, B.L.; Forcier, Janice I.; Donisi, Carl M.; & Cooper, Marina. 1969. Nutritional influences of Mexican-American food in Arizona. JADA 55: 557-561.

4415. Kiihara, Hitoshi, ed. 1955. Land and crops of Nepal Himalayas; scientific results of the Japanese expeditions to Nepal Himalaya, 1952-1953. Ky-oto: Kyoto University Fauna and Floral Research Society.

4416. Kikuchi, William K. Hawaiian aquacultural system. Ph.D. dissertation. Anthropology. University of Hawaii. 1973.

The principal functions of aquaculture, or the cultivation of seaweeds, molluscs, fish, crustaceans, and marine animals in salt, brackish, and fresh water environments, is to produce a food supply in quantity through controlled sea farming. In prehistoric Hawaii, true aquaculture was typified by fishponds, complemented by the use of fishtraps, weirs, dams, and artificial fish shelters. Native taxonomy generally considered all of these to be sources for seafood and did not distinguish between the cultivation and the trapping of fish. By modern standards, the indigenous aquacultural system produced low yields, estimated at three hundred fifty pounds of fish per annum. The system was not intended to be an intensive source of food for the populace, but rather conspicuous ownership of food sources increasingly became a symbol of high status within Hawaiian society. This study traces the probable origin, development, and decline of functional acquaculture in the Hawaiian Islands.

4417. Kilbride, Philip. An ethnographic description of household structure and domestic activities in a Mexican peasant community. Master's thesis. Anthropology. Pennsylvania State Unversity. 1968.

4418. Kilburn, John W. Catfish farming in the mid-South; its distribution and potential growth. Ph.D. dissertation. Geography. Hattiesburg: University of Southern Mississippi. 1972.

4419. Kim, Dai You & Defngin, Francis. Taro cultivation in Yap. In Taro cultivation practices and beliefs. Pars 2. The eastern Carolines and Marshall Islands. By Trust Territory of the Pacific Islands. Office of the Staff Anthropologist. 1960. Pp. 48-68.

Preparation of taro; taboos: pp. 63-68.

4420. Kimball, Marie Goebel. 1938. Thomas Jefferson's cook book. Richmond: Garrett & Massie. Reprint. Charlottesville, Virginia: University Press of Virginia. 1976.

Contains reference to Jefferson as a gourmet.

4421. Kimura, Kunihiko; Hagiya, Shukuko; & Kitano, Shinsei. 1959. Effect of war on stature. [In Japanese, with English summary.] JZ 57: 82-89.

4422. Kincaid, Jean, et al. 1968. Infant feeding practices among mothers in eastern Kentucky. Maternity and Infant Care Project. Frankfort: Kentucky State Department of Health Information.

4423. Kinch, Edward. 1882. List of plants used for food or from which foods are obtained in Japan. ASJ-T 11: 1-30.

4424. King, A. A study of the Italian diet in a group of New Haven families. Master's thesis. Yale University. 1935.

4425. King, Ann Culmer. Acceptance and non-acceptance of American culture on the part of married and non-married Indian students at the University of Mississippi. Master's thesis. Anthropology. University of Mississippi. 1969.

4426. King, Aramita. 1969. Extension of Guide to Good Eating: acceptable foods of some racial and ethnic groups in the United States. San Francisco: Dairy Council of California.

4427. King, Arthur. 1907. Influence of an excessive meat diet and fertility. DMJ 1: 1029.

Evidence contra-indicating role of meat intake in predisposing to high fertility.

4428. King, Charles Glen. Nutrition in relation to flavor and world food acceptance. In Flavor chemistry symposium. Proceedings. 1961. Camden, New Jersey. 1961. Pp. 97-107. Camden, New Jersey: Campbell Soup Co.

Includes reference to variation in cultural patterns in relation to food acceptance. Mentions the development of Incaparina, and the role played by anthropologist Richard N. Adams and his wife in recording food preferences in highland Guatemalan villages. (p. 106).

4429. King, Clyde Lyndon. 1913. Municipal markets. AAPSS-A 50: 102-117.

4430. King, Glenn E. A cross-cultural model for the sociospatial organization of hunters-gatherers. Paper presented at 77th Annual Meeting of the American Anthropological Association. 14 to 18 November, 1978. Los Angeles, California.

4431. King, Kendall, W. 1964. Development of all-plant food mixtures using crops indigenous to Haiti: amino acid composition and protein quality. EB 18: 311-322.

4432. King, Kendall W. Nutrition research in Haiti. In Research and resources of Haiti. Papers of the conference. 1969. Pp. 347-370. New York: Research Institute for the Study of Man.

History of nutrition research since 1958.

4433. King, Kendall W.; Dominique, G.; Uriodain, W.; Fougere, W.; & Beghin, Ivan D. 1968. Food patterns from dietary surveys in rural Haiti. JADA 52: 114-118.

4434. King, Larry L. 1970. "If a Bayou baby sticks his finger down a crayfish hole before he's six months old, he's a cajun." Holiday 47: 70-73.

Food of Louisiana Acadian French: pp. 72,73.

4435. King, William (LL.D. Student of Christ Church [College] Oxford). 1708. The art of cookery; in imitation of Horace's Art of Poetry, with some letters to Dr. Lister and others, occasion'd principally by the title of a book published by the Doctor, being the works of Apicius Coelius... To which is added Horace's Art of Poetry in Latin. London: B. Lintott.

4436. Kinsley, Herbert M. 1894. One hundred recipes for the chafing dish. New York: Gorham Manufacturing Co.

Includes illustrations of chafing dishes and accessories.

4437. Kinzey, Warren. The canine tooth in human evolution. Paper presented at 69th Annual Meeting of the American Anthropological Association. 19 to 22 November, 1970. San Diego, California.

4438. Kirk, N. 1958. Nutrition in native peoples; some observations on the food habits of Nauruans. Health 8: 79-82.

4439. Kirkpatrick, E.L. & Sanders, J.J. The cost of living among colored farm families of selected localities of Kentucky. Tennessee, and Texas. A preliminary report. Mimeographed. Bureau of Agricultural Economics. Washington, D.C. United States Department of Agriculture. January. 1926. Cited in United States Department of Agriculture. Bureau of Agricultural Economics. Agricultural Economics Bibliography. No 10. January, 1926. P. 25.

4440. Kirkup, James. 1962. These horned islands. A journal of Japan. New York: Macmillan.

Contains observations on foods, food uses, and restaurants throughout: pp. 35, 42, 50-51, 56-58, 71-74, 79-80, 82, 86, 107, 137-138, 153, 177, 196, 245-246, 324, 348.

4441. Kirn, Leon. 1884. L'alimentation du soldat. [The soldier's diet.] Paris: L. Baudoin.

Also in JSciM mai-octobre. (1884).

4442. Kirwan, Andrew Valentine. 1864. Host and guest. A book about dinners, dinner giving, wines and desserts. London: Bell & Daldy.

4443. Kisban, Eszter. 1962. Verbreitung des Fruchtebrotes in Ungarn. [Distribution of fruit-bread in Hungary.] AE No. 11. Pp. 119-142.

4444. Kisban, Eszter. 1963. A nepi taplalkozas alakulasanak problemai. [The problem of change in popular diet.] MHag 5: 189-203.

4445. Kisban, Eszter. Zum Problem der Systeme der Milchverarbeitung in Sudosteuropa. [The problem of the diary production systems in southeast Europe.] In Congres International des Etudes Balkaniques et Sud-est Europeenes. Premiere. Sofia. Resumes des communications. 1966. Pp. 26-37.

4446. Kisban, Eszter. 1967. A jogurt helye es szerepe a delkelet-europai tejfeldolgozasi rendszerekben. [Place and role of the dairy product yoghurt within the dairy system of southeastern Europe.] Ethnografia 78: 81-94.

4447. Kisban, Eszter. Die Historische Bedeutung des Joghurts in den Milchverarbeitungs-systeman Sudosteuropas [The historical significance of yoghurt in the dairy production systems of southeastern Europe.] In Viehwirschaft und Hirtenkultur. Ethnographische Studien. Edited by L. Foldes. 1969. Pp. 517-530. Budapest: Akademiai Kiado.

4448. Kisban, Eszter. Bericht uber den gegenwartigen Stand der Nahrungs-forschung in Ungarn. [Study of the present state of food habits in Hungary.] Paper presented at the First International Symposium on Ethnological Food Research. 21 to 25 August, 1970. Lund: Folklivsarkivet. University of Lund.

4449. Kitchin, A.H. & Passmore, R. 1949. The Scotsman's food: an historical introduction to modern food administration. Edinburgh: E. & S. Livingstone.

4450. Kiticyna. 1927. Chleb, pitanie Kostroskogo kraya. [Bread and food habits in Kostrom Province.] KNOIM-K Pp. 92-104.

Kostroma is located approximately two hundred fifty kilometers northeast of Moscow.

4451. Kitto, John. 1848. The olive, vine, and palm: embracing an illustration of the numerous allusions in Scripture to these trees and their produce. Edinburgh.

4452. Kittrell, Flemmie P. A study of Negro infant feeding practices in a selected community of Greensboro, North Carolina. Ph.D. dissertation. Cornell University. 1935.

4453. Klaarbergen, F.T. van & Zoethout, Kosten H. 1965. Summary of results of studies of nutrition in monasteries from 1953-1961. [In Dutch.] Voeding 26: 104-112.

4454. Klatskin, G.; Slater, W.T.; & Humm, F.D. 1947. Gynaecomastia due to malnutrition. 1. clinical studies. ADMedS 213: 19-29.

Investigation of thirty-six cases of gynaecomastia among U.S. prisoners released from Japanese prisoner-of-war camps in Philippines, after World War II.

4455. Klausner, Samuel Z. 1979. Social order and energy consumption in matrifocal households. HEcol 7: 21-39.

This article includes brief data relating to food, food consumption, and cooking in housholds supported by either welfare or by the mother's earnings. Data are derived from published statistics, and interviews for households in Camden, New Jersey; data were gathered in 1969, 1970, and 1973.

4456. Kalutzke, Paul. 1922. Nutzpflanzen und Nutztiere Chinas. Weltwirtschaftliches Abhandlung. [Useful plants and animals of China. Essay on world commerce.] Hanover: C.E. Poeschel.

4457. Klees. Die erforschung der Volksnahrung in Luxemburg. [Ethnological food research in Luxemburg.] Paper presented at the First International Symposim on Ethnological Food Research. 21 to 25 August, 1970. Lund: Folklivsarkivet. Lund University.

4458. Klein, David R. 1966. Waterfowl in the economy of the Eskimos on the Yukon-Kuskokwim Delta, Alaska. Arctic 19: 319-336.

4459. Klein, Philip. 1920. Prison methods in New York State. CU-SHEPL 90 (1).

Prison foods: pp. 155-170.

4460. Klein, Robert E. & Yarbrough, Charles. 1972. Some considerations in the interpretation of psychological data as they related to the effects of malnutrition. ALN 22: 40-48.

Cultural congruence of cognitive tests used in assessing effects of malnutrition upon learning and behavior potential.

4461. Klenger, J.L.; Frieden, T.Y.; & Sullivan, R.A. 1970. Mealtime manual for the aged and handicapped. Institute of Rehabilitative Medicine. New York: New York University Medical Center.

4462. Klick, Mary V.; Hollender, H.A.; & Lachance, Paul A. 1967. Foods for astronauts. JADA 51: 238-245.

Reviews menus, and forms of preparation and feeding for foods used in National Aeronautics and Space Administration Gemini, Apollo, and Project Mercury flights.

4463. Klicka, Mary V.; Lachance, Paul A.; & Hollender, Herbert A. 1968. Space feeding. USA-FCI-RDA-AR 20(1): 53-70.

High altitude feeding requirements; development of space foods; bite size foods; edible coatings; rehydratable foods; food production and development; testing; nutritional evaluation of dehydrated foods; menus; nutrient intakes - Gemini flights; nutritional findings and problems of space flight; nutrient requirements for Apollo.

4464. Klier, Karl Manus. 1953. Das Hochzeitsgebacke "Ach, Herr Jegerle." [The wedding pastry called "Ach, Herr Jegerle."] VH 1: 5.

4465. Klier, Karl Magnus. 1963. Speisezettel der bischoflichen Hofkuche zu Linz (um 1860). [Bill of fare of an episcopal court kitchen from Linz (around 1860). HJSL Pp. 199-206.

4466. Kliewe, H. 1969. Wein und Gesundheit. [Wine and health.] Neustadt a.d. Weinstrasse: Meininger.

Contains a section on the history of wine: Pp. 9-16.

4467. Kligler, I.J.; Geiger, A.; Bromberg (Bavly), Sarah.; & Gurevich, D. 1931. An inquiry into the diets of various sections of the urban and rural population of Palestine. PES-B 5(3).

Includes discussion of dietary patterns of rural and urban Muslim and Jewish populations. A glossary of Arabic food names is included.

4468. Kliks, Michael. Palaeodietetics: a review of the role of dietary fiber in preagricultural human diets. In Fiber in human nutrition. Edited by Gene A. Spiller & R.J. Amens. 1976. Springfield, Illinois: Charles C. Thomas, Publisher.

Suggests that a high-residue diet of plant tissues has had a selective effect on the evolution of the human gastrointestinal tract, with functional alterations occurring since the development of agriculture within the past ten to twenty thousand years. Also in Topics in dietary fiber research. Edited by Gene A. Spiller. 1978. Pp. 181-202. New York; London: Plenum Press.

4469. Kling, A. 1976. Comportement alimentaire et contrainte par les prix. [Cost as a constraint on food habits.] ANA 30: 447-452.

4470. Kloos, Helmut. 1978-1979. Food and medicinal plants used by Armenian-Americans in Fresno, California. Ethnomedizin 5: 127-140.

4471. Kloos, P. 1971. A note on vegetable food of the Maroni River Caribs. Sur Lan 19:63-67.

4472. Kloss, Cecil Boden. 1903. In the Andaman and Nicobars. London: John Murray.

Food habits: pp. 246-248.

4473. Klunzinger, C.B. 1878. Upper Egypt: its people and its products. A descriptive account of the manner, customs, superstitions, and occupations of the people of the Nile Valley, the desert, and the Red Sea coast, with sketches of the natural history and geology. New York: Scribner, Armstrong.

Descriptions of native coffee house and beer-shop: pp. 24-27; 28-30; description of a village kitchen: pp. 43-44; a Turkish meal in Egypt, its and after dinner ablution: pp. 54-61; a Coptic meal during a fast: pp. 83-85. Gardening, field and garden plants, ancient and modern: pp. 140-144; diet of the common people: pp. 158; 160; foods of the Easter week celebration: pp. 182-183; foods used in birthday ceremonies: pp. 186; food and cooking utensils of desert Ababdeh (Abadi-Bedya Bedouin): pp. 251-259; preparation and use as food of fish and shell-fish: pp. 307, 309.

4474. Knapp, A.W. 1920. Cocoa and chocolate. Their history from plantation to consumer. London: Chapman and Hall.

4475. Knickerbocker Mills. 1942. A short study of spices, published for its friends on the occasion of its hundredth anniversary. [New York]: Knickerbocker Mills.

4476. Knight, C. Gregory. 1974. Ecology and change. New York: Academic Press.

Agricultural intensification and nutrition: pp. 137-145.

4477. Knight, H.L. 1909. Food habits and customs of Central African natives. JHE 1: 356-362.

4478. Knodel, J. & Walle, E van de. 1967. Breast feeding, fertility and infant mortality: an analysis of some early German data. PStud 21: 109-131.

4479. Knorzer, K.-H. 1971. Prahistorische Mohnsamen in Rheinland. [Prehistoric poppy seeds in Rhineland.] BJ 171: 34-39.

4480. Knott, Eustace Reynolds, compilor. 1915. Knott's popcorn book. Boston: E.R. Knott Machine Company.

4481. Knowlton, F.H. 1919. Description of a supposed new fossil species of maize from Peru. WAS-J 9: 134-136.

A specimen obtained in Cuzco, by Dr. W.F. Parks, of St. Louis, Missouri.

4482. Knox, Kirvin L. Nutrition education and changing food habits. Paper presented at 77th Annual Meeting of the American Anthropological Association. 14 to 18 November, 1978. Los Angeles, California.

4483. Knox, Robert. 1681. An historical relation of the Island Ceylon in the East Indies: together with an account of the detaining in captivity of the author...and of the author's miraculous escape. London: R. Chiswell. Reprint. CHJ 6 (1-4). (1956-1957).

Food: pp. 18-19; 22-23; 138-141.

4484. Knudson, K.E. Resource fluctuation, productivity, and social organization on Micronesian coral islands. Ph.D. dissertation. University of Oregon. 1970.

4485. Knutsson, Karl Eric. 1972. Malnutrition and the community. In Nutrition. A priority in African development. Edited by Bo Vahlquist. 1972. Pp. 46-61. Stockholm: Almqvist & Wiksells. The Dag Hammarskjold Foundation.

Observations by a social anthropologist on the need for analysis of the cultural environment prior to implementation of applied nutrition programs.

4486. Knutsson, Karl Eric & Mellbin, Tore. 1969. Breast-feeding habits and cultural context (A study in three Ethiopian communities.) JTPECH 15: 40-49.

The three communities are Meremite, Garbicho, and Arji Galla. Length of breast feeding for male and female infants is studied.

4487. Knutsson, Karl Eric & Selinus, Ruth. 1970. Fasting in Ethiopia. An anthropological and nutritional study. AJCN 23: 956-969.

Effect of Orthodox Christian fasts upon infants and young children, due to elimination of animal protein.

4488. Kobbe, W.H. 1950. Rice instead of bread. RJ 53: 77.

4489. Kobert, Rudolph. 1897. Ueber Kvass und dessen Bereitung. [On kvass and its manufacture.] Halle: Tauche & Grosse.

4490. Koch, Klaus-Friedrich. 1970. Warfare and anthropology in Jale society. Anthropologica 12: 37-58.

West New Guinea.

4491. Koch, M.P. Das "Erfurter Kartauserregimen": Studien zur diatetischen Literatur des Mittelalters. [The Carthusian regimen of Erfurt: Studies on the dietetic literature of the Middle Ages.] Ph.D. disseration. Rheinische Friedrich-Wilhelms-Universitat Bonn. 1969.

4492. Koch, Theodor. 1899. Die anthropophagie der sudamerikanischen Indianer. [Anthropophagy among South American Indians.] IAE 12: 78-110.

4493. Kodicek, E.H. & Young, F.G. 1969. Captain Cook and scurvy. RSL-NR 24: 43-63.

4494. Koehler, Franz A. 1958. Special rations for the armed forces. Quartermaster Corps Historical Studies. Series 2, No. 6. Historical Branch. Office of the Quartermaster General. Washington, D.C.: Department of the Army.

4495. Koehler, Margaret H. 1973. Recipes from the Portuguese of Provincetown. Riverside, Connecticut: Chatham Press.

4496. Koenig, J. 1889. Chemische Zusammensetzung der menschlichen Nahrungs-und Genussmittel. Nach vorhandenen Analysen mit Angabe der Quellen zusammengestellt. [The chemical composition of human foods and stimulants. Compiled according to existing analyses, and with a listing of sources.] Berlin: Springer.

4497. Kolbohm, Ted E. Growth and development of fish-pond culture: a care study of modern catfish farming, Imperial Valley, California. Master's thesis. Geography. Temp: Arizona State University. 1972.

4498. Kohler, Ludwig. 1931. Gebrateuer Fisch und Honigsheim. [Broiled fish and honey comb.] ZDPV 54: 289-293.

A debated New Testament passage (Luke 24:42), verified by observation on the practice of serving honeycomb with fish in Portugal, where Arabic influence was marked; as well as in modern Palestine.

4499. Kohler, R.L. 1975. Distinction entre la restauration et neo-restauration. L'evolution de l'industrie francaise des restaurants depuis 1970 et ses perspectives d'avenir. Les principaux facteurs qui ont contribue a la croissance rapide de ce domaine. Les possibilite's q' offre ce marche aux fournisseurs candiens. [The difference between food-catering and new food-catering. The evolution of the French restaurant industry since 1970 and its plans for the future. The principal factors which have contributed to the rapid growth of this sector. The possibilities which this market offers to Canadian suppliers.] Com Can 126: 43-45.

4500. Kohlmayer, Johann. 1963. Vom Korn zum Bauernbrot. [From grain to farm bread.] KL No. 9. Pp. 6-8.

4501. Kolata, G.B. 1974. Kung hunter-gatherers: feminism, diet and birth control. Science 185: 932-934.

4502. Kondo, Akitani. 1972. Nihon no chojuson tanmeison. [Long-life villages in Japan.] Tokyo: Sanrodo.

Contains discussion of relationship between longevity and the intake of miso, a fermented soybean paste.

4503. Konig, J. 1904. Chemie der Menschlichen Nahrungs - und Genussmittel. 2. Die Menschlichen Nahrungs-und Genussmittel, ihre Herstellung Zusammensetzung und Beschaffenheit. [Chemistry of human foods and condiments. 2. Human foods and condiments, their preparation, composition, and properties.] Berlin: Julius Springer.

4504. Konig, J. & Bettels, J. 1905. The carbohydrates of marine algae and products made from them. [In German.] ZUNG 10: 457-473.

Comparison of chemical structure of edible bird's nests, and marine algae.

4505. Konlande, J.E., & Robson, John R.K. 1972. The nutritive value of cooked camas as consumed by Flathead Indians. EFN 1: 193-195.

Camasia quamash, a major root food of a Native American group of Montana, U.S.A. has been previously analyzed in the raw form and shown to be without nutritive value. This report shows that modern experimentation with cooked camas reveals useful amounts of carbohydrates. The authors emphasize the danger of recommending substitutions of indigenous foods before analyses are done on both raw and cooked forms in order to determine whether processing effects chemical changes favorable to the nutrient content of the food. A description of traditional camas preparation is included.

4506. Konner, Melvin Joel. Infants of a foraging people. Ph.D. dissertation. Anthropology. Harvard University. 1973.

4507. Koos, Earl Lomon. 1943. Factors influencing our diets. In The nutrition front. Report of the New York State Joint Legislative Committee on Nutrition. Legislative document No. 64. Pp. 30-36. Albany.

A review of the influence of family food patterns, ethnicity, and the psychological meaning food upon food choice.

4508. Koos, Earl Lomon. A study of the use of the friendship pattern in nutrition education. In The problem of changing food habits. Report of the Committee on Food Habits. 1941-1943. National Research Council. 1943. NRC-B No. 108. Pp. 74-81.

Results of an attempt to use ethnically-bounded friendship networks, in New York, during World War II, are described and the ineffectiveness of the technique as a teaching channel are analyzed. One hundred forty-four homemakers, representing Irish, Italian, and Hungarian groups, in the Kipps-Bay Yorkville area of Manhattan participated.

4509. Kooser, J.H. & Blankenhorn, M.A. 1941. Pellagra and the public health. A dietary survey of Kentucky mountain folk in pellagrous and nonpellagrous communities. JAMA 116: 912-915.

4510. Kopczynska - Jaworowska, Bronisawa. 1961. Owcze sery zdobione z karpat. [Ornamented sheep's-milk cheeses from the Carpathian region.] EPol 5: 197-226.

4511. Kopczynska-Jaworska, Bronislawa. Gebruhte Schafkase in den Karpaten. [Ewe's cheese in the Carpathian Mountains.] In Viehwritschaft und Hirtenkultur. Ethnographische Studien. Edited by L. Foldes. 1969. Pp. 531-546. Budapest: Akademiai Kiado.

4512. Korff, Sameul I. 1966. The Jewish dietary code. FTech 20: 76-78.

4513. Kortizer, Richard T. 1968. An analysis of the cause of tooth loss in an ancient Egyptian population. AA 70: 550-553.

Cites toughness, abrasiveness of cereal diet.

4514. Korn, Shulamit R. Decktor. Strategies and resources for household economics in the Tonga Islands. Paper presented at 72nd Annual Meeting of the American Anthropological Association. 1 December, 1973. New Orleans, Lousiana.

4515. Korner, B. 1962. Rauschgetranke und trinksitten in Ostasien. [Intoxicating drinks and drinking customs in East Asia.] GGBB-J Pp. 178-197.

4516. Kose, Mursel. 1965. Tandir. TFA 9: 3714-3719.

Tandir is a type of bread-baking oven of cupola construction. This article focuses on the town of Kars, in northeastern Turkey, located at 40. 35N, 43. 05E.

4517. Kosikowski, Frank V. 1968. College course in international food development. JDS 51: 242-245.

4518. Kostelny, A. 1935. Folk foods of a Slovakian village. JADA 11: 99-104.

4519. Koster, H. 1937. Japanese diet. [In German.] DMW 63: 719-721.

4520. Kostial, I. 1940. O slovenski in srbohrvatski mlekarsk teminologi. [On Slovenian and Serbocroatian folk terminology in the dairy industry.] Etnolog 13: 125-128.

4521. Kotani, Yoshinobu. Environmental factors in the shift to rice cultivation in Japan. Master's thesis. Anthropology. University of Wisconsin. 1968.

4522. Kotchetkova, Z. The influence of environment on diet. In Deuxieme Congres International d'Hygiene Alimentaire et de l'Alimentation Rationelle de l'Homme. 4-8 Octobre, 1910. Bruxelles. Rapports et Communications. 1910. Vol. 1. Section 1. Pp. 261-264.

On the basis of studies made in rural and urban Belgium, the United States, and elsewhere, it is concluded that migrating persons will rapidly adapt their diets to conditions prevailing in their new home.

4523. Kothe, H. 1952. Wie alt sind Kannibalismus und Krieg? [How ancient are cannibalsim and war?] Urania 15: 241-246.

4525. Kother, J. 1964. La memoire du ventre. Histoire de la gourmandise francaise. [Memoirs of a stomach. History of French gourmandise.] Brussels: Pierre de Meyere.

4525. Kotnis, Manorma. Industrial nutrition: some observations on canteens in industry. In First Asian Congress of Nutrition. 22 January - 2 February 1971. Proceedings. Edited by P.G. Tulupe & Kamala S. Jaya Rao. 1972. Pp. 826-827. Hyderabad: Nutrition Society of India.

4526. Kottak, Conrad P. Subsistence and exchange in cultural adaptation in Madagascar. Paper presented at 68th Annual Meeting of the American Anthropological Association. 20 to 23 November, 1969. New Orleans, Louisiana.

The contributory roles of environment and ecology, including subsistence, on the one hand, and interregional contact on the other, including exchange of various items, are examined in relation to the development of covergent, parallel, and divergent socio-cultural forms in Madagascar.

4527. Kottak, Conrad Phillip. McDonald's as myth, symbol and ritual. Paper presented at 75th Annual Meeting of the American Anthropological Association. 17 to 21 November, 1976. Washington, D.C.

Especially over the past three decades, changes in transportation and communication have nurtured a number of ostensibly commercial institutions which, together, make an overwhelming contribution to those shared aspects of U.S. national culture that override region, class and ethnic group. The present paper focuses on one such institution - McDonald's, a successful fast-food franchise business. Similarities between McDonald's and organized religions are examined in its context as an eating place contrasted with competitor food outlets; in the uniformity of physical structure; costume, and behavior of employees; and in the nature of advertising, designed to incorporate a variety of persons, regardless of socially signficant variation among them.

4528. Kotz, Nick. 1969. Let them eat promises. The politics of hunger in America. Englewood Cliffs: Prentice-Hall.

4529. Kouhestani, Akhtar; Ghavifekr, Hossein; Rahmanian, Munire; Mayurian, Heshmat; & Sarkessian, Nazenik. 1969. Composition and preparation of Iranian breads. JADA 55: 262-266.

Compares Iranian breads with American and Arabic breads.

4530. Koundjy, E. 1927. Les menus dans l'histoire. [Menus in history.] Pres Med No. 12. Pp. 187-188.

Especially ancient Hebraic, Egyptian, Greek, and Roman; Middle Ages; diet of Louis XIV.

4531. Kowalska-Lewicka, Anna. Die milchwirtschaft in den Polnischen Karpaten. [Dairy economy in the Polish Carpathians.] In Viehwirtschaft und Hirtenkultur. Ethnographische Studien. Edited by L. Foldes. 1969. Pp. 696-705. Budapest: Akademia Kiado.

4532. Kowalska-Lewicka, Anna. Der hunger und die Magie des Uberflusses der Nahrung in der traditionellen Kultur der polnischen Karpaten. [Famine, and the magic of overabundance of food in the traditional culture of the Polish Carpathians.] Paper presented at First International Symposium on Ethnologic Food Research. 21 to 25 August, 1970. Lund: Folklivsarkivet. Lund University.

4533. Kowalska-Lewicka, Anna. Die polnischen ethnographischen Untersuchungen im 19. und 20. Jahrhundert uber die Volksernahrung. [Polish ethnographic research in the 19th and 20th Centuries on food folkways.] Paper presented at First International Symposium on Ethnologic Food Research. 21 to 25 August, 1970. Lund: Folklivsarkivet, University of Lund.

4534. Kraft Foods Company. 1954. World of cheeses: guide to the world's favorite cheeses. Chicago: Kraft Foods Co., Education Department.

4535. Kralj-Cercek, L. 1956. The influence of food, body build and social origin on the age at menarche. HB 28: 393-406.

4536. Kramarz, Inge. 1972. The Balkan cookbook. New York: Crown Publishers.

4537. Kramer, Amihud & Szczesniak, Alinas, eds. 1973. Texture, measurements of food; psycophysical fundamentals, sensory, mechanical, and chemical procedures, and their interrelationships. Dodrecht; Boston: Reidel Publishing Co.

4538. Kramer, Augustin. 1905. Die Gewinnung und die Zubereitung der Nahrung auf den Ralik-Ratakinseln (Marshall-inseln). [Food production and preparation on the Ralik-Ratak Islands. [Marshall Islands].] Globus 88[9]: 140-146.

4539. Kramer, Augustin. 1926. Palau. Hamburgische Wissenschaftliche Stiftung. Ergebnisse der Sudsee-Expedition 1908-1910. Ethnographie: B. Mikronesien. Volume 3. Part 2. [Palau. Hamburg Scientific Institute. Results of the South sea-Expedition 1908-1910. Ethnography: B. Micronesia.] Hamburg: Friederichsen, De Gruyter.

Food production and consumption: pp. 41-107.

4540. Kramer, Augustin. 1932. Truk. Hamburgische Wissenschaftliche stiftung und Notgemeinschaft der Deutschen Wissenschaft. Ergebnisse der Sudss-Expedition 1908-1910. Ethnographie: B. Mikronesien. Volume 5. Part 2. [Truk. Hamburg Scientific Institute and Emergency Association of the German Institute. Results of the South Sea expedition. 1908-1910. Ethnography: B. Micronesia.] Hamburg: Friederichsen, de Gruyter.

Cookery, plant food, hunting, and animal food, fish: pp. 122-146.

4541. Kramer, Augustin & Collins, S.A. 1897. Uber den Bau der Korallenriffe und die Planktonverteilung an den samoanischen Kusten nebst vergleich bemerk uber den Palolo-Wurm. [On the structure of coral reefs and the plankton distribution along the Samoan coast, together with parallel notes on the palolo worm.] Kiel: Lipsius & Fischer.

4542. Kramer, Milton. et al. 1969. Brief food deprivation: reflection in dreams. Psychopathology 6: 249.

4543. Krannhals, H. 1884. Ueber das kumysahnliche Getrank "Kephir" und uber den "Kephir-pilz. [On a similar drink to kefir and on the kefir bacterium.] DAKM 35: 1837.

4544. Krant, H.; Lehmann, G.; & Bramsel, H. 1939. Statistics of nutritional requirements for individual trades. [In German.] <u>Arbeitsphysiologie</u> 10: 440-458.

4545.   Krause, K. 1915. Wild plants used as food. [In German.] <u>DLG-M</u> 30: 315-319.

4546.   Krause, K.E.H. 1881. Wann ist die Bohne (Phaseolus) in Mecklenburg eingefuhrt? [When was the bean (Phaseolus) brough to Mecklenburg? <u>AVFNM</u> 34: 232-235.

    Mecklenurg is located in the German Democratic Republic at 53. 52N, 11. 27E., close to the Balkan Ocean.

4547. Krause, Marie V. 1966. Chapter Thirteen. Geographic and cultural dietary variations. In <u>Food, nutrition and diet therapy</u>. Philadelphis, London: W.B. Saunders Co.

    Reviews information on changes in food patterns in the United States; provides synopses of regional food patterns in the United States. Also provides brief outlines of food patterns for the following ethnic dietaries: Belgian, British, Bulgarian, Czechoslovakian, Danish, Dutch, French, German, Greek, Hungarian, Italian, Japanese; Jewish dietary restrictions and holiday observances; Puerto Rican; Roman Catholic dietary restrictions and holiday observances; Roumanian, Syrian, and Yugoslavian.

4548.   Kraybill, Nancy. Changing dietary patterns and levels of lactase activity in Americans of Asian descent. Paper presented at 76th Annual Meeting of the American Anthropological Association. 29 November to 3 December, 1977. Houston, Texas.

    Thirty-one Americans of Asian decent were studied in Chicago, Illinois, during Spring, 1975, and during Spring and Summer, 1976. Levels of lactase activity were established using the lactose tolerance test. Eating habits were determined through the use of diet histories, three-day recalls, and nutritional interviews. Principal components analysis and multiple regression were used to examine the relationship of dietary lactose to levels of lactase.

4549.   Krebs, Roland. 1953. <u>Making friends is our business: 100 years of Anheuser-Busch</u>. St. Louis, Missouri [?]: Anheuser-Busch.

    Anheuser-Busch is the United States' largest beer brewery.

4550.   Kretzinger, Hilda. 1968. <u>The picture of Krio life, Freetown 1900-1920</u>. <u>AEL</u> No. 11.

    In the chapter "Traditional dishes," the author describes dining etiquette and customs, records recipes and provides data on cultural history of food in the village of Waterloo, Sierra Leone.

4551.   Kridberg, Marjorie. 1975. <u>Food on the frontier: Minnesota cooking from 1850 to 1900</u>. St. Paul: Minnesota Historical Society Press.

4552.   Kriegbaum, Lawrence L. <u>The origin of primitive American agriculture and its relations to the early agriculture of Arizona</u>. Master's thesis. University of Arizona. 1920.

4553.   Krieger, Herbert William. Aboriginal land utilization and food economy in the Antilles. In <u>Eighth American Scientific Congress. 10 to 18 May, 1940. Washington, D.C. Proceedings. Volume Two. Anthropologic Sciences</u>. 1942. Pp. 141-142. Washington, D.C. Department of State.

    Outline of pre-Columbian Arawak and non-Arawak food resources.

4554.   Krieger, Herbert W. 1942. <u>Peoples of the Philippines</u>. <u>SI-WBS</u> No. 4.

    Plate 6, photograph No. 2. illustrates the method of cooking rice in a green bamboo stem, in Rizal Province, Luzon.

4555.   Krishnaswamy, N. 1951. Origin and distribution of cultivated plants of South Asia: millets. <u>IJGPB</u> 11: 67-74.

4556.   Krochmal, Arnold. 1955. Olive-growing in Greece. <u>EB</u> 9: 228-232.

4557.   Krochmal, Arnold. 1967. Cassava in the New World. <u>WC</u> 19: 74-75.

4558.   Kroeber, Alfred Louis. The food problem in California. In <u>The California Indians</u>. Edited by Robert F. Heizer & Mary Anne Whipple. 1951. Pp. 233-236. Berkeley: University of California Press.

    Review of food resources available to California Native American cultures.

4559.   Kroeber, Alfred Louis & Barrett, S.A. 1960. <u>Fishing in the northwestern California</u>. <u>UCal-AR</u> 21(1).

4560.   Krom Prachasongkhro. 1962. <u>Report on the socio-economic surve of the hill tribes in northern Thailand</u>. Department of Public Welfare. Bangkok: Ministry of the Interior.

4561.   Krondl, Marion Magdalena & Boxen, Gloria G. Nutrition behavior, food resources, and energy. In <u>Gastronomy. The anthropology of food and food habits</u>. Edited by Margaret Louise Arnott. 1975. Pp. 113-120. Paris, The Hague: Mouton Publishers. World Anthropology.

    In the sedentary life style of industrial societies, humans contribute little of their own energy to food getting. In technologically undeveloped groups, food intake is seen as almost entirely dependent on physiological signals, internal cues. In highly technologized societies, external (cognitive) cues take on greater significance in affecting food intake. The authors discuss the role of the external, culturally-derived stimuli and how the study of these can be incorporated into the overall study of nutritional status.

4562.   Kronenberger-Fentzen, Hanna.   1959.   Die alte kunst der Sussen Sachen.   Backformen und Waffeleisen vergangener Jahrhunderte.   [The old art of confectionery.   Backing forms and waffle-irons from ancient times.] Hamburg: Broschek.

4563.   Krulish, E.   1909.   Aboriginal methods of preparing corn for food by the American Indians of Arizona and New Mexico.   DHG 25: 55-57.

   Based on author's personal observations.

4564.   Krulish, E.   1913.   Sanitary conditions in Alaska.   USPHR 28: 544-551.

   Notes that natives bury fish heads to permit putrefaction, after which the heads are used as food.

4565.   Kubijovyc, Volodymyr, ed.   1970.   Ukraine. A concise encyclopedia. Reprint. Toronto: University of Toronto Press.

   Storage and preparation of food: pp. 295-297.

4566.   Kubista, A.B.   1966.   The noble nopales. True West 14: 33.

   Fruit of the cactus Opuntia sp.

4567.   Kubo, T. 1931.   Diet peculiar to southern China, seen in Chinese literature.   [In Japanese.] Nanpo 1: 21-27.

4568.   Kuenn, D.J.   Man, food, and insects as an ecological problem. In 16th International Congress of Zoology. 20 August - 27 August, 1963. Washington, D.C. Proceedings. Vol. 7. Nature. man, and pesticides. Edited by John A. Moore. 1964. Pp. 4-13.

4569.   Kuhn, Alvin Boyd.   1940.   Chapter Twelve. Ambrosia and nectar. In The lost light. Elizabeth New Jersey: Academy Press.

   Bread, wine and other foods in Egyptian, Babylonian, and Christian ritual, with comparisons from other religions.

4570.   Kuhnau, Joachim.   Food cultism and nutrition quackery in Germany. In Food cultism and quackery. Symposia of the Swedish Nutrition Foundation. Vol. 8. Edited by Gunnar Blix. 1970. Pp. 59-68. Uppsala: Almqvist & Wiksells.

4571.   Kuhnlein, H.V. & Calloway, Doris H. 1977. Contemporary Hopi food intake patterns. EFN 6: 159-173.

   Discusses the economic, geographic, and socio-cultural variables which have been responsible for the declining use of Hopi traditional foods. Includes an extensive list of plant foods, tables of frequency of food use, and meals comprised exclusively of traditional foods.

4572.   Kumlien, Ludwig. 1882. Fragmentary notes of the Eskimo of Cumberland Sound. SI-MC 23: 11-46.

   Northwest Territories. Food uses of whale skin; seal testes, spinal cord; intestine of Logopus and Somateria spectabilis; fatty excrescence at base of upper mandible of male S. spectabilis: pp. 20-22.

4573.   Kunz, L. Die traditionelle Milch-und kasewirschaft in Mittel-und West-mahren.   [Traditional dairy and cheese economy in central and west Mahren.] In Viehwirtschaft und Hirtenkultur. Ethnographische Studien. Edited by L. Foldes. 1969. Pp. 706-734. Budapest: Akademia Kiado.

4574.   Kup, Karl.   1963.   A medeival codex of Italy. Plants, simples, food and diet are outlined in Jacuinum Sanitatis. NH 72[10]: 30-41.

4575.   Kuper, Hilda.   1960.   Indian people in Natal. Pietermaritzberg: At the University Press.

   Diet: pp. 34-35; post-partum diet: pp. 149-150; ritually impure foods: p. 203; sample food purchases, and diet of one family: p. 238; food classification: i.e. 'hot-cold': pp. 250-251; the kulwutra (sour porridge) ceremony: pp. 288-289.

4576.   Kupper-Sonnenberg, G.A. 1962. Balkanisches Festagsbackwerk (Gebildebrot), Ornementik, Symbolik, Stellung in Festbrauch. [Balkan holiday bake-craft (decorated bread). ornamets, symbolism, their place in holiday custom.] ZE 87: 93-114.

4577.   Kuschke, B.M.   1944.   Food habits in Rhode Island. RI-AES-B No. 291.

4578.   Kuttruff, L. Carl.   Late Woodland settlement and subsistence in the lower Kaskasia River Valley. Ph.D. dissertation. Anthropology. Southern Illinois University, Carbondale. 1974.

   Illinois.

4579.   Kuwabara, Jitzuzo. 1928. On P'ou Shoukeng... a man of the Western regions, who was the superintendent of the Trading ships' Office in Ch'uan-chou...towards the end of the Sung dynasty, together with a general sketch of trade of the Arabs in China during the T'ang and Sungeras. Part 2. Memoirs of the Research Department of the Toyo Bunko No. 2. Tokyo: Oriental Library.

   Muslim cooking in China: pp. 48-50.

4580.   Kwon, T.W. Compilor. 1972. Fermented foods in Korea. An annotated bibliography, 1917-1971. Food Resources Laboratory. Seoul: Korea Institute of Science and Technology.

4581.   Laade, W. 1966. Notes on the use of plants as food, medicine, cosmetics, aphrodisiacs, etc. at Saibai, Duan, and Boigu, Torres Straits. Canberra: the author.

4582.   Labarge, Margaret Wade. 1966. Chapter Five. The spice account. Chapter Six. Wine and beer. Chapter Seven. Cooking and serving meals. In A baronial household of the Thirteenth Century. New York: Barnes & Noble, University Paperbacks No. 62.

4583. La Barre, Weston. 1938. Native American beers made from plant substances. AA 40: 224-234.

4584. La Barre, Weston. 1947. Potato taxonomy among the Aymara Indians of Bolivia. Acta Am 5: 83-103.

4585. La Barre, Weston. 1948. The Aymara Indians of the Lake Titicaca plateau, Bolivia. AA 50: 53-66.

Includes notes on diet and food preparation.

4586. Labatut, Edmond. 1880. Les repas chez les Romains. [Roman meals.] Paris: E. Thorin.

4587. Labbe, Marcel. 1921. L'education alimentaire des infants. [Dietary education of children.] RSci 59: 481-490. Also translated in SI-AR for the year 1921. Pp. 549-564 [1922].

Nutrition education in school lunch room; diet as preventive health care; public health nutrition in France.

4588. Labouret, Henri. L'alimentation des indigenes en Afrique Occidentale Francaise. [Diet of natives in French West Africa.] In L'alimentation indigene dans les colonies francaises. Protectorats et territoires sous mandat. Edited by G. Hardy and C. Richet. 1933. Pp. 139-154. Paris: Vigot Freres.

Begins with a geographical summary of the area, and proceeds to review of pastoralist, agricultural, and forest groups. A brief discussion of oil sources follows, with conclusory remarks on malnutrition.

4589. Labouret, Henri. 1937. La geographie alimentaire en Afrique occidentale. [The geography of diet in West Africa.] AGeo 46: 591-610.

4590. Labouret, Henri. 1938. L'alimentation des autochtones dans les possessions tropicales. [Native diet in the tropical possessions.] Africa 11: 160-173.

Diet in the tropical colonies of France, Great Britain, Italy, and Belgium.

4591. Labouret, Henri. 1938. The food and nutrition of African natives. Africa 11: 354-356.

A note introducing the bibliography submitted by Labouret for his article: L'alimentation des autochtones dans les possessions tropicales. Africa 11: 160-173.

4592. Labouret, Henri. 1957. La geographie alimentaire en Afrique Occidentale. [Dietary geography in West Africa.] AGeo 66: 591-610.

4593. Lacey, Mary G. 1923. Food control during forty-six centuries. SM 16: 623-637.

Covers ancient Egypt, China, Athens, Rome; Great Britain, Netherlands, India, Colonial United States, and France (ca. 1200-1793). Reprint. Chicago: American Meat Institute. July, 1973.

4594. Lacroix, P. 1876. Manners, customs and dress during the Middle Ages, and during the Renaissance period. London: Chapman and Hall.

Food and cookery: pp. 105-177.

4595. La Flesche, Francis. 1924. Ethnology of the Osage Indians. SI-MC 76[10].

Green maize gathering, and preparation; water chinkapin (Nelumba lutea); persimmon cakes; squash: pp. 104, 106-107.

4596. Lafon, Ciro Rene. 1969-1970. Notas de etnografia Huichairena. [Ethnographic notes on the Huichaira.] Runa 12: 273-328.

Argentina. Agriculture, dairy products: pp. 281-284; beverages: pp. 314-315.

4597. Lafont, R. 1950. Formes d'utilisation pour l'alimentation des produits de la peche dans les eaux continentales du Cambodge. [Food use of fish products in continental Cambodian waters.] In Communications presentees au Premieres sessions du Conseil Indo-Pacifique des Peches. Phnom-Penh.

4598. Lagemann, J.H. 1904. Edible bulbs. CHS-J 19:9.

4599. Lagercrantz, Sture. 1953. Forbidden fish. Orientalia 2: 3-8.

4600. Lagerstedt, Torsten. 1949. Mat och dryck i Sverige pa 1600-talet. [Food and drink in Sweden in the 17th Century.] H Bild 2: 326-349.

4601. Laguna, Frederica de. 1972. Under Mount Saint Elias: the history and culture of the Yakutat Tlingit. Part One. SI-CA Vol. 7.

Food and its preparation: pp. 391-410. Food getting and processing; Yakutat foods; domestic utensils; food in the 18th and 19th centuries; meat of land animals; birds and birds eggs; seal meat; flenzing and processing; methods of cooking and preserving; seal oil; meat of other seal mammals; fish; salmon; smoking salmon; other fish; preserving fish; fish eggs; fish heads; herring spawn; lachon oil; "beach food" (seaweed, marine invertebrates); plant food: roots, bark, berries, green plants. Some native recipes for modern foods. Food taboos: p. 514; smoking feast for a dead person: pp. 533-534. Food restrictions of shaman: p. 683. Food tabus in relation to the spirit worlds: p. 835.

4602. Laigue, Estienne de. Singulier traicte contenant la propriete de tortues, escargotz, grenoilles, et artichaulz [Singular treatise containing the properties of turtles, snails, frogs, and artichokes.] Paris: Galliot du Pre; Pierre Vidoue.

Permit for publication is dated 19 August, 1530. See Catalogue General de Livres Imprimes de la Bibliotheque Nationale. Vol. 86. P. 622. Paris: Imprimerie Nationale.

4603.   Laing, Jeannie M.   The modes of grinding and drying corn in old times. Paper presented at the meeting of the British Association. Aberdeen. 1885.

4604.   Laird, Carobeth. 1976. The Chemehuevis. Banning, California: Malki Museum, Morongo Indian Reservation.

Extensive data on food supply, food preparation and food use throughout.

4605.   Lal, B.M. & Rao, K.R.   1956.   The food value of some Indian lichens. JSIR 15: 71-73.

4606.   Lal, B.S.   1954.   Changes in dietary habits and physique of aboriginals in Santhal Parganas, a district in Bihar. IJMR 42: 167-179.

This is a resurvey of ten villages inhabited by the Santhal and Pahari tribes; the original survey was done in 1938-1939. Data on food habits are recorded.

4607.   Lamb, Jr., Charles W.   1975. High school students perceptions of fish as a menu item. MFRev 37(10): 25-27.

Data base is sixty-six responses from Austin, Texas home economics students. Favorable responses in several dimensions are reported.

4608.   Lamb, Corrinne. 1935. The Chinese festive board. Peiping: H. Veitch.

Contains proverbs; notes on table etiquette; kitchens; ordering meals. Recipes included.

4609.   Lamb, M.W. & Corrington, M.T.   1946. A further analysis of food selections of 80 families in Lubbock, Texas. JADA 22: 134-138.

4610.   Lambert, L. 1950. Les coquillages comestibles. [Edible shell fish] Paris: Presses Universitaires de France. Serie 'Que sais-je?'

4611.   Lambert-Lagace, L. 1976. Entretien avec le chef cuisinier francais Michel Guerard portant sur la nouvelle cuisine francaise a la fois gastronomique et respectueuse des regles de la dietetique. [Interview with major French cook Michel Guerard bearing upon the new French cookery which is both gourmet and yet mindful of the rules of dietetics.] Chatelaine 17: 50-51.

4612.   Lambrechts, A. & Bernier, G.   1960. Enquete alimentaire parmi les populations rurales du Haut-Katanga. [Dietary survey among rural populations of Upper-Katanga.] PSC No. 51. Pp. 3-25.

4613.   Lampe, P.H.J. 1936. Popular notion prevailing in Surinam in regard to certain forbidden foods as factors in the etiology of leprosy. [In Dutch] DVNI-M 25: 80-88.

4614.   Lampinen, Aino. 1951. Ohrarieska. Kotiseutu Pp. 12-21.

An unleavend barley bread of Finland.

4615.   Lamprey, Louise. 1940. The story of cookery. New York: Frederick A. Stokes.

4616.   Lamson, Herbert Day. 1935. Chapter Two. The standard of living in China. In Social pathology in China; a source book for the study of problems of livelihood, health and the family. Shanghai: Commercial Press.

Contains information on food consumption and expenditures for food.

4617.   Lancelot. 1667. Dissertation sur l'hemine de vin, et sur la livre de pain de S. Benoist, & des autres anciens religieux. Ou l'on fait voir que cette hemine n'estoit que le demi-setier, & que cette livre n'estoit que de douze onces: ou l'on represente l'esprit des peres, & des saints fondateurs d'ordres, touchant le jeune et la temperance, etc. [Dissertation on the hemina of wine, and on the pound of bread of S. Benoist, and of other old clerics. Where one is shown that the hemina is but a demi-setier and the pound only twelve ounces: in which are portrayed the character of the priests and founding saints of religious orders, touching on fasting, temperance, etc.] Paris: chez Charles Savreux.

The hemina is an ancient Roman measure of volume, containing 27 centiliters; the demi-setier is an ancient measure of volume equivalent to one quarter of a liter. Contains information on the dietary of religious orders during fasts and Lent; and on their uses of wine.

4618.   Landa, Jose A. Nutrition education: seven major components. In Communication and behviour change. 8th International Conference on Health and Health Education. 1969. Buenos Aires. Proceedings. 1971. Pp. 286-289. Geneva: International Journal of Health Education.

The seven components mentioned are the biological, economic, social, anthropological-cultural, ecological, and hygienic.

4619.   Landar, Herbert J. 1964.   Seven Navajo verbs of eating. IJAL 30: 94-96.

4620.   Landberg, Leif C. Subsistence patterns of the Chumash Indians of Southern California. Master's thesis. Anthropology. University of Arizona. 1963.

4621.   Landes, Ruth. 1947. The city of women. New York: Macmillan.

Food habits of matriarchal candomble group in Bahia, Brazil: pp. 33, 56, 68, 69, 71, 93, 94, 95, 118-121, 125.

4622.   Lando, Richard P. Pigs, buffalos and men: an analysis of ceremonial meat distribution at Toba Batak feasts.   Paper presented at 75th Annual

Meeting of the American Anthropological Association. 17 to 21 November, 1976. Washington, D.C.

The detailed rules for the ceremonial distribution of meat at feasts of a localized Toba Batak group is considered a symbolic map of the varying status relationships which may be expressed between an individual and his affinal, wife-giving clans in different ceremonial contexts. This system of meat division is considered in light of the present controversy over whether or not the Batak possess a prescriptive, assymetrical marriae alliance system. These data are from one-and-one-half years fieldwork at Lake Toba, Sumatra (located at approximately 2. 20N, and 3.0N, and 98. 20E, and 99. 0E) during 1974-1975.

4623.   Landsberger, B. 1922. Zur Mehlbereitung im altertum. [Flour preparation in antiquity.] OL 25: 340-341.

Refers to several old Babylonian inscriptions, and to the seah, a measure used for barley.

4624.   Landtman, Gunnar. 1927. The Kiwai Papuans of British New Guinea. London: Macmillan.
Myth. British New Guinea: acquisition of food supply for human race: p. 74; origin of yams, sweet potatoes, taro: p. 87.

4625.   Lane, V. 1956. Tennesse vittles. FQ 11: 42-43.

4626.   Lanessan, Jean Marie Antoine de 1884. Flore de Paris (phanerogames et cryptoames), contenant la description de toutes les especes utiles ou nuissible, avec l'indication de leurs proprietes medicales, industrielles et economiques. [Flora of Paris (phanerogams and cryptogams), containing the description of all useful or noxious species, with an indication of their medical, industrial and economic properties.] Paris: O. Doin.

4627.   Lanessan, Jean Marie Antoine de. 1886. Les plantes utiles des colonies francaises. [Useful plants of the French colonies.] Paris: Imprimerie Nationale.

4628.   Lang, Andrew. 1907. Seething the kid. Man No. 103. Pp. 180-182.

Discusses the taboo against boiling the meat of a young animal in the maternal milk. Cites Christian scripture, and ethnographic data.

4629.   Lang, R.R. 1939. Nutritional studies in a region of Puerto Rico. AMPR-B 31: 113-132.

4630.   Langdon, Steve. The interaction of subsistence and cash economies in subarctic Alaska. Paper presented at 72nd Annual Meeting of the American Anthropological Association. 1 December, 1973. New Orleans, Louisana.

4631.   Langdon, Steve. Technology and ecological knowledge: the development of fishing systems in southeastern Alaska. Paper presented at 75th Annual Meeting of the American Anthropological Association. 17 to 21 November, 1976. Washington, D.C.

Posits that technology, to a large extent, mediates and structures human ecological knowledge. Comparisons are drawn between the aboriginal technology for taking salmon in southeastern Alaska, and two modern gear types used in the same pursuit – with reference to the epistemological models of salmon behavior that are required by and produced by their use. The author show how knowledge of salmon behavior currently emphasizes the ocean phase of the fish's development while, aboriginally, the stream phase was paramount in human knowledge about this food resource.

4632.   Langdon, Thomas A. Food restrictions in the medical system of the Barasana and Taiwano of Colombia. Paper presented at 75th Annual Meeting of the American Anthropological Association. 17 to 21 November, 1976. Washington, D.C.

This paper deals with a part of the medical system which related to food restrictions and the shaman's chanting over food and other substances to prevent misfortunes (mostly illnesses). The relevant data are presented and the processes analyzed by which such misfortunes are caused and prevented-processes which are related to a world-view, implicit in the medical system, concerning the balance between humans and nature.

4633.   Langdon, William Chauncy. 1941. Everyday things in American life, 1776-1876. New York: Charles Scribner's Sons.

The dining room and its furniture; hearty meals; the pantry; the kitchen; early cookbooks: pp. 183-207.

4634.   Lange, Charles H. 1950. Notes on the use of turkeys by Pueblo people. El Pal 57: 204-209.

4635.   Lange, Charles H. 1959. Chapter Five. Preparation of food and diet. In Cochiti: a New Mexico pueblo past and present. Austin: University of Texas Press.

4636.   Lange, Frederick W. 1971. Marine resources: a viable alternative for the prehistoric lowland Maya. AA 73: 619-639.

4637.   Lange, Frederick W. 1973. Lowland Maya subsistence and marine resources: a reply. AA 75: 908-910.

Questions validity of attempting to explain prehistoric lowland Maya subsistence in terms of a model applicable to other New World civilizations.

4638.   Langford, William S. 1941. The psychological aspects of feeding in early childhood. JADA 17: 208-216.

4639. Langier, J.D. 1970. Economical and nutritional diets using scarce resources. Graduate school of Business Administration. Division of Research. East Lansing: Michigan State University.

Use of computer in prioritizing diet components on the basis of cost and nutrient content. Focus area is northeast Brazil.

4640. Langkavel, B. 1881. Das Hunde-Essen bei den verschiedenen Volkern. [Dog-eating among various peoples.] Auslander 54: 658-660.

4641. Langley, Doreen. Part Four. Food consumption and dietary levels. In New Guinea Nutrition Survey Expedition. Report. Edited by Eben H. Hipsley & F.W. Clements. 1947. Pp. 92-142. Canberra: Australia. Department of External Territories.

Meal preparation; food patterns; infant feeding: pp. 97-105. List of principal food eaten, and methods of preparation: pp. 112-132.

4642. Langley, Doreen. 1953. Nutrition survey of the kingdom of Tonga. Suva, Fiji: South Pacific Health Service.

4643. Langley, Doreen. 1954 [?]. Dietary surveys and growth records in Fijian village, Nadurai, June 1952-November 1953. Suva, Fiji: South Pacific Health Service.

Data is recorded relative to gardens; fishing; food; wild and cultivated foods; meal patterns; kitchens; food preparation and cooking techniques; recipes; and infant feeding practices.

4644. Langman, Ida Kaplan. 1964. A selected guide to the literature on the flowering plants of Mexico. Philadelphia: University of Pennsylvania Press.

A basic annotated bibliography. Includes extensive entries pertaining directly or indirectly to food plants, their production, use, and chemical composition.

4645. Langton, Joy. 1937. Cannibal feast. London: Herbert Joseph.

4646. Langworthy, Charles Ford. 1905. Notes on food and diet in Cuba. DCSM 10: 1-8; 77-79.

4647. Langworthy, Charles Ford. Progress report of investigations in human nutrition, 1906-1910. In Deuxieme Congres International d'Hygiene Alimentaire et de l'Alimentation Rationnelle de l'Homme. 4-8 Octobre, 1910. Bruxelles. Vol. 1. Section 1. 1910. 185-235. Brussels: M. Weissenbruch.

4648. Langworthy, Charles Ford. 1911. Food customs and diet in American homes. USDA-OES-C No. 110.

Discusses briefly the origin of food habits; physiology of absorption; relation of exercise to diet; dietary standards; U.S. regional food habits. Poorly documented.

4649. Langworthy, Charles Ford. 1916. Homemade fireless cookers and their use. USDA-FB 791.

4650. Lanham, Willie Gertrude. The relation of past and present diets to the physical condition of a group of aged people. Master's thesis. Greensboro: Woman's College of the University of North Carolina. 1944.

4651. Lankester, Edwin. 1832. Vegetable substances used for the food of man. London Society for the Diffusion of Useful Knowledge. Library of Entertaining Knowledge. London: Charles Knight.

4652. Lankester, Edwin. 1859. Guide to the food collections of the South Kensington Museum, London. London: Printed by G.E. Eyre & W. Spottiswoode.

An analysis of all common foods used by mankind, based on material held at the South Kensington Museum. The Guide was begun by Dr. Lyon Playfair, and continued by Lankester, under government financial support.

4653. Lankester, Edwin. 1861. On food; being lectures delivered at the South Kensington Museum. London: R. Hardwicke. Reviewed in BMJ 2: 389, 390. (12 October, 1861).

4654. Lankester, Edwin. 1867. On prison and workhouse dietaries. BMJ 2: 380-382.

Considers optimum nutrition on basis of then-current knowledge of physiology. Brief account of actual diets.

4655. Lantis, Margaret. 1962. The child consumer; cultural factors influencing his food choices. JHE 54: 370-375.

4656. Lantz, D.E. 1908. Deer farming in the United States. USDA-FB No. 330.

Deer and elk as potential domestic food animals.

4657. Lantz, Edith M. & Wood, Patricia. 1958. Nutrition of New Mexican Spanish-American, and Anglo adolescents. 1. Food habits and nutrient intake. JADA 34: 138-144.

Home production and preservation of food; meal patterns; consumption of different food groups.

4658. Lantz, Edith M & Wood, Patricia. 1958. Nutritional condition of New Mexican children. JADA 34: 1199-1207.

Food habits; nutrient intake; serum analysis; anthropometric data.

4659. Lanza, F. 1975. Problemi prospettive della ricerca agricolo-alimentare. [Problems and prospects in food-agriculture research.] ISA-A 6: 311-328.

Better uses of natural resources, including inventory, and storage of plant genetic material: pp. 320, 321.

4660.   Lanzkowsky, Philip.   1959.   Investigation into aetiology and treatment of pica. ADC 34: 140-148.

Reviews the literature on pica briefly, and describes an investigation of twelve children suffering from this phenomenon. Iron deficiency anemia was the main deficiency found, and rapid disappearance of pica invariably followed treatment with iron.

4661.   La Picque, Louis.   1896.   Documents ethnographiques sur l'alimentation minerale.   [Ethnographic documents on mineral nutrition.] Anthropologie 7: 35-45.

Salt.

4662.   La Picque, Louis.   1908.   Sur l'explication physiologique de l'usage du sel, discussion, contre Bunge de certains documents ethnographiques.   [On the physiological explanation of the use of salt, argument against Bunge, based on certain ethnographic documents.] P-SB-CRHSM 64: 1011-1014.

4663.   La Picque, Louis.   1936.   L'alimentation dans le monde et la Societe des Nations.   [World nutrition and the League of Nations.] AM-B 115: 103-106.

4664.   Lappe, Frances Moore.   1971.   Diet for a small planet. New York: Ballantine Books.

The first popular cook book based on the concept of the combination of plant and dairy product amino acids as an option to reliance on red and white meat protein sources. Includes numerous recipes and text on scientific lacto-ovo-vegetarianism.

4665.   Laquer, G.L.; Mickelsen, O.; Whiting, Marjorie Grant; & Kurland, L.T.   1963.   Carcinogenic properties of nuts from Cycas circinalis L. indigenous to Guam. NCI-J 31: 919-951.

4666.   Larkin, Frances & Sandretto, Anita.   1970. Dietary patterns and the use of commodity foods in a Potawatami Indian community. JHE 62: 385-388.

4667.   Larkin, V. de P.   1953.   Favism. Report of a case and brief review of the literature. JPed 42: 453-456.

4668.   Larsen, Henry & Larsen, May.   1964.   The forests of Panama. London: George G. Harrap & Co.

Food habits (with recipes): pp. 64-67.

4667.   Larsen, L.D.   1917.   Miscellaneous food crops on sugar plantations. Haw Plant 16: 382-396.

Banana, pigeon pea [Cajanus cajan] are mentioned. Descriptions are given of gardens grown by various nationalities living and working on sugar cane plantations in Hawaii (Oahu).

4668.   Larsen, Nils Paul. Prevalence of diseases on the Hawaiian sugar plantations and methods for their control. In Far Eastern Association of Tropical Medicine. Tenth Congress. 26 Novembra a 2 Decembre, 1938. Comptes rendus. 1939. Pp. 333-360. Hanoi: Imprimerie d'Extreme Orient.

4669.   Larsen, Nils Paul.   1947.   Le taro et la patate contre les cereales alimentaires et leur influence sur la sante et la carie dentaire aux Hawaii. [Taro and sweet potato as opposed to food cereals and their influence on health and dental caries in Hawaii.]   Translated from English by Bertrand Juanez. SED-B &; 388-406.

4670.   Larson, T.A.   1965.   History of Wyoming Lincoln: University of Nebraska Press.

Pioneer food of the 1860's and 1870's: pp. 199-200.

4671.   Lasas, V. 1933.   Diet of Lithuanians.   [In Lithuanian.] AMFVMUK 1: 253-298.

4672.   Lasas, V. 1933.   Nutrition of the people of Lithuania. [In Lithuanian.] AMFVMUK 1:91-190.

4673.   Lasas, V. 1938.   Average diet of Lithuanians. [In Lithuanian.] AMFVMUK 5: 1-12.

4674.   Lasch, R. 1898.   Uber geophagie.   [On geophagy.] AGWS-M 28: 214-222.

4675.   Lasker, Gabriel Ward. 1952. Note on the nutritional factor in Howell's study of constitutional types. AJPA 10: 375-379.

4676.   Lassabliere, P.   1920.   La lait condensee. [Condensed milk.]   2nd, revised edition. A. Maloine et Fils.

Historical data included: pp. 1-42.

4677.   Lassche, J.B. & Weits, J. 1963. Research on the eating habits in northeast Polder.   [In Dutch.] Voeding 24: 152-161.

4678.   Latham, Michael. 1965. Human nutrition in tropical Africa.   Rome: Food and Agriculture Organization of the United Nations.

Food habits and their influence on nutritional status: pp. 11-19; recipes for infants and young children: pp. 222-227; home preservation of food: pp. 238-240.

4679.   Latham, Michael C. 1972. Planning and evaluation of applied nutrition programmes. FAO Nutrition Studies.   No. 26.   Rome: Food and Agriculture Organization of the United Nations.

The comments on collecting information (pp. 60-61) are basic to the publication, which elaborates upon them throughout.

4680.   Lathrap, Donald W. Manioc and the rise of civilization in the New World. Paper presented at

70th Annual Meeting of the American Anthropological Association. 18 November, 1971. New York City.

In contrast to the hypothesis concerning the synchronicity of rise of New World civilizations and appearance of efficient patterns of maize agriculture, a growing body of evidence is accumulating that root crop agriculture and, specifically, manioc cultivation provided the context in which the first civilizing influences appeared in both Mesoamerica and the Central Andes. This evidence is reviewed together with its implications concerning nature and time depth of the tropical forest culture pattern.

4681.   Lathrop, Elise. 1926. Early American inns and taverns. New York: Robert M. McBride.

4682.   Latini, Mildred. 1971. Food is a point of view, in nutrition education in the school food service-challenge, change and commitment. In Proceedings of the Western Regional School Food Service Seminar. 21 June to 2 July, 1971. Department of Food and Nutrition. College of Family Life. Logan: Utah State University.

Diversity of food habits, and their relation with economics, food choice and consumption. Stresses importance of interdisciplinary approach for understanding food habits.

4683.   Latour, Olga Fernandez. 1960. Datos sobre el folklore de la villa de Belen. [Data on the folklore of the town of Belen.] INIF-C 1: 129-142.

Describes preparation of various breads, and a type of wine.

4684.   Latsky, Johan Michael. 1950. Dietary habits on Finnish Lapland. Rome: Food and Agriculture Organization of the United Nations.

4685.   Latsky, Johan Michael. 1955. Dietary habits in Finnish Lapland. Some personal investigations. SAMJ 29: 794-796.

4686.   Latterner-Stoffel, E.G. 1958. Le lait dans l'histoire de Lorraine. [Milk in the history of Lorraine.] Sarrebourg: Unicoolait.

4687.   Lattimore, Owen. 1930. High Tartary. Boston: Little, Brown.

Foods (raisins, walnuts, mutton) in Turkestan: pp. 167-168; pilau and its etiquette: p. 170; a meal of boiled lamb, and its delicacies: pp. 238-239.

4688.   Laubengayer, Grace W. An historical survey of the relations of pediatrics and nutrition to the development of artificial methods of feeding infants. Master's thesis. Cornell University. 1935.

4689.   Lauber, Doris E. The nutritionist and a deaf-blind child. In Institute on Nutrition Services in Mental Retardation Programs. March 20, 21, and 22, 1963. Cincinnati, Ohio. A report. 1963. Pp.

27-28. Welfare Administration. Children's Bureau. Washington, D.C.: Department of Health, Education, and Welfare.

4690.   Laubscher, B.J.F. 1951. Sex, custom, and psychopathology. London: Routledge & Kegan Paul.

Southeastern Cape Tembu Bantu food tabus: pp. 82-84.

4691.   Laudermilk, J. 1945. Mexicans call it tuna. DM 8: 13-15.

Fruit of Opuntia sp. cactus.

4692.   Laufer, Berthold. The introduction of maize into Eastern Asia. 15e Congres International des Americanistes. 10-15 Septembre 1906. Quebec. Compte rendu. 1907. Vol. One. Pp. 223-257. Quebec: Dussault & Proulx.

Concludes that maize reached China not via the coastal areas, through Portuguese or Spanish contact, by rather overland, via Tibet, about A.D. 1540 being introduced first into Szechuan Province.

4693.   Laufer, Berthold. Note on the introduction of the ground-nut into China. In 15e Congres International des Americanistes. 10 au 15 Septembre 1906. Quebec. Compte Rendu. Vol. 1. 1907. PP. 259-262. Quebec: Dussault & Proulx.

Concludes the Arachis hypogaea, the peanut, was introduced into China, in Fukhien, sometime prior to A.D. 1573, by Fukhienese sailors or traders, who obtained the seed probably in the Philippines or the Malay Archipelago.

4694.   Laufer, Berthold. 1926. Ostrich egg-shell cups of Mesopotamia and the ostrich in ancient and modern times. FMNH-AL No. 23.

4695.   Laufer, Berthold. 1928. Geophagy. FMNH-P-AS 18: 99-198.

4696.   Laufer, Carl. 1966. Nahrungszubereitung und Genussmittel der Baining (Neuebritannien). [Food preparation and stimulants of the Baining (New Britain).] SGAE-B 42: 59-77.

4697.   Laulan, Robert. 1955. Bonaparte mangeat-il vraiment si bien a l'Ecole Militaire? [Did Bonaparte really eat that well at the Ecole Militaire?] IH 17: 123.

4698.   Lauman, Laura. Evaluation of food information found in periodicals. Master's thesis. Denton: Texas State College for Women. 1944.

4699.   Launay, Robert G. The pig and the Prophet. Paper presented at 76th Annual Meeting of the American Anthropological Association. 29 November to 3 December, 1977. Houston, Texas.

As Muslims, the Diola (Guinea Coast) do not eat pork. They possess a corpus of folktales concerning the pig, some of which appear to explain the prohibition of pork. These tales

call to mind explanations of other alimentary as well as sexual prohibitions which,
taken together, can be compared in an attempt to discern structural parallels and
transformations. However, these relations
cannot be interpreted as a cause of the
various prohibitions. Rather, they must be
seen as a tentative attempt to relate historically disparate traditions within a single
intellectual framework.

4700. Laurent, Stephen. 1959. The diet that
made the Red Man. NHA No. 9. Pp. 6-9.

4701. Lauwe, P. Chombart de; Lauwe, M. Chombart de; & Benoit, O. 1954. Etude sur certaines
motivations de comportement alimentaire. 1. Menages ouvriers: legumes, crudites, conserves.
[Studies of some motivations of food behavior. 1.
Workers households: vegetables, raw foods, preserves.] P-INH-B 9: 119-132.

4702. Lavanway, Priscilla. Relation of nutritional
status to motility, intellectual performance, and
personality of a group of Iowa school children.
Master's thesis. Iowa State College. 1949.

4703. Laverty, M. 1945. In a Spanish   kitchen;
abridged. Cath Dgst 9: 62-65.

4704. Law, P.G. 1957. Nutrition in the Antarctic.
The Annie B. Cunning Lectures on Nutrition. No. 9.
Sydney: The Royal Australasian College of Phsyi-
cians.

Reviews historical data on expedition dietaries, and current practices.

4705. Lawrence, Jeremy Charles Dalton. 1957.
The Iteso, fifty years of change in a Nilo-Hamitic
tribe of Uganda. Oxford: Oxford University Press.

Food and drink: Pp. 118-125.

4706. Lawrence, Julia F.   Food supply in the
Marshall Islands. Master's thesis. Yale University.
1943.

Covers agriculture, meat supply, sea food,
food preparation and preservation.

4707. Lawrence, Robert John. 1965. Aboriginal
habitat and economy: some examples and problems.
Canberra: Australian National University.

Australian Aborigines.

4708. Lawrence, Robert John. 1968. Aboriginal
habitat and economy. Occasional Paper No. 6
Department of Geography School of General Studies. Canberra: Australian National University.

4709. Lawson, A. & Moon, P. 1938. A clay
adjunct to potato dietary. Nature (L)141: 40.

Quechua. Capochica Peninsula, Puno Department, southeastern Peru. Certain Andean peoples consume a whitish earth clay
with indigenous tubers.

4710. Lawson, R.M. 1957. The nutritional status
of a rural community on the lower Volta, Gold
Coast. WASA-J 3: 123-129.

4711. Lazarsfeld, Paul F. 1934. The psychological
aspect of market research. BRev 13: 54-71.

4712. Lea, David A.M. Abelam land and susten-
ance: swidden horticulture in an area of high
population density, Maprik, New Guinea. Ph.D.
dissertaiton. Australian National University. 1964.

4713. Leach, Helen M. 1969. Subsistence patterns in prehistoric New Zealand; a consideration of
the implications of seasonal and regional variability
of food resources for the study of prehistoric economics. Studies in Prehistoric Anthropology. Vol. 2.
Anthropology Department. Dunedin, New Zealand:
Otago University.

4714. Leachman, Douglas. 1951. Bone grease.
Am An 16: 355-356.

Process of extraction of oil from bone marrow for cooking and pemmican preparation.
Reference areas are North American midwest, and Canadian Yukon.

4715. Leacock, Seth. 1964. Ceremonial drinking
in an Afro-Bazilian cult. AA 66: 344-354.

Use of alcohol by members of the Batuque
cult, for curing and ceremonial purposes, in
Belem, Para State, Brazil. The nature of
the cult is described, and additional material recorded relating to ceremonial drinking,
cult beliefs and problem drinkers, and the
functions of drinking in the cult, e.g. integration, reduction of anxiety, extension of
trance experience.

4716. League for International Food Education.
1976. Small-scale intensive food production. Report of a workshop on improving the nutrition of the
most economically disadvantaged families. Washington, D.C.: League for International Food Education.

4717. League of Nations. Health Organization.
1937. Intergovernmental conference of Far Eastern
countries on rural hygiene. Preparatory papers.
Report of French Indo-China, No. CH 1235. Geneva: League of Nations.

Composition of food; and preparation methods: pp. 74-80.

4718. League of Nations. Health Organization.
1937. Intergovernmental Conference of Far Eastern
Countries on Rural Hygiene. Preparatory papers:
National Reports: Report of the Netherlands Indies,
No. CH 1235 (j).
Dietary, and food preparation methods: pp.
118-129.

4719. League of Nations. Health Organization.
1937. Intergovernmental Conference of Far Eastern
Countries on Rural Hygiene. Preparatory papers.
Report on health organization in Ceylon, No. CH
1235(d). Geneva: League of Nations.

Composition of food and preparation methods: pp. 40-42.

4720.   League of Nations. International Labor Office. 1936. Worker's nutrition and social policy. Studies and reports. Series 13. [Social and economic conditions] No. 23. Geneva: League of Nations.

Includes data on socio-economic aspects of nutrition.

4721.   League of Nations. 1939. European conference on rural life. General technical documentation. Rural dietaries in Europe. Annex: report on bread, prepared under the auspices of the Health Committee. Geneva: League of Nations.

1. Dietaries. 2. Food. 3. Bread.

4722.   League of Nations. 1939. European conference on rural life, 1939. National monographs drawn up by governments. No. 11. Latvia. Geneva: League of Nations.

Preparation of food; use of major foodstuffs: pp. 74-78.

4723.   League of Nations. 1939. European conference on rural life. National monographs drawn up by governments. No. 23. Yugoslavia. Geneva: League of Nations.

Rural nutrition, with brief account of regional diets: pp. 72-73.

4724.   League of Nations. 1939. Rural dietaries in Europe. LN-HO-B 8: 470-497.

4725.   Leary, James B. Food taboos and level of culture: a cross-cultural study. In Cross-cultural studies of factors related to differential food consumption; final report. United States Public Health Service Grant No. A-3557. New Haven, Connecticut: Human Relations Area Files. 1961.

4726.   Leary, P.M. 1969. The diet of Pedi school children. SAMJ 43: 792-795.

4727.   LeBeuf, Jean-Paul & LeBeuf, A.M.D. Systemes classificatoires africains. [African classificatory systems.] Paper presented at 9th International Congress of Anthropological and Ethnological Sciences. 28 August to 8 September, 1973. Chicago, Illinois.

Examines a complex system among the Kotoko of Lake Chad, comprising fundamental divisions based on gender, air, fire, earth, water; and ancillary numbered categories. Included in this system are edible grains, and other food plants.

4728.   Lebhar, Godfrey M. 1963. Chain stores in America: 1859-1962. New York: Chain Store Publications.

Retail businesses with multiple outlets, local, regional, and national. Data on food supermarkets throughout.

4729.   Lebault, Armand. 1910. Le table et le repas a travers les siecles. [The table and meals through the centuries.] Paris: L. Laveur.

A history of dining; utensils, ceremonies and entertainments at table among ancient peoples; and the French; preceded by a study of primitive gastronomic customs, and of the role of meals in civilization.

4730.   Le blanc, Maria. 1960. Personalite de la femme Katangaise. [Personality of the Katanga woman.] Studia Psychologica. Louvain: Publications Universitaires.

As food provider: pp. 55-66.

4731.   Lebon, J. & Choussat, J. 1948. Une epidemie de lathyrisme en kabylie. [An epidemic of lathyrism in Kabyle.] Pres Med 37: 450-451.

Northeastern Algeria.

4732.   Le Bovit, Corinne B. & Clark, Faith. 1956. Household practices in the use of foods; three cities, 1953. United States Department of Agriculture. Agriculture Research Service. Household Economic Research Branch. Washington, D.C.: United States Department of Agriculture.

4733.   Lebuis, Francois. Le complex culturel de la peche de subsistence a Nemiska au Nouveau Quebec. [Subsistence fishing culture-complex at Nemiska, New Quebec.] Master's thesis. Anthropology. Universite de Montreal. 1971.

4734.   Lechler, George. 1944. Nutrition of Paleolithic man. MASAL-P 30: 499-510.

4735.   Lechmanan, C. A socio-economic study of the Muthuvans in the K.D. Hills, Deveculan District. Master's thesis. Social Work. University of Madras. 1964.

Kerala State, India.

4736.   Leclerc, Henri. 1925. Lel fruits de France: historique, dietetique et therapeutique. [The fruits of France: in history, dietetics, and therapy. 2nd. ed. rev.] Paris: Masson & Cie.

4737.   Lecler, Henri. 1929. Les epices, plantes condimentaires de la France et des colonies. [Spices, condiment plants of France and the colonies.] Paris: Masson et Cie.

4738.   Leclerc, Henri. 1941. Les legumes de France; leur histoire, leurs usages alimentaires, leurs vertus therapatiques. [Vegetables of France; their history, their food use, their therapeutic virtues.] 3rd revised edition. Paris: Legrand.

4739.   Leclerc, Henri. 1943. La vesce (Vicia sativa, L.) dans l'alimentaiton humaine. [Vetch (Vicia sativa, L.) in human diet.] Pres Med 51: 188.

4740.   Lecler, Henri. 1954. A propos du poischiche (Cicer arietinum, L.) Son emploi dans l'alimentation et en therapeutique. [Concerning the chick

pea, (Cicer arietanum, L.) its use in diet and therapeutics.] Pres med 62: 2522.

Use as a dietetic.

4741.   Le Clercq, Jacques. 1925. The decay of the
cook. Am Merc 6: 200-203.

Criticism of American food by a French
writer. Includes historical references.

4742.   Lecoeur, C. & Lecoeur, M. 1946. Initiation
a l'hygiene et a la morale de l'alimentation chez les
Djerma et les Peuls de Niamey (Niger). [Initiation
to food hygiene and ethics of diet among the Djerma
and the Peul of Niamey (Niger). IFAN-B 8: 164-180.

4743.   Le Cointe, Paul. 1934. A Amazonia Brasileira. 3. Arvores e plantas uteis.)Indigenas e
acclimadas). [The Brazilian Amazon. 3. Useful
trees and plants. (Native and introduced).] Belem-
Para: Livraria Classica.

Food products and their uses are noted.

4744.   Le Conte, J. 1846. Observations on geophagy. SMSJ 1: 417-444.

4745.   Lecoq, Raoul. 1926. Food value of flours or
meals prepared from the leguminosae. [In French.]
SSHAARH-B 14: 273-286.

4746.   Lecoq, Raoul. 1926. L'histoire du malt.
[The history of malt.] Paris: Vigot.

4747.   Lederer, Jean. 1957. Le probleme alimentaire des noirs au Congo Belge. [Dietary problems
of Belgain Congo natives.] Rev Nou 26: 285-297.

4748.   Lederer, Jean. 1964. Problemes sociaux de
l'alimentation. [Social problems of diet.] Louvain:
Editions Mauwelaerts.

Reviewed by Yvonne Verdier in E Rur Nos.
22-23-24: 274 (1966).

4749.   Ledesma, Antonio Colmenero de.   1631.
Curioso tratado de la naturaleza y calidad de chocolate, divido en quatro puntos. En el primero se trata
que sea chocolate; que calidad tenga el cacao, y los
demas ingredientes.   En el segundo, se trate la
calidad que resulta de todo ellos.   En el tercero se
trata el modo de hazerlo, y de quantas maneras se
toma en las Indias, y qual dellas es mas saludable. El
ultimo punto trata de la quantidad, y como se ha de
tomar, y en que tiempo, y que personas. [Curious
treatise on the nature and quality of chocolate,
divided into four parts. In the first is treated what
chocolate is; the character of cacao in addition to
its composition. In the second part is considered the
resulting characteristics of the latter in combination. In the third part is treated the manner of
preparing chocolate and how it is drunk in the
Indies, and which of them is most healthful. The
last part treats of the quantity, and how it is drunk,
when, and with whom.] Madrid: Fransisco Martinez.

4750.   Lee, Alice K.Y.   1935.   Some forms of
Chinese etiquette in Hawaii. SPH 1: 37-39.

Includes comments on eating etiquette, and
attitudes toward food.

4751.   Lee, Bung Chong. 1936. The Chinese store
as a social institution. SPH 2: 35-38.

Classification of Chinese foods into categories, i.e. delicacies, and ordinary foods: p.
33, footnote 5.

4752.   Lee, Chan.   History of rice with special
reference to Louisiana. Ph.D. dissertation. Geography.   Baton Rouge: Louisiana State University.
1960.

4753.   Lee, D.S. 1966. Confessions [of a] ranch-
cook: "never saw a homely cowboy". Southwestern-
er April. P. 15.

4754.   Lee, Dorothy Demetrocopoulos. 1957. Cultural factors in dietary choice. AJCN 5: 166-170.

4755.   Lee, Jeanette Barbour [Perry]. 1926. If
you must cook. New York: Dodd, Mead.

Presentation of coooking principles from an
artistic rather than a mechanical point of
view.

4756.   Lee, Jim. 1969. Jim Lee's Chinese cookbook. New York: Harper & Row.

Historical data interspersed between recipes.

4757.   Lee, Ki Yull; Song, Chung Suk; Yang, Jae
Mo; Kim, Myung Ho; Soh, Chin Thack; & Thomson,
James Claude. 1962. Dietary of Korean farmers.
JHE 54: 205-211.

Survey of Sangsair village, Kyunggie Province, ca. 23 km from Seoul. Description of
typical Korean foods, and eating patterns: p.
207.

4758.   Lee, Melvin; Alfred, Braxton M.; Birkbeck,
John A.; Desai, Indrajit D.; Meyers, Gordon S.;
Reyburn, Rejeanne G.; & Carrow, Anne.   1971.
Nutritional status of British Columbia Indian popu-
lations. 1. Ahousat and Anaham Reserves. School
of Home Economics. Vancouver: The University of
British Columbia.

The Ahousat Reserve is a Nootka community, located on Flores Island, west of Vancouver Island, at 49. 9N, 126. 1W. Anaham
Reserve is a Chilcotin community, located
approximately seventy miles west of Williams Lake, at 52. 5N, 123. 6W. Ahousat
food patterns and typical menus; food expenditures: pp. 31-50. Anaham food patterns: pp. 50-54. Survey data collected in
1968.

4759.   Lee, Norman E. 1960. Harvests and harvesting through the ages. New York: Cambridge
University Press.

4760.   Lee, Richard Borshay. Subsistence ecology of Kung Bushmen. Ph.D. disseration. Anthropology. University of California, Berkeley. 1966.

Produces evidence that the hunter-gatherer life style is not as impoverished or precarius as heretofore assumed. Demonstrates the Dobe Kung leas an unexpectedly comfortable and secure existence even during periods of severe drought. As with other hunter-gatherers, the Kung possess one super-abundant staple - in this instance the mongongo (Manetti) nut of the tree Ricinodendron rautanenii, which is a rich source of protein.

4761.   Lee, Richard Borshay. 1969. Eating Christmas in the Kalahari. NH: 14-22.

Kung Bushman culture.

4762.   Lee, Richard Borshay. Kung Bushman subsistence: an input-output analysis. In Environment and cultural behavior. Ecological studies in cultural anthropology. Edited by Andrew P. Vayda. 1969. Pp. 47-79. Garden City: Natural History Press.

Quantitative analysis of energy, time, and caloric expenditure among a South African hunter-gatherer group. A favorable energy-cost/nutrition-benefit is demonstrated and the traditional anthropological view of hunter-gatherer cultures as impoverished is challenged. Absence of material wealth is discounted as an indicator of success in subsistence, and it is suggested that hunter-gatherers may enjoy more leisure time per capita than groups at other levels of subsistence activity.

4763.   Lee, Richard Borshay. 1973. Mongongo: the ethnography of a major wild food source. EFN 2: 307-321.

Riconodendron rautanenii, Schinz is a staple wild nut of the Dobe area Kung San (Bushment), who live in the area of northeastern Botswana (Namibia border). The importance of mongongo for this hunter-gatherer group is examined in fine detail; with nutrient analysis, collecting and processing techniques, yields, production and carrying capacity all described. A mongongo song text is also included.

4764.   Lee, T'ao. 1940. Historical notes on some vitamin deficiency disease in China. CMJ 58: 314-323.

4765.   Lee, W.Y. & Lee, Y.F. 1947-1948. Vitamin C content of Shanghai winter vegetables. PNHB 16: 227-230.

4766. Leechman, Douglas. 1972. Camas - a sumptuous feast. Beaver 303: 4-6.

Role of camas lily in northwestern Native American diet; description of gathering, processing, and storage.

4767.   Leed, Theodor W. & German, Gene A. 1973. Food merchandising: principles and practices. New York: Chain Store Publications.

4768.   Leeds, Albert R. 1887. Food for invalids. In New Jersey. Dairy Commissioner. Annual Report. Trenton. Pp. 37-47.

4769.   Leeper, Mary Eunice. Foods used by two groups of aged persons. Master's thesis. Ohio State University. 1944.

4770.   Lefebvre, J. 1972. Quelques expressions et locutions francaises qui relevent du langage de la gastronomie ou de l'art culinaire. [Some French expressions and turns of speech which relate to gastronomy or culinary art.] VL 247. Pp. 578-581.

4771.   Lefevre, M.P.C. 1965. Alimentation des populations africaines au Sud du Sahara. [Diet of African populations south of the Sahara.] Enquetes bibliographiques 13. Brussels: Centre du Documentation Economique et Sociale Africaine.

4772.   Lefft, Harold H. 1957. Some nutritional and therapeutic aspects of wine and cognac. 170: IRMGPC 170:361-368.

Enumeration of effects of moderate alcohol intake upon digestion, metabolism, and in cooking: pp. 362-364.

4773.   Le Forestier du Boisdelaville. 1865. Fungiphage du Canton de Laigle (Orne). [Fungus eating in Laigle Canton (Orne). Alencon: E. de Broise.

France.

4774.   Legendre, A. 1932. On Japanese diet [In French.] P Med 40: 309.

4775.   Legendre, A.F. 1910. Les Lolos de Kientchang, a l'ouest de la Chine. [The Lolos of Ch'ien chiang, western China.] [In English.] SI-AR for the year 1911. Pp. 569-586.

Mention of a kind of pemmican prepared from meat which is pulverized and dissolved in water prior to eating: pp. 583-584. Reference area is Szechuan.

4776.   Legendre, A.F. 1935. Le "Chan Si". L'alimentation des ses inhabitants. [Shensi, the diet of its inhabitants.] P Med 43: 461.

4777.   Legey, Francoise. 1935. Chapter Twelve. Food. In The folklore of Morocco. Translated by Lucy Hotz. London: George Allen & Unwin.

4778.   Le Gros Clark, Frederick. The school child and school canteen. Mimeographed. Hertforshire, England: Hertfordshire County Council. 1942.

A copy of this item is on deposit at the Centre du Documentation of the Comite International pour l'Anthropologie de l'Alimentation et des Habitudes Alimentaires. Laboratoire d'Ethnobotanique. Museum National d'Histoire Naturelle, Paris. Document 74.

4779. Les Gros Clark, Frederick. Soviet forms in communal feeding. A comparative study. Mimeographed. Harpenden, Hertfordshire, England: no publisher cited. 1942.

A copy of this item is on deposit at the Centre du Documentation of the Comite International pour l'Anthropologie de l'Alimentation et des Habitudes Alimentaires. Laboratoire d'Ethnobotanique. Museum National d'Histoire Naturelle, Paris. Document P. 272.

4780. Le Gros Clark, Frederick. The school child's taste in vegetables. Mimeographed. Hertfordshire, England: Hertfordshire County Council. 1943.

A copy of this item is on deposit at the Centre du Documentation of the Comite International pour l'Anthropologie de l'Alimentaiton et des Habitudes Alimentaires. Laboratoire d'Ethnobotanique. Museum National d'Histoire Naturelle, Paris. Document 73.

4781. Le Gros Clark, Frederick. 1944. Food habits and how to change them. Lancet 247: 53-55.

4782. Le Gros Clark, Frederick. 1947. The vicious circle of austerity: adjusting our food habits. Lancet 252: 721-722.

4783. Le Gros Clark, Federick. 1953. The weaning of the human child. Nutrition 7: 59-63.

4784. Le Gros Clark, Federick. 1968. Food habits as a practical nutrition problems. WRND 9: 56-84.

Food in culture; relationship of food habits to health. Sociological and economic problems involved in applied change, with illustrative examples from the literature. Concludes 'Food habits is basically a scientific or medical category' pp. 83.

4785. Le Gros Clark, Frederick & Brinton, L.Noel. 1936. Chapter Six. World's great food problem. Chapter Seven. The great food problem - Soviet solution. Chapter Eight. Milk, bread, meat. Chapter Nine. Customs of feeding socially. Chapter Ten. Catering on the large scale. Chapter Eleven. State inspection of food. Chapter Twelve. Cooks, managers and so forth. Chapter Thirteen. Man and his food - the work of the laboratories. Chapter Fourteen. Man and his food - the mass and the individual. Chapter Fifteen. Physical condition of the people. Chapter Sixteen. Flow of food production in the U.S.S.R. Chapter Seventeen. Men at mealtime. Chapter Eighteen. Children at mealtime. In Men, medicine and food in the U.S.S.R. London: Lawrence & Wishart.

4786. Le Gros Clark Frederick & McKay Helen S. Allocation of food within the family cirlce. A study of the consumption habits of forty working-class families. Mimeographed. Harpenden, Herfordshire, England: no publisher cited. 1940.

A copy of this item is on deposit at the Centre du Documentation of the Comite International pour l'Anthropologie de l'Alimentation et des Habitudes Alimentaires. Laboratoire d'Ethnobotanique. Museum National d'Hitoire Naturelle, Paris. Document P. 263.

4787. Lehmayer, Dorothy Margaret. Home visiting as a means of changing food habits: a six-month study of five families on limited food budgets. Master's thesis. Cornell University. 1942.

4788. Lehrer, Adrienne. 1972. The cooking vocabularies and the culinary triangle of Levi-Strauss. A Ling 14: 155-171.

4789. Leigh, R. Wood. 1937. Dental morphology and pathology of pre-Spanish Peru. AJPA 22: 267-296.

Agriculture and food: pp. 268-270.

4790. Leininger, Madeleine. Some cross-cultural and non-universal functions, beliefs, and practices of food. In Dimensions of nutrition. Proceedings of the Colorado Dietetic Association Conference. 1969. Fort Collins, Colorado. Edited by Jacqueline Dupont. 1970. Pp. 155-179. Boulder: Colorado Associated University Press.

A theoretical article which suffers only from lack of supportive documentation.

4791. Leis, Philip E. 1964. Palm oil, illicit gin and the moral order of the Ijaw. AA 66: 828-838.

A shift to distilling gin from previous production of palm oil was made by consensus, without concomitant change of moral values in the Ijaw village of Ebama, southern Nigeria.

4792. Lejeunne, F. 1962. Medizin und diat in alten Portugiesischen sprachwort. [Medicine and diet in old Portuguese proverbs.] MErn 3: 15-16, 41, 64-65, 100, 119, 142-143, 167, 187, 213, 234-235, 258-259, 287.

4793. Lekkerkerker, C. Quelques aliments vegetaux protohistoriques en Indonesie. [Some protohistoric Indonesian plant foods.] In Institut International d'Anthropologie. 3e Session. 20-29 Septembre 1927. Amsterdam. 1928. Pp. 512-516. Paris: Libraire E. Nourry.

Provides a research methodology for determining food uses utilizing archeological, ethnological and linguistic data, for five sequential subsistence phases, i.e., non-agricultural; root culture; cereal or grain culture; native grains and rice on temporary or permanent fields; and rice cultivation on permanent fields together with expansion of artificial irrigation of rice fields.

4794. Lelong, M.H. 1946. Ces hommes qu'on appelle anthropophages. [These men called cannibals.] Paris: Alsacia.

4795. Lema, N.T. 1963. Tribal customs in infant feeding. 2. Among the chagga. EAMJ 40: 370-375.

4796.   Lemert, Edwin M. 1964. Forms and pathology of drinking in three Polynesian societies. <u>AA</u> 66: 361-374.

> Festive drinking in Tahiti and Bora Bora (Society Islands); ritual-disciplined drinking on Atius, Rarotonga, and Aitutaki (Cook Islands); secular drinking in Samoa. For each area, alcohol abuse and its consequences are explored.

4797.   Lemery, Louis. 1704. <u>A treatise of all sorts of foods, both animal and vegetable; also of drinkables.</u> London: T. Osborne.

4798.   Lemon, James T. 1967. Household consumption in Eighteenth Century America and its relationship to production and trade: the situation among farmers in Southeastern Pennsylvania. <u>AH</u> 4: 59-70.

> Incudes extensive information on food habits, their production and consumption, with brief indication of costs for some commodities.

4799.   Lent, D. <u>Meal patterns and food purchasing practices of 204 members of the Arizona Federation of Business and Professional Women.</u> Master's thesis. University of Arizona. 1968.

4800.   Lentnek, Barry A. <u>A geography of the subsistence economy of El Llano, Aguascalientes, Mexico.</u> Ph.D. dissertation. Geography. Baltimore, Maryland: Johns Hopkins Unviersity. 1966.

4801.   Leon, Jorge. Area de origen y dispersion inicial del cultivo del cacao. [Area of origin and initial dispersal of cultivated cacao.] In <u>33o Congresso Internacional de Americanistas. 20-27 Julio 1958. San Jose, Costa Rica. Aetas. Vol. One.</u> 1959. Pp. 251-258. San Jose, Costa Rica: Lehmann.

> Evidence indicates <u>Theobroma cacao</u> to have originated in the tropical Mexico, northern Guatemala area, with dispersal advancing from the Pacific Coast north to Colima, and on the Atlantic Coast north to Veracruz.

4802.   Leon, Jorge. 1964. The "maca" (<u>Lepidium meyenii</u>, Walp.). A little-known food plant of Peru. <u>EB</u> 18: 122-127.

> Use as food: p. 127; notes plant is also reputed to facilitate reproduction.

4803.   Leon, Jorge.   1964.   <u>Plantas alimenticas Andinas.</u> [Andean food plants.] Boletin No 6. Lima: Instituto Interamericano de Ciencias Agricolas Zona Andina.

4804.   Leonard, J. 1966. The 1964-65 Belgian trans-Saharan expedition. <u>Nature</u> (L) 209: 126-128.

> Contains an expanded note on the use of algae as food. The alga is <u>Spirulina</u> <u>platensis</u> (Cyanophycea), called <u>dihe</u>, harvested from Lake Chad, and sold in cakes. Analysis indicated the algae is a rich source of protein.

4805.   Leonard, Jonathan Norton. 1970. <u>American cooking: New England, with supplementary chapters on the cooking of eastern Canada.</u> New York: Time-Life Books. Foods of the World.

4806.   Leonard, Jonathan Norton. 1971. <u>American cooking - the Great West.</u> New York: Time-Life Books. Foods of the World.

4807.   Leonard, Jonathan Norton. 1973. <u>The first farmers.</u> New York: Time-Life Books.

> Concerned largely with emergence of agriculture in the Near East. Discusses livestock domestication, and contemporary, non-industrialized farming groups.

4808.   Leonard, Warren H. 1957. World population in relation to potential food supply. <u>SM</u> 85: 113-125.

4809.   Leonard, Warren H. & Roberts, Raymond. 1949. <u>Tea in Japan.</u> Supreme Commander for the Allied Powers. Natural Resources Section. Report No. 125.   Tokyo: General Headquarters of the Supreme Commander for the Allied Powers.

> Historical and cultural aspects of tea use: pp. 9-11. Publication available in photocopy form from United States National Archives, Washington, D.C.

4810.   Leonardi, Piero. 1958. L'alimentzione dell'uomo paleolitico dell'Italia padana. [The diet of Paleolithic populations in the Po River Valley area of Italy.] <u>Min Med</u> 49: 1673-1676.

4811.   Leong, P.C. 1953. The nutritive value of coconut toddy. <u>BJN</u> 7: 253-259.

4812.   Leopold, A. Carl & Ardrey, Robert. 1972. Early man's food habits. <u>Science</u> 177: 833-835.

4813.   Leopold, A. Carl & Ardrey, Robert. 1972. Toxic substances in plants and the food habits of early man. <u>Science</u> 176: 512-514.

4814.   Lepkovsky, Samuel. 1947. The effect of the nature of the food eaten upon the desire for food. <u>FTech</u> 1: 26-29.

> Variables considered are: the role of nutritional adequacy; physiological behavior of food in the gastrointestinal tract; effect of food on the flow of the digestive secretions; effect of food on the composition of the circulating body fluids; rate of movement of food through the gastrointestinal tract; role of bulk; effect of deleterious components in food.

4815.   Lerche, Grith. 1969. Kogegruber i New Guineas hojland. [Cooking pits in the New Guineas highlands.] <u>Kuml</u> 1969. Pp. 196-209.

4816.   Lerche, Grith. Notes on different types of "bread" in northern Scotland: bannocks, oatcakes, scones, and pancakes. In <u>Gastronomy. The anthropology of food and food habits.</u> Edited by Margaret Louise Arnott. 1975. Pp. 326-336. Paris, The Hague: Mouton Publishers, World Anthropology.

Describes preparation (including recipes), and food use of oatcakes, wheat muffins; informal record of daily menu patterns in included.

4817. Leren, G. 1953. Christmas food and food habits in Trondelagen in olden days. Landbruksti-dende 59: 976-978.

Norway.

4818. Leriche, Albert. 1949. Le couscous sa preparation. [Couscous - its preparation.] NA No. 44. Pp. 106-107.

A North African food comprised of steamed bulgur wheat, meat, and vegetables.

4819. Leriche, E. 1943. La ration alimentaire. [Dietary allowances.] IIEH-BT 5: 79-84.

4820. Lerner, Franz. 1964. Aber die Biene nur findet die Sussigkeit. Kleine Kulturegeschichte des Honigs. [The bee always finds the sweetness. A brief cultural history of honey.] Dusseldorf: Econ-Verlag.

4821. Lery, F. 1962. L'alimentation. [Diet.] Paris: Editions du Seuil.

4822. Lesko, Leonard H. 1978. The wine wisdom of King Tutankhamon. SMFW-B 20: 3-4.

A brief, historical review of wine in ancient Egyptian culture, its production, qualities, and uses in medical practice.

4823. Leslau, Wolf. 1965. Ethiopians speak. 1. Harari. University of California Publications. Near Eastern Studies Vol. 7. Berkeley and Los Angeles: University of California Press.

Food and its preparation: Pp. 88-97.

4824. Leslie, Eliza. 1847. The Indian meal book: comprising the best receipts for the preparation of that article. Philadelphia: Carey and Hart.

Maize.

4825. Le Soeuf, W.H.D. 1916. Aboriginal culinary methods and kitchen middens. VGJ 32: 1-11.

4826. Lessinger, Johanna M. Produce vendors in the Princes Town market, Trinidad. Master's thesis. Anthropology. Brandeis University. 1968.

4827. Lestradet, H. & Machinot, S. 1976. Le comportement alimentaire de l'infant francais. [Dietary behavior of French children.] ANA 30: 185-194.

4828. Lestrange, Monique de 1952. Le sel dans l'alimentation des Coniagui de Guinee. [Salt in the diet of the Coniagui of Guinea.] Con Med 74: 815-816.

French Guinea.

4829. Letard, Etienne. Le riz et ses derives dans l'alimentation des animaux domestiques. [Rice and its by-products in the nutrition of domestic animals.] In Sixieme Congres International d'Agriculture Tropicale et Subtropicale. 15-19 juillet, 1931. Paris. Vol. 2. Pp. 445-448. Paris: Secretariat General de l'Association Scientifique Internationale d'Agriculture des Pays Chauds et de Son Comite Francais.

4830. Le Testu, G. 1940. Note sur les cultures indigenes dans l'interieur du Gabon. [Note on native cultivation in the interior of Gabon.] RBAAT 20: 540-556.

Enumerates food plants, and discusses the nature of settlements and their kinship, which members of the group are responsible for gardening; techniques used to protect gardens from animals; cultivation and harvesting tools; fallow periods; choice of garden area; and traditions, rites, and taboos pertaining to agriculture.

4831. Letheby, Henry. 1876. Sale of diseased meat as human food. Extract from the weekly report of the medical officer of the City of London. London: M. Lownds.

4832. Letourneau. 1887. Sur l'anthropophagie en Amerique. [On anthropophagy in America.] SAP-B 10: 777-780.

Reports on anthropophagy among the Blackfoot, the ancient Aztecs, and Native Chileans. A discussion follows, relating to the validity of the Chilean example and anthropophagy in general.

4832. Letourneau. 1888. La femme et l'anthropophagie en Polynesie. [Woman and canniabalism in Polynesia.] SAP-B 11: 133-136.

New Zealand, Nukuhiva, Tahiti.

4833. Lett, Lewis. 1935. Sweet potatoes: A Papuan day. Cornhill 152: 315-321.

4834. Leung, Woot-tsuen-wu; Pecot; R.K.; & Watt, Bernice K. 1952. Composition of foods used in Far Eastern Countries. USDA-AH No. 34.

4835. Leurquin, Philippe. 1958. Economie de subsistence et alimentation au Ruanda-Urundi. [Subsistence economy and diet in Ruanda-Urundi.] Zaire 12: 3-35.

4836. Leurquin, Philippe. 1960. Le niveau de vie des populations rurales du Ruanda-Urundi. [The standard of living of rural populations in Ruanda-Urundi.] Publications de l'Universite Lovanium de Leopoldville. Louvain: Institut de Recherches Economiques et Sociales.

Food quality: p. 189; quantity of food available in various regions: p. 192; 231; production of indigenous beers: p. 210; seasonal variation in diet: P. 237; daily diet of a Hutu farmer: p. 241.

4837.   Leverton, Ruth N. & Coggs, Maud. 1931. Food choices of Nebraska children. JHE.

4838.   Leverton, Ruth M. & Marsh, Alice G. 1939. Comparison of food intakes for weekdays and for Satuday and Sunday. JHE 31: 111-114.

Also available as Nebraska Agricultural Experiment Station Paper No. 216. This study shows a significant difference for weekdays as compared with Saturday and Sunday in the food intake of college women on self-selected diets. Results stress the need to consider no less than one calendar week as the smallest time unit for studies of food consumption or metabolism.

4839.   Levey, Martin. 1959. Food and its technology in ancient Mesopotamia: the earliest chemical processes and chemicals. Centaurus 6: 36-51.

A major resource for food habits information at this period. The data provided should permit some extrapolation to general dietary patterns and their nutritional value. Includes data on military rations and famine food.   Food preparation techniques are recorded, and staple foods covered under the following sections: cereals; vegetables; fruit; meat; dairy products; spices; wine and beer; miscellaneous foods; and preservation; utensils and containers.

4840.   Levin, C.M. 1934. A study of Jewish food habits. JADA 9: 389-396.

4841.   Levin, Simon S. 1963.   A philosophy of infant feeding. Springfield, Illinois: Charles C. Thomas Publisher.

Chapters Two and Three: 'Breast milk', and 'Historical perspectives' contain historical and ethnographic data; however, regrettably, the book includes no documentation.

4842.   Levin, Solomon Isaac & Boyden, Edward A. 1940. The Kosher code of the Orthodox Jew; being a literal translation of that portion of the Sixteenth-Century codification of the Babylonian Talmud which describes such deficiencies as render animals unfit for food (Hilkot terefot, Shulhan gharuk); to which is appended a discussion of Talmudic anatomy in the light of the science of its day and of the present time.   Minneapolis: The University of Minnesota Press; New York: Herman Press.

4843.   Levine, Arthur S. 1939. Nutrition vs. heredity in determining stature. Growth 3: 53-59.

Affirms the role of nutrition in influencing modification of height.

4844.   Levine, Donald N. 1965. Wax and gold. Tradition and innovation in Ethiopian culture. Chicago and London: University of Chicago Press.

Diet of the Amhara peasant: pp. 58-61; socialization of young women to food-related tasks; pp. 98-99; Chapter Six: 'Orality and the search for leadership' explores, and attempts to interpret, the role of food and drink in Amhara culture in terms of Freudian dogma.

4845.   Levine, V.E.   1929.   The importance of nutrition in child hygiene. SM 38: 554-559.

4846.   Levine, V.E. 1955. The epidemic of scurvy among the Indians of the Omaha tribe, 1844-1845. AJDD 22: 294-295.

4847.   Levinson, F. James & Berg, Allan D. 1969. Proposal to combat malnutrition in India - with a grain of fortified salt. F Tech 23: 70-73.

Fortification of salt with Vitamin A, and iron.

4848.   Levi-Strauss, Claude. 1952. The use of wild plants in tropical South America. EB 6: 252-270. Also in Handbook of South American Indians. 1950. Edited by Julian H. Steward. SI-BAE-B No. 143. Vol. 6. Pp. 465-486.

4849.   Levi-Strauss, Claude. 1955. I starved with the world's most primitive tribe. Realites No. 58: 59-61.

The Nambicuara of Brazil's Mato Grosso.

4850.   Levi-Strauss, Claude. 1978. The origin of table manners. Introduction to a science of mythology: 3. Translated by John & Doreen Weightman. London: Jonathan Cape.

A wide variety of food-related behavior is contained throughout the volue, in the course of structural interpolation of myth. 'A short treatise on culinary anthropology': pp. 471-495, is given over to analysis of various cooking processes (boiling, roasting, frying) and their significance in mythocosmology. A subsection addresses 'the origin of digestion.'

4851.   Levron, J. 1975. Caracteristiques des habitudes alimentaires des francais qui vecurent sous le regne de Louis XV. [Characteristics of the food habits of the French under the reign of Louis XV.] Historia No. 42. Pp. 63-70.

4852.   Levy, L.F. & Fox, F.W. 1935. The antiscorbutic value of some South African foodstuffs. SAMJ 9: 181-186.

4853.   Levy, L.F.; Weintroub, D. & Fox, F.W. 1936. Food value of some common edible leaves. SAMJ 10: 699-707.

Listed by botanical family, with food preparation and use recorded.

4854.   Levy, R.C. 1917. La ravitaillement du nord de la France et de la Belgique. [The provisioning of northern France and Belgium.] RDM 42: 417-444.

Food relief during W.W.I.

4855.   Lewicki, Tadeusz & Johnson, Marion. 1974. West African food in the Middle Ages. London, New

York: Cambridge University Press.

4856.   Lewin, Kurt.   Forces behind food habits and methods of change.   In The problem of changing food habits.   Report of the Committee on Food Habits.   1941-1943.   National Research Council. 1943. Pp. 35-64. NRC-B No. 108.

Includes exposition of the author's classic 'channel' theory, which models food in culture as moving through various production, processing, transportation, marketing, preparation, and consumption channels latter are seen as controlled by 'gate-keepers', through whom modification in food habits ideally would be made, by means of an understanding of their 'psychology' or role orientation. Also contains details of experiments in altering dietary behavior through refinement of group decision-making techniques.

4857.   Lewis, Albert.   1923.   The use of sago in New Guinea.   Chicago Natural History Museum. Popular series: Anthropology Leaflet No. 9. Chicago: Chicago Natural History Museum.

4858.   Lewis, Federick.   1934. The vegetable products of Ceylon. A guide to their identification and economic uses.   Colombo: Associated Newspapers of Ceylon.

4859.   Lewis, H.E.; Masterson, J.P.; & Ward P.G. 1957. The food value of biltong (South African dried meat) and its value on expeditions. BJN 11: 5-12.

4860.   Lewis, Henry T.   The role of fire in the domestication of plants and animals in southwest Asia. Paper presented at 69th Annual Meeting of the American Anthropological Association. 19 to 22 November, 1970. San Diego, California.

4861.   Lewis, J.P.   1883.   Tamil customs and ceremonies connected with paddy cultivation in the Jaffna district. RASC-J 304-333.

Peninsula northern Ceylon.

4862.   Lewis, Jane & Tamrat, Rahel.   Dietary practices of Ethiopians living in Los Angeles. Paper presented at 77th Annual Meeting of the American Anthropological Association.   14 to 18 November 1978. Los Angeles, California.

4863.   Lewis, L. James. The effect of diet changes in allergies. Ph.D. dissertation.   University of Pittsburgh. 1943.

4864.   Lewis, R. 1970. The Korean tea room: its function in Korean society. SSR 55: 53-62.

4865.   Lewis, R.K.   Hadchite: a study of emigration in a Lebanese village.   Ph.D.   dissertation. Columbia University. 1967.

Food gathering; baking; and foods consumed are described briefly.

4866.   Lex, Barbara W. Social death of the alcoholic: extrusion from the family. Paper presented at the 77th Annual Meeting of the American Anthropological Association.   14 to 18 November, 1978. Los Angeles, California.

4867.   Leyton, G.B. A survey of the effects of slow starvation on man. Ph.D. dissertation. Cambridge University. 1946.

A medical officer, Leyton was captured during World War II and was interned in concentration camps in Libya, Italy, and Germany.

4868.   Li, Chiao-ping. 1948. Chapter Four. Salt. Chapter Nine. Vegetable oils and fats.   Chapter Eleven.   Sugars.   Chapter Fourteen. Soybean products. Chapter Fifteen.   Alcoholic beverages and vinegar. In The chemical arts of old China. Easton, Pennsylvania: Journal of Chemical Education.

4869.   Li, Hui-lin. 1969. The vegetables of ancient China. EB 23: 253-260.

4870.   Li, Hui-lin. 1970. The origin of cultivated plants in Southest Asia. EB 24: 3-19.

4871.   Liang, Ch'ing-hsiao. 1941. Shina shokuryo shi. [History of food in China.]   Translated by K. Ito. Tokyo: Daito Shuppan-sha.

4872.   Lias, Marie Brau de Saint Pol. 1884. De France a Sumatra par Java, Singapour et Pinang: les anthropophages. [From France to Sumatra, by way of Java, Singapore and Penang: the anthropophagii.] Paris: H. Ondin.

4873.   Lichtenfelt, Hans. 1905. Food consumption in southern Italy. [In German.] PAGPMT 107: 57-80.

4874.   Lichtenfelt, Hans. 1913. Die geschichte der Ernahrung.   [The history of diet.]   Berlin: George Reimer. Reviewed in ZEM 5: 157-158.

4875.   Lichtenstein, F. 1951. Uber die Bedeutung und die Funktionen der Naturfarben in der menschlichen Nahrung. [The significance and function of the natural colors in human food.] ZG 73: 9-16.

4876.   Lieb, C.W. 1929. The effects on human beings of a twelve month's exclusive meat diet. JADA 93.

4877.   Lieberman, Leslie Sue. Diet, natural selection and adaptation in human populations. Paper presented at 75th Annual Meeting of the American Anthropological Association.   17 to 21 November, 1976. Washington, D.C.

This paper examines the significance of digestive enzyme polymorphisms in relation to specific dietary elements and the dietary histories of populations. The most well-documented example of genetotrophic adaptation is the relationship between lactase sufficiency and adult milk drinking in populations with a history of dairying. An investigation is made of the complex and recent

changes in genotype-dietary interactions w-
hich have led to the increasing prevalence
of metabolic abnormalities such as obesity,
diabetes, coronary heart disease, gout, and
hypertension.

4878.   Lieberman, Leslie Sue & Keleher, Brendan.
Medico-nutritional practices in a Puerto Rican community.   Paper presented at 72nd Annual Meeting of
the American Anthropological Association.   1 December 1973.   New Orleans, Louisiana.

4879.   Liebig, Justus von. 1867. Food for infants: a
complete substitute for that provided by nature.
Translate by Elise von Lersner-Ebersburg.   2nd ed.
London: J. Walton.

4880.   Liedgren, Rut. 1956. Kulinariska studier i
1800-talets Stockholm.   [Culinary study of 19th
Century Stockholm.] Fataburen Pp. 49-66.

4881.   Lief, Alfred.   no date.   A close-up of
closures. History and progress. New York: Glass
Container Manufacturers Institute.

Caps, lids and other seals for bottles and
jars.

4882. Liener, Irvin E. 1962. Toxic factors in
edible legumes and their elimination. AJCN 11:
281-298.

4883.   Liener, Irvin E. ed. 1969. Toxic constituents of plant foodstuffs. Food Science and Technology. A series of monographs, vol. 6. New York:
Academic Press.

4884.   Lierbreich, O.   1905. The value of condiments in the diet. [In German.] TM 18: 65-68.

Stimulating effect of condiments in the
diet. Abstracted in ZUNG 9: 368.

4885.   Lieske, Rudolph.   1914.   Brasilianische
Studien.   3.   Jamin-bang, das Brot der Kaingan-
Indianer.   [Basilian studies. 3. Jamin-bang, Kaingan
Indian bread.] JWB[P] 53: 516-526.

Bacterial and chemical analysis of a bread
prepared from both unripe and mature maize, using an acid fermentation process.

4886.   Lieurade. 1932. Enfants rouge du Cameroun. [Red babies of Cameroon.] SPE-B 25: 46.

Kwashiorkor in N'Gaoundere.

4887.   Ligers, Z. 1953. L'economie d'acquisition: la
cueillite, la chasse et la peche en Lettonie. [Sub-
sistence economy: hunting, gathering, and fishing in
Estonia.] Paris.

4888.   Light, Luise. 1965. In praise of vegetables.
New York: Charles Scribner's Sons.

4889.   Lightfoot, William E. 1973. "I hardly ever
miss a meal without eating just a little": traditional
sorghum-making in western Kentucky. MSF 1: 7-17.

Production; processing; marketing and cultural role of sorghum.

4890.   Lima, Oswaldo Goncalves de 1955.   El
empleo de la sal de cenizas por los indigenas brasil-
enos. [The use of ash salt by Brazilian natives.]
Mex Ant 8: 353-364.

4891.   Lima, Oswaldo Goncalves de. 1959. El
maguey y el pulque en los codices Mexicanos. [Ma-
guey and pulque in the Mexican codices.] Mexico
City: Fondo de Cultura Economica.

4892.   Lin, S.Y. 1940. Salf manufacture in Hong
Kong. HKV 10: 34-38.

Describes the leaching, and solar methods.
Diagrams, illustrations of tools, and one
plate of photographs are included.

4893.   Lin, S.Y. 1966. General aspects of fish
culture in Southeast Asia. IFC 4: 2-18.

4894.   Lin, Yueh-hwa.   1947. Liang-shan-I-chia.
[The Lolo of I-chia.]   Translated by Ju-shu Pan.
Shanghai: Commercial Press.

English translation prepared by Human Relations Area Files, New Haven, Connecticut.

4895.   Lin, Yu-t'ang.   1937. My country and my
people. New York: Reynal and Hitchcock. A John
Day Book.

Chinese food and beverages: pp. 335-344.

4896.   Linares, Olga F. Comments on the mode of
production in some tropical societies. Paper presented at 73rd Annual Meeting of the American
Anthropological Association.   19 to 24 November,
1974. Mexico City.

4897.   Linares, Olga F. 1976. "Garden hunting" in
the American tropics. HEcol 4: 331-349.

Using faunal analysis, this article outlines a
coastal mammalian harvesting pattern at a
site called Cerro Brujo, in Bocas del Toro
Province, Panama. Evidence is presented to
support the view that the biomass of a few
terrestrial mammals was larger when associated with human settlement that when
not. Archeological data suggests that these
animals fed regularly on cultivated crops
and were hunted in house gardens and cultivated fields. By concentrating the supply of
carbohydrates and animal protein, "garden
hunting" may have eliminated seasonability
and scheduling problems, and also functioned as a substitute for animal domestication.

4898.   Lincoln, Waldo. 1929.   Bibliography of A-
merican cookery books, 1742-1860. AAS-P 39: 85-
225.

4899.   Lindau, G. 1904. Uber das Vorkommen des
pilzes de Taumellolchs in altagyptischen Samen.
[Occurrence of Lolium temulentum fungi in ancient
Egyptian seeds.] KPAW-B-S Part 2: 1031-1036.

Found with rye grass and darnel.

4900.   Lindblom, Gerhard. 1941. Drinking Tubes, especially in Africa. Ethnos 6: 48-74.

Tubes used for drinking water; beer; palm and rice wine.

4901. Lindebloom, G.A. 1966. Een pleidooi tot verbertering der volksvoeding uit de vorige eeuw. [A plea for the improvement of national diet over that of the last century.] Voeding 27: 1-5.

4902. Lindenblaum, Shirley. The "last course": nutrition and antropology in Asia. In Nutrition and anthropology in action. Edited by Thomas K. Fitzgerald. 1976. Pp. 141-155. Assen, Amsterdam: Van Gorcum.

This article focuses primarily on the Indian subcontinent. Various examples of the influence of symbolism in indian daily life are examined and the relation of some of these to food behavior and nutritional status noted. The "hot" "cold" food classification system is considered in detail, and brief sections review the population and food relationship; malabsorption; specific nutrient deficiencies; and the nutritional status of widows.

4903. Lidenfeld, Jacqueline. Communicative patterns in a French marketplace. Paper presented at 75th Annual Meeting of the American Anthropological Association. 17 to 21 November, 1976. Washington, D.C.

In this preliminary study, based on data collected at an open air market, the focus is on verbal communication between participants. Particular attention is focused on two of the speech components listed in Hymes' model for the ethnography of communication, namely "norms of interaction" and "norms of interpretation". The object is to show that an in-depth analysis of natural conversation can reveal interesting social functions of speech, as well as some of the covert features of interpersonal relations and cultural knowledge.

4904. Lindet, Leon. 1920. Evolution des industries qui transform les produits agricoles: introduction au cours professe a l'Institut National Agronomique. [Evolution of agricultureal products processing industries: introduciton to the course taught in the National Institute of Agronomy.[Paris: Librairie de l'Enseignement Technique.

4905. Lindley, Edith Rose. An evaluation of student growth when the goal-seeking method is employed in teaching a food unit. Master's thesis. Dention: North Texas State Teachers College. 1948.

4906. Lidqvist, K. 1960. On the origin of cultivated lettuce. Hereditas 46: 319-350.

4907. Lindsay, 1887. The dietary of the poor. BMJ 2: 671, 672.

Food of Belfast working class. Cites overconsumption of tea, meat, and potatoes.

4908.   Ling, shun-sheng & Ruey, yih-fu.   1947. Hsang-hsi Miao-tsu Tiao-cha Pao-kao. [A report on an investigaiton of the Miao of Western Hunan.] Translated by Lien-en Tsao. AS-IHP-M Series A. No. 18.

Food habits: pp. 104, 106-110. Based on field work done in 1933.

4909.   Linao, A.L. & Bautista, A.P. 1965. Survey of food preparation and common cooking practices in metropolitan Manila, Ilocos Mountain Province, and Cagayan Valley - Batanes region. PJN 18: 184-203.

4910.   Lingenfelter, Sherwood G. Liminality, eating classes and the ritual process in Yap. Paper presented at the 75th Annual Meeting of the American Anthropological Association. 17 to 21 November, 1976. Washington, D.C.

This paper describes the dynamic communal-ritual context of the initiation to higher levels of eating ranks in the total pattern of structure and communities in the traditional social life of Yap. The paper analyzes the ritual process to discern the importance of the ranks in the total pattern of structure and communities. Ritual is shown to be of major significance in creating both local and regional solidarity, with individuals, and society itself as a unit, passing through transition and structural re-newal in its annual ritual. The paper concludes with some suggestions regarding the consequences of the collapse of ritual that functions to renew both structure and communities in a social system.

4911.   Linne, Carol von. 1965. Om chokhladdrychken. [On chocolate drinking.] Fabel's Linneserie. Stockholm: Fabel.

4912.   Linocier, Geoffroy. 1584. Histoire des plantes, traduite du Latin en francois a laquelle sont adjoustees celles des simples aromatiques, animaux a quatre pieds, oiseaux, poissions, serpens...ensemble les distillations. [History of plants, translated from Latin to French to which are added aromatic medicinal plants, four legged animals, birds, fish, serpents...distillations included.] Paris: C. Mace.

4913.   Linsenmeyer, Helen Walker. 1972[?]. From fingers to finger bowls. A sprightly history of California cooking. Edited by Richard F. Pourade. San Diego: Union Tribune Publishing Co.

4914.   Linstedt, Helgo. 1938. Food consumption habits in the Far East. IRA 29: 399E-413E.

4915.   Listedt, Helgo. 1939. Food consumption habits in China. IRA 30: 363E-413E.

4916.   Linstedt, Helgo. 1945. Rural dietaries in Europe. IRA 36: 77E-109E.

4917. Linstedt, Helgo. 1946. Rural dietaries in the Middle East. IRA 37: 57E-78E.

4918. Linton, Ralph. 1924. The signficance of certain traits in North American maize culture. AA 26: 345-349.

4919. Linton, Ralph. 1927. Rice, a Malagasy tradition. AA 29: 654-660.

Legends concerning the origin of rice; its cultivation; preparation; rice post-harvest thanksgiving cermoney and its associated foods.

4920. Liong, L.S. 1953. Termite trapping. [In Dutch.] Ent B 14: 220-222.

4921. Lipp, Frank. Ethnobotany of the Chinantec Indians, Oaxaca, Mexico. Master's thesis. Anthropology. Hunter College of the City of New York. 1968.

4922. Lippe-Stokes, Susan. 1973. Eskimo story-knife tales: reflection of change in food habits. EFN 2: 27-34.

Story-knife tales are generally told by girls from early childhood (about five years of age) throught adolescence. The stories are told to groups. Story tellers accompany their tales with illustrations made in the mud. In aboriginal times, the illustrations were made with an elaborately-carved ivory "story-knife". In modern times, a metal butter-knife or ice-cream stick is used. Typical traditional tales are rich in ethnographic details concerning social structure and subsistence activities. In 1968, eighty-three story-knife tales were collected in seven Kuskokwim River villages in the Kuskokwim River Delta regions of southwestern coastal lowland Alaska. The Kuskokwim traditional food quest pattern is describes and the stories concerning food procurement are evaluated, and separated into three categories: traditional (reflecting no modern influences); transitional (reflecting some modern influences),and modern. The implications of the changes in dietary patterns for the nutritional status of the Kuskokwim are considered. Suggestions are made for use of children's stories or other indigenous narratives as an aid for collecting information on dietary patterns in areas where communication with inhabitants is difficult.

4923. Lippold, Lois K. Aboriginal animal resource utilization in Woodland Wisconsin. Ph.D. dissertation. Anthropology. University of Wisconsin, Madison. 1971.

4924. Lipscomb, M. 1966. Early days of hospital dietetics. JADA 49: 103-109.

4925. Lipton, Michael, ed. & Longhurst, Richard, rapporteur. 1975. Food problems in South Asia, 1975-1990. IDSUS-C NO. 78.

4926. Lira, Jorge A. 1948. Elaboracion de la chicha amarilla. [Preparation of yellow chicha.] INT-R 1: 115-117.

A maize beer. Description obtained from two women of Kaykay, Paucartambo, Peru, about two hundred kilometers northeast of Lima.

4927. Lissauer. 1896. Kuchenabfalhaufen von Rutzau am Putziger Wiek, Kreis Putzig, Westpreussen. [Kitchenmiddens of Rutzau on Putziger Bay, Putzig District, west Prussia.] NDA Part 2. P. 20.

4928. Litman, T.J.; Cooney, J.P.; & Stief, R. 1964. The views of Minnesota school children on food. JADA 45: 433-440.

4929. Little, Inc., Arthur D. 1958. Flavor research and food acceptance. New York: Rheinhold.

4930. Littman, Enno. 1910. Publications of the Princeton Expedition to Abyssinia. Vol. 2. Tales, customs, names, and dirges of the Tigre tribes. Leyden: E.J. Brill.

Foods and beverages: pp. 227-232; food taboos: pp. 236-240.

4931. Liu, J. Heng. Dietary habits of the Chinese In A brief review of food and nutrition in five countries. 1944. Pp. 18-22. United States Department of Agriculture. War Food Administration. Washington, D.C.: Government Printing Office.

A concise overview of Chinese food uses, and preparation techniques, with comments on nutritional deficiencies and food production.

4932. Liversidge, Joan Eileen Annie. 1957. Kitchen in Roman Britain. ANL 6: 83-85.

4933. Livet, Roger. 1969. Geographie de l'alimentation. [Geography of diet.] Paris: Les Editions Ouvrieres.

Begins with a discussion of calories from a physiological perspective, with examples of caloric requirements for various nations; discusses the nature of nutritional surveys, and compares fluctuations in caloric intake in various nations from 1948-1964. The relationship between income and caloric intake is observed. Similar discussion follows relating to protein, lipids, vitamins, carbohydrates, and calcium. Dietary balance is addressed, with definitions given for undernutrition and malnutrition. Part Three is devoted to a region by region analysis of world nutritional status, illustrated with carefully conceptualized graphs. Typical dietary patterns are described. A final section considers solutions to world nutrition problems and the influence of cultural patterns upon nutritional status.

4934. Livingstone, Daneil A. Interactions of food production and changing vegetation in Africa. Paper presented at 77th Annual Meeting of the American Anthropological Association. 17 November, 1978. Los Angeles, California.

> Reviews the state of research into the paly-
> nology of food crops in Africa. Concludes
> that certain identification of more than only
> a few plants (baobab tree, bottle gourd, and
> bambara ground nut) plants is currently not
> possible, and that data on the history of
> food production in Africa will come from
> archeology not palynology.

4935.   Llama, Juan Roca y R. 1932. Estudio del frijol como alimento. [Study of the bean as food.] Mexico City: Instituto Nacional de Biologia.

4936.   Llewellyn, Sian. 1972. The love spoon: a selection of recipes from Wales. Swanson, Wales: Celta International.

4938.   Lobera de Avila, Luis. 1556. Bancket der Hofe und Edelleut. Des gesunden lebens Regiment. Von eygenschafft, nutz und schedlichkeyt alles so zu Menschlicher speise, tranck, und gebrauch, in Keuchen, Keller und Apotecken, auch zu leibs mancherly von noten. [Banquets of courts and noblemen, rules for a healthy life. Of properties, benefits, and harmfulness of all things necessary for human consumption and for use in kitchen, cellar, and pharmacy, as well as for various bodily afflictions.] Franckfurt am Main: C. Egendtt.

4939.   Lobisch, W.F. 1894. Die Ernahrungsfrage in ihrer anthropologischen und ethnologischen Bedeutung. [The nutrition question in its anthropological and ethnological meaning.] AGWS-M 24: 108-111.

4940.   Lobotka, V. 1959. Susiarne a susenie ovocia v banovskom okrese. [Drying-kilns and the drying of fruit in the district of Banovce.] SN 7: 590-612. Banovce is located in southeastern Czechoslovakia, at 48.43 N., 18.15 E.

4941.   Lockhart, H.A. 1954. Food attitudes - a part of nutrtion education. NR 12: 161-162.

4942.   Lockhead, Marion Cleland. 1934. The Scots' household in the 18th Century. Moray Press, Edinburgh.

4943.   Lodewyckx, C. 1944. L'alimentation de l'indigene. [Native diet.] Aequatoria 8: 29-31.

4944.   Lodian, L. 1905. Some tea curiosities. Interesting facts concerning compressed tea, the Russian dry cup of tea, tea tablets, Chinese virgin tea, tea made exclusively from the flowers of the tea plant, and Japanese compressed tea here presented for the first time. TCTJ 9: 212-214.

4945.   Lodian, L. 1918. The fats of fighters. SA 118: 229.

> Various types of cooking fats used by na-
> tional armies: cocoanut butter, horse lard,
> goose grease, goat fat, pig lard, butter, oil,
> cheese, rice, ghee, white chocolate, cocoa
> butter.

4946.   Loeb, Edwin Meyer. Cannibalism. Master's thesis. Yale University. 1921.

4947.   Loeb, Edwin M. Cannibalism. In Encyclopedia of the social sciences. Edited by Edwin R. Seligman et al. 1930. Vol. 3. Pp. 172-173. New York: Macmillan.

4948.   Loeb, Edwin Meyer. 1943. Primitive intoxicants. QUSA 4: 387-398.

4949.   Loeb, Ellla-Marie. Flora and fauna of the Kaunyama Ambo Banut of Southwest Africa. Paper presented at 77th Annual Meeting of the American Anthropological Association. 14 to 18 November, 1978. Los Angeles, California.

4950.   Loeb, M.B. 1951. The social functions of food habits. JAN 4: 227-229.

4951.   Loew, Oscar. 1896. Ueber einige japanische Nahrungsmittel. [On certain Japanese foods.] DGNVOT-M 6: 352.

> Nomenclature of different food plants ana-
> lysis of edible yam Dioscorea japonica.

4952.   Loew, Oscar. 1906. Some unusual Japanese food products. [In German.] 11: 109-111.

> Use of young sprouts and flowers of various
> plants; fresh water algae [e.g. Nostoc phyl-
> loders], and several insects. Reference is
> made to some soy bean products, and to
> Japanese food customs.

4953.   Loewenthal, L.J.A. 1938. The effect of the addition of milk to the diet of school boys in Buganda. EAMJ 15: 34-45.

4954.   Lofgren, Alberto. 1895. Ensaio para uma synomia dos nomes populares das plantas indigenas do estado de Sao Paulo. [Preliminary glossary of popular native plant names in Sao Paulo State.] CGGSP-B No. 10.

> Food uses of plants indicated.

4955.   Logan, Michael H. 1072. Humoral folk medicine: a potential aid in controlling pellagra in Mexico. Ethnomedizin 1: 397-410.

> The adherence to humoral folk medicine
> may provide a mechanism for cultural inter-
> vention in the control of pellagra, through
> the utilization of certain foods for medicin-
> al purposes.

4956.   Logaras, G. Dietary survey of small-income families of Athens during the famine period 1941-1942. [In Greek.] Athens: Commission to the Academy of Athens. October, 1942.

4957.   Logaras, G. 1947. Some statistical, clinical, and experimental data on malnutriton in Greece. APed 36: 100-105.

4958.   Loir, A. 1906. The food of natives [In French.] RSci 5: 590-592.

Diet of native laborers in South Africa; native foods and food habits.

4959.   Lolli, Giorgio. 1960.   Social drinking.   Cleveland: World Publishing co.

4960.   Lolli, Giorgio. The cocktail hours: physiological, psychological, and social aspects.   In Alcohol and civilization.   Edited by Salvatore Pablo Lucia. 1963. Pp. 183-199. New York; San Francisco; Toronto, London: McGraw-Hill.

4961.   Lolli, Giorgio; Serriani, Emidio; Balboni; Claudia; & Mariano, Aldo. 1953.   Further observations on the use of wine and other alcoholic beverages by Italians and Americans of Italian extraction. QJSA 14: 395-405.

4962.   Lolli, Giorgio; Serriani, Emidio; Banissoni, Ferrucio; Golder, Grace; Mariani, Also; McCarthy, Raymond G., & Toner, Mary. 1952. The use of wine and other alcoholic beverages by a group of Italians and Americans of Italian extraction. QJSA 13: 27-48.

4963.   Lolli, Giorgio; Serianni, Emidio; Golder, Grace M., & Luzzato-Fegis, Pierpalo. 1959.   Alcohol in Italian culture: food and wine in relation to sobriety among Italians and Italian Americans. Glenco: Freepress.

Indicates that drinking is viewed as a form of eating, an attitude which may be partly responsible for the relative sobriety associated with alcohol intake in Italian culture.

4964.   Lombard, Lucinda Haynes. 1919. The purple water-avena Geum rivale. A Bot. 24: 129-131.

The root stocks of this plant were steeped, and an infusion sweetened and drunk with cream added, in late 18th Century Colonial North America.

4965.   Lomborg, Ebbe. 1963. A grave from Stubberup on Lolland: human sacrifice and cannibalism in the Bronze Age. Kuml 1953. Pp. 29-30.

Lolland is a large island off the southwestern coast of Denmark.

4966.   London, British Museum.   Department of Manuscripts. MS. 32, 248[2].   Mos mensae: rules for behaviour at table, in Latin hexameters.

4967.   London. Library of the Royal Empire Society.   Bibliography on nutrition in India [by D.H. Varley]. 1937.

4968.   London.   Public   Record   Office. J3440/460/1. Great Britain. Foreign Office. Egyptian and Ethiopian Department.   Correspondence. Note on native food supplies at Harrar [1938].

4969.   London.   Public   Record   Office. L/1788/1788/405 [file]. Great Britain. Foreign Office.   Librarian's Department.   Correspondence. Use of wood flour (flour dust) in bakeries: Danish inquiry. [1933].

4970.   London. Society for the Diffusion of Useful Knowledge. 1829. Description and history of vegetable substances used in the arts and in domestic economy. Timber trees: fruits. Library of Entertaining Knowledge.

4971.   London Times.   1936. Food in Britain: a special survey published by the Times. A supplement issued with the Times on all aspects of food in Britain. 21 January.

4972.   Long, A.L.   1913.   Egg delicacies of the Orient. Pp. 9: 494-496.

Describes methods for preparing various preserved eggs in China; and the Philippine balut: a boiled egg containing a partially developed duck embryo.

4973.   Longely, A.E.   1938.   Chromosomes of maize from North American Indians. JAR 56: 177-195.

A knowledge of the morphological structure of the chromosomes of Zea mays L. and closely-related wild Gramineae is thought to contribute to an understanding of the origin and distribution of this cereal. A collection was made of maize from thirty-three Native North American tribes of the United States. An analysis revealed a previously unknown form of the tenth chromosome. Correlations between chromosome characteristics and geographic source of maize seed are noted.

4974.   Longman, D.P. 1965. Working with Pueblo Indians in New Mexico. JADA 47: 470-473.

4975.   Longree, Karla. 1945.   Soya beans and peanuts.   Hampton, Virginia: Hampton Institute Press.

4976.   Lonn, Ella. 1933.   Salt as a factor in the Confederacy. New York: W. Neale.

4977.   Loo, C.C.   1968.   A collection of Far Eastern recipes using coconut. Food and Agriculture Organization of the United Nations.   World Health Organization. International Childrens' Education Fund-Protein Advisory Group of the United Nations meeting: 9 September to 13 September. Protein Advisory Group document 9/7. Appendix 1. Rome: Food and Agriculture Organization of the United Nations.

4978.   Loomis, H.M. 1914. Food products from the soybean. AFJ 9: 472-475.

Methods of preparing several Japanese foods including shoyu, tofu, oil, and miso.

4979.   Lopez, J. Gongora y & Lopez, N. Young. 1952. La alimentacion humana en Colombia. 2,3, [Human diet in Colombia. 2,3.] Ag Trop 8: 41-47; 25-36.

4980.   Lopez, Matas A. 1954.   Enlatado, curado y otros metodos de preservacion del pescado y elabor acion de subproducts. [Canning, curing and other methods of preserving fish and processing by-products.] Rome: Food and Agriculture Organization of the United Nations.

Part One covers history, principles, and processing of fish as food. Part Two considers meal and oils.

4981.   Lorand, A. Le regime alimentaire rationnel pour les pays tropicaux. [The rational diet for tropical countries.] In Congres International de Medicine Tropical et d'Hygiene. Cairo. December, 1928. Comptes rendus. 1929. Vol. 5. Pp. 387-390.

Recommends a predominantly vegetarian diet.

4982.   Lorenzo y Deal, J. 1937.   Frozen human milk. [In Spanish.] APU 8: 733-737.

4983.   Loret, Victor.   1887. La flore pharaonique d'apres les documents hieroglyphiques et les specimens de-couverts dans les tombes. [Pharaonic flora from hieroglyphic documents and specimens discovered in the tomb.] Paris: J.-B. Bailliere.

4984.   Loret, Victor. 1893. Recherches sur plusiers plantes, connues des anciens Egyptiens. [Researches on numerous plants known to the ancient Egyptians.] Paris: E. Bouillon.

4985.   Lorey, Eustach de & Sladen, Douglas. 1907. Queer things about Persia.   Philadelphia: J.B. Lippincott; London: Eveleigh Nash.

Persian meals, foods, and etiqueete: pp. 82-85.

4986.   Lorry. 1954.   Essai sur les alimens, pour servir de commentaire aux livres dietetiques d'Hippocrate. [An essay on foods, to serve as a commentary on the dietetic writing of Hippocrates.] Paris: chez Vincent.

This book is divided into three parts: a study of food in general; food in relation to the body; and food material in the different realms of nature.

4987.   Losonczi, E. 1958.   Social anthropology in health education with particular reference to nutrition. WIMJ 7: 206-210.

4988.   Louis-Sylvestre, J. 1976. Les mecanismes de selection alimentaire chez l'homme: preferences et aversions. [Mechanisms of food selection in man: preferences and aversions.] ANA 30: 331-340.

4989.   Lourie, Reginald S.; Layman, Emma M.; & Millican, Frances K. 1963. Why children eat things that are not food. Children 10: 143-146.

Pica in children represents a craving early in life which has many of the dynamic characteristics of the cravings which later in life form the basis for the common addictions.

4990.   Louthan, Bruce D. Anasazi occupation near Chippean ridge: site types, settlement patterns and subsistence southwest of the Abajo Mountains, San Juan County, Utah. Master's thesis. Anthropology. Provo, Utah: Brigham Young University. 1977.

4991.   Loveland, Franklin O. The significance of salt in the cosmology and mythology of the Rama Indians of Nicaragua. Paper presented at 70th Annual Meeting of the American Anthropological Association. 19 November, 1971. New York City.

Hypothecates salt as the substance which sustains life in Rama mythology and cosmology. A corollary of this hypothesis is that the fundamental structural marker in the Rama categorization of the world is the presence or absence of salt. A new dimension is added to Levi-Strauss' basic opposition between raw and cooked, that of salted and unsalted food.

4992.   Loveland, Franklin O. Rama cosmography, subsistence activities and culture contact. Paper presented at 74th Annual Meeting of the American Anthropological Association.   2 to 6 December, 1975. San Francisco, California.

4993.   Lovewell, Caroline Barnes Forbes; Whittemore, Francis Dean; & Lyon, Hannah Wright. 1908. The fireless cooker.   Directions for making and using fireless cookers, with recipes. Topeka: Home Publishing Co.

4994.   Low, Immanuel. 1934. Die Flora der Juden. [The flora of the Jews.] Vol. Four. Vienna: Verlag der Kohut-Foundation.

Plants in Jewish cookery: pp. 314-316.

4995.   Lowenberg, Miriam E. 1948. Food preferences of young children. JADA 24: 430.

4996.   Lowenberg, Miriam E. 1970. Socio-cultural basis of food habits. FTech 24 (7): 27-30.

Explores the relationship between food choices and cultural patterns. Theories of motivation, and perception are considered, particularly in regard to changing food practices.

4997.   Lowie, Robert H. Chapter Seven. Subsistence. In General anthropology.   Edited by Franz Boas. 1938. New York: D.C. Heath.

Includes general categories of subsistence; appraisal of the hunting stage; cultivation; domesticated animals; pastoral nomadism; economic determinism of culture.

4998.   Lowndes, Henry.   1865.   Remarks on the diet suitable after childbirth. BMJ 2: 600-604.

Review of historical sources; notes on author's own practices.

4999.   Lu, T.H.   1934.   Nutrition of Chinese in Manchuria; actual food consumption and average diet. MIZ 20: 73-74.

5000. Lu, T.H. 1934. Nutrition of Chinese in Manchuria; Chinese diet in a region of Mukden. MIZ 20: 22-23.

5001. Lu, Yu. 1974. The classic of tea. Translated by Francis Ross Carpenter. Boston: Little, Brown & Co.

   Cha-no-yu, the Japanese tea ceremony.

5002. Lucas, A. Castillo de. 1939. Refranerillo de una comida espanola. [Proverbs of a Spanish-meal.] SME 2: 544-547.

   Spanish proverbs relating to foods, eating, and alcoholic beverages.

5003. Lucas, A. Castillo de. 1956. Ideas sobre la nutricion en la folkmedicina. [Ideas about nutrition in folk medicine.] REEADN 5: 748-762.

5004. Lucas, Anthony T. 1959. Nettles and charlock as famine food. CSB-J 1: 137-146.

5005. Lucas, Anthony T. 1960. Irish food before the potato. Gwerin 3: 8-43.

5006. Lucas, Anthony T. Ethnological research on food in Ireland. Paper presented at First International Symposium on Ethnological Food Research. 21 to 25 August, 1970. Lund: Folklivsarkivet, University of Lund.

5007. Lucas, Jannette May. 1945. Indian harvest; wild food plants of America. Philadelphia, New York: J.B. Lippincott Co.

5008. Lucia, Salvatore Pablo. The antiquity of alcohol in diet and medicine. In Alcohol and civilization. Edited by Salvatore Pablo Lucia. 1963. Pp. 151-166. New York, San Francisco, Toronto, London: McGraw-Hill.

5009. Lucia, Salvatore Pablo. Chapter Three. Wine as food. In Wine as food and medicine. New York: The Blakiston Co.

5010. Luckwill, Leonard C. 1943. The evolution of the cultivated tomato. RHS 68: 19-25. Lycopersicum sp. (Solanaceae).

   Historical data trace the tomato from its native habitat in the eastern Andean region. Includes accounts of its early description in Europe, and notes the primitive form is still cultivated near La Paz, in Bolivia.

5011. Luczak, C. 1953. Przemsky spozywyczy miasta Poznanie w 18 wieka. Naklad Poznanskiego Towar. [Dietary of the city of Poznan in the Eighteenth Century. Expenditures for commodities.] Poznan: Przyjaciol Nauk.

5012. Ludvikova, Miroslava Lidova. 1963. Strawa v jizni casti Drahanske vysocny. [Food in the southern part of the Drahanske plateau.] CMM-AM 48: 161-198.

   Yugolslavia.

5013. Luerssen, Artur, & Kuhn, M. 1908. Yoghurt, die bulgarische Sauermilch. [Yoghurt, the Bulgarian sour milk.] ZBPIH 20: 234-248.

5014. Lugger, Otto. 1898. The Orthoptera of Minnesota. Minn-AES-AR for the year 1897. Pp. 91-375.

   Undocumented reference to use of salted cockroaches as human food: p. 126.

5015. Lumholtz, Karl Sofus. 1902. Unknown Mexico; a record of five year's exploration among the tribes of the Western Sierra Madre; in the tierra caliente of Tepic and Jalisco; and among the Trascos of Michoacan. New York: Charles Scribner's Sons.

   Food: pp. 6, 15, 35-40; mescal hearts: p. 169; concept of principal deity a cook of mescal: pp. 169, 181; distillation: pp. 182-186; maize wrapped around arrows and baked: pp. 205, 206; tortillas: P. 249; maize beer: P. 271; maize feast: pp. 279-281; meal in an inn at Ahualulco: P. 316; ice cream: P. 322; atole as a remedy for itching due to poisoning: P. 358; maize being ground for prisoners in Queretaro (illustration): P. 446.

5016. Lumholtz, Karl Sofus. 1912. New trails in Mexico. An account of one year's exploration in northwestern Sonora and southwestern Arizona. 1909-1910. New York: C. Scribner's Sons.

   Mention of harvest and uses of Saguaro [Carnegeia gigantea] cactus fruit among Native Americans in southern Arizona.

5017. Lumholtz, Carl Sofus. 1919. A great native festival in central Borneo. SMag 66: 449-459.

5018. Luna, Seminario A. 1956. Contribucion al estudio bromatologico de las llamadas "leches vinagres" que se consumen en Lima. [Contribution to the chemical study of what are called sour milks which are consumed in Lima.] UNMSML-FFB-A 7: 181.

5019. Lunan, John. 1814. Hortus Jamaicensis; or, a botanical decription (according to the Linnean system) and an account of the virtues &c. of its indigenous plants hitherto known, as also of the most useful exotics. Compiled from the best authorities, and alphabetically arranged. Jamaica: Printed at the office of the St. Jago de la Vega Gazette.

5020. Lundell, Cyrus Longsworth. 1938. Plants probably utilized by the Old Empire Maya of Peten and adjacent lowlands. MASAL-P 24: 37-56.

5021. Lunsford, Lorine. A nutrition education project in the Gilmer public schools. Master's thesis. Denton: Texas State College for Women. 1944.

5022. Luomala, Katharine. 1938. Chapter Eight. Food. In Navaho life of yesterday and today. Western Museum Laboratories. National Park Service. Berkeley, California: United States Department of the Interior.

5023. Luomala, Katherine. 1953. Ethnobotany of the Gilbert Islands. BPBM-B No. 213.

5024. Luomala, Katherine. 1965. Humourous narratives about individual resistance to food distribution customs in Tabiteuea Gilbert Islands. JAF 78: 28-45.

5025. Lurie, Nancy Oestereich. 1971. The worlds' oldest on-going protest demonstration: North American Indian drinking patterns. PHS 40: 311-322.

5026. Lussana, F. & Frua, Carlo. 1856. Memoria su la pellagra. [Memorial on pellagra.] Milan: Bernardoni

5027. Lussier, Betty. 1957. Amid my alien corn. Philadelphia, New York: J.B. Lippincott.

Farming in the Lukus Valley, Spanish Morocco.

5028. Lutz, Henry Frederick. 1922. Viticulture and brewing in the ancient Orient. Leipzig: J.C. Hinrichs for G.E. Stechert & Co., New York.

5029. Luyken, R. 1961. Vorderingen op het gebied van voedingsonderzoek in Nieuw Guinea. [Progess in the area of nutrition surveys in New Guinea.] NGS 5: 93-103.

Review of surveys undertaken since 1953.

5030. Luyken, R.; Luyken-Koning, F.W.M.; & Van Dam-Bakker, A.I.W. 1959. Nutrition survey on Windward Islands [Netherland Antilles]. 1. The daily diet and the results of chemical blood examinations. TGM 11: 49-56.

Includes data on mean food inatake of two hundred seventy-nine families [Black, and European], rural and urban on the Islands of St. Maarten, Saba, and St. Eustatius.

5031. Luzzato-Fegis, Pierpalo & Lolli, Giorgio. 1957. The use of milk and wine in Italy. QJSA 18: 35-381.

This paper contains data on attitudes towards food; commensalism; dietary quality, and quantity and appropriate use of both beverages, in terms of age, and meals.

5032. Lyman, A.R. 1930. Pahute biscuits. UHQ 3: 118-120.

5033. Lynn, C.W. 1937. Agriculture in north Mamprusi. GC-DA-B No. 34.

Diet; famine foods: pp. 10,11.

5034. Lyon, Arthur Bates. 1933. History of infant feeding. AJDC 46: 359-374.

5035. Lyon, Ernest. 1904. Esculent tubers and vegetables in Liberia. USDCL-MCR 74: 407.

5036. Ma, Wen-chao; Ni, Yin-yuan; & Kao, Hsieh-ching. A comfortable and spontaneous cure of the opium habit by means of a lecithin diet. Far Eastern Association of Tropical Medicine. Ninth Congress. Nanking, October 2-8, 1934. Transactions. 1935. Vol. 2. pp. 381-387.

Administration of twenty to thirty grams of soy bean lecithin orally three times daily after meals.

5037. Maack, R. 1962. Unknown Indians in western Parana. [In German.] Kosmos 58: 385-394.

5038. Maas, W. 1951. La vie quotidienne d'un paysan polonais de nos jours. [Daily life of a modern Polish farmer.] RPP 6: 172-185.

5039. Mabson, Richard Rous. 1881. Forty-five year's history of the tea trade. compiled from...Sillar & Company's statistics. London: Sillar & Co.

5040. Macabies, Jean. 1951. Valeur alimentaire des vins de 8 a 12°. [Nutritional value of wines from 8% to 12%.] Paris: Comite National de Propagande en Faveur du Vin.

5041. MacAdam, W.E. 1882. On the results of chemical investigation into the composition of the 'bog butter', and of 'adipocere' and the 'mineral resins'; with a notice of a cask of bog butter found in Glen Gell, Morvern, Argyllshire, and now in the Museum. SAS-P 4: 204-223.

5042. Macaranas, Natividad M. A survey of the methods of preparation of the less generally known edible plants of the Philippines. Master's thesis. Home Economics. Diliman, Quezon City: University of the Philippines. 1952.

Lists 245 plants in six categories: 1. vegetable and salad; 2. flavoring and souring meat and fish; 3. edible fruits eaten fresh or as sweets; 4. nuts and seeds eaten raw, roated, boiled, or as deserts; 5. used in deserts, or in meant or fish dishes; 6. edible grains, or cereals used as beverages.

5043. Macauley, Thurston. 1931. The festive board. A literary feast. London: Methuen & Co.

Selections in prose and verse on the arts of cooking and dining.

5044. MacBride, Gail. 1941. Eating in the Everglade country. A Cook 45: 623-626.

5044. McCarthy, F. Desmond. 1975. Nutrition, food, and prices in Pakistan. M.I.T. International Nutrition Planning Program Paper. No. 4. Cambridge, Massachusetts: Massachusetts Institute of Technology. June.

Analyzes some of the issues involved in determining nutritional status. The empirical work related to West Pakistan and is largely based on the household surveys conducted by the government of that country. [After Foster.] 1978. p. 49.

5045. Mac Caughey, Vaughan. 1916. The seaweeds of Hawaii. AJB 3: 474-479.

5046.   Mac Caughey, Vaughan. 1917. Food plants of the ancient Hawaiian. SM 4: 75-80.

5047.   Mac Caughey, Vaughan. 1918. The native bananas of the Hawaiian Islands. PWorld 21: 1-12.

Reviews the role of bananas in native Hawaiian diet; methods of propagation, food uses; the kapu on bananas as women's food. The characteristics and Hawaiian names of twenty-two varieties are also given.

5048.   Mac Caughey, Vaughan & Emerson, Joseph S. 1913-1914. The kalo in Hawaii. HFA 10: 186-193 et se.; 11: 17-23 et seq.

Taro.

5049.   Mac Cauley, Clay. 1887. The Seminole Indians of Florida. SI-BAE-AR for the year 1883-1884.

Food: pp. 504, 505; manner of eating (etiquette, and time): pp. 505, 506.

5050.   Macchiavello, A. & Cifuentes, O. 1939. Rural nutrition in Choapa Valley. [In Spanish.] RCHMP 2: 265-323.

Chile.

5051.   Mac Crone, I.D. 1937. A note on "tsamma" and its use among the Bushmen. BStud 11: 251-252.

Citrullus vulgaris.

5052.   Mac Culloch, J.A. Cannibalism. In Encyclopedia of religion and ethics. Edited by James Hastings. 1951. Vol. 3. Pp 194-209. New York: Charles Scribner's Sons.

5053.   Mac Donald, James. 1878. Food from the far west; or, American agriculture with special reference to the beef production. London: William p. Nimmo.

5054.   MacDonald, Shoemaker. 1940. Pioneer bakers of Paradise. PPac 52: 11-12.

Hawaii.

5055.   MacDougald, Jr., Duncan. Aphrodisiacs and anaphrodisiacs. In The encyclopedia of sexual behavior. Edited by Albert Ellis and Albert Abarbanell. 1964. pp. 145-153. New York: Hawthorn Books.

Rold of food in the history of aphrodisiacs: pp. 146-149.

5056.   MacDougall, Alan Ross, ed. 1942. And the Greeks, a book of Hellenic recipes and culinary lore. New York: Near East Foundation.

5057.   MacDougall, Alice Foot. 1928. Eating aesthetically. Forum 394-397.

Restaurant decor and atmosphere.

5058.   Mace, C. 1969. Food habits and nutritional problems in Indonesia. A synopsis from documents available at the Food and Agriculture Organization of the United Nations Headquarters. Rome: Food and Agriculture Organiztion. July.

5059.   MacFarlane, A.D.J. Population and economy in central Nepal: a study of the Gurungs. Ph.D. dissertation. University of London. 1972.

Includes a food consumption component. Author observes that population pressure is causing a change in diet away from animal protein sources towards cereal-derived carbohydrates. Includes some data on seasonal food availability. [After Schofield. 1975: 196.]

5060.   MacFarlane, Eileen W. Erlanson. 1937. Rates of growth of non-vegetarian and vegetarian children of Trivandrum, Travancore. Cur Sci 6: 149-151.

Kerala State, southwestern India.

5061.   MacFarlane, Janet R. 1954. Recipes: New York pastry. NYFQ 10: 218-225.

Twenty recipes.

5062.   MacFarlane, Janet R. 1955. Early and late New York state recipes: a miscellany. NYFQ 11: 305-309.

Twelve recipes from the 18th to 20th Centuries.

5063.   MacFarlane, Janet R. 1955. Recipes: nineteenth century bread recipes. NYFQ 11: 69-72.

Fourteen recipes for biscuits, French bread, rolls, buns, wafers, cake, muffins, rice and corn meal bread, from New York, since 1795.

5064.   Machado, Deirdre Meintel. Religious feasts in Cabo Verde: an example of emigrant traditionalism. Paper presented at 77th Annual Meeting of the American Anthropological Association. 14 to 18 November, 1978. Los Angeles, California.

5065.   MacKay, Alistair I. 1950. Farming and gardening in the Bible. Emmaus, Pennsylvania: Rodale Press. Reprint. New York: Pyramid Books. 1970.

5066.   MacKay, Ian F.S.; Stafford, Doreen; Wilson, Kathleen; & Fox, Helen. 1958. Dietary survey of Jamaican children. JADA 34: 603-610.

Includes food composition table; descriptions of local foods; cooking methods; preservation techniques; and typical dietaries.

5067.   MacKay, Robert. 1961. An anthology of the potato. Dublin: Hodges, Figgis.

5068.   MacKenzie, Margaret. Self-esteem and self-hatred: cultural epidemiology of Samoan and American obesity. Paper presented at 75th Annual Meeting of the American Anthropological Association. 17 to 21 November, 1976. Washington, D.C.

> In the United States, substantial obesity is a manifestation of stress, a disease of desperation, a symbol of powerlessness. In rural Western Samoa, instead of being defined as a disease, obesity is likely to be seen as a natural accompaniment of aging, a symbol of dignity, wisdom, and honor. Because Samoans almost certainly neither perceive nor use obesity as an expression of stress - the manifestations of which take other forms - the most severe pain obese people in the United States feel they suffer is not likely to be found associated with obesity in Samoa. Data derive from research in Berkeley, California, and Summer 1976 research in Samoa.

5069. Mackenzie, Margaret. Gathering anthropological data about food. Paper presented at 76th Annual Meeting of the American Anthropological Association. 29 November to 3 December, 1977. Houston, Texas.

> Provides examples which indicate how anthropological techniques may be applied to nutrition research to improve interpretation of the sociocultural contexts of food in particular societies.

5070. Mackie, W.W. 1943. Origin, dispersal and variability of the lima bean, Phaseolus lunatus. Hilgardia 15: 1-29.

5071. MacKinnon, C. Frances. 1955. Changing food habits - the dietitian's dilemma. JADA 31: 566-569.

5072. MacLachlan, E.S. The diet pattern of the South. Master's thesis. Unversity of North Carolina. 1933.

5073. MacLachlan, Morgan D. Shrimping as a professional sport. Paper presented at 77th Annual Meeting of the American Anthropological Association. 14 to 18 November, 1978. Los Angeles, California.

5074. MacLeod, William C. 1933. Mortuary and sacrificial anthropology on the Northwest Coast of North America and its cultural-historical sources. SAmP-J 25: 335-366.

5075. MacMechen, E.C. 1918. Wild game as a war weapon. A neglected means of increasing and conserving our meat. SA 118: 88-89.

> Cost of maintaining elk, buffalo, and other game animals.

5076. Macmillan, Donald Baxter. 1918. Food supply of the Smith Sound Eskimos. AMJ 18: 161-176.

> Animal foods; hunting and egg gathering methods; food preparation.

5077. Macmillan, H.F. 1908. Breadfruit of the tropics. Trop Ag 31: 428-429.

> Artocarpus sp.

5078. MacMillan, H.F. 1908. Select edible Garcinia fruits. Trop Ag 31: 230-231.

> Magosteen.

5079. MacNeish, Richard S. 1954. The development of civilization in Meso-America, Tamaulipas, Mexico. APS-Y for 1954. pp. 323-326.

5080. MacNeish, Richard S. 1955. Ancient maize and Mexico. Archaeology 8: 108-115.

5081. MacNeish, Richard. Chapter Twelve. The food-gathering and incipient agriculture stage of prehistoric Middle America. In Natural environment and early cultures. Edited by Robert C. West. In Handbook of Middle American Indians. Edited by Robert C. Wauchope. 1964. Vol. 1. pp. 413-426. Austin: University of Texas Press.

5082. MacNeish, Richard S. A summary of the subsistence. In The prehistory of the Tehuacan Valley. Vol. 1. Edited by D.S. Byers. 1967. Austin: University of Texas Press.

5083. MacNeish, Richard S. & Nelken, A. 1961. Le Mexique et les debuts de l'agriculture au nouveau monde. [Mexico and the appearances of agriculture in the New World.] Anthropologie 65: 349-353.

5084. MacNicol, Mary. 1967. Flower cookery. The art of cooking with flowers. New York: Fleet Press Corp. Reprint. New York: Collier Books. 1972.

5085. MacPherson, A. 1964. Scotch whisky. SGM 80: 99-106.

5086. MacPherson, H.A. 1897. A history of fowling. Edinburgh: O. Douglas.

5087. Macrae, D.M. The Bechuanaland Protectorate, its people and prevalent diseases, with a special consideration of the effect of tropical residence and food in relation to health and disease. M.D. thesis. Glasgow University. 1920.

5088. MacVikar, Neil. 1946. The people's food. Recent discoveries and their application in South Africa. Pamphlet No. 9. Johannesburg: South African Institute of Race Relations.

> Held by Missionary Research Library, New York. Pamphlet Af. - S.

5089. Macy, Icie Gertrude., et al. 1951. Nutrition fronts in public health. New York: Vitamin Foundation.

5090. Madariaga, B. 1966. El regimen alimenticio del hombre prehistorico. [The dietary regime of prehistoric man.] SEOrto-A 12: 83-86.

5091. Maddox, George L.; Back, Kurt W.; & Leiderman, Veronica R. 1968. Overweight as social deviance and disability. JHSB 9: 287-298.

5092. Madison, William [May-Z huc-Ke-Ge-Shig 1940] Man-no-min (wild rice), Ojibway's native food recipes. Minneapolis, Minnesota: privately printed.

5093. Madsen, William. 1955. Hot and cold in the universe of San Francisco Tecospa, Valley of Mexico. JAFS 68: 123-139.

    Food classification: pp. 126, 127.

5094. Madueno, Augusto p. 1942. La realidad indigena - ensayos y apuntes. [Native life - essays and notes.] WP 2: 56.

    Folk drinks of the Peruvian Andes.

5095. Mafeking. Botswana National Archives. V4/3. A note summarizing the present position of nutrition at African schools in the Bechuanaland Protectorate [By H.J.E. Dumbrell.] no date.

5096. Mafeking. Botswana National Archives. S295/8. Malnutrition amongst the children of the Bakwena tribe [by H.W. Dyke]. Mafeking. 23 September 1932.

5097. Mafeking. Botswana National Archives. SA 28/3. Investigation into malnutrition among the native children of the Ngwato Reserve. [By A. Austin Morgan] 30 October 1935.

5098. Mafeking. Botswana National Archives. S428/5/2. The anti-scorbutic properties of bojalwa [kaffir beer] [by Bernard T. Squires.] 16 November, 1938.

5099. Mafeking. Botswana National Archives. S 428/5/2. Method of manufacture of bojalwa [by Bernard T. Squires.] 16 November, 1938. Kaffir beer.

5100. Mafeking. Botswana National Archives. SM87. Report upon malnutrition in two areas of the northeastern Protectorate. [by Bernard T. Squires.] 1939.

5101. Mafeking. Botswana. National Archives. S429/1 or V4/3. Notes on native diet, dietary deficiency, and its results in the Bechuanaland Protectorate. Colonial Empire Nutrition Report. Paragraphs 1-21 [by J.W. Stirling & Bernard T. Squires]. 6 March, 1940.

5102. Mafeking. Botswana National Archives. V4/3. The present practice in regard to the consumption of animal protein in the Bechuanaland Protectorate. 12 March 1940 [BY J.H.N. Hobday.]

5103. Mafeking. Botswana. National Archives. S42 9/1. Report of the Economic Advisory Council Committee on Nutrition in the Colonial Empire; conference at Mafeking. 14 March 1940.

5104. Mafeking. Botswana National Archives. S. 428/5/3. Interim report on nutrition in the Bechuanaland Protectorate. 14 October 1940.

5105. Mafeking. Botswana National Archives. S429/6. Report on visit to Chobe area and Caprivi Strip in connection with assessment of nutritional status of African children [by Bernard T. Squires.] 1 February, 1945.

5106. Mafeking. Botswana National Archives. S500/19. Bantu dietary. Report. [Government of the Bechuanaland Protectorate.] 11 April 1950.

5107. Mafeking. Botswana National Archives. S 428/5/2 or S 428/5/3. Report upon investigations into malnutrition [by Bernard T. Squires.] 7 February 1939.

5108. Magee, H.E. 1959. Nutrition and public health. London, New York, Toronto: Pitman Medical Publishers.

5109. Magelby, Richard; Niehaus, Robert; & Rowland, Sandra. 1975. Poverty and malnutrition in developing countries and regions. Prepared by United States Department of Agriculture, Economic Research Service, Foreign Department Division for United States Department of State, Agency for International Development, Office of Agriculture, June.

    The objective of this document is to develop and maintain a data and analysis system for rural development, planning, programming, and evaluation with particular emphasis on food production, nutrition, employment, and income distribution problems. [After Foster. 1978. p. 53.]

5110. Mager, J.; Razin, A.; & Hershko, A. Favism. In Toxic constituents of plant foodstuffs. Edited by Irvin E. Liener. 1969. pp. 293-318. New York, London: Academic Press.

    Favism refers to an acute hemolytic anemia following ingestion of broad beans (fava, haba) or inhalation of pollen of the Vicia faba plant. The area of greatest prevalence of reaction to V. faba is in the insular and littoral regions of the Mediterranean (Balearic Islands Greece, Israel, southern provinces of Italy, Sardinia, Sicily, Spain, Syria, and Turkey.)

5111. Maget, Marcel. 1948. Le pain bouilli a villar-d Arene, Hautes-Alpes. [The boiled bread of Villar-d Arene, Hautes-Alpes.] ATP 45: 1-39.

    France. Detailed description of preparation technique.

5112. Maggiolo, Marcio Veloz. 1971-1972. Sobre un posible caso de geofagia en las Antilla precolombinas. [On a possible case of geophagy in the pre-Columbian Antilles.] RDAA 2: 128-146.

5113. Magistocchi, G. 1940. Vino como alimento. [Wine as food.] BA 8:44.

5114. Magnen, J. Le., ed. 1962. Vocabulaire tecnique des characteres organoleptiques et de la degustation des produits alimentaires. [Technical glossary of terms relating to the organoleptic characteristics and the mastication of food products.] Paris: Centre Nationale de la Recherche Scientifique.

5115.   Magness, III, T.H. The conch: an expandable folk food of the Bahamas. Master's thesis. Geography. University of Wisconsin at Madison. 1969.

5116.   Mahadevan, Indira. 1961. Belief systems in food of the Telugu speaking people of the Telangana region. IJSW 21: 387-396.

    Andhra Pradesh State, India.

5117.   Mahalandbis, p.C. 1943. An inquiry into the prevalence of drinking tea among middle-class Indian families in Calcutta. Sankhya 6: 283-312.

5118.   Mahapatra, L.K. 1955. Food quest among the Pauri Bhuiyan. E Anth 9: 48-52.

    Social change in North Orissa, among a group of shifting cultivators.

5119.   Maheshwari, p. & Singh, Umrao. 1965. Dictionary of economic plants in India. New Delhi: Indian Council of Agricultural Research.

5120.   Maiden, Joseph Henry. Human foods and food-ajuncts. Paper read at the Linnean Society of New South Wales. 30 May, 1888.

    Australian Aborigines.

5121.   Maiden, Joseph Henry. 1889. Australian indigenous plants providing human foods and food adjuncts. LSNSW-P 3 [series 2, Part 1]: 481-556.

5122.   Maiden, Joseph Henry. 1889. The useful native plants of Australia, [including Tasmania]. London: Kegan Paul, Trench, Trubner co.

    Human food and food adjuncts: pp. 1-69.

5123.   Maiden, Joseph Henry. 1898. Some plant-foods of the Aborigenes. An article written for New South Wales children. AGNSW 9: 349-354.

5124.   Maiden, Joseph Henry. 1899. Native food plants. AGNSW 10: 117-130; 279-290; 618-629; 730-740.

5125.   Maiden, Joseph Henry. 1901. Some Australian food adjuncts. AGNSW 12: 1518-1532.

    Water sources from plants; infused or decocted beverages; lerp and manna (sources of natural sweeteners); honey flowers; spices.

5126.   Maier, O.F.A. de. 1956. La coca, alimento y vicio del aborigen americano. [Coca: food and vice of the American aborigene. REd : 752-757.

5127.   Maierbrugger, Mathias. 1964. Besonderheiten der Karntner Bauernkost. [Characteristics of Carinthian peasant food.] KL No. 1. pp. 8-9.

5128.   Maillard, J. 1954. L'evolution de l'alimentation de la population autochtone en Indochine.

[Evolution of the diet of the indigenous population of Indochina.] MCMonde 10: 3290-3294.

5129.   Mainello, Emilia D. A study of the effect of dietary changes on a selected group of school children. Master's thesis. Syracuse University. 1947.

5130.   Major, Roasabel. A study of the food habits of sixty Negro adults of Turner Station, Maryland. Master's thesis. Washington, D.C.: Howard University. 1948.

5131.   Majumdar, Dhirendra Nath. 1931. The economic life of the Hos. MIndia 11: 57.

    Kolhan, Bihar State, India.

5132.   Majumdar, Dhirendra Nath. 1931. Economic life of the Korwas. ISCA-P 18: 415.

    India.

5133.   Majumdar, Dhirendra Nath. 1936. Food and feeding among the Austric tribes. ISCA-P 23: 395.

5134.   Majumdar, Dhirendra Nath. 1950. The affairs of a tribe. Uttar Pradesh: Ethnographic and Folk Culture Society.

    The Ho of Kol. Insects as food: pp. 2-3; general description of diet, meal times: pp. 73-82.

5135.   Majumdar, S.K. 1972. Vegetarianism: fad, faith, or fact? AS 60: 175-179.

5136.   Malbrant, p. 1941. Le probleme de l'alimentation des indigenes en Afrique Equatoriale Francaises. [Dietary problems of natives in French Equatorial Africa.] SRC-B No. 28. pp. 99-132.

5137.   Malcolm, Sheila. 1950. Preliminary report on research conducted in New Ireland, Territory of Papua and New Guinea. South Pacific Commission. Research Council. Projects H.2-H.5. Nutrition and alimentation. Report No. 1.

5138.   Malcolm, Sheila. 1951. Preliminary report on research conducted in Trobriand Islands, Papua. South Pacific Commission. Research Council. Projects H.2-H.5. Nutrition and alimentation. Report No. 4. [Noumea: South Pacific Commission.]

    Children's diets.

5139.   Malcolm, Sheila. 1951. Preliminary report on research conducted in urban areas of Rabaul, New Britain. South Pacific Commission. Research Council. Projects H.2.-H.5. Nutrition and alimentation. Report No. 3. [Noumea: South Pacific Commission.]

5140.   Malcolm, Sheila. 1951. Rapport preliminaire sur les recherches effectuees en Nouvelle-Bretagne. [Preliminary report on research done in New Britain.] Commission du Pacifique Sud. Projects H.2.-H.5. La nutrition et l' alimentation. Rapport No. 2. [Noumea]: Commission Pacifique Sud.

5141.   Malcolm, Sheila   1954. L'alimentation et la nutrition dans le samoa americaine. [Diet and nutrition in American Samoa.] SPC-TP No. 63.

5142.   Malcolm, Sheila H. 1954. Diet and nutrition in Americans Samoa. SPC-TP No. 63.

5143.   Malcolm, Sheila. 1955. Diet and nutrition in the Trust Territory of the Pacific Islands. SPC-TP No. 83.

5144.   Malcolm, Sheila H. A study of food intake in two areas of New Guinea (with special emphasis on breast feeding and diets of mothers and children). Food and Agriculture Organization of the United Nations. Report No. 885. Mimeographed. FAO 58/6/4644. Rome: Food and Agriculture Organization of the United Nations. 1958.

5145.   Malcolm, Sheila & Massal, Emile. 1955. Etudes sur las nutrition et l'alimentation dans les establissements francaises de l'Oceanie. [Studies on the nutrition and diet of the French Settlement of Oceania.] SPC-TP No. 85.

5146.   Maldonado, Koerdell M. 1947. Estudios etnobiologicos 3. Contribuciones mexicanas al concocimiento de la etnobiologia del maiz y de la historia de la agricultura en Mexico. [Ethnobological studies. 3. Mexican contributions to the knowledge of the ethnobiology of maize and of the history of agriculture in Mexico.] INAH-A 2: 137-141.

5147.   Maletto, S.; Mussa, p.p.; & Luna, F.S. 1973. Banana meal as food and as animal feed. [In Italian.] FMVT-A 20: 67-85.

    Composition and digestability of various types of whole banana meal, banana pulp meal, and banana peel meal.

5148.   Malherbe, Marguerite. 1941. A study of some Indian family diets in Durban. SAJE 9: 22-44.

5149.   Malinovski, T. 1959. O ranosredovjecnim Slavenskim posudama za przenje zita. (Ealry medieval slav vessels for grain roasting.) E Preg 1: 51-58.

5150.   Malinowski, Bronislaw. 1915. The natives of Mailu: preliminary results of the Robert Mond research work in British New Guinea. RSSA-TP 39: 494-706.

    Food preparation, utensils: pp. 545-553.

5151.   Malinowski, Bronislaw. 1922. Argonauts of the western Pacific. An account of native enterprise and adventure in the archipelagoes of Melanesian New Guinea. London: Reprint. New York: E.p. Dutton & Co., Inc. 1961. Dutton Paperback. D74.

    Includes descriptions of the significance of food withing the kula exchange complex. Importance of yams is noted, as well as ceremonial food distribution, pig butchering, sago processing, and preparation for feasts. Food payment to canoe-builder and associated specialists; and communal garden-clearing groups: pp. 160-163; food as an object of wealth, and as a primary cultural focus; significance of yams: pp. 170-172. Food exchange obligations: p. 174. Other food data included throughout.

5152.   Malinowski, Bronislaw. 1935. Coral gardens and their magic. A study of the methods of tilling the soil and of agricultural rites in the Trobriand Islands. 2 vols. New York, Cincinnati, Chicago: American Book Company.

    Volume One. The description of gardening. Volume Two. The language of magic and gardening. Includes extensive reference to ceremonial and other aspects of food in Trobriand society.

5153.   Malinowsi, Bronislaw.   Chapter Eleven. Problems of native diet in their economic setting. In The dynamics of culture change. An inquiry into race relations in Africa.   Edited by Phyllis M. Kaberry. 1945. New Haven: Yale University Press.

    Chapter related specifically to indigenous diet during the 1930's. Examines large-scale feeding of indigenous laborers; introduction of new crops; and introduction of European food habits.

5154.   Malkin, Borys. 1956. Seri ethno-zoology: a preliminary report. DJA 2: 73-83.

5155.   Mallock, M.M. 1894. Old English cookery. QR 178: 82-104.

5156.   Mallowe, Charles & McLaughlin, Jr., T., eds. 1971. Food marketing and distribution: selected readings. New York: Chain Store Publications.

    Forty-one articles covering manufacturing, market research; marketing strategies; promotions; and private labels.

5157.   Malo, David. 1951. Hawaiian antiquities. 2nd ed. BPBM-SP No. 2.

    Eating under the kapu system: pp. 27-30; food and drink in Hawaii: pp. 42-44.

5158.   Malone, Kemp.   1960.   Bonnyclabber. Celtica 5: 142.

    Etymological note concerning a dairy food.

5159.   Maloiy, G.M.O. 1965. African game animals as a source of protein. NAR 35: 903-908.

5160.   Maloney, Thomas J. Progress, anthropologists and appropriate technology: are we closet native evolutionists? Paper presented at 76th Annual Meeting of the American Anthropological Association. 29 November to 3 December 1977. Houston, Texas.

    Unlike professionals in other applied sciences, anthropologists do not assume that people of other cultures are unskilled and without useful knowledge. Yet in dealing with rural populations in developing countries, we frequently accept such assumptions, especially when we observe or participate in technology change programs. Can "progress" be made in meeting basic material needs by retaining and improving traditional, "empirically-based" technology and new sociopolitical structure with engagement in national and international markets? Open-pan sugar production in Central America illustrates the dilemma.

5161. Maltby, Lucy Mary. Suggested place and extent of nutrition education in public schools in Grades 1 through 12. Ph.D. dissertation. Syracuse, New York: Syracuse University. 1945.

5162. Mancini, F. 1959. La consommation en Italie et, plus particulierement celle des produits alimentaires. [Consumption in Italy, particularly of food products.] QN 19: 283-354.

5163. Mangat, Hardilal Singh. Marketing of groundnut with special reference to Ludhiana District. Master's thesis. Punjab Agricultural University. 1966.

The peanut, Arachis hypogaea, L., in Punjab State, India.

5164. Mangelsdorf, Paul Christoph. 1948. The role of pod corn in the origin and evolution of maize. MBG-A 35: 377-406.

A comparative morphological study illustrating the possibility of the evolution of modern maize from a wild pod form.

5165. Mangelsdorf, Paul Christoph. 1949. New evidence on the origin and evolution of maize. Science 109: 444.

Abstract of a paper presented at a meeting of the National Academy of Sciences, in 1949.

5166. Mangelsdorf, Paul Christoph. 1951. Hybrid corn. SA 185: 39-47.

5167. Mangelsdorf, Paul Christoph. 1954. New evidence on the origin and ancestry of maize. Am An 19: 409-410.

Data from Bat, and Cebollita Caves, New Mexico; and La Perra, Tmaulipas, Mexico.

5168. Mangelsdorf, Paul Christoph. 1958. Ancestor of corn. Science 128: 1313-1320.

Includes discussion of Bat Cave, New Mexico; and Mexican pollen data.

5169. Mangelsdorf, Paul Christoph. 1958. The mutagenic effect of hybridizing maize and teosinte. CSH-BL-SQB 23: 409-421.

5170. Mangelsdorf, Paul Christoph. 1958. Reconstructing the ancestor of corn. APS-P 102: 454-463.

Also in SI-AR for the year 1959. pp. 495-507 (1960).

5171. Mangelsdorf, Paul Christoph. 1974. Corn, its origin, evolution and improvement. Cambridge: Harvard University Press. Belknap Press.

5172. Mangelsdorf, Paul Christoph & Cameron, James W. 1942. Western Guatemala a secondary center of origin of cultivated maize varieties. HU-BML 10: 217-255.

All of the eighteen chromosome-knob positions known in maize and an addition three positions not previously reported were encountered. The greatest diversity was found in a small area in the Department of Huehuetenango where low-knob and high-knob varieties occur in close proximity. This is also the area in which teosinte is found growing in the wild.

5173. Mangelsdorf, Paul Christoph & Lister, Robert H. 1956. Archaeological evidence on the evolution of maize in northwestern Mexico. HU-BML 17: 151-177.

5174. Mangelsdorf, Paul Christoph; MacNeish, Richard S.; & Galinat, Walton C. 1956. Archaeological evidence on the diffusion and evolution of maize in N.E. Mexico. HU-BM-L 17: 125-150.

5175. Mangelsdorf, Paul Christoph; MacNeish, Richard S., & Galinat, Walton C. 1964. Domestication of corn. Science 143: 538-545.

5176. Mangelsdorf, Paul Christoph; MacNeish,Richard S., & Galinat, Walton C. 1967. Prehistoric maize, teosinte, and tripsacum from Tamaulipas, Mexico. HU-BML 22: 33-62.

5177. Mangelsdord, Paul Christoph & Oliver, Douglas L. 1951. Whence came maize to Asia? HU-BML 14: 263-291.

Concludes that, as of the writing, the authors had discovered no tangible evidence of any kind - botanical, archaeological, ethno graphic, linguistic, ideographic, pictorial or historical - of the existence of maize in any part of the Old World before A.D. 1492.

5178. Mangelsdorf, Paul Christoph & Reeves, Robert G. 1939. The origin of Indian corn and its relatives. Tex-AES-B No. 574.

5179. Mangelsdorf, Paul Christoph & Reeves, Robert G. 1945. The origin of maize: present status of the problem. AA 47: 235-243.

5180. Mangelsdorf, Paul Christoph & Reeves, Robert G. 1959. The origin of corn. 1. Pod corn, the ancestral form. HU-BML 18: 329-353.

5181. Mangelsdorf, Paul Christoph & Reeves, Robert G. 1959. The origin of corn. 3. Modern races, the product of teosinte introgression. HU-BML 18: 389-406.

5182.   Mangelsdorf, Paul Christoph & Reeves, Robert G. 1959. The origin of corn, 4. Place and time of origin. HU-BM-L 18: 413-427.

5183.   Mangelsdorf, Paul Christoph & Sanoja O., Mario. 1965. Early archaeological maize from Venezuela. HU-BML 21: 105-112.

5184.   Mangelsdorf, Paul Christoph & Smith, Jr., C. Earle. 1949. A discovery of remains of primitive maize in New Mexico. JHer 40: 39-43.

5185.   Mangelsdorf, Paul Christoph & Smith, C. Earle. 1949. New archaeological evidence of evolution in maize. HH-BM-L 13: 213-247.

Discussion of material from Bat Cave, New Mexcio, dated at ca. 2500 B.C. to 3000 B.C. The maize excavated from the lower cave strata is pod corn and pop corn, not teosinte-derived, and the most primitive known to the time of excavation. Later Strata revealed teosinte introgression.

5186.   Mangelsdorf, Paul Christoph & Willey, Gordon R. Origins of agriculture in Middle America. In Natural environment and cultures. Edited by Robert C. West. In Handbook of Middle American Indians. Edited by Robert Wauchope. 1964. Vol. 1. pp. 427-455.

5187.   Mani, G.S.; Lily, G.; Balasubramanian, S.C.; & Basu, K.p. 1955. Composition and nutritive value of some indigenous milk products. IJMR 43: 237-242.

5188.   Mann, E.J. 1967, compilor. Evaluation of the world food literature: results of an international survey. Farnham Royal: Great Britain. Commonwealth Agricultural Bureaux.

This publication presents the results of an international project, as a preliminary step toward establishment of an abstracing and documentation service for food science and technology. Over two thousand periodicals were searched, evaluated, and classified, according to commodity and aspect.

5189.   Mann, G.V. 1978. The Masai: milk and the yogurt factor: an alternate explanation. Atherosclerosis 29: 265.

5190.   Mann, I. 1960. The conversion of unproductive animals from overstocked areas into high protein food. EAMJ 37: 343-377.

5191.   Mann, I. 1964. Vitamin content and amino acid composition of some African game animals. JAFC 12: 374-376.

5192.   Mann, Virginia R. Food practices of the Mexican-American in Los Angeles County. Revised Edition. Los Angele: Los Angeles county Health Department. Mimeographed. 1966.

Prepared to assist nurses, dietitians, and nutritionists working with Mexican-Ameri-cans. Contains suggestion for low-sodium and low-caloric diets.

5193.   Mannin, E. 1955. Food in Burma. VNews 34: 94-97.

5194.   Manning, Frank E. Drinking at sea: a Canadian case. Paper presented at 76th Annual Meeting of the American Anthropological Association. 29 November to 3 December, 1977. Houston, Texas.

5195.   Manzi, L. 1968. La cucina e le malattie nel secolo 14. [Cookery and the invalid inthe 14th Century.] GBVI 61: 405-409.

5196.   Maples, William R. Crop predation by baboons. Paper presented at 70th Annual Meeting of the American Anthropological Association. 21 November, 1971. New York City.

Discusses and analyzes data gathered over a two year period in East Africa. Raiding techniques, and social organization of raiding troops are explained, stressing the adaptive nature of that organization in a particular ecological situation.

5197.   Maraini, Fosco. 1952. Secret Tibet. Translated by Eric Mosbacher. New York: Viking Press.

Millet beer (chang): pp. 53, 188; yak butter and roasted barley flour [tsampa]: p. 95; tea: p. 112; a typical Tibetan meal; pp. 117-118; a monastery meal: p. 166; a Tibetan feast: p. 188; yak milk and its products: pp. 267-268.

5198.   Maramba, Manuela G. 1960. The economics of food and nutrition in the United States Trust Territory of the Pacific Islands, April 25 - June 2, 1959. SPC-TIC No. 39.

5199.   March, E.F. A dietary study of two thousand families on relief in Texas. Master's thesis. University of Texas. 1935.

5200.   Marchant, Alexander. 1942. From barter to slavery: the economic relations of Portuguese and Indians in the settlement of Brazil, 1500-1580. JHUSHPS Vol. 60 No. 1. Manioc: pp. 64-65; flour imports to and provisioning of Bahia (1544-1553): pp. 87-90; 111-113.

5201.   Marchione, Thomas J. Nutritional and cultural aspects of food-import banning by Third World countries. Paper presented at 75th Annual Meeting of the American Anthropological Association. 17 to 21 November, 1976. Washington, D.C.

This paper is an exploration of the cultural and nutritional issues arising form the postwar movement in Third World countries toward government policies which ban food imports or otherwise encourage a shift from foreign to domestic food sources. Secondary data are presented from Zambia, Guyana, Jamaica and other countries recently adopting such policies. Original longitudinal data on Jamaica's efforts to promote the consumption and production of locally-grown food are also presented, which include socioeconomic, dietary, and anthropometric data collected on preschool children and their households in 1973 and 1975.

5202. Marchione, Thomas J. Interfamilial versus intrafamilial factors in child nutritional status. Paper presented at 76th Annual Meeting of the American Anthropological Association. 29 November to 3 December, 1977. Houston, Texas.

The thesis that child nutritional status is a function of differential child care within households is explored in this paper, by examining the relative importance of intrafamilial and interfamilial variances. The effects on young child malnutrition of birth order in relation to expressions of ideal family size and intrafamilial kin and care environments are compared with effects of socio-economic household conditions such as income, land use and employment status of household providers in a sample of two hundred Jamaican children under five years of age. Some implications of results for national policies are considered.

5203. Marchoux. 1933. L'alimentation des indigenes aux colonies. [Native diet in the colonies.] AM-B pp. 751-766.

5204. Marcuse, Adolf. 1894. The Hawaiian Islands. Translated by Helen H. Smith. SGM 10: 9-22.

A Hawaiian feast: pp. 12-13.

5205. Marescalchi, Aruturo. 1942. Storia dell alimentazione e dei piaceri della tavola. [History of eating and of the pleasures of the table.] Milan: Garzanti.

5206. Marett, Robert Randolph de la. Food rites. In Essays presented to C.G. Seligman. Edited by Edward Evan Evans-Ritchard; Raymond Firth; Bronislaw Malinowski; & Isaac Schapera. 1934. pp. 197-208. London: Kegan Paul, Trench, Trubner & Co, Ltd.

A critque of Jane Harrison's theory concerning the evolution of ritual commensalism, in her book Themis.

5208. Maretu. 1911. A word about cannibalism at Rarotonga. JPS 20: 196-209.

5209. Margo, Joan. The food supply problem of the California gold mines, 1848-1855. Master's thesis. History. University of California, Berkeley. 1947.

5210. Marin, Louis. 1925. Questionnaire d'ethnographie. Table d'analyse en ethnographie. [Ethnographic questionnaire. Analytic ethnographich table.] Alencon France: Laverdure.

Includes sections on food habits and geophagy.

5211. Marinov, Vassil. Berichte uber den Gegenwartigen Stand der Ethnologische Nahrungs forschungen (Methoden und Aufgaben) in Bulgaria. [Study on the present state of ethnological food research (methods and results) in Bulgaria. Paper presented at First International Symposium on Ethnological Food Research. 21 to 25 August, 1970. Lund: Folklivsarkivet, University of Lund.

5212. Marinov, Vassil. Die nahrung beiden Nomadistienden Karakatschanen in Bulgarien. [Diet of the Karakachan nomads in Bulgaria.] Paper read at the First International Symposium on Ethnological Food Research. 21 to 25 August, 1970. Lund: Folklivsarkivet, University of Lund.

5213. Mariscotti, Ana Maria. 1959. La alimentacion tipica en la Quebrada Humahuaca y la Puna y algunas interesantes costumbres con ellas relacionadas. [Typical diet in the Quebrada de Humahuaca and Puna and some interesting customs associated with it.] REd 4: 387-396.

Northern Argentina.

5214. Market Research Corporation of America. 1965. Evaluation of youth beverage consumption habits. Report No. FCC-ERD-65-11. Economic Research Department. Lakeland: Florida Citrus Commission.

Considers citrus and other beverages.

5215. Markevitch, Marie Alexandre. 1941. The epicure in Imperial Russia. San Francisco: Colt Press.

5216. Markham, Jean E. 1966. Sociological aspects of alcohol and food deviations. NYAS-A 133: 814-819.

An extremely perceptive analysis of major psycho-social characteristics of United States culture which may cause cognitive conflict and predispose of alcohol and food abuse.

5217. Markley, Klare Stephen. 1950-1951. Soybeans and soybean products. 2 vols. New York: Interscience.

5218. Marks, Stuart A. Profile and process: subsistence hunters in a Zambian community. Paper presented at 73rd Annual Meeting of the American Anthropological Association. 19 to 24 November, 1974. Mexico City.

5219. Markus, Michal. 1961. Fruit collecting in the Upper Hron Valley district. [In Czechoslovakian.] SN 9: 190-242.

5220. Markus, Michal. Gegenwartiger Stand und Ergebnisse der Volksnahrungsforschung in der Tschechoslowakei. [Present state and results of ethnological food research in Czechoslovakia.] Paper presented at the First International Symposium on Ethnological Food Research. 21 to 25 August, 1970. Lund: Folklivsarkivet. Lund University.

5221. Markus, Michal. Gemeinsame Probleme und Aufgaben der Volksnahrungsforschung in Karpaten-Raum. [Common problems and tasks in ethnological food research at the Carpathian region.] Paper presented at First International Symposium on Ethnological Food Research. 21-25 August, 1970. Lund: Folklivsarkivet. Lund University.

5222. Marquez, D.R. 1962. Food from the wilds. Mirror 13 January. pp. 6-7.

5223. Marres, Paul. 1950. La vigne et le vin en France. [Vineyard and wine in France.] Paris: Armand Colin.

5224. Mars, J.A. & Tooley, E.M., eds. 1959. The Kudeti book of Yoruba cookery. 8th edition. Lagos: C.M.S. (Nigeria) Bookshops.

5225. Marsh, Dick E. 1969. Two contemporary Papago recipes of indiegnous plants, and American Southwest botanical implications. Kiva 34: 242-245.

        Use of the following Amaranths and Opuntiae: A. blitoides, A. cruentes, A. palmeri, A. retroflexus; O. abrorescens, O. camachica, O. echinocarpa, O. engelmannii, O. fulgida, O. plumbea, O. polyacantha, O. spinosios, O. versicolor, O. whipplei by the Cocopah, Hopi, Navajo, Papago, Tewa and Zuni. The two 'recipes' are for amaranth and opuntia, respectively.

5226. Marsh, Elizabeth F. Dietary studies of families on relief. Master's thesis. Austin: University of Texas. 1935.

5227. Marshall, Dorothy. 1956. English people in the Eighteenth Century. London, New York, Toronto: Longmans, Green.

        Squire's food: p. 120; middle-class menus and budgets: pp. 128-129; diet of the poor: pp. 170-171; excise officers' food expenditures: p. 272; food riots: pp. 195-196.

5228. Marshall, Dorothy. Chapter Twelve. Manners, meals, and domestic pastimes. In Johnson's England. An account of the life and manners of his age. Edited by A.S. Turberville. 1965. Oxford: Clarendon Press.

5229. Marshall, Guy A.K. 1902. Five years' observations and experiment (1896-1901) on the bionomics of South African insects, chiefly directed to the investigation of mimicry and warning colors. ESL-T pp. 397-398.

        Notes an "eye-like" warning-marking developed in Choerocampa larvae when presented to a baboon as food, and the baboon's negative reaction.

5230. Marshall, Harry Ignatius. Chapter Nine. Food and its preparation. In The Karen people of Burma. 1922. OSU-B 26 No. 13.

5231. Marshall, James. 1958. Elbridge A. Stuart: founder of Carnation Company. Los Angeles: Carnation Company.

        Carnation is a major United States producer of diversified food products.

5232. Marshall, Laurence K. & Marshall, John K. 1971. Bitter melons. 16mm film, sound and color. Thirty minutes. Watertown, Massachusetts: Documentary Educational Resources.

        Hunting, gathering and obtaining water by the San Bushman, of the Kalahari Desert, southern Africa.

5233. Marshall, Laurence K. & Marshall, John K. 1972. Debe's tantrum. 16mm film, sound and color. Nine minutes. Watertown, Massachusetts: Documentary Educational Resources.

        Preparations for food gathering among the °Kung Bushman, of the Kalahari Desert, southern Africa.

5234. Marshall, Laurence K. & Marshall, John K. 1972. Wasp's nest. 16mm film, sound and color. Twenty minutes. Watertown, Massachusetts: Documentary Educational Resources.

        Food gathering by Bushman women and children, in the Kalahari Desert, southern Africa.

5235. Marshall, Laurence K. & Marshall, John K. The meat fight. 16mm film, sound and color. Fourteen minutes. Watertown, Massachusetts: Documentary Educational Resources.

        Records a controversy which arises during the distribution of meat, among a Bushman group, in the Kalahari Desert of southern Africa.

5236. Marshall, Mac. 1978. Weekend warriors: alcohol in a Micronesian culture. Palo Alto: Mayfield Publishing Co.

        Drinking among young males in Truk.

5237. Martens, Ethel G. 1966. The need for social anthropological outlook in community nutrition programs. CNN 22: 112-119.

        The author provides suggestions to professional nutrition personnel regarding the facilitation of inter-cultural communication. Examples from the author's experience, and from the literature lend support to the methods proposed.

5238. Martial, J.E. 1931. Contribution a l'etude de l'alimentation du tirailleur Senegalais en Afrique Occidentale Francaise. [Contribution to the study of the diet of the Senegalese rifleman in French West Africa.] AMPC 29: 516-532.

5239. Martial, J.E. 1937. L'alimentation indigene en Afrique Occidentale Francaise. [Native diet in French West Africa.] AMPC 35: 648-687.

5240.   Martin, Abbott C. 1929.   Patriotism and fried chicken. <u>Sewanee</u> 37: 34-37.

Observation on apparent similarity between the food of southeastern United States, and Syria.

5241.   Martin, Alexandre. 1827. <u>Manuel de l'amateur de melons; out, l'art de reconnaitre et d'acheter de bons melons. Precede d'une histoire de ce fruit, avec un traite sur sa culture.</u> [Manual for the melon-lovers; or, the art of recognizing and buying good melons. Preceded by a history of the fruit, with a treatise on their cultivation.] Paris: Aug. Udron.

5242.   Martin, Alexandre. 1828. <u>Manuel de l'amateur de cafe, ou l'art de prendre toujours de bon cafe, ouvrage contenant plusieurs procedes nouveaux.</u> [Manual for the coffee-lover; or, the art of always having good coffee, a work containing many new processes.] Paris: Audot.

5243.   Martin, Alexandre. 1829. <u>Manuel de l'amateur des truffes; ou, l'art de obtenir des truffes. Au moyen des plants artificiels, dans les parcs, bosquets, jardins, etc.; etc.; precede d'une histoire de la truffe et d'anecdotes gourmandes et suivi d'un traite sur la culture des chapignons. 2nd edition.</u> [Manual for the truffle-lover; or, the art of obtaining truffles. Through means of artificial plantings, in parks, groves, gardens, etc.; etc.; preceded by a history of the truffle and by gourmand anecdotes, and followed by a treatise on the cultivation of mushrooms.] Paris: Leroi; Audin.

5244.   Martin, Annie. 1890. Chapter Eleven. How we fared. In <u>Home life on an ostrich farm.</u> London: Philip.

Account of cookery on a Karoo farm in South Africa in the 1880's.

5245.   Martin, Calvin. 1974. The European impact on the culture of a northeastern Algonquian tribe: an ecological interpretation. <u>WMQ</u> 31: 3-26.

Discusses the functional relationship of subsistence and environment. A variety of foods are noted, including some game; fish; seal; molluscs; moose-bone grease; wild geese. Ritual practices relating to hunting and eating are considered from a functional-ecological perspective.

5246.   Martin, Claro & Sulit, Jose I. 1955. Stuides on the preparation of salted fish paste (bagoong) from dried <u>dilis</u> [<u>Stolephorus indicus</u>]. <u>PJF</u> 3: 39-45.

5247.   Martin, Franklin W. & Ruberte, Ruth M. 1975. <u>Edible leaves of the tropics.</u> Mayaguez Institute of Tropical Agriculture, United State Department of Agriculture, Agriculture Research Service, Southern Region/United States Department of State, Agency for International Development. Mayaguez, Puerto Rico: Antillean College Press.

An exhaustive study of leaves suitable for food and beverages; their nutritional value, methods of preparation, and cultivation techniques.

5248.   Martin, Jean. 1978. <u>Infant feeding 1975: attitudes and practice in England and Wales. A survey carried out on behalf of the Department of Health and Social Security.</u> Office of Population Censuses and Surveys. Social Survey Division. London: Her Majesty's Stationery Office.

Purposes of this survey were to establish the incidence and prevalence of breast feeding over the first year of life; to describe current practices in infant feeding, especially the time of introduction of solid food; determine factors responsible for decline in breast feeding; and to investigate why women who commence breast feeding shortly change to bottle feeding.

5249.   Martin, M.K. 1969. South American foragers: a case study in cultural devolution: <u>AA</u> 243-260.

5250.   Martin, Paul S. & Schoenwetter, J. 1960. Arizona's oldest cornfield. <u>Science</u> 132: 33-34.

5251.   Martin, Paul S. & Sharrock, Floyd W. 1964. Pollen analysis of prehistoric human feces, a new approach to ethnobotany. <u>Am An</u> 30: 168-180.

5252.   Martin, Wilard W. 1962. <u>Twelve full ounces.</u> New York: Hold, Rhinehart & Winston.

Story of Pepsi-Cola.

5253.   Martins, W. 1955. <u>Um Brasil diferente; ensaio sobre fenomenos de aculturacao no Parana.</u> [A different Brazil; essay on the phenomena of acculturation in Parana.] Sao Paulo: Edicoes Anhembi.

Food: pp. 312-336. Introduced foods: German (apfel strudel); Syria, Lebanon (yoghurt); Japan (chama se kaki).

5254.   Martinet, M. Territoires Africains sous mandat. Togo et Cameroun. [African territories under mandate. Togo and Cameroon.] In [<u>L'alimentation indigene dans les colonies francaises. Protectorats et territoires sous mandats.</u> Edited by G. Hardy & C. Richet. 1933. pp. 262-289. Paris: Vigot Freres.

Covers food habits; food preparation (includes several native recipes); staple crops, spices, beverages and colonial intervention in native diet. Data on chemical composition of various native foods is appended.

5255.   Martinez, Celia & Chavez, Adolfo. 1967. Los habitos de la alimentacion infantil en una comunidad indigena. [Infant diet in a native community.] <u>RMS</u> 29: 223-242.

5256.   Martinez, Maximino. 1959. [<u>Plantas utiles de la flora Mexicana.</u> [Useful plants of the Mexican flora.] Mexico: Ediciones Botas.

5257.   Martini, I.   1957.   Curiosities in foods of animal origins; fish and other tropical animals.   [In Italian.] VI 8: 1153-1166.

5258.   Martinique.   Service de l'Agriculture.   1943. Valeur nutritive des aliments en usage a la Martinique.   [Nutritive value of some foods used in Martinique.]   Fort-de-France: Imprimerie Officielle.

5259.   Martiny, Benno.   1871.   Die Milch, ihre Wesen und Ihre Verwerthung.   [Milk, its nature and its utilization.]   Danzig: Kasemann.

5260.   Martiny, Benno.   1895.   Kirne und Girbe. Eine Beitrag zur Kulturgeschichte besonder zur Geschichte der Milchwirtschaft.   [Churn and thresher. A contribution to culture history, especially to the history of dairy economy.]   Berlin: Gelbstverlag.

5261.   Martiny, Benno. 1909.   Geschichte der Rahmgewinnung. 1. Die Aufrahmgewinnung Geshichte, ihrer Entwicklung von der fruhsten zeiten bis zu Gegenwart.   [History of cream-making. 1. From the history of cream-making, its development from the earliest times to the present.] Leipzig: M. Honsius Nachverlag.

5262.   Martyn, Charles, compilor.   1906.   Food and culinary utensils of the ancients.   Compiled from standard historical works.   New York: The Caterer Publishing Co.

5263.   Marx, Otto M.   1968.   Diet in European psychiatric hospitals, jails, and general hospitals in the first half of the 19th Century according to travellers' reports.   JHM 23: 217-247.

        The first third of this article discusses early views on dietetics, after which the travellers' reports are cited.   An Appendix includes details of foods served, with costs and/ or quantities indicated.

5264.   Marzell, H.   1964.   Zauberpflanzes-hexentranke.   [Magic plants - enchanted drinks.] DJV 10: 403-404. Also in ZV 61: 118 [1965].

5265.   Marzhowska, M. & McLoughlin, L.   1928. Polish food habits.   JADA 4: 142-148.

5266.   Masefield, G.B.   1938.   The production of native beers in Uganda.   EAMJ 5: 361-364.

        Preparation of sorghum beer by the Baganda, and its use; and Kiganda banana beer.

5267.   Masefield, G.B.; Wallis, Michael; Harrison, S.G.; & Nicholson, B.E.   1969.   The Oxford book of food plants.   London: Oxford University Press.

5268.   Maskell, Henry Parr.   1927.   The taverns of old England.   New York: John Day.

        Comments on food, alcoholic beverages and coffee throughout.

5269.   Maslansky, E.   1935.   The Jewish dietary laws.   MWJ 42: 182-185.

5270.   Maslansky, E. 1941.   Cultural factors influencing attitudes of Jewish mothers toward eating habits.   MWJ 48: 113-116.

5271.   Maslow, Abraham H.   1933.   Comparative behvior of primates.   6.   Food preferences of primates.   JCPP 16: 187-197.

5272.   Mason, Francis.   1882-1883.   Burmah: its people and productions. 3rd ed. Rewritten and editibed by W.   Theobald. 2 vols. Hertford: Austin.

        Volume Two. Botany.

5273.   Mason, Gregory.   1936.   Native American food.   NH 37: 309-318.

        Cassava, tomato, potato, maize, lima bean, sweet potato, squash, turkey, pineapple.

5274.   Mason, J. Alden.   1912.   The ethnology of the Salinan Indians.   UCal-PAAE 10 No. 4.

        A central California group, which inhabited an area including southern Monterey, San Luis Obispo, and parts of San Benito Counties. Food: pp. 117-123.

5275.   Mason, J. Alden.   1920. The Papago harvest festival.   AA 22: 13-25.

5276.   Mason, J. Alden.   1952.   Notes and observations on the Tepehuan.   AmInd 12: 33-54.

        Tesquino, a maize beer: pp. 45-46.

5277.   Mason, Lynn.   Hopi domestic animals.   Senior thesis. Dartmouth College.   1965.

5278.   Mason, Otis Tufton.   1891.   The ulu or woman's knife of the Eskimos.   SI-AR for the year 1890. pp. 411-416.

5279.   Mason, Otis Tufton.   1896.   Migration and the food quest: a study in the peopling of America. SI-AR for the year 1894. pp. 523-539.

        Struggle for existence; migration and its motives: food areas and food supply; food and migration in America; the roads to America; a hypothetical case; necessary conditions; a definite proposition; abundance of food; the naval possibilitis; ocean currents and food supply; prevailing winds and food; encouragements and discouragements; the race problem; the problems of sociology; American and Asiatic languages; similarities in arts; the witness of archaeology; religion and folklore; the testimony of ethnographers and others.

5280.   Mason, Otis Tufton. 1900. Chapter Two. The food bringer. In Woman's share in primitive culture.

        Food gathering and preparation activities in the western United States (Native American); Malay peninsula; Arctic (Eskimo); Mexico; Guiana.

5281.   Mason, Otis Tufton. 1903. Sugar making in Sumatra. AA 5: 176.

5282.   Masquelier, J.   Le vin dans l'alimentaiton humaine. [Wine in human diet.] In Traite d'oenologie [Treatise on enology.] 2 vols. By J. Riberau-Gayon Peynaud. 1961. Vol. 2. pp. 93-148. Paris: Librairie Polytechnique Charles Beranger.

5283.   Massal, Emile. 1954. Dietary and nutritional problems in the Pacific. SPC-TP No. 59.

5284.   Massal, Emile. 1955. Fish: a valuable Pacific island food. SPC-QB 5: 18-19.

5285.   Massal, Emile. 1956. A survey of...subsistence problems in the South Pacific. SPC-QB 6: 34-35.

Impact of Western diet on food habits of Pacific Islanders. Emphasizes the necessity for agronomists and nutritionists to cooperate in the selection of nutritious staple subsistence plants.

5286.   Massal, Emile. 1958. Nutrition and the Papuan child. SPC-QB 8: 39-40.

5287.   Massal, Emile & Barrau, Jacques.   1956. Food plants of the South Sea Islands. SPC-TP No. 94. Reprint 1973.

Staple food crops and supplementary food plants, with compositional analyses and nutritive values included.

5288.   Massal, Emile & Barrau, Jacques.   1954. Pacific subsistence crops. Breadfruit. SPC-QB 5: 24-26.

5289.   Massal, Emile & Barrau, Jacques. 1955. Pacific subsistence crops. Cassava. SPC-QB 5: 15-18.

5290.   Massal, Emile, & Barrau, Jacques.   1955. Pacific subsistence crops. Sweet potato. SPC-QB 5: 10-13.

5291.   Massal, Emile & Barrau, Jacques.   1956. Quelques plantes alimentaires monis connues des iles du Pacifique. [Several little-known food plants of the Pacific Islands.] CPS-BT 6: 24-27.

5292.   Massal, Emile & Barrau, Jacques.   1956. Some lesser-known Pacific food plants. SPC-QB 6: 17-18.

Gnetum gnemon; Setaria palmifolia; Hibiscus manihot.

5293.   Massam, J.A.   1927. The cliff dwellers of Kenya. London: Seeley, Service & Co,

Note on Elgeyo food: pp. 87-88.

5294.   Masseyeff, R.; Pierme, M.-L. & Bergeret, B. Enquetes sur l'alimentation au Cameroun: 2. Sous-division de Batouri. [Dietary inquiry in the Cameroon: 2. Batouri. [Dietary inquiry in the Cameroon: 2. Batouri Subdivision.] Mimeographed. Yaounde: Institut de Recherches Scientifiques du Cameroun. 1960.

Batouri is in eastern Cameroon, at 4 .26 N, 14 27 E. The villages included in the survey are Bokindja, Kagnol; Kombe-Tiko; and Tikondi, Leta. Foods, their preparation and nutrient composition, kitchen facilities, meal patterns and child feeding practices are described.

5295.   Masseyeff, R.; Pierme, M.-L. & Bergeret, B. 1960. Une enquete sur l'alimentation dans la region de Batouri. [Dietary inquiry in the Batouri region.] REC 1: 6-70.

Cameroun.

5296.   Masseyeff, R.; Perisse, J.; Serre, A.; Temolieres, J.; & Claudian J. 1957. Considerations methodologiques sur les enquetes alimentaires en Afrique Noire, a propos de quelques enquetes recentes parmi les populations de l'union francaise. [Methodological considerations on dietary surveys in Black Africa, relevant to several recent inquiries among the populations of the French Union.] P-INH-B 12: 737-765.

5297.   Massieu; H. Guillermo; Cravioto, R.O.; Cravioto, O.Y.; & Figueroa, F. de M. 1959. Nuevos datos sobre comestibles mexicanos. [New data on the nutritive value of some edible Mexican insects.] SBP-A 16: 91-104.

5298.   Massieu; Guillermo; Guzman, J.; Cravioto, Rene; & Calvo, J. de la T. 1951. Nutritive value of some primitive Mexican foods. JADA 27: 212-214.

Ahuautle [aguaucle] are the eggs of several species of aquatic Hemiptera: Krizousacorixa femorata, Guer.; K. azteca, Jaca; Corisella Texcocana, Jacz., and C. mercinaria, Say. Axayacatl is a mixture of aquatic Hemiptera and their larvae: K. azteca, Jaca.; K. femorata, uer; Notonecta unifasciata; C. mercinaria, Say. Jumiles, also Hemiptera: Euschistus zopilotensis, Distant.; Edessa mexicana, Stal., and Afizies sulfatus are eaten raw, fried, or roasted. Acociles, a Crustacean, Cambarus moctezumi, are boiled before being eaten. Gusanos de maguey [meocuiles] are worms of the Aegiale [Acentrocneme] hesperiaris butterfly, which develop on the agave plant. They are fried in lard and eaten in tortillas. Charales [xuili] are fish [Chirostoma jordani, Woolman] of Lake Patzcuaro.

5299.   Massola, A. 1964. Food of the Aborigines. VNat 80: 323.

5300.   Masson, Richard. 1950. Wild plants for food and medicine. Tararua 4: 45-50.

5301.   Massy, Jules-Henry-Robert de. 1861-1862. Des halles et marches et du commerce des objets de consommation a Londres et a Paris. Rapport a son excellence M. Le Ministre d'Agriculture. [Market places and markets and trade in comestibles in London and Paris. Report to his excellency the

Minister of Agriculture.] 3 vols. Paris: Imprimerie Imperiale.

5302. Masters, Thomas. 1844. The ice box: being a compendius and concise history of everything connected with ice... London: Simpkin, Marshall & Co.

5303. Masumdar, R.C. & Puzalker, A.D. 1957. The history and culture of the Indian people. The Vedic age. London: George Allen & Unwin.

Food & drink: pp. 457-458.

5304. Masuoka, Jitsuichi. 1945. Changing food habits of the Japanese in Hawaii. ASR 10: 759-765.

The primary objective of this study of Japanese sugar cane plantation families on the Island of Maui was, in the authors words, not to obtain a cross-section of foods most commonly used by the Japanese of Hawaii, but to measure objectively the forces that bring about changes in the food habits of a people. Among the factors and motives identified are availability of food; convenience and ease of preparation; change in types of plantation work; influence of advertising and pressure of salesmen; relinquishing of traditional intitutional control over certain kinds of food; new items of food introduced by the second generation from public schools; and changing attitudes of second generation toward food, and Japanese folkways, mores and intitutions. The author lived in the plantation community for almost eight years, prior to coming to the Mainland.

5305. Mata, Leonardo J. 1978. The children of Santa Maria Cauque: a prospective field study of health and growth. Cambridge: M.I.T. Press.

Guatemala. Study of a long-term nutritional assessment and intervention program.

5306. Mata, Leonardo & Mohs, E. 1976. Cambios, culturales y nutricionales en Costa Rica. [Cultural and nutritional changes in Costa Rica.] BMHI 33: 579-593.

5307. Mathew, K.M. 1964. Kerala cooking. Kottayam: Mahorama Publishing Co.

Hints on Kerala cooking: pp. 7-11.

5308. Mathews, D.S. 1955. The ethnological and medical significance of breast feeding: with special reference to the Yorubas of Nigeria. JTPECH 1: 9-24.

Observations on psychological and physiological variables related to lactation.

5309. Mathews, John Duncan. Kuru: a puzzle in cultural and environmental medicine. Medical dissertation. University of Melbourne. 1971.

Kuru is a slow-acting, fatal virus of the central nervous system, endemic among the Fore Tribe of New Guinea. The virus is transmitted through anthrophagic ingestion of brains.

5310. Mathews, John Joseph. 1961. The Osages. Norman: University of Oklahoma Press.

Use of acorns, persimmons: pp. 488-489.

5311. Mathews, Susan J. 1929. Food habits of Georgia rural people. G-AES-B No. 159.

Diets are analyzed for calorie, protein, calcium, phosphorous and iron contents; sources of nutrients are recorded, together with an indication of the percentage of each nutrient derived from each source; nutritive value of diets of forty-five land owners and forty-five tenants are contrasted; seasonal variation in nutrient intake is examined; and food production is considered in relation to food consumption.

5312. Mathias, M. The impact of industrialisation and urbanisation on food consumption patterns in developing countries referene - India. In First Asian Congress of Nutrition. 22 January. - 2 February 1971. Hyderbad, India. Proceedings. Edited by p.G. Tulpule & Kamala S. Jaya ao. 1972. pp. 742-750. Hyderbad: Nutrition Society of India.

Describes social, economic, and cognitive variables determining trends in change in food consumption; provides statistics concerning consumption of food types in Maharashtra; income distribution; and awareness of nutrition concepts.

5313. Mathias, Peter. 1959. The brewing industry in England, 1700-1830. Cambridge: Cambridge University Press.

5314. Mathias, Peter. 1967. Retailing revolution: a history of multiple retailing in the food trades based upon the allied suppliers group of companies. London: Longmans.

Businesses including Liptons'; Home and Colonial Stores; and Maypoles. Analyzes the business strategy involved in building up one of the largest retailing organizations in the European food trade.

5315. Mathieu, A. 1951. L'hospitalite laotienne. [Laotian hospitality.] SE 26:4.

5316. Mathur, Kripa Shanker. 1964. Caste and ritual in a Malwa village. New York: Asia Publishing Co.

Caste food habits: pp. 123-129.

5317. Mathur, R.N. 1954. Insects and other wild animals as human food. IF 80: 427-432.

5318. Maticetov, Milko. 1954. "Poprtnik". ['Ritual Christmans breads.'] S Etno No. 6-7. pp. 223-239.

5319.   Matignon, J.J.   1909.   The diet of the Chinese. [In French.] RHPS 31: 120-125.

North China.

5320.   Matignon, J.J. & Salm, J. 1908. L'alimentation a Java. [Diet in Java.] RHPS 30: 471-484.

Provides nutritional analysis of diets of various groups (e.g. soldiers, hospital patients), with observations on local foods and food habits; restaurants; and food vendors. Recounts details of experiments involving prisoners, undertaken to determine causal relationship between intake of polished rice and beri-beri.

5321.   Matter, Sharleen & Wakefield, Lucille M. 1971. Religious influence on dietary intake and physical condition of indigent, pregnant Indian women. AJCN 24: 1097-1106.

Sample includes, Hindu, Muslim, and Christian populations.

5322.   Matthews, Washington.   1886.   Navajo names for plants. AN 20: 767-777.

Listed by botanical family. A few plants named are used for food.

5323.   Matthews, Washington. 1897. Navajo legends. AFS-M No. 5.

Food use of maize; cheese: pp. 183, 229, 248.

5324.   Matthews, Washington. 1902.   The night chant. AMNH-M No. 6.

Ritual foods: pp. 189, 218, 309.

5325.   Mauranges, p. 1960. Enquete alimentaire en Mauretanie. [Dietary survey in Mauritania.] Sem Med 36: 476-480.

5326.   Maurel, E. 1914.   Influence des climats et des saisons sur les besoins alimentaires. [Influence of climate and season on dietary needs.] P-AS-CRHS 158: 1201-1204.

5327.   Maurizio, Adam. 1927. Die Geschichte unserer Pflanzennahrung von die Urzeiten bis zu Gegenwarten. [History of our food plants from early times to the present.] Berlin: p. Parey.

5328.   Maurizio, Adam. 1931. Histoire d'alimentation vegetale chez l'homme. [History of Man's food plants.] RBAAT 11: 159-168.

5329.   Maurizio, Adam.   1938.   Les bases des regimes alimentaires traditionels. [The bases of traditional dietaries.] In Premier Congres International de Folklore. Travaux. 23-28 aout, 1937. Publications du Department et du Musee National des Arts et Traditions Populaires. Tours: Arrault & Cie.

5330.   Mawe, John 1816. Travels in the interior of Brazil. Philadelphia: M. Carey; Boston: Wells & Lilly.

Diet in Minas Gerais: pp. 29; 120-121; 130; 136-137.

5331.   May, Earl Chapin. 1937. The canning clan; a pageant of pioneering americans. New York: Macmillan.

5332.   May, Jacques Meyer. 1957. The geography of food and cooking. IRMGPC 170: 231-239.

Using as his departure point the influence of diet on patterns of disease, the author provides a wide range of (undocumented) examples of human food uses, and the ecological factors determining them, which affect medical well-being. Emphasis is placed on the geographical context of food availability. The article is popular and informal, and contains such questionable statements as "In other areas we find that cakes and waffles of porridge and gruel are heated on a hot stone. Here the sun is used as fuel.", with no reference to time, place, or culture.

5333.   May, Jacques Meyer. 1959. The geography of milk. JMFT 22: 137-141.

5334.   May, Jacques Meyer. 1963. The ecology of malnutrition in five countries of eastern and central Europe: East Germany, Poland, Yugoslavia, Albania, Greece. New York: Hafner Publishing Co.

5335.   May, Jacques Meyer. 1965. The ecology of malnutrition in middle Africa: Ghana, Nigeria, Republic of the Congo, Rwanda, Burundi, and the former French Equatorial Africa. New York: Hafner Publishing Co.

5336.   May, Jacques Meyer. 1966. The ecology of malnutrition in central and southern Europe: Austria, Hungary, Roumania, Bulgaria, Czechoslovakia. New York: Hafner Publishing Co.

5337.   May, Jacques Meyer. 1967. The ecology of malnutrition in northern Africa: Libya, Tunisia, Algeria, Morocco, Spanish Sahara and Ifni, Mauretania. New York: Hafner Publishing Co.

5338.   May, Jacques Meyer & Jarcho, Irma. 1961. The ecology of malnutrition in the Far and Near East: food resources, habits, and deficiencies. New York: Hatnfer Publishing Co.

5339.   May, Jacques Meyer & McLellan, Donna L. 1968. The ecology of malnutrition in the French speaking countries of West Africa and Madagascar: Senegal, Guinea, Ivory Coast, Togo, Dahomey, Cameroon, Niger, Mali, Upper Volta, and Madagascar. New York: Hafner Publishing Co.

5340.   May, Jacques Meyer & McLellan, Donna L. 1970. The ecology of malnutrition in eastern Africa: Equatorial Guinea, the Gambia, Liberia, Sierra Leone, Malawi, Rhodesia, Zambia, Kenya, Tanzania, Uganda, Ethiopia, and the French Territory of Afars and Issas, the Somali; Republic and Sudan. New York: Hafner Publishing Co.

5341.   May, Jacques Meyer & McLellan, Donna L. 1971. The ecology of malnutrition in seven countries of southern Africa and in Portuguese Guinea: the Republic of South Africa, South West Africa (Namibia), Botswana, Lesotho, Swaziland, Mozambique, Angola, Portuguese Guinea. New York: Hafner Publishing Co.

5342.   May, Jacques Meyer & McLellan, Donna L. 1972. The ecology of malnutrition in Mexico and Central America: Mexico, Guatemala, British Honduras, Honduras, El Salvador, Nicaragua, Costa Rica, and Panama. New York: Hafner Publishing Co.

5343.   May, Jacques Meyer & McLellan, Donna L. 1973. The ecology of malnutrition in the Caribbean: the Bahamas, Cuba, Jamaica, Hispaniola (Haiti and the Dominican Republic), Puerto Rico, the Lesser Antilles, and Trinidad and Tobago. New York: Hafner Press.

5344.   May, Jacques Meyer & McLellan, Donna L. 1974. The ecology of malnutrition in eastern South America. Venezuela, Guyana, Surinam (and the Netherlands Antilles), French Guiana, Brazil, Uruguay, Paraguay, and Argentina. New York: Hafner.

5345.   May, Jacques Meyer & McLellan, Donna L. 1974. The ecology of malnutrition in western South America. Colombia, Ecuador, Peru, Bolivia, and Chile. New York: Hafner.

5346.   Mayani, Zecharia. 1962. Chapter Five. Meals and the kitchen. Chapter Six. The tavern. Chapter Seven. At market. In The Etruscans begin to speak. Translated by Patrick Evans. New York: Simon & Schuster.

5347.   Mayard, Constantin. 1940 Cuisine des pays chauds. [Cookery for the tropics.] Santiago, Chile: Imprenta Molina Lackington.

5348.   Maybee, G.R. 1939. Flavour in food; classification and comparison of tastes. CCPI 23: 115-118.

5349.   Mayberry, Reuben H., & Lindeman Robert D. 1963. A survey of chronic disease and diet in Seminole Indians in Oklahoma. AJCN 13: 127-134.

        Dietary patterns: pp. 130-131.

5350.   Maybury-Lewis, Pia. Diet and health in an acculturated tribe. In The thirty-second International Congress of Americanists. 1956. Copenhagen. Proceeding. 1958. pp. 190-197. Copenhagen: Munksgaard.

        Food supply; nutritional value of diet; mealtimes; significance of meat in changing food habits; ritual use of food; and food exchange among the Sherente of central Brazil.

5351.   Mayer, Andre. 1955. Alimentation et societes. [Nutrition and society.] EO-M 38: 360-372.

5352.   Mayer, Andre. 1956. Nutrition and society. Food and Agriculture Organization of the United Nations. World Food Problems Series. Rome: Food and Agriculture Organization of the United Nations.

5353.   Mayer, E. Reciprocity, self-sufficiency and market relations in a contemporary community in the Central Andes of Peru. Ph.D. dissertation. Ithaca, New York: Cornell University, 1974.

5354.   Mayer, Jean. 1965. The nutritional status of American Negroes. NR 23: 161-163.

        Includes review of food consumption patterns.

5355.   Mayer, Jean; Dwyer, Joanna; & Feldman, Jacob J. 1970. The social psychology of dieting. JHSB 2: 269-287.

5356.   Mayhall, Mildred p. 1962. The Kiowas. Norman: University of Oklahoma Press.

        Mesquite beverage: pp. 101-102.

5357.   Maynard, Araujo, Aleu. 1952. Dulces caipiras. [Country sweets.] T-RPC 4: 20-24.

        Eleven recipes for confections from Sao Luis de Paraitinga, Brazil.

5358.   Maynard, L. 1911. Preparation of salmon caviar. USDCL-DCTR 14: 615-617.

5359.   Maynard, Leonard A. 1936. Improvement of diet of Chinese farm family. CMJ 50: 425-433.

5360.   Mayo, W.C. 1936. Man and his diet; man composed to carnivora (meat eaters) and herbivora (vegetarians). MHQ 5: 5-10.

5361.   Mayaorga, Wenceslao. El mani. [The peanut.] Bachelor's thesis. Natural Sciences. Lima: Universidad Mayor de San Marcos. 1888.

5362.   Mazer, A. 1959. Enquete-sondage alimentation-nutrition faite dans le Hodh (Mauretanie). [Dietary-nutritional survey done in the Hodh (Mauretania). P-INH-B 14: 951-965.

5363.   Mazess, Richard B. 1968. Hot-cold food beliefs among Andean peasants. JADA 53: 109-113.

5364.   Mazess, Richard B. & Baker, p.T. 1964. Diet of Quechua Indians living at high altitude: Nuno, Peru. AJCN 15: 341-351.

        Geophagy (earth used as condiment); ash-paste cake made with coca; chuno negro: a form of dehydrated potato.

5365.   Mazieres, B. 1954. Etude geographique de l'alimentation dans le Departement du Lot entre 1840 et 1880. [Geographic study of diet in the Department of Lot between 1840 and 1880.] RGPSO 25: 293-312.

        Southern France.

5366.   Mazois.   La cuisine et la table romaine. [Roman cooking and dining.] In Les classiques de la table. Petite bibliotheque des ecrits les plus distingues publies a Paris sur la gastronomie et la vie elegante. 3rd revised edition.   Anonymous. 1844. Paris: Imprimerie de Bethune.

5367.   McAdams, W. The salt-kettles and pans of the Mound Builders. Paper presented at the Thirty-fifth meeting of the American Association for the Advancement of Science. 1886. Buffalo, New York.

5368.   McAhron, Albert R. The material culture of the Southwestern Indians as seen by the early Spanish explorers: 1536-1634. Master's thesis. University of Notre Dame. 1952.

5369.   McAlpine, D. 1903-1904.   Blackfellow's bread. VJA 2: 1012-1020.

An underground fungus (Polyporus mylittae, C & M), eaten raw by certain Australian Aboriginal tribes.

5370.   McArthur, Margaret. Food consumption and dietary levels of the Aborigines at the settlements. In Records of the Australian American Scientific Expedition to Arnhem Land. Volume Two. Anthropology and nutrition.   Edited by Charles Percy Mountford. 1960. pp. 14-26. Melbourne: Melbourne University Press.

5371.   McArthur, Margaret. Food consumption and dietary levels of groups of Aborigines living on naturally occurring-foods. In Records of the Australian-American Scientific Expedition to Arnhem Land. Volume Two. Anthropology and nutrition. Edited by Charles Percy Mountford. 1960. pp. 90-135. Melbourne: Melbourne University Press.

5372.   McArthur, Margaret. Report of the nutrition unit. In Records of the Australian-American Scientific Expedition to Arnhem Land. Volume Two. Anthropology and nutrition. Edited by Charles Percy Mountford. 1960. pp. 1-13. Melbourne: Melbourne University Press.

Ethnohistorical and current anthropological background for study of Arnhem Land Aborigine nutritional status.

5373.   McArthur, Margaret. Report on an assignment in Malaya. Mimeographed.   World Health Organization of the United Nations.   Regional Office fo the West Pacific.   Manila: World Health Organization. 1962.

Includes are data on food attitudes.

5374.   McBryde, Felix Webster.   1945.   Cultural and historical geography of southwest Guatemala. SI-ISA-P No. 4.

Preparation of cultivated food plants: pp. 134-149.

5375.   McCall, Daniel F. Ethnobotany and history. Paper submitted to the Third Conference on African History and Archaeology. 3 to 7 July, 1961. School of Oriental and African Studies, University of London.

5376.   McCann, Mary B. & Trulson, Martha F. 1957. Our changing diet. JADA 33: 358-365.

Diachronic changes in food consumption patterns in the United States.

5377.   McCarrison, Robert. Relative values of the national diets of certain Indian races. In Seventh Far Eastern Association of Tropical Medicine. Congress in British India. 1927. Transactions.   Vol. Three. 1928. pp. 322-323. Calcutta: Thacker.

An experiment in comparative ethnodietetics. Laboratory animals were fed diets characteristic of various regional cultures. Results correlated well with known nutritional status of groups whose diets were used.

5378.   McCarrison, Robert. 1932. Problems of nutrition in India. NARev 2: 1-12.

5379.   McCarthy, Frederick D. 1943. Hunters and gardners of New Guinea. AMM 8: 76-81.

5380.   McCarthy, Frederick D. 1944. The coconut palm and its uses in Oceania. AMM 8: 234-238.

5381.   McCarthy, Frederick D. 1958. Aborigines: domestic and economic life, material culture. Australian Encyclopedia Vo. 1.

Food habits: pp. 29-37; 40-45.

5382.   McCarthy, Frederick D.& McArthur, Margaret. 1960. The food quest and the time factor in aboriginal economic life. In Records of the American-Australian Scientific Expedition to Arnhem Land.   Volume Two.   Anthropology and nutrition. Edited by Charles p. Mountford. 1960. pp. 145-194. Melbourne: Melbourne University Press.

5383.   McCay, C.M. 1933. Is longevity compatible with optimum growth? Science 77: 410-411.

Notes that modern nutrition is governed by the belief that ideal diet is that which produces optimum growth. It is pointed out that such a philosophy is appropriate in animal nutrition, where breeding is for meat and slaughter occurs shortly after maturity. In this case, rapid growth implies efficient feed conversion. The same orientation in child nutrition, however, does not take into account experimentation demonstrating a relationship between early rapid growth and short life span in laboratory rats. Concludes that longevity and rapid growth may be incompatible.

5384.   McCay, C.M. 1944. Increasing the use of plant proteins. FASEB-FP 3: 128-130.

Estimates one-third of the animal protein consumed in the United States could be replaced by plant protein without serious repercussion to agriculture.

5385. McCay, D. 1910. Investigations on Bengal dietaries with some observations on the influence of dietary on the physical development and well-being of the people of Bengal. Scientific memoirs by officers of the Medical and Sanitary Departments of the Government of India, No. 37. Calcutta: Government Printing Press.

5386. McCay, Jeanette Beyer. Some psychological factors affecting the appetite of nursery school children. Master's thesis. Ithaca, New York: Cornell University. 1934.

5387. McCay, Jeanette Beyer. Behavior relating to nutrition of sixty-six nursery school children. Ph.D. dissertation. Home Economics. Ithaca, New York: Cornell University. 1939.

5388. McClure, Ruth Alice. A study of native plants used for food by Indians on the North American deserts. Master's thesis. University of Idaho. 1966.

5389. McCollum, Elmer Verner. Malnutrition through errors in the combination of foods In: Association of Dairy, Food & Drug Officials. Twentieth Annual Meeting. August 7-11, 1916. Detroit, Michigan. pp. 61-68.

Need to achieve a nutritionally balanced diet through selection of nutritionally complementary foods.

5390. McCollum, Elmer Verner. 1957. A history of nutrition. The sequence of ideas in nutrition investigation. Boston: Houghton Mifflin.

5391. McCollum, Elmer Verner. 1964. From Kansas farm boy to scientist; The autobiography of Elmer Verner McCollum. Lawrence: University of Kansas Press.

5392. McCollum, Elmer Verner; Simmonds, N.; & Pitz, W. 1916. The vegetarian diet in the light of our present knowledge of nutrition. AJPhy 41: 333-360.

5393. McCord, C.p. 1972. Scurvy as an occupational disease. 6. Scurvy among the whalers. JOMed 13: 543-548.

5394. McCord, C.p. 1972. Scurvy as an occupational disease. 12. Scurvy in the early American colonies. JOMed 14: 551-559.

5393. McCord, Jr., Thomas T. An economic history of the Mescalero Apache Indians. Master's thesis. University of New Mexico. 1946.

5396. McCord, William & McCord, Joan; with Gudeman, Jon. 1960. Origins of alcoholism. Palo Alto: Stanford University Press.

5397. McCormick, Robert. 1943. Wing talk, how to cook the strange flora and fauna of the Pacific Islands. Collier's 112: 21.

5398. McCracken, Robert D. Cultural genetics and dietary behavior. Paper presented at 69th Annual Meeting of the American Anthropological Association. 19 to 22 November, 1970. San Diego, California.

5399. McCracken, Robert D. 1971. Lactase deficiency: an example of dietary evolution. CAnth 12: 472-517.

Lactase deficiency is characterized by insufficient or absent capacity to secrete the enzyme lactase, which is required to metabolize the milk sugar (lactose) present in most dairy products. This paper explores the phenomenon of variable lactase secretion among various gene pools, and offers hypotheses explaining the differences. The author concludes that prior to domestication of animals and the development of dairying, the normal condition among adult humans was lactase deficiency. With the introduction of lactose into the adult diet in certain cultures, however, new selective pressures were created which favored the genotype for adult lactase production.

5400. McCrae, Janet E. The ecology of malnutrition in a Buganda village. Master's thesis. University of London. 1966.

Based on questionnaire dietary survey, socio-economic data are anlysed and graded and their significance in promoting or precipitating malnutrition interpreted. All children under five years of age, in the village of Buso were studied for one year. Covers incidence of protein calorie malnutrition and methods of assessment. Describes the village and customs affecting etiology of malnutrition. Quantitative information on households is recorded to assess factors affecting malnutrition, e.g. housing, water supply, sanitation. Includes data on children's food consumption; measurement of crop acreage; food bought and sold; attitudes toward health and feeding; food storage; and livestock.

5401. McCulloch, W.E. 1929. Inquiry into dietaries of Hausa and town Fulani of northern Nigeria, with some observations of effects on national health, with recommendations arising therefrom. WAMJ 3: 8-22.

5402. McCulloch-Williams, Martha. 1913. Dishes and beverages of the old South. New York: McBride, Nast & Co.

Preparation; equipment; available food supply.

5403. McCullogh, J.W.S. 1941. Food in the highlands and islands of Scotland. CanCJ 20: 37.

5404. McCurdy, Betty Joan. A proximate analysis of a Maori food: the Karaka berry. Master's thesis. Home Science. University of Otago. 1947.

Corynocarpus laevigata, Forst. Seeds of this plant are poisonous when raw, but suitable for eating after prolonged soaking or steaming. (A dictonary of plant names. By H.L.

Gerth van Wijk. Vol. 1. 1911. p. 378. The Hague: Martginus Nijhoff.)

5405. McCusker, John J. 1973. Weights and measures in the Colonial sugar trade: the gallon and the pound and their international equivalents. WMQ 30: 599-624.

Trade among New Englanders, British, Dutch, French, Portuguese and Danes during the 17th and 18th Centuries.

5406. McCutcheon, Mary. Taro cultivation in Palau: a study of extensification. Paper presented at 77th Annual Meeting of the American Anthropological Association. 14 to 18 November, 1978. Los Angeles, California.

5407. McDonald, Barbara S. 1963. Gingivitis-ascorbic acid deficiency in the Navajo, 3. Dietary aspects. JADA 43: 332-335.

5408. McDonald, Barbara S. 1965. Nutrition on the Navajo. Second edition. United States Public Health Service. Washington, D.C.: Government Printing Office.

5409. McDowell, Nancy. Food taboos in an East Sepik village. Paper presented at the 76th Annual Meeting of the American Anthropological Association. 29 November to 3 December, 1977. Houston, Texas.

Food taboos in Bun do not constitute a coherent, integrated conceptual system, and any understanding of their symbolic meaning should not derive from an analysis of them as a system of prohibitions. Food taboos have different meanings in different contexts, and only by examing all of a taboo's associated elements does its symbolic significance become clear. An extensive discussion of two such taboos illustrates that more is understood of them when analyzed in context than by relating them to one another.

5410. McEvoy, J.p. 1943. Survive at sea by eating and drinking fish: (suggestion of Gifford Pinchot, reinforced by Charles Nordhoff). RD April. pp. 27-30.

5411. McFadden, E.S. & Sears, E.R. 1946. The origin of Triticum spelta and its free-threshing hexaploid relatives. JHer 3: 81-90; 107-116.

5412. McGanity, William J. 1969. Nutrition survey in Texas. TMed 65: 40-49.

5413. McGee, W.J. 1897. The Siouan Indians. SI-BE-AR for year 1893-1894. pp. 153-204.

Dog flesh as a prestige food: p.171.

5414. McGee, W.J. 1898. The Seri Indians. SI-BE-AR for the year 1895-1896. pp. 1-344.

Early comments on Seri food habits: pp. 91-92. Food and food getting: pp. 180-214. This section discusses availability of water; utensils, hunting equipment, turtle-hunting the use of live pelican decoys for obtaining fish; use of fish and shellfish; hunting; fire-making; use of bow-and-arrow; small game; plant food; use of undigested cactus seeds dried fecal matrix; estimate of quantitative food intake by food type.

5415. McGloshan, N.D. 1969. A diet survey in Kalene Hill area. MJZ 2: 179-187.

Kalene Hill is located at 11.10' S. 24.12' E., in Zambia.

5416. McGonagle, Roberta L. Prehistoric use of food plants in northwestern Nevada. Ph.D. dissertation. Anthropology. University of Missouri, Columbia. 1975.

5417. McGowan. 1871-1872. On the mutton wine of the Mongols and analagous preparations of the Chinese. RAS-NCB-J 7: 237-240.

5418. McGrew, John. Colonial wine-making in Maryland. Paper presented at Bicentennial Symposium on Heritage of Agriculture in Maryland. July 30, 1976. National Agriculture Library Beltsville, Maryland.

5419. McGrew, John R. 1975. Thomas Jefferson: viticulturist and enophile. AWSJ 7: 58.

5420. McGuire, L.M. 1946. Old World foods for New World families. Detroit: Wayne State University Press.

5421. McHenry, E.W. 1939. Nutrition in Toronto: CPHJ 30: 4-13.

5422. McKay, C.G.R. 1953. The rising of the Palolo. SPC-QB 3: 35.

The sea worm Palolo viridis.

5423. McKay, David A. 1971. Food, illness, and folk medicine: insights from Ulu Trengganu, West Malaysia. EFN 1: 67-72.

The existence of indigenous food classification systems often has a functional relationship with indigenous medical practices. In this study, such a relationship is described and effects on nutritional status examined. Reference to xerophthalmia is made in the context of restriction of intake of carotene-containing foods, based on local perception of what foods are and are not appropriate for certain manifest symptoms of disease. The author provides suggestions for effective cross-cultural research in relation to nutrition and health-care delivery.

5424. McKay, David A. & Wade, T.L. 1970. Nutrition, environment, and health in the Iban longhouse. SEAJTMPH 1: 68-77.

Includes information on frequency of fish, meat and egg consumption, and incidence of nutritional deficiency symptoms.

5425.   McKay, Hughina & Brown, Mary Ann. 1931. Foods used by rural families in Ohio during a three year period. O-AES-B No. 492.

5426.   McKee, H.S. 1956. Fish sauces and pastes are palatable and nourishing. SPC-QB 6: 16-17.

5427.   McKee, H.S. 1957. Food plants of the South Sea Islands. SPC-QB 7: 43-45.

5428.   McKee, H.S. 1957. Some food problems in the Pacific Islands. SPC-TP No. 106.

5429.   McKee, H.S. 1957. Some practices of the Pacific Island peoples in handling and storing foodstuffs. AJS 20: 69-71.

5430.   McKee, John. 1951. Bibliography of South African cookery. University of Capetown. School of Librarianship. Bibliographical Series. Vol. 41 No. 1. Capetown: University of Capetown.

5431.   McKendry, Maxime. 1973. Seven centuries of English cooking. Edited by Arabella Boxer. London: Wiedenfeld & Nicolson.

5432.   McKenzie, John C. 1965. The composition and nutritional value of diets in Manchester and Dukinfield in 1841. Lanc Cas-T 72: 123-140.

   Study of the first known dietary survey to be made in Britain.

5433.   McKenzie, John C. Recent developments in social science related to nutrition and dietetics. In Fourth International Congress of Dietetics. 12 July to 16 July, 1965. Stockholm. Proceedings. 1965. pp. 38-46. Stockholm: Ivan Haegstrom Trykkeri.

5434.   McKenzie, John C. 1967. Social and economic implications of minority food habits. PNS 26: 197-205.

5435.   McKenzie, John C. & Mumford, Pamela. 1964. Food habits of West Indian immigrants. PNS 23(2): xlii, xliii.

5436.   McKenzie, John C. & Yudkin, John. 1963. The food we fancy. NSci 17: 280-281.

5437.   McKey, Doyle. 1974. Ant-plants: selective eating of an unoccupied Barteria by a Colobus monkey. Biotropica 6: 269-270.

   Description of feeding activity by Colobus satanas in the Douala-Edea Faunal Reserve, in southern Cameroun. The evolutionary-ecological role of stinging ants in relation to herbivore subsistence is examined.

5438.   McKnight, Robert K. & Obak, Adalbert. Yam cultivation in the Palau District. In Yam cultivation in the Trust Territory of the Pacific Islands. Office of the Staff Anthropologist. 1959. pp. 14-37. Anthropoligical Working Papers No. 4. Agana: Trust Territory of the Pacific Islands.

   Food preference; social value (Sonsorol): pp. 21-32.

5439.   McKnight, Robert K.; Obak, Adalbert; & Emesiochl, M. 1960. Breadfruit cultivation practices and beliefs in Palau. Trust Territory of the Pacific Islands. Office of the Staff Anthropologist. Anthropological Working Papers No. 7. Agana: Trust Territory of the Pacific Islands.

   Food use: pp. 11-17.

5440.   McLaren, Donald S. 1974. The great protein fiasco. Lancet 15 July. pp. 93-96.

   Criticism of the "protein-gap" as fallacious. Indicates concept was based on erroneous generalization that childhood malnutrition throughout the world consisted of kwashiorkor, due to correct but limited observations in atypical situations such as rural Africa during the 1930's where kwashiorkor was originally observed.

5441.   McLaren, Donald S. Chapter Three. Historical perspective of nutrition in the community. In Nutrition and the community. Edited by Donald S. McLaren. 1976. pp. 25-34. London, New York, Sydney, Toronto: John Wiley & Sons.

   How ancient are nutritional disorders: pp. 23-28.

5442.   McLaughlin, Terence. 1979. If you like it, don't eat it. Dietary fads and fancies. New York: Universe Books.

   History of unorthodox dietetic thought from Pythagoras to modern times.

5443.   McLay, E.R. Lack of appetite in one hundred pre-school children. Master's thesis. University of Chicago. 1924.

5444.   McLemore, Richard Aubrey, ed. 1973. A history of Mississippi. Vol. 1. Jackson: University & College Press of Mississippi.

   Food substitutes used during War between the States. p. 507.

5445.   McLeod, Ellen. An experiment in nutrition with children in the early elementary grades. Master's thesis. Tallahassee: Florida State College for Women. 1943.

5446.   McLester, James S. 1935. Nutrition and the future man. JAMA 104: 2144-2147.

   Discusses the role of nutrition in upgrading the public health and well-being. Emphasizes the need for physicians to have a basic understanding of nutrition, and to also be able to prescribe diets within the financial means of the patient. Acknowledges the significance of culturally determined food habits, as well as the place of political and economic factors as they affect the cost of food.

5447.   McLester, James S. 1942. War and the nutrition of the nation. SMA-J 36: 219-220.

Rations developed by Army Quartermaster Corps; President's National Nutrition Conference for Defense.

5448.   McLuney, Katie. Food likes and dislikes of five age groups. Master's thesis. Denton: Texas State College for Women. 1942.

5449.   McMahan, Ruby Nell. The effect of certain poster presentations on the food acceptance of elementary school children. Master's thesis. Denton: North Texas State Teachers College. 1948.

5450.   McMaster, D.N. 1962. The distribution of traditional types of food storage containers in Uganda. UJ 26: 154-160.

5451.   McMetting, R. 1964. Beer as a locus of value among the West African Kofyar. AA 66: 375-384.

Nigeria.

5452.   McMichael, Edward. Ethnobotanical material from the Ohio Valley. In Twenty-first Southeastern Archaeological Conference. November 6-7, 1964. New Orleans, louisiana. Proceedings. Edited by Stephen Williams. 1965. pp. 36-37. SAC-B No. 3.

Mentions sunflower seeds, acorn, and hickory nuts in Middle Wodland sites, and sunflower and maize in late prehistoric excavations.

5453.   McNabb, J. 1929. Disease incidence and diet of natives at Lake Magadi. KEAMJ 6: 212-221.

5454.   McNeil, Blanche & McNeil, Edna V. 1936. First foods of America. Los Angeles; San Francisco; New York: Suttonhouse, Ltd.

A collection of recipes for Mexican foods, dating from the Conquest to the 1930's; supplemented by folklore, songs about food, and glimpses of Mexican life.

5455.   McNeil, Charles. 1942. An alphabet of breast feeding. BMJ 2: 271-273.

Difficulties and remedies of breast feeding written for phsyicians and nurses who counsel new mothers.

5456.   McNeill, Florence Marian. 1929. The Scots kitchen: its traditions and lore with old time recipes. London, Glasgow: Blackie & Son.

5457.   McNeil, Florence Marian. Food and drink. In Scotland. A description of Scotland and Scottish life. Edited by Henry William Meikle. 1947. pp. 237-242. London: Thomas Nelson & Sons.

5458.   McNeil, Florence Marian. 1954. The festive foods of Scotland. Scot Mag 50(12) 32-34.

5459.   McNeil, Florence Marian. 1956. The Scots cellar: its tradition and lore. Paterson: Edinburgh.

Traditional drinks of Scotland.

5460.   McPhee, W.R. 1956. Acquired hemolytic anemia caused by ingestion of fava beans. AJCPath 26: 1287-1302.

5461.   Mead, Charles W. 1921.   Indian corn or maize. NH 21: 409-413.

History of maize in the Western Hemisphere; some early recipes included.

5462.   Mead, Charles W. 1922. Tapioca, a familiar food of unfamiliar origin. NH 22: 468-470.

Use in South America.Describes detoxification process of bitter cassava (Manihot utilissima, L.), and mentions a sweet species Manihot dulcis, var. Aipi Pax. Includes photographs of processing equipment.

5463.   Mead, George Richard. The Indians of the Redwood belt of California: an ethnobotanical approach to culture area. Ph.D. dissertation. Sociology and Anthropology. Washington State University. 1971.

Redefines 'culture area' as 'cultural space' which is delineated in terms of the degree of similarity between tribes as reflected by their culturally determined preferences for botanical materials. 'Cultural space' is seen as being non-contiguous.

5464.   Mead, Margaret. 1934.   How the Papuan plans his dinner. NH 34: 377-388.

5465.   Mead, Margaret. 1942. Reaching the last woman down the road. JHE 34: 710-713.

Suggestions for national nutrition education methods and procedures.

5466.   Mead, Margaret. 1943. The anthropological approach to dietary problems. NYASci-T 5: 17-182.

A summary of the findings of the National Research Council's Committee on Food Habits, as of 1943.

5467.   Mead, Margaret. 1943. Changing food habits. In The nutrition front. Report of the New York State Joint Legislative Committee on Nutrition. Legislative document No. 64. pp. 37-43. Albany.

Emphasizes need for nutrition education during wartime, and in urbanized societies generally. Notes there is no automatic mechanism in human societies which ensures an adequate diet. Notes that greater flexibility in thinking about meal patterns and food subsitutions is required, rather than changes in food habits as such, to effect improved nutritional status, especially in war time.

5468.   Mead, Margaret. 1943. Committee on food habits. PB 20: 290-293.

5469.   Mead, Margaret.   1943.   Dietary patterns and food habits. JADA 19: 1-5.

5470.   Mead, Margaret.   1943.   Factor of food habits. AAPSS-A 225: 136-141.

5471.   Mead, Margaret. 1943. Food therapy and wartime food problems. JADA 19: 201-202.

5472.   Mead, Margaret. The problem of changing food habits. In The problem of changing food habits. Report of the Committee on Food Habits. 1941-1943. National Research Council. 1943. pp. 20-31. NRC-B No. 108.

Reviews the early efforts of the Committee on Food Habits to coordinate information as a basis for making recommendations directed toward changing the dietary pattern of American culture during World War II. Suggestions for studying food behavior, and results of studies in medicine, psychology, and group communications of significance to dietary change are included.

5473.   Mead, Margaret.   1943.   The problem of changing food habits, with suggestions for psychoanalytic contributions. MC-B 7: 57-61. Also in Etc. 1: 47-50. (1943)

5474.   Mead, Margaret.   Changing food habits in the post-war period. In Nutrition for young and old. Legislative document No. 76. New York State Joint Legislative Committee on Nutrition. 1946. pp. 60-64.   Albany: New York State Joint Legislative Committee on Nutrition.

5475.   Mead, Margaret. Significant aspects of regional food patterns. In Conference on food acceptance research. 6 December to 7 December, 1945. United States War Department. Food and Container Institute. Research and Development Branch. Military Planning Division. Committee on Food Research. 1946. Quartermaster Corps Manual 17-9. pp. 64-67.

5476.   Mead, Margaret. Cultural contexts of nutritional patterns.   In Centennial: collected papers presented at the centennial celebration. Washington, D.C., September 13-17, 1948. 1950. pp. 103-111. Washington, D.C.:   American Association for the Advancement of Science.

A very concise review of the theory and methods of the National Research Council's Committee on Food Habits, which was concerned with domestic nutrition intervention in the United States during World War II. Although Mead has summarized the Committee's work in numerous other publications, this article is perhaps the most succinct and comprehensive.

5477.   Mead, Margaret.   1948.   Cultural contexts of nutritional patterns. Science 108: 598-599.

5478.   Mead, Margaret.   1949. Cultural patterning of nutritionally relevant behavior. JADA 25: 677-680.

Food expectations in various ethnic contexts, and how these expectations may be changed.

5479.   Mead, Margaret. 1950. Food and the family. United Nations Educational, Scientific and Cultural Organization. Food and People Series No. 1. New York: Manhattan Publishing Co.

5480.   Mead, Margaret. 1957. We don't like what we don't eat. Cypress MJ 9: 90-93.

5481.   Mead, Margaret.   1960.   The changing American food pattern. LYH October pp. 140-141, 161-165.

5482.   Mead, Margaret. The contribution of cultural anthropology to nutrition. Background paper prepared for the Conference on Malnutrition and Food Habits. 9 to 14 September, 1960. Cuernavaca, Mexico.

5483.   Mead, Margaret.   1964.   Anthropology - a human science. New York: Van Nostrand Paperbook.

Cultural contexts of nutrition patterns: pp. 175-193.

5484.   Mead, Margaret. 1964. Food habits research: problems of the 1960's.   National Research Council.   Publication No. 1225. Washington, D.C. National Academy of Sciences. National Research Council.

5485.   Mead, Willliam Edward. 1931. The English medieval feast.   Boston & New York: Houghton Mifflin.

5486.   Mead, Joaquin. 1948. Iziz centl (el maize). Origenes y mitologia, illus. de codices y monumentos, prolog de Enrique Juan Palacios. [Iziz centli (maiz). Origins and mythology, illustrated by codices and monuments.   Prologue by Enrique Juan Palacios.] Mexico: no publisher. Also published an AMH-M 14(1): 1-31. [1955]

5487.   Meakin, Budgett. 1906. Life in Morocco and glimpses beyond. New York: E.p. Dutton.

Restaurant foods, and etiquette: pp. 102-106; market foods; aged butter; food vendords: pp. 125-132.

5488.   Meaney, F. John. Nutritional factors in socioeconomic group differences during child growth: genetic and environmental considerations. Paper presented at 77th Annual Meeting of the American Anthropological Association. 14 to 18 November, 1978. Los Angeles, California.

5489.   Medlock, Wilyjen A. A study of the diet of the Southern Negro in Charlotte, North Carolina. Master's thesis. New York   Teachers College of Columbia University. 1927.

5490.   Medsger, Oliver Perry. 1939. Edible wild plants. New York: Macmillan.

5491. Medway. 1958. Food bone in Niah Cave. A preliminary report. Sar MJ 8: 627-636.

Niah is located at 3.48N., 113.47E., in Sarawak. Discusses bird, turtle, monitor lizard, fish and mammal archeo-osteological material; a c[14] date of 40,000 B.P. has been determined for the oldest stratum.

5492. Meek, Charles Kingsley. 1925. The northern tribes of Nigeria. Vol. 1. Oxford: Oxford University Press.

Food, food preparation, beverages, etiquette: pp. 135-141.

5493. Meek, Charles Kingsley. 1931. Tribal studies in northern Nigeria. London: Kegan Paul, Trench, Trubern & Co.

Food of the Katab: pp. 47-48; Yungur initiation-fast-breaking food: p. 452.

5494. Meggitt, Mervyn J. 1957. Notes on the vegetable foods of the Walbiri of central Australia. Oceania 28: 143-145.

5495. Meggitt, Mervyn J. 1958. Salt manufacture and trading in the western highlands of New Guinea. AusMJ 12: 309-313.

5496. Meggitt, Mervyn J. Aboriginal food-gatherers of tropical Australia. In Ecology of man in the tropical environment. 9th Technical Meeting. September, 1973, Nairobi. International Union for Conservation of Native and Natural Resources. Proceedings and Papers. 1964. pp. 30-37. Morges, Switzerland: International Union for Conservation of Native and Natural Resources.

5497. Mehta, B.H. Social and economic condition of Chodras, an aboriginal tribe of Gujaret. Master's thesis. Sociology. University of Bombay. 1933.

5498. Meikeljohn, M.F.M. 1962. Wild birds as human food. PNS 21: 80-83.

5499. Meillasoux, Claude. 1964. Antrhopologie economique des Gouro de Cote d'Ivoire. De l'economie de subsistence a l'agriculture commerciale. [Economic anthropology of the Guro of the Ivory Coast. From subsistence economy to commercial agriculture.] Le Monde d'Outre-Mer. Passe et Present. Premiere serie. Etudes No. 27. Paris: Mouton & Cie.

5500. Mejia Xesspe, M.T. 1931. Kausay alimentacion de los indios. [Kausay Indian diet.] Wira 1: 9-24.

Study of pre-Hispanic Peruvian food, based largely on data taken from early dictionaries, and vocabularies. A glossary is given for food words in the Quechua, Aymara and A'kavo languages.

5501. Melhus, I.E. & Chamberlain, I.M. 1953. A preliminary study of teosinte in its region of origin. ISC-JS 28: 139-164.

5502. Melich, Janos. 1963. "Palata". MNyelv 59: 351.

Hungarian fig pastry.

5503. Melichar, H. 1956. Zum Kochen mit heissen Steinen auf Sardinian. [Cooking on hot stones in Sardinia.] ZOV 59: 129-135.

5504. Melikoff, p.G. & Rosenblatt, M. 1907. Le brynsa, fromage russe de lait de brebis. [Brynsa, a Russian sheep milk cheese.] JAPrat 71: 814-815.

5505. Mello, Antonio da Silva. 1942. Alimentacao -instinto - cultura. Perspectiva para uma vida mais feliz. [Diet instinct - culture. Prospect for a happier life.] Rio de Janeior: Jose Olympio.

5506. Mello, Antonio da Silva. 1945. Alimentacion, instinto y cultura. [Diet, instinct and culture. Tanslated from the 2nd Brazilian edition by Arturo Leon Lopez. Buenos Aires: Orientacion Integral Human. Sociedad de Resp. Limitida.

5507. Mello, J.A. Gonsalves e. 1954. Notas acerca da introducao de vegetais exoticos em Pernambuco. [Notes on the introduction of foreign plants to Pernambuco.] IJNPS-B 3: 33-64.

Historical data on food and non-food plants, and their areas of origin.

5508. Mellot, Jean. 1968. Qu est-ce qu'un boulanger? [What is a baker?] VL No. 199. p. 630.

5509. Melsted, Bogi Thorarsen. 1907. En nokkur ordh um slaturhus og saudhakjot. [The specific word for slaughterhouse, and mutton.] Reykjavik: Ikke i Bog.

5510. Mencher, Joan p. Rice cultivation and the female: some South Asian perspectives. Paper presented at 75th Meeting of the American Anthropological Association. 17 to 21 November, 1976. Washington, D.C.

In areas of intensive cultivation, females play unsuspectedly crucial roles, both as laborers and (at times) as supervisors of labor. Furthermore, in areas with significant left-oriented political organizations, women laboreres form a markedly large part of labor movements than men (up to eighty per cent, in some areas). The relatively low number of women who appear as labor leaders, or as agricultural professionals has, perhaps, masked the importance of women in agriculture, which has several implications for the social relations of production, as well as for the political mobilization of agricultural laborers, in these areas.

5511. Mendel, Lafayette B. 1932. The changing diet of American people. JADA 8: 47-55. Also in JAMA 99: 117-120 (1932).

Reviews food patterns in the United States during the Nineteenth Century. Based on excerpts from cookboods and travel literature. Considers the nutritional significance of the increase in sugar intake and other refined foods; and the value of knowledge of nutritional biochemistry to health, for physicians.

5512. Mendelson, Myer. 1964. Deviant patterns of feeding behavior in man. FASEB-FP 23: 69-72.

Focus is on obesity and anorexia nervosa.

5513. Mendelson, R.A. Parents, peers and mass media; their influence on children's food behavior. Master's thesis. Nutritional Science. Cornell University. 1974.

5514. Mendenhall, George E. 1954. Poppy and lettuce in northwest-Semitic covenant making. ASOR-J 133: 26-30.

5515. Mendes, Helen. 1971. The African heritage cookbook. New York: Macmillan.

Includes discussion of influence of Black African food habits on U.S. cookery.

5516. Mendizabal, M.O. de. 1928. Influencia de la sel en la distribucion geografica de los grupos indigenas de Mexico. [Influence of salt on the geographical distribution of native Mexican groups.] Mexico: Imprensa del Museo Nacional de Arqueologia, Historia y Etnografia.

5517. Menendez-Ramos, R. 1937. Agriculture of Puerto Rico and its relation to medico-social problems. [In Spanish.] AMPR-B 29: 11-22.

5518. Menzes, M.L.F. 1962. Edible insects on palm trees. [In Portuguese.] GA 14: 277-279.

5519. Menjaud, Henri. 1967. When famine ravaged Europe. FFH September-October. pp. 16-23.

Socio-historical overview of food and agriculture in medieval Europe.

5520. Mennonite Central Committee. 1929. Feeding the Hungry. Russian famine 1919-1925; Mennonite relief operations under the auspices of Mennonite Central Committee. Edited by p.C. Hiebert & Orie O. Miller. Scottdale, Pennsylvania: Mennonite Central Committee.

5521. Mentz, Elize. The hygiene of food. In Manual for public health nurses. Edited by Charlotte Searle. 1967. pp. 231-248. Pretoria: South African Nursing Association.

5522. Mercader, Cesar. n.d. [1964?] Freedom from cassava. A medico-legal study of Republic Act 657 on cassava law. Vol. 1. Dumanjug, Cebu, Philippines: the author.

Criticizes legislation encouraging cassava production. Brings forward cassava toxicity and limited nutritional value in arguing against production and use.

5523. Mercier, Andre 1943. Le baobab, enquete d'ethnographie botanique. [The baobab, ethnobotanical inquiry.] MC Octobre. pp. 3-15; Novembre. pp. 171-175.

Adansonia digitata.

5524. Mericer, Andre-Louis. 1946. Enquete sur les vegetaux dans le folklore et l'ethnographie, suivie d'une bibliographie sur le culte des arbres et les plantes dans le folklore et l'ethnographie. [Inquiry on vegetables in folklore and ethnography, followed by a bibliography on tree and plant worship in folklore and ethnography.] Ethnographie No. 38. pp. 45-49.

5525. Mercier, Andre-Louis. 1952. Enquete sur les vegetaux dans les folklore et l'ethnographie. Flore populaire. 1. Les herbes (suite) [2]. [Inquiry on vegetables in folklore and ethnography. Popular flora. 1. Herbs. (continued) (2).] Ethnographie No. 47. pp. 86-113.

5526. Mercier, Andre-Louis. 1953. Les vegetaux dans le folklore et l'ethnogrophie. Les herbes populaire de France (Suite). [Vegetables in floklore and ethnography. The popular herbs of France. [continued].[Ethnographie No. 48. pp. 48-61.

5527. Mercier, Andre-Louis. 1954. Les vegetaux dans le folklore et l'ethnographie. Les herbes populaires de France [suite]. [Vegetables in folklore and ethnography. The popular herbs of France (continued). Ethnographie No. 49. 82-92.

5528. Mercier, Andre-Louis. 1955. Les vegetaux dans le folklore et l'ethnographie. Les herbes populaires de France (suite). [Vegetables in folklore and ethnography. The popular herbs of France. (continued). Ethnographie No. 50. pp. 148-158.

5529. Mercier, Andre-Louis. 1956. Les vegetaux dans le folklore et l'ethnography. [The popular herbs of France.] Ethnographie No. 51. pp. 125-136.

5530. Mercier, Andre-Louis. 1957. Les vegetaux dans le folklore et l'ethnographie. Les epices. [Vegetables in folklore and ethnography. Spices.] Ethnographie No. 52. pp. 87-106.

5531. Mercier, Andre-Louis. 1959. Les vegetaux dans le folklore et l'ethnographie. Les epices et plantes condimentaires. [Vegetables in folklore and ethnography. Spices and condiment plants.] Ethnographie No. 53. pp. 97-115.

5532. Mercier, Andre-Louis. 1960. Les vegetaux dans le folklore et l'ethnographie. Les epices et plantes condimentaires. [Vegetables in folklore and ethnography. Spices and condiment plants.] Ethnographie No. 54. pp. 91-109.

5533. Mercier, Andre-Louis. 1961. Les vegetaux dans le folklore et l'ethnographie. Les epices et plantes condimentaires. Les moutardes. [Vegetables in folklore and ethnographie. Spices and condiment plants. Mustards.] Ethnographie No. 55. pp. 108-123.

5534. Mercier, Andre-Louis. 1962. Les vegetaux dans le folklore et l'ethnographie. Les epices et plantes condimentaires. [Vegetables in folklore and

ethnography. Spices and condiment plants.] Ethnographie No. 56. pp. 101-115.

5535.   Mercier, Andre-Louis. 1963. Les vegetaux
dans les folklore et l'ethnographie. Les epices et
plantes condimentaires. [Vegetables in folklore and
ethnography. Spices and condiment plants.] Ethnographies No. 57. pp. 149-171.

5536.   Mercier, Andre-Louis. 1964-1965. Suite de
l'enquete sur les vegetaux dans le folklore et l'ethnographie. Les agrumes. [Continuation of the
inquiry on vegetables in folklore and ethnographie.
The citrus fruits.] Ethnographie Nos. 58-59. pp.
137-142.

5537.   Merigot, Madame.   Annee 3.   [1775] La
cuisiniere republicaine qui enseigne la maniere d'accomoder les pommes de terre; avece quelques avis
sur les soins necessaires pour les conserver. [The
Republican cookbook in which is taught the manner
of cooking potatoes; with several suggestions on the
care necessary to preserve them.]   Paris: Merigot
jeune.

5538.   Merle. 1958.   Des chenilles comestibles.
[Edible worms.] NA No. 77. pp. 20-23.

5539.   Merlo, M. 1961. Cooked rice for the
athletes of antiquity. [In Italian.] Riso 10: 25-26.

5540.   Merrett, Mary Jo. Diet in relation to health
and some common diseases. Master's thesis. Denton: North Texas State College. 1942.

5541.   Merriam, C.H. 1918. The acorn, a possibly
neglected source of food. NGM 34: 129-137.

   Uses of acorns by California Native American groups.

5542.   Merriam, Willis B. 1944. The role of pemmican in the Canadian northwest fur trade. APCG-
YB 17: 34-38.

5543.   Merrill, Elmer Drew. 1909. Medical survey
of the town of Taytay. 5. Principal foods utilized by
natives, with list of fruits, vegetables, pot herbs,
and condiments found in market of said town. PJS 4
[B]: 219-223.

   Phillipines.   Review of dietary pattern.
   Taytay is a suburb, located approximately
   ten kilometers east of Manila.

5544.   Merrill, Elmer Drew. 1920. Comments on
Cook's theory as to the American origin and prehistoric Polynesian distribution of certain economic
plants, especially Hibiscus tiliaceus, Linnaeus. PJS
17: 377-384.

   A portion of this article is given over to
   criticism of the theory advanced by Orator
   Fuller Cook concerning the probable New
   World origin of the coconut (Cocos nucifera,
   L.).

5545.   Merrill, Elmer Drew. 1933. Crops and
civilization. TBC-B 60: 323-329.

5546.   Merrill, Elmer Drew. 1931. The phytogeography of cultivated plants in relation to assumed
pre-Columbian Eurasian-American contacts. AA 33:
375-382.

5547.   Merrill, Elmer Drew. The problem of econ-
omic plants in relation to man in pre-Columbian
America. In Fifth Pacific Science Congress. 1933.
Canada. Proceedings. 1934. Vol. 1. pp. 759-769.
Toronto: University of Toronto Press.

   Argues against any general dissemination of
   economic food plants between Eurasia and
   America before European discovery of
   America.

5548.   Merrill, Elmer Drew. 1938. Domesticated
plants in relation to the diffusion of culture. BR 4:
1-20.

   Largely devoted to a refutation of cult, and
   single-course diffusionist theories of culture. The latter half of the article is a
   reprise of scientific evidence relating to the
   origin and distribution of food plants.

5549.   Merrill, Elmer Drew. 1943. Emergency and
poisonous plants of the islands of the Pacific; review. Science 98: 10.

5550.   Merrill, Elmer Drew. 1945. Chapter Ten.
Jungle foods. In Plant life of the Pacific worlds.
Washington, D.C.: Press of the Infantry Journal.

5551.   Merrill, Lucius H. 1906. Indian corn as food
for man Me-AES-B No. 131.

   Includes mention of food uses of maize
   among early New England colonists; recipes
   for several maize meal products are given
   (johnny-cake; brown bread, and hoe-cake).

5552.   Merritt, Albert Newton. 1920. War-time
control of distribution of foods. A short history of
the Distribution Division of the United States Food
Administration, its personnel and achievements.
New York: Macmillan.

5553.   Meskill, Jane M. Some Brazilian plants in
the early Colonial period. Master's thesis. Columbia University. 1966.

   Native food plants; some information on
   preparation and use.

5554.   Mesnard, J. & Rose, E. 1920. Recherches
complementaires sur la fabrication du nuoc-mam.
[Further researches on the manufacture of nuoc-
mam. IPI-A 34: 622-649.

   Nuoc-mam is a fish oil condiment used in
   Indochina.

5555.   Messedaglia, Luigi. 1932. Per la storia dell'
agicoltura e dell alimentazione. [Toward a history
of agriculture and diet.] Piacenza: Federazione
Italiana dei Consorzi Agrari.

5556.   Messenger, A.H. 1934. An old-time Maori
feast. Walkabout December. pp. 49-55.

5557. Messer, Ellen. 1972. Patterns of "wild" plant consumption is Oaxaca, Mexico. EFN 1: 325-332.

Considers the significance of uncultivated plants as a nutritional supplement to the maize-legume-cucurbit complex of Meso-american native diet. The uses of such plants in the diet are described, and the effect of irrigation and agriculture on the availability of wild plants is examined in San Sebastian Abasolo, located fifteen kilometers ESE of Oaxaca City, along the Rio Salado.

5558. Messer, Ellen. Zapotec plant knowledge: classification, uses and communication about plants in Mitla, Oaxaca, Mexico. Ph.D. dissertation. Anthropology. University of Michigan, Ann Arbor. 1975.

5559. Messer, Ellen. Cultivation and cognition: plants and archaeological research strategies. Paper presented at 75th Annual Meeting of the American Anthropological Association. 17 tp 21 November, 1976. Washington, D.C.

Ethnobotany can provide several types of information for archeologists. Contemporary land use and plant use studies may help in the interpretation of paleoethnobotanical and settlement pattern diets. Ethnobotanical models may also be used in planning sampling, and recovery procedures; and to learn more about plant production and consumption strategies. In addition, the economic botany, ethnotaxonomic, and ethnoecological studies combined by the ethnobotanist can add to the archaeologist's understanding of the choice of particular plants for cultivation, construction and ritual. The foregoing are illustrated, with reference to data from the Valley of Oaxaca, Mexico.

5560. Messer, Ellen. The ecology of vegetarian diet in a modernizing Mexican community. In Nutrition and anthropology in action. Edited by Thomas K. Fitzgerald. 1976. pp. 117-124. Assen, Amsterdam: Van Gorcum.

Examines some of the dietary changes and nutritional consequences of specialization in agriculture and the economic demise of the subsistence farm, with particular reference to the Zapotec community of Milta, in the eastern extension of the Valley of Oaxaca, in the Mexican State of Oacaca (located at 16.56' N, 96.19' W). Dietary patterns gathered, uncultivated plants, food customs and nutritional knowledge are considered and evaluated in relation to their potential significance for future directed change in both the agricultural and public health nutrition sectors.

5561. Messer, Ellen. Traditional and non-traditional maize diet in Mitla, Oaxaca, Mexico. Paper presented at 77th Annual Meeting of the American Anthropological Association. 14 to 18 November, 1978. Los Angeles, California.

5562. Mestdagh. 1913. La culture du mais par les indigenes de l'Ubangui (Congo Belge). [Cultivation of maize by the natives of Ubangi [Belgian Congo]. BACB 4: 884-890.

Preparation of rice flour; p. 888.

5563. Metais, Pierre. 1962. L'alimentation vegetale des Melanesiens de Nouvelle-Caledonie. [Vegetable diet of the Melanesians of New Caledonia.] QPMV 10: 53-72.

5564. Metraux, Alfred. 1936. Les Indiens Uru Cipaya de Carangds: moyens de subsistance; la preparation des aliments. [The Uru-Chipaya Indians; means of subsistence; food preparation.] SAP-J 28: 159-167.

5565. Metraux, Alfred. 1937. Une feodalite cannibale en Polynesie (les iles Gambier, et l'oeuvre du p. Laval). [A cannibal feudal system in Polynesia (the Gambier Islands and the work of p. Laval).] RParis 44: 637-661.

5566. Metraux, Alfred. 1940. Ethnology of Easter Island. BPBM-B No. 160.

Myth: acquisition of vegetables and cereals: p. 364; myth: origin of yams (sweet potatoes, taro): p. 317; myth: origin of cannibalism: p. 377. Agriculture and cookery: pp. 151-164; feasts: 343-351.

5567. Metraux, Alfred. Warfare, cannibalism, and human trophies. In Handbook of South American Indians. SI-BAE-B No. 143. Edited by Julian H. Steward. 1949. Vol. 5. pp. 383-409.

5568. Metraux, Alfred. 1957. One man's meat is another man's - taboo. UC 10: 10-11.

5569. Metraux, Alfred. 1959. Voodoo. Translated by Hugo Charteris. London: Andre Deutsch, Ltd. Reprint. London: Sphere Books. 1974.

The place of food in vodun ritual is extensive. Specific references are found on pp. 176-178 [(offerings); p. 187 (song); and pp. 224, 225 [the feast of yams].

5570. Metraux, Alfred. The cannibalistic Tupinamba of Brazil. In The Americans on the eve of discovery. Edited by Harold E. Driver. 1964. pp. 61-68. Englewood Cliffs, New Jersey: Prentice-Hall.

5571. Metraux, Alfred. Tupinamba - war and cannibalism. In Readings in anthropology. Edited by Jesse D. Jennings & Ernest Adamson Hoebel. 1966. pp. 177-180. New York: McGraw-Hill.

5572. Metraux, Rhoda. Popular beliefs about the relationship between specific foods and morale. Mimeographed. Committee on Food Habits. Washington, D.C.: National Academy of Sciences. National Research Council. 21 July, 1942.

5573. Meurs, G.J. van. 1964. Elmer Verner McCollum. Voeding 25: 587-599.

5574. Mexico. Instituto de Nutrologia. 1959. Encuesta nutricional del Municipio de Cuatepec, Guerrero. [Nutritional inquiry in the Municipality of Cuatepec, Geurrero.] Mimeographed.

5575. Mexico. Instituto Nacional de la Nutricion. Encuestas nutricionales en Mexico. [Nutrition surveys in Mexico.] Mimeographed. Mexico City: Instituto Nacional de la Nutricion. 1965.

Data on food taboos, and preferences recorded for various communities surveyed.

5576. Mexico City. Museo Nacional de Mexico. Relacion de Huetlalpan. Descripcion del puelbo de Gueytlalpa y su jurisdiccion. [Report of Hutelalpan. Description of the village of Gueytlalpa and its territory.]

Notes that cacaguasuchil is added to chocolate so that the [systematic] 'coldness' of the cacao may not be injurious.

5577. Mexico City. Universidad Nacional Autonoma de Mexico. Instituto de Biologia. Las plantas alimenticias y comestibles utilizadas en Mexico. [Plants used for food in Mexico] [by Cassiano Conzatti.] 1919-1922.

5578. Meyer, E. 1954. Native feeding on farms. WHH 6: 176-177.

South Africa

5579. Meyer, Frank Nichols. 1911. Agricultural explorations in the fruit and nut orchards of China. USDA-BPI-B No. 204.

5580. Meyer, Frank Nicholas. 1911. Chinese plant names. These characters refer to plants collected by Mr. Meyer during his explorations in North China from 1905 to 1908 inclusive and are romanized in accordance with the Wade system. New York: Chinese and Japanese Publishing Co. Electrotyped for the Office of Foreign Seed and Plant Introduction, Bureau of Plant Industry. [United States.] Department of Agriculture.

5581. Meyer, Frank Nicholas. 1916. China, a fruitful field for plant exploration. USDA-YB for the year 1915. pp. 205-224.

5582. Meyer, Kurt. 1947. Saatgutuntersuchungen bei Heil-und Gewurzpflanzen. [Investigations of seeds of medicinal and condiment-yielding plants.] Pharmazie 2: 320-330.

5583. Meyer-Rochow, V.B. 1973. Edible insects in three different ethnic groups of Papua and New Guinea. AJCN 26: 673-677.

Orthoptera, Odonata, Anoplura, Hemiptera, Homoptera, Coleoptera, Lepidoptera, Siphonaptera, Hymenoptera, Arthropods other than insects.

5584. Meyers, Amy Louise. The preparation of animal growth studies to be used in public nutrition teaching. Master's thesis. Ohio State University. 1943.

5585. Mezincescu, M.D. 1939. Nutrition of the rural population of Roumania. [In Roumanian.] RSMed 28: 829-869.

5586. M'hamsadji, N. 1955. Le material de cuisine dans les regions d'Aumale et de Sidi-Aisa. [Foodstuffs in the regions of Aumale, and Sidi-Aissa] IEO-A 13: 5-29.

Both regions are located in north-central Algeria, inland from the Mediterranean about one hundred kilometers, at 36.10' N, 3.41' E, and 35.53' N, 3.45' E, respectively.

5587. Michael, Pamela & Michael, Maurice. 1977. Food for lovers. New York, London: Paddington Press.

Largely a book or recipes, but illustrated with reproductions of classical art - both Occidental and Oriental - which combine the erotic with eating.

5588. Michael, W.H. 1909. Pickled tea. USDCL-DCTR No. 3444: 15.

A preparation of fermented or pickled tea leaves. The leaves are soaked in oil, and seasoned with dried fish and garlic. In some regions, a beverage is made from this tea. Burma, and the Shan States.

5589. Michalakowna, Barbara. 1964. Pozywiene. [Food consumption.] KLW 2: 401-445.

Poland. English summary: pp. 696-697.

5590. Michalowski, Michael. 1957. Plantas comestibles del Paraguay. [Edible plants of Paraguay.] Servicio Tecnico Inter-americano de Cooperacion Agricola. Asuncion: Ministerio de Agricultura y Ganaderia.

5591. Michelsen, Ralph C.; Albrecht, Jacques; & Kjonegaard, Vernon H. The Kiliwa: hunters and gatherers of Baja California. Film. Screened at 73rd Annual Meeting of the American Anthropological Association. 19 to 24 November, 1974. Mexico City.

5592. Michie, G. & Fenton, Alexander. 1963. Cheese-presses in Angus. SS 7: 47-56.

Scotland.

5593. Mickey, Joseph B. 1972. Old, old Western recipes used before 1867. Edited and compiled from an original wagon-train and settler's handbook, 1867. 4th edition. Ottawa, Kansas: no publisher cited.

5594. Mickey, Karl B. 1946. Health from the ground up. Chicago: International Harvester Company.

Relationship of soil quality to nutritional value of crops.

5595. Mickey, Margaret Portia. 1944. The Hai P'a Miao of Kweichow. WCBRS-J 15: 57-78.

Ordinary and ceremonial foods: pp. 62-63.

5596. Mickey, Margaret Portia. 1947. The Cowrie Shell Miao of Kweichow. H-PMAAE-P 32 No. 1.

Food habits: pp. 236; 24a,b; 34a; 35a,b; 38a; 39a; 40a; 72a,b; 73a,b; 74a; 796.

5597. Mida's Trademark Bureau, comp. 1910. Confectionary trade-marks. Chicago: Criterion Publishing Co.

5598. Miege, J.L. 1952. L'importance economique des ignames en Cote d'Ivoire. [The economic importance of yams in the Ivory Coast.] RBAAT Nos. 353-354. pp. 144-155.

5599. Miege, J.L. 1957. Origine et developpement de la consomation du the au Maroc. [Beginnings and development of tea consumption in Morocco.] BESM 20: 377-398.

5600. Miege, J.L. & Lefort, M. 1949. Le manioc en Cote d'Ivoire. [Manioc in the Ivory Coast.] In Congres du manioc et du plantes feculentes tropicales des territoires de l'Union francaises. Marseilles: Imprimerie de A. Lesstrohan.

5601. Miklau, Lia. 1964. Die "karntner Bauerin" und das "Eierdampfl" in der Karntner Bauerkuche. [The "Carinthian Farmer's Wife" and the "egg dumpling" in Carinthian country cooking.] KL No. 1. pp. 3-4.

5602. Miklouho-Maclay, N. de. 1885-1886. List of plants in use by the natives of the Maclay-Coast, New Guinea. LSNSW-P 10: 346-354.

Cultivated plants, forest food-plants.

5603. Milam, D.F. 1942. A nutritional survey of small North Carolina community. AJPH 32: 406-412.

5604. Milam, D.F. & Anderson, Richmond K. 1944. Nutrition survey of an entire rural county in North Carolina. SMedJ 37: 597-605.

Wayne County.

5605. Milam, D.F. & Darby, William J. 1945. The average diet of a Southern county and its effects on nutritional status. SMedJ 38: 117.

North Carolina.

5606. Milanich, Jerald T. Dietary scarcity: a stimulus for warfare among New World horticulturalists. Paper read at 74th Annual Meeting of the American Anthropological Association. 2 to 6 December, 1975. San Francisco, California.

5607. Milanich, Jerald T. & Weisman, Brent. Deer, maize and warfare in the historic southeast United States. Paper presented at 73rd Annual Meeting of the American Anthropological Association. 19 to 24 November, 1974. Mexico City.

5608. Mildbraed, J. 1913. Ergebnisse, wissenschaftliche der deutschen Zentral-Afrika-Expedition unter Fuhrung Adolf Friedrich, Herzog zu Mecklenburg. Vol. 2. Von den Bulus genutzte wildwachsende pflanzen der Sudkamerunner Waldlandes. [Scientific report of the German Central Africa Expedition led by Duke Adolf Friedrich of Mecklenburg. Vol. 2. The useful wild forest plants of the Bulu of southern Cameroun.] KBGMB-D-N.

5609. Milella, A.A. 1936. Food of peasants in Bari Province. [In Italian.] FMed 22: 955-981.

Northeastern Italy.

5610. Miles, Douglas. 1965. Consumption and local mobility in Upper Mentayan villages. Oceania 36: 121-131.

Records changes in diet occurring as the result of migration from upper to lower zone, in a Bornean village. Chart of an informal diet survey is given, together with description of the nature of meals, and staple foods.

5611. Miles, G.p.L. 1938. Rapid approximation of the computation of diet in the field. Man 38: 67-68.

Refers to the studies of Orr & Gllks (1931), Richards & Widdowson (1936) among others and states that "...some survey of nutrition should become almost a 'sine qua non' for the anthropological field worker; more especially if, as Malinowkski suggests, he is to approach culture by means of the theory of primary needs and to ascertain to what extent these needs are met by the particular culture under observation." Suggests that the anthropologist include as a field reference tool food composition tables for calculation of approximate dietary values.

5612. Miles, J.D. 1965. The drinking pattern of the Bantu in South Africa. Research Series, 18. Pretoria: National Bureau of Educational and Social Research.

5613. Milev, N. & Demirewa, M. 1964. Influence of economic and social factors on the biological value of the diet. [In German.] Nahrung 8: 611-620.

5614. Milgrom, J. 1963. Biblical diet laws as an ethical system. Food and faith. Interpretation 17: 288-301.

5615. Milk Research Council, Inc. & University of Newark Research Centre. 1938. Milk drinking habits among young people. A psychological study. no place cited: Milk Research Council, Inc. & University of Newark Research Centre.

Questionnaires were responded to by 5,227 high school students in the Evander Childs, James Monroe, and Theodore Roosevelt schools. Four hundred fifteen of the students were interviewed who disliked milk, as were two hundred seventeen of their mothers. The study is comprised of a general survey of milk consumption and sections addressing reasons for dislike of milk; the mother's role; what children dislike about milk; individuals who like milk but do not drink it; milk nausea; other beverages consumed by the students; indices for the measure of milk consumption; early feeding difficulties; comparison of mothers' and students responses. Held by National Agricultural Library. No. 389 1M592.

5616.   Millepierres, Francois. 1966. De quelques legumes. [About some vegetables.] VL No. 166. pp. 17-25.

Includes a section of etymologies of various garden vegetables; and a section titled "legumes et litterature" [i.e. "vegetables and literature".]

5617.   Miller, Amy Bess & Fuller, Persis. 1970. The best of Shaker cooking. New York: Macmillan. Collier Books; London: Collier Macmillan.

Shaker foods, kitchens, dining habits: pp. 1-11.

5618.   Miller, C.M. 1967. Food habits and nutritional deficiency, a study of diet in Central Africa. Master's thesis. Hamilton, Ontario: McMaster University. 1967.

5619.   Miller, Carey D. no date. The influence of foods and food habits upon stature and teeth of the ancient Hawaiians. Hi-AES-MP No. 94. [unpublished]

5620.   Miller, Carey D. 1927. Food value of poi, taro, and limu. BPBM-B No. 37.

History and use of the Hawaiian starchy staple (Colocasia esculenta); and seaweed, before contact and during the present.

5621.   Miller, Carey D. 1929. Food values of breadfruit, taro leaves, coconut, and sugar cane. BPBM-B No. 64.

Precontact and modern uses by Hawaiians.

5622.   Miller, Carey D. 1932. The foods of the ancient Hawaiians. M-P Mag 44: 337-342.

5623.   Miller, Carey D. 1933. Japanese foods commonly used in Hawaii. Hi-AES-B No. 66.

5624.   Miller, Carey D. 1936. Some fruits of Hawaii. Hi-AES-B No. 77.

5625.   Miller, Carey D. 1938. A study of the dietary values and standard of living of forty-four Japanese families in Hawaii. UHi-RP 18 No. 2.

5626.   Miller, Carey D. 1945. The thiamine content of Japanese soybean products. JADA 21: 430-432.

Tofu, aburage, miso.

5627.   Miller, Carey D. 1947. Foods and food habits in the Hawaiian Islands. JADA 23: 766-768.

Emphasis on introduced food affecting precontact diet.

5628.   Miller, Carey D. The nutritive value of some native foods compared with highly milled cereals. In 7th Pacific Science Congress. Proceedings. 1949. Christchurch, New Zealand. Proceedings. Vol. 7. 1953. pp. 428-429.

Compares thiamine, riboflavin, niacin, and calcium values in wheat, rice, sweet potato, breadfruit, and taro (leaves and corm).

5629.   Miller, Carey D.; Bazore, Katherine; & Robbins, Ruth C. 1936. Some fruits of Hawaii. Their composition, nutritivi value and use. Hi- AES-B No. 77.

5630.   Miller, Carey D.; Branthoover, B.; Sekiguchi, Nao; Denning, Helen; & Bauer, Adelia. 1956. Vitamin values of foods used in Hawaii. Hi-AES-TB No. 30.

5631.   Miller, Carey d. & Lind, H.Y. 1942. Food for health in Hawaii. Hi-AES-B No. 88.

5632.   Miller, Carey D.; Louis, Lucille; & Yanazawa, Kisako., 1946. Foods used by Filipinos in Hawaii. Hi-AES-B No. 98.

5633.   Miller, Carey D.; Louis Lucille; & Yanazawa, Kisako. 1947. Vitamin values of foods in Hawaii. Hi-AES-TB No. 6.

5634.   Miller, Carey D.; Murai, Mary; & Pen, Florence. 1956. The use of pandanus fruit as food in Micronesia. PSci 10: 3-16.

5635.   Miller, Carey D. & Robbins, Ruth C. 1940. Chemical analysis and vitamin assay of opihi, the Hawaiian limpet. PJS 71: 141-163.

Helcioniscus exaratus, Nuttall, and Helicioniscus argentatus, Sowerby. Samples analyzed were from the Honolulu fish market, as well as taken fresh from the ocean. Brief, historical data on use as food are included.

5636.   Miller, Carey D.; Robbins, Ruth C.; & Haida, Kisako. 1934. The nutritive value of the mountain apple Eugenia malaccensis or Jambosa malaccensis. PJS 53: 211-221.

Samples analyzed are from the Hawaiian Islands.

5637.   Miller, Carl F. Prehistoric irrigation systems in Arizona. Master's thesis. University of Arizona. 1929.

5638.   Miller, Carl F. 1960. The use of Chenopodium seeds as a source of food by the early people in Russel Cave, Alabama. SoIS 1: 31-32.

Early Woodland Horizon, ca. 3000 B.C.

5639.   Miller, Cora & Kaumvakli, Theodora. 1955. Food intake of Greek farm families. JADA 31: 269-272.

5640.   Miller, D.S. 1972. Seasonal variations in food intake in two Ethiopian villages. PNS 31: 32A-33A.

5641.   Miller, E. Joan Wilson. 1968. The Ozark culture region as revealed by traditional materials. AAG-A 58: 51-77.

Foods: p. 73.

5642.   Miller, Edward Y. (Mrs.), trans. 1905. Manners and customs of the Tagbanuas and other tribes of the Island of Palawan. SI-MC 48: 514-558.

Philippines. Feasts (lunar; thanksgiving; post-harvest); feast foods, beverages, and their preparation: pp. 524-525; food in the marriage ceremony: p. 530.

5643.   Miller, Jr., Gerrit. 1931. Mammals eaten by Indians, owls and Spaniards in the coast region of the Dominican Republic. SI-MC 82: 1-16.

5644.   Miller, Marc. Ethnicity and occupational socialization: Italian fishermen in New England. Paper presented t 77th Annual Meeting of the American Anthropological Association. 14 to 18 November, 1978. Los Angeles, California.

5645.   Miller, Mary Ann. 1971. The relationship between employee breakfast-eating habits and visits to industrial health facilities. OHN 19: 7-12.

A study of eighty subjects revealed that those who ate an inadequate breakfast, or no breakfast on a given morning tended to visit the health unit requesting care for either an illness or injury, more often than those who ate an adequate breakfast.

5646.   Miller, Raymond W. 1959. The fine art of human relationships applied to changing worldwide dietary patterns. CST 1: 123-128.

A popular article which discusses world hunger; need for nutrition education; difficulties in communicating scientific facts. Includes a section 'How food habits affect human behavior.' Mentions National Research Council Committee on Food Habits, and its Bulletin No. 108.

5647.   Miller, Sanford A. The kinetics of nutritional status: diet, culture, and economics. In Diet of man: needs and wants. Edited by John Yudkin. 1978. Pp 187-208. London: Applied Science Publishers.

A discussion of the impact of population growth, environment, immigration, and standard of living on human food behavior and health. Concludes that future problems of societies' food demands will require the collaboration of nutritionist, anthropologist, sociologist, food technologist, economist, planner, politician, statesman and food industry.

5648.   Milliau, E. 1895. Des huiles comestibles. [Edible oils.] Marseilles: Berthelet et cie.

5649.   Millican, F.K.; Layman, E.M.; Lourie, R.S., Takahashi, I.Y.; & Dublin, C.C. 1962. The prevalence of ingestion and mouthing of nonedible substances by children. CH-CP 18: 207-214.

5650.   Million, H.L. 1926. Old Roman cookbook. Classic 21: 443-450.

5651.   Millis, Jean. 1956. The influence of economic level on the feeding of Chinese infants in the first year of life. JTPECH 2: 103-108.

Contains information on food patterns, and food beliefs related to infant feeding among Chinese in Singapore.

5652.   Millis, Jean. 1959. The feeding of Chinese, Indian, and Malay infants in Singapore. QRP 14: 42-48.

5653.   Mills, J.p. 1926. The Ao Nagas. London: Macmillan & Co.

Food: pp. 142-148.

5654.   Mills, Reva. A study of low-cost adequate diets in a state institution. Master's thesis. Ohio State University. 1944.

5655.   Millsaps, F. Eileen. The basis of our food habits. Master's thesis. Home Economics. Ithaca, New York: Cornell University. 1948.

5656.   Milne, Lorus J. & Milne, Margery J. 1949. Sugar season in the South. NH 58: 460-462.

Manufacture of cane sugar syrup in southeastern United States.

5657.   Milne, William. 1860. On some of the plants used as food by the Feejee Islanders. BSE-T 6: 263-265. Also in ENPJ 10: 151-153 (1859).

5658.   Milojcic, Vladimir; Boessneck, Joachim; & Hopf, Maria. 1962. Die Deutschen Ausgrabungen auf der Argissa-Magula in Thessalien. 1. Das Prakeramische Neolithicum Sowie die Tier-und Pflanzenreste [Beitrage zur ur-und fruhgeschichtlichen Archaologie des Mittelmeer-Kulturaumes]. Vol. 2. [German excavations at Argissa-Maghula in Thessaly. 1. The preceramic Neolithic as well as the animal and plant remains. [Contribution to prehistoric and hsitorical archaeology of the Mediterranean culture area.]. Bonn: Habelt.

5659.   Miloradovich, Milo. 1954. Pickling spices: yesterday and today. Herbarist No. 20. pp. 5-8.

5660.   Miloslavevic, S.M. 1928. Bacijanje na Sar-planini. [Milk industry in the Sara Mountains.] GSND 3: 209-236.

5661.   Miner, William Harvey. 1917. The American Indians. Cambridge: at the University Press.

Cooking and preparing mescal: p. 122.

5662.   Minich, Virginia; Okcuoglu, Ayhan; Arcasoy, Ayten; Suhru, Cin; Yurukoglu, Orhan; Renda, Fevzi; & Demirag, Bahtiyar. 1968. Pica in Turkey. 2. Effects of clay upon iron absorption. AJCN 21: 78-86.

5663.   Minino, Matilde Candelario de. Factores culturales en la alimentacion Dominicana. [Cultural factors in Dominican Republic diet.] In Seminario de nutricion del nino y la familia. Santo Domingo, Republica Dominicana. 10-15 de abril de 1967. 1968. pp. 194-199. Montevideo: Instituto Interamericano del Nino.

5664.   Minj, B. Economic life of the Birhor. Master's thesis. Anthropology. Ranchi University. 1958. India.

5665.   Mirenda, Rose. Experimental cookery affects food habits. Paper prepared for Third International Congress of Food Science and Technology. 9 to 14 August, 1970. Washington, D.C.

5666.   Mintz, Sidney W. 1955. The Jamaican internal marketing pattern. SES 4: 95-103.

5667.   Miracle, Marvin p. 1958. Maize in tropical Africa agriculture. Trop Ag 35: 1-15.

5668.   Miracle, Marvin p. 1961. "Seasonal hunger": a vague concept and an unexplored problem. IFAN-B 23: 273-283.

5669.   Miracle, Marvin p. 1964. Traditional agricultural methods in the Congo Basin. Food Research Institute. Palo Alto, California: Stanford University Press.

Includes information on traditional methods of preservation of foods; and production of beverages based on maize, palm, bamboo, and sugar cane.

5670.   Miracle, Marvin p. 1965. The introduction and spread of maize in Africa. JAH 6: 39-55.

5671.   Miracle, Marvin p. Chapter Eight. Maize in African diets. In Maize in tropical Africa. 1966. Madison, Milwaukee, London: University of Wisconsin Press.

5672.   Miracle, Marvin p. 1967. Agriculture in the Congo Basin: tradition and change in African rural economies. Madison: University of Wisconsin Press.

5673.   Miranda, Faustino. 1952. La vegetacion de Chiapas. [The flora of Chiapas.] 2 vols. Tuxtla Guitierrez, Chiapas: Departamento de Prenso y Turismo. Seccion Autografica.

5674.   Miranda, Fransisco, de p. The economics of Mexican nutrition. In A brief review of food and nutrition in five countries. 1944. pp. 1-5. United States Department of Agriculture. War Food Administration. Washington, D.C.: Government Printing Office.

A concise account of production; consumption; public health and economic apsects of nutrition in Mexico for the late 1930's and early 1940's. Brief mention of staple foods, and food patterns is included.

5675.   Mischlich, A. 1930. Ueber die Kolanuss in Afrika. [On the Kola nut in Africa.] KRund Nos. 7-12. pp. 152-163; 212-215.

5676.   Mishra, Baldep. 1963. The agricultural system, diet and dietary habits of Konds - a tribe of Orisssa. Vanyajati 11: 135-140.

India.

5677.   Mitaritonna, O. 1968. Problemi alimentari e indicazioni dietetiche nell'opera di A.S. Tissot. [Food problems and dietetic instructions in the works of A.S. Tissot.] CPSM 19: 45-57.

5678.   Mitchell, G.H. & Sherman, R.W. 1955. History of prepackaging fresh fruits and vegetables. Department of Agricultural Research and Rural Sociology. Wooster: Ohio Agricultural Experiment Station.

5679.   Mitchell, H.H. 1913. Does a low-protein intake produce racial inferiority? Science 38: 156-158.

5680.   Mitchell, H.H. & Edman, Marjorie. 1951. Nutrition and climatic stress with special reference to man. Springfield Illinois: Charles Thomas.

Effects of extreme heat, cold, and high altitude on human nutritional requirements. Based on a report prepared for the United States Quartermaster Food and Container Institute for the Armed Forces.

5681.   Mitchell, H.S. 1930. Nutrition survey in Labrador and northern Newfoundland. JADA 6: 29-35.

5682.   Mitchell, H.S. et al. 1954. Selected list of references on national food patterns and recipes. Chicago: American Dietetic Association.

Cited in Fundamentals of normal nutrition. By Corinne H. Robinson. 1968. p. 238. New York: Macmillan Co.

5683.   Mitchell, H.S. & Joffe, Natalie F. 1944. Food patterns of some European countries: background for study programs and guidance for relief workers. JADA 20: 676-687.

5684.   Mitchell, John D.; Brand, Janette; & Halbisch, Jeanette. 1977. Weight gain inhibition by lactose in Australian aboriginal children - a controlled trail of normal and lactose hydrolysed milk. Lancet 1: 500-502.

Research findings indicate that the effect of lactose intolerance must be considered when planning nutritional rehabiliation programs for children regardless of degree of nutritional deficiency.

5685.   Mitchell, K. 1936. China as a dietitian sees it. JADA 12: 121-129.

5686.   Mitra, Babu Rajendrala 1870. On the gypsies of Bengal. ASL-M 3: 120-133.

The Bediyas. Cooking utensils, food and drink: pp. 125-126. Cooking is stated to be the exclusive duty of the husband.

5687.   Mitra, Babu Rajendralala. 1872. Beef in ancient India. RASB-J 41: 174-196.

5688.   Mitra, Babu Rajendralala. 1872. A picnic in ancient India. RASB-J 41: 340-353.

5689.   Mitra, Babu Rajendralala. 1873. Spiritous drinks in ancient India. RASB-J 42: 1-23.

5690.   Mitra, D.D. 1938. Dietary habits of some communities living at Calcutta. IMG 73: 280-282.

5691.   Mitra, D.D. 1939. A study of the diet of the Bengali Hindus and their nutrition. IMG 73: 280-283.

5692.   Mitra, K. 1940. Dietary and physique of aboriginals in Santal Parganas, a district of Bihar. IJMR 28: 117-132.

5693.   Mitra, K. 1942. Diet and nutritional state of aboriginal (Hos) tribe. IJMR 30: 91-97.

5694.   Mitra, K. 1947. The food habits of the Muslims of Bihar and the nutritional state of their children. IJMR 35: 29-37.

5695.   Mitra, Sarat Chandra. 1893. Note on the use of locusts as an article of diet among the ancient Persians. ASB-J 3: 178-182.

5696.   Mitra, Sarat Chandra. 1905. Note on clay eating as a racial characteristic. ASB-J 7: 284-290.

5697.   Mitra, Sarat Chandra. 1927. Note on the use of ferns as an article of food in the district of Rangpur, northern Bengal. ISC-P 14: 303.

5698.   Mitra, Sarat Chandra. 1930. A note on the prevalence of cannibalism among the Birhars of Chota Nagpore. ISC-P 7: 397.

5699.   Mix, H. 1960. Die Entwicklung der Nahrungsausgaben nach Verbraucher-gruppen. [Evolution of food expenditure by consumption groups.] Agrarwirtschaft 9: 305-310.

5700.   Miyamoto, Keitaro. 1958. Clothing, food and housing of Oroks and Gilyaks. [In Japanese.] MK 22: 5-14.

Siberia.

5701.   Mize, Jessie Julia. Methods for studying the home management aspects of kitchen storage space for farm homes. Ph.D. dissertaiton. Ithaca, New York: Cornell University. 1952.

5702.   Mize, Jessie Julia; Koll, Mary; & Warren, Jean. 1953. Design of kitchen storage for farm homes from home management considerations. JHE 45: 105-109.

5703.   Modi, J.J. 1926. An American tribe and its buffalo and an Asiatic tribe and its fish. ASB-J 13: 432-437.

5704.   Modrzewski, T. & Modrzewski, M. 1969. Szkorbut i witamina C a odkrycia geograficzne (kartka z dziejow medycyny.) [Scurvy and vitamin C from geographial disclosures (From medical history files)]. WiadLek 22: 589-595.

5705.   Mohammad, Abdul Aziz bin. Rice in Malaya. Thesis. Economics. University of Singapore. 1949.

5706.   Mohanty, Purna Chandra. 1967-1968. Food habits of a tribal community. Adibasi 9(3): 20-25.

5707.   Mohr, J.C. van der M. 1965. Insects eaten by the Karo-Batak people (a contribution to entobromatology). [In Dutch.] EntB 25: 101-107.

5708.   Mohr, R. 1960. Einige Notizen uber die Tangale von Biliri. [A note on the Tangale of Bilire.] Anthropos 55: 860-870.

Cannibalism in a Nigerian group.

5709.   Mohrer, Jonathon. 1979. Breast and bottle feeding in an inner-city community: an assessment of perceptions and practices. Med Anth 3: 124-145.

Analyzes variables associated with breast feeding among low-income urban women. Sample of one hundred forty-one mothers in Hartford, Connecticut is data base.

5710.   Moine, F. 1976. Les habitudes alimentaires des francais, la nouvelle tendence vers la simplicite des menus. [French food habits, the new tendency towards simpler meals.] La Vie No. 1628. pp. 16-17.

5711.   Moir, H.C. 1936. Some observations on the appreciation of flavour in foodstuffs. CI 55: 145-148.

5712.   Mol, p. 1937-1938. Munani. NAf No. 11. pp. 501-503.

"Munani" designates meat or fish food among the people of the Lake Bangweulu region, Zambia, 11.15' S, 29.45'E.

5713.   Moldenhawer, Konstanty. 1959. Zboza chlebowe, rosliny straczkowe i konopie z okresu latenskiego i rzymskiego z okolic Krakowa. [Cereals, vegetables, and hemp of the La Tene and Roman periods derived from excavations near Cracow.] Prz Arch 11: 23-30.

5714.   Molle, Andre. 1964. Fromages d'Auvergne. [Cheeses of Auvergne] Collection Le Touriste en Auvergne No. 42. Clermont-Ferrand: Editions de Bussac.

5715.   Mollenhauser, H.p. 1954. The passion fruit. FMan 29: 149-152.

Includes historical data.

5716.   Moliner, Rafael Romero. 1949. Notas sobre alimentacion del indigena de Fernando Poo. [Notes on the diet of the natives of Fernando Poo.] Africa [M] 6: 17-21.

5717.   Molnar, Stephen. Cultural influences on the incidence of periodontal diseases among prehistoric populations. Paper presented at 69th Annual Meeting of the American Anthropological Association. 19 to 22 November, 1970. San Diego, California.

5718.   Molnar, Stephen. The use of prehistoric human teeth as a source of environmental information. Paper presented at 70th Annual Meeting of the American Anthropological Association. 19 November, 1971. New York City.

Notes dental caries, periodontal abscesses, and tooth wear seem to vary greatly between prehistoric populations; also developmental defects in the enamel and dentine, probably due to dietary differences, occur more frequently in certain populations than in others.

5719.   Moloney, Alfred.   1887. Sketch of the forestry of West Africa, with particular reference to its present principal commercial products. London: Sampson Low, Marston, Searl & Rivington.

West African economic plants with foods uses indicated: pp. 269-458.

5720.   Molony, Carol H. 1975. Systematic valence coding of Mexican "hot" - "cold" food. EFN 4: 67-74.

The qualitative characteristics "hot" and "cold" assigned to foods in many areas of Spanish-speaking Latin America are derived from the quadripartite Hippocratic humoral system of medicine. Most researchers have found consistency lacking in the labeling of foods according to this set of categories. In this research report, the author describes a systematic code for assigning foods to categories, based on fieldwork in the Zapotec peasant community of Diaz Ordaz, near Oaxaca, Mexico. The determining causes of food quality are described.   The author concludes that greater consistency in valence might be discovered, provided one obtains data on the qualifying variables of environment of growth and method of preparation of a food.

5721.   Monckton, H.S.   1965. An historical survey of English ale and beer. Tech Qtly 2: 221-229.

Prehistory; influence of the early church; from Domesday to the Assize of bread and ale; later Middle Ages; from ale to beer; Tudor period; beer duty; Stuart period; technological development; Nineteenth and Twentieth Centuries.

5722.   Moninger, M.M. 1932. The Hainanese Miao and their food supply. LSJ 11: 521-526.

5723.   Monnot, R. 1961. Le pommier. [Apple trees.] VL No. 116. pp. 562-567.

Historical and etymological data.

5724.   Monod, T. 1949. Plantes alimentaires indigenes de l'Afrique de l'Ouest. [Native food plants of West Africa.] NA No. 43. pp. 69-70.

5725.   Monrad, J.H. 1912. Finnish egg cheese. HD 44: 588.

Sour curd or sour-milk cheeses containing eggs.

5726.   Monroe, Day & Kyrk, Hazel. 1940. Food buying and our markets. Revised edition. New York: M. Barrows.

5727.   Monroy, Fernando Anaya. 1966. La antropofagia entre los antiguos Mexicanos. [Anthropophagy among the ancient Mexicans.] ECN 6: 211-218.

5728.   Montag, G. & McRoberts, K. 1971, Application of linear programming to menu planning by computer. CDA-J 32: 64-69.

5729.   Montagnac,p. 1961. Cactacees alimentaires dans le sud de Madagascar. [Edible cacti of southern Madagascar.] B Mad No. 6. pp. 609-620.

5730.   Montagu, Montagu Rhodes Ashley. 1937. Cannibalism and primitive man. Science 86: 56-57.

5731.   Montagu, Montague Rhodes Ashley. 1957. Nature, nurture and nutrition. AJCN 5: 237-242.

Consideration of how diet is influenced by culture, the obstacles encountered in efforts to change food patterns; and a suggestion that re-establishment of the family meal could improve nutritional status.

5732.   Montague, Rhodes Ashley. 1961. Chapter Seven. A brief excursion into cannibalism. In Man in process. Cleveland: World Publishing Company.

Questions the assumption that cracked, charred human bones, in archeological contexts; or the use of crania as drinking vessels, are sufficient proof of cannibalism.

5733.   Montefiore, C.G. 1896. Dr. Wiener on the dietary laws. JQR 8: 392-413.

Jewish religious dietary restrictions.

5734.   Monteil, Vincent. 1064. L'Islam noir. [Black Islam.] Paris: Editions du Seuil.

Includes information concerning edible plants introduced into sub-Saharan Africa by the Muslims.

5735. Monteir, Mario Ypiranga. 1963. Alimentos preparados a base da mandioca. [Foods based on manioc.] RBF 3: 37-82.

5736. Montell, Gosta. 1937. Distilling in Mongolia. Ethnos 2: 321-332.

5737. Montemayor, J.M. A sociological analysis of a Goan village community. Ph.D. disseration. University of Delhi. 1970.

Includes brief data on types of foods consumed by Catholics and Hindus. The village studied is Loliem.

5738. Montetn, M.p. 1910. Les scenes de boucherie dans les tombes de l'ancien empire. [Butchering as depicted in tombs of the Old Empire.] IFAO-B 7: 41-65.

Egypt.

5739. Monteuuis, Albert. 1907. L'alimentation et la cuisine naturelle dans le monde. [Food habits and natural diet in the world.] Brussels: H. Lamartin.

5740. Montgomery, Edward. The significance of nutritional data in socio-cultural research: examples from southern India. Research communication. In First Asian Congress of Nutrition. 22 January - 2 February, 1971. Hyderabad, India. Proceedings Edited by p.G. Tulpule & Kamala S. Jaya Rao. 1972. pp. 851, 852. Hyderabad: Nutrition Society of India.

Suggests that analysis of behaviorally-defined social groups which distribute and consume food regularly ('alimentary groups') can provide a better understanding of nutritional levels than analysis of traditionally-defined groups such as 'family', 'household', 'kinship', 'caste', or 'village'. Memberships of 'alimentary groups' are defined, how these groups transect other social units, the foods they characteristically distribute, and the measurable differences in nutritional levels that relate to group membership are described.

5741. Montgomery, Edward. Problems in the study of human energy expenditure. Paper presented at 72nd Annual Meeting of the American Anthropological Association. 1 December, 1973. New Orleans, Louisiana.

5742. Montgomery, Edward, Chapter Four. Contributions to the study of food-related cultural variability. In Progress in human nutrition. Vol. Two. Edited by Sheldon Margen & Richard A. Ogar. 1978. Westport, Connecticut: AVI Publishing co.

In this article, the author reviews a sample of the literature pertaining to human food-related behavior, and provides an analysis of the theoretical and methodological categor-

ies within which the studies cited may be placed. Considered are distributional studies based on geographical area; functionalist-oriented works; food as an expression of culture pattern; food habits as expressions of socio-economic variables; ecological, and structuralist approaches.

5743. Montgomery, Edward & Bennett, John W. Anthropological studies of food and nutrition: the 1940's and the 1970's. In The uses of anthropology. Edited by Walter W. Goldschmidt. 1979. pp. 124-144. Washington, D.C.: The American Anthropological Association.

This article provides an historical review of the involvement of anthropologists in the United States in theoretical and applied research in the area of human food behavior. The author suggests why this involvement has peaked, waned, and been reactivated, and provides illustrative examples of relevant research from the literatures of several disciplines. Optimism is expressed concerning the potential for interdisciplinary communication among researchers involved with various facets of human behavior.

5744. Montgomery, Edward & Johnson, Allen. 1977. Machiguenga energy expenditure. EFN 6: 97-105.

The Machiguenga are a Native Latin American group living along tributaries of the upper Amazon near the base of the Andes in southeastern Peru; they are hunter-gatherer-horticulturalists. Included in this report is a brief description of Machiguenga diet; and data on energy expenditure and time allocation in the context of food-related activities.

5745. Monticelli, Juan V. 1939. Regimen de alimentacion de los antiguos peruanos. [Diet of the ancient Peruvians.] RGA 11: 216-220.

5746. Montreal. Grand Council of Crees (of Quebec). A discussion and analysis of potential food intake and nutritive value of Waswanipi Cree Indian diets [by Carol S. Farkas & H.A. Feit]. 1974.

5747. Montreal. Health and Welfare Canada. Preliminary diet survey of Cree population of northwest Quebec [by C. Pass]. 1976.

5748. Mood, Fulmer. 1937. John Winthrop, Jr. on Indian corn. NEQ 10: 121-133.

Methods of preparation, Native American, and colonist: pp. 129-132.

5749. Mood, John D. A folk botany of Guam: an ethnobotanical study of the Guamanian-Chamorro. Master's thesis. Anthropology. Agana, Guam: University of Guam. 1976.

5750. Moodie, R.L. 1930. Teeth, jaws, and palates in pre-Pueblo Indians from New Mexico. PDG 38: 127-145.

5751.   Moodie, R.L. 1930. What bad teeth did to a pre-historic Indian. Hygeia 8: 551-552.

5752.   Moody, F.W. 1949. Oatbread. YDS-T 8: 20-30.

5753.   Moon, A. 1824. Catalogue of the indigenous and exotic plants growing in Ceylon, distinguishing the several esculent vegetables, fruits, roots and grains: together with a sketch of the division of genera and species in use amongst the Singhalese: also an outline of the Linaean sexual system of botany, in the English and Singhalese languages. Colombo: Wesleyan Mission Press.

5754.   Mooney, James. 1896. The Ghost-Dance religion and the Sioux outbreak of 1890. SI-BE-AR for the year 1892-1893. pp. 653-1136.

Arapaho songs relating to food: pp. 961 (fruit); 9991 (pemmican); Paiute millet (Oryzopsis membranacea); Sioux pemmican preparation and song: 1066-1067; Sioux cooking songs: 1073-1074. Kiowa berry preparation song: p. 1087.

5755.   Mooney, James. 1900. Myths of the Cherokee. SI-BAE-AR for the year 1897-1898. pp. 3-548.

Native American belief that the qualities of (animal) food are absorbed by those who eat the food: p. 472.

5756.   Mooney, James. 1901. Our last cannibal tribe. HMM 103: 550-555.

The Tonkawa.

5757.   Mooney, James. 1902. Die Tonkawas, der letzte Kannibalenstamm in den Vereinigten Staaten. [The Tonkawa, the last cannibal tribe in the United States.] Globus 82: 76-79.

5758.   Moore, Daniel G. 1974. Shoot me a biscuit: stories of yesteryear's roundup cooks. Tucson: University of Arizona Press.

5759.   Moore, Frank William. The foundations of New World agriculture. Ph.D. dissertation. Columbia University. 1960.

5760.   Moore, Frank William. 1964. Methodologic problems of cross-cultural dietary research. JADA 45: 418-419.

Reviews the development of categories used in the Human Relations Area Files' Food Habits Survey (1964).

5761.   Moore, Frank W. Food habits in non-industrial societies. In Dimensions of nutrition. Proceedings of the Colorado Dietetic Association Conference. 1969. Fort Collins, Colorado. Edited by Jacqueline Dupont. 1970. pp. 182-221. Boulder: Colorado Associated University Press.

Based on data contained in Volume One of the Human Relations Area Files Food Habits Survey (1964). Article is an excellent introductory overview of world food use patterns.

5762.   Moore, Geneva. A study of the food habits of a selected group of Negro farm families in Caddo Parish, Shreveport, Louisiana. Master's thesis. Home Economics. Washington, D.C.: Howard University. 1953.

5763.   Moore, H.R. 1960. Indian figs...desert fruit. ADW 24 April. pp. 50-51.

Cactus fruit.

5764.   Moore, Harriet Bruce. 1952. Psychologic facts and dietary facts. JADA 28: 789-794.

Discusses symbolic dimension of food; reasons for lay persons attitudes toward food; attitudes of the upper middle-class; effects of early food experiences on food beliefs; food preferences in illness; eating as a subliminating activity; psychological uses of food and appetite; prestige nature of food.

5765.   Moore, Harriet Bruce. 1957. The meaning of food. AJCN 5: 77-82.

An exploration of the role of food in human culture, and its deep psychological significance. Illustrated with examples both documented and traditional.

5766.   Moore, James A. The effects of information methods in hunter-gatherer society. Paper presented at 77th Annual Meeting of the American Anthropological Association. 14 to 18 November, 1978. Los Angeles, California.

5767.   Moore, M.p. 1974. Secular aspects of the sacred cow: the productivity of some Indian farm animals. IDSUS-C 58.

5768.   Moore, Marion Elizabeth. Nutrition education in the elementary school: an evaluation of selected activities used in the primary and Fifth grades. Master's thesis. University of Chicago. 1947.

5769.   Moore, Oscar K. 1948. The coconut palm - mankind's greates provider in the tropics. EB 2: 19-144.

Brief reference to food use of cocounut oil, and shredded coconut meat.

5770.   Moore, Percy; Kruse, H.D.; & Tisdall, F.F. 1943. Nutrition in the North, a study of the state of nutrition of the Canadian bush Indian. Beaver 273: 21-23.

5771.   Moore, p.E., et al. 1946. Medical survey of nutrition among northern Manitoba Indians. CMAJ 54: 223-233.

5772.   Moore, S.T. A historical study of trends in the methodology and content of adult education programs in nutrition in the United States. Ph.D. dissertation. Michigan State University. 1965.

5773.   Moore, T. 1850. Sacred botany. Part 1. On hyssop. GMB for 1850. pp. 37-38. The tamarask, manna; pp. 77-78; the lentil: pp. 141-142; the terebinth, nuts: pp. 162-163. Part 2. The cereals. GMB for 1851. pp. 135-136.

Terebinth is Pistacia Terebinthus, the pistacio The tamarisk noted is Tamarix mannifera, Ehrenb.

5774.   Moore, W. Robert. 1950.   Feast day in Kapingamarangi. NGM 97: 523-537.

5775.   Moose, J. Robert. 1911. Village life in Korea. Nashville: M.E. Church.

Brief mention of basic diet; preparation of kimchee, a pickled vegetable condiment; use of hot water as beverage poured into rice.

5776.   Mora, Alejandrino Borroto. 1967. Decentralizacion del mercado unico de la Habana. [Decentralization of Havana's only market.] EFolk No. 4. pp. 79-98.

5777.   Moraes (filho), Alexandre Jose de Mello. 1886. Os ciganos no Brasil; contribuicao etnografica. [The gypsies of Brazil; ethnographic contribution.] Rio de Janeiro: B.L. Garnier.

5778.   Moragne, Lenora. Influence of household differentiation on food habits among low-income urban Negro families. Ph.D. dissertation. Home Economics. Cornell University, 1969.

Two factors precipitated interest in this work: an absence in the literature of systematic research on food habits among Black American families residing in large urban areas, and a questioning of whether there exist varying degrees of diversity among the life styles of such a low-income population. Results of statistical correlation analysis showed a significantly positive degree of concurrency between indicators of household structure and food habits; that is, families showing complexity in household structure tended also to practice the more complex food habits. Further analysis was completed to identify indicators of household structure that best serve as determinants or predictors of complexity in food habits. The presence of two or more female adults rather than one, and residing in public project apartments rather than private tenements were the two household structure measures that best predicted food habits diversity. Findings from this study provided implications for nutrition education and further research in the area of food practices among low-income groups.

5779.   Moran, Emilio F. An energetic view of manioc culture in the Amazon. Paper presented at 9th International Congress of Anthropological and Ethnological Sciences. 28 August to 8 September, 1973. Chicago, Illinois.

Analysis of community energy flow and its effect on manioc yields.

5780.   Moran, Emilio F. Food, development and man in the tropics. In Gastronomy. The anthropology of food and food habits. Edited by Margaret Louise Arnott. 1975. pp. 169-186. Paris; The Hague: Mouton Publishers. World Anthropology.

Taking as an example rural Brazil, this study makes suggestions as to how small industries could be developed to produce enriched manioc. Agricultural, economic, and sociological significance of manioc as well as manioc processing are considered.

5781.   Moraru-Popa, Georgeta. Havest tools in Romania. Paper presented at 9th International Congress of Anthropological and Ethnological Sciences. 28 August to 8 September, 1973. Chicago, Illinois.

Use of the sickle and scythe for grain harvesting, in the late 19th and first half of the 20th Centuries.

5782.   Morcasitas de Pozas, Isabel. 1951. Estudio sobre la alimentacion en el poblado de Acacoyahua. [Dietary study in the town of Acacoyahua.] INAH-A 5: 153-176.

5783.   Morcos, Sabry Riad 1966. A review of the state of nutrition in the United Arab Republic. EPHA-J 41: 151-174.

5784.   Morcos, Sabry Riad & Boctor, Aamal Morgan. 1959. The use of Dolichos lablab and Lathyrus sativus in the making of taamiah [bean cakes] in Egypt. BJN 13: 163-167.

Taamiah is a fermented bean paste, which is fried after processing. The paste is cut into small pieces. Seasoning in the paste includes onions, garlic, pasrley, coriander, pepper, and salt.

5785.   Morcos, Sabry Riad & Morcos, W.R. 1977. Diets in ancient Egypt. PFNS 2: 457-471.

5786.   Moreau, J. 1940. Une scene d'anthropophagie en Egypte en l'an 127 de notre ere. [A cannibalistic scene in Egypt, in A.D. 127.] Chronique 30: 275-289.

5787.   Moreno, Angel Turrado. 1945. Etnografia de los Indios Guaraunos .[Ethnography of the Guarauno Indians.] Caracas: Litografia y Tipografia Vargas.

Cookery, food: pp. 44-50; beverages: pp. 125-129.

5788.   Moreno, Jose Antonio. 1949. Formas actuales de antropofagia en los territorios espanoles del Golfo de Guinea. [Contemporary forms of anthropophagy in Spanish territories in the Gulf of Guinea.] An Etno 1: 187-204.

5789.   Moreno, Jose Antonio. 1951. Formas de antropofagia en lost territorios espanoles del Golfo de Guinea. [Forms of anthropophagy in Spanish territories in the Gulf of Guinea.] IEF-A 17: 69-85.

5790. Moreno-Black, Geraldine. Diet, home range and behavior of Colobus angolensis: mechanisms of resource partitioning. Paper presented at 76th annual Meeting of the American Anthropological Association. 29 November to 3 December, 1977. Houston, Texas.

Data collected in Kenya, on a troop of Colobus angolensis indicate that patterns of activity, movement and interspecific interaction are distinctive and differ from those of the Cercopithecinae species. Information on diet gathered by direct observation and fecal analysis indicate that dietary constituents and foraging patterns also differ. This differential utilization of resources and habitat appears to be effective in maintaining existence without competition between the species.

5791. Morettini, Alessandro. 1950. Olivicoltura. [Olive cultivation.] Rome: Ramo Editore degli Agricoltori.

5792. Morey, Geoffrey. 1931. Among the cannibals in Australia. Empire 53: 124-128.

5793. Morey, Nancy Booker. A study of the food habits and health of farm families in Tompkins County, New York. CU-AES-B No. 563.

This monograph provides data on two hundred and eight farm families, studied in the summer of 1928. Extensive data on food consumption is recorded. Includes a section of 'refusal of foods in the family diet': pp. 36-39.

5794. Morgan, Lewis H. 1901. League of the Ho-de-no-sau-nee or Iroquois. New York: Dodd Mead & Co. Reprint 2 vols. New Haven: Human Relations Area Files. 1954.

Food. Vol. 1. pp. 190, 191, 310, 320, 321, 336. Vol. 2. pp. 160, 188, 249, 274.

5795. Morgan, W.B. 1959. The distribution of food crop storage methods in Nigeria. JTG 13: 58-64.

5796. Morgenstern, L. 1882. Die menschliche Ernahrung und die culturhistorische Entwicklung der Kochkunst. [Human diet and the cultural-historical development of the art of cooking.] Berlin: Stuhr.

5797. Morimoto, Kokichi. 1918. Chapter Three. General studies of diets. Chapter Four. Actual status of food consumption. Chapter Five. National diet of Japan. Chapter Six. Comparison of rice and wheat as the principal food. Chapter Seven. Improvement of food consumption. In The standard of living in Japan. JHUSHPS Vol. 36.

5798. Morisue, Y. 1967. Shokumotsu shi; Nipponjin no shokuseikatsu no hatten. [History of food; the development of food habits of the Japanese.] Revised edition. Tokyo: Daichi Shuppan.

5799. Moritz, L.A. 1958. Grain-mills and flour in classical antiquity. Oxford: at the Clarendon Press.

Contents: the Homeric mill; the donkey; finds of early corn grinders; mortars; terracotta figures; the saddle-quern in classical Greece; the 'hopper-rubber'; Greek rotary mills; mills and millers in Plautus' comedies; the Pompeian donkey mill; Pompeian mill in other parts of the [Roman] Empire; animal mills and slave mills; rotary hand mills; the geared mills; water-mills. Grain products other than fine meal and flour; the production of different grades of meal; sieves and sifted flour in classical Greece; Roman flour sieves; grades of meal and flour; three-grade and four-grade milling; Pliny's extraction rates; bread yield from wheat and flour; Roman flour in the First Century A.D.

5800. Mornet, p. & Gilbert, Y. 1948. Rapport sur la production et l'utilisation du lait en Afrique Occidentale Francaise. [Report on the production and use of milk in French West Africa.] SEIAAOF-B Octobre-Decembre. pp. 59-78.

5801. Morrell, L. Ross. A suggested method for locating aboriginal garden areas. In Twenty-first Southeastern Archaeological Conference. November 6-7, 1964. New Orleans, Louisiana. Proceedings. Edited by Stephen Williams. 1964. pp. 38-41. SAC-B No. 3.

Describes results of aerial photography of the Texas #1 site, on the eastern side of the Kaskaskia River floodplain, in Clinton County, Illinois. Three types of film were used: Panatomic X (black-and-white); infrared; and [unspecified] color films. Disucsses wide furrows - thought to be of agricultural significance - revealed by the infrared film.

5802. Morren, Jr. George E.B. Woman the hunter. Paper presented at 72nd Annual Meeting of the American Anthropological Association. 29 November, 1973. New Orleans, Louisiana.

5803. Morris, D. 1887. Tree tomato. GB-RBGK-KB No. 8 pp. 2-6.

5804. Morris, H.S. 1953. Report on a Melanau sago-producing community in Sarawak. GB-CO-CRS No. 9.

Preparation of sago biscuit: pp. 29-30.

5805. Morris. p.F. 1943. Some vegetable foods of the Wimmera and Mallee. VNat 59:167-170.

Australian Aborigene groups. Polygonaceae, Chenopodiaceae; Amaranthaceae; Aizoaceae; Portulacaceae; Cruciferae; orchids; roots; tubers; gums; piths; greens; water; beverages; and sugar.

5806. Morris, Robert T. 1927. Edible acorns for man, livestok, and fowls. NNG-RP Eighteenth Annual Meeting. pp. 35-43.

Enumerates edible acorn varieties of the world.

5807.   Morrison, H.   1935.   Trichiniasis among Jews. NEJM 213:531-532.

5808.   Morrison, Marjorie M. An elementary cookbook and food guide written to meet the needs of households of low socio-economic status in the mill area of Knoxville, Tennessee. Master's thesis. University of Tennessee. 1944.

5809.   Morrow, Launa. An evaluation of food acceptance when students participate in lunchroom activities. Master's thesis.   Denton: North Texas State College. 1949.

5810.   Morrow, Linda, M. A study of the food and feeding habits of young children in a Mexican village. Master's thesis. Ithaca, New York: Cornell University. 1966.

5811.   Mors, p.O.   1958.   Grasshoppers as food in Buhaya. AQ 31:56-58.

Bukoba District, Tazania.   Use as gifts; prohibition against their consumption by women; methods of cooking.

5812.   Morse, Edward S.   1884.   Kitchens of the East. AAAS-P 32:426.

Notes on stoves in Japan, China and Singapore.

5813.   Morse, Katherine. 1920. What and how they ate in the days of Elizabeth. Sewanee 28:93-100.

Literary excerpts.

5814.   Morse, W.R.   1928.   Observations on the anthropology of the peoples of the West Chino-Tibetan Borderland, the Marches of the Mantsi. LSJ 5:313-344.

Food and its preparation: tsamba, a mixture of coarse ground barley and tea boiled together with butter and rolled in to a ball: pp. 324-325.

5815.   Mortillet, Adriaen de; Nadaillac, Marquis de; Lagneau, Gustave; Fauvelle; Sanson, Andre. 1888.   Suite de la discussion sur l'anthropophagie. Continuation of the discussion on antropophagy.] SAP-B 11:72-82.

Anthropophagy in Neolithic times and later; includes extracts from the classic writers of Greece and Rome.

5816.   Morton, Julia Frances.   1962.   Wild plants for survival in south Florida.   Miami: Hurricane House.

5817.   Morton, Julia Frances. 1967. Cadushi (Cereus repandus, Mill.).   A useful cactus of Curacao. EG 21:185-191.

Includes a recipe for cadada, an Aruban cadushi-powder soup; and for funchi - a maize-meal porridge.

5818.   Moscoso, C.G.   1956.   West-Indian cherry - richest source of natural vitamin C. EB 10: 280-294.

Malpighia punicifolia, L.

5819.   Moseley, Lloyd W. 1972. Customer service, the road to greater profits. New York: Chain store Publications.

Written by a former executive of a large retail-chain food store in the eastern United States.

5820.   Moseley, M.R.   Reaction of pre-school children to food.   Master's thesis.   University of Chicago. 1925.

5821.   Moseley, Michael E. 1975. The maritime foundations of Andean civilization.   Menlo Park, California: Benjamin/Cummings.

Food; laws; tools; and people: pp.39-58.

5822.   Moseman, A.H.   1963.   The role of plant science in the improvement of nutrition. FASEB-FP 22: 145-147.

5823.   Moser, Ada, M. 1935. Food consumption and use of time for food work among farm families in the South Carolina Piedmont.   SC-AES-B   No. 300.

This research was performed in the counties of Abbeville, Chester, Greenwood, Oconee, and Spartanburg.   Part One covers food consumption in Black and Caucasian families, with nutrient analysis by food source; cash value of diets; home-produced foods; and costs of diets.   Part Two studies time devoted to meal preparation and clean-up and factors influencing time use; meal preparation and service practices; typical menus; time in relation to menus; and nutritive adequacy in relation to time used.

5824.   Moser, Ada M.   1942.   Food habits of South Carolina farm families. SC-AES-B No. 343.

5825.   Moser, Ada M.   1950.   Some dietary attitudes and ideas among rural school children in South Carolina. SC-AES-B No. 402.

5826.   Moser, Ada M.   1953.   Menu patterns and food preferences in South Carolina.   SC-AES-B No. 406.

5827.   Moser, Ada M. 1953.   Use of food by farm families in the tobacco farming area of South Carolina. SC-EAS-B No. 402.

5828.   Mosher, Stephen Westley.   1979.   Birth seasonality among peasant cultivators: the interrelationship of workload, diet and fertility. HEcol 7:151-181.

Presents an hypothesis that links the productive cycle to conceptions through the intervening variable of diet. Hypotheses is suggested as explaining seasonablity of conceptions and births in populations that experience significant seasonal variation in diet. The community studied is a fishing village located forty kilometers east of Taipei, Taiwan.

5829.   Mosley, H.N. 1877. Notes on the various plants made use of as food and as implements, clothing, etc. by the natives of the Admiralty Islands. LSL(B)-J 15: 80-82.

5830.   Mosley, May. 1948-1949. Son-of-gun or rascal. NMFR 3:26-27.

A stew of beef giblets, (sweetbreads, heart, liver, tongue, brains, and testicles) made in southwestern United States, when fat calves or suckling yearlings are range-butchered.

5831.   Mosqueda, A. 1961. Venezuelan cornbread or "arepa"; its enrichment. [In Spanish] AB 13:157-165.

5832.   Mossell, Sadie Tanner. 1921. Standards of living of 100 Nego migrant families in Philadelphia. AAPSS-A 98: 173-218.

5833.   Mosseri, V.M. 1922. Sur l'origine du riz et l'histoire de sa culture en Egypte. [On the origin of rice and the history of its cultivation in Egypt.] UAE-B 20:5-15.

5834.   Mossinger, Friedrich. 1954. Seltene Gebildbrote. [Unusual-shaped baked goods.] HBV 45:34-62.

5835.   Motoyama, Tekishu. 1958. Inshoku jiten. [Dictionary of food and drink in Japan.] Tokyo: Heibon-sha.

5836.   Motoyama, Keisen. Inshoku. [Eating and drinking.] In Nihon minzoku Zush. [Japanese floklore Illustrated.] Vol. Seven. Tokoyo: tokyoto.

5837.   Moulin, L. 1975. L'Europe a table. [Europe at the dinner table.] Brussels: Elsevier.

5838.   Moulinier, R. 1906. Alimentation chez des Indo-chinois transportes dans des climats froids. [Diet of Indo-chinese moved to cold climates.] P-SB-CRHSM 57:210-211.

5839.   Mountford, Charles Percy. 1939. Aboriginal methods of fishing and cooking as used on the southern coast of Eyre's Peninsula, South Australia. Mankind 2:196-200.

5840.   Mountford, Charles Percy 1960. Records of the American-Australian scientific expedition to Arnhem Land. Volume Two. Anthropology and nutrition. Melbourne: Melbourne University Press.

5841.   Mourant, A. E., ed. 1963. Man and cattle: proceedings of a symposium on domestication. RAI-GBI-OP No. 18.

5842.   Moussy, Martin de. 1867. [Note on scurvy in Montevideo, during the sieges 1842-1851, and 1813-1814.] [In French.] SAP-B 2 [second series] :37-39.

Details of diet during the siege are given, in relation to the occurrence of ascorbic acid deficiency.

5843.   Mouton, J. & Sillans, R. 1954. Les cultures indigenes dan les regions forestieres de l'Oubangui-Chari Departement de la Lobaye. [Native crops inthe forest areas of Ubangi-Shari (Lobaye Department).] MCM-A Vol.2.

5844.   Moynier, M.M. 1836. De la truffle: traite complet de ce tubercule. [About the truffle: complete treatise on this tubercule.] Paris: Barba; Legrand & Bourgougnioux.

5845.   Mrak, Emil M. 1967. Some of the developments in food production and their impact on nutrition. JN 91 [Supplement 1] : 55-61.

5846.   Muazzam, M.G. & Khaleque, K.A. 1959. Effects of fasting in Ramadhan. JTMH 62: 292-294.

5847.   Mudge, Gertrude Gates 1923. Italian dietary adjustments. JHE 15: 181-185.

Thirty-eight weekly dietary records were secured from families at three different income levels, residing in New York City, Boston, Detroit, and Memphis, Tennessee. Food expenditure data, meal cost, calorie cost, and patterns of food category (cereals, dairy products, meat, produce, oils) use are recorded. Nutritional evaluation of diets is included.

5848.   Mudge, Gertrude Gates 1924. Polish dietary studies. M Hosp 22: 503-504.

5849.   Mueller, Ferdinand von. 1885-1886. Appendix. Edible fruits from the Maclay Coast, New Guinea. LSNSW-P 10: 335-358.

5850.   Mugellano, Antonio Cocchi. 1743. Del vitto Pitagorico per uso della medicina. [The Pythagoream regime, for use in medicine.] Florence: Francesco Moucke.

The Pythagorean regime was based upon abstinence from consumption of any flesh.

5851.   Mugrditchian, Helen Wadsworth. 1954. Food and eating habits in Lebanon. JADA 30: 48-50.

Food preparation; shopping for food in the bazaars; hospitality and food etiquette in Arabic-speaking countries.]

5852. Muhammad, Elijah. 1963. How to eat to live. Chicago: Muhammad's Mosque No. 2.

An exposition of dietary principles developed by the leader of the Black Muslim organization in the United States. Much of the material is dervied from classic Islamic and

Judaic dietary dogma, interpolated by the author who has added procriptions of his own.

5853.   Muhammad Shaikh, Jan. Varietal classification of Arachis hypogaea, L. Masters thesis. Tandojam, India: University of Sind. 1970.

Peanut varieties.

5854.   Muir, John. 1911. My first summer in the Sierra. Boston: Houghton Mifflin Co.

Contains a description of fooduse of carpenter-ant gasters by the Digger Tribe, a Native American group in California.

5855.   Mukhopadhyay, Carol C. Current foodways of Asian Indians residing in Los Angeles. Masters thesis. Anthropology. California State University at Los Angeles. 1971.

5856.   Mukwaya, A. The marketing of staple foods in Kampala, Uganda. In Markets in Africa. Edited by Paul Bohannan & George Dalton. 1962. pp. 643-666. Evanston, Illinois: Northwestern University Press.

5857.   Mulder, Gerrit Jan. 1847. De voeding van de neger in Suriname. [Food of the Surinam Negro.] Rotterdam: H.A. Karmers:

5858.   Mulder, Gerrit Jan. 1854. De Voeding van Nederlanders. [The diet of Netherlanders.] Rotterdam: H.A. Kramers.

5859.   Mulder, Gerrit Jan. 1863. De La bierre, sa compositon chimique, sa fabrication, son emploi comme boisson... [Beer, its chemical composition, production, and use as a beverage...] Translated by August Delondre, from the Dutch with the authors' approval. 2nd edition. Paris: J.-B. Bailliere et fils.

5860.   Muller, H. 1890. Sur les debris de cuisine (sambaquis) du Bresil.   [On the kitchen refuse (sambaqui) of Brazil.] In Congres International des Americanistes. Compte-rendu de la septieme session. Berlin, 1888. pp. 459-462. Berlin: Librairie W. H. Kuhl.

5861.   Muller, Hans G. 1973. An introduction to food rheology. New York: Crane, Russak.

Organoleptic factors in food technology.

5862.   Muller, R.F.   1966.   Die Bewertung von Geschmack und Ernahrung in der alten Indischen Medizin. [The evaluating of taste and nutrition in ancient Indian medicine.] FPF 17: 202-204.

5863.   Muller, Wilhelm. 1917 . Yap. Hamburgische Wissenschaftliche Stiftung. Ergebnisse der Sudsee-Expedition 1908-1910. Ethnographie: B. Mikronesien.   Vol. 2. Part 2. [Yap. Hamburg Scientific Institute. Results of the South Sea expedition. 1908-1910. Ethnography B. Micronesia .

5864.   Mulon, Marianne. Les premieres recettes medievales. [The first medeival recipes.] In Pour une histoire de l'alimentation. Edited by J.J. Hem-

ardinquer. 1970. pp. 236-240. Paris: Colin.

5865.   Multhauf, R.p. 1978. A history of common salt.   Baltimore: The Johns Hopkins University Press.

5866.   Mundel, G., Fischel, J. & Varsano, D. 1961. Malnutrition in infants in Israel. (A sociological, clinical and biochemical investigation). JTP 7:23-28.

5867.   Munroe, Robert L. & Munroe, Ruth H. Effects of food deprivation among the Logoli, Gusii, and Kipsigis. Paper presented at the 67th Annual Meeting of the American Anthopological Association. November 21 to 24, 1968. Seattle, Washington.

Based on Allan Holmberg's 1969 study of food deprivation among the Siriono of Brazil, this paper seeks to test Holmerg's hypothesis that similar conditions in other cultures would produce similar food concerns. The three groups studied live within 100 miles of each other, in Kenya, on the Equator, west of Lake Victoria, in similar ecological niches. Population densities (and therefore available farmland) differ significantly i.e. Logoli=1252 persons per square mile; Gusii = 638; and Kipsigis = 270. The land shortage among Logoli is associated with food shortages, which in turn lead to greater food concerns than among their neighbors. Preliminary analysis of folk tales shows Logoli mentioning food consumption more often. Dream reports are analyzed for food content. In experimental setting, given 10 food items and 10 non-food items to try to remember briefly, the Logoli recall more comestible items than do the Kipsigis.

5868.   Munroe, Robert L.; Munroe, Ruth H.; Nerlove, Sara B.; & Daniels, Robert E. 1969. Effects of population density on food concerns in three East African soicietes. JHSB 10: 161-171.

Logoli, Gusii, and Kipsigis, of Kenya.

5869.   Munsell, Hazel E. 1944. Food and nutritional problems in Puerto Rico. JADA 20: 305-307.

5870.   Munsell, Hazel E.; Castillo, Raul; Zurita, Clemencia; & Portilla, Jose M. 1953. Composicion de algunos alimentos de origin vegetal del Ecuador. [Composition of some Ecuadorean vegetable foods.] OSP-B 35[1]: 26-64.

5871.   Munsell, Hazel E.; Castillo, Raul; Zurita, Clemencia; & Portilla, Jose M. 1953. Production, uses and composition of foods of plant origin from Ecuador. FR 18: 319-342.

5872.   Munsell, Hazel E.; Williams, Louis O.; Guild, Louise p.; Kelley, Lucille T.; & Harris, Robert S. 1950.   Composition of food plants of Central America. 7. Honduras. FR 15: 421-438.

5873.   Munsell, Hazel E.; Williams, Louis O.; Guild, Louise p.; Kelley, Lucille T.; McNally, Anne M.; Harris, Robert S. 1950. Composition of food plants of Central America. 6. Costa Rica. FR 15: 379-404; 8. Guatemala. 15: 439-453.

5874.   Munsell, Hazel E.; Williams, Louis O.; Guild, Louise P.; Troescher, Cynthia B.; & Harris, Robert S. 1950. Composition of food plants of Central America. 5. Nicaragua. FR 15: 355-365.

5875.   Munsell, Hazel E.; Williams, Louis O.; Guild, Louise P.; Troescher, Cynthia B.; Nightingale, Gertrude; Harris, Robert S. 1949. Composition of food plants of Central America. 1. Hondura. FR 14: 144-164; 2. Guatemala. 15: 16-33; 3. Guatemala. 15: 34-42.

5876.   Munsell, Hazel E.; Williams, Louis O.; Guild, Louise P.; Troescher, Cynthia B.; Nightingale, Gertrude; Kelley, Lucille T.; & Harris, Robert S. 1950. Composition of food plants of Central America. 4. El Salvador. FR 15: 263-296.

5877.   Munsey, Cecil. 1972. The illustrated guide to the collectibles of Coca-Cola. New York: Hawthorn Books.

5878.   Munson, A.H. & Calloway, Doris Howes. 1960. Absence of radioprotection in cabbage-fed swine. Quartermaster Food and Container Institute for the Armed Forces. Report 29-60.

Eighty-two swine were exposed to 11 different doses of Co^{60} gamma radiation. Exposures ranged from 75 to 1650 roentgens measured in air. All animals exposed to over 525 roentgens were divided into 2 dietary groups. Basal diet was supplemented with dehydrated cabbage in one group and dehydrated white potatoes in the other. No differences in the response attributable to sex or diet were noted.

5879.   Munson, Patrick J. The origins and antiquity of maize-beans-squash agriculture in eastern North America: some linguistic implications. In Variation in anthropology: essays in honor of John Charles McGregor. Edited by Donald Ward Lathrap & Jody Douglas. 1973. pp. 107-135. Urbana, Illinois: Illinois Archaeological Survey, Inc.

Based on language group studies, the author concludes 1. "Sweet" maize was the earliest variety used by Algonquian speakers; 2. Ojibwa-Ottawa-Potawatomi were the first Central Algonquian speakers to obtain Flint maize and beans. 3. Among Algonquian speakers, original use of squash and gourds was as utensils (dippers or containers), rather than as food. 4. Northern and Southern Iroquoian terms for squash may be related. 5. The crop triad may have been either known to the proto-Siouan speakers or all Siouan-speaking groups may have shared a contiguous and relatively small area at the time the three crops were introduced. 6. Maize and squash may have been cultivated by proto-Muskogean speakers. 7. The similarity of the words for maize in all the Caddoan languages, as well as the archaeological data which indicates that some of the Caddoan groups have divided prior to ca. A.D. 1000, indicated a fair antiquity of maize among these peoples. 8. There are no linguistic indications that the food complex of maize-beans-squash was being grown by proto-Tunican speakers.

5880.   Munstererberg, M. 1935. Confection with a past. Cath World No. 142. pp. 299-305.

5881.   Murai, G. 1933. Alimentation indigene dans les colonies francaises. [Native diet in the French colonies.] Paris: Vigot.

5882.   Murai, Mary M. 1954. Food patterns in the Caroline and Marshall Islands. JADA 30: 154.

A concise nutritional ethnography.

5883.   Murai, Mary; Pen, Florence; & Miller, Carey D. 1958. Some tropical South Pacific Island foods. Honolulu: University of Hawaii Press.

5884.   Murai, Mary; Pen, Florence, & Miller, Carey D. 1958. Some tropical South Pacific Island foods. Hi-AES-B No. 110.

5885.   Muramatsu, S. 1912. On the preparation of natto. Eighth International Congress of Applied Chemistry. Original communications. Vol. 18. pp. 251-263. TIU-CA-J 5: 81-94.

Methods and materials used in the preparation of a fermented Japanses soy cheese. T-IU-CA-J 5: 81-94.

5886.   Murata, Kiku; Ikehata, Hideo; & Miyamoto, Teijiro. 1967. Studies on the nutritional value of tempeh. JFS 32: 580-586.

Traditional Indonesian fermented soy bean curd.

5887.   Muratori, G. 1966. Andrea Bacci e il suo trattato sui vini. [Andrea Bacci and his treatise on wine.] PSMed 10: 23-27.

5888.   Muraz, G. L'alimentation indigene en Afrique Equatoriale Francaise. [Native diet in French Equatorial Africa.] In L'alimentation indigene dans les colonies francaises. Protectorats et territories sous mandat. Edited by G. Hardy & C. Richet. 1933. pp. 177-211. Paris: Vigot Freres.

Opens with a general consideration of the public health aspects of nutrition; diet in relation to work; and demographic variables characteristic of the region. Agricultural techniques and basic crops are described. Dairy products, fruits, spices and other ancillary foods are enumerated, followed by sections on fish and game. Regional dietary patterns are outlined. An interesting section covers the food ration provided Chinese laborers brought to Africa to work on the "Congo-Ocean' railroad building project. A review of famine; specific nutrient deficiencies; and general nutritional status of the region terminate the article.

5889.   Murdoch, John. 1891. Ceremonial cannibalism in East Africa. AA 4 [old series]: 299, 300.

Upper portion of sacrificial victim's skull is used as a drinking vessel for a beverage called pombo, among the Wado, of Tanganyika.

5890.   Murdoch, John. 1892. Ethnological results of the Point Barrow Expedition. SI-BE-AR for the year 1887-1888. pp. 1-446.

Means of subsistence: (substances used for food; food preparation methods; time and frequency of eating; beverages): pp. 61-65. Utensils used in food preparation, water carrying, and eating: pp. 86-105. Point Barrow is at the extreme northern peninsular area of Alaska, on the Beaufort Sea.

5891.   Murdock, George Peter, ed. 1943. Cross cultural survey. Food and water supply in the Marshall Islands. Institute of Human Relations. Strategic Bulletins of Oceania, No. 4. New Haven: Yale University.

cf. Lawrence (1943).

5892.   Murdock, George Peter. 1960. Staple subsistence crops of Africa. GR 50: 523-540.

5893.   Murdock, George Peter. The current status of the world's hunting and gathering peoples. In Man the hunter. Edited by Richard Borshay Lee & Irven DeVore. 1968. Chicago: Aldine Publishing Co.

5894.   Murie, Olaus J. 1935. Alaska-Yukon caribou. USDA-BBS-B No. 54.

Note on the warble fly [Oedemagena tarandi] eaten by the Eskimo: p. 10.

5895.   Muriel, C.E. 1901. Appendix to Report on Sudan forests. 2nd ed. Cairo: Al-Mokattam Printing Office.

Food use of fruit: pp. 23-24.

5896.   Murphy, George H. 1905. New German food products. USDCL-MCR No. 291 P. 103.

5897.   Murphy, Gladys Hagan & Wertz, Anne W. 1954. Diets of pregnant women: influence of socioeconomic factors. JADA 30: 34-38.

5898.   Murphy, John. 1942. National nutrition plan. Print 199: 19.

Cooperation between industry and government, during World War II, to develop a nutrition program for workers.

5899.   Murray, A.W. 1924. The Chinese banana in the Pacific. JHer 15: 235, 236.

Its introduction to Samoa.

5900.   Murray, J. 1964. Manna in the desert; Turkana Desert. W Mission 14: 14-19.

The Turkana area is in western Kenya, west of Lake Arthur.

5901.   Murray, J.H.P. 1939. The Papuan instrument called 'pombo' and the drink called 'hanni'. Man 39: 48.

Use of an intoxicating beverage in the Purari River region of Papua, New Guinea.

5902.   Murray, Jacqueline. 1970. The first European agriculture; a study of the osteological and botanical evidence until 2000 B.C. Edinburgh: Edinburgh University Press.

5903.   Murray, Janet. 1963. Food in Scottish song. Scot Mag 59: 19-21.

5904.   Murray, Thomas A. Subsistence change in northwestern Costa Rica: some suggestions from settlement patterns. Paper presented at 74th Annual Meeting of the American Anthropological Association. 2 to 6 December, 1975. San Francisco California.

5905.   Murray, Thomas A. The protein factor in the prehistory of northwestern Costa Rica. Paper presented at 77th Annual Meeting of the American Anthropological Association. 14 to 18 November, 1978. Los Angeles, California.

5906.   Muse, Marianne & Gillum, Isabelle. 1931. Food consumption of fifty Vermont farm households. VI-AES-B No. 327.

5907.   Musgrave, Anthony. 1926. Turtle's eggs as food. AMM 2: 422.

In New Guinea; Santa Cruz Islands, and Capricorn Islands. The Santa Cruz Islands are in the eastern Solomon Group; the Capricorns are located within the Australian Great Barrier Reef, on the Tropic of Capricorn at approximately 153 .OE.

5908.   Musgrave, W.E. & Richmond, George F. 1907. Infant feeding and its influence upon infant mortality in the Philippine Islands. PJS 2 [B. Medical Sciences] : 361-385.

This study is a very comprehensive one, and doubtless one of the earliest of its kind in the literature. The authors' review of available health statistics leads them to conclude that more than seventy-five percent of infant deaths in Manila are primarily due to dietetic error. Child feeding practices of native and non-native mothers are described and an analysis of thirty samples of human milk - ten each from three groups: two Filipino (higher and lower socio-economic classes) and one from resident North Americans - are given. An extensive section is given over to the analysis of animal milks and proprietary foods used for infant feeding. The authors are rigorous in their emphasis that infant feeding be approached scientifically, and recommend exact indication of contents be provided by manufacturers. A final section provides formulas for achieving the proper dilution of milk as to percentages of milk and cream for children of different ages.

5909. Mustacci, P. 1971. Cesare Bressa (1785-1836) on dirt-eating in Louisiana. JAMA 218: 229.

Analysis of Bressa's unpublished manuscript 'De la disolution scorbutique'. ['Scorbutic degeneration.']

5910. Muto, S.; Muzuno & Kobayashi, Y. 1969. Dietary patterns of Japanese and American pre-school children in Tokyo. JADA 55: 252-256.

5911. Myers, Alice. 1944. Breadfruit and fafa in the Marshalls. CSM-M 4 March. P. 5.

Includes preparation description for fish soup; a banana/coconut cream confection; dried bread fruit. Earth ovens are also described.

5912. Mytinger, Beverly Griss. Interpersonal opinion leadership, seekership and neutrality in food. Ph.D. dissertation. Health Sciences. University of California at Los Angeles. 1969.

Examines interpersonal influence in food-related behavior in a Hawaiian Homestead community (Nanakuli, Island of Oahu). The formal leader who was active and interested in the food area was found to be an opinion leader on the subject in the social network, but was not necessarily a very active opinion leader. On the other hand, an opinion leader who was an expert in a specific area of food, because of this expertness, often had leadership which extended beyond the immediate social network, into the entire community.

5913. Na Conce. 1951. Peruvian creole cookery. The art of cooking Peruvian fod. Lima: Talleres Graficos G.A. Quinoz.

Bilingual Spanish-English edition.

5914. Nadaillac, Marquis de. 1885. L'anthropophagy et les sacrifices humains. [Anthropophagy and human sacrifice.] RDM 66: 405-434.

5915. Nadaillac, Marquis de; Mortillet, Gabriel de; & Le Tourneau. 1888. Suite de discussion sur l'anthropophagie [Continuation of the discussion on anthropophagy.] SAP-B 11: 27-46.

Review of historical accounts of, and archaeological evidence for cannibalism.

5916. Nag, D.S. 1958. Tribal economy (an economic study of the Baigas]. Delhi: Bharatiya Adimjati Sevak Sang.

5917. Nagarajan, V. Neurolathyrism. In First Asian Congress of Nutrition. 22 January - 2 February 1971. Hyderabad, India. Proceedings. Edited by P.G. Tuluple & Kamala S. Jaya Rao. 1972. pp. 641-647. Hyderabad: Nutrition Society of India.

The continued ingestion of Lathyrus sativus grain, particularly in central India, predisposes to various extremes of paralysis in the legs, as a consequence of the action of the neurotoxin 3-(N)- oxalyl aminoalanine (possibly upon the pyramidal tract of the spinal cord). Suggestions for prevention and control of lathyrism, through plant breeding and grain detoxication are made.

5918. Nagy, Jeno. 1964. Fank, panko. MNyelv 60: 352-355.

Two Hungarian words for 'pancake', and 'apple fritter'.

5919. Nagy, Lajos K. 1964. A tej feldogozasa zsadanyban. [Dairy economy in Zsdany [Bihar County]. Ethnografia 75: 607-609.

Hungary.

5920. Naik, Thakorall Bhanabhai. Bhils: a study in primitive social economy. Ph.D. dissertation. Lucknow University. 1951.

India.

5921. Nairobi. African Medical and Research Foundation. The food and growth of Gogo children [by R. Shaffer and Finkelstein.] 1964.

5922. Nakashima, Leslie S. 1933. Industrial use of Hawaiian limu is conceivable. PRI-J 8: 14. Hawaiian edible seaweed.

Also in HS-B 26 December (1931).

5923. Namikawa, S. 1906. Fresh-water algae as human food. T-IU-CA-B 7: 123-124. Abstracted in JCS 90: 884 (1906).

5924. Nanavati, M.B. no date. Bhadkad: social and economic survey of a village, a comparative study [1915 and 1955]. Bombay: Indian Society of Agricultural Economics.

Comparative caste menus are recorded, and changes in food consumption noted between the two surveys: e.g. rice, dhal, wheat, vegetables, milk, ghee and tea are consumed in greater quantities. [After Schofield 1975: 105.] The village studied is Bhadkad, in Kaira District in the State of Gujarat, located southwest of Ahmadabad, at approximately 22 .55 N., 72 .50 E.

5925. Napel, Rolf. 1969. Entwicklungstendenzen der Lebensmittelverpackung. [Trends in the evolution of food packaging.] LInd 16: 91-93.

5926. Narr, Karl J. 1956. Early food-producing populations. In Man's role in changing the face of earth. Edited by William L. Thomas, Jr. 1956. pp. 134-151. Chicago: University of Chicago Press.

5927. Naselli, Carmelina. 1953. "Empanadilla," un dolce spagnolo in Sicilia e in Argentina. ["Empanadilla", a Spanish confection in Sicily and in Argentina.] Catania: G. Crisafulli.

5928. Nash, G.V. 1909. The Kafir bread plants. NYBG-J 10: 275-277.

Description of several farinaceous plants, notably Encephalartos caffer, used by South African natives for making bread-like cakes. Preparation method described.

5929. Nash, Manning. 1958. Machine age Maya. The industrialization of a Guatemalan community. Research Center in Economic Development and Cultural Change, The University of Chicago. Glencoe, Illinois: The Free Press.

Location of kitchen in typical homes in Estancia: p. 34, 36, 37. Food: p. 38. Weekly food consumption: quantity and monetary value of four families: p. 39.

5930. Nash, Robert Alan. The Chinese shrimp fishery in California. Ph.D. dissertation. University of California at Los Angeles. 1973.

A history from 1850.

5931. Natal Fisheries Advisory Board. 1915. Natal food fishes; how to select and how to cook them. Durban: Natal Fisheries Advisory Board.

Varieties of fishes; seasonal availability; recipes.

5932. Nathanael, W.R.N. The history of vinegar production and the use of coconut toddy as a raw material. CCQ 3: 135-139.

Conversion of coconut toddy to vinegar and alcohol, in Ceylon.

5933. National Academy of Sciences. 1975. Underexploited tropical plants with promising economic value. Report of an ad hoc panel of the Advisory Committee on Technology Innovation. Board on Science and Technology for International Development. Commission on International Relations. Washington, D.C.: National Academy of Sciences.

Of thirty-six plants described, twenty-three are food plants; in the categories; cereals; roots and tubers; vegetables; fruits; and oilseeds. Food uses; research needs; and contacts for germ plasm supply are included.

5934. National Academy of Sciences. 1975. The winged bean: a high-protein crop for the tropics. Washington, D.C.: National Academy of Sciences.

Psophocarpus tetragonolobus, L. [DC].

5935. National Research Council. Food and Nutrition Board. 1944. Symposium on nutrition surveys. December 2, 1944. Washington, D.C. Washington, D.C.: National Research Council.

5936. National Research Council. Committee on Food Habits. 1945. Manual for the study of food habits. Report of the Committee on Food Habits. NRC-N No. 111.

During World War II, in the United States, a wide range of social scientists were involved in the coordinated study of the population's eating habits. This concerted effort related to the desire to discover means by which dietary modifications, necessitated by wartime restrictions, scarcity, and rationing, could be effected with a minimum of cognitive dissonance, in view of the multi-ethnic nature of the population, regional differences in dietary patterns, variation in income, and the existence of illnesses in which dietary control was a significant consideration. One major result of the research of the Committee on Food Habits is this procedural monograph. The Manual major foci are: food patterns; social organization of food; ideology of food; enculturation to food habits; material culture and technology of food; food pathology; stability and change in food behavior; food-related studies within a cultural context; techniques used in observational studies of food habits. Section 5, 'Experimental methods in the field of food habits' contains reviews of laboratory experiments designed to test various psycho-physiological variables related to food choice; preference; hunger; and dietary change. An extensive bibliography of six hundred eighty-two items is appended providing a resource for data on experimental psychology, nutritional status, and ethnic food patterns.

5937. National Soft Drink Association. 1963. Liquids for living: a discussion of the relationship between good health and an adequate liquid intake. Washington, D.C.: National Soft Drink Association.

5938. Native Harvesting Research. 1976. Research to establish present levels of harvesting by native peoples of northern Quebec. 2 vols. Vol. 1. A report on the harvests by the James Bay Cree. Montreal: James Bay and Northern Quebec Native Harvesting Research Committee.

5939. Native Harvesting Research. 1976. Research to establish present levels of harvesting by native peoples of northern Quebec. 2 vols. Vol. 2. A report on the harvests by the Inuit of northern Quebec. Montreal: James Bay and Northern Quebec Native Harvesting Research Committee.

5940. Naumann, L. 1887. Systematik der Kochkunst: Internationales Kochlehrbuch fur Haushaltungen aller Staende zur Benutzung beim Ertheilen von Unterricht sowie zum Selbstudium; desgleichen zur Orientierung fur Arzte. [Taxonomy of the culinary art: international textbook on cooking for households of all social classes; for use in teaching and in independent study; also for the information of physicians.] Dresden: Schofeild.

Preparation and use of ten edible South African plants: p. 52.

5941. Navarro del Aguila, Victor. 1944. Comidas tradicionales del Cusco. [Traditional foods of Cuzco.] WP 3: 10-12.

Lechon; moraya; phasi; llatan; tamale.

5942. Navia, J.M.; Lopez, M.H.; Cimadevilla, E.M.; Fernandez, A. Valiente; Clement, I.D.; & Harris, Robert Samuel. 1955. Nutrient composition of Cuban foods. 1. Food of vegetable origin. FR 20: 97-113.

5943. Nazeer, Mian M. 1964. An analysis of the food and food habits of our people. Com Ind 8: 16-20.

Pakistan.

5944. Nazeer, Mian M. 1964. The food and food habits of the Pakistans. EInt 17: 715-720.

5945. Nazir-ud-Din. Classifiation of groundnut varieties. Master's thesis. West Pakistan University. 1962.

The peanut, Arachis hypogaea, L.

5946. N'doye, Thianar. 1967. A propos du rapport F.A.O. (W.R. Aykroyd et Joyce Doughty) sur les legumineuses dans l'alimentaiton humaine. [Concerning the F.A.O. report (W.R. Aykroyd and Joyce Doughty) on legumes in human diet.] Seventh International Congress of Nutrition. 1966. (Hamburg). Proceedings. Volume 3. pp. 289-293.

5947. Neale, Margaret Kennedy Mumford. The composition of peanut meal and its uses as a diabetic food. Master's thesis. University of Chicago. 1920.

5948. Neal, Marie Catharine. 1940. Edible weeds in Hawaii. PPac 52: 5-6.

5949. Neal, Marie Catharine. 1965. In gardens of Hawaii. BPBM-SP No. 50. Revised edition.

Contains references to food use of indigenous and introduced plants.

5950. Neger F.W. & Vanino, L. 1903. Der Paraguay-Thee. [Paraguay tea.] Stuttgart: F. Grub. Reviewed in ZUNG 7: 637 (1904). Yerba mate.

5951. Negri, G. Viti fossili e viti preistoriche in Italia. [Prehistoric and fossil grape vines in Italy.] In Storia della viti e del vino in Italia. Edited by A. Marescalchi & G. Dalmasso. Vol. 1. Milan: Arti Grafiche Gualdoni.

5952. Neguse, Admasu. 1956. Food of the Kottu Gallas. AA-UC-ES-B 5: 33-39.

Ethopia.

5953. Nelson, Alexander. 1951. Medical botany: a hand-book for medical men and all who are concerned in the use of plants. Edinburgh: Livingstone.

5954. Nelson, D.C. Taxonomy and origins of Chenopodium guinoa and Chenopodium Nuttaliae. Ph.D. dissertation. Bloomington: University of Indiana. 1968.

5955. Nelson, Edward William. 1899. The Eskimo about Bering Strait. SI-BAE-AR for the year 1896-1897. pp. 3-518.

The technique of manufacturing dippers, ladles, and spoons is described on pp. 65-72; pestles, blubber hooks and carriers, and oil, and water bags are described on pp. 73, 74; root picks and bone breakers: p. 75; knives: pp. 85, 86; typical foods, their preparation, cooking, and preservation: pp. 267-270. Description of famine on St. Lawrence Island 1879-1880: pp. 269-270.

5956. Nelson, Linda Jean. Daily acitivity patterns of peasant homemakers. Ph.D. dissertation. Michigan State University. 1966.

Costa Rica.

5957. Nelson, Sarah. Chulum period villages on the Han River in Korea: subsistence and settlement. Ph.D. dissertation. Anthropology. University of Michigan. 1973.

5958. Nemethy, Endre. 1949. Ket regi kemenesaljai nagybojti teszta: a male es szalados. [Two traditional Lenten foods in Kemenesalja.] Ethnografia 60: 281-282.

5959. Nemoy, Leon, ed., trans. 1942. From the "Kitab al-Anwar" of Yaghqub al Qirqisani. MLeaves 4: 96-102.

Excerpt from the writings of a 10th Century Karaite author. Proscribed foods: pp. 10-101.

5960. Nenquin, Jacques. 1961. Salt. A study in economic prehistory. Dissertationes Archaeologicae Gaudenses. Vol. Six. Brugge, Belgium: De Tenpel.

5962. Nequatewa, Edmund. 1943. Some Hopi recipes for the preparation of wild plant foods. Plateau 16: 18-20.

5963. Nequatewa, Edmund. 1946. The place of corn and feathers in Hopi ceremonies. Plateau 19: 15-16.

5964. Netherly, Patricia. Fish, corn and cloth: intra-regional specialization on the north coast of Peru. Paper presented at 74th Annual Meeting of the American Anthropological Association. 2 to 6 December, 1975. San Francisco, California.

5965. Netolitzky, Friz. 1912. Hirse und Cyperus aus dem prahistorischen Agypten. [Millet and cyperus in prehistoric Egypt.] BBZ 29[2]: 1-11.

5966. Netolitzky, Fritz. 1913. Supplement to the discussion of foods and medicines of the ancient Egyptians. [In German.] ZUNG 26: 425-427.

Discussion of present-day Egyptian food customs similar to those believed to have been practiced in antiquity. Several forms of preserved fish are described which appear to be similar to the garum of the ancient Romans.

5967.   Netolitzky, Fritz. 1930. Unser wissen van den Alten Kulturpflanzen. Mitteleuropas. [Our knowledge of ancient central European cultivated plants.] DAI-RGK-B 20: 30-32.

5968. Netting, Robert. 1977. Cultural ecology. Menlo Park, California: Benjamin/Cummings.

Nutrition: pp. 11, 19, 44, 50, 57, 70, 73, 84, 88.

5969. Neumann, Charlotte. The nutritional problems of young African children. Paper presented at 77th Annual Meeting of the American Anthropolical Association. 14 to 18 November, 1978. Los Angeles, California.

5970. Neumann, Holm Wolfram. 1960. The identification of a sample of unmodified faunal remains from Angel site. IAS-P 70: 46. Abstract.

Faunal food remains from a Middle Mississippian site in Southwestern Indiana.

5971. Neuman, Robert . 1961. Domesticated corn from a Fort Walton mound site in Houston County, Alabama. Fla Anth 14: 75-80.

5972. Neumann, Rudolf Otto. 1932. Der einfluss der Mode auf die Ernahrung. [The role of fashion in nutrition.] BV 32: 146-149.

Popular trends in food habits.

5973. Neumann, Thomas W. A biocultural approach to salt taboos: the case of the southeastern United States. CAnth 18: 289-308.

5974. Neuville, H. 1931. Cannibalisme et carences alimentaires. [Cannibalism and dietary deficiencies.] Anthropologie 41: 552-556.

Suggests nutrient deficiency is not a basis for anthropophagy.

5975. Neverman, Hans. 1933. St. Matthias-Gruppe. Hamburgische Wissenschaftliche Stiftung und Notgemeinschaft der Deutschen Wissenschaft. Ergebnisse der Sudsee-Expedition 1908-1910. Ethnographie: A. Melanesien. Volume 2. Part 2. [St. Matthias Group. Hamburg Scientific Institute and Emergency Association of the German Institute. Results of the South Sea-Expedition 1908-1910. Ethnography: A. Melanesia.] Hamburg: Friederichsen, De Gruyter.

Food: pp. 83-107.

5976. Neverman, Hans. 1934. Admiralitats-Inseln. Hamburgische Wissenschaftliche Stiftung und Notgemeinschaft der Deutschen Wissenschaft. Ergebnisse der Sudsee-Expedition 1908-1910. Ethnographie: A. Melanesien. Volume 3. Part 2. [Admirally Islands. Hamburg Scientific Institute and Emergency Association of the German Institute. Results of the South-Sea Expedition. 1908-1910.

Ethnography: A. Melanesia] Hamburg: Friederichsen, De Gruyter.

Food: pp. 155-210.

5977.   New, Peter Kong-Ming & Priest, Rhea Pendergrass. 1967. Food and thought: a sociologic study of food cultists. JADA 51: 13-18.

5978.   Newberry, John Strong. 1887. Food and fibre plants of North American Indians. New York: D. Appleton.

5979.   Newberry, John Strong. 1888. Food and fibre plants of the North American Indians. PSMo 32: 31-46.

Food plants: pp. 37-38; 41-42.

5980.   Newberry, P.E. 1928. The pig and the cult animal of sete. JEA 14: 211-225.

Ancient Egypt.

5981.   Newcomb, Franc Johnson. 1940. Origin legend of the Navajo eagle chant. JAF 53: 50-77.

This article includes abundant references to foods and food preparation.

5982.   Newcomb, Franc Johnson. 1964. Hosteen Klah. Norman: Univesity of Oklahoma Press.

Navajo food: pp. 7, 56, 69, 76, 79.

5983.   Newcomb, Robert M. The husbandry of pepper, ginger, and cardamon on the Malabar Coast of India before the Sixteenth Century. Ph.D. dissertation. Geography. University of California, Los Angeles. 1958.

5984.   Newcombe, Ken. 1976. The energetics of vegetable production in Asia, old and new. Search 7: 423-430.

5985.   Newcombe, Ken. 1976. Energy use in the Hong Kong food system. Ag Eco 2: 253-276.

5986.   Newcombe, Ken. 1977. Nutrient flow in a major urban settlement: Hong Kong. H Ecol 5: 179-208.

Current and potential nutrient recycling are examined, together with phosphorous flow and loss. A comparison is made between land-based forage-area demands of Hong Kong, and Sydney, Australia. Patterns of food production and nutrient recycling are proposed, with the aim of optimizing resource utilization in close association with contemporary urban settlements.

5987.   New Haven, Connecticut. Human Relations Area Files. AE3: Sino-Tibetan border peoples. Die Mewu Fan-tse von Ch'inghai. [The Mewu Fantzu of Ch'inghai.] by Hans Stubel. Translated by Frieda Schutze.] 1954.

A Tibetan people living ca. 200 miles from Koko Nor, on both sides of the Kansu-Ch'inghai border. Food habits: pp. 26-27.

5988.   Newman, James L. 1975.   Dimensions of Sandawe diet. EFN 4: 33-39.

Lists and describes uses of staple foods, relishes, and food supplements. The Sandawe occupy central Tanzania and are probably linguistically related to the Khoisan [Bushman-Hottentot] peoples.

5989.   Newman, L.F. 1940.   Diet and race. Man 40: 73-74.

Abstract of a paper presented at a special meeting of the Royal Anthropologial Institute, 24 February, 1940, Cambridge, England.   Stresses the importance of critical work on the phsyiology of food, and dietetics as factors in the development of culture.   Notes a great deal of information on food and agriculture in the past could be obtained from epic and folk-stories. Discusses Armitage (1922).

5990.   Newman, L.F. 1046.   Some notes on foods and dietetics in the Sixteenth and Seventeenth Centuries. RAIGBI-J 76: 39-49.

Discusses the felt need on the part of the educated classes for what might be called 'popular scientific lterature'. Covers classic texts of the period; food, health, hygiene; the Hippocratic humours; food prices and production; food preferences; bread; dietetic disorders, and nutritional values of diets; dietetic knowledge and prejudices; diet and medicine.

5991.   Newman, M.V. 1927.   Hawaiian staff of life. GH 20.

Poi, a fermented starchy staple prepared from the boiled, mashed corm of Colocasia esculenta, called taro in the Hawaiian language.

5992.   Newman, Marshall Thornton. 1960. Adaptations in the physique of American aborigines to nutritional factors. HB 32: 288-313.

5993.   Newman, Marshall Thornton. 1961. Biological adaptation of man to his environment: heat, cold, altitude and nutrition. NYAS-A 91: 617-633.

In the section 'Bodily adjustments to nutrition' (pp. 627, 629), the author provides examples of adaptations of populations to apparently insufficient quantities of specific nutrients without pathological effects; also considered are Bergmann's rule in relation to small body-size in the tropics; and the results of hyperalimentation.

5994.   Newman, Marshall Thornton. 196 Ecology and nutritional stress in man. AA 64: 22-34.

Where deficiency diseases principally attributable to a single nutrient are apparent, these diseases have strong ecological and usually seasonal associations. Concomitant cultural correlates are observable, insofar as socioeconomic variables are characteristic of certain ecological zones.

5995.   Newman, Marshall Thornton.   Nutritional adaptation in man. In Physiological anthropology. Edited by Albert Damon. 1975. New York: Oxford Univesity Press.

5996.   Newman, Thomas Stell.   Aboriginal Hawaiian agriculture: the archaeological evidence. Paper presented at 67th Annual Meeting of the American Anthropological Association.   21 to 24 November, 1968. Seattle, Washington.

Compares and contrasts the relative stability of maritime as against terrestrial ecosystems and presents an analysis of the only two tableland field systems in the State which have survived modern land use, at Lapakahi, and Kealekekua Bay (approximately 19.29N, 155 05W), on the Island of Hawaii.   Analytic data is based on area photogrammetric mapping and archaelogical investigations, and are correlated with palynological, pedological, ethnographic and ecological data to provide an initial description of a major type of Hawaiian agriculture.   A tentative sequence of Hawaiian cultural adaptation to the terrestrial ecosystem is suggested based on the presented data.

5997.   Newman, Thomas Stell. Mauka-makai fishing and farming on the Island of Hawaii in A.D. 1788. Ph.D. dissertation. Anthropology. University of Hawaii. 1970.

5998.   Newton, Delores. A tuber in the pot...Paper presented at 70th Annual Meeting of the American Anthropological Association.   18 November, 1971. New York City.

Recipes are a significant aspect of cultural variation and are subject to the same forces for conservation and of change as other aspects of culture. For example, William O. Jones, of the Stanford University Food Research Institute, has noted a single pattern in the African use of manioc in the structure of the meal: it is the starch over which some kind of sauce is poured. The mannner in which it, and other foods are structured in the meal form should be considered worth recording and analyzing for South American cultures, too. Examples of manioc recipes from a Timbira tribe (the Krikati) of northeastern Brazil are offered here for initial comparative discussion.

5999.   New York. Academy of Medicine. Manuscript 1 (Phillips 275). De re culinaria [by Apicius]

Probably from Fulda, 9th Century.

6000.   New York State. Joint Legislative Committee on Nutrition. 1944. Consolidated Report. Food in war and peace. Legislative document No. 73.

Part 1. This hungry world. Part 2. 1944 food problems. Part 3. School lunches. Part 4. Our daily bread. Part 5. Food behind bars.

6001.   Ng, Kwei-chu. Chinese restaurant workers in London. Master's thesis. London School of Economics. 1964.

6002.   Nghi, Nguyen Nhu. 1960. Contibution a l'etude du 'nuoc-mam' condense au Vietnam. [Contribution to the study of the 'nuoc-mam' paste of Vietnam.] Indo-Pacific Fisheries Council. Eighth Session Proceedings. Section 2. pp. 79-81. Bangkok: Food and Agriculture Organization of the United Nations. Regional Office for Asia and the Far East.

6003.   Niaudet, J. 1976. Les depenses des Francais pour leur alimentation. [Expenditures for food by the French] ANA 30: 429-437.

Shows an increase in food budget since 1959, in relation to population growth; changes in food quality; size of area of residence (city, town). Notes increase in meals consumed away from home, and emphasizes that "Consumption, until recent years, was considered an instantaneous act, without duration. If consumers were only driven by finding the same product at the lowest price, there would be no difference in prices for the same product - which is not the case. Time is to be incorporated in the theory of consumers' choices" (p. 437).

6004.   Niceforo, Alfredo. 1905. Les classes pauvres; recherches anthropologiques et sociales. [The poor classes: anthropological and sociol research.] Paris: V. Giard & E. Briere.

Contains brief data on food habits.

6005.   Nichol, E.P. 1956. Notes on some African vegetables in Sierra Leone. SLS 6:66-70.

6006.   Nicholas, R.C. 1965. Charqui. WW 29:35-38.

Preparation of dried meat.

6007.   Nicholls, Lucius. 1961. Tropical nutrition and dietetics. Revised by H.M. Sinclair, and Derrick Brian Jelliffe. London: Bailliere, Tindall and Cox.

Food habits; food for special groups; religiously defined foods; attitudes toward and beliefs about food: pp.331-368.

6008.   Nichols, Dorothy Emma. A comparison of a foods curriculum with the food practices of a selected group of high school girls at McCune, Kansas. Master's thesis. Education and Psychology. Kansas State College. 1942.

6009.   Nichols, Linda. Change and nutrition: the anthropologist's roles. Paper presented at 77th Annual Meeting of the American Anthropological Association. 14 to 18 November, 1978. Los Angeles, California.

6010.   Nichols, Narcissus. The nutritive value of the diets of a small Negro group. Master's thesis. Indiana University. 1946.

6011.   Nichols, Thomas Low. 1873. Count Rumford; how he banished beggary from Bavaria. London: Her Majesty's Health Office.

Biological data on Benjamin Thompson.

6012.   Nickerson, Grace P. 1929. The giant cactus, sahuaro. Los Angeles: Trade Printing Co.

Use as food by Papago of Arizona: pp. 21-23.

6013.   Nickerson, Norton H. 1935. Variations in cob morphology among certain archaeological and ethnological races of maize. MBG-A 40:79-111.

Basket Maker; Pima-Papago; and early levels at Ventana Cave, in Arizona.

6014.   Nickerson, Norton, H; Rowe, N.H. & Richter, E.A. Native plants in the diets of northern Alaskan Eskimos. In Man and his food. Edited by C. Earle Smith, Jr. 1973. pp. 3-28.

6015.   Nickles, Harry G. 1969. Middle Eastern cooking. New York: Time-Life Books. Foods of the World.

6016.   Nicod, Michael. A method of eliciting the social meaning of food. Master's thesis. Anthropology. University of London. 1974.

6017.   Nicol, B.M. 1949. Nutrition of Nigerian peasant farmers, with special reference to the effects of vitamin A and riboflavin deficiency. BJN 3:25-43.

Cookery and food preparation: p.27.

6018.   Nicol, B.M. 1953. Protein in the diet of the Isoko tribe of the Niger Delta. PNS 12: 66-69.

6019.   Nicolardot, Lois. 1868. Histoire de la table. Curiosites gastronomiques de tous les temps et de tous les pays. [History of the table. Gastronomic curiosities of all times and all nations.] Paris: E. Dentu.

6020.   Niehoff, Arthur 1967. Food habits and the introduction of new foods. WAS-J 57:30-37.

6021.   Niehoff, Arthur. Cultural influences in nutrition projects. Paper presented at 67th Annual Meeting of the American Anthropological Association. 21 to 24 November, 1968. Seattle, Washington.

6022.   Niehoff, Arthur. 1969. Changing food habits. JNE 1:10-11.

6023.   Niehoff, Arthur. Food habits and cultural patterns. In Food, science, and society. A symposium held in February, 1968, sponsored by the Nutrition Foundation, Inc., the Northern California Section of the Institute of Food Technologists, and the University of California, Berkeley, Department of Nutritional Sciences. 1969. pp. 54-68. New York: The Nutrition Foundation.

Article gives examples of errors made by technical assistance volunteers in attempting to introduce new foods into traditional cultures.

6024.   Nielsen, Richard M. An experimental study of the effects of food consumption on message acceptance. Master's thesis. Home Economics. Provo, Utah: Brigham Young University. 1976.

6025.   Niemann, Theodore. 1884. Homoopatisches burgerliches kochbuch. Eine Zusammenstellung von Speisen und Getranken, welche wahrend einer homoopathischen Kur ohne Nachtheil genossen werden durfen. Homeopathic cookbook for home cooking. A listing of foods and beverages which may be consumed without adverse effects while under homeopathic treatment.] Eranienburg: Frenhoff.

6026.   Niethammer, Carolyn. 1974. American Indian food and lore. New York: Collier Books.

Contemporary recipes for traditional Native American foods, with related anthropological data, derived from the historical literature.

6027.   Nietschman, Barney. Between land and water: the subsistence ecology of the Miskito Indians, Eastern Nicaragua. Ph.D. dissertation. University of Wisconsin, Madison. 1970.

6028.   Nietschmann, Barney. 1972. Hunting and fishing focus among the Miskito Indians. HEcol 1:41-67.

6029.   Nigh, Ronald B. Nutritional strategies in historical and contemporary Mayan communities in Chiapas, Mexico. Paper presented at 77th Annual Meeting of the American Anthropological Association. 14 to 18 November, 1978. Los Angeles, California.

6030.   Nijholt, J.A. 1964. Report of the survey on cassava production and processing in Ceylon. Food and Agriculture Organization of the United Nations. Agricultural Engineering Branch. Land and Water Development. Rome: Food and Agricultural Organization of the United Nations.

6031.   Nikitine, Basile. 1956. Les Kurdes. [The Kurds.] Paris: Imprimerie Nationale.

Dietary: pp. 95-97.

6032.   Nikitine, Basile. 1956. La pomme de terre dans le folklore russe. Avec les raisons sociales et religieuses qui rendirent sa culture impopulaire dans le pays. [The potato in Russian folklore. With sociological and religious reasons for the unpopularity of its cultivation in the country.] Ethnographie. No. 51 pp. 95-114.

6033.   Nikolaev, A.B. 1963. On the utilization of wild medicinal, food, fodder, and other economically valuable plants of the far north Soviet Union. PNorth 6:207-217.

6034.   Niles, George MacCallum. 1912. Sitophobia: a digestive phantasm. Med Rec 81:987-989.

Analyzes psychological, physiological, and sociological bases of fear of or aversion to food.

6035.   Nims, Amy Elizabeth. Chinese life in San Antonio. Master's thesis. San Marcos, Taxas: Southwest Texas State Teachers College. 1941.

Superficial account of food habits, and gardening: pp. 31-33.

6036.   Nimuendaju, Curt. 1940. The Kupa, a cultivated plant of the Timbira of Brazil. In Sixth Pacific Science Congress. Proceedings. 1939. Vol. 4. Antrhopology, zoology, entomology, botany, forest resources, soil resources, climatology. pp. 131-134. Berkeley: Unversity of California Press.

A ground plant (Cissus sp.), with edible stems, which are baked in earth ovens. Eastern Timbira.

6037.   Nimuendaju, Curt. 1946. The eastern Timbira. Edited and translated by Robert H. Lowie. UCal-PAAE Vol. 41.

Fruit, nuts, palm, kupa (Cissus sp): pp. 59, 73.

6038.   Nino, Milagrosa Gabriel de. An appraisal of several methods of egg preservation. Master's thesis. Pharmacy. University of Santo Tomas. 1955.

Philippines.

6039.   Nipperdey, H. 1886. The industrial products and food-stuffs of the Congo. SGM 2: 483-487.

6040.   Nishimura, Y. 1897-1898. The chemistry of soja sauce manufacture. T-IU-CA-B 3: 191-206.

6041.   Nissen, H.W. & Crawford, M.P. 1936. A preliminary study of food-sharing behavior in young chimpanzees. JCPP 22: 383-419.

6042.   Nixon, C.W.W. 1943. Food, poverty and bad cooking. MTT 4: 4-7.

6043.   Niyogi, S.P.; Narayana, N.; & Desai, B.G. 1934. Nutritive value of Indian vegetable foodstuffs. IJMR 22: 373-382.

6044.   Niyogi, S.P.; Narayana, N.; & Desai, B.G. 1934. The nutritive value of ragi (Eleusine coracana). IJMR 22: 373-382.

6045.   Niyogi, S.P. & Sukhatankar, D.R. 1939. A dietary survey in Bombay. IMG 74: 674-679.

6046.   Nizzardini, G. & Joffe, Natalie F. Italian food patterns and their relationship to wartime problems of food and nutrition. Committee on Food

Habits. Mimeographed. Washington, D.C.: National Research Council. 1942.

6047. Noble, Donald G. 1963. The indispensable potato. ScotMag 79: 263-272.

6048. Notling, Fritz. 1910. The food of the Tasmanian Aboriginse. RST-PP pp. 279-305.

Begins with review of evidence provided by earlier writers, followed by analysis of linguistic evidence. Part 3 contains an extensive list of plant and animal foods by family genus, and species. Part 4 (pp. 296-305) is devoted to a nutritional evaluation of Tasmanian aboriginal diet, based on then-current knowledge, and estimates of dietary patterns.

6049. Noice, Harold H. 1939. Back of beyond. New York: G.P. Putnam's Sons.

Tariana of Brazil. Food: sauba (leafcutter) ants; tapir; manioc preparation: pp. 120-124.

6050. Nomura, H. 1954. Insects as food. Fauna 13: 36-39.

6051. Nordenskiold, Erland. 1920. The changes in the material culture of two Indian tribes under the influence of new surroundings. Comparative ethnographical studies. 2. Goteborg: Elanders Boktyckeri Aktiebolag.

The Chiriguano, and Chane of southern Bolivia and northern Argentina. Food preparation utensils: pp. 51-57.

6052. Nordholm, Patricia L. The effects of a monotonous diet on the eating habits of preschool children. Master's thesis. Michigan State University. 1932.

6053. Nordland, Odd. 1968. Brewing and beer traditions in Norway. The social anthropological background of the brewing industry. Oslo: Universitetsforlaget.

6054. Nordland, Odd. Traditional beer in Scandinavia. Paper read at the First International Symposium on Ethnological Food Research. 21 to 25 August, 1970. Lund: Folklivsarkivet, University of Lund.

Norway.

6055. Nordland, Odd. 1971. Traditional beer in Scandinavia and some reflections on taste. EScan 1971. pp. 166-171.

Brief review of the place of beer in Norwegian life and folklore, and substances used in flavoring beer. A distributional map of implements used in filter-vat straining, and of juniper flavoring is included.

6056. Norman, Edward C. 1958. Group discussion in changing food habits. JADA 1187-1189.

Description of a project in-progress at Sara Mayo Hospital in New Orleans, among pregnant, low-income group women.

6057. Norris, Theodore. The aboriginal utilization of the small cacti in the American Southwest. Master's thesis. University of New Mexico. 1939.

6058. Norsander, Goran. 1971. Herringssupe. Zum ethnologischen Asperkt eines Gerichtes. [Herring soup. An ethnological evaluation.] EScan 1971. pp. 171-184.

A distributional study, focusing on Sweden.

6059. Norse, G.T. 1975. Seasonal hunger of Ngowi and Ntumba of central Malawi. Africa 45: 1-11.

6060. North American Congress on Latin America. 1975. U.S. grain arsenal. NACLA's Latin America & Empire Report. 9 No. 7. New York, Berkeley: North American Congress on Latin America.

An examination of the United States' largest grain merchants and their commercial and political influence domestically and overseas.

6061. Norwak, Mary. 1975. Kitchen antiques. New York: Praeger.

6062. Noter, R. de. 1932. Les colocases dits "taros" au point de vue alimentaire. [The Colocaceae called "taro", from a nutritional point of view.] Nature (P) No. 2772. pp. 35, 36.

6063. Nougaret, A.M. & Jardin, C. 1964. Questions alimentaires aupres des groupes melanesiens et polynesiens de Noumea. [Dietary matters concerning some groups of Melanesians and Polynesians in Noumea.] Noumea, New Caledonia: Organisation de Recherche des Territoires d'Outre-Mer.

6064. Novak, Vilko. Ljudska prehrana v Prekmurju. [Folk food in Prekomurge.] Dissertation. University of Ljublyana. Yugoslavia. 1947.

Northeastern Yugoslavia.

6065. Novak, Vilko. Uber die milchwirtschaft bei den Volkern Jugoslawiens. [On dairy economy among the Yugoslavian people.] In Viehwirtschaft und Hirtenkultur. Ethnographische Studien. Edited by L. Foldes. 1969. pp. 574-599. Budapest: Akademiai Kiado.

6066. Nowak, Michael. Income and subsistence patterns in Eskimo communities. Paper presented at 73rd Annual Meeting of the American Anthropological Association 19 to 24 November, 1974. Mexico City.

6067. Nowak, Michael. Inflation: its role in a subsistence society. Paper presented at 74th Annual Meeting of the American Anthropological Association. 2 to 6 December, 1975. San Francisco, California.

6068.   Nowak, Michael. 1975. Subsistence trends in a modern Eskimo community. Arctic 28: 21-34.

6069.   Nowlis, V. 1941. The relation of degree of hunger to competitive interaction in chimpanzees. JCPP 32: 91-115.

6070.   Nowlis, V. 1942. Sexual status and degree of hunger in chimpanzee competitive interaction. JCPP 34: 185-194.

6071.   Nuckolls, Jr., G.N. An analysis of demand and price relationships between peanuts and cashew nuts in the United States, with emphasis on the salted nut trade. Master's thesis. Virginia Polytechnic Institute. 1961.

6072.   Nurge, Ethel. 1957. Infant feeding in the village of Guinhangdan, Leyte, Philippines. JTPECH 3: 89-96.

This study was performed by an anthropologist, and emphasizes the dynamics of culture change. Included are data on diets during pregnancy, breast-feeding patterns, bottle-feeding, supplementary foods, methods of food preparation, food beliefs and feeding practices.

6073.   Nurge, Ethel. Problems and approaches to the study of hunger and malnutrition. Paper presented at 68th Annual Meeting of the American Anthropological Association. 20 to 23 November, 1969. New Orleans, Louisiana.

Suggests areas or guidelines for research in which anthropologists and other social scientists are needed to help study personal, social and cultural factors related to hunger and malnutrition.

6074.   Nylen, Anna-Maja. 1963. Vara brod-traditioner. [Our bread traditions.] Al-Kron 20: 41-57.

6075.   Nyirenda, A.A. 1957. African market vendors in Lusaka: with a note on the recent boycott. HPBCA 22: 31-63.

6076.   Nyswander, D.B. 1943. Psychological factors associated with eating. NYJD 13: 10-14.

6077.   Nzekwu, Onura. 1961. Kola nut. N Mag 71: 298-305.

6078.   Nzekwu, Onura. 1963. Banda - the secret of Ibo concentration in Maiduguri. N Mag 79: 248-253.

Smoking and drying techniques in fish preservation.

6079.   Oakes, Sadie. Techniques used in helping a 6th grade group to develop food habits that build strong bones and teeth. Master's thesis. University of Alabama. 1945.

6080.   Oates, Frank. 1939. A note on earth-eating in the southern province. TNR 7: 113.

Geophagy among some native people of Nyarumba, Tanganyika.

6081.   Oberdorfer, M.J. 1938. Ernahrungs-studien unter den Ibostamen Sudost-Nigeriens. [Dietary studies among the Ibo tribe of southeastern Nigeria.] ASTPTEK 42: 245-252.

6082.   Oberg, Kalervo. 1940. Social economy of the Tlingit Indians. Private edition distributed by the University of Chicago libraries.

This publication is an excerpt (pp. 133-161) of the author's doctoral dissertation.

6083.   Oberg, Kalervo. 1949. The Terena and the Caduveo of southern Mato Grosso, Brazil. SI-ISA-P. No. 9.

Food (palm shoots, algaroba flour, palm nuts): p. 9; manioc: pp. 24-25; cane sugar and syrup: p. 25; maize foods, sweet potatoes: pp. 25-26; cara (a tuber), beans, rice, bananas: p. 26.

6084.   Oberg, Kalervo. 1973. The social economy of the Tlingit. Seattle: University of Washington Press.

Based on Oberg's doctoral dissertation, with additional material.

6085.   Oberg, Kalervo & Van Dijk, F. 1960. The fisherman of Surinam. Paramaraibo: Surinam-American Technical Cooperative Service.

6086.   O'Bern, Daniel. [Pseud. Mangin, Arthur]. 1860. Le cacao et le chocolat consideres aux points de vue botanique, chimique, physiologique, agricole, commercial, indstriel et economique...suivi de la legende du cacahuatl par Ferdinand Denis, conservateur de la Bibliotheque Sainte-Genevieve. [Cacao and chocolate considered from the botanical, chemical, physiological, agricultural, commercial, industrial and economic points of view...followed by the legend of Cacahuatl by Ferdinand Denis, Curator of the Bibliotheque Saint-Genevieve. Paris: Guillaumin & Cie.

6087.   Oberti, Federico. 1957. Repudiados y excomulgados por tomar mate. [Rejections and indictments against drinking mate.] La Prensa 3 Novembre.

6088.   Oberti, Federico. 1960. Disquisiciones sobre el origin de la bombilla. [Disquisition on the origin of the bombilla.] INIF-C 1: 151-158.

Etymology and origin of the tube used to drink yerba mate.

6089.   Obeyesekere, G. 1963. Pregnancy cravings (Dola-Duka) in relation to social structure and personality in a Sinhalese village. AA 65: 323-342.

Food rejections and cravings: pp. 336-341.

6090.   Obold, Walter L. 1959. What little rats drink, and how they grow: a discussion of some of the nutritional aspects of soft drinks, as demonstrated by animal experiments. Washington, D.C.: American Bottlers of Carbonated Beverages.

6091. Obolensky, Alexander P. 1972. Food. Notes on Gogol. University of Manitoba. Department of Slavic Literature. Readings in Slavic Literature No. 8. Winnipeg: Trident Press.

Food in the writing of Russian novelist Nikolai Visil'evich Gogol (1809-1852).

6092. O'Brien, Patricia J. 1972. The sweet potato: its origin and dispersal. AA 74: 342-365.

Traces the distribution of the plant throughout the Old World and Polynesia. Posits kumara to have been introduced into Quechua dictionaries by Spaniards "to reflect the educated Spaniard's knowledge of sweet potato terms".

6093. Ochse, J.J. 1948. Experience is their laboratory. SM 66: 70-72.

Diet in Indonesia.

6094. Ochse, J.J., with Backhuizen van den Brink, Reinier Cornelius. 1931. Vegetables of the Dutch East Indies (edible tubers, bulbs, rhizomes and spices included). Survey of the indigenous and foreign plants serving as pot-herbs and side dishes. Translated by Cornelis Andries Backer. Department of Agriculture, Industry and Commerce of the Netherlands East Indies. Buitenzorg: Archipel Drukkerij.

6095. O'Connell, Mary Frances. A study of the influence of nutrition knowledge on the food selection habits of high school students. Master's thesis. Greensboro: Woman's College of the University of North Carolina. 1943.

6096. Oddy, Derek J. Assessments of the diets. In The dietary surveys of Dr. Edward Smith, 1862-3. Edited by T.C. Barker; Derek J. Oddy; & John Yudkin. 1970. London: Staples Press.

Great Britain.

6097. Oddy, Dereky J. The diets of the 1860's. In the dietary surveys of Dr. Edward Smith, 1862-3. Edited by T.C. Barker, Derek J. Oddy; & John Yudkin. 1970. London: Staples Press.

Great Britain.

6098. Oddy, Derek J. A nutritional analysis of historical evidence: the working-class diet, 1880-1914. In The making of the modern British diet. Edited by Derek J. Oddy & D.S. Miller. 1976. London: Croom Helm.

6099. Oddy, Derek J.; & Yudkin, John. 1969. An evaluation of English diets of the 1860's. PNS 28: 13A-14A.

6100. Odom, W.P. 1953. A study of food habits of primitive and modern Latin America. MNutr 6: 4-9.

6101. Ogbu, John U. Food economy and consumption habits in [a] changing community. Paper presented at 9th International Congress of Anthropological and Ethnological Sciences. 28 August to 8 September, 1973. Chicago, Illinois.

Northern Malawi. Organization of food economy; fluctuation of food supply in a Poka village; effects of these variables upon outward labor migration, and the introduction of cash coffee cropping.

6102. Ogbu, John U. 1973. Seasonal hunger in tropical Africa as a cultural phenomenon. Africa 43: 317-332.

Argues in favor of seasonal hunger as cultural not a biophysical phenomenon. Data from two African villages: Chakaka (Poka), Malawi; and Onicha (Ibo), Nigeria.

6103. O'Gorman, J.J. 1930. Fransiscans in Mexico in the Sixteenth Century: Sahagun's book on the manners and customs of the Mexican Indians. ERev 81: 262-263.

6104. Oiso, Toshio. Post-war changes in food consumption patterns in Japan. In First Asian Congress of Nutrition. 22 January - 2 February, 1971. Hyderabad, India. Proceedings. Edited by P.G. Tulpue & Kamala S. Jaya Rao. 1972. pp. 275-284. Hyderabad: Nutrition Society of India.

Detailed analysis of data derived from the Japanese National Nutrition Survey, which was begun in 1946. Statistics are for rural as well as urban populations. Changes in nutrient intake are also tabulated.

6105. Oiso, Toshio. Problems in organization and implementation of school meal programmes in Japan. In First Asian Congress of Nutrition. 22 January - 2 February 1971. Hyderabad, India. Proceedings. Edited by P.G. Tulpue & Kamala S. Jaya Rao. 1971. pp. 172-176. Hyderabad: Nutrition Society of India.

Provides background on the history and operation of Japanese government -subsidized child feeding programs.

6106. Ojiambo, Julia A. 1967. A background study of the Abasama of Busia District - Western Province, Kenya. A preliminary study, 1965-1966. Nutriton 21: 216-221.

6107. Ojiambo, Julia A. 1967. Maternal and infant dietary practices in the Abasama of Busia District, Western Province, Kenya. A preliminary study, 1966-1967. EAMJ 44: 518-523.

6108. Oka, Monica Odinckezo. 1972. Black Academy cookbook; a collection of authentic African recipes. Buffalo, New York: Black Academy Press.

6109. Okamura, K. Uses of algae in Japan. In Fifth Pacific Science Congress. 1933. Canada. Proceedings. 1934. Vol. Four. pp. 3153-3161. Toronto: University of Toronto Press.

Extensive reference to algae used for food.

6110.   O'Kane, Walter Collins.   1957.   Sun in the sky. Norman: University of Oklahoma Press.

Hopi foods: pp. 79-94.

6111.   Okcoglu, Ayhan; Arcasoy, Ayten; Minich, Virginia; Tarcon, Y.; Suhru, Din; Yurukoglu, Orhan; Demirag, Bahtiyar; & Renda, Fevzi. 1966. Pica in Turkey. Part 1. The incidence and association with anemia. AJCN 19: 125-131.

Looks at multivariate causes of clay and dirt-eating, and their possible association with anemia.

6112.   Oke, O.L. 1966. Chemical studies on some Nigerian foodstuffs: gari. Nature (L) 212: 1055-1056.

Gari is prepared by grating cassava (Manihot utilissima), which is then detoxified through fermentation. After drying, the product is fried. The conversion by fermentation is described, and food uses of gari mentioned. Industrial production potential is noted, and the process described.

6113.   O'Kelly, Michael J. An ancient Irish method of cooking meat. In 4° Congresos Internacionales de Ciencios Prehistoricas y Protohistoricos. 21 - 27 de Abril, 1954. Madrid. Actas. Edited by A. Beltran. 1956. pp. 615-619. Zaragaza: Libreria General.

Experiment in cooking meat in an excavated open-air trough.

6114.   O'Kelly, M.J. 1954. Excavations and experiments in ancient Irish cooking places. RSAI-J 84: 105-155.

6115.   Okiy, G.E.O. 1960. Indigenous Nigerian food plants. WASA-J 6: 117-121.

6116.   Okumura, J. 1897-1898. Contributions to the chemistry of sake brewing. T-IU-CA-B 3: 207-220.

6117.   Olascoaga, Jose Quintin. 1952. Bases para ampliar la politica alimenticia mexicana. [Bases for amplifying Mexican nutrition policy.] Nutriologia 1: 83-97.

6118.   O'Laughlin, Bridget. Mbum beer-parties and structure of production and exchange in an African social formation. Ph.d. dissertation. Anthropology. Yale University. 1973.

6119.   Olcott, H.S. & Schaffer, M.B. 1965. Food from the sea. FTech 19: 774-777.

6120.   Olcott, Henry Steele. 1858. Sorgo and imphee, the Chinese and African sugar canes...their origin, varieties, and culture. New York: A.O. Moore.

6121.   Olden, Sarah Emilia. 1923. Shoshone folklore. Milwaukee: Morehouse Publishing co.

Pemmican; berries used as food: pp. 33-34; 203.

6122.   Oliva, Alberto. 1939. Nuove tracce dell' alta civilta delle neolitico 'umbro' desunte da ritrovamenti vegetali delle caverne di Belverde. [New traces of early Neolithic Umbrian civilization derived from plant discoveries from Belverde Cave.] IAg 76: 15-24.

6123.   Oliveira, J.F. Santos. 1974. The nutritional value of some foods consumed on San Tome Island. EFN 3: 237-242.

Sao Tome is located almost on the Equator at 0.25 N., 6.35 E. A small section of this paper described the preparation and use of a variety of typical San Tomean foods of plant origin.

6124.   Oliveira, J.F. Santos; Carvalho, J. Passos de; Sousa, R.F.X. Bruno de.; & Simao, M. Madalena. 1976. The nutritional value of four species of insects consumed in Angola. EFN 5: 91-97.

Macrotermes subhyalinus (Isoptera; Imbrasia ertli (Lepidoptera); Usta terpischore (Lepidoptera); and Rynchophorus phoenicis (Coleoptera). Methods of preparation noted briefly.

6125.   Oliver, Douglas L. 1942. A case of change in food habits in Bougainville, British Solomon Islands. AAnth 1: 34-36.

Case study of efforts to introduce new foods into traditional dietaries. This article points up how colonial administration's lack of understanding concerning native social structure and food habits resulted in failure to successfully introduce new crops.

6126.   Oliver, Douglas L. 1949. Economic and social uses of domestic pigs in Siuai, southern Bougainville, Solomon Islands. HU-PMAAE-P 29(3).

Butchering, cooking, and eating pigs: pp. 24-25.

6127.   Oliver, R. 1975. Les principaux evenements qui ont marque l'histoire de la cuisine francaise au cours des siecles; ce qu'elle est aujourd'hui et l'avenir qui est reserve. [The principal events marking the history of French cuisine over time; its present state, and its possible future.] Historia No. 42. pp. 2-8.

6128.   Oliver, R. 1976. Art culinaire et civilisation: quelques reflexions. [Some reflections on culinary art and civilization.] ANA 30: 427-428.

6129.   Oliver, W.R.B. 1931. An ancient Maori oven on Mount Egmont. JPS 40: 73-80.

6130.   Ollivier-Beauregard, G.-M. 1898. La vigne et le vin dans l'antiquite' egyptienne. [Vines and wine in ancient Egypt.] Bordeaux: Feret et fils. Also in: ANNSBLAB-A 56: 273-297 (1894).

6131.   Olmsted, W.H. 1925. The teaching of dietetics to medical students and interns. Diet Ad Ther 3: 533-537.

Comments on the ignorance of the general practitioner regarding dietetics; describes an experimental third year program of twenty-two hours' dietetic instruction; and encourages relocation of the hospital kitchen closer to the ward, to facilitate more convenient contact between physician and dietitian.

6132.   Olsson, Alfa. 1947. Kostvanor bland fiskare i Bohuslan. [Diet of Bohuslan fisher folk.] Folk-Liv 11: 5-32.

Sweden.

6133.   Olsson, Alfa. 1954. Faroiska kostvanor. [Diet of the Faroese.] Rig 37: 79-91.

Meat, fish, grains; seasonal availability of food; food preservation, on the Danish Faroe Islands.

6134.   Olsson, Alfa. 1958. Om Allmogens Kosthall. Studier med utgangspunkt fran vastnordiska matvanor. [On peasant diet. Studies with a starting point from western Scandinavian foodstuffs.] Institutit for Vastsvensk Kulturforskning. Goteborg: Elanders Boktryckeri Akt ebolag.

6135.   Olsson, Alfa. 1961. Koagulerad mjolk i aldre tiders hushallning. Nagra synpunkter pa producter och metoder. [Coagulated milk in old time home-making. Some points of view on production and methods.] Rig 44: 113-124.

6136.   Olsson, Alfa. Nordic bread research. In 6 Congres International des Sciences Anthropologiques et Ethnologiques. 30 juillet - 6 aout 1960. Vol. 2. Ethnologie (Vol. 2.). 1964. pp. 249-252. Paris: Musee de l'Homme.

Scandinavian research into the history of grain smoking, bread preservation, bread storage culture areas, and uses of bread as food.

6137.   Olszyna-Marzys, A.E. 1962. Food in Iran. Teheran: Central Public Health Laboratory.

6138.   Omeliansky, V.L. 1923. Aroma-producing microogranisms. JBact 8: 393-419.

Discussion of knowledge of chemical processes underlying aroma-production by bacteria, and application of such processes to food industry.

6139.   Onabamiro, Sanya Dojo. 1953. Food and health. Penguin West African Series. London: Penguin Books.

6140.   Onate, Burton T. 1964. Use of census results, maps and lists in food consumption studies in the Philippines. Phil Stat 13: 158-203.

6141.   O'Neale, Lila M. & Whitaker, Thomas W. 1947. Embroideries of the early Nazca Period and the Crops depicted on them. SJA 3: 294-321.

6142.   O'Neil, Dennis Harold. San Jorge, a late terrace site on the Sabana de Bogota, Colombia. Ph.D. dissertation. Anthropology. Michigan State University. 1972.

6143.   O'Nell, Carl. Manifest orality and thirst in dreams: a cross-cultural study in oral frustration: Master's thesis: University of Chicago. 1964.

6144.   Onstadt, M. The effect of a mid-morning lunch upon the subsequent behavior of preschool children. Master's thesis. Iowa State College. 1936.

6145.   Oomen, Henricus Adrianus Petrus Canisius. 1956. Le repas de la mere et de l'enfant dans les iles du Pacifique. [Maternal and infant diets in the Pacific Islands.] CPS-BT 6: 1-8.

6146.   Oomen, Henricus Adrianus Petrus Canisius. 1958. The diet of the adult Papuan. [In Dutch.] Voeding 19: 323-342.

6147.   Oomen, Henricus Adrianus Petrus Canisius. 1958. Nutrition and environment of the Papuan child. TGM 10: 337-340.

6148.   Oomen, Henricus Adrianus Petrus Canisius. 1958. Voeding en milieu van het Papoeakind. [Diet and environment of the Papuan child.] The Hague: Staatsdrukkerij en Uitgeverijbedrijf.

6149.   Oomen, Henricus Adrianus Petrus Canisius. 1959. Poor food patterns in New Guinea. NGS 3: 35-46.

6150.   Oomen, Henricus Adrianus Petrus Canisius. 1961. The nutrition situation in western New Guinea. TGM 13: 321-335.

6151.   Oomen, Henricus Adrianus Petrus Canisius. 1971. Ecology of human nutrition in New Guinea. Evaluation of subsistence patterns. EFN 1: 1-16.

Indigenous agriculutre, and food-getting patterns are described against the geographical background. The nutritional qualities of primary and secondary foods are examined and evaluated. Food preparation and eating practices are described, and the efficiency of diets based on various staples (sago, yams, sweet potatoes) compared.

6152.   Oomen, Henricus Adrianus Petrus Canisius & Malcolm, Sheila. 1958. Nutrition and the Papuan child: a study in human welfare. SPC-TP. No. 118.

6153.   Oomen, Henricus Adrianus Petrus Canisius; Spoon, W.; Heesterman, J.E.; Ruinard, J.; Luyken, R.; & Slump, P. 1961. The sweet potato as the staff of life of the highland Papuan. TGM 13: 55-66.

Because of the heavy reliance on the sweet potato (Ipomoea batatas) and other starchy foods (sago, taro, yam, banana) in Papua New Guinea communities, a study of the composition of popular I. batatas clones was undertaken. The low real protein value (average 2.5% to 3.0% dry weight basis) leads the authors to suggest efforts be made to selectively breed sweet potatoes for increased protein values.

6154.   Opler, Morris Edward. 1941. An Apache lifeway. Chicago: University of Chicago Press.

Foods: 354-376; 428, 429.

6155.   Oppenheim, Leo. 1950. On beer and brewing techniques in ancient Mesopotamia. AOS-J-S No. 10.

6156.   Oppenheim, Leo & Hartman, Louis F. 1945. The domestic animals of ancient Mesopotamia according to the thirteenth tablet of the series Har.ra = hubullu. JNES 4: 152-177.

6157.   Oppenheimer, H.R. 1931. Flora Transiordanica. 1. Revision critique des plantes recoltees et partiellement determinee par Aaron Aaronsohn an cours de ses expeditions (1904-1908) en Transjordanie et dans le Wadi el - Araba. Avec des journaux de voyages d'Aaron Aaronsohn. [Transjordanian flora. 1. Critical revision of plants collected and partially identified by Aaron Aaronsohn in the course of his expeditions (1904-1908) in Transjordan and in the Wadi el-ghAraba.] Geneva: Imprimerie Jent S.A.

This monograph contains an unusual biographical preface relating to Aaronson who, in addition to being an accomplished professional in the field of economic botany, was also apparently a significant influence in Middle East campaigns during World War I.

6158.   Oradilla, A.: Linares, F.; & Manor, G. Analytical studies of a wild, high-yielding yucca (Jatropha manioth). Paper presented at Third International Congress of food Science and Technology. 9 August to 14 August, 1970. Washington, D.C.

Protein content of native Colombian yucca.

6159.   Orbe, G. Rubio. 1956. Punyaro. Estudio de antropologia social y cultural de una comunidad indigena y mestiza. [Punyaro, Socio-anthropological and cultural study of a native and mestizo community.] Quito: Casa de la Cultura Ecuatoriana.

Includes mention of foods produced and consumed in the community. Punyaro is located in the Valle de Otavalo (approximatley 0.13 N., 78.25 W.) in the Province of Imbabura, Ecuador.

6160.   Orenstein, A.J. & Hoernle, A.W. 1938. The diets of natives employed on the Witwatersrand gold mines. Africa 9: 218-226.

6161.   Organ, John. 1960. Rare vegetables for garden and table. London: Faber & Faber.

6162.   Organ, John. 1963. Gourds: decorative and edible, for garden, craftwork and table. Newton Centre, Massachusetts: C.T. Bradford.

6163.   Orlove, Benjamin. A mixed agricultural transhumance economy and techniques of mico-environmental variation in the Andes. Paper presented at 72nd Annual Meeting of the American Anthropological Association. 29 November, 1973. New Orleans, Louisiana.

6164.   O'Rourke, D.E.; Quin, J.G.; Nicholson, J.O.; & Gibson, H.H. 1967. Geophagia during pregnancy. OG 29: 581-584.

Incidence of geophagia was found to be fifty-five percent among a random sample of two hundred women living within a one-hundred mile radius of Atlanta, Georgia. Substances ingested included clay and corn starch.

6165.   Orr, John Boyd. 1936. Food, health and income. London: Macmillan.

6166.   Orr, John Boyd. 1936. Problems of African native diet. Foreward. Africa 9: 145-146.

6167.   Orr, John Boyd. 1937. Food, health and income; report on a survey of adequacy of diet in relation to income. 2nd edition. London: Macmillan.

6168.   Orr, John Boyd & Gilks, J.L. 1931. Studies on nutrition, the physique and health of two African tribes. GB-PC-MRC-SRS No. 155.

Extensive metabolic studies of the vegetarian Akikuyu, and the carnivorous Masai. Points up the relationship between nutritional status and diet as well as the importance of anthropological factors influencing food intake.

6169.   Orr, Kathryn. 1967. About Hawaiian foods and ancient food customs. U HI-CES-HEC No. 343.

6170.   Orraca-Tetteh, R. Protein rich foods in Ghana. Paper presented at the 3rd International Congress of Food Science and Technology. 9 August to 14 August, 1970. Washington, D.C.

6171.   Ortega, J.J. Consumer attitudes towards wine. Master's thesis. Oenology. University of California at Davis. 1972.

6172.   Ortleib, Heinz-Dietrich. Eingeborenernahrung und ernahrungs-politik im tropischen Afrika. [Primitive diet and the politics of food in tropical Africa.] Dissertation. Universitat Hamburg. 1940.

6173.   Osborn, Alan J. Prehistoric utilization of marine resources in coastal Peru: how much do we understand? Paper presented at 76th Annual Meeting of the American Anthropological Association. 29 November to 3 December, 1977. Houston, Texas.

Intensive exploitation of marine foods such as shellfish, fish, birds, and sea mammals first appears in the archaeological record in Peru during the late preceramic periods (Preceramic V and VI), along the northcentral coast. The archaeological literature concerning marine resource exploitation in coastal Peru contains a number of basic assumptions regarding the character of marine productivity; the nutritional value of aquatic foods; and low costs of procurement; which have remained unchallenged. The purpose of this paper is to examine these assumptions and to assess our understanding of past coastal adaptations.

6174.   Osborn, Chase Salmon 1924. Madagascar. Land of the man-eating tree. New York: Republic Publishing co.

Malagasy diet: pp. 245-246; New Year's foods: pp. 260-263; harvest festival foods: p. 280. Chapter Thirty. Embryos, silkworms, and locusts as food.

6175.   Osborn, Clare Winston. A nutrition course for the Fourth Grade. Master's thesis. State University of Iowa. 1945.

6176.   Osborn, Rosalie. 1963. Observations on the behavior of the mountain gorilla. In The primates. The proceedings of the symposium held on 12th - 14th April, 1962. pp. 29-37. Symposia of the Zoological Society of London. No. 10. London: published by the Society.

Food: p. 32.

6177.   Osborn, T.W.B. & Noriskin, J.N. 1937. Data regarding native diets in southern Africa. SAJS 33: 605-610.

6178.   Osborne, W.H.   1953.   Northwest Indian berry rights. NM 46: 482-484.

6179.   Ortiz, Fernando. 1966. La cocina afro-cubana. [Afro-cuban cuisine.] Cas Am 6: 63-69.

6180.   O Se, Michael. 1948. Old Irish cheeses and other milk products CHAS-J 53: 82-87.

6181.   Osgood, Cornelius. 1951. The Koreans and their culture. New York: The Ronald Press.

Contains extensive data on food preparation.

6182.   Osgood, Cornelius.   1963.   Chapter Ten. Production and enjoyment of food. In Village life in old China. A community study of Kao Yao, Yunan. New York: The Ronald Press.

6183.   Osgood, Cornelius. 1971. The Han Indians. A compilation of ethnographic and historical data on the Alaska-Yukon boundary area. YUPA No. 74.

Food: pp. 98-116. Supported by excerpts from the ethnographic, historical and biological literatures.

6184.   Oshima, Harry. T. 1967. Food consumption, nutrition and economic development in Asian countries. EDCC 15: 397.

6185.   Oshima, Kintaro. 1905. A digest of Japanese investigations on the nutrition of man. USDA-OES-B No. 159.

Preparation and uses of Japanese foods: pp. 18-47.

6186.   Osio, T. 1976. History of food and diet in Japan. FNS 2: 35-48.

6187.   Ostoya, Paul. 1964. La prehistorie revele l'origine du mais. [Prehistory reveals the origin of maize.] SProg 3353: 329-335.

6188.   Ostrander, C.R.   1958.   Acculturation in the diet of indigenous American Samoans. SD-AS-P 37: 102-106.

6189.   Ostrowski, Z. Le probleme de sous-alimentation en Afrique et la maladie kwashiorkor. [The problem of malnutrition in Africa and kwashiorkor.] Unviersity of Warsaw. 1965.

6190.   Oswalt, Wendel H. 1957. A western Eskimo ethnobotany. UAlas-AP 6: 16-36.

6191.   Oswalt, Wendell H.; with Mann, Gloria; & Satterthwait, Leonn.   1976.   An anthropological analysis of food-getting technology. New York, London, Sydney, Toronto: John Wiley & Sons.

This study is unique in the literature, consisting of the detailed examination of eleven hundred and seventy-five elements used to obtain food, in thirty-six societies. The purpose of this presentation is to identify structural styles of forms in terms of their number of parts, on the basis of a classification according to the most important way in which it was utilized to obtain food. The forms are also evaluated and compared, and ranked in terms of their overall complexity. The cultural sample is represented by four subsistence categories (foragers, farmers, root-crop farmers, cereal-crop farmers) chosen from five ecological-geographical area-types: desert, tropics, temperate, subarctic and arctic.

6192.   Otele, A. 1959. Les boissons fermentees de l'Oubangui-Chari. [Fermented drinks of Ubangi-Shari.] Liasons 67: 34-42.

Native beers and wines: lakpoto: maize beer; bilbili: millet beer; samba ti fondo: banana beer: peke: bamboo wine: gbongo (kangoya): palm wine.

6193.   Othick J. The cocoa and chocolate industry in the nineteenth century. In The making of the modern British diet. Edited by Derek J. Oddy & D.S. Miller. 1976. London: Croom Helm.

6194.   Ottawa, Canada. Department of Indian Affairs. Office of Medical Service. Foodways of the Fort Nelson Indians [by John Joseph Honigmann]. 1943.

This manuscript is listed in National Research Council (1945); and in Gottlieb & Rossi (1961). In personal correspondence with the author (ca. 1969), it was indicated that this manuscript had been lost; however, the data are incorporated into Honigmann (1946).

6195. Otten, Charlotte M. 1967. On pestilence, diet, natural selection, and the distribution of microbial and human blood group antigens and antibodies. CAnth 8: 209-226.

6196. Ottino, Paul. 1963. Les economies paysannes malgaches du Bas Mangoky. [Malagasy peasant economies of Lower Mangoky.] Paris: Editions Levrault.

6197. Oudschans-Dentz, Fred. 1942. Bannanen en 'bacoven'. [Bananas and bake ovens.] WIG 24: 246-250.

Musa paradisiaca, and Musa sapientum.

6198. Outlaw, Eunice Bryan. A study to determine the effect of a nutrition program on the eating habits of a group of First Grade children. Master's thesis. Greensboro: Woman's College of the University of North Carolina. 1943.

6199. Outram, A.A. 1967. Mice as food. YN 9: 3.

6200. Ouzounellis, Theodore. 1970. Some notes on quail poisoning. JAMA 211: 1186-1187.

Suggests that Biblical quail poisoning incident (Old Testament: Exodus 16; Numbers 11:33) may have been the result of acute myoglobinuria (aggravated by fatigue) in individuals with an enzyme abnormality of the red corpuscles. A modern case of quail poisoning on the Greek Island of Lesbos is described.

6201. Overholser, Winfred & Havsgaard, Arleen G. 1957. Special problems of food and cooking today: psychiatry IRMGPC 170: 351-356.

Outline of one dietitian's view of the role of food service in psychiatric facilities.

6202. Ovington, J.D., ed. 1963. The better use of the world's fauna for food. Symposia of the Institute of Biology. No. 11. London: The Institute of Biology.

6203. Owen, George M.; Nelsen, Carl E.; Kram, Kathryn M.; & Garry, Philip J. Nutrition survey of White Mountain Apache preschool children. In Nutrition growth, and development of North American Indian children. Based on a conference co-sponsored by the National Institute of Child Health and Human Development, Indian Health Service, American Academy of Pediatrics Committee on Indian Health. Edited by William M. Moore; Marjorie M. Silveberg; & Merrill S. Read. 1972. pp. 91-112. Department of Health, Education, and Welfare. Publication No (NIH) 72-26. Washington, D.C.: Government Printing Office.

6204. Owen, Hera Ware. 1973. Bat soup and other recipes from the South seas. Seattle: Graphics Press.

Palau Islands. Song delineating uses of coconut: p. 12.

6205. Oxford, Arnold Whitaker. 1909. Notes from a collector's catalogue; with a bibliography of English cookery books. London: John and Edward Bumpus.

Bibliography section: pp. 39-109.

6206. Oyarzun, Aureliano. 1945. Antropofagia de los Fueginos. [Anthropophagy among the Fuegians.] MHN-R 1: 492-496.

6207. J.P. 1935. Le probleme alimentaire au Congo Belge. [The dietary problem in the Belgian Congo.] R Auc 10: 106-107.

6208. Packard, Jr., Alpheus Springer. 1877. Part Five. Edible Insects. In Half-hour recreations in natural history. Division first: half-hours with insects...Parts 1-8. (no more published). Boston: Estes & Lauriat.

Includes reference to food use of locusts by Arabs, and in Bushman groups.

6209. Packman, Ana Begue. 1938. Early California hospitality; the cookery customs of Spanish California, with authentic recipes and menus of the period. Glendale, California. Arthur H. Clark.

6210. Paddock William C. Cultural influence affecting a crop improvement program for an underdeveloped country. In 33 Congreso Internacional de Americanistas. 20 -27 Julio 1958. San Jose, Costa Ria. Actas. Vol. One. 1959. pp. 283-294. San Jose, Costa Rica: Lehmann.

Emphasizes the importance of recognizing indigenous practices and attitudes in applied agricultural projects. Uses as an example the improvement of maize quality in Guatemala.

6211. Page, Edward Beynon & Kingsford, P.W. 1971. The master chefs; a history of haute cuisine. London. Edward Arnold. New York: St. Martins (1972).

6212. Page, Louise, & Friend, Bertha. 1978. The changing United States diet. BioScience 28: 192-197.

Based on statistics gathered by the United States Department of Agriculture, this study covers changes in food consumption patterns, and nutrient levels for the years 1909-1913 to 1976. Specific attention is given to consumption of energy derived from various food groups. A closing section looks at future trends, and the variables which may influence these.

6213. Pages, R.P. 1928. La flore domestique du Ruanda. Les plantes alimentaires. [Domestic flora of Ruanda. Food plants.] BACB 19: 116-131.

Bananas; grains; sweet potatoes; pot herbs; Cucurbita sp.; root plants; mushrooms; fruits; spice and condiment plants; recently imported plants. Some foods of animal origin are mentioned. Vitamin resources in native diet are considered.

6214.   Pahlen, Alejo von der. 1977. Cubio (Solanum topiro, Humb. & Bonpl.), uma fruteira da Amazonia. [Cubio (Solanum topiro, Humb. & BOnpl.(, an Amazonian fruit.] AAM 7: 301-307.

Use as food: p. 301.

6215.   Pailleux, A. & Bois, Desire. 1899. Les potager d'un curieux histoire, culture et usages de 250 plantes comestibles; peu connues ou inconnues. [Vegetables with a strange history: cultivation and uses of 250 little-known or unknown edible plants.] 3rd edition. Paris: Librairie Agricole de la Maison Rustague.

6216.   Painter, Michael D. Alternatives to subsistence agriculture in two districts of Huancayo Province, Peru. Master's thesis. University of Florida. 1977.

6217.   Pak, Hwaja Suh. Departure from traditional food patterns among Korean-Americans. Master's thesis. De Kalb: Northern Illinois University. 1970.

6218.   Pal, R.K. 1939. A review of the literature on the nutritive value of pulses. IJAS 9: 133-144.

6219.   Palad, Jose Garcia; Abdon, Isabel, C.; Lontoc, Aurea V.; Dimaunahan, Leonardo B., Eusebio, Emerina C.; and Santiago, Natividad. 1964. Nutritive value of some foodstuffs processed in the Philippines. PJS 93: 355-373.

Description, and analysis (with methods of preparation) of two hundred and eighteen locally processed foods most of which are dessert or snack items, prepared from rice, maize, and cassava.

6220.   Palay, Simin. 1932. Autour de la table beanaise. [sic] Tradition, coutumes, terminologie, proverbs et dictons. [Around the Bearn table. Tradition, customs, terminology, proverbs and sayings.] Paris: H. Didier.

Bearn is the southwestern-most province of France.

6221.   Pales, Leon. 1946. Alimentation et nutrition. Rapport No. 2. Soudan occidental. [Diet and nutrition. Report No. 2. Western Soudan.] Organisation de Recherches pour l'Alimentation et la Nutrition Africaines. Dakar: Direction General de la Sante Publique.

6222.   Pales, Leon. 1946. Les etudes d'anthropologie, d'alimentation et de nutrition dans les populations de l'Afrique Occidentale Francaise. (Mission dirigee par le Medecin Lieutenant-Colonel Pales). [Anthropological, dietetic and nutrition studies among the populations of French West Africa. (Mission directed by Doctor Lieutenant-Colonel Pales). NA No. 30. pp. 23-24.

6223.   Pales, Leon. 1947. Note additionnelle sur les huiles de poisson. [Furthern note on fish oil.] ORANA-R No. 3. pp. 268-270.

6224.   Pales, Leon. 1950. Les sels alimentaires; sels mineraux, problemes des sels alimentaires en A.O.F. [Dietary salt, mineral salts; problems of alimentary salts in French West Africa.] Dakar: Direction Generale de la Sante Publique.

6225.   Pales, Leon. 1955. L'alimentation en AOF. Milieux et enquetes techniques, rations, avec le concours de Marie Tassin de Saint Fereuse. Preface d'Andre Mayer. [Diet in French West Africa. Social contexts and survey techniques, food allotments, with the cooperation of Marie Tassin de Saint Fereuse Preface Preface by Andre Mayer.] Dakar: Organisation de Recherches pour l'Alimentation et la Nutrition Africaines.

6226.   Pales, Leon. 1956. Les problemes alimentaires africains. [African dietary problems.] MTM 12: 3011-3015.

6227.   Palkovich, Ann M. Evaluating the nutritional status of a prehistoric population: skeletal biology and demography. Paper presented at 74th Annual Meeting of the American Anthropological Association. 2 to 6 December, 1975. San Francisco, California.

6228.   Palkovich, Ann M. A demographic approach to the modeling of disease processes in prehistoric populations. Paper presented at 75th Annual Meeting of the American Anthropological Association. 17 to 21 November, 1976. Washington, D.C.

A model recently developed for urban populations evaluated various causes of death in linear combinations, yielding specific, age-dependent profiles for each cause. This application of this cause-of-death or epidemiological model to archeological and ethnohistorical data, from the American Southwest, evidences marked nutrition-related morbidity and mortality in prehistoric and historic groups. This model appears to be an important analytic device for evaluating the nutritional status of, and disease patterns evident in, a population.

6229.   Palmer, Edward. 1871. Food products of the North American Indians. USDA-RC for the year 1870. pp. 404-428.

Sections: roots, and tubers; dried fruits and nuts; berries; fleshy fruits; seeds; miscellaneous cultivated fruits; animal food with vegetable substances. Reprinted in WA 10: 2-31 (1966).

6230.   Palmer, Edward. 1874. The berries of Rhamnus croceus as Indian food. AN 8: 247.

Use of R. croceus in pemmican.

6231.   Palmer, Edward. 1874. Die Vegetabilischen Nahrungsmittel der Indianer in Nordamerika. [The vegetable foods of North American Indians.] Translated by Ludwig Wittmack. VBGKPS-M 17: 22-28, 76-84, 133-136, 154-175, 236-240.

6232.   Palmer, Edward. 1878. Plants used by the Indians of the United States. AN 12: 593-606.

Covers fruits and nuts, seeds, pollen, leaves, stems and roots of sixty-eight plants, together with manner of preparation and use. Also in AJPharm 50: 539-548.

6233.   Palmer, Edward. 1883. On plants used by the natives of North Queensland. RSNSW-JP 17: 93-113.

6234.   Palmer, Edward. 1889. Opuntia fruit as an article of food. WASci 6: 67-69.

6235.   Palmer, Edward. 1890. Customs of the Coyotero Apaches. Zoe 1: 161-172.

Comments on eatings times; food sources; cooking techniques; and a fermented maize beverage: pp. 167-170.

6236.   Palmer, Edward. 1891. Chia. Zoe 2: 140-142.

Various food uses of Salvia sp. (Labiatae) in the southwestern United States, and in Mexico.

6237.   Palmer, Edward. 1891. The use of broken pottery among Indians. Zoe 2: 73, 74.

As food plates, food containers, eating utensils, and cooking-pot cover: p. 73.

6238.   Palmer, Eve & Pitman, Norah. 1972. Trees of Southern Africa covering all known indigenous species in the Republic of South Africa, Southwest Africa, Botswana, Lesotho, and Swaziland. 3 vols. Cape Town: A.A. Balkema.

Trees and food: Vol. 1. pp. 225-246.

6239.   Palmer, Jane Margaret. 1974. No fancy cuisine...its Cambodian. SS-BA 3 March. Section C. pp. 11-12.

Cambodian food habits with recipes.

6240.   Palmieri, Richard P. The yak in Tibet and adjoining areas. Its economic uses, social relationships, and religious functions. Master's thesis. Geography. University of Texas, Austin. 1970.

6241.   Palmieri, Richard P. Domestication and exploitation of livestock in the Nepal Himalaya and Tibet: an ecological, functional, and culture historical study of yak and yak hybrids in society, economy, and culture. Ph.D. dissertation. Geography. University of California, Davis. 1976.

6242.   Palmqvist, Lars. 1946-1947. Om matbredning och maltidsseder i Hammerdal. [Food preparation and table etiquette in Hammerdal.] Fornvardaren 9: 49-105.

Hammerdal is located in northcentral Sweden at 63.35 N, 15.20 E.

6243.   Pancho, J.V. 1961. Wild rice. AIL 23:4.

6244.   Pangborn, Rose Marie. Relationship of taste and other oral functions to food acceptability. Paper presented at Third International Congress of Food Science and Technology. 9 August to 14 August, 1970. Washington, D.C.

6245.   Pangborn, Rose Marie. 1975. Cross-cultural aspects of flavor preferences. FTech 29(6): 34, 36.

A brief review of the significance of tastes - singly, and in combination - in different cultural food traditions. "These preferences should receive serious attention", writes the author, "not only because of their economic importance but also because of their intrinsic value to the cultural identity of the individual and to the society in which he lives."

6246.   Pangborn, Rose Marie & Bruhn, Christine M. 1971. Concepts of food habits of 'other' ethnic groups. JNE 2: 106-110.

Results of investigation to determine knowledge of ethnic food habits among food service personnel; students; nutritionists; and migrant laborers, need to include training in ethnic food patterns in courses designed for professional foods and nutrition students.

6247.   Pangkatana, P. Traditional methods of food processing for infants in Papua-New Guinea. Research communication. In First Asian Congress on Nutrition. 22 January - 2 February 1971. Hyderabad. India. Proceedings. Edited by P.G. Tulpule & Kamala S. Jayo Rao. 1972. pp. 801, 802. Hyderabad: Nutrition Society of India.

Mentions breast-feeding; solid foods, and pre-mastication.

6248.   Panhuys, L.C. van. The trafe-superstition in Surinam. Twenty-first Congress of Americanists. August 12-16; 1924. The Hague. Proceedings. 1924. Part One. pp. 182-185. Leiden: E.J. Brill.

Reports a belief among Surinam Blacks holding that leprosy can be prevented by certain food avoidanes. Examines the occurrence of the belief in Surinam. French Sudan, and sub-Saharan Africa but does not mention foods.

6249.   Pankhurst, R. 1966. The great Ethiopian famine of 1888-1892: a new assessment. JHM 21: 95-124; 271-294.

6250.   Pankhurst, R. 1966. Some factors influencing the health of traditional Ethiopia. JES 4: 31-70.

Includes observations on the influence of diet on health.

6251.   Pan, Ku. 1950. Han shu. Food and money in ancient China. The earliest economic history of China A.D. 25. Han shu 24, with related tests. Han shu 91, and Shih-chi 129. Translated and annotated by Nancy Lee Swann. Princeton: Princeton University Press.

From Imperial Chinese court records 3rd Century B.C., to A.D. 25

6252.   Panoff, F. 1970. Food and feces: a Melanesian rite. Man 5: 237-252.

The Maenge of Jacquint Bay, east New Britain.

6253.   Paradise, Viola I. 1921. Sipping and sniffing. SMag 70: 577-583.

Tasting tea, and coffee.

6254.   Parahym, Orlando. 1940. O problema alimentar no sertao. [The problem of diet in the interior.] Recife: Imprensa Industrial.

6255.   Pardo A, Marta Eugenia. Patrones de alimentacion de la mujer embarazada en una comunidad de bajo nivel economico. [Dietary patterns of pregnant women in a low-income community.] Paper presented at 73rd Annual Meeting of the American Anthropological Association. 19 to 24 November, 1974. Mexico City.

Costa Rica.

6256.   Parham, B.E.V. 1940. Minor food plants of the Fijian and Indian. FSSI-TP pp. 12-18.

6257.   Parham, B.E.V. 1940-1941. Fijian ferns and fern alies. FSSI-TP pp. 19-25.

Food uses of ferns: p. 20.

6258.   Parham, B.E.V. 1942. Some useful plants of the Fiji Islands. Parts 1-2. F-DA-AJ 13: 39-47.

6259.   Parham, Richenda H.B. 1943. Fiji native plants with their medicinal and other uses. PS-M No. 16.

Includes annotation concerning food plants.

6260.   Paris. Museum National d'Histoire Naturelle. Laboratorie d'Ethnobotanique. Comite International pour l'Anthropologie de l'Alimentation et des Habitudes Alimentaires Centre de Documentation. Letter concerning the effects of Western influence upon Eskimo diet [by Frederick Machetanz.] 10 January 1947.

6261.   Paris, John. 1922. Chapter Eleven. A geisha dinner. In Kimono. New York: Boni & Liveright.

Japan.

6262.   Pariser, E.R., & Hammerle, O.A. 1966. Some cultural and economic limitations on the use of fish as food. F Tech 20(5): 61-64.

Notes that fish is an unexploited resource. Traces the history and symbolism of, and attitudes toward, fish: problems involved in preservation, storage and acceptance; and the role of food technology in overcoming prejudice toward fish.

6263.   Park, Martha. 1954. Teaching food preparation twenty-five years ago to Young Eskimo men. JADA 30: 785-786.

This description of a cross-cultural learning situation should be studied as an example of ethnocentrism in perception.

6264.   Parker, Arthur Caswell. 1910. Iroquois uses of maize and other plant foods. NYSM-B No.144. Reviewed by Frank Gouldsmith Speck in AA 13: 136. Reprinted in Parker on the Iroquois. Edited by William N. Fenton. 1968. Syracuse, New York: Syracuse University Press.

6265.   Parker, E.H. 1897. Diet and medicine in China. Cornhill 75: 175-183.

6266.   Parker, George F. 1940. Iowa pioneer foundations. Iowa City: State Historical Society of Iowa.

Choice and preparation of food: pp. 66-76; cookery: pp. 76-79.

6267.   Parker, J.R. 1954. Grasshoppers. A new look at an ancient enemy. USDA-FB No. 2064.

Used as food: p. 8.

6268.   Parker, Luther. 1929. Daughters of Sinukuan: how the water vine came to be. Phil Mag 26: 88.

Philippines.

6269.   Parker, Robert William. 1884. Food and rickets. BMJ 1:808-809.

Implicated artificial feeding; poor maternal health; lack of breast feeding; heredity; and poor hygiene.

6270.   Parker, S.L. Folic acid content of diets in Puerto Rican and Black women living in the New York City. Master's thesis. Nutritional Sciences. Ithaca, New York: Cornell University. 1974.

6271.   Parkinson, R.W. 1955-1957. Food problems of the Gilbertese. FS-TP 6: 61-73.

6272.   Parkinson, Sydney. 1773. Journal of a voyage to the South Seas, in His Majesty's Ship, the Endeavor, etc. London: Stanfield Parkinson.

Includes mention of plants used for food: pp. 37-50.

6273.   Parrow, E. 1905. Chuno, a frozen potato produce from Bolivia. [In German.] ZSpir 28: 405. Abstracted in ZUNG 12: 672 (1906).

6274. Parrish, John B. 1971. Implications of changing food habits for nutrition educators. JNE 3: 140-146.

6275. Parry, John W. 1945. The spice handbok. New York: Chemical Publishing Co.

Spices; aromatic seeds; herbs.

6276. Parry, John W. 1954. Spices through the ages. New York: Chemical Publishing Co. Reviewed in FMan 29(11):438 (1954).

6277. Parsley, Rosa Frances. A study of the expenditure for food of some urban Latin American families on work relief in Austin Texas. Master's thesis. Austin: University of Texas. 1935.

Studies expenditures for food in relation to fulfillment of dietary requirements.

6278. Parsons, James J. 1962. The green turtle and man. Gianesville: University of Florida Press.

Cultural attitudes towards turtle meat and eggs: pp. 6-15; the epicures and the turtle trade: pp. 15-22.

6279. Parsons, Jeffrey R. & Psuty Norbert P. 1975. Sunken fields and prehispanic subsistence on the Peruvian coast. Am An 40: 259-282.

Data presented suggest a relatively minor field system, developed late in the prehispanic sequence in natural topographic lows.

6280. Partride, Michael. 1974. Farm tools through the ages. Boston: New York Graphic Society.

6281. Pascual, Conrado R. Social and cultural factors in malnutrition. In First Asian Congress of Nutrition. 22 January - 2 February 1971. Hyderabad, India. Proceedings. Edited by P.G. Tuluple & Kamala S. Jaya Rao. 1972. pp. 560-570. Hyderabad: Nutrition Society of India.

In this paper, the author provides illustrations from Asian life which indicate the complexities which may be encountered when nutrition intervention programs are brought to target populations. The strength of social organization, community structure, the influence of elders, demands of away-from-home labor, the impact of urbanization and industrialization–all together affect nutritional status. The need for collaboration between nutritional science and social scientists is emphasized.

6282. Passalacqua, M. 1862. Recherches sur les plantes trouvees dans les tombeaux egyptiens. [Researches on the plants found in the Egyptian tombs.] ASN 8: 418-423.

6283. Passin, Herbert & Bennett, John W. Social processes and dietary change. In The problem of changing food habits. 1941-1943. 1943. pp. 113-123. NRC-B No. 108.

A summary of procedural-methodological considerations, with descriptive data relating to the study of the food habits among established and immigrant groups in a southern Illinois community. The authors provide historical background, before describing current dietaries, both of which are analyzed in terms of the concepts of core, secondary, and peripheral food items.

6284. Paterson, A.R. 1940. Nutrition and agriculture. EAMJ 17: 51-59.

6285. Pathansali, D. & Soon, Min Kong. 1960. Some aspects of cockle (Anadora granosa) culture in Malaysia. Indo-Pacific Fisheries Council. Eighth Session. Section 2. pp. 26-31. Bangkok: Food and Agricultural Organization of the United Nations. Regional Office for Asia and the Far East.

6286. Patino, Victor Manuel. 1950. Noticia sobre el Borojo, una neuva especie frutal de la cost Colombiana del Pacifica. [Note on the Borojo, a new species of fruit from the Colombian Pacific Coast.] ACCEFN-R 7: 478-481.

As food: p. 481.

6287. Patino, Victor Manuel. 1958. Platanos y bananos en America equinoccial. [Plantains and bananas in equinoxial America.] RCAnt 8: 295-337.

6288. Patino, Victor Manuel. 1961. El maiz matambre de la planicie de Popayan. [Nourishing maize of the Popayan plain.] RCAnt 10: 121-148.

Popayan is located in southeastern Colombia, at 2.27 N., 76.32 W.

6289. Patino, Victor Manuel. 1962. Edible fruits of Solanum in South American historic and geographic references. HU-BML 19: 215-286.

6290. Patino, Victor Manuel. Importancia de los frutales en las alimentacion y en la vida y costumbres de los pueblos Americanosa de la parte equinoccial. [The importance of fruit in the diet, life and customs of tropical American peoples.] In 35 Congreso Internacional de Americanistas. 1962. Mexico. Actas y Memorias; Vol. Three. 1964. pp. 169-175. Mexico: Editorial Libros de Mexico.

Notes that fruit has been overloooked by previous writers who have developed classification categories of ethnic groups based on staple food type. A list of cultivated fruit plants is given, according systematic botanical nomenclature, followed by a discussion of the ecological causes of fruit abundance; times of harvest; harvest celebrations; and fruit in myth.

6291. Patino, Victor Manuel. 1964. Plantas cultivadas y animales domesticos en America Equinoccial. Tomo 2. Plantas alimenticias. [Cultivated plants and domesticated animals in equinoctial America. Book 2. Food plants.] Cali, Colombia: Imprenta Departmental.

6292.   Patnaik, M. 1934. Iodine content of Indian foodstuffs. IJMR 22: 249-262.

6293.   Paton, Diarmid Noel, & Findlay, Leonard. 1926. Poverty, nutrition and growth: Studies of child life in cities and rural districts of Scotland. GB-PC-MRC-SRS No. 101.

Part Five is a detailed record of the dietary component of the study. A comparison of breast versus artificial feeding is included.

6294.   Patrick, Ralph. 1968. Social and nutritional determinants of food habits. In Nutrition education conference. Proceedings. 20 February to 22 February, 1967. Washington, D.C. USDA-MP 1075. P. 15.

Outline of text only. Text indicated as not available.

6296.   Patwardhan, Vinayak Narayan. 1962. Pulses and beans in human nutrition. AJCN 11: 12-30.
Methods of consumption of legumes in India: pp. 15-17.

6297.   Patwardhan, Vinayak Narayan & Darby, William J. 1972. The state of nutrition in the Arab Middle East. Nashville, Tennessee: Vanderbilt University Press.

After a general review of the geographical and sociological characteristics of the culture area, food habits, consumption and production are studied. Individual nutrient deficiency diseases are then considered followed by a description of infant feeding practices, child growth and development. An extensive section (Chapter Twelve) is devoted to diets and dietary habits. Review of nutritional status of various Middle Eastern populations rounds out the volume.

6298.   Patwardhan, Vinayak Narayan & Jagannathan, S.N. 1962. A review of nutrition studies in India (1951-1956). ICMR-SRS No. 37.

6299.   Paul, Charlie. 1902. American and other iced drinks. Recipes. London: McCorquodale.

6300.   Paul, Gemini. 1958. Sherdukpens. 2. Habitat, migrations and tribal drink. 4. Village council, land taxes, and food. Vanyajati 6: 61-69; 153-156.

6301.   Paul, John Robert. 1973. Soft drink bottling, a history with special reference to Illinois. Springfield: Illinois State Museum Society.

6302.   Pauwels, Marcel. 1948. Au Ruanda: quand et comment mangent-ils? [When and how do they eat in Ruanda?] Grands lacs 64: 51-54.

East Africa.

6303.   Pavlov, J.P. 1902. The work of the digestive glands. London: Charles Griffin & Co.

The classic study of behavior modification through conditioning. Focus is on hunger and appetite response, using the dog as experimental subject.

6304.   Pavy, Frederick William. 1874. A treatise on food and dietetics physiologically and therapeutically considered. London: J. & A. Churchill.

Includes a list of dietaries of principal British hospitals.

6305.   Paz, Octavio. 1972. Eroticism and gastrosophy. Daedalus 101: 67-85.

6306.   Peak, H. 1857. Case of cachexia africana. NOMSJ 13: 299-300.

Geophagy.

6307.   Pearl, Raymond. 1920. The nation's food. A statistical study of a physiological and social problem. Philadelphia: W.B. Sannders.

6308.   Pearl, Raymond & Matchett, Esther Pearl. 1918. Reference handbook of food statistics in relation to the war. United States Food Administration. Statistical Division. Washington, D.C.: Government Printing Office.

World War I.

6309.   Pearlman, Steven R. Factors in the transition to agriculture. Paper presented at 75th Annual Meeting of the American Anthropological Association. 17 to 21 November, 1976. Washington, D.C.

Despite the general assumption that, if given the opportunity, hunters-gatherers will become producers, it would appear that many factors are operating to inhibit that transition. Examination of ethnographic and archeological data shows that mechnaisms for minimizing stress and conflict in hunters-gatherers are sacrificed in the transition to agriculture, and compounded by further limitations on behavior. Two models are presented to explain the development and spread of agriculture. The first is Boserup's population growth model, modified to accommodate data concerning controls of reproductive rate in hunters-gatherers. The second is an ecological competition model.

6310.   Pearson, J.M. Interrelationship of home environment and industrial employment, including methodological study of family food practices. Ph.D. dissertation. Iowa State University. 1974.

6311.   Pease, H.D. 1932. The oyster--modern science comes to the support of an ancient food. JCED 9: 1675-1712.

Introduction contains brief historical data.

6312.   Peccano, Alessandro. 1627. Del Bever Freddo libro uno, con problemi intorno alla stessa materia. [A book about cold beverages, with problems bearing upon said subject.] Verona: A. Tamo.

6313.   Pechnik, Emilia. 1956. Complementacao de alimentos. [Complementarity of foods.] ABN 12: 9-17.

6314.   Pechnik, Emilia & Rebeiro, G.L.   1959. Contribuicao ao estudos dos alimentos da regiao amazonica. [Contribution to the study of foods of the Amazon region.] ABN 15: 15-24.

6315.   Peckolt, Theodore. 1871-1884. Historia das plantas alimentares do Brasil. [History of Brazilian food plants.] Rio de Janeiro: N. & H. Laemmert.

6316.   Peckolt, Theodor.   1886.   Die cultivirten Mandiokpflanzen Braziliens.   [The cultivatated manioc plants of Brazil.] PRund 4 (April -August): 57-59; 129-134; 147-149; 201-205; 227-229.

Notes food uses, includes chemical analyses.

6317.   Pederson, P.O.   1939.   Ernahrung und Zahncaries primitiver und urbanisierter Gronlander. [Diet and dental caries in non-urban and urbanized Greenlanders.] DGIM-V 51: 661-668.

6318.   Peery, Wilson Kimsey. 1949. And there was salmon. Portland, Oregon: Binfords and Mort.

6319.   Peet, Stephen D. 1885. Ancient agricultual works in America. AAnt 7: 13-38.

6320.   Pegge, Samuel, ed.   1780. The forme of cury, a roll of ancient English cookery, compiled about A.D.   1390, by the master-cooks of King Richard II.   Presented afterwards to Queen Elizabeth, by Edward, Lord Stafford, and now in the possession of Gustavus Brander, Esq.   Illustrated with notes, and a copious index or glossary. A manuscript of the editor, of the same age and subject, with other congruous matters are subjoined... London: J. Nichols.

6321.   Pekkarinen, Maija.   1970. Methodology in the collection of food consumption data. WRND 12: 145-171.

Compares the relative merits of the basic methods: weighing; food accounts; and interview (dietary recal). A valuable introduction for the social scientist.

6322.   Pelc, L. & Podzimkova-Rieglova, M.   1934. Nutrition of a Slovak agricultural family according to records of its food consumption during one year. [In French.] IHPET-T 5: 129-162.

6323.   Peller, Lili e. 1943. Eating in groups in war time. MHyg 27: 188-197.

Group feeding of children and its effects upon their emotional development.

6324.   Pellet, Peter L. 1976. Nutritional problems of the Arab world. EFN 5: 205-215.

Overview of regional diet: pp. 207-209.

6325.   Pellet, Peter L. & Jamalian. Observations on the protein-calorie value of Middle Eastern foods and diets.   In Man, food and agriculture in the Middle East. Edited by Fuad Sarruf. 1969. pp. 621-648. Beirut: The American University of Beirut.

Overview of Middle Eastern diets: pp. 621-622; mountain-village diets of children: pp. 638, 642.

6326.   Pellet, Peter L. & Shahdiervan, S. 1970. Food consumption tables for use in the Middle East. Beirut: American University.

6327.   Pellow, Deborah. 1978. Women in Accra. Options for autonomy. Algonac, Michigan: Reference Publications.

Food: pp. 98-99, 141-142, 144.

6328.   Pelras, Christian. 1974. "Herb divine": le riz chez les Bugis (Indonesie) "[Divine plant": rice among the Bugi (Indonesia).] E Rur Nos. 53-54-55-56. pp. 357-374.

6329.   Pelshenke, Paul. 1936. Geback aus deutschen Gauen. Eine Leistungsschau des Backerhandwerks. [Baking from German districts. A review of baking handicrafts.] Berlin: Reichsinnungsverband des Backhandwerks.

6330.   Pelshenke, Paul. 1941. Die Backhilfs-mittle. Herstellung, Wirkungen, Zusammen-setzung und Anwend... [Baking technology. Production, results, assembly, and utilization....] Berlin: Parey.

6331.   Pelshenke, Paul 1949. Geback aus Deutschen Landen. Seine Herstellung, Geschichte und Verbreitung. [Baking in German-speaking lands. Its production, history and distribution.] Alfeld: Gilderverlag.

6332.   Pelter, Karl J. 1947. Economic plants of Truk. For Ag 11: 74.

Native uses of breadfruit (Artocarpus communis)   as food.   Also in EB 2: 219-221 (1948).

6333.   Peltier, Maurice A.G. Considerations sur l'amplitude varietal de voandzu (Voandzeia subterranea, Thou.) a Madagascar en fonction de l'origine de l'espece. [Considerations on the wide variety of Voandzu (Voandzeia subteranea, Thou.) in Madagascar, in terms of the species origin.]   In Huitieme Congres International de Botanique. 1954. Paris. Rapports et Communications.   Parvenus avant le Congres aux Sections 14, 15, & 16. 1954. pp. 50-51.

Food value: p. 51.

6334.   Pelto, Gretel H. Patterns of food use in New England households. Paper presented at 76th Annual Meeting of the American Anthropological Association. 29 November to 3 December, 1977. Houston, Texas.

Food use patterns were explored intensively in a sample of households in a New England rural area. Data were collected on sociocultural variables, as well as diet behavior, using a twenty-four hour diet check list and a one-week food serving estimate. Information on food preferences, nutrition knowledge, shoppping and eating schedules and reported health status were also gathered. Special diets (e.g. low sodium; low fat) were also noted. Patterns of intracultural diversity in dietary behavior are explored in relation to socioeconomic status, education, health status and other variables.

6335. Pelto, Gretel H. Dietary modernization in west Finland. Paper presented at 77th Annual Meeting of the American Anthropological Association. 14 to 18 November, 1978. Los Angeles, California.

6336. Pelto, Gretel & Kandel, Randy. Vegetarianism and health food use among young adults in south New England. Paper presented at 72nd Annual Meeting of the American Anthropological Association. 1 December, 1973. New Orleans, Louisiana.

6337. Pelton, Robert w. 1974. Chapter Eighteen. Voodoo omens about eating. Chapter Twenty-five. Voodoo omens about salt. Chapter Thirty. Voodoo omens about kitchens. In Voodoo sign and omens. South Brunswick, New Jersey & New York: A.S. Barnes & Co. London: Thomas Yoseloff Ltd.

6338. Pelzer, Louis. 1936. Pioneer stage-coach travel. MVHR 23: 3-26.

The word slumgullion in reference to typical food of adobe houses: p. 24.

6339. Pena, A.J. 1961. Earth as food. [In Portuguese.] GAA 6: 94.

6340. Pende, Nicola. 1935. Alimentation et biotype individuel. [Diet and individual biotype.] Nutriition (P) 5: 269-286.

Relationship between diet and endocrine system influence on personality.

6341. Pendleton, Charles. 1946. Illicit whiskey-making. TFS-B 12: 1-16.

Tennessee.

6342. Pendered, A. 1930. Kubika wawa. Beer making. Nada 9: 30.

Notes, with native texts, on the production of beer among the population of southern Rhodesia.

6343. Penhallow, David Pearce. 1882. Note on a few of the useful plants of northern Japan. AN 16: 119-121.

Food plants: Lilium bulbiferun; Lappa major, Gaert.; Pitasiles japonicus, Miq.; Trapa bispinosa, Roxb., var. incisa (an Ainu plant); Actinidia arguat; Arundinaria japonica.

6344. Penn, William. 1885. A further account of the Province of Pennsylvania and its improvements for the satisfaction of those that are adventurers, and inclined to be so. PMHB 9: 63-81.

Mentions introduction of malt into the Province for beer brewing.

6345. Penn, William. 1903. Recipe for dried apples, pears and plums. PMHB 27: 373.

6346. Pennell, Elizabeth Robbins. 1903. Flamboyant period in cookery. Cornhill 87: 493-505.

6347. Pennell, T.L. 1909. Among the wild tribes of the Afghan frontier. A record of sixteen years close intercourse with the natives of the Indian marches. Philadelphia: J.B. Lippincott; London: Seeley & Co.

Kitchens and food provided to Hindu religious mendicants; food offerings to animals: pp. 225-226.

6348. Penney, Annette C. Cooking with wine at the white House. In Jefferson and wine: the wine connoisseur and wine grower. Edited by R. de Treville Lawrence, Sr 1976. The Plains, Virginia: Vinifera Wine Growers Association.

6349. Pennington, Campbell, W. The material culture of the Tarahumara and their environment. Ph.d. dissertation. Geography. University of California, Berkeley. 1959.

6350. Pennington, Campbell W. 1977. The Tepehuan of Chihuahua. Their material culture. Salt Lake City: University of Utah Press:

Food: pp. 45, 90, 91, 104-105; 264-265; blood as foood: pp. 130, 156, 157, maize: pp. 48, 49, 50, 52, 89, 99-100; 101, 102, 103, 136, 143, 264; domestic animals: pp. 152, 155-157; 313-315; fish: pp. 133-135, 285; vegetables: pp. 90, 91, 93; insects, reptiles: pp. 142-143; 144, 309; wild animals: pp. 119, 123-128; 130, 285; birds: pp. 114-117; wild plants: pp. 54, 84, 135-142, 293-309.

6351. Penny, Newton Mack. Peanut marketing in Georgia. Ph.d. dissertation. Cornell University. 1951.

6352. Penso, G. 1950. I prodotti della pesca. [Fish products.] 2nd edition. Milano: Ulrico Hoepli.

6353. Penso, G. 1953. Les produits de la peche. [Fish products.] Translated by P. de Montera. Paris: Vigot Freres.

6354. Penton, Anne. 1973. Customs and cookery in the Perigord and Quercy. Newton Abbot: David & Charles.

Regions in Southcentral and west-central France.

6355. Pequignot, G. 1976. La consommation alimentaire des adultes en France. [Adult food intake in France.] ANA 30: 175-184.

6356. Percival, John. 1936. Cereals of ancient Egypt and Mesopotamia. Nature (L) 138:270-273.

6356.   Percival, Olive. 1904. About sake, and the pleasing art of sake-sets. Craftsman 6:150-153.

Japanese rice wine and its ceramic serving vessels.

6357.   Peregrino, Junior. 1951. Alimentacao e cultura. [Diet and culture.] Biblioteca Brasileira de Nutricao No. 2. Sao Paulo: Servicio de Alimentacao da Previdencia Social.

6358.   Pereira Junior, J.L. Algumas concieracoes sobre...o regimen das classes abastadas do Rio de Janeiro em seus alimentos e bebidas. [Some considerations on...the diet of the well-to-do classes of Rio de Janeiro: their foods and beverages.] Medical thesis. Faculty of Medicine of Rio de Janeiro.

6359.   Pereira Salas, Eugenio. 1943. Apuntes para la historia de la cocina chilena. [Notes on the history of Chilean food.] Santiago de Chile: Imprenta Universitaria.

Traditional Chilean food and beverages; preparation; manner of serving, table utensils; dining customs; fusion of indigenous, Spanish and foreign traditions.

6360.   Peretti, G. 1957. Studi sulla nutrizione in Sardegna. Gli abitudini alimentari della popolazione rurale in Sardegna, in un paeso economicamenta depresso. [Studies on nutrition in Sardinia. Food habits of a Sardinian population in an ecomonically depressed area.] SItalBS-B 33:36-38.

6361.   Perez, M. Perez y. Contribucion al estudio de algunos de los alimentos Mexicanos. [Contribution to the study of some Mexican foods.] Thesis. Universidad Nacional de Mexico. 1943.

6362.   Perez, M.R. Gonzalez; Castell, M.E., & Espinosa, J. 1960. Estudios sobre la alimentacio espanola. Habitos alimenticios de la poblacion de Madrid. [Studies on diet in Spain. Food habits of the population of Madrid.] INIA-B 20: 185-212.

6363.   Perez, Vidal Jose. 1947. Conservas y dulces Canarias. [Preserves and sweets of the Canary Islands.] RF 3:236-255.

Pipotes, rapadura, alfajor, bienmesabe, hojulea, marquesote, sopa de miel, turrones, and others.

6364.   Perez-Llano, George Albert. 1944. Lichens, their biological and economic significance. BR 10: 1-65.

As food: pp.33-34. Also in HU-CLCBFH No. 215.

6365.   Perez-Llano, George Albert. 1948. Economic use of lichens. EB 2: 15-45.

Human food uses of lichens: pp. 23-25. Nutritional value of lichens: pp.25-26. Notes that the Biblical manna, of the Old Testament may have been Lecanora esculenta, Evers. Other uses, for Iceland, Japan,

Turkey and among Native Americans, are recorded, with data on preparation.

6366.   Perisse, Julien. 1958. Une enquete alimentaire sur les populations agricoles du Togo. A: Principes generaux et conduite de l'enquete. B: une enquete alimentaire sur la population Ouatachi du Sud-Togo. [Dietary survey of the agricultural populations of Togo. A: general principals and conduct of the survey. B: a dietary survey of the south Togo population of Ouatachi.] P-INH-B 13: 945-1020.

Part B contains data of frequency of consumption of various foods; meal patterns; food hygiene and food taboos.

6367.   Perisse, Julien. 1958. La consommation des legumineuses au Togo. [Consumption of legumes in Togo.] Cote de Classement No. 4019. Paris: Office de la Recherche Scientifique et Technique d'Outre-Mer.

6368.   Perisse, Julien. 1958. Habitudes alimentaires (Togo). [Food habits (Togo).] P-INH-B 13: 984-990.

6369.   Perisse, Julien. L'alimentation en Afrique intertropicale: etude critique a partir des donnees des enquetes de consommation, 1950-1965. [Diet in intertropical Africa: critical study based on data from consumption surveys, 1950-1965.] Ph.D. Dissertation. Universite de Paris. 1966.

6370.   Perisse, Julien. 1972. Is Homo economicus returning to a "Stone Age" diet? NNLet 10(1):1-3.

Diversification of staple diets and staple foods in relation to the level of industrialization of a given nation.

6371.   Perisse, Julien; Adrian, J.; Rerat, A., & Le Berre, S. 1959. Bilan nutritif de la transformation du sorgho en biere. Preparation, composition, consommation d'ne biere au Togo. [Nutritional balance in the transformation of sorghum to beer. Preparation, and consumption of a native Togo beer.] ANA 13:1-15.

Ethnographic and nutritional study of a beer manufactured from Sorghum vulgare, among three groups in Togo (the Moba, and two groups of Cabrai). The beer was found nutritionally deficient, except in riboflavin and vitamin B12.

6372.   Pekins Hidalgo, Guillermo E. 1948. Comidas regionales de la Provincia de Corrientes. [Regional foods of Corrientes Province.] INT-R 1:118-121.

Northeastern Argentina.

6373.   Perkins Hidalgo, Guillermo E. 1961. La cocina tradicional de Corrientes. [Traditional cuisine of Corrientes.] INIF-C 2: 31-49.

Corrientes Province, northeastern Argentina.

6374.   Perlo, Victor. 1953. The Negro in southern agriculture. New York: International Publishers.

United States. Nutrition: pp.46-51.

6375.   Perigault, Jean. 1932. L enfer des noirs: cannibalisme et fetichisme dan la brousse. [The Black's hell: cannibalism and fetishism in the bush.] Paris: Nouvelle Librairie Francaise.

6376.   Perrot, Marguerite. 1961. Le mode de vie des familles bourgeoises, 1873-1953. [Middle class family life style, 1873-1953.] Paris: Colin.

France.

6377.   Perroud, A.P. 1930. Les Indiens du Perou: l'anthropophagie. [The Indians of Peru: anthropophagy.] SAP-BM 11:16-20.

6378.   Peru. Servicio Coopertivo Interamericano de Produccion de Alimentos. Direccion de Extension Agricola. 1953. Recetas a base de quinua. [Recipes based on quinua.] Lima: Servicio Cooperativo Interamericano de Produccion de Alimentos.

6379.   Perusini, Antonini Giuseppina. 1963. Mangiar friulana. [The cuisine of Friulia.] Venice: Neri Pozza.

Friulia is in northeastern Italy, near the Yugoslavian border, due west of Ljubljana.

6380.   Peryam, David R. 1960. Food attitudes in an unusual environment. Interim Report. United States Army. Quartermaster Food and Container Institute for the Armed Forces. Quartermaster Research and Engineering Command. Chicago: Quartermaster Food and Container Institute for the Armed Forces.

6381.   Peryam, David R. 1962. Food attitudes in an unusual environment. Report No. 2-62. United States Army. Quartermaster Food and Container Institute for the Armed Forces. Quartermaster Research and Engineering Command. Chicago: Quartermaster Food and Container Institute for the Armed Forces.

6382.   Peryam, David R. 1963. The acceptance of novel foods. FTech 17(6):33-39.

Reviews the background of food habits research, and the psychological significance of food patterns and preferences. Describes experiments with military personnel in which innovation of novel foods was undertaken, and evaluates the results of these experiments.

6383.   Peryam, David R.; Pilgrim, Francis J.; & Peterson, Martin S., eds. 1954. Food acceptance testing methodology. A symposium sponsored by the Quartermaster Food and Container Insitute for the Armed Forces. Quartermaster Research and Development Command. U.S. Army Quartermaster Corp. 8-9 October, 1953. Chicago, Illinois. National Research Council. Committee on Foods. Advisory Board on Quartermaster Research and Development. [Washington, D.C.]:

6384.   Peryam, David R.; Polemis, Bernice W.; Kamen, Joseph M.; Eindhoven, Jan; & Pilgrim, Francis J. 1960. Food preferences of men in the U.S. Armed Forces. Department of the Army. Quartermaster Research and Engineering Command. Chicago: Quartermaster Food and Container Institute for the Armed Forces.

Particularly relevant for the study of food habits are Chapters Seven, Eight, and Nine: characteristics of the respondents; classification of the foods; and preference in relation to food class.

6385.   Pesce, H. 1941. Geography of leprosy and geography of food in Peru. [In Spanish.] RMPeru 13:658-666.

6386.   Peske, G. Richard. Earthen ridge-furrow systems in the Upper Great Lakes. Paper presented at 67th Annual Meeting of the American Anthropological Association. 21 to 24 November, 1968. Seattle, Washington.

Presents evidence of pre-Columbian cultivated-field system, believed to have been "garden beds" constructed for maize agriculture. Area extent of the ridge-furrows indicates a semi-sedentary to sedentary village life.

6387.   Peslouan, O. Lucas de. 1976. Evolution des consommations de glucides et de saccharose dans la population francaise. [The evolution of carbohydrate consumption among the French.] ANA 30:129-140.

Examines the food use of dietary starches, and sugar. Includes statistics on sugar intake and comparisons with other industrialized nations.

6388.   Petard, Paul. 1956. Le cocotier et ses produits dans les iles francaises de l Oceanie. [The coconut palm and its products in the French Islands of Oceania.] Nature (P) No. 3260. pp. 494-498.

6389.   Petard, Paul. 1957. Le pandanus en Polynesie. [The pandanus in Polynesia.] Nature(P) No. 3264. pp. 150-153.

Includes reference to food use.

6390.   Petard, Paul. Quelques plantes utiles de la Polynesie francaise. Pteridophytes et monocotyledones. [Some useful plants of French Polynesia. Pteridophytes and monocotyledons.] Ph.D. dissertation. Pharmacy. Universite de Marseilles. 1960.

6391.   Peters, Frank E. 1952. The value of coconut as a human foodstuff. CCQ 3:201-205. Also in SPC-QB 2:29-33.

6392.   Peters, Frank E. 1954. Analysis of South Pacific Foods. SPC-QB 4: 6-7.

Describes technical facilities of the South Pacific Commission for analysis of nutritive values of Pacific Island foods.

6393.   Peters, Frank E. compilor. 1954. Bibliography of the nutritional aspects of the coconut. SPC-TP No. 58.

6394.   Peters, Frank E., compilor. 1956. Bibliography of the nutritional aspects of the coconut. Revised edition. SPC-TP No. 95.

6395.   Peters, Frank E. 1957. Chemical composition of South Pacific foods; an annotated bibliography. SPC-TP No. 100.

Included are compositional tables with nutrient analyses of common Oceanic foods.

6396.   Peters, Frank E. 1958. The chemical composition of South Pacific foods. SPC-TP No. 115.

6397.   Peters, Frank E. 1959. La composition chimique des aliments du Pacifique Sud. [Chemical composition of some South Pacific foods.] QPMV 5:313-343.

6398.   Peters, Frank E. & Wills, Pamela. 1956. Dried breadfruit. Nature(L) 178: 1252.

6399.   Peterson, William J. 1937. Steamboating on the Upper Mississippi. The water way to Iowa. Iowa City: The State Historical Society of Iowa.

Food on riverboats, during the mid-Nineteenth Century: pp. 358-361.

6400.   Peterson, Harold L. 1958. American knives, the first history and collector's guide. New York: Charles Scribner's Sons.

6401.   Peterson, Mary A. Indian and Alaska low-income groups. Infant and child feeding practices among low-income reservation and rural American Indian and Alaska Native families. In Practices of low-income families in feeding infants and small children, with particular attention to cultural subgroups. Edited by Samuel J. Fomon & T.A. Anderson. 1972. pp. 101-112. Washington, D.C.: U.S. Department of Health, Education, and Welfare.

Includes breast and formula feeding; solid foods. Alaska studies: seasonal factors; nutrient intakes; solid food supplements. Nutrition survey of White Mountain Apache preschool children: dairy foods; meat and poultry; legumes; grains; fruit; vegetables; fats and oils; sweets; beverages; and food availability.

6402.   Peterson, Nicolas. 1968. The pestle and mortar: an ethnographic analogy for archaeology in Arnhem Land. Mankind 6: 657-570.

6403.   Peterson, Susan B. Decisions in a market: a study of the Honolulu fish auction. Ph.d. dissertation. Anthropology. University of Hawaii. 1973.

6404.   Peterson, Susan B. Language of the Honolulu fish market. Paper presented at 72nd Annual Meeting of the American Anthropological Association. 1 December, 1973. New Orleans, Louisiana.

6405.   Peterson, W. 1964. Stonehenge on the desert. ADW 26 January. pp. 15-17.

Early kitchen utensils, in Arizona.

6406.   Petrakis, Nicholas L. & Wilson, Christine S. Breast cancer and diet: some crosscultural differentials. Paper presented at 75th Annual Meeting of the American Anthropological Association. 17 to 21 November, 976. Washington, D.C.

Diets of traditional groups differ from those of technologically advanced peoples in amounts of grains, pulses, and types of fats and vegetable products eaten. Incidence of breast and other forms of cancer parallels these differences, being lower in populations consuming greater quantities of cereals and other less processed foods. These facts fit a biochemical model that implicates low levels of two nutrients removed from grains in processing, plus increased amount of polyunsaturated fat in precancerous tissue damage. Acculturation to Western diets thus may present another hitherto unrecognized hazard to health.

6407.   Petrov, B.D. 1969. Ocherki istorii pitaniia v Rossii. Ocherk pervyi. [Historic essay on nutrition in Russia.] VP 28:81-85, 91-95.

6408.   Petrovic, A. 1939. Contributions to the study of the Serbian gypsies Part 2: the eating of carrion. GLS-J 18:24-34.

6409.   Pett, L.B. Nutrition survey methods as applied to Pacific Coast Canadian Indians. In Seventh Pacific Science Congress. 2 February to 4 March, 1949. Auckland and Christchurch, New Zealand. Proceedings. Vol. 7. (Anthropology, Public Health and Nutrition, and Social Sciences). 1953. pp. 149-151. Christchurch: Pegasus Press.

6410.   Pettit, Anna Stockton. Arachis hypogaea, L. Ph. D. dissertation. New York: Columbia University. 1895.

The peanut.

6411.   Pfanner, David Eugene. Rice and religion in a Burmese village. Ph.D. dissertation. Ithaca, New York: Cornell University. 1962.

This study is concerned with a description and analysis of the economy and religion of a Burman community in the Pegu District. The structure of village economy is based on production of rice and peanuts, for village consumption and sale. The relationship of religious roles and economic behavior is shown in the influence of the Buddist monk through the teaching and support of Buddhist values which have an effect on economic activities.

6412.   Pfizmaier, August. 1871. Alte Nachtrichten und Denkwurdigkeiten von einigen Lebensmitteln Chinas. [Old accounts and memoirs of foodstuffs in China.] KAWW-PHK-S 67: 413-466.

6413.   Pharaon, Hasan M.; Darby, William J.; Shammout, Hani A.; Bridgforth, Edwin B.; & Wilson, Christine S.   1965.   A year-long study of the nutriture of infants and pre-school children in Jordan. JTPECH-M No. 1.

Breast-feeding and weaning: pp. 20-21.

6414.   Phelps, David Sutton. 1964. A possible case of cannibalism in the Early Woodland period of eastern Georgia. Am An 30: 199-202.

6415.   Philby, Harold St. John B. 1933. The empty quarter, being a description of the Great South Desert of Araba known as Rub al Khali. New York: Henry Holt.

Food as a subject of conversation: p. 42; camel fetus as food: p. 283; raw meat eaten: p. 302; dates eaten with butter, or milk: p. 315.

6416.   Philby, Harold St. John B. 1952. Arabian highlands. Ithaca, New York: Cornell University Press.

Cost of staple foods at the oasis of Bisha (approximately 20.0 N., 42.0 E.) in the year 1932: p. 38; a camp banquet: p. 135; food prices in the market of Khamis Mushayt (18 .9 N., 42.45 E.): p. 137; wheat doughnut, mutton gravy, honey and clarified butter: p. 243; foods of Jewish community at Najran (17.31 N., 44 .19E.): pp. 278, 281; mutton: p. 305; wheat porridge: p. 329; pomegranate: p. 389; Daum-palm fruit: p. 441; diet of Raha Valley population: p. 445; raw maize: p. 618; coffee-husk beverage: p. 639.

6417.   Philhower, Charles A. 1940. Agriculture and the foods of the Indians of New Jersey. NJHS-P 58: 93-102; 192-202.

6418.   Philip, C. 1960. Will fried bees replace your sirloin steak? ABJ 100: 444.

6419.   Philips, Velma & Howell, E. Laura. 1920. Racial and other differences in dietary customs. JHE 41: 396-411.

Expenditures for foods, and caloric intake in 105 low-income families of Italian, Black, and Eastern European Jewish origin, in New York City. Includes typical menus, and some data on food costs.

6420.   Philips, Will. Food sources in China, Manchuria and Mongolia during prehistoric times. Master's thesis. Geography. University of California, Berkeley, 1965.

6421.   Phillips, Doris E. & Bass, Mary A. 1976. Food preservation practices of selected homemakers in east Tennessee. EFN 5: 29-35.

Reviews commonly used techniques, and attitudes towards food preservation among fifty homemakers.

6422.   Phillips, Ediwn Percy. 1917. A contribution to the flora of the Leribe Plateau and environs; with a discussion on the relationships of the floras of Basutoland, the Kalahari, and the southeastern regions. SAM-A 16: 1-379.

Basutoland.   Included annotated list of plants giving native names and uses. The Leribe Plateau is currently within the boundaries of northeastern Lesotho.

6423.   Phillips, Henry. 1822. History of cultivated vegetables; comprising their botanical, medicinal, edible, and chemical qualities; natural history; and relation to art, science, and commerce. 2 vols. London: Henry Colburn & Co.

Includes a wide range of food and condiment plants, with documented and undocumented references to history, etymology, origin and use.

6424.   Phillips, Margaret G. & Dunn, Mildred M. 1961. Toward better understanding of other people: their folkways and foods. NO 9: 498-499.

Description of an 'International Festival' planned and presented by first year students at Massachusetts Memorial Hospital, Boston, Massachusetts.

6425.   Phillips, Ulrich B. 1914. A Jamaica slave plantation. A HRev 14: 543-558.

Geophagy: p. 546.

6426.   Phillips, William John. 1940. The fishes of New Zealand. Vol. 1. New Plymouth, New Zealand: Thomas Avery & Sons.

Contains references to fish used by the Maori.

6427.   Phillips, William John. 1954. Maori drinking cup as used in Otago. JPS 63: 167-169.

6428.   Phillips, William John. 1956. Making fire and cooking food. TAH 4: 24-25.

Maori.

6429.   Phillips, William John. 1956. Mutton birding at Bay of Islands. JPS 65: 363.

The decline in food use of the grey-faced petrel (Pterodroma macroptera. Gouldi).

6430.   Phipps, Frances. 1972. Colonial kitchens and their gardens. New York: Hawthorn Books.

6431.   Piazza, Walter F. A mandioca e sua farinha; aspectos culturais na ilha de Santa Catarina. [Manioc and manioc flour; cultural aspects on the Island of Santa Catarina.] Mimeographed. Faculdade Catarinense de Filosofia. Curso de Geografia e Historia. Cadeira de Antropologia Cultural. Florianopolis: Universidade Catarinense 1956.

Origin, dispersal, legends, cultivation, food use. Santa Catarina is located on the coast of Brazil, at Florianopolis, at approximately 27.35 S. 48.31 W.

6432. Pichot, Paul Alimentation du paysan sous l'ancien regime. [Peasant diet under the old regime.] Medical thesis. No. 136. Universite de Paris. 1908.

Prior to 1791.

6433. Pick, Jr., H.L. Research on taste in the Soviet Union. In M.R. Kare and B.P. Halpern, eds. 1961. The physiological and behavioral aspects of taste. pp. 117-126. Chicago: University of Chicago Press.

6434. Pickering, Charles. 1879. Chronological history of plants: man's record of his own existence, illustrated through their names, uses, and companionship. With a preface by SSP. and short biographical notices of the author. Boston: Little, Brown & Co.

Divided into nine sections: (1) the colonization of Egypt [4000 B.C. - 3469 B.C.]; (2) early kings of Egypt [3769 B.C. -1873 B.C.]; (3) the Shepherd kings [1873 B.C. - 1614 B.C.]; (4) the Pharaohs [1614 B.C. - 664 B.C.]; (5) Greek ascendancy [664 B.C. - 200 B.C.]; (6) Roman dominion [200 B.C. - A.D. 79]; (7) early Christian period [A.D. 79 - A.D. 640]; (8) early Moselm period; (9) reign of commerce. This encyclopedic work is arranged, as its title indicates, chronologically, with each binomial botanical entry complemented by historical, etymological, and geographical data, together with mention of the plant's use as food where relevant.

6435. Pickersgill, Barbara. 1969. The archaeological record of chili peppers (Capsicum sp.) and the sequence of plant domestication in Peru. Am An 34: 54-61.

6436. Picon-Reategui, E. 1968. Food requirements of high altitude Peruvian natives. Penn SUDA-OPA No. 1. pp. 538-554.

6437. Picon-Reategui, E. Food and nutrition of high altitude populations. In The biology of high altitude peoples. Edited by Paul T. Baker. 1977. pp. 219-249. Cambridge: Cambridge University Press.

6438. Pidlaoan, F.O. Santos & Pidlaoan, Nazario. 1931. The nutritive value of balut. 1. Studies of calcium. 19: 659-664.

Balut is a duck or other poultry egg with a partially-developed embryo, eaten in the Philippines.

6439. Piedallu, Andre. 1916. Legumes sauvages. [Wild vegetables.] Brochures Larousse A-15. Paris: Larousse.

6440. Piedallu, Andre. 1923. Le sorgho, son histoire, ses applications. [Sorghum, its history and uses.] Paris: Challamel.

6441. Pierson, Donald. 1951. Cruz da Almas, a Brazilian village. SI-ISA-P No. 12.

Wild fruit: p. 34; ica (female sauva ant) eaten when carrying her eggs: pp. 34-35.

6442. Piette, E. 1896. Les plantes culivees de la periode de transition au Mas-d'Azil. [Cultivated plants at the transition period at Mas-d'Azil.] Anthropologie 7: 1-17.

Quercus sp.; Crataegus oxyacantha; Prunus spinosa; Corylus avellana; Castanea vesca; Triticum vulgare; Prunus avium; Juglans regia.

6433. Piette, Leontine. Speise und Trank der Eingeborenen im tropischen Afrika. [Food and drink of the aborigines of tropical Africa.] Ph.D. dissertation. Universitat Koln. 1925.

6444. Pignede, Bernard. 1966. Les Gurungs, une population himalyenne du Nepal. [The Gurung, a Himalayan group of Nepal.] Le Monde d'Outre-Mer. Passe et Present. Premiere Serie 21. The Hague; Paris: Mouton & Co.

Food habits: pp. 88-94.

6445. Pijoan, Michel. 1942. Cyanide poisoning from choke-cherry seeds. AJMS 204: 550-553.

In attempt to increase vitamin C intake among the Shoshone, the medical nutritionist encouraged increased consumption of the choke cherry (Prunus melanocarpa), a popular traditional dietary item. Ten days later, a fourteen year old woman was brought to the area hospital in a coma. Laboratory tests were successful in revealing the nature of the illness. The patient passed away within twenty-four hours; however, autopsy revealed huge quantities of fresh choke cherry seeds in the gastrointestinal tract. The young woman had apparently spent several days in the mountains and, in her hunger, had chewed the fresh seeds together with the fruit. Laboratory analysis indicated a break-down of amygdalin in the seeds to cyanide. Four similar cases occurred, but were saved once the cause of illness was known. The author concludes "We were forced to advise the natives to beware of the seeds, little realizing that in doing so we were actually advising them not to touch the fruit as a whole. In tampering with their culture or advising them to do something which they did not understand, we had defeated our purpose and caused one death."

6446. Pijoan, Michel. 1942. Food availability and social function. NMQR 12: 418-423.

Reviews occurrences of malnutrition in several New Mexico communities. Emphasizes the importance of considering the preexisting ethnological background of a population in programs of nutritional intervention; and of informing the target group of the evolutionary processes in the culture which make changes necessary.

6447.   Pijoan, Michel. The importance of a cultural approach in ameliorating nutritional defects in the Southwest. In The application of anthropology to problems of nutrition and population. pp. 13-22. [Minutes of Liason Session.] Mimeographed. United States National Research Council. Committee on Food Habits. Washington, D.C.: National Academy of Sciences. 15 April, 1944.

6448.   [Pijoan, Michel.] (United States Navy Department. Office of the Chief of Naval Operations. Military Government Section. Central Division. Naval Medical Research Institute. Bureau of Medicine and Surgery. 15 August 1944. Civil Affairs guide. Far eastern nutritional relief (Japanese culture). OPNAV 13-18. Washington, D.C.: United States Navy Department.

This guide originally classified as a Restricted document, deals with anticipated emergency nutritional requirements during projected occupation of Japan, after the end of World War II. Requirements published were intended to cover a period of from two to three months. A proposed basic ration is give, with a provisional emergency nutritional plan. The second part of the guide describes Japanese food habits and dietary. Includes cautions against introducing certain Western foods in the occupied nation.

6449.   Pijoan, Michel. 1946. The health and customs of the Miskito Indians of northern Nicaragua: interrelationships in a medical program. Mexico City: Ediciones del Instituto Indigena Interamericano.

6450.   Pijoan, Michel. 1957. Estado Sanitario y costumbres de los indios mosquitos del norte de Nicaragua: como se relacionan esos dos dos aspectos en una progama medico. [State of health, and customs of the Miskito Indians of northern Nicargua: interrelationships in a medical program.] NI 2:61-77.

Includes description foods.

6451.   Pijoan, Michel & Elkin, C.A. 1944. Secondary anemia due to prolonged and exclusive milk feeding among Shoshone Indian infants. JN 27 67-75.

When missionaries criticized premastication of infant food as unhygienic the practice was abandoned among Native American groups. With its abandonment, however, a potentially important source of dietary iron - supplementary to breast milk - was also lost. In spite of risk of tuberculosis infection, a return of premastication was recommended. This paper describes how and why.

6452.   Pijoan, Michel; Elkin, C.A.; & Eslinger, C.O. 1943. Asorbic acid deficiency among Papago Indians. JN 25:491-496.

6453.   Pijoan, Michel & Carrera, Antonio Goubaud. no date. Observations on food patterns and body economy in Canon de Taos.

This study was made during the Southwest Project, conducted in Arizona, Colorado and New Mexico, during the early 1940's. The manuscript was submitted for publication to the University of New Mexico Press, but withdrawn before publication, by the senior author (Pijoan), due to disatisfaction with methodology involved in the biochemical evaluation. (Personal conversation with Pijoan, 1976).

6454.   Pijoan, Michel & Roskelly, R.W. 1943. Nutrition and certain related factors of Spanish - Americans in northern Colorado. Denver: Rocky Mountain Council on Inter-American affairs; Des Moines: Western Policy Committee.

Study of nutritional status of Spanish-speaking American migrant workers in the suburban Fort Collins and Fort Lupton areas. Specific consideration is given to socio-cultural and historical variables affecting food habits and attitudes toward health and nutrition. Concludes the presence of a vitaminoses and malnutrition among low-income migrants is related to cultural food patterns, but that acculturation toward a proper dietary is difficult. Recommends nutrition education through schools and local channels. Photocopy held by New Mexico State Library. (Vertical files). Santa Fe.

6455.   Pilgrim, Francis J. 1957. The components of food acceptance. Conference notes. Chicago: United States Army. Quartermaster Food and Container Institute.

6456.   Pilgrim, Francis J. 1957. The components of food acceptance and their measurement. AJCN 5:171-175.

6457.   Pilgrim, Francis J. 1961. What foods do people accept or reject? JADA 38:439-443.

6458.   Pilgrim, Francis J. & Kamen, Joseph M. 1959. Patterns of food preferences through factor analysis. JM 24: 68-71.

6459.   Pilgrim, Fraancis J. & Kamen, Joseph M. 1963. Predictors of human food consumption. Science 139: 501-502.

Suggests that three-fourths of the variation in percentage of enlisted military personnel, who take the foods at the serving table, is predictable from knowledge of food preferences, the subjective satiety or "fillingness" of the food, and the amount of two major nutrients -fat and protein - the food contains. Research was accomplished at Truax Air Force Base Wisconsin. Resondents were 400 airmen.

6460.   Pilgrim, K. 1962. Deutsche und russische Trinksitten und andere Merkwurdigkeiten des 17 -

Jahrhunderts aus der Moskowitischen und Persianischen Reisebeschreibung des Adam Olearius. [German and Russian drinking habits and other curious facts of the 17th Century drawn from Adam Olearius account of his travels to Moscow and Persia.] GGBB-J pp.9-31.

6461.   Pille, G. 1955. Essai d une politique alimentaire en Afrique noire (aspect biologique et scientifique). [Attempt at a food policy in Black Africa (biological and scientific aspects).] REMVPT 8:217-222.

6462.   Pillsbury, Richard. 1968. The production of sun-dried shrimp in Louisiana. J Geog 63:251-258.

6463.   Pimstone, S.M.; Wittmann, W.; Hansen, J.D.C.; & Murray, P. 1966. Growth hormone and kwashiorkor. Lancet 2:777.

6464.   Pina, Luis da. A fauna maritima e fluvial na alimentacao Portuguesa do seculo 18. [Sea and coastal fauna in 18th Century Portuguese diet.] In Congreso Internacional de Etnografia. Promovido pela Camara Municipal de Santo Tirso de 10 a 18 de Julho de 1963. Actas. Vol. Three. 1965. pp. 509-548. Porto: Imprenta Portuguesa.

    Includes historical data relating to fish as food, and a list of food fish, with nutritional values for several entries.

6465.   Pinchot, Gifford B. 1966. Whale culture - a prospect. PBM 10: 33-43.

6466.   Pinder, Davenia V. Food practices of fifty rural families in Chesterfied County, Virginia. Master's thesis. Virginia State College. 1946.

6467.   Pinho, Jose de. Sur des graines trouvees dans la station eneolithique de Pepim-Amarante. [On the grains discovered at the Neolithic site of Pepim-Amarante. In 15 Congres International d Anthropologie & d Archeologie Prehistorique. 21-30 Septembre 1930. Coimbre & Porto, Portugal. Actes du Congres. 1931. pp. 356-358. Paris: Librairie E. Nourry.

    Discovery of a species of fava in a megalithic zone which the author believes to be the place of origin of the type. The fava in question in unknown in modern time.

6468.   Pio, I orn. 1956. Mad pa Alstrup omkring 1900. [Provisionings in Alstrup, ca. 1900] Folkeminder 2:88-94.

    Denmark.

6469.   Pires, Joao Murca & Schultes, Richard Evans. 1950. The identity of ucqui. HU-BML 14:87-96.

    Edible fruit of the genus Pouteria (Sapotaceae), used by natives of the upper Rio Negro Basin of Brazil.

6470.   Pires de Lima, Fernando de Castro. 1959. A arte popular em Portugal. [Portuguese popular art.] Vol. One. Lisbon: Editorial Verbo.

Includes notes on Portuguese sweet pastries.

6471.   Pires de Lima, Fernando de Castro. 1964. O vinho verde na etnografia. [Green wine in ethnography.] RE 2:11-24.

6472.   Pirie, Norman W. 1962. Indigenous foods. ASci 18: 467-475.

6473.   Pirie, Norman. 1969. Food resources: conventional and novel. Harmondsworth; Baltimore: Penguin Books.

6474.   Pirkova - Jakobson, S. & Joffe, Natalie F. Some Central European food patterns and their relationship to wartime problems of food and nutrition. Czech and Slovak food patterns. Mimeographed. Committee on Food Habits. Washington, D.C.: National Research Council. February, 1943.

6475.   Pirtle, T.R. 1926. History of dairying. Chicago: Mojonnier Bros. Co.

    Cross-cultural study.   Reviewed in JDS 10:192 (1927).

6476.   Pisanelli, Baldassare. 1586. Trattato della Natura de Cibi, et del Bere. [Treatise on the nature of food and beverages.] Venice: G. Alberti.

6477.   Pisanelli, Baldassare. 1596. Traite de la nature des viandes et due boire, avec leurs vertus, vices, remedes et histories naturelles, utile et delectable a quiconque desire vivre en sante. [Treatise on the nature of foods and beverages, with their advantages, disadvantages, therapeutic values, and natural histories, useful and delightful for whoever wishes to live healthfully.] Arras: G. Bauduyn.

6478.   Pisani, S. 1954. La dieta nelle stazioni termal. [Diet in a thermal unit.] A Med Hyd 22:9-25.

6479.   Pittier, Henry Francois. 1908. Ensayo sobre las plantas usuales de Costa Rica. [Essay on the common plants of Costa Rica.] Washington, D.C.: H.L. & J.B. McQueen.

6480.   Pitzkhelauri, G.Z. 1969. L Kornaro i ego "traktat o trezvoi zhizni. [Luigi Cornaro and his "Treatise on the sober life."] VP 28:86-88. July-August.

6481.   Piuz, A.M. Alimentation populaire et sous-alimentation au 17 siecle, le cas de Geneve et de sa region. [Common diet and malnutrition in the 17th Century, the case of Geneva and its environs.] In Pour une histoire de l' alimentation. Edited by J.J. Hemardinquer. 1970. pp. 129-154. Paris: Colin.

6482.   Plaen, Guy de. 1969. Le role du vin de palme dans la vie sociale et religieuse. [The role of palm wine in the social and religious life.] Africa (T)15:81-86.

6483.   Plakut, Casimir. 1950. Backwoods Indians. IS 30:54-55.

Contains illustration of tapping for maple syrup.

6484. Planalp, Jack M. Religious life and values in a north Indian village. Ph.d. dissertation. Cornell University. 1956.

Ritual food pollution and purity: pp. 50-64.

6485. Plantz, D.V. 1966. Maricopa County food prices in historical perspective. ABB 13:3-9.

Arizona.

6486. Platt, Benjamin Stanley. 1936. Approach to infant feeding problems in China. CMJ 50:410-424.

6487. Platt, Benjamin Stanley. 1955. Some traditional alcoholic beverages and their importance in indigenous African communities. PNS 14:115-124.

6488. Platt, Benjamin Stanley. 1956. The soya bean in human nutrition. CI 18:843-847.

6489. Platt, Benjamin Stanley. 1962. Tables of representative values of foods commonly used in tropical countries. GB-PC-MRC-SRS No. 302.

6490. Platt, Benjamin Stanley & Gin, S.Y. 1938. Chinese methods of infant feeding and nursing. ADC 13:343-354.

6491. Platt, W. 1937. Some fundamental assumptions pertaining to the judgement of food flavors. FR 2:237-249.

6492. Plattner, Stuart. Do richer Indians eat better and grow taller? Paper presented at 72nd Annual Meeting of the American Anthropological Association. 1 December, 1973. New Orleans, Louisiana.

6493. Plenert, W. 1965. Sauermilchen in der Sauglingsernahrung. [Sour milks in infant nutrition.] Ernahr 10:605-610.

6494. Plummer, Orlay. Task and the oil palm nut. Paper presented at 76th Annual Meeting of the American Anthropological Association. 29 November to 3 December, 1977. Houston, Texas.

The implications of the notion of task in Brunswikian psychology, for the anthropological study of decision-making, are explored. The notion's distinctions between the requirements for the correct performance of a task, the patterns of the data, and the forces generating that pattern are applied in an economic analysis of the organization and decisions of wild oil palm harvesting, a major source of income for a certain Ghanaian village. A specific model of the phenomenon of the economic actor(s) is offered. The relation between this approach and the micro-economic and cognitive approaches is then discussed.

6495. Podolsky, Edward. 1927. Jewish contribution to the hygiene of the digestive tract. MJR 205:49-50.

Exegeses from Hebraic holy literature relating to food hygiene. Includes a list of allowed and forbidden foods according to the laws of Moses, arranged according to species.

6496. Poggi, P. 1966. Sull'indirizzo dietetico praticato al principio del 19 secolo presso l'Ospedale Civile di Piacenza. [On the course in dietetics practiced at the beginning of the 19th Century at the Civil Hospital in Piacenza.] PSMed 10:87-93.

Piacenza is in northcentral Italy, at 45. 03N., 9. 41E.).

6497. Poglayen-Neuwell, Stephen. 1920. Das Wunder der Brot - und Fischvermehrung in der altchristlichen Kunst unter besonderer berucksichtigung zweirer elfenbeinbehalter aus dem Museo-Civico zu Livorno und dem South Kensington Museum. [The miracle of the loaves and the fishes in early Christian art, with special reference to two ivory boxes from the Museo-Civico at Livorno and the South Kensington Museum. MKunst No. 2. pp.98-107.

6498. Pogolsky, A.L. 1909. The diet of the Russian peasantry. VM-HR 7:37.

6499. Pohath-Kehelpannala, T.B. 1907. Poison in food plants, especially cassava. Trop Ag 28:161-164.

Manihot utilissima. Use as food; poisonous characteristics; symptoms of poison; Sinhalese native remedies. Other poisonous food plants are listed.

6500. Pohl, Mary. The contribution of hunting to present-day village nutrition. Paper presented 73rd Annual Meeting of the American Anthropological Association. 19 to 24 November, 1974. Mexico City.

With reference to the Maya Lowlands.

6501. Pohren, D.F. 1972. Adventures in taste: the wines and folk foods of Spain. Moron de la Frontera (Sevilla): Society of Spanish Studies.

6502. Poleman, T.T. 1961. The food economics of urban middle Africa. The case of Ghana. SU-FRI-S 2:121-175.

6503. Poliakoff, J. 1954. La noix de coco. [The coconut.] Oleagineux 9:87-93.

Distribution; preparation and uses of coconut products.

6504. Pollard, Charles Louis. 1902. Plants used for Cuban confectionery. PWorld 5:131-132.

6505. Pollard, Samuel. 1921. In unknown China. Philadelphia: J.B. Lippincott.

Food habits of the Lolo of West China: pp. 108-110.

6506. Pollnac, Richard B. Psychocultural adaptation to alternative fishing types in southern New England. Paper presented at 77th Annual Meeting of the American Anthropological Association. 14 to 18 November, 1978. Los Angeles, California.

6507.   Pollock, Ivan Lester 1923. The food administration in Iowa. 2 vols. Iowa City: State Historical Society of Iowa.

World War I.

6508.   Pollock, Nancy J.   Breadfruit and bread-
winning on Namu Atoll, Marshall Islands.   Ph.d.
dissertation. Anthropology. University of Hawaii.
1970.

A study of the transition between traditional subsistence and cash economy in Micronesia.   Considers the influence of land
tenure and residence rules on accessibility
to crop items (breadfruit, pandanus, copra,
fish) the sale of which provides the cash
that permits the purchase of non-traditional
staples such as rice, flour, tea and sugar.
Observes the persistence of the traditional
ethic of food sharing and communal labor.
Concludes that multiple options (through
matrilineal, or other consanguineal inheritance, or through an affine) to land tenure
and land use - which in turn permit access
to cash crop resources, are the bases for a
transition between traditional and cash
economies without the traditional ethic or
social structure suffering damage.

6509.   Pollock, Nancy J. 1974. Breadfruit or rice.
Dietary choice on a Micronesian atoll. EFN 3:107-
115.

Studies the constraints operating to deter
mine food availability on Namu an atoll of
the Marshall Islands (located at 8.0' N., 168.
08 E.).   Availability of both local and purchased foods is shown to be dependent upon
the quantities of native-grown breadfruit
(Artocarus altilis), pandanus (Pandanus tect-
orius, Park), and coconuts, (Cocos nucifera
L.) which later are a cash crop, the sale of
which providing the income to buy imported
foods. Increasing population makes the pre-
carious dependence on limited food sources
a threat to nutritional status and survival.
Meals, eating patterns, food preparation,
infant and child feeding practices, snacking,
food preferences and seasonal variation are
described.

6510.   Pollock, Nancy J.   The risks of dietary
change: a Pacific atoll example. In Gastronomy.
The anthropology of food and food habits. Edited by
Margart Louise Arnott. 1975. pp. 121-130. Paris: the
Hague: Mouton Publishers. World Anthropology.

Namu Atoll, in the Marshall Islands group, is
dependent on both indigenous and imported
food resources, although minimal reliance is
placed on purchased foods, owing to irregu-
lar shipping and cargos.   The author
analyzes the problems of the atoll population in relation to potential for cash income,
the aforementioned food resources, and increasing population. New food adaptations,
(i.e. imported, purchased items) are added
to the native subsistence repertoire, rather

than substituted for them, which the author
perceives as a stratey to ward off an ever-
present fear of hunger.

6511.   Pomeroy, Ralph.   1975.   The ice cream
connection. All you'd love to know about ice cream.
New York, London: Padington Press, Ltd.

Ice cream in the United States and Europe.
A socio-historical study.

6512.   Pomiane, Edouard de. 1929. Cusine juive,
ghettos modernes. [Jewish cookery modern ghettos.] Paris: Albin Michel.

Recipes from Poland, France, and Algeria.

6513.   Poncet. 1937. Diet and social problems;
need for education about food. [In French.] RHMS
16:33-47.

6514.   Pond, J.A.   Foods and beverages.   Paper
read at the "Popular Lecture" of the Auckland
Institute.   12 September 1887.   Cited in NZI-TP
20:459.

6515.   Ponde, A. 1966. Los primeros tiempos en la
historia de la nutricion.   [Earliest period in the
history of nutrition.] PMArg 58:854-863.

6516.   Poole, Fitz John Porter.   The ethnosemantics of Yemen: food prohibitions, food transactions and taro as cultigen, food and symbol among
the Bimin-Kuskusmin. Paper presented at the 76th
Annual Meeting of the American Anthropological
Association.   29 November to 3 December, 1977.
Houston, Texas.

Taro taboos provide models for an elaborate
system of food prohibitions.   In focusing
upon prescribed permitted and proscribed
taro transactions in ritual contexts, the
ethnosemantics of taro as "plant" and "food"
are analyzed, compared and articulated with
the ethnosociology of social personae, who
transact in this "idiom", through an "etho-
genealogical" taxonomy of taro which, as in
the genealogical linkage of persons, is predi-
cated on a symobolic sharing of ancestral
substance.

6517.   Poole, Peter.   Wildlife cropping in East
Africa: present problems, and future prospects.
Master's thesis. Geography. New York: Columbia
University. 1968.

6518.   Popenoe, Paul B. 1914. Meat production in
the swamps. JHer 5:37-37.

Suggest the pygmy hippotamus (Hippotamus
amphibious) be bred in swamp areas of
southeastern United States. Notes the salted, cured flesh (zee koe speck) is prized by
South African Cape Colony population.

6519.   Popenoe, Paul B.   1914.   Origin of the
banana. JHer 5:273-280.

6520.   Popenoe, F. Wilson. 1912. The cherimoya in California. With notes on some other Anonaceous fruits. PCJEB 2:277-300.

6521.   Popenoe, F. Wilson. 1912. Feijoasellowiana; its history, culture and varieties. PCJEB 2:217-242.

      Native to Brazil, Argentina, Paraguay, Uruguay, known as 'guayabo' or 'guayabo del pais'.

6522.   Popenoe, F. Wilson. 1918. Avocados as food in Guatemala. JHer 9:99-107.

6523.   Popenoe, F. Wilson. 1919. Batido and other Guatemalan beverages prepared from cacao. AA 21:403-409.

6524.   Popenoe, F. Wilson. 1919. Useful plants of Copan. AA 21:125-138.

      Honduras. Includes cereals and vegetables; fruits, beverage plants; seasonings and flavorings.

6525.   Popenoe, F. Wilson. 1921. The native home of the cherimoya. JHer 12:331-336.

6526.   Popenoe, F. Wilson. 1921. The "Pejibaye", a fruit with high food value in Costa Rica. PAU-B 53:449-462.

      Fruit of the palm tree Guilielma utilis Oerst.

6527.   Popenoe, F. Wilson. 1924. Economic fruit-bearing plants of Ecuador. SI-USNH-C 24:101-134.

6529.   Popova, N.L. & Asherova, M.E. 1962. Vlian-iye nurusheniya ritma pitaniye na nekotoriye pokaz-atelii lipoidnogo obmyena. [Effects of disturbing the rhythm of eating, on some indices of lipid metabolism.] VP 21:20-25.

      Study of Tadzhik Muslims during Ramadan, when food may be eaten only after sunset.

6530.   Popovici, Zaharia & Angelescu, Victor. 1954. La economia del mar y sus relaciones con la alimentacion de la humanidad. [Ocean resources and their relation to human nutrition.] 2 vols. MACNBR-PECD No. 8.

6531.   Poppe, E. 1913. Notes on food and diet in Katanga. [In French.] SCB-B 27:33-36.

6532.   Poppe, Johann Heinrich. 1834. Die Bierbra-uerei auf der hochsten Stufe der jetzigen Vervollko-mnung. [Beer brewing at the highest level of its present perfection.] Tubingen:

6533.   Porcher, Francis Peyre. 1863. Resources of the Southern field and forests, medical, economical and agricultural. Being also a medical botany of the Confederate States; with practical information on the useful properties of the trees, plants, and shrubs. Prepared and published by the order of the Surgeon General, Richmond, Virginia. Charleston: Steam Power Press of Evans & Cogswell.

6534.   Poree-Maspero, Eveline. 1962. Chapter Two. Le riz et les saisons. [Rice and the seasons.] In Etude sur les rites agraires des Cambodgiens. Vol. One. Paris; The Hague: Mouton.

6535.   Porphyrius. 1965. Porphyry on abstinence from animal food. Translated by Thomas Taylor. Edited by Esme Wynne-Tyson. New York: Barnes & Noble.

6536.   Porsild, Alf Erling. 1953. Edible plants of the Arctic. Arctic 6:15-34.

      Vitamin values, preparation, use, and storage of forty plants used as food by Eskimo, Chukchi, and European populations.

6537.   Porter, C.E. 1914. Some edible fishes of Chile, with a description of the new species. SCA-A 77:185-210.

6538.   Porter, J.H. 1883. Cannibalism. ASW-T 2:119-120.

6539.   Porter, Kenneth W. 1965. Humor, blasphemy and criticism in the 'Grace' before meat. NYFLQ 21:3-18.

6540.   Porter, R. Howard. 1950. Mate. South American or Paraguay tea. EB 4:37-51.

      Methods of preparation: pp. 49-51.

6541.   Porteres, Roland. 1951. Note pour servir a une introdution a l'histoire de l'alimentation veg-etale dans les regions mantagneuses forestieres de l'Ouest - Africain (des Monts de Lima au massif des Dan.) [Introductory note to the history of vegetable diet in the forested mountain regions of West Africa (from the Lima hills to the Dan plateau). Premiere Congres International de l' Afrique Occidentale. Comptes-Rendus. pp. 71-80. Dakar: Institut Francais de l' Afrique Noire.

6542.   Porteres, Roland. 1955. L'introduction du mais en Afrique. [Introduction of maize to Africa.] JATBA 2:221-231.

6543.   Porteres, Roland. 1956. L'etat des recher-ches sur la nutrition et l'alimentation au Senegal. [The state of research on nutrition and diet in Senegal.] JATBA 3:769-778.

6544.   Porteres, Roland. Les appellations pour "manioc" dans l'Ouest africain. [West African names for manioc.] In 6 Congres International des Sciences Anthropologiques et Ethnologiques. 30 juillet - 6 aout 1960. Vol. 2. Ethonologie (Vol. 2) 1964. pp. 45-46. Paris: Musee de l'Homme.

6545.   Porteres, Roland. 1964. Le palmier Ronier (Borassus aethiopum, Mart) dans la province du Baoule (Cote d'Ivoire). [The Ronier palm (Borassus aethiopum, Mart.) in the Ivory Coast province of Baoule).] JATBA 11:499-514.

      Food uses include the fruit, and palm cabbage (terminal bud). An extensive description of palm wine production makes up the largest portion of this paper.

6546.   Porterfield, Jr., W.M. 1951. The principle Chinese vegetable foods and food plants of Chinatown. EB 5:3-37.

6547.   Portisch, Hugo. 1967. Red China today. Greenwich, Connecticut: Fawcett Crest Books.

Information on diet and digestion in a Peking 'palace of culture': p. 214; use of garlic as a theatre snack: p. 223; restaurant prices: p. 232; food markets: 317-319; food habits: pp. 319-321.

6548.   Pose, G. 1963. Nutrition and the endocrine system. 1. The influence of nutrition on the thyroid gland. [In German.] Ernahr 8:241-262.

6549.   Posner, Lewis L.B.; McCottry, Catherine M.; & Posner, A. Charles. 1957. Pregnancy craving and pica. OG 9:270-272.

Reviews occurrence of food craving among six hundred women in third trimester of pregnancy. A frequency order table is included. Corn starch was the most desired food.

6550.   Pospisil, Leonard. 1963. Kapauku Papuan economy YUPA. No. 67.

An exceedingly detailed monograph touching upon practically all major aspects of food production and consumption. Part Four covers agricultural practices, including plant cultivation; site selection; the nature of gardens; and shifting cultivation. Part Five describes animal husbandry, with focus on pigs and chickens. Part Six examines fishing, hunting, and gathering. Part Seven is concerned with distribution, and includes data on markets and trading. Part Nine is devoted to such topics as regulation and attitudes pertaining to eating; with descriptions of food preparation. A section 'Problem of nutrition in Botukebo' (pp. 373-379) includes results of two food intake surveys: one of sixty-three persons for one day, and one of twenty persons for six days. The village of Botukebu, in which the author resided for eighteen months, is located the Kamu Valley, Papua New Guinea.

6551.   Post, Lauren, C. 1933. The domestic animals and plants of French Louisiana as mentioned in the literature, with references to sources, varieties and uses. LHQ 16:554-586.

6552.   Postmus, S. 1956. Nutrition work in Burma. [In Dutch.] Voeding 17:403-415.

6553.   Postmus, S. 1956. Nutrition work in Burma, past and present. PNS 15:35-40.

6554.   Postmus, S. 1965. Mikkel Hindhede en de minimum eiwitbehoefte. [Michael Hindhede and the minimum protein requirement.] Voeding 26:129-137.

6555.   Postolka, August & Toscano, Anton. 1893. Die animalischen nahrungs - und Genusmittel des Menschens. [Human food of animal origin, together with stimulants.] Vienna: Moritz Perls.

6556.   Potgieter, Martha & Morse, Ellen. 1955. Food habits of children. JADA 31:794-796.

6557.   Potgieter, Martha & Nakatani, Kiyo. 1954. Diet and health in rural Hawaii. Hi-AES-TB No. 21.

6558.   Potter, Sulamith Heins. 1977. Family life in a northern Thai village. Study in the structural significance of women. Berkeley, Los Angeles, London: University of California Press.

Food habits, purchasing food, food preparation, meals: pp. 71-74; 78-81.

6558.   Potter, Thomas I. 1930. Some Trinidadian "honey plants". ASTT-P 30:173-183.

6560.   Pottier, R. 1956. Le probleme de l' alimentation des autochtones en Afrque Occidentale Francaise. [Nutrition problems among the natives of French West Africa.] EMO-M No. 66. pp. 66-71.

6561.   Pottsmith, Marie Holst. 1960. Pioneering years in Hamlet, Oregon: Finnish community. OHQ 61:5-45.

Includes reference to Finish food during the early 20th Century.

6562.   Pourchet, Maria Julia. Subnutricao da crianca indigena. [Malnutrition in native children.] Am Ind 20: 103-110.

Native Brazilian Kaingang, in Parana.

6563.   Powdermaker, Hortense. 1932. Feasts in New Ireland, the social function of eating. AA 34:236-247.

Covers social function of eating; social organization; frequency of feasts; preparations for a feast; description of a feast; trade after a feast; food exchange (reciprocity); women's speeches about their husbands as a successful or unsuccessful food providers; daily meals; non-feast related food behavior.

6564.   Powell, G.H. 1968. Cooking methods from the past. RNFS No. 11. pp. 16-19.

6565.   Powell, M.N. 1928. Diet of coolies in Changsha. CJP No. 1. pp. 129-133.

6566.   Powers, G.F. 1935. Infant feeding: historical and modern practice. JAMA 105:753.

6567.   Powers, Stephen 1877. Tribes of California. USDI-USGGSRMR-CNAE No 3.

Food (Yurok): fish; acorn gruel; algae: pp. 49, 50. (Kelta): soap root (Chlorogalum pomeridianum), and its detoxificaton; wild potato, berries, fish: pp. 92-92; (Wailakki): camas, wild potato: p. 115; (Yuki): earthworm soup: p. 130; (Pomo): plant and animal foods; sea food, kelp: pp. 150,151; &

Gualala): preparation of wild oats, acorns: pp. 187,188: (Patwin): Ranunculus californicus processed into flour, wild sun flower and grass seeds: p. 220; (Wintun) fish roe, manzanita berry beverage preparation; clover, inner bark of yellow pine: pp. 234, 235; (Modok): wokas and camas root: pp. 255, 256; (Achomawi) poor quality of Hot Springs' tribes diet: p. 269; (Nishinam): acorn mush as travel food: p. 322; (Miwok): comments on need to conserve food, made by the orator Old Sam: p. 353. (Yokuts): plant, insect, and animal food: pp. 378, 379. Chapter Thirty-eight: Aboriginal botany, includes a list of plant foods and uses. Some animal foods are also listed. Also in CAS-P 5:373-379 (1873-1875).

6568. Poyner, George V. & Andrews, Margaret S. 1976. Development of household food behavior models. Report prepared for the Agency for International Development under Contract No. AID/Ta-C-1318. Silver Spring, Maryland: Poyner International Inc.

Investigates and evaluates methods for analyzing economic factors which influence family food consumption. Linear programming models are used: one of urban household food consumption and another for rural households. Fieldwork done in Bolivia, Colombia, the Dominican Republic, and Guatemala. [After Foster. 1978. P. 48.]

6569. Prade, G. 1975. Situation actuelle de la cuisine francaise; les principaux noms qui se d'egagent ce domaine. [The current state of French cuisine; the most significant names to emerge from the field.] Historia No. 42. pp.114-122.

6570. Pradeau, Alberto Francisco. 1974. Pozole, atole, and tamales; corn and its uses in the Sonora - Arizona region. JAriz H 15:1-7.

6571. Prado, Estuardo. 1942. La dietetica del lactante en Quito. [Diet of nursing children in Quito.] Quito: Editorial Quito.

Sociological and medico-nutritional study of health status.

6572. Prain, D. 1898. The mustards cultivated in Bengal. AL No. 1. pp. 1-80.

6573. Prain, D. & Burkill, Isaac Henry. 1936. An account of the genus Dioscorea in the East. BGC-AR 14:193.

6574. Prakash, O.M. 1961. Food and drinks in ancient India. Delhi: Mushi Ram Manohar Lal Nai Sarak.

6575. Prasad, Rajendra. 1958. Vegetarianism in India. IAC 6:339-346.

6576. Prato, Katharina. 1904. Die suddeutsche Kuche. [South German cookery.] Revised by Viktorine Von Leitmaier. Gratz: Verlagsbuchhandlung "Styria".

6577. Prema, C.B. Report of a community nutrition project on the dietary and nutrient intake of nineteen selected families in the village of Veerapundipur. Master's thesis. University of Madras. 1967.

As a component of a nutrition education project a preliminary diet survey was made, which includes data on meal patterns; food taboos; beliefs related to food and cooking; foods consumed during illness; food storage; and preservation; food purchasing and cooking methods. The village studied is in the Coimbatore District of the south Indian State of Tamil Nadu.

6578. Prentice, Ezra Parmalee. 1939. Hunger and history the influence of hunger on human history. New York: Harper and Brothers.

6579. Prentiss, Sara W. & Jones, Mary Cover. 1930. The observation of food habits in young children. CEd 7:14-17.

6580. Prescott, Della R. 1922. A day in a colonial home. Edited by John Cotton Dan. Boston: Marshall Jones. United States.

Food, kitchen utensils: pp. 8-12, 27-29, 33, 54-55, 57, 58, 61, 63, 66, 69, 70.

6581. Prest, W.H. 1904-1905. Edible wild plants of Nova Scotia. NSIS-P 11: 387-416.

Popular description of plants which have little commercial value but which may be used for food in case of necessity.

6582. Preston, David A. 1963. Weavers and butchers: a note on the Otavalo Indians of Ecuador. Man 63:146-148.

Socio-economic status, and trade practices of butchers: p. 148.

6583. Pretty, G.L. 1965. Two stone pestles from western Papua and their relationship to prehistoric pestles and mortars from New Guinea. SAM-R 15:119-130.

6584. Prezzolini Giuseppi. 1955. Spaghetti dinner. A history of spaghetti eating and cooking. New York: Abelard Schuman.

6585. Price, L. 1917. Horse flesh as human food. AVMA-J 51:679-692.

6586. Price, Richard. 1966. Caribbean fishing and fisherman: a historical sketch. AA 68:1363-1383.

Discusses Island Carib fishing techniques, and the influence of European technology thereupon. The social position of the Black fishing slaves is considered in detail, with special attention to their elite status, and transition to freedom.

6587. Price, Richard. 1966. Fishing rites and recipes in a Martiniquan village. CStud 6:3-24.

6588.   Price, Weston Andrew. 1936. Field studies among some African tribes on the relation of their nutrition to the incidence of dental caries and dental arch deformities. JA Dent A 23:876-890.

6589.   Price, Weston Andrew. 1939. Light from primitive races on relation of nutrition to individual and national development. JA Dent A 26:938-948.

6590.   Price, Weston Andrew. 1939. Nutrition and physical degeneration. A comparison of primitive and modern diets and their effects. New York, London: P.B. Hoeber. Reprint. Santa Monica, California. Price - Pottenger Foundation. 1970.

6591.   Prichard, H. Hesketh. 1902. Through the heart of Patagonia. New York: D. Appleton & co.

   Food uses of guanaco, and ostrich blood: pp. 87, 100.

6592.   Priestland, Gerald. 1972. Frying tonight. The saga of fish and chips. London: Gentry Books.

6593.   Prithard, Jack Lee. Kwakiutl potlatching and Ponapean feasting: an examination of the potlatch and of potlatch parallels. Master's thesis. Ohio State University. 1972.

6594.   Proca, G. & Kirileau, G.T. 1938. Diet of rural population in Rumania. [In Rumania.] RSMed 27:607-623.

6595.   Procter, R.A.W. 1926. The Kikuyu market and Kikuyu diet. KMJ 3: 15-22.

6596.   Proctor, Richard Anthony. 1884. The universe of suns, and other scientific gleanings. London: Chatto & Windus.

   Contains a section on the infuence of food on civlization.

6597.   Prohaska, Janos. 1963. Abarle, aballe vagy abale. ["Boille, boyle or boil".] N Nyelv 87:578-598.

   Hungarian word for 'boil'.

6598.   Proudfit, Fairfax Throckmorton & Robinson, Corinne Hogden. Chapter Fourteen. Food patterns of various cultural groups. In Nutrition and diet therapy. Eleventh ed. New York: Macmillan.

   Groups included are Mexican, Chinese, Black American, Orthodox Jewish. Tables are given for Italian, and Near Eastern (Armenian, Syrian, Turkish, and Greek) food patterns.

6599.   Provancher, Leon. 1874. [Locusts.] NCan 6:270.

   Locusts as human food. References to use in Irag, and Syria.

6600.   Pruitt, Ida. 1945. A daughter of Han. The autobiography of a Chinese working woman. Palo Alto: Stanford University Press.

Food and cooking: pp. 8, 13, 56, 102, 167-168, 226, 238. New Year's food: pp. 12, 13, 80-81, 89-90, 238.

6601.   Publow, Charles A. 1910. Fancy cheese in America. From the milk of cows, sheep and goats. Chicago: American Sheep Breeder Co.

6602.   Pukui, Mary Kawena. Poi making. In Polynesian culture history: essays in honor of Kenneth P. Emory. Edited by Genevieve A. Highland, et. al. 1967. BPBM-SP No. 56.

6603.   Puleston, Dennis Edward. Brosimum alicastrum as a subsistence alternative for the Classic Maya of the central southern lowlands. Master's thesis. University of Pennsylvania. 1968.

6604.   Puleston, Dennis E. 1971. An experimental approach to the function of Classic Maya chultuns. Am An 36:322-334.

   Experimental techniques have provided a breakthrough for the functional analysis of Maya chultuns. While deep, cistern-like chultuns, common at certain sites in the northern lowlands, have been shown to be functional for water storage smaller, lateral-chambered chultuns, characteristic of certain parts of the southern lowlands, probably had a different function. Excavation and examination of the latter features, in light of a whole range of possibilities, suggest that they were constructed to be used for food storage. Experimental studies, however, reveal them to be unsuitable for the storage of most tradtional foods, including maize. At least one local food crop, the seed of the ramon (Brosimum alicastrum) appears to be ideally suited for long-term storage under these conditions. Chambers constructed beneath platforms in the northern lowlands may have been used for the storage of maize.

6605.   Puleston, Dennis E. Ancient Maya settlement patterns and environment at Tikal, Guatemala: implicatons for subsistence models. Ph.D. dissertation. Anthropology. University of Pennsylvania. 1973.

6606.   Puleston, Dennis E. Experimental agriculture as a method of testing models of ancient subsistence systems. Paper presented at 73rd Annual Meeting of the American Anthropological Association. 19 to 24 November, 1974. Mexico City.

   With reference to the Maya lowlands.

6607.   Puleston, Olga S. & Doyle Margaret. The use of model diets for the study of ancient Maya food patterns. Paper presented at 70th Annual Meeting of the American Anthropological Association. 19 November, 1971. New York City.

   Through use of modelling, the authors investigate the diet and nutrition of the lowland Maya. Using modern Maya diets as a starting point, model diets are calculated in terms of a variety of possible staples and combinations of foods known to have been available, based on archaeological and historical evidence. The lowland Maya diet is examined as a possible pressure contributing to the Late Classic Maya collapse.

6608.   Pulgar Vidal, Javier. 1954. Breves datos sobre la historia del curi. [Brief data on the history of the curi.] SGC-B 12:117-124.

Distribution of the Cavia cobaya, Schreb. in Columbia. Evidence of its early use as food by indigenous groups.

6609.   Pumpian - Mindlin, E. 1954. The meanings of food. JADA 30:576-580.

Covers cultural conditioning; experiences of infancy; symbolic meaning of food; food as reward; prestige value of food; meaning of food in adolescence; food during illness; and how the dietitian can respond to patients' individual psychological needs concerning food.

6610.   Purcell, F.M. 1939. Diet and ill-health in the forest country of the Gold Coast. London: H.K. Lewis.

West Africa.

6611.   Pyke, Magnus. 1952. Townman's food. London: Turnstile Press.

Written in lay persons' terms, this book provides an understandable, and easily-read description of the role of nutrition and industrial food technology in the production of breads, meat, fish, poultry, eggs, dairy products, sweeteners, vegetables, fruit and fruit preserves. Could serve as a useful resource in non-technical courses on food habits, with appropriate up-date.

6612.   Pyke, Magnus. 1961. The effects of industrialization, recent food legislation and advertising on food habits in Britain. PNS 20:46-51.

Concludes tht industrialization appears to be affecting British food habits by changing the social environment, and influencing the food industries, but believes that advertising and recent legislation have little permanent effect. Discusses the possible effects of women's employment in industry upon changes in food habits.

6613.   Pynaert, L. 1952. La patate douce, son origine et la facon de la conserve chez les primitifs. [The sweet potato, its origin and methods of its preservation among primitive peoples.] BACB No. 1. pp. 209-210.

6614.   Quackenbush, G.G. & Shaffer, J.D. 1960. Collecting food purchase data by consumer panel. Methodological report of the Michigan State University Consumer Panel, 1951-1958. Department of Agricultural Economics. Technical Bulletin No. 279. East Lansing: Michigan State University. Agricultural Experiment Station.

6615.   Quarterly Journal of Studies on Alcohol. 1942. Alcoholic beverages as a food and their relation to nutrition. QJSA-LS No. 8.

6616.   Queen, George So. 1957. Culture, economics, and food habits. JADA 33:1044.

An informal essay, by an historian, which seeks to resolve the question: does culture, or ecology determine food habits?

6617.   Quemener, E. Quelques considerations sur l'Inde Francais et l'alimentation des indigenes. [Some considerations on French India and the diet of its natives.] In L'alimentation indigene dans les colonies francaises. Protectorats et territories sous mandats. Edited by G. Hardy & C. Richet. 1933. pp. 291-305. Paris: Vigot Freres.

Karikal, Pondicherry, Yanaon, Chandernagor, and Mahe. Briefly reviews local agriculture, livestock raising, fishing, and food-related industry (sesame oil extraction, rice exporting). Notes variation in diet according to religion (Hindu, Islam). Preparation of rice; hours of mealtime; food in marriage ceremonies; and fasts are described.

6618.   Querault, A.M. & Biron, P. Rapport du gouvernement de la Republique Malgache concernant les problemes laitieres dans la Republique Malgache. Mimeographed. [Report of the government of the Malagasy Republic concerning milk problems in the Malagasy Republic.] Rome: Food and Agriculture Organization of the United Nations. 1961.

6619.   Querino, Manuel Raymundo. 1954. Arte culinaria na Bahia. [Culinary art of Bahia.] Seria miniatura. Vol. 1. Salvador: Livraria Progresso.

Bahia State is located in northeast central Brazil.

6620.   Quick, Horace F. Geographic dimensions of human ecology. In Dimensions of Nutrition. Proceedings of the Colorado Dietetic Association Conference. 1969. Fort Collins, Colorado. Edited by Jacqueline Dupont. 1970. pp. 133-152. Boulder: Colorado Associated University Press.

Infuence of environment on human food production, physiology, and nutrient requirements.

6621.   Quijada Jara, Sergio. 1955. Algunas comidas tipicas del valle del Mantaro. [Some typical foods of the Mantaro Valley.] APF 1:86-93.

Describes preparation of twelve traditional Peruvian foods.

6622.   Quilici, P.A. 1921. Les eaux d'alimentation de la ville de Bastia. [The nutritive waters of Bastia.] Montpellier: Imprimerie Firmin et Montane.

Corsica.

6623.   Quimby, George Irving. 1963. A maple sugar camps 200 years ago. CNHM-B 34(3):6-7.

6624. Quin, P.J. 1959. Foods and feeding habits of the Pedi with special reference to identification, classification, preparation and nutritive value of the respective foods. Johannesberg: Witwatersrand University Press.

The author's doctoral dissertation. The Pedi live in northern Transvaal, and are kin to the Tswana, and Sotho. This study covers Pedi agriculture and crop plants; edible wild foods (animal, plant, and insect); dietary, fire, and food classifications; modern tendencies in African dietary; and Pedi health. Reviewed in HPBCA 26:77-80 (1959); A Studies 19:102-103 (1960); Man February P. 30. (1960).

6625. Quin, P.J. 1964. Foods and feeding habits of the Pedi. SAMJ 38:961-971. Abstracted in NARev 30. Abstract No. 5161.

6626. Quinn, Vernon. 1943. Chapter Seven. Edible fruits and nuts. In Seeds, their place in life and legend. New York: Frederick A. Stokes.

6627. Quintana, Epaminondas. 1944. El ingente problema del maiz en su aspecto agrcola y nutitivo. [The enormous problem of maize: its nutritional and agricultural aspects.] Am Ind 4:129-132.

6628. Quiogue, Elena S. 1960. Dietary patterns and food habits. NN 13:19-27.

Philippines.

6629. Quiogue, Elena S. Review of food consumption surveys in India. In First Asian Congress of Nutrition. 22 January - 2 February 1971. Hyderabad, India. Proceedings. Edited by P.G. Tulupe & Kamala S. Jaya Rao. 1972. pp. 216-239. Hyderabad: Nutrition Society of India.

Focus is largely on the Philippines, with coverage for India, Iran, Korea, Japan, East and West Pakistan.

6630. Quisumbing, Eduardo. 1948. Aromatic plants in the Philippines used as ingredients or for flavoring. PPA-J 35:49-53.

6631. Quisumbing, Eduardo. 1956. Elmer Drew Merrill. PJS 85:181-188.

A biographical obituary. Dr. Merrill was an United States botanist who spent many years in the Philippines working in the field of economic botony. Much of his work dealt with identification, and description of tropical food plants, and phytogeography.

6632. Raab, Patricia Verdi. The nutrition of the Maidu and Maya Indians: a comparison. Master's thesis. University of Texas. 1959.

6633. Rabbitt, James A. 1940. Rice in the cultural life of the Japanese people. ASJ-T 19:187-258.

Sacredness of rice; rice in religion; socioeconomic role of rice; rice in the yearly cycle.

6634. Rabeyrin, C 1936. Comment ils mangent. [How they eat.] Grands Lac 52:321-327.

Food habits of the Warundi of Azire.

6635. Rabinowitch, Ralph D. & Fischhoff, Joseph. 1952. Feeding children to meet their emotional needs. A survey of the psychologic implications of eating. JADA 28:614-628.

6636. Rabot, C. 1890 De l'alimentation chez les Lapons. [Diet of the Lapps.] Anthropologie 1:187-200.

Food supply, food preparation, plants, fish, game.

6637. Rachilda. 1938. De gebruiken en de kleederdracht van de Bapedi. [Food uses and costume of the Bapedi.] DZA No. 51. pp. 143-144.

Contains notes on food preparation.

6638. Rachman, S. The modifications of attitudes and behavior. In Malnutrition is a problem of ecology. Edited by Paul Gyorgy and Otto L. Kline. 1970. pp. 132-141. Bibliotheca "Nutritio et Dieta" No. 14. Basle; New York: S. Karger.

The author provides an overview of theory and method in the field of behavior modification and attitude change. A fictitious example is given of introducing a new food into a village in a developing nation, with step-by-step elucidation of procedure. Examples of changes of food habits in Thailand and Haiti are included; and favorable comment is made regarding Kurt Lewin's (1943) group discussion method of food habits change.

6639. Ract, G. 1958. Enquete sur la consommation alimentaire dans la region de l'Est. [Survey of food consumption in the east of France.] P-INH-B 13:99-121.

6640. Radell, David Richard. 'Mom 'n pop' grocery stores in the Boyle Heights section of Los Angeles, California: a study of site and situation. Master's thesis. Geography. California State University, Los Angeles. 1961.

6641. Radin, Paul. 1914. Some aspects of puberty fasting among the Ojibwa. CGM-B 2:69-78.

6642. Radin, Paul. 1923. The Winnebago tribe. SI-BAE-AR for the year 1915-1916. pp. 35-550.

Berry-picking: p.116; wild rice gathering: p.116; preparation of food (meat; wild rice; maize; squash, fruit): pp. 116-118; preservation of food: p. 118; a Winnebago "menu": p. 118; utensils used for preparing and eating food: pp. 118, 119. clan feasts: pp. 318-328.

6643.   Radke, Marian & Klisurich, Dayna. 1947.
Experiments in changing food habits. JADA 23:403-
409.

> Following the work of Lewin (1943), this
> study reports on two experiments designed
> to effect changes in food habits. Experi-
> ment One involved feeding among new-born
> infants of low-income mothers in University
> Hospital, State University of Iowa. Experi-
> ment Two involved efforts to increase home
> milk consumption among low-income house-
> wives in Cedar Rapids, and Iowa City, Iowa.
> It was found that group decision methods
> were significantly more effective in leading
> mothers and housewives to change than
> were individual instruction or lectures.

6644.   Radley, Jack Augustus. 1968. Starch and its
derivatives. 4th edition. New York: Barnes &
Noble.

6645.   Radovic, Bosiljka. 1955. Pecon'e rakie u
nashem narodu. [Brandy-distilling in our country.]
MEB-B 18:69-112.

> Serbia.

6646.   Rael, Juan B. 1937. The theme of the theft
of food by playing godfather in New Mexican folklore. Hispania 20:231-234.

6647.   Raghaviah, V. 1968. Chapter Four. Food
gathering nomads. In Nomads. New Delhi: Adimjati Sevak Sang.

6648.   Raglan, Fitz Roy Richard Somerset. 1939.
Food classification in N.E. New Guinea. Man 39:36.

> Mountain Arapesh.

6649.   Ragonese, A.E. & Martinez Crovetto, R.
1947. Plantas indigenas de Argentia con frutos o
semillas comestibles. [Native plants of Argentina
with edible fruit or seeds.] Buenos Aires: Ministerio de Agricultura.

6650.   Raichelson, Richard M. Coumarin -contain-
ing plants used by Native Americans having albumin
polymorphisms. Paper presented at 76th Annual
Meeting of the American Anthropological Association. 29 November to 3 December, 1977. Houston,
Texas.

> Albumin Naskapi and Mexico are two poly-
> morphic variants of normal serum albumin
> A, found only in certain Native American
> populations. The polymorphisms differ from
> albumin A, and seemingly from each other,
> in their ability to bind the coumarin drug
> Warfarin. A catalogue of cumarin-contain-
> ing plants present in the environments of
> those Native American populations is being
> prepared. It includes the following informa-
> tion: scientific and common name; descrip-
> tion; habitat; the ways in which plants are
> used in the diet and medical system of the
> culture; relative abundance of the plants in
> the region; and the comparative use of these
> plants in scientific medicine.

6651.   Rainey, Froelich. 1941. Native economy and
survival in arctic Alaska. A Anth 1:9-14.

> Discusses the effects of decimation of cari-
> bou herds; introduction of reindeer, and the
> unlikelihood of reindeer becoming a basic
> food animal.

6652.   Raith, L.M. 1955. Hand-made Continental
chocolates and pralines. Translated by the British
Baker staff from the Swiss [sic] original. London:
MacLaren & Sons.

> Brief historical data; otherwise primarily
> devoted to recipes.

6653.   Rakocevic, M. 1952. Mljekarstvo na Sinja-
jevini i mjere za njegova unapredenje. [Dairy
economy of Sinjajevina and the regulations regarding its improvement.] Stocarstovo 6:120-129.

> Sinjajevina is a mountainous region in south-
> western Yugoslavia.

6654.   Rakshit, J.N. 1916. Rice, as prepared food
in Bengal. AJI 11:174-198.

6655.   Ramain, Paul. 1946-1947. Essai de mycog-
astronomie. [Essay on fungus-eating.] Rev Myc-S
11:97-101; 12:4-18; 29-38; 75-82.

6656.   Ramain, Paul. 1952. Rumino-mycophagie.
[Ruminant fungus-eating.] Rev Myc-S 17:106-107.

> Field mushrooms (Trichlomes), eaten by
> livestock, with a recipe for use in a seafood
> stew.

6657.   Ramanamurthy, P.S.V. 1969. Physiological
effects of "hot" and "cold" foods in human subjects.
IJND 6:187-191.

> Description of laboratory experiments de-
> signed to determine possible physiological
> bases underlying the "hot" - "cold" food
> classification system in India.

6658.   Ramirez, Miguel Justino. 1952. Pachuco.
Folklore(L) 3:776-779.

> Food and drink in Piura, a Department of
> northeastern Peru.

6659.   Rammstedt, O. 1913. The importance of
maize as human food. [In German.] ZOC 19:288-
294; 305-316; 327-334.

> Includes data on use of maize in various
> cultures.

6660.   Ramos Espinoza, Alfredo. 1937. Diet of a
Mexican child. [In Spanish.] Medicina 17:337-343.

6661.   Ramos Espinosa, Alfredo. 1940. Badly-fed
native child (Indian). [In Spanish] Medicina
20:223-229.

6662.   Ramos Espinosa, Alfredo. 1940. El frijol en
el alimentacion. [Beans in the diet.] OSP-B
19:989-992.

Urges the growing of beans in rural districts due to the legume's valuable nutrient contribution to largely vegetable-based diet in Mexico.

6663.   Ramos Espinoza, Alfredo. 1942. Folklore de alimentacion y turismo.   [Folklore of diet and tourism.]   OSP-B 21:239-241.

6664.   Ramos Espinosa, Alfredo. 1942. Folklore y alimentacion.   [Folklore and diet.]   Medicina 22:601-608.

6665.   Ramos Espinosa, Alfredo. 1943. El folklore y el alimentacion.   [Folklore and diet.]   SFM-A 2:195-205.

Nutritive value, and savor of Mexican folk foods.

6666.   Ramos Espinosa, Alfredo. 1944. La alimentacion en Mexico. [Diet in Mexico.]   PSeg 8:380-382.

6667.   Ramos Espinosa, Alfredo. 1944. Bases para un estudio geografico de la alimentacion en Mexico. [Bases for a geographical study of diet in Mexico.] Am Ind 4:65-72.

6668.   Ramos Espinosa, ALfredo. 1946. Las cosas de la alimentacion en la historia de Sahagun. [Diet in Sahagun's History.] SGHG-A 21:149-156.

Sahagun's acount is the earliest European history of pre-Hispanic Mexican civilization, with reference to the Aztec.

6669.   Ramos Espinosa, Alfredo. 1952. Un tema de sociologia. El drama nutriologico de nuesto pueblo. [A sociological theme.   The nutritional drama of our people.]   Nutriologia 1:107-109.

6670.   Ramos Espinosa, Alfredo. 1953. Alimentacion popular - ninos del campo.   [Common diet - peasant children.] Medicina 33:65-67.

6671.   Ramsbottom, J. 1953. Mushrooms and toadstools. PNS 12:39-44.

6672.   Randal, Judith. 1967. FPC. New hope for undernourished. Bio Science 17:257-258.

Fish protein concentrate; malnutrition and learning ability.

6673.   Randiga, Henry.   The banana regions of East Africa: the regional distribution and cultural significance of a traditional food crop.   Master's thesis.   Geography.   Bowling Green: Western Kentucky University. 1971.

6674.   Randoin, Lucie. 1937. La questionnaire des enquetes nationales sur l' alimentation.   [National dietary surveys' questionnaires.]   SSHAARH-B 25:245-260.

6675.   Randoin, Lucie. 1951. Les problemes souleves par l'alimentation des Nord-Africains travaillant dans la Metropole. [Nutrition problems arising among North Africans working in France. CNord Nos. 18-19.

6676.   Randoin, Lucie & Le Gallic, Pierre. 1938. Les besoins alimentaire varient - ils avec les races? [Do nutritional requirements vary with groups?] RAnth 63:5-17.

6677.   Randolph, L.F. 1952. New evidence on the origin of maize. An 86:193-202.

On the basis of archaelogical and botanical evidence, this article postulates a Mexican or southwestern United States origin for maize, at time between five to ten thousand years BP.   The progenitor of cultivated maize is suggested as having been intermediate between maize of the Bat Cave era and its closest relatives, Euchlaena and Tripsacum.

6678.   Randolph, L.F. History and origin of corn. 2.   Cytogenetic aspects of the origin and evolutionary history of corn. In Corn and its improvement. Edited by George F. Sprague. 1955. pp. 16-57. New York: Academic Press.

6679.   Range, P. 1942. Salz in Afrika. [Salt in Africa.] Tropenpflanzer 45:257-265.

6680.   Ranjan, M.P. 1944. Lathyrism. Antiseptic 41:652-653.

6681.   Rank, Gustav. 1953-1954. Var vardagsrot. [Our common-place roots.] Folk-liv 17-18:62-70.

Edible plant roots.

6682.   Rank, Gustav. 1956. Om aldre mjolkhushallning; Baltikum. [On early milk economy in the Baltic.] SEst 4:165-200.

6683.   Rank, Gustav. 1957-1958. Die gemeinschaftliche Kaserbereitung in Schweden. [Cooperative cheese-production in Sweden.] Folk-liv 21-22:115-133.

6684.   Rank, Gustav. 1961. Vilken roll har tatorten spelat i mjolkhushallningen? Folktro kontra vetande. [What role does butterwort play in milk economy? Popular belief versus scientific knowledge.] Folk-liv 24:65-75.

Pinguicula vulgaris. It has been used as substitute for rennet (Fernald, Kinsey, & Rollins. 1958:339.)

6685.   Rank, Gustav. 1963. Mjolets och mjolkens roll i de gamla varmlandska matvanorna, sarskilt hos finnarna. [The role of flour and milk in the old food habits of the Province of Varmland, especially among the Finns.] SB-L-VL 3:50-57.

6686.   Rank, Gustav. 1964. Om aldre ostkultur i ovre Sveriges fjalltrakter. [On former cheese culture in the mountainous country of north Sweden.] Norveg 11:35-44.

6687.   Rank, Gustav. 1964. Gammal ost. [Cheese in olden times.] GK 4:47-56.

6688.   Rank, Gustav. Verbreitungsverhaltnisse einiger Milchprodukte im eurasischen Raum. [Distribution relation of a milk product the Eurasian area.] Paper presented at the First International Symposium on Ethnological Food Research. 21 to 25 August, 1970. Lund: Folklivsarkivet. Lund University.

6689.   Ransom, Jay Ellis. 1946. Aleut natural-food economy. AA 48:606-623.

A review modern Aleut food getting. A list of animal (and a few plants foods) together with descriptions of fishing; sealing and whaling; butchering and disposition of game; seasonal migratory game; food avoidances; preparation of food; hunting ceremonies; and dietary changes due to acculturation.

6690.   Ranson, John E. 1923. The place of dietetics in a community health program. Diet Ad Ther 1:3-5.

6691.   Rao, D.H. & Balasubramanian, S.C. 1966. Socio-cultural aspects of infant feeding practices in a Telegana village. TGM 18:353-360.

Includes review of food habits and food taboos of lactating women. The village studied is Boduppal, in the Indian State of Andhra Pradesh.

6692.   Rao, M.V. Radhakrishna. 1934. Normal dietary in Vizagapatnam. IMG 69:142-144.

Infant feeding in Andhra Pradesh State, India. Also in IJ Ped 1:159-165.

6693.   Rao, S.L.N.; Malathi, K.; & Sarma, P.S. 1969. Lathyrism. WRND 10:214-238.

6694.   Rao, V.N. Madhava. 1965. The jackfruit in India. Farm Bulletin. No. 34. New Delhi: Indian Council of Agricultural Research.

6696.   Raphael, Dana. 1973. The role of breast-feeding in a bottle-oriented world. EFN 2:121-126.

This paper posits four socio-economic classes with different problems and values with regard to breast-feeding: the total breast-feeder (village); the emerging bottle feeder (town); the elite bottle feeder (city); and the breastfeeder in a bottle feeding world (suburban). The sociological bases for these categories are examined within the context of newly Westernized nations.

6697.   Raphael, Dana. L973. The tender gift: breast feeding. Englewood Cliff, New Jersey: Prentice-Hall.

6698.   Raphael, Dana. A sociobiological approach to human lactation. Paper presented at 74th Annual Meeting of the American Anthropological Association. 2 to 6 December, 1975. San Francisco, California.

6699.   Raponda-Walker, A. & Sillans, R. 1961. Plantes utiles au Gabon. Essai d'inventaire et de concordance des noms vernaculaires et scientifiques des plantes spontanees et introduites, description des especes, proprietes, utilisations economiques, ethnographiques et artistiques. [Useful plants of Gabon. Attempt at an inventory and concordance of vernacular and scientific names of native and introduced plants, descriptions of species, properties and economic, ethnographic, and artistic uses.] Paris: P. Lechevalier.

6700.   Rappaport, Roy A. Ritual in the ecology of a New Guinea people: an anthropological study of the Tsembaga Maring. Ph.D. dissertation. Columbia University. 1966.

6701.   Rappaport, Roy A. Pigs for the ancestors: ritual in the ecology of a New Guinea people. New Haven: Yale University Press.

6702.   Rappaport, Roy A. 1971. The flow of energy in an agricultural society. SA 225:117-122, 127-132.

An input-output analysis of Tsembaga gardening on the east bank of the Simbai River, in the central New Guinea Highlands. Gardening and animal husbandry tasks are described. "Combining all the input and comparing input with yield", author writes "I found that the Tsembaga received a reasonable short-term return on their investment. The ratio of yield to input was about 16.5 to 1 for the taro-yam gardens and about 15.9 to 1 for the sweet potato gardens". This was in a festival year, with dwellings at a distance from the gardens. "If the normal residential patterns [dwellings dispersed among the gardens] had been in effect ratios would have risen respectively to 20.1 to 1 and 18.4 to 1." "...the ratio of energy yield to energy input in Tsembaga pig husbandry is certainly no better than two to one and is probably worse than one to one".

6703.   Rasmussen, Holger. 1959. The baking of bread in southern Italy. Kuml pp. 166-194.

6704.   Rasmussen, M.P.; Quitslund, F.A.; & Cake, E.W. 195. Hucksters and pushcart operators as retailers of fruit. CorU-AES-B No. 820.

An apparently unique item in the literature. This report studies the economics, and briefly the history and sociology of produce vendors in New York City. It is illustrated with black and white photographs.

6705.   Rattray, Alexander. 1879. Bible hygiene, or health hints by a physician. London: Hodder & Stoughton; Philadelphia: P. Blakiston.

6706.   Rattray, Alexander. 1903. Divine hygiene. Sanitary science and sanitarians of the sacred scriptures and mosaic code. 2 vols. London: James Nisbet.

6707.   Rattray, Jeanette Edwards. 1953. Sunday samp on Long Island. NYFLQ 9:190-195.

Samp is a food of Algonquian origin, here described as made from maize, or hominy with white beans and salt pork.

6708.   Ratzel, Friedrich. 1887. Zur Beurtheilung der Anthropophagie. [Towards a judgement on anthropophagy.] AGWS-M 17:81-85.

6709.   Rau, Charles. 1884. Prehistoric fishing in Europe and North America. SI-CK No. 509.

6710.   Rau, E. 1958. Le juge et le sorcier: les mangeurs d'hommes. [The judge and the sorcerer: man eaters.] Ann Af 1958. pp. 179-206.

6711.   Rau, Santha Rama. 1969. The cooking of India. New York: Time-Life Books. Foods of the World.

6712.   Raven, H.C. 1934. "Makanan malayu", some of the foods in common use among the natives of Borneo and Celebes. NH 34:176-182.

6713.   Rawson, G.S. 1966. A short guide to fish preservation with special reference to West African conditions. Rome: Food and Agriculture Organization of the United Nations.

6714.   Rawson, Ian G. & Berggren, G. 1973. Family structure, child location and nutritional disease in rural Haiti. JTPECH 19:288-298.

Includes discussion of meal patterns, and staple foods. Transference of children from natal household to another residence is identified as a significant variable in the etiology of malnutrition.

6715.   Rawson, Ian G. Etiology of malnutrition in Central Costa Rica. Paper presented at 73rd Annual Meeting of the American Anthropological Association. 19 to 24 November, 1974. Mexico City.

6716.   Rawson, Ian G. Cultural components of diet and nutrition in rural Costa Rica. Ph.D. dissertation. Anthropology. University of Pittsburgh. 1975.

6717.   Rawson, Marion Nicholl. 1927. Chapter Eleven. Board, sideboard and pantry. Chapter Twelve. Pioneer knives, forks and spoons. In The story of early American arts and implements. New York, London: The Century Co. United States.

6718.   Ray, G. 1948. Les industries de l'alimentation. [Food industries.] "Que sais-je?" series. Paris: Presses Universitaires de France.

Historical, and methodological.

6719.   Ray, Jogischandra. 1933-1934. Food and drink in ancient India. M India 13:15-38.

6720.   Raymond, Armand-Eugene-Antoine. L'alimentation aux pays chauds (Etude d' hygiene coloniale). [Diet in the tropics.] (Study of colonial hygiene.] Medical dissertation. No. 63. Universite de Bordeaux. 1909.

6721.   Raymond, Charlotte. 1939. Food customs from abroad. Mass DPH-P No. 7051.

6722.   Raymond, Irving Woodworth. 1927. The teaching of the early Church on the use of wine and strong drink. CU-SHEPL No. 286.

6723.   Raymond, Nathaniel C. Authority and division of labor in collecting - hunting societies. Paper presented at 74th Annual Meeting of the American Anthropological Association. 2 to 6 December, 1975. Sn Francisco, California.

6724.   Raymond, W.D. 1938. Native materia medica. TNR 5:72-75.

Includes notes on alcoholic beverages.

6725.   Rea, F. 1963. Il favismo. [Favism.] Pediatria 71:1301-1309.

6726.   Read, Bernard Emms, 1939. Common food fishes of Shanghai. Shanghai: Mercury Press. Printed under the auspices of the Royal Asiatic Society. North China Branch.

6727.   Read, Bernard Emms & Wagner, W. 1940. Shanghai vegetables. CJ 33:206-220; 259-271.

6728.   Read Bernard Emms & Wagner, W. 1940. Shanghai vegetables. Shanghai: China Journal Publishing Co.

6729.   Read, Carveth. 1914. On the differentiation of man from the anthropoids. Man No. 91. pp. 181-186.

The influence of hunting and the development of a meat diet on the evolution of Homo sapiens.

6730.   Read, Catherine E. Animal bones and human behavior - approaches to faunal analysis in archeology. Ph.D. dissertation. Anthropology. University of California, Los Angeles. 1971.

6731.   Read, Kenneth E. The relationship between food, population, and social structure in primitive societies. Ph.D. dissertation. University of London. 1948.

6732.   Read, Margaret H. 1938. Native standards of living and African culture change. Illustrated by examples of the Ngoni highlands of Nyasaland. Africa. 11(3).

6733.   Read, Margaret H. 1941. The basis of nutrition in tribal society. Man 41:89. Summary of a paper presented at Royal Anthropological Institute, 24 May, 1941.

Discusses land as a basis for food supply in Nyasaland; tribal views of nutrition; what "food" is, and the nature of satiety. Notes the effect of decline in belief in the supernatural on motivation to work for food supply. Defines nutrition as "...the relation of diet to physical health".

6734.   Read, Margaret H. Cultural factors in relation to nutritional problems in the tropics. In Fourth International Congresses on Tropical Medicine and Malaria. Washington, D.C., 10 May to 18

May, 1948. Proceedings. Vol. 2. pp. 1196-1201. Washington, D.C.: Department of State.

> Cultural attitudes toward food; cultural attitudes toward health and disease in relation to diet.

6735. Read, Margaret H. Sociological and psychological bases for food habits. Second International Congress of Dietetics. 10-14 September, 1956. Rome. Proceedings. 1956. pp. 165-171.

> Examines the relationship between sociology, food habits, economics, and class structure. "If better nutrition programmes could be associated with less physical toil for the women, more opportunities for them to meet and talk and make money, and more recognition of their part as generous hosts, then I think these programmes would make a good start."

6736. Read, Margaret H. The role of the anthropologist. In Changing food habits. By John Yudkin and John Crawford McKenzie. 1964. pp. 46-61. London: MacGibbon & Kee.

> Focuses specifically on applied nutrition projects in tropical areas.

6737. Read, Merrill Stafford. Nutrition and ecology: crossroads for research. In Malnutrition is a problem of ecology. Edited by Paul Gyorgy and Otto L. Kline. 1970. Bibliotheca "Nutritio et Dieta" No. 14. Basle; New York: S. Karger.

> In this paper, the author provides an overview of nutrition-related research within one of the National Institutes of Health of the United States Department of Health, Education and Welfare. The subject areas focused on are family size; nutrition during pregnancy; breast feeding; critical periods in malnutrition and mental development; nutrition among preschoolers, and the elderly; environmental variables associated with malnutrition (physiological, sociological, psychological); and nutrition education. In concluding comments, the author notes that "Particular attention needs to be given to scientists oriented toward interdisciplinary studies involving teams having diverse capabilities" (p. 214).

6738. Reade, Arthur. 1884. Tea and tea drinking. London: Low.

6739. Reagan, Albert B. 1928. Plants used by the Bois Fort Chippewa (Ojibwa) Indians of Minnesota. WArch 7:230-248.

6740. Reagan, Albert B. 1929. Plants used by the White Mountain Apache Indians of Arizona. W Arch 8:143-161.

> Includes a note on the use of maize smut, a fungus (Utsilago maydis) as food eaten with honey.

6741. Reagan, Albert B. 1934. Various uses of plants by West Coast Indians. WHQ 25:133-137.

6742. Reagan, Sydney. Peanut price support programs, 1933-1952, and their effect on farm income. Ph.D. dissertation. Harvard University. 1953.

6743. Real, Enrique Suarez del. 1962. El problema alimenticio en Mexico; datos bioquimicos y planeamientos socio-politicos. [The problem of diet in Mexico; biochemical data and socio-politico changes.] RMS 24:367-381.

6744. Rebeiro, G.L. & Pechnik, Emilia. 1956. Contribuicao ao estudo dos alimentos da regiao amazonica. [Contribution to the study of foods of the Amazon region.] ABN 12:7-40.

6745. Recalde, Fabian. Cultural and educational factors in nutrition promotion. In Communication and behavior change. 8th International Conference on Health and Health Education. 1969. Buenos Aires. Proceedings. 1971. pp. 278-282. Geneva: International Journal of Health Education.

> Points out the necessity to integrate nutrition into total health education activities; the value of a multidisciplinary approach; the education of the consumer in areas of food hygiene, and selection of nutritionally sound foods. Outlines the various steps in planning nutrition education programs.

6746. Recordon, G. 19885. L'hippophagie, son histoire, son avenir, son etude au point de vue de l'hygiene publique. [Eating horse flesh: its history, its future, its study from the point of view of public hygiene.] Paris: Asselin & Houzeau.

6747. Reddy, Vinodini & Pershad, Jitender. Lactase deficiency in Indians. In First Asian Congress of Nutrition. 22 January - 2 February 1971. Hyderabad, India. Proceedings. Edited by P.G. Tulpule & Kamala S. Jaya Rao. 1972. pp. 751-756. Hyderabad: Nutrition Society of India.

> Little data exist regarding lactose intolerance among Indian children. This report indicates that while lactose intolerance occurs in Indian children, this fact does not necessarily imply clinical milk intolerance. The authors conclude that high incidence of lactose deficiency should not be used as an argument against the distribution of skim milk to undernourished populations in Asian countries.

6748. Redfield, Margaret Park. 1929. Notes on the cookery of Tepoztlan, Morelos. JAF 42167-196.

> Begins by distinguishing between indigenous, and introduced (European) foods, and lists pre-Columbian foods still in village use. Introduced foods are also listed. Utensils and techniques and procedures for making tortillas, tamales, moles (sauces) atoles, and gruels are next described. The place of grinding, and associated physical problems (swelling of the knees) is examined, followed by a consideration of ritual foods. The

article concludes with nine pages of recipes, as recorded in Spanish, from local informants.

6749. Redfield, Sarah P. 1906. The hay box cookbook. Chicago: the author.

6750. Redgrove, Herbert Stanley. 1933. Spices and condiments. London: Isaac Pitman & Sons.

6751. Reed, Charles A. 1959. Animal domestication in the prehistoric Near East. Science 130:1029-1039.

6752. Reed, Charles A. 1961. Osteological evidences for prehistoric domestication in southwestern Asia. ZTZ 76:31-38.

6753. Reed, Charles A. 1962. Snails on a Persian hillside. Postilla 66:1-20.

An Iraqi archeological site dating circa 12000 B.P., indicating use of snails for food. Edible snails are still found in the site area.

6754. Reed, E. David. Nutrition study of Spanish-American group. Fort Lupton, Colorado: Farm Labor Center. 1943. Unpublished.

Cited in Nutrition and certain related factors of Spanish-Americas in northern Colorado. By Michel Pijoan and R.W. Roskelly. 1943. P. 7. Denver: Rocky Mountain Council on Inter-American Affairs; Des Moines: Western Policy Committee.

6755. Reed, H.C. 1941. How early Polynesians used the now neglected pia plant. PIM 11:27-28.

6756. Reed, Joe Dudey. The early basis of subsistence of the Indians of the Plains area. Master's thesis. University of New Mexico. 1941.

6757. Reed, Minnie. 1906. The economic seaweeds of Hawaii and their food value. Hi-AES-AR for the year 1906. pp. 59-88.

Native methods of preparing and serving limu (seaweed) for food: pp. 65-70.

6758. Reed, Minnie. 1914. Ocean vegetables. M-PM 8:14-23.

Hawaiian seaweeds.

6759. Reed, William. 1866. The history of sugar and sugar-yielding plants. London: Longmans, Green.

6760. Rees, J. Aubrey, 1910. The grocery trade. 2 vols. London: Duckworth.

6761. Reese, A.M. 1917. Reptiles as food. SM 5:545-550.

Encourages greater utilization of reptiles for food.

6762. Reese, A.M. 1918. Alligators as food. Science 47:640.

Experimental acceptance test in Morgantown, Virginia.

6763. Reese, LaVerne. Food service in the Negro colleges in Texas. Master's thesis. Institutional Management. Iowa State College. 1947.

6764. Reeves, Robert G. 1953. New "evidence" on the origin of maize. AN 87:157-159.

A letter concerning the article by L.F. Randolph in AN 86:193-202 (1952).

6765. Reeves, Robert G. & Mangelsdorf, Paul C. 1959. The origin of corn. 2. Teosinte, a hybrid of corn and tripsacum. HU-BML 18:357-387.

6766. Regel, C. Ethnobotanique et vegetation. Lithuania (Kaunas), Poland, Iraq. [Ethnobotany and flora. Lithuania (Kaunas), Poland, Iraq.] In Huitieme Congres International de Botanique. 1954. Paris. Rapports et Communications. Parvenus avant le Congres aux Sections 14, 15 & 16. 1954. pp. 34,35.

Draws attention to the persistence of plant use over time.

6767. Regelson, Stanley, Cuisine in a southIndian village. Paper presented at 68th Annual Meeting of the American Anthropological Association. 20 to 23 November, 1969. New Orleans, Louisiana.

6768. Regelson, Stanley. Caste identity and the theory of "customary foods". Paper presented at 69th Annual Meeting of the American Anthropological Association. 19 to 22 November, 1970. San Diego, California.

6769. Regelson, Stanley. Food behavior in a Hindu village in South India. Ph.D. dissertation. Anthropology. Columbia University. 1971.

6770. Regelson, Stanley. The bagel: a "secular" ritual among American Jews. Paper presented at 73rd Annual Meeting of American Anthropological Association. 19-24 November, 1974. Mexico City.

6771. Reh, Emma. Food economics on the Papago Indian Reservation. Typescript. Office of Indian Affairs. Washington, D.C. United States Department of the Interior. 1942.

This study was undertaken as part of the Southwest Project conducted jointly by the U.S. Department of Interior and the Department of Anthropology of the University of Chicago. It is composed of the following sections: a general introduction; a description of the Papago Reservation; descriptions of Chiawuli Tak village, Sells, Arizona, and Bigfields, and overview of traditional Papago food habits; review of food habits in three reservation villages, nutritional evaluation of Papago dietary; suggestions for nutritional improvement and impications of the study for research in other areas. Copy in library of compilor

6772.   Reh, Emma; Benitez, S.; & Flores, Mariana. 195. Estudio de la dieta en Centro America. [Study of diet in Central America.] RCMG 2(4):2-22.

6773.   Reh, Emma; Castellanos, Aurora; & Rueda, Yolanda Bravo de. 1954. Estudio de la dieta y de las condiciones de vida existentes entre los trabajadores de una plantacion azucarera de Guatemala. [Study of the diet and living conditions of workers on a Guatemalan sugar plantation.] OSP-B 38:32-52.

6774.   Reh, Emma & Fajardo, Gloria. 1955. Condiciones de vida y de alimentacion de algunos grupos de poblacion urbano y rural de la Zona Central de Honduras. [Living conditions and diet of some rural and urban groups of the Central Zone of Honduras.] In Estudios nutricionales en Honduras. [Nutritional studies in Honduras.] 1955. pp. 7-48. Tegucigalpa: Ministerio de Sanidad y Beneficencia.

6775.   Reh, Emma & Fernandez, C. 1955. Condiciones de vida y de alimentacion en cuatro grupos de poblacion de la Zona   Central de Costa Rica. [Living conditiones and diet in four groups of the Central Zone of Costa Rica.] OSP-B-S(2) 39(4) 66-89.

6776.   Rehnburg, Mats, compilor. 1963. Svenska gastabud fran all tider.   En antologi om svenska mat- och dryckesseder sammanstalld.   [Swedish feasts. An anthology of food and drinking habits from all periods. Stockholm: Forum.

6777.   Rehnburg, Mats. 1965. Gustav Adolfsbakelser. [Gustav Adolf-cakes.] G Kal 5:56-80.

   Cakes with the likeness of Gustav II (died 1632), sold on the day of the death of a Swedish king. These cakes were first made in Goteborg at the end of the 19th Century, and have become widely diffused.

6778.   Reich, Edward. 1860-1861.   Die Nahrungs - und Genussmittelkunde historisch naturwissenschaflich und hygienisch begrundet. The historic, natural science, and hygienic bases of human food science.] 2 vols. Gottingen: Vandenhoek & Ruprecht's Verlag.

6779.   Reichard, Gladys Amanda. 1939.   Dezba. New York: J.J. Augustin.

   Navajo food preparation: pp. 19-32.

6780.   Reichard, Gladys. 1944.   The story of the Navajo Hail chant. New York: the author.

   Food.   pp. 19, 81-83, 103, 127, 135, 137, 139, 141, 143.

6781.   Reichart, E.L. & Downs, P.A.   1942.   The manufacturer of Cornhusker cheese.   Neb-AES-B No. 342.

6782.   Reichel, Alicia Dussan de. 1953. Practicas culinarias en una poblacion mestiza de Colombia. [Culinary practices in a Colombian mestizo community.] RCF 2: 05-136.

   Food habits of Atanquez. Santa Maria.

6783.   Reichnitz, Wilhelm. 1959. The earth oven: a method of cooking in the Torres Straits Islands. Man 59:21.

6784.   Reid, Ira de A. 1939. The Negro immigrant. His background, characteristics and social adjustment, 1899-1937. CU-SHEPL No. 449.

   Foods of West Indian immigrants: pp. 129-131.

6785.   Reid, J.   1907.   Leprosy and fish. BMJ 2:852-853.

6786.   Reid, Margaret Gilpin. 1943.   Food for people. New York: John Wiley & Sons.

   Food economics, production, and legislation in the United States.

6787.   Reidhead, Van A. The role of vitamin, mineral and energy requirements in prehistoric food production. Paper presented at 74th Annual Meeting of the American Anthropological Association. 2 to 6 December, 1975. San Francisco, California.

6788.   Reidhead, Van A. & Limp, William F. Nutritional maximization: a multifaceted nutritional model for archeological research. Paper presented at the 73rd Annual Meeting of the American Anthropological Association. 19 to 2 November, 1974. Mexico City.

6789.   Reilly, Conor. 973. Heavy metal contamination in home-produced beers and spirits. EFN 2:43-47.

   Analyses were made of more than one hundred thirty beers and spirits from different regions of Africa, India, Europe and Canada. A high proportion of home-produced alcoholic drinks were found to contain zinc (0.10 to 68.0 mg per litre); iron (0.2 to 245 mg per litre), and copper (0.10 to 58.0 mg per litre).   Little lead was found.   The metals were traced largely to the use of galvanized metal drums which have replaced traditional wooden, clay, or gourd vessels. Largest number of samples are from Zambia.

6790.   Reim, Helmut. 1962. Die Insektennahrung der australischen ureinwohner.   Eine Studie zur Fruhgeschichte menschlicher Wirtschaft und Ernahrung. [Insect food of the Australian Aborigine. A study on the early history of human economy and nutrition.] Museum fur Volkerkunde, Leipzig. Veroffentlichungen No. 13. Berlin: Akademie-Verlag.

6791.   Rein, Georg Kurt. 1909. 1911. Die im englischen Sudan, in Uganda, und dem nordlichen Kongostaate wild und halbwild wachsenden nutzpflanzen. [The wild and semi-wild useful plants growing in the Anglo Sudan, Uganda, and the northern Congo.] Tropenpflanzer 13:374-379; 532-539; 15:217-220; 387-393.

6792.   Reina, Reuben E. 1967. Milpas and milperos: implications for prehistorical times. AA 69:1-20.

A study of the contemporary maize producing system among descendants of the Itza, of Peten, Guatemala. Conclusions are drawn from the study which are related to the possibility that food shortages were involved in the collapse of southern lowland Maya religious center.

6793. Reinberg, Alain. 1974. Chronology and nutrition. Chronobiologia 1:22-27.

Both nutrition and chronobiology are involved in attempts to solve phyiological problems related to food intake such as eating habits, energy metabolism, and nutritional balance. This article reviews the research accomplishedusingchronobiologicalmethodology in the following areas: (1) circadian and other rhythms in spontaneous behavior of food intake; (2) the synchronizing effects of timed and restricted duration of food availability; (3) the observed persistence of most, if not all, circadian rhythms during fasting or very restricted diet (Chossat phenomenon); (4) bioperiodic changes of nutrient metabolism.

6794. Reinbold, Bela. 1907. A taplalkozas nehany kerdese. [Some questions on eating.] EMEVEK 2:109-116.

6795. Reinburg, Pierre. 1923. Gastronomie equatorienne. [Gastronomy in Ecuador.] RETP 4:123-138.

Basic foods and food preparations of native, Quechua-speaking population.

6796. Reinhardt, Albert. 1964. In einer schwarzwalder Schnappsbrauerei. [In a Black Forest schnapps distillery.] Der Lichtgang 14:40.

6797. Reinilaa, Anna-Maria. 1971. On a diet of woman in childbed in Finland. Ethnomedizin 1:227-239.

History, geographical distribution, and composition of tradition Finnish post-partum foods, especially "voimura", prepared from cubed bread, cooked in butter.

6798. Reinking, Otto August. Philippine edible fungi. In Minor products of the Phippine forest. PI-DANR-BF-B No. 22. Edited by William H. Brown. 1921. Vol. 3. pp. 103-147.

Food uses and methods of cooking: p. 147.

6799. Reinman, Fred M. 1967. Fishing: an aspect of Oceanic economy; an archaeological approach. Field: Anth 56 No. 2.

Preservation of sea foods: pp. 192-194.

6800. Reis, Carlos Manuel dos Santos. 1964. Contribuicao para o estudo de nutricao dos povos da Guine portuguesa. 1. Inquerito etnografico a alimentacao materno-infantil. [Contribution to the study of the nutrition of the people of Portuguese Guinea. 1. Ethnographc inquiry on maternal-child feeding.] IMT-A 21:123-130.

6801. Reis, Carlos Manuel dos Santos & Costa, F. Coutinho da. 1961. A alimentacao dos Manjacos. [Mandyako diet.] BCGP 16:377-504.

6802. Reisinger, Keith; Rogers, Kenneth D. & Johnson, Ogden. Nutritional survey of Lower Greasewood, Arizona Navajos. In Nutrition, growth and development of North American Indian children. Based on a conference co-sponsored by the National Institute of Child Health and Human Development, Indian Health Service, American Academy of Pediatrics, Committee on Indian Health. Edited by William M. Moore; Marjorie M. Silverberg; & Merrill S. Read. 1972. pp. 65-90. Department of Health, Education and Welfare. Publication No. (NIH) 72-26. Washington, D.C.: Government Printing Office.

6803. Reko, Blas Pablo. 1945. Mitobotanica Zapoteca. [Zapotec mythobotany.] Tacubaya, D.F., General Leon 9. No publisher cited.

Plants in Zapotec mythology. References to food plants included.

6805. Remington, C.L. 1946. Insects as food in Japan. Ent N 57:119-121.

Orthoptera, Ephemeroptera, Plecoptera, Trichoptera, Odonata, Coleoptra, Lepidoptera, Hymenoptera.

6806. Remington, Roe E. 1936. The social origins of dietary habits. SM 43:193-204.

6807. Renaud, E.B. 1934. The infuence of food on Indian culture. SF 10:97-101.

Native North American.

6808. Renaud, Jules. 1875. L'office du roi de pologne et les mets nationaux lorrains, fragments d'une etude sur les moeurs epulaires de la Lorraine. [The king of Poland's household and the regional food of Lorraine, fragments of a study on the mealtime customs of Lorraine.] Nancy: Wiener.

6809. Rendon, Silvia. 1953. Fue el maiz originario de America? [Did maize originate in America? Am Ind 12: 223-230.

Cites evidence for maize in America, Asia and Africa. Concludes its origin to have been in Transcaucasia or the Danube Valley.

6810. Rendon, Silvia. 1954. Fue el maiz originario de America? [Did maize originate in America? SGC-B 12:107-115.

Cites evidence for maize in America, Asia and Africa. Concludes its origin to have been in Transcaucasia or the Danube Valley.

6811. Renew, Audrey. 1968. Some edible wild cucumbers (Cucurbitaceae) of Botswana. BNR 1:5-8.

6812.   Renfrew, Jane M.   Palaeoethnobotany and the Neolithic Period in Greece and Bulgaria.   Ph.D. dissertation. University of Cambridge. 1969.

6813.   Renfrew, Jane M.   1973.   Palaeoethnobotany.   The prehistoric food plants of the Near East and Europe. New York: Columbia University Press.

Wheat, barley, millets; pulses: horsebean, field peas, lentils, bitter vetch, grass pea, chick pea; flax; cultivated and wild fruit; nuts; edible wild plants.

6814.   Renner, Hans Deutsch. 1944.   The origin of food habits. London: Faber & Faber.

6815.   Renouard, Yves. 1953.   O grande comercio do vinho na Idade Media. [The great wine trade of the Middle Ages.] Sao Paulo: Industria Grafica J. Magalhaes.

6816.   Renouard, Yves. 1958. Le grande commerce du vin au Moyen Age. [The extensive wine commerce of the Middle Ages.] IH 20:47-53.

6817.   Replogle, Wayne F. 1956.   Yellowstone's Bannock Indian trails. Yellowstone Interpretive Series No. 6. Yellowstone National Pak, Wyoming; Yellowstone Library and Museum.

Shoshone foods: p. 51.

6818.   Republica Argentina.   Ministerio de Salud Publica de la Nacion. 1951.   Politica alimentaria Argentina.   Conferencias pronunciadas en la campana de educacion alimentaria.   29 de abril de 1949. Buenos Aires. [Argentine food policy. Addresses made in the field of nutrition education April 29, 1949. Buenos Aires. Buenos Aires: Departmento de Talleres Graficos.

This volume opens with a thirty-two page statement by General Juan Domingo Peron, endorsing the conference and outlining a nutrition policy for Argentina. Subsequent statements address nutritional status; production, consumption; distribution; and specific foods and their place in Argentine diet.

6819.   Restat, Jorge Mardones. 1933. El problema de la alimentacion. [The problem of diet.] RMA 1:367-378.

Nutritional aspects of Chilean food habits.

6820.   Retief, G.P. 1971.   The potential of game domestication in Africa, with special reference to Botswana. SAVMA-J 42:119-127.

6821.   Reuss, C. 1960. L'evolution de la consommation des boissons alcoolisees en Belgique, 1900-1958. [Evolution of the consumption of alcoholic beverages in Belgium, 1900-1958.] IRES-B 26:85-124.

6822.   Reutlinger, Shlomo, & Selowsky, Marcelo. Undernutrition and poverty. Magnitude and target group oriented policies. International Bank for Reconstruction and Development. Bank Staff Working Paper No. 202.   April.   Washington, D.C.: International Bank for Reconstruction and Development. 1975.

6823.   Reutlinger, Shlomo & Selowsky, Marcelo. 1976.   Malnutrition and poverty. Magnitude and policy options.   World Bank Staff. Occasional Papers. No. 23. Baltimore: John's Hopkins University Press.

Focuses on income distribution and cost-effectiveness of some intervention policies.

6824.   Reynaud, G. 1907. Geophages et geophagie. [Earth-eaters and earth eating.] Mars Med 46:677-682.

6825.   Reynolds, Ellen A. 1926.   The relation between dietary habits and health of children in rural sections of Virginia. VPI-VAES-B No. 250.

This study is concerned largely with the effects of diet on dental and skeletal health and, therefore, with the consumption of milk as a calcium source. Five hundred and seventy-six Caucasian and three hundred and twenty-three Black children are surveyed. All children are rural. Results of total dietary status, and of comparative Caucasian/Black dietary status are given, with explanations provided for some notable differences. Differential consumption of common foods is reported.

6826.   Reynolds, Philip Keep. 1951.   Earliest evidence of banana culture. AOS-J-S No. 12. Pacific Islands.

Includes data on literary evidence from India, Greece, Rome, and China; archeological evidence from India and Java; and evidence of distribution and cultivation in Oceania, Africa, the Canary Islands, and in the Western Hemisphere. A concluding chapter is concerned with linguistic evidence relating to the etymology of the word musa.

6827.   Reynosa, Alvaro. 1881.   Agricultura de los indigenas de Cuba y Haiti. [Agriculture of the natives of Cuba and Haiti.] Paris: E. Leroux.

6828.   Rhett, Blanche Salley, compilor. 1934. Two hundred years of Charleston cookery. Cooking recipes gathered by B.S. Rhett. Edited by Lettie Gay. New York: Random House.

6829.   Rhodes, Reuby Tom. The influence of cocoa beverage on the metabolism of six preschool children. Master's thesis. Luabbock, Texas: Texas Technological College. 1944.

6831.   Ribeiro, Joaquim. 1952.   A historia da alimentacao no periodo colonial. [History of food habits during the colonial period.] Colecao Ensaio o Debate Alimentar. Rio de Janeiro: Servico de Alimentacao da Previdencia Social.

Brazil.

6832. Rice, Arthur B. 1909. Cannibalism in Polynesia. AA 11:487.

Abstract of paper providing historical and comparative aspects.

6833. Rice, Arthur B. 1910. Cannibalism in Polynesia. AAOJ 32:77-87.

6834. Rice, G.D. 1923. Singular foods of the Filipinos. SA 84:35.

6835. Rice, Glen Eugene. Were the first Mogollon sedentery farmers? Paper presented at 73rd Annual Meeting of the American Anthropological Association. 19 to 24 November, 1974. Mexico City.

United States. Southwest archeology.

6836. Rice, T.B. 1944. The emotional factor in nutrition. Hygeia 22:100-101.

6837. Rice, William Hyde. 1923. Hawaiian legends. BPBM-B No. 23.

Myth: origin of cooking (Hawaii):p.21; (Marquesas): pp. 104, 128.

6838. Rich, E.E. 1976. The fur traders: their diet and drugs. Beaver Summer. pp. 25-30.

6839. Richard, C. 1959. Le chao. Fromage de soja fermente, sale et alcoolise. [Chao. A fermented, salted, alcoholic soy cheese. SEIC-B 34:317-324.

Viet-nam.

6840. Richardin, Marie-Ernest-Edmond. 1907. La cuisine francaise du 14me au 20e siecle. L'art du bien manger. [French cookery from the 14th to the 20th Century. The art of fine dining.] Paris: Nilsson.

6841. Richards, Audrey Isabel. 1932. Hunger and work in a savage tribe. A functional study of nutritional among the Southern Bantu. London: George Routledge & Sons.

Interrelationship of food habits with other social institutions in Bemba society, northeastern Rhodesia. Introductory material considers nutrition as a biological process and as a social activity. Food is then examined in relation to the socialization of the child; to paternal authority; and its role within the kin group. Details of the subsistence cycle are reviewed; followed by consideration of the significance of kinship in relation to economic organization. A final; extensive section is devoted to food symbolism in Bemba culture: its sacred character; sacrificial function; symbol of union; taboos; its association with the female principle; and role in filial dependence.

6842. Richards, Audrey Isabel. 1939. Land, labour and diet in Northern Rhodesia. An economic study of the Bemba tribe. Oxford: Oxford University Press.

A study of the Bemba. Foods habits in their total sociological context. More detailed than Richards' study of 1932, including results of her collaboration with Widdowson in 1936. Part One covers the Bemba people, material culture; social organization; environment and an overview of diet. Part Two studies native views on food; eating and drinking; storage methods; kitchens; and food preparation. Part Three examines the kinship network and domestic economics as food production; distribution; and exchange are involved therein. Part Four describes the intracacies of garden ownership; granary rights; budgeting; magic rites and types of exchanges. Part Five is concerned with land tenure; cultivation; hunting and fishing. Part Six discusses religion and magic in economic life; and division of labor and work rhythm.

6843. Richards, Andrey Isabel. 1956. Chisungu. A girl's initiation ceremony among the of Northern Rhodesia. London: Faber & Faber.

Food in ritual: pp. 84-87; 142-145; food exchange: pp. 44-46; additional references to food in daly life and ritual: passim.

6844. Richards, Audrey Isabel & Widdowson, Elsie M. 1936. A dietary study in northeastern Rhodesia. Africa 9: 166-196.

Possibly the earliest study involving a social scientist and a nutritionist in assessing the interrelationship between culturally determined food habits and clinical/biochemical nutritional status.

6845. Richards, Darrel J. 1967. Food staples of the coast Indians. Totem Pole 50:38-39.

6846. Richardson, Anna Euretta. 1917. Cotton seed flour as a human food. Austin: University of Texas.

6847. Richardson, Frank Howard. 1921. The nutrition class idea - retrospect and a prospect. A Ped 38:237-245.

Report of an out-patient nutrition education and diet clinic for children at Brooklyn Hospital, New York.

6848. Richardson, D.J. J. Lyons & Co. Ltd., caterers and food manufacturers, 1894-1939. In The making of the modern British diet. Edited by Derek J. Oddy & D.S. Miller. 1976. London: Croom Helm.

6849. Richardson, Sheila. 1959. The Forfar bridie. Scot Mag 55:45.

A Scots baked confection.

6850. Riches, P. 1964. Nardoo - the clover fern. SANat 38:63-64.

6851. Richet, Charles (fils) & Hardy, Georges. 1933. L'alimentation indigene dans les colonies francaises, protectorats et territoires sous mandat. [Native diet in the French colonies, protectorates and territories under mandate.] Paris: Vigot Freres.

6852.   Richter, Anita. A study of food preservation and storage practices of 100 families in Lavaca County. Master's thesis. University of Texas. 1945.

6853.   Richter, Curt P. 1939. Transmission of taste sensation in animals. ANA-T 65:49-50.

6854.   Richter, Curt P. 1941. Alcohol as food. QJSA 1:650-662.

6855.   Rick, Charles M. & Anderson, Edgar F. 1949. On some uses of maize in the Sierra of Ancash. MBG-A 36:405-412.

South central Peru.

6856.   Ridell, Francis A. 1960. Honey Lake Paiute ethnography NSM-AP No. 4.

Subsistence: pp. 32-41.

6857.   Riddell, W. 1943. The domestic goose. Antiquity 17:148-155.

6858.   Ridder, Clara Ann. Basic distances in 100 farm homes for preparing and serving food and washing dishes. Ph.D. dissertation. Ithaca, New York: Cornell University. 1950.

6859.   Ridder, Clara Ann. 1952. Basic distances in 100 farm homes for preparig and serving food and washing dishes. CU-AES-B No. 879.

This study reports the distances between major work places in farm kitchens and the distances at which homemakers stored frequently used items of food and equipment from the places where the latter are used. The study reveals some of the limitations imposed by home interior layout, as well as the homemaker's practices in assembling materials for six common tasks, i.e. paring and boiling potatoes; opening and heating a homecanned vegetable; frying eggs; mixing cake, or cookie dough; making and serving coffee; cleaning up. Data were gathered from visits to one hundred farm homes. An analysis of factors contributing to loss of time/efficiency is made. The findings of this research have both ergonomic and time-motion applications.

6860.   Rideau, A. 1975. Presentation d'un test destine a' approfondir le caractere d'un enfant a partir de son comportement alimentaire. [Introduction of a test intended to determine an infant's personality from its food behavior.] Psychologie No. 66. pp. 6-10.

6861.   Ridley, H.N. 1912. Spices. London: Macmillan.

6862.   Ridley, H.N. 1930. The dispersal of plants throughout the world. Ashford, Kent, England: L. Reeve.

6863.   Riehm, Karl. 1961. Prehistoric salt-boiling. Antiquity 35:181-191.

6864.   Riepma, S.F. 1970. The story of margarine. Washington, D.C.: Public Affairs Press.

6865.   Riesenfeld, Alfons: Fruchtbarkeitsriten in Melanesien. [Fertility rites in Melanesia.] Ph.D. dissertation. Universitat Wien. 1937.

6866.   Rietz, Carl A. & Wanderstock, Jeremiah. 1965. A guide to the selection, combination, and cooking of foods. 2 vols. Westport, Connecticut: AVI.

Provides potentially useful data for an ethnoscientific analysis of food categories and practices.

6867.   Rife, Dwight W. 1931. Primitive man's diet in the Mesa Verde area. MVN 2:17-18.

6868.   Riis, Jacob A. 1898. Feast days in Little Italy. Century 58:491-499.

New York City; immigrant Italian neighborhood.

6869.   Riis - Olesen, H.A. 1956. Den ulovlige braendevinsbraending. [Unlawful brandy distilling.] T Arbok pp. 104-124.

6870.   Riley, Charles V. 1876. Locusts as food for man. AAAS-P Twenty-fourth meeting. August, 1875. pp. 208-214.

Contains account of experiments in cooking locusts for food. Similar data by Riley are found in USGGS-ST-UC No. 14 (1878).

6871.   Riley, Charles V. 1877. The locust plague in the United States: being more particularly a treatise on the Rocky Mountain locust or so-called grasshopper, as it occurs east of the Rocky Mountains, with practical recommendations for its destruction. Chicago: Rand McNally.

Includes notes on locusts used as human food.

6872.   Riley, Charles V. 1883. Insects as food for man. AN 17:546-547.

6873.   Riley, E. Baxter. 1923. Sago-making on the Fly River. Man 23:145-146.

Production of sago pulp or starch from the trunk of the sago palm. The Fly River is located in West Irian, New Guinea.

6874.   Riley, Robert A. How sociocultural variables affect food consumption: the Guatemalan case. Paper presented at 70th Annual Meeting of the American Anthropological Association. 21 November, 1971. New York City.

A dietary survey of four communities in different microenvironments within the Valley of Guatemala revealed that food intake was less influenced by habitat than by cultural and socio-economic variables. The dietary data were collected by using an inventory-recall questionnaire technique and the results compared between and within the communities. The results of the survey suggest that the relationship between cultural phenomena and environmental factors, expressed in terms of the ecological approach, should be re-evaluated in view of the effect of urbanism on rural communities in disparate ecosystems.

6875. Riley, Thomas J. Agricultural transformations in a Hawaiian valley. Paper presented at 69th Annual Meeting of the American Anthropological Association. 19 to 22 November, 1970. San Diego, California.

6876. Riley, Thomas J. The wet and dry in a Hawaiian valley: the archeology of an agricultural system. Ph.D. dissertation. Anthropology. University of Hawaii. 1973.

6877. Rimoli, Renato O. 1971-1972. Restos alimenticios en los yacimientos arqueologicos de la Republica Dominicana. [Food remains in the archaeological deposits of the Dominican Republic.] RDDA 2:68-78.

6878. Ripley, P.O. 1971. Nutrition notes from Ghana. CNN 27:85-90.

Describes food patterns; preferences; and preparation techniques. Does not specify areas.

6879. Rippey, Charles D. Evolving settlement-subsistence patterns in the Zagros region of Iraq and Iran. Master's thesis. Anthropology. University of Arizona.

6880. Rist, Edouard & Khoury, Joseph. 1902. Etudes sur un lait fermente comestible. Le "leben" d' Egypte. [Study on an edible fermented milk. Egyptian "leben".] IP-A 16:65-84.

6881. Ristorcelli, A. 1938. Diet and familial customs of the people of Nefzaoua, Tunisia. [In French.] IPT-A 27:78-84.

6882. Ritchie, J. 1940. A keg of 'bog butter' from Skye, and its contents. SAS-P 75:5-22.

6883. Ritchie, Jean S. 1967. Learning better nutrition. FAO Nutritional Studies 20. Rome: Food and Agricultural Organization of the United Nations.

Cultural and psychological influences on food patterns: pp. 28-34; social organization in relation to changes in food habits: pp. 40-53; changing food habits: pp. 54-68.

6884. Ritchie, T. Russel. 1927. Diet. MJA [Supp. 5]: 2:160. September 10.

A comparison of Samoan and Maori diets.

6885. Ritchie, William A. The development of aboriginal settlement patterns in the northeast and their socio-economic correlates. In Twenty-first Southeastern Archaeological Conference. November 6-7, 1964. New Orleans, Louisiana. Proceedings. Edited by Stephen Williams. 1965. pp. 25-29. SAC-B No. 3.

Includes reference to prehistoric food-plant remains excavated at archaeological sites in New York State. Mentioned are acorns, maize, beans, pumpkin, and squash.

6886. Ritenbaugh, Cheryl. 1978. Model course. 4. Nutritional anthropology. MANews 9:23-29.

A course outline, with readings provided for biocultural and sociocultural dimensions of human food uses. Changing group food behavior, and a number of specific topics (e.g. obesity, pica) are given emphasis.

6887. Ritson, Joseph. 1802. An essay on abstinence from animal food as a moral duty. London: Richard Phillips.

6888. Ritzenthaler, Robert E. 1966. Piki bread of the Hopi Indians of Arizona. Lore 16:102-105.

6889. Ritzenthaler, Robert E. & Ritzenthaler, P. 1962. Cameroons village: an ethnography of the Bafut. MPM-PA No. 8.

Description of foods, their preparation, and meal patterns included.

6890. Rivera M. Irene. 1938. Importancia economica del maiz. Estudio sistematico e historico y datos acerca de su cultivo. [The economic importance of maize. Historical and systematical study with data regarding its cultivation.] UNacMex-IB-FDC No. 29.

The section titled 'El maiz entre los antiguos Mexicanos' ('Maize among the ancient Mexicans') contains a list of Nathuatl place names which have reference to maize; as well as Aztec glyphs depicting maize, or objects related to it. Data on maize and its use as food reported from older sources (Acosta, and Sahagun).

6891. Rivera, Trinita. Diet of a food-gathering people, with chemical analysis of a salmon and saskatoons. In Indians of the urban northwest. Edited by Marian Wesley. Smith. 1949. pp. 19-36.

Samples of Coast Salish foods were obtained on Seabird Reserve, British Columbia, in the summer of 1945. Nutritional values for dried, sockeye and spring salmon; and dried Juneberry (Amelancier alnifolia are given. Preservation techniques are described.

6892. Rivera, Virginia Rodriguez. 1965. La comida en el Mexico antiguo y moderno. [Meals in ancient and modern Mexico.] Coleccion Pormaca. Mexico City: Editorial Pormaca.

6893.   Rivolier, J. 1955. Froid et altitude dans leur rapport avec alimentation.   [Coldness and altitude - their relationship to diet.]   ANA 9:135-177.

6894.   Robbins, M. Leon. Tea, Camellia sinensis, in North America. Paper presented to the 247th Annual Meeting of the American Society of Horticultural Sciences. Tropical Region. 5 December to 10 December, 1956. Puerto Rico.

Contains an historical note on tea-growing in North Carolina.

6895.   Robbins, Michael C. 1977. Problem-drinking and the integration of alcohol in rural Baganda. Med Anth 1(3):1-24.

6896.   Robbins, Michael C. & Pollnac, Richard B. 1969. Drinking patterns and acculturation in rural Buganda. AA 71:276-284.

Suggests increasing acculturation generates a trend toward informal drinking behavior, and the elaboration of drinking settings. Marginal populations are the heaviest alcohol users. Data on beverage preference are included, together with indications for additional research procedures for refining the observations presented.

6897.   Robbins, Wilfred William; Harrington, John Peabody; & Freire - Marreco, Barbara. 1916. Ethnobotany of the Tewa Indians. SI-BAE-B No. 55.

Data from Santa Clara and San Ildelfonso Pueblos in New Mexico; and Hano Vaillage, Hopi Reservation, Arizona.

6898.   Roberson, Catherine D. Food involvement and attitudes to body size: the influence of race and socio-economic level. Master's thesis. Northern Illinois University. 1970.

6899.   Robert, P. Une operation-pilote: l'etude du ravitaillement de Paris au temps de Lavoisier. [A pilot-project: study of the provisioning of Paris in Lavoisier's time.] In Pour une histoire de l'alimentation. Edited by J.J. Hemardinquer. 1970. pp. 60-67. Paris: Colin.

6900.   Roberts, D.F. 1978. Climate and human variability. Menlo Park: Benjamin/Cummings.

Nutrition: pp. 6, 17, 19, 31, 38, 62, 64, 65, 70.

6901.   Roberts, Jr., Frank H. 1946. Carter's thesis in the light of archaeology: the Southwest. Am An 11:266-269.

Review of George Francis Carter (1946). Plant geography and culture history in the American Southwest. VFPA No. 5.

6902.   Roberts, H. 1903. The tramp's handbook. London & New York: John Lane.

Includes notes on camp cookery; and unusual sources of edibles in Great Britain.

6903.   Roberts, Jean D. 1932. Cacti and culinary art. PA 12:13. February.

6904.   Roberts, John B. 1963. Sources of information and food buying decisions. UKy-AES-SCS-B No. 85.

Effects of age of shopper; income; education; and media influence on consumer food planning and purchases.

6905.   Roberts, John M. 1951. Three Navajo households. HU-PMAAE-P 40 No. 3.

Blue corn bread: pp. 44; alcoholic beverages: p. 46.

6906.   Roberts, K.S. 1959. A Fifteenth Century Portuguese cookbook. KFLQ 6:179-182.

6907.   Roberts, L.M. 1968. World prospects for increasing foods of plant origin. AVMA-J 153:1843-1847.

6908.   Roberts, Lydia Jean. 1929. The nutrition and care of children in a mountain county of Kentucky. USDL-CBP. No. 110.

6909.   Roberts, Lydia Jean. 1929. The psychologists study eating habits. CS 7:35-38.

6910.   Roberts, Lydia Jean. 1944. Nutrition in Puerto Rico. JADA 21:298-304.

6911.   Roberts, Lydia Jean. 1948. The road to good nutrition. Diets for children. Federal Security Agency. Children's Bureau. Washington, D.C.: Government Printing Office.

6912.   Roberts, Lydia Jean & Stefani, Rosa Luisa. 1949. Patterns of living in Puerto Rican famiies. Rio Piedras: University of Puerto Rico.

Family diets: pp. 143-206.

6913.   Roberts, R. 1973. The classic slum. Salford life in the first quarter of the century. Harmondsworth, Middlesex, England: Penguin Books.

Data on food habits and their change after World War I are included.

6914.   Roberts, R.G. 1955. Coral atoll cookery. JPS 64:227-232.

Describes staple foods and their preparation on the Ellice Islands atoll of Funafuti. Included are utensils; cooking ovens; coconut palm toddy (fresh or boiled), derived from the flower spathes); coconut paste (poi), and confections; coconut embryo; Alocasia indica; Colocasia antiquorum; banquet puddings; fish; breadfruit; sweet potato; bananas; birdsnest fern (Asplenium nidus).

6915.   Roberts, William Kemuel. 1914. Health from natural foods. An argument for the fruitarian diet. Sunnyvale, California: no publisher cited.

6916.   Robertson, William O. 1961. Breast feeding practices: some implications of regional variations. AJPH 51:1036-1042.

Concludes breast feeding is influenced by multivariate cultural factors, as opposed to maternal personality alone. Lowest percentage of breast feeding was noted for New England, with the highest percentage in Mountain, and Pacific Coast states.

6917.   Robineau, C. 1967. Culture materielle des Djem de Souanke. [Material culture of the Ndjem of Souanke.] OM 7:37-50.

Congo/Cameroun. Describes banana mortar and pestles; peanuts; and gourd seeds. Souanke is located at 2.03 N, 14.02 E.

6919.   Robinson, Corinne Hogden, with Lawler, Marilyn R. 1972. Chapter Fourteen. Factors influencing food habits and their modification. Chapter Fifteen. Cultural food habits in the United States. In Normal and therapeutic nutrition. New York: The Macmillan Co.

These chapters examine, respectively, physiological, psychological, social, age, gender, and illness variables in relation to food acceptance; and regional, and ethnic (Jewish, Puerto Rican, Mexican, Italian and Near Eastern [Armenia, Syria, Greece, Turkey]), and Chinese food patterns.

6920.   Robinson, F.N. Notes on the Irish practice of fasting as a means of distraint. In Putnam anniversary volume. Anthropological essays presented to Frederick Ward Putnam in honor of his seventieth birthday, April 16, 1909, by his friends and associates. 1909. pp. 567-583. New York: G.E. Stechert & Co.

Fasting as a religious practice; as a means of notifying a debtor of high rank, before seizure of property; as a guarantee or pledge of good surety; as a means of aggression against or coercion of an enemy.

6921.   Robinson, P. 1957. Infant feeding in Burma. QRP 12:14-15.

6922.   Robinson, P. 1957. Infant feeding in Ceylon. QRP 12:208-209.

Describes traditions and customs.

6923.   Robinson, P.   1959.   Infant feeding in Afghanistan. QRP 14:244-245.

6924.   Robinson, R.K. & Cadena, Maria A. 1978. The potential value of yoghurt-cereal mixtures. EFN 7:131-136.

Typical Middle Eastern sun-dried mixtures (kishk, tarhana) are described as to preparation, storage, and nutritive value. The po-

tential these foods have for conserving limited supplies of unprocessed milk is stressed.

6925.   Robinson, William D.; Payne, George C.; & Calvo, Jose. 1944. A study of the nutritional status of a population group in Mexico City. JADA 20:289-297.

Eighty-seven families comprise the sample population. Food staples and dietary patterns, with food consumption statistics, and nutritional value of dietary; pp. 289-291.

6926.   Robson, John Robert Keith. 1974. The ecology of malnutrition in a rural community in Tanzania. EFN 3:61-72.

This article describes the remote and immediate causes of protein deficiency among the Songea Ngoni, subsistence farmers in southwest Tanzania. Seasonal availability of foods, infant feeding practices are examined, and the plight of this group highlighted in terms of previous political events and the impact of these latter on cultural values and subsistence orientation.

6927.   Robson, John Robert Keith. 1976. Commentary: changing food habits in developing countries. EFN 4:251-256.

Discusses the cognitive; sociological; political; agricultural; and nutritional variables to be considered in introducing new foods. Includes examples of both successful and unsuccessful introductions.

6928.   Robson, John Robert Keith. Fruit in the human diet. Fruit in the diet of prehistoric man and of the hunter-gatherer. JHN 32:19-26.

6929.   Robson, John Robert Keith; Carpenter, G.A.; Latham, Michael C.; Wise R.; & Lewis P.G. 1962. The district team approach to malnutrition. Maposeni nutrition scheme. JTPECH 8:60-75.

6930.   Robson, John Robert Keith; Konlande, J.G.; Larkin, Frances; O'Connor, P.A. & Hsi-yen, L. 1974. Zen macrobiotic dietary problems in infancy. Pediatrics. 53:326-329.

6931.   Robson, John Robert Keith with Larkin, Frances A.; Sandretto, Anita M.; & Tadayyon, Bahram. Chapter Seven. Food habits: cultural determinants and methodology of change. In Malnutrition. Its causation and control (with special reference to protein calorie malnutrition). 1972. pp. 563-594. New York, London, Paris: Gordon & Breach.

6932.   Robson, John Robert Keith & Wadsworth, G.R. 1977. The health and nutritional status of primitive populations. EFN 6:187-202.

A general overview of Bushman; Australian Aborigene; Papua New Guinean; Andean Peruvian; and circumpolar food patterns is provided as a basis for generalizations concerning cardiovascular disease nutrient deficiency; infectious disease and cancer among non-urban, non-industrialized groups cited.

6933.   Robson, John Robert Keith & Yen, Douglas E. 1976. Some nutritional aspects of the Philippine Tasaday diet. EFN 5:83-89.

The Tasaday are a recently-contacted group inhabiting caves in the South Cotabato forest, Mindanao Island. Food resources are described, together with food getting, preparation, and eating practices. Limited food composition and nutrient value data are provided for staple foods.

6935.   Rochas, Victor de. 1862. La Nouvelle Caledonie et ses habitants: productions, moeurs, cannibalisme. [New Caledonia and its inhabitants: productions, manners, cannibalism.] Paris: F. Sartoris.

6936.   Roche, J.; Vzan, M. & David, M. 1952. Enquetes alimentaires en Tunisie. 2. Ville de Sousse. 1951. [Dietary investigations in Tunisia. 2. City of Ssa, 1951.] BEST 67:52-56.

Susa is located in northeastern Tunisia, on the Mediterranean coast, at 35 50' N., 38'E.

6937.   Rock, Joseph F. 1913. The indigenous trees of the Hawaiian Islands. Honolulu: Published under patronage.

Contains scattered data on economic botany, including use of fruit and nuts as food.

6938.   Rockwell, Jane. 1957. Some gourmet recipes from explorer's cookbooks. CNHM-B 28:3-6.

New Ireland; Palau.

6939.   Roden, Claudia. 1974. A book of Middle Eastern food. New York: Random House. Vintage Book V-948.

The introduction contains documented discussion of the history of Near Eastern cuisine, the sociology of food and its uses, Islamic dietary laws, and an account of regional food preferences.

6940.   Rodert, E.E. Food practices of Arabic-background families living in East Valley Health District. Mimeographed. County of Los Angeles. Department of Health. 1969.

6941.   Rodinson, Maxime. Ghidha'. [Food and feeding.] In Encyclopedia of Islam. Edited by B. Lewis; Ch. Pellat & J. Shaacht. 1965. Vol. 2. pp. 1057-1072. Leiden: E.J. Brill; London: Luzac & Co.

Part One. Food of the pre-Islamic period: pp. 1057-1062. Part Two. Pre-Islamic southern Arabia: pp. 1060, 1061. Part Three. Regulations concerning food in early Islam: pp. 1061-1062. Part Four. Food in the traditional Muslim world: pp. 1062-1072.

6942.   Rodrigo, J.A.G. 1887-1888. Arrowroot cultivation and preparation. Trop Ag 7:833-834.

6943.   Rodrigues, Evandro J.V. Bebidas cafreis. [Kaffir beverages.] Ph.D. dissertation. Lisbon: Instituto Superior de Ciencias Sociais e Politica Ultramarina. 1950.

6944.   Rodrigues, F.C. 1953. Nutrition of the natives of Vilanculos. [In Portuguese.] IMT-A 10:1229-1255.

Vilanculos is located on the Mozambique Indian Ocean coast, at 22 01S., 35 19E.

6945.   Rodriques, L.A. 1944. Breve historia de la cerveza. [A short history of beer.] PSeg 8:369-378.

6946.   Rodriguez, S.B. 1941. Campaign against group consumption of mate. [In Spanish.] BSPub 2:164-168.

Uruguay.

6947.   Rodriguez-Minon, J.L. 1953. Nutritive value of the most common dishes in the Spanish cuisine. [In Spanish.] REEADN 12:276-286.

6948.   Rodriguez de Mendoza, Virginia R. 1950. Comidas de origen judio muy acostumbradas. [Foods of Jewish origin common in Mexico.] TI No. 72. pp. 20-21.

Foods of Sephardic Jews.

6949.   Rodriguez Rivera, Virginia. 1943. Algunas comidas de Mexico de fines del siglo 19. [Some foods of late 19th Century Mexico.] SFM-A 2:173-180.

6950.   Rodseth, F. 1958. More African taboos. Nutrition. 13:30-34.

6951.   Rodway, James & Aiken, James. 1913. Some of our food fishes. Timehri 3:43-50.

6952.   Roepke, W. 1952. Insects from Java used as human food and as medicine. [In Dutch.] Ent B 14:172-174.

6953.   Roflo, Tarcela Etulle. Bamboo in the economy and folk life of the municipality of Tabgon, Cebu. Master's thesis. Anthropology. University of San Carlos. 1964.

Bamboo as food: pp. 126, 127.

6954.   Rogers, Ann. 1968. A Basque Story cook book. New York: Charles Scribner's Sons.

6955.   Rogers, Dvid J. Botanical considerations on the origin of Manihot esculenta. Paper presented at 70th Annual Meeting of the American Anthropological Association. 18 November, 1971. New York City.

6956.   Rogers, Edward S. 1967. Subsistence areas of the Cree-Ojibwa of the eastern subarctic: a preliminary study C-NMM-CE No. 5 B No. 204. pp. 59-90.

6957.   Rogers, Edward S. & Black, Mary B. 1976. Subsistence strategy in the fish and hare period, northern Ontario: the Weagamow Ojibway, 1888-1920. JAR 32:1-43.

> Proposes a "home base" model and related zones of exploitation which are seen as able to 'expand' and 'contract' according to variations in resource availability. Field data; together with archival material are used to reconstruct settlement and demographic patterns; environmental conditions; and specific food-getting techniques.

6958. Rogers, Fred B. 1968. Sixty years of meat inspection. AJPH 58:214-215.

6959. Rogers, L.A. 1911. Fermented milks. USDA-BAI-C No. 171. Also in USDA-BAI-AR No. 26. (1909).

> Medical-therapeutic value of fermented milk is considered, followed by a discussion of the various forms of such dairy products (buttermilk, kefir, kumiss, yoghurt). A recipe for producing kefir, in the absence of kefir "grains' is given. Some ethnographic data is included.

6960. Rogers, L.S. 1922. Notes on the occurrence of umu (ovens) in the Warepa district, Otago. JPS 31:155-157.

> New Zealand.

6961. Rogers, Susan F. 1915. Colonial cookery terms. DN 4:239.

> United States of America.

6962. Rohde, Eleanour Sinclair. 1939. Rose recipes. London: Routledge.

> Reprinted as Rose recipes from olden times. New York: Dover Publications. 1973.

6963. Roheim, Geza. 1954. Cannibalism in Duau, Normandy by Islands, D'Entrecastaux Group, Territory of Papua. Mankind 4:487-495.

6964. Rohrl, Vivian J. 1970. A nutritional factor in Windigo psychosis. AA 72:97-101.

> The witiko, or windigo, is a mythical monster with cannibalistic characteristics, found in northern Algonkian folklore. Tales are recorded both about the monster and people who have, or have almost, reached this condition. The condition has been manifest among the Chippewa, Creek, and other northern Algonkian peoples. The possibility of a nutritional etiology is explored; specifically the possibility of deprivation of animal fat. The traditional "treatment" which includes the ingestion of fat, or fatty meat, most frequently of the bear, is examined in relation to the nutritional biochemistry of fat and its role in B complex metabolism.

6965. Rojas, Alfonso Villa. 1964. Los Chontales de Tabasco. [The Chontales of Tabasco.] Am Ind 24:29-48.

Food habits: pp. 40-48. Mexico.

6966. Rojas, Bernardo Valenzuela. 1971. La cocina campesina. Estudio etnografico del anejo Chileno de la vivienda campesina del Valle Central De Chile (Region Aconcagua – Concepcion). [Country kitchen. Ethnographic study of an old Chilean of the rural lodgings of the Central Valley of Chile (Aconcagua-Concepcion region.)] AFC No. 9. pp.43-58.

6967. Rojas, Isidro. Breve estudio sobre la higiene de los antiguos pobladores de la Mesa Central. [Short study on the hygiene of ancient populations of the Central Mesa.] In Congreso Internacional de Americanistas. Actas de la Undecima Reunion. Mexico – 1895. 1897. pp. 65-73. Mexico City: Agencia Tipografia de F. Diaz de Leon.

> Data on food habits of early inhabitants of the Central Mesa of Mexico: pp. 65-70.

6968. Rojas, Ulises. 1946 - 1974. Las plantas y sus productos. [Plants and their products.] USCarl-PT No. 2. pp. 493-540; No. 5. pp. 127-169. No. 6. pp. 187-202; No. 7. pp. 117-135.

> Medicinal and culinary uses. Listed alphabtically by Spanish common name, and latin binomial. Lists food plants.

6969. Rola-Butrillos, Nena. Chapter Four. Food practices. Chapter five. Food likes, dislikes, and beliefs. In Food management practices of homemakers in the rural areas. Study series 12. Community Development Research Council. Quezon City: University of the Philippines.

6970. Rolfs, P.H. 1923. "Brazilian ant eaters." FEnt 7:26-28.

> Atta sexdens, L. a species of ant consumed as food by certain groups in the Brazilian interior.

6971. Rolland, M.-F.; Chabert, C. & Serville, Y. 1977. La consommation du pain et de ses substituts. [Consumption of bread and its substitutes.] ANA 30:105-118.

> France.

6972. Rolland, M.-F.; Chabert, C.; & Serville, Y. 1979. Le choix des pains. [The choice of bread.] ANA 32:1285-1300.

> French consumption of bread has declined over the past forty years; the general tendency among consumers is toward long loaves with a maximum of crust and golden-brown color. Bread is seen as an accessory to other main foods, rather than as a major meal component, as in times past, wheat bread is the traditional preference.

6973. Rolland, M.-F. Serville, Y. 1976. Le consommateur face au changement. [The consumer vis-a-vis change.] ANA 30:467-480.

Enumerates factors operating to inhibit change (habit conservatism; nostalgia for the past; suspicion of industrially-prepared food; fear of food pollution; love the art of good cooking); and those which favor change (higher standard of living; the desire to save time; evolution of cooking practices; need for variety and quality). Concludes "...the consumer will accept things which give a maximum of pleasure for the least effort. He will also accept something which by its taste, prestige, convenience, and safety contributes to a better life". (p. 479).

6974.   Romer, Bela. Brot und Fladen im Pannon-ischen gebiet Jugoslawiens vom Standpunkt eines ethnologen und lebensmittelchemikers. [Bread and flat cakes in the Pannonia region of Yugoslavia from an ethnological and food chemistry point-of-view.] Paper presented at the First International Symposium on Ethonological Food Research.   21 to 25 August, 1970. Lund: Folklivsarkivet. Lund University.

6975.   Romero-Rojas, B.   1956.   El consumo de bebidas alcoholicas en Colombia. [The consumption of alcoholic beverages in Colombia.] EE No. 82. pp. 49-76.

6976.   Romney, Kimball & Romney, Romaine. 1966. The Mixtecans of Juxtlahuaca, Mexico. New York: John Wiley & Sons.

Food: pp. 34-38.

6977.   Romunde, Leonardus Hendrikus van.   1911. Der voeding der Trappisten.   [The diet of Trappists.] Utrecht: den Boer. Also in KAWA-VGVW-N-A 19: 1406-1407. (1910-1911).

6978.   Rooke, T.C.B.   1855.   Report on the sweet potato (Convolvulus batata). RHAS-T 2(2):38-43.

Includes a table giving Hawaiian names of sweet potato varieties, and soil type best suited for each.

6979.   Roosevelt, Anna. History of aboriginal subsistence in a floodplain region of northern Amazonia. Paper presented at 76th Annual Meeting of the American Anthropological Association.   29 November to 3 December, 1977. Houston, Texas.

The existence of dense populations, at Contact, in the greater Amazonian floodplains, is usually attributed to the high productivity of tropical forest subsistence in this habitat. Archeological, ethnohistoric, and ecological evidence, however, suggests that these densities, might better be explained by the productivity of the habitat for intensive seed crop cultivation.   An archeological project designed to test this hypothesis was carried out in a floodplain region of the middle Orinoco River, and preliminary analysis of the data recovered shows a temporal correlation between the inception of maize and legume cultivation and the development of high population density.

6980.   Roosevelt, G.W.   1905.   Hop sprouts as vegetables. USDCL-MCR No. 297. Pp. 59.

Belgium.

6981.   Roosman, Raden Selamat. 1970. Coconut, breadfruit and taro in Pacific oral literature. JPS 79: 219-232.

6982.   Root, Waverly Lewis. 1968. The cooking of Italy. New York: Time-Life Books. Foods of the World.

6983.   Root, Waverly, Lewis. 1971. The food of Italy. New York: Atheneum.

An historical and regional study of Italian foods and food patterns.

6984.   Root, Waverly Lewis & De Rochemont, 1976. Eating in America. A history. New York: William Morrow.

6985.   Roper, Marilyn Keyes. A study in intra-human killing in the Pleistocene. Master's thesis. Anthropology. University of Pennsylvania. 1968.

6986.   Roper, Marilyn Keyes. 1969. A survey of the evidence for intrahuman killing in the Pleistocene. CAnth 10:427-448

Data from Krapina site, Yugoslavia; and Brno site, Czechoslovakia.

6987.   Roquia, F.D. & Dosado, Y.G. 1961. The wild rice varieties of Bukidnan. AIL 23:28.

Mindanao, Philippines.

6988.   Rorer, Sarah Tyson Heston. 1883. How to use olive butter. A collection of valuable cooking recipes. Philadelphia: W. Butcher's Sons.

6989.   Rorer, Sarah Tyson Heston. 1883. Recipes used in Illinois corn exhibit model kitchen, Woman's Building. Columbian Exhibition, Chicago. Philadelphia: G.H. Buchanan.

6990.   Roscher, W.H. 1883. Nektar und ambrosia. Mit eine Anhang uber die Grundbedeutung der Aphrodite und Athene. [Nectar and ambrosia. With an appendix on the underlying meaning of Aphrodite and Athene.] Leipzig: Teubner.

6991.   Roscoe, John. 1965. The Baganda. 2nd edition. London: Frank Cass.

Food, food habits, brewing: pp. 435-442.

6992.   Rose, E. 1918. Food sauces of Europeans and Indo-Chinese compared. [In French.] BAEI 21:525-532.

6993.   Rose, E. 1918. Le nuoc-mam du Nord (nord centre-Annam et Tonkin), composition chimique et fabrication. [Nuoc-man in the north (northcentral Annam and Tonkin], chemical composition and manufacture.] BAEI 20:955-973.

6994.   Rose, E. 1919. Etude comparee de diverses sauces alimentaires. [Comparative study of different alimentary sauces.] IP-A 33:292-300.

6995.   Rose, E. 1919. Le nuoc-mam, condiment national indochinois. [Nuoc-mam, national condiment of Indochina.] IP-A 33:275-281.

6996.   Rose, Giles. 1682. The perfect school of instructions for officers of the mouth, shewing the whole art of a master of the household, a master carver, a master butler...a master cook...with pictures displaying the whole arts. London: printed for R. Bentley & M. Magnes.

6997.   Rose, Joseph Nelson. 1899. Notes on useful plants of Mexico. USDA-DB-USNH-C 5:209-225.

Extensive data on food plants and their uses.

6998.   Rose, Mary Swartz. 1937. Racial food habits in relation to health. SM 44:257-267.

6999.   Rosedale, John Louis. The education of school teachers in nutrition. In Ninth Far Eastern Association of Tropical Medicine. Congress Nanking. 2 October to 8 October. 1934. Transactions. 1935. Vol. 2. Pp. 799-805. Nanking: National Health Administration.

Focus is on Malayan classrooms. Includes suggested diets; and chemical demonstrations illustrating digestion and protein metabolism for the elementary dietetics curriculum.

7000.   Rosedale, John Louis. 1936. The improvement of local dietaries. Malay M 11:151-153.

7001.   Rosemburg, Tobias. 1953. Los "mitotes" de Oreste. The household festivals of Oreste.] ATF-B 2:96-100.

Traditional foods and beverages of Chile.

7002.   Rosen, E. 1904. Anatomische Wandtafeln der vegetabilischen - und Genussmittel. [Anatomical charts of vegetables and stimulants.] Breslau: J.U. Kern.

7003.   Rosen, G.; Johnson, L.; Halberg, F.] & Sargent, II., F. 1976. Free-running individualized circannual rhythms in human infants' weight gain and carbohydrate, fat and protein intake. Chronobiologia 1: 76-77. Abstract of a paper presented at 10th International Congress of Nutrition. August, 1975. Kyoto.

Analysis of Davis' (1928) research on infant self-selection of diet indicates a high probability that individualized circanual rhythms in human food preference are built into homo sapiens by evolution.

7004.   Rosenberg, Ellen M. Ecological [demographic] effects of sex-differential nutrition. Paper presented at 72nd Annual Meeting of the American Anthropological Association. 1 December, 1973. New Orleans, Louisiana.

Supporting the position with extensive excerpts from the ethnographic literature, the author concludes that extreme sex-differential diets reflect underlying societal attitudes toward controlling group size. If increase is desired, women's diets will be supplemented. If the goal is limitation, women, and sometimes children, will be affected by receiving insufficient animal protein.

7005.   Roseberry, C.H. 1910. Experiences in raising Virginia deer. ABM 1:50-52.

Experiment in domestication of wild deer for meat.

7006.   Rosendahl, Paul. Aboriginal agriculture and residence pattern in upland Lapakahi, Island of Hawaii. Ph.D. dissertation. Anthropology. University of Hawaii. 1972.

7007.   Rosengarten, Jr., Frederic. 1969. The book of spices. Wynnewood, Pennsylvania: Livingston Publishing Co. Reviewed in Herbarist 1970. Pp. 54-55.

7008.   Rosenstein, L. 1973. La psychologie de l'extreme famine. Manguers de cadavres et mangeur d'hommes. The psychology of extreme famine: corpse and man eaters.] CND 8:291-297.

Records of the famine in the Volga provinces, during 1921-1922.

7009.   Rosewater, Nathan. 1925. Superior health and longer life of the Jew—blood will tell. Diet Ad Ther 3:56-59.

A highly subjective defense of Hebraic dietary code.

7010.   Rosner, Frd. 1970. The Biblical quail incident. JAMA 211:1544.

Letter to the Editor concerning sudden death following ingestion of quail as reported in the Old Testament (Exodus 16; Numbers 11:33).

7011.   Ross. 1965. Nagot om kaffe - historia, odling och anvadning. [A little about coffee - history, cultivation and use.] SFT 69:680-689.

7012.   Ross, C. 1924. Family dinner in Korea. LA No. 323. Pp. 123-125.

7013.   Ross, Eric Barry. Hunting taboos: metempsychosis versus cost-benefit. Paper presented at 75th Annual Meeting of the American Anthropological Association. 17 to 21 November, 1976. Washington, D.C.

In contrast to many other Amazonian populations, the Achuara Jivaro practice a solitary mode of hunting, combined with a focus on small and intermediate-sized game; dietary prohibitions apply to large terrestial quadrupeds (deer, tapir), believed to be reincarnations of the dead. The organization of hunting among the Achuara is examined in terms of a fauna, weapons, fishing potential, non-aquatic game productivity, horticultural output and settlement pattern. It is proposed that a cost-benefit model based on such variables is best able to explain the occurrence of dietary specialization typified by such taboos.

7014.   Ross, Eric Barry. 1978. Food taboos, diet, and hunting strategy: the adaptation to animals in Amazon cultural ecology. C Anth 19:1-36.

Food taboos viewed as a functional response to restrict maximization of protein sources to those most useful to a culture.

7015.   Ross, Hubert Barnes. The diffusion of the manioc plant from South America to Africa; an essay in ethnobotanical culture history. Ph.D. dissertation. Columbia University. 1954.

7016.   Ross, June Anne. Introducing peanut butter into Chimbu infant diet. In An integrated approach to nutrition and society. The case of the Chimbu. Report of the symposium held at the Thirty-seventh Congress of the Australia and New Zealand Association for the Advancement of Science. 20 to 24th January. NGRU-B No. 9.

7017.   Ross, Mary A. 1956. Nutrition and home economics programme in Egyptian villages. PNS 15:30-35.

Studies foods; preparation techniques; female labor in-put; cooking facilities; household equipment; in the village of Aghour Soughra, Qalyubia Province, north of Cairo.

7018.   Ross, Mary A. 1964. An applied nutrition program in action. CNN 20(1):1-6.

Describes a program carried out in Botswana, under the aegis of the Food and Agriculture Organization of the United Nations, and the United Nations International Children's Education Fund.

7019.   Ross, Winifred. The present day dietary habits of the Papago Indians. Master's thesis. University of Arizona. 1944.

Based on fieldwork done at Sells and Ajo, Arizona during the year 1940-1941, this report includes nutrient analysis of the following edible desert plants cholla cactus; mescal pulp; sahuaro cactus preserve; sahuaro cactus seeds; mesquite beans (Prosopis sp.); fruit of Opuntia sp.; tansy mustard; Salvia columbaris; yucca fruit. Protein, lipids, kcals, ash and calcium values are given. High calcium values were uniformly found [possibly due to the underlying caliche of desert soils in the area.]

7020.   Rossi, Clemente. 1888. Gastromicologia ossia nozioni popolari sopra una gran parte delle migliori specie de funghi mangerecci, sul modo di cucinarli e conservarli. [Mycological gastronomy, or popular knowledge of a large number of the best species of edible fungi, and the manner of cooking and preserving them.] Milan: Agnelli.

7021.   Rossi, Peter H. 1958. Progress report. Study of the bases for changing food attitudes. Contract No. DA19-129-QM-1117. P-1114-Rpt #1. Period: 15 May 1958 - 14 July 1958. Research and Engineering Command. Quartermaster Food and Container Institute for the Armed Forces. Chicago: Quartermaster Corps, United States Army.

This report is a preliminary version of Gottlieb and Rossi (1961 q.v.). The 1961 version is unchanged.

7022.   Rossmann, Bruno. 1942. "Kamajahu", ein estnisches Volksnahrungsmittel. ["Kamajahu", an Estonian national food.] ZUL 84:34-36.

A traditional food prepared from rye, oats, barley, peas, and beans.

7023.   Rossmann, Jr., Edward David. From the secular meal to the Holy Table: the problem of food in the fiction of J.K. Huysmans. Ph.D. dissertation. Romance Languages. University of Rochester. 1969. Abstracted in DAI 30[A] (9): 3957

7024.   Rostlund, Erhard. 1952. Freshwater fish and fishing in native North America. UCal-PG Vol. 9.

Part One includes food value of principal species of freshwater fish. Part Two covers aboriginal fishery and fishing methods, with information on equipment. Section Twelve is concerned with fish preservation.

7025.   Rostron, Primrose. 1964. The food they cried in Paris. CL 136 (3535):1528.

Folklore of food vendors in Nineteenth Century Paris. The cries of coffee, vinegar, pastry, fruit, cocoa, and milk sellers are referred to.

7026.   Roth, Henry Ling; Butler, Marion E.; & Walker, James Backhouse. 1890. The aborigines of Tasmania. London: Kegan Paul, Trench, Trubner. Reprint. Hobart: Fullers Bookshop Pty. 1968.

7027.   Roth, Walter Edmund. 1901. Food: its search, capture, and preparation. NQE-B No. 3.

Australian Aborigines. Reviewed by James Edge-Partington in Man No. 51. Pp. 94-95 (1903).

7028.   Roth, Walter Edmund. 1912. On the native drinks of the Guianese Indians. Timehri 2:128-134.

7029.   Roth, Walter Edmund. 1915. An inquiry into the animism and folklore of the Guiana Indians. SI-BAE-AR for the year 1908-1909. Pp. 103-386.

Belief concernings eating food after nightfall: pp. 184, 185; 295 (No. 276). Restrictions on food intake: p. 294 (No. 244); p. 295 (No. 247); p. 296 (No. 248); p. 297 (No.

297). "The Lucky [cooking] Pot": pp. 302, 303; food sanctions related to the preparation of hunting poison: p. 304; "honey bee and the sweet drinks": p. 305. Food restrictions during puberty: pp. 308-316, passim.

7030. Roubakine, A. 1933. Social factors of diet in the past. [In French.] SSHAARH-B 21:30-67.

7031. Roueche, Berton. 1966. Cultural factors and drinking patterns. NYAS-A 133. 846-855.

Opens with a brief review of the history of alcoholic beverages to the discovery of distillation. Also included are brief accounts of the origin of "aqua vitae", brandy, gin, whiskey, scotch, rum, rye and bourbon.

7032. Rougemont, W. 1933-1934. Die Entstehung der yerba mate. [The origin of yerba mate.] Lasso 1:26-31.

Ilex paraguayensis.

7033. Roughley, Thomas. 1823. The Jamaica planter's guide, or a system for planting and managing a sugar estate or other plantations on that island, and throughout the British West Indies. London: Printed for Longman, Hurst, Rees, Orme & Brown.

Includes a passage on geophagy among Negro slaves. The habit of earth-eating was considered fatal and some of the observed symptoms are described.

7034. Roulx, L. 1937. L'alimentation en Haiti. [Diet in Haiti.] Hai-SNHAPS-B No. 14.

7035. Roumain, Jacques. 1942. Contribution a l'etude de l'ethnobotanique precolombienne des Grandes Antilles. [Contribution to the study of the pre-Columbian ethnobotany of the Greater Antilles.] Hai-BE-B 1:1-72.

Includes plants used as food.

7036. Rouse, John E. 1970. World cattle. 2 vols. Norman: University of Oklahoma. Press.

Major breeds of cattle in eighty-five countries.

7037. Rouse, Jr., Parke, 1968. Chapter Ten. Food, drink, and merriment. In Planters and pioneers. Life in Colonial Virginia. New York: Hastings House. Toronto: Saunders.

7038. Rousseau, Jacques. L'alimentation vegetal des Amerindiens chausseurs du nord-est de l'Amerique. [Plants in the diet of Ameridian hunters of the American Northwest.] In Huitieme Congres International de Botanique. 1954. Paris. Rapports et Communications. Parvenus avant le Congres aux Sections 14, 15 & 16. 1954. P. 34. Paris: Andre

Groups covered are the Eskimo, Montagnais, and Naskapi.

7039. Rousseau, Jacques & Raymond, Marcel. 1945. Etudes ethnobotaniques Quebecoises. [Quebec ethnobotanical studies.] IBUM-C No. 55.

7040. Rousseaux, Y. La gastronomie a Paris sous le Consulat et l'Empire. [Parisian gastronomy under Consulate and Empire.] Thesis. Sorbonne. 1962.

7041. Roussel-Botreau. 1943. Note sur l'alimentation du paysan du delta tonkinois et l'amelioration qu'il est possible d'y apporter. [Note on the diet of the Tonkin Delta peasant and its possible improvement.] IIEH-BT 5:59-66.

7042. Roust, Norman Linnaeus. 1967. Preliminary examination of prehistoric human coprolites from four western Nevada caves. In Papers on Great Basin archeology. UC-AS No. 70. UCARF Pp. 49-88.

This report is concerned with the identification of undigested materials, including numerous plant and animal food remains. Sites excavated include Lovelock Cave, Humboldt Cave, and Hidden Cave, all located in Churchill County; and a dry rock shelter located in Pershing County, Nevada. This article carries a Preface by Robert F. Heizer, which provides a brief history of coprolite research based on the Nevada sites' excavations.

7043. Rout, Ettie A. Hornibrook. 1926. Maori symbolism. New York: Harcourt, Brace.

Food as medicine (diet and its relation to health): pp. 29-33.

7044. Rout, Ettie A. Hornibrook. 1926. Native diet, with numerous practical recipes. Preface by Sir W. Arbuthnot Lane. London: Heinemann.

Maori. New Zealand.

7045. Rutledge, W. Scoresby & Routledge, Katherine. 1910. With a prehistoric people. The Akikuyu of British East Africa. London: Edwin Arnold.

Food and food preparation: pp. 49-65.

7046. Roux, Jean-Paul. 1967. Le lait et le sein dans les traditions Turques [Milk and breast in Turkish tradition.] L'Homme 7:48-63.

7047. Rowland, A.C. 1940. Hue fafaru° the dreadful experience of a sensitive man in Tahiti. PIM 10:36.

Includes reference to marinating fish.

7048. Rowntree, Jennie I. 1950. Influences on children's food habits. JHE 42: 805-807.

Mother's attitudes during infancy; teacher, parental, and other adult attitudes in introducing new foods; role of 4-H clubs, advertisers, food industry.

7049.   Roxas, M.L. & Collado, E.G.   1922.   A preliminary critical study of the Filipino diet. PIMA-J 2:171-185.

7050.   Roy, Carmen, ed.   1973.   Presentation du Centre Canadien d'Etudes sur la culture tradition-elle - An introduction to the Canadian Center for Folk Culture Studies.   [Edition bilangue -bilingual edition.]   CCFCS-P No. 7.

Materials relating to culinary anthropology (English text):   Pp.   29, 30, 31, 33, 38; (French text); pp.   73, 74, 75, 77.

7051.   Roy, D.M. 1951.   A note on field investiga-tions of an outbreak of lathyrism in Madhya Pradesh 1945.   IMG 86:263-265.

7052.   Roy, J.K. & Biswas, R.   1964.   Proteins in the diets of some Indian tribes. SCult 30:126-129.

7053.   Roy, J.K. & Rao, R.K.   1956.   Diet survey amongst the tribes of Madhya Pradesh.   Part 1. Baigas and Gonds of Madhya Pradesh.   I-DA-B 5(2).

7054.   Roy, J.K. & Rao, R.K. 1962.   Diet of some tribes of India.   IJMR 50:905.

7055.   Roy, J.K. & Rao, R.K. 1962.   Investigation on the diet of the Muria of Bastar District.   I-DA-B 6:33-45.

7056.   Roy, J.K. & Rao, R.K. 1967.   Studies on the seasonal variation of diet of a semi-agricultural community in West Bengal: effect of the recent flood. I-AS-B 12:97-107.

7057.   Roy, J.K. & Roy, B.C. 1967.   Food sources, diet and build of the people of Great Nicobar.   I-AS-B 16:313-342.

Local foods; their preparation; nutritional assessment of the population.   A similar article, title changed slightly, appears in IJMR 57:958-964 (1969).   Great Nicobar Is-land lies northeast of Sumatra, at approxi-mately 7.O N, 94.O E.

7058.   Roy, Ramesh Chandra.   An economic study of the two tribes of Bihar.   Master's thesis. Anthro-pology. Ranchi University. 1958.

India.

7059.   Roy, Sarat Chandra. 1915.   The Oraons of Chota Nagpur: their history, economic life, and social organization.   Calcutta: Brahmo Mission Press.

Food, and drink; religious restrictions per-taining to food: pp. 162-170.

7060.   Roy, Sarat   Chandra & Roy,   Ramesh Chandra. 1937.   The Kharias.   Ranchi: Man in Indian Office.

Food habits of a tribe occupying western Assam, Bengal, Bihar, and Orissa: pp. 81-90.

7061.   Royle, John Forbes. 1844. On the hyssop of Scripture. RSL-P 5:510-520.

Identified as Capparis spinosa, Scheele.

7062.   Royle, John Forbes. 1849.   On the identifi-cation of the mustard tree and the hyssop of Scrip-ture.   London: W. Clowes & Sons.

The plant which has been translated as hyssop (Hyssopus officinalis) is identifed as the caper (Capparis spinosa), which grows in the Jordan and Kedron Valleys, and in Eqypt. The mustard tree may be Sinapis sp., or khardal, a tree which grows near the Sea of Galilee.

7063.   Royle, John Forbes. 1846. On the hyssop of Scripture. RASGBI-J 8:193-221.

Capparis spinosa, Scheele.

7064.   Roys, Ralph L. 1931.   The ethnobotany of the Maya. TulU-MARS-P No. 2.

7065.   Rubel, Paula G.   & Rosman, Abraham. Yams for the ancestors, pigs for the ancestors: transformational relationships between exchange structures. Paper presented at 75th Annual Meeting of the American Anthropoligical Association.   17 to 21 November, 1976.   Washington, D.C.

Many New Guinea societies are characteriz-ed by the symbolic elaboration of the theme of fertility and reproduction. Within a sing-le society, this theme is expressed through different structures, particularly structures of exchange. These structures are homolo-gous and are related to one another by means of transformations.   We intend to explore these transformational relationships in several New Guinea societies.   The Abelam have two structures of exchange: one involving women, the other involving long yams. One represents an inverse trans-formation of the other. The Kuma, Chimbu, and the Maring offer pigs to ancestors, and give pork to affines who are exchange part-ners. These two structures of exchange are also inverse tranformations of one another.

7066.   Rubinstein, Robert L.   Men, women and hermaphroditic pigs in the New Hebrides.   Paper presented at 76th Annual Meeting of the American Anthropological Association.   29 November to 3 December, 1977.   Houston, Texas.

Traditional public culture of Malo Island (15. 40S., 167. 10E.), New Hebrides, was charac-terized by a system of achievable, ranked eating classes for men, each class entered by killing a specific number of pigs. Many of the classes necessitated the killing of hermaphroditic pigs. An analysis of the ritual significance of these mutants is offer-ed.   It is posited that, in the pig-killing system, men symbolically appropriated the power of human regenesis. Pigs required for such regeneration had both male and female characteristics.

7067.   Rubner, Max. 1902. Die Gesetze des Energie verbrauchs bei der Ernahrung. [The laws of energy consumption in nutrition.] Leipzig & Vienna; F. Deutchke. English edition: Natick, Massachusetts: United States Army Research Institute of Environmental Medicine and Development. Edited by Robert J.T. Joy. 1968. Available in microfiche form from United States Department of Commerce. National Technical Information Service, Springfield, Virginia.

7068.   Rubner, Max. 1914. Uber moderne Ernahrungsreformen. [Concerning modern nutrition reforms.] Munich, Berlin: R. Oldenbourg.

7069.   Rubner, Max. 1913. Wandlungen in der Volksernahrung. [Transition in national nutrition.] Leipzig: Akademie Verlags.

7070.   Rubner, Max & Schulz. 1913. Das "belegte Brot" und seine Bedeuting fur die Volkernahrung. ["Vassal bread" and its meaning for national diet.] AHyg 81:260-271.

7071.   Rudder, Eugene F. 1899. Cannibalism in Queensland. SMan 2:40-41.

7072.   Ruddle, Kenneth. 1973. The human use of insects: examples from the Yukpa. Biotropica 5:94-101.

Among the Yukpa-Yuko of Venezuela and Columbia, insect foods have retained their importance in the less acculturated communities, where these foods help to compensate for the general deficiency of animal proteins and other vital protective substances. The manner of collecting, and food use of twenty-two genera and seven orders is described. Fieldwork was done between 1969 and 1971, in the area comprising the Sierra de Perija, the Serrania de Valledupar, and the Serrania de los Motilones between 9.O N, and 10. 3 N.

7073.   Ruddle, Kenneth & Chesterfield, Ray. 1977. Education for traditional food procurement in the Orinoco Delta. University of California Publications in Ibero Americana Vol. 53. Berkeley: University of California Press.

This study analyzes the training of children to procure food through traditional cultivation and complementary activities and shows how such education forms an integral part of the local human ecosystem in a traditional Venezuelan campesino community. The study focuses on the Isla de Guara, a small island of the Orinoco delta, located in the State of Monagas, opposite the town of Tucupita, capital of the Federal Territory of the Delta Amacuro. Included are data on hunting; fishing; food distribution; repair of equipment; division of labor; time involved in task training; and identification of flora and fauna with local and Latin names provided.

7074.   Ruddle, Kenneth; Johnson, Kenneth; Townsend, Patricia; Townsend, K.; & Reese, John D.

1978. Chapter Two. Traditional extraction and preparation of sago. In Palm sago. A tropical starch for marginal lands. Honolulu: University of Hawaii Press. An East-West Center Book.

7075.   Rudofsky, Bernard. 1965. The kimono mind; an informal guide to Japan and the Japanese. New York: Doubleday.

Food; its preparation. etiquette; attitudes: pp. 164-199.

7076.   Rudolph, N. 1948. Nahrung und Rohstoffe aus dem Meer. [Food and raw materials from the sea.] Stuttgart: Wissenschaftliche Verlag.

A book criticized for the absence of a bibliography; but noted to be rich in historical references.

7077.   Rudra, M.N. & Kant, L. 1950. A field investigation into lathyrism. IMG 85:415-418.

7078.   Rue, E. Aubert de la. Saint-Pierre et Miquelon. [Saint-Pierre and Miquelon.] In L'alimentation indigene dans les colonies francaises. Protectorats et territories sous mandats. Edited by G. Hardy & C. Richet. 1933. Pp. 345-350. Paris: Vigot Freres.

Concerned largely with available fish. Reference is made to edible wild plants, and to gardening. No mention is made of nutritional status, or food patterns.

7079.   Ruffer, Marc Armand. 1919. Food in Egypt. IEM Vol. 1. [new series.]

A study of animal, and plant foods in ancient Egypt.

7080.   Ruhe, Adolf. Kulturgeschichte Untersuchungen zur afrikanischen Milchwirtschaft. [Culture-historical investigation on African milk economy.] Ph.D. Disseration. Universitat Hamburg. 1940.

7081.   Ruiz, Felipe Gonzalez. 1933. La antropofagia en los Indios del continente americano. [Anthropophagy among Indians of the New World.] Estudio 2:240-245.

7082.   Ruoppila, Viekko. 1939. Vuodenajat ja ravinto. [Food and the seasons.] Kotiseutu Pp. 130-134.

Karelia, Finland.

7083.   Rusby, Henry H. 1906-1907. ...wild food plants of the United States. CLA 9:718-719; 10:66-69; 202-204; 220; 328-330; 436-438; 533-535; 11:82; 456; 546.

Arranged according to month of availability.

7084.   Rusby, Henry H. 1914. Tropical vegetable foods. NYBG-J 15:107-112.

Abstract of a lecture concerning consumption of vegetable foods in tropical climates.

7085. Rusby, Henry H. 1933. Jungle memories. New York: McGraw Hill Book Co. Whittlesey House.

Preparation of fish among the Araua, Ibon River region, Brazil: p. 278; Andean food plants available in the La Paz markets in 1885: pp. 38-41; illustrations of Inga sp.; Oxalis tuberosa; Tropaeolum tuberosum; Annona murcata, Zea mais: plate 4.

7086. Russell, Charles M. 1958. Last of the buffalo meat. Montana 1:14.

Illustration.

7087. Russell, Frank. 1908. The Pima Indians. SI-BAE-AR for the year 1904-1905. Pp. 3-389.

The food supply: pp. 66-78. This section opens with comments on the tendency of Pima diet to produce overweight individuals. Food preparation is described, followed by a list of staple foods and the manner in which these are processed. A chemical analysis of the mesquite bean is given on p. 74. Animals used for food are listed on pp. 80-83, together with the ways in which these are prepared for food. Agricultural methods and crops: pp. 86-92. Utensils used for food processing, or consumption (wooden mortar, pestle; bread tray; fork; ladle): pp. 99-101; saguaro fruit hook: p. 103; stone metates, manos, pestles: pp. 108-110; baskets for grain storage: pp. 143, 144, sieve baskets, food bowls: pp. 145, 146.

7088. Russell, G. 1954. There are many different customs for eating lamb. NWG 44:35.

7089. Russell, Jeffrey Burton. 1968. Medieval civilization. New York: John Wiley.

Food: pp. 487-489.

7090. Russell, John. 1867. The boke of nurture...the boke of keruyng [printed by Wynkyn de Worde...the boke of nurture by Hugh Rhodes. Edited by Frederick J. Furnivall. Bungay, England: The Roxburghe Club.

Food habits of an English noble household of the Fifteenth Century.

7091. Russell, R. 1905. Strength and diet. A practical treatise with special regard to the life of nations. London, New York, Bombay: Longmans, Green & Co.

An encyclopedic work which begins by discussing the merits and appropriateness of animal versus vegetarian diet, and proceeds to a review of diet in history. Chapter Seven 'Diet of races and nations: a general conspectus' is a world-wide ethnographic compilation of food habits. Additional data is provided for dietary practices among religious sects; armies; and in workhouses and prisons. Chapter Eleven is devoted to a disussion of the relationship between diet and the frequency of cancer. Implicated, with corroborative statistics; are excessive meat, coffee, and tea consumption. The data provided throughout the book are fully documented.

7092. Russell, R. Scott, ed. 1966. Radioactivity and human diet. Oxford: Pergamon Press.

7093. Russell, Vilena. A survey of the eating habits of women employed in the Bureau of Ships, Navy Department, Washington, D.C. Master's thesis. University of Txas. 1945.

7094. Rutchik, Rose. 1956. A Kosher dietary department. Hosp Man 82(5): 42-43.

Hospital food service for Jewish patients who observe traditional religious dietary regulations.

7095. Rutishauser, I. H. 1963. Custom and child health in Buganda. Part Four. Food and nutrition. TGM 15:138-147.

Kiganda culture.

7096. Rutland, Joshua. 1895. Eating worms. JPS 4: 207.

Maori. Note on use by elderly Maori man, using fish-bait worm.

7097. Rutot, Aime. 1907. Le cannibalisme a l'epoque des cavernes en Belgique. [Cannibalism during the period of cave occupation in Belgium.] SPF-B 4: 318-326.

7098. Ruus, Poul. 1964. Af et gammelt land-bryggeris saga. P. Kjeldgaard's bryggeri i Fjerritslev. [From the saga of an old country brewer. P. Kjellgaard's brewery in Fjerritslev.] T Arbok Pp. 349-360.

Fjerritslev is located in northwestern Denmark at 57. o6'N., 9. 17E.

7099. Ruyle, J.B. 1938. The effect of the use of maple sugar on the teeth of the prehistoric Indian. N D Health 4:5-9.

Speculative article based on the examination of four hundred crania from central and southern Illinois.

7100. Rwegelera, G.C.C. & Lema, N.T. 1963. Tribal customs in infant feeding 1. Among the Haya. 2. Among the Chagga. EAMJ 40:366-369, 370-375.

7101. Ryan, Brice. 1958. Sinhalese Village. Coral Gables: University of Miami.

Meals and meal times: pp. 38-39.

7102. Ryan James G. 1977. Human nutritional needs and crop breeding objectives in the Indian semi-arid tropics. Hydera bad: International Crops Research Institute for the Semi-Arid Tropics.

Calories, calcium, copper, iron, zinc, vitamins A, and the B complex are the major deficiencies among low-income Indian groups, rather than protein.

7103. Ryder, M.L. 1969. Can one cook in a skin? Antiquity 40:225-227.

Account of an experiment using a sheep skin, based on references to such use in the historical literature. Failure of the water to boil leads to the question: what techniques may have been used historically to effect boiling. Illustration on Plate 40 (facing page 215.

7104. Ryder, M.L. 1969. Paunch cooking. Antiquity 43: 218-220.

Account of an experiment using a sheep's rumen, suspended over flame by a tripod.

7105. Saalfrank, Ingrid. The lexical field of cooking terms in German. Master's thesis. University of Arizona. 1969.

7106. Sabry, Z.I. 1961. Protein foods in Middle Eastern diets. National Academy of Sciences, National Research Council. Publication No. 843. Washington, D.C. National Academy of Sciences.

7107. Saccas, A. 1951. A propos de quelques champignons sur mais. [Concerning several fungi of maize.] RPVEAF 30:161-196.

7108. Saccas, A. 1952. Principaux champignons parasites du mais (Zea mais,L.) en Afrique Equatoriale Francaise. [Principal parasites of maize (Zea mais, L.) in French Equatorial Africa.] AT 7:5-42.

7109. Sack, J. 1912. Vegetables and other products used as food in Surinam. [In Dutch.] P Week 49: 105-113; 129-136.

7110. Sackett, Marjorie. 1962. Folk recipes in Kansas. MF 12: 81-86.

7112. Sackett, S.J. 1972. Folk recipes as a measure of inter-culteral penetration. JAF 85: 77-81.

Examines culture contact in the town of Concordia, Kansas, characterized by a fair range of ethnic diversity. Interviews revealed little inter-cultural penetration.

7113. Sacramento. California State Archives. Letter to George S. Evans, Adjutant General of California. December 20, 1864. [by John G. Mc Cullough.]

McCullough, as Attorney General of California, opines that "cooks of African descent...are entitled to receive from the State the same bounties as volunteers." Reference is to service during the War Between the States.

7114. Sadoun, Roland; Lolli, Giorgio; & Silverman, Milton. 1965. Drinking in French culture. Rutgers Center of Alcohol Studies. New Brunswick: Rutgers University.

7115. Sadow, S.E. 1928. Jewish ceremonials and food customs. JADA 4:91-98.

7116. Saffirio, Luigi. Monophagy in the European Upper Paleolithic. In Gastronomy. The anthropology of food and food habits. Edited by Margaret Louise Arnott. 1975. Pp. 79-88. Paris; The Hague: Mouton Publishers. World Anthropology.

Assumes a predominantly animal protein diet for Cro-Magnon populations, based on available archaeological evidence. Discusses the nutritional implications of such a diet and compares same with traditional circumpolar diets both of which the author sees as functional in the context of climates characterized by low temperatures. A contrast is made with the high lipid-high protein monodiet (camel's milk) of Somali herders, who apparently exhibit no adverse effects as a result of this regimen.

7117. Safford, William Edwin. 1902. Guam and its people. SI-AR-BR for the year 1901. Pp. 493-508.

Food plants, food preparation, cooking methods.

7118. Safford, William Edwin. 1905. The useful plants of the island of Guam. SI-CUNH Vol. 9.

Aboriginal food habits: pp. 98-99; data on preparation of various food plants is found in section titled "Descriptive catalogue of plants": pp. 170-404.

7119. Safford, William Edwin. 916. An economic Amaranthus of ancient America. Science 44:870.

A mustard seed used as food by the Aztecs, called huautli.

7120. Safford, William Edward. Food plants and textiles of ancient America. In Second Pan American Scientific congress. December 27, 1915 to January 8, 1916. Proceedings Vol. 1. Section 1. Anthropology. Edited by Glen Levin Swiggett. 1917. Pp. 146-159.

Maize; quinoa, beans, Lupinus sp.; peanuts; gourds; Annona sp; Solanum muricatum; Cyphomandra sp. Caryocar Amygdaliforme; acrodiclidium Puchury-minor (a substitute for nutmeg); various roots and tubers; Theobroma cacao; Ilex Paraguayensis.

7121. Safford, William E. The isolation of ancient America as established by the cultivated plants and the languages of its aborigenes. In Vigesimo Congreso Internacional de Americanistas. 20 a 30 de Agosto de 1922, Rio de Janeiro. Annaes. 1924. Vol. 1. Pp. 167-171. Rio de Janeiro: Imprensa Nacional.

In support of "isolation", the author states that "...all of the cultivated plants encountered at the time of its discovery had been evolved from endemic species... [and] ... none of these American plants had found its way to Europe, Asia, or Africa before the time of Columbus". In support of the Southeast Asian origin of the coconut, the author notes the absence of the coconut crab Birgus latro in America.

7122. Safford, William Edwin. 1925. Foods discovered with America. SM 21: 181-186.

7123. Safford, William Edwin. 1926. Potato of romance and reality. SI-AR for 1925. Pp. 509-532.

7124. Sagan, Eli. 1974. Cannibalism: human aggression and cultural forms. New York; Evanston; San Francisco; London: Harper & Row. Harper Torchbooks.

7125. Sagna, A. 1962. Recettes culinaires Senegalaises. [Senegalese culinary recipes.] Dakar: Societe Africaine d'Edition.

7126. Saha, A.L. 1968. Dietary and nutritional patterns in certain rural areas of India. IDA-J 3: 8-15.

7127. Saha, T.K.; Chatterjee, S.B. & Chaudhuri, R.N. 1960. Lathyrism in a rural area of West Bengal. CSTM-B 8:98-99.

7128. Sahu, D.R.N. & Bose, A.N. 1932. The calcium content of the common dietaries in India. IMG 67:140-141.

7129. Saillans, Maurice Edmond (Curnonsky). 1936. Anthologie de la gastronomie francaise. [Anthology of French gastronomy.] Paris: Editions Delagrave.

7130. Saint Blanquat, H. de. 1960. L'alimentation medieval: une reve de ripaille. [Medieval diet: a dream of feasting.] Equilibre 4: 13-16.

7131. Saint-Germain, J. 1975. Characteristiques des habitudes alimentaires des francais qui vecurent sous le regene de Louis XIV. [Characteristics of the food habits of the French under the reign of Louis XIV.] Historia No. 42. Pp. 52-62.

7132. Saint-Pere, M. 1923. La culture et le traitement du riz dans le cercle de Guidmaka. [Cultivation and processing of rice in the Guidimaka Circle.] CEHS-AOF-B P. 376.

7133. Sakamoto, Nobuko. 1977. The People's Republic of China Cookbook. New York: Random House.

Recipes translated from three major contemporary Chinese Mainland cookbooks. In addition to explanations of the characteristics of regional cuisines, basic preparation methods are described. Major restaurants currently operating and their specialities are listed for each region.

7134. Sakr, Ahmad H. Amio acid patterns of some wild edible plants growing in Lebanon. Master's thesis. Beirut: American University. 1961.

7135. Sakr, Ahmad H. 1971. Dietary regulations and food habits of Muslims. JADA 58: 123-126.

7136 Saksena, R.R. 1953. Food habits of India. JADA 29:1009.

Brief sketch of regional foods, and preparation techniques.

7137. Salaman, Redcliffe N. 1943. The influence of the potato on the course of Irish history. Dublin: Browne & Nolan.

7138. Salaman, Redcliffe N. 1946. The early European potato: its character and place of origin. LSL (B)a-J 53:1-27.

Concludes that there is one species of potato with the chromosome formula 2n=48 called Solanum Andigenum, and that the term Solanum tuberosum is convenient for indicating specialization which has overtaken varieties derived from S. andigenum group forms in Europe, the Island of Chiloe, off the southwestern coast of Chile, and the Chilean mainland. The place of origin of the European potato is suggested as being in the northern extremity of the distribution area of S. andigenum with Columbia the most likely location. It is most probable the potato left some northern port in South America, possible Cartagena, and that at least one importation reached Spain, at the port of Seville, not later than 1569.

7139. Salaman, Redcliffe N. 1949. The history and social influence of the potato. Cambridge: Cambridge University Press.

7140. Salaman, Redcliffe N. 1952. The social influence of the potato. SA 187 (6):50-52.

A brief history of the potato in Peru, and Europe.

7141. Salamone, L. 1957. Primi risultati de una inchiesta alimentare in Sicilia. [First results of a dietary inquiry in Sicily.] SIBS-B 33: 1278-1280.

7142. Salas, Julio Cesar. 1919. El mito de la antropofagia. [The myth of anthropophagy.] Indica 1: 126-130.

7143. Salas, Julio Cesar. 1921. Los indios caribes: estudio sobre el origen del mito de la antropofagia. [The Carib Indiams: study on th origin of the myth of anthropophagy.] Barcelona: Talleres Graficos Lux.

7144. Salas, Mariano Picon. 1953. Pequena historia de la arepa. [Short history of arepa] El Farol 14:2-5.

The Venezuelan 'tortilla', made of maize but thicker, and smaller in diameter.

7145. Sale, J.W. & Skinner, W.W. 1919. Composition and food value of bottled soft drinks. USDA-YB for the year 1918. Pp. 115-122.

Disscusses method of manufacture, and includes data on consuption.

7146. Saletore, Bhasker Anand. 1934. Social and political life in Vijayanagra Empire (A.D. 1346 -A.D. 1646). 2 Vols. Madras: B.G. Paul.

Food: Vol. 1 Pp. 305 - 308.

7147. Saleun, G. 1949. L'alimentation et la nutrition pour les territoires d'Afrique. [Diet and nutrition for the African territories.] CFI No. 114. Pp. 24-25.

7148. Salisbury, R.; Hyman, J.; Elberg, N.; & Elliot, R.; Tanner, A.; & Spence, J.A. 1972. Not by bread alone. The subsistence economies of the people of Fort George, Paint Hills, Eastmain, Great Whale, Fort Chilmo, and Nitchequon Band from Mistassini. Prepared for the James Bay Task Force of the Indians of Quebec Association and the Northern Quebec Inuit Association. Montreal.

7149. Salledo, Maria Ju[p?]anda. Utilization of the fresh-water fish of the Bicol Region. Master's theses. Home Economics. Phillippine Women's University. 1957.

Philippines.

7150. Salonen, Armas. 1961. Die Hausgerate der alten Mesopotamier. Nach Sumerisch-Akkadischen Quellen. Eine lexikal und Kulthurgeschichtliche Untersuchungen. [Household utensils of ancient Mesopotamia. From Sumerian-Akkadian sources. A lexical and culture-historical investigation.] Helsinki: Suomalainen Tiedakatemian Toimituksia.

7151. Salzmann, L.F. 1914. Medicval cookery. Blackwoods's 196: 765-773.

Determination of some old English foods and cookery techniques.

7152. Sammapuddhi, K 1962. Some food plants in the forests of Thailand. In Ninth Pacific Science Congress. 18 November to 9 December, 1957. Chulalongkorn University, Bankok. Proceedings (Botany) Vol. 4. Pp. 309-311.

7153. Sampaio, A.J.de. 1944. A alimentacao sertaneja e do interior da Amazonia. Onomastica da alimentacao rural. [Diet in the Brazilian out-back and in the interior of the Amazon region. List of names of rural food.] Biblioteca Pedagogia Brasileira. Series 5a. Vol. 238. Sao Paulo: Companhia Editora Nacional.

Regional food habits, with sketches of cooking utensils and food preparation methods.

7154. Sampalmieri, A. 1968. Francesco Calori, medico condottto bolognese studiose della pellagra. [Francesco Calori, municipal doctor of Bologna and specialist on pellagra.] CPSM 17: 175-181.

7155. Sampson, Dexter R. 1954. On the origin of oats. HU-BM-L 16: 265-303.

Part Four: "Oats and man", provides a brief review of archaeological evidence, and the historical literature. No conclusive statement as to the origin of oats, the author writes, can be made, beyond broad generalizations.

7156. Sampson, H.C. 1936. Cultivated crop plants of the British Empire and Anglo-Egyptiana Sudan (tropical and subtropical). GB-RBGK-BMI-AS No. 12.

7157. Samson, Jr., Pablo. 1966. Food consumption demonstration survey. Stat Rep 8: 713.

Review of a demonstration survey carried out in Barrio San Guillermo of Morong, Rizal, Phillipines, for participants of the Food and Agriculture Organization of the United Nations Training Center on Food Consump tion Surveys for Asia and the Far East, 3 November to 8 November, 1964.

7158. Samuelson, G., et al. 1971. An epidemiological study of child health and nutrition in a northern Swedish county. 6. Relationship between general and oral health, food habits, and socioeconomic conditions. AJCN 42: 1361-1373.

7159. Sancho, Nieves de Hoyos. 1947. Gazpachos, migas y sopas de ajo. [Gazpachos, croutons and garlic soups.] El Espanol No. 233.

7160. Sandell, H.J. The effect of a mid-morning lunch upon the subsquent behavior of nursery school children. Master's thesis. Iowa State College. 1938.

7161. Sanders, Cynthia. Diet, nutrition, and biculturation among Vietnamese refugees residing in a mid-western city. Master's thesis, Anthropology. Lawrence, Kansas: University of Kansas. 1977.

7162. Sanders, George P. 1969. Cheese varieties and descriptions. USDA - HB No. 54. Revised.

An alpabetical description of the history, manufacture, chemical composition and area of origin of over four hundred cheeses.

7163. Sanderson, Stewart F. Magic formulae used in fishing. Paper presented at 9th International Congrss of Anthropological and Ethnological Sciences. 28 August to 8 September, 1973. Chlcago, Illinois.

A survey of songs and formulae believed to attract fish, in use among Breton fishermen; in the Marquesas; Philipines; Cook Islands; Hudson Bay; Greenland, and scattered examples from the Mediterranean to Scandinavia.

7164. Sandin, Benedict. 1961. Gawai antu: Sea Dyak feast of the departed spirits. SARMJ 10: 170-190.

Palm beverage; rice foods: pp. 175, 179.

7165. Sando, Gene. Methods for determining food preferences of elementary school children. Their development and use. Master's thesis. Ohio State University. 1948.

7166. Sands, Louisa B. 1956. Indian bread N MEX 34: 22-23.

7167. Sands, Louisa B. 1957. Good eating Indian style. N MEX 35: 59.

7168. Sandre. 1907. Report on the manufacture and sale of vermicelli called song-than and ho-tieu. [In French] SEIC-B 10: 805-808. Noodles manufactured from Phaseolus radiatus, Dolichos albus, Oryza sativa, and Manihot esculenta.

7169. Sandstead, Harold R.; McGanity, William J.; Smith, Hugh H.; McKinely, Pauline; Tineche, Laverne; & Darby, William J. 1956. A study of the dietary background and nutriture of the Navajo Indian. 3. Physical findings. JN 60: 35-62.

7170. Sanford, R.N. 1937. The effects of abstinence from food upon imaginal process: a further experiment. JP 3: 145-159.

In a preliminary experiment, ten children, when presented with words for association and ambiguous pictures for interpretation, gave significantly more "food responses" (responses associated with food) immediately before a regular meal than they gave shortly after a regular meal. This result was taken as evidence in support of the hypothsis that imaginal processes depend upon the needs of the organism.

7171. San Francisco, California. American Indian Historical Society. American Indian use of plants. A comprehensive bibliography with an instructional module component for classroom discussion. Prepared for American Indian Historical Society. [by Hurly Parkhurst (Sac &Fox)]. March 31, 1971.

7172. Sangar, S.p. 1962. Domestic life in the 16th Century as reflected in the literature of Sur Das. IHQ 38: 29-43.

Food and beverages: pp. 38-41. India.

7173. Sanielevici, H. 1912. Die Ernahrung als Hauptfaktor der Rassen-Differenzierung.[Diet as a primary factor in racial differences.] AAnz 41: 523-525.

7174. Sanjur, Diva. undated. Puerto Rican food habits. 35mm slide set. Visual Communications Office. Ithaca, New York: Cornell University.

7175. Sanjur, Diva. undated. Puerto Rican food habits : a sociocultural approach. (looseleaf notebook). Duplicating services, MVR Hall. Ithaca, New York: Cornell University.

7176. Sanjur, Diva M. A sociocultural approach to the study of infant feeding practices and weaning habits in a Mexican community. Ph. D. dissertation. Ithaca, New York: Cornell Universithy. 1968.

7177. Sanjur, Diva. 1974. Food ideology systems as conditioners of nutritional practices. ALN 24: 47-64.

Studies the influence of the 'hot-cold' classification system on nutrition in three Spanish-speaking communities; particularly in regard to childhood illness; pregnancy; and post-partum sequence. Stresses the need to understand food beliefs, and the need to help people improve rather than change their food havits.

7178. Sanjur, Diva M.; Cravioto, Joaquin; Rosales, L.; & Van Veen, Andre G. 1970. Infant feeding and weaning practices in a rural pre-industrial setting - a socio-cultural approach. A P Scan-S No. 200.

Mexico.

7179. Sanjur, Diva M.; Cravioto, Joaquin; & Van Veen, Andre G. 1970. Infant nutrition and socio-cultural influences in a village in central Mexico. TGM 22: 443-451.

7180. Sanjur, Diva M.; Cravioto, Joquin; Van Veen, Andre G., & Rosales, L. 1971. La alimentacion des los lactantes y el destete en un medio rural preindustrial. Estudio desde el punto de vista sociocultural. [Infant feeding and weaning practices in a rural, pre-industrial setting. A socio-cultural approach.] OSP-B 71: 281-339.

Study of one hundred twenty-five infants in a village located sixty-five miles southwest of Mexico City. Charcteristics of the pre-industrial social setting are examined, and correlated with nutritional, health, and disease variables.

7181. Sanjur, Diva & Scoma, A.D. 1971. Food habits of low-income children in northern New York. JNE 2: 85-95.

7182. Santa Maria, Julio V. 1935. Algunas observaciones sobre la alimentacion hospitalaria. [Some observations on hospital diets.] RMV 1: 395-406.

Considers economic, dietetic, culinary and physiological aspects. Daily consumption figures are included for several Chilean hospitals.

7183. Santa Maria, Julio V. 1941. Caracteristicas de alimentacion en Chile. [Characteristics of dietary in Chile.] RMC 69: 308-322.

7184. Santa Maria, Julio V. 1949. Caracteristicas de nuestros habitos alimentarios. [Characteristics of our food habits.] RMA 2: 71-83.

Lists typical Chilean foods, beverages, and cookery methods. Comments on causes of regional variations.

7185. Santandrea, S. 1961. Alimentazione Africana come primo, peggio di prima. [Nutrition in Africa: as before-worse than before.] Nigrizia 7: 32-34.

7186. Santiana, Antonia. Dental abrasion among South American Indians. [Author's summary of text.] In Thirtieth International Congress of Americanists. 18-23 August, 1952. Cambridge, England. Proceedings. [1953] Pp. 249.

Notes that the primary reason for dental abrasion is found in diet, especially that which is composed of roots, tubers, especially raw, semi-raw, or toasted maize; and of semi-raw flesh which may contain sand and other foreign matter.

7187. Santos, F.O. 1930. Problems in Filipino nutrition. PIMA-J 10: 121-129.

7188. Santos, F.O. Studies on the plane of nutrition of families of laborers in Calabanga, Camarones Sur. Paper read at 4th Philippine Science Convention. 23 February, 1937.

7189. Santos, F.O. & Adriano, F.T. 1929. The chemical composition of Philippine food material. Manila: Public Welfare Association.

7190. Santos, F.O. & Demetrio, J.K. 1939. Studies on the food of Labourers' families in Macrohon, Leyte. Pag 28: 15-24.

7191. Santos,F.O. & Pidlaoan, N.A. 1933. Food of male inmates of Bilibid Prison. PIMA-J 13: 493-501.

7192. Santos, F.O. & Pidlaoan, N.A. 1937. The chemical analysis of the food of the children in Welfareville. PAg 25: 812-816.

Welfareville is a government child-care institution located in San Felipe Neri, Rizal, ten kilometers from Manila. Sample menu for one week is included. Study samples were recorded during a six months period, January to July, 1934. Children are minor offender males, aged 10-21 years.

7193. Santos Reis, C. & Coutinho da Costa, F.M. 1961. A alimentacao dos Manjacos. [Diet of the Mandyaka.] BCGP 16: 377-0504.

7194. Sapper, Karl Theodor. 1902. Speise und Trank Der Kekchiindianer. [Food and drink of the Kekchi Indians.] Globus 80: 259-k263.

Guatemala.

7195. Saarasin, Fritz. 1926-1927. Uber den Kannibalismus in New-Kaledonia. [On cannibalism in New-Caledonia.] SGAE-B 3: 9-13.

7196. Sarcinella, F. 1939. Problems of nutrition of natives in Italian East Africa. [In Italian.] RSAOI 1: 83-107.

7197. Sariola, Sakari. 1954. Drinking patterns in Finnish Lapplan. Helsinki: Finnish Foundation for Alcohol Studies.

7198. Sarmento, A. 1953. Nutrition of the Huambos. [In Portuguese.] IMTR-A 10: 1113-1127.

Portuguese Angola.

7199. Sarson, H.S. 1943. Fermented liquors in old-time cooking. Nature (L) 152; 386.

7200. Sasportas, Leon, 1924. La "popoi" des iles Marquises [The popoi of the Marquesas Islands.] RETP 5: 80-82.

Preparation of popoi; and the text of the French song sung during the preparation of breadfruit which is allowed to ferment before being eaten.

7201. Sastroamidjojo, S. 1954. Egg as foodstuff for man. HZ 61: 357-377.

7202. Sato, T., Et at. 1968. Factor analysis of nutrient - intake in some districts in Shikoku with special reference to the relationship between factor - loading matrix of nutrients and food habits. TJEM 15: 165-175.

7203. Sauer, Carl O. American agricultural origins: a consideration of nature and culture. In Essays in anthropology presented to A.L. Kroeber. Edited by Robert H. Lowie. 1936. Pp. 279-297. Berkely: University of California Press.

7204. Sauer, CArl O. 1950. Cultivated plants of South and Central America. In Handbook of South American Indians. SI-BAE-B No. 143. Vol. Six Pp. 487-544.

7205. Sauer, Carl O. Age and area of America cultivated plants. In 33° Congreso Internacional de Americanistas. 20-27. Julio 1958. San Jose, Costa Rica. Actas. Vol One. 1959. Pp. 215-229. San Jose, Costa Rica: Lehamann.

Reviews the areas of origin of New World food crops, the geographical and ecological bases of the limits of their distribution: causes and effects of vegetative planting; the relationship of the nutritive value of domesticated crops (largely carbohydrate) to available protein resources; the diversity of starch foods; limits of vegetative planting; development and dispersal of Mesoamerican seed plants.

7206. Sauer, Carl O. 1969. Seeds, spades, hearths, and herds: the domestication of animals and foodstuffs. 2nd edition. Cambridge: Massachusetts Institute of Technology Press.

7207. Sauer, Jonathan Deininger. 1950. The grain amaranths: a survey of their history and classification. MBG-A 37: 561-632.

History, cultivation, and use in the Old and New Worlds. Includes data indicating possible food use in the southwestern area of the United States: p. 563.

7208.   Sauer, Jonathan Deininger. 1969. Identity of archaeological grain amaranths from the Valley of Tehuacan, Puebla, Mexico. Am An 43: 80-81.

7209.   Saul, Frank P.   Disease and the ancient Maya: Some biocultural ramifications. Paper presented at 9th International Congrss of Anthropological and Ethnological Sciences.   28 August to 8 September, 1973.   Chicago, Illinois.

Selected aspects of the differentiation of the Maya are reviewed, using skeletal remains from Altar de Sacrificios, Seibal, and other sites.   Vogt's "genetic model" and Comas' findings of "somatic heterogeneity" are discussed in respect to the author's research on chronological context; skeletal indications of continuity and discontinuity; and disease patterns. The biocultural ramifications of disease (especially nutritional disease) in the Maya are emphasized. Pathological lesions (enamel hypoplasia, porotic or spongy hyperostosis, ossified subperiosteal hemorrhages in conjunction with periodontal degeneration, etc.) are examined in the light of their disease implications.   Decline in stature is contrasted with dental genetic continuity and tentatively related to diet and social class. Cultural factors are considered both in regard to setting the scene for the advent of disease and in regard to the effects of disease upon Maya culture in relation to its decline.

7210.   Saunders, Charles Francis.   9134.   Useful wild plants of the United States and Canada.   New York: Robert M. McBride.

7211.   Saunier, P. 1976.   Les determinants economiques et sociaux de la nourriture dans le long terme: l'alimentation des familles ouvrieres urbaines. [Socio-economic determinants of nutrition over the long-term: the diet of urban working-class families.] ANA 30: 439-446.

Examines and compares urban French working-class diet with that of Great Britain and Germany from ca. 1900 to early 1972. Food prices are seen to be dependent on specific economic restraints.   Changes in food sources of nutrients; population size; salary size; family size; agriculture; and housing costs are considered.

7212.   Sauvage, H.-E.   Note sur un Kjoekkenmoedding situe pres de L'embouchure de la Somme. [Note on a kitchen-midden located near the mouth of the Somme.] In 5^e Congres International d'Anthropologie et d'Archeologie Prehistorique. 1871. Bologne. Compte Rendu. Bologna: Imprimerie Fava et Garagnani.

Includes a list of animals' remains.

7213.   Sauvage, H.-E. La peche dans le Midi de la France pendant l'epoque du Renne.   [Fishing in the south of France during the reindeer age.]   In 7^e Congres International d'Anthropologie S& d' Archeologie Prehistoriques 1874.   Stockholm.   Compte Rendu. Vol. One. 1876. Pp. 55-61. Stockholm: P.A. Norstedt & Soner.

Reviews the occurence of fishing and species of fish in various areas of the world, and concludes with a discussion of archaeological and other evidence of fishing in the Midi.

7214.   Savage, Landor, A. Henry. 1895, Corea or Cho-sen, the land of morning calm.   London: William Heineman.

Brief description of rice preparation, and of foods mixed with rice.

7215.   Savard, Remi. 1965. La differentiation des activites sexuelles et alimentaires; (representations mystiques esquimaudes et indiennes.) [Diffenentiation of sex-role and food activities; Eskimo and Indian mystic displays.] Anthropologica (0) 7: 39-58.

A structural analysis based on Eskimo and Native American Mythic material.

7216.   Save, K.J. 1945.   The Warlis. Bombay: Padma Publishing Co.

An aboriginal tribe of the Thana District, Bombay State.   Food habits: pp. 10-11.

7217.   Saw, Chee Leng. Spice cultivation in early Penang, 1786-1835. Bachelor's thesis. History. University of Singapore. 1957.

Malaysia.

7218.   Sawa, S. 1900-1902.   Note on hamanato, a kind of vegetable cheese. T-IU-CA-B 4: 419-426.

7219.   Sawamura, S. The diet of the Japanese. In Deuxieme Congres International d'Hygiene Alimentaire et de L'Alimentation Rationelle de l'Homme. 4-8 Octobre, 1910. Bruxelles. Rapports et Communications. 1910. Vol. 1. Section 1. Pp. 215-230.

Lists vegetable and animal foods; alcoholic beverages; and spices. National food consumption statistics for 1908 are given. Methods of cooking and meals patterns are described and a nutrient analysis of some Japanese foods is given.

7220.   Saxena, Ranvir Prakash.   Tribal economy in Madhya Bharat.   Ph.D. dissertation. Economics. Agra University. 1957.

Bhil culture.

7221.   Saxena, Ranvir Prakash. 1964. Tribal economy in Central India. Calcutta: K.L. Mukopadhyay.

Food preparation among the Bhils of Madhya Bharat: Pp. 24-25.

7222.   Sayce, R.U.   1946.   Food through the ages.
MC-PC-T   49: 1-25.

Great Britain.

7223.   Sayce, R.U. 1948-1949.   Food from the
highland zone of Britain in the 18th Century. Folk-
liv 12-13: 199-207.

7224.   Sayers, G.;   Lipschitz, D.A.; Sayers, M.;
Seftel, H.C.; Bothwill, T.H.; & Charlton, R.W. 1974.
Relationship between pica and iron nutrition in
Black Johannesburg adults. SAMJ 48: 1655-1660.

7225.   Scarborough, J. 1970.   Diphilus of Siphnos
and Hellenistic medical dietetics.   JHM   25: 194-
201.

7226.   Schaefer, Arnold E.   1966.   Observations
from exploring needs in national nutrition programs.
AJPH 56: 1088-1096.

Reviews results of nutrition surveys undertaken by the United States Interdepartmental Committee on Nutrition for National
Defense in various nations. Emphasizes the
relationship between public health agencies
and nutrition education on the broadest
scale.

7227.   Schaefer, Arnold E.   1969.   The national
nutrition survey. JADA 4: 371-375.

7228.   Schaefer, Arnold E. & Johnson, Ogden C.
1969. Are we well fed? NT 4: 2-11

7229.   Schaefer, Otto. 1959. Medical obsevations
and problems in the Canadian arctic.   Part Two.
CMAJ 81: 386-393.

Section One 'Nutrition and nutritional deficiencies' notes the deleterious effects of
Western diet; and a change from breast to
bottle feeding on Eskimo diet.   Suggests
that discontinuance of breast-feeding effects lactation-stimulation/ovulation-suppr-
ession relationship by shortenting the lactation period with concommitant increase in
childbirths.   Shortening of lactation period
is also implicated in breast cancer increase.
Comments on the practice of pre-mastication of infant food as a source of supplementary minerals.   Reference community is
Pangnirtung Northwest Territories, Canada.

7230.   Schaefer, Otto. Changing dietary patterns
of Indian and Inuit.   Nutritional consquences and
opportunities for imporvement. Paper presented at
Medial Services Nutrition Policy Planning Seminar.
Ottawa. Health and Welfare, Canada. 1977.

7231.   Schaefer, Robert B. 1978.   Factors affecting food behavior and quality of husbands' and
wives' diets. JADA 72: 138-143.

Interviews among couples in two non-metro-
politan towns in the midwestern United
States indicated the wife, and her awareness
of her food preferences, were primary
influences on family diet quality.   Wives

considered cost to be a major influence on
dietary quality, and the greater the concern
for cost, the poorer the observed diet.

7232.   Schaeffer, Claude Everett. The subsistence
quest of the Kutenai; a study of the interaction of
culture and environment. Ph.D Dissertation. University of Pennsylvania. 1940.

7233.   Schaeffer, Hans-Helmut. 1963. Pflanzen
der Kanarischen Inseln - Plants of the Canary
Islands. Bilingual edition. English section translated by F.J. McKie.   Lubeck: Wullenwever-Druck
Heine K.G.

Edible plants and fruit noted.

7234.   Schaik, Theodora F.S.M. van. 1964. Food
and nutrition relative to family life. JHE 56:225-
232.

Reviews the various cultural, sociological,
psychological and economic variables which
determine quantity, and quality of, and attitudes toward food in the home; appetite;
and nutritional status. The author observes
that in advisory work and education, account should be taken of the changing function of the family with regard to nutrition
and the changing culture.

7235.   Schaller, George B.   The behavior of the
mountain gorilla. In Primate behavior: field studies
of monkeys and apes. Edited by Irven DeVore. 1965.
New York: Holt, Rhinehart & Winston.

Mentions geophagy amog gorillas.

7236.   Schapera, Isaac. 1968. The Tswana. Ethnographic survey of Africa. Southern Africa. Part 3.
London: International African Institute.

Food production: pp. 21-25.

7237.   Schapera, Isaac & Goodwin, A.J.H.   Work
and wealth: foodstuffs.   In The Bantu-speaking
tribes of South Africa.   Edited by Isaac Schapera.
1937. London: G. Routledge & Sons.

Commodities and their production; foodstuffs; horticulture; animal husbandry; hunting:
pp. 131-142; household utensils: pp. 145-148;
produce: pp. 159-160.

7238.   Schapiro, H.L. 1919. Jewish dietary problems. JHE 11:47-59.

Dietary habits deriving from religious food
prescriptions. Contains suggestions for dietary modification within the framework of
permitted foods.

7239.   Scharfbillig, Christian. 1948. Genussmittel
als Arzneien: Tee.   [Condiments as therapeutics:
tea.] Kosmos 44:245-248.

7240.   Scheben, B. 1880. Die Kunst der Brauer in
Koln in ihren innern Wesen und Wirken, nebst den im
Jahre 1603 erneuerten uralten Ordnungen und dem
1497 Amtsbriefe. Nach meist ungebrudten Quellen

berarbeiten.   [The brewer's art at Cologne; its essence and function.   Together with the ancient regulations as renewed in 1603, and the official charter of 1497.   Based largely on sources never before used.] Koln: Boisseree.

7241.   Schechter, Elaine J.   Time devoted to housework and its division by sex and age: a videotape analysis. Presented at Annual Meeting of the American Anthropological Association. 14 to 18 November, 1978. Los Angeles, California.

7242.   Scheinfeld, Sandra J.P.   Malnutrition and poverty in the United States: a Chicago case study. Ph.D. dissertation.   Geography.   University of Chicago. 1976.

7243.   Scheltema, Anne Marie Peter August. 1936. The food consumption of the native inhabitants of Java and Madura.   Translated by A.H. Hamilton. Report A. in the International Research Series of the Institute of Pacific Relations issued under the auspices of the National Council for the Netherlands and the Netherlands Indies. Batavia: Ruygrok & Co.

> This is a socio-economic study. A brief overview of native diet is contained in the Introduction. Historical material is covered in Chapter Two.   Changes in diet with respect to specific foodstuffs are examined in Chapter Three. Data on food consumption of various occupational groups are presented in Chapter Four (pp. 31-35). Chapter Five looks at factors influencing diet.

7244.   Schenk, Sara M. & Gifford, Edward Winslow. 1952. Karok ethnobotany. UCal-AR 13:377-392.

7245.   Schery, Robert W. 1947. Manioc - a tropical staff of life. EB 1:21-25.

7246.   Schery, Robert W. 1952. Part Four. Plants and plant parts used primarily for food and beverage. In Plants for man. New York: Prentice-Hall.

7247.   Shevchenko, M.G. 1968. Iz istorii razvitiya sanitarnogo nadzora v oblasti gigieny pitaniya posle Velkoi Oktyabr'skoi sosialisticheskoi revoliutsii. [From the history of the development of sanitary inspection in the area of food hygiene after the Great October Revolution.] VP 27(3): 7-11.

7248.   Scheving, L.E.; Burns, E.R.; Pauly, J.E.; Tsai, S.; & Halberg, F. 1976.   Meal scheduling, cellular rhythms and the chronotherapy of cancer. Chronobiologia 1:80. Abstract of a paper presented at 10th International Congress of Nutrition. August, 1975. Kyoto.

> Cell division for all mammalian tissues is characterized by prominent circadian oscillation, which has been repeatedly documented for both the synthesis and mitotic stages of the cell cycle.   Normally, in rodents, these rhythms are synchronized to the environmental light-dark cycle; in man, the social routine plays a dominant role. Many of those engaged in cell kinetic investiga-

tions have paid little or no attention to this inherent fluctuation. We have demonstrated that, in vivo, cell cycle time cannot reliably be determined without considering this basic rhythmic phenomenon.   More recently, it has been demonstrated in mice that by restricting the daily availability of food to four hour spans, one can override the synchronizing effect of the light-dark cycle; and the prominent circadian DNA synthesis rythms in bone marrow, duodenum, and spleen will become synchorinized to meal timing. Such information can be used advantageously in shielding those organs that normally are adversely affected by radiotherapy and chemotherapy. Synchronizing by meal timing may make chronotherapy of cancer logistically feasible for man.

7249.   Schiedlausky, G. 1961. Tee, Kaffee, Schokolade, ihr Eintritt in die europaische Gesellschaft. [Tea, coffee, and chocolate, their appearance in European culture.] Bilder aus deutscher Vegangenheit. Vol. 17. Munich: Prestel.

7250.   Schieffelin, Edward L.   Sorry, brother, I don't eat that° Food taboos: the implication for symbolic systems in social process. Paper presented at 9th International Congress of Anthropological and Ethnological Sciences.   28 August to 8 September, 1973. Chicago, Illinois.

> The Kaluli people of the Australian Territory of Papua communicate affection and friendship through giving and sharing food, particularly meat. However, although they live in a tropical forest abundant with game, they also prohibit the eating various types of animals. These taboos are explained in terms of their own understanding of the operation of natural processes, together with their fear of ill-health if taboos are not respected.

> Since food is a symbolic medium of the expression of personal identification between people, however, food prohibitions affect relations on the social level, inhibiting certain relationship and channeling others in a way that promotes affinal ties over other kinds of bonds in the society. Kaluli explanations of food taboos, as well as the final ties these taboos promote revolve about Kaluli concepts of women as dangerous and debilitating on the one hand, and as the domestic wife, on the other. Management of food is seen as the symbolic means by which both views of woman are reconciled.   Further, it is through women that the entire society is articulated, in terms of reciprocity in food.

7251.   Schiemann, Elisabeth. 1951. New results on the history of cultivated cereals. Heredity 5: 305-318.

> Aspects covered are: gene centers; modes of evolution; wheat from collections made in the Hindu Kush (mid-30's); and barley (Tibet, 1934);   criticism of Vavilov's gene-center

theory; biological understanding of the gene centers in mountains (temperature shocks as mutation inducing); the identity of center of origin with center of diversity; the importance of Vavilov's work; origin of hexaploid wheats; new material from archeological sources: Near East; Egypt; Europe; the origins of agriculture.

7252.   Schindlmayr, A. & Goszner, G. 1952. Kuchengewr uz. [Cooking spices.] Munich: J.F. Schreiber.

7253.   Schlegel, H.G., et al. 1970. Microorganisms in the service of human nutrition.   [In German.] ZBPIH 212:303-317.

7254.   Schlegal, Stuart A.   The Tiruray zodiac: The celestial calendar of a Philippine hill people. Paper presented at 68th Annual Meeting of the American Anthropological Association.   20 to 23 November, 1968. New Orlean, Louisiana.

The Tiruray are a swidden farming group inhabiting the Cotabato Cordillera of southwestern Mindanao. Their calender is described as well as its role in making critical agricultural decisions. The problem of the drift of sidereal from solar time is considered, and the Tiruray solution is clarified.

7255.   Schlegel, Stuart A. & Guthrie, Helen A. 1973. Diet and the Tiruray shift from swidden to plow farming. EFN 2: 181-191.

The Tiruray are a Philippine group whose traditional habitat has been the forested hills of the Cotabato Cordillera, Southwestern Mindanao.   With exploitation of the forests, their mode of agriculture is changing.   This paper studies two Tiruray communities, one of which still follows the traditional life style of swidden farming, with access to wild game and plants; the other of which is now in a deforested area, and consequently dependent on external markets for purchasable foods. A comparison of the dietaries of the two communities reveals that the greater variety of foods among the traditional swidden group is not nutritionally superior to that of the peasant group - a fact which is in contradiction to the feelings of the latter group. An extensive list of Tiruray animal and plant foods is given, together with the portions of each used.   Nutritive values of diets of both groups is compared with recommended daily allowances established at the national level.

7256.   Schleiden, M. I.   1873.   Die Kofe. Geschichte und Symbolik in ethnographie und kultur historie, [Coffee. History, and symbolism in ethnography and culturehistory.] Leipzig: Engelmann.

7257.   Schleiden, M.I. 1875.   Das Salz. Seine Geschichte, seine symbolik und seine Bedeutung in Menschenleben. [Salt.   Its history, its symbolism, and its meaning in human life.] Leipzig: Skizze.

7258.   Schlesier, E. 1961. Zum Problem einer Sago-verwertenden Kulturschicht auf Neu-guinea. [On the problem of a sago-using cultural stratum of New Guinea.[ZE 86: 224-233.

7259.   Schlettwein - Gsell, D. 1968. Changes in the nutrition of single women after the age of 70. [In German] Gerontologia 14: 216-223.

7260.   Schloser, Frank. 1906. The greedy book. A gastronomical anthology. London: Gay and Bird.

7261.   Schluckebier, Friedrich Wilhelm. 1964. Allerlei Kummer Mit Kase. Betrachtung ubver ein altherkommliches Nahrungsmittel.   [The trouble with cheese.   Reflections on a traditonal food.] HKG Pp. 57-58.

7262.   Schlutter, Otto B. 1916.   Beer bees. DN 4: 307.

Etymology of bee Old English baes (=Old Teutonic *bait-ti fermentum.)

7263.   Schmid, Robert.   Cinematographie de la faim.   [Hunger in the cinema.]   In Economie alimentaire du globe.   Essai d' interpretation. Michel Cepede & Maurice Lengelle. 1953. Pp. 626-632. Paris: Librairie de Medicis.   Editions M.-Th. Genin.

The first section lists popular, commercial films, in which hunger is the main, or one of the primary themes.   The second section lists films in which hunger is a theme used in support of propagandistic or quasi-propagandistic ends. A third section enumerates films in which hunger is portrayed from a sociological perspective. A fourth listing gives the titles of films in which hunger is an ancillary focus. Sixteen millimeter films on the subject of nutrition and health are next indicated, followed by films illustrating nutrition problems in relation to world economics.   A final section lists films showing the distribution of food to populations suffering from famine or malnutrition.

7264.   Schmideberg, Melitta.   1938.   Intellectual inhibition and disturbances in eating. IJP-A 19: 17-22.

Application of psychoanalytic theory to food-related problems.

7265.   Schmidt, C. Rowena. 1925. The psychology of child nutrition. JHE 17: 260-264.

Study done at Detroit's Merrill-Palmer Nursery School. Indicates food habits are acquired, not inherited.   Notes significance of children's imitation of adult food behavior.

7266.   Schmidt, C. Rowena.   1929.   Good food habits for children. USDA-L. No. 42.

North American attitudes toward food habits socialization.

7267.   Schmidt, E. 1937. Controle de l'alimentation au moyen age. [Control of food in the Middle
Ages.] Nature (P) 65: 129-130.

7268.   Schmidthaus, Karl. 1964. Aus Berichten
des Archivs fur Westfalische Volkskunde, Munster
(Westfalia). Essen und Trinken. Der Tageslauf im
Haushalt. [From the reports of the Archives for
Westphalian Folklore, Munster (Westphalia). Eating
and drinking. Daily course of the household.] RWZV
11: 89-102.

7269.   Schmitt, F. 1927. Les parfums employes
dans l'alimentation. [Perfumes sused in food.] RPC
30: 161-166, 203-207; 321-326.

7270.   Schmitt, Martin. 1952. "Meat's meat:" An
account of flesh-eating habits of Western Americans. WF 11: 185-203.

  Food eaten by pioneers in Western United
  States.

7271.   Schmitz, Carl A. 1958. Zum Problem des
Kannibalismus in nordlichen Neuguinea. [On the
problem of cannibalism in northern New Guinea.]
Paideuma 6: 381-410.

7272.   Schmitz, Carl A. 1960. Kannibalismus und
Todeszauber auf New guinea. [Cannibalism and
death magic of New Guinea.] UWT 60: 590-603;
619-620.

7273.   Schmitz, Robert. 1912. Les Baholoholo
(Congo Belge) [The Baholoholo (Belgian Congo).
Brussels: Albert Dewit; & Institut International de
Bibliographie.

  Types of food: pp. 49-50; food preparation:
  pp. 53-54; kitchen utensils and equipment:
  p. 55, meals: p. 57; taboos: p. 59; condiments: p. 61; beverages: pp. 63-64; anthropophagy: p. 65; geophagy: p. 65; preservation
  of food: pp. 67-68; fishing: pp. 103-106;
  agriculture: pp. 107-108; animal husbandry:
  p. 109; nutrition(i.e. work capacity and food
  intake): p. 593.

7274.   Schmutzer, R. 1936. Food and its consumption in a monastery two hundred years ago. [In
German.] SAGMN 29: 321-327.

7275.   Schnake, M.L. Growth patterns of preschool
children as influenced by minor illness and food
habits. Master's thesis. Nutritional Sciences.
Ithaca, New York: Cornell University. 1974.

7276.   Schnegg, Hans. 1952. Die Hefereinzucht.
[Pure yeast culture.] Nureburg: Brauwelt Verlag.

  Yeast culture; history; isolation; shipment.

7277.   Schnell, Raymond. 1957. Plantes alimentaires et vie agricole de L'Aftique noire. Essai de
phytogeographie. [Food plants and agricultural life
of Black Africa. Essay in phytogeography.] Paris:
Editions Larose.

7278.   Schneour, Elie A. 1974. The malnourished
mind. Garden City, New York: Doubleday. Anchor
Press.

  Presents evidence in support of the relationship between nutrition and intellectual development.

7279.   Schoener, Marguerite, compilor. 1942. Historical references on baking; bread customs; super-
sitions and folklore. Chicago: American Institute of
Baking.

7280.   Schoenwetter, J. Pollen analysis of human
paleofeces from Upper Salt's Cave. In The archaeology of the Mammoth Cave area. Edited by P.J.
Watson. 1974. New York: Academic Press.

7281.   Schofield, Eunice M. 1972. Food and cooking of the working class about 1900. HSLC-T 123:
151-168.

7282.   Schofield, Eunice M. 1975. Working class
food and cooking in 1900. Folklife 13: 13-23.

7283.   Schofield, Sue. 1971. Seasonal factors
affecting nutrition in different groups and especially
preschool children. JDev 11: 23-40.

7284.   Schofield, Sue. 1975. Village nutrition
Studies. An annotated Bibliography. Edited by C.M.
Lambert. [Brighton] : Institute of Development
Studies at the University of Sussex.

  An extremely valuable resource for concise
  synopses of dietary and nutritional status
  surveys for rural populations throughout the
  world. North America, Western Europe, Australia, New Zealand, and Japan are not
  included.

7285.   Schofield, Sue. 1979. Development and the
problems of village nutrition. London: Croom Helm.

  Studies methods of collecting data on nutrition for the purpose of administering aid at
  the village level. The question of food
  classification is addressed and villages are
  identified by type of main food staple; type
  of village economy; value of food consumption, and village location. Seasonal nutritional problems are also examined.

7286.   Schonfeld-Leber, Barbel. Marine algae as
human food in the Pacific region. Master's thesis.
Davis: University of California. 1977.

7287.   Schonfeld-Leber, Barbel. 1979. Marine
algae as human food in Hawaii, with notes on other
Polynesian Islands. EFN 8:47-59.

  Considers the morphological, nutritional and
  dietary aspects of seaweed in Hawaiian diet,
  and elsewhere in the Western Pacific. Incipient Hawaiian limu (seaweed) cultivation,
  cleaning, preservation, and preparation are
  described.

7288.   Schorger, A.W. 1965. The beaver in early
Wisconsin. WASAL-T 54:147-179.

As food: pp. 149-150.

7289.   Schorger, A.W. 1967-1968. The wild honey-bee in early Wisconsin. WASAL-T 56:49-64.

Food use of honey (Native American): pp. 50; (European): pp. 51-52.

7290.   Schott, Rudiger. Anfange der Privat- und Planwirtschaft-Wirtschaftsordnung und Nahrungsv-erteilung bei Wildbeutervolkern. [Beginnings of home-and planned economy, organization of econo-my and food distribution among hunting and gather-ing peoples.] Ph.D. dissertation. Universitat Bonn. 1954.

7291.   Schotte-Lindsten, Ann-Sofi. 1964. Ran och vaflor. [Waffles and "hippen".] GK 4:92-108.

Ran ("hippen") are thin, wafer-shaped cakes, rolled together, eaten in Sweden.

7292.   Schouteden, Wery J. 1939. Souvenirs d'Afri-que.   Makalekesse, petit village.   [Memories of Africa, the hamlet of Makalekess.] UFC-B 101:59-62.

Included is a description of palm wine in the region of Moanda, Gabon (l. 32 S., 13.17 E).

7293.   Schrader, Otto Herman. 1883. Thier-und Pflanzengeographie im Licht der Sprachforschung mit besonderer Rucksicht auf die Frage nach der Urheimat der Indogermanischen. [Animal and plant geography in the light of linguistics with special consideration to the question of the original home of Indogermanic culture.] Berlin: C. Habel.

7294.   Schram, Ferenc. 1964. Simai Kristof kezira-tos szakacskonyve. [The Simai Kristof [1742-1833] manuscript cookbook.] Ethnografia 75:578-598.

7295.   Schram, Louis M.J. 1954. The Monguors of the Kansu-Tibetan frontiers: their origin, history, ad social organization. APS-T 44:1-138.

Food habits: pp. 114a; 117a, b.

7296.   Schranil, J. Anthropophagie et inhumations rituelles dans les fonds de cabanes de plus recent age du bronze en Boheme. [Anthropophagy and ritual burials in the foundations of shelters of the recent Bronze Age in Bohemia.] In Institut Interna-tional d'Anthropologie. 3[e]Session. 20-29. Septem-bre 1927. Amsterdam. 1928. Pp. 383-388. Paris: Librairie E. Nourry.

7297.   Schreiber, G. 1962. Der Wein als Heiltrank. Zur Volkskunde Medizingeschichte. Kulturgeschi-chte.   [Wine as a healing beverage. Its folklore, medical history, culture history.] RWZV 9:39-55.

7298.   Schrire, Carmel. The implications of mo-dern hunter-gatherer history. Paper presented at 77th Annual Meeting of the American Anthropologi-cal Association. 14 to 18 November, 1978. Los Angeles, California.

7299.   Schroeder, C.A. 1968. Sociological aspects of the jicama in Mexico. Ethnos 33:78-89.

Pachyrrhizus erosus (yam bean). Ethnogra-phic and botanical history: food use in Mexico and the United States; as a pinata favor; in the seed-fertility ceremonies of the Otomi; as a ritual altar offering on Dia de los Muertes (All Saints and All Souls' Days).

7300.   Schroder, Dominik. 1952-1953. Zur religion der Tujen des Sininggebietes (Kukonor). [On the religion of the Tujen of the Sining Region (Koko Nor).] Anthropos 47:1-79; 620-658; 822-870; 48: 202-259. Translation by Richard Reuse. New Haven: Human Relations Area Files. n.d.

Food habits: pp. 74, 119, 163, 22-223, 236. Koko Nor (now Ch'ing-hai hu (Lake Ching-hai) is located in Tsinghai Province, People's Republic of China..

7301.   Schuck, Cecelia; Wenberg, Burness G. & Talcott, Margaret I. 1962. Nutritive value of the boarding school diets of Sioux Indian children. FASEB-FP 21:387.

Survey of seven to fourteen year old stu-dents - male and female. Eight boarding schools were surveyed for a total of twenty-four days. Dietary values were reported as having little variation.

7302.   Schuh, Doris D. ; Moore, A.N. & Tuthill, B.H. 1967. Measuring food acceptability by freque-ncy ratings. JADA 51:340-343.

7303.   Schulein, J. von. 1935. Die Bierhefe als Heil-Hahr-und Futtermittel. [Brewer's yeast as remedy, food, and fodder.] Dresden: Steinkopf.

7304.   Schullerus, P. 1916. Pflanzen in Glaube und Brauch der Siebenburger Sachsen. [Plants in belief and custom in Siebenburg Saxony.] AVSL 40:69-188; 348-426.

7305.   Schulte, Marie Jacobson. 1942. Fruits of the desert. CSJ 1:55-64.

Use of cactus fruit by Native Americans in the southwestern United States.

7306.   Schulte, Marie Jacobson. 1942. The lure of the desert. CSJ 1:70-73.

Continuation of CSJ 1:55-64.

7307.   Schulte, V.R. Relationship between the belief in food fallacies and the educational attain-ment levels of upper class home makers in New York City. Ph.D. dissertation. New York Universi-ty. 1962.

7308.   Schultes, Richard Evans. 1957. The genus Quararibea in Mexico and the use of its flowers as a spice for chocolate. HU-BML 17:247-264.

7309.   Schultes, Richard Evans. 1958. A little-known cultivated plant from northern South America. HU-BML 18:229-244.

Solanum Tipiro, HBK., cultivated as fruit in Colombian Amazon.

7310.　Schultes, Richard Evans. 1977. Diversas plantas comestiveis nativas do noroeste da Amazonia. [Various edible native plants of the northwest Amazon.] AAm 7:317-327.

Plants of the genuses Erythroxylon, Hevea, Micrandria, Vaupesia, Macoubea, Marata, Calathea, Pourouma, Pouteria, and others.

7311.　Schultes, Richard Evans & Romero-Castaneda, R. 1962. Edible fruits of Solanum in Colombia. HU-BML 19:235-286.

7312.　Schultz, E. 1964. Chapter Four. Food and its preparation. In Proverbial expressions of the Samoans. Translated by Brother Herman. 1965. Polynesian Paperbacks No. 1. Wellington, New Zealand. The Polynesian Society.

7313.　Schultze, Rudolph. 1867. Geschichte des Weins und der Trinkgelage. Ein Beitrag ur allgemeinen Kultur-und Sittengeschichte, nach den besten Quellen bearbeitet und popular dargestellt fur das deutsche Volk. [History of wines and carousing. A essay on the general history of culture and customs based on the most excellent sources, and popularly described for the German people.

7314.　Schulz, T. 1952. A human needs diet in April 1952. OUIS-B 14:177-182.

7315.　Schulz, T. 1952. A human needs diet in November 1952. OUIS-B 14:423-429.

7316.　Schulze, Louis. 1891. The aborigines of the Upper and Middle Finke River: their habitats and customs, with introductory notes on the physical and natural history features of the country. Translated by J.G.O. Tepper. RSSA-TP 14:210-246.

Food: pp. 231-234. Northern Territory, Australia.

7317.　Schulz, August. 1913. Die Geschichte der Kultivierten Getriede. [The history of cultivated cereals.] Halle: L. Nebert.

7318.　Schulze, W. 1953. Gewurze und sonstige Wurzmittel. [Spices and former means of spicing.] Leipzig: Fachbuch Verlag.

7319.　Schumacher, Max George. The northern farmer and his markets. Ph.D. dissertation. University of California, Berkeley. 1948.

7320.　Schuman, Clyde B. 1927. Nutrition's place in community welfare. HSS 15: 424-431.

Activities of Red Cross nutrition outreach in New York City, St Joseph, Missouri, and in Humboldt County, California.

7321.　Schuman, Clyde. 1943. War developments in nutrition. JESoc 16:309-318.

Maintenance of nutritional status in the United States and Great Britain during World War II.

7322.　Schutte, O. 1907. Cooking utensils injurious to health. PP 3:163-169.

Possible dangers from the use of metal and cooking utensils other substances, with special reference to conditions in various countries.

7323.　Schutz, Howard W. & Kamen, Joseph M. 1958 Response set in the measurement of food preferences. JApsych 42:175-177.

7324.　Schutz, Howard G. & Pilgrim, Francis J. 1953. Psychophysiology in food acceptance research. JADA 29:1126-1128.

Reprinted and condensed from FCIAFAD-AR 4(3) (1952).

7325.　Schutz, Howard G. & Pilgrim Francis J. 1958. A field study of food monotony. Psych Rep 4:559-565.

7326.　Schutz, Howard G.; Rucker, M.H.; & Hunt, Judy D. 1972. Hospital patients' and employees' reactions to food-use combinations. JADA 60:207-212.

7327.　Schutzmeister, P. Der Mensh auf den Atollen der Sudsee in seiner Abhangigkeit von der Landschaft hinsichtlich Siedlung, Wirtschaft und Verkehr. [Man on the atolls of the Pacific; his dependence on the land with regard to settlement, economy, and transport.] Ph.D. dissertation. Universitat Hamburg. 1932.

7328.　Schwartz, Herbert J. The world food problem. Ph.D. dissertation. Geography. New York: Add Teachers College of Columbia University. 1951.

7329.　Schwartz, Noel & Foster, Dean. 1957. Methods of rating quality and intensity of the psychological properties of food. FTech 11(9):15-20.

7330.　Schwarz, Edouard. 1859. Die Nahrungsmittel der Tahitier. [Food of the Tahitian.] KKGAW-Z 15:570-572.

7331.　Schwarz, Richard Williams. John Harvey Kellogg: American health reformer. Ph.D. dissertation. University of Michigan. 1964.

7332.　Schwede, Madge L. 1970. The relationship of aboriginal Nez Perce settlement patterns to physical environment and to generalized distribution of food resoures. NARN 4:129-136.

Studies the relationship between several environmental variables: size of streams; and immediate availability of fish; game and root resources.

7333.　Schweigrat, F. & Weichers, S.G. 1959. Herstellung und Trocknung von Magou und sein Werft fur die Ernahrung. [The preparation and drying of magou and its nutritional value.] VZ 4:712. Reprinted in FISA May-June 1960.

Magou or mahewu is a fermented food prepared by South African Bantus, by boiling thin maize porridge and adding wheat flour to it. After approximately thirty-six hours, lactic acid, and butyrate are formed. When dried, magou may keep for up to one year.

7334. Shweigert, B.S. Technological advances and their effect on food habits and food uses. In Food, science, and society. A symposium held in February, 1968, sponsored by Northern California Section of the Institute of Food Techologists, and the University of California, Berkeley, Department of Nutritional Sciences. 1969. Pp. 18-23. New York: The Nutrition Foundation, Inc.

7335. Schweight, B. 1953. Servicemen's food preferences. JADA 29:592.

7336. Schweinfurth, Georg. 1870. Vegetationsskizzen vom Bachr-el-Ghasl. [Glimpses of the vegetation from Bahr al-Ghazl. BZ 28:81-88.

Mentions economically useful plants from an area in the Anglo-Egyptian Sudan.

7337. Schweinfurth, Georg. 1871. Berichte uber die botanischen ergebnisse der ersten Niam-Niam reise. [Report on the botanical results of the first Niam-Niam expedition.] BZ 29:301-317; 324-341; 351-366; 372-376.

Contains notes on the principal cultivated plants.

7338. Schweinfurth, Georg. 1883. The ancient flora of Egypt. Nature(L) 28:109-114.

Finds at Deir el-Bahari. Food plants mentioned include dates, raisins, lichen (Parmelia furfuracea) used in modern times to flavor bread; and leaves of the watermelon vine.

7339. Schweinfurth, Georg. 1891. Aegyptens answartige Beziehungen hinsichtlich der Culturegewachse. [Egyptian foreign relations with regard to cultivated plants.] ZE 23:649-669.

7340. Schweinfurth, Georg. 1900. Einige von der freien Natur Sudwest-Afrikas dem Naturmenschen dargebotene vegetabilische Nahrungsmittel. [Some wild food plants of the natives of southwest Africa.] ZE 32:354-359.

7341. Schweinfurth, Georg. 1908. Ueber die von A [aron] Aaronsohn ausgefuhrten Nachforschungen nach dem wilden Emmer (Triticum dicoccoides, Kcke). [Aaron Aaronsohn's investigation into wild emmer (Triticum dicoccoides, Kcke.] DBGB 26a [Part 4]: 309-324.

7342. Schweizerisches Museum fur Brot und Geback, Luzern. 1963. Fuhrer. [Guide.]

Guide to the Swiss Museum for Bread and Baking, Lucern.

7343. Schwerin, Karl H. 1970. Apuntes sobre la yuca y sus origenes. [Points on yuca and its origins.] AVS-BI No. 7.

Discusses preparation methods, and toxicity.

7344. Schwerin, Karl H. Techniques of manioc preparation and the identification of manioc types. Paper presented at 70th Annual Meeting of the American Anthropological Association. 18 November, 1971. New York City.

A survey of South American manioc-using cultures was made to determine the variety and distribution of techniques for processing the tuber. This data is then used to determine whether or not, and to what extent techniques of processing are related to classification of cultigen type (particularly the distinction between "bitter" and "sweet") as recognized by native cultivators.

7345. Schwerin, Karl H. Agriculture in the swamps - Karinya drained field cultivation. Paper presented at 73rd Annual Meeting of the American Anthropological Association. 19 to 24 November, 1974. Mexico city.

7346. Schwitzgebel, Robert L. & Gray, Jeffrey. 1977. A nutritional source of reading disabilty. JIR 23(3):3-4.

Satire. Suggests that ingestion of soup and breakfast cereal products containing alphabet letters may be eulexic.

7347. Schwitzer, Matej Karel. 1956 Margarine and other food fats: their history, production, and use. London: Leonard Hill; New York: Interscience.

7348. Scola, R. 1975. Food markets and shops in Manchester, 1770-1870. JHG 1:153-168.

7349. Scollon, Jr., Robert W. 1956. The relative effectiveness of several film variables in modifying attitudes: a study of the application of films for influencing the acceptability of foods. Technical Report NAVTRA-DEVCEN 269-70-60. Port Washington, New York: Navy Special Devices Center.

7350. Scott, D. 1826-1831. On the mustard plant mentioned in the Gospel. WSE-M 6:430-442.

7351. Scott, Edward M. 1956. Nutrition of the Alaskan Eskimos. NR 14:1-3.

7352. Scott, Edward M. & Heller, C.A. 1962. Nutrition of a northern population. In Conference on medical and public health in the Arctic and Antarctic. Document No. 18. P. 18. Geneva: World Health Organization.

7353. Scott, Edward M. & Heller, C.A. 1968. Nutrition in the Arctic. AEH 17:603-617.

7354. Scott, Eugenie C. Dental attrition in pre-Columbian Peru. Paper presented at 72nd Annual Meeting of the American Anthropological Association. 1 Decemer, 1973. New Orleans, Louisiana.

7355.   Scott, Eugenie C.   Dental variation and subsistence changes in pre-Columbian coastal Peru. Ph.D. dissertation.   Anthropology.   University of Missouri, Columbia. 1974.

7356.   Scott, H.S. 1937. Education and nutrition in the colonies. Africa 10:458-471.

7357.   Scott, James Maurice. 1964. The tea story. London: Heinemann. Also published as The great tea venture. New York: Dutton. 1965.

7358.   Scott, Leslie M. 1941. Indian women as food providers and tribal counselors. OHSQ 42:208-219.

7359.   Scott, M.P.   1972.   Some aboriginal food plants of the Ashburton District, Western Australia. WAN 12:94-96.

7360.   Scott, R.R. 1934. The preparation of maize flour in Tanganyika territory.   SAMJ 8:399-402. Reviewed in NARev 4:369.

7361.   Scott Blair, K.R. 1969. Rheology: a brief historical survey. JTS 1:14-18.

7362.   Scribner, Robert Leslie & Hemphill, William Erwin. 1958. A denial of liberty: after 1906 the average citizen was given less opportunity to consume poison unknowingly, a fact that was reflected in the altered tenor of newspaper advertisements. VC 7:19-22.

   The Pure Food and Drug Act, promulgated by Dr. Harvey Wiley, was initially passed in 1906.   The legislation was the first such to regulate chemicals added to foods and pharmaceuticals either as preservatives or adulterants.

7363.   Scrimsher, Leda Scott.   Native foods used by the Nez Perce Indians of Idaho.   Master's thesis. University of Idaho. 1967.

7364. Scroggie, Helen H.M.   The sociology of Ngwaketse diet.   Master's thesis.   University of South Africa. 1946.

7365.   Scudder, Thayer. 1971.   Gathering among African woodland savannah cultivators: a case study: the Gwemba Tonga. ZP No. 5.

7366.   Seabrook, William B. 1929.   The magic island. New York: Harcourt, Brace.

   Salt and zombies; Haitian confections: p. 96.

7367.   Seabrook, William B. 1930. Adventure in Arabia, among Bedouins, Druses, whirling dervishes, and yezidee devil worshippers.   New York: Blue Ribbons Books.

   Bedouin meal and its etiquette: pp. 38-39; a Bedouin breakfast: pp. 40, 72; camel milk, cheese: pp. 71, 72; coffee: p. 72; camel meat: p. 97-98; a Druse meal: p. 173.

7368.   Seabrook, William B.   1931. Jungle ways. New York: Harcourt, Brace.

   Cooking utensils, and food of the Geure of the Sassandra River, Ivory Coast: pp. 153-154; preparation of an aphrodisiac beverage using dried shell fish, and red pepper: pp. 157-158; Guere preparation techniques for human flesh: pp. 160-164; general discussion of anthropophagy: pp. 151-153; 164-167.

7369.   Seaforth, Compton E. 1962. The ackee - Jamaica's national fruit. J-SRC-IB 3:51-53.

   Blighia spadia, Kon.

7370.   Seale, Alvin. 1911. The fishery resoures of the Philippine Islands. Part 4. Miscellaneous marine products. PJS 6 [D]:283-319.

   Edible sea weeds: pp. 308-309.

7371.   Seale, Alvin. 1912. Notes on Philippine Islands edible molluscs. PS 7 [D]:273-281.

7372.   Seaman, Arlie. 1952. The Indian root festival. Hebarist No. 18. P. 5.

   Correspondence regarding the root festival of the Warm Spring Native Americans of Oregon.

7373.   Seaton, Richard W. & Gardiner, Bertram W. 1959.   Acceptance measurement of unusual foods. FR 24:271.

7374.   Sebillot, Paul. 1891. Traditions et superstitions de la boulangerie. [Traditions and superstitions of baking.] Paris: Lechevalier.

7375.   Sebillot, Paul. 1967. Chapitre Six. Moeurs epulaires.   [Meal-time customs.]   In Coutumes populaires de la Haute-Bretagne. Les litteratures populaires de toutes les nations. Vol. 22. Paris: G.P. Maisonneuve & Larose.

7376.   Sebrell, William H.; Smith, S.C., et al. 1954. Appraisal of nutrition in Haiti. AJCN 7:538-584.

7377.   Secundus, Dick Humelbergius. 1829. Apician morsels; or, tales of the table, kitchen, and larder; containing a new and improved code of eatics; select Epicurean precepts; nutritive maxims, reflections, anecdotes &c. Illustrating the veritable science of the mouth; which includes the art of never breakfasting at home, and always dining abroad. New York: Collins & Hannay; Philadelphia: Lea & Carey.

7378.   Segal, Edwin S. Subsistence participation and division of labor.   Paper presented at 77th Annual Meeting of the American Anthropological Association.   17 November, 1978.   Los Angeles, California.

   Using the standard Cross-Cultural Sample, and the Ethnographic Atlas as data bases, this paper focuses on the question: what is the relationship between gender-based division of labor in subsistence, and division of labor for other technological activities? In conclusion, it is stated that division of labor is a complex phenomenon having at least two and probably more than two dimensions; and, the simple assertion that the principal basis for division of labor being phenotypic gender does not explain anything.

7379.   Seegers, S. 1954.   Through Latin America with knife and fork. Americas 6:9-11.

7380.   Seekirchner, A.   Der Alkohol in Afrika. [Alcohol in Africa.] In Atlas Africanus. Edited by Leo Frobenius. 1931. Vol. Eight. Pp. 44-47. Berlin; Leipzig: W. de Gruyter & Co.

Fermented bverages.

7381.   Seeman, Mark F. Culture contact, subsistence, and pigs: reanalysis of Haddon's theses on the Torres Straits. Master's thesis. Anthropology. University of Cincinnati. 1971.

7382.   Seerly, Norma R.   A social system analysis of the changing food practices of the Teton-Dakota Indians, 1800-1900. Master's thesis. South Dakota State University. 1965.

7383.   Seger, Nancy L. A study of infant-feeding practices as used with Cornell's 45 practice house babies from 1920 to 1944. Master's thesis. Ithaca, New York: Cornell University. 1945.

7384.   Seguin, Robert Louis. 1963. Les moules du Quebec. [The mussels of Quebec.] MNC-B 188.

7385.   Segura Millan, R. 1942. Dietary conditions in Mexican rural communities. JADA 18:521-522.

Describes typical foods, dietary and meal patterns of adult Mexican peasants, of about thirty-five years of age, working eight hours daily moderate labor.

7386.   Seifrit, Emma. 1961. Changes in beliefs and food practices in pregnancies. JADA 39:455-466.

Opens with a review of some non-Western cultural beliefs; and continues on to highlight ideas held in classical Greece and Rome. Eighteenth and Nineteenth Century medical views are discussed, and modern nutritional practices outlined in detail.

7387.   Seim, Einar. 1964. Shetland food in former times. SFB 4:13-16.

7388.   Seler, Cacilie. 1909. Mexicanische kuche. [Mexican cookery.] ZVV 19:369-381.

7389.   Self, Huber. The peanut industry in Oklahoma. Master's thesis. Oklahoma State University. 1947.

7391.   Seligmann, C.G. & Seligmann, Brenda Z. 1911. The Veddas. Cambridge: Cambridge University Press.

Henebedda food taboos: p. 102; food avoidance: pp. 178-180; 334; honey: pp. 326-329.

7392.   Selinus, Ruth, et al. 1971. Dietary studies in Ethiopia. 2. Dietary patterns in two rural communities in N.E.   Ethiopia.   A study with special attention to the situation in young children. ASMU 76:17-38.

7393.   Selinus, Ruth, et al. 1971. Dietary studies in Ethiopia. 3. Dietary studies among the Sidamo ethnic group. A study on villagers in the Ensete monoculture area in S. Ethiopia with special attention to the situation in young children. ASMU 76:158-178.

7394.   Selivanovna, Nina Nikolaevna. 1933. Dining and wining in old Russia. New York: E.P. Dutton.

7395.   Selk, Paul. 1963. Eten und drinken. Eine volkskundliche Plauderei. [Eating and drinking. A folkloric chat.] SH-MHV 15:36-37.

7396.   Selling Lowell Sinn. 1943. Psychology and industrial nutrition programs. Food in relation to mental processes. Indust Med 12:69-73.

Discusses effects of dietary adequacy upon workers' attitudes; variables influencing food habits; and the importance of supervision of employee feeding.

7397.   Selling, Lowell Sinn. 1946. Behavior problems of eating. JO 16:163-169.

Eating as behavior; eating patterns; eating as a source of conflict; emotions at mealtimes.

7398.   Selling, Lowell Sinn & Ferraro, Mary Anna. 1945. The psychology of diet and nutrition. New York: W.W. Norton.

7399.   Selowsky, Marcelo & Taylor, Lance. The economics of malnourished children: a study of disinvestment in human capital. University of Minnesota. Department of Economics. Center for Economic Research. Discussion Paper. No. 13. Minneapolis: University of Minnesota. December, 1971.

Investigates ways to measure private and social benefit of alleviating childhood malnutrition. Specific reference is made to low-income population in Santiago, Chile.

7400.   Selsam, Millicent Ellis. 1955. The plants we eat. New York: William Morrow.

For younger readers.

7401.   Selye, Hans. 1957. Lathyrism. Rev Canad 16:1-82.

History and geographic distribution of lathyrogenic plants. Lathyrogenic compounds. Clinical manifestations of lathyrism; stimuli which influence lathyrism; pathogenesis of lathyrism.

7402.   Semler, Henrique. 1913. Plantas uteis do deserto. [Useful plants of the desert.] Servico de Informacoes e Divulgacao. Rio de Janeiro: Ministerio da Agricultura, Industria, e Commercio.

7403. Semple, Ellen Churchill. 1921. Geographic factors in the ancient Mediterranean grain trade. AAG-A 11:47-74.

7404. Semple, Ellen Churchill. 1922. The influence of geographic conditions upon ancient Mediterranean stock-raising. AAG-A 12:3-38.

7405. Senaveratine, John M. 1919-1920. Milk-drinking in ancient Ceylon. CALR 5:18-19.

7406. Senft, E. 1906-1907. Some Japanese vegetable food materials with special reference to preserved army stores. [In German.] PPrax 5:481-491; 6:1-8; 49-56; 81-89; 122-132; 163-168; 208-220.

   Preserved foods used during the Russo-Japanese war. A list of principal food plants is included.

7407. Sen Gupta, P.N. 1953. The dietaries of the primitive tribes of India. March 6:60-65.

7408. Sen Gupta, P.N. 1959. Investigations into the dietary habits of the aboriginal tribes of Abor hills (north-eastern frontier). Part 2. Minyong and Pangi. I-DA-B 3:155-173.

7409. Sen Gupta, P.N. &Rao, R.K. 1957. Studies on the living conditions, dietary habits and nutritional status of the Tripura, Bangkhal, and Biang tribes of Tripura State. I-DA-B 6:1-19.

   Northeast Indian frontier.

7410. Sengupta, S.C. & Chakravorty, S.K. 1960. Studies in rural change: first-point village surveys. No. 2. Binanoi (Cooch Behar District) 1956-1957. Agro-Economic Research Center. Santiniketan, West Bengal: Visva-Bharati University.

   Includes detailed food expenditure data for religious and occupational groups. Cooch Behar District is located in northeastern West Bengal, at approximately 26.25N., 80. 50E.

7411. Senn, Charles Herman, ed. 1896. Ye art of cookery in ye olden time. London: Universal Cookery and Food Association.

7412. Sense, Eleanora. 1942. American's nutrition primer. What to eat and why. New York: M. Barrows.

7413. Sense, Eleanora. 1960. Chapter Five. Nutrition etiquette. Chapter Six. Communication in nutrition. Chapter Eight. Anxiety and nutrition. In Clinical studies in nutrition. Philadelphia; Montreal: J.B. LIppincott Co.

   These chapters deal respectively with mealtime environment; presentation of food; and feeding handicapped patients; communication between dietitian and patient in hospital contexts; and the causes of and solutions for stress, as these relate to feeding and diet therapy. All three chapters communicate definite cultural values, and maybe studied for both their professional and sociological contents.

7414. Serebriakov, V.A. & Baratov, K.B. 1960. Change in diet of rural inhabitants of Tajikistan, following their migration from mountainous regions to valley areas. [In Russian.] VP 19:9-12.

7415. Sergent, M.G. 1955. Une solution immediate a la malnutrition de l'africain: la recuperation du sang de boeuf. [An immediate solution to African malnutrition: the recovery of beef blood.] AVF-B 28:183-188.

7416. Sergo, E. 1964. Rakospalota nepi taplalkozasa. [The common food of Rakospalota.] NeKoz 9:190-256.

   Hungary.

7417. Serjeant, Richard. 1964. A man may drink: aspects of a pleasure. London: Putnam.

7418. Serjentson, Mary Sidney. 1938. The vocabulary of cookery in the Fifteenth Century. OEA-ES 23:25-37.

7419. Serpenti, Laurentius Maria. 1965. Cultivators in the swamps. Social structure and horticulture in a New Guinea society. Assen: Van Gorcum.

   Frederick-Hendrick Island, West New Guinea.

7420. Service, Elman & Service, Helen S. 1954. Tabati: Paraguayan town. Chicago: University of Chicago Press.

   Beliefs about food; common recipes: pp. 306-316.

7421. Serville, Yvonne & Bleyer, R. 1976. L'apport des enquetes de motivation pour la connaissance du comportement alimentaire. [Contribution of studies on motivation to knowledge of dietary behavior.] ANA 30:195-210.

   Reviews research in France on variables influencing food selection, including organoleptic factors; infuence of food on health; and convenience of preparation. Observes that food is strongly interrelated with needs for affection; communication; distraction; creativity; and security.

7422. Serville, Yvonne, & Tremolieres, Jean. 1967. Recherches sur le symbolisme des aliments et la signification du repas familial. [Research on food symbolism and the significance of the family meal.] CND 2:49-58.

   Importance of the day's meals in modern city life; differences in diet from a generation ago; modern procedures and traditional foods; mealtime atmosphere.

7423. Sery, P. 1972. Debut d'implantation de la restauration industrielle en France. [First introduction of industrial feeding in France.] NObs No. 424. Pp. 38-40.

7424. Sessions, Doris. 1959. Cooks of yesterday. Arizona 14:36-41.

7425. Sessler, W.M. & Spoon, W. 1952. Over het gebruik van wilde salie op de Beneden Windse Eilanden. [On the use of sage in the lower Windward Islands.] WIG 33:49-52.

7426. Setchell, William Albert. 1907. Limu. UCP-B 2:9-113.

Limu is the generic Hawaiian word for edible seaweeds. This article includes ethnographic material on their uses; etymological data; island of provenience; and some interesting notes on classification (p. 95), for a large number of algae.

7427. Setchell, William Albert. 1924. American Samoa. CIW-DMB 20 Part 20.

An ethnobotanical study. Food plants, and cooking techniques: pp. 192-196.

7428. Seth, V. 1971. Feeding habits of infants and preschool children in urban, semiurban and rural community. IJPed 8: 452-455.

India.

7429. Seurat, Leon Gaston. 1905. Flore economique de la Polynesie francaise. [Economic flora of French Polynesia.] SNAF-B Pp. 310-326; 355-359; 369-376.

7430. Seurat, Leon Gaston. 1905. Resources alimentaires tirees du regne animal des indigenes de la Polynesie francaise. [Food resources drawn from the animal kingdom by the natives of French Ploynesia.] MCM 3: 539-551.

7431. Seyffert, Carl. 1911. Die Pflege der Zahne Bei naturvolkern. [The care of teeth among primitive peoples.] DMZ 11: 842-858.

7432. Syeffert, Carl. 1931. Einige beobachtungen und Bemerkungen uber die Ernahrung der naturvolker. Ein Beitrag zur Geschichte der Ernahrung. [Some observations and notes on the nutrition of aboriginal peoples. An essay on the history of nutrition.] ZE 63: 53-85.

7433. Seymour, Thomas Day. 1907. Chapter Seven. Homeric food. In Life in the Homeric age. London: Macmillan. Reprint. New York: Biblo & Tannen. 1963.

7434. Seymoure, Robert David. Food habits of the White Mountain Apache Indians. Fort Apache Reservation, Arizona. Mimeographed. Report prepared for Project Apache of the Good Samaritan Hospital, Phoenix, Arizona. 18 November, 1973.

7435. Seymoure, Robert David. Present-day food habits of the White Mountain Apache Indians. Mimeographed. Phoenix, Arizona: Project Apache of the Good Samaritan Hospital. 1974.

7436. Shack, Dorothy N. 1969. Nutritional processes and personality development among the Gurage of Ethiopia. Ethnology 8: 292-300.

7437. Shack, Dorothy N. Taster's choice: social and cultural determinants of food preferences. In Diet of man: needs and wants. Edited by John Yudkin. 1978. Pp. 209-224. London: Applied Science Publishers.

Discusses values influencing procuring food; food as an ethnic marker; conspicuous consumption of food; food as an ideological marker; the role of commercial advertising in influencing food use; eating habits of childhood; obesity; significance of food for patients in hospital; symbolism of food sharing.

7438. Shack, William A. 1971. Hunger, anxiety and ritual: deprivation and spirit possession among the Gurage of Ethiopia. Man 6: 30-45.

7439. Shack, William A. Anthropology and the diet of man. In Diet of man: needs and wants. Edited by John Yudkin, 1978. Pp. 261-280. London: Applied Science Publishers.

Taking the works of Audrey Richards (1932; 1939) as points of departure, this article exemplifies the close correspondence between social systems and dietary systems posited by Richards, and how this correspondence directly effects nutritional status. Cases in point are the dietaries of three Ethiopian groups: the Christian Amhara and Tigrinya; and the non-Christian Gurage. Parallels are drawn between the religiously imposed dietary asceticism of Christian fasts, and the culturally-determined restraints on food intake among the Gurage -in spite of the fact that all three groups possess food surpluses. Further examples of the central role of food in various neoreligious and political movements are given in support of the central thesis of the importance of studying the sociological aspects of diet in attempting to understand social change.

7440. Shakespear, John. 1912. The Lushei Kuki clans. London: macmillan.

Food and beverages of a Burman people: pp. 36-38.

7441. Shakman, Robert A. 1974. Nutritional influences on the toxicity of environmental pollutants. AEH 28: 105-113.

Pesticides and air pollution may act synergistically to increase the effects of dietary deficiencies. Endrin, parathion, and captan are indicated as markedly hazardous in diets characterized by general protein, or specific amino acid deficiencies. Endrin is used in cotton production in poorer countries where the population is likely to be short of protein.

7442. Shallenberger, R.S. & Acree, T.E. 1967. Molecular theory of sweet taste. Nature (L) 216: 480-482.

7443. Shamel, A.D. & Popenoe, F. Wilson. 1916. The pitanga. JHer 7: 179-185.

A Brazilian fruit, Eugenia uniflora, L. As food: p. 184.

7444. Shammas, Elia & Adolph, William H. 1950. Nutritive value of parboiled wheat used in the Near East. JADA 30: 982-983.

7445. Shand, Philip Morton. 1928. A book of food. New York: Alfred A. Knopf.

A subjective, gourmet appreciation of British, and other national cuisines. Each chapter focuses on a specific food, or food preparation (e.g. soup; desserts.).

7446. Shaner, Richard H. 1963. Distillation and distilleries among the Dutch. P Folk 13: 39-42.

Pensylvania Dutch.

7447. Shankman, Paul. 1969. Le roti et le bouilli: Levi-Strauss' theory of cannibalism. AA 71: 54-69.

7448. Shantz, H.L. 1922. Urundi, territory and people. GR 12: 329-337.

Contains data on animal and vegetable foods; markets and marketing; and food preparation.

7449. Deleted

7450. Sharada, K. A Socio-economic survey of the Kannikars - a tribe in Kerala. Master's thesis. Social work. University of Delhi. 1959.

7451. Sharaga, S. The effect of television advertising on children's nutrition attitudes, nutrition knowledge an eating habits. Ph. D. dissertation. Nutritional Sciences. Ithaca, New York: Cornell University. 1974.

7452. Sharma, K.N. Hindu sects and food patterns in northern India. In Aspects of religion in Indian society. Edited by L.P. Vidyarthi. 1961. Pp. 45-58. Meerut: Kedar Nath Ram Nath.

7453. Sharma, S.C. 1972. Land use and nutrition in the village Manikapur in the central upland of the Yamuna Chambal Doab. GRI 34: 369-385.

Manikapur is located at 26.44N., 78. 54#., in Uttar Pradesh, India. This article describes crop patterning, and nutritional status. The dietary deficiencies which exist lead the author to make suggestions concerning the possibility of increasing crop yields through irrigation, manuring, and changes in crop patterning.

7454. Sharman, Anne. Social and economic aspects of nutrition in Padhola, Bukedi District, Uganda. Ph. D. dissertation. University of London. 1970.

Contains a disscussion of the division of labor in Padhola, and the conditions under which increasing demands will be made on a woman's time. The influence of socio-economic variables upon medical and nutritional status are examined.

7455. Sharon, Irving M. 1965. Sensory properties of food and their function during feeding. FTech 19: 35-36.

Discusses the sensory interrelationships and morphological factors involved in eating, and their influences on food preferences and nutritional status.

7456. Sharpe, H.G. 1906. Fireless cooking. USA - RCG Pp. 114-118.

7457. Sharsmith, Carl W. 1946. A visit with Ta-Bu-Ce. YNN 25: 126-129.

Mentions use of dried larvae of Ephydra hians as food.

7458. Shattuck, George Cheever, ed. 1933. The penninsula of Yucatan; medical, biological, meteorological and sociological studies. CIW-P No. 431.

Food: pp. 67-71.

7459. Shattuck, George Cheever & Benedict, Francis Gano. 1931. Further studies on the basal metabolism of Maya Indians in Yucatan. AJP 96: 518-528.

7460. Shaw, Mary Margaret. 1933. 1933. The basal metabolism of some American Indian girls. JADA 9: 120-123.

Compares Native American students enrolled at the United States Indian School at Flandreau, South Dakota with Caucasian students at South Dakota State University.

7461. Shawcross, Kathleen. 1977. Fern-root, and the total scheme of 18th Century Maori food production in agricultural areas. JPS 76: 330-352.

7462. Shawcross, Wilfred. 1967. An evaluation of the theoretical capacity of a New Zealand harbour to carry a human population. T-JAUFC 13: 3-11.

7463. Shawcross, Wilfred. 1967. An investigation of prehistoric diet and economy on a coastal site at Galatea Bay, New Zealand. PS-P 33:107-131.

7464. Shenkel, James Richard. Cultural adaptation to the molusk: a methodological survey of shellmound archeology and a consideration of the shellmounds of the Marismas Nacionales, west Mexico. Ph. D. dissertation. Anthropology. State University of New York, Buffalo. 1970.

7465. Shenton, James P. 1971. American cooking: the Melting Pot. New York: Time Life Books. Foods of the World.

7466. Shepard, Ronald & Newton, Edward. 1957. The Story of Bread. London; Routledge & Kegan.

7467. Shephard, R.J. 1978. Human physiological work capacity. Cambridge; Cambridge University press.

Nutrition and physical work capacity; pp. 81-89.

7468. Sherman, Hartley Embrey. 1929. Relative vitamin A content of four Oriental foods. PJS 38: 1-7.

Chinese persimmon; flower of day lily (Hemerocallus flava, L.); tofu.

7469. Sherman, Hartley Embrey & Wang, Tsan-ch'ing. 1929. Chemical analyses of thirty-seven Oriental foods. PJS 38: 67-79.

7470. Sherman, Henry Clay. 1931. Emergency nutrition. New York: American Child Health Association.

7471. Sherman, Henry Clay. 1932. Nutrition in the present emergency. RCC 11: 619.

Importance of balanced diet, and economical purchasing of food during historic Depression era.

7472. Sherman, Henry Clay. 1938. Nutritional improvement in health and longevity. SM 40: 97-107.

7473. Sherman, Henry Clay; Campbell, H.L.; & Lanford, C.S. 1938. Experiments of the relation of nutriion to the composition of the body and the length of life. Science 88: 436.

7474. Sherman, Henry Caly & Gillett, Lucy H. 1917. The adequacy and economy of some city dietaries. Publication 121. New York; New York Association for Improving the Condition of the Poor.

7475. Sherman, M. 1906. Manufacturing of foods in the tenements. CComm 15: 669-672.

7476. Sherson, Erroll. 1931. The book of vegetable cookery - usual and unusual. London: Frederick Warne.

7477. Shevchenko, M.G., & Khazanova, V.V. 1968. Molok; molochnie produkti Danii (po materialam poezdki). [Milk and dairy products of Denmark (based on materials gathered during a trip).] VP 27: 86-89.

7478. Shewell-Cooper, Wilfred Edward. 1962. Plants and fruits of the Bible. London: Longman & Todd.

7479. Shibusawa, Keizo, ed., compilor. 1958. Chapter Three. Food and Drink. In Japanese life and culture in the Meiji era. Translated by Charles S. Terry. Tokyo: Obunsha,

Traditional diet; production and consumption of the principal foods at the end of the Tokugawa period; influence of the opening of the country on eating habits: new foods; beverages; beer; wine; other alcoholic beverages; ice; ways of eating; including types of restaurants (Japanese, Chinese, Western) and the inclusion of beef and chicken in menus; parties and dining out. The city and modernization of eating habits. the spread of new foods and eating habits to the provinces; general trends; specific foods and beverages; Western cuisine; conclusion.

7480. Shiflett, Peggy A. 1976. Folklore and food habits. JADA 68: 347-350.

Discusses magical properties attributed to food; planting and preparing food; New Year's day; Shrove Tuesday; Maundy Thursday; Good Friday; St. Martin's Day, Christmas; foods and folk medicine; food taboos.

7481. Shih, C.Y. 1925. Studies in Chinese economic botany. CEM 2(9):24-29; (10):36-43; (11): 23-26; (12):37-44; (13):30-44; (15):38-53.

7482. Shih, Ko-ching & Ying, C. 1958. American brewing industry and the beer market: a statistical analysis and graphic presentation. Morton Grove, Illinois: the authors.

History of brewing; role of brewing industry in national economy; national, regional, and local brewers; market conditions in various states; list of U.S. brewers.

7483. Shimoda, Y. 1965. Nihonjin no Shokusei katsushi. [History of eating habits of the ancient Japanese.] Tokyo: Koseikan Publishing Co.

7484. Shimooka, C. Products for foodstuffs and special use. In Agriculture in Japan. 1908. Pp. 157-161. Tokyo: Imperial Japanese Government.

Scattered throughout this and other sections are data on kinds and amounts of plant and animal food products used in Japan; current food habits compared with those of earlier times, and other food-related subjects.

7485. Shkopkova, M.M. 1950. Vyzhiva a hlediska socialni anthropologie. [Nutrition from the point of view of social anthropology.] AS-Z 3: 41-44; 61-64.

7486. Short, J.B. 1928. The butcher's shop: a study of a country butcher's business. Oxford: Clarendon Press.

7487. Shortall, J.P. 1960. It's food for princes and potentates. there's an export drive on beche-de-mer. PIM 30: 49-52.

7488. Shotwell, R.L. 1958. The grasshopper your sharecropper. M-AES-B No. 714.

Locust as human food; pp. 5-6.

7489. Shourie, K.L. 1939. A survey of diet and nutrition in Najafgarh, Delhi Province. IJMR 26: 907-920.

7490. Shourie, K.L. 1945. An outbreak of lathyrism in central India. IJMR 33: 239-247.

7491.   Showalter, H.A. 1945.   Taste and flowers. FC 5: 9-11.

7492.   Showalter, W.J. 1929.   Exploring the wonders of the insect world. NGM 56: 1-90.

Illustrations of Philippine Ifugao collecting and cooking locusts: pp. 39, 41.

7493.   Shulsinger, Stephanie Cooper.   1971.   Kitchen tin. Relics 4: 20-23.

Historic tinware of the United States.

7494.   Shurtleff, William & Aoyagi, Akiko.   1975. The book of tofu.   Food for mankind Brookline, Massachusetts; Autumn Press.

History; technology; food value; and uses of soybean curd; and its products.

7495.   Shurtleff, William & Aoyagi, Akiko.   1976. The book of miso Hayama-shi Kanagawa-ken, Japan: Autumn Press.

History; technology; and use of fermented soybean paste.

7496.   Shurtleff, William & Aoyagi, Akiko.   1977. The book of kudzu.   A culinary and healing guide. Brookline, Massachusetts; Autumn press.

Pueraria thunberfiana (Pachyrhizus thunbergianus) a leguminous plant, the root of which is used as a thickening agent in Japan, China, and Korea.   Preparation techniques and recipes for kudzu included in a general discussion of the economic uses of the plant.

7497.   Sidibe, Manby.   1929.   Les sorciers mangeurs d'hommes au Soudan francais.   [Cannibal sorcereers in the French Sudan.]   Outre-Mer 1: 22-32.

7498.   Sievert, R.J. 1948.   The uses of Hevea for food in relation to its domesticaiton.   MBG-J 35: 117-121.

Hevea, the classical source of natural rubber, also produces a seed which is used for food by native Brazilian groups in the Rio Negro region. The seeds contain a toxin when fresh, and are procesed to remove this. This article considers a possible sequence in the domestication of some species of Hevea, both in relation to its source as food, and as a source of rubber.

7499.   Siegal, Morris & King, Margaret.   Food habits of Spanish-Americans at Cundiyo, New Mexico. National Research council. Washington, D.C.: National Academy of Sciences. 1943.

7500.   Siegel, Paul S.   1957.   The repetitive element in the diet. AJCN 5: 162-164.

7501.   Siegal, Paul S. & Brandtley, J.J. 1955.   the relationship of emotionality to the consumatory response of eating. JEP 42: 304-306.

7502.   Siegel, Paul S. & Pilgrim, Francis J.   1958. The monotony effect in food acceptance. AJPsy 71: 756-759.

Experiment with college students, results of which confirm the hypothesis which posits that monotony in eating is associated with repeated occurrence of a food; monotony in eating dissipates slowly; high initial level of acceptance slows growth of monotony; monotony is partly a function of personality; monotony results in lowered acceptance of food.

7503.   Siggaard, N.   1941.   Diet of Danish population in former times.   [In Danish.]   ULaeg 103: 519-521.

7504.   Sigismund, Rheinhold.   1884.   Die Aromata in ihrer Bedeutung fur Religion, Sitten, Gebrauche, Handel und Geographie des Alterthums bis zu den Ersten Jahrhunderten unserer Zeitrechnung.   [Aroma, its meaning in religion, manners and customs, commerce and geography from antiquity to the first centuries of our era.]   Leipzig: C.F. Winter.

7505.   Sillans, R.   1953.   Sur quelques plantes alimentaires spontanees de l'Afrique Centrale.   [On some naturally-occurring African food plants.]   IEC-B No. 5. Pp. 77-100.

7506.   Silva, Armando Bordalo da 1949.   Aspectos antropo-sociais da alimentacao na Amazonia.   [Anthropo-sociological aspects of diet in the Amazon region.]   IAEP-P No. 1.

7507.   Silva, M.A. de A. 1955.   The nutrition problem in Mozambique.   [In Portuguese.]   IMT-A 12: 691-712.

7508.   Silva, R.A. de.   1974.   Eating cigarette ashes in anemia AIM 80:115.

7509.   Silva, Walter.   1946.   A alimentacao dos selvagens brasileiros.   [The diet of Brazilian indigenes.]   ACiba 13: 154-157.

7510.   Silvan, L. 1956.   Composition and character of the diet in Guipuzcoa.   [In Spanish.]   AB 8: 393-407.

7511.   Silverberg, Margorie M.; Read, Merrill S.; & Moore, William M. Part Six. Nutrition research and community service among Native American populations.   Summary and recommendations.   In Nutrition, growth and development of North American Indian children. Edited by William D. Moore; Marjorie M. Siverberg; & Merrill S. Read. 1972. Pp. 219-231.   DHEW Publication No. 72-26).   Washington, D.C. Department of Health, Education, and Welfare.

Includes the recommendation that indigenous foods, hunting and fishing sites be preserved, protected and restocked.

7512.   Silverman, Milton.   A study of drinking habits.   Paper presented to the College of Agriculture, University of California at Davis. 1960.

7513.   Silvert, Henrietta Meta.   Food lore of the North American Indian. Master's thesis. Louisiana State University. 1930.

History of Native North American food uses, and their influence on the diet of European colonists.

7514.   Silvestre, Antonio Melico. 1953. Contribuicao para o estudos da alimentacao do indigenas das nossas provincias ultramarinas. [contribution to the study of nutrition of the natives in our overseas provinces.] IMT-A 10: 1545-1553.

Analysis of food legumes.

7515.   Silvestri, G.   1953.   At table with the descendants of Cangrande. [in Italian.] APC 3: 28-31.

Food habits and cookery in Verona.

7516.   Simeons, A.T.W. 1968.   Food: facts, foibles, and fables; the origins of human nutrition. New York: Funk & Wagnalls.

A popular introduction, covering the evolution of dietary needs in relation to species and environment. Chapters Three, Four, and Five discuss, respectively, primate feeding; early hominid feeding; and the Neolithic Revolution. The ancient classical cultures (China, India, Greece, Rome); modern food, and prospects for the future, are also considered.

7517.   Simmonds, Peter Lund. 1854. The commercial products of the vegetable kingdom, considered in their various uses to man and in their relation to the arts and manufactures; forming a practical treatise and handbook of reference for the colonist, manufacturer, merchant, and consumer, on the cultivation preparation for shipment, and commercial value, &c. of the various substances obtained from trees and plants, entering into the husbandry of tropical and sub-tropical regions, etc.   London: T.F.A. Day.

Covers cocao, coffee, tea, sugar, wheat, maize, rice, root crops, cinnamon and other spices; and oil-bearing plants.

7518.   Simmonds, Peter Lund. 1859. The curiosities of food; or the dainties and delicacies of different nations obtained from the animal kingdom. London: Richard Bentley.

7519.   Simmons, D.C. 1966. Eating and its correlatives in Uyo Ibibio proverbs. NField 31: 180-184.

Nigeria. Lists thirty-one proverbs relating to meals and eating.

7520.   Simmons, D.R. 1968.   Man, moa, and the forest. RSNZ - T 2: 115-127.

Forest habitat inferred from gizzards of two moas (Emeus sp. and Dinornis Sp.) found in marl. The moa was an important food source, until drier climate caused recession of forests. Hunting gave way to shore-dwelling, fishing, and agriculture in the 14th and 15th Centuries on the North Island of New Zealand, where the populaion was less constrained by a chnaging ecology than were the South Islanders.

7521.   Simon, Andre Louis. 1906-1909. History of the wine trade in England. 3 vols. London: Wyman & Sons.

7522.   Simon, Andre Louis. 1944.   Section Six. Birds and their eggs. In a concise encyclopedia of gastronomy. London: Wine & Food Society.

7523.   Simon, Andre Louis. 1952. A concise encyclopedia of gastronomy; complete and unabridged. New York: Harcourt, Brace.

7524.   Simon, Billy. 1972.   Ethnocuisine: cactus jelly. Affword 2: 36-37.

Prepared from the fruit of Opuntia sp.

7525.   Simon, Edmund. 1914.   The introduction of the sweet potato into the Far East. ASJ-T 42: 711-724.

7526.   Simonini, Riccardo. 1900.   La geophagia nell' infanzia. [Geophagy in infancy.] Corriere 11: 712,728, 745, 762, 776, 792, 810, 822.

7527.   Simonsson, Sten. 1956.   Om olbrygdens uppkomst i Norden. [On the origin of beer brewing in Scandinavia.] NK 13: 236-253.

7528.   Simoons, Frederick John. 1954. The non-milking area of Africa. Anthropos 49: 58-66.

7529.   Simoons, Frederick John. 1956. The role of ensete in Ethiopia. GR 46: 271-272.

Ensete ventricosum, the 'false bannana'.

7530.   Simoons, Frederick John. 1958. The distribution and origin of widely-held prejudices against certain animal foods in the Old World. AAG-A 48:289.

7531.   Simoons, Frederick John. 1958. The use and rejection of hippoptamus flesh as food in Africa. TNR 51: 195-197.

7532.   Simoons, Frederick John. 1960. Northwest Ethiopia, peoples and economy. Madison: University of Wisconsin Press.

Food: pp. 23,30, 31, 48, 67, 90; famine: pp. 28, 34, 108, 110-113, 114, 116-119, 126, 128-133, 137, 138-139, 149, 152, 160-172.

7533.   Simoons, Frederick John, 1961. Eat not this flesh: food avoidances in teh Old World. Madison: university of Wisconsin Press.

Reviewed in AAPSS-A 343: 187-188 (1962).

7534.   Simoons, Frederick John. 1966. The geographic approach to food prejudices. FTech 20: 274-276.

7535.   Simoons, Frederick John. 1966. Some contributions of the Stanford Food Research Institute relevant to geography and African studies. GR 56: 588-591.

7536.   Simoons, Frederick John. 1969. Primary adult lactose intolerance and the milking habit: a problem in biological and cultural interrelations. Part 1. Review of the medical research. AJDD 14:819-836; Part 2. A cultural historical hypothesis. 15:695-710 (1970).

7537.   Simoons, Frederick John. 1970. The traditional limits of milking and milk use in southern Asia. Anthropos 65:547-593.

7538.   Simoons, Frederick John. 1971. The antiquity of dairying in Asia and Africa. GR 61:431-439.

7539.   Simoons, Frederick John. 1973. The determinants of dairying and milk use in the Old World: ecological, physical, and cultural. EFN 2:83-90.

This paper examines the various reasons for the failure of dairying and use of milk of domestic animals in parts of the Old World where milkable animals were available. Among the reasons cited are the occurrence of intolerance to lactose; as well as ecological and technological variables.

7540.   Simoons, Frederick John. 1974. Contemporary research themes in cultural geography of domesticated animals. GR 64:559-576.

7541.   Simoons, Frederick John. 1974. Fish as forbidden food: the case of India. EFN 3:185-201.

Fish avoidance is examined in the light of three probable influences: the view of fish as unclean; the belief in the sanctity of water and, by extension, in the sanctity of fish found therein; and the principles of non-violence (ahimsa) and its cosequent vegetarianism.

7542.   Simoons, Frederick John. 1974. The purificatory role of five products of the cow in Hinduism. EFN 3:21-34.

Of the five products, three are important food products: milk, milk curd, and clarified butter (ghee). The author examines the history of, and practices relating to these bovine products seeing them as a classic example of the influence of religious beliefs on the use of food. An extensive section of the paper is given over to a discussion of the food categories kachcha (inferior cooked) and pakka (superior cooked) foods.

7543.   Simoons, Frederick John. 1974. Rejection of fish as human food in Africa: a problem in history and ecology. EFN 3:89-105.

A possible Cushite origin for African fish avoidance is examined, and a cause hypothesized as deriving from pastoralists' dominance of sedentary groups and from pastoralists' adequate protein supplies from cattle-herd resources.

7544.   Simoons, Frederick John. 1978. Traditional use and avoidance of foods of animal origin: a culture historical overview. BioScience 28:178-184.

Flesh foods in human diet; pork avoidance and Near Eastern tradition; beef avoidance; cow slaughter and the sacred cow concept of Hinduism; horsemeat as food in Western Europe; rejection of fish as human food in Africa and Asia; dairying; milk use; and lactose malabsorption.

7545.   Simoons, Frederick J.; Johnson, J.D.; & Kretchmer, Norman. 1977. Perspectives on milk-drinking and malabsorption of lactose. Pediatrics 59:98-109.

7546.   Simpson, George Eaton. 1940. The vodun service in northern Haiti. AA 42:236-254.

Food offerings to vodun deities (the Twins): pp. 238, 240.

7547.   Simpson, I.A.; Cheek, Elizabeth; & Chai, Soh-chin. 1956. Applied nutrition in Malaysia. A collection of papers issued for the use of participants at a training course in applied nutrition. 24 November to 4 December. Kuala Lumpur: Institute for Medical Research.

7548.   Simpson, John Frederick Norman Hampson. [pseud. John Hampson.] 1944. The English at table. London: William Collins.

7549.   Simpson, Ruth D. 1953. The Hopi Indians. South M-L 25.

The food quest: pp. 50-57.

7550.   Sims, Laura S. 1978. Food-related value orientations, attitudes, and beliefs of vegetarians and non-vegetarians. EFN 7:23-35.

Four hundred eighty-seven questionnaire replies are analyzed, approximately one-fourth of which were from self-reported vegetarians. Results indicate the vegetarian group adhered more strongly than non-vegetarians to food-related value orientations of ethics, religion, and health. Vegetarians believed in "health" foods, and distrusted food processing and additives. Non-vegetarians showed greater agreement with the overall importance of "nutrition".

7551.   Sinclair, Dorothy 1954. Food habit and other dietary surveys. Part One. CNN 10:57-58.

A very informal, popular discussion for surveys, and some of the methods used in conducting them.

7552.   Sinclair, H.M. 1953. The diet of Canadians Indians and Eskimos. PNS 12:69-82.

7553.   Sing, Raghbir. A comparative study of the nutritional anthropometric measurements of the

Punjabis and the Tamilians. Paper presented at the 9th International Congress of Anthropological and Ethnological Sciences. 28 August to 8 September, 1973. Chicago, Illinois.

7554.   Singaravelu, S. 1966.   Social life of the Tamils - the classical period. Department of Indian Studies. Monograph Series. Kuala Lumpur: University of Malaya.

Food: pp. 23-32.

7555.   Singer, J. 1927. Taboos of food and drink. OC 41: 368-380.

7556.   Singh, Chandra. 1961. Dietetic habits of Gonds in Hoshangabad. Vanyajati 9:163-165.

South central Madhya Pradesh, India.

7557.   Singh, Indrajit. 1944.   The Gondwana and the Gonds. Lucknow: Universal Publishers.

Food quest: pp. 18-22.

7558.   Singh, Madan Mohan. 1967. Chapter Five. Food and drink. In Life in north-eastern India in pre-Mauryan times (with special reference to 600 B.C. - 325 B.C.). Delhi: Varanasi; Patna: Motilal Banaridasu.

7559.   Singh, Shew Shunder [munshi] & Gunanand, Pandit [Shri], translators. 1958. History of Nepal. With an introductory sketch of the country and people of Nepal by the editor Daniel Wright. Cambridge, England: Cambridge University Press.

Translation of Vansavali, or genalogical history of Nepal according to Buddhist recension. Notes on food: pp. 17-18.

7560.   Singh, R., et. al. 1971. Diet survey in village Gauri in Lucknow District. IAMS-A 7:103-128 (Part 1); 7:201-215 (Part 2).

Part 1 contains observations on comparative nutritional deficiencies of different religious, caste, and occupational groups. Part 2 provides food and nutrient intake data for different caste, religious, and social groups [sic] compared with recommended allowances published by the Indian Council of Medical Research. [After Schofield. 1975:173.] The village studied is located in the Indian State of Uttar Pradesh.

7561.   Singh, S. 1937. Preparation of beer by the Loi-Manipuris of Sekami. ISC-P 21:411.

Assam. Northeastern Indian frontier.

7562.   Siniscalco, M. 1961. Favism and thalassaemia in Sardinia and their relationship to malaria. Nature (L) 190:1179-1180.

7563.   Sinoda, O. 1977. The history of Chinese food and diet. PFNS 2:483-497.

7564.   Sipple, Horace, L. 1955. Nutrition education, opportunity and responsibiity. FTech 9:563-565.

Potential role of food science in nutrition education.

7565.   Siqueira, Rubens de & Pechnik, Emilia. 1954. Analise de alimentos consumidos pelos indios do Xingu. [Analysis of foods eaten by the Xingu Indians.] ArqB 2:75-80.

Brazil. Arachis nambiquarae; Mauritia vinifera, M.; Caryocar brasilensis. Food preparation methods, and uses noted.

7566.   Sircar, D.C. 1965. A study in Hindu folklore of Bengal. A letter. Folk Lore (C) 6:294-295.

7567.   Siskind, Janet. Manioc, maize or plantains. Paper presented at 70th Annual Meeting of the American Anthropological Association. 18 November, 1971. New York City.

Land with good drainage is a crucial factor in manioc cultivation, and its availability influences decisions on apportioning land and labor between manioc and other subsistence crops. The decisions made vary from one ecologial niche to another along a range from relatively high land to flood plain. A comparison is made between two groups of Panoan-speaking societies of the tropical Brazilian forest, one of which has only recently left the high, interfluvial environment, while the other has spent generations producing crops along the flood plain.

7568.   Sisters of Ravanica Serbian Orthodox Church. 1955. Serbian cookery. A collection of traditional Serbian recipes contributed by Serbian-Americans of the Detroit community. Detroit: Sisters of Ravanica Serbian Orthodox Church.

7569.   Skeat, William Walter. 1902. The wild tribes of the Malay Peninsula. GB-RAIGBI-J 32:124-128. Also in SI-AR for the year 1902. Pp. 463-478.

Neutralization of yam toxicity: p. 467.

7570.   Skidmore, Susan. 1969. Jewish gastronomy. Wine No. 142. Pp. 32-39.

7571.   Skinner, Alanson. 1921. Material culture of the Menominee. Heye Foundation. Indian notes and Monographs. No. 20. New York: Museum of the American Indian.

Food preparation: pp. 142-208.

7572.   Skinner, Alanson. 1923. Some Wyandot corn foods. M-PM-YB 3:109-112.

7574.   Skogen, Kenneth H. A study of the food practices, economic position, and conception of health on the Pine Ridge Indian Reservation. Master's thesis. South Dakota State University. 1965.

7575. Sladden, D.E. 1933. Transference of induced food-habit from parent to offspring. Part 1. L-RS-PT 114:441-449.

This study is concerned with insects; it may, however, be of heuristic value, in relation to consideration of inheritance in more complex life forms.

7576. Sladden, D.E. & Hewer, H.R. 1938. Transference of induced food habit from parent to offspring. Part 3. L-RS-Pt 126:30-44.

7577. Slater, Charles C. 1956. Baking in America. Vol. 1. Market organization and competition. Northwestern University Studies in Business History. Evanston: Northwestern University Press.

7578. Slater, L.E. 1953. Taste thermometer brings food in focus. FE 26:41-43.

7579. Sloane, Hans. 1707-1725. Voyage to the islands of Madeira, Barbados, Nieves [sic], St. Christopher's and Jamaica, with the natural history of the last of these islands, to which is prefix'd an introduction, wherein is an account of the inhabitants, air, waters, diseases, trade, &c. of that place, with some relations concerning the neighboring continent, and islands of America. Illustrated with figures of the things described which have not been heretofore engraved; in large copper-plates as big as the life. 2 vols. London: printed by B.M. for the author.
   Vol. 2. P. 204: field crickets as food.

7580. Sloimovici, A. 1973. Ethnocuisine de la Burgogne. [Ethnocuisine of Burgundy.] Guillou: Cormarin.

7581. Slome, Cecil. 1960. Culture and the problem of human weaning. JTPECH 6:23-34.

7582. Slotkin, J.S. 1954. Fermented drinks in Mexico. AA 56:1089-1090.

Calls attention to accounts of beverages in the Mexican, and ethnographic literatures.

7583. Sluiter, E. 1960. Voedingsmiddelen uit de Bijbel. [Foods of the Bible.] Voeding 21:47-51.

7584. Slutsky, Herber. An ecological study of mortality among Guatemalan pre-school children; with special emphasis on protein malnutrition and kwashiorkor. Ph.D. dissertation. Urbana: University of Illinois. 1959.7585.

7585. Small, John K. 1922. Wild pumpkins. Have we found the original home for this garden esculent? NYBG-J 19-23.
   Notes on uses by Native American groups: pp. 22-23.

7586. Small, John K. 1930. Okeechobee gourd. NYBG-J 31:10-14.

Pepos okeechobeensis, native to the area of Lake Okeechobee, Florida (located at approximately between 81.02'W., and 82.0. W., and 26.2.N.,and 27.5.N). The author notes that the presence of this Cucurbit, a variety of Pepo moschata, usually indicates a former Indian campsite.

7587. Smead, P.F. Pakistan's date industry, history and progress. Paper presented at Third International Congress of Food Science and Technology. Third. 9 August to 14 August, 1970. Washington, D.C.

7588. Smeds, H. 1955. The ensete planting culture of eastern Sidamo, Ethipia. The role of the ensete-plantations in the local economy and their significance in the cultural geography of Ethiopia. Acta Geog 13:1-40.

Ensete ventricosum, the 'false banana' plant is the staple food of the Gurage people of the midlands of southwest Ethiopia. The center stem, and root are a source of starch, made into bread, or allowed to ferment underground. The plant bears no fruit, its common name notwithstanding.

7589. Smets, G. 1934. L'alimentation et les institutions d'une peuplade sauvage. [Diet and institutions of a savage people.] IRCB-B 5:684-695.

Commentary on Audrey Richards' (1932) Bemba study.

7590. Smetzer, Brbara, 1969. Night of the Palolo. NH 78:64-71.

Eunice viridis as a food in Samoa. Description of the life cycle; preparation as food, annual 'rising'; and folklore of an ocean annelid.

7591. Smidth, J.K. 1876. Historical observation on the conditions of the fisheries among the ancient Greeks and Romans, and on their mode of salting and pickling fish. USCFF-RC for 1873-4 and 1874-5.

Includes background on Greek and Roman fishing techniques; fish used as food; salting of fish; lobster; fish; oyster; and snail ponds. Data derived from classical authors.

7592. Smith, A.K.; Backles, J.J.; Hesseltine, C.W.; Smith, M; Robbing, D.J.; & Booth, A.N. 1964. Tempeh. Nutritive value in relation to processing. CChem 41:173.

An Indonesian food, prepared from fermented soy beans.

7593. Smith, Alice Henderson. 1919. A historical inquiry into the efficacy of lime juice for the prevention and cure of scurvy. JRoyAMedC 32:93-116; 188-208.

In the context of British Navy operations; with brief reference to several arctic expeditions.

7594. Smith, Andrew. 1895. A contribution to South African materia medica, chiefly from plants in use among the natives. Lovedale, South Africa: J.C. Jutta.

7595. Smith, Bruce David. Middle Mississippian exploitation of animal populations. Ph.D. dissertation. Anthropology. University of Michigan, Ann Arbor. 1973.

A uniform, valley-wide pattern of exploitation was found to exist within central section of the Mississippi Valley. From the period commencing A.D. 900 to European contact, a group of thirteen species/species-groups accounts for at least ninety-five percent of the projected meat yield at each site (white-tailed deer; raccoon; turkey; migratory waterfowl; fish; beaver; opossum; rabbit; aboriginal dog; squirrel; black bear; and wapit;. Patterns of exploitation are analyzed based on frequency of faunal remains.

7596. Smith, Jr., Claude Earle. 1950. Prehistoric plant remains from Bat Cave. HU-BML 14:157-180.

Bat cave is located in west central New Mexico, on the edge of the Plains of San Augustin, in Catron County. This report, includes identification of cultivted as well as uncultivated food plants.

7597. Smith, Jr., Claude Earle. 1965. Agriculture, Tehuacan Valley. Field-Bot 31 No. 3.

Mexico. Modern and prehistoric techniques. Includes discussion of diffusion of botanical materials between the Old and New Worlds. Accepts diffusion only in the instance of sweet potato (Ipomoea batatas, Poir.) across the Pacific.

7598. Smith, Jr., Claude Earle. 1969. Additional notes on pre-conquest avocadoes in Mexico. EB 23:135-140.

Analysis of cotyledons an whole seeds of Persea americana, Mill. unearthed during archeological excavations in the Oaxaca Valley. The author believes that, if the avocado materials are non-intrusive, there is no indication of selective plant breeding.

7599. Smith, C.W. An economic study of the peanut industry. Ph.D. dissertation. Texas A & M University. 1949.

7600. Smith, Cecil-Woodham. The great hunger: Ireland, 1845-1849. In European diet from pre-industrial to modern times. Edited by Robert Forster & Elborg Forster. 1975. New York: Harper & Row. Harper Torchbooks. No. 1863.

7601. Smith, Charline Galloway. Diabetes among the Upland Yuman Indians. Paper presented at 68th Annual Meeting of the American Anthropological Association. 20 to 23 Novemer, 1968. New Orleans, Louisiana.

7602. Smith, Charline Galloway. Diabetes as a physiological adaptation among the Upland Yuman Indians. Paper presented at 69th Annual Meeting of the American Anthropological Association. 19 to 22 November, 1970. San Diego, California.

7603. Smith, Charline Galloway. Culture and diabetes among the upland Yuman Indians. Ph.D. dissertation. Anthropology. University of Utah. 1971.

7604. Smith, Dama Margaret [White Mountain] 1933. Indian tribes of the Southwest. Palo Alto: Stanford University Press.
    Foods: pp. 6, 20, 44, 47-48, 57, 60, 74, 90, 117, 123, 127, 155.

7605. Smith, Daphne. An experiment in nutrition education. Master's thesis. Denton: Texas State College for Women. 1945.

7606. Smith, Dorothy W. 1934. Kiowa Indian recipes. United States Department of the Interior. Office of Indian Affairs. Division of Extension. Anadarko, Oklahome: Kiowa Indian Agency.

7607. Smith, E.J. 1962. Man eats insect. QNat 16(5-6):92.

Australia. Xyleutes boisduval, a giant wood-moth.

7608. Smith, Edward. 1864. Practical dietary for families, school, and the laboring classes. London: Walton & Maberly. Reviewed in BMJ 1:67, 68 (21 January , 1864; BMJ 1:130 4 February, 1864).

Dr. Smith urged the distribution of handbills among the poor, headed "The cheapest and best kinds of food".

7609. Smith, Edward. 1866. Dietaries for the inmates of workhouses. Report to the President of the Poor Law Board of Dr. E. Smith. GB-PP Session 1866. Vol. 35.

7610. Smith, Edward. 1903. Foods. International Scientific Series. No. 3. New York: D. Appleton.

Contains a large number of references to food habits in various cultures, but lacks documentation.

7611. Smith, Elmer L. 1970. Shenandoah Valley cooking. Recipes and kitchen lore. Lebanon, Pennsylvania: published for Shenandoah Valley Folklore Society by Applied Arts Publishers.

7612. Smith, Elmer L., compilor. 1972. Early American butter prints. A wealth of rural folk art designs from wooden molds and prints. Lebanon, Pennsylvania: Applied Arts Publishers.

7613. Smith, Elmer L. 1975. Country cooking. Recipes and utensils from rural America. Lebanon, Pennsylvania: Applied Arts Publishers.

7614. Smith, Elmer L. 1977. The country store of yesterday. Lebanon, Pennsylvania: Applied Arts Publishers.

7615. Smith, Eric Alden. Optimal foraging theory and the study of human hunters-gatherers. Paper presented at 77th Annual Meeting of the American Anthropologial Association. 14 to 18 November, 1978. Los Angeles, California.

7616.   Smith, Erminnie A. Significance of flora to the Iroquois. Paper presented at the Thirty-fourth Meeting of the American Association for the Advancement of Science. 26 August to 1 September, 1885. Ann Arbor, Michigan.

7617.   Smith, Eva Prudhomme. 1972. Cajun cooking from the Bayou country. Midlothian, Texas: Midlothian Mirror.

   Southwestern Louisian, Southeastern Texas. Food of Acadian settlers.

7618.   Smith, G.H. Income and nutrition in the Guatemalan highlands. Master's thesis. University of Oregon. 1972.

7619.   Smith, H.B. 1940. Vancouver brands tiger meat. CGNF 59:12.

7620.   Smith, Harlan I. Primitive industries as a normal college course. In Putnam anniversary volume. Anthropological essays presented to Frederick Ward Putnam in honor of his seventieth birthday, April 16, 1909, by his friends and associates. 1909. Pp. 486-520. New York: G.E. Stechert & Co.

   A course which included study of primitive subsistence techniques; food preparation; and agriculture. The outine for this section is contained on pp. 501-506.

7621.   Smith, Helen V. 1961. Michigan wildflowers. CIS-B No. 42.

   Contains brief reference to use of plants as food among Native Americans of Michigan. Data are derived from files of the University of Michigan Museum of Anthropology.

7622.   Smith, Henry Ecroyd. 1869. Notice of Romano - British culinary vessels, discovered in North Wales. HSLC-T 9:19-44.

   A site near Abergele, Denbighshire.

7623.   Smith, Hugh G. 1904. The seaweed industries of Japan. USDCL-USDA-B 24:135-165.

   Extensive descriptive data on food use of Japanese seaweeds.

7624.   Smith, Hugh G. 1904. The utilization of seaweeds in the United States. USCDL-USDA-B 24:169-181.

   Contains brief data on food uses of seaweeds.

7625.   Smith, Huron Herbert. Botanizing among the Ojibwe. M-PM-YB 3:38-47.

7626.   Smith, Huron Herbert. 1923. Ethnobotany of the Menominee Indians. M-PM-B 4:1-174.

7627.   Smith, Huron Herbert. 1928. Ethnobotany of the Meskwaki Indians. M-PM-B 4:175-326.

7628.   Smith, Huron Herbert. 1932. Ethnobotany of the Ojibwe. M-PM-B 4:327-525.

7629.   Smith, Huron Herbert. 1933. Etnobotany of the Forest Potawotomi Indians. M-PM-B 7 No. 1.

7630.   Smith, Ilee. Analysis of the food ration of the Iowa State Penitentiary for the years 1935 to 1941 inclusive. Master's thesis. Iowa State College. 1942.

7631.   Smith, J. Cecil. 1931. Hair eating and pica in children. BJCD 28:282-289.

7632.   Smith, J. Cecil & Halstead, James A. 1970. Clay ingestion (geophagia) as a source of zinc for rats. JN 100 973-980.

7633.   Smith, Joseph Russell. 1919. The world's food resources. New York: Henry Holt.

7634.   Smith, Joseph Russell. 1929. Tree crops - a permanent agriculture. New York: Harcourt Brace.

   Includes a discussion of acorns (Quercus sp.) as human food.

7635.   Smith, Philip E.L. Man, the subsistence farmer: new directions in society and culture. In Progress in human nutrition. Vol. 2. Edited by Sheldon Margen & Richard Ogar. 1978. Pp. 27-41.

   Examines the consequences of horticulture and agriculture, characterized by the 'Neolithic Revolution', upon the development of human culture. Demographic and epidemological results of sedentary food production are hypothesized (e.g. population growth; increase in contagious disease, and nutritional deficiency). Changes in social and political organization are seen as occurring due to increased population density, and speculation is offered regarding cognitive and symbolic attitudes in art and religion as direct or indirect spin-offs of sedentary food production.

7636.   Smith, Robert O. 1947. Fishery resoures of Micronesia. USDI-FWS-FL No. 239.

   Preparation methods: p. 9.

7637.   Smith, Robinson. 1917. Food values and the rationing of a country. London: Commission for Relief in Belgium.

7838.   Smith, Robinson. 1918. Rationing through commercial channels, together with a sample breadcard. London: Commission for Relief in Belgium.

7639.   Smith, S. Percy. 1911. Did the Maoris know of rice? JPS 20:100.

   Data from Maori legend, and Rarotongan linguistic evidence are offerred as a possible basis for such knowledge.

7640.   Smith, Thomas Lyon. 1946. Brazil: people and institutions. Baton Rouge: Louisiana State University Press.

   Diet: pp. 363-372.

7641.   Smith, Victor E. 1959. Linear programming models for the determination of palatable human diets. JFE 41:272-283.

The author shows how least-cost diets may be developed, using a dietary-survey data base, and with consideration for human factors such as palatabilty and need for variety.

7642.   Smith, Victor E. & Yoghoobi-Rahmatabadi. 1973. The nutritional efficiency of improved methods in Nigerian agriculture. Econometrics Workshop Papers. No. 4302. East Lansing: Michigan State University.

Indicates altering certain traditional practices would increase, rather than decrease the cost of improving national nutritional status.

7643.   Smith, W. 1864. Hyssop. GCAG for 1864. Pp. 895-896.

Hyssopus officinalis was once a popular kitchen and tea herb.

7644.   Smith, W.; Powell, Elizabeth, K.; & Ross, S. 1955. Manifest anxiety and food aversion. JASP 50:101-104.

7645.   Smith, William Carlson. 1925. The Ao Naga tribe of Assam. London: Macmillan.

Food; cooking utensils: pp. 31-35.

7646.   Smith, W.H. & Smith, E.M. 1935. Native diet in Zanzibar. EAMJ 12:246-251.

7647.   Smithson, Carma Lee. 1959. The Havasupai woman. UU-AP No. 38.

Food: pp. 147-151.

7648.   Smyth, R. Brough. 1878. Aborigines of Victoria: with notes relating of the habits of the natives of other parts of Australia. 2 vols. London: Trubner.

Note on the use of skulls of departed relatives as drinking vessels: Vol. One. P. 30.

7649.   Snapper, I. 1955. Food preferences in man. Special cravings and aversions. NYAS-A 63:92:106.

7650.   Snow, L.F. & Johnson, S.M. 1978. Folklore, food, female reproductive cycle. EFN 7:41-49.

Forty women attending a public clinic in Ingham County, Michigan; responded to a questionnaire concerning the advisabilty of dietary changes during menstruation, pregnancy, and the puerperium; and about their attitudes toward clay - and starch-eating practices. Results show that a majority of respondents held one or more dietary folk beliefs linked to the various phases of the reproductive cycle and that many of these beliefs are nutritionally unsound.

7651.   Snow, Phyllis Roberta. Managerial aspects of freezer use with emphasis on cooked and prepared foods. Ph.D. dissertation. Ithaca, New York: Cornell University. 1956.

7652.   Snyder, Charles R. 1958. Alcohol and the Jews. Yale Center of Alcohol Studies. New Haven: Yale University Press.

7653.   Snyder, Charles R. Culture and Jewish sobriety: the in-group and out-group factor. In Society, culture, and drinking patterns. Edited by David Joshua Pittman & Charles R. Snyder. 1962. New York: Wiley & Sons.

7654.   Snyder, Clara Gebhard. 1957. Breads of many lands. Chicago: National Committee on Boys and Girls Club Work.

7655.   Snyder, Clara Gebhard. 1959. Holiday breads. Chicago: National Committee on Boys and Girls Club Work.

7656.   Snyder, M.E. A nutritive evaluation of the food consumed by three children when fed by the conventional method and by the Davis technique. Master's thesis. Iowa State College. 1936.

7657.   Snyder, Mary Leon. A diet change for the Eskimo: a challenge to their culture. Master's thesis. St. Louis, Missouri: St. Louis University. 1962.

7658.   Snyder, Sally. The spirit-power-wealth-food syndrome: a psychoanalytic interpretation of the potlatch. Paper presented at 70th Annual Meeting of the American Anthropological Association. 20 November, 1971. New York City.

A psychoanalytic interpretation of the potlatch gives it new significance within a coherent world view and value system, which underlie the manipulation of wealth as given descriptively by standard socioeconomic analyses. Conclusions are based on the data of Skagit ethnography and are supported in part by Erikson's Yurok data, and writings of Mauss and neo-Freudians. Resolutions presented for the Skagit case may pertain, as well, as to the entire North Pacific Coast potlatch area.

7659.   Snyder, Thomas E. 1927. Odd and curious facts about termites or white ants. M-P Mag 34:337-342.

7660.   Soberheim, M. 1912. Das Zuckermonopol unter Sultan Barsbai. [The sugar monopoly under Sultan Barsbai.] Z Assyr 27:75-84.

Al-Malik al-Ashraf abu al-Nasr Barsbai was Mamluk Sultan of Egypt from A.D. 1422 to 1438.

7661.   Society of Chemical Industry. 1968. Rheology and texture of foodstuffs. Monograph No. 27. London: Society of Chemical Industry.

7662. Soderstrom, Jan. 1937. Some notes on poi and other preserved vegetables in the Pacific. Ethnos 2:235-242.

Focused largely on fermented taro (Hawaii) and breadfruit (Marquesas, Tahiti). Food preservation methods in Micronesia and Melansia are mentioned beiefly. Also refers to Maori preservation of pigeon. Hawaiian taro processing equipment (poi-pounders) are illustrated.

7663. Soejarto, Djaja D. 1965. Baccaurea and its uses. HU-BML 21:65-104.

A species of Euphorbiaceae used as food in Malaysia and Borneo. The fruit is eaten raw, or cooked and fermented to produce a liquor.

7664. Soekirman. 1974. Priorities in dealing with nutrition problems in Indonesia. Cor U-INMS No. 1.

7665. Sofer, C.; Janis, I.; & Wishlade, L. 1964. Social and psychological factors in changing food habits. In Changing food habits. Edited by John Yudkin and John Crawford McKenzie. 1964. Pp. 90-108. London: MacGibbon & Kee.

7666. Sogandares, Lucila & Barios, G. de. 1955. Estudio dieteticos en Panama. 1. La mesa provincia de Veraguas. [Dietary studies in Panama. 1. The plateau province of Veraguas.] OSP-B-S(2) Pp. 38-46.

7667. Sogandares, Lucila de.; Barrios, G. de; & Corco, E.Z. de. 1955. Estudios dieteticos en Panama. 2. Barrio El Charillo. Ciudad de Panama. [Dietary studies in Panama. 2. Barrio El Charillo, Panama City.] OSP-B-S(2) Pp. 47-53.

7668. Sokolowsky, Alexander. 1903. Kannibalismus. [Cannibalism.] GVES-B 1901-1902. Pp. 19-22.

7669. Solenberger, Robert R. 1967. The changing role of rice in the Marianas Islands. Micronesica 3:97-103.

An aboriginal crop, rice, is no longer cultivated, but still highly valued and imported.

7670. Soler, Paul. 1979. The dietary prohibitions of the Hebrews. NYRevB 26(10):24-31.

7671. Solien de Gonzalez, Nancie L. 1963. Breast-feeding, weaning, and acculturation. JPed 62:577-581.

Guatemalans of European ancestry.

7672. Solien de Gonzales, Nancie L. 1963. Patterns of diet, health and sickness in a Black Carib community. TGM 15:422-430.

Food production; preparation; infant diet; diet during lactation: pp. 423-428. The community studied is Livingston, Guatemala. Includes data on food beliefs; meal times; snack foods; etiquette; hygiene; and typical meal patterns.

7673. Solien de Gonzalez, Nancy L. Changing dietary patterns of North American Indians. In Nutrition, growth and development of North American Indian children. Based on a conference co-sponsored by the National Institute of Child Health and Human Development, Indian Health Service, American Academy of Pediatrics Committee on Indian Health. Edited by William M. Moore; Marjorie M. Silverberg; & Merrill S. Read. 1972. Pp. 15-33. Department of Health, Education, and Welfare. Publication No. (NIH) 72-26. Washington, D.C.: Government Printing Office.

Covers ethnohistorical record; European influence; introduction of horses and guns; herd animals; furtrapping; population shifts and containment; factors causing deprivation: ethnographic record; the Southwest; Pueblo tribes; Papago, Yuma, and Navajo; Eastern Woodland groups; California, Plains, Northwest Coast, Arctic and subarctic tribes, Eskimo; and dietary taboos.

7674. Somanader, S.V.O. 1960. The water-lily as food and medicine. CTo 9:19-23.

7675. Somers, A.N. 1892. Prehistoric cannibalism in America. PSi 42:203-207. Also in WArch 19 [Series 1]: 20-24. (1920).

Human osteological material excavated at a mound-builder site, Aztalan, Wisconsin.

7676. Sonafrank, Jr., E. Allen. Computerized analysis of nutritional data. Paper presented at 76th Annual Meeting of the American Anthropological Association. 29 November to 3 December, 1977. Houston, Texas.

Drawing from the work of nutrition scientists, dietitians, and medical researchers, and from the development and generalization of interactive computer software to analyze nutritional data from the Upper Amazon basin, this paper elucidates considerations which are useful in formulating projects for the collection of adequate data; identifying lacunae in a date base which must be filled prior to processing; and designing or choosing a computer system flexible enough to carry out the analysis.

7677. Sonnenfeld, Joseph. Changes in subsistence among the Barrow Eskimo. Ph.D. dissertation. Geography. Baltimore, Maryland: Johns Hopkins University. 1957.

7678. Sontag, Lester Warren & Wines, Janet 1947. Relation of mothers' diets to status of their infants at birth and in infancy. AJOG 54:994-1003. Also in AC-FRI-P 45:3-12 (1946-1947).

7679. Soos, Aladar. 1932. Evolutionary periods in human diet. [In Hungarian.] Or Het 76:341-344.

7680. Soper, Fred L. INCAP - An innovation in

international collaboration. In Fourth Armed Forces International Nutrition Conference. August 24-31, 1960. Washington, D.C., Denver, Chicago. Interdepartmental Committee on Nutrition for National Defense. 1960. Pp. 115-119. Bethesda Maryland: National Institutes of Health.

This contribution is a history of the Instituto de Nutricion de Centro America y Panama.

7681.   Sopher, David Edward.   Turmeric in the color symbolism of southern Asia and the Pacific Islands. Master's thesis. University of California, Berkeley. 1950.

7682.   Sopher, David Edward.   1964.   Indigenous uses of turmeric (Curcuma domestica) in Asia and Oceania. Anthropos 59:93-127.

After a botanical description, the following subject areas are examined in detail: turmeric in domestic rites in India and elsewhere; as a dye and pigment; as condiment and coloring matter in food; in magic and folk medicine, in agricultural rites.

7683.   Sordinas, Augustus.   Old and new olive-oil machines in Corfu, Greece: an ethnographic case study of rapid technical and cultural change. Paper presented at 68th Annual Meeting of the American Anthropological Association.   20 to 23 November, 1969. New Orleans, Louisiana.

Fieldwork was carried out in 50 villages on the island of Corfu to gather data for the construction of a typology of pre-industrial olive-oil workshops on the island (A.D. 17th to 20th Centuries). Data show that simple wooden presses and primitive, horse-drawn rotary mills (all gigantic and cumbersome) lingered in the economy until the end of World War II. The form and function of this equipment indicate an equilibrium between the availability of cheap peasant labor and these low-yielding primitive machines. After World War II, the rapid introduction of electrification and modern technology upset this equilibrium and revolutionized production rates. The economy was reoriented. The available peasant labor now released from the rigidity of the earlier social organization, found new outlets in the industrial demands of the Greek cities, and Germany. The gathered data indicate the following polarity: the old men (here called "rejectors") still cling to their antiquated values regarding the pre-industrial machines. The young (here called "acceptors") overtly despise these machines and demonstrably orient their values toward urbanized village economies and the new power symbolized by the industrial machines. This paper aims to show statistically these correlations and the significance of this age-group polarity.

7684.   Sordinas, Augustus. 1971. Old olive oil mills and presses on the island of Corfu, Greece.   An essay on industrial archeology and the ethnography

of agricultural implements.   Memphis SU-ARC-OP No. 5.

7685.   Sordinas, Augustus.   Wild plant-gathering for subsistence in the villages of Corfu, Greece. Paper presented at 70th Annual Meeting of the American Anthropological Association.   21 November, 1971. New York City.

This paper emphasizes the neglected role of wild plants in the economy of settled farming villages. An attempt is made to examine critically the often artificially polarized concepts of subsistence farming and gathering activities, not as theoretical formulations but, rather, as variable ecological adaptations in the subsistence routine of the traditional farming village.

7686.   Sorel, Francois.   L'alimentation des indigenes en Afrique Occidentale Fancaise   [Diet of natives in French West Africa.]   In L'alimentation indigene dans les colonies francaises.   Protectorats et territoires sous mandat. Edited by G. Hardy & C. Richet. 1933. Pp. 155-176. Paris: Vigot Freres.

Opens with a general discussion of the role of food in the cultures of French West Africa. A region by region review follows (i.e. the Sahara, Sudan, Guinea). A description of typical workers' and soldiers rations' closes the article.

7687.   Sorenson, E. Richard & Gajdusek, Daniel Carleton. 1969. Nutrition in the Kuru Region. 1. Gardening, food handling, and diet of the Fore people. A Trop 26:281-330.

Ecology; cannibalism; sweet potato cultivation; traditional garden products; pigs: domesticated animals; hunting and gather-ing; introduced foods; native-made salt; daily meals; casual eating; feasts, dietary fluctuations; and cash crops among a group of eastern New Guinea highlanders. This monograph in nutritional anthropology derives from research on the aetiology of kuru, a slow-acting, neural virus associated with the ingestion of human tissue, in mortuary cannibalism practiced until the late 1950's among Fore groups.

7688.   Soret, Marcel. 1959. Les Kongo nord occidentaux. [The northeastern Kongo culture.] Institut International Africain. Monographies Ethnologiques. Paris: Presses Universitaires de France.

Food habits: pp. 53-55.

7689.   Sotheby & Company. 1965. Catalogue of the Westbury collection of cookery books...sold by auction by Sotheby & Co. 22 February 1965, and the following day. London: Sotheby & Co.

7690.   Soto, William Reuben & Fonseca, Ana Cecelia de. Patrones reales e ieales de ingestion de bebidas alcoholics en el area metropolitana. [Real and ideal patterns of alcoholic beverage consumption in the metropolitan area.] Paper presented at 73rd Annual Meeting of the American Anthropological Association. 19 to 24 November, 1974. Mexico City.

Costa Rica.

7691. Sound, K.K. 1968. Infant and toddler feeding practices in a village around Primary Health Care Centre, Najafgarh (Delhi). MMJ 14:641-650.

Najafgarh is located at 28.37N., 76. 59 E.

7692. Sound, K.K. & Lal, A. 1969. Production and consumption patterns of milk in a small community. ASI 24:729-734.

Data on methods of milk use (largely in tea); and in cooking; and attitudes toward milk consumption are recorded. The village studied is Kair, in Delhi Union Territory.

7693. Southern Pacific Company. 1928. General instructions covering service by dining car waiters. San Francisco: Southern Pacific Company. August 15.

7694. Southworth, Mary E., compilor. 1906. One hundred and one Mexican dishes. New York: San Francisco: Paul Elder.

7695. Souza, A.H. 1955. Caijuna. RBQ 39:218.

Processed cashew juice, and its food value.

7696. Souza, Antonio Jose de. Do regimen das classes pobres e dos escravos na cidade do Rio de Janeiro em seus alimentos e bebidas. [On the diet of the poor and of the slaves in Rio de Janeiro: their foods and beverages.] Medical thesis. Faculty of Medicine of Rio de Janeiro. 1822.

7697. Souza, Robert Adrian. Differentials in consumption patterns among major ethnic groups on Oahu. Master's thesis. Business Administration. University of Hawaii. 1965.

7698. Souza-Novelo, N. 1950. Plantas alimenticias y plantas de condimento que viven en Yucatan. [Food plants and condiment plants growing in Yucatan.] Merida: Instituto Tecnico Agricola Henequenero.

7699. Sowerby, Arthur de C. 1931. The edible bird's nest swift. CJ 14:135-137.

The bird the saliva of which produces the nest used in Chinese cookery.

7700. Soyer, Alexis. 1853. The pantropheon, or history of food and its preparation, from the earliest ages of the world. London: Simpkin, Marshall; Boston: Ticknor, Reed & Fields.

7701. Soyer, Nicolas. 1911. Soyer's paper-bag cookery. New York: Sturgis & Walton.

7702. Spalding, Walter. 1957-1958. O sol no populario gaucho. [Salt in gaucho folklore.] CCF-B 8:60-72.

Rio Grande do Sul, Brazil.

7703. Spangle, Paul & Sutton, Myron. 1949. The botany of Montezuma Well. Plateau. 22:11-20.

East central Verde Valley, Arizona. Includes list of plants identified.

7704. Spannaus, Gunther. 1954-1955. Ernahrung und Ess-Sitten bei den Ndau in Sudost-Afrika. [Diet and etiquette among the Ndau in southeast Africa.] Tribus 4-5:69-77.

7705. Sparkes, Brian A. & Talcott, Lucy. 1964. Pots and pans of classical Athens. Excavations of the Athenian Agora. Picture Books No. 1. Princeton: American School of Classical Studies at Athens.

7706. Sparks, Jack P. The spatial context of a rural Guatemalan diet. Master's thesis. Pennsylvania State University. 1966.

7707. Spath, Georges. Geschichte des Braugewerbes im Kanton Luzern. [History of the brewing trade in the Canton of Lucern.] Ph.D. dissertation. Zurich: Volkswirtschaftliche Universitat. 1952.

7708. Specht, Franz Anton. 1887. Gastmahler und Trinkgelager bei den Deutschen von den altesten Zeiten bis ins neunte Jahrhundert, ein Beitrag zur Deutschen Kulturgeschichte. [Banquets and drinking bouts among the Germans from the earliest times until the 19th Century, a study in German culture history.] Stuttgart: J.H. Cotta.

7709. Specht, R.L. & Mountford, Charles P., eds. 1958. Records of the American-Australian scientific expedition to Arnhem Land. Vol. 3. Botany and plant ecology. Melbourne: Melbourne University Press.

7710. Specht, R.L. An introduction to the ethnobotany of Arnhem Land. In Records of the American-Australian scientific expedition to Arnhem Land. Vol. 3. Botany and plant ecology. Edited by R.L. Specht & Charles P. Mountford. 1958. Pp. 479-503. Melbourne: Melbourne University Press.

7711. Speck, Frank Gouldsmith. 1909. Ethnology of the Yuchi Indians. UPenn-UM-AP 1(1).

Food preparation: pp. 42-45.

7712. Speck, Frank Gouldsmith. 1941. Gourds of the southeastern Indians. Boston: New England Gourd Society. United States.

7713. Speck, Frank Gouldsmith. 1942. The Tutelo spirit adoption ceremony. Pennsylvania Historical Commission. Harrisburg: Commonwealth of Pennsylvania Department of Public Instruction.

Food: p. 30.

7714. Speck, Frank Gouldsmith & Dexter, R.W. 1948. Utilization of marine life by the Wampanoag Indians of Massachusetts. WAS-J 38:257-265.

7715. Spector, D.H. & Calloway, Doris Howes. 1960. Modification of the response of guinea pigs to whole-body irradiation by dietary supplementation with raw plant materials. Quartermaster Food and Container Institute for the Armed Forces. Report 28-60.

Exposure to 400 r.w.b x-irradiation resulted in 99% mortality in 10-15 days of young male guinea pigs fed basal diet of bran and oats plus ascoric acid. Supplementation with green plant materials, notably from the Brassicas, for 2 weeks before irradiation, and during 30 days after irradition reduced mortality to 46%. Other categories of foods showed marginal or no beneficial effects. Pre-feeding of cabbage to time of radiation exposure delayed onset of death; post-irradiation supplementation yielded a lower total mortality. These effects were additive. Supplements which were beneficial promoted improved growth, but superior weight gains did not guarantee decreased radiosensitivity. Supplements providing vitamin A uniformly extended survival time but did not consistently influence mortality.

7716.   Spector, Harry & Peterson, Martin S., eds. 1954. Nutrition under climatic stress. A symposium sponsored by the Quartermaster Food and Container Institute for the Armed Forces. Quartermaster Research and Development Command. U.S. Army Quartermaster Corps. National Academy of Sciences. Washington, December 4-5, 1952. Washington, D.C.: National Academy of Sciences-National Research Council.

Comprises four sessions of papers: 1. Practical problems of service operations under climatic stress; 2. Animal experimentation; 3. Human experimentation; 4. Summary of present knowledge - need for more research.

7717.   Speed, J.G. 1900.   Food and foreigners in New York. HW 44:846-847.

7718.   Speight, W.L. 1943. Food through the ages. Cath Dgst 7:47-49.

7719.   Spencer, Baldwin.   Chapter Eleven. Food restrictions. In Native tribes of the Northern Territory of Australia. 1914. London: Macmillan.

The Kakadu tribe. Boys and youths; women in pregnancy; husbands; young men passing through ober and Jamba ceremonies; removal of restrictions; and among the Port Essington natives.

7720.   Spencer, Herbert & Collier, James.   1873. Spencer's descriptive sociology; a cyclopaedia of social facts. No. 1. English. New York: D. Appleton.

Food: p. 58.

7721.   Spencer, Herbert & Collier, James.   1881. Spencer's descriptive sociology; a cyclopaedia of social facts. No. 8. French. New York: D. Appleton.

Food: pp. 143-144.

7722.   Spencer, Herbert & Duncan, David.   1874. Spencer's descriptive sociology; a cycolopaedia of social facts, No. 3 Negrito races, and Malayo-Polynesian races. New York: D. Appleton.

Food: pp. 54-55.

7723.   Spencer, Herbert & Duncan, David.   1875. Spencer's descriptive sociology; a cyclopaedia of social facts. No. 4. African races. New York: D. Appleton.

Food: P. 42.

7724.   Spencer, Herbert & Duncan, David.   1876. Spencer's descriptive sociology; a cyclopaedia of social facts. No. 5. Asiatic races. New York: D. Appleton.

Food: Pp. 51-52.

7725.   Spencer, Herbert & Duncan, David.   1878. Spencer's descriptive sociology: a cyclopaedia of social facts. No. 6. American races. New York: D.Appleton.

Food: p.49.

7726.   Spencer, Herbert & Scheppig, Richard. 1874. Spencer's descriptive sociology; a cyclopaedia of social facts.   No. 2.   Mexicans, Central Americans, Chibchas, and Peruvians. New York: D. Appleton.

Food: pp. 64-65.

7727.   Spencer, Herbert & Scheppig, Richard. 1880. Spencer's descriptive sociology; a cyclopaedia of social facts. No. 7. Hebrews and Phoenicians. New York: C. Appleton.

Food: pp. 111-112.

7728.   Spencer, Joseph E. 1935. Salt in China. GR 25: 353-366.

7729.   Spencer, Joseph E. 1942.   The Szechwan village tea house. J Geog 41: 52-58.

7730.   Spencer, K.S. 1919. An old-time method of yeast-making. A Cook 23: 520-521.

7731.   Sperber, Daniel. 1965. Cost of living in Roman Palestine. JESHO 8: 248-271.

7732.   Sperling, H. 1955. Die sozio-okonomische Bedeutung der pysiologischen Nahrungsmittelbewertung. [The socio-economic significance of the physiological evaluation of food.] SJGVV 4: 53-62.

7733.   Speth, John D. Subsistence and settlement system of Olduvai Autralopithecines: Some preliminary hypotheses. Paper presented at 74th Annual Meeting of the American Anthropological Association. 2 to 6 December, 1975. San Francisco, California.

7734.   Spezzafumo, O.   1940.   Enquete sur l'alimentation dans la population italienne ouvriere de Tunis. [Dietary inquirey among an Italian working population of Tunis.] IPT-A 29: 113-125.

7735.   Spicer, D.G. 1926. Health superstitions of the Italian immigrant. Hygaeia 4:266-269.

Food prejudices; frying; use of black coffee: pp. 266, 268.

7736.   Spier, Leslie. 1928. Havasupai ethnography. AMNH-PA 29:81-408.

Wild foods: pp. 105-180; food preparation: pp. 114-123.

7737.   Spier, Leslie 1933.   Yuman tribes of the Gila River. Chicago: University of Chicago Press.

Food: mesquite flowers: pp. 51, 79; ironwood nuts: pp. 53-54; cholla beans: p. 54; opuntia fruit: p. 54; mescal: p. 55; saguaro fruit: pp. 56-57; black-eyed peas, beans, pumpkin: pp. 63-64; fowl, turtle honey, insects: pp. 72-73; fish: pp. 77-78.

7738.   Spier, Leslie & Sapir, Edward. 1930. Wishram ethnography. UWash-PE 3:151-300.

Acorn as food, berries; nuts; moss; roots: pp. 182-186.

7739.   Spier, Robert F.G. 1951. Some notes on the origin of taro. SJA 7:69-76.

7740.   Spier, Robert F.G.   1958.   Food habit of Nineteenth-Century Chinese. Cal H SQ 37:79-84; 129-136.

Documents maintenance of traditional food habits through importation, agriculture, and fishing enterprises.

7741.   Spiers, Marguerite L.   1929.   The social worker and dietitics. HSS 19:441-444.

Covers economic insufficiency; broken homes; alcoholism; drug addiction; mental disabilty; superstition; ethnic and religious beliefs; environmental problems; foster homes; lack of home or family. Encourages closer cooperation between social worker and dietitian, especially where diet regulation is critical to health.

7742.   Spiess, Arthur. Dorset Eskimo subsistence patterns. Paper presented at 75th Annual Meeting of the Ameican Anthropological Association. 17 to 21 November, 1976. Washington, D.C.

Reports on the application of recent advances in osteoarcheology to survey of Labrador Eskimo sites from Okak Bay, and reproduces the main features of the ethnographically-known subsistence and settlement cycle. Evidence from Labrador and the Belcher Islands, elicited with the same techniques, suggests that Dorset settlement and subsistence strategies were very similar to those of ethnographically-known non-whale-hunting Eskimos of the eastern Arctic.

7743.   Spiller, Brian. 1955.   The story of beer. 1. The first five thousand years. Geog Mag 28:86-94; 2. The rise of the English brewing trade; 28:143-154; 3. From brewery to bar; 28:169-181.

7744.   Spillman, W.J. Teosinte. In Cyclopedia of farm crops. A popular survey of crops and cropmaking methods in the United States and Canada. By Liberty Hyde Bailey. 1922. New York: Macmillan.

7745.   Spinden, Herbert J. The origin and distribution of agriculture in America. Nineteenth International Congress of Americanists. December 27-31, 1915. Washington, D.C. Proceedings. Pp. 269-276.

Comments on the association of pottery with agriculture in relation to sedentary societies. Discusses various arguments for and against Old versus New World origins of certain food plants, e.g. coconut; common gourd; maize. Types of agriculture are considered in relation to ecological zone: e.g. arid; humid tropical.

7746.   Spinden, Herbert J. 1928. Thank the American Indian. SA 138:330-332.

Food plants.

7747.   Spinden, Herbert J. 1946. Food plants of the Indians of the Guatemalan highlands. AArb-J 27:395-400.

A sketch of commonly-used foods, with interspersed comments on food habits.

7748.   Spindler, Evelyn B. 1967. Food for family survival.   Leader's guide.   USDA-DHE-FES & DD-OCD.

Pamphlet keyed to film loop relating to problems of food protection, storage, etc. in the event of nuclear attack.

7749.   Spindler, Evelyn B. 1967. Script for "Food for family survival". USDA-DHE-FES & DD-OCD.

7750.   Spindler, Evelyn B. & Camp, Susan B. 1967. Food for family survival. Suggestions for the extension worker. USDA-DHE-FES & DD-OCD.

7751.   Spinks, G.P. 1963. Pilot survey of food consumption and expenditure patterns in two settlements in Port Moresby. PNGAJ 16:21-36.

7752.   Spooner, E.C.R. 1957. Food habits. FTA 9:359, 361, 363, 403.

An informal approach concerned primarily with food taboos and food avoidance. Text of an after-dinner speech.

7753.   Spooner, F. Regimes alimentaires d'autrefois: proportions et calculs en calories. [Diets in former times: quantities and caloric calculations.]

In Pour une histoire de l'alimentation. Edited by J.J. Hemardinquer. 1970. Pp. 35-42. Paris: Colin.

7754. Sprague, Claire D. 1973. Making it with bread. PH 17:1-8.

History of the Genoa Bakery, in Stockton, California, from A.D. 1918.

7755. Sprauve, M.E. & Dodds, M.L. 1965. Dietary survey of adolescents in the Virgin Islands. JADA 47:287-291.

7756. Spruill, Julia Cherry. 1972. Women's life and work in the Southern colonies. New York: W.W. Norton Co.

Housewives and their helpers: pp. 276-277; food advertising: pp. 282-283.

7757. Squiller, Joseph. 1859. Des subsistances militaires, de leur qualite de leur falsification, de leur manutention et de leur conservation, et etude sur l'alimentation de l'homme et du cheval, appliquee, plus specialement au soldat et a cheval de troupe. [Military supplies, their quality, falsification, management, and preservation; and study of the feeding of men and horses, applied most specially to soldiers and troop horses.] Anvers: Dumaine.

7758. Squires, Bernard T. 1943. Malnutrition amongst Tswana children. A Studies 2:210-214.

7759. Squires, Bernard T. 1956. Nutrition in the Bechuanaland Protectorate. CAFJ 2:112-118.

Provides background on ecological variables impinging on food supply. Dietary patterns, and staple foods are described and evaluated in terms of their nutritional adequacy. Nutritional status is profiled, and dietary deficiencies recorded.

7760. Sreenivasmurthy, V. & Krishnamurthy. 1959. Place of spices and aromatics in Indian dietary. FS 8:287-288.

7761. Srinavas, M.N. 1961. Sociological aspects of Indian diet. ASI 16:246-248.

7762. Srivastava, P. An investigation of the factors associated with food procurement in selected rural families. Master's thesis. Lady Irwin College. University of Delhi. 1967.

Studies factors associated with food procurement in rural families; i.e. caste; occupation; land-holding; food taboos; and education. Home production of food increased in proportion to size of land holdings. Village studied is Nangloi, in Delhi Union Territory. [After Schofield 1975:103].

7763. Stadelman, Raymond. 1940. Maize cultivation in northwestern Guatemala. CIW-CAAH 6:85-205.

7764. Staden, Hans. [i.e. Johann von.] Killing and eating one's enemy in Sixteenth Century Brazil. In Primitive Heritage. Edited by Margaret Mead &

Nicolas Calas. 1953. Pp. 494-494. New York: Randon House.

A full account of Staden's adventures is found in Hans Staden: the true history of his captivity, 1557. Translated and edited by Malcolm Letts. 1928. London: G. Routledge & Son.

7765. Stahel, Gerold. 1942. De nuttige planten van Suriname. [The useful plants of Surinam.] S-DL-B No. 57.

7766. Stahel, Gerold. 944. Notes on the Arawak Indian names of plants in Surinam. NYBG-J 45:268-275.

7767. Stahel, Gerold. 1946. Soybeans. NYBG-J 47:21-285.

Food uses in Asia, and Surinam.

7768. Stahl, Gunther. 1932. Die Geophagy. [Geophagy.] ZE 63:346-374.

7769. Stair, John B. 1897. Palolo, a sea worm eaten by Samoans. JPS 6:141-144.

7770. Stamer, Heinrich. 1964 Aus dem Dorfbuch Brunstorf (2). Ueber das Essen. [From the Brunstorf village-book (2). On eating.] LHeim 44:50.

7771. Stamm, Emily K. & Wiehl, Dorothy G. 1942. Medical evaluation of nutritional status. 8. The school lunch as a method of improving diets of high school students. MMFQ 20:83-96.

7772. Stampa, Manuel Carrera. 1961. Comida tipica de Mexico. [Typical Mexican foods.] AMH-M 20:21-41.

Regional Mexican foods.

7773. Stan, Anisoara. 1951. The Romanian cookbook. New York: Citadel Press.

7774. Standing Bear, Luther. 1928. My people the Sioux. Edited by E.A. Brininstool. Boston: Houghton Mifflin. Reprint. Lincoln: University of Nebraska Press. 1975.

Food: pp. 21-23.

7775. Standley, Paul C. 1912. Some useful native plants of New Mexico. SI-AR for the year 1911. Pp. 447-462.

Includes edible plants.

7776. Standley, Paul C. 1926. Trees and shrubs of Mexico. SI-USNH-C No. 23.

This encylopedic monograph includes scattered references to food materials throughout. Nahuatl, Spanish, Latin, and English names are given.

7777. Stanfield, Sott. 1961. A chronology of precontact subsistence crops in the southwest. UOkla-DA-PA 2:1-12.

Maize, *Phaseolus* sp., cucurbits.

7778.   Stanford, Karin B.   A country store in Jacksonian America: a study of purchase patterns in St. Mary's County, Maryland.   Master's thesis. Anthropology. District of Columbia: George Washington University. 1976.

7779.   Stanilaus, I.V.S. 1908. Kefir and its preparation. AJP 80:20-26.

Kefir is a fermented milk product.

7780.   Stanislawski, Dan.   1970.   Landscapes of Bacchus: the vine in Portugal. Austin: University of Texas Press.

7781.   Stanislawski, Dan.   1975.   Dionysius westward: early religion and the economic geography of wine. GR 65:427-444.

7782.   Stanley, Louise & Yeatman, Fanny Walker. 1929. Reindeer recipes. USDA-L No. 48.

Included is an introductory historical note regarding marketing of reindeer meat in the United States.

7783.   Stanley, S. 1966.   Ensete in the Ethiopian economy. EGJ 4:30-37.

Ensete ventricosum, or 'false banana'.

7784.   Stanner, W.E.H.   1933.   Ceremonial economics of the Mulluk Mulluk and Madngella tribes of the Daly River, North Australia. A preliminary paper. Oceania 4:156-175; 458-471.

Foods, and their preparation in ceremonial exchange between respective relatives of bride, and bridegroom: pp. 466-470.

7785.   Stanton, J.R.; Doughty, Joyce; Orraca-Tetteh, R.; & Steele, W.   1966.   Grain legumes in Africa. Rome: Food and Agriculture Organization of the United Nations.

Eating beliefs; preparation: pp. 18-23.

7786.   Stanton, W.R. & Willett, F. 1963. Archaeological evidence for changes in maize type in West Africa: an experiment in technique. Man 63:117-123.

Analysis based on variation of ceramic sherds decorated with impressions of maize-kernels.

7787.   Stastna, J. 1959. Strava textilnich delniku v usti nad Orlici a okoli od Ronce minuleho stoleti do prvni svetove valky. [Food of textile workers in Usti Orl and the surrounding region since the end of the last century to World War I.] Cesky Lid 46: 130-158.

Czechoslovakia.

7788.   Stathopoulo, T. 1925. The use of preserved olives as food. [In French.] J P Chim 8: 280-285.

Greece.

7789.   Stavrakis, Olga & Cassidy, Claire M. Methods for quantifying nutrition and subsistence data. Paper presented at 73rd Annual Meeting of the American Anthropological Association. 19 to 24 November, 1974. Mexico city.

With reference to the Maya lowlands.

7790.   Steager, Peter William. Food in its social context on Puluwat, Eastern Caroline Islands.   Ph. D.   dissertation.   Anthropology.   University of California, Berkeley. 1971.

Food classification system (cooked/uncooked): pp. 65-68; edible and inedible foods: pp. 79-96; organoleptic factors involved in dietary choice: pp. 97-100; food supply: pp. 127-139; food distribution: pp. 140-145; food preparation; cookery; equipment: pp. 147-159; food preparations: pp. 159-167; animal food preparation: pp. 167-168; food preferences : pp. 168-171; food consumption; eating rituals; who eats with whom; host-guest relationships: pp. 180-185; time and place of eating: pp. 185-186; personal and interpersonal behavior during eating: pp. 186-190.

7791.   Stearns, W.T. 1965.   The origin and later development of cultivated plants. RHS 90: 279-341.

7792.   Stechishin, Savella.   1957.   Traditional Ukrainian cookery. Winnipeg: Trident Press.

7793.   Steckle, J. 1972. Effects of industrialization on food consuption patterns in two Ewe villages.   Institute of Statistical, Social and Economic Research. Technical Publication Series. No. 20. Legon, Ghana: University of Ghana.

The two villages studied are Juapong, located in the Tonga District, in which income is based on industrial wage labor; and Vane, located in the Ho District (6. 38 N., O. 38E.), which is primarily agricultural. Schofield (1975:26) remarks that data reported on food practices are extremely detailed.

7797.   Steel, Thomas. 1893. Cannibals and cannibalism. VNAT 10: 4-10, 26-30.

Fiji, and New Zealand Maori.

7798.   Steen, Charlie R. & Jones, Volney Hurt. 1941. Prehistoric lima beans in teh Southwest. El Pal 48: 197-203.

Upper Tonto Ruin, Arizona. Includes background on origin, and New World cultivation.

7796.   Steenmeijer, Folkert. 1957. Chaper three. Foods and dietary customs. In Food and Nutrition of Arubans. Utrecht: Schotanus & Jens.

Maize, wheat, and Sorghum vulgare are grain staples, and the comoposite foods prepared from them are described. Breads and soups are then enumerated, followed by a list of fruits, vegetables, legumes, dairy products, fats, oils, animal foods (including seafood) and beverages. Family food customs are indicated, with special mention of infant feeding practices, and food habits of school children. The remainder of the monograph is comprised of sociological background data, and data deriving from nutritional surveys, analyses, and recommendations based on the latter.

7797. Steenstrup, Johan Japetus Smith. 1886. Kjokkenmodinger. Eine gedrangte Darstellung dieser Monumente sehr alter Kulturstadien, mit 3 Holzschnitten und 1 Kupfertafel. [Kitchenmiddens. A concise statement on these monuments of a very old cultural level, with three wood cuts and one copperplate. Copenhagen: Hagerup.

7798. Steeves, Taylor, A. 1952. Wild rice - Indian food and a modern delicacy. EB 6: 107-142.

A comprehensive botanical, historic and economic study. Food uses; harvesting; and Native American mythic material are recorded.

7799. Stefaniszyn, Bronislaw. 1964. The material culture of the Ambo of Northern Rhodesia. RLM-OP No. 16.

Food: pp. 41-53.

7800. Stefansson, Vilhjalmur. 1920. Food tastes and food prejudices of men and dogs. SM 11: 540-543.

7801. Stefansson, Vilhjalmur. 1935-1936. Adventures in diet. Harper's 171: 668-675. 172: 46-54; 178-179.

7802. Stefansson, Vilhjalmur. 1937. Food of the ancient and modern stone age man. JADA 13: 102-119.

Account of the author's experiences with Eskimo populations of the Mackenzie River, Northwest Territories. Subjects covered include vegetable foods, fish; meat; meat and fish preservation; cooking techniques; use of blood as food; mastication of food; comments on dentition.

7803. Stefansson, Vilhjalmur. 1944. The diets of explorers. MSurg 95: 103.

Cites examples of individuals who have eaten flesh diets exclusively for long periods without suffering ill effects.

7804. Stefanson, Vilhjaalmur. 1944. Pemmican. M Surg 95: 89-98.

A history of the use, varieties and manufacture of a dried meat product developed by Native North Americans.

7805. Stefansson, Vilhjalmur. 1956. The fat of the land. New York: Macmillan. An expanded version of Stefansson's book Not by bread alone. New York: Macmillan. 1946.

Concerned largely with the place of meat, and animal fat in the diet of Artic populations, with some references to meat diet in other area of the world. A wide range of travel literature is cited in support of the author's own observations as an explorer. Several chapters are concerned with pemmican. in addition, a detailed account is included of the author's experimental, long-term diet on which only flesh was eaten.

7806. Stefansson, Viljhalmur. Food and food habits in Alaska and northern Canada. In Human nutrition: historic and scientific. New York Academy of Medicine. Institute of Social and Historical Medicine. Monograph 3. Edited by Iago Goldston. 1960. Pp. 23-60. New York: International Universities Press.

7807. Steffen, Max. 1883. Die Landwirtschaft bei den altamerikanischen Kulturvolkern. [Agriculture among ancient American aborigenes.] Leipzig: Duncker und Humbolt.

7808. Steffensen, Jon. 1958. Stature as a criterion of the nutritional level of Viking Age Icelanders. Islen Forn 1958. Pp. 39-51.

7809. Steggerda, Morris. 1943. Some ethnological data concerning one hundred Yucatan plants. SI-BAE-B 136: 189-226.

The majority of the plants recorded here are medicinal, however, there are a few which are used for food, or food-related purposes (containers, wrappers). One hundred plants are listed, which were collected by the author in the vicinity of Chichen Itza.

7810. Steggerda, Morris & Benedict, Francis Gano. 1932. Metabolism in Yucatan: a study of the Maya Indian. AJP 100: 274-284.

7811. Steggerda, Morris & Carpenter, Thorne M. 1939. The food of the present-day Navajo Indians of New Mexico and Arizona. JN 18: 297-305.

A review of sixty-six common foods, with nutrient analysis; informal quantitative food consumption data are recorded. Food plants are identified only by common English names.

7812. Steggarda, Morris & Cranston, Harriet. 1935-1936. Anthropology and human genetics. CIW- DG-RE No. 35.

Includes data on dental caries; nutrition.

7813. Steggerda, Morris & Eckardt, Ruth B. 1941. Navajo foods and their preparation. JADA 17: 217-225.

Maize and maize meal; breads, dumplings and mush; vegetables; fruits; nuts; and berries; grass and weed seeds (including Amaranthus retroflexus, L.) ; and meats. Navajo, Latin, and English plant names are included.

7814.   Stehle, Henri. Ethnobotanique precolombienne dans l'archipel caraibe. [Precolombian ethnobotany of the Caribbean archipelago.] In Huitieme Congres International de Botanique. 1954. Paris. Rappports et Communications. Parvenus avant le Congres aux Sections 14,15, & 16. 1954. Pp. 35-36.

7815.   Stehle, Henri & Stehle, Mme. 1963. Le ravets de la Guadeloupe; ces commensaux indesirables. [The turnips of Guadelupe; those undesirable table companions.] B Pedag 1: 37-40/

7816.   Steidl, Rose E. Arrangement of spearate electric range surface units and ovens. Department of Household Economics and Management. New York State College of Home Economics. Ithaca, New York; Cornell University. Unpublished report. 1954.

7817.   Steidl, Rose E. Effects of multiple water and drainage facilities on work involved in family meal preparation and cleanup. Ph. D. dissertation. Ithaca, New York: Cornell University. 1957.

7818.   Steidl, Rose E. 1958. Use of time during family meal preparation and cleanup. JHE 50: 447-450.

Laboratory studies indicate time cost for the preparation of complex meals (breakfasts, lunches, dinners) was greater than for cleanup, in a ratio of sixty percent to forty percent, even though menus and test conditions varied. The author emphasizes that test conditions and home conditions are different, insofar as home tasks are subject to interruption, and urges that home studies of time cost in meal preparation and clean-up be undertaken.

7819.   Steidl, Rose E. 1960. Supplementary sinks in home kitchens. CorU - AES-B No. 374.

The purpose of this investigation was to determine the possible usefulness of additional sinks with limited cold water and drainage facilities and if these would change work patterns during family meal preparation, service, and clean-up, in order to reduce effort. Various arrangements of sinks were experimented with, and their effects analyzed and evaluated.

7820.   Steidl, rose E. 1961. Family in the Kitchen. Cor U - HEMRR   No. 6.

Detailed informtion about the movement of family members in and out of the kitchen during meal preparation and cleaning is limited. Little is known also about the help received, and the number and type of interruptions homemakers have as they work in their kitchens. This report investigates these variables, and their relevance for planning functional and versatile kitchen space.

7821.   Steidl, Rose E. 1961. Using kitchen storage space before and after the addition of functional storage devices. Cor U-HEMRR No. 5.

This report summarizes a relatively small but detailed study planned to compare the work at storage areas in identical home kitchens before and after adding functional storage devices. In addition, information was sought about the costs of altering existing storage areas and changes in linear footage of shelving.

7822.   Steidl, Rose E. 1962. Trips between centers in kitchens for 100 meals. An examination of methods of analysis and relationships to kitchen planning and description of work. CorU-AES-B No. 971.

This monograph has as its purpose an analysis of variables affecting the arrangement of equipment, work, and storage space in the kitchen.

7823.   Steidl, Rose E. 1963. Continuity of household work. Cor U-AES B No. 383.

A study of variables affecting work task sequence undertaken to clarify factors important in work planning and control. Contains statistics relating to meal preparation and related activities.

7824.   Steidl, Rose E. 1963. Research methods for study of human costs of household work: development and use at Cornell University. Cor U AES B No. 988.

This monograph is concerned with time and motion studies, and with the ergonomics of household design. A 'slow motion' film recording technique, termed "memomotion" is described for the documenting of time-motion studies. According to the introductory section "Only the methods developed or used at the Cornell University Agricultural Experiment Station and in the Department of Household Economics and Manageement are included. They were used most often in the Study of the function and design of kitchens" (p.5).

7825.   Steigelmann, W. 1962. Der Wein in der Bibel. [Wine in the Bible.] Neustadt a.d. Wein.: Meininger.

7826.   Stein, Lothar. 1964. Arabische Kaffeekochkunst. [The art of Arabian coffee preparation.] LMV-M No. 4 Pp. 13-14.

7827.   Steinberg, Rafael. 1969. The cooking of Japan. New York: Time-Life Books. Foods of the World.

7828.   Steinberger, A. Die Neuerungen des Polizeitierarztes Dr. Michael Stangassinger. Ein beitrag Zur Entwicklung der Fleischund Lebensmittel hugiene in Munchen in der Mitte des 19 Jahrhunderts. [The innovations in veterinary policing of Dr. Michael Stangassinger. A contribution to the development of meat and food hygiene in Munich during the mid-19th century.] Ph.D. dissertation. Munich: Ludwig - Maximilians Universitat. 1967.

7829. Steininger, G. Russell & Van de Velde, Payul. 1935. Chapter Fourteen. Beans on horseback. In Three dollars a year. Being the story of San Pablo Cuatro Venados, a typical Zapotecan Indian village that hangs on a slope of the Sierras in southwestern Mexico. New York: Delphic Studios Reprint. Detroit: Blaine Ethridge. 1971.

Tabulation of foods consumed, and their costs: p. 114.

7830. Steinkraus, B.; Yap, B.H.; Van Bauren, J.P.; Providenti, M.I.; & Hand, D.B. 1960. Studies on tempeh - an Indonesian soybean food. FR 25: 777.

7831. Steinmetz, Rudolph S. 1896. Endokannibalismus. [Endocannibalism.] AGWS - M 26: 1-60.

Refers to the custom of eating deceased parents or other consaguines. The author concludes that endocannibalism is an analogue of what has been observed among other animals; exocannibalism, on the other hand, is a result of moral, religious and social causes.

7832. Stemler, Ann B. Comments on the evidence for a relatively late transistion from food collecting to food production in sub-Saharan Africa. Paper presented at 77th Annual Meeting of the American Anthropological Association. 14 to 18 November, 1978. Los Angeles, California.

7833. Stene, Jessie Anderson & Roberts, Lydia Jean. 1928. A nutrition study on an Indian reservation. JADA 3: 216-222.

A survey of sixty-seven families on the Crow Creek Sioux Reservation, Fort Thompson, South Dakota. Describes staple foods, dietary pattern, and nutritional adequacy of diets.

7834. Stenholm, Nancy. An inquiry into past and present agriculture in Palestine. Master's thesis. Anthropology University of Washington. 1966.

7835. Stenning, Derrick J. 1957. Tranhumance, migratory drift, migration; patterns of pastoral Fulani nomadism. GB-RAIGBI-J 878: 57-73.

Ecological and subsistence variables and their influence.

7836. Sternberg, W. 1906. Geschmak und Geruch. Physiologie Untersuchungen uber den Geschmacksinn. [Taste and smell-physiological investigation on the sense of taste.] Berlin: J. Springer. Reviewed in BMJ No. 2393: 1309 (1906).

7837. Sternberg, W. 1915. Sense impression and appetite. [In German] IBPTESV 5: 421-433.

Stimulation of appetite by visual, tactile, olfactory, and taste variables.

7838. Stern-Montagny, Hubert. 1939. Walnut oil in Switzerland. NNGA-RP Pp. 101-102. 30th Annual Meeting.

Preparation and food use of pethee in French -speaking Switzerland.

7839. Stevenson, Fredrick J. 1948. The potato-a leading world crop. For Ag 12: 211-216.

Historical data: pp. 211-216.

7840. Stevenson, G.T. 1960. Introduction to foods and nutrition. New York: John Wiley & Sons.

Effect of cultural background on meal plans: Pp. 414-417.

7841. Stevenson, H.N.C. 1937. Feasting and meat dividion among Zahan Chins of Burma. GB-RAIGBI-J 67: 15-32.

7842. Stevenson, James. 1883. Illustrated catalogue of the collections obtained from the Indians of New Mexico and Arizona in 1879. SI-BE-AR for the year 1880-1881. Pp. 307-465.

Zuni mortars, pestles: pp. 340-342. Zuni water vases: pp. 343-347; Zuni water jugs and jars: pp. 347-349; Zuni pitchers: pp. 349-350; Zuni eating bowls: pp. 350-358; Zuni cooking vessels: pp. 358-360; Zuni condiment cups: pp. 363-364; Zuni foods: p. 372. Wolpi grain grinders: pp. 376-377; Wolpi martars and pestles: p. 377; Wolpi water vases: pp. 378-381; Wolpi cups: p. 382; Wolpi eating bowls: pp. 382-384; Wolpi cooking vessels: p.385; Wolpi ladles: pp. 385-387; Wolpi water baskets and othe woven items related to food use: pp. 389-391. Laguna water vases: pp. 399-401; Laguna water jugs and jars: p. 401; Laguna pitcher: pp. 401,402; Laguna eating bowls: pp. 403, 404; Acoma water vases: pp. 404,405; Acoma pitchers and eating bowls: p. 405; Cochiti water vessels: pp. 405-408; Cochiti eating bowls: p. 408; Santo Domingo water vessels: p. 409; Tesuke metates, mortars: p. 410; Tesuke water vases: 410-413; Tesuke water jugs and jars: p. 413; Tesuke pitchers: p. 413; Tesuke eating bowls: pp. 413,414; Tesuke cooking vessels: p. 414; Santa Clara water vases: p. 415; Santa Clara Eating bowls: p. 415; Santa Clara cooking vessels: p. 416; San Juan eating bowls: pp. 416, 417; Jemez water vessel: p. 417; Canon de Chelly water vessels: pp. 419,420; Canon de Chelly bowls and cooking vessels: p. 420. The Catalogue is fully illustrated throughout with pen and ink drawings of representative objects in the collection; several of the illustrations are in color.

7843. Stevenson, Matilda Coxe. 1894. The Sia. SI-BE-AR for the year 1889-1890. Pp. 1-157.

Food in the Rain Ceremonial of the Knife Society: pp. 104, 105; food during the process of childbirth, and following parturition: pp. 137, 140.

7844.   Steveson, Matilda Coxe.   1904.   The Zuni Indians. Their mythology, esoteric fraternities, an ceremonies. SIBAE-AR for the year 1901-1902. Pp. 3-608.

Food and drink: pp. 361-369. Bread bakinga and the manufacture of baking stones receives primary attention.   Meat and plant foods, and beverages are considered, together with meal times and etiquette.

7845.   Stevenson, Paul Huston. 1934. Interrelation of biometric and clinical methods in the appraisal of nutritional status. CMJ 48: 1295-1312.

7846.   Steveren, W.A. Van; Tiggelman-Krugten, V.A.H.; Ferrier, B.; Maggilavry, C.J.; & Dubois, G. 1971. Food habits of infants and preschool children in Surinam. JADA 58: 127-132.

Covers breast feeding; number of meals; food taboos (treef, or trafe=Hebrew Tereefa: 'forbidden foods', derived from presence of early Jewish plantation owners in Surinam).   Staple foods are enumerated for Hindu, Creole, Javanese, and Black populations.

7847.   Steward, Julian H.   1937.   Ethnological reconnaisance among the desert Shoshones. SI-MP No. 3407.

Included is an illustration of Shoshone seed-gathering and winnowing.

7848.   Steward, Julian H.   1938.   Basin-plateau aboriginal sociopolitical groups. SI-BAE-B No. 120.

Plant foods: pp. 21-33.

7849.   Steward, Julian, ed. 1956. People of Puerto Rico. Chapaign: University of Illinois Press.

Diet; seafood beliefs: pp. 363, 401; eating habits: pp. 254, 383; 'hot'-'cold' food categories: pp. 155, 217, 229, 288, 363, 401; food in Canemelar: pp. 383-384, 400-401; food in Nocora: pp. 284, 288-289, 312-313; milk in diet: pp. 113, 130, 401; diet on sugar hacienda: p. 345; maize meal: pp. 200, 209.

7850.   Stewart, C.E. 1886. A visit to Badghis in 1833, and then to the Herat Valley in 1885. SGM 2: 129-144.

Northwestern Afghanistan.   Bread-baking; dried watermelon as a sugar source: p. 132; onagere flesh as food: p. 139.

7851.   Stewart, Gertrude. 1958. Manila cookbook Manila: [Manila] Evening News.

Information on regional foods of the Manila area.

7852.   Stewart, Kenneth M. 1957. Mohave fishing. MKey 31: 198-203.

7853.   Steyn, D.G. 1949. Vergiftiging van mens en dier, mit giftplante, voedsel en drink wanter. [Poisoning of himans and animals by giftplants, food and drinking water.] Pretoria: van Schaik.

7854.   Stickney, Gardner P. 1896. Indian uses of wild rice. AA 9: 115-121.

Describes harvesting, preparation, and other roles of Zizania aquatica among Native American groups in the Great Lakes region.

7855.   Stickney, Gardner P. The use of maize by Wisconsin Indians. Milwaukee. Parkman Club Publications 13 March 1897.

7856.   Stiebeling, Hazel K. 1939. food habits, old and new. USDA YB pp. 124-130.

7857.   Stiebeling, Hazel K. 1941. The National Research Council's Committee on Food Habits. JHE 33: 541-543.

Includes a list of Committee members; and details of research projects.

7858.   Stiebeling, Hazel K.; Day, Monroe; Coons, Callie M.; Phipard, Esther F.; & Clark, Faith. 1941. Family food consumption and dietary levels - five regions. USDA-MP No. 405.

7859.   Stiebling, Hazel K.; Day, Monroe; Phipard, Esther F.; Adelson, Sadye F.; & Clark, Faith. 1941. Family food consumption and dietary levels - Five regions. USDA-MP 452.

7860.   Stiebling, Hazel K. & Phipard, Esther F. 1939. Diets of families of employed wage earners and clerical workers in cities. USDA-C No. 507.

7861.   Stiebeling, Hazel K. & Ward, Medora. 1933. Diets at four levels of nutritive content and cost. USDA-C 296.

7862.   Stimpson, Edwin G. A nutritive Study of Vigna sinensis (Black-eyed pea variety).   Ph. D dissertation. University of Maryland. 1937.

7863.   Stini, William A. Adaptive strategies of human populations under nutritional stress. Paper presented at 9th International Congress of Anthropological and Ethnological Sciences. 28 August to 8 September, 1973. Chicago, Illinois.

7864.   Stini, William A. The error of policies which induce the maximization of human growth. Paper presented at 75th Annual Meeting of the American Anthropological Association. 17 to 21 November, 1976. Washington D.C.

The wide range of qualitative and quantitative variations in dietary intake which permits human survival is evidence of the high degree of adaptability which our species has maintained. Perhaps the least characteristic dietary pattern in human history is the currently widespread one of sustained overabundance of "high quality" nutrients. The stimulation of early growth associated with this very recent development has been often called "optimization", a term which may be inappropriate in view of its effects on world food supplies, as well as potential ill-effects on individual susceptibility to certain degenerative conditions.

7865. Stini, William A. Nutritional stress and sexual dimorphism in evolutionary perspective. Paper presented at 76th Annual Meeting of the American Anthropological Association. 29 November to 3 December, 1977. Houston, Texas.

The capacity to produce viable offspring is an essential element of a species' adaptation. Support of a fetus and later of the nursing infant places a heavy demand on the female mammal. A variety of mechanisms have evolved in our own species to permit such support even when the mother herself is underfed. As a result of this aspect of human adaptation, different strategies have been evolved by males and females subjected to nutritional inadequacy. Physiological components of the female strategy are contrasted to those charaterizing males, in the light of their evolutionary significance.

7866. Stini, William A. Early nutritional experiences and human health. Paper presented at 77th Annual Meeting of the American Anthropological Association. 14 to 18 November, 1978. Los Angeles, California.

7867. Stitt, Kathleen. 1958. Fat consumption in Alabama. JADA 34: 496-500.

Amount and kind of fat; houshold practices in culinary use; frequency of serving fried foods; fat as a seasoning for vegetables.

7868. St. John, Harold. 1954. The Hawaiian variety of Dioscorea pentaphylea, an edible yam. JPS 63: 27-34.

7869. Stobnicka-Szczglowa, H. 1963. Opinions on th division of the daily diet into meals. [In Polish] RPZH 14: 287-290.

7870. Stockdale, F.a. 1918. Food of the island. Trop Ag 51: 131-142.

Ceylon.

7871. Stocker, Harry E. & Frueauff, Herman T. 1938. The Moravian Indian mission on White River. Diaries and letters. May 5, 1799 to Novembver 12, 1806. Indiana Historical Collections. Vol.23. Traslated by Samuel C. Zeller. Edited by Henry Lawrence. Indianapolis: Indiana Historical Bureau.

Geographagy among Native Americans (Mississippi) :P. 287.

7872. Stocker, Hector E.F. 1941. La dietetica en la epoca de Hipocrates. [Dietetics in Hippocrates' time.] PMArg 28: 1266-1279.

A review of the Hippocratic canon pertaining to diet in relation to health and disease.,

7873. Stockholm. Nordic Museum. Maltning och brygd. [Malting and Brewing.] Questionnaire issued by the Nordic Museum, Stockholm, for the purpose of collecting information on Scandinavian brewing traditions [by John Grandlund].

7874. Stoddard, Natalie. 1970. Micmac Foods. Halifax, Nova Scotia: Halifax Natural Science Museum.

7875. Stokar, Alter von. 1958-1959. Uber die Ernahrung inder Eiszeit. [Nutrition during the Ice Age.] Quartar 10-11: 59-62.

7876. Stoklund, Bjarne. 1956. Hostkage og Julerente. [Harvest cakes and Christmas gifts.] Budstikken Pp. 13-24.

7877. Stoler, Richard C. Simulation of a hunter-gatherer subsistence strategy. Paper presented at 72nd Annual Meeting of the American Anthropological Association. 29 November, 1973. New Orleans, Lousiana.

7878. Stolz, F. 1815. Kochbuch der Israeliten, oder praktische Anweisung, wie man nach den judischen Religionsgrunden alle Gattungen der feinsten Speisen kauscher bereitet. [The Jewish cookbook, or a practical guide for the Kosher preparation of all manner of fine dishes according to the Jewish religious laws.]

7879. Stone, Benjamin Cecil. The wild and cultivated Pandanus of the Marshall Islands. Ph.D. dissertation. University of Hawaii. 1960.

Includes descriptions of preparation and use as food.

7880. Stone, Doris Z. 1949. The Boruca of Costa Rica. HU-PMAAE-P 26 No. 2.

Foods: pp. 7-9.

7881. Stone, Doris Z. 1956. Data on maize in Talamanca, Costa Rica; an hypothesis. SAmP-J 45:189-194.

Proposes that maize was introduced into this area from Mexico.

7882. Stone, Doris Z. 1962. The Talamancan tribes of Costa Rica. HU-PMAAE-P 43 No. 2.

Food: pp. 13-16.

7883. Stone, Doris Z & Balser, Carlos. 1957. Grinding stones and mullers of Costa Rica. SAmP-J 46:165-179.

Discussion of pre-Columbian foods: tubers, cacao; fruit of the pejivall palm; and maize (consumed by northern Nahuatl and Chorotega migrants), all of which were processed by grinding.

7884. Stone, Margaret. 1943. Bean people of the cactus forest. DM 6:5010.

Illustration of gathering saguaro fruit: p. 8.

7885.   Stone, R.H. 1932. After the hunt. Hygeia 10:984-987.

Included are recipes for venison; pigeon; rabbit; squirrel; wild duck; pheasant; quail; squab.

7886.   Stonor, C.R. & Anderson, Edgar. 1949. Maize among the hill peoples of the Assam. MBG-A 36:355-404.

The varieties and food uses of maize are enumerated, culture by culture, and the position is taken that transfer of a primitive and unaggressive race of maize may have occurred through trans-Pacific contact via Polynesian navigators. Indicates a need for an approximate survey of the Asian maizes, and for more critical taxonomic data on cultivated plants.

7887.   Storbeck, D. 1967. Quo vadis medicina? 6. A medical dilemma: preservation of more human lives than the inadequate economic basis allows. Hippokrates 38:477-483.

7888.   Storck, John & Teague, Walter Dorwin. 1952. Flour for man's bread. A history of milling. Minneapolis: University of Minnesota Press.

7889.   Storer, F.S. & Rolfe, G.W. 1904. Observations on a malt glucose known as midzuame, made in Japan. IB-B 3:80-94.

Includes historical data.

7890.   Storni, Julio S. 1938. Vegetales que utilizaban nuestros indigenas para su alimentacion. [Vegetables used by our natives for food.] Tucuman: Universidad de Tucuman.

7891.   Storni, Julio S. 1939. Hortus guaranensis. Toponimias, alimentos, elementos, instituciones. [Hortus guaranensis. Place names, foods, elements, institutions.] Tucuman: Universidad de Tucuman.

The section headed 'Alimentos. Procedimentos Utiles afines. (Foods. Processes. Related uses.) translates Guarani words related to food. Includes data on food preparation.

7892.   Storni, Julio S. 1939. Sugestiones fitoargueologicas vinculadas a la alimentacion. [Phytoarcheological suggestions based on food habits.] Tucuman: edicion del autor.

7893.   Storni, Julio S. 1942. Bromatologia indigena. Solucion precolombiana del problema alimenticio. [Native food science. Precolombian solution to the nutrition problem.] Tucuman: the author.

7894.   Storni, Julio S. 1944. Hortus guaranensis. Flora. [Guarani garden flora.] Universidad Nacional de Tucuman. Gabinete de Etnologia Biologia. Publicacion No. 354. Tucuman: Universidad de Tucuman.

Catalogue of Guarani plants. Includes systematic description; Guarani and Latin names; and indication of use.

7895.   Storvick, Clara A.; Schaad, Bernice; Coffey, Ruth E.; & Deardorff, Mary B. 1951. Nutritional status of selected population groups in Oregon. Part 1. Food habits of native born and reared school children. MMFQ 29:165-185.

7896.   Story, R. 1958. Some plants used by the Bushmen in obtaining food and water. USAfr-DA-DB-M No. 30.

7897.   Story, R. Plant lore of the Bushmen. In Ecological studies in southern Africa. Edited by D.H. Davis. 1964. The Hague: W.W. Junk.

7898.   Stouff, Louis. 1970. Ravitaillement et alimentation en Provence aux 14 et 15 siecles. [Food supply and diet in Provence during the 14th and 15th Centuries.] Paris: Mouton.

7899.   Stout, A.B. 1914. Vegetable foods of the American Indians. NYBG-J 15:50-60.

7900.   Stout, S.D. 1970. Survival nutrition. Aerospace Studies Institute. Bulletin No. 8. Maxwell Air Force Base, Alabama: Air University.

7901.   Straatmans, W. 1967. Ethnobotany of New Guinea in its ecological perspective. JATBA 14:1-20.

7902.   Stram Associates, Michael A. 1975. Milk substitutes; protein-fortified citrus juices and breakfast drinks; and protein sodas: legal, market demand, nutritional, and technical analysis. Chicago: Michael S. Stram Associates.

7903.   Stangeways, T.G. 1953. Food and flowers. HK-DAFF-B No. 3.

Traditional method of artificial egg incubation in south China: pp. 47-52.

7904.   Strangway, Alice K. 1961. Malnutrition in Angola. JADA 39:585-589.

7905.   Stransky, E. 1968. Scurvy: with special considerations on infantile scurvy. A historical review. PJPed 17:46-74.

7906.   Strantz, M. von. 1877. Unsere Gemusse. Mit Anschluss der Kastanie, Olive, Kaper, der Wein- und Hopfenrebe. Kulturhistorische und gastronomische Skizzen. [Our vegetables. Including chestnut, olive, capers, grapes, and hops. Cultural, historical, and gastronomical sketches.] Berlin: Enslin.

7907.   Strathern, Barbara. 1969. Why is the Pueraria a sweet potato? Ethnology 8:189-198.

Notes on the ethnobotanical taxonomies of the Medlpa (Melpa) of Mount Hagen, central New Guinea highlands.

7908.   Strauch, R. 1896. Das Huhnerei als nahrungsmittel und des Conservierung. [Hen's eggs as food and their preservation.] Bremen: M. Heinsius.

7909.   Straus, Robert. 1966. Public attitudes regarding problem drinking and problem eating. NYAS-A 133:792-802.

Both behaviors elicit such reactions as stereotyping; humor; denial; rejection rationalization; and/or anxiety. In both behaviors, reactions may vary according to gender, age, and subculture. The author feels that these attitudes also reflect the confusion regarding an appropriate conceptual model, which in turn, has hampered effective study of and response to the problems – there being rather a number of conflicting conceptual models, each of limited dimension: moral, psychological, medical, public health, socio-cultural, and biological.

7910.   Strauss, W. 1958. Changes in food habits in the Yemenite and Iraqi communities in Israel. Jerusalem. Israel Institute of Applied Social Research.

7911.   Strauss, W. & Shatan Herzeberg, M. 1955. A preliminary investigation into the food habits of Oriental Jewish communities with special reference to the changes enforced by immigration to Israel. Department of Hygiene. Jerusalem: Hebrew University Medical School.

7912.   Streeter, George L.; Park, E.A.; & Jackson, Deborah. 1937. Hereditary vulnerability to dietary defects in the development of bone. Science 85:437.

Abstract. Indicates that heredity is a definite etiological factor in abnormal bone development, based on experiments with laboratory rats on rachitic diets.

7913.   Streeter, J.M. & Murry, C.M. 1976. Carcinogenic properties of some common foods. JIR 22(3):12-13.

Satire of research attempting to correlated causes and effects on the basis of questionable samples; and indictment of assumed validity of use of rats as valid experimental animals upon which to base extrapolitions to human behavior and susceptibility.

7914.   Streuver, Stuart. The "flotation" process for recovery of plant remains. In Twenty-first Southeastern Archaeological Conference. November 6-7, 1964. New Orleans, Louisiana. Proceedings. Edited by Stephen Williams. 1965. Pp. 32-35. SAC-B No. 3.

Describes a method of obtaining plant material from excavated soil. Results using the technique suggest "that the commonly accepted idea that food plant remains are poorly preserved in sites of the eastern United States is not valid." Food plant remains from the Apple Creek site (area unspecified) are mentioned.

7915.   Streuver, Stuart & Rackerby, Frank. Evolution and subsistence in the Interior-Riverine area of the eastern United States. Paper presented at 68th Annual Meeting of the American Anthropological Association. 20 to 23 November, 1968. New Orleans, Louisiana.

Archeological evidence points up sharp evolutionary development at the beginning of the Middle Woodland period (ca. 200 B.C.) in the Interior Riverine. Explanations are sought for: (1) the distributions and meaning of the four Middle Woodland regional traditions; (2) the distribution and selective participation of Middle Woodland groups in the Hopewell Interaction Sphere; (3) the apparent differential rate of cultural evolution within the Hopewell Interaction Sphere; and (4) the implied differences in form of ecological adaptation between local Middle Woodland groups in the Interaction Sphere and others. To explain these developments, their distribution must be treated in ecological context and viewed against recent hypotheses about the development of agriculture in the eastern Woodlands. Several factors during the later Archaic set the stage for plant manipulation in the Early and Middle Woodland periods in certain riverine situations.

7916.   Strieck, F. 1964. Entwicklung der Diatkuchen in Deutschland. [Development of dietetic cooking in Germany.] Internist 5:315-316.

7917.   Striker, Cecil. 1934. Diets: a discussion of certain metabolic principles and their application to otolaryngology. Laryngology 44:625-641.

7918.   Strodtbeck, Fred L. The latent intellective factors in the food cycle. In Malnutrition, learning and behavior. Edited by Nevin S. Scrimshaw & John E. Gordon. 1968. Pp. 363-374. Cambridge, Massachusetts; London, England: The Massachusetts Institute of Technology Press.

Using examples from the ethnographic and psychological literatures, this paper illustrates in a lively, and unique way how food in various cultures structures food-getting and eating behavior, and the effects such structuring may have on personality, and attitudes toward food. Also notes the need to consider cultural food behavior in introducing new foods.

7919.   Stromsky, K.R. Die Zahnpflege in der diatetischen Literatur von der Romantik bis zum Aufkommen des naturwissenschaftlichen Denkins in der Medizin. [Dental hygiene in the dietetics literature from the Romantic to the rise of natural scientific thought in medicine. Ph.D. dissertation. Rheinische Friedrich-Wilhelms Universitat Bonn. 1969.

7920.   Strong, F.M. 1956. Lathyrism and odoratism. NR 14:65-67.

Review of toxic substances in the leguminous plants Lathyrus sativus, L. cicerca; L. clymenum and L. ordoratus.

7921.   Strong, F.M. 1966. Naturally-occurring toxic factors in plants and animals used as food. CMAJ 94:568-573.

7922. Strong, W.M. 1936. Feeding of native laborers in Papua. Port Moresby: Government Printer.

7923. Strouse, Solomon. 1928. Food and food habits. NYAM-B 4 [Series 2]: 1274-1279.

Criticizes the habit of extrapolation from results of dietary experiments with laboratory animals to humans; takes the position that genetics, and not food habits, is the primary determinant of longevity.

7924. Strub, Augustine. 1954. Harvesting wild rice. IS 34:125.

Illustration.

7925. Strubing, G.E. 1964. "Buch der Natur", die alteste deutschsprachige Quelle zur Geschichte der menschlichen Ernahrung. [The "Book of Nature" the oldest historical source on nutrition in the German language.] Ernahr 9:190-211.

A book by Konrad von Megenberg.

7926. Strubing, G.E. 1967. Knoblauch in alten Zeiten zur Diatetik und Ernahrung der Menschen. [Garlic in olden days in human dietetics and nutrition.] Ernahr 12:585-623.

7927. Strydom, S. 1969. The preparation of edible wild fruit and plant samples for analysis and some difficulties encountered in such analysis. SAMJ 43:1530-1532.

7928. Stuart, Bradley R. 1945. Pug-a-roo gathers mescal. MKey 19:79-80.

Gathering and preparation of Agave utahensis, Engelm. by the southern Paiute.

7929. Stuart, David E. Yahgan subsistence ecology, mobility and social-organizational patterns. Paper presented at 73rd Annual Meeting of the American Anthropological Association. 19 to 24 November, 1974. Mexico City.

7930. Stuart, Herbert H. 1957. Observation of effect of diet on teeth of prehistoric man. Screenings 6:3-4.

7931. Stuart, J.D. 1918. Queer foods from the Orient. Travel 32:31-35.

7932. Stuart, James W. Isthmus Nahuat food classification: guidelines for good nutrition. Paper presented at 77th Annual Meeting of the American Anthropological Association. 17 November, 1978. Los Angeles, California.

Describes a quadripartite taxonomy of foods, which cognitively insure that only those foods highest in complementary protein are considered to comprise a meal and may be eaten together.

7933. Stuart, James W. Subsistence ecology of the Isthmus Nahuat Indians of southern Vera Cruz, Mexico. Ph.D. dissertation. Anthropology. Riverside, California: University of California. 1978.

Describes and analyzes the subsistence system, and suggests some implications for prehistoric cultural developments in the area. Chapters are devoted to environment, agriculture; hunting and gathering; diet; and subsistence-system productivity. Includes description and analysis of food classification system.

7934. Stuart-Fox, D. 1973. Bees and beetles are feast. HAd 28 June Section F. P. 5.

Orthoptera, Odonata, Coleoptera, Hymenoptera.

7935. Stubbs, Ansel Hartley. 1971. Wild mushrooms of the central Midwest. Lawrence: University of Kansas Press.

7936. Stubbs, F.J. 1913. Notes on rare fishes sold for food in East London. Zoologist 4:377-381.

7937. Stubbs, Ron D. An investigation of the edible and medicinal plants used by the Flathead Indians. Master's thesis. Anthropology. University of Minnesota. 1966.

7938. Stull, Donald D. Modernization and symptoms of stress: attitudes, accidents and alcohol use among urban Papago Indians. Ph.D. dissertation. University of Colorado. 1973.

7939. Stunkard, A. 1968. Environment and obesity: recent advances in our understanding of regulation of food intake in man. FASEB-FP 27:1367-1373.

7940. Sturrock, David. 1940. Tropical fruit from southern Florida and Cuba and their uses. Jamaica Plain: The Arnold Arboretum of Harvard University.

7941. Sturtevant, Edward Lewis. 1879. Indian corn. NYSAS-T 33:37-74.

7942. Sturtevant, Edward Lewis. 1885. Indian corn and the Indian. AN 19:225-234.

Reviews the historical literature in Icelandic, English, French, Swedish, Spanish) describing maize and other staple Native American crops in North America.

7943. Sturtevant, Edward Lewis. 1885. Kitchen garden esculents of American origin. AN 19(5): 444-457; (6): 542-553; (7): 658-669.

7944. Sturtevant, Edward Lewis. 1889. History of garden vegetables. AN 23:665-677.

7945. Sturtevant, Edward Lewis. 1918-1919. Sturtevant's notes on edible plants. Edited by U.P. Hendricks. NY-AES-AR 27(2) Part Two. Reprint. New York: Dover Publications, (as Sturtevant's edible plants of the world.) 1972.

7946. Sturtevant, William C. Historic Carolina Algonkian cultivation of Chenopodium or Amaranthus. In Twenty-first Southeastern Archaeological Conference. November 6-7, 1964. New Orleans, Louisiana. Proceedings. Edited by Stephen Williams. 1965. Pp. 64-65. SAC-B No. 3.

Based on an eye-witness description by Thomas Heriot, in 1586, and published in The Roanoke Voyages (Hakluyt Society, 1955), the author suggests either of these plants may be Heriot's 'hearbe'. Of particular interest is Heriot's comment that the ashes of the burnt stalk were used as a [salt-like] seasoning. If Amaranthus, this would be the first documented evidence of its cultivation for food use north of Mexico.

7947. Sturtevant, William C. Preliminary annotated bibliography on eastern North American Indian agriculture. In Twenty-first southeastern Archeological Conference. November 6-7, 1964. New Orleans, Louisiana. Proceedings. Edited by Stephen Williams. 1965. Pp. 1-24. SAC-B No. 3.

7948. Sturtevant, William C. Studies in ethnoscience. In Transcultural studies in cognition. Edited by Antone Kimball Romney & Roy Goodwin D'Andrade. AA 66 (3 [Part 2]). 1964. Pp. 99-131.

Describes production of starch similar to that of sago. The sap and fruit of the palm are also eaten. Structural in relation to diet, with particular reference to Thomas (1960): pp. 119-120.

7949. Stuyvenberg, J.H. van., ed. 1969. Margarine. An economic, social and scientific history, 1869-1969. Liverpool: Liverpool University Press.

7950. Suarez, A. Mosqueda. 1954. La arepa criolla. [The creole arepa.] AVN 5:407-423.

The arepa is a thick maize cake, made in Venezuela, smaller in diameter than a tortilla.

7951. Suarez, Maria-Matilde, 1966. Les utilisations du palmier 'moriche' (Mauritia flexuosa, L.f.) chez les Warao de l'Orenoque, territoire Delta Amacuro, Venezuela. [Use of the 'moriche' palm (Mauritia flexuosa, L.f.) by the Warao of the Orinoco River, Amacuro Delta Territory, Venezuela.] JATBA 13:33-38.

7952. Subba Rao, G.N. 1965. Uses of seaweed directly as human food. IPFC-RS 2:1-32.

7953. Subrahmanyan, V.; Moorjani, M.N.; & Bhatia, D.S. 1954. A milk substitute from ground nuts. FMan 29:271-275.

7954. Subramanian, S. Sankara. 1965. Lichens and their food value. IJND 2:217-222.

Food prepared from lichens: p. 219.

7955. Subramanyan, V. & Srinavasan, M. 1954. Unfamiliar food resources - the agave. MCFTRI-B 3:137-139.

7956. Suero C., Victor. Estudio sobre habitos alimentarios y consumo de alimentos en el pais. [Study on dietary habits and food consumption in the nation.] In Seminario de nutricion del nino y la familia. Santo Domingo. Replublica Dominicana, 10-15 de abril de 1967. 1968. Montivideo: Instituto Interamericano del Nino.

Socio-economic survey; beliefs related to foods: p. 128.

7957. Suesskind, S. 1944. Favism or bean disease. [In Hebrew.] Harefuah 26:227-230.

7958. Sugiura, Kenichi. 1949. The relation between distribution and ownership: emphasis on foods of uncivilized peoples. [In Japanese.] JZ 1:3-13.

7959. Sulit, Mamerto D. 1932. Native methods of preparing nami (Dioscorea hispida Dennst.) tuber as food. PAg 20:637-641.

7960. Sullam, V.B. 1945. Food and agriculture in the Trieste region of Italy. For Ag 9:190-192.

7961. Sullenberger, Tom. 974. Ajax meets the jolly green giant. JAF 87:53-65.

Observations on the use of folklore and myth in American mass marketing, with several references to food advertising.

7962. Sullivan, H.R. & Goldsworthy, N.E. 1954. Some dietetic and nutritional factors in relation to the prevention of dental caries, including a reference to difficulties in effecting changes in food habits. Paper presented at Australian and New Zealand Association for the Advancement of Science. Thirtieth meeting. 13 January to 20 January, 1954. Abstracted in SPC-QB 4:31 (1954).

A control experiment among children in Bowral, New South Wales. Implicates excessive intake of refined carbohydrates in etiology of dental caries. Discusses necessity of considering socio-anthropological factors when considering attempts to modify food habits.

7963. Sullivan, Louis R. 1923. New light on the races of Polynesia. Asia 23: 17-20.

Illustration of poi making.

7964. Sulochana, R. Evaluation of the benefits of an applied nutrition programme for pre-school children in a village. Master's thesis. University of Madras. 1969.

Records data on food use frequency; food prohibitions; meal planning; food storage and preservation practices; cooking methods; and weaning practices. The village studied is Samichettipalayam, in the Coimbatore District of the south Indian State of Tamil Nadu.

7965. Sundararaj, D. Daniel & Balasubramanyan, Girija. 1959. Guide to the economic plants of South India. Madras: Amudha Nilayam.

Edible plants included.

7966.   Sundstrom, Sigfrid. 1909. Untersuchungen uber die Ernahrung der Landbevolkerung in Finland. [Investigation on the diet of the rural population in Finland.] BKFNF-UFVS 67. No. 1.

Includes data on regional dietary patterns, and food preparation.

7967.   Surface, Frank Macy. 1928. The grain trade during the war, being a history of the Food Administration Grain Corporation and the United States Grain Corporation. New York: Macmillan.

The Food Administration Grain Corporation was established by Executive Order, on August 14, 1917, for the purpose of buying, selling and storing wheat, flour, meal, beans and potatoes.

7968.   Surface, Frank M. & Bland, Raymond L. 1931. American food in the world war and reconstruction period. Operations of the organizations under the direction of Herbert Hoover, 1914-1924. Stanford, California. Stanford University Press.

Exhaustive economic and statistical review of United States food relief to European nations. Includes details of commodities, distribution to local districts; committees; kitchens; and dates of steamer sailings. A bibliography of related publications is included.

7969.   Suto, Kenzo. 1913. Die Ernahrung der Japaner. [The diet of the Japanese.] Med Klin 9:1885-1888.

7970.   Suttles, Wayne. 1951. The early diffusion of the potato among the Coast Salish. SJA 7:272-288.

Historical, ethnographic and linguistic evidence, supplemented by details on potato in the native culture. Suggests that Salish acceptance of the potato may indicate that food-gathering societies "...may be set up so that they can take over food producing without wholesale change."

7971.   Sutton, Horace; Hanes, Phyllis; Sturges, Lena; Ratteree, LeClare Church, Ruth Ellen; Crisswell; & Brown, Philip S. 1973. Is there really an American cuisine? SR 20 November.

Brief profiles of regional cuisine in the Continental United States.

7972.   Suzuki, Akira. 1966. On the insect-eating habits among wild chimpanzees living in the savannah woodlands of western Tanzania. Primates 7:481-487.

7973.   Suzuki, Akira. 1971. Carnivority [sic] and cannibalism observed among forest-living chimpanzees. JZ 79:30-48.

7974.   Suzuki, K. 1891. Beverages of the South Sea Islanders. [In Japanese.] KZ 23:135-137.

7975.   Suzuki, K. 1891. Cooking and candy-making among South Sea Islanders. [In Japanese.] KZ 23:98-100.

7976.   Swaminathan, M. 1966. Lathyrism; its aetiology and prevention. IJND 3:100-103.

7977.   Swanholm, Carl E. A chemical study of the bitter principle of pia (Tacca leontopetaloides (L.) O. Ktze). Doctoral dissertation. University of Hawaii. 1959.

Use of pia starch as food: p. 2.

7978.   Swank, Edith Elliott. 1943. The story of food preservation. Pittsburgh: H.J. Heinz Co.

7979.   Swank, George R. Ethnobotany of the Acoma and Laguna Indians. Master's thesis. University of New Mexico. 1932.

Rio Grande Pueblo cultures of New Mexico.

7980.   Swanson, P. 1965. Charles Ford Langworthy; a biographical sketch. (August 9, 1864 to March 3, 1932). JN 86:3-16.

7981.   Swanton, John R. 1922. Early history of the Creek Indians and their neighbors. SI-BAE-B No. 73.

Foods: pp. 358-360.

7982.   Swanton, John R. 1931. Social and ceremonial life of the Chocktaw Indians. SI-BAE-B No. 103.

Food preparation: pp. 38, 47-49.

7983.   Swanton, John R. 1946. The Indians of the southeastern United States. SI-BAE-B No. 137.

Foods and food habits: pp. 351-381.

7984.   Sweeney, G. 1947. Food supplies of a desert tribe. Oceania 17:289-299.

Food staples of the Walbiri, an Australian Aborigine group. Lists fruit, roots, seeds, honey, eggs, insects, marsupials, lizards, reptiles. Food preparation techniques, and water sources are described. Extensive information is given on the yala or 'desert yam' which, after maturation, yields tubers the year 'round.

7985.   Sweeney, Katherine H. 1949. The Biblical prophets and sugar cane. Herbarist No. 15. Pp. 40-43.

Historical account of sugar cane in Asia Minor.

7986.   Sweeney, Mary. 1942. Changing food habits. JHE 34:457-462.

The author was an executive member of the Committee on Food Habits of the National Research Council. This article reviews the Committee's research work and some of its conclusions concerning the cultural and psychological meanings of food.

7987. Sweet, Clifford. 1936. Voluntary food habits of normal children. JAMA 107:765-768.

Observations by a physician on approaches
to mediating real and imagined dietary problems which parents observe in infants and
children. Includes reference to Davis (1928,
1930, 1933). Emphasizes the physician's role
in childhood nutrition education, and concludes "Healthy children, if allowed to do
so, will voluntarily choose an adequate diet
from a well supplied family table" (p. 767).

7988. Sweet, Muriel. 1962. Common edible and
useful plants of the West. Healdsburg, California
Naturegraph Publishers.

7989. Swern, Perry W. 1923. Hospital architecture
and the department of dietetics. Diet Ad Ther 1:10-
16.

Stresses the importance of consulting with
the dietitian in planning hospital food preparation facilities.

7990. Swet, C.J. 1972. Antipollution systems. A
universal solar kitchen. Silver Spring, Maryland:
Johns Hopkins University Applied Physics Laboratory.

7991. Swinnerton, Frederick, 1901.   Neolithic
'fire-holes' or outside cooking places. YLM 3:570.

7992. Swynnerton, R.J.M. 1937. The 'oyster' or
Kweme nut. EAAJ 2:444-446.

Telfairea pedata. Used in East Africa in
cookery; and subsequent to childbirth on the
basis of its reported ability to effect early
contraction of the pelvis. Used by th Wakamba of Kenya as a lactagene.

7993. Sykes, Ella C. 1910. Persia and its people.
New York: Macmillan.

Food etiquette: pp. 70-72; rural dietaries:
pp. 211, 213; wine-making: p. 216; rosewater: p. 220; camel meat as food: p. 245;
vegetables and fruit: pp. 258-259.

7994. Szabadfalvi, Jozsef. 1960-1961. A debreceni
mezeskalasos mesterseg. [Gingerbread makers of
Debrecen.] Deri Muz 2:91-141.

Debrecen is city in eastern Hungry, adjacent
to the Rumanian border.

7995. Szabadfalvi, Jozsef. 1963. Die Metberei-
tung in Ungarn. [Preparation of mead in Hungary.]
AE 12:265-294.

7996. Szabo, T., Attila.   1963.   Panko.
[Pancakes.] M Nyelv 59:475-478.

7997. Szczawinski, Adam F. & Hardy, George A.
1962. Guide to common edible plants of British
Columbia. British Columbia Provincial Museum.
Department of Recreation and Conservation. Handbook No. 20. Victoria: A. Sutton, Queen's Printer.

7998.   Szczesniak, A.S. & Kahn, E.L. 1971. Consumer awareness of and attitudes to food texture.
JTS 2:280-295.

7999.   Szegedy-Maszak, Andrew, translator. 1970.
"Heraclides to Petepsais, about an order of food."
ASP-B 7:67-70.

A Third (?) Century Greek papyrus (Metropolitan Museum inventory 25.8), mentioning
lupine, chick pea, and fenugreek.

8000.   Szilady, Z. 1934.   Diofank oshonossaga.
[Native home of our nut trees.] Term Koz 66:137-
146.

8001.   Szromba, Zofia. 19363. Pozywienie ludnosci
wieskiej w starych siolkowicach z koncem 19 i w 20
wieku. [Food of rural folk in old hamlets in the late
19th, and 20th Centuries.] SNS 1:131-176.

Poland.

8002.   Tabrah, F.L., & Hauck, Hazel M. 1963.
Some aspects of health and nutritional status, Awo
Omamma, Nigeria. JADA 43:321-326.

8003.   Tackholm, Laurent. Tackholm, Vivi; Tackholm, Gunnar; & Drar, Mohammed. 1941. Flora of
Egypt. Volume 1. Pteridophyta, Gymnospermae,
and Angiospermae. Part Monocotyledones: Typha-
ceae - Graminae. FU-FS-B No. 17.

Contains an extensive bibliography on the
literature pertaining to archaeological remains of cereal grains, and other food
plants.

8004.   Tackholm, Vivi. Ancient Egypt, landscape,
flora and agriculture. In The Nile, biology of an
ancient river. Edited by Julian Rzoska. 1976. Pp. 51-
68. The Hague: W. Junk. Monographiae Biologicae
Vol. 29.

Early Egyptian agriculture: pp. 58-59; cereals: p. 61; pulses: pp. 62; oil plants: pp.
62, 63; vegetables: pp. 63-64.

8005.   Taft, Donald R. 1923. Two Portuguese communities in New England. CU-SHEPL No. 127.

Food habits: pp. 68-71.

8006.   Taguchi, Tatsuo. 1941. Kaza-matsuri [Wind
rites.] Tokyo: Kokin-Shoin.

Essays on beliefs and rites relating to meteorological phenomena and effects, especially in the domain of agriculture: winds,
typhoons, rains, snow, etc. Weather fore-
casting, prayers, ceremonies, rites designed
to assure favorable weather; for requesting
rain.

8007.   Takahashi, Eiji. 1966. Growth and environmental factors in Japan. HB 38:112-130.

Nutrition and growth-in-height: pp. 123-129. Observes that the curve for growth-in-height included for the sample studied is very similiar to that of the logarithm curve of post-World War II milk production. Implicates the influence of calcium intake on long bone development. Notes that the traditional Japanese diet was 60% cereal-based, with concomitant deficiency in calcium intake.

8008.   Takaishi, M. 1908. Young bees as a delicacy. T-IU-CA-B 7:641.

Discussion, and analysis of young bees, and bee larvae used for food in Japan.

8009.   Takeuchi, Kumpei. 1939. The culinary art in Japan. ConJ 8:396-405.

8010.   Takeuchi, T. 1907. On the composition of the shoots of Aralia cordata. T-IU-CA-B 7:465-468.

Analysis of an asparagus-like vegetable eaten both raw and cooked in Japan.

8011.   Talcott, Margaret I. Study of dietaries and nutritional status of adolescent Indian girls in boarding schools of the Dakotas. Master's thesis. South Dakota State University. 1960.

8012.   Talcott, Margaret & Schuck, C. 1961. Diets and nutritional status of adolescent Indian girls in boarding schools of the Dakotas. SD-AS-P 40:245-246.

8013.   Talman, A.L. 1936. Origin of chop suey. Ave 43:275-276.

8014.   Tallman, Frank F. 1947. Food and the mentally ill. JADA 23:6-7.

Behavioral responses relating to eating in behavioral malfunctions.

8015.   Talve, Ilmar. Die Nahrungsforschung in Finnland. [Food research in Finland.] Paper presented at the First International Symposium on Ethnological Food Research. 21 to 25 August, 1970. Lund: Folklivsarkivet. University of Lund.

8017.   Tambiah, S.J. 1969. Animals are good to think and good to prohibit. Ethnology 8:423-459.

Structural analysis of permitted animal food sources: pp. 433-452; ritual architecture and kitchens: p. 432. Reference community is Phraan Muan, a village in northeastern Thailand.

8018.   Taminiau, P.L.M.M. 1937. Nutrition of Trappist monks. [In Dutch.] GBKLP 34:375-387.

8019.   Tamiya, H. The role of algae as food. In Symposium on algology. Proceedings. 1960. Pp. 379-382. New Delhi: Indian Council of Agricultural Research.

8020.   Tamura, Heiji. 1971. Shoyu no hon. [Book of shoyu.] Tokyo: Shibata Shoten.

Included are historical data on the production of soy sauce, and several other products derived from soy bean fermentation (e.g. miso, hishio, and tamari.)

8021.   Tan, M.G., et al. 1970. Social and cultural aspects of food patterns and food habits in five rural areas in Indonesia. National Institute of Economic and Social Research (Lipi) and Directorate of Nutrition. Djakarta. [?]: Department of Health, Republic of Indonesia.

Includes data on locally-grown foodstuffs; daily meal patterns; frequency of consumption of foods; infants' and children's diets; weaning patterns; food beliefs and taboos; ritual meals; expenditure patterns. The villages studied are Badjang and Seloredjo (Blitar District, East Java: located at approximately 8.06S., 112.12E.); Bangsri and Djerukoswit (Karanganjar District, central Java); Karangtengan and Tjidjenkol (Sukabumbi District west Java; located at approximately 6.55S., 106.50E.); Tandjung Agund and Burai (Ogan Komerigan Ilir District, south Sumatra), and Sembung and Kerobakan (Badung District, Bali).

8022.   Tanaka, Chozaburo. 1967. Progress in the development of economic botany and knowledge of food plants. EB 21:383-387.

A review of the major historical literature in botany relating to plants used as human food. Includes a report on the author's compilation of food plants.

8023.   Tanaka, Chozaburo. 1976. Tanaka's cyclopedia of edible plants of the world. Edited by Sasuke Nakao. Tokyo: Keigaku Publishing Co.

A listing of more than ten thousand food plants. Common and Latin names are given. Food uses indicated for some entries, together with geographical location.

8024.   Tanaka, Chozaburo & Odashima, Kijiro. 1938. Vegetable resources of south China. STA-J 10:61-124.

Classified list of economic plants, with Japanese names, and distribution by province. Also as Tu-HI-Con No. 23.

8025.   Tanaka, Chozaburo & Odashima, Kijiro. 1939. A material for the study of vegetable resources of the Hainan Island. Trop Hort 9:103-133. Also in TU-HI-Comm 82:1-31 (1939).

8026.   Tanaka, Jack S. 1967. Two new togan varieties for Hawaii. HiFS 16:8.

Benincasa hispida; Chinese preserving melon. Includes information on food use.

8027. Tanaka, Jiro. Subsistence ecology of central Kalahari San. In Kalahari hunter-gatherers. Edited by Richard Lee & Irven DeVore. 1976. Pp. 98-119. Cambridge: Harvard University Press.

8028. Tanaka, Sen'o. 1974. Tea ceremony. Translated by T. Nishikama. Tokyo: Kodansha.

Japanese ritual tea preparation, and its place in Japanese life.

8029. Tandon, G.L. 1938. Preparation of lemon-barley water. PFJ 2: 296.

8030. Tang, P.S. & Chang, L.H. 1939. Calculation of Chinese rural dietary from crop reports. CJP 14: 497-508.

8031. Tannahill, Reay. 1973. Food in history. New York: Stein & Day.

Contents include the prehistoric period; the Near East and Europe 3,000 B.C. to A.D. 1000; Hellenic and Roman diets; Europe after the decline of the Roman Empire; Asia to the Middle Ages; the Arabic world; Europe from A.D. 1,000; Hellenic and roman Europe from A.D. 1000 to A.D. 1500; the age of exploration A.D. 1490-1800; and the modern world: 1800 to present.

8032. Tannahill, Reay. 1975. Flesh and blood: a hisory of the cannibal complex. New York: Stein & Day.

8033. Tanner, R.E.S. 1956. A preliminary inquiry into Sukuma diet in the Lake Province, Tanganyika Territory. EAMJ 33: 305-324.

8034. Tannous, Afif I. 1943. Food production and consumption in the Middle East. For Ag 7: 243-255.

Foods, and preparation techniques: pp. 251-255.

8035. Tannous, Afif I. 1944. Agricultural production and food consuption in Iran. For Ag 8: 27-42.

8036. Tantaquidgeon, Gladys. 1942. A Study of Delaware Indian medicine practice and folk beliefs. Pennsylvania Historical Commission. Harrisburg: Commonwealth of Pennsylvania Department of Public Instruction.

8037. Tanzania. National Nutrition Unit. 1969. Report of a dietary survey in Kisarawe District: 20th - 26th September 1968. Mimeographed. Tanzania Nutrition Committee Report. Series 7A. Dar es-Salaam [?]: Tanzania National Nutrition Unit.

The village of Kidugalo (6.49S., 38. 12E.) was studied. Breast-feeding practices; meal patterns; food taboos; food preparation techniques; and storage methods are described.

8038. Tappen, Neil C. Functional studies of mandibles of fossil man. Paper presented at 73rd Annual Meeting of the American Anthropological Association. 19 to 24 November, 1974. Mexico City.

8039. Tapsell, Enid. 1946. Original kumara. JPS 56: 325-332.

Based on information from older Maoris, early types of sweet potatoes are described, and the locales where they were grown, prior to 1941, identified.

8040. Tao, Chau-minh. 1931. Sach an chay. [Vegetariansim among the Buddhists.] Collection Tha-linh-hoc. Saigon: Durc-luru-phurong.

8041. Tarenetzkj, A. 1896. Der gebrauch des Saki in Japan und das Opium rauchen in China. [The use of Sake in Japan and opium smoking in China.] Arch Anth 26: 185.

Review of a paper read at the St. Petersburg Anthropological Society.

8042. Tarnowski, W. 1969. Meal-time eating against continuous food intake. BND 11: 142-147.

8043. Tartaglia, Louis J. Maritime subsistence strategies: a technological approach. Paper presented at 74th Annual Meeting of the American Anthropological Association. 2 to 6 December, 1975. Sn Francisco, California.

8044. Tassoni, G. 1958. Gastronomia mantovana. [Gastronomy in Mantua.] Lares 24: 5-21.

Italy.

8045. Tastevin, R.P. 1925. A necrophagia nos Cachinauas. [Eating the dead among the Cashinawa.] Missionario: 5: 19-20.

8046. Tastevin, R.P. Constant. 1954. Preparation et utilisation de manioc dans la region du moyen Amazone et de ses affluents. [Preparation and use of manioc in the region of the central Amazon and its tributaries.] Ethnographie No. 49. pp. 53-59.

8047. Tastevin, R.P. Constant 1955. Le merveilleux developpement de l'agriculture, toujours "precolombienne", des indiens insoumis de L'amazonie bresilienne. [The remarkable development of agriculture, always "precolumbian", of the unpacified Brazilian Indians in Amazonia.] RAnth 1 [new series]: 169-177.

Manioc; Taro; sweet potato; peanuts; banana; and various minor plants are mentioned, with some mention of preparation. Cultures referred to include Tupi, Cuniba, and Cashinawa.

8048. Tatum, Lise S. Seasonality and scheduling: a subsistence model for historic nomadic bison hunters. Master's thesis. Anthropology. Iowa City, Iowa: University of Iowa. 1976.

8049. Taube, Edward. 1951. Wild rice. SM 73: 368.

8050.   Tautain L.F. 1896. Sur L'anthropophagie et les sacrifices humains aux Isles Marquises. [On anthropophagy and human sacrifices in the Marquesas Islands.] Anthropologie 7: 443-452.

8051.   Tax, Sol. 1962. Changing consumption in Indian Guatemala. PAnth 9: 15-26.

Staple food consumption: pp. 17,17; a table of per capita weekly consumption (grams) of various foods in rural Guatemala is given on p. 19.

8052.   Taylor, A.E. 1918. International and national food control. AAPSSA 78: 149-156.

8053.   Taylor, Albert A.; Finkelstein, Beatrice; & Hayes, Robert E. 1960. Food for space travel. "An examination of current capabilities and future needs." ARDC TR 60-8/ July. Unclassified. Headquarters. U.S. Research and Develpment Command. Andrews Air Force Base. Washington, D.C.: United States Air Force.

Describes feeding in short and extended space flights. Preflight feeding provisions are described as well as partially regenerative systems and, finally, the requirements of a closed ecology are considered. One section is given over to a discussion of permissable pre-flight foods. Varied menus are offered for short, medium, and long range flights, in an ascending order of variety, consumer acceptance and support equipment.

8054.   Taylor, Annie. 1894. My experiences in Tibet. SGM 10: 1-8.

Tsampa: a mixture of tea, barley flour and butter; ba: solidified tsampa: p.5.

8055.   Taylor, Barbara Howland. 1969. Mexico: her daily life and festive breads. Edited by Ruth S. Lamb. Claremont, California: Creative Press.

8056.   Taylor, Bayard. 1855. A visit to India, China, and Japan, in the year 1853. New York: G.P. Putnam; London: Sampson Low, & Son.

Dinner prepared for Commodore Perry by the Japanese Regent: pp. 385-386.

8057.   Taylor, Douglas. 1950. The meaning of a dietary and occupational restrictions among the Island Carib. AA 52:343-349.

Fasting and the couvade; in menstruation; as a requirement for those aspiring to be chiefs; or shamans.

8058.   Taylor, Douglas. Historical implications of linguistic data on the foods of the Island Carib and Black Carib. In 33 Congreso Internacional de Americanistas. 20-27 Julio 1958. San Jose, Costa Rica. Actas. Vol. One. 1959. Pp. 294-308. San Jose, Costa Rica: Lehmann.

Detailed comparative etymological study which includes extensive data on foods;

their preparation; and uses. Mention is also made of European loanwords incorporated into Native Caribbean dialects.

8059.   Taylor, Lawrence. 1976. Coffee: the bottomless cup. New York: Alfred Publishing Co.

8060.   Taylor, Lawrence. Fishing and social change in southwest Donegal in the 19th Century. Paper presented at 77th Annual Meeting of the American Anthropological Association. 14 to 18 November, 1978. Los Angeles, California.

8061.   Taylor, R.M.S. 1934. Maori foods and methods of preparation. NZDJ 30:88-96. November.

Based on previously published literature.

8062.   Taylor, Ronald L. & Carter, Barbara J. 1976. Entertaining with insects or: the original guide to insect cookery. Santa Barbara, California: Woodbridge Press Publishing Co.

8063.   Taylor, Sue; Shelor, Nancy; & Abdelnour, Nancy. 1972. Nutritional ecology: a new perspective. L Alpha 4:47-59.

Effects of environment upon nutritional status; cultural response to ecology as reflected in food habits.

8064.   Tays, George. 1938. Mariano Guadelupe Vallejo and Sonoma. A biography and a history. Chapter 10. Distinguished visitors from Sonoma and events from 1839 to 1844. CHSQ 17:141-167.

A typical California breakfast of the period: pp. 142-143.

8065.   Tedder, J.L.O. 1956. Breadfruit drying in the Reef Islands. SPC-QB 6:21-22.

Banks Islands, New hebrides group located at 13.35S., 167.30E.

8066.   Teesdale, M.J. 1897. Manna. Nature (L) 55:349.

8067.   Teesdale, M.J. 1897. The manna of the Israelites. SG 3:229-232.

8068.   Tegengren, Jacob. 1939. Forntida forestallningar om brod och sad. [Old ideas relating to bread and cereals.] Vasabladet No. 28. P. 8.

8069.   Teicher, Morton I. 1960. Windigo psychosis: a study of a relationship between belief and behavior among the Indians of northeastern Canada. Seattle: American Ethnological Society.

8070.   Teichert, Kurt. 19061907. Ueber eine als Zur bezeichnend Mehlteiggarung. [Zur, a typical fermented grain dough.] ZBPIH 2 [Abteilung 17(2)] : 376-378.

A polish food zur, made from fermented rye flour batter. After fermenting, the dough-like substance is cooked in hot water. A study of the fermenting bacterial agent is included.

8071.   Teit, James Alexander. 1930. Ethnobotany of the Thompson Indians of British Columbia. Edited by E.V. Steedman. SI-BAE-AR for the year 1927-1928. Pp. 441-522.

8072.   Teit, James Alexander. 1930. The Salishan tribes of the Westen Plateau. Edited by Franz Boaz. SI-BAE-AR for the year 1927-1928.

Subsistence: pp. 88-97; 341-348.

8073.   Teitelbaum, Joel Mathless. Land use and nutristructural change among Berbers of the Moroccan Atlas. Paper presented at 72nd Annual Meeting of the American Anthropological Association. 1 December, 1973. New Orleans, Louisiana.

8074.   Teitelbaum, Joel Mathless. Ramadan in Tunisian villages: fast or feast? Paper presented at 73rd Annual Meeting of the American Anthropological Association. 19 to 24 November, 1974. Mexico City.

8075.   Teitelbaum, Joel Mathless. American school feeding in a culture bind. Paper presented at 75th Annual Meeting of the American Anthropological Association. 17 to 21 November, 1976. Washington, D.C.

School food service has become institutionalized in American education. Examination of a southern school shows decreasing population and rising foodwaste by pupils. These phenomena are seen as the results of change in perceived food preferences of school children, parents, and teachers of diverse ethnic and social backgrounds. Bureaucratic rigidities and political constraints limit the food programs from above. A cultural bind exists at the level of food symbolism in the United States. Nutritional outcomes are measured in relation to food choices outside the "captive" boundaries to school cafeterias.

8076.   Teitelbaum, Joel Mathless. Human versus animal nutrition: a "development" project among Fulani cattlekeepers of the Sahel of Senegal. In Nutrition and anthropology in action. Edited by Thomas K. Fitzgerald. 1976. Pp. 125-140.

This paper analyzes in detail the potential nutritional ramifications of transforming a subsistence society into a "cashcrop" system through use of bushland for raising cattle to supply urban protein demands. After a thorough account of current practices, and a review of the project, the author makes recommendations calculated to avoid the consequences of a plan that initially ignores the felt needs and threatens the integrity of Fulani sciety.

8077.   Teleki, Geza. The predatory behiavior of chimpanzees in eastern Africa. Paper presented at 72nd Annual Meeting of the American Anthropologi-cal Association. 1 December, 1973. New Orleans, Louisiana.

8078.   Telford, Emma Paddock. 1912. Stanford paper bag cookery. New York: Cupples and Leon.

8079.   Tellez, Herrero, Luis. 1946. Lo que se come en Bolivia. [What is eaten in Bolivia.] La Paz: Sanabria.

8080.   Temgwe, Noah. Experiences of peanut feeding in the Chimbu District. In An integrated approach to nutrition and society. The case of Chimbu. By Eben H. Hipsley. Report of the symposium held at the Thirty-seventh Congress of the Australian and New Zealand Association for the Advancement of Science, 20 to 24th January. NGRU-B No. 9. Pp. 104-108.

Introduction of peanut butter into infant diet, in a highland New Guinea culture, in an effort to alleviate protein malnutrition. The project of which the account is part, exemplifies how nutrition intervention can be successfully accomplished through inter-disciplinary teamwork.

8081.   Tempir, Z. 1964. Beitrage zur altesten geschichte des pflanzenbaus in Ungarn. [Contribution to the oldest history of plant cultivation in Hungary.] AAH 16:1-2.

8082.   Tennent, James Emerson. 1860. Ceylon 2 vols. London: Longman, Green. Longman, & Robert.

Curry: Vol. 1. Pp. 76-77; 437. Vol. 2. Pp. 160-161.

8083.   Teply, Lester Joseph. 1965. Entrevista sobre los problemas de nutricion infantil en los paises en vias de desarollo. [Interview on the problems of infant nutrition in developing nations.] Des Ec 2:52-54.

8084.   Tercero, Dorothy. 1939. Adventures in taste. PAU-B 73:573-579.

Latin American food. Some recipes included.

8085.   Terra, G.J.A. 1964. The significance of leaf vegetables, especially of cassava, in tropial nutrition. TGM 16:97-108.

Recipes for cassava: pp. 104-105.

8086.   Tesi, G.; Boutourline, E.; Kerr, G.R.; Hegsted, D. Mark; El Lozy, M.; Ghamry, M.; Stare, Frederick J.; Kallal, Z.; Turki, M.; & Hemaidan, N. 1975. Economic aspects of food, protein, and energy consumption in a region of southern Tunisia. EFN 4:5-14.

Staple foods of the area bordering Chott el Djerid, a salt lake in west central Tunisia: pp. 9, 10.

8087.   Teti, M. 1935. Nutrition in rural districts in hilly regions of Calabria. [In Italian.] FMed 21:505-518.

8088.   Teuteberg, Hans-Jurgen. Wandlungen des Fleischkonsums in Deutschland. [Changes in meat consumption in Germany.] Paper presented at the First International Symposium on Ethnological Food Research. 21 to 25 August, 1970. Lund: Folklivsarkivet. University of Lund.

8089.   Teuteberg, Hans-Juergen. 1971. Variation in meat consumption in Germany. EScan 1971. Pp. 131-141.

Historic, socio-economic, and statistical study.

8090.   Teuteberg, Hans Jurgen. The general relationship between diet and industrialization. In European diet from pre-industrial to modern times. Edited by Robert Forster & Elborg Forster. 1975. New York: Harper & Row. Harper Torchbooks No. 1863.

8091.   Thackeray, Franklin A. 1953. Sand food of the Papagos. DM 16:22. (April).

Ammobroma sonorae is a plant parasitic on various other desert plants. The stem is dug from sand dunes, and eaten after roasting, by the southern Papago, and Cocopa. The stem is also a source of moisture. A sonorae occurs in the Arizona-Sonora Desert.

8092.   Thackeray, Franklin A. & Leding, A.R. 1929. The giant cactus of Arizona. JHer 20:401-414.

Carnegeia gigantea, the saguaro; its fruit, and the fruit of other cacti used by Native Americans in Arizona.

8093.   Thapa, Jeewan Kumar. 1966. Primitive maize with the Lepchas. JT 3:29-31.

8094.   Theen, Lutz. 1964. Kindjees poppen. AHGB-J 28:68-72.

Bentheim Christmas pastry. Bentheim is located in northwestern Germany, and was formerly in the Prussian province of Hannover.

8095.   Theil, P. 1976. La curieuse histoire du sucre et de la place qu'il a prise dans l'alimentation. [The curious history of sugar and the place it has taken in the diet.] Historia No. 53. Pp. 92-95.

8096.   Theodoratus, Robert James. Chapter Six. The coffee house. In The influence of the homeland on the social organization of a Greek community in America. Ph.D. dissertation. Anthropology. University of Washington. 1961.

8097.   Theroux. Madagascar et Reunion. In L'alimentation indigene dans les colonies francaises. [Native diet in the French colonies.] By Georges Hardy & Charles Richet (fils). 1933. Pp. 217-240. Paris: Vigot Freres.

8098.   Thich-Nu. 1934. Sach day nau da an chay. [The preparation of vegetarian meals among the Buddhists.] Saigon: Tin-durc thu-xa.

8099.   Thiele, Ernst. 1959. Waffeleiser und Wafelgebacke in Mitteleuropa. [Waffle irons and waffle baking in Central Europe.] Koln: Oda Verlag.

8100.   Thienfont, D. & Vandervelden, M. 1962. Coutumes du Ruanda-Urundi au sujet des viandes. [Ruanda-Urundi custom relating to meat.] Africa 7:12-17.

8101.   Thimmayamma, B.V.S.; Satyanarayana, K.; Rao, Parvati K.; & Swaminathan, M.C. 1973. The effect of socio-economic differences on the dietary intake of urban population in Hyderabad. IJND 10:8-13.

8102.   Thion, L. Le vin de palme. [Palm wine.] In Sixieme Congres International d'Agriculture Tropicale et Subtropicale. 15-19 juillet, 1931. Paris. Vol. 2. Pp. 413-422. Paris: Secretariat General de L'Association Scientifique Internationale d'Agriculture des Pays Chauds et de son Comite Francais.

Describes method of tapping the palm tree; the fermentation process, and gives a chemical analysis of the product. Comments on native nomenclature for types of palm wine (malafu), in the Mauymbe region of the Congo, are included.

8103.   Thion, L. 1946. A propos des termites au point de vue alimentaire. [Termites from a dietary point of view.] BACB 37 865-868.

8104.   Thion, L. 1946. Contribution a l'etude du probleme alimentaire indigene au Congo. [Contribution to the study of the native diet problem in the Congo.] BACB 37:829-864.

8105.   Thiroux, A. 1937. L'hygiene de l'alimentation dans les colonies francaises. [Food hygiene in the French colonies.] Pres Med 45:847-849.

8106.   Thirumurthi, Hemalatha R. & Longenecker, J.B. 1966. Nutrition considerations of biological variation. NYASci-A 134:873-884.

Emphasizes that "one should not be arbitrary about dietary recommendations. The use of mean requirements has obvious limitations and is an unfortunate necessity". "The entire subject of ranges in nutritional requirements, with respect to all items, needs to be fathomed both on an extensive as well as intensive scale so that we become aware of the general facts of biochemical individuality. It is wrong to tacitly assume that the human population is made up largely of individuals who have about average needs and that a minority exhibit what may be considered abnormal values. The chance that any individual will be average with respect to all nutrients is slim. There is the likelihood that the typical individual exhibits some values which are far removed from the average. Thus individuals have distinctive patterns of nutritional requirements and vary several-fold from one another in specific needs. Many persons undoubtedly suffer from deficiencies unidentified by present techniques and many diseases of obscure origin may ultimately be found to be nutritionally related" (pp. 882-883).

8107.   Thomas, Anthony E. Overweight and ethnicity: cultural mechanisms regulating food intake and energy expenditure among adolescents in an urban environment. Paper presented at 70th Annual Meeting of the American Anthropological Association. 21 November, 1971. New York City.

Overweight and obesity in adolescents tend to be both physically and socially disabling, whereas in adult populations the onset of obesity is not as socially and psychologically impairing. As in other chronic illnesses, wherein the afflicted are stigmatized and isolated (e.g. drug addiction, alcoholism) sociocultural mechanisms related to the continuance of the physical malady are paramount. The distribution of preadolescent and adolescent overweight across ethnic groups and social class was plotted, and a panel of hypotheses was formulated for identifying preadult populations which exhibit greater risk to the onset of obesity.

8108.   Thomas, Brynmor & Hargrave, J. 1931. The composition of kitchen waste. GB-MA-J 38: 366-373.

Data collected from hotels; restaurants; and first-and second-class cafes.

8109.   Thomas, D.R. 1927. A note on vegetable ghee (vanaspati) with a short experiment on its food value. IJMR 14:659-666.

8110.   Thomas, Edith M. 1915. Mary at the farm and book of recipes. Compiled during her visit to the Pennsylvania Germans. Norristown, Pennsylvania: John Hartenstine.

8111.   Thomas, Ernest . 1873. Le marche aux bestiaux de la Villette et les abattoirs de la ville de Paris, guide historique et pratique de l'approvisionner, de l'acheteur. [The livestock market of Villette, and the slaughterhouse of the city of Paris, historical and practical guide for stocking-up, and for the consumer.] Paris: Librairie Agricole de la Maison Rustique.

8112.   Thomas, Gertrude Ida. 1941. Foods of our forefathers. Philadelphia: F.A. Davis.

8113.   Thomas, L.L. Kitchen gardening in Baton Rouge, Louisiana. Master's thesis. Geography. Louisiana State University. 1970.

8114.   Thomas, Louis-Vincent. 1960. Essai d'analyze structurale appliquee a la cuisine diola. [Study of structural analysis applied to Diola cuisine.] IFAN-B 22:328-345.

8115.   Thomas, Louis-Vincent. 1963. L'usage du lait chez les Diola (Basse Casamance). [The use of milk among the Diola (lower Casamance.) NA No. 98 Pp. 39-42.

Milk as a beverage; and in other foods.

8116.   Thomas, Louis-Vinent. 1965. Essai sur la conduite negro-africaine du repas (l'alimentation comme fait humain total). [Essay on Black African eating behavior. (Eating as a uniquely human occurrence.)] IFAN-B 2 [series B]: 573-635.

Ecological, biological, and psychological aspects of ritual food preparations; consecration of eating; and symbolism of foods.

8117.   Thomas, Margaret E. 1961. Green things to eat. Herbarist No. 27. Pp. 45-48.

Edible herbs.

8118.   Thomas, R.E. 1937. The sacred meal in the older Roman religion. Chicago: University of Chicago Press.

8119.   Thomas, S. 1965. A report of a community nutrition project in Rajannagar village of Bhavanisagar Block of Coimbatore District, with special reference to pre-school children. Madras: University of Madras.

A nutrition education project integrated with a dietary survey of forty-five village families of which fourteen families with pre-school children were selected for further study. Data on meal patterns; staple foods; and cooking methods are recorded.

8120.   Thome, K.E. 1966. Swedish food habits. VN 43:140.

8121.   Thompson, B.J. 1942. Some culinary returns from the Bible. Ave 55:295-298.

8122.   Thompson, Basil. 1896. A fishing party. NRev 14:229-240.

8123.   Thompson, Benjamin. [Count Rumford.] 1796-1812. Essays, political, economical and philosophical. London: T. Caddell Junior & W. Davies. Published in parts.

8124.   Thompson, Betty Preston. 1954. Two studies in African nutrition. An urban and a rural community in Northern Rhodesia. R-LP No. 24.

8125.   Thompson, Gladys Scott. 1959. Chapter Seven. The kitchen and its clerk, 1653-1667. Chapter Eight. After 1667. In Life in a noble household. Ann Arbor: University of Michigan Press. Ann Arbor Paperback AA 27.

England.

8126.   Thompson, Henry. 1879. Food and feeding. New York: Harper & Brothers. Reviewed in BMJ 1.: 859 (7 June, 1879). Reprint. New York: F. Warne. 1880.

8127.   Thompson, J. 1895. On pica or dirt-eating in children. EHR 3:81-94.

8128.   Thomson, James Claud. Nutrition in Iran; report on a preliminary nutritional assessment survey of seven different geographical areas in Iran. Mimeographed. Tehran: World Health Organization. 1952.

8129.   Thompson, Laura. 1945. Native culture of the Marianas. BPBM-B No. 185.

Food habits data included.

8130.   Thompson, Patricia. A survey of factors affecting diet in the Swahili community of Lamu, Kenya. Paper presented at 77th Annual Meeting of the American Anthropological Association. 14 to 18 November, 1978. Los Angeles, California.

8131.   Thompson, Peter Anthony. 1906 Chapter Eight. Rice and fish. In Lotus land. Being an account of the country and people of southern Siam. Philadelphia: J.B. Lippincott; London: T. Werner Laurie.

Rice agriculture; and subsistence fishing. Includes data on rice land surveys; and net-fishing techniques.

8132.   Thompson, Reginald Campbell. 1949. A dictionary of Assyrian botany. London: The British Academy.

Based on cuneiform texts, this work identifies plants known to the Assyrians, most of which have an indicated medical use. Foods uses are also recorded.

8133.   Thompson, Steven & Thompson, Mary. 1972. Wild food plants of the Sierras. Berkeley, California: Dragtooth Press.

8134.   Thompson, Vance. 1914. Eat and grow thin. A collection of hitherto unpublished Mahdah menus and recipes. A list of "forbidden" foods. New York: E.P. Dutton.

8135.   Thompson, Virginia. 1941. Thailand. The new Siam. New York: Macmillan.

Contains an overview of Thai dietary; nutritional value; and causes of changing food consumption.

8136.   Thomson, Donald F. 1938. The Australian native woman as food producer. ILN 22 October: pp. 730-731.

8137.   Thomson, Donald F. 1939. The seasonal factor in human culture, illustrated from the life of a contemporary nomadic group. PS-P 5:209-221.

This Wik-Monkan of northeastern Queensland. Includes data on foods, preparation equipment and tecniques.

8138.   Thomson, Donald F. 1950. The Australian aboriginal as hunter and food gatherer. Walk 16:29-31.

8139.   Thone, Frank. 1931. Human ant eaters. SNL 19:288.

Leaf cutter ants used as food by Native Brazilians.

8140.   Thone, Frank. 1932. They all get eaten anyhow. SNL 22:210-211.

Mentions monkey's use of spiders for food.

8141.   Thonner, Franz. 1908. Die Blutenpflanzen Afrikas. Eine anleitung zum Bestimmen der Gattlungen der Afrikanischen Siphonogam. [The flowering plants of Africa. An analytical key to the genera of African phanerogams.] Berlin: R. Friedlander & Sohn.

An English edition, translated by the author, titled The flowering plants of Africa, was published in 1915, by Dulau & Co. of London. Reprint. Weinheim: J. Cremer. 1962. Frequent mention is made in text of food and beverage use of plants.

8142.   Thorndike, L. 1934. Medieval saucebook, with Latin text. Speculum 9:183-190.

Excerpt of Latin text, in English translation.

8142.   Thornton, Thomas Perry. 1957. Grobianische Tischzuchten. [Boorish table manners.] Berlin: E. Schmidt.

8143.   Thornton, Thomas Perry. 1957. Hofische Tischzuchten. [Courtly table manners.] Berlin: E. Schmidt.

8144.   Thouvenot, Claude. Evolution des habitudes alimentaires en mileau rural Lorrain. [Evolution of food habits in rural Lorraine.] In 93^e Congres National des Societes Savantes. 4 9 avril, 1967. Tours, France. Actes. 1968. Pp. 289-300. Paris: Imprimerie Jemmapes.

8145.   Thouvenot, Claude. 1969-1970. Apport de la geographie a l'etude du comportement alimentaire: le pain paysan dans la France de l'Est. [Contribution of geography to the study of food behavior: the peasant bread of eastern France.] Geo Med 1:71-96.

8146.   Thouvenot, Claude. 1970. Le pain paysan dans la France rurale. Evolution et technologie. [Peasant bread in rural France. Evolution and technology.] CND 4:13-21; 5:17-20.

8147.   Thouvenot, Claude. 1971. La viande dans les Campagnes Lorraines. [Meat in Lorraine.] A Geo 80(439):288-329.

Meat consumption was formerly limited for several reasons (disposition of meat for cash; problems of meat preservation), then seems to have increased after 1860 in towns, and among a minority of well-to-do people who began to eat boiled beef on Sundays. Between 1870 and 1914, factory workers in the country regularly began to buy butcher's meat, followed by a demand by farm servants. Between World War I and II vehicles permitted meat deliveries by butchers, with a concomitant appearance of very fat, boiled meat on Sundays, among lower in come groups. After 1950, consumption of retail butcher's meat increased to several times a week among non-farmers, and subsequently among farmers as well. Greater demand occurred for better cuts of meat and rural meat consumption increased as a result of preservation made possible by freezers.

8148. Thouvenot, Claude. Les habitudes alimentaires dans la France du Nord-Est. [Food habits in north-east France.] Ph.D. dissertation. Universite de Nancy. 1975. (March).

Alsace, and Lorraine Departments.

8149. Thouvent, Claude. 1978. Studies in food geography in France. SSMed 12 (ID [Medical Geography]): 43-54.

Focusing on the Departments of Lorraine, and Alsace, this study reviews the socio-economic and historical variables affecting food consumption, and then narrows to a study of specific foods, illustrating consumption patterns using maps of France.

8150. Thrum, Thomas G. 1879. Varieties of sweet potato. THA Pp. 30-31.

Fifty varieties of indigenous Hawaiian sweet potato, described on the basis of color and quality.

8151. Thrum, Thomas G. 1880. Varieties of taro. THA Pp. 28-29.

Hawaiian names of twenty-nine varieties of Arum esculentum.

8152. Thrum, Thomas G. 1887. Some important and favorite taro varieties and their use. THA Pp. 63-65.

Notes that some varieties were reserved for use by priests of the Hawaiian religion.

8153. Thrum, Thomas G. 1892. Manoa Valley. THA Pp. 110-116.

Thrum quotes from the legend of Punahou Spring, in which tender shoots of the popolo, aheahea, pakai, laulele, and sweet potato vines are said to have been eaten by two children while waiting for a patch of potatoes to develop. Aheahea is Chenopodium sandwicheum, a pot-herb also called aweweo. These were cooked by rolling hot stones around them in a covered gourd, a method of cooking called hakui by the Hawaiians.

8154. Thrum, Thomas G. 1914. Pepeiao. THA Pp. 201-202.

Pepeia akua is a fungus used in Chinese cuisine. It was gathered from the decayed limbs and trunks of the kukui tree (Aleurites moluccaensis). After sun-drying, the fungus was baled and shipped to the Orient. Export declined in the 1870's and ceased after 1886.

8155. Thrum, Thomas G. 1923. Leaf uses of the Hawaiians. THA Pp. 21-23.

Taro leaves were used as a sort of spinach; sweet potato vine leaves of a certain maturity furnished the palula of native Hawaiian diet.

8156. Thrum, Thomas G. 1924. Hawaiian salt making. THA Pp. 112-117.

8157. Thudicum, J.L.W. 1895. The spirit of cookery: a popular treatise on the history, science, practice, and medical and ethical import of culinary art. London: Baillere, Tindall & Cox; New York: Frederick Warne.

8158. Thuillier, G. Note sur les sources de l'historie regionale de l'alimentation pour la France du 19 siecle. [Note on sources of French regional diet history for the 19th Century.] In Pour une histoire de l'alimentation. Edited by J.J. Hemardinquer. 1970. Pp. 212-227. Paris: Colin.

8159. Thurman, Sue Bailey, ed. 1958. The National Council of Negro Women presents the historical cookbook of the American Negro. Washington, D.C.: Corporate Press.

8160. Thurston, H.D. 1969. Tropical agriculture: a key to world food crises. Bioscience 19:29.

8161. Tibbles, William. 1912. Foods, their origin, composition, and manufacture. London: Bailliere, Tindall & Cox.

8162. Tibesar, Antonine S. 1950. Salt trade among the montana Indians of the Touma area of eastern Peru. PMan 23:103-108.

Focus is on activities of the last quarter of the Seventeenth Century, involving the Campa and Amuesha; the Conibo, Piro; Mochobo; and Rema.

8163. Tierney, Gail D. 1973. Plants and man in prehistoric Catron County. El Pal 79:28-38.

Review of plant materials from salvage archeology sites in southwestern New Mexico.

8164. Tieu, Nguyen-Cong. 1935. Nhung loai an duoc o xu Bac-ky. [Edible insects of Tonkin.] Khoa No. 24. Pp. 287-289.

8165. Tiltack, Curt. 1964. Alte Koch-und Haushalts-Rezepte. [Old cookery, and household recipes.] HK-OH-J 8:168-172.

8166. Timmons, Gayle Curinne. Food plans for two-member veterans families at Oregon State College. Master's thesis. Oregon State College. 1947.

8167.   Timothy B.   1897.   The origin of manna. Nature(L) 55:440.

8168.   Tindale, Norman B.   Ecology of primitive Aboriginal man in Australia.   In Biogeograhy and ecology in Australia.   Monographiae Biologicae No. 8.   Edited by A. Keast; R.L.   Crocker; & C.S. Christian.   1959.   Pp. 36-51.

Ecological implications in dietary restrictions: p. 40; water and food availability as criteria for tribal territoriality: pp. 40, 41; effects of introduced plants and animals on native subsistence: p. 46; interaction between native culture and environment on native subsistence: p. 50.

8169.   Tindale, Norman B.   1966.   Insects as food for the Australian Aborigines.   ANH 15:179-183.

8170.   Ting, Y.   1959.   Notes on the Neolithic rice husks unearthed in Hupei.   [In Chinese, with English summary.]   Kaogu 4:31-34.

8171.   Tingle, Lilian E.   1907.   Food notes -Shantung, north China.   BCSM 12:155-159.

8172.   Tinker, Sylvester & Tinker, Alice.   1955. Authenticated American Indian recipes.   Pawhuska, Oklahoma: S. McLain.

Osage.

8173.   Tipton, Alice S.   1916.   New Mexico cookery. Santa Fe: State of New Mexico Land Office. Reprint. Santa Fe, New Mexico: Richard J. Polese. 1965.

8174.   Titcomb, Margaret.   1967.   The foods of ancient Hawaii.   HS-B Section E.   27 September. Pp. 3, 4.

8175.   Titcomb, Margaret & Pukui, Mary Kawena. 1951.   Native use of fish in Hawaii.   PS-M No. 29.

8176.   Titiev, Misha.   1937.   The Hopi method of baking sweet corn.   MAS-AL-P No. 23.   Pp. 87-94.

8177.   Titley, A.L.   1948.   A yam festival in Ashanti.   GC-DA-N 2:7-8.

8178.   Tizzano, A.   1956.   La geografia dell' alimentazione.   [The geography of food.]   Dif Soc 35:7-45.

8179.   Tobey, James A. 1932. Wholesome nutrition in times of Depression.   HSS 25:269-270.

Suggestions for obtaining balanced diet in limited income.

8180.   Tobias, E. Silva M.M. 1956. Contribution to the study of the nutritive value of the Alagoan suvuvu (Mytilus mundahuensis, Duarte).   [In Portuguese.]   RBQ 41:192.

A mussel found in the Brazilian State of Alagoas.

8181.   Tobias, Gregoria A.   Preparation of edible kapok seed oil from local kapok plant.   Master's thesis.   Pharmacy.   Manilla: University of Santo Tomas. 1957.

Philippines.

8182.   Tobier, N. & Steinberg, I.   1966.   Fletcherism.   Early Twentieth Century food fad.   NYJM 66:2687-2689.

A fad based on extensive mastication of foods.

8183.   Todhunter, E. Neige.   1964.   Dietetics in the Shakespearean plays.   JADA 44:285-286.

8184.   Todhunter, E. Neige.   1964.   Some classics of nutrition and dietetics.   JADA 44:100-108.

8185.   Todhunter, E. Neige.   1965.   Russell Henry Chittenden.   Ala JMS 2:337-341.

8186.   Todhunter, E. Neige.   1965.   Some aspects of the history of dietetics.   WRND 5:32-78.

8187.   Togamau.   1940.   Preparation and use of niutolo and suau'u manogi oils.   NMP 3:503-505.

Coconut oils. Fiji.

8188.   Toklas, Alice B.   1958.   Aromas and flavors of past and present.   New York: Harper Brothers.

8189.   Tolbert, Frank X.   1966.   A bowl of red.   A natural history of chili.   Garden City, New York: Doubleday.

8190.   Tolerton, Burt & Rauch, Jerome.   1949. Social organization, land tenure and susbsistence economy of Lukonor, Nomoi Island.   Coordianted Investigation of Micronesian Anthropology (CIMA) No. 26.

CIMA fieldwork was conductd in Guam and in islands of the Trust Territory in Micronesia (1947-1949)   with transportation and facilities contributed by the Navy Department.   Studies in anthropology as well as human and economic geography were carried out in cooperation with universities, museums, and research institutions under this project of the Pacific Science Board of the National Research Council, aided by financial assistance from the Viking Fund and other private sources.   CIMA operated with finacial assistance from Contract N7-onr-291, Task Order IV between the Office of Naval Reasearch and the National Academy of Sciences.   The Nomoi Islands are located at 5.0 N., 153. 0 E., in the Central Carolines. Diet: p. 15; chart of seasonal changes in Lukonor food supply: p.   16; seasonal variation: pp. 17, 18. Subsistence economy: pp. 97-98; agriculture: pp. 98-108; bread fruit: pp. 108-112; conconut: p. 113. taro, arrowroot, bananas: pp. 113-114; animal food sources: pp.   114-116; fish, fishing and fishing technology: pp. 116-127. Ritual and magic related to food production: pp. 128-130; food in boy's puberty ceremonies; food in fish trap-setting rituals: pp. 130-137. Food distribution: (intra-and inter-lineage) : pp. 138-139; non-lineage food exchange and feasts: pp. 139-146; food preparation, and cooking techniques: pp. 146-148; beverages: p. 148; food etiquette: p. 148. Division of labor (subsistence-related) pp. 149-155; food as payment for loans of equipment: p. 175.

8191.   Tolkowsky, S. 1930. The history of the cultivation of citrus fruits in Palestine. P-DAF-AL Series 4. Horticulture No. 22.

8192.   Tolkowsky, S. 1937. Hesperides, a history of the culture and use of citrus fruits. London: John Bale Sons & Curnow.

8193.   Tolley, H. 1948. Population and food supply. CB 11: 217-224.

8194.   Tomkinson, G. 1938. High tea in New foundland. Dal Rev 18: 67-72.

8195.   Tooker, Elizabeth. 1964. An ethnography of the Huron Indians. SI-BAE-B No. 190.

    Food preparation: pp. 67-70.

8196.   Tookey, H.L. & Gentry, H.S. 1969. Proteinase of Jarilla chocola, a relative of papaya. Phytochemistry 8: 989-991.

    Jarilla chocola is a perennial herb which grows wild in northwestern Mexico. Its fruit and starchy roots are sold for food in native markets. Juice of both fruit and root contain a proteinase resembling papain.

8197.   Toor, F. 1935. Cooking and sweets of the Mexican Indians with Spanish translation. MFolk No. 74-77.

8198.   Topper, Martin David. The daily life of a traditional Navajo household: an ethnographic study in human daily activities. Ph. D. Dissertation. Anthropology. Northwestern University. 1972.

8199.   Toronto Nutrition Committee. 1967. Food customs of new Canadians. Toronto: toronto Nutrition Committee.

    Includes Chinese, Czech, German, Greek, Hungarian, Italian, Jewish, Dutch, Polish, Portuguese, Spanish, Ukranian, and West Indian. Consideration is given to possible modification as required by unavailability of certain foods in the Toronto area.

8200.   Torrance, E. Paul. 1955. Food prejudice and survival. United States Air Force Survival Training School. Crew Research Laboratory. (AFP and TRC). Survival Reasearch Field Unit. Laboratory Note 55-LN-210. Reno, Nevada: Stead Airforce Base.

8201.   Torres, L. & Manso, L. 1903. Estudo comparativo de alguns indices para appreciacao de farinhas de peixe e peixe seco. [Comparative study of some indices for the evaluation of fish meals and dried fish.] NMCBP 36: 1-16.

    Nutritive value of two Portuguese African foodstuffs.

8202.   Torres, Rosa Marina. 1959. Dietary patterns of the Puerto Rican people. AJCN 7: 349-355.

8203.   Torry, William I. Location patterns, sociability and food production among the Gabra. Paper presented at 74th Annual Meeting of the American Anthropological Association. 2 to 6 December, 1975. San Francisco, California.

8204.   Tothill, John Douglas, ed. 1948. Agriculture in the Sudan, being a handbook of agriculture as practiced in the Anglo-Egyptian Sudan, by numerous authors. Oxford: Oxford University Press.

8205.   Totsuka, K. 1933. Coconut taboos in the South Sea Islands. [In Japanese.] SI 1: 245-251.

8206.   Tournemille, Jean. 1963. La pomme et la poire. [The apple and the pear.] VL No. 139. Pp. 554-556.

8207.   Toutain, J.C. 1971. La consommation alimentaire en France de 1789 a 1964. [Consumption of food in France from 1789 to 1964.] ESoc 5: 1909-2049.

8208.   Touzet, Henri-Paul. Note sur la geophagie en Portugal. [Note on geophagy in Portugal.] In 15^e Congres International d'Anthropologie & d'Archeologie Prehistorique. 21-30. Septembre 1930. Coimbre & Porto, Portugal. Actes du Congres. 1931. Pp. 666-668. Paris Librairie E. Nourry.

    Draws attention to a report in the literature indicating the ingestion of a talc-like, clayey schist in the Portuguese village of Penacove, ca. 25km from Coimbre.

8209.   Towle, Harvey P. 1925. Diet in diseases of the skin. HSS 11: 146-155.

    Review of most common dermatological complaints, and the relationship of various foods to them, e.g. acne, psoriasis, impetigo, eczema, urticaria. Also discusses diabetes.

8210.   Towle, Margret Ashley. 1952. The pre-Columbian occurrence of Lagenaria seeds in coastal Peru. HU-BML 15: 171-184.

    Lagenaria siceraria.

8211.   Towle, Margaret Ashley. 1952. Plant remains from a Peruvian mummy bundle. HU-BML 15: 223-245.

    Paracas site. Included are maize, peanuts, manioc, gourds.

8212.   Towle, Margret Ashley. 1961. The ethnobotany of pre-Columbian Peru. VFPA No. 30.

Food plants and their uses are noted throughout.

8213.   Townsend, Jeanne. 1964.   Unexploited crops in Bolivia. WC 16(3): 67-68.

Ullucu (Ullucus tuberosus); oca (Oxalis tuberosum); anu (tropaeolum tuberosum); quinoa (Chenopodium quinoa); Kanahua (Chenopodium palidicauk).   Refers briefly to F.A.O. - administered, agricultural research at Lake Titicaca.

8214.   Townsend, John Kirk.   1839. Narrative of a journey across the Rocky Mountains, to the Columbia River; with a visit to the Sandwich Islands, Chili, &c. with a scientific appendix.   Philadelphia: H. Perkins; Boston: Perkins and Marvin.

Includes a description of a camas (Camasia esculenta) feast in central Idaho.

8215.   Townsend, Patricia Kathryn Woods. Subsistence and social organization in a New Guinea society. Ph. D. Dissertation. University of Michigan. 1969.

This study deals with the relationship between subsistence, population, and social organization among the Heve people of the Wogamus River area.   Heve subsistence is based on hunting, gathering, pig husbandry, and horticulture.   The emphasis of this study is on sago, which provides eighty-five percent of the diet.   Sago work is evaluated in terms of ratio of labor and energy input to output.   The results of quantitative studies of food consumption are reported.   From data on sago yields, the carrying capacity of the Heve area is estimated.   The actual population is shown to fall substantially below the carrying potential, and it is suggested that protein resources are a significantly limiting factor.   Social and cultural aspects of subsistence are covered, including food taboos; division of labor; and food-related ritual and mythology.

8216.   Townsend, Patricia Kathryn Woods. 1971. New Guinea Sago gatherers. A study of demography in relation to subsistence. EFN 1: 19-24.

Among the people living along the Wogamus River, a tributary of the upper Sepik River, both infanticide, and post-partum taboos (on sexual intercouse) which lasts for two years, are seen as practiced to ensure the adequate nutrition of older siblings.   As population grows to the point where there is pressure on game, fish, and vegetable foods, other than the always abundant sago, the people are more likely to limit their families.

8217.   Townsend, Petricia Kathryn Woods Liao, Shu chung; & Konlande, J.E. 1973. Nutritive contributions of sago ash used as a native salt in Papua New Guinea. EFN 2: 91-97.

In New Guinea, the Sanio-Hiowe group of the Wogamus River do not have a supply of naturally occurring salt.   They have, however, developed a technique for preparing a salty ash by reduction of the midribs of the sago plant (Metroxylon sp) by burning.   The procedure is described.   The ash is not added to food, but consumed by itself, irregularly during the day, in quantities estimated not to exceed two grams.   Chemical composition of the ash is given.   It is suggested that the alkalinity of the ash may help to spare protein in a diet deficient in this nutrient.   Reference is made to plant salt products produced elsewhere.

8218.   Tracy, H.C. 1918.   The food habits of a people without nerves. A Cook 22: 644-646.

Armenia.

8219.   Trager, James. 1970. The enriched, fortified, concentrated, country-fresh, lip-smaking, finger-licking, international, unexpurgated foodbook. New York: Grossman.

Food history; nutrition; hygiene; and technology.

8220.   Traglia, G.   1956. Milk in cookery in the Seventh Century. [In Italian.]   ML 10: 753-754.

8221.   Tranmere, E.C. 1969.   Can one cook in a skin: Antiquity 43: 217-218.

Example of pit-cooking of kangaroos, by Aborigines in Australia.   The disemboweled animal is placed in a preheated pit, and hot sand and embers raked over, with no damage to the skin, beyond scorching.

8222.   Trant, hope.   1954.   Food tabus in East Africa. EAAJ 20: 223. Also in Lancet 267: 703-705. (1954)

8223.   Traven, Bruno. 1970. The carretera. New York: Hill & Wang.

A novel depicting the life of wagoneers in Chiapas, Mexico. Food habits: pp. 144-145; 168; 188-189.

8224.   Treat, Ida. 193. South-Sea adventure in the kitchen. Geog Mag 6(4) : 245-258.

An informal, romantic account of Tahitian staple foods, and food preparation. Illustrated with numerous black-and-white photographs.

8225.   Trecker, Patricia Grinager. The anthropology of eating.   Paper presented at 73rd Annual Meeting of the American Anthropological Association. 19 to 24 November, 1974. Mexico City.

8226.   Treganza, Adan E. 1947. Possibilities of an aboriginal practice of agriculture among the southern Diegueno. Am Ant 12: 169-173.

8227.   Tregear, Edward. 1888. The knowledge of cattle amongst the ancient Polynesians. NZI-TP 21: 447-476.

Based largely on liniguistic eveidence. References to Tahiti, and the Marquesas Islands.

8228.   Treide, Barbara. 1967. Wildpflanzen in der Ernahrung der Grundbevolkerung Melanisiens. [Wild plants in the diet of Melanesian aborigines.] Berlin: Akakemie Verlag.

8229.   Tremeau de Rochebrune, Alphonse. 1879. recherches d'ethnographie botanique sur la flore des sepultures peruvienne d'Ancon. [Ethnobotanical researches on the flora of the Peruvian graves at Ancon.] Paris: Masson. Also in SLB-A 3: 343-358.

8230.   Tremeau de Rochebrune, Alphonse. 1883-1884. De l'emploi des mollusques chez les peuples anciens et modernes. 1. Amerique. 2. Mollusques des sepultures de l'Equateur et de la Nouvelle-Grenade. [On the use of molluscs by ancient and modern peoples. 1. America. 2. Molluscs from graves in Ecuador and New Grenada.] Paris: E. Leroux.

8231.   Tremeau de Rochebrune, Alphonse. 1896-1899. Toxicologie africaine, etude botanique, historique, pharmacologique, posologique... sur les vegetaux toxiques et suspects propres au continent africain et aux isles adjacentes. [African toxicaology, botanical, historical, ethnographic, chemical, physiological, threapeutic, pharmacologic, and dosologic study on toxic and toxicologically-suspect plants in Africa and its adjacent islands.] Paris: O. Doin.

8232.   Tremolieres, Jean. Socio-economic implications of food habits. In First International Congress on Food Science and Technology. September 18-21, 1962. London. Proceedings. Vol. 5. Food science and technology. Edited by James Mail Leitch. 1967. Pp. 221-234.

Consumption factors; food in family life; marketing.

8233.   Tremolieres, Jean. 1969. L'alimentation comme ordinateur de la societe. Sur les relations du tissu social et de l'individu. [Food habits as regulator of society. On the relations between the social fabric and the individual.] Con Med 86: 87-93; 95-96.

Interrelationship between food production and consumption and the psychological, social, economic, scientific, and medical aspects of life. Emphasizes the strong influence of family and sex-role upon food habits in a culture. Criticizes the effects of industrialization upon the cohesion of traditional agricultural societies: "By transforming its way of eating one transforms the culture." Observes that certain food taboos represent an effort to reject the civilization which produces the food: e.g. pork, at first rejected by desert nomads as being a food of their enemy: the Egyptian farmer; and the myth of health foods as a reaction against industrial life.

8234.   Tremolieres, Jean. Nutrition and underdevelopment. In Progress in human nutrition. Vol 1. Edited byt Sheldon Marge. 1971. Pp. 1-28. Westport, Connecticut: AVI.

8235.   Tremolieres, Jean & Baquet, R. 1967. Le comportement alimentaire de l'homme. [Human dietary behavior.] MMed No. 508. Pp. 759-763.

8236.   Tremolieres, Jean & Claudian, Jean 1954. Algunos aspectos de los habitos alimenticios del hombre. [Some aspects of human food habits.] AVN 5: 425-462.

8237.   Tremolieres, Jean; Claudian, Jean; & Desroches, H.C. Contribution des enquetes sociologiques sur l'alimentation a l'etude du comportement alimentaire de l'homme. [The contribution of sociological investigations of diet to the study of human food behavior.] In Present Problems in Nutrition Research Symposium. 1-4 October, 1952. Basel Edited by F. Verzar. 1953. Pp. 13-35. Basel-Stuttgart: Verlag Birkhauser.

8238.   Tremolieres, Jean; Claudian, Jean, & Desroches, H.C. 1953. Contribution des enquetes alimentaires a l'etude du comportement alimentaire de l'homme. [Contribution of dietary surveys to the study of human food behavior.] Experientia 9. [Supp. 1].

Report of a sociologically-oriented food consumption survey carried out in Paris during the period ca. 1944-1954. Discusses food consumption patterns, as affected by socio-economic variables, and observes the existence of food habits patterns along rural-urban, geographical, and professional lines.

8239.   Tremolieres, Jean; Serville, Yvonne; & Jacquot, Raymond. 1958. Manuel elementaire d'alimentation humaine. Tome 1. Les bases de L'alimentation. [Basic handbook of human nutrition. Vol. 1. The foundations of diet.] Paris: Editions Sociales.

Part One provides a history of diet. Part Six covers the psychology of eating including taste; sequence of meal components; and structure of the meal.

8240.   Tremolieres, Jean; Serville, Yvonne; & Jacquot, Raymond. 1958. Manuel elementaire d'alimentation humaine. Tome 2. Les aliments. [Basic handbook of human nutrition. Vol. 2. Foods.] Paris: Editions Sociales.

The conclusion of this volume touches upon food in modern society; trends in the recent evolution in food habits; and woman's time expended on food preparation.

8241.   Trenchard, Thomas (Lord) The inter-relationship of marketing and nutrition. In Diet of man: wants and needs. Edited by John Yudkin. 1978. Pp. 225-241. London: Applied Science Publishers.

De-emphasizes the influence of advertising upon consumer food choice, and makes a claim for the case that changes in consumer food preferences are largely unpredictable, in spite of costly market research. Article is largely concerned with a review of historical changes in British food consumption patterns during the past one hundred years

8242.   Tressider, Argus John.   1960.   Cylon New York: D. Van Nostrand.

Food: pp. 545-55.

8243.   Triay, Jose E.   1914.   Nueve manual del cocinero criollo.   Con un prologo del Dr. Gonzalo Arostegui y del Castillo; contiene unas mil formulas de todos los platos de la cocina criolla, y de las cocinas espanola, francesa, italiana, alemana e inglesa, que se acostumbra servir en las mesas de Cuba; adiciniado con un tratado de pasteleria y dulceria. [New handbook of Creole cookery with a prologue by Dr. Gonzalo Arostegui y del Castillo; contains a thousand recipes for all Spanish, French, Italian, German, and English cookery that one is accustomed to have served at Cuban tables; a treatise on baking and confectionery is added. Havana: Moderna Poesia.

8244.   Trillin, Calvin.   1974.   American fried: adventures of a happy eater.   New York: Coubleday

Essays on the author's experiences in searching for sources of quality regional foods. Specific attention is given to Kansas City; New York; Martha's Vineyard; and New Orleans.

8245.   Trimborn, Hermann.   1938.   Die Kannibalismus im Caucatal.   [Canniblaism in Cauca.]   ZE 70: 310-330.

Cauca is a division in southwestern Colombia, in the lower Cordillera Occidentale.

8246.   Tringham, Ruth 1971.   Chapter Three.   The earliest food producers, 5500-3800 B.C.   In Hunters, fishers and farmers of eastern Europe, 6000-3000 B.C.   London: Hutchinson University Library.

8247.   Tripathi, M.   1935-1936.   A few fasts, festivities and observances in Orissa.   MIndia 15:37-59; 16:156-182.

8248.   Trolli, Giovanni.   1936.   L'alimentation chez les travailleurs indigenes dans les exploitations commerciales, agricoles, industrielles et minieres au Congo.   [Native workers' diets in commercial, agricultural industrial and mining operations in the Congo.]   Africa 9:197-217.

Sub-Saharan African colonies.

8249.   Troin, J.F.   1963.   Observations sur les souqs de la region d'Azrou et de Khenifra.   [Observations on the markets of the region of Azrou and Khenifra.]   RGM Nos. 3-4.   Pp. 109-120.

Azrou and Khenifra are located in north-central Morocco at 33.27N., 5.14W.; and 33.0 N., 5.40 W., respectively.

8250.   Troost, G. & Wanner, E.   1951.   Weinprobe-Weinausprache.   [Wine sampling - wine glossary.]   Frankfurt am Main: Rehingauer Weinzeitung.

Glossary of technical terms in wine sampling; with suggestions on how to arrange a taste-panel.

8251.   Trouborst, A.A.   Bananenbier in Burundi.   [Banana beer in Burundi.]   16 mm film.   Gottingen: Institut fur den Wissenschaftlichen Film.

Shows the preparation of a fermented beverage based on bananas.

8252.   Trowell, Margaret & Wachsmann, K.P. 1953.   Tribal crafts of Uganda.   London: Oxford University Press.

Food utensils: pp. 105-107.

8253.   Troxel, Kathryn.   1955.   Food of the overland emigrants.   OHQ 56:12-26.

8254.   Truax, Grace H.   1957.   Down our way: our daily bread.   KFR 3:45-48.

Reminiscences of food patterns at Chaplin, eastern Nelson County, Kentucky. Mentions underground storage of pumpkin, squash, turnips, parsnips, apples, and cabbage. Includes one pie and one cake recipe.

8255.   Truc-Vien. 1933.   Van-de nuoc-mam.   [The question of nuoc-mam.]   Saigon: Imprimerie Tin-duc-thu-xa.

8256.   Truex, Nancy W.   Interaction at a supermarket checkout stand.   Paper presented at 72nd Annual Meeting of the American Anthropological Association.   30 Nov.ember, 1973.   New Orleans, Louisiana.

8257.   Trull, Fern Coble.   The history of the Chinese in Idaho from 1864 to 1910.   Master's thesis.   History.   University of Oregon.   1946.

Role of Chinese as mine, and railroad cooks, and restaurateurs: pp. 56-61.

8258.   Trulson, Martha F.   1959.   The American diet-past and present.   AJCN 7:91-97.

Surveys trends in increase and decrease in consumption of specific nutrient sources.

8259.   Trulson, Martha F. & McCann, Mary B. 1959.   Comparison of dietary survey methods.   JADA 35:672-676.

Sources of consumption data; individual food intake "diary"; food weighment; questionnaires; dietary history interviewing.

8260.   Truswell, A.S. & Hansen, J.D.L. 1968.   Medical and nutritional studies of Kung Bushmen in north-west Botswana: a preliminary report.   SAMJ 42:1338-1339.

8261.   Tryon, Thomas. 1684. Plants of the West
Indies. 1. Tryon's friendly advice to the gentlemen
planters of the East and West Indies. Brief treatise
of the principal fruits and herbs that grow in Barba-
does, Jamaica, and other plantations in the West
Indies. London: Andrew Sowle.

8262.   Tsangridis, G. & Veziris, C.D. 1952. Contribution a l'etude de l'alimentation du peuple grec
pendant la periode 1941-1945. [Contribution to the
study of the dietary of the Greek people during the
period 1941-1945. Pres Med 60:1361-1362.

8263.   Tseng, Chao-lun. 1948. Liang-Shan I-chu
Kai Huang. Ta Liang- Shan I-Chu K'ao-cha Chi.
[The Lolo District in Liang-Shan. A selection from
an account of an investigation trip to Liang Shan.]
Translated by Josette M. Yeu, for the Human Rela-
tions Area Files.

         Food habits and utensils: pp. 10-11; 17.
         Szechuan Province, China.

8264.   Tseng, Cheng-kwei. 1933. Gloiopeltis and
other economic seaweeds of Amoy, China. LSJ
12:43-63.

         Food uses: pp. 56-60.

8265.   Tseng, Cheng-kwei. 1935. Economic seaweeds of Kwangtung Province, south China. LSJ
14:93-104.

         Edible species: pp. 101-102.

8266.   Tseuschiner, I. 1962. A peep at foreign
foods - Germany. FSA 38:62-66.

8267.   Tsuru, Sueo. 1901. Ainu no inshokumotsu ni
tsuitse. [Ainu food and drink.] JZ 16:398-400.

         Ainu foods, and methods of preservation.

8268.   Tsuzuki, Y. & Yamashita, A. 1969. History
of the chemistry of taste in Japan. [In Japanese.]
KKenkyu 8:1-12.

8269.   Tuan-Sanh. 1933. Nos reportages illustres:
la crise du nuoc-mam. [Our illustrated reports: the
nuoc-mam crisis.] ANI No. 10. P. 37.

8270.   Tubiana, M.-J. 1961. Le marche de Hili-ba:
moutons, mil, sel et contrabande. [The market at
Hili-ba: sheep, millet, salt and contraband.] CEA
2:196-243.

8271.   Tubiana, M.-J. 1963. A propos du cannibais-
me au Senegal. [Concerning cannibalism in Senegal.] L'Homme 3:130.

8273.   Tuchakov, J. 1964. Use of wild palnts as
nutritive supplement in the Besna Kobila Mountains
during lean and war years. Srp AN [Medicine] - G
17:53-93.

         Southeastern Yugoslavia 42. 31N., 22.11E.

8274.   Tugby, Elsie. The manufacture of sugar
from the sugar palm in Upper Mandailing, Sumatra.
In Ninth Pacific Science Congress. 18 November to

9 December, 1957. Bangkok, Thailand. Proceedings.
Vol. Four (Botany). 1962. Pp. 266-269. Bangkok:
Chulalongkorn University.

8275.   Tuggle, H. David. Prehistoric agricultural
growth: a Hawaiian example. Paper presented at
73rd Annual Meeting of the American Anthropological Association. 19 to 24 November, 1974. Mexico
City.

8276.   Tunis, Edwin. 1959. Indians. Cleveland;
New York: World Publishing Co.

         Food of woodland hunters: p. 42; Plains
         groups: pp. 98-99; illustration of pinon nut
         p. 108; illustration of camas (Camasia escu-
         lenta) plant: p. 111; method of cooking piki
         bread (Hopi): p. 119.

8277.   Tupper, August M. 1884. Anthropophagy.
BMSJ 236-237.

         Account of blood drunk from a corpse, by
         crew of an American schooner in 1882. Abs-
         tracted from Boston Sunday Globe, January
         8, 1882.

8278.   Turbia, M. 1937. Eating in China. Cath
Dgst 1:20-23.

8279.   Turbot, Charles R. 1953. Beche-de-mer
trepang. FS-TP 2:14-154.

         Trepang is a Malay word for dried, smoked
         sea cucumbers (family Holothuriidae) of
         which a number of species are used for food
         in southern Japan; the Philippines; and In-
         donesia. The animals are cut open, cleaned,
         often boiled to desalt them, and sun-dried.
         In Samoa, the 'cucumber' is eaten raw; in
         the Philippines, roasted. It is stated to have
         a protein content of 50 to 60 percent (basis
         not stated). [After Grzimek's Animal Life
         Encyclopedia. 1974. Vol. 3. Pp. 323, 324.
         New York: Van Nostrand Reinhold Co.]

8280.   Turbott, I.G. 1949. Diets, Gilbert and Ellice
Islands colony. JPS 58:36-46.

         Lists staple plant and animal foods, with
         nutritional values for some local and impor-
         ted items. The variability of meal times is
         mentioned at length; and infant foods are
         enumerated. Average daily Gilbertese diets
         are outlined, with quantities consumed, in a
         concluding Appendix.

8281.   Turbott, I.G. 1954. The value and importance of Portulaca as a native food in the Phoenix
Islands, central Pacific. Mankind 4:495-500.

         Food value, methods of collection; prepara-
         tion and preservation of Portulaca lutea.
         The Phoenix group is located just below the
         Equator at approximately 170.0 W.

8282.   Turbott, I.G. 1954. Portulaca: a specialty
in the diet of the Gilbertese in the Phoenix Islands,
central Pacific. JPS 63:77-85.

8283. Turkin, V.A. 1954. Inspolzovaniye dukora-stushshchniye poldovoyagodnich i orekoglodnich rastenii. [Utilization of wild fruits, berries, and nuts.] Moscow: Foreign Lanuguages Publishing House.

8284. Turnbull, Pauline. 1929. Praenestine 'asom-fero". Language 5:15-18.

Verification of 'boiling' as opposed to 'roast-ing' as depicted on the Praeneste cista.

8285. Turner, II., Christy, G. 1967. Bite marks in tule quids of prehistoric Nevada Indians. In Papers in Great Bain archeology. UCal-AS No. 70. UCARF Pp. 117-122.

Quids are the fibrous residue discarded after chewing plant materials, often for the pur-pose of extracting juice and sugars. In this instance, the chewed ends of the desert bulrush (Scirpus sp.) recovered from Love-lock Cave, were cast in a water-based algin-ate impression material revealing sufficient detail to estimate approximate age, tooth wear, and absence of caries activity. Such quids provide an indirect means for obtain-ing phenotypic and pathological data for dental studies of prehistoric populations, in the absence of actual dental remains.

8286. Turner, G.A. 1 909. The diet of South African natives in their kraals. Pretoria: Govern-ment Printing Office.

8287. Turner, Jessie C. & Alexander, Agnes B. 1912. How to use Hawaiian fruits. 2nd ed. Honolu-lu: Paradise-Pacific Print.

8288. Turner, Lucien M. 1894. Ethnology of the Ungava District, Hudson Bay Territory. SI-BE-AR for the year 1889-1890. Pp. 159-350.

Food and its preparation: pp. 232-234.

8289. Turney, Omar A. 1929-1930. Prehistoric irrigation. AzHR 2(1):12-52, (2):11-52; (3):9-45; (4):33-73.

8290. Turney-High, Harry Holbert. 1933. Cooking camas and bitterroot. SM 36:262-267.

8291. Turney-High, Harry Holbert. 1937. The Flathead Indians of Montana. AAA-M No. 48.

Butchering (of bison): pp. 119, 120; the eco-nomics of meat: pp. 120, 121; meat curing: pp. 121, 122; cooking: 127-129; eating eti-quette, utensils: p. 129.

8292. Turney-High, Harry Holbert. 1941. Ethno-graphy of the Kutenai. AAA-M No. 56.

The search for food: pp. 33-53. Plant foods: pp. 33-35; hunting; butchering; pem-mican preparation; fishing: pp. 35-41; bird hunting: pp. 41-44; fishing: pp. 44-52; food distribution (meat, fish): pp. 52-53; seasonal availability of food: pp. 53-55; wooden

containers: pp. 78, 79; meal times: pp. 122-123; etiquette: pp. 124-125.

8293. Turril, W.B. 1952. Wild and cultivated oli-ves. GB-RBGK-KB No. 3. 1951. Pp. 437-442.

Historic, economic, mythologic, origin and distribution data.

8294. Tuzin, Donald F. Carnivorousness and car-nality in Ilahita. Paper presented at the 76th Annual Meeting of the American Anthropological Association 29 November to 3 December, 1977. Houston, Texas.

A full account of Arapesh taboos and pros-criptions surrounding meat consumption must take account of the symbolic equation - highly ramified in this culture but also reported in many other places - between meat-eating and coitus. After providing evidence from myth, ritual and other con-texts that this association is locally salient, the paper shows how proper awareness of this symbolic dimension improves our under-standing of meat consumption patterns as a demarcator of gender and generational cat-egories among these people.

8295. Tweeddale, Constance. Diet, disease and living conditions among Canadian Indians. Master's thesis. Sackville, New Brunswick: Mount Allison University. 1939.

8296. Twyman, R.W. 1971. Clay eater. A new look at an old Southern enigma. JSH 37:439-448.

8297. Tyau, Min-ch'ien tuk-sung. 1920. London through Chinese eyes. London: Swarthmore Press.

Observations on English cuisine and restaur-ants: pp. 112-129.

8298. Tylor, Edward B. 1865. Chapter 9. Fire, cooking and vessels. In Researches into the early history of mankind. London: Murray.

8299. Uchendu, Victor C. The cultural and eco-nomic factors influencing food habits in sub-Saharan Africa. Paper presented at Third International Congress of Food Science and Technology. 9 August to 14 August, 1970. Washington D.C.

8300. Uchida, Ruriko. The music of rice planting in Chindo Island (Korea). paper presented at 9th International Congrss of Anthropological and Ethno-logical Sciences. 28 August to 8 September, 1973. Chicago, illinois.

Chindo Island is located in the Tadohae Sea, southwest of the Korean Peninsula. The rice planting, weeding, and harvesting music is described, and compared with similar per-formances in the Japanese district of Chug-oku.

8301. Udo, Reuben K. 1971. Food deficit areas of Nigeria. GR 61: 415-430.

8302.   Uebel, F.   1965.   The salt tax at the begining of the Ptolemaic period. ASP-B 3: 20, 21.

Abstract of a paper presented at the annual meeting of the American Society of Papyrologists.

8303.   Ukers, William Harrison. 1936.   The romance of tea. An outline of tea and tea-drinking through sixteen hundred years. New York; London: Alfred A. Knopf.

Genesis of tea; tea's conquest of the Orient; tea comes to Europe and America; the ocean-going tea trade; tea cultivation; processing; tea commerce; tea manners and customs; tea and the fine arts; chemical and medical aspects of teea; brewing tea.

8304.   Ullrich, Wolfgang. 1970.   Ernahrung und Verhaaltenweisen des Nahrungswerbes der Prahominiden und fruhen Euhominiden.   [Nutrition and food-getting patterns of prehominids and early proto-hominids.] E-AZ 11: 55-60.

8305.   Ulmer, Mary & Beck, Samuel E.   1951.   Cherokee cooklore. To make my bread. Cherokee, North Carolina: Museum of the Cherokee Indian.

Traditional Cherokee foods and methods of preparation.

8306.   Underhill, Ruth Murray. 1946. Workaday life of the Pueblos. Edited by Willard W. Beatty. Indian life and customs. No. 4.   United States Department of the Interior. United States Indian Service. Phoenix Arizona: Phoenix Indian School.

Food preparation: 30-64.

8307.   Underhill, Ruth Murray. 1953. Here come the Navajo.   United States Department of the Interior.   Bureau of Indian Affairs.   Lawrence, Kansas: Haskell Insititute.

Food preparation: pp. 54-66.

8308.   Underwood, Frances W. 1960.   The marketing system in peasant Haiti. YUPA   No. 60.

Contains numerous references to food throughout.

8309.   United Kingdom. Ministry of Overseas Development. 1963. The changing pattern of economic activity in a Gambian Village. Overseas Research Publication No. 2. London: Her Majesty's Stationery Office.

Examines the change in staple food from millet to rice.

8310.   United Nations Educational, Scientific and Cultural Organization.   1953.   New Horizons at Tzentzenhuaro. Paris, UNESCO.

Illustration of a Tarascan kitchen: Plates 3,5.

8311.   United States Department of Agriculture. 1935. Economic and social problems and conditions of the southern Appalachians. USDA-MP No. 205.

Includes dietary data.

8312.   United States Department of Agriculture. 1943. Manual of industrial feeding. Food Distribution Administration. Nutrition and Food Conservation Branch. Washington, D.C. Gorvernment Printing Office.

As part of the Defense program, during World War II, a special program on industrial nutrition was developed.   This pamphlet reviews the requirements of in-plant nutrition, and includes nutrition education recommendations; sample menus; discussion of national dietary problems; and food preparation instructions for preserving maximum food value.

8314.   United States Department of Agriculture. 1959. Food. USDA-YB

Nutrients; food for health; food requirements; quality; preparation; costs; trends; programs.

8315.   United States Department of Agriculture. 1961. Family food stockpile for survival. USDA-HGB No. 77.

Food protection, preservation and selection, in the event of nuclear attack.

8316.   United States Department of Agriculture & The Nutrition Foundation, Inc. 1973. Workshop on the role of Land Grant institutions in applied human nutrition. Washington, D.C.: The nutrition Foundation, Inc.

Empahsizes usefulness of develoment of multidisciplinary curricula in the training of nutrition professionals.

8317.   United States Department of the Air Force. 1969. Survival. Training edition. Air Force Manual 64-3.   Washington, D.C.: Govenment Printing Office.

Edible plants: A1-12 to A1-104.

8318.   United States Department of State. Agency for International Development. 19632. Food for peace around the world. Manual for leaders in community feeding programs. Resources Division. Publications and Technical Information Branch. Washington, D.C.: Agency for International Development.

Covers nutrition; sanitation; equipment construction, and quantity recipes.

8319.   United States. Department of State. Agency for International Development. 1973. Planning national nutrition programs: a suggested approach. Vol. Two. Case Study. Office of Nutrition. Bureau for Technical Assistance. Washington, D.C.: Agency for International Development. 30 March.

This publication is a companion to Forman (1973), and illustrates the methodology suggested in teh latter. Specific reference is to the nutrition system of Ecuador.

8320.   United Sttes. Department of State. Agency for International Development. Technical Assistance Bureau. Office of Nutrition. 1974. Nutrition education in child feeding programs in developing countries. Washington, D.C.: Agency for International Development.

8321.   United States Department of State. Agency for International Development. 1976. An initial inventory of A.I.D. information science projects and activities in food and nutrition areas. Technical Assistance Bureau. Washington D.C.: Agency for International Development.

This inventory is divided into four parts. Section One presents A.I.D. information science projects, bureau-by-bureau, which are concerned wholly, or in part, with the food and nutrition developmental areas. Section Two contains A.I.D. food and nutrition contracts within which various information controls are implemented as sub-components. Section Three contains A.I.D. -funded contracts and grants which support development of international agricultural research centers and their programs. Section Four presents A.I.D. -funded food and nutrition grants under Section 211 (d) of the Foreign Assistance Acts of 1966, as ammended. [After Foster. 1975. P. 51.]

8322.   United States. General Accounting Office. 1978. Food. Reports, legislation and information sources. A guide issued by the Comptroller General. Document Report No. 78-37. May. Washington D.C.: General Accounting Office.

Contains more than five hundred citations and abstracts of food-related documents released by the General Accounting Office, Office of Technology Assessment; Congressional Budget Office; Congressional Research Service; and Congresssional Committees from July 1973 through September 1977. Topics covered include domestic feeding programs; food safety and quality; nutrition; food production resources; farm marketing; distribution; price supports; food aid; trade policy; population control and food policy; congressional documents on food (Committee prints); Federal information sources and systems on food (listed by agency and title); recurring reports to the Congress; Federal program evaluations on food; major food legislation. Indexed by subject; agency; organization; Congressional committee; and names of individual members of Congress.

8323.   United States House of Representatives. Fifty-second Congress. First session (1891-1892). 1895. Miscellaneous Document No. 340. Part 15. Vol. 50 Part 6.

Pissoina, a wheat based alcoholic beverage: p. 220.

8324.   United States Public Health Service. 1954. Some observations on the nutritional status of Alaskan natives. Anchorage: Arctic Health Research Center.

8325.   United States Senate. Forty-fourth Congress. Second session. 1877. Report of the Joint Special Committee to Investigate Chinese Immigration. Washington, D.C.: Government Printing Office.

Food: pp. 226, 882.

8326.   United States Senate. Sixty-first Congress. Second session. 1911. Reports of the Immigration Commission. Immigrants in industries (in twenty-five parts). Part 25. Japanese and other immigrant races in the Pacific Coast and Rocky Mountain States (in three volumes: Vol. 1.). Japanese and East Indians. Washington D.C. Government Printing Office.

Cost of meals in Japanese restaurants: pp. 124, 284; also see Table 66, p. 383, for statistics concerning capital, profits, employees of Japanese restaurants. Diets of immigrant Hindus and Muslims: p. 342.

8327.   United States Senate. Seventy-fourth Congress. 1939. Survey of conditions of the Indians in the United States. Hearings before a Subcommittee on Indian Affairs. Part 36. Alaska. Washington, D.C.: Government Printing Office.

Comments on reindeer meat, with recipes: pp. 20305-20311.

8328.   United States Senate. Subcommittee on Employment, Manpower, and Poverty. Labor and Public Welfare Committee. 1969. Hunger and malnutrition in America. Hearings before the Subcommittee on Nutrition and Human Needs. Washington, D.C.: Government Printing Office.

8329.   United States. Superintendent of Documents. 1911. Checklist of United States public documents. Third edition. Volume One. Washington, D.C.: Government Printing Office.

Publications relating to introduction and distribution of plants and seeds from abroad: pp. 259-261; 268.

8330.   University of California. Extension Media Center. 1961. Pine nuts: a food of the Pauite and Washo Indians of California and Nevada. 16 mm film sound and color. Thirteen minutes. Berkeley, California: University of California. Extension Media Center.

Harvesting, preparation, and eating acorns among the Paviotso of Nevada. Reviewed by Harold E. Driver in AA 68:597 (1966).

8331.   University of California. Extension Media Center. 1962. Acorns: the staple food of the California Indians. 16 mm film, sound and color.

Twenty-eight minutes. Berkeley, California: University of California. Extension Media Center.

> Acorn gathering and processing, by southwest Pomo women and children. The processed acorn is prepared into a mush. Reviewed by Harold Driver in AA 68:596 (1966).

8332. University of California. Extension Media Center. 1965. The beautiful tree - chishkale. 16 mm film, sound and color. Twenty minutes. Berkeley, California: University of California. Extension Media Center.

> Details of gathering, storage, and preparation of acorns into a bread-like form, among the southwestern Pomo. Also includes footage on broiling of meat, and fish on hot stones and coals. Reviewed by Harold E. Driver in AA 68:596, 597 (1966).

8333. University of Ibadan. Food Science and Applied Nutrition Unit. Report of nutrition studies of mid-western Nigeria. Mimeographed. Fellowship Course in Food Science and Applied Nutrition Papers. No. 6. Ibadan: University of Ibadan. 1966.

> Three villages (Ibusa, Unoghovo, and Eguare) are studied. Methods of serving food; household authorities on food; infant feeding practices; food preferences and taboos; seasonal variations; storage methods and food sources, are described.

8334. Uno, Enku. 1940. Religious rites and ceremonies concerning rice planting and eating in Malaya. [In Japanese.] Toyo Bunko Ronso Series A. Vol. 28. Tokyo: Toyo Bunko.

8335. Unver, A. Suheyl. 1948. Tarihte 50 Turk yemegi. [Fifty Turkish foods in history.] Istanbul: Universite Tip Tarihi Enstitusu Yayinlari.

8336. Unver, A. Suheyl. 1958. Food and medical vignettes from Turkey. IRMGPC 171: 52-57.

> Includes a section on dietary habits of the Turks in the Fifteenth Century.

8337. Uotani, Tsunekichi. 1936. Gyoryori. [Cooking fish.] Tokyo: Shuhoen.

8338. Urban, Manfred. Die Haustiere der Polynesier Ein Beitrag zur Kulturgeschichte der Sudsee. [Domestic animals in Polynesia. A contribution to the culture history of the South Seas.] Ph.D. dissertation. Gottingen: Georg-August Universitat. 1961. Reprint. Gottingen: Hantzschel. Volkerkundliche Beitrag zur Ozeanistik. Vol. Two. 1961.

8339. Urena, Pedro Enriguez. 1938. Para la historia de los indigenismos. Papa y batata; el enigma del aje; boniato; caribe; palabras antillanas. [Toward the history of native words. Potato and sweet potato; the msystery of the yam; sweet potato; caribe; Antillean words.] Bibloiotaca de Dialectologia Hispanoamericana. Instituto de Filologia. Buenos Aires: Facultad de Filosofia y Letras de la Universidad de Buenos Aires.

8340. Urguart, I.A.N. 1951. Some notes on jungle Punans in Kapit District. Sar MJ 5:495-533.

> Sago flour foods: pp. 513-514.

8341. Uruguay. Biblioteca del Poder Legislativo. Alimentos. (Material existente en la Biblioteca). [Food. (Materials existing in the Library).] Mimeographed. Montevideo, Uraguay. 1948.

> A three part bibliography covering books; journals; and year books; articles; newpapers, and popular magazines.

8342. Useem, John. Report on Yap and Palau. economic urvey. 1946. Honolulu: U.S. Commercial Company. October.

> This report is a post-World War II evaluation of Yap and Palauan economy, undertaking to provide the United States military government with data upon which to base post-war planning. Yap: basic food (indigenous): p. 26; imported foods desired: pp. 28, food utensils: p. 30. Agricultural products, and domestic animals, fishing: pp. 49-51. Palau: diet: p. 82; projected imported food needs: p. 87; agricultural products: pp. 113-115; livestock fishing: pp. 115-116.

8343. Usha, M.S. Report of a community nutrition project conducted in Maddampayam village, Coimbatore District. Master's thesis. University of Madras. 1968.

> Data on the followng aspects of food habits are recorded: expenditures for food; meal patterns; diets during infancy; childhood, adolescence; pregnancy; lactation and old age; child feeding practices; diet during illness; types of home-produced foods; food preservation and storage techniques; and cooking methods. Village studied is located in the south Indian State of Tamil Nadu.

8344. Usha, T.M. A report on the community nutrition project conducted in Kalappanaickenpalayam village. Master's thesis. University of Madras. 1964.

> A dietary survey was conducted on a random sample of fifty families as part of a nutrition education project. Data were collected on methods of cooking; food waste; and food preservation. The village studied is located in the south Indian State of Tamil Nadu.

8345. Uusivirta, Hilkka. Festspeisen in der Stadt Pori, 1880-1900. [Feast foods in the city of Pori, 1880-1900.] Paper presented at the First International Symposium on Ethnological Food Research. 21-25 August, 1970. Lund: Folklivsarkivet. Lund University.

> Finland.

8346. Uvarov, B.P. 1944. The locust plague. JEE 37:93-99.

> Locusts used as food in the near East: p. 95.

8347.   Vaerst, Friedrich Christian Eugen von. 1851. Gastrosophie oder die Lehre von den Freunden der Tafel. [Gastrosophy, or instruction for friends of the table.] Leipzig: Avenarius & Mendelsohn.

8348.   Vahlquist, Bo. 1975.   Evolution of breast-feeding in Europe. JTPECH 21:11-16.

8349.   Vaizey, J. 1960. The brewing industry. 1886-1951: an economic study. London: Pitman.

        Great Britain.

8350.   Vajkai, Aurele. 1947. A magyar nepi taplal-kozas kutatasa. [Research on popular food habits in Hungary.] Budapest: Edit. Teleki Pal Tudomanyos Intezet.

8351.   Vakarelski, C.   Milchverarbeitung und Milchprodukte bei den Bulgaren. [Milk production and milk products among the Bulgarians.] In Viehw-irtschaft und Hirtenkultur. Ethnographischen stud-ien. Edited by L. Foldes. 1969. Pp. 547-573. Budapest: Akademiai Kiado.

8352.   Valaoras, V.G. 1946. Some effects of famine on the population of Greece. MMFQ 24:215-235.

8353.   Valassi, Kyriake. 1962. Food habits of Greek-Americans. AJCN 11:240-248.

        Provides   detailed   descriptions   of   major Greek food preparations; staple foods and meal patterns; as well as the adaptability of these patterns to therapeutic diets.

8354.   Valcarcel, Luis E. 1948. El alimentos en el antiguo Peru. [Food in ancient Peru.] RMN 17: 3-33.

        The first portion of this article is concerned with a general overview of the sociological and physiological significance of food in culture (pp. 3-17). The second part discus-ses the roles of social organization and agriculture in providing an abundant food supply for pre-Hispanic Preu. The third section examines specific food crops; their distribution; terminologies; and occurence in place names.

8355.   Valdecanas, D.C. 1972. Beliefs and prac-tices in food and nutrition of some rural women. PJN 25: 43-52.

8356.   Valenti, A. 1904. Aromatici e nervini nell' alementazione. [Aromatics and stimulants in the diet.] Milan: Ulrico Hoepli.

        Method of production; sources; physiologi-cal effect of salt, vinegar, sugar pepper, ginger, and other condiments. Also, coffee, tea, alcohol. Reviewed in BMJ no. 2268: 1433 (1904).

8357.   Valentine, Betty Lou & Valentine, Charles A. Poor people, good food, and fat babies: observa-tions on dietary behavior and nutrition among low-income, urban Afro-American infants and children.

In Practices of low-income families in feeding in-fants and small children with particular attention to cultural sub-groups. Edited Samuel J. Fomon & T.A. Anderson. 1972. Pp. 59-69. Washington, D.C.: U.S. Department of Health, Education, and Welfare.

        Reference area is northeastern United States. Community studied is given a ficti-tious name (i.e. "Blackston").

8358.   Valenzuela Rojas, Bernardo. 1957. Apuntes breves de comidas y bebidas de la region de Cara-hue. [Brief points o fooods an beverages in the region of Carahue.] AFC No. 8. Pp. 90-105.

        Carahue is located in southwest-central Chile, approximately fifty km from the coast, at 38.435., 73.12W.

8359.   Valeri, Renee. Study of traditional food supply in the southwest of France. Paper presented at the First International Symposium on Ethnologi-cal Food Research. 21 to 25 August, 1970. Lund; Folklivsarkivet. Lund University. Also in EScan 1971. Pp. 86-95.

        Describes the roles of maize, and confit (preserved pork, or their meat); the role of food exchange in the system of mutual ser-vices rendered among neighbors, and the persistence of folk beliefs in relation to planting, slaughtering and other food practi-ces. Also noted is the significance of time in relation to food spoilage, and the changes in attitudes toward traditional foods with an increasingly improved standard of living.

8360.   Vallaeys, G. 1948. Le Coix Lacryma-Jobi. [Coix Lacryma - Jobi] . BACB 39: 247-304.

        'Job's tears', a leguminous plant used for food. uses: pp. 257-271.

8361.   Valldejuli, Carmen Aboy. 1975. The art of Caribbean cookery.   Garden City, New York: Doubleday.

8362.   Valles, marie-Therese. 1968. Motivation and process of change or alteration of habits. CNN 24(1): 1-8.

        A discussion of the theories of Kurt Lewin as applied to modification of food habits.

8363.   Vamszer, G. 1942. A szekely juhturo keszitese. [Manufacture of Szekely sheep cheese.] Erdely 39: 40-43.

8364.   Van Arsdale, May B. 1916. Elizabethan hospitality. CU-TCR 17: 177-183.

8365.   Van Arsdale, May B.; Monroe, Day; French, Lucille G.; Colman, Anna; New York City Food Aid Committee. 1918. Tested international recipes. CU-TCR 19:68-86.

        Recipes collected by the New York City Food Aid Committee from New York City immigrant neighborhoods, and tested in Columbia University Teachers College experimental cookery classes. Costs for meals and meal servings is given.

8366. Van Buskirk, J.D. 1923. Some common Korean foods. RAS-KB-T 14: 1-8.

Dietary habits, and food preparation procedures.

8367. Vance, J.L. 1896. Forbidden foods of all nations. CurLit 19: 314.

8368. Van Cleft, Kathleen. A survey of the foods of the Fort Apache Indians. United States Department of Health, Education and Welfare. Office of Health. Indian Health Service. Phoenix: Phoenix Area Office. December, 1958.

8369. Van Daelle, G. 1939. Sur une affection de carence et de desequilibre dietetique observee au Congo ("buaki" des indigenes). [A disease of dietary insufficiency and imbalance observed in the Congo ("buaki").] SBMT-A 18:653-669.

Includes clinical observations of cases treated for kwashiorkor.

8370. Van de Graft. Le pain et les gateaux de Saint Nicolas. [The bread and cakes of Saint Nicholas.] In Institut International d' Anthropologie. 3^e Session. 20-29 Septembre 1927. Amersterdam. 1928. Pp. 530-534. Paris: Librairie E. Nourry.

Traces the history of Saint Nicholas, from a pagan diety through Christianity; the calendrical significance of his celebration; and the folklore surrounding the associated baked goods.

8371. Vandenbergh, J.G. 1963. Feeding activity and social behavior of the tree shrew Tupaia glis, in a large outdoor enclosure. FP 1:199-207.

8372. Vandeputte, Henri. Le regime alimentaire dans les prisons belges. [Diet in Belgian prisons.] In Deuxieme Congres International d'Hygiene Alimentaire et de l'Alimentation Rationnelle de l'Homme. 4-8 Octobre, 1910. Bruxelles. 1910. Vol. 1. Section w. Pp. 37-38. Brussels: M. Weissenbruch.

8373. Van der Bogert, Frank. 1927. Sweet-eating -its history and effects. HSS 15:324-334.

8374. Van der Heever, L.W. 1967. Some public health aspects of meat and milk. SAMJ 41:1240-1243.

8375. Van Der Kuyp, Edwin. 1962. Literatuuroverzicht betreffende de voeding en de voedingsgewooten van de Boslandcreool in Suriname. [Overview of the diet and food habits of the Surinam Bush Negro.] NWIG 41:205-271.

8376. Van der Post, Laurens. 1970. African cooking. New York: Time-Life Books. Foods of the World.

Food customs and recipes of sub-Saharan Africa; illustrated with color photographs.

8377. Van der Ven, J. 1956. Lekkere boerenmelkkost en onsmakelijke namen. [Tasty peasant milk foods and unsavory names.] Coop Melk 12:136-139.

8378. Van der Wijst, M.A. 1963. Chichorei. [Chickory.] RV-BM 26:7-11.

8379. Van der Woude, A.M. 1963. De consumptie van graan, vlees en boter in Holland op het einde van de achttiende eeuw. [Consumption of cereals, meat, and butter in Holland at the end of the Eighteenth Century.] AAGB 9: 127-153.

8380. Vanderyst. 1928. Jardin agrostologique de Kisantu. [Pastoralist garden at Kisantu.] C-RGCB-BSBEC 2:20-36.

Use of major grains in the Belgian Congo. Kisantu is located at 5.08S., 15.09E., in Zaire.

8381. Vanderyst. 1929. Le vin de palme ou malafou. [Palm wine, or malafu.] C-RGCB-BSBEC 1:653-658.

8382. Van Dress, Michael C. 1965. Estimated number of days' supply of food and beverages in establishments that serve food for on-premises consumption: a Civil Defense study. USDA-ERS (in cooperation with Department of Defense Office of Civil Defense) - MRR No. 707.

Stocks of food by major food type and storage type shown for states and counties in Metropolitan. Statistical Areas; other counties; and independent cities.

8383. Van Duzen, J.; Carter, James P.; Secondi, J.; & Federspiel, C. 1969. Protein and calorie malnutrition among preschool Navajo Indian children. AJCN 22:1362-1370.

8384. Vangala, R.R., et. al. 1969. Studies on the amino acid composition of some African legumes. [In German.] IZV 39:203-209.

8385. Vann, D.M. 1951. Meals for Navajos. Smoke 3:5-b.

8386. Vanoverberg, Morice. 1936. Iloko kitchen. PJS 60:1-10. Philippines.

This article comprises a list of Iloko terms denoting food; food preparation, techniques, and related cookery terms. The terms are entered by substantives which contain a verbal particle, with derived forms included.

8387. Van Staveren, W.A.; Tiggelman-Krugten, V.A.H.; Ferrier, B.; Maggilavry, C.J.; & Dubois, G. 1971. Food habits of infants and preschool children in Surinam. JADA 58:127-132.

8388. Van Stone, James W. 1963. The Snowdrift Chipewyan. Northern Co-ordination and Research Centre. Publication 63-4. Ottawa: Department of Northern Affairs and National Resources.

Food, and food preparation: pp. 26-28.

8389.   Van Syckle, C.   Changes in food consumption in the United States, and certain factors affecting it. Master's thesis.   Iowa State College. 1941.

8390.   Van Syckle, C.   1945. Some pictures of food consumption in the United States. Part 1.   1630-1860. JADA 31:1143-1146.

8391.   Van Veen, Andre G.   1941. Chemisch onderzoek over pedah, en gezouten vischproduct.   [Chemical investigation of pedah, a salted fish product.] INI 8:128-137.

        Indonesia.

8392.   Van Veen, Andre G.   1942. Nutrition (especially in the tropics). ARBio 11:391-414.

        The section titled 'Food stuffs' reviews the literature concerned with nutritional value of various tropical foods.

8393.   Van Veen, Andre G.   1950.   Nutritional deficiencies in Indonesia before the war.   [In Dutch.]   DNIMT 2:121-127.

        Observations on the influence of ecology on food consumption, prior to World Warr II.

8394.   Van Veen, Andre G.   1953. Fish preservation in Southeast Asia.   In Advances in food research. Vol. 4.   Pp. 209-231. New York: Academic Press.

8395.   Van Veen, Andre G.; Graham, D.C.W.; & Steinkraus, K.H.   1968.   Fermented rice - a food from Ecuador. ALN 18:363-373.

        Report on the microbiological aspects of this food, noting a preponderance of Aspergillus flavus, A. candidus, and Baccillus subtilis.   No aflatoxin was detected in the fermented rice samples, and aflatoxin was not formed on a wheat medium.

8396.   Van Zeist, W.   1970.   Prehistoric and early historic food plants in the Netherlands.   Paleohistoria 14:42-173.

8397.   Van Zeist, W. & Bottema, S.   1971.   Plant husbandry in early Neolithic Nea Nikomedia, Greece.   ABNeer 20:524-538.

        Triticum monococcum, Triticum dicoccum. Hordem vulgare var nudum, Lens culinaris, Pisum sativum, Vicia ervilia, Quercus sp., Cornus mas, and Prunus spinosa were identified at a date of ca. 5470 B.C.

8398.   Van Zeist, W. & Casparie, W.A.   1968.   Wild einkorn wheat, and barley from Tell Mureybit in northern Syria. ABNeer 17:44-53.

8399.   Vara, Albert C.   1970.   Food and beverage industries: a bibliography and guidebook.   Management Information Guide.   No. 16.   Detroit: Gale Research Co.

8400.   Vargas, Luis A.   Hot-cold food categories in Mexico and their use in nutrition education.   Paper presented at 75th Annual Meeting of the American Anthropological Association.   17 to 21 November, 1976. Washington, D.C.

        The food classification system attributing 'hot' and 'cold' qualities to foods has been little-used in nutrition education, being considered unscientific, and hampered by too many local inconsistencies in attribution. After studying the subject in villages near Mexico, a basic program was designed for use in general, as well as infant nutrition education. The 'hot'-'cold' system was applied directly in the program, in order to promote the consumption of nutritionally-adequate foods among underprivileged suburban mothers, and university employees. The results are evaluated and presented in this paper.

8401.   Varlet, F.   1956. Fabrication et composition de l'alcool de Bangui.   [Manufacture and composition of alcohol at Bangui.]   NA No. 71.   Pp. 74-75.

        Bangui is located in the southwestern portion of the Central African Republic, at approximately 4.10N., 18.25E.

8402.   Vasantha, P.S.   The nutritional status of expectant women in a village.   Master's thesis. University of Madras. 1969.

        Food taboos, and methods of food preparation are briefly described for twenty families in the village of Samichettipalayam, Coimbatore District.   Tamil Nadu State, India.

8403.   Vasey, Daniel Eugene.   The pub and English social change.   Ph.D. dissertation.   Anthropology. Carbondale: Southern Illinois University. 1974.

        Traditionally, the public house is a predominantly working class institution.   As a whole, the study supports the position that workers, even the most affluent, are not being assimilated into the middle class. Field work was conducted in 1970-1971, in Bolton, Lancashire, England.

8404.   Vasey, George.   1847.   Illustrations of eating, displaying the omnivorous character of man; and exhibiting the natives of various countries at feeding time.   London: J.R. Smith.   Reprint. Pasadena, California: Grant Dahlstrom. 1971.

        A collection of brief accounts of food habits from diverse parts of the world.   No documentation supports these data. Based on their nature, and the date, it would appear these were taken from traveler's accounts. Includes a chapter on geophagy which contains a number of unusual references.

8405.   Vassal, Joseph.   L' alimentation indigene en Indochine.   [Native diet in Indochina.]   In L'alimentation indigene dans les colonies francaises.   Protectorats et territoires sous mandats.   Edited by G. Hardy & C. Richet. 1933. Pp. 308-32.   Paris: Vigot Freres.

Overview of diet of various groups inhabiting the peninsula with special attention to fishing industry. A final section, written by Gabrielle M. Vassal, discusses child feeding practices in Annam.

8406.   Vatelle, Alcibiades & Vatelle, Yolande. 1951.   Grammaire de gastronomie sentimentale. [Grammar of sentimental gastronomy.] Toulon: Editions Provencia.

8407.   Vaughn, W.T.   1940.   Why we eat what we eat. SM 50:148-154.

8408.   Vavich, M.G.; Kemmerer, A.R.; & Hirsch, J.S. 1954. The nutritional status of Papago Indian children. JN 54:121-132.

Sketch of diet pattern: pp. 123, 124. Survey conducted on Papago Reservation, Sells, Arizona.

8409.   Vavilov, Nikolai I.   1926.   Studies on the origin of cultivated plants. [In Russian.] TPBGS 16:139-144.

8410.   Vavilov, Nikolai I. 1931. Mexico and Central America as the principal center of origin of cultivated plants of the New World.   [In Russian.] TPBGS 26. No. 3.

8411.   Vavilov, Nikolai I. The world centre of the origin of agriculture, and soil map of the world. In Second International Congress of Soil Science. July 20-31, 1932. Leningrad - Moscow. Proceedings and Papers. Vol. 4. 1932. Pp. 81-85. Moscow: State Publishing House of Agricultural, Cooperative, and Collective Farm Literature.

8412.   Vavilov, Nikolai I. 1949-1950.   The origin, variation, immunity and breeding of cultivated plants. CB 13. Nos. 1-6.

World centers of origin of most important plants: pp. 20-54.

8413.   Vayda, Andrew P. 1960 Maori women and Maori cannibalism. Man 60:70-71.

Distinguishes contexts in which women may have eaten human flesh.

8414.   Vayda, Andrew P. 1970. Reply to 'Limited nutritional value of cannibalism'. AA 72:1462-1463.

Reply to the note by Garn & Black AA 72:269-270 (1970).

8415.   Vayda, Andrew P.; Leeds, Anthony; & Smith, David B. The place of pigs in Melanesian subsistence. In 6e Congres International des Sciences Anthropologiques et Ethnologiques. 30 juillet a 6 aout 1960. Paris. Vol. 2. Ethnologie. (Vol. 1). 1963. Pp. 653-658. Paris: Musee de l'Homme.

8416.   Vayda, Andrew P.; Smith, D.B.; & Leeds, Anthony. The place of pigs in Melanesian society. In American Ethnological Society. Annual Spring Meeting. Proceedings. Edited by V. Garfield. 1961. Pp. 69-79. Seattle: University of Washington Press.

8417.   Veber, M. 1975. Histoire de la cuisine francaise au Moyen Age. [History of French food in the Middle Ages.] Historia No. 42. Pp. 37-44.

8418.   Vega, Ana Huidobro de la.   1953. El cochayuyo en en el alimentacion popular Chilena. [Cochayuyo in Chilean popular diet.] ATF-B 2:105-106.

Culinary use of the gigantic algae Durvillea utilissima.

8419.   Vega-Yap, Gloria & Alcantara, R.O. 1961. Purchasing patterns, consumption habits, and preferences for rice and corn. PAg 45: 1-28.

Philippines.

8420.   Vehling, Joseph Dommers. 1936. Apicius. Cookery and dining in Imperial Rome. A bibliography, critical review and translation of the ancient book known as Apicius de re coquinaria. Chicago: Walter M. Hill.

The introductory Review examines food in antiquity; comments of other writers on Apicius; the influence of Apicius' cookery upon the Western world; Apician terminology; earlier editions. The bibliographic section describes known manuscript and other versions of the Apician material.

8421.   Vehling, Joseph Dommers. 1937. Medical aspects of Apicius. Hygeia 15:517-520.

Medical aspects of cookery as contained in the classic Roman cookbook.

8422.   Velasquez, M., Rogerio. 1960. La fiesta de San Fransisco de Asis en Quibdo. [The fiesta of Saint Francis of Asisi in Quibdo.] RCF 2:15-37.

Contains description of foods eaten, and recipes. Quibdo is located in west-central Colombia, at 5.40N., 76.38W.

8423.   Velez, Ismael. 1946 Wild pineapples in Venezuela. Science 104:427-428.

Mentions cultivation of edible varieties by the Piaroa.

8424.   Velez Boza, Fermin. 1948. Alimentacion y nutricion en Venezuela (Capitula de alimenacion indigena). [Diet and nutrition in Venezuela (Resume of native diet).] RMSAS 13:56-57.

8425.   Velez Boza, Firmin. 1961. Un metodo para el estudio de los habitos alimenticios humanos. [A method for the study of human food habits.] AVN 11:55-65.

Describes a form for the recording of individual foods and food preparations for use during dietary or food habits surveys.

8426.   Velez Boza, Fermin & Baumgartner, Juan. 1962. Estudio general clinico y nutricional en tribus indigenas del Territorio Federal Amazonas de Venezuela. [General and clinical nutritional study of native tribes in the Federal Amazon Territory of Venezuela.] AVN 12:143-225.

8427.   Velez-Boza, Fermin & Gonzalez, Magdalena. 1961.   Los alimentos basicos utilizados en algunas poblaciones de Venezuela.   [The staple foods of some Venezuelan communities.] AVN 11:31-54.

Reviews results of a dietary and nutritional survey of seven hundred seventy-eight families of middle-and working class, in urban, suburban and semi-rural areas.   Main foods used are listed and analyzed into a core group common to seventy-five percent of the families surveyed.   Percent of nutrients supplied by these basic foods is analyzed.

8428.   Vellard, J. 1939.   Une civiliaation du miel. Les indiens Guayakis du Paraguay. [A honey civilization.   The Guayaki Indians of Paraguay.] Paris: Librairie Gallimard.

Honey; edible ants; palm fruit; game, fish; fruit; anthropophagy: pp. 77-89; utensils: p. 100.

8429.   Vendeix, Marius-Joseph. 1933.   Fetes des semailles et de moissons chez les paysans Senoufou. [Planting and harvest festivals among Sen farmers.] CEHS-AOF-B Pp. 161-167. Janvier-Mars.

The Senoufo people inhabit the Bondoukou region of the northeast-central area of the Ivory Coast.

8430.   Venkatachalam, Peruvemba Sitarama J. A study of the diet, nutrition and health of the Chimbu natives (with supporting papers). Medical dissertation. University of Sydney. 1959.

8431.   Venkatachalam, Peruvemba Sitarama J. 1962.   A study of the diet, nutrition and health of the people of the Chimbu area (New Guinea Highlands).   Australia.   Territory of Papua and New Guinea. Department of Public Health. Monograph No. 4. Port Moresby: W.S. Nicholas, Government Printer.

Chimbu diet; available foods, vegetable and animal; cooking facilities; meal patterns; diets of pregnant and lactating women; food consumption; dietary deficiencies: pp. 6-10.

8432.   Venkataratnam, L. 1959.   Sitaphal, annona and other fruits in India. I-MFG-FIU-DE-B.

Annona squamosa (sitaphal, sharifa); Annona cherimola (cherimoya); Annona reticulata (bullock's heart); Annona muricata (soursop). History of Annona sp. in India, and South America: p. 3; food uses: pp. 26-29; 31-34.

8433.   Venturello, Manuel Hugo. 1905.   Manners and customs of the Jagbanuas and other tribes of the island of Palauan, Philippines. Translated by Mrs. Edward Y. Miller. SI-MC 48:514-558.

Fermented rice beverage (pangassi); rice and fruit 'appetizer' (amit): p. 524.

8434.   Vera, Juana G. Infantes. Historia y utilizacion moderna de algunas plantas nativas del Peru, representadas en las ceramica, tejidos, pinturas, ornamentos, folklore, en la epocas preincaica e incaica. [History and modern use of some Peruvian native plants represented in pre-Inca and Inca ceramics, weaving, paintings, ornaments and folklore.] In 6 Congres International des Sciences Anthropologiques et Ethnologiques.   30 juillet - 6 aout 1960. Paris. Vol. 2. Ethnologie (Vol. 2). 1964. Pp 3338. Paris: Musee de l'Homme.

Food plants represented: Zea mais L.; Phaseolus lunatus L.; Manihot utilissima Pohl.; Solanum tuberosum L.; Cana edulis; Arachis hypogaea; Ipomoea batatas; Polymnia sonchifolia; Ullucus tuberosus; Oxalis tuberosus; Tropaelum tuberosum R. & P.

8435.   Verall, F.M. 1936.   Traditional Christmas fare. Cath Wld 144:345-350.

8436.   Verdat, Marguerite. Iles du Pacifique occidental: Nouvelle Caledonie et Hebrides. [Eastern Pacific islands: New Caledonia and New Hebrides.] In L'alimentation indigene dans les colonies francaises.   Protectorats et territoires sous mandats. Edited by G. Hardy and C. Richet. 1933. Pp. 371-379. Paris: Vigot Freres.

With regard to New Caledonia, the author cites legend, folklore, and early missionary accounts as sources for data on food habits prior to European contact. Staple vegetable, and sea foods are mentioned, and reference to agriculture and its rituals is made. Comments on the New Hebrides are brief, noting a similarity in staple crops to New Caledonia, and occurrences of anthropophagy.

8437.   Verdier, Yvonne. 1969. Pour une ethnologie culinaire. [Toward a culinary ethnology.] L'Homme 9:49-57.

An overview of the role of food in cultural life opens this paper.   A precis and criticism of Audrey Richards functionalism (1932, 1939) follows; succeeded by a synopsis of Levi-Strauss' application of structuralism to human food-related thought and activities. Additional discussion centers on food classification systems; food and human sexuality; food, magic and medicine; ceremonial aspects of food; and food in relation to cultural identity.

8438.   Verdoorn, Inez C. 1938. Edible wild fruits of the Transvaal. USAfr-DAF-DB-PIS-B No. 29.

8439.   Verdot, C. 1833. Historiographie de la table; ou, abrege historique, philosophique, anecdotique et litteraire des substances alimentaires et des objets qui leur relatifs, des principales fetes, moeurs, usages et coutumes de tous les peuples anciens et modernes. [Historiography of the table; or historical, philosophical, anecdotal, and literary summary of foods and of objects relative to them, of principal feasts, manners, practices, and customs of all peoples, ancient and modern. Paris: the author.

8440.   Verghese, E.J. 1952. Food value of coconut products. ICJ 5:119-129.

8441.   Verghese, I. 969. The Kota. I-AS-B Vol 12 No. 2.

Food: pp. 110-113. India.

8442.   Vergnaud, H. 1942. Resources of the Asiatic bean (soybean) for human diet. [In French.] CInd 48:126. Abstracted in CA 37:6049.

8443.   Vermeer, Donald E. Agricultural and dietary practices among the Tiv, Ibo, and Birom tribes, Nigeria. Ph.D. dissertation. University of California, Berkeley. 1964.

This monograph privides evidence in support of the view that dietary habits derive, in part, from underlying physiological needs -in this instance, hot tropical conditions. A food classification system defining food commonly noted to produce a sensation of heat, following ingestion (grains, and meat) and non-heat inducing (generally carbohydrates) is uncovered and described. Specific verbs are also noted which designate those foods "eaten" (principally the starchy staples), and those foods "bitten" or "chewed" (such as meat). The practice of geophagy among pregnant Tiv women is noted. Salt is customarily added to the clays ingested which, according to the author "...increases the basic radical of the body fluids and thereby promotes water retention, a condition which may be beneficial to pregnant women dehydrated from copious sweating under tropical environments and from such diseases as dysentery".

8444.   Vermeer, Donald Eugene. 1966. Geophagy among the Tiv of Nigeria. AAG-A 56:197-204.

8445.   Vermeer, Donald E. 1971. Geophagy among the Ewe of Ghana. Ethnology 10:56-72.

8446.   Vermeer, Donald E. & Fratz, Dennis A. 1975. Geophagy in a Mississippi county. AAG-A 65:414-424.

8447.   Verneau, R. 1896. L'alimentation chinoise. [Chinese food habits.] Anthropologie 7:502.

Comments on Chinese foods, and the number of items comprising a meal.

8448.   Verneau, R. 1897. La cynophagie au Soudan. [Cynophagy in the Sudan.] Anthropologie 8:742.

Reference to use of dogs as food by the Banmana (Bambara), in the eastern Sudan.

8449.   Verrier, Elwin. 1939. The Baiga. London: John Murray.

Liquor: pp. 44-46; food preparation; food in folk songs: pp. 46-52.

8450.   Verrill, Alpheus Hyatt. 1937. Strange insects and their stories. Strange stories from Nature Series. London: George G. Harrap.

Insects as human food: pp. 153-158.

8451.   Verrill, Alpheus Hyatt. 1946. Chapter Thirteen. Strange foods. In Strange customs, manners, and beliefs. Boston: L.C. Page.

8452.   Verrill, Alpheus Hyatt, & Barnett, Otis W. 1937. Foods America gave the world; the strange, fascinating and often romantic histories of many native American food plants, their origin and other interesting and curious facts concerning them. Boston: Little, Page; Toronto: Reginald Saunders.

8453.   Verzar, F. Nutrition as a factor against addiction. In Third International Congress of Nutrition. September 13-17, 1954. Amsterdam. 1954. Pp. 277-305. Amsterdam: Stichting tot Wettenschapelijke 's-Gravenhage. Voorlichting op Voedingsgebied.

Discussion of the possible prevalence of Andean coca use as a means for inhibiting chronic hunger. Discussion which follows paper refers to Catha edulis use among Yemeni immigrants to Israel.

8454.   Vestal, Paul Anthony. 1938. Cucurbita moschata found in pre-Columbian mounds in Guatemala. HU-BML 6:65-68.

Carbonized peduncle of C. moschata found in Construction P. Burial 37, Room 54, Structure A-V, at Uaxactun, Peten, dated at ca. A.D. 900.

8455.   Vestal, Paul Anthony. 1940. Notes on a collection of plants from the Hopi Indians region of Arizona made by J.G. Owens in 1891. HU-BML 8:153-168.

Lists fifty food plants from seventeen botanical families, and their uses. Latin, Hopi, and common English names are also given. Seeds of Amaranthus blitoides S. Watson are indicated as a base for 'mush'.

8456.   Vestal, Paul Anthony. 1954. Ethnobotany of the Ramah Navajo. HU-PMAAE-P 40. No. 4.

8457.   Vestal, Paul Anthony & Schultes, Richard Evans. 1939. The economic botany of the Kiowa Indians as it relates to the history of the tribe. Cambridge: Botanical Museum of Harvard University.

8458.   Vetschera, Traude. 1974-1975. Zur ernahrung der Mina von Rajasthan. [On the nutrition of the Mina of Rajasthan.] Ethnomedezin 3:313-333.

South India. Low protein intake and impure water constitute public health problems. Staple foods are enumerated.

8459.   Viault, Elsie Rosine. Maize - its cultivation and preparation as food by the Indians of the Southwest and the area east of the Mississippi. Master's thesis. Columbia University. 1921.

8460.   Vicaire, Georges. 1890. Bibliographie gastronomique. [Gastronomic bibliography.] Paris: chez P. Rouquette et fils. Reprint. London: Derek Verschoyle Academic Bibliographic Publications. [later purchased by Andre Deutsch Ltd.] 1954.

An exhaustive annotated bibliography covering almost exclusively the literature in French, with a small number of entries in English, German, and Latin. The scholarship of this work is painstaking, with a comprehensive range of literatures represented, from cookbooks and gastronomic fiction through the medical, botanical, and historical publications. It is also valuable for its coverage of ephemeral serial literature published in England and France. As a source for the study of European food habits, and attitudes toward food, from the Renaissance to the last quarter of the Nineteenth Century, it is recommended.

8461.   Vickers, W.J. 1944. A nutritional economic survey of wartime Palestine, 1942-1943. Palestine: Department of Health.

Compares and contrasts dietaries of Jewish and Islamic populations. Comments on patterns of food use, along a rural-urban continuum, and among Oriental and European Jewish, and Islamic populations, can be found in the Foreword, and under the headings for the various nutrients: e.g. carbohydrates, fats, etc. See also Section Five: Some particular local food customs and analyses. Of interest is protein value of 11.9 g per 100g for thyme powder and 28.9g per 100g for mulukiya powder (Jew's mallow, Corchorus olitorius) which is also high in calcium. Data on food expendtures are contained throughout.

8462.   Vickers, William T. Native Amazonian subsistence in a changing habitat: the Siona-Secoya of Ecuador. Paper presented at 75th Annual Meeting of the American Anthropological Association. 17 to 21 November, 1976. Washington, D.C.

The Siona-Secoya are a semi-nomadic tropical forest tribe practicing swidden horticulture and hunting-gathering. Low population density and frequent fissioning of settlements are characteristic. Dietary surveys at the new village of Shushufindi indicate an adequate level of nutrition under the traditional adaptation with a mean daily intake (all age groups) of twenty-two hundred kilocaries and eighty grams of protein. Hunting and fishing provide eighty-one percent of dietary protein; however, quantitative analysis of hunting at Shushufindi reveals a forty-one percent decline in the mean kill pattern as a response to declining hunting yields.

8463.   Vickery, Kenton Frank. 1936. Food in early Greece. UIll-B No. 34.

8464.   Victorin, F. Marie & Rousseau, Jacques. 1944-1945. Reconstitution de l'Ambrosia prehistorique des Ozarks. [Reconstruction of the prehistoric Ambrosia of the Ozarks.] UMontr-IB-C No. 56. Pp. 66-72.

An experiment in genetic manipulation of Ambrosia trifida, L. Common names: bloodweed; great bitterweed; great ragweed; horseweed; wild hemp.

8465.   Vida, G. Levi della. 1957. Il motivo del cannibalismo simulato. [The motive for feigned cannibalism.] RSO 32:741-748.

8466.   Vidal, Jean-Paul. 1964. Le mate. [Mate.] VL No. 146. Pp. 250-254.

Yerba mate, a South American tea plant. Ilex paraguayensis.

8467.   Vignati, Milciades Alejo. 1960. Dos comidas Araucanas en el ambito Pampa-Patagonia [Two Araucanian foods of the Pampa-Patagonia boundary.] INIF-C 1:143-149.

The custom of eating blood, and raw viscera by the Araucanians.

8468.   Vignoli & Cristau, B. 1950. Le gari, produit alimentaire a partir du manioc. Analogie et differences avec le tapioca. [Gari, a food prepared from manioc. Similarity to and difference between tapioca.] CColon No. 8. Pp. 303-308.

8469.   Vijayalakshmi, R. A report on a community nutrition project conducted in Rajannagar village with special reference to expectant mothers. Master's thesis. University of Madras. 1965.

A socio-economic and dietary survey was made of forty-three families. Nine of these families included expectant mothers, and were chosen for more detailed study. Information on all forty-three families was recorded on patterns of food expenditure; staple foods; cooking methods; food preservation and storage techniques; and special diets.

8470.   Vilkuna, Kustaa. 1939. "Kaka soker maka". ["Every cake has its make."] Rig Pp. 177-186.

English summary included.

8471.   Vilkuna, Kustaa. 1945. Brodet och bakningens historia: Finland. [History of bread and baking in Finland.] Folk-liv 9:17-56.

8472.   Villafuerte, Carolos. 1959. Estampas catamaquenas; el pan casero. [Catamarcan impressions: home-made bread.] La Prensa 5 Julio.

Catamarca Province is in northeast-central Argentina.

8473.   Villalta, Jorge Gaston Blanco. 1948. Antropofagia ritual americana. [Ritual anthropophagy in the Americas.] Buenos Aires: Emece.

8474.   Villamil, J.C. 1935. Feeding a child after weaning in rural Yucatecan communities. [In Spanish.] RMY 18:132-136.

8475.   Villaneuva, Amaro. 1960. El mate; arte de cebar. [Mate; the art of brewing it.] 2nd edition. Buenos Aires: Compania General Fabril Editora.

Special memorial edition for the sesquicentennial of the May Revolution.

8476.   Villanova, Arnaldus de. 1943. The earliest printed book on wine, now for the first time rendered into English and with an historical essay essay by H.E. Sigerist. With fasimile or original edition, 1478. New York: Schuman's.

8477.   Villas-Boas, Claudio & Villas-Boas. Orlando. Atracao dos Indios Txukahamai. [Attracting the Txukahamai Indians.] In Relatorio da atividades do Servico de Protecao aos Indios durante o ano 1954. 1955. Pp. 79-88. Rio de Janeiro: Ministerio da Agricultura.

Food habits of the Me-kranoti: pp. 83-85.

8478.   Vileneuve, Roland. 1962. Le cannibalisme. [Cannibalism.] Aesculape 45:7-46.

8479.   Villeneuve, Roland. 1965. Histoire du cannibalisme. [History of cannibalism.] Paris: Le Livre Club de Librairie.

8480.   Villiers, A. 1947. Une manne africaine-les termites. [An African manna: termites.] Nature (P) No. 3140. Pp. 239-240.

8481.   Vilmorin-Andrieux et Compagnie. [Parisian grain merchants.] 1883. Les plantes potageres. Description et culture des principaux legumes des climats temperes. [Garden plants. Description and cultivation of the principal temperate climate vegetables.] Paris: Vilmorin - Andrieux et Cie.

8482.   Vilppula, Hilkka. 1946. Finsk ost. [Finnish cheese.] Fataburen Pp. 83-92.

8483.   Vincze, Istvan. 1959. Ungarische Weinkelter. [Hungarian wine press.] AE 8:99-132.

8484.   Vinogradov, N. 1959. Prjaniki. O russkom prjanicnom iskusstve. [Gingerbreads. The Russian gingerbread art.] DISSSR 6:34-36.

8485.   Violant y Simorra, Ramon. 1956. Panes rituales infantiles y juveniles en el nordeste y levante espanol. [Ritual breads for infants and chilren in northeastern and Levantine Spain.] RDTP 12:300-359.

8486.   Viravaidhya, Vira. Methods of increasing protein in mung bean pudding with peanut instead of coconut. In Ninth Pacific Science Congress. 18 November to 9 December, 1957. Bangkok, Thailand. Proceedings. Vol. Five. 1959. Pp. 139-141. Bangkok: Chulalongkorn University.

8487.   Virchow, Rudolph. 1894. Funde bei der Ausgrabung des Nordostsee - Kanals in Holstein. [Discovery during the excavation of the North Sea Canal in Holstein.] NDA [supp. ZE] Part 4: pp. 59-60.

Occurrence of grains of Cratopleura halsatica, a plant not local to the area of the Baltic Canal.

8488.   Virey, Julien - Joseph. 1820. Histoire naturelle des medicamens, des aliments et des poisons, tire de trois regnes de la nature, etc. [Natural history of medicines, foods, and poisons, derived from the three kingdoms of nature, etc. Paris: Remont et fils.

8489.   Vis, H.L. 1967. Situation nutritionnelle dans le Bushi et la Bukavu (Notes preliminaires). [The nutritional situation in Bushi and Bukavu (preliminary notes).] IRSAC-C 2:31-47.

Belgian Congo.

8491.   Vishnu-Mittre. The archaeobotanical and palynological evidence for the early origin of agriculture in South and Southeast Asia. Paper presented to the 9th International Congress of Anthropological and Ethnological Sciences. 28 August to 8 September, 1973. Chicago, Illinois.

Notes that the earliest evidence of rice for Southeast Asia does not allow definite identification as to a wild or domesticated form. Cautions that utmost care be exercised in extrapolating from archaelogical and palynological materials.

8492.   Vishnu-Mittre. The archaeobotanical and palynological evidence for the early origin of agriculture in South and Southeast Asia. In Gastronomy. The anthropology of food and food habits. Edited by Margaret Louise Arnott. 1975. Pp. 13-21. Paris, The Hague: Mouton Publishers. World Anthropology.

Notes definite evidence of highly-evolved cultivars to ca. 3000 B.C., and ambiguity of pollen material which decreases its usefulness as a dating variable. Earliest evidence from Southeast Asia suggests a hunter-gatherer stage rather than domestication.

8493.   Vitols, M.M. 1968. Culture patterns of drinking in Negro and White alcoholics. DNS 29:391-394.

8494.   Vittorelli, Jacopo & DeRogatis. 1803. I maccheroni. Poemetto giocoso. [Maccaroni. A humorous little poem.] Venice: Graziosi.

8495.   Vivian, R.P., et al. 1948. The nutrition and health of the James Bay Indian. CMAJ 59:505-518.

8496.   Vizetelly, H. 1882. A history of champagne, with notes on the other sparkling wines of France. London: Sotheran.

8497.   Voegelin, Erminie Wheeler. 1938. Tubatulabal ethnography. UCal-AR 2:1-90.

Ethnobiology: pp. 10-22. Yearly food-cycle; food preferences; and rejections; preparation of animal food; fish and molluscs; food plants and plant gathering; preparation of plant foods and beverages; manufactured foods and gum; meals; meal-times; food beliefs; salt; food storage and preservation; staple foods and yearly consumption; water supply.

8498.　Voelcker, A.F. 1907. Some common errors in the diet and general hygiene of children. BMJ 1:181-185.

The section on 'Diet and feeding' contains a outline of then current infant and child feeding practices. The author encourages breast-feeding.

8499.　Vogel, Virgil J. 1970. American Indian medicine. Norman: University of Oklahoma Press.

Diet: pp.249-253.

8500.　Vogt, Carl. Anthropophagie et sacrifieces humaines. [Anthropophagy and human sacrifices.] In 5 Congres International d'Anthropologie et d'Archeologie Prehistoriques. 1871. Bologne. Compte Rendu. 1873. Pp. 295-328. Bologna: Imprimerie Fava et Garagnani.

An extensive review, based on historical and ethnographic documentation.

8501.　Vogt, Carl. 1894-1895. Ueber die Nahrung in verschiedenen Klimaten. [On nutrition in various climates.] Arch Anth 23:467-483.

8502.　Vogt, Evon Z. Tortillas for the gods: Zinacanteco ritual symbols. Paper presented at 69th Annual Meeting of the American Anthropological Association. 19 to 22 November, 1970. San Diego, California.

8503.　Volhard, Ewald. 1937. Kannibalismus. [Cannibalism.] Studien zur Kulturkunde Vol. 5. Stuttgart: Strecker & Schroder. Italian edition: Il cannibalismo. Turin: Einaudi. 1949.

8504.　Volkonsky, M.I. 1934. Mongolian milk products. CJ 21:117-130.

8505.　Volunteers in Technical Assistance. 1977. Evaluation of solar cookers. Mt. Rainier, Maryland: Volunteers in Technical Assistance.

8506.　Volunteers in Technical Assistance. 1977. Solar cooker instruction manual. Mt. Rainier, Maryland: Volunteers in Technical Assistance.

Instructions for constructing a cooking apparatus utilizing the reflected heat of the sun.

8507.　Von Bokay, J. 1935. Use of pottery feeding vessels in the Roman period - archaeological discoveries in Hungary. [In Hungarian.] Or Het 79:106-108.

8508.　Von Bokay, J. 1936. Ancient Roman pottery feeding vessels. [In German.] WMW 86:743-747.

8509.　Von Bokay, J. 1937. Earthen feeding vessels of the Bronze Age found in Hungary. [In German.] JKind 148:226-228. Infant feeding vessels.

8510.　Von Bunge, Gustav. 1908. Die Kochsalz-Surrogate der Negerstamme. [Cooking-salt substitutes of some Black tribes.] ZBiol 51:105-114.

Chemical analyses of plant-ash "salts" from the French Congo; Congo Free State; the Lake Chad area; and Nigeria. African groups mentioned include the Kanembu, and Kanuri.

8511.　Von Gerard, H. 1912. The narra fruit. A botanical wonder in the desert of South Africa. AJUSA 3:102-106.

Acanthosicyos horrida, a cucurbit which grows in the desert sand dunes inland from the west coast of the Union as South Africa. Protected by sharp thorns, the roots of these plants sometimes grow forty to sixty-five feet below the desert surface to reach moisture. Both the seeds and flesh of the fruit are used for food by the Hottentot.

8512.　Von Hagen, Victor Wolfgang, ed. 1948. The green world of the naturalists. A treasury of five centuries of natural history in South America. New York: Greenburg.

Contained in some of the selections are descriptions of various indigenous foods, and their preparation, recorded by early explorers.

8513.　Von Hagen, Victor Wolfgang. 1949. The bitter cassava eaters. NH 58: 120-124.

Photostudy of cassava preparation by the Macaguaje of Colombia.

8514.　Von Haller, Albert. 1966. Was werden wir morgen essen?: ein blick auf die Ernahrung der Zukunft. [What will tomorrow's food be? A glimpse into the nutriton of the future.] Dusseldorf: Econ-Verlag.

8515.　Von Lissauer, A. 1908. Archaoloigische und anthropologische Studien ueber die Kabylen. [Archaeeological and anthropological studies of the Kabyle.] ZE 40:501-529. Also in English translation as The Kabyles, in SI-AR for the year 1911. Pp. 523-538.

Soksa (Kabyle couscous): p. 533.

8516.　Von Muller, F. List of vegetables commonly eaten by the natives of Victoria. In Aborigines of Victoria: with notes relating to the habits of the natives of other parts of Australia. 2 vols. Edited by R. Brough Smith. 1878. Vol. 1. P. 212.

8517.　Von Muller, F. 1936. Uber die Diatetik. [Concerning dietetics.] DMW 62:1-5.

Surveys the history of dietetics from Hippocrates to the present. Mentions important earlier books on food and nutrition. Special reference is made to therapeutic dietetics. Some current dietary regimens are considered.

8518. Von Rechenberg, Carl. 1890. Die Ernahrung der Handweber in der Amstshauptmannschaft Zittau. Gedrukt mit Unterstutzungen. d. Koniglich Sachsen Gesellschaft der Wissenschaften. [Nutrition of handweavers in the District of Zittau, Saxony. Printed with support from the Royal Saxon Society of Science.] Leipzig: Hirzel.

An early socio-anthropologically-oriented dietary study, based on interviews with workers, and employers. Both questionnaires and direct observation are used, and dietary data are shown against the perspective of general living conditions.

8519. Von Richter, Wolfgang. 1970. Wildlife and rural economy in S.W. Botswana. BNR 2: 85-94.

8520. Von Schaafhausen, Reimar. 1952. Adlay, or Job's tears. EB 6:216-227.

Coix Lacryma-Jobi. Use as food: pp. 217-218. Cites uses in the Philippines, Ceylon, Brazil, China, and Japan.

8521. Von Schultz, A. 1910. Food and living conditions of Central Asian tribes. [In German.] JPGA-M 56:250-254.

Notes on the pastoral, nomadic Khirgiz; and the sedentary, agricultural Tajik. Refers to a flour made of dried mulberries, by the Tajik.

8522. Von Tyszka. 1934. Die Ernahrung der verscheidenen Volker. [The dietaries of various peoples.] MW 8:1213-1216. Also in KWoch 14:593-599. (1935).

8523. Von Tyszka. 1934. Die Ernahrung der Volker der Welt. [Food habits of the world's people.] Umschau 38:949-951.

8524. Vosseler, J. 1908. Eier konservierung in den Tropen. [Egg preservation in the tropics.] Pflanzer 4:129-136. Abstracted in CA 3:1780 (1909); CZen 79:1214 (1908).

8525. Vries, M. de. 1962. Menuverbetering op de Nederlands - New Guinea. [Dietary improvement in Netherlands New Guinea.] NGS 6:34-42.

8526. Vuillet, Jean. 1906. Les kolatiers et les kolas. [Kola trees and kola nuts.] Paris: Challamel.

8527. Vukina, R. 1949. Proizvodnya durmitorskog sira. [The production of Durmitor cheese.] Stocarstvo 3:323-326.

Reference is to a mountainous area in southwestern Yugoslavia.

8528. Waal, Marinus de. 1951. Keukenkruid en specerij. Naam herkomst, spijzen en dranken, geneeskunst, proza en poezie, de Bijbel, Grieken en Romeinen, bestanddeelen, plantlore. [Cooking herbs and spices. Etymologies, eating and drinking, therapy, prose and poetry, the Bible, Greece and Rome, composition, plantlore.] Zutphen: W.J. Thieme.

8529. Waddel, Jack O. The place of the cactus wine ritual in the Papago Indian ecosystem. Paper presented at 9th International Congress of Anthropological and Ethnological Sciences. 28 August to 8 September, 1973. Chicago, Illinois.

Examines the rainmaking function of the ritual, as well as its role in reaffirming community affinal relationships; specifying communities where potential spouses can be found; defining the broader relationships with more distant communities; animating and expressing important features of landscape; emphasizing gender roles; calling attention to kinship identities; renewing egalitarian principles of recurrent sharing of basic goods; and stressing the importance of seniority. Also considered are the adaptive features of the ritual, and how it functions as a means of coping with changes occurring in the Papago Reservation community culture.

8530. Waddell, Jack O. From tank to townhouse: probing the impact of a legal reform on drinking styles of urban Papago Indians. Paper presented 74th Annual Meeting of the American Anthropological Association. 2 to 6 December, 1975. San Francisco, California.

8531. Waddell, L.A. 1899. Among the Himalayas. New York: New Amsterdam Book Co; Westminster: Archibald Constable.

Millet beer, and an ode to the reed straw used to sip it: pp. 75-76. Lepcha foods: p. 98.

8532. Wade, Nicholas. 1974. Bottle feeding: adverse effects of a Western technology. Science 184:45-48.

Reviews the economic cost to developing nations where breast feeding is abandoned in favor or commercial formulas; causes of decline in breast-feeding; and the nature of commercial formula-producers' marketing practices.

8533. Wade, Richard C. 1964. Slavery in the cities. The South 1820-1860. New York: Oxford University Press Paperback GB209.

Slave diet: 132-134.

8534. Wade, William Richard. 1842. A journey to the northern island of New Zealand: interspersed with various information relative to the country and the people. Hobart: W. Pratt & George Rolwegan.

Includes references to Maori foods, and a list of New Zealand plants, with their Maori names.

8535. Wadsworth, G.R. 1961. Some historical aspects of infant feeding practices. NN 14:4-8.

8536. Wagener, Shirley. 1976. Asian foods and fermentation. USDA-OC-FHN No. 8. Pp. 2-4.

Notes that fermented legume-grain products improves digestability, enhance keeping quality, and prolong shelf-life where salt and spices are added. Fermentation improves flavor and appearance, and can shorten cooking time and may improve nutritional value. Mentioned are rice beer; palm wine; idli: fermented rice and black gram flour dumplings or cakes, popular in South India; and jalebies, pretzel-like, syrup-filled confections made of deep-fried, fermented wheat-flour dough, also eaten in India.

8537. Waggoner, George Andrew. 1905. Stories of old Oregon. Salem: Statesman Publishing Co.

Note on fern pie, prepared by early settlers of Sweet Home Valley: pp. 60-63.

8538. Wagley, Charles & Galvao, Eduardo. 1949. The Tenetahara Indians of Brazil. CU-CA No. 35.

Manioc: pp. 38-40.

8539. Wagner, Catherine Allen. Quechua drinking. Paper presented at 77th Annual Meeting of the American Anthropological Association. 14 to 18 November, 1978. Los Angeles, California.

8540. Wagner, F., ed. 1955. Das Getrankebuch. [The drink book.] Giessen: Fachbuchverlag Dr. Pfanneberg.

A review of the history, technology and commerce of alcoholic and non-alcoholic beverages.

8541. Wagner, Philip M. Food as ritual. In Food and civilization. A symposium. Edited and compiled by Seymour Farber; Nancy L. Wilson; & Roger H.L. Wilson. 1966. Pp. 60-82. Springfield, Illinois: Charles C. Thomas.

An informal, undocumented potpourri of examples of the role of food in religious and secular ritual; ceremony and celebration.

8542. Wahler, M. 1938. Die deutsche Volksnahrung. [German national diet.] Leipzig: W. Pessler.

8543. Wahren, Max. 1953. Bread through the ages. Bern: Verlag des Schweizerischen Backer-und Konditoren Meistervierbandes. Quadrilingual edition, with versions in German, French and Italian. Reviewed in WFood No. 92. Pp. 262-263.

8543. Wahren, Max. 1960. Die Backvorrichtungen des Altertums in Orient unter Berucksichtigung ihres Weiterbestheens in der Gegenwart. [Ancient Oriental baking apparatus from the point of view of their continued existence in the present.] BGeb 14:86-96.

8544. Wahren, Max. 1961. Typologie in altagyptischen Brote und Geback. [Typology of ancient Egyptian breads and baked goods.] BGeb 15:1-13; 28-32.

8545. Wahren, Max. 1964. Das Brot in fruhchristlicher Zeit. [Bread in the pre-Christian era.] BGeb 18:213-230.

8546. Wainwright, G.A. 1940. Cannibalism in modern Egypt. Man 40:160.

8547. Wake, C.S. 1873-1875. Cannibalism. Anthropologia 1:571-578.

8548. Wakefield, Elmer G. & Dellinger, Samuel C. 1936. Diet of the Bluff dwellers of the Ozark Mountains and its skeletal effects. AIM 9:1412-1418.

Analyses of coprolitic material indicating diet of sumac fruit; acorns; meat; fish; vegetable matter, and insects, which may have been accidentally ingested.

8549. Wakeland, Claude. 1959. Mormon crickets in North America. USDA-TB No. 1202.

As human food: p. 4.

8550. Waldmann, E. 1975. The ecology of the nutrition of the Bapedi, Sekhukuniland. EFN 4:139-151.

Sekhukuniland is a Bantu reserve in the northeastern Transvaal region of South Africa. The native people of this area, the Bapedi, have nutritionally inadequate diets resulting in sub-optimal growth and protein-calorie malnutrition. Bapedi diet is described, including infant feeding practices. The effects of environment, detriblization, food beliefs, and disease on infant nutritional status are a major focus of this article.

8551. Waldo, Myra. 1967. Dictionary of international food and cooking terms. New York: Macmillan.

8552. Waldron, Ralph Augustus. The peanut (Arachis hypogaea), its history, physiology, and utility. Ph.D. dissertation. University of Pennsylvania. 1918.

8553. Waldron, Ralph Augustus. 1919. The peanut (Arachis hypogaea) - its history, histology, physiology, and utility. UPenn-BL-CBLMA 4:301-338.

The section on history and geographical distribution discusses the probability of a Brazilian origin, and discounts the presence of peanut in the Old World before European contact with South America in the Fifteenth and Sixteenth Centuries. The matter of the two-seeded Brazilian, and three-seeded Peruvian types is also considered.

8554. Walker, A. 1929. Feuilles potageres. [Pot-herbed leaves.] SRC-B No. 10 Pp. 100-121. Food of the Fan (Pahouin), the Cameroun.

8555. Walker, A. 1930. Le bananier. (variete, usage). [The banana plant: (varieties, uses)]. SRC-B 12:131-143.

The banana plant in the religious and material life of native groups in French Equatorial Africa.

8556. Walker, A. 1939. Les plantes a "sel" au Gabon. ["Salt" plants of Gabon.] RBAAT 19: 121-123.

Latin and vernacular names, and descriptions of various plants, the ash of which, (after drying and burning) is used as a condiment. The ash is put in water, and the remaining material, after evaporation, is the "salt".

8557. Wlaker, A. 1952. Plantes orrginaires d'Amerique par ordre d'anciennete dans l'ancien monde. Comment ces plantes se sont-elles reproduites chez les Africins? Peut-on suivre leur expansion d'apres les noms indigenes? [Plants of American origin by order of their ancientness in the Old World. How are these plants propagated in Africa? Are their native names a clue to the sequence of their disseminations?] RBAAT 32: 278-287.

8558. Walker, A. 1953. Emploi ou usages de feuilles de vegetaux. [Use of vegetable leaves.] RBAAT 33: 178-180.

As food utensils, and food: p. 179.

8559. Walker, A. 1953. Preparation du manioc et du vin d'Ananas au Gabon et en Amazonie. [Preparation of manioc and of pineapple wine in Gabon, and the Amazon region.] RBAAT 33: 86.

Among the Nambicuara of the Brazilian Mato Grosso; and an African group residing near th Ogouee Delta of Gabon.

8560. Walker, A. Les noms des vegetaux chez les Gabonais. [The names of vegetables among the Gabonais.] In Huiteme Congres International de Botanique. 1954. Paris. Rapports et communications. Parvenus avant le Congres aux Sections 14,15, & 16. 1954. Pp. 39-45.

8561. Walker, A.R.P.; Fletcher, D.C.; Strydom, E.S.P.; & Andersson, M. 1955. Food preparations used in weaning urban Bantu infants. BJN 9: 38-41.

8562. Walker B. 1969. The end of an Ice Age. Ice harvesting as an occupation. AEH 19: 144-148.

8563. Walker, B.N.O. [Hen-toh, Wyandot.] Mondah-min, and the Red Man's world; old uses of Indian corn as food. JHE 10: 444-451.

Legends and recipes. Also in Chron Okla 35: 194-203. (1957). Contains a Native American legend on the origin of maize.

8564. Walker, George. 1885. The costume of Yorkshire illustrated by a series of forty engravings being facsimiles of original drawings with descriptions in English and French. Leeds: Richard Jackson.

Contains several plates ilustrating food habits preparation of oatcakes; cranberry gathering; dairying; Midsummer evening meal.

8565. Walker, Harley Jesse. The changing nature of man's quest for food and water as relted to snow, ice, and permafrost in the American Arctic. Ph. D. dissertation. Louisiana State University. 1960.

Analyzes the nature, distribution, and availability of food and water sources and the techniques and equipment that were developed aboriginally to obtain them. Increased mechanization in relation to water supply, and increased importation of food are gradually loosening the bond between these needs and the snow-ice, permafrost variables, with a resultant loss of familiarity with traditional appropriate technologies.

8566. Walker, Harley Jesse 1962. Man in the Arctic. The changing nature of his quest for food and water as related to snow, ice, and permafrost. Maxwell Air force Base: Alabama Desert Tropic Information center.

8567. Walker, Iain C. 1975. Cooking in a skin. Antiquity 49: 216-217.

Reference to use of skins for cooking, in early 18h Century Scotland.

8568. Walker, J.D. 1962. Nutritional survey in the Cook Islands. Nutrition 16: 15-20.

8569. Walker, Phillip L. Great ape feeding behavior and incisor morphology. Ph. D. dissertation. Anthropology. University of Chicago. 1973.

8570. Walker, Vera. 1943. Case studies of nutrition. Other Florida children. AAPSS-A 225: 57-58.

Profiles of two children, one from rural northwestern Florida; one from urban northeastern Florida. Typical food intake is reported.

8571. Wallace, Alfred Russell. 1853. Palm trees of the Amazon and their uses. London: John Van Voorst.

Brief reference to food uses.

8572. Wallace, Benny Joe. 1967. Gaddang rice cultivation: a ligature between man and nature. PSR 15: 114-122.

8573. Wallace, Benny Joe. Pagan Gaddang agriculture: the focus of ecological and cultural change. Ph. D. dissertation. University of Wisonsin. 1967.

8574.   Wallace, Benny Joe. 1970. Shifting cultivation and plough agriculture in two Pagan Gaddang settlements. Monograph 11. Manila: National Insitute of Science and Technology.

8575.   Wallace, Ernest & Hoebel, Ernest Adamson. 1952. The Comanche Norman: University of Oklahoma Press.

Food preparation: pp. 30, 60, 70-75.

8576.   Wallace, John A. Dietary adaptations of Australopithecus and early Homo. Paper presented at 9th International Congress of Anthropological and Ethnological Sciences. 28 August to 8 September, 1973. Chicago, Illinois.

Observations on tooth wear and dental morphology are presented as evidence that the South African early hominids represent two lineages: Australopithecus and Homo. All South African early hominids except five from Sterkfontein and two from Swartkrans are assigned to Australopithecus. The five from Sterkfontein and the two from Swartkans are classified as Homo. A functional analysis of the dentition suggests that Australopithecus and early Homo had different adaptations for crushing and grinding food. Australopithecus seemingly crushed and ground the food mostly with their teeth. Early Homo apparently crushed and ground the food mainly outside the mouth, with stone tools.

8577.   Wallace, John A. Dietary adaptations of Australopithecus and early Homo. In Paleoanthropology. Morphology, and paleoecology. Edited by Russell M. Tuttle. 1975. Pp. 202-223. Chicago: Aldine.

8578.   Wallen, Richard. 1943. Sex differences in fod aversions. JAPsych 27: 228-298.

8579.   Wallen, Richard. 1945. Food aversions of normal and neurotic males JASP 40: 77-81.

8580.   Wallen, Richard. 1948. Food aversions in behavior disorders. JConP 12: 310-312.

8581.   Walsh, E. 1949. Nutritionists and social workers cooperate on mutual problems. JADA 25: 681-683.

8582.   Walsh, Joseph. 1896. Tea: its history and mystery. 3rd edition. Philadelphia: the author.

8583.   Walsh, Mary Edward. An evaluation program to measure the ability of students to apply principals of nutrition. Master's thesis. Greensboro: Woman's College of the University of North Carolina. 1943.

8584.   Walsh, P. 1900. On the occurrence of Cordyline terminalis in New Zealand. NZI-TP 33: 301-306.

8585.   Walsh, P. 1902. The cultivation and treatment of the kumara by the primitive Maoris. NZI-TP 35: 12-24.

Sweet potato.

8586.   Walter, Eugene. 1971. American cooking: southern style. New York: Time-Life Books. Foods of the World.

Delaware, Maryland, Virginia, West Virginia, North and South Carolina, Kentucky, Tennessee, Florida, Georgia, Alabama, Mississippi.

8587.   Walter, Richard. 1956. Canary Island adventure. A young family's quest for the simple life. New York: E.P. Dutton.

Typical foods of the Angostura Valley, and food prices: pp. 99-106.

8588.   Walters, Joseph David. 1963. Detection of nutritional imbalances. JAN 16(1) 29-32.

Investigations encompassing general medical and nutritional history; extensive use of a questionnaire; skin examination in toto, laboratory procedures; and X-ray and fluoroscopy combine to evaluate the nutritional status of the patient and provide clues to the therapy in each case. Includes illustrative case histories.

8589.   Walters, Joseph David. 1963. Supplementation. JAN 16(1): 10-16.

Emphasis is placed on the need to study each patient as an individual. Recovery time depends on cooperation of the patient and his or her family, as well as upon the ability to obtain and utilize proper nutritional supplementation. Includes illustrative case histories.

8590.   Walters, Joseph David. 1964. Chronic fatigue: metabolic and nutritional aspects. JAN 17(2-3): 126-140.

Although chronic fatigue may often seem to be elusive in its detection and treatment, it is posible to extend investigations more fully than usual. Various physical examinations and laboratory tests are of help in diagnosis and treatment. Successsful therapy requires a combination of dietary modification, nutritional supplementation, endocrine therapy and habit correction. Emphasizes total therapeutic measures. Includes illustrative case histories.

8591.   Walters, Joseph David. 1971. Updating the matabolic-nutrition examination. JAN 23(1-2): 34-43.

Using as its point of departure an excerpt from the AMA statement on 'Nutrition teaching medical schools' (JAMA 183: 955, 1963) "It is necessary to think more in terms of disturbances of the metabolic and biochemical reactions of the body. Nutritional diagnosis implies evaluation of biochemical changes within and outside the cell, as well as abnormalities of function and structure of the organs and tissues of the body.", this article enumerates a series of tests and examinations designed to provide a comprehensive profile of nutritional status from structural-functional, biochemical, and behavioral perspectives.

8592.   Walton, Alan Hull. 1958. Aphrodisiacs from legend to prescription. Westport: Associated Booksellers.

Part 2, The cookery of love, discusses foods and spices believed to possess aphrodisiac powers; includes recipes.

8593.   Walton, J.   1953.   Pestles, mullers and querns from the Orange Free State and Basutoland. SAAB 8: 32-39.

8594.   Wang, Chi-che.   The chemistry of Chinese preserved eggs and edible birds' nests.   Ph. D. dissertation. University of Chicago. 1918.

8595.   Wang, Chi-che. 1920. Is the Chinese diet adequate? JHE 12: 289-293.

Description of popular Chinese foods, but with little reference to geographic regions. Focuses largely on use of eggs, with additional reference to legumes, cereals, and leafy vegetables.

8596.   Wang, Chi-che. 1921. The isolation and the nature of the amino sugar of chinese edible birds' nests. JBChem 49: 441-452.

8597.   Wang, Hsing-ju.   1948.   Hainan Tao Chih Miao jen.   [The Miao people of Hainan Isand.] Translated for the Human Relations Area Files by Te-kong Tong.   Chung-Kuo Pien-chaing Yen-chu Shin.   [Institute for Chinese Frontier Studies.] Series B. No. 2. Canton: Chu-tai University.

Rice Preparation: p. 42.

8598.   Wang, Hwa L. & Hesseltine, Clifford W. Oriental fermented foods. Paper presented at the Seminar on Protein Food Promotion. 22 November to 1 December, 1970. Bangkok: Institute fo Food Research and Product Development, Kasetsart University.

Miso, hamanatto, sufu, natto, tempeh.

8599.   Wang, Hwa L., & Hesseltine, Clifford W. 1970. Sufu and lao-chao. JAFC 18: 573-575.

Description of manufacure, and chemical analysis of two fermented Chinese foods: sufu, fermented soy bean curd; and lao-chao, fermemnted, glutinous rice.

8600.   Wang, Hwa L.; Ruttle, Doris E.; & Hesseltine, C.W. 1969. Antibiotic activity of a fermented soybean food: tempeh. FASEB-FP 28:304. Abstrct 261.

Rhizopus oligisporus, which ferments an Indonesian soy food, manifests positive activity against some microorganisms, including gut bacteria.

8601.   Wang, P.W. 1922. Chinese nuts - walnut. NNGA-RP 13th Annual Meetng. Pp. 120-121.

Use of walnut 'milk' (extract) for infants; brief mention of other Chinese food uses of nuts.

8602.   Warburg, Otto.   1903.   Kunene-Sambesi-Expedition, H. Baum.   [The H. Baum Kunene-Zambesi Expedition.

Contains an annotated list of plants, classified by use. Portuguese West Africa.

8603.   Ward, Artemas. 1923. The encyclopedia of food. The stories of the foods by which we live. How and where they grow and are marketed; their comparative values and how best to use and enjoy them. New York: Baker & Taylor.

8604.   Ward, C. Osborne. 1907. The ancient lowly. Vol. 1. A history of the ancient working people from the earliest-known period to the adoption of Christianity by Constantine. Chicago: Charles H. Kerr.

Army suppliers; unions of winemakers; bakers; sutlers; oil grinders; pork butchers: pp. 382-387; trades system: how Rome was supplied with food; trade unions of fish salters; cooks; pretasters; milkmen; cooking utensil makers; stewards: pp. 389-400.

8605.   Ward, Melbourne. 1942. Primitve man and his larder. AMM 8:52-56.

Observes the practice of tabooing large tracts of jungle land on Murray Island (Torres Straits) which become reserves from which plants may be transplanted to native gardens.   Discusses marine food sources particularly the mangrove swamp, lagoons and mudflats.   Animals mentioned are the Stone Fish (Cyanceja horrida); oysters; crab (Seylla serrata, and Portunus pelagicus); mud skipper Periophtalmus koelreuteri); also notes use of White Mangrove fruit (Avicenna officialnis), and its method of prepraration. Cooking methods are described briefly. Mentions the Curry Fish (Holothuria Scabral). Reference is unspecific, but appears to include Australian Aborigine groups, and other Oceanic peoples.

8606.   Ward, Melbourne. 1943. New Guinea menu. Army August: Pp. 28-31.

8607.   Ward, Melbourne. 1952. Folklore of the coconut. AMM 10:319-321.

8608.   Ward, Steven C. Oro-facial form and masticatory force distribution in selected primates: an experimental analysis. Ph.D. dissertation. Anthropology. St. Louis, Missouri: Washington University. 1974.

8609.   Ward, William Theophilus Thomas. A preliminary survey of the economic and social life of the Mortlock Islands people, eastern Carolines, Trust Territory of Micronesia. Master's thesis. University of the Philippines. 1955.

8610.   Warner, J.N. 1962. Sugar cane; an indigenous Papuan cultigen. Ethnology 1:405-411.

8611.   Warner, Richard. 1791. Antiquitates culinariae, or curious tracts relating to the culinary affairs of the old English, with a preliminary discourse, notes, and illustrations by the Reverend Richard Warner, of Sway, near Lymington, Hants. London: Printed for R. Blamire, Strand.

Contains "The Forme of Cury" and "Ancient Cookery".

8612.   Warren, Jean. 1940. Use of time in relation to home management. CorU-AES-B No. 734.

Variation in time used for food preparation, and dishwashing: pp. 42-44; 68-70; food preservation: p. 53; household cooperation in food-related activities: p. 66. Data gathered from more than five hundred farm households in Genesee County, New York.

8613.   Washburne, Chandler. 1961. Primitive drinking. A study of the uses and functions of alcohol in preliterate societies. New York & New Haven: College and University Press Publishers.

8614.   Washington, D.C. United States Department of the Interior. Office of Indian Affairs. Diet and nutrition of the Papago Indians. [by James B. Watson & Michel Pijoan.] 1943.

8615.   Wason, Elizabeth. 1962. Cooks, gluttons and gourmets: a history of cookery. Garden City, New York: Doubleday.

Includes recipes.

8616.   Wasson, Edmund A. 1914. Religion and drink. New York: Burr Printing House.

8617.   Watanabe, Hitoshi. 1969. Famine as a population check. Comparative ecology of northern peoples. UTo-FS-J [Section 5. Anthropology.] 3:237-252.

8618.   Watanabe, T.; Yukawa, K.; Sakamoto, A. 1968. Nutritional intake and longevity. International comparative study. AMN 13:44-66.

Demographic data representing thirty nations. Influence of nutritional intake upon life span is indicated to change for better or worse at a mean of 3000 kcal, where the ratio of energy from animal sources was 35% to 40%; the protein intake at ca. 90 grams; and the fat intake ca. 50 grams to 60 grams.

8619.   Wateff, S. 1940. National diet and popular remedies in Bulgaria. [In German.] WMW 90:792.

8620.   Waterlow, J.C. Observations on the metabolism of adaption to low protein intakes. In First Asian Congress of Nutrition. 22 January - 2 February 1971. Hyderabad, India. Proceedings. Edited by P.G. Tulpule & Kamala S. Jaya Rao. 1972. Pp. 515-524. Hyderabad: Nutrition Society of India.

Provides limited evidence of a regulation or adaptation tending to maintain the circulating albumin mass by changes in three factors which vary independently and must be independently controlled - the rates of snythesis and catabolism, and the rate of net transfer between the intravascular and extravascular pools.

8621.   Waters, Joseph H. 1962. Some animals used as food by successive cultural groups in New England. ASC-B 31:32-46.

8622.   Watson, Ernest. 1923. The principle articles of Chinese commerce. China. The Maritime Customs. 2. Special Series. No. 38. Shanghai: Statistical Department of the Inspectorate General of Customs.

Exported food products: pp. 295-578; and passim; classification of teas: 553-563.

8623.   Watson, James B. Hopi foodways. A study in the cultural, nutritional, and environmental factors in the diet of the Hopi people. Master's thesis. Anthropology. University of Chicago. 1942.

8624.   Watson, James B. 1943. How the Hopi classify their food. Plateau 15:49-52.

Description of the uh:ngala concept - a category inclusive of the non-agricultural Hopi food products. Uh:ngala foods traditionally included meat, wild and domestic; relish plants; and condiments.

8625.   Watson, James B. 1964. A previously unreported root crop from the New Guinea highlands. Ethnology 3:1-5.

Report on a species of Pueraria discovered in the Kainantu subdistrict of Australian New Guinea. Food preparation is described.

8626.   Watson, James B. 1968. Peuraria: names and traditions of a lesser crop of the central highlands. New Guinea. Ethnology 7:268-279.

8627.   Watson, James B. Sweet potatoes in the central highlands of New Guinea. Paper presented at 74th Annual Meeting of the American Anthropological Association. 2 to 6 December, 1975. San Francisco, California.

8628.   Watson, James B. 1977. Pigs, fodder and the Jones effect in post-Ipomoean New Guinea. Ethnology 16:57-70.

Looks at the adoption of sweet potato as pig feed in the central highlands of New Guinea after A.D. 1600. One consequence of this innovation was increase in the size of pig herds. The relationship of pigs to native diet is examined briefly: pp. 61-63.

8629. Watson, James B. & Pijoan, Michel. A casual inquiry into Hopi foodways. 1943.

This manuscript was written as part of the Southwest Project (see Eggan & Pijoan 1943; and Freedman 1976.)

8630. Watson, Lyell. 1971. The omnivorous ape. A zoologist looks at man, the omnivore, and what his eating habits reveal about his origins. New York: Coward, McCann & Geoghegan.

8631. Watson, R.P. 1907. Influence of an excessive meat diet on fertility. BMJ 1:193-194.

Case history from South Africa indicating a possible role of high meat intake predisposing to high fertility.

8632. Watson, Virginia Drew. 1955. Archaeology and proteins. AmAn 20:288.

Calls attention to the fact that faunal remains may not, in every instance, be a reliable basis from which to extrapolate to dietary protein intake. Cites examples from modern dietary practices of the Agarabi of New Guinea.

8633. Watt, George. 1889-1896. Dictionary of the economic products of India. 6 Vols. London: W.H. Allen.

8634. Watt, George. 1908. The commercial products of India. London: John Murray.

8635. Watt, W. 1895. Cannibalism as practiced on Tanna, New Hebrides. JPS 4:226-230.

8636. Watters, R.F. 1958. Cultivation in old Samoa. EG 34:338-351.

8637. Watts, Edith Ballard & Watts, John. 1954. Jessie's book of Creole and deep south recipes. New York: Viking Press.

Recipes of Jesse Willis Lewis.

8638. Waugh, Frederick Wilkerson. 1916. Iroquois foods and food preparation. C-DM-GS-M No. 86. AS No. 12.

8639. Way, A.S. 1930. Food hygiene of the Middle Ages. LQR No. 305. Pp. 40-52.

Review of "Mensa Philosophica", a treatise on health and food, written ca. A.D. 1230, by Michael Scott.

8640. Waygood, W.A. 1943. Naturally-occurring flavors of foodstuffs. CI 62:59-61.

After a brief discussion of the differences between taste and flavor sensations, foods are considered in seven groups and a brief outline is given for each group regarding

information available on the chemical constituents responsible for their flavors.

8641. Weatherwax, Paul. 1918. The evolution of maize. TBC-B 45:309-342.

8642. Weatherwax, Paul. 1919. The ancestry of maize - a reply to criticism. TBC-B 46:275-278.

8643. Weatherwax, Paul. 1923. The story of the maize plant. Chicago: University of Chicago Press.

8644. Weatherwax, Paul. 1936. The origin of the maize plant and maize agriculture in ancient America. In Symposium on prehistoric agriculture. UNM-B No. 296. AS 1(5):11-18.

8645. Weatherwax, Paul. 1950. The history of corn. SM 71:50-60.

8646. Weatherwax, Paul. 1954. Indian corn in Old America. New York: Macmillan.

8648. Weaver, A.L. & Spittell, J.A. 1964. Lathyrism. Mayo. 39:485-489.

8649. Weaver, Sally, M. 1972. Medicine and politics among the Grand River Iroquois. A study of the non-conservatives. NMC-PE No. 4.

Food patterns: p. 110.

8450. Webb, Kempton Evans. Food supply of Belo Horizonte. Ph.D. dissertation. Syracuse, New York: Syracuse University. 1958.

Belo Horizonte is located in Minas Gerais State, Brazil, at 19.54S., 43.54W.

8651. Webb, Kempton Evans. 1959. Geography of food supply in central Minas Gerais. Foreign Field Research Program. Office of Naval Research. Report No. 4. National Research Council. Division of Earth Sciences. Publication 642. Washington, D.C.: National Academy of Sciences. National Research Council.

8652. Webb, Kempton Evans. 1959. Origins and development of a food economy in central Minas Gerais. AAG-A 49:409-419.

8653. Webb, L.J. 1973. Eat, die and learn - the botany of the Australian Aborigenes.

8654. Webb, M.J., ed. 1937. Early English recipes, selected from the Harleian. ms [No.] 279 of about A.D. 1430. London: Macmillan.

8655. Weber, C.W. 1969. Protein evaluation of two species of cucurbitaceae seeds. SEBM-P 130:761-765.

8656. Weber, Donald S. 1973. Health and disease effects upon hill tribes of southeast Asia. UNCol-MA-MS No. 31.

Malnutrition: p. 10; goitre: p. 12; rice and nutrition: pp. 20-21.

8657. Weber, George F. 1954. Animal names, anatomical terms and some ethnozoology of the Flathead Indians. WAS-J 42:345.

8658. Webster, Helen Noyes. 1940. Tea herbs in early America. Herbarist No. 6. Pp. 34-41.

8659. Wechsberg, Joseph. 1968. The cooking of Vienna's Empire. New York: Time-Life Books. Foods of the World.

8660. Weckler, Joseph Edwin. 1947-1949. Land and livelihood on Mokil. An atoll in the eastern Carolines. Coordinated Investigation of Micronesian Anthopology. Final Report. No. 11.

CIMA fieldwork was conducted in Guam and in islands of the Trust Territory in Micronesia (1947-1949) with transportation and facilities contributed by the Navy Department. Studies in anthropology as well as human and economic geography were carried out in cooperation with universities, museums, and research institutions under this project of the Pacific Science Board of the National Research Council, aided by financial assistance from the Viking Fund and other private sources. CIMA operated with financial assistance from Contract N7 - onr 291, Task Order 4 between the Office of Naval Research and the National Academy of Sciences; Cookery: p. 13; coconuts: p. 14; food preparation after church: p. 15; meals lunch: pp. 17-19; food for cooperative work groups: pp. 22-23; food gifts: p. 23. first fruits: ceremony: pp. 45-46.

8661. Wedemeyer, Ivon. 1972. Mais. Rausch und Heilmittel im Alten Peru. [Maize, inebriation and curing in ancient Peru.] Ethnomedizin 2:99-112.

Explores the place of maize in cult and ritual; and its modern significance in the form of chicha, an alcoholic beverage.

8662. Wegman, Myron E.; Marchante, R.F.; & Kramer, M. 1942. Mortality and infant feeding in Puerto Rico. PRJPHTM 17:228-243.

8663. Wehmeyer, A.S.; Lee, Richard Borshay; & Whiting, Marjorie. 1969. The nutrient composition and dietary importance of some vegetable foods eaten by °Kung Bushmen. SAMJ 43:1529-1530.

8664. Wehrmann, M. 1892. Zur Geschichte des Bieres in Pommern. [On the history of Pomeranian beer.] ZK 3 [new series.] (2). No. 2977.

8665. Weidenreich, Franz. 1939. Did Sinanthropus pekinensis practice cannibalism? GSC-B 19:49-63.

8666. Weigley, E.S. 1964. Food in the days of the Declaration of Independence. JADA 45:35-40.

8667. Weigmann, H.; Gruber, T.; & Huss, H. 1907. Ueber armenisches Mazun. [On Armenian madzoon.] ZBPIH 19:70-87.

Microbiological analysis of Armenian yoghurt.

8668. Weinstein, M.S. 1976. What the land provides. An examination of Fort George subsistence economy and the possible consequences on it of the James Bay Hydroelectric Project. Report of Fort George Resource Use Study. Montreal: Grand Council of the Crees (of Quebec).

8669. Weiss, Brian. Selling a subsistence system. Paper presented at 73rd Annual Meeting of the American Anthropological Association. 19 to 24 November, 1974. Mexico City.

8670. Weiss, Caroline Dreyfous. 1948. Sesame, with emphasis on an unusual use in Louisiana. Herbarist No. 14. Pp. 43-45.

Use in pralines, a sugar or syrup-based candy.

8671. Weiss, Harry B. 1954. The history of applejack of apple brandy in New Jersey from Colonial times to the present. Trenton: New Jersey Agricultural Society.

8672. Weiss, Pedro. 1953. Los comedores peruanos de tierra; datos historicos, sociales y geograficos, nombres de las tierras comestibles, interpretacion fisiologica de la geofagia y la pica. [Earth-eaters of Peru; historical, sociological and geographical data; names of edible earths; physiological explanation of geophagy and pica.] Peru Ind 5:12-21.

8673. Weiss, Theodore J. 1970. Food oils and their uses. Westport, Connecticut: AVI.

8674. Weitlaner, Roberto J. 1952. Sobre la alimentacion Chinanteca. [Chinatec diet.] INAH-A 5: 177-195.

8675. Welinder, Stig. Agriculture, inland-hunting and sea-hunting in the western and northern region of the Baltic, 6,000 to 2,000 B.C. Paper presented at 9th International Congress of Anthropological and Ethnological Sciences. 28 August to 8 September, 1973. chicago, Illinois.

Largely deveoted to a consideration of seal-hunting in Denmark, southern and central Sweden, and southern Finland.

8676. Wellers, J.D.V. 1963. Pica. CMD 3(5): 1-10.

Includes a section on historical works. Extensively documented.

8677. Wellin, Edward. 1955. Cultural factors in nutrition. NR 13: 129-131.

Discusses the relevance of cultural factors for dietary surveys; experimental nutrition; and the investigation of the epidemiology of malnutrition.

8678. Wellin, Edward. 1955. Maternal and infant feeding practices in a Peruvian village. JADA 31: 889-894.

Influence of cultural concepts on infant nutrition. Nutrition education is evaluated in terms of pre-existing coginitive categories, and the extent to which it is congruent with these determines the extent of acceptance (synthesis) or rejection.

8679.   Wellin, Edward, & Muchapina, A.G.   Child feeding and food ideology in a Peruvian village. Mimeographed report prepared by the ICA Anthropology Project. Document MH/AS/160. 154. World Health Organiozation. 1953.

8680.   Wellman, F. Creighton. 1907. On the food plants cultivated by the Umbundu-speaking natives of Portuguese West Africa. JTM 10: 157-160.

8681.   Wellman, F. Creighton.   1908.   Notes on some Angolan insects of economic or pathologic importance. EN 19: 26-33.

The giant cricket Brachytrypus membranaceous , Drury (Orthoptera) is eaten, the legs and wings being removed before cooking: pp. 29-30. Schistocera peregrinatoria, L. (Orthoptera) is roasted, then boiled and dried and stored for future use: pp. 30,31. Chrysobothris fatalis, Har. (Coleoptera) used as food: p. 32.

8682.   Wells, A.H. 1916. Possibilities of gulaman dagat as a substitute for gelatin in food.   PJS 11: 267-271.

A Philippine seaweed used in salad, and sold as a gelatin substitute.

8683.   Wells, C.V. 1942. America's changing food consumption, 1909-1941. JHE 34: 463-467.

8684.   Wells, Kenneth. 1971. Ethno- cuisine: pit barbecue and beans. Affword 1: 22-23.

Origin of barbecue cookery and procedure.

8685.   Wells, Kenneth. 1972. Ethno-cuisine: 'son of a bitch' stew. Affword 2: 24-25.

A stew composed of beef glandular meats, traditionally eaten by range hands at round-up time.

8686.   Welsch, Roger L. 1966.   A treasury of Nebraska pioneer folklore.   Lincoln: University of Nebraska Press.

Pioneer cookery: p. 307-328.

8687.   Welsch, Roger L. 1971. We are what we eat: Omaha food as symbol. KFQ 16: 165-170.

8688.   Wendler, J. 1911. Zur Feuer-und Nahrungsbereitung der Mashall Insulaner. [About fire and food preparation of the Marshall Islands.] BArch 1: 269-276.

8689.   Wendt, George V. 1936. Kost und Kultur. [Food and culture.] DMW 62: 1984.

An informal overview of the various roles of food in human life.

8690.   Weknam, Nao S. & Wolff, Robert J. 1970. A half-century of changing food habits among Japanese in Hawaii. JADA 57: 29-32.

Indicates a change from a carbohydrate, vegetable-based diet to one characterized by high protein and fat. Dental caries and coronary heart disease are concomitants of the change. Staple foods of the older dietary pattern, and socio-cultural variables influencing change, are recorded.

8691.   Wenkam, Nao S. & Miler, Carey D. 1965. Composition of Hawaii fruits. Hi-AES-B No. 135.

8692.   Wentworth, Edward N. 1947. Meat in the diet of westward explorers and imigrants   Mid-Am 29: 75-91.

8693.   Wentworth, Edward N. 1956. Dried meat: early man's travel ration. AH 30: 2-10.

8694.   Werge, Robert Wendell. Agricultural development in Clear Creek: strategies and economic roles in a Dominican settlement. Ph. D. dissertation. University of Florida. 1975.

Studies the contrast between modern and traditional farming in a mountainous area of the Dominican Republic. Agricultural development has eliminated subsistence economy and self-sufficiency among small farm holdings, forcing much of the population to rely on marginal cash employment for survival.

8695.   Werge, Robert Wendell. Potato anthropology: a model for applied analysis of tropical food production. Paper presented at 75th Annual Meeting of the American Anthropological Association. 17 to 21 November, 1976. Washington, D.C.

As a response to world food shortages, attention in tropical agricultural development has been focused on increasing the production of basic food crops such as rice and cassava. A mumber of international agricultural centers have been developed to help direct research and training programs for such crops. Most of these centers have social science components in which anthropologists can have a significant input. This paper describes a model for anthropological analysis which stresses data collection, information flow and the manipulation of jargons. Besides presentation of the model, case studies will describe how the model is implemented aty the International Potato Center, Lima, Peru.

8696.   Werge, Robert Wendell 1979. Potato processing in the central highlands of Peru. EFN 7: 229-234.

Three potato products of the Andean highlands are described, with particular attention to processing methods of chuno, a dried product which is first frozen, and then leached in running streams to remove bitter glycoalkaloids; papa seca, a boiled, then sun-dried food; and potato starch. The use of these foods in the diet is mentioned. Data recorded in the Province of Concepcion, in the Mantaro Valley.

8697.   Werlauff, Erik Christian. 1807. Historiske Efferetninger om Hestekiods Brug til Menneskefode i Norden i aeldere og nyere Tider. Haedret med Videnskabernes Selskabs Solvmedaille. [Historical knowledge of horse meat use as human food in Scandinavia in early and modern times. Honored by the Scientific Society's silver medal.] Copenhagen: Saerskildt aftrykt af Vindenskabernes Selskabs Skrifter.

8698.   Werlin, J. 1963. Wein rezepte aus einer Sudtiroler Sammelhandschrift. [Wine recipes from a manuscript collection of the south Tirols.] AK 45:243-252.

8699.   Werner, A. 1906. The native races of the British Empire. The natives of British central Africa. London: Archibald Constable.

Food of children and convalescents: p. 108; general diet: pp. 136-141.

8700.   Werner, H. 1908. Anschwellung der Ohrspeicheldrusengegend bei von Wurzelnahrung lebenden Eingeborenen Afrikas. [Swelling of the parotid gland area among native Africans subsisting on root crops.] ASTPTEK 12:510.

8701.   Werner, Jaffe. 1947. El valor alimenticio del ajonjoli. [Nutritive value of sesame.] Ven-MAG-DG-C No. 30.

8702. Werner, Otmar. 1964. Wie heissen die Kuchlein, die aus geriebenen, rohen Kartoffeln bereitet und in der Pfanne gebacken werden? Eine wortgeographische studie aus der Arbeitzstelle des Ostfrankischen Worterbuchs. [What is the name of the chicken dish which is cleverly prepared from raw potatoes and pan-baked? A study in linquistic geography employing East Franconian dictionaries.] VL-J 24:411-455.

8703.   Wernert, Paul. 1936. La antropofagia ritual y la caza de cabezas en las epocas actual y paeolitica. [Ritual anthropophagy and the case of modern and Paleolithic skulls.] In Pro 10:47-53.

8704.   Wessman, James W. Labor, value and price on a Puerto Rican sugar cane hacienda. Paper presented at 76th Annual Meeting of the American Anthropological Association. 29 November to 3 December, 1977. Houston, Texas.

This study considers Karl Marx's labor theory of vaue as it applies to price formation on a Puerto Rican sugar can hacienda, in 1911. This hacienda provides a good opportunity to examine the labor factor in pricing, because there were several stages of transaction involved, i.e., purchasing sugar cane from growers, and selling raw sugar and molasses to buyers. This stage progres-

sion permits consideration of possible deviations in applying the labor theory of value, especially those introduced by the seasonality of sugar cane cultivation and processing.

8705.   West, Louis C. 1931. Roman Britain: the objects of trade. Oxford: Basil Blackwell.

Honey: p. 24.

8706.   West, Robert C. 1948. Cultural geography of the modern Tarascan area. SI-ISA-P No. 7.

Maize, and wheat foods; vegetables: pp. 39-42, 44.

8707.   Westacott, R. 1911. Paper-bag cookery. USDLC-DCTR 14:1009.

A note on the type of paper bags used in this method of cookery.

8708.   Westbury, Richard Mortland Tollemache. 1963. Handlist of Italian cookery books. Florence, Italy: L.S. Olschki.

8709.   Westenburg, J. 1941. De Visschery-Produkten van Indo-China. [The fishery products of Indo-China.] Communiction No. 6. Batavia: Institute of Seafisheries.

8710.   Westenburg, J. Fishery products of Indo-China. A compilation of the literature up to the Japanese invasion. In Indo-Pacific Fisheries Council. Proceedings. 17 April to 28 April, 1950, Cronulla, New South Wales. 1951. Sections 2 & 3. Pp. 125-150. Bangkok: Food and Agriculture Organization of the United Nations.

8711.   Wester, P.J. 1913. Additional notes on roselle. PARev 6:223-227.

Hibiscus sabdariffa. Includes recipes.

8712.   Wester, P.J. 1920. The cultivation and uses of roselle. PARev 13:89-99.

8713.   Wester, P.J. 1920. The mango. PI-BA-B No. 18. 2nd edition.

Popular and native Philippine preparation techniques: pp. 56-57.

8714.   Wester, P.J. 1921. Additional notes on adlay. PARev 14:159-167.

Coix lachrymae-jobi or 'Job's tears'. A Philippine food grain. Summary of data on food value; methods of cooking; and food uses.

8715.   Wester, P.J. 1921. The food plants of the Philippines. PARev 14:206-384.

8716.   Wester, P.J. 1922. The breadfruit. JHer 13:129-135.

Includes myth material from Polynesia, and historical data on its dispersion by Captain Bligh of H.M.S. Bounty.

8717.   Wester, P.J.   1924.   Food plants of the Philippines. PI-BA-B No. 39.   3rd edition.

8718.   Westervelt, William Drake. 1906. Honolulu salt beds. PPac 19:43-46.

An industry operated by Chinese in the Kalihi district of Oahu.

8719.   Westervelt, William Drake, collector, compilor, translator. 1915. Legends of old Honolulu. Boston: M.L. Millard.

Refers to food use of limu (edible fresh, or salt-water algae), in the context of old Hawaiian folk-tales.

8720.   Wetterstrom, Wilma E. Nutrition and paleo-demography at Pueblo, Arroyo Hondo. Paper presented at 74th Annual Meeting of the American Anthropological Association 2 to 6 December, 1975. San Francisco, California.

New Mexico.

8721.   Wetterstrom, Wilma E. Reconstructing prehistoric subsistence patterns: material evidence and conceptual reconstructions.   Paper presented at 75th Annual Meeting of the American Anthropological Association. November 17 to 21, 1976. Washington, D.C.

Archeological material from Pueblo Arroyo Hondo, near Santa Fe, New Mexico, which includes plant and animal remains, as well as ecological information about these resources, suggest which foods people ate and the potential carrying capacity of the area. However, construction of a detailed quantitative model of these subsistence patterns requires equal attention to reconstruction of the folk classification system which distinguishes foods from non-foods; established priorities separating heavily exploited staples from occasionally-gathered snacks; and determined the methods by which foods were obtained.

8722.   Wewerka, Franz. 1964. Essen und Trinken in Karnten. [Eating and drinking in Carinthia.] KL No. 1. 1-3.

8723.   Weyh, Maria Elizabeth. 1939. Rheinische Gebildbrote.   Sieben Karten zu ihrer Verbreitung. [Decorated breads of the Rhineland. Seven maps showing their distribution] RV 9:105-148.

8724.   Wharton, H.J. & Duesselmann, W.   1947. Favism. A short review and report of a case. NEJM 236:974-977.

8725.   Wharton, J.C. 1977. Tempest in a fleshpot: the formulation of a physiological rationale for vegetarianism. JHM 32:115-139.

8726.   Wharton, James. 1973. The bounty of the Chesapeake. Fishing in Colonial Virginia. Charlottesville: University Press of Virginia.

Includes details of Native American, and European preparation technology, with notes on commerce.

8727.   Whatley, Bonnie L. Subsistence practices in the Woodland Period. Paper presented at the 76th Annual Meeting of the American Anthropological Association. 29 November to 3 December, 1977. Houston, Texas.

Analysis of botanical and faunal remains from habitation sites in the lower Illinois River Valley permits characterization of the Woodland subsistence base and inference regarding environmental and nutritional stress. Evidence for change within the period is also present. Against this background, resource exploitation data from early Woodland sites are described in detail The diversity in proportional representation of species at early Late Woodland sites is seen to reflect localized exploitation, a pattern of crucial importance in explaining changing Woodland subsistence strategies.

8728.   Wheat, Margaret M. 1958. Pinenut hunt: an ancient Indian skill survives. NHP No. 2. Pp. 10-13.

8729.   Wheatley, Christine. Food stamps and hunger. Paper presented at 69th Annual Meeting of the American Anthropological Association.   19 to 22 November, 1970. San Diego, California.

8730.   Wheatley, Paul.   1965.   A note on the extension of milking practices in Southeast Asia during the First Millennium. Anthropos 60:577-590.

Examines the history and influence of Hindu and Buddhist civilization in mainland and island Southeast Asia, and the related presence of milk cow herds which produced the sacred butter with which temple statues were annointed.

8731.   Wheeler, Gerald Clair William Camden. 1926. Mono-Alu folklore. Bugainville Strait. Western Solomon Islands.   London: G. Routledge & Sons.

Myth (Solomon Islands: Buin): acquisition of food supply of human race: p. 59.

8732.   Whelan, William Joseph & Whitaker, Desmond Arnold. 1952. A new South African beverage plant. Helichysum nudifolium, Less. var. quinquinerve (Thumb.) Moes. SAJMS 17:77-78.

8733.   Wherry, Edgar Theodore. 1913. Does a low-protein diet produce racial inferiority?   Science 37:908-909.

8734.   Whetham, E.H.   1970.   The London milk trade: 1900-1930. URead-IAH-RP No. 3.

8735.   Whetten, Nathan L. 1962. Chapter Ten. Diet and nutrition. In Guatemala. The land and its people. New Haven; London: Yale University Press.

8736.   Whitacre, J. 1934. The diet of Texas school children. Tex-AES-B No. 489.

8737.   Whitaker, Meredith. A study of the adequacy of diets selected by industrial workers on the day and night shifts. Master's thesis. Greensboro: Woman's College of the University of North Carolina. 1944.

8738.   Whitaker, Thomas W. 1948. Lagenaria: a pre-Colombian cultivated plant in the Americas. SJA 4:49-68.

   Botanical, archaelogical, and ethnographic study. Indicates common use of the gourd Lagenaria siceraria (Molina) Standl. as a food container.

8739.   Whitaker, Thomas W. 1956. The origin of the cultivated Cucurbita. AN 90:171-176.

8740.   Whitaker, Thomas W. 1957. Archaeological Cucurbitaceae from a cave in southern Baja California. SJA 13: 144-148.

8741.   Whitaker, Thomas B. & Bird, Junius B. 1949. Identification and significance of the cucurbit materials from Huaca Prieta, Peru. AMNH-N 1426: 1-15.

8742.   Whitaker, Thomas W. & Carter, George Francis. 1946. Critical notes on the origin and domestication of the cultivated species of Cucurbita. AJB 33: 10-15.

   Provides archaeological evidence of the New World origin of Cucurbita pepo, C. maxima, and C. moschata. A domesticated form of C. pepo from the southwestern United States is described for the first time, and it is shown to be distinct from domesticated species of the Atlantic Coast region of the eastern United States.

8743.   Whitaker, Thomas W. & Cutler, Hugh C. 1966. Food plants in a Mexican market. EB 20: 6-16.

8744.   Whitaker, Thomas W.; Cutler, Hugh C.; & MacNeish, Richard S. 1957. Cucurbit materials from three caves near Ocampo, Tamaulipas. Am An 22: 352-258.

8745.   Whitcomb, E.S. 1926. Food education. Hygaeia 4: 641.

   Potential role of nutrition education in school lunch programs.

8746.   White, Charles A. Kjoekken moeddings de l'Amerique du Nord. [Kitchen-middens of North America.] In 5ᵉ Congres International d'Anthropologie et d'Archeologie Prehistorique. 1871. Bologne. Compte Rendu 1873. Pp. 379-391. Bologna: Imprimerie Fava et Garagnani.

   Includes two lists of animal remains found in North American middens; and a brief bibliography of relevant publications prior to 1866.

8747.   White, E.G. 1947.   Kaffir beer. Johannesburg: Radford Adlington.

   A beer brewed from maize.

8748.   White, Florence. 1931. Traditional cooking in the north-east of England. SR 152:155.
8749.   White, Florence. 1931. Traditional dishes of the south-west. SR 152: 457-458.

   England.

8750.   White, Florence. 1934. Flowers as food. Recipies and lore from many sources. London; Toronto: Jonathan Cape.

8751.   White, Florence. 1952. Good English food. Local and regional. Famous food and drink of yesterday and today, recorded with recipes. London: Jonathan Cape.

8752.   White, H.P. 1956. Internal exchange of staple foods in the Gold Coast. EG 32: 115-125.

8753.   White, H.S.; Collazos, C.; White, P.L.; Huenemann, Ruth Lois; Benites, R.; Castellanos, A.; Bravo, E.; Moscoso, I.; Dieseldorf, A. 1954. Dietary surveys in Peru. 2. JADA 30: 856-864.

   Food consumption and meal pattern data include description of commonly eaten foods with statistics for average daily consumption and seasonal availability.

8754.   White, Herbert. 1919-1920. Do the Sinhalese drink milk? CALR 5: 16-18.

8755.   White, James J. I am not yet tired of Korean food. In The feel of Korea. A symposium of American comment. Edited by In-Hah Jung. 1966. Pp. 184-194. Seoul: Hollym Corporation.

   Comments on Korean food by a U.S. American residing in Korea. Attitudes of Americans to Korean food; observations on food-related customs. Notes that the table on which the meal is served in Korea is actually a "plate", refuse being placed on it and removed, in contrast to the practice in the West of removal of the plate itself, but leaving the table in place.

8756.   White, John. 1925. The moa in Maori tradition. PS-J 34: 170-174.

   The moa is an extinct land bird once inhabiting parts of New Zealand. Its food use, and methods of preparation for eating are described on pp. 172,173.

8757.   White, Kenneth Douglas. 1963. Wheat farming in Roman times. Antiquity 37: 207-212.

8758.   White, Kenneth Douglas. 1970. Roman farming. London: Thames; Ithaca, New York: Cornell University Press.

8759.   White, Lynn. Food and history. In Food, man, and society. Edited by Dwain N. Walcher;

Norman Kretchmer; & Henry L. Barnett. 1975. Pp. 12-30. New York, London: Plenum Press.

The first part of this contribution discusses the availability of protein foods in Medeival northern Europe and the ramifications of this and the agricultural revolution of the Ninth to Eleventh Centuries upon the development of society in the region. Part Two looks at the global pattern of the history of food.

8760. White, P.L. 1964. Diet and the driver. 1964. PFPMP-J 13: 253-256.

8761. White, Philip L.; Alvistur, Enrique: Dias, Cesar; Vinas, Eduardo; White, Hilda S.; & Collazos, Carlos. 1955. Nutrient content and protein quality of quinua and canihua, edible seed products of the Andes Mountains JAFC 3: 531-534.

Quinua (Chenopodium quinoa, Willd.), and canihua (Chenopodium pallidicule) are traditional seed foods of highland Andean natives. Experiments with laboratory rats indicate these plant products have a protein quality equal to that of whole dried milk.

8762. White, Rose P. 1956. The sourdough biscuit. WF 15: 93-94.

Eastern New Mexico and western Taxas; preparation and historical anecdote.

8763. White, Ruth L. 1943. Case studies of nutrition. Boston's problem children. AAPSS-A 225: 63-65.

Sketches briefly the food habits of a fourteen year woman; a seven year old Irish girl; and a nine year boy of Italian-American parentage. Nutritional deficiencies are recorded.

8764. White, Taylor. 1912. The kuri or Maori dog. JPS 21: 137-138.

Brief mention of its use as human food.

8765. White, Theodore Elmer. 1952-1953-1954-1955. Observations on the butchering techniques of some aboriginal peoples. AmAn 17: 337-338. No. 1. Antelope. 19: 160-164. No.2. Bison. 19: 254-264. Nos. 3,4,5,6. Small vs. large game; bison. 21: 170-178. Nos. 7,8,9. Dog bone; bison and elk bone.

Reference is to archeo-osteological materials dervied from Native North American sites.

8766. White, Theodore Elmer. 1953. A method of calculating the dietary percentages of various food animals utilized by aboriginal peoples. AmAn 18: 396-398.

Includes a conversion table, from which pounds of usable protein may be determined, based on average live weight figures, extrapolating from osteological materials.

8767. Whitehead, George. 1924. In the Nicobar Islands. London: Seeley, Service.

Foods: pp. 64-68.

8768. Whitehill, Jane Revere Coolidge. 1963. Food, Drink, and recipes of early New England. Old Sturbridge Village Booklet Series. No. 16. Sturbridge, Massachusetts: Old Sturbridge Village.

8769. White House Conference on Child Health and Protection. 1932. Growth and development of the child. Part three. Nutrition. New York, London: The Century Company.

Dietary adaptations for geographic and racial factors (Slovak; Chinese; Japanese): pp. 452-456. Eating habits in children: pp. 506-511. Psychological factors: pp. 512-519.

8770. White House Conference on Child Health and Protection. Committee on Medical Care for Children. 1932. Nutrition service in the field. Child health centers: a survey. New York: The Century Company.

Surveys the role of the nutritionist; need for nutrition education; nutrition services provided by various public health and medical agencies. A review of child health centers in the United States, territories and possessions is included. A review of the Conference can be found by Henry Schumacher in HSS 26: 235, 236 (1932).

8771. Whiteman, Josephine. 1961. Dietetics in Fiji. Nutrition (L) 15: 35-38.

8772. Whiteman, Josephine. 1961. Food habits in Nigeria. Nutrition (L) 15: 136-140.

8773. Whiteman, Josephine. 1962. The food economy of the Gilbert Islands. Nutrition (L) 16: 111-114.

8775. Whiteman, Josephine. 1964. Food and nutrition amongst school children of a Libyan oasis. Nutrition (L) 18: 1418.

8776. Whiteman, Josephine 1965. Customs and beliefs relating to food, nutrition and health in the Chimbu area. TGM 17: 301-316.

Includes descriptive data on attitudes toward foods; eating; food preparation; and cooking of a highland New Grinea group..

8777. Whiteman, Josephine 1966. The function of food in society. Nutrition (L) 20: 4-8.

8778. Whiteman, Josephine. 1966. A study of beliefs and attitudes toward food in a New Guinea low-cost housing settlement. TGM 18: 157-166.

8779. Whiting, Albert N. 1947. Starch and soot eating among southern rural Negroes in North Carolina. JNegro 16: 610-612.

8780. Whiting, Alfred F. 1936. Hopi Indian agriculture. 1. Background. MNA-MN 8: 51-53.

8781.   Whiting, Alfred F.   1937.   Hopi Indian agriculture 2: seed sources and   distibrution.   MNA-MN
10: 13-16.

8782.   Whiting, Alfred F.   1939.   Ethnobotany of
the Hopi.   MNA-B No. 15.

8783.   Whiting, J.D.   1911.   Bedouin desert bread.
USDCL-DCTR 14: 630.

> Bread made from the seed of Samh (Mesem-
> brianthemum forskahilii) , a small plant
> which grows wild over desert areas where no
> cultivation is practiced due to insufficient
> rainfall.

8784.   Whitmore, Helen B.   1946. Vanilla-bean production and trade.   ForAg 10: 11-16.

> Historical data: pp. 11-12.

8785.   Whiting, Marjorie Grant.   A cross-cultural
nutrition survey of 118 societies, representing the
major cultural and geographic areas of the world.
D.Sc.   dissertation.   School of Public Health.
Harvard University.   1958.

8786.   Whitney, Cornelius Vanderbilt (Mrs.) 1977.
Potato chip cookbook.   Lexington, Kentucky: Maple
Hill Press.

8787.   Whitney, John Morgan.   1893.   Among the
ancient Hawaiians.   DC 35: 900-906.

> Discussion of dental conditions in relation to
> native diet.

8788.   Whitney, Leo D.; Bowers, F.A.I.; & Takahashi, M. 1939.   Taro varieties in Hawaii.   Hi-AES - B
No. 84.

8789.   Whittemore, Margaret & Neil, Berniece.
1929. Time facors in the business of homemaking in
rural Rhode Island.   RI-AES-B No. 221.

> Preparation and clearing away of food: pp.
> 9-11; fuels used in cooking: p. 21; buying
> bread: p. 22.

8790.   Whyte, Robert Orr.   1972.   The Gramineae,
wild and cultivated, of monsoonal and equatorial
Asia. APer 15: 127-151.

8791.   Whyte, Roberyt Orr.   1974.   An environmental interpretation of the origin of Asian cereals.
IJGPB 34A: 1-11.

8792.   Whyte, Robert Orr.   1975.   An environmental interpretation of the origin of Asian food
legumes. IJGPB 35: 61-68.

8793.   Whyte, Robert Orr.   1977.   The botanical
Neolithic Revolution HEcol 5: 209-222.

> Article suggests, on the basis of geological
> and   paleoclimatological   evidence,   that
> annual grasses and legumes did not appear
> as significant components of the vegetation
> of Asia until the Neothermal, ca. 11,000
> years B.P. The new combination of environ-
> mental   factors   which   then   became
> operative induce a widespread physiologi-
> cal and genetic change from a perennial to
> an annual habit in ecoclimatic zones, in
> which annual types of ancestral perennials
> had not earlier occurred in any number.
> The annual prototypes of the Asian cereals
> and grain legumes therefore became rather
> suddenly and abundantly available to primi-
> tive groups. Once this botanical revolution
> had occurred throughout the isoxerother-
> mic zones around the inner core of Asia,
> progress toward what came to be called
> civilization, based on increasingly econom-
> ic agricultural ecosytems involving cultiva-
> tion and domestication of crops, followed
> in a gradual step-by-step manner.

8794.   Whyte, W.F.   1948.   Chapter One.   The
restaurant in American society.   In Human relations
in the restaurant industry.   New York: Mc Graw-Hill
Book Co.

8795.   Wickes, Ian G.   1953.   A history of infant
feeding.   1.   Primitive peoples; ancient works;
renaissance writers.   ADC 28: 151-158.

8796.   Wickes, Ian G.   1953. A history of infant
feeding. 2. Seventeenth and Eighteenth Centuries.
ADC 28: 232-240.

8797.   Wickes, Ian G.   1953.   A history of infant
feeding.   3.   Eighteenth and Nineteenth Century
writers. ADC 28: 332-340.

8798.   Wickes, Ian G.   1953.   A history of infant
feeding.   4.   Nineteenth Century continued.   ADC
28: 416-422.

8799.   Wickes, Ian G.   1953.   A history of infant
feeding.   5.   Nineteenth Century concluded and
Twentieth Century.   ADC 28: 495-502.

8800.   Wickizer, V.D. & Bennett, Merril K.   1941.
The rice economy of monsoon Asia.   Palo Alto:
Stanford University Press.

8801.   Wiedfelt, O.   1914.   Wirtschaft, rechtliche
und soziale Grundtatsachen und Grund-formen der
Ataylan auf Formosa.   [Basic domestic economy,
judicial, and sociological data on the Atayal of
Formosa.] DGNVOT-M [Part C]: 7-55.

> Includes an enumeration of staple foods,
> and cooking techniques.

8802.   Weigelmann, Gunter.   1964.   Speiseeis in
volkstumlichen Festmahlzeiten.   [Ice cream in popular festival times.] DLR [section 7] . Pp. 201-204.

8803.   Weigelmann, Gunter.   Stand und Aufgaben
der ethnologischen Nahrungsforschung in Deutschland.   [State and problems of ethnologic food research in Germany.] Paper presented at the First
International Symposium on Ethnological Food Research.   21 August to 25 August, 1970.   Lund:
Folklivsarkivet. Lund University.

8804.   Weigelmann, Gunter, Was ist der spezielle
Asp kt ethnologischer Nahrungsforchung? [What is

the special nature of ethnologic food research?] Paper presented at the First International Symposium on Ethnologic Food Research. 21 August to 25 August, 1970. Lund: Folklivsarkivet. Lund University.

8805.   Weil, D.G. & Palmer, C.E. 1939. Summer diets of the poor in Washington, D.C. MMFQ 17: 5-28.

8806.   Wieland, E. 1938.   Raw and cooked human milk. [In German.] SMW 68: 79-80.

8807.   Wiener, Adolf 1895. Die Judischen Speisegesetze nach ihren verschieden Gesichtspunkten zum ersten male wissenschaftlichmethodisch geordent und Kritisch beleuchtet. [The Jewish dietary laws: their different aspects arranged and critically examined for the first time according to scientific methods.] Bresalu: S. Schottlaender

8808.   Wiens.   1907   Infant feeding and infant mortality among the Chinese. [In German] ARGERG 4: 224-227.

Based in part on the author's personal observations.

8809.   Wiet, Gaston.   1955.   Les marchands d'epices sous les sultans Mamlouks.   [Spice merchants under the Mamluk sultans.] CHE 7: 81-147.

Egypt

8810.   Wiklund, Karl Bernhard. 1902. Lapp customs and injunctions concerning food and cookery. [In Swedish.] NMUAH-M 1899-1900 Pp. 1-12.

8811.   Wilbert, Johannes.   1972.   Survivors of El Dorado. Four Indian cultures of South America. New York: Praeger.

Cooking (Goajiro): p. 174; (Makiritare) : p. 149; (Warao): p. 93; (Yanoamo)S: p. 76; food quest (Goajiro):P pp. 172-174; (Makiritare): pp. 140-149; (Warao) : pp. 80-97; (Yanoamo): pp. 33-45.

8812.   Wildeman, Emile de. 1934. Documents pour l'etude de l'alimentation vegetale de l' indigene au Congo Belge. [Documents for the sutdy of vegetable diet of Belgian Congo natives.] IRCB -ARSC - SSNM -M Vol. 2. No. 4.

8813.   Wildeman, Emile de. 1936. La probleme de L'alimentation de l' indigene au Congo Belge. [The probem of native diet in the Belgian Congo.] MColon 27: 134-154.

8814.   Wildeman, Emile de. 1938. Dioscorea alimentaires et toxiques (morphologie et biologie). Espece et varietes congolaises. [Edible and toxic Dioscorea (morphology and biology). Species and varieties in the Congo.] IRCB-ARSC-SSNM-M Vol. 6. No. 3.

8815.   Wildeman Emile de. 1939. Alimentation des indigenes.   Enquetes   botanico-agronomiques. [Native diet. Botanic-agronomic surveys.] RBAAT 19: 107-121.

A discussion of native tropical African nutritional status and the various means by which it may be improved.

8816.   Wildeman, Emile de & Trolli, Giorgio. 1939. Notes sur les plantes medicinales et alimentaires du Congo Belge. (Missions du Fondation Reine Elisabeth Pour l'Assistance Medicale aux Indigenes.) [Notes on medicinal and food plants of the Belgian Congo. (missions of the Queen Elizabeth Foundation for Medica Assistance to the Indigenes.)].   IRCB-ARSC-SSNM-M No. 3.

8817.   Wilder, A.P. 1909. Food products in China. USDCL-DCTR No. 3847. Pp. 14-16.

Notes on diet in Southern China.

8818.   Wilder, Gerrit Parmile. 1928. The breadfruit of Tahiti. BPBM-B No. 50.

Preparation for food: pp. 15,18.

8819.   Wilder, Russel M. 1923. Rationing a canoeing party. Diet Ad Ther 1: 26-28.

Dietetic evaluation of provisions used during a wilderness expedition.

8820.   Wilder, Russell M. & Keys, Thomas E. Unusual foods of high nutritive value. Handbook of nutrition: 14. JAMA 120:529-535.

Reviews a variety of little-used domestic foods, as well as foods from other cultures which the authors believe to be favorable to good health and which might be introduced into the diet of the United States.

8821.   Wilhaber, Robert. 1950. Schneckenzucht und Schneckenspeise.   [Clams and clam eating. ASTP 46:119-184.

8822.   Wiley, Harvey. 1895. The synthetic food of the future. ACS-J 17:155-178.

Role of chemistry in synthesizing natural products.

8823.   Wilkerson, Fred W. 1929. Dietetic difficulties in the South. MCMA 12:1479-1489.

Neither malaria nor hookworm, but malnutrition is seen as "the curse of the South", a view based on the author's clinical observations. Urges physicians to counsel patients on proper selection of diet and correct food preparation.

8824.   Wilkerson, Fred W. 1933. Dietary errors in the southern United States. SMedJ 26:1062-1065.

8825.   Wilkie, H.F. 1947. Beverage spirits in America: a brief history. New York: Newcomen Society of England, American Branch.

8826. Wilkinson, Joseph G. 1868. Hospital expenditure in London and the Provinces, being an analysis of the working expenses of forty-six London and Provincial hospitals for the year 1868. London.

Includes financial aspects of hospital diets.

8827. Will, George F. Indian agriculture at its northern limits in the Great Plains region of North America. In Vigesimo Congresso de Americanistas. 20 a 30 de Agosto de 1922, Rio de Janeiro. Annaes. 1924. Vol. 1. Pp. 203-205. Rio de Janeiro: Imprensa Nacional.

8828. Will, George F. & Hyde, George E. 1917. Chapter Four. Corn as food. In Corn among the Indians of the upper Missouri. St. Louis. Missouri: William Harry Mino Co. Reprint. Lincoln: University of Nebraska Press. Bison Book No. 165.

8829. Will, George F. & Spinden, Herbert J. 1906. The Mandans. HU-PMAAE-P 3:81-219.

Agriculture; hunting; and fishing; including reference to foods and food use: pp. 117-122.

8830. Willard, Mary Jean. A study of the diet and nutritional status of Latin American women. Master's thesis. Austin: University of Texas. 1942.

8831. Wille, Otto. 1949. Handbuch der Fischkonservierung. [Handbook of fish preservation.] Hamburg: Hans A. Keune.

Survey of the industry in Germany.

8833. Willett, R.C. 1934. An ususual infant diet and its questionable effects upon dentitiion. IJOrth 20:432-444.

'Home-brew', i.e. home-brewed beer.

8834. Williams, A.W. Dietary patterns in three Mexican villages. Paper presented at 69th Annual Meeting of the American Anthropological Association. 19 to 22 November, 1970. San Diego, California.

8835. Williams, Bobby Joe. A model of hunting-gathering societies and some genetic consequences. Ph.D. dissertation. University of Michigan. 1965.

Investigates the results of mating structures of hunters-gatherers, using a computer simulation of Bithor society (Bihar State, India). Results of simulation indicate that, in general, gene frequency distributions are more stable in such a system than is commonly supposed in the "small breeding isolate" model of Paleolithic society. Concludes that polymorphisms are evenly maintained, either through heterozygote advantage or through areal reversals in selective advantage. The effective population number of such groups is equal to or larger than the census number and, consequently, genetic drift would not be as important as an evolutionry force as commonly supposed.

8836. Williams, Cicely D. 1933. Nutritional disease of childhood associated with maize diet. ADC 8:423-433.

Early description of kwashiorkor, among young children of the Gold Coast. Family customs, and food habits are described which are causal of the deficiency syndrome.

8837. Williams, Cicely D. 1935. Kwashiorkor: nutritional disease of children associated with maize diet. Lancet 2:1151-1152.

8838. Williams, Cicely. Varieties of unbalanced diet and their effect on nutrition. In Science and mankind. No. 1. Hunger and food. Edited by Josue de Castro. 1858. Pp. 40-50. London: World Federation of Scientific Workers.

8839. Williams, Edwin. 1963. Frozen foods, biography of an industry. Boston: Cahner's.

Historical, from 1930's to the 1960's.

8840. Williams, Emiy. 1908. Housekeeping in Egypt. BCSM 12:317.

Includes description of diet and food preparation.

8841. Williams, F. Revor. 1950. Chapter One. A brief history of confectionery. In Chocolate and confectionery. London: Leonard Hill.

8842. Williams, Faith M. & Lockwood, Julia E. 1930. An economic study of food consumed by farm and village families in central New York. CorU-AES-B No. 502.

In-depth analysis of cash cost of food, nutrition, and metabolic energy. Nutritional adequacy of diets is also evaluated. Study covers the period 1925-1927.

8843. Williams, Faith Moore. 1940. Nutrition is a eugenics problem. JHer 31:521-526.

Comments on nutrition as an environmental variable affecting on the public health and national well-being.

8844. Williams, Faith Moore; Stiebeling, Hazel K.; Swisher, Idella G.; & Weiss, Gertrude Schmidt. 1937. Family living in Knott County, Kentucky. USDA-TB 576.

Data collected over the period February, 1929 to March 1, 1930. Food purchases, their costs; quantity; consumption; production; and nutritional evaluation of diet: pp. 31-44.

8845. Williams, Francis X. 1944. A survey of insect pests of New Caledonia. HPR 48:93-124.

Mentions an edible longicorn beetle which inhabits decaying trees (e.g. Aleurites moluccana, Wild.

8846. Williams, George D. & Benedict, Francis G. 1928. The basal metabolism of Mayas in Yucatan. AJP 85:634-649.

8847. Williams, Howard. 1883. The ethics of diet. A catena of authorities deprecatory of the practice of flesh-eating. Manchester: F. Pitman.

8848. Williams, J. 1892. New England corn cake. Critic 21:126.

8849. Williams, Martha McCulloch. 1907. The peacock edible. CLA 13:252.

Directions for preparing and cooking peafowl.

8850. Williams, R.O. & Williams, Jr., R.O. 1941. The useful and ornamental plants in Trinidad and Tobago. 3rd edition, revised. Port-of-Spain: A.L. Rhodes, Government Printer.

8851. Williams, Robert Ramapatnam. 1952. Rice in Asiatic diets. JADA 28:209-212.

8852. Williams, Roger J. 1956. Human nutrition and individual variability. BRNR 17:11-26.

Statement of Williams' concept of the "genetotrophic effect", which posits biochemical individuality in need for nutrients; absorptive capability; enzyme secretion; nutrient synthesis.

8853. Williams, Ruth O. & Brush, Miriam K. 1965. Family food habits in the Virgin Islands. JHE 57:641-645.

Meal patterns and daily menus recorded. Brief socio-economic background data is given. Analysis of a typical meal is included.

8854. Williams, Sue Rodwell. 1973. Chapter Thirteen. Cultural, social and psychological infuences on food habits. In Nutrition and diet therapy. Saint Louis: C.Y. Mosby.

8855. Williams, Thomas Rhys, 1972. Introduction to socialization. Human culture transmitted. St. Louis, Missouri: C.V. Mosby Co.

Observations on diet included under: ethnographic reports of voluntary control of drives (hunger); diverse ways of meeting human metabolic requirements; and cultural patterns and voluntary meeting of metabolic requirements.

8856. Williams, Thomas Thackery. An economic analysis of Negro food habits in Tuskegee, Alabama. Ph.D. dissertation. Ohio State University. 1951.

Food consumption and expenditure data for seven days among one hundred twenty-nine randomly selected Black white collar workers revealed regional southern food patterns (rice, grits, pork, chicken, and vegetables). Home meal consumption was preferred.

8857. Williams, W.L. 1913. Kumara lore. JPS 22: 36-41.

New Zealand Maori ceremonies associated with sweet potato planting, harvesting and storage.

8858. Williamson, Hugh Anthony. Populaton movement and food gathering economy of northern Labrador. Master's thesis. Geography. McGill University. 1964.

Eskimo.

8859. Williamson, Jesse. 1956. Salt and potashes in the life of the Cewa. N Journal 9: 82-87.

8860. Williston, Samuel Wendell. 1883. Dipterous larvae from the western alkaline lakes and their use as human food. CAAS-T 6: 87-90.

8861. Willoughby, Charles C. 1906. Houses and gardens of the New England Indians. AA 8: 115-132.

Food-related utensils and containers: pp. 123-124; gardens and garden crops: pp. 128-132.

8862. Wills, Pamela A. 1958. Salt consumption by natives of th trritory of Papua and New Guinea. PJS 87: 169-177.

Thirteen samples of indigenous plant-ash salts are analyzed for all or some of the following constituents: chlorine, iodine, magnesium, potassium, sodium, and sulphate. Preparation methods are described for the following areas: Bougainville Island; Morobe District; Sepik District; eastern highlands; Madang District; Wissel Lakes; Milne Bay Area; and Kokoda District.

8863. Willson, R.G. 1963. Manna in the desert was known to Indians. ADW 15 December. Pp. 42-43.

8864. Willson, kR.G. 1966. Dynamite got rid of cooks. ADW 13 February. Pp. 40-41.

8865. Wilm, Paul. 1926. Notes on Mongol economy and modern dairy farming in Chahor. CEM 3: 281-293.

Preparation of dairy products: pp. 286-288.

8866. Wilmot, J.S. & Batjer, M.Q. 1960. Chapter Two. Food habits. In Food and the family. Chicago: J.B. Lippincott.

8867. Wilmsen, Edwin N. & Meyers, J. Thomas. 1972. The mercury content of prehistoric fish. EFN 1: 179-186.

The importance of archaeological data for establishing baselines for modern environmental evaluation is examined. Eight samples of fish from midland North America, and nine samples from pre-Inca coastal Peru are analyzed. Twelve of the prehistoric samples contained mercury in quantities ranging from 0.014 ppm to 9.463 ppm. Modern samples were used as controls.

8868.   Wilson, A.M. 1877. The wines of the Bible: an examination and refutation of the fermented wine theory. London; Glasgow: Hamilton.

8869.   Wilson, Anna May 1953. What to eat on a tropic isle. TH 31 (6): 30.

> In formal account of tropical foods; typical diet; nutrition research (meeting with Dr. Lydia Jean Roberts, and Ester Zayas).

8870.   Wilson, A.T.M. 1961. Nutritional change: some comments from social research. PNS 20: 133-137.

> Concludes: "There is little doubt that all-round nutritional knowedge could, with advantage, be developed; but there is, equally, little reason to doubt that much of the knowledge we already possess is not being effectively applied. In part this is due, I believe, to the slowness with which social science research in this field has developed; and although I must declare a bias, I feel that if there are any particularly urgent research needs, I would include among them study of the social and cultural aspects of nutritional change" (p. 137).

8871.   Wilson, C. Anne. 1973. Food and drink in Britain from the Stone Age to recent times. London: Constable.

8872.   Wilson, Christine Shearer; Food beliefs and practices of Malay fishermen; and ethnographic study of diet on the east coast of Malaysia. Ph. D. dissertation. University of California, Berkeley. 1970.

8873.   Wilson, Christine Shearer. 1971. Food beliefs affect nutritional status of Malay fisherfolk. JNE 21: 96-98.

8874.   Wilson, Christine Shearer. 1973. Food habits: a selected annotated bibliography. JNE 5. No. 1. Supp. 1. Jan.-Mar.

> A handbook of references mainly in English, from 1928 through 1972. In the author's words in her Introduction "This present work, in additon to bringing the literature up to date, will hopfully be more readily available to a wider audience - increasing in numbers - as various disciplines come together to work in this area which impinges on so many of them" (p.40).

8875.   Wilson, Christine Shearer. 1973. Food taboos of childbirth: the Malay example. EFN 2: 267-274.

> The diets of fifty women (prima - and multiparas), from the community of RuMuda, in Trengganu, (located about one hundred miles south of the Malaysia-Thai border) were studied over a period of sixteen months. On the basis of the felt influence of 'hot' and 'cold' characteristics, certain foods are removed from the diet of the post-parturient women for a period of forty days. This article studies these food prohibitions, and indicates the possible nutritional ramifications resulting from them.

8876.   Wilson, Christine Shearer. Nutrition in two cultures: Mexican-American and Malay ways with food.   Paper presented at 9th International Congreess of Anthropological and Ethnological Sciences. 28 August to 8 September, 1973. Chicago, Illinois.

> Compares similarities in food classification ('hot'/'cold' properties); foods consumed; and nutritional value of diets in southern California, and Malaysia, where data were collected.

8877.   Wilson, Christine Shearer. 1974. Child following: technic for learing food and nutrient intakes. JTPECH 20: 9-14.

> A relatively simple technic of learning the total daily food and nutrient intake of a toddler child, who eats as well as snacks away from home during part of the day, has been divised and proved sstaisfacory in use in a Malay village. It consists of following behind the child for his/her entire waking day, and recording the amounts of all of the food he/she eats. The method is suggested for use in studies of traditional societies, but is seen as ammenable to adaptation to other contexts and age levels. Qualificaions as to application of the method are included.

8878.   Wilson, Christine Shearer. Nutrition in two cultures: Mexican-American and Malay ways with food. In Gastronomy. The anthropology of food and food havits.   Edited by Margaret Louise Arnott. 1975. Pp. 131-144. Paris; The Hague: Mouton Publisher. World Anthropology.

> In this paper, the author compares similarities in staple foods, eating patterns, and food beliefs, and some historical reasons for some of these cogruences. In conclusion, suggestions are made for improving upon traditional dietary recording techniques through the innovation of methods used by social scientists.

8879.   Wilson, Christine Shearer. 1975. Rice, fish, and coconuts - the bases of southeast Asian flavors. FTech 29(6): 42-44.

> A sketch of Malaysian food patterns, and of foods and food prepartions characteristic of Southeast Asia.

8880.   Wilson,   Christine   Shearer.   Reasearch methods in nutritional anthropology: approaches and techniques.   In Nutrition and anthropoloigy in action. Edited by Thomas K. Fitzgerald. 1976. Pp. 62-68. Assen, Amsterdam: Van Gorcum

> A review of research procedures, from the various disciplines which impinge upon social and natural science approaches to the study of human nutrition.

8881.   Wilson, Christine Shearer.   Person-following: a way to learn what an individual eats.   Paper presented aat 76th Annual Meeting of the American Anthropological Association. 29 November to 3 December, 1977. Houston, Texas.

The author generalizes that, after weaning, if allowed, children will eat what is offered at various times and places, away or at home. Conventional dietary survey methods cannot determine total food intake within such circumstances; as a child may eat wild foods; at shops; or homes; as a result, under-reporting of nutrients consumed occurs. To overcome this problem, techniques are suggested for following a child or adult all day, in order to achieve accurate dietary intake records.

8882.   Wilson, Christine. 1978. Contributions of nutrition science to anthropological research. FASEB-FB 37: 73-76.

Examples of field research, in which nutrition and anthropological techniques have been or might be combined for more productive results than if each discipline worked independently of the other. Concludes that greater collaboration between nutrition and anthropology professionals could contribute to resolution of a variety of health problems involving food and culture in the United States and elsehere.

8883.   Wilson, Christine Shearer & Anderson, James N. 1968. Socioeconomic status and nutrient intakes in a Phillippine Village. FASEB-P 27: 680 [Abstract No., 2609.]

Records of food intake revealed that lower status families consumed varieties of indigenous greens which have low status in the community as food sources. These plants contain substantial amounts of calcium, vitamin A, and ascorbic acid; and lesser amounts of iron, and the B-complex. Diets of higher status families were inadequate in these nutrients. Interviewing in the community's households was done by a member of each household. The authors feel these important plant nutrient sources (because of the low esteem in which they are held as food) might not have been reported consumed to an outside investigator. On the basis of this feeling, the authors suggest the need for developing anthropological techniques to assist in the cross-cultural evaluation of dietary status.

8884.   Wilson, Christine Shearer. 1979. Food - custom and nurture. An annotated bibliography on sociocultural and biocultural aspects of nutrition. JNE 11. No. 4. S. No. 1.

This publication is an update of the author's earlier compliation (Wilson 1972). New titles have been added to the latter, some omitted, and some retained. Major categories under which citations are entgered include; sociocultural factors; environmental factors; biologic factors; psychologic aspects; foodways; implications; methodology. An author index is appended.

8885.   Wilson, Eddie W. 1961. The gastronomic wilderness. LW No. 75. Pp. 20-23.

A popular article on wild foods of North America with documented references to their uses by Native Americans and early explorers.

8886.   Wilson, Eddie W. 1950. The gourd in the Southwest. MKey 24: 84-88.

Food and utensil uses mentioned.

8887.   Wilson, Ellen Gibson. 1971. A West African cook book.   An introduction to good food from Ghana, Liberia, Nigeria and Sierra Leone.   New York: M. Evans.

8888.   Wilson, Gilbert Livingstone. 1917. Agriculture of the Hidatsa Indian. An Indian interpretation. UMinn-B-SSS No. 9.

Utsilago maydis a maize fungus, as food: p. 42; varieties of maize, and their uses: pp. 58-59; 60-67; breeding for new varieties: p. 66; sqash, cooked with squash blossoms: pp. 76-80; beans: pp. 85-86; European vegetables: pp. 119-120.

8889.   Wilson, H. Clyde. 1956. A new interpretation of the wild rice district of Wisconsin. AA 58: 1059-1064.

Refutes Jenks (1900) inclusion of Sak, Kickapoo, Fox, Mascouten, and Potawatome as wild rice gatherer's as well as his theory that wild rice was the basis for support of the high population density reported in the area northwest of Green Bay.

8890.   Wilson, J.S.G. 1966. The economic survey of the New Hebrides. GB-MOD-ORP DNo. 15.

Native subsistence agriculture: pp. 159-168.

8891.   Wilson, Jose. 1971. American cooking: the Eastern heartland; New York, New Jersey, Pennsylvania, Ohio, Michigan, Indiana, Illinois. New York: Time-Life Books. Foods of the World.

8892.   Wilson, Mary Margaret & Lamb, Mina W. 1968. Food beliefs as related to ecological factors in women. JHE 60:115-118.

How effective is nutrition education in combating food fallacies? This study suggests that although homemakers with home economics and nutriion training are not free from misconceptions about food, they are less acceepting than their peers in other disciplines. However, in this study, the largest group of participants who accepted false beliefs about food were college graduates.

8893. Wilson, Norman L. 1972. Notes on traditional Foothill Nisenan food technology. UCalD - CAR-P No. 3. Pp. 32-38.

8894. Wilson, Peter J. 1976. Chapter Three. La pensee alimentaire. In Our wits beginning. U Otago-DA-SPA No. 10.

Prehominid discrimination of available food types and its effects upon and implicaitons for hominid evolution.

8895. Wilson, R.L. 1959. Evidence in empty bottles. El Pal 66: 120-123.

Drinking habits at Fort Union, New Mexico, a frontier military post during the latter half of the 19th Century, as revealed by archeological excavation.

8896. Wilson, T. 1916. The use of wild plants as food by Indians. ON 30: 17-21.

Roots, shoots, leaves and berries used by native Americans of British Columbia.

8897. Wiltrock, Marion A. 1942. Food plants of the Indians. NYBG-J 43: 57-71.

8898. Windle, Jan. Feeding of infants in Japanese and American miiddle-class families. Master's thesis. Anthropology. Washington, D.C.: The American Unversity. 1968.

8899. Wing, Elizabeth S. Prehistoric fishing in the Carribbean. Paper presented at 67th Annual Meeting of the American Anthropological Association. 21 to 24 November, 1968. Seattle, Washington.

8900. Wing, Elizabeth S. Animal domestication in the Andes. Paper presented at the 9th International Congress of Anthropological and Ethnological Sciences. 28 August to 8 September, 1973. Chicago, Illinois.

8901. Wing, Elizabeth. Zooarcheology, diet and pre-Columbian relationships. Paper presented at 73rd Annual Meeting of the American Anthropological Association. 19 to 24 November, 1974.

8902. Wing, Elizabeth S. & Hammond, Norman. 1974. Fish remains in archaeology: a comment on Casteel. AMAn 39: 133-134.

Comment on the contention that fish remains can yield informantion on territorial exploitation; and the possibility of expanding this concept to include inferences about the technology required for the subsistence activity involved.

8903. Winner, D. 1945. Rationing during the Montana gold rush in 1864-65 PNQ 36: 115-120.

Food rationing.

8904. Winship, George Parker. 1896. The Coronado Expedition, 1540-1542. SI-BE-AR for the year 1892-1893. Pp. 339-598.

Food of the Pueblo tribes (uncooked meat): p. 506; blood: p. 527; maize grinding: p. 559.

8905. Winslow, C.E.A. & Herrington, L.P. 1936. Influence of oders on appetite. AJH 23: 143-156.

8906. Winstedt, Richard O. 1920. Rice ceremonies in Negeri Sembilan. FMSM-J 9: 122-128.

Malaysia

8907. Winstedt, Richard O. 1920. Rice ceremonies in Upper Perak. FMSM-J 9: 116-121.

Malaysia

8908. Winter, Elizabeth Kathleen. The nutritional adequacy of the diet of young Indian children of Okalahoma. Master's thesis. University of Oklahoma. 1958.

8909. Winter, Evelyne. 1972. Mexico's ancient and native remedies. Mexico City: Editorial Tournier.

Herbal remedies and others; includes abundant references to food used as medicine.

8910. Winter, Johanna Maria Van. 1966. Feestmalen in vroeger tyd. [Baquets in former times.] Voedingsniews No. 49. Pp. 658-671.

8911. Winter, Joseph C. Aboriginal agriculture in the Southwest and Great Basin. Ph.D. dissertation. Anthropology. University of Utah. 1974.

8912. Winter, Joseph C. & Wylie, Henry G. 1974. Palaeoecology and diet at Clydes Cavern. AmAn 39:303-315.

During the Fremont occupation, this Utah site is thought to have functioned as a farming and collecting station. Maize horticulture, and utilization of wild grass seeds is indicated by coprolite sequence and alluvial chronology.

8913. Winterhalder, Bruce. Optimal foraging in a patchy environment: an analysis of Cree hunting and gathering. Paper presented at 77th Annual Meeting of the American Anthropological Association. 14 to 18 November, 1978. Los Angeles, California.

8914. Winters, Jet Corrine. 1931. Comparative dietary studies of American children of nursery school age. AJPH 21:1003-1012.

Compares Hispanic-American; Black-American; and Anglo-American diets.

8915. Winters, Jet Corine. 1932. Diet of Mexicans living in Texas. JADA 8:47-55.

Analysis the nutritional adequacy of the diets of sixty-five Hispanic-American families living in San Antonio, and Austin, Texas. Includes description of dietary patterns;

food expenditure data; prenatal diets, and diets of preschool children.

8916.   Winters, Jet Corine. 1931. A report on the health and nutrition of Mexicans living in Texas. UTex-B No. 3127. BRSS-S No. 21.

8917.   Winton, Ivor. Prolegomena to the diffusion of winemaking in antiquity. Master's thesis. Geography. University of British Columbia. 1975.

8918.   Winton, Marianne Yvonne. The secular essential nature of diet of some South American Indian. Ph.D. dissertation. University of California, Berkeley, 1969.

Studies Native South American cultures in Colombia, and the Gran Chaco region of Argentina and Paraguay. The processes of biological evolution are currently affecting the evolution of Native South America populations. One factor influencing the processes is the availability of food in the cultural and physical environments. A survey of published information on food; its occurrence; and customary use among Native South American groups of Colombia and the Gran Chaco revealed that the subject had not been systematically studied. The available accounts do contain data that can be used as starting points and directions to structure future studies in human evolution with these contemporary people.

8919.   Winton, Marianne Yvonne. 1970. Nutritional adaptation of some Columbian indians. AJPA 32: 293-297.

Surveys food resources agriculture and hunting/fishing; and plant gathering) of the Choco, Kogi, Ika, Motilon, Guahiro, Guahibo, and Cubeo, with observations on the nutritional adequacy of diets.

8920.   Wise, John H. Food and its preparation. In Ancient Hawaiian civilization. A series of lectures delivered at the Kamehameha Schools. Edited by Helen Pratt. 1933. Pp. 95-103. Honolulu: the Kamehameha Schools. Reprint. Rutland, Vermont; Tokyo: Charles E. Tuttle. 1965.

8921.   Wise, John H. 1938. Hawaiian foods. HS-B 6 January; 13 January; 20 January; 27 January; 3 Fevruary; 10 February.

Based on a lecture delivered at the Kamehameha School titled "Food of early Hawaii".

8922.   Wiser, Charlotte Viall. 1937. The foods of a Hindu village of north India. AO-UP-SERB-B No. 2. Republished as 'The foods of and Indian village of north India.' MBG-A 42. No. 4. 1955.

The community studied is karimpur, located at 29.9N. Data were recorded during the years 1926-1931. Describes plant and animal food sources; spices; food costs; care of food at harvest time; food storage and preservation; food processing and preparation equipment; foods prepared from cereals;

legumes; green vegetables; fruit; animal foods-with description of preparation; feast foods; food taboos; prison diet in Agra and Oudh; the research of Robert McCarrison; availability of foods on a seasonal basis; survey of diets of four families of different castes; nutrition education. Two final sections discuss problems of food supply; use; and nutrition and their amelioration.

8923.   Wishard, John G. 1908. Twenty years in Persia. A narrative of life under the last three shahs. New York, Chicago, Toronto, London; Edinburgh: Fleming H. Revell.

Menu of a prosperous physician: p. 114; staple foods: pp. 115-116; fooods and food habits of prosperous Persians (Teheran): pp. 183-188.

8924.   Wishahy, Abdel Ghany. 1958. el labat: an Egytian vegetable milk. Review of the literature on vegetable milks. EMA-J 41: 433-438.

El labat is prepared from white sesame seed, chick pea, and cane sugar; for flavoring, rose water is added.

8925.   Wishahy, Abdel Ghany. 1958. Problems of dried milks in Egypt; preparation of similar formulae at home to feed the Egyptian infants. EMA-J 41: 353-360.

8926.   Wiskemann, Heinrich. 1859. Die Antike Landwirtschaft und das Thunen'sche Gesetz aus den alten Schriftstellen. [Ancient agricuture and Thunen's law from Old Testament passages] Liepzig: S. Hirzel.

8927.   Wissler, Clark. 1910. & Material culture of the Blackfoot Indians. AMNH-PA 5. Part 1.

Food preparation: pp. 21-27.

8928.   Wissler, Clark. 1918. idian corn is a world food. AMJ 18: 25-29.

8929.   Wiswe, Hans. 1964. Die Branntweinshale. Studien um ein Speisebrauchtum. [The brandy cup. Studies of a food custom.] BDVA 8: 61-82.

8930.   Wittfogel, Karl 1931. Wirtschaft und Gesellschaft Chinas. Erstes Teil. Produktions und Zirkulationsprozess. [Chinese economy and society. Part One. Production and circulation.] Leipzig: C.L. Hirschfield.

8931.   Witthoft, Felix Der Salz in Ozednien. [Salt in Oceania.] Ph. D. Dissertation. Hamburg Universitat. 1939. Reprint. Wurzburg: Buchdruckerei R. Mayr. 1939.

8932.   Witthoft, John. 1946. The Cherokee green corn medicine and the Green Corn Festival. WAS-J 36: 213-219.

North Carolina.

8933.   Wittmack. L. 1880.   Ubver antiken Mais aus Nord-und Sud-Amerika.   [On ancient maize from North and South America.]   ZE 12: 85-97.

8934.   Wittmack, L.   Die Nutzpflanzen der alten Peruaner.   [The useful plants of the ancient Preuvian.]   Septieme Congres International des Americanistes.   1888, Berlin.   1890. Pp. 325-348.   Berlin: Librairie W.H. Kuhl.

Cereals and other bread sources; tubers; vegetables; fruit.

8935.   Witzig, Louise.   1953.   Figurliches Festgeback.   [Shaped holiday baked goods.]   Heimatleben 26: 72-75.

8936.   Woenig, Franz.   1886.   Die pflanzen im alten agypten.   Ihre heimat, Geschichte, Kultur und Ihre mannigfache Verwendung im sozialen Leben, im Kultus, sitten, gerbrauchen, medizin, runst.   Nach den eigenen bildlich Darstellungen der alten Aegypter, pflanzenresten aus Graberfunden zeugnissen alter schrifttsteller und den Ergebinssen der Neuren forschungen.   Mit zahlreichen Original Abbildungen.   [Plants in ancient Egypt.   Their provenience, cultivation, and their various uses in social life, cult, customs, brewing, medicine, art.   From the original graphic descriptions of the ancient Egyptians; plant remains from the burial finds; evidence of ancient writers, and the results of the latest research.   With numerous original illustration.   Leipzig, Friederich.

8937.   Wohlcke, Manfred.   1974-1975.   Ernahrung und gesundheit in einem entwicklungsland: Brasilien.   [Nutrition and health in a developing nation: Brazil]   Ethnomedizin 3: 81-109.

The areas of nutrition, health, aspirations, medical assistance and domestic hygiene are examined, with supporting statistics.   The author suggests a model for development (desenvolvimento) based on conditions obtaining in Brazil.

8938.   Wohltman, Ferdinand.   1904.   Kultur-und vegetations bilder aus unseren Deutschen Colonien.   [Illustrations of the vegetation and plant life of our German colonies.]   Berlin: Suserott.

8939.   Wohltman, Ferdinand.   1904.   Pflanzung und Siedlung auf Samoa.   Erkundungsbericht an das Kolonia wirtschaft komitee zu Berlin.   [Plantation and colony in Samoa.   Exploratory report of the Colonial Economy Committee of Berlin.]   Berlin: E.S. Mittler & Sohn.

8940.   Wolberg, Lewis Robert.   1936.   The psychology of eating.   London: George C. Harrap; New York: Robert M. McBride; Toronto: George J. McLeod.

Reviewed in BRD 1937: 1067; SOR 1 June: 10 (1937); LT-LS 19 June: 466 (1937).

8941.   Wolf, Carl B.   1945.   California wild tree crops.   Santa Ana Canyon, Orange County, California: Rancho Santa Ana Botanic Garden of the Native Plants of California.

Refers to Native American use of products of the Joshua Tree (Yucca brevifolia); oak (Quercus sp.); and California 'buckeye' (Aesculus californica) for food Undocumented.

8942.   Wolf, Faith J.   A study of the diets of homemakers in a West Virginia mining community.   Master's thesis.   Ohio State University.   1948.

8943.   Wolf, R.   1884.   Kochbuch fur israelitischen Frauen...mit genauer Answeisung zur Fuhrung einer religios-judischen Haushaltung.   [Cookbook for Jewish women, with detailed instrutions for setting up and conducting a religious Jewish household.]

8944.   Wolfe, C.B.   1961.   Kwashiorkor on the Navajo Indian reservation.   HFHMB 9:566-569.

8945.   Wolfe, Kenneth A.   Foraging behavior of the Arashiyama West Japanese macacques.   Paper presented at 73rd Annual Meeting of the American Anthropological Association.   19 to 24 November, 1974.   Mexico City.

8946.   Wolfe, Linda.   1972.   The cooking of the Caribbean Islands.   Revised edition.   New York: Time-Life Books.   Foods of the World.

8947.   Wolff, M.P.   1884.   Food for the millions.   A plan for starting public kitchens.   With statistical tables, calculations of the prices of thirty-six dishes, statement of the starting expense, the yearly current expenditure, the gross and net profits of a public kitchen, and a ground-plan.   London: S. Low, Marston, Searle & Pivington.

8948.   Wolff, R.J.   Food habits in Malaya: observations and comments.   Mimeographed.   University of California International Center for Medical Research and Training.   Kuala Lumpur: Institute for Medical Research.   1963.

8949.   Wolff, R.J.   1965.   Meanings of food.   1965.   TGM 17:450-451.

8950.   Wong, Sau-chun.   1937.   Chinese temples in Honolulu.   SPH 3:27-35.   Also in Community forces in Hawaii.   Readings from Social Process In Hawaii.   Edited by Bernhard L Hormann.   1968.   2nd edition.   Honolulu: Sociology Club Publication.   University of Hawaii.

Refers to propitiatory foods used in worship, including jai, a vegetable preparation eaten during the New Year feast, and by vegetarian nuns and monks.

8951.   Wong, Wesley.   The folk medicine of Blanchisseuse, Trinidad.   Master's thesis.   Anthropology.   Cambridge, Massachusetts: Brandeis University.   1967.

8952.   Wood, Alice L.   1955.   The history of artificial infant feeding.   JADA 31:472-482.

Early records of wet-nursing and artificial feeding; Europe: Middle Ages to 1800; early Nineteenth Century; first proprietary foods;   preservation and modification of milk; evol ution of the feeding bottle; sanitary milk supply; deficiency diseases.

8953.   Wood, Arthur William. Food in the Jamaican economy, 1900-1950. Ph.D. dissertation. Stanford University. 1956.

Seeks to determine whether the economic level of the people of Jamaica has been adversely affected by growing population pressure over the period stated. The general pattern of the dietary and an approximation of the per capita daily supply of calories and protein are presented in a food balance sheet for the average annual food supply for 1946-1950. Changes in per capita supplies of a number of important foods are deduced from import statistics plus estimates of domestic supplies of a few important foods over the first five decades of the Twentieth Century. Changes in population growth, age, and gender composition are examined in order to provide a basis for assessing the significance of changes in the food supply.

8954.   Wood, Bertha M.   1929.   Foods of the foreign-born; in relation to health. 2nd ed. Boston: M. Barrows & Company.

Recipes of immigrant Americans, with nutritional evaluations.

8955.   Wood, Charles L. 1959. How the chaplain and the dietitian can cooperate JADA 35: 821-822.

Possible role for clergy to interpret food restrictions and provide therapeutic spiritual support for hospital patients.

8956.   Woodbury, Richard Benjamin. 1961. Climatic changes and prehistoric agriculture in the Southwestern United States. NYAS-A 95: 705-709.

Review of archeological evidence for staple food production in relation to climate fluctuation.

8957.   Woodbury, Richard Benjamin 1961. Prehistoric agriculture at Point of Pines, Arizona. ASS-M 26(3). Part 2.

8958.   Woodbury, Richard Benjamin.   1961.   A reappraisal of Hohokam irrigation. AA 63: 550-560.

Account of archeological excavations of the canals, and some theoretical interpretations of evidence regarding origin and function. Southern Arizona.

8959.   Woodbury, Robert Morse. 1942. Food consumption and dietary surveys in the Americas; results - methods. Report presented by the International Labour Office to the Eleventh Pan American Sanitary Conference. 7-18 September, 1942. Rio de Janeiro. Montreal: International Labour Office.

8960.   Woodman, H.M. 1947. Nutrition in the African tsetse-fly areas. EAMJ 24: 315-336.

8961.   Wooodman, H.M. 1950. Nutrition in the southern Sudan. RSTMH-T 44: 231-232.

8962.   Woodruff, C.W. & Hoerman, K. 1960. Nutrition of infants and preschool children in Ethiopia. USDHEW-PHR 75: 724-730.

8963.   Woods, C.D. & Mansfield, E.R. 1904. Studies of the food of Maine lumbermen. USDA-OES-B 149.

Provides a descriptive background of the lumber camp; the lumbering operation; daily routine; food preparation; with nutritional and metabolic analyses of the recored diets.

8964.   Woods, Ruth. 1951-1952. The problem of rice eating populations in the Orient. BRNR 12: 115-120. 13: 13-28.

8965.   Woodward, Mary Margaret. A recommended educational program in nutrition, based on a survey of selected rural families in Josephine County, Oregon. Master's thesis. Oregon State College. 11943.

8966.   Woodward, P. Attitudes toward the use of soybeans as food. United States. Mimeographed. Committtee on Food Habits. National Research Council. Washington, D.C. : National Academy of Sciences. October, 1943.,

8967.   Woodward, Siiri. Anexamination of Palestinian protoneolithic cultural materials and environment in the light of the broader problem of the evolution of food production and settled life in southwest Asia. Master's thesis Anthropology. University of Pennsylvania. 1964.

8968.   Woodworth, Robert H. 1943. Economic plants of St. John, U.S. Virgin Islands. HU-BML 11: 29-54.

Food plants: pp. 30-35.

8969.   Woodworth, W.M. 1907. The palolo worm. Eunice viridis (Gray). HU-MCZ-B 51. No. 1.

A sea worm used for human food. This report provides a review of accounts of the food use of E. viridis published in European languages; a full zoological description of the worm; and ethnographic data on its use as food in Samoa, and Fiji.

8970.   Woolfe, Jennifer A.; Wheeler, Erica F.; Dyke, Wilhelmina van; & Oraca-Tetteh, R. 1977. The vaue of the Ghanaian trditional diet in relation to the energy needs of young children. EFN 6:175-181.

Includes descriptions of staple food preparations: p. 176; typical meals: p. 177; and staple foods and food combinations: p. 180.

8971.   Woolsey, Anne I., & Hole, Frank. Pollen evidence of subsistence and environment in ancient Iran: palynology supplements paleobotanical studies and adds data on problems on problems of domestication and prehistoric land use. Paper presented at

77th Annual Meeting of the American Anthropological Association. 14 to 18 November, 1978. Los Angeles, California.

8972.   Woolston, F.P.   1973.   Ethnobotanical items for the Wellesly Island, Gulf of Carpentaria. UQn-AM-OP No. 1. Pp. 95-103.

Wellesly Island is located off the extreme northwestern coast of Queensland, Australia.

8973.   Worl, Rosita.   An ethnoscientific analysis of the contemporary Tlingit potlatch system within a changing social structure. Paper presented at 73rd Annual Meeting of the American Anthropological Association. 19 to 24 November, 1974. Mexico City.

8974.   Worthington, E.B.   1936.   On the food and nutrition of African natives. Africa 9:150-165.

Review of clinical and sociological nutrition activities.

8975.   Worthington, E.B. & Cazanne, J.L.F.   1937. The food and nutrition of African. IIALC-M No. 13.

8976.   Wrangham, R.W.   Feeding behavior of chimpanzees in Gombe National Park, Tanzania. In Primate ecology; feeding and ranging behavior of lemurs, monkey and apes. Edited by T.H. Clutton-Brock. 1977. London: Academic Press.

8977.   Wrench, Guy Theodore.   1946.   Chapter Three. The Roman foods. Reconstruction by way of the soil. London: Faber & Faber Ltd.

A review of Roman diet based on data contained in Hintze (1934). The author characterizes Roman diet as lacto-vegetarian, until the period of empire when, for the upper class, a great variety of imported foods, especially animal protein, became available. The diet of the lower urban classes apparently retained a whole meal, vegetarian character.

8978.   Wreszinski, Walter.   1926. Backerei. [Baking.] ZASA 61:1-15.

Excerpts from Egyptian hieroglyphic writings on the art of baking.

8979.   Wright, A.C.A.   1949.   Maize names as indicators of economic contacts. UJ 13:61-81.

Documents the points of origin; directions of dispersal; and relative age of maize in Africa by means of comparative linguistics.

8980.   Wright, Carlton E.   1962.   Food buying: marketing information for consumers. New York: Macmillan.

Consumer; food; family spending; food expenditures; food supply and transportation; food markets; changes in eating habits; seasonal supply: influence on cost; food bargains; cost per serving; planning and shopping for meals.

8981.   Wright, Jr., Henry E.   Natural environment of early food production north of Mesopotamia. Science 161:334-339.

Discusses climate changes, ca. 11,000 B.P., which may have permitted a change from food collecting to primitive farming. Data base is palynological material.

8982.   Wright, Henry T.; Bokonyi, Sandor; Flannery, Kent V.; & Mayhall, John. 1969. The administration of rural production in an early Mesopotamian town. UMich-MA-AP No. 38.

Based on archeological excavation of a site at Ur; and data from cuneiform documents. Extensive information on early food production technology, food resources; and agricultural practices.

8983.   Wright, Lawrence. 1964. Home fires burning: the history of domestic heating and cooking. London: Routledge.

8984.   Wright, Mabel Osgood. 1926. My New York kitchen days in the Sixties, Jefferson Market, street cries, wedding cake, etc. New York: Macmillan.

8985.   Wright, Richardson Little. 1927. Hawkers and walkers in early America. Strolling peddlers, preachers, lawyers, doctors, players, and others from the beginning to the Civil War. Philadelphia: J.B. Lippincott.

Street cries of: seafood; fruit, vegetables, hominy, pepper, sweet potatoes, hot maize, pastry, gingerbread peddlers: pp. 235-238; Gullah chicken peddlers; porgy peddlers in Charleston, South Carolina: pp. 239-240; confections: New Orleans: p. 240.

8986.   Wright, S. 1847. Dirt eating. Enormous quantity of Fuller's earth eaten in the space of a year-and-a-half. MTimes 16:265-267.

8987.   Wright, W.G. 1913. Edible flowers. PP 9:141-142.

Lily flowers,; pickled banana blossom (China); dried Calligonum polygonoides (Afghanistan).

8988.   Wright-St. Clair, R.E. 1969. Early accounts of Maori diet and health. NZMJ 70:327-331; 415-419.

8989.   Wright-St. Clair, R.E. 1972. Diet of the Maoris of New Zealand. EFN 213-223.

This paper provides a description of native New Zealand food patterns as recorded by early voyagers and other observers during the Eighteenth and Nineteenth Centuries. The state of Maori health at contact, and its slow degeneration as a result of increased use of non-indigenous foods, is recorded.

8990.   Wu, H. 1927. Chinese diet in the light of modern knowledge of nutrition. CSPR 11:56-81.

Presents data in support of the view that the Chinese population as qualitatively underfed.

8991. Wu, H. & D.Y. 1928. Study of dietaries in Peking. CJP 1:135-152.

8992. Wu, Hsien. Nutritional deficiencies in China and southeast Asia. In Fourth International congresses on Tropical Medicine and Malaria. Washington, D.C., 10 May to 18 May, 1948. Proceedings. Vol. 2. Pp. 1217-1224. Washington, D.C.: Department of State.

8993. Wuerffel, Stella. 1968. Nutrition work among the Sioux. JADA 53:113.

Reviews traditional diet, and the effects of refined Western diet on nutrition and present health.

8994. Wuhr, Hans. 1961. Altes Essgerat. Loffel, Messer, Gabel. [Old eating utensils. [Tablespoons, knives, forks.] Darmstadt: Schneekluth.

8995. Wurmbach, Anne Marie. 1960. Kuchen. Fladen, Torte; eine-wort-und sachkundliche untersuchung. [Flatcakes; a specialized philological inquiry.] ZV 61:20-40.

Etymologies; usage; and distribution of three words for a flat cake.

8996. Wurtenberger, Otto. 1917. Die erdnuss (Arachis hypogaea). Ihre geschichte, geographische verbreitung und wirtshcaftliche bdeutung. [The groundnut (Arachis hypogaea). Its history, geographical distribution, and agricultural significance.] BeiTrop 213:27-201.

8997. Wurzburg, O.B. 1952. Root starches other than those of white and sweet potato. EB 6:211-215.

Tapioca (manioc); sago; and arrowroot. Contains information on processing and food use; chemistry; and production, yield, and importation statistics.

8998. Wyatt, Laura Jane. A review of methods used in nutrition education. Master's thesis. University of Minnesota at St. Paul. 1947.

8999. Wyckoff, D. Daryl & Sasser, W. Earl. 1979. The Chain restaurant industry. Lexington, Massachusetts: Lexington Books.

A selection of case studies of corporate situations and management decision-making processes regarding restaurant industry issues. Businesses included are Victoria Station, Inc.; Benihana of Tokyo; Brighton Fish Pier; Wendy's Old Fashioned Hamburgers; Waffle House, Inc.; MacDonald's Corp.; and Dobbs House.

9000. Wyczanski, Andrezej. 1960. Uwagi o konsumpcji zwaynosci w Polsce 16 w. [Remarks on the consumption of foodstuffs in Poland during the 16th Century.] KHKM 8:15-39.

9001. Wylie, J.C. 1903. Mrs. Washington's "Book of Cookery". PMHB 27:436-440.

Extracts froma cookbook written by Mrs. Frances Parke Curtis and handed down through the family of the first president of the United States.

9002. Wyman, Leland Clifton, & Bailey, Flora L. 1964. Navajo Indian ethnoentomology. Albuquerque: University of New Mexico Press.

The only insect mentioned as used for food is the cicada: pp. 41-42.

9003. Wyman, Leland Clifton & Harris, Stuart K. 1951. Ethnobotany of the Kayenta Navajo. An analysis of the John and Louisa Wetherill ethnobotanical collection. UNM-PB No. 5.

9004. Wyndham, W.T. 1890. Australian aborigines, varieties of food and methods of obtaining it. RSNSW-TP 24:112-120.

9005. Wynne-Tyson, Jon. 1975. Food for a future: the ecological priority of a humane diet. London: Davis-Poynter.

Supports the view that vegetarianism is the appropriate alternative to current animal-protein based diets.

9006. Xabregas, J. & Nunes, P. 1959. Legumes in native Angolan diet. [In Portuguese.] Agros 42:324-325.

9007. Xolocotzi, Efraim Hernandez. 1949. Maize granaries in Mexico. HU-BML 13:153-192.

An indepth historical-geographical study of maize storage technology and architecture. The article is illustrated with photographs of modern structures, and by several reproductions from the Codex Mendoza, and from Sahagun.

9008. Yabuka, Isao. no date. The special foods of Tokyo. Tokyo: Foreign Affairs Association of Japan.

9009. Yacovleff, Eugenio & Herrera, Fortunata L. 1934. El mundo vegetal de las antiguos peruanos. [The plant world of the ancient Peruvians.] RMN 3:241-322.

9010. Yamada, Ryuji. 1959. The research group of rice culture-and-its-peoples, in Southeast Asia. SJin 2:65-67.

9011. Yamaguchi, Sadao, ed. 1938. Sanson seikatsu no kenkyu. [The study of mountain village life.] Tokyo: Minkondensho no kai.

Includes a chapter on food which covers the names of meals; meal composition; food preparation; festival meals; religious significance of ceremonial banquets.

9012. Yanagita, Junio. 1940. Momen izen no koto. [Before the use of cotton.] Tokyo: Sogen-sha.

Mochi (glutinous) rice, and rice mortars; meals and ceremonial meals; history of the mortar (usu) used to prepare mochi; uses of mochi in Japanese cookery; ritual significance of mochi; pp. 95-137. Changes in the manner of drinking sake; ancient method of brewing sake; ritual consumption of sake: pp. 181-198. [In Japanese.]

9013.   Yanagita, Kunio.   1940.   Shokumotsu to shinzo. [Food and the heart.] Sogen sensho. Vol 45. Tokyo: Sogen-Sha.

Contains five articles on food. One. Ritual mochi (glutinous) rice cake preparation: pp. 1-32. Two. Mochi as remedy; its use in soup. Three. Ritul use of sake (rice wine) and salt in marriages on Amami Oshima Island. Four. Noon meal and mid-afternoon meal. Five. Meal preparation and meal sequence.

9014.   Yanagita, Kunio.   Individual freedom concerning foods. [In Japanese.] In Meji-Taisho shi. Vol. four. Seison Hen. [History of the Meiji and Taisho Periods. Vol. Four. Social conditions.] Revised edition. 1971. Pp. 39-77. Tokyo: Asahi-shinbunsha.

Discusses the followig subjects: nutrition and civilization; coookery in antiquity; role of women in development of foods and cooking; rice in Japanese diet; preparation of fish, and Japanese-style meats; meals eaten away from home.

9015.   Yang, En-fu. Nutritional evaluation of cereal diets, with general discussion of nutrition problems in China. In Science and mankind. No. 1. Hunger and food. Edited by Josue de Castro. 1958. Pp. 83-92. London: World Federation of Scientific Workers.

9016.   Yang, M.G.   Mickelsen, Olaf; Campbell, M.E.; Laqueur, G.L.; & Keresztesy, J.C. 1966. cycad flour used by Guamanians: effects produced in rats by long-term feeding. JN 90: 153-156.

Use of cycad flour produced in Guam, and detoxified by local methods of soaking, did not cause lesions. Indications are that local detoxification procedures, if properly performed, removes the carcinogenic glucoside cycasin.

9017.   Yang, M.G. & Mickelsen, Olaf. Cycads. In toxic constituents of plant foodstuffs. Edited by Irvin E. Liener. 1969.   Pp. 159-167. New York, London: Academic Press.

Leaves, seeds, stems, and tuberous underground portions of cycads are used as food in the Malay Peninsula, parts of the Philippines, Indonesia, and Guam. A toxic principle cycasin is present in the seeds which is carcinogenic although, where used as food, the seeds are soaked to eliminate the toxin.

9018.   Yanovsky, Elias. 1936. Food plants of the North American Indians. USDA-MP No. 237.

9019.   Yanovsky, Elias & Kingsbury, M.   1938. Analyses of some Indian food plants. AOAC-J 21: 648-665.

Native North American.

9020.   Yarnell, Richard A. 1963. Comments on Streuver's discussion of an early "Eastern agricultural complex". AmAn 28: 547-548.

9021.   Yarnell, Richard A. 1964. Aboriginal relationships between culture and plant life in upper Great Lakes region. U Mich-AM-AP No.23.

9022.   Yarnell, Richard A. 1965. Early Woodland plant remains and the question of cultivation. Fla Anth 18: 77-82.

9023.   Yarnell, Richard A. Wild Plant remains. In The McGraw site, a study in Hopewellian dynamics. Edited by Olaf H. Prufer. 1965. CleveMNH-SP Vol. 4, No. 1 Pp. 113-114.

9024.   Yarnell, Richard A. Evidence from Salt's Cave for independent evolution of plant cultivation in eastern North American woodlands. Paper presented at 70th Annual Meeting of the American Anthropological Association. 20 November, 1971. New York City.

Recent excavations in the vestibule of Salt's Cave, Mammoth Cave National Park, Kentucky, have resulted in the discovery of a stratigraphic sequence of deposits, some of which contain evidence of human occupation. Economic plant remains in the upper occupational strata include hickory nut, gourd, squash, sunflower, sumpweed (Iva annua), Chenopodiaceae; and Maygrass. The lower occupation levels include essentially the same remains but with the conspicuous absence of gourd and squash, and should probably be considered late Archaic in origin.

9025.   Yarnell, Richard. Intestinal contents of the Salt's Cave mummy and analysis of the initial Salt's Cave flotation series. In The archaeology of the Mammoth Cave area. Edited by P.J. Watson. 1974. New York: Academic Press.

9026.   Yates, Lucy M. 1908. Food and fare in Italy. Epicure 15: 72.

9027.   Yde, J. 1957. The agricultural level of the Waiwai Indians. Timehri 36: 23-35.

Amazonian Brazil.

9028.   Yearsley, Ellen. 1960. Nutrition in the Canadian north. NAB 7: 30-33.

Dietary patterns of Anglo-Canadian and Eskimo populations at Frobisher Bay, Baffin Island, recorded during the year 1958-1959. Comments that Eskimo nutritional problems have occurred as a result of "haphazard and badly managed integration with Southern culture: (p.32).

9029.   Yee, Rhoda. 1977. Dim sum San Francisco, California: Taylor & Ng.

An illustrated recipe book for steamed or fried dumplings served in Chinese luncheon or tea parlors. The etiquette of the tea houses is explained, and anecdotes relating to dim sum included.

9030.   Yen, Douglas E. 1959. The use of maize by the New Zealand Maoris. EB 13: 319-127.

The only European vegetable introductions which have been absorbed by the Maoris as standard items are potatoes, squash, and maize. The one use of maize developed by the Maoris which has been considered unique is the process of fermenting in water prior to eating. This process is similar to one occurring in the Sierra of Ancash, Peru. A brief description of water processing of other Maori foods (both plant and marine) is included.

9031.   Yen, Douglas E. 1960. the sweet potato in the Pacific: the propagation of the plant in relation to its distribution. JPS 69: 368-375.

9032.   Yen, douglas E. 1961. The adaptation of Kumara by the New Zealand Maori. JPS 70: 338-348.

9033.   Yen, Douglas. Indigenous food processing in Oceania. Paper presented at 9th International Congress of Anthropological and Ethnological Sciences. 28 August to 8 September, 1973. Chicago, Illinois.

Discusses the extraction and preparation of sago (Metroxylon sp.); the pounding of root-, and tree-crops; the fermentation of root-, and tree-crops; the geographical distribution of plants and processing techniques, in terms of adequacy; population; and the attainment of surplus, and attempts to view them in the light of their influences on social organization.

9034.   Yen, Douglas E. Indigenous food processing in Oceania. In Gastronomy. The anthropology of food and food habits. Edited by Margaret louise Arnott. 1975. Pp. 147-168. Paris; the Hague: Mouton Publishers. World Anthropology.

Three basic processes are defined: pounding, fermenting, and drying, and their distribution charted. Consideration is given to the possible historical influences responsible for Oceanian food technology. Two areas in the Pacific are examined: Santa Cruz, in the eastern Solomon Islands, and Anuta, a small Polynesian outlier in Melanesia, in relation to food production and distribution, and cultural and environmental factors influencing the former. The Santa Cruz Islands are located at approximately 166.0W., 15.0S.

9035.   Yengoyan, Aram. Sugar and poverty. Paper read at 74th Annual Meeting of the American Anthropological Association. 2 to 6 December, 1975. San Francisco, California.

9036.   Yeo, Eileen & Thompson, E.P. 1972. The unknown Mayhew. New York: Schocken books.

Diets of London working class (by occupation) during the year 1849-1850: passim; prices of foods (retail) in London, during the year 1849-1850: pp. 481-483.

9037.   Yesner, David. Nutrition and cultural evolution: patterns in prehistory. Paper presented at 72nd Annual Meeting of the American Anthropological Association. 1 December, 1973. New Orleans, Louisiana.

9038.   Yesner, David. Nutrition and population dynamics of hunter-gatherers. Paper presented at 74th Annual Meeting of the American Anthropological Association. 2 to 6 December, 1975. San Francisco, California.

9039.   Yetly, Elizabeth Ann D. A causal-mode analysis of food behavior. Ph. D. dissertation. Iowa State University. 1974.

9040.`   Yien, Shih-chi. 1918. Beans and bean products. Biology Department. Shanghai: Soochow University.

9041.   Ying, Li-yu & Grandvoinnet, L. 1912. Le soja, sa culture. Ses usages alimentaires, therapeutiques, agricoles et industriels. [The soybean. Its food, therapeutic, agricultural and industrial uses.] Paris: Challamel.

9042.   Ying, Ting. 1959. Examination of rice husk found in red baked earth of the Neolithic period in the Chiang Han Plain. KKHP 4: 31-34.

9043.   Yo, Ba-ba. 1937. Actual food consumption and average diet of   natives of Formosa. [In Japanese.] TIZ 36: 2585-2588.

9044.   Yoder, Don. 1971. Historical sources for American foodways research and plans for an American foodways archive. EScan 1971. Pp. 41-55.

Focuses specifically on the cookery and food habits of the Pennsylvania "Dutch", with suggestions for the collection of regional food habits data, and a national food museum.

9045.   Yoder, Don. 1972. Folk cookery, folklore and folklife. Chicago: University of Chicago Prewss.

9046.   Young, E.G. 1941.   A dietary survey in Halifax. CPHJ 32: 236-240.

Nova Scotia, Canada.

9047.   HYoung, E.G. 1942. Food consumption and preferences of families with low-incomes in Halifax NS. CPHJ 33: 480-485.

Nova Scotia.

9048.   Young, Elizabeth. A study of food consumption at the University of Tennesses cafeteria, 1938-1947. Master's thesis.   University of Tennessee. 1948.

9049.   Young, Katherine. A study of some of the food storage practices used by 75 families in Travis county Texas. Master's thesis. University of Texas. 1944.

9050.   Young, E.G.   1948.   Canadian dietary patterns. RSC-PT. 42: 1-23.

9051.   Young, J.H. 1968. The science and morals of metabolism: catsup and benzoate of soda. JHM 23: 86-104.

> Account of Harvey Wiley's experiments with sodium benzoate, a once popular food preservative, which preceded passage of the historic Pure Food and Drug Act of 1906.

9052.   Young, Michael W. 1971. Fighting with food: leadership, values and social control in a Massim Society. London, New York: Caambridge University Press.

> Explores the role of food in redressing wrongs, through abutu food exchanges and redistributions. Offenses are publicized, and shame effected by giving a recipient more and better food than can be immediately returned. Goodenough Island, D; Entrecastaux Archipelago, New Guinea. Reviewed by Sharon W. Young. AA 76: 602, 603. (1974).

9053.   Young, Paul Thomas. 1948. Appetite, palatability, and feeding habits, a criticial review. PB 45:289-320.

> A review of research related to the physiology of food intake. Discusses bodily needs and homeostasis (dietary requirements); nutritive instincts; dependence of food acceptance upon the organic state; sickness and health; hunger and thirst; satiation and deprivation in food selection; palatability and the environmental determinants of food acceptance; experimental methods for the anlaysis of food acceptance; motiviation of food-seeking and food selecting behavior; (local-stimulus theory of internal drive); the nature of specific food-seeking drives and food-selecting behavior; basis of feeding habits; affective psychology and the science of nutrition.

9054.   Young, Paul Thomas. 1949. Food-seeking drive, affective process, and learning. Psych Rev 56:98-121.

9055.   Young, Paul Thomas. 1957. Psychological factors regulating the feeding process. AJCN 5:154-161.

> Concludes that appetite, as a combination psycholoigcal and psysiological varaibles, cannot be relied upon too strongly as a guide to correct nutrition, and that nutritional

science must supplement the innate patterns of food selection. Strictly scientifically-planned diets, however, must also take into account the importance of the psychological dimenson in dietary choice.

9056.   Young, Stella. Slaughtering a goat and using it Navajo fashion. Mimeographed. A school project set up and developed at the Charles H. Burke Indian School, Deparment of Home Economics, Fort Wingate, New Mexico. 1934.

9057.   Young, Stella. Growing and using Indian corn Navajo fashion. Bulletin 4. Mimeographed. Fort Wingate, New Mexico: Charles H. Burke Indian School. 1936.

9058.   Young, Stella. Native plants used by the Navajo. U.S. Department of the Interior. Office of Indian Affairs.   Home Economics Department. Mimeographed.   Fort Wingate, New Mexico: Wingate Vocational High School. 1938.

9059.   Younger, William Anthony. 1966. Gods, men, and wine. London: Wine and Food Society.

> History of wine and wine-making.

9060.   Yousif, Mamoun. 1967. Nutritional study of Hag Yousif rural community. (Sudan). TGM 19:192-198.

9061.   Yudkin, John. 1956. Man's choice of food. Lancet 270:645-649.

> Enumerates factors which determine food choices: availability factors (geography; season; economics; food technology; fuel); social factors (religion; social customs; social class; education in nutrition and hygiene; advertising); physiological factors (heredity; allergy; therapeutic diets; food acceptability; nutritional needs). Considers the role of physical status (age; pregnancy; pathology), in relation to dietary choice. Discusses satiety in relation to cultural transmission of dietary patterns.

9062.   Yudkin, John. History and the nutritionist. In Our changing fare. Edited by T.C. Barker; John C. McKenzie; & John Yudkin. 1966. London: MacGibbon & Kee.

9063.   Yudkin, John. Physiological determinants of food choice. In Diet of man: needs and wants. Edited by John Yudkin. 1978. Pp. 24-260. London: Applied Science Publishers.

> In this paper, the first section discusses factors of food availiability and economic means as antecedent variables determining the food choice. Further discussion focuses upon perception of particular foods as health-giving ("health foods"); and evidence for a nutritional instinct; followed by a review of classic experiments concerned with food choice among laboratory animals and human subjects. The author emphasizes the importance of organoletpic qualities as decision-making criteria in the evolution

and maintenance of food habits; and implies that there is little basis for assuming that humans -in the face of a wide range of both nutritionally high and low quality foods-will instinctively select a beneficial diet.

9064.   Yudkin, John & McKenzie, John Crawford. eds.   1964.   Changing food habits.   London: MacGibbon & Kee.

9065.   Yukawa, Genyo. Uber die absolut vegetarische Ernahrung japanishcher Bonzen. 1 & 2. [On the exclusively vegetarian diet of Japanese monks.] Parts 1 & 2.] AVSPD 15:471-524; 609-646.

Exhaustively supoorted by statistics on food consumption.

9066.   Yukawa, Genyo. 1913. Bericht uber die absolut vegetarische Ernahrung japanischer Bonzen. 3 & 4. [Report on the exclusively vegetarian diet of Japanese monks. Parts 3 & 4.] AVSPD 19:356-370.

9067.   Yutaka, Jono. 1927. The vitamin content of a few food plants in Manchuria. JOM 6:55.

Plants analyzed include kaoling (Andropogon sorghum); hoan-pao-mi (Zea mays, L.); shao-mi (Setaria italica).

9068.   Zabilka, Gladys. 1963. Chapter Nine. Food. In Customs and cultures of the Philippines. Tokyo; Rutland, Vermont: Charles E. Tuttle.

Contains three recipes, and brief descriptions of some fruits and vegetables.

9068.   Zaborowski, A. Marie, & Zaborowski, G. Cannibalisme et avitaminose. [Cannibalism and avitaminosis.] In 15^{e} Congres International d'Anthropologie & d'Archelogie Prehistorique. 20-27 Septembre 1931. Paris. 1933. Pp. 645-657. Paris: Libraire E. Nourry.

Discusses the possibility that, under certain circumstances, cannibalism may be a response to vitamin deficiencies. Includes references to cases of psychopathological cannibalism in Europe during the 19th Century, and their association with certain somatopathological conditions.

9070.   Zaky, Ahmed & Zaky, Iskander 1942. Ancient Egyptian cheese. E-SAnt-A 41: 295-313.

9071.   Zaneveld, Jacques S. 1959. The utilization of marine algae in tropical south and east Asia. EB 13; 89-131.

Notes food uses throughout.

9072.   Zapletal, Vincenz. 1920. Der Wein in der Bibel. Kulturgeschichtliche und exegetische Studie. [Wine in the Bible. Culture-historical and exegetical study.] Biblische Studien. Vol. 20. Freiburg i. B.

9073.   Zappacosta, Mariea E. 1957. La vitivinicultura de Mendoza. [The grape wine culture of Mendoza.] IL-A 6: 375-425.

The Department of Mendoza is located in northwest-central Argentina.

9074.   Zarur, George de Cerqueira Liete. Seafood gatherers in Mullet Springs: economic rationality and the social system. Ph. D. dissertation, Anthropology. University of Florida. 1975.

This dissertation attempts to explain the differential economic behavior of seafood gatherers of different social classes in a small village on the Gulf Coast of Florida. It was observed that those seafood gatherers who have access to external markets are those whose behavior conforms to the traditional view of "economic rationality", in the sense that they organize production in a way that results in a maximization of profit and a minimization of costs . This is possible by cooperation of those gatherers in productive activities with members of their kinship groups or with hired help. Those gatherers who do no have access to external markets tend not to work with others and act in a way that may be considered "economically irrational". The Mullet Spring gatherers' behavior is compared with studies of peasantries which have observed "economically rational" behavior.

9075.   Zaunick, R. 1917. Uber "mehlerde" in Anhaltischen 1617. [Earth-flour as used in Anhalt 1617. NatWoch 16: 496.

Anhalt was a former state in central Germany, the capital of which was Dessau. In 1863, its several principalities were united in one duchy.

9076.   Zdanovski, N. 1947. Pasnjarstvo i mjelkarstvo u sjenicko-pesterskom kraju. [Pasture conditions and dairy economy in the Sjenica-Pester region.] Stocarstvo 1: 468-474.

Sjenica is located in southcentral Yugoslavia at 43.16N., 20.0E.

9077.   Zega, A. & Majstorovie, R. 1899. Der mais als Vlksnahrung in Servien. [Maize in Serbian national diet.] CZ 23: 544-545.

9078.   Zeitlin, Judith F. Strategies of subsistence and exchange production among local groups of the southern Isthmus of Tehuantepec. Paper presentd at 77th Annual Meeting of the American Anthropological Association. 14 to 18 November, 1978. Los Angeles, California.

9079.   Zelekin, K.D. 1907. Uksus u russkih krestyan. [Vinegar among Russian peasants.] EO 84: 71-74.

9080.   Zeller, H. 1913. Indian edible swallow's nests. [In German] HSZPC 86: 85-106.

9081.   Zenlea, B.J. 1934. There is a cocoa for every use. FI 6: 102.

9082. Zerries, Otto. 1960. El endocannibalismo en la America del Sur. [Endocannibalism in South America.] MP-R 12: 125-175.

9083. Zetterstrom, M.H. 1962. Psychological factors influencing food habits of the elderly. MHyg 47: 479-485.

9084. Zeuner, Frederick Eberhard. 1963. A history of domesticated animals. London: Hutchinson & Co. Reprint. New York: Harper Brothers. 1964.

Includes animals used as food sources.

9085. Zhukovskij, Petr Mikhailovich. 1968. Cultivated plants and their wild relatives. Translated by P.S. Hudson. Farnham Royal, Bucks., England: Commonwealth Agricultural Bureaux.

This is an abridged version of the author's larger work, written in Russian (1950). this translation provides synopses of information on the origin and distribution, of a large number of food plants. Includes historical documentation.

9086. Zeigler, Francis. J. 1897. Banquets of the olden time. Lippincott 60: 689-694.

Poorly documented description of dining and gourmandise in ancient Greece and Rome.

9087. Ziemann, H. 1937. Nutrition questionnaire conerning natives of Africa. [In German.] ASTPTEK 41: 695-697.

9088. Zigmond, Maurice Louis. Ethnobotanical studies among Califonia and Great Basin Shoshoneans. Ph. D. dissertation. Yale University. 1941.

9089. Zihlman, Adrienne. Woman the gatherer: women as shapers of human adaptation. paper presented at 77th Annual Meeting of the American Anthropological Association. 14 to 18 November, 1978. Los Angeles, Claifornia.

9090. Zimerly, Anna L. 1907. Fruits of Alaska. A-YM 3: 344-345.

9091. Zimerman, Carle C. 1931. Chaper Twelve. Food and diet. In Siam, rural economic survey, 1930-1931. Bangkok: The Bangkok Times Press.

9092. Zingg, Robert M. 1934. American plants in Philippine ethnobotany. PJS 54: 221-273.

Staple food plants introduced from America: pp. 227-233 Less important North American food plants: pp. 233-238. Unimportant South American food plants; pp. 238-241. American fruit in the Philippines: pp. 244-259. Includes historical, etymological ethnographic, and food preparation data.

9093. Zoborowski, G. 1931. Quelques vices singuliers provoques chez les animaux et chez l'homme par des carences alimentaires. [Several singular vices provoked by dietary deficiencies in animals and humans.] SSHAARH-B 29: 24-28.

Observation on the possible relation of avitaminosis to the eating of offspring in mammals (including humans, documented during times of famine); and the pecking phenomenon of chickens; pica; and nailbiting.

9094. Zohary, Daniel & Hopf, Maria 1973. Domestication of pulses in the Old World. Science 182: 887-894.

Revues evidence on place of origin and time of domestication of the pea, Pisum sativum, lentil (Lens culinaris), broad bean (Vicia faba), bitter vetch (Vicia ervilia), and chick pea (Cicer arietanum). Posits pea and lentil as "founder" crops of Old World Neolithic Agriculture, domesticated probably in the Near East, simultaneously with wheats and barley (ca. 6000 B.C.), and bitter vetch. Evidence as to place of origin, and time of domesication of the broad bean and chick pea are fragmentary, the wild progenitors not having been satisfactorily identified. Both the lattter plants emerge as important foods in Bronze Age cultures of the Near East and Europe.

9095. Zohary, Michael. 1962. Plant life of Palestine, Isreal and Jordan. CB No. 33. New York: The Ronald Press.

Native plants in everyday use: pp. 212-214,

9096. Zollner, N. 1969. Friedrich von Muller, 1858-1941. Ueber die fettsucht. [Friedrich von Muller, 1858 - 1941. On obesity.] Internist 10: 83-36.

9097. Zottola, Georges. 1962. Tortillas and beans. WH 25: 24-31.

Reportage on a journey through Mexico and Guatemala describing efforts of FAO, WHO, UNICEF, and UNESCO to combat malnutrition. Includes interesting background data on early experiments with INCAPARINA, not available in more technical reports on the project.

KEY WORD INDEX

Numbers refer to entry numbers in the bibliography.

AARONSOHN, AARON, 6157, 7341.

ABASAMA CULTURE, 6106, 6107.

ABELAM CULTURE, 4712, 7065.

ABOR HILLS, 3325, 3326, 7408.

ABORTION, 2595.

ABSINTHE, 3978.

ABSORPTION, 5662, 7067, 7536, 7539, 7544, 7545.

ABURAGE, 5626.

ACADIAN CULTURE, 2046, 4433, 7617.

Acanthosicyos horrida, 8511.

ACCRA (GHANA), 2134, 6327.

Acentrocneme hesperiaris, 401

ACEROLA, 1647.

ACHIOLI CULTURE, 868.

ACHOMAWAI CULTURE, 6567.

ACHUARA JIVARO CULTURE, 7013, 7014.

ACKEE, 7369.

ACOMA PUEBLO CULTURE, 1807, 7842, 7979.

ACORN, 1368, 1539, 1806, 2308, 3024, 3129, 3130,
    3253, 3942, 5310, 5452, 5541, 5806, 6567,
    6885, 7634, 7738, 8331, 8332, 8548, 8941.

Acrodiclidium Puchury-minor, 7120.

Actinidia arguta, 6343.

ACTIVITY, 1749, 5888, 5956.

ADAIR, JOHN,   24.

ADAMS, RICHARD N., 4428.

Adansonia digitata 909, 1544, 4934, 5523.

ADAPTATION, 1284, 7863, 7864, 7915, 8577, 8919,
    9089.

ADDICTIONS, 4989, 5036, 8453.

ADENA CULTURE, 3154.

ADLAY, 8520, 8714.

ADMINISTRATION, 99, 458, 1384, 2632, 3402, 3403,
    4449, 4785, 6507, 8999.

ADMIRALTY ISLANDS, 5829, 5976.

ADOLESCENTS, 3657, 3729, 3949, 6609, 7755, 8011,
    8012, 8107, 8343.

ADVERTISING, 1501, 2207, 3229, 3230, 3278, 3335,
    4256, 5304, 6612, 7048, 7362, 7437, 7451,
    7756, 7961, 8241, 9061.

Aegiale hesperiaris, 5298.

Aesculus Californicus, 8941.

AFARS AND ISSAS, 5340.

AFFECTION, 7421.

AFGHANISTAN, 285, 3505, 6347, 6923, 7850, 8987.

Afizies sulfatus, 5298.

AFLATOXIN, 8395.

AFRICA,   79,   155,   359,   542, 836, 956, 990,
    1006, 1046, 1068, 1390, 1454, 1490, 1491,
    1544, 1547, 1682, 1744, 1785, 1849, 1851,
    1911, 1994, 2003, 2036, 2027, 2049, 2058,
    2135, 2141, 2187, 2463, 2482, 2536, 2559,
    2786, 2855, 2974, 2981, 3066, 3133, 3203,
    3677, 3970, 4017, 4022, 4037, 4120, 4121,
    4127, 4128, 4158, 4251, 4152, 4253, 4285,
    4303, 4337, 4591, 4678, 4934, 5153, 5159,
    5190, 5191, 5440, 5515, 5538, 5667, 5668,
    5671, 5672, 5892, 5969, 5998, 6102, 6108,
    6120, 6166, 6172, 6189, 6226, 6284, 6443,
    6461, 6482, 6287, 6542, 6588, 6679, 6789,
    6804, 6809, 6815, 6826, 6950, 7015, 7080,
    7277, 7356, 7380, 7415, 7505, 7528, 7531,
    7535, 7538, 7544, 7723, 7785, 8116, 8141,
    8231, 8384, 8557, 8700, 8815, 8974, 8975,
    8979, 9087.

AFRICA (CENTRAL), 49, 354, 569, 729, 781, 1362,
    1363, 1373, 1474, 1550, 1733, 1736, 1897,
    1956, 1970, 1971, 2140, 2182, 2478, 2613,
    2637, 2884, 3042, 3380, 3604, 3742, 3832,
    4087, 4111, 4216, 4229, 4232, 4477, 4747,
    4943, 5136, 5335, 5618, 5843, 5888, 6039,
    6075, 6213, 6302, 6531, 6634, 6917, 7273,
    7337, 7688, 8251, 8699.

AFRICA (EAST), 9, 131, 138, 293, 474, 475, 827,
    891, 984, 1077, 1078, 1323, 1601, 1668, 1669,
    1850, 1912, 1916, 1963, 2051, 2247, 2378,
    2379, 2424, 2425, 2517, 2518, 2680, 2816,
    2835, 2990, 2991, 2992, 3035, 3036, 3037,
    3171, 3221, 3223, 3380, 3497, 3552, 3822,
    4139, 4142, 4218, 4294, 4358, 4486, 4487,
    4705, 4795, 4823, 4836, 4844, 4953, 5189,
    5196, 5201, 5218, 5266, 5293, 5400, 5415,
    5450, 5453, 5640, 5790, 5856, 5867, 5868,
    5889, 5900, 5921, 5952, 6080, 6106, 6107,
    6168, 6249, 6250, 6302, 6422, 6517, 6673,
    6724, 6732, 6733, 6895, 6896, 6991, 7045,
    7095, 7100, 7116, 7196, 7365, 7392, 7393,
    7436, 7438, 7439, 7448, 7449, 7529, 7543,
    7588, 7646, 7783, 7972, 7992, 8033, 8037,
    8130, 8203, 8222, 8252, 8960, 8962.

AFRICA (GERMAN EAST), 1255.

5197, 5277, 5383, 5767, 5830, 5841, 5980,
6156, 6240, 6241, 6350, 6551, 6601, 6617,
7036, 7065, 7293, 7540, 7687, 7782, 8076,
8111, 8215, 8227, 8327, 8342, 8359, 8415,
8416, 8628, 8730, 9056, 9084.

ANIMALS (NON-DOMESTICATED), 1219, 1370, 1490,
1667, 1794, 1994, 2003, 2075, 2174, 2424,
2502, 2548, 2701, 3192, 3263, 3431, 3540,
3570, 3607, 3656, 3694, 3727, 3862, 4345,
4393, 4656, 5075, 5159, 5190, 5191, 5245,
5317, 5414, 5755, 5888, 6202, 6350, 6465,
6517, 6518, 6624, 6636, 6689, 6820, 7005,
7250, 7255, 7332, 7573, 7595, 7619, 7736,
7885, 8428, 8519.

ANISE, 2781.

ANKOLE CULTURE: (see NYANKOLE).

ANNAM, 1890, 3301, 6993, 8405.

ANNELIDS, 1839, 1898, 2823, 4541, 5422, 7590,
7769, 8969.

Annona cherimola, 8432.

Annona muricata, 7085, 8432.

Annona squamosa, 8432.

Annona reticulata, 8432.

Annona sp. , 3703, 6520, 7120, 8432.

ANOPLURA, 3788, 5583.

ANOREXIA NERVOSA, 1034, 1130, 1311, 5512.

ANTARTIC, 4351, 4704.

ANTHROPOLOGY, 343, 351, 608, 1734, 1824, 2602,
2632, 2738, 2743, 2802, 2803, 2804, 2912,
2926, 2931, 3036, 3089, 3101, 3106, 3798,
4099, 4142, 4182, 4278, 4366, 4485, 4486,
4487, 4618, 4939, 4987, 4997, 5069, 5237,
5372, 5466, 5482, 5647, 5743, 5840, 6004,
6053, 6073, 6168, 6494, 6736, 7050, 7485,
7506, 7962, 8225, 8695, 8882, 8883.

ANTHROPOLOGY (APPLIED), 32, 33, 343, 670, 910,
1384, 2137, 2741, 2804, 2996, 3340, 4132,
4133, 4135, 4136, 4137, 4138, 4139, 4485,
5160, 5237, 5476, 6009, 6125, 6446, 6447,
6736, 6927, 7970, 8076.

ANTHROPOLOGY (ECONOMIC) 3089.

ANTHROPOMETRY, 717, 1127, 2180, 3968, 4658,
4675, 5201, 7553.

ANTHROPOPHAGY, 59, 88, 144, 207, 223, 233, 234,
281, 295, 354, 556, 557, 561, 595, 596, 602,
603, 605, 706, 760, 766, 812, 823, 868, 891,
916, 919, 931, 968, 982, 1046, 1057, 1082,
1313, 1342, 1343, 1362, 1363, 1364, 1378,
1502, 1629, 1633, 1637, 1861, 1880, 1897,
1909, 1993, 2064, 2089, 2155, 2156, 2244,
2351, 2400, 2401, 2469, 2517, 2518, 2551,
2561, 2682, 2825, 2858, 2887, 2937, 2040,

3061, 3073, 3074, 3108, 3251, 3274, 3279,
3280, 3461, 3496, 3537, 3568, 3577, 3663,
3681, 3687, 3819, 3825, 3858, 3862, 3895,
3925, 3989, 4097, 4388, 4490, 4492, 4523,
4645, 4794, 4832, 4872, 4946, 4947, 4965,
5052, 5074, 5208, 5309, 5565, 5566, 5567,
5570, 5571, 5698, 5708, 5727, 5730, 5732,
5756, 5757, 5786, 5788, 5789, 5792, 5889,
5914, 5915, 5974, 6206, 6375, 6377, 6414,
6538, 6708, 6710, 6830, 6832, 6833, 6934,
6935, 6963, 6964, 6985, 6986, 7008, 7071,
7081, 7097, 7124, 7142, 7143, 7195, 7271,
7272, 7273, 7296, 7368, 7447, 7497, 7668,
7675, 7687, 7764, 7794, 7831, 8031, 8045,
8050, 8245, 8271, 8413, 8414, 8436, 8465,
8473, 8477, 8478, 8479, 8500, 8503, 8546,
8547, 8635, 8665, 8703, 9069, 9082, 9093.

ANTIBIOTICS, 8600.

Antigonon leptopus, 338.

ANTIQUES, 1832, 6061, 6400.

ANTOFAGASTA (CHILE), 3075.

ANU, 3802, 3804, 8213.

ANUTA, 9034.

ANXIETY, 7438, 7644, 7909.

APACHE CULTURE, (WESTERN), 591, 1254, 1674,
3715, 4018, 4157, 6154, 6235, 6740, 8368.

APHRODISIACS, 2055, 5055, 7368.

APICIUS, 142, 289, 290, 1013, 1803, 2205, 4435,
5650, 5999, 8420, 8421.

APOCYNACEAE, 1423.

APPALACHIA, 1811, 8311, 8942.

APPERT, FRANCOIS, 3232.

APPETITE, 2281, 3809, 3992, 4060, 4330, 4561,
4814, 5386, 5443, 5764, 6303, 7234, 7837,
8905, 9053, 9055.

APPLES, 2166, 3732, 4071, 6345, 8206, 8671.

APPROPRIATE TECHNOLOGY, 2388, 8565.

AQUA VITAE, 7031.

ARABIA, 3681, 4388, 6415, 6416, 6941, 7367,
7826.

ARABIAN SEA, 3305.

ARABIC CULTURE, 4498, 4529.

ARABIC LANGUAGE, 4467, 6940.

ARACEAE, 498, 509, 1848.

Arachis hypogaea, 221, 292, 8434, 8552, 8996.

Arachis nambiquarae, 7565.

1951, 2054, 2126, 2149, 2217, 2462, 2463, 2512, 2592, 2675, 2730, 2760, 2817, 3069, 3070, 3078, 3182, 3228, 3308, 3366, 3519, 3571, 3584, 3591, 3624, 3658, 3847, 3887, 3924, 3994, 4071, 4072, 4084, 4105, 4218, 4323, 4324, 4383, 4413, 4473, 4569, 4582, 4583, 4617, 4683, 4772, 4822, 4836, 4839, 4891, 4900, 4926, 4961, 4962, 4963, 5009, 5015, 5028, 5031, 5040, 5099, 5313, 5197, 5223, 5266, 5276, 5282, 5213, 5418, 5419, 5451, 5642, 5721, 5859, 5887, 6053, 6054, 6055, 6116, 6118, 6130, 6155, 6171, 6192, 6235, 6342, 6344, 6348, 6356, 6371, 6471, 6501, 6722, 6789, 6815, 6816, 6945, 6991, 7199, 7262, 7297, 7316, 7380, 7479, 7521, 7527, 7561, 7582, 7663, 7743, 7782, 7825, 7830, 7993, 7996, 8041, 8102, 8250, 8251, 8381, 8433, 8476, 8483, 8496, 8531, 8536, 8604, 8661, 8664, 8698, 8747, 8833, 8917, 9012, 9013, 9059, 9072.

BEVERAGES (HERBAL) 152, 583, 746, 1181, 1569, 2082, 2248, 2732, 3112, 3233, 3374, 3573, 3870, 3410, 4244, 4864, 5125, 5950, 6087, 6540, 6946, 7032, 7643, 8466, 8475, 8658.

BEVERAGES (NON-ALCOHOLIC), 235, 353, 411, 668, 691, 692, 731, 746, 749, 1123, 1178, 1181, 1423, 1531, 1662, 1761, 1891, 2025, 2449, 2728, 2867, 3058, 3059, 3131, 3250, 3352, 3860, 3977, 4164, 4397, 4911, 4964, 5214, 5356, 5588, 5599, 6515, 5775, 5937, 6090, 6301, 6738, 6829, 6894, 7239, 7249, 7902, 7953, 8028, 8601, 8868, 8924, 8925.

BHANG, 1537.

BHIL CULTURE, 5920, 7220, 7221.

BHOJANA KUTUHALA (INDIAN TREATISE ON DIETETICS), 3087.

BHUIYA CULTURE, 5118.

BIAFRA, 276.

BIANG CULTURE, 7409.

BIBLE, 334, 1700, 1770, 2054, 2257, 2274, 2462, 2837, 3182, 3265, 3292, 3550, 3700, 3849, 3964, 4179, 4398, 4399, 4451, 4498, 4628, 5065, 5614, 5773, 6200, 6365, 6497, 6705, 6706, 7010, 7061, 7062, 7350, 7063, 7478, 7583, 7825, 7985, 8066, 8067, 8121, 8167, 8528, 8868, 8926, 9072.

BIBLIOGRAPHY, 156, 370, 429, 514, 688, 1070, 1099, 1302, 1361, 1739, 1745, 2086, 2100, 2136, 2306, 2411, 2547, 2711, 2712, 2744, 2800, 2832, 2903, 2979, 3057, 3081, 3152, 3157, 3168, 3187, 3202, 3254, 3581, 3598, 3754, 3906, 4580, 4591, 4644, 4771, 4898, 4967, 5188, 5430, 5484, 5524, 5936, 6205, 6393, 6394, 6395, 6886, 7021, 7284, 7689, 7947, 7968, 8003, 8322, 8341, 8399, 8420, 8421, 8460, 8708, 8710, 8746, 8874.

BIHAR (INDIA), 816, 1587, 2224, 2347, 4606, 5131, 5692, 5694, 7058, 7060, 8835.

BIMIN-KUSKUSMIN CULTURE, 6516.

BINJI CULTURE, 2884.

BIOCHEMICAL INDIVIDUALITY, 2280, 4814, 4877, 6340, 6650, 6676, 7939, 8106, 8588, 8589, 8590, 8593.

BIOCHEMISTRY, 2632, 2754, 3036, 3185, 4814, 4877, 5866, 6168, 6340, 6463, 6650, 6743, 6747, 6964, 7442, 7473, 7536, 7601, 7602, 7603, 7939, 8356, 8591, 8620, 8582.

BIOGRAPHY, 302, 437, 799, 1011, 1041, 116, 1503, 1804, 2563, 3232, 5231, 5331, 5391, 6011, 6631, 7154, 7980, 8185.

BIOLOGY, 331, 626, 652, 1256, 2139, 2673, 2936, 2963, 3194, 3332, 4618, 6886, 7909, 8116.

BIPEDALISM, 3727.

BIRDS, 761, 893, 1160, 1620, 1841, 2153, 2452, 2453, 2975, 3431, 3710, 4458, 4572, 4601, 5086, 5498, 6173, 6200, 6350, 6429, 6591, 6857, 7010, 7520, 7522, 7595, 7662, 7699, 7737, 7885, 7908, 8292, 8756, 8849.

BIRD'S NEST (EDIBLE), 442, 4504, 7699, 8594, 8596, 9080.

Birgus latro, 604, 7121.

BIRHOR CULTURE, 5664, 5698, 8835.

BIROM CULTURE, 8443.

BIRTH ORDER, 5202.

BIRTH (SEASONALITY), 5828.

BISHA OASIS (ARABIA), 6416.

BISMARCK ARCHIPELAGEO, 3400, 4041, 5975.

BISMARCK MOUNTAIN RANGE, 1168.

BITTERSWEET VINE, 4249.

BLACK AMERICANS, 272, 353, 820, 878, 1066, 1143, 1565, 1905, 2023, 2085, 2092, 2191, 2193, 2194, 2196, 2197, 2199, 2200, 2344, 2370, 2406, 2410, 2830, 2944, 3079, 3186, 3249, 3339, 3526, 3706, 3796, 3890, 4054, 4165, 4167, 4173, 4186, 4189, 4274, 4439, 4452, 5030, 5130, 5354, 5489, 5762, 5823, 5832, 5852, 6010, 6270, 6374, 6419, 6598, 6763, 6784, 6825, 7113, 8159, 8313, 8357, 8493, 8533, 8779, 8856, 8914.

BLACK CARIB CULTURE, 7672, 8058.

BLACK-EYED PEA, 7862.

BLACKFOOT CULTURE, 2529, 4212, 4213, 4214, 4215, 4832, 8927.

BLACK SURINAM CULTURE, 7480.

Blechnum serrulatum, Rich. , 451.

6358, 6431, 6441, 6469, 6521, 6562, 6619,
6744, 6831, 6970, 6979, 7073, 7085, 7153,
7402, 7443, 7498, 7506, 7509, 7565, 7567,
7640, 7695, 7696, 7702, 7764, 8045, 8046,
8047, 8047, 8139, 8180, 8477, 8520, 8538,
8553, 8559, 8571, 8650, 8651, 8652, 8937,
9027.

BREAD, 70, 76, 145, 226, 282, 322, 323, 324,
325, 326, 348, 350, 394, 437, 439, 465, 478,
634, 635, 939, 940, 941, 962, 965, 992, 1005,
1014, 1031, 1036, 1079, 1140, 1157, 1236,
1246, 1316, 1349, 1351, 1352, 1353, 1540,
1636, 1714, 1758, 1760, 1952, 2023, 2099,
2102, 2111, 2165, 2270, 2320, 2641, 2726,
5990, 6387, 6497, 6611, 6703, 6797, 6971,
6972, 6974, 7070, 7166, 7279, 7338, 7342,
7466, 7638, 7654, 7655, 7754, 7796, 7813,
7844, 7850, 7888, 8055, 8068, 8145, 8146,
8471, 8472, 8485, 8543, 8544, 8545, 8723,
8762, 8783, 8789.

BREADFRUIT, 499, 1179, 2810, 3377, 3899, 4337,
5077, 5288, 5439, 5621, 5628, 5911, 6332,
6398, 6508, 6509, 6914, 6981, 7200, 7662,
8065, 8190, 8716, 8818.

BREADNUT, 1781.

BREAKFAST, 76, 148, 793, 1382, 1631, 2534, 2698,
2851, 3433, 3616, 4053, 4241, 5645, 7331,
7367, 7818, 7902, 8064.

BREAST-FEEDING, 71, 136, 435, 601, 844, 938,
1109, 1267, 1727, 2008, 2588, 2990, 3003,
3137, 3230, 3321, 3451, 3661, 4141, 4145,
4221, 4235, 4478, 4486, 4841, 4982, 5144,
5248, 5308, 5455, 5709, 6072, 6269, 6293,
6401, 6413, 6451, 6696, 6697, 6698, 6737,
6916, 7229, 7671, 7846, 8037, 8348, 8498,
8532, 8806.

BRESSA, CESARE, 5909.

BREWING, 464, 487, 571, 885, 2054, 2369, 3069,
3070, 3382, 3571, 3645, 3658, 4218, 4549,
5028, 5313, 6053, 6054, 6055, 6116, 6155,
6371, 6532, 6789, 6991, 7098, 7240, 7482,
7527, 7707, 7873, 8349, 8936, 9012.

BRISTOL INFIRMARY, 612.

BRITISH COLUMBIA, 29, 484, 3016, 3189, 3190,
3288, 3845, 4758, 6891, 7970, 7997, 8071,
8072, 8896.

BRITISH GUIANA (see: GUYANA).

BRITISH HONDURAS, 2904, 5342.

BRITTANY, 4002, 7163.

BROILERS, 885.

BROILING, 8332.

BRONZE AGE, 3634, 3642, 3789, 4965, 7296, 8509,
9094.

BROOKLYN (BOROUGH, NEW YORK), 12, 2174, 6847.

Brosimum alicastrum, 6603, 6604.

Bryonia alba, L., 1304.

Bryonia dioica, Jacq., 1304.

BUAKI (NUTRITIONAL PATHOLOGY, AFRICA), 8369.

BUANG CULTURE 3060.

BUDDHIST FAITH, 779, 780, 1112, 2208, 3844,
6411, 8040, 8098, 8730.

BUDGETS, 149, 4787, 5227, 6003, 6482, 8980.

BUENOS AIRES (ARGENTINA), 1272.

BUFFALO (MAMMAL), 318, 2679, 2723, 4352, 4714,
5075, 5703, 7086, 8048.

BUGANDA, 4139, 4149, 4953, 5400, 6896, 7095.

BUGINESE, 6328.

BUGRE CULTURE, 2977.

BUIN (SOLOMON ISLANDS), 8731.

BUKAVU (ZAIRE), 8489.

BULBS, 4598, 6094.

BULGARIA, 3247, 4547, 5013, 5211, 5212, 5336,
6812, 8351, 8619.

BULLOCK'S HEART (FRUIT), 8432.

BULOD CULTURE, 4181.

BULRUSH, 618, 8285.

BULU CULTURE, 5608.

BUNGWALL (FERN), 451.

BUREAUCRACY, 8075.

BURGUNDY, 1861, 7580.

BURI PALM, 3010.

BURMA, 223, 1643, 3188, 3429, 3815, 3955, 5193,
5230, 5272, 5588, 6411, 6552, 6553, 6921,
7440, 7841.

BURUNDI, 5335, 8251.

BUSAMA CULTURE, 3438.

BUSHMAN CULTURE, 1322, 2175, 2302, 3222, 3438,
3618, 5051, 5232, 6208, 6932, 7896, 7897,
8027, 8260, 8663.

BUSHONGO CULTURE, 4125.

BUSINESS HOURS, 178.

BUTCHERING, 171, 173, 174, 360, 464, 520, 549,
738, 1214, 1370, 2074, 2124, 2311, 2679, 2829,
2946, 3027, 3307, 3358, 4218, 4601, 5151,

CANADA (PRAIRIE PROVINCES), 7232, 8292.

Cana edulis, 8434.

CANAGUA (see: CANIHUA).

CANARY ISLANDS, 2106, 4222, 6362, 6826, 7233, 8587.

CANDOMBLE CULT (BRAZIL), 546.

CANIHUA, 432, 8213, 8761.

Cannabis sativa, 1537, 3530.

CANNIBALISM (see: ANTHROPOPHAGY).

CANNING, 817, 1290, 4277, 5331.

CANOE BIRCH, 2583.

CANOE-BUILDING, 5151.

CANON DE CHELLY (ARIZONA), 7842.

CANON DE TAOS (NEW MEXICO), 6453.

CANTONESE, 485.

CAPE COLONY (SOUTH AFRICA), 948.

CAPE MALAY CULTURE, 2984, 2986.

CAPERS, 960, 7061, 7062, 7063, 7906.

CAPE VERDE ISLANDS, 5064.

Capparis spinosa, 7061, 7062, 7063.

CAPRICORN ISLANDS, 5907.

Capsicum sp., 3703, 3829, 6435.

CAPTAN, 7441.

CARABAO, 2288.

CARAHUE (CHILE), 8358.

CARBOHYDRATE, 4504, 6387, 7062, 8461.

CARBON-14, 1950, 3240, 3241, 3638.

CARDAMON, 5983.

CARIB CULTURE (ANTILLEAN), 3801, 3805, 6586, 7143, 8057, 8058.

CARIB CULTURE (CENTRAL), 2549, 3496.

CARIBBEAN, 583, 601, 959, 1121, 1418, 1462, 1485, 1536, 1576, 1617, 1623, 1737, 1751, 1783, 1902, 1967, 2059, 2089, 2170, 2365, 2479, 2564, 2615, 2688, 2735, 2737, 2745, 2761, 2771, 2810, 2811, 3099, 3132, 3211, 3230, 3254, 3333, 3334, 3413, 3496, 3754, 3801, 3805, 3837, 3886, 3898, 4009, 4144, 4150, 4221, 4240, 4241, 4400, 4431, 4432, 4433, 4553, 4563, 4629, 4646, 4826, 5019, 5030, 5066, 5112, 5115, 5201, 5202, 5258, 5343, 5435, 5517, 5569, 5643, 5663, 5666, 5776, 5817, 5869, 5942, 6179, 6425, 6504, 6559, 6587, 6638, 6714, 6784, 6827, 6877, 6910, 6912, 7033, 7034, 7035, 7143, 7174, 7175, 7369, 7376, 7546, 7579, 7755, 7796, 7814, 7815, 7849, 7940, 7956, 8057, 8058, 8202, 8243, 8261, 8308, 8339, 8361, 8662, 8694, 8704, 8850, 8853, 8869, 8899, 8946, 8951, 8953, 8968.

CARIBBEAN-CANADIANS, 8199.

CARIBOU, 1207, 2576, 3882, 4160, 4714, 5894, 6651.

Carica papaya, 3703.

CARNATION COMPANY, 5231.

Carnegeia gigantea, 467, 3217, 5016, 8092.

CARNEGIE INSTITUTION OF WASHINGTON, 1559, 1560, 1561, 1562.

CAROLINE ISLANDS, 536, 537, 538, 1968, 2129, 2640, 3392, 4419, 5882, 7790, 8609, 8660.

CAROTENE, 3268, 3269, 3811, 5423.

CARPATHIAN MOUNTAINS, 3317, 4510, 4511, 4531, 4532, 5221.

Carpodacus, sp. 1160.

CARRIER CULTURE, 3845.

CARRION, 3261, 3727, 6408.

CARRYING CAPACITY, 1778, 1787, 2223, 2465, 4712, 4763, 5867, 7462, 8215, 8721.

CARTAGENA (COLUMBIA), 7138.

CARVING, 1464, 2979, 6996.

Carya illinoensis, 2670.

Caryocar amigdaliforme, 7120.

Caryocar brasilensis, 7565.

Caryocar sp., 1397.

CASABE, 1349, 1351, 1352.

CASE HISTORIES, 8588, 8589, 8590, 8724.

CASH ECONOMY, 4630, 6508, 6509, 6510, 8694.

CASHEW, 1466, 1838, 4196, 6071, 7695.

CASHINAWA CULTURE, 4389, 8045, 4847.

CASSAVA, 131, 406, 1456, 2582, 2709, 2990, 3837, 3838, 4055, 4337, 4557, 5273, 5289, 5522, 6030, 6112, 6219, 8085, 8513, 8695.

Castanea vesca, 6442.

CHILD REARING, 518, 847, 1152, 1416, 1572, 2302, 2321, 2441, 3657, 3944, 3946, 3947, 4153, 4288, 4506, 4845, 6714, 6908, 6909, 7073, 7160, 7265, 7987.

CHILDREN, 272, 920, 966, 1034, 1095, 1112, 1121, 1152, 1220, 1311, 1359, 1535, 1574, 1576, 1578, 1687, 1726, 1766, 1798, 1843, 1879, 1914, 2016, 2147, 2200, 2220, 2292, 2302, 2344, 2346, 2370, 2380, 2407, 2412, 2441, 2658, 2689, 2691, 2696, 2698, 2748, 2791, 2792, 2838, 2874, 2918, 3103, 3110, 3171, 3185, 3275, 3339, 3350, 3521, 3667, 3672, 3828, 3840, 3911, 3941, 3944, 4059, 4144, 4200, 4288, 4321, 4354, 4506, 4655, 4660, 4702, 4726, 4827, 4837, 4928, 4989, 4995, 5066, 5096, 5097, 5105, 5129, 5138, 5201, 5202, 5234, 5443, 5449, 5488, 5514, 5649, 5684, 5694, 5825, 5910, 5969, 6052, 6144, 6147, 6148, 6152, 6203, 6293, 6297, 6323, 6412, 6556, 6562, 6579, 6747, 6802, 6829, 7004, 7170, 7181, 7265, 7275, 7283, 7392, 7393, 7400, 7437, 7451, 7584, 7631, 7758, 7846, 7895, 8119, 8127, 8383, 8408, 8485, 8736, 8763, 8775, 8837, 8877, 8908, 8962, 8970.

CHILE, 690, 1025, 1830, 2294, 3075, 3754, 3999, 4000, 4832, 5050, 5345, 6206, 6359, 6537, 6819, 6966, 7001, 7138, 7182, 7183, 7184, 7399, 8358, 8418.

CHI'LI PROVINCE (CHINA), 1183.

CHILI CON CARNE, 523, 1797, 8189.

CHIMBU CULTURE, 423, 425, 1113, 3438, 7016, 7065, 8080, 8430, 8431, 8776.

CHIN CULTURE, 7841.

CHINA, 5, 10, 42, 43, 45, 120, 121, 122, 123, 124, 125, 126, 127, 128, 129, 214, 229, 269, 270, 274, 279, 312, 442, 443, 460, 540, 724, 802, 1040, 1041, 1042, 1181, 1183, 1281, 1493, 1494, 1526, 1528, 1529, 1530, 1532, 1533, 1536, 1552, 1568, 1569, 1570, 1573, 1580, 1593, 1600, 1643, 1715, 1724, 2025, 2039, 2255, 2318, 2375, 2461, 2463, 2654, 2789, 2805, 2890, 2891, 3178, 3179, 3216, 3273, 3350, 3351, 3352, 3367, 3420, 3494, 3582, 3684, 3698, 3708, 3709, 3716, 3717, 3791, 3793, 3794, 3807, 3815, 3826, 3851, 3886, 3897, 3901, 3903, 3928, 3930, 3931, 3932, 4158, 4296, 4342, 4456, 4567, 4579, 4593, 4608, 4616, 4692, 4693, 4756, 4764, 4765, 4775, 4776, 4892, 4894, 4895, 4908, 4915, 4931, 4944, 4972, 4999, 5000, 5036, 5319, 5359, 5417, 5579, 5581, 5595, 5596, 5685, 5722, 5812, 5814, 5987, 6120, 6182, 6265, 6412, 6487, 6490, 6505, 6547, 6565, 6600, 6726, 6727, 6728, 7133, 7295, 7300, 7481, 7496, 7699, 7728, 7729, 7903, 8024, 8025, 8030, 8154, 8171, 8263, 8264, 8265, 8278, 8447, 8520, 8594, 8595, 8597, 8598, 8599, 8601, 8622, 8808, 8817, 8930, 8987, 8990, 8991, 8992, 9015, 9029, 9040.

CHINA ANCIENT, 1488, 1489, 1491, 1553, 2994, 3785, 3900, 3902, 3929, 3934, 4868, 4869, 4871, 6251, 6420, 7516, 7563, 8170, 9042.

CHINANTEC CULTURE, 4921, 8674, 8808.

CHINDO ISLAND, 8300.

CHINESE-AMERICANS, 485, 3080, 3266, 3267, 3562, 3563, 3599, 3912, 4069, 4176, 4750, 5930, 6035, 6546, 6598, 6919, 7740, 8013, 8257, 8325, 8718, 8769, 8950.

CHINESE-CANADIANS, 8199.

CHINESE LANGUAGE, 1494, 1495, 1595, 5580.

CHINESE (OVERSEAS), 1528, 3839, 3912, 5651, 5652, 5888, 6001.

CHIOS ISLAND (GREECE), 308.

CHIPPEWA CULTURE (see: OJIBWA).

CHIRICAHUA APACHE CULTURE, 1433.

CHIRIGUANO CULTURE, 6051.

CHIRIMOYA FRUIT, 3703.

Chirostoma jordani, Woolmann, 5298.

CHITTENDEN, RUSSELL HENRY, 8185.

CHLORINE, 8862.

Chlorogalum pomeridianum, 6567.

CHOCO CULTURE, 297, 8918, 8919.

CHOCOLATE, 296, 464, 932, 977, 1177, 1182, 1196, 1957, 2057, 2096, 2327, 2328, 2342, 2911, 3156, 4474, 4749, 4911, 4945, 5576, 6086, 6193, 6652, 7249, 7308, 7776, 8841.

CHOCTAW CULTURE, 1252, 1325, 1938, 3943, 7982.

CHODHARA CULTURE, 5497.

CHOKE CHERRY, 6445.

CHOLESTEROL, 3968.

CHOLLA, 7019, 7737.

CHONTAL CULTURE, 3485, 6965.

CHOP SUEY, 8013.

CHORTI CULTURE, 1560, 3660.

CHOTA NAGPUR (INDIA), 7059.

CHOTT EL DJERID (TUNSIA), 8086.

CHOU-DA-CHINE, 1848.

CHRISTIAN FAITH, 739, 4569, 5321, 6434, 6497, 6722, 7480, 8370, 8435.

COLLEGE STUDENTS, 1673, 1883, 3791, 3792, 4425, 4838, 7502, 8166, 8892, 9048.

Colocasia antiquorum, 756, 3404, 6914.

Colocasia esculenta, 80, 160, 239, 610, 1231, 3072, 3753, 3899, 5620, 5991, 6602.

COLOGNE (KOLN, GERMANY), 7240.

COLOMBIA, 633, 1061, 1062, 1201, 1421, 2081, 2130, 2216, 2235, 2301, 2503, 2548, 2696, 2697, 2874, 3754, 4105, 4632, 4979, 5345, 6142, 6158, 6286, 6568, 6608, 6782, 6975, 7072, 7138, 7309, 7311, 8245, 8422, 8513, 8811, 8918, 8919.

COLOR, 2776, 3521, 3624, 4405, 4875, 7682, 8150.

COLORADO, 112, 2779, 3975, 4309, 6454, 6867.

COLORADO RIVER, 1430, 2716, 4184.

COLUMBIAN EXPOSITION, 3123, 3212, 6989.

COLUMBUS, CHRISTOPHER, 4126, 4128.

COMANCHE CULTURE, 1360, 8575.

COMITE NATIONAL DE SECOURS ET D'ALIMENTATION, 3683.

COMMANDER ISLANDS, 3927.

COMMENSALISM, 5031, 7790.

COMMERCE, 166, 171, 344, 411, 644, 707, 727, 830, 833, 839, 925, 935, 1265, 1312, 1344, 1381, 1401, 1411, 1505, 1695, 1761, 1771, 1817, 1818, 1895, 2099, 2218, 2242, 2304, 2479, 2636, 2700, 2732, 2749, 2766, 2769, 2870, 3033, 3058, 3099, 3166, 3201, 3230, 3236, 3246, 3405, 3413, 3464, 3579, 3770, 3824, 4051, 4084, 4119, 4130, 4197, 4203, 4224, 4254, 4257, 4392, 4549, 4728, 4767, 4798, 5039, 5156, 5231, 5313, 5314, 5405, 5597, 5726, 5819, 6060, 6071, 6086, 6193, 6278, 6351, 6403, 6404, 6423, 6640, 6760, 6815, 6816, 7319, 7389, 7403, 7482, 7486, 7521, 7577, 7614, 7743, 7967, 8162, 8303, 8322, 8349, 8532, 8540, 8705, 8726, 8734, 8809, 8931, 9074.

COMMITTEE ON FOOD HABITS (UNITED STATES OF AMERICA - NATIONAL RESEARCH COUNCIL), 240, 244, 3340, 5466, 5468, 5472, 5476, 5646, 7857, 7896.

COMMUNAL LABOR, 5151, 8660.

COMMUNICATION, 1711, 5646, 5766, 6024, 6404, 6415, 6424, 6735, 7413, 7421.

COMMUNITIES, 428.

COMPETITION, 3058, 3464, 6069, 6070, 6309, 7577.

COMPUTERIZATION, 440, 1792, 4194, 4268, 4639, 5728, 6568, 7641, 7676.

CONCENTRATION CAMPS, 2912, 4867.

CONCEPCION PROVINCE (PERU), 8696.

CONDIMENTS, 146, 818, 876, 960, 1032, 1033, 1058, 1530, 1600, 1808, 1974, 2267, 2320, 2366, 2697, 2768, 2891, 3013, 3078, 3250, 3273, 3311, 3312, 3313, 3432, 3587, 3716, 3724, 3980, 3993, 4016, 4102, 4218, 4282, 4304, 4337, 4503, 4884, 5246, 5426, 5530, 5531, 5532, 5533, 5534, 5535, 5543, 5582, 5775, 6002, 6040, 6213, 6423, 6435, 6524, 6750, 6992, 6993, 6994, 7273, 7682, 7698, 7760, 7842, 8020, 8255, 8269, 8356, 8624.

CONFECTIONS, 76, 278, 464, 814, 1025, 1348, 1352, 1704, 1755, 1837, 1838, 1919, 2048, 2096, 2178, 2502, 2566, 2623, 2624, 2625, 2626, 2627, 2700, 2781, 2819, 3156, 3208, 4368, 4464, 4562, 5061, 5253, 5357, 5502, 5597, 5880, 5911, 5918, 5927, 6219, 6363, 6401, 6470, 6504, 6652, 6777, 6849, 6914, 7366, 7524, 7876, 7975, 7892, 7994, 8094, 8197, 8243, 8370, 8484, 8536, 8670, 8841, 8985.

CONFERENCES, 1744, 2026, 2710.

CONGO, 20, 781, 1897, 2182, 3042, 4111, 4125, 4216, 5669, 5672, 6039, 6791, 7337.

CONGO (BELGIAN), 47, 48, 766, 1265, 1358, 1646, 1736, 1750, 2884, 3372, 3832, 4590, 4612, 4730, 4747, 5562, 5843, 6192, 6207, 6531, 7273, 8104, 8369, 8380, 8812, 8813, 8814, 8816.

CONGO FREE STATE, 8510.

CONGO (FRENCH), 569, 2140, 4590, 5136, 5843, 6917, 7132, 7688, 8102, 8510, 8555.

CONIAGUI CULTURE, 4828.

CONIBO CULTURE, 2548, 8162.

CONNECTICUT, 4424, 5709.

CONSERVATION (ECOLOGICAL), 8605.

CONSPICUOUS CONSUMPTION, 29, 639, 831, 2360, 2415, 2416, 2467, 3288, 3845, 6593, 7437, 7658, 8973.

CONSULTING, 2934.

CONSUMER BEHAVIOR, 3278, 3770, 3850, 3860, 4197, 4270, 4272, 4655 4767, 6171, 6614, 6904, 6973, 7421, 7998, 8241, 8980.

CONTAINERS, 564, 611, 1022, 1080, 1489, 2222, 2226, 2296, 2297, 2400, 2506, 2598, 2601, 3099, 3235, 3517, 3860, 3961, 4103, 4183, 4218, 4379, 4694, 4839, 4881, 5149, 5450, 5732, 5889, 6088, 6237, 6356, 6427, 6789, 7029, 7087, 7622, 7648, 7809, 7842, 8292, 8298, 8507, 8508, 8509, 8738, 8861, 8885, 8929, 8952.

CONVALESCENCE, 648, 2705, 8699.

CONVENIENCE FOODS, 3464.

Convulvulus batatas, 6978.

COOK, JAMES (NAVIGATOR), 1705, 4493.

COOK, ORATOR FULLER, 604.

COOKBOOK WRITING, 2794, 3202.

COOKERY, 11, 31, 141, 142, 143, 163, 184, 185, 254, 259, 279, 282, 289, 290, 308, 309, 336, 353, 370, 372, 373, 400, 415, 416, 417, 419, 443, 474, 506, 512, 515, 523, 536, 546, 566, 568, 576, 582, 591, 607, 620, 648, 661, 682, 704, 730, 763, 773, 783, 789, 820, 895, 918, 922, 952, 962, 1013, 1014, 1052, 1056, 1058, 1060, 1091, 1099, 1165, 1176, 1189, 1192, 1195, 1208, 1259, 1289, 1294, 1329, 1348, 1352, 1361, 1419, 1425, 1452, 1478, 1485, 1596, 1614, 1615, 1617, 1624, 1632, 1666, 1713, 1728, 1740, 1788, 1794, 1801, 1810, 1902, 2011, 2015, 2038, 2042, 2055, 2127, 2141, 2163, 2172, 2208, 2226, 2238, 2278, 2279, 2290, 2303, 2306, 2316, 2323, 2335, 2337, 2343, 2345, 2361, 2414, 2440, 2444, 2458, 2473, 2502, 2508, 2558, 2562, 2567, 2570, 2571, 2635, 2645, 2651, 2660, 2661, 2662, 2663, 2664, 2667, 2677, 2701, 2721, 2733, 2756, 2794, 2795, 2812, 2814, 2819, 2850, 2882, 2896, 2913, 2944, 2951, 2955, 2956, 2979, 2984, 2985, 2986, 2987, 2994, 3009, 3025, 3029, 3031, 3056, 3078, 3081, 3104, 3127, 3129, 3130, 3168, 3172, 3175, 3202, 3208, 3213, 3245, 3287, 3330, 3347, 3348, 3357, 3368, 3416, 3419, 3422, 3423, 3436, 3453, 3454, 3462, 3463, 3514, 3515, 3526, 3527, 3544, 3563, 3572, 3577, 3580, 3581, 3585, 3586, 3587, 3597, 3599, 3600, 3652, 3661, 3665, 3678, 3694, 3699, 3707, 3715, 3728, 3732, 3741, 3758, 3764, 3768, 3787, 3791, 3843, 3844, 3847, 3853, 3855, 3858, 3886, 3893, 3920, 3931, 3934, 3952, 4021, 4026, 4086, 4094, 4103, 4109, 4149, 4163, 4178, 4259, 4296, 4298, 4306, 4341, 4347, 4348, 4382, 4402, 4411, 4420, 4435, 4436, 4455, 4495, 4536, 4540, 4550, 4551, 4554, 4579, 4582, 4594, 4601, 4611, 4615, 4625, 4633, 4643, 4649, 4664, 4668, 4678, 4703, 4714, 4730, 4741, 4755, 4756, 4772, 4805, 4806, 4815, 4816, 4824, 4850, 4888, 4898, 4909, 4913, 4936, 4945, 4977, 4993, 4994, 4997, 5015, 5043, 5056, 5061, 5062, 5066, 5084, 5092, 5111, 5155, 5195, 5224, 5225, 5244, 5254, 5307, 5332, 5347, 5357, 5366, 5397, 5420, 5430, 5431, 5454, 5456, 5461, 5503, 5515, 5537, 5551, 5566, 5587, 5593, 5617, 5650, 5661, 5665, 5686, 5754, 5787, 5796, 5808, 5817, 5839, 5864, 5911, 5913, 5940, 5956, 5962, 5999, 6015, 6025, 6026, 6036, 6042, 6108, 6113, 6114, 6126, 6128, 6129, 6179, 6204, 6205, 6209, 6211, 6235, 6237, 6263, 6266, 6320, 6346, 6348, 6354, 6372, 6373, 6378, 6379, 6428, 6501, 6564, 6569, 6575, 6576, 6577, 6584, 6587, 6600, 6619, 6621, 6652, 6656, 6711, 6748, 6749, 6783, 6798, 6837, 6840, 6866, 6870, 6902, 6903, 6906, 6914, 6938, 6939, 6954, 6961, 6962, 6982, 6983, 6989, 7017, 7020, 7029, 7044, 7103, 7104, 7105, 7110, 7117, 7125, 7129, 7130, 7133, 7151, 7182, 7184, 7199, 7252, 7260, 7281, 7282, 7294, 7312, 7322, 7377, 7379, 7388, 7394, 7411, 7418, 7420, 7424, 7427, 7456, 7465, 7476, 7492, 7493, 7496, 7515, 6568, 7570, 7571, 7606, 7611, 7613, 7617, 7645, 7689, 7692, 7694, 7699, 7701, 7705, 7760, 7773, 7782, 7790, 7792, 7816, 7827, 7842, 7851, 7867, 7878, 7885, 7891, 7916, 7948, 7964, 7975, 7990, 7991, 8009, 8013, 8062, 8078, 8084, 8085, 8098, 8110, 8119, 8134, 8142, 8153, 8157, 8159, 8165, 8171, 8172, 8173, 8176, 8189, 8190, 8197, 8221, 8240, 8243, 8254, 8284, 8290, 8291, 8297, 8298, 8305, 8332, 8337, 8343, 8344, 8361, 8365, 8376, 8386, 8420, 8421, 8422, 8430, 8431, 8469, 8505, 8506, 8528, 8536, 8563, 8567, 8586, 8592, 8605, 8611, 8615, 8637, 8638, 8646, 8654, 8659, 8660, 8673, 8684, 8686, 8707, 8708, 8714, 8748, 8749, 8750, 8751, 8768, 8776, 8786, 8789, 8801, 8810, 8811, 8849, 8887, 8891, 8943, 8946, 8954, 8983, 9001, 9012, 9014, 9029, 9045, 9068.

COOKHOUSES, 1190.

COOKIES, 735.

COOK ISLANDS, 610, 2842, 2843, 3039, 3853, 3968, 4796, 7163, 8568.

COOKS, 105, 885, 1045, 1503, 2563, 2850, 3436, 3678, 4611, 4753, 4785, 6211, 6996, 7113, 7424, 8257, 8604, 8864.

COPAN (HONDURAS), 6524.

COPLAS, 2440.

COPPER, 1060, 6789, 7102.

COPROLITES, 92, 1159, 1301, 1862, 2704, 2840, 2841, 3628, 5251, 7042, 8548, 8912.

COPROPHAGIA, 972, 5414.

COPTIC CULTURE, 4473.

Corchorus olitorius, 8461.

Cordeauxia edulis, Hemsl, 3223.

Cordyline terminalis, 8584.

CORFU (GREECE), 4404, 7683, 7684, 7685.

Corisella mercinaria, Say., 5298.

Corisella Texcocana, Jacz, 5298.

CORNARO, LUIGI, 1822, 6480.

CORN LAWS, 2489.

CORN (MAIZE) STARCH, 2408, 2409, 2410, 6164, 6547.

CORNELL UNIVERSITY, 7383.

Cornus mas, 8397.

CORPORAL PUNISHMENT, 177.

CORPORATE ACTIVITIES, 8999.

CORSICA, 439, 6622.

Corylus avellana, 6442.

COSMOGRAPHY, 4992.

COSMOLOGY, 716.

COSSACK CULTURE, 4185.

COSTA RICA, 528, 787, 3158, 5306, 5342, 5873, 5904, 5905, 5956, 6255, 6479, 6526, 6715, 6716, 6775, 7690, 7880, 7881, 7882, 7883.

COST-BENEFIT ANALYSIS, 7013.

COST-OF-LIVING, 164.

Costus speciosus, 3868.

COTTAGE CHEESE, 2036.

COTTON, 4218, 6846.

COUMARIN, 6650.

COURTSHIP, 1531.

COUSCOUS, 3418, 4818, 8515.

COUVADE, 8057.

COVENANT-MAKING, 5514.

COWBOYS, 31, 1789, 4753, 5758, 5830.

COWRIE SHELL MIAO CULTURE, 5596.

CRAB, 451, 7121, 8605.

CRACOW, 5713.

CRANBERRY, 1242, 1259, 8564.

Crataegus oxyacantha, 6442.

Cratopleura halsatica, 8487.

CREAM, 77, 4964, 5261, 6511.

CREATIVITY, 7421.

CREE CULTURE, 710, 1829, 2573, 2824, 3438, 5747, 5938, 6956, 6964, 7148, 8495, 8668, 8913.

CREEK CULTURE, 2060, 7981.

CREOLE CULTURE, 1801, 1902, 2508, 2571, 3357, 3586, 3886, 4086, 7846, 8243, 8637.

CRESS, 2781.

CRETE, 4404.

CRICKET, 7579, 8549, 8681.

CRIME, 1612.

CROATIA, 4520.

CRO-MAGNON CULTURE, 7116.

CROP VALUE, 1556.

CROP YIELD, 837, 1863, 5779, 6702, 6907, 6979, 7042, 8030, 8997.

CROP ZONATION, 1149.

CROSS-CULTURAL RESEARCH, 774, 1106, 1108, 1158, 1622, 1792, 1852, 1869, 1902, 1923, 2223, 2561, 2855, 3061, 3228, 3258, 3412, 3438, 3929, 3957, 4040, 4136, 4138, 4297, 4335, 4428, 4430, 4640, 4725, 4741, 4790, 5237, 5240, 5423, 5760, 5761, 6143, 6191, 6246, 6387, 6475, 6632, 6830, 6832, 6884, 7344, 7378, 7518, 7553, 8297, 8439, 8522, 8523, 8613, 8618, 8784, 8795, 8883, 8914, 9074.

A CROSS CULTURAL SUMMARY (BOOK), 1106, 1107, 1108.

Crotolaria pumila, 3106.

Croton megalobotrys, 3034.

CRUCIFERAE, 2282, 5805.

CRUSTACEA, 5298, 7368.

CUBA, 622, 1424, 4646, 5343, 5776, 5942, 6179, 6504, 6827, 7940, 8243.

CUBAN-AMERICANS, 1155.

CUBEB, 960.

CUBEO CULTURE, 8918, 8919.

CUCUMBER, 6811.

Cucumis melo, 909.

CUCURBITACEAE, 1385, 1386, 1432, 1877, 1948, 2238, 3063, 3517, 3829, 4368, 4595, 4934, 5241, 5273, 5557, 5879, 6162, 6213, 6811, 6885, 7586, 7777, 8511, 8655, 8739, 8740, 8741, 8742, 8744.

Cucurbita maxima, 8742.

Cucurbita moschata, 8454, 8742.

Cucurbita pepo, 8742.

CUICATEC CULTURE, 3880.

CULTURE, 392, 434, 652, 672, 827, 849, 1070, 1139, 1253, 1256, 1323, 1414, 1512, 1558, 1601, 1635, 1673, 1784, 1820, 1872, 1938, 1940, 1987, 2001, 2002, 2050, 2131, 2203, 2588, 2803, 2929, 2930, 2931, 2991, 3101, 3103, 3117, 3124, 3140, 3194, 3254, 3255, 3256, 3257, 3270, 3332, 3435, 3465, 3492,

ENCYCLOPEDIE FRANCAISE, 914.

ENDOCRINE SYSTEM, 6340, 6548, 8590.

ENDRIN (PESTICIDE), 7441.

ENDURANCE, 2650, 4208.

ENERGY USE, 353, 608, 659, 1749, 2139, 2398, 2763, 3276, 3548, 3549, 4376, 4561, 4762, 5741, 5744, 5779, 5984, 6702, 7067, 8107, 8970.

ENERGY (FOOD PRODUCTION-RELATED), 925, 4007, 4376, 4762, 5779, 5984, 5985, 6702, 7073, 7273, 8215, 8842, 8983.

ENGLAND, 73, 134, 163, 185, 192, 195, 350, 373, 612, 750, 751, 1025, 1181, 1244, 1306, 1615, 1678, 1796, 1817, 2015, 2306, 2313, 2314, 2463, 2663, 2817, 2862, 2863, 2864, 3252, 3281, 3284, 3364, 3406, 3498, 3581, 3633, 3749, 3856, 4346, 4347, 4831, 5155, 5227, 5228, 5248, 5268, 5301, 5313, 5431, 5432, 5435, 5485, 5721, 5813, 5990, 6096, 6097, 6098, 6099, 6320, 6592, 6913, 7090, 7151, 7348, 7387, 7418, 7486, 7521, 7548, 7608, 7609, 7743, 7936, 8108, 8125, 8183, 8297, 8364, 8403, 8564, 8611, 8654, 8748, 8749, 8751, 8826, 8947, 9036.

ENMITY, 6920.

ENRICHMENT, 437, 1079, 1527.

ENSETE, 7529, 7588, 7783.

Ensete ventricosum, 7588.

ENVIRONMENT, 1574, 2219, 2964, 3143, 3264, 3332, 3916, 3963, 3992, 4162, 4209, 4210, 4521, 4526, 5488, 5647, 6147, 6148, 6163, 6349, 6605, 6620, 6737, 6874, 7232, 7332, 7933, 7939, 8007, 8063, 8550, 8623, 8791, 8792, 8843, 8971, 8981, 9033, 9034.

ENVIRONMENTAL CHANGE, 892, 2972, 7520, 8573, 8668, 8793, 8956.

ENZYMES, 4877, 6200.

EPHEMEROPTERA, 6805.

Ephydra hians, 7457.

EPICS, 781.

EPIDEMIOLOGY, 458, 2376, 6228, 7158, 8677.

EQUINOX (VERNAL), 3807.

Ereuntes occidentallis, 1160.

ERGONOMICS, 1892, 3614, 3615, 3616, 3617, 6858, 6859, 7816, 7824.

ERITREA, 4218.

Erminia harmsiana, DeWild., 731.

Erminia polyadenia, Hauman., 731.

Erythroxylon coca, 2333.

Erythroxylon sp., 7310.

ESKIMO, 132, 1279, 1612, 1894, 2428, 2576, 2818, 2910, 3019, 3021, 3298, 3561, 3609, 3655, 3656, 3882, 3923, 3990, 4160, 4376, 4458, 4572, 4922, 5076, 5278, 5280, 5890, 5894, 5955, 6014, 6066, 6068, 6190, 6260, 6263, 6536, 6651, 7038, 7215, 7229, 7351, 7352, 7353, 7552, 7657, 7673, 7742, 7802, 7805, 7806, 8288, 8565, 8858, 9028.

ESTONIA, 4887, 7022.

ETHICS, 7550, 7887.

ETHIOPIA, 2247, 3795, 3822, 3972, 4218, 4486, 4487, 4823, 4844, 4862, 4930, 4968, 5640, 5952, 6249, 6250, 7392, 7393, 7436, 7438, 7439, 7529, 7532, 7543, 7588, 7783, 8962.

ETHNICITY, 1109, 1110, 1269, 1612, 1673, 1740, 2109, 2394, 2406, 2521, 2608, 2802, 3138, 3266, 3267, 3360, 3515, 3558, 3665, 3749, 3840, 3912, 4175, 4426, 4507, 4547, 4667, 5420, 5434, 5478, 5644, 5682, 5936, 6246, 6290, 6419, 6424, 6676, 6721, 6919, 6998, 7050, 7112, 7173, 7437, 7697, 7717, 7840, 7909, 8075, 8107, 8365, 8954.

ETHNOBOTANY, 337, 501, 516, 593, 609, 665, 716, 882, 976, 1062, 1073, 1427, 1650, 1746, 1786, 1811, 1850, 1877, 2496, 2560, 2575, 2599, 2605, 2738, 2821, 3054, 3249, 3320, 3509, 3517, 3598, 3618, 3703, 3739, 3754, 3859, 3917, 3965, 3974, 4046, 4242, 4258, 4310, 4312, 4313, 4505, 4921, 5023, 5251, 5375, 5452, 5463, 5523, 5558, 5559, 5749, 6190, 6516, 6567, 6766, 6803, 6812, 6813, 6897, 7015, 7035, 7039, 7064, 7244, 7427, 7594, 7625, 7626, 7627, 7628, 7710, 7814, 7894, 7897, 7901, 7907, 7979, 8071, 8212, 8132, 8228, 8229, 8456, 8457, 8782, 8909, 8972, 9003, 9088, 9092.

ETHNOBIOLOGY, 3144, 3906, 3964, 5146, 8497.

ETHNOCENTRISM, 4139, 4143, 4741, 6263, 7009.

ETHNODIETETICS, 378, 1030, 5377, 6246, 8909.

ETHNOGRAPHIC ATLAS (BOOK), 590, 1106, 7378.

ETHNOGRAPHY, 1198, 1199, 4099, 4237, 4278, 4313, 4628, 4661, 4662, 5210, 5279, 5524, 5525, 5526, 5527, 5528, 5529, 5530, 5531, 5532, 5533, 5534, 5535, 5536, 5996, 6309, 6371, 6402, 6699, 7091, 7256, 7299, 7918, 7970, 8231, 8738, 8969, 9092.

ETHNOLOGY, 4793, 4939, 8437, 8803, 8804.

ETHNOMEDICINE, 337, 1945, 4632, 4955, 5003, 5423, 7480, 8909, 8951.

ETHNOSCIENCE, 119, 122, 2414, 2560, 2602, 2605, 2765, 2844, 3125, 3218, 3739, 3859, 3917,

6133, 6401, 6509, 6510, 6689, 6793, 6926,
7056, 7082, 7083, 7283, 7449, 8048, 8137,
8190, 8333, 8753, 8922, 8980, 9061.

FOOD AVERSION, 86, 392, 1267, 2016, 2642, 3161,
3441, 4988, 5448, 5480, 5615, 5990, 6034,
6457, 6535, 6969, 7530, 7644, 7649, 8200,
8233, 8578, 8579, 8580.

FOOD AVOIDANCE, 2595, 2596, 2597, 2975, 4275,
5793, 5852, 6089, 6248, 6535, 6689, 7391,
7533, 7534, 7541, 7543, 7544, 7752, 8017,
8497.

FOOD BEHAVIOR, 149, 867, 912, 1131, 1191, 1991,
2220, 2321, 2509, 2765, 2803, 2832, 2917,
2927, 2931, 2932, 3083, 3210, 3304, 3354,
3365, 3544, 3661, 3795, 4006, 4047, 4166,
4200, 4205, 4218, 4237, 4326, 4790, 4827,
4902, 4952, 5387, 5472, 5513, 5514, 5647,
5741, 5820, 5936, 6198, 6305, 6563, 6769,
6808, 6860, 6898, 6909, 6933, 7231, 7265,
7375, 7397, 7445, 7451, 7790, 7918, 8114,
8115, 8116, 8145, 8148, 8149, 8235, 8238,
8371, 8976, 9039.

FOOD BELIEFS, 62, 122, 310, 371, 389, 419, 601,
640, 936, 998, 999, 1056, 1161, 1169, 1580,
1630, 1833, 1902, 1926, 1964, 2055, 2148,
2168, 2203, 2215, 2257, 2274, 2483, 2493,
2514, 2595, 2596, 2597, 2697, 2713, 2739,
2927, 2975, 3065, 3120, 3194, 3195, 3419,
3544, 3741, 4135, 4157, 4790, 4842, 4902,
5055, 5116, 5213, 5572, 5651, 5755, 5764,
5825, 5852, 5977, 6007, 6072, 6337, 6539,
6576, 6887, 6969, 7029, 7130, 7177, 7250,
7307, 7312, 7331, 7368, 7386, 7420, 7550,
7650, 7785, 7849, 7956, 8021, 8355, 8359,
8497, 8550, 8679, 8778, 8847, 8872, 8873,
8875, 8876, 8878, 8892, 9063.

FOOD BUYING, 2246, 2304, 2356, 2562, 3189, 3190,
3770, 3850, 3860, 3862, 3863, 4575, 4799,
5726, 5851, 6334, 6558, 6576, 6614, 6904,
7231, 7471, 8256, 8419, 8789, 8980.

FOOD (CARBOHYDRATE), 749, 1100, 2147, 3903,
4337, 4505, 4897, 4938, 5059, 6153, 6387,
6702, 7003, 7205, 7962, 8690.

FOOD (CEREMONIAL ASPECTS), 640, 2133, 2600,
2657, 2679, 2806, 2828, 2834, 2849, 2857,
2904, 3004, 3022, 3059, 3077, 3193, 3304,
3324, 3528, 3529, 3541, 3544, 3557, 3569,
3613, 3624, 3707, 3814, 3896, 3898, 3899,
3908, 3987, 4083, 4101, 4181, 4223, 4569,
4575, 4622, 4632, 4729, 4910, 4919, 5151,
5152, 5206, 5324, 5487, 5569, 5595, 5981,
6328, 6411, 6534, 6593, 6617, 6633, 6642,
6748, 7115, 7480, 7713, 7843, 8021, 8118,
8177, 8190, 8334, 8429, 8437, 8451, 8502,
8660, 8857, 8906, 8907, 8932, 8950, 8973,
9011.

FOOD CHEMISTRY, 1597, 2057, 2282, 2288, 2461,
2610, 3013, 3033, 3145, 3730, 3748, 3883,
3999, 4093, 4331, 4496, 4503, 4504, 4882,
4883, 4885, 5018, 5635, 5859, 6040, 6086,
6112, 6116, 6138, 6316, 6371, 6891, 6974,
6993, 7269, 8268, 8303, 8391, 8594, 8596,

8599, 8640, 8822, 8997, 9051.

FOOD CLASSIFICATION SYSTEMS, 122, 127, 544, 545,
652, 715, 1169, 1630, 1833, 1926, 2080, 2257,
2274, 2483, 2560, 2596, 2605, 2739, 2990,
3525, 3528, 3529, 3964, 3995, 4132, 4133,
4137, 4319, 4409, 4575, 4727, 4751, 4842,
4902, 4910, 5093, 5116, 5269, 5363, 5423,
5576, 5614, 5720, 5733, 5852, 6484, 6495,
6624, 6648, 6657, 6866, 7009, 7066, 7177,
7238, 7426, 7542, 7670, 7790, 7849, 7878,
7907, 7932, 7933, 8400, 8437, 8443, 8622,
8624, 8807, 8875, 8876.

FOOD (COLD), 3807.

FOOD COMBINATIONS, 2345, 2430, 2431, 4275, 4299,
4300, 5389, 6313, 6866, 7326, 8970.

FOOD COMPOSITION, 43, 51, 52, 179, 196, 330,
340, 351, 401, 402, 612, 652, 703, 815, 845,
862, 950, 1100, 1952, 1965, 2057, 2252,
2288, 2461, 2563, 2683, 2761, 2777, 2784,
2801, 2852, 2866, 3217, 3223, 3399, 3432,
3449, 3490, 3494, 3560, 3563, 3748, 3869,
4019, 4020, 4139, 4262, 4412, 4496, 4503,
4529, 4644, 4717, 4719, 4749, 4814, 4834,
4883, 5018, 5066, 5147, 5187, 5287, 5404,
5611, 5629, 5635, 5636, 5859, 5870, 5871,
5872, 5873, 5874, 5875, 5876, 5908, 6112,
6316, 6326, 6395, 6396, 6397, 6423, 6489,
6891, 6933, 7019, 7087, 7145, 7189, 7192,
7469, 7510, 8010, 8102, 8161, 8391, 8528,
8594, 8596, 8599, 8663, 8691.

FOOD CONSERVATION, 2983, 3300, 5075, 6567.

FOOD CONSUMPTION, 30, 78, 212, 218, 297, 317,
324, 328, 330, 332, 333, 347, 459, 517, 522,
571, 652, 749, 865, 939, 944, 1036, 1037,
1102, 1111, 1162, 1184, 1220, 1224, 1295,
1337, 1457, 1487, 1507, 1635, 1642, 1714,
1735, 1736, 1845, 1864, 1887, 2023, 2063,
2071, 2085, 2120, 2121, 2123, 2133, 2196,
2281, 2299, 2589, 2688, 2689, 2711, 2712,
2763, 2891, 2983, 3305, 3345, 3412, 3464,
3465, 3552, 3566, 3651, 3774, 3841, 3860,
3957, 3958, 3976, 3997, 4319, 4539, 4561,
4616, 4682, 4725, 4732, 4798, 4838, 4873,
4914, 4915, 4999, 5201, 5214, 5311, 5312,
5354, 5370, 5371, 5376, 5414, 5425, 5589,
5640, 5674, 5699, 5740, 5746, 5797, 5823,
5827, 5837, 5906, 5924, 5929, 6003, 6024,
6030, 6104, 6140, 6212, 6322, 6330, 6355,
6367, 6369, 6387, 6550, 6568, 6629, 6639,
6818, 6874, 6925, 6971, 6972, 7145, 7157,
7219, 7243, 7274, 7421, 7692, 7751, 7753,
7790, 7793, 7811, 7829, 7858, 7956, 8034,
8035, 8051, 8088, 8089, 8107, 8135, 8147,
8149, 8207, 8215, 8232, 8233, 8236, 8241,
8258, 8259, 8280, 8379, 8389, 8390, 8393,
8419, 8430, 8431, 8497, 8683, 8753, 8842,
8844, 8881, 8959, 9000, 9043, 9047, 9048,
9065.

FOOD CONSUMPTION FREQUENCY, 416, 478, 479, 517,
577, 578, 601, 660, 675, 920, 1059, 1220,
1337, 1507, 1622, 1736, 2023, 2133, 2181,
2357, 2586, 2629, 2870, 2988, 3157, 3295,
3548, 3549, 3661, 3671, 3720, 3847, 4239,

5796, 5797, 5798, 5810, 5824, 5827, 5837,
5851, 5855, 5857, 5858, 5863, 5881, 5883,
5884, 5936, 5943, 5944, 5952, 5955, 5966,
5972, 5976, 5987, 6004, 6007, 6008, 6015,
6020, 6026, 6035, 6046, 6052, 6064, 6076,
6100, 6110, 6125, 6127, 6128, 6154, 6169,
6181, 6182, 6183, 6185, 6186, 6194, 6220,
6239, 6246, 6290, 6294, 6297, 6302, 6310,
6320, 6357, 6359, 6362, 6368, 6379, 6424,
6443, 6444, 6448, 6466, 6474, 6514, 6547,
6556, 6558, 6579, 6596, 6611, 6612, 6616,
6624, 6625, 6628, 6634, 6636, 6658, 6662,
6668, 6691, 6711, 6719, 6721, 6732, 6735,
6769, 6771, 6780, 6782, 6793, 6794, 6800,
6806, 6807, 6814, 6831, 6841, 6842, 6843,
6844, 6851, 6855, 6856, 6883, 6909, 6912,
6919, 6931, 6932, 6939, 6941, 6946, 6965,
6969, 6982, 6983, 6984, 6991, 6998, 7019,
7021, 7037, 7050, 7060, 7091, 7093, 7115,
7129, 7131, 7135, 7136, 7146, 7153, 7158,
7169, 7172, 7174, 7175, 7181, 7193, 7194,
7202, 7216, 7219, 7265, 7266, 7268, 7275,
7281, 7282, 7295, 7300, 7330, 7334, 7364,
7375, 7377, 7379, 7394, 7395, 7408, 7421,
7432, 7433, 7434, 7435, 7436, 7437, 7439,
7440, 7451, 7452, 7480, 7484, 7499, 7513,
7515, 7532, 7548, 7549, 7552, 7558, 7563,
7574, 7575, 7580, 7604, 7610, 7645, 7677,
7688, 7717, 7721, 7722, 7723, 7724, 7725,
7726, 7740, 7747, 7752, 7770, 7774, 7796,
7799, 7806, 7811, 7846, 7849, 7856, 7863,
7870, 7874, 7892, 7923, 7956, 7971, 7981,
7983, 7987, 8005, 8018, 8021, 8063, 8084,
8114, 8120, 8129, 8144, 8145, 8146, 8147,
8148, 8149, 8171, 8218, 8219, 8223, 8232,
8233, 8235, 8236, 8237, 8238, 8240, 8244,
8254, 8263, 8266, 8267, 8276, 8278, 8280,
8286, 8291, 8292, 8299, 8303, 8325, 8353,
8357, 8358, 8366, 8368, 8375, 8376, 8387,
8404, 8407, 8436, 8447, 8451, 8447, 8451,
8461, 8477, 8514, 8522, 8523, 8542, 8595,
8614, 8629, 8630, 8674, 8689, 8772, 8774,
8775, 8810, 8836, 8853, 8854, 8856, 8866,
8871, 8872, 8880, 8923, 8948, 8963, 8974,
8975, 9053, 9063, 9083, 9091.

FOOD HABITS CHANGE, 62, 133, 264, 476, 478, 579,
628, 652, 678, 836, 914, 940, 1050, 1168,
1224, 1346, 1501, 1528, 1639, 1658, 1673,
1683, 1714, 1736, 1765, 1766, 1767, 1780,
1872, 2109, 2136, 2181, 2183, 2196, 2198,
2216, 2220, 2455, 2602, 2802, 2867, 2882,
2898, 2901, 2936, 2938, 3064, 3084, 3125,
3142, 3157, 3171, 3266, 3286, 3340, 3394,
3490, 3528, 3567, 3589, 3702, 3721, 3727,
3774, 3791, 3814, 3841, 3846, 3862, 3916,
4004, 4042, 4264, 4326, 4328, 4329, 4365,
4444, 4482, 4522, 4547, 4781, 4784, 4787,
4856, 4863, 4922, 4996, 5059, 5063, 5071,
5129, 5153, 5248, 5304, 5306, 5350, 5472,
5473, 5474, 5476, 5478, 5481, 5511, 5560,
5610, 5627, 5731, 5838, 5904, 5936, 6009,
6022, 6056, 6125, 6168, 6212, 6217, 6260,
6274, 6283, 6335, 6406, 6445, 6454, 6508,
6590, 6612, 6638, 6643, 6689, 6736, 6883,
6886, 6913, 6927, 6931, 6973, 7021, 7068,
7069, 7161, 7177, 7229, 7230, 7243, 7349,
7355, 7382, 7414, 7422, 7479, 7657, 7665,
7673, 7677, 7910, 7911, 7962, 7986, 8073,
8199, 8240, 8258, 8309, 8359, 8362, 8389,

8390, 8683, 8690, 8870, 8980, 8989, 8993,
9028, 9064.

FOOD HABITS (HISTORY), 307, 311, 336, 348, 349,
360, 397, 413, 427, 461, 476, 477, 479, 504,
515, 522, 532, 549, 567, 568, 573, 574, 597,
615, 620, 627, 644, 651, 660, 685, 725, 734,
748, 775, 795, 806, 850, 854, 858, 875, 881,
887, 899, 902, 906, 914, 918, 923, 929, 932,
936, 956, 962, 1048, 1083, 1088, 1133, 1147,
1170, 1191, 1195, 1206, 1213, 1225, 1227,
1242, 1247, 1248, 1251, 1263, 1299, 1305,
1332, 1336, 1366, 1400, 1405, 1415, 1425,
1475, 1483, 1488, 1504, 1509, 1543, 1596,
1615, 1640, 1678, 1728, 1729, 1738, 1759,
1760, 1803, 1810, 1834, 1846, 1847, 1866,
1917, 1918, 1832, 1942, 1954, 1987, 1991,
1992, 1998, 2022, 2024, 2038, 2041, 2042,
2076, 2123, 2148, 2164, 2166, 2177, 2184,
2185, 2186, 2189, 2205, 2224, 2237, 2269,
2296, 2297, 2305, 2312, 2313, 2314, 2319,
2320, 2364, 2381, 2382, 2383, 2384, 2403,
2426, 2427, 2438, 2446, 2456, 2463, 2464,
2488, 2497, 2523, 2525, 2550, 2563, 2610,
2615, 2637, 2652, 2721, 2722, 2734, 2745,
2753, 2812, 2817, 2820, 2840, 2848, 2853,
2854, 2862, 2863, 2907, 2960, 2982, 2993,
3026, 3084, 3092, 3097, 3136, 3143, 3159,
3183, 3194, 3255, 3256, 3261, 3296, 3297,
3347, 3349, 3370, 3386, 3453, 3479, 3480,
3520, 3532, 3550, 3556, 3574, 3575, 3579,
3581, 3602, 3619, 3630, 3631, 3632, 3633,
3634, 3635, 3636, 3637, 3638, 3639, 3640,
3643, 3644, 3646, 3678, 3690, 3699, 3701,
3727, 3766, 3767, 3772, 3774, 3775, 3776,
3883, 3884, 3929, 3934, 3960, 3961, 3979,
3982, 3994, 3999, 4000, 4021, 4024, 4037,
4057, 4058, 4102, 4104, 4115, 4118, 4161,
4193, 4203, 4204, 4228, 4254, 4298, 4340,
4341, 4342, 4402, 4408, 4468, 4483, 4524,
4530, 4550, 4562, 4574, 4579, 4586, 4600,
4615, 4670, 4686, 4729, 4734, 4736, 4756,
4812, 4813, 4851, 4855, 4868, 4871, 4874,
4901, 4922, 4998, 5034, 5090, 5155, 5205,
5206, 5227, 5228, 5260, 5261, 5262, 5303,
5327, 5328, 5346, 5365, 5366, 5402, 5431,
5486, 5519, 5539, 5555, 5593, 5650, 5748,
5796, 5798, 5799, 5813, 5880, 5905, 5926,
5960, 5966, 5989, 5990, 5999, 6019, 6061,
6096, 6097, 6099, 6113, 6114, 6127, 6155,
6227, 6276, 6320, 6331, 6407, 6412, 6420,
6430, 6432, 6434, 6475, 6476, 6511, 6564,
6566, 6574, 6578, 6746, 6776, 6787, 6814,
6840, 6890, 6892, 6906, 6928, 6939, 6945,
6949, 6967, 6983, 6984, 7037, 7040, 7080,
7089, 7090, 7091, 7116, 7130, 7131, 7137,
1738, 7139, 7140, 7151, 7162, 7172, 7222,
7223, 7243, 7249, 7256, 7270, 7279, 7317,
7330, 7347, 7348, 7386, 7387, 7394, 7411,
7418, 7424, 7434, 7463, 7466, 7479, 7483,
7484, 7494, 7495, 7503, 7513, 7516, 7538,
7542, 7554, 7563, 7583, 7591, 7600, 7614,
7635, 7673, 7679, 7700, 7708, 7718, 7727,
7731, 7733, 7743, 7753, 7770, 7787, 7832,
7839, 7856, 7875, 7893, 7898, 7906, 7925,
7926, 7970, 7978, 7999, 8003, 8004, 8020,
8031, 8064, 8088, 8089, 8112, 8118, 8125,
8132, 8144, 8148, 8149, 8157, 8158, 8161,
8165, 8174, 8183, 8188, 8192, 8207, 8212,
8219, 8220, 8239, 8258, 8298, 8304, 8335,

HILO (HAWAII), 4257.

HIMALAYA MOUNTAINS,   7336, 1212, 1628, 3146,
    3590, 4238, 4415, 5059, 5197, 6240, 6241,
    6444, 7559, 8054, 8093, 8531.

HINDHEDE, MICHAEL, 6554.

HINDU-AMERICANS, 8326.

HINDU FAITH, 393, 736, 1472, 1511, 1514, 1515,
    1902, 2224, 2901, 3327, 3528, 3529, 3879,
    4409, 5321, 5691, 5737, 5767, 6347, 6484,
    6617, 6769, 7440, 7452, 7542, 7544, 7566,
    8730.

HINDU KUSH, 7251.

HIPPOCRATES, 573, 4986, 7872.

HIPPOPOTAMUS, 2424, 3540, 6518, 7531.

Hippopotamus amphibious, 6518.

HISHIO, 8020.

HISPANIC AMERICANS, 22, 848, 920, 978, 998,
    1066, 1134, 1347, 1565, 1630, 1926, 2045,
    2201, 2344, 2421, 2808, 3029, 3030, 3109,
    3155, 3390, 3653, 3892, 3962, 4201, 4392,
    4414, 4567, 5192, 5412, 6277, 6454, 6570,
    6598, 6646, 6754, 6919, 7499, 8173, 8876,
    8878, 8914, 8915, 8916.

DE HISTORIA STIRPIUM (BOOK), 1124.

HISTORY OF THE AMERICAN INDIAN (BOOK), 1124.

HITTITES, 3344.

HO CULTURE, 2347, 5131, 5134, 5693.

HOABINHIAN, 3147, 3148.

HOHOKAM CULTURE, 4184, 8958.

HOHOKAM TRAIL, 915.

HOLOCENE, 3148.

Holothuria scabral, 8605.

HOLOTHURIIDAE, 8279.

HOLSTEIN (GERMANY), 8487.

HOMEOPATHY, 184, 6025.

HOMER, 1823.

HOMINY, 8985.

HOMOPTERA , 559, 974, 1063, 1064, 2501, 3788,
    5583.

Homo sapiens, 6759.

HONDURAS, 840, 1531, 1762, 5342, 5872, 5875,
    6524, 6774.

HONEY, 334, 529, 743, 827, 1619, 1758, 2149,
    2177, 2444, 2512, 2787, 2788, 3812, 3847,
    4218, 4498, 4820, 5125, 6416, 6740, 7391,
    7737, 7984, 7995, 8428, 8705.

HONG KONG, 119, 121, 123, 124, 125, 126, 127,
    128, 129, 1053, 2031, 3698, 4892, 5985, 5986.

HONOLULU, 1109, 1110, 4257, 5635, 6403, 6404,
    8719, 8950.

HOOKWORM, 2974.

HOOVER, HERBERT C., 1398.

HOPEWELLIAN CULTURE, 1949, 7915, 9023.

HOPI CULTURE, 157, 462, 588, 1119, 1387, 1558,
    1718, 2421, 2447, 2599, 2600, 2720, 2725,
    3905, 4571, 5225, 5277, 5962, 6110, 6888,
    7549, 7842, 8176, 8276, 8455, 8623, 8624,
    8629, 8780, 8781, 8782.

HOPPIE, W.D., 241.

HOPS, 6980, 7906.

HORACE, 4435.

Hordeum vulgare var. nudum , 8397.

HORMONES, 6463.

HORSES, 2717, 4183, 4945.

HORSE CHESTNUT, 1304.

HORSE MEAT,   193, 194, 728, 738, 777, 846, 966,
    1309, 2069, 2070, 2071, 2072, 2073, 2074,
    2115, 2329, 2870, 2978, 3206, 6585, 6746,
    6918, 8697.

HORTICULTURE,   504, 570, 628, 640, 708, 894,
    1080, 1124, 1168, 1325, 1809, 1877, 1956,
    2249, 2445, 2450, 2515, 2557, 2716, 2762,
    2975, 3052, 3153, 3399, 3538, 3648, 3709,
    3751, 3823, 3862, 3863, 3954, 4293, 4371,
    4473, 4643, 4667, 4830, 4897, 5065, 5247,
    5379, 5606, 5744, 6035, 6191, 6482, 7013,
    7078, 7237, 7635, 7687, 8113, 8462, 8861,
    8912.

HOSHANGABAD (INDIA), 7556.

HOSPITAL FOOD, 612, 1051, 1262, 1496, 1536,
    2394, 3138, 4039, 4924, 5263, 5320, 6304,
    7182, 7326, 7437, 8826, 8955.

HOSPITAL FOOD SERVICE, 12, 1536, 1590, 2394,
    6131, 6201, 7094, 7413, 7989.

HOSPITALITY, 4283, 5851, 7790, 8364.

HOSPITALS, 2021, 6424, 7989, 8826, 8955.

HOT - COLD FOOD CLASSIFICATION SYSTEM, 122, 652,
    1630, 1833, 1926, 2596, 2739, 3465, 3525,
    3528, 3529, 4575, 4902, 5093, 5363, 5576,
    5720, 5990, 6657, 7177, 7849, 8400, 8875.

IRON AGE, 1006, 3632, 3789.

IROQUOIS CULTURE, 599, 2273, 5794, 6264, 7616, 8638, 8649.

IRRIGATION, 161, 1385, 2376, 2385, 3388, 3880, 4793, 5557, 5637, 8289, 8958, 8982.

IRRITABILITY, 1572.

Irvingia Gabonensis, 359.

ISABEL ISLAND, 610.

ISLAMIC FAITH, 284, 288, 773, 1532, 1914, 2203, 2224, 2414, 3275, 3291, 4073, 4406, 4407, 4467, 4579, 4699, 5321, 5694, 5734, 5846, 6434, 6529, 6617, 6939, 6941, 7135, 8461.

ISLAND OF CHILOE, 7138.

ISLETA PUEBLO CULTURE, 4242.

ISOKO CULTURE, 6018.

ISOPTERA 559, 974, 1063, 1923, 2501, 6124.

ISRAEL, 578, 579, 580, 877, 3305, 3306, 4262, 5110, 5866, 7910, 7910, 8453, 9095.

ISTHMUS NAHUAT CULTURE, 7932, 7933.

ISTHMUS OF TEHUANTEPEC (MEXICO), 9078.

ITALIAN-ALGERIANS, 7734.

ITALIAN - AMERICANS, 240, 1565, 1966, 2023, 2147, 2790, 4186, 4424, 4508, 4961, 4962, 4963, 5644, 5847, 6046, 6419, 6598, 6868, 6919, 7735, 8763.

ITALIAN - CANADIANS, 8199.

ITALY, 266, 414, 436, 439, 539, 747, 864, 911, 952, 1051, 1165, 1273, 1407, 1455, 1822, 1887, 1896, 1934, 1952, 2306, 2439, 2463, 3290, 3505, 3603, 4547, 4574, 4810, 4867, 4873, 4961, 4962, 4963, 5031, 5110, 5162, 5609, 5927, 5951, 6046, 6360, 6379, 6496, 6703, 6982, 6983, 7141, 7154, 7515, 7960, 8044, 8087, 8220, 8494, 8708, 8774, 9026.

ITESO CULTURE, 4705.

ITZA CULTURE , 6792.

IVAI RIVER, 2585.

IVORY COAST, 5598, 5600, 6545, 7368, 8429.

JABUTICABA, 2777.

JAIN FAITH, 4307.

JAIPUR (INDIA), 3676.

JAK FRUIT, 1 4076, 6694.

JAKUN CULTURE, 2514.

JALE CULTURE, 4490.

JALEBI, 8536.

JALISCO (MEXICO), 4368.

JAMAICA, 403, 458, 609, 1418, 1485, 2007, 2008, 2013, 2564, 2761, 3211, 4150, 4563, 5019, 5066, 5201, 5202, 5343, 5666, 6425, 7033, 7369, 7579, 8261, 8953.

Jambosa malaccensis, 5636.

JAMES BAY (ONTARIO), 8495.

JAMES I (MONARCH), 3442.

JANJERA CULTURE, 3972.

JAPAN, 10, 23, 205, 214, 229, 236, 273, 345, 391, 552, 553, 554, 555, 595, 973, 1399, 1600, 1959, 2225, 2617, 2849, 2860, 2971, 2976, 3231, 3233, 3354, 3432, 3569, 3571, 3572, 3573, 3716, 3717, 3791, 3940, 4002, 4006, 4010, 4040, 4042, 4085, 4102, 4275, 4296, 4339, 4340, 4341, 4342, 4421, 4423, 4440, 4502, 4519, 4521, 4547, 4774, 4809, 4944, 4951, 4952, 4978, 5001, 5626, 5797, 5798, 5812, 5835, 5836, 5885, 5910, 6040, 6104, 6105, 6116, 6185, 6186, 6261, 6343, 6356, 6365, 6448, 6629, 6633, 6805, 7075, 7202, 7218, 7219, 7406, 7479, 7483, 7494, 7495, 7496, 7623, 7827, 7889, 7969, 8006, 8007, 8008, 8009, 8010, 8020, 8028, 8041, 8056, 8267, 8268, 8279, 8337, 8520, 8598, 8599, 8898, 9008, 9011, 9012, 9013, 9014, 9065, 9066.

JAPANESE-AMERICANS, 1109, 2460, 3912, 5304, 5623, 5625, 8326, 8690, 8769.

Jarilla chocola, 8196.

JARMAN-BELL, 2965.

Jatropha manioth, 6158.

JAVA 421, 1012, 1732, 2404, 2405, 3748, 3839, 3858, 5320, 6952, 7243, 8021.

JAVANESE (OVERSEAS), 7846.

JAW, 684, 1321, 2523, 3747, 5750, 6588, 8038.

JEFFERSON, THOMAS, 4420, 5419, 6348.

JEMEZ PUEBLO CULTURE, 1786, 7842.

JERICHO, 792, 2265, 3593.

JERUSALEM, 709, 3306.

JERUSALEM ARTICHOKE, 551, 2102.

JESUIT ORDER, 81, 409.

JEWISH FAITH, 709, 811, 949, 1019, 1334, 1413, 1690, 1982, 2124, 2473, 2834, 3059, 3065,

3104, 3213, 3305, 3700, 3707, 3995, 4049,
4052, 4179, 4261, 4333, 4467, 4512, 4547,
4840, 4842, 4994, 5269, 5270, 5733, 5807,
6416, 6419, 6495, 6512, 6598, 6770, 6919,
6948, 7009, 7094, 7115, 7238, 7570, 7652,
7653, 7670, 7878, 7896, 7910, 7911, 8199,
8462, 8807, 8943.

JEW'S MALLOW, 8641.

JICAMA, 3703, 7299.

JICAMA DE BARYTA, 888.

JICAQUE, 1643.

JIMI VALLEY (PAPUA NEW GUINEA), 1168.

JIVARO (CULTURE),   715, 716, 718, 719, 1643,
2548, 7013, 7014.

JOB'S TEARS, 8360, 8520, 8714.

JOCHELSON, WALDEMAR, 4043.

JOGJAKARTA (INDONESIA), 421.

JOHANNESBURG (SOUTH AFRICA), 3659.

JOJOBA, 2210.

JONES, WILLIAM O., 5998.

JORDAN, 3593, 3594, 6413, 7062, 9095.

JOSHUA TREE, 8941.

JOURNALISM (FOOD-RELATED), 3713.

JOY OF COOKING (COOK BOOK), 607.

Juglans regia, 3005, 6442.

JUJUBE, 3377.

JULIAN THE APOSTATE, 323.

JUNEBERRY 6891.

JUNGLE, 5550.

JUNJO (JAMAICAN = 'mushroom'), 1418.

KABYLE CULTURE, 4731, 8515.

KACHARI CULTURE, 2470.

KACHIN CULTURE, 3429.

KAFA CULTURE, 3972.

KAFFIR CULTURE, 295, 1246, 1497, 5928, 6943,
8747.

KAGURU CULTURE, 632.

KAIBAB PAIUTE CULTURE, 4367.

KAINGANG CULTURE, 4885, 6562.

KAIPAROWITS PAIUTE CULTURE, 4367.

KAKADU CULTURE, 7719.

KALAHARI DESERT, 1043, 3255, 3256, 3257, 3259,
3260, 3262, 3263, 3438, 4760, 4761, 4762,
4763, 5232, 5233, 5234, 5235, 8027.

KALAPALO CULTURE, 544, 545.

KALULI CULTURE, 7250.

KAMAJAHU, 7022.

KAMIYA CULTURE, 2716.

KAMAPALA (UGANDA), 5856.

KAMPOCHORA, 308.

KANAHUA: (see: CANIHUA).

KANEMBU CULTURE, 8510.

KANGAROO, 3462, 8221.

KANIKKARAN CULTURE, 7450.

KANSAS, 1000, 1496, 4174, 6008, 7110, 7112.

KANSAS CITY, KANSAS, 4174.

KANSU PROVINCE (CHINA), 7195.

KANURI CULTURE, 8510.

KAPAUKU CULTURE, 2223, 3438, 6550.

KAPINGAMARANGI, 1190, 5774.

KAPOK, 8181.

KARAKATCHAN CULTURE, 5212.

KARANKAWA CULTURE, 2953.

KAREN CULTURE, 5230.

KARIMOJONG CULTURE, 2379.

KARO BATAK CULTURE, 5707.

KAROK CULTURE, 7224.

KARS (TURKEY), 4516.

KARUT (MILK PRODUCT), 3871.

KASHMIR, 1628.

KATAB CULTURE, 5493.

KATANGA (ZAIRE), 729, 731, 732, 4612, 4730,
6531.

KATCHINAS, 2600.

KATSUOBUSHI, 3716.

KATZ, JOHAN RUDOLF, 635.

KAUAI (HAWAII), 2385, 3948, 4343.

KAUNYAMA AMBO CULTURE, 4949.

KAYENTA NAVAJO CULTURE, 9003.

KEFIR, 770, 1136, 3384, 3401, 4543, 6959, 7779.

KEKCHI CULTURE, 1561, 7194.

KELLOGG, JOHN HARVEY, 1382, 7331.

KELP, 6567.

KELTA CULTURE, 6567.

KENTROCHORA (GREECE), 308.

KENTUCKY, 1877, 2410, 3142, 3191, 4243, 4422, 4439, 4509, 4889, 6908, 7280, 8254, 8586, 8844, 9024, 9025.

KENYA, 131, 827, 844, 1073, 1202, 1886, 2990, 3036, 3171, 3221, 5189, 5293, 5340, 5790, 5867, 5868, 5900, 6106, 6168, 7749, 8130, 7992, 8130, 8203.

KERALA (INDIA), 3103, 3305, 4735, 5307, 7450.

KETCHUP, 818.

KHAMIS MUSHAYT (ARABIA), 6416.

KHARIYA CULTURE, 7060.

KHASI CULTURE, 3328.

KHOA (MILK PRODUCT), 2048.

KIANGSU PROVINCE (CHINA), 3420.

KICKAPOO CULTURE, 8889.

KIDNEY BEAN, 1385.

KIGANDA CULTURE, 667, 5266, 7095.

KIKUYU CULTURE, (see: AKIKUYU).

KILIMANJARO, 9.

KILIWA CULTURE, 5591.

KING COUNTY (WASHINGTON STATE), 614.

KINSHIP, 639, 1689, 2336, 3538, 4622, 4830, 5740, 6508, 6841, 6482, 7065, 7250, 8190, 8529, 9074.

KIOWA CULTURE, 764, 5356, 5754, 7606, 8457.

KIOWA APACHE CULTURE, 4258.

KIPSIGIS CULTURE, 5867, 5868.

KIRGIZ CULTURE, 8521.

KISSELKOMLEKO (MILK PRODUCT), 3247.

KITCHEN-MIDDENS, 690, 838, 2019, 2020, 3407, 4825, 4927, 5860, 7212, 7797, 8746.

KITCHENS, 55, 266, 1248, 1865, 1892, 1937, 2355, 2446, 2460, 3056, 3581, 3614, 3615, 3616, 3617, 3678, 3801, 3831, 3904, 4230, 4473, 4608, 4633, 4643, 4703, 4932, 5294, 5346, 5617, 5812, 5929, 6337, 6347, 6405, 6430, 6858, 6859, 7816, 7820, 7821, 7822, 7824, 7990, 8017, 8125, 8310.

KIVA, 2600.

KIVU, 1358.

KIWAI CULTURE, 4624.

KLAMATH CULTURE, 1857, 1858.

KNEE INJURY, 6748.

KNIVES, 6400.

KNOXVILLE (TENNESSEE), 5808.

KOBUK RIVER (ALASKA), 3019.

KODIAK ISLAND, 233, 3848.

KOFYAR CULTURE, 5451.

KOGI CULTURE, 8918, 8919.

KOJI (SOY BEAN PRODUCT), 3717.

KOKO NOR (CHINA), 7300.

KOLA NUT, 5675, 6077, 8526.

KONA (HAWAII), 2460.

KONDH CULTURE, 5676.

KONGO CULTURE, 7688.

KONIAG ESKIMO, 3848.

KONING, MARTINE WITTOP, 3271.

KOREA, 924, 1357, 1974, 3356, 3409, 3791, 3904, 4304, 4580, 4757, 4864, 5775, 5957, 6181, 6629, 7012, 7214, 7496, 8300, 8366, 8755.

KOREAN-AMERICANS, 6217.

KORWA CULTURE, 5132.

KOTA CULTURE, 8441.

KOTOKO CULTURE 4727.

KRAO CULTURE, 4550.

KRIKATI CULTURE, 5998.

Krizousacorixa azteca, Jacz., 5298.

Krizousacorixa femorata, Guer., 5298.

LUCKNOW (INDIA), 7560.

LUKONOR (NAMOI ISLAND, MICRONESIA), 8190.

LUMBERMEN, 2047, 8963.

LUMMI CULTURE, 5956.

LUNCH, 1572, 1631, 1743, 4241, 6144, 7160, 7818, 8660, 9029.

LUNDA CULTURE, 3034.

Lupinus sp., 7120, 7999.

LUSAKA (ZAMBIA), 6075.

LUSHAI-KUKI CULTURE, 7440.

LUXEMBOURG, 4457.

LUZON ISLAND, 3242, 3341, 3693, 8572, 8573, 8574.

Lycopersicum esculentum, 3703, 4153.

Lycopersicum sp., 5010.

LYDGATE JOHN, 3199.

LYSINE, 4331.

MAASTRICHT (NETHERLANDS), 571.

MACABO (FOOD PLANT, ARACEAE), 1848.

MACAGUAJE CULTURE, 8513.

MACCARONI, 8494.

MACHIGUENGA CULTURE, 2548, 4207, 5744.

MACKENZIE RIVER, 7802.

Macoubea sp., 7310.

MACROBIOTIC DIET, 1112, 2483, 2780, 4302, 6930.

MACUSI CULTURE, 2549.

MADAGASCAR, 399, 1141, 2064, 2065, 2066, 2360, 2555, 4226, 4526, 4919, 5339, 5729, 6174, 6196, 6333, 6618, 8097.

Madaria sp., 3942.

MADEIRA, 3173, 4185.

MADHYA PRADESH (INDIA), 2376, 2845, 4014, 7051, 7053, 7055, 7059, 7556.

MADRAS (INDIA), 186.

MADURA (INDONESIA), 7243.

MADZOON (ARMENIAN = 'yogurt'), 2332, 2466.

MAFAFFA FOOD PLANT, ARACEAE), 1848.

MAGHREB (REGION, NORTH AFRICA), 439.

MAGIC, 1056, 6842, 7163, 7480, 8190, 8437.

MAGNESIUM, 8862.

MAGOU (FERMENTED CEREAL PRODUCT), 7333.

MAGUEY, 401, 651, 664, 879, 1328, 3887, 4891.

MAHARASHTRA (INDIA), 4295, 4327, 5312.

MAHRATTA (INDIA), 196, 1084.

MAIDU CULTURE, 3130, 6632.

MAILU CULTURE, 5150.

MAIMONIDES, 2995.

MAINE, 2047, 2269, 3577, 8963.

MAIN-ET-LOIRE (FRANCE), 1038.

MAIZE, 21, 28, 108, 109, 110, 111, 112, 113, 114, 115, 116, 117, 118, 160, 256, 468, 471, 526, 586, 600, 611, 651, 688, 731, 791, 808, 906, 969, 984, 1076, 1080, 1119, 1120, 1180, 1218, 1247, 1260, 1261, 1265, 1300, 1368, 1382, 1385, 1388, 1390, 1393, 1465, 1497, 1588, 1715, 1717, 1718, 1719, 1720, 1767, 1778, 1780, 1863, 1873, 1874, 1876, 1904, 1913, 1929, 1930, 1931, 1845, 1947, 1948, 1950, 1951, 2180, 2283, 2359, 2384, 2387, 2389, 2395, 2408, 2409, 2410, 2459, 2465, 2494, 2495, 2506, 2579, 2583, 2615, 2676, 2679, 2707, 2723, 2779, 2809, 2828, 2857, 2878, 2879, 2880, 2904, 2990, 3032, 3135, 3241, 3290, 3342, 3472, 3507, 3508, 3515, 3547, 3624, 3660, 3688, 3703, 3764, 3793, 3924, 3975, 4017, 4034, 4083, 4120, 4121, 4122, 4124, 4125, 4126, 4127, 4128, 4129, 4180, 4191, 4246, 4247, 4331, 4337, 4368, 4377, 4378, 4383, 4413, 4480, 4481, 4563, 4595, 4680, 4692, 4824, 4885, 4918, 4926, 4973, 5015, 5080, 5146, 5164, 5165, 5166, 5167, 5168, 5169, 5170, 5171, 5172, 5173, 5174, 5175, 5176, 5177, 5178, 5179, 5180, 5181, 5182, 5183, 5184, 5185, 5250, 5273, 5276, 5323, 5452, 5461, 5486, 5501, 5551, 5557, 5562, 5562, 5607, 5667, 5669, 5670, 5671, 5748, 5817, 5831, 5879, 5963, 5964, 5971, 6013, 6083, 6164, 6187, 6192, 6210, 6219, 6235, 6264, 6288, 6350, 6386, 6416, 6542, 6549, 6604, 6627, 6642, 6659, 6677, 6678, 6707, 6740, 6764, 6765, 6792, 6809, 6855, 6888, 6890, 6905, 6979, 6989, 7085, 7107, 7108, 7120, 7144, 7186, 7333, 7360, 7517, 7567, 7572, 7745, 7763, 7777, 7786, 7796, 7813, 7849, 7855, 7881, 7886, 7941, 7942, 7950, 8093, 8176, 8211, 8359, 8419, 8434, 8459, 8563, 8638, 8641, 8642, 8643, 8644, 8645, 8646, 8647, 8661, 8706, 8747, 8756, 8828, 8832, 8836, 8848, 8888, 8904, 8912, 8928, 8932, 8933, 8979, 8985, 9007, 9030, 9057, 9067, 9077.

MALABAR (INDIA), 1643, 5983.

MALABSORPTION, 4902.

MAPLE, 2583.

MAPLE SUGAR, 261, 1241, 1476, 3690, 3814, 6483, 6623, 7099.

MAPS, 677, 1316, 1460, 5996, 6140, 8149, 8723.

MARANON RIVER, 716, 719.

Maranta arundinacea, L., 406.

Maranta, sp., 7310.

MARASMUS, 2330, 4008.

MARGARINE, 6864, 7347, 7949.

MARIANAS ISLANDS, 2882, 7669, 8129.

MARICOPA CULTURE, 1430.

MARINE RESOURCES, 106, 147, 222, 386, 391, 444, 755, 757, 765, 867, 895, 1153, 1383, 1450, 2384, 2340, 2823, 3219, 3220, 3395, 3409, 3665, 3698, 3726, 3738, 3965, 4002, 4032, 4102, 4234, 4343, 4416, 4473, 4504, 4541, 4601, 4610, 4636, 4637, 4706, 5073, 5115, 5422, 5635, 5821, 5930, 5931, 5996, 6109, 6119, 6173, 6285, 6311, 6352, 6353, 6426, 6426, 6462, 6464, 6465, 6506, 6530, 6537, 6567, 6689, 6726, 6757, 6758, 6799, 7076, 7078, 7286, 7287, 7370, 7462, 7463, 7487, 7623, 7624, 7636, 7714, 7849, 7936, 8019, 8043, 8264, 8265, 8279, 8436, 8605, 8821, 9030, 9074.

MARING CULTURE, 1167, 1168, 1169, 3438, 4047, 6700, 6701, 7065.

MARKETING RESEARCH, 2356, 2934, 3278, 4711, 5156, 5214, 6614, 7902, 8241.

MARKETS, 171, 174, 279, 285, 845, 1070, 1160, 1200, 1556, 1738, 1846, 1847, 1999, 2173, 2386, 2387, 2398, 2479, 2789, 3132, 3252, 3516, 3985, 4218, 4257, 4339, 4429, 4826, 4903, 5160, 5301, 5346, 5353, 5666, 5776, 5851, 5856, 6075, 6403, 6416, 6547, 6550, 6558, 6595, 7085, 7255, 7348, 7448, 7482, 7577, 7936, 8111, 8249, 8270, 8308, 8603, 8743, 8980.

MARMA CULTURE, 733.

MARONI RIVER CARIB CULTURE, 4471.

MARQUESAS ISLANDS, 886, 2068, 2080, 3414, 4185, 6837, 7163, 7200, 8050, 8227.

MARRIAGE, 29, 1755, 2460, 4304, 4425, 4464, 4622, 5642, 6617, 7784, 9013.

MARROW-BONE, 2451.

MARSEILLE, (FRANCE), 796, 1037.

MARSHALL ISLANDS, 4538, 4706, 5882, 5891, 5911, 6508, 7879, 8688.

MARSUPIALS, 7984.

MARTHA'S VINEYARD, 8244.

MARTINIQUE, 1181, 2326, 2771, 4400, 5258, 6587.

MARXIAN THEORY, 8704.

MARYLAND, 784, 5130, 5418, 7778, 8586.

MASAI CULTURE, 3036, 3171, 5189, 6168.

MASATO (YUCCA PRODUCT, PERU), 2393.

MASCOUTEN CULTURE, 8889.

MAS D'AZIL (FRANCE), 6442.

MASSA CULTURE, 2925.

MASSACHUSETTS, 1242, 2023, 4495, 6424, 7714, 8244, 8763.

MASSAGE, 2367.

MASSIM CULTURE, 9052.

MASTIC, 960.

MASTICATION, 1188, 1321, 2295, 2650, 3747, 4158, 5114, 7802, 8182, 8285, 8608.

MATERNAL-CHILD HEALTH, 486, 1144, 1414, 1415, 1727, 2121, 2392, 2409, 2417, 3142, 3203, 3254, 3255, 3256, 3257, 3451, 4135, 4998, 5144, 5897, 6107, 6145, 6577, 6800, 8678.

MATHUVAN CULTURE, 4735.

MATLATZINCA CULTURE, 1253, 2496.

MATO GROSSO (BRAZIL), 544, 545, 2303, 4849, 5350, 6083, 8560.

MATRIFOCALITY, 4455, 4621.

MAUI (HAWAII), 4257, 5304.

MAUNDY THURSDAY, 7480.

MAURITANIA, 1613, 2594, 3452, 5325, 5337, 5362.

Mauritia flexuosa, 7951.

Mauritia vinifera, M., 7565.

MAYA CULTURE, 1069, 1074, 1075, 1417, 2030, 2688, 2859, 2904, 3660, 5929, 6029, 6500, 6607, 6632, 6792, 7064, 7458, 7459, 7789, 7809, 7810, 8846.

MAYA (ANCIENT), 147, 444, 624, 996, 1065, 1069, 1257, 1781, 1863, 2262, 2465, 2511, 3006, 3718, 4636, 4637, 5020, 6603, 6604, 6605, 6606, 6607, 6792, 7209.

MBEERE CULTURE, 1073.

MBUM CULTURE, 6118.

MBUNDU CULTURE, 8680.

MBUTI CULTURE (see: BAMBUTI).

MCCARRISON, ROBERT, 378, 8922.

MCCOLLUM, ELMER VERNER, 5391, 5573.

MEAD (BEVERAGE), 7995.

MEAL COST, 5847, 8365.

MEAL PATTERNS, 57, 425, 1087, 1220, 2276, 2277, 3186, 3318, 3651, 4094, 4104, 4329, 4643, 4567, 4757, 4799, 5294, 5467, 6366, 6576, 6577, 6714, 6889, 7219, 7385, 7672, 7840, 8021, 8037, 8119, 8239, 8343, 8353, 8430, 8431, 8447, 8753.

MEALS, 398, 568, 584, 629, 723, 736, 801, 866, 946, 1025, 1151, 1188, 1258, 1271, 1281, 1424, 1425, 1493, 1494, 1635, 1639, 2274, 2276, 2277, 2414, 2509, 2845, 2975, 2982, 3193, 3465, 3616, 3795, 3847, 3862, 4011, 4047, 4085, 4102, 4135, 4153, 4173, 4207, 4275, 4298, 4633, 4729, 4816, 4985, 5015, 5031, 5197, 5228, 5346, 5610, 5710, 5823, 5847, 5998, 6261, 6509, 6539, 6558, 6563, 6808, 6892, 6972, 7012, 7101, 7273, 7367, 7375, 7397, 7413, 7422, 7519, 7687, 7790, 7817, 7818, 7819, 7846, 7869, 7932, 7964, 8021, 8064, 8118, 8195, 8447, 8660, 8755, 8756, 8853, 8970, 9011, 9012, 9013, 9014.

MEALS (LOW COST), 192, 3515, 8166.

MEALS (SEATING ARRANGEMENT), 4405.

MEAL SERVICE, 962, 2384, 2457, 2856, 2979, 3100, 3616, 3678, 4582, 4608, 5823.

MEAL-TIMES, 183, 536, 1025, 1635, 2697, 3113, 3678, 3738, 3847, 5049, 5134, 5350, 5890, 6235, 6302, 6334, 6529, 6617, 7029, 7101, 7248, 7672, 7844, 7869, 8042, 8280, 8292, 8497.

MEASUREMENT (PSYCHOLOGICAL), 3281.

MEASUREMENT (VOLUME), 4617, 4623, 5405.

MEAT, 188, 191, 199, 202, 206, 209, 334, 462, 520, 683, 701, 703, 719, 739, 766, 722, 1017, 1058, 1066, 1188, 1207, 1219, 1264, 1358, 1370, 1464, 1513, 1624, 1666, 1671, 1721, 1847, 1895, 1920, 1997, 2069, 2070, 1071, 2072, 2073, 2074, 2080, 2097, 2099, 2124, 2167, 2233, 2234, 2311, 2320, 2384, 2424, 2451, 2458, 2502, 2602, 2629, 2688, 2749, 2863, 2891, 2946, 2990, 3078, 3285, 3307, 3327, 3425, 3516, 3607, 3729, 3767, 3826, 3829, 3847, 3979, 4013, 4052, 4053, 4102, 4161, 4218, 4227, 4298, 4307, 4319, 4345, 4352, 4390, 4427, 4601, 4622, 4628, 4706, 4775, 4785, 4818, 4831, 4839, 4859, 4876, 4907, 5042, 5075, 5235, 5350, 5360, 5383, 5424, 5687, 5807, 6006, 6113, 6133, 6168, 6278, 6401, 6415, 6518, 6535, 6585, 6611, 6642, 6729, 6746, 6958, 6964, 7005, 7091, 7116, 7186, 7250, 7270, 7479, 7486, 7531, 7544, 7595, 7619, 7782, 7802, 7803, 7804, 7805, 7811, 7813, 7828, 7841, 7844, 7993,

8100, 8147, 8291, 8292, 8294, 8332, 8374, 8379, 8443, 8548, 8624, 8631, 8692, 8693, 8766, 8847, 8904, 9014, 9056.

MECHANIZATION, 8565.

MECKLENBURG (GERMANY), 575, 4546.

MEDELLIN (COLUMBIA), 2235.

MEDIA, 1501, 1635, 5514.

MEDICAL SCHOOLS, 2699, 6131.

MEDICI, 3442.

MEDICINE, 122, 649, 849, 1146, 1178, 1480, 1590, 1833, 1926, 1985, 1987, 2021, 2436, 2437, 2699, 3525, 3548, 3549, 3620, 3629, 3739, 3798, 3861, 3900, 3902, 4008, 4215, 4740, 4822, 4878, 5472, 5517, 5850, 5862, 5953, 5990, 6265, 6478, 6959, 7043, 7225, 7297, 7386, 7594, 7887, 7909, 7919, 8036, 8157, 8233, 8303, 8421, 8588, 8589, 8590, 8909, 8931.

MEDITERRANEAN PEOPLES, 349, 439, 508, 4035, 5346, 7727.

MEDITERRANEAN REGION, 4222, 4332, 4556, 5110, 6200, 7163, 7403, 7404, 7562.

MEDLPA CULTURE, 7907.

MEGARHA CULTURE, 4040.

MEGENBERG, KONRAD VON, 7925.

MEIJI PERIOD (JAPAN), 7479.

ME-KRANOTI CULTURE, 8477.

MELANAU CULTURE, 4089, 4091.

MELANESIA, 494, 495, 954, 1604, 1681, 2644, 3251, 3282, 3365, 3778, 3780, 4041, 4159, 4293, 4696, 5150, 5151, 5563, 5657, 5829, 5975, 6063, 6252, 6256, 6257, 6258, 6259, 6563, 6783, 6865, 6934, 6935, 6938, 7066, 7195, 7381, 7662, 8065, 8187, 8228, 8415, 8416, 8635, 8731, 8771, 8845, 8890, 9052.

MELLOCA (FOOD CROP, ANDES MOUNTAINS), 3802, 3804.

MELONS, 909, 3829, 5241, 8026.

MEMPHIS (TENNESSEE), 5847.

MENARCHE, 772, 3019, 4535.

MENDE CULTURE, 541, 3820.

MENDOZA (ARGENTINA), 9073.

Mennispermum cocculus, 2390.

MENNONITE DENOMINATION, 5520.

MENOMINI CULTURE, 3814, 7571, 7626.

MISSISSIPPIAN CULTURE (PREHISTORIC) 628, 1765, 1766, 1767, 2539, 2556, 2752, 5970, 7595.

MISSISSIPPI VALLEY 3017, 3227, 7595.

MISSOURI, 1624, 1866, 1903, 7320.

MISSOURI RIVER, 3050.

MISTASINI CULTURE, 2572.

MIWOK CULTURE, 6567.

MIXTEC CULTURE, 1831, 6976.

MNONG GAR CULTURE, 1746.

MOA, 2153, 7520, 8756.

MOANDA (GABON), 7292.

MOBA CULTURE, 6371.

MOCHI (RICE VARIETY), 3068, 9012, 9013.

MOCHOBO CULTURE, 8162.

MOCTEZUMA, 114.

MODELING, 149, 4194, 4268, 6494, 6605, 6606, 6607, 6788, 7013, 7877, 8048, 8835.

MODERNIZATION, 601.

MODOC CULTURE, 1643, 6567.

MOGH CULTURE, 733.

MOGOLLON CULTURE, 1076, 6835.

MOHAVE CULTURE, 1430, 4081, 7852.

MOHAVE DESERT, 1506.

MOKIL, 8660.

MOLDAVIA (ROUMANIA), 381.

MOLASSES, 480, 481, 3828.

MOLOKAI (HAWAII), 137.

MOLUCCAS ISLANDS, 2171.

MOLLUSCA, 147, 451, 792, 1153, 1243, 3219, 3220, 3322, 3665, 3738, 4343, 4416, 4610, 5245, 5635, 6311, 7371, 7384, 7464, 8180, 8230, 8497, 8605, 8821.

MONEY, 2364.

MONGOLIA, 3108, 3531, 5417, 5736, 6420, 8504, 8865.

MONGONGO NUT, 4760, 4763.

MONGUOR CULTURE, 7295, 7300.

MONI CULTURE, 4040.

MONKS, 779, 780, 2208, 2355, 2532, 4453, 5197, 6411, 7274, 8950, 9065, 9066.

MONOCOTYLEDONS, 6390.

MONOCROPPING, 652.

MONO ISLAND, 564.

MONOPOLIES, 7660.

MONOTONY, 6052, 7325, 7500, 7502, 7641.

MONTAIGNAIS CULTURE, 7038.

MONTANA, 1671, 8291, 8903.

MONT-CENIS (FRANCE), 905.

MONTEVIDEO (URUGUAY), 5842.

MONTEZUMA'S WELL (ARIZONA), 7703.

MONTREAL (CANADA), 2162.

MOON, 5642.

MOOSE, 5245.

MORALE, 5572.

MORBIDITY, 2888.

MORELOS (MEXICO), 1308, 6748.

MORICHE PALM, 7951.

MORMON FAITH, 335.

MOROCCO, 1140, 1534, 3086, 3314, 3418, 3446, 3447, 4052, 4128, 4777, 5027, 5337, 5487, 5599, 8073, 8249.

MORTALITY, 2317, 2417, 2888, 6228, 6445, 7010.

MORTALITY (CHILDHOOD), 601, 3653, 4221, 4478, 5908, 7584, 8662, 8808.

MORTLOCK ISLANDS, 8609.

MORTUARY PRACTICES, 2601, 2679, 3814.

MOSHAWENG TLOKWA CULTURE, 3260, 3262, 3263.

MOSS 2451, 7738.

MOSURR, 2583.

MOTHERS, 978, 1109, 2008, 2026, 2588, 4221, 4422, 5144, 5270, 5615, 5709, 6145, 6577, 6643, 6801, 6916, 7048, 8400.

MOTILONES MANSOS CULTURE, 8918, 8919.

MOTLEY, WILLARD, 1270.

MOTT FARM, 981.

MOUND BUILDER CULTURE, 5367, 7675.

7182, 7324, 7836, 8126, 8356, 8373, 8725, 8905, 9053, 9055, 9063.

PHYTOGEOGRAPHY, 5546, 7251, 8603.

Phytolacca dodecandra, 2837.

PIA, 7977.

PIACENZA (ITALY), 6496.

PIAROA CULTURE, 1839, 8423.

PICA, 272, 1135, 1512, 1798, 2715, 3163, 3261, 3275, 3339, 3798, 4185, 4660, 4989, 5649, 5662, 6111, 6549, 6886, 7224, 7508, 7631, 8127, 8672, 8676, 8779, 9093.

PICKLING, 5659, 5775.

PICNICS, 2345, 2617, 5688.

PICTORIUS, GEORGIUS, 2438.

PIDAN, 862, 3420.

PIDGIN ENGLISH, 1369.

PIE, 249, 8537.

PIGEON, 7885.

PIGEON PEA, 243, 4667.

PIGS, 640, 1056, 1768, 1996, 2067, 2203, 2762, 3751, 5151, 5878, 5980, 6126, 6550, 6700, 6701, 7065, 7066, 7381, 7687, 8215, 8415, 8416, 8628.

PIG WEED, 4373.

PIJOAN, MICHEL, 2421.

PIKI, 462, 6888, 8276.

PILAGA CULTURE, 3685.

PILGRIMAGE, 4117.

PIMA CULTURE, 116, 591, 1429, 2942, 3714, 3715, 4018, 4080, 6013, 7087.

PINADU (FRUIT PASTE), 449.

PINATA, 7299.

PINEAPPLE, 137, 909, 1407, 1722, 3377, 3703, 4206, 5273, 8423, 8559.

PINE NUTS, 950, 1312, 2371, 3505, 3771, 8276, 8330, 8728.

Pinguicula vulgaris, 6684.

Pinus monophylla, 2371.

PIRO CULTURE, 8162.

PISSOINA (WHEAT BEVERAGE), 8323.

Pistacia terebinthus, 5773.

Pisum sativum, 8397, 9094.

PITANGA (FRUIT), 7443.

Pitasiles japonicus, Miq., 6343.

PITCHER PLANT, 1172.

PITH, 5805.

PLANTAIN, 160, 4139, 4149, 6287, 7567.

PLANTATIONS 87, 1333, 1559, 1711, 2059, 2771, 2819, 3048, 3077, 3828, 4667, 4668, 5304, 6773, 7033, 7849, 7896, 8704, 8939.

PLANT BREEDING, 1194, 1718, 1886, 2543, 2720, 3057, 5822, 5917, 6153, 7102, 7598, 8026, 8888.

PLANT COLLECTING, 1600, 2738, 4293, 4973, 5579, 5581, 6157, 6631, 7251, 7927.

PLANT DISTRIBUTION, 502, 503, 604, 657, 658, 1385, 1389, 1390, 1420, 1491, 1850, 1972, 2098, 2305, 2531, 2615, 2643, 2670, 2878, 2886, 3038, 3088, 3174, 3295, 3456, 3505, 3523, 3547, 3603, 3611, 3645, 3731, 3755, 3756, 3888, 4036, 4120, 4121, 4122, 4124, 4125, 4126, 4127, 4128, 4129, 4154, 4184, 4204, 4313, 4356, 4555, 4692, 4693, 4801, 4973, 5010, 5070, 5173, 5174, 5177, 5546, 5547, 5548, 5670, 6431, 6503, 6673, 6809, 6826, 6862, 6901, 7015, 7121, 7138, 7205, 7251, 7277, 7293, 7597, 7662, 7745, 8024, 8293, 8354, 8557, 8716, 8979, 8996, 9031, 9033, 9085.

PLANT-FOOD MIXTURES, 4431.

PLANT INTRODUCTION, 3793, 3888, 4120, 4121, 4122, 4124, 4125, 4126, 4127, 4128, 4129, 4184, 4204, 4356, 4546, 5010, 5153, 5177, 5507, 5546, 5547, 5548, 5579, 5670, 5734, 5899, 6542, 6809, 6826, 7121, 7138, 7525, 7597, 7881, 7886, 7970, 8329, 8487, 8557, 8628, 8716, 8832, 8979.

PLANTS, 27, 101, 107, 132, 157, 321, 355, 368, 405, 407, 426, 430, 431, 446 447, 470, 472, 490, 495, 497, 505, 555, 569, 570, 609, 618, 632, 651, 667, 668, 719, 729, 748, 798, 834, 837, 840, 851, 887, 888, 909, 1020, 1040, 1042, 1076, 1085, 1090, 1094, 1156, 1171, 1174, 1175, 1194, 1225, 1227, 1230, 1250, 1256, 1360, 1389, 1395, 1455, 1495, 1583, 1584, 1621, 1692, 1698, 1746, 1772, 1775, 1783, 1800, 1810, 1811, 1825, 1901, 1913, 1946, 1970, 1984, 2005, 2061, 2065, 2068, 2079, 2087, 2159, 2182, 2202, 2205, 2228, 2249, 2265, 2305, 2372, 2402, 2445, 2498, 2531, 2564, 2603, 2609, 2631, 2738, 2773, 2774, 2807, 2811, 2821, 2869, 2905, 2971, 2975, 2983, 3078, 3133, 3147, 3179, 3221, 3249, 3254, 3310, 3315, 3317, 3323, 3344, 3435, 3439, 3459, 3491, 3493, 3502, 3502, 3557, 3578, 3603, 3635, 3637, 3644, 3689, 3691, 3723, 3724, 3733, 3801, 3803, 3805,

RICHARDS, AUDREY ISABEL, 3082, 4237, 7589, 8437.

Ricinodendron rautanenii, Schinz. 4760, 4763.

RICKETS, 6269, 7912.

RIDDLES, 1964.

RIO GRANDE DO SUL (BRAZIL), 7702.

RIO GRANDE RIVER, 848, 971, 1786, 1929, 1930, 3892.

RIO DE JANEIRO (BRAZIL), 2403, 6358, 7696.

RIO DE LA PLATA, 7894.

RIO MUNI (EQUATORIAL GUINEA), 1377.

RIO NEGRO (BRAZIL), 6469, 7498.

RIOTING, 5227.

RITUAL, 306, 389, 393, 552, 554, 600, 639, 641,
  642, 652, 674, 759, 921, 969, 1342, 1343,
  1725, 1732, 1851, 1870, 2364, 2600, 2633,
  2679, 2834, 2849, 2857, 2946, 3304, 3324,
  3529, 3569, 3573, 3707, 3987, 4181, 4384,
  4569, 4796, 4830, 4910, 5001, 5206, 5324,
  5350, 5559, 5569, 6700, 6701, 6770, 6843,
  7066, 7438, 7480, 7682, 8006, 8021, 8028,
  8116, 8190, 8215, 8294, 8334, 8436, 8451,
  8473, 8485, 8502, 8529, 8541, 8661, 9012,
  9013.

RITUAL PURITY, 639, 3065, 3465, 3528, 3529,
  4575, 6484.

RIVERBOATS, 6399.

RIVERS, 2772, 7915.

ROASTING, 4850, 5298, 8279, 8284.

ROBERTS, LYDIA JEAN, 799, 8869.

Robinia pseudoacacia, 2461.

ROCHESTER (NEW YORK), 2052.

ROCKY MOUNTAINS, 3471, 6916.

RODENTS, 2135, 2868, 3051, 6199.

ROMAN CATHOLIC FAITH, 4547, 5737, 5958.

ROME (ANCIENT), 142, 143, 146, 257, 289, 290,
  349, 448, 574, 875, 895, 902, 1013, 1366,
  1400, 1643, 1803, 1964, 2041, 2148, 2166,
  2205, 2527, 2563, 2753, 2778, 3174, 3322,
  3236, 3581, 3605, 3645, 3696, 3789, 3907,
  4110, 4390, 4530, 4586, 4593, 4617, 4932,
  5366, 5650, 5713, 5799, 5815, 5966, 5999,
  6434, 6535, 7386, 7516, 7591, 7622, 7700,
  7731, 8031, 8118, 8284, 8420, 8421, 8507,
  8509, 8528, 8604, 8705, 8757, 8758, 8977.

ROME (ITALY), 2433.

RONIER PALM, 6545.

ROSELLE, 3377, 8711, 8712.

ROSES, 3139, 6962.

ROSEWATER, 814, 7993, 8924.

ROSSEL ISLAND, 3251, 6934.

ROUEN (FRANCE), 701.

ROUERQUE (FRANCE), 3160.

ROUNDWORM, 2334.

ROYAL BRITISH NAVY, 7593.

ROYAL MUSEUM (BERLIN), 1020.

RUANDA, 50, 1668, 1669, 3743, 4835, 4836, 6213,
  6302, 8100.

RUE, 960.

RUM, 1142, 3524, 7031.

RUMANIA, 381, 663, 1346, 2339, 4025, 4547, 5336,
  5585, 5781, 6594, 7773.

RUMFORD, BENJAMIN (COUNT) (see: THOMPSON,
  BENJAMIN).

Running, 268.

RUPERT'S HOUSE (CANADA), 4396.

RURAL POPULATIONS, 1830, 1887, 1938, 1939, 1941,
  2084, 2085, 2122, 2191, 2192, 2193, 2194,
  2195, 2196, 2197, 2199, 2200, 2292, 2339,
  2360, 2497, 2503, 2566, 2587, 2588, 2628,
  2647, 2688, 2744, 2864, 2894, 2921, 3030,
  3068, 3186, 3191, 3383, 3822, 3838, 3893,
  3975, 4011, 4012, 4013, 4014, 4094, 4105,
  4150, 4200, 4290, 4403, 4404, 4433, 4467,
  4509, 4522, 4561, 4563, 4612, 4710, 4721,
  4723, 4724, 4916, 4917, 5050, 5311, 5585,
  5604, 5672, 5701, 5702, 5780, 5823, 5824,
  5825, 5826, 5827, 5906, 6104, 6134, 6293,
  6317, 6322, 6325, 6334, 6401, 6432, 6466,
  6557, 6568, 6594, 6662, 6696, 6714, 6774,
  6825, 6874, 6895, 6908, 6926, 7052, 7054,
  7126, 7175, 7176, 7177, 7178, 7179, 7180,
  7284, 7285, 7385, 7392, 7428, 7613, 7614,
  7692, 7706, 7762, 7966, 7993, 8001, 8124,
  8051, 8146, 8147, 8149, 8236, 8308, 8355,
  8359, 8427, 8461, 8474, 8570, 8612, 8779,
  8789, 8834, 8842, 8965, 9060.

RURAL TO URBAN TRANSITION 2657, 2659, 3341,
  3342.

RUSSIAN ORTHODOX CHURCH, 2568.

RUSSO-JAPANESE WAR, 7406.

RUST (PLANT DISEASE), 256.

RUTACEAE, 1549.

RWANDA, 5335.

TAMALE, 462, 3835, 6570, 6748.

TAMARASK, 927.

TAMARI (SOY BEAN PRODUCT), 8020.

TAMARIND, 3869.

Tamarix mannifera, Ehrenb., 5773.

TAMAULIPAS (MEXICO), 1300, 4314, 5079, 5167, 5176, 8744.

TAMIL NADU (INDIA), 343, 415, 416, 435, 2595, 2596, 2597, 3064, 4329, 6576, 6577, 7964, 8343, 8344, 8402.

TAMIR CULTURE, 4861, 7553, 7554.

TANGALE CULTURE, 5708.

TANGANYIKA, 631, 891, 1900, 1916, 2835, 2990, 3078, 3221, 3497, 4358, 4795, 5889, 5921, 5988, 6080, 7100, 7360, 8033.

TANGSA CULTURE, 2374.

TANSY MUSTARD, 1368, 7019.

TANZANIA, 1077, 1078, 2493, 2680, 2681, 2835, 3552, 4040, 4294, 4358, 5340, 5811, 6926, 7972, 8037.

TAPE RECORDERS, 1711.

TAPIOCA, 1227, 4337, 5462, 8468, 8997.

TAPIR, 7013.

TAPIRAPE CULTURE, 1365.

Tapirira edulis, 1010.

TARAHUMARA CULTURE, 680, 4383, 6349.

TARALLI (BREAD: NAPLES), 1952.

TARASCAN CULTURE, 592, 8310, 8706.

TARIANA CULTURE, 6049.

TARN-ET-GARRONNE (FRANCE), 1038.

TARO, 80, 239, 509, 610, 756, 1848, 2080, 3072, 3077, 3224, 3404, 3546, 3753, 3899, 4236, 4337, 4419, 4624, 4669, 5048, 5406, 5566, 5620, 5621, 5628, 5991, 6153, 6516, 6602, 6702, 6914, 6981, 7662, 7739, 7963, 8047, 8151, 8152, 8155, 8190, 8788.

TASADAY CULTURE, 6933.

TASMANIA, 405, 919, 1163, 1322, 3919, 4031, 6048, 7026.

TASMANIAN ABORIGINES, 405, 919, 1163, 1322, 3735, 3736, 4031, 6048, 7026.

TASTE, 841, 1072, 1367, 1696, 1706, 1799, 1973, 3282, 3283, 2391, 2642, 2909, 3015, 3258, 3466,

3680, 4060, 4152, 4169, 4317, 5862, 6244, 6245, 6253, 6433, 6853, 7442, 7491, 7578, 7836, 8239, 8268, 8640.

TATARS, 3238.

TATOO, 1199.

TAVERNS, 166, 167, 885, 1980, 2766, 2767, 2969, 4325, 4681, 5268, 5346, 8403.

TAWSUG CULTURE, 2530.

TAX, SOL, 1559, 1560, 1561, 1562.

TAXATION, 2489, 2770, 8302.

TAYTAY (PHILLIPINES), 330, 5543.

TEA, 148, 200, 223, 229, 253, 691, 692, 839, 985, 1058, 1181, 1236, 1493, 1528, 1569, 1602, 2052, 2057, 2327, 2328, 2331, 2342, 2355, 2617, 2732, 2849, 3233, 3410, 3246, 3531, 3573, 3620, 3977, 4102, 4164, 4241, 4282, 4809, 4864, 4907, 4944, 5001, 5039, 5117, 5588, 5599, 5814, 5924, 6253, 6508, 6738, 6894, 7092, 7239, 7249, 7357, 7517, 7692, 8028, 8054, 8194, 8303, 8582, 8622.

TEA HOUSES, 2617, 4864, 7729, 9029.

TEA (SOUCHONG), 3410.

TEACHERS, 800.

TEAM RESEARCH, 422, 423, 6929.

TECHNOLOGY, 106, 774, 2386, 2719, 3276, 3409, 4254, 4297, 4376, 4389, 4631, 5160, 6191, 6586, 7539, 7683, 8043, 8694, 8902, 9007.

TECUITLATL, 1644, 2553.

TEEN AGERS, 614, 3949.

TEFF, 4218.

TEHERAN (IRAN), 8923.

TEHUACAN (MEXICO), 1300, 5082, 7208, 7597.

TELEVISION, 1635, 3278, 3335, 7451.

TELLIER, CHARLES ALBERT, 3232.

TEMNE LANGUAGE, 1231.

TEMPEH (SOY BEAN PRODUCT), 3355, 3716, 3717, 5886, 7592, 7830, 8598, 8600.

TEMPERANCE, 4617.

TENETEHARA CULTURE, 8538.

TENNESSEE, 1865, 2363, 3240, 4439, 4625, 5808, 6341, 6421.

TEN STATE NUTRITION SURVEY, 7227, 7228.

TEOSINTE, 586, 2879, 2880, 3547, 5169, 5176, 5181, 5185, 5501, 6765, 7744.

8603, 8663, 8690, 8706, 8756, 8812, 8883, 8888, 8934, 8935, 9068.

VEGETABLES (ORIENTAL), 845, 1554, 1595, 3068, 3582, 3709, 4102, 4765, 4858, 4869, 6423, 6546, 6727, 6728, 7476, 8010, 8595.

VEGETARIANISM, 69, 180, 199, 202, 210, 211, 215, 739, 772, 1112, 1203, 1672, 1902, 2483, 2563, 2780, 2901, 3445, 3457, 3676, 3721, 4087, 4307, 4322, 4357, 4664, 4981, 5060, 5135, 5360, 6392, 5850, 6168, 6336, 6535, 6574, 6887, 7091, 7440, 7541, 7550, 8040, 8098, 8725, 8847, 8950, 8977, 9005, 9065, 9066.

VENDEE (FRANCE), 1642.

VENDING MACHINES, 3841.

VENEZUELA, 337, 1039, 1080, 1348, 1349, 1350, 1351, 1352, 1839, 2130, 2490, 2844, 3116, 3303, 3613, 5183, 5344, 5787, 5831, 7072, 7073, 7144, 7950, 7951, 8016, 8423, 8424, 8426, 8427, 8811.

VENTANA CAVE (ARIZONA), 6013.

VERACRUZ (MEXICO), 4801.

VERMONT, 3769, 5906.

VERONA, 7515.

VEST, 1014.

VETCH, 4739.

Vicia ervilia, 8397, 9094.

Vicia faba, 5110, 9094.

Vicia sativa, 1298, 4739.

VICOS (PERU), 1709.

VIENNA (AUSTRIA), 8659.

VIETNAM, 1028, 1746, 1808, 1889, 1890, 1908, 2338, 3148, 3301, 3408, 6002, 6839, 6993, 6995, 7041, 7168, 8164, 8255, 8269, 8405.

VIETNAMESE-AMERICANS, 7161.

Vigna sinensis, 7862.

VILANCULOS (MOZAMBIQUE), 6944.

VINBER, 2583.

VINEGAR, 82, 168, 169, 170, 960, 1123, 2768, 3812, 4868, 5932, 7025, 8356, 9079.

VINES, 909, 956, 2126, 2217, 2358, 2580, 3994, 4451, 5028, 5951, 6130, 8153, 8155.

VINEYARDS, 2358, 5223, 7780.

VIRGINIA, 798, 1296, 1312, 1748, 2830, 3145, 3363, 3960, 6466, 6825, 8586, 8726.

VIRGIN ISLAND (UNITED STATES), 1121, 2735, 4240, 4241, 7755, 8853, 8968.

VIRUS, 281, 3073, 3074, 5309, 7687.

VISAYAN CULTURE, 3513.

VITAMIN A, 466, 2688, 2693, 3268, 3269, 4847, 6017, 7102, 7468, 8883.

VITAMIN B-COMPLEX, 366, 377, 387, 437, 1065, 1288, 1527, 1571, 1921, 2031, 2688, 2693, 2852, 3135, 3495, 3902, 3903, 4331, 4955, 5026, 5320, 5626, 6371, 7102, 6964, 7154, 8883.

VITAMIN C, 1552, 1647, 2666, 2685, 2688, 2760, 2839, 3268, 3269, 3711, 4493, 4765, 4846, 4852, 5098, 5393, 5394, 5407, 5704, 5818, 5842, 6452, 7593, 7905, 8883.

VITAMIN D, 391, 6269.

VITAMIN DEFICIENCY, 2426, 2427, 2568, 2693, 2760, 2839, 3135, 3495, 3711, 3902, 4764, 4846, 4847, 4955, 5026, 5098, 5320, 5393, 5394, 5407, 5704, 5842, 6017, 6269, 6452, 6454, 7102, 7154, 7593, 7905, 7912, 9069, 9093.

VITAMINS, 1100, 1816, 1886, 2427, 2637, 2675, 2852, 2858, 3931, 4092, 4938, 5191, 5630, 5633, 5635, 6213, 6536, 6787, 9067.

Vitis vinifera, 909.

Voandzeia poissoni, A. Chev. , 1546.

Voandzeia subterranea, Thou. , 6333.

VODUN, 546, 2089, 5569, 6337, 7546.

VOIMURU (FINLAND, FOOD PREPARATION), 6797.

VOLTA RIVER, 4710.

VOLVULUS (SMALL BOWEL), 284.

VORARLBERG PROVINCE (AUSTRIA), 4005.

VOREIOCHORA (GREECE), 308.

WADO CULTURE, 5889.

WAFFLE IRONS, 8099.

WAFFLES, 7291, 8099.

WAGE LABOR, 652, 1450.

WAGES, 7113, 7793.

WAILAKI CULTURE, 6567.

WAILUKU (HAWAII), 4257.

WAIWAI CULTURE, 9027.

WAKAMBA CULTURE, 7992.

WALAPAI CULTURE, 4081.

WALBIRI CULTURE, 5494, 7984.

WALES, 980, 2662, 3645, 4002, 4936, 5248, 7622, 7991.

WALNUT, 814, 2132, 2520, 3005, 7838, 8601.

WALPI (see: HOPI CULTURE).

WAMPANOAG CULTURE, 7714.

WAPITI, 7595.

WAR BETWEEN THE STATES, 1686, 4976, 5444, 7113.

WARBLE-FLY GRUBS, 2576, 5894.

WARAO CULTURE, 3613, 7951, 8811.

WAREHOUSING, 1265.

WARFARE, 2223.

WARLI CULTURE, 7216.

WARM SPRINGS SAHAPTIN CULTURE, 7372.

WARUNDI CULTURE, 6634.

WASHINGTON, D.C., 272, 589, 2655, 2742, 3339, 8805.

WASHINGTON STATE, 614, 1667, 1980, 2416, 3320.

WASHO CULTURE, 3438, 8330.

WASWANIPI CREE CULTURE, 2573, 5746.

WATER, 67, 76, 217, 238, 610, 673, 1164, 1172, 1197, 1859, 2316, 2368, 2871, 2975, 3291, 3569, 3847, 4373, 4900, 5125, 5232, 5410, 5414, 5805, 5890, 5891, 6268, 6604, 6622, 7541, 7817, 7819, 7842, 7853, 7896, 7984, 8168, 8458, 8497, 8565, 8566, 9030.

WATER CHINKAPIN, 4595.

WATER LILY, 1858, 7674.

WATERMELON, 3063, 7338, 7850.

WEANING, 66, 622, 749, 844, 938, 1030, 1115, 1727, 2033, 2033, 2034, 2035, 2635, 2990, 3832, 4783, 6413, 6577, 7176, 7178, 7179, 7180, 7581, 7671, 7964, 8474, 8561.

WEAVING, 8434.

WEIGHT GAIN, 3034, 5684, 7003.

WEIGHT REDUCTION, 187, 5355, 8134.

WEIGHTS, 2479, 4617, 5405.

WELLESLY ISLAND, 8972.

WELLINGTON (NEW ZEALAND), 755.

WESTERN HEMISPHERE, 307, 688, 708, 1138, 1342, 1392, 1722, 1772, 1774, 3279, 3444, 3517, 3731, 3888, 4104, 4229, 4313, 4331, 4557, 3637, 4680, 4749, 4832, 5083, 5461, 5544, 5606, 5759, 6809, 6826, 7081, 7120, 7121, 7122, 7207, 7675, 7745, 7807, 8230, 8303, 8452, 8473, 8644, 8738, 9092.

WEST INDIES, 713, 1617, 1751, 2365, 2479, 3230, 3254, 3496, 3754, 3886.

WEST IRIAN (NEW GUINEA), 6873, 8525.

WESTPHALIA (GERMANY), 7268.

WEST VIRGINIA, 1486, 3041, 8586, 8942.

WETHERILL, JOHN & WHETHERILL, LOUISE, 9003.

WHALE-BONE, 636.

WHALES, 765, 1015, 1016, 1676, 4572, 6465.

WHALING, 5393, 6689.

WHANGANUI (NEW ZEALAND), 3319.

WHEAT, 145, 160, 256, 323, 410, 747, 929, 967, 1775, 1842, 2098, 2783, 3013, 3033, 3201, 3290, 3418, 3455, 3634, 3638, 4110, 4298, 4816, 4818, 5628, 5797, 5924, 6416, 6813, 7251, 7333, 7444, 7517, 7796, 8323, 8398, 8510, 8536, 8706, 8757, 9094.

WHISKEY, 3215, 3378, 3583, 5085, 6341, 7031.

WHITE MEO CULTURE, 801.

WHITE MOUNTAIN APACHE CULTURE, 2521, 2522, 6203, 6401, 6740, 7434, 7435.

WHITE RIVER APACHE CULTURE, 3924.

WHITE SEA, 1164.

WIDOWS, 4902.

WIFE, 7231.

WIKMUNKAN CULTURE, 8137.

WILDERNESS ACTIVITIES, 8819.

WILD ONION, 4373.

WILD RICE, 1483, 1547, 1701, 2112, 2143, 2583, 2865, 2872, 3474, 3814, 3821, 4155, 4156, 4199, 4255, 4373, 5092, 6642, 7792, 7798, 7854, 7924, 8049, 8889.

WILEY, HARVEY, 7362, 9051.

WILLAMETTE VALLEY (OREGON), 2716.

WILLIAMS, ROBERT RAMAPATNAM, 437.

WILLIAMS-WATERMAN FUND, 437.

WIMMERA CULTURE, 5805.

WIND, 8006.

WINDIGO PSYCHOSIS, 812, 3568, 6964, 8069.

WINDMILLS, 679.

WINDWARD ISLANDS, 7425.

WINE, 25, 70, 166, 186, 273, 442, 815, 956, 1045, 1271, 1399, 1568, 1573, 1700, 2099, 2126, 2217, 2270, 2358, 2462, 2463, 2592, 2668, 2675, 2730, 2749, 2781, 2873, 2979, 3059, 3099, 3182, 3215, 3378, 3571, 3994, 4071, 4072, 4084, 4323, 4324, 4397, 4398, 4399, 4442, 4466, 4569, 4582, 4617, 4683, 4772, 4822, 4859, 4900, 4961, 4962, 4963, 5009, 5028, 5031, 5040, 5113, 5223, 5282, 5417, 5418, 5419, 5887, 6116, 6130, 6171, 6192, 6348, 6356, 6471, 6501, 6722, 6815, 6816, 6192, 6348, 6356, 6471, 6501, 6722, 6815, 6816, 7297, 7313, 7479, 7521, 7781, 7825, 7993, 8041, 8250, 8476, 8483, 8496, 8529, 8604, 8698, 8868, 8917, 9012, 9013, 9059, 9072.

WINELAND THE GOOD, 2583.

WINE-TASTING, 8250.

WINGED BEAN, 5934.

WINNEBAGO CULTURE, 6642.

WINNOWING, 1140.

WINTER, 866, 928, 1533, 1864.

WINTUN CULTURE, 6567.

WISCONSIN, 1864, 2648, 4923, 7288, 7289, 7675, 7855, 8889.

WISHRAM CULTURE, 7738.

WITOTO CULTURE, 2245, 2548.

WOKAS, 6567.

WOLPI (see: WALPI)

WOLVES, 636.

WOMEN, 511, 589, 731, 772, 778, 987, 1238, 1239, 1347, 1673, 1711, 1795, 1914, 2185, 2186, 2408, 2409, 2410, 2417, 2487, 2503, 2581, 2588, 2595, 2596, 2597, 2666, 2750, 2786, 2864, 2954, 2955, 3004, 3120, 3132, 3242, 3298, 3368, 3719, 4142, 4238, 4261, 4535, 4730, 4832, 4838, 4844, 5047, 4234, 4280, 5510, 5778, 5802, 5811, 6056, 6327, 6558, 6563, 6600, 6612, 6691, 6735, 6797, 6843, 7004, 7017, 7065, 7093, 7250, 7259, 7358, 7454, 7460, 7647, 7719, 7756, 8011, 8012, 8136, 8240, 8355, 8413, 8830, 8892, 9014, 9089.

WOOD, 2152, 4969, 6789.

WOODLAND CULTURE, 628, 1765, 1766, 1767, 1787, 1877, 2556, 2638, 4578, 4923, 5452, 5638, 6414, 7915, 8727, 9022.

WORK EFFICIENCY, 659, 2398, 6858, 6859, 7816, 7817, 7819, 7822.

WORK HOUSES, 7091, 7609.

WORKLOAD, 5828, 7273, 7467.

WORK PATTERNS, 940, 947, 6842, 6858, 6859, 7073, 7241, 7817, 7819, 7822, 7823, 7824, 8198.

WORLD FOOD CONFERENCE, 2714.

WORLD HEALTH ORGANIZATION OF THE UNITED NATIONS, 9097.

WORLD'S FAIR, 250.

WORLD WAR I, 53, 420, 1162, 1398, 2036, 2544, 2655, 3107, 3484, 3683, 3920, 4361, 4362, 4363, 4364, 4854, 4945, 5075, 5552, 6157, 6308, 6507, 6913, 7637, 7638, 7967, 7968, 8147.

WORLD WAR II, 589, 595, 598, 794, 865, 1016, 1072, 1292, 1394, 2439, 2448, 2912, 3128, 3195, 3286, 3340, 3402, 3403, 3512, 3705, 3841, 4189, 4275, 4454, 4508, 4782, 4867, 4956, 5447, 5467, 5471, 5476, 5572, 5898, 5936, 6046, 6104, 6442, 6474, 7321, 7396, 7683, 8007, 8147, 8262, 8312, 8342, 8352, 8393, 8461.

WORMS, 286, 1898, 2823, 4541, 5298, 5422, 5538, 6567, 7096, 7590, 7769, 8969.

WORRY, 4044.

WYANDOT CULTURE, 7572.

WYOMING, 4670.

XANGO CULTURE, 1731.

Xanthosoma sp. 3898.

XEROPHTHALMIA, 2568, 5423.

XIKRIN TRIBE, 2826.

XINGU CULTURE, 7565.

XUILI, 5298.

Xyleutes boisduval, 7607.

YAHGAN CULTURE, 7929.

YAK, 5197, 6240, 6241.

YAKUT CULTURE, 4183.

YAKUTAT TLINGIT CULTURE, 4601.

YALA, 7984.

YALE UNIVERSITY, 2650.

YAM BEAN, 3703, 7229.

ABOUT THE COMPILER

ROBERT L. FREEDMAN has contributed to such journals as *Current Anthropology*, *International Migration*, and *World Review of Nutrition and Dietetics*.